HOLT

AMERICAN GOVERNMENT

ANNOTATED TEACHER'S EDITION

Steven Kelman

HOLT, RINEHART AND WINSTON

A Harcourt Classroom Education Company

Austin • New York • Orlando • Atlanta • San Francisco • Boston • Dallas • Toronto • London

Editorial

Sue Miller, *Director*
Steven L. Hayes, *Executive Editor*
Robert Wehnke, *Managing Editor*
Paul Rubinson, *Associate Editor*
Sue Minkler, *Assistant Editorial Coordinator*

TECHNOLOGY RESOURCES

Rob Hrechko, *Editor*
Annette Saunders, *Editor*

FACT CHECKING

Bob Fullilove, *Editor*
Jenny Rose, *Associate Editor*

COPY EDITING

Julie Beckman-Key, *Senior Copy Editor*
Katelijne A. Lefevere, *Copy Editor*

Editorial Permissions

Janet Harrington, *Permissions Editor*

Art, Design, and Photo

BOOK DESIGN

Diane Motz, *Senior Design Director*
Teresa Carrera-Paprota, *Designer*
David Hernandez, *Designer*

IMAGE ACQUISITIONS

Joe London, *Director*
Elaine Tate, *Art Buyer Supervisor*
Joyce Gonzalez, *Art Buyer*
Tim Taylor, *Photo Researcher Supervisor*
David Knowles, *Photo Researcher*

TECHNOLOGY DESIGN

Susan Michael, *Design Director*
Kimberly Cammerata, *Design Manager*
Grant Davidson, *Designer*

MEDIA DESIGN

Curtis Riker, *Design Director*

GRAPHIC SERVICES

Kristen Darby, *Manager*
Jeff Robinson, *Senior Ancillary Designer*

COVER DESIGN

Pronk & Associates

New Media

Dave Bowman, *Operations Manager*
Armin Gutzmer, *Director of Product Development*
Jessica A. Bega, *Senior Project Manager II*
Cathy Kuhles, *Technical Assistant*
Nina Degollado, *Technical Assistant*

Pre-Press & Manufacturing

Gene Rumann, *Production Manager*
Leanna Ford, *Production Coordinator*
Clary Knapp, *Production Coordinator*
Jevara Jackson, *Manufacturing Coordinator, Book*
Rhonda Farris, *Inventory Planner*
Kim Harrison, *Manufacturing Coordinator, Media*

Cover: *The Capitol Building in Washington, D.C., the seat of American government.*

It's All About

The first step to success in the social studies classroom is capturing and sustaining the interest of your students. *HOLT AMERICAN GOVERNMENT* is designed to be open and friendly to all students, so that they develop an enthusiasm for learning and an appreciation for the past.

HOLT AMERICAN GOVERNMENT offers

- **Built-in Reading Support**
- **Technology with Instructional Value**
- **Standardized Testing and Skill Building**
- **The Best Teacher Management System in the Industry**

CITIZENSHIP IN ACTION engages your students' critical-thinking skills by showing them how certain issues have played out in local, state, and federal governments and asks them to participate in the political process.

RELEVANCE

CNNfyi.com™ is a site designed to give students in grades 6–12 access to people, places, and environments around the globe while offering "real-world" articles, career and college resources, and online activities.

CNNfyi.com > News

John Adams: A force for independence

July 3, 2001
Web posted at 5:45 PM EDT (2145 GMT)

SOURCE
Lesson plan for parents and educators — Click here

By Todd Leopold
CNN

(CNN) -- On July 4, the United birthday -- the anniversary of It's a celebration that wouldn't actions of a frequently ignored Fou

"Adams hasn't received the attention h David McCullough, author of the rece "And (Thomas)

An oil-on-wood portrait of John Adams, circa 1821, by Gilbert Stuart.

In-Text Features Put Government into Perspective

- Careers in Government
- Comparing Governments
- Citizenship in Action
- Case Studies
- Linking Government and Geography
- Linking Government and Economics
- Linking Government and History
- Linking Government and Journalism
- Linking Government and Philosophy
- Linking Government and Psychology
- Linking Government and Sociology

Reading in the

At Holt, we don't assume that students know how or have any desire to make sense of what they're reading, and we develop our programs based on that assumption. We don't just ask students questions about content, we give them strategies to get to that content. Through design, research, and the help of experts like Dr. Judith Irvin, we make sure students' reading needs are covered with our programs.

Helping Students Make Sense of What They're Reading

An Essay by Dr. Judith Irvin, Ph.D. Reading Education

Who in middle and high schools helps students become more successful at reading and writing informational text? When I ask this question of a school faculty, the Language Arts/English teachers point to the social studies and science teachers because they are the ones with this type of textbook. The social studies and science teachers point to the Language Arts/English teachers because they are the ones that "do" words.

I advocate teachers taking an active role in helping students learn how to use text structure and context to understand what they read. Through consistent and systematic instruction that includes modeling of effective reading behavior, teachers can assist students in becoming better readers while at the same time helping them learn more content material.

The strategies in this book are designed to assist students with getting started, maintaining focus with reading, and organizing information for later retrieval. They engage students in learning material, provide the vehicle for them to organize and reorganize concepts, and extend their understanding through writing.

When teachers combine the teaching of reading and the teaching of content together into meaningful, systematic, and corrected instruction, students can apply what they have learned to understanding increasingly more difficult and complex texts as they progress through the school years.

Content Area

READING STRATEGIES FOR THE SOCIAL STUDIES CLASSROOM

Reinforce reading skills while teaching historical concepts. This resource contains a number of widely-tested and widely-accepted strategies to use with struggling and reluctant readers. Developed by Dr. Judith Irvin, Ph.D. Reading Education.

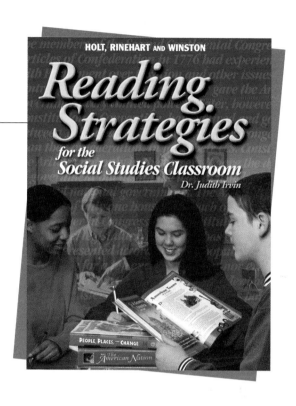

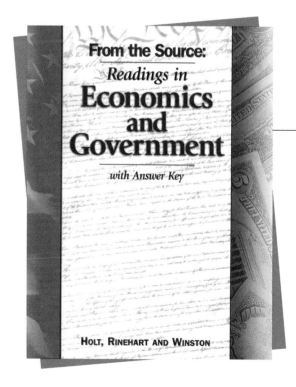

FROM THE SOURCE: READINGS IN ECONOMICS AND GOVERNMENT

These primary source readings, historical documents, legal statutes, and speeches—from notable figures such as Adam Smith, John Maynard Keynes, and David Ricardo—have brief introductions and critical-thinking questions that help students understand where these concepts originated.

Get Your Students

Your students love activities that get them involved with the content. That's why Holt offers active-learning resources that link directly to program content and provide a multitude of different lessons for large-group, small-group, and individual projects.

CHALLENGE/ENRICHMENT ACTIVITIES

These worksheets extend lessons through complementary activities and provide students with extra practice in critical thinking and researching economic issues.

SIMULATIONS AND STRATEGIES FOR TEACHING AMERICAN GOVERNMENT

Engage your students with alternative lesson plans that pique their interest, such as mock trials, Senate debates, interviews, city council meetings, and more.

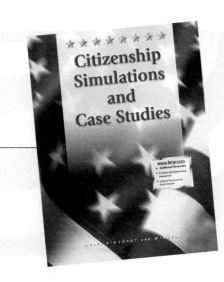

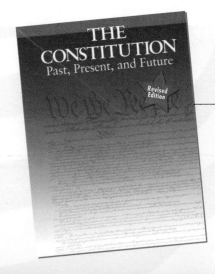

PRIMARY SOURCES

Through readings, literature excerpts, political cartoons and more, students will gain insight into the nation's past by examining period accounts and first person voices. Not only will these resources provide excellent preparation for standardized assessment, but they will expose your students to the real people and events that helped shape our country.

Involved in Learning

PUBLIC POLICY LABS

These cooperative-learning projects challenge students to synthesize learning objectives and put them into practice. They also provide students with the opportunity to apply the information and ideas they have learned in the unit to a real-world situation.

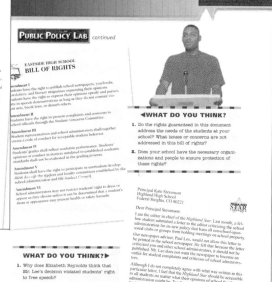

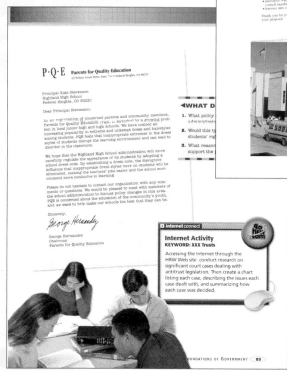

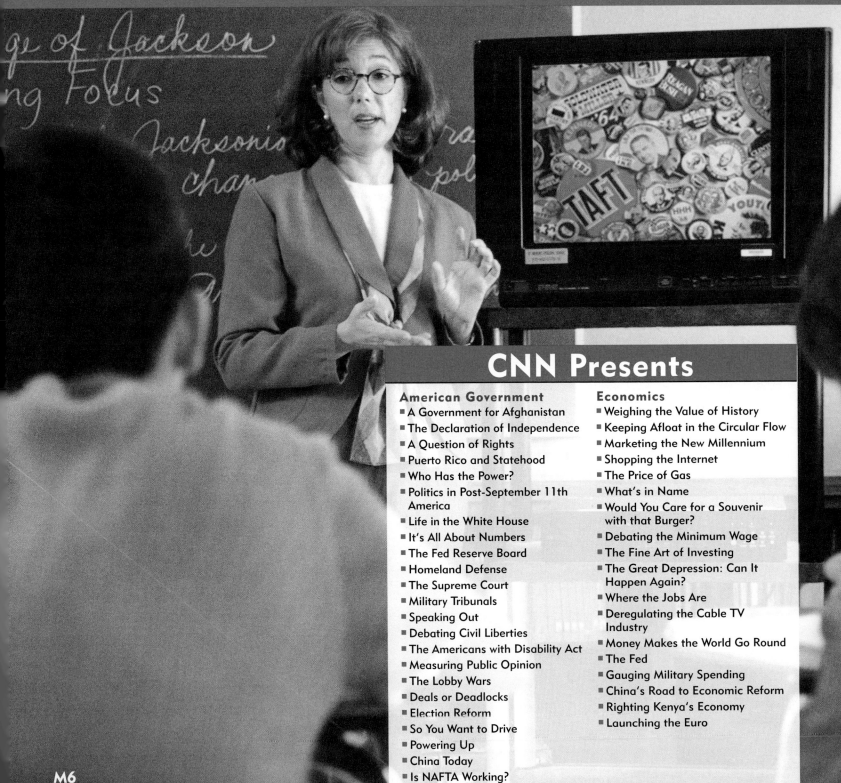

Joining Forces

CNN Presents

to Enrich your Classroom

CNNfyi.com

At **CNNfyi.com**, students will love exploring news stories written by experienced journalists as well as student bureau reporters complete with links to homework help and lesson plans.

CNN PRESENTS VIDEO LIBRARY

The **CNN PRESENTS** video collection tackles the issue of making content relevant to students head on. Real-world news stories enable students to see the connections between classroom curriculum and today's issues and events around the nation and the world.

CNN PRESENTS...

- **America: Yesterday and Today, Beginnings to 1914**
- **America: Yesterday and Today, 1850 to the Present**
- **America: Yesterday and Today, Modern Times**
- **American Government**
- **Economics**
- **Geography: Yesterday and Today**
- **September 11, 2001: Part One**
- **September 11, 2001: Part Two**
- **World Cultures: Yesterday and Today**

Holt is proud to team up with CNN/TURNER LEARNING to provide you and your students with exceptional current and historical news videos and online resources that add depth and relevance to your daily instruction. This information collection takes your classroom to the far corners of the globe without students ever leaving their desks!

Your Multi-talented Classroom

AWARD WINNER!

HOLT RESEARCHER CD-ROM: ECONOMY AND GOVERNMENT

This fully searchable database tool includes biographies, state and nation profiles, Supreme Court cases, national and international organizations, and statistics. This outstanding research resource comes with an easy-to-use search engine, a link to **www.hrw.com**, a glossary, and a graphing tool.

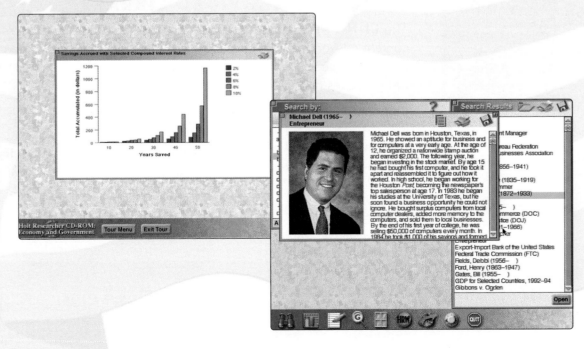

needs Multimedia Tools

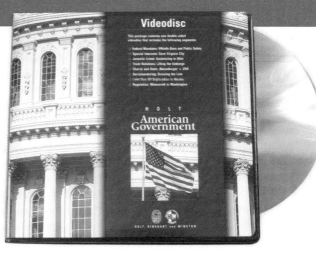

HOLT AMERICAN GOVERNMENT VIDEODISC PROGRAM

This visual resource presents in-depth case studies about topics such as government mandates for a rail-highway safety program. Each case study enables you to present information and engage students in a whole new way.

AMERICAN CIVICS CITIZENSHIP SKILLS VIDEOCASSETTE AND VIDEODISC

Informative and enlightening, these eight segments include "The Roles of a Citizen," "The Critical Consumer," and "The Citizen and Local Media"; all designed to enhance how you teach citizenship skills.

Technology with

go.hrw.com FOR TEACHERS

Throughout the *Annotated Teacher's Edition,* you'll find **Internet Connect** boxes that take you to specific chapter activities, links, current events, and more that correlate directly to the section you are teaching. Through **go.hrw.com** you'll find a wealth of teaching resources at your fingertips for fun, interactive lessons.

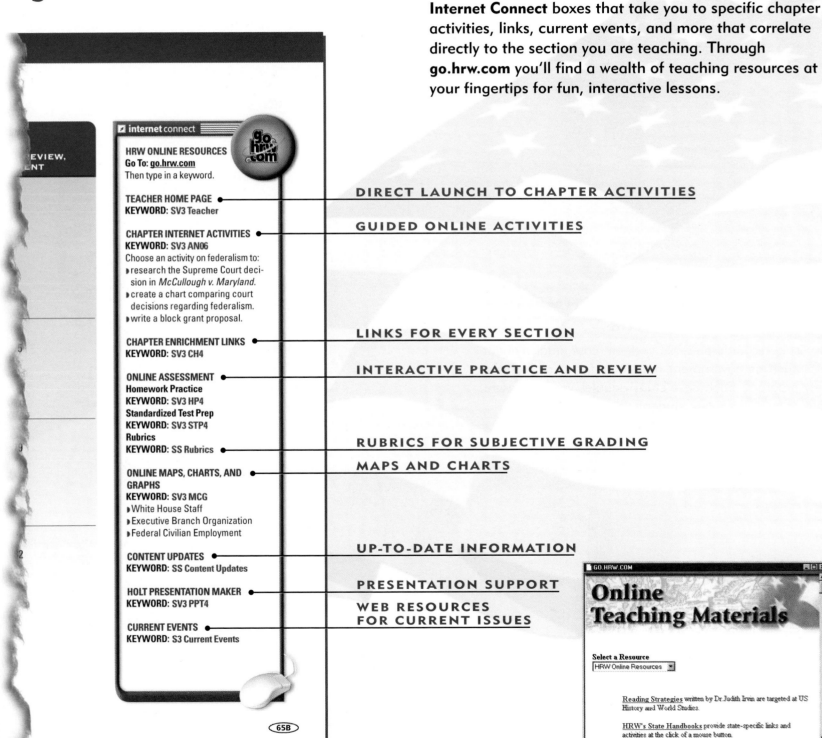

internet connect

HRW ONLINE RESOURCES
Go To: go.hrw.com
Then type in a keyword.

TEACHER HOME PAGE
KEYWORD: SV3 Teacher

CHAPTER INTERNET ACTIVITIES
KEYWORD: SV3 AN06
Choose an activity on federalism to:
▸ research the Supreme Court decision in *McCullough v. Maryland.*
▸ create a chart comparing court decisions regarding federalism.
▸ write a block grant proposal.

CHAPTER ENRICHMENT LINKS
KEYWORD: SV3 CH4

ONLINE ASSESSMENT
Homework Practice
KEYWORD: SV3 HP4
Standardized Test Prep
KEYWORD: SV3 STP4
Rubrics
KEYWORD: SS Rubrics

ONLINE MAPS, CHARTS, AND GRAPHS
KEYWORD: SV3 MCG
▸ White House Staff
▸ Executive Branch Organization
▸ Federal Civilian Employment

CONTENT UPDATES
KEYWORD: SS Content Updates

HOLT PRESENTATION MAKER
KEYWORD: SV3 PPT4

CURRENT EVENTS
KEYWORD: S3 Current Events

65B

DIRECT LAUNCH TO CHAPTER ACTIVITIES

GUIDED ONLINE ACTIVITIES

LINKS FOR EVERY SECTION

INTERACTIVE PRACTICE AND REVIEW

RUBRICS FOR SUBJECTIVE GRADING

MAPS AND CHARTS

UP-TO-DATE INFORMATION

PRESENTATION SUPPORT

WEB RESOURCES FOR CURRENT ISSUES

GO.HRW.COM

Online Teaching Materials

Select a Resource
HRW Online Resources

Reading Strategies written by Dr. Judith Irvin are targeted at US History and World Studies.

HRW's State Handbooks provide state-specific links and activities at the click of a mouse button.

Instructional Value

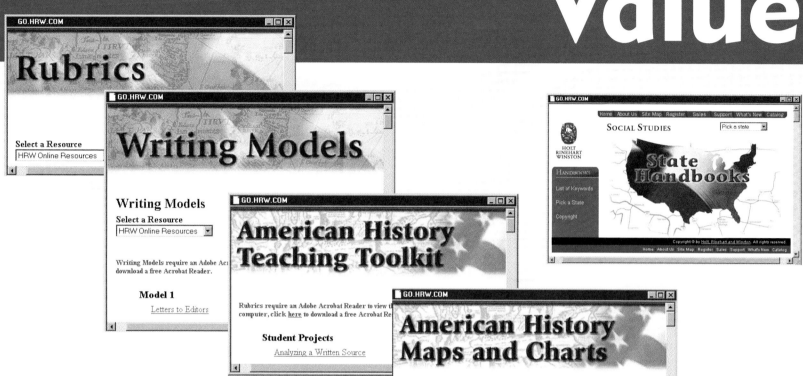

ONLINE TEACHING SUPPORT

Teacher materials on **go.hrw.com** offer you multiple resources for keeping content current. From **American History Maps and Charts** to **State Handbooks,** we've got it all.

CLASSROOM PRESENTATION SUPPORT

Animated lecture notes help add visual support to your classroom presentations.

CHAPTER 4

Powers and Responsibilities

HOLT **AMERICAN GOVERNMENT**

Powers of the Federal Government

- **Expressed powers–specifically granted in the Constitution**
- **Implied powers–suggested by the expressed powers**
- **Elastic Clause–allows Congress to stretch powers not specifically granted or denied by the Constitution**
- **Inherent powers–naturally belong to any nation's government**

HOLT, RINEHART AND WINSTON

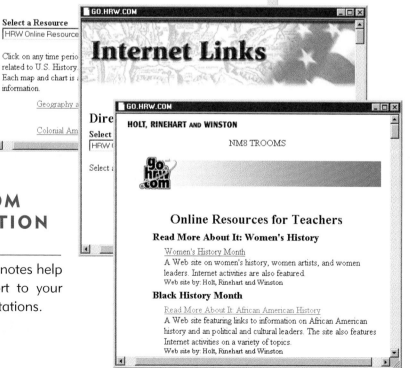

HOLT, RINEHART AND WINSTON

NM8 TROOMS

Online Resources for Teachers

Read More About It: Women's History

Women's History Month
A Web site on women's history, women artists, and women leaders. Internet activities are also featured.
Web site by: Holt, Rinehart and Winston

Black History Month

Read More About It: African American History
A Web site featuring links to information on African American history and an political and cultural leaders. The site also features Internet activities on a variety of topics.
Web site by: Holt, Rinehart and Winston

Technology that

Supreme Court Watch Online at go.hrw.com

The Holt American Government program includes an online resource that offers students up-to-date and comprehensive news about important Supreme Court events.

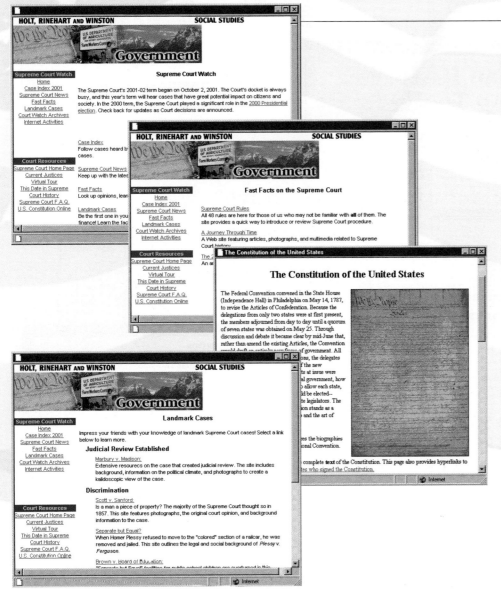

SUPREME COURT WATCH

- Case Index
- Supreme Court News
- Fast Facts
- Landmark Cases
- Court Watch Archives
- Internet Activities

Students may also visit pre-selected Court Resources including:

- Supreme Court Home Page
- Current Justices
- Virtual Tour
- This Date in Supreme Court History
- Supreme Court F.A.Q.

Delivers Content

HOMEWORK PRACTICE

This helpful tool allows students to practice and review content by chapter anywhere there is a computer.

HRW ONLINE ATLAS

This helpful online tool contains over 300 well-rendered and clearly labeled country and state maps. The clean design and easy-to-use navigational tools make accessing information simple. These maps are continually updated so you can rest assured that you and your students have the latest and most accurate geographical content available. Maps are available in English and Spanish.

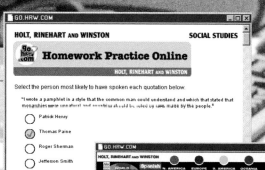

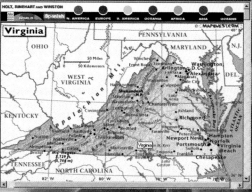

M13

Unique Teacher's

In-Text Chapter Planning

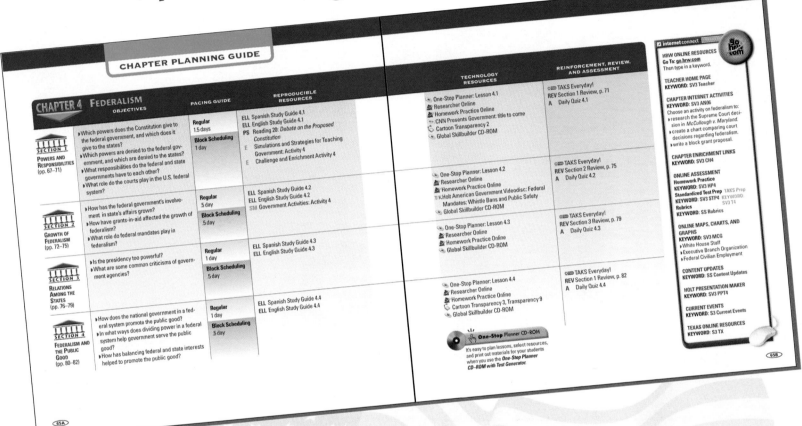

Program Resources at Your Fingertips

Primary Sources
- The Constitution: Past, Present, and Future
- From the Source: Readings in Economics and Government

Teaching Support
- Reading Strategies for the Social Studies Classroom
- Challenge/Enrichment Activities
- Reteaching Activities
- Simulations and Strategies for Teaching American Government
- Transparency Resources

Review and Assessment
- Daily Quizzes
- Chapter Tests
- Spanish Study Guides
- Social Studies Skills Review
- Unit Tests and Unit Lab Activities
- Alternative Assessment Handbook
- English Study Guides

Management System

Everything you need is on one disc!

Energize

CHAPTER 4
Powers and Responsibilities

AMERICAN GOVERNMENT

Objectives:

- Which powers does the Constitution give to the federal government, and which does it give to the states?

- Which powers are denied to the government, and which are denied to the states?

- What responsibilities do the federal and state governments have to each other?

- What role do the courts play in the U.S. federal system?

HOLT, RINEHART AND WINSTON

Presentations That Benefit Learning

Animated lecture notes can be accessed with ease when you use Holt's **Presentation** tool found on the *One-Stop Planner CD-ROM*. This resource helps you spice up your presentations and gives you ideas to build on. You'll find Microsoft® PowerPoint® presentations that include lecture notes and animated graphic organizers for each chapter and section of your text.

Your Classroom Presentations

LESSON 4.1 POWER AND RESPONSIBILITIES
TEXTBOOK PAGES 67–71

HOLT PRESENTATION MAKER
Access Illustrated LECTURE NOTES using Microsoft® PowerPoint® on the One-Stop Planner CD-ROM

OBJECTIVES
▶ List the powers given to the federal government and to the state governments by the Constitution. ★8D, 10B
▶ List the powers denied to the federal government and to the state governments by the Constitution. ★8D, 10D
▶ Identify the responsibilities that the federal and state governments have to each other. ★6D, 10B
▶ Describe the courts' role in the federal system. ★8D, 10C

MOTIVATE
Divide students into small groups. Give each group a large piece of butcher paper and three different colored markers. Have each group define the terms *expressed*, *implied*, and *inherent*. Ask groups to identify examples in their own lives in which they have had either expressed permission, implied permission, or inherent ability to do something. Have students write their ideas on the butcher paper using a different color for each of the three examples. Let each group read from their paper and discuss the reasons for placing each example under the category that they chose. Explain that in this section students will learn what powers and responsibilities the federal and state governments are given or denied by the Constitution. ★21A, 22A

TEACH

Building a Vocabulary
In spiral notebooks, have students create a Political Dictionary to be used throughout the course. This dictionary can be used as an activity at the start of each new section; also be used as a modification device for students having difficulty or sheltered English students during tests and homework assignments. For words the students will be expected to know for this section, list on the board. Have students list, define, and give an example of each terms, using information provided in the text or on the *Researcher Online ROM*. ★22A

65C

Learning from Visuals
Divide students into six groups. Assign each of the words *expressed*, *implied*, and *inherent* to two groups. For each pair of groups with the same topic have one group cover the federal role and the other cover the states' role. Have students make a poster depicting the powers given to the level of government they were assigned. Encourage students to use such tools as newspapers, magazines, and computers. Have each group display and discuss the powers listed on their poster. Tell students that in the next activity they will learn about the powers denied the government. ★10B, 22A, 22D

Hypothesizing
List the powers denied to the federal government on one side of the chalkboard and those denied to the states on the other. Ask students to brainstorm what might happen if federal and state governments held the powers that are denied to them by the Constitution. Use examples from the Articles of Confederation to show what could happen when powers are poorly distributed. Have students share their examples with the class. Discuss the importance of denying certain powers to each level of the government. Tell students that in the next activity they will learn about the responsibilities that come with these powers. ★8D, 10D

Comparing and Contrasting
Write the headings *Powers* and *Responsibilities* on the board. Ask students to debate the difference between power and responsibility in their own lives. Guide them in distinguishing between the two, and list examples of each on the board. Lead a discus-

Drawing Conclusions
Divide students into groups of three. Tell students that two members of the group are to play games of tic-tac-toe, and the third member should act as the referee. Explain that the rules of the game are standard but that certain special rules apply, such as no touching of the table or desk when it is not a player's turn, no saying words with more than one syllable, no looking at other teams, and no touching a player's own face. Have the referees watch for any violations and record occurrences on a piece of paper. After students have had the opportunity to play a few rounds, have them discuss the similarities between the referees in their games and the role of the courts in the federal system. Try to point out that both the game and the courts are based on interpreting the rules. ★8D, 10C

CLOSE
Ask students to consider the example they wrote during the Motivate activity. Have them brainstorm why it is important for the government to have expressed, implied, and inherent powers. Ask students to identify powers that are denied to the federal government. Lead a discussion regarding how the balance of powers in their own lives is similar to those in the federal and state governments. ★10D, 22A

OPTIONS

Gifted Learners
Encourage students to learn more about federalism in other countries using the Country Profiles section on the *Researcher Online* and other resources. Students may write a paper or complete a project for extra credit in which they compare the division of powers in other countries to the division of power in the United States. ★21A, 22B, 22D

Students Having Difficulty/Sheltered English Students
 Have students examine current newspapers and magazines for examples of powers exerted by one level of government that are denied to the other levels, such as the federal government printing new dollar bills. Encourage students to share these articles with the class by making a collage for each type of power, or have students create a list of these powers in their Government Notebook. ★10D, 22D

Gifted Learners
Have students write a short paper describing a Supreme Court case that involves a conflict of interest between a state government and the federal government. Students should include the state involved, what the conflict was, the decision in the case, and what impact the decision had. Encourage students to use the Supreme Court Docket section on the *Researcher Online* and other resources to gather information. ★10C, 22B, 22D

Logical-Mathematical Learners
Discuss with students that sometimes concurrent powers are used to manage large projects, such as highway construction and running public universities. Have students research projects that the federal government and state governments are working on together. Have students write a short paper describing the project. Be sure to have students discuss the amount of money being spent by both the federal and state governments. They should also describe any other commitments that either level of government has made to the project. ★10B, 22B, 22D

REVIEW
Have students complete the Section 1 Review on page 71. Use the answers in the Annotated Teacher's Edition to assess student mastery of this section.

ASSESS
To assess student mastery of this section, have students complete Daily Quiz 4.1 in *Daily Quizzes with Answer Key*. For additional assessment options, see *Portfolio and Performance Assessment for Social Studies* on the *Teaching Resources CD-ROM*.

ADDITIONAL RESOURCES
Cornell, Saul. *The Other Founders: Anti-Federalism and the Dissenting Tradition in America, 1788-1828.* 1999. University of North Carolina Press.
Durland, William. *William Penn, James Madison and the Historical Crisis in American Federalism (Studies in American History; Vol 28).* 2000. Edwin Mellen Press.
Wills, Gary. *Explaining America: The Federalist.* 2001. Penguin USA.

65D

CHAPTER PLANNING GUIDE

Each chapter in the *Teacher's Edition* is preceded by this unique interleaf section. This two-page teacher's guide tells you what classroom resources are available. Working on Chapter 6 this week? No problem. Just check the listing of available print and technology resources for Chapter 6 to help plan your lessons.

Side Column Annotations that Spark Curiosity

■ **Case Studies**
■ **Careers in Government**
■ **Citizenship in Action**
■ **Comparing Governments**
■ **Linking Government to Other Curricula**

INTERACTIVE PRACTICE ACTIVITIES

SECTION 2 REVIEW

1. Identify and explain:
- revenue sharing
- grant-in-aid
- categorical grant
- block grant
- federal mandate

2. Categorizing: The federal government is increasingly involved in states' affairs. In the web below, list four examples, past and present, of increased federal involvement.

Increasing Federal Involvement

Homework Practice Online
keyword: SV3 C04S2

3. Finding the Main Idea
a. What are the forms of federal mandates?
b. What are the two kinds of grants-in-aid and what do they fund?

4. Writing and Critical Thinking

Drawing Conclusions: Write a paragraph explaining your opinion of the federal role in states' affairs. Does the federal government have too much control? Too little?

Consider the following:
- How has the role of the federal government in states' affairs expanded?
- What benefits do states derive from the federal government?
- What drawbacks are there to federal involvement?

THIS SUPERIOR TEST GENERATOR REALLY WORKS!

REVIEW OF MAIN IDEAS

CHAPTER 4
Review

Writing a Summary

Using standard grammar, spelling, sentence structure, and punctuation, write a summary of the information in this chapter.

Identifying People and Ideas

Identify the following terms and explain their significance.

1. expressed power
2. implied power
3. inherent power
4. categorical grant
5. block grant
6. federal mandate
7. enabling act
8. act of admission
9. extradition
10. interstate compact

Understanding Main Ideas

SECTION 1 *(pp. 67–71)*

1. What powers does the Constitution give to state governments and what powers does it give to the federal government?

2. What powers does the Constitution deny state and federal governments?

3. What branch of government serves as referee in disputes between state and local governments

SECTION 2 *(pp. 72–75)*

4. How has federal involvement in states' affairs changed?

5. How do federal grants-in-aid support state governments?

6. What three basic forms do federal mandates take?

SECTION 3 *(pp. 76–79)*

7. How are states admitted into the United States?

8. How do states work together in the federal system?

SECTION 4 *(pp. 80–82)*

9. How does federalism promote the public good?

10. How does the distribution of power between state and federal governments promote the public good?

Reviewing Themes

1. **Constitutional Government** The concept of limited government is an important principle of the U.S. political system. In what ways does the federal system limit government?

2. **Political Processes** Not everyone agrees on the role of the federal government. What arguments do opponents of federal mandates use to support their position?

3. **Constitutional Government** Why have interstate compacts grown more numerous and more important in the past century?

4. **Public Good** How does having a central authority in the form of the federal government promote the public good?

Thinking Critically

1. **Supporting a Point of View** Some people argue that the federal government has become too involved in state and local affairs. Do you agree with that assessment? Why or why not?

Writing about Government

Review the list of government powers that you wrote in your Government Notebook at the beginning of the chapter. Given what you have learned, how would you revise your list? Do you need to switch some of the powers you listed to other levels of government? Record your revisions in your Notebook.

CRITICAL-THINKING REINFORCEMENT

OPPORTUNITIES FOR WRITING REINFORCEMENT

Every Student

Building Social Studies Skills

Interpreting Political Cartoons

Study the image below. Then use it to help you answer the questions that follow.

Berry's World

Better
downsize!

FEDERAL BUREAU-CRA-CY

© 1993 by NEA, Inc.

1. How does the cartoonist portray the federal government in this cartoon?

   a. It is the fierce defender of freedom and democracy.

   b. It interferes too much in the affairs of state and local governments.

   c. It is a bloated bureaucracy that needs to slim down.

   d. It spends too much time eating junk food at the mall.

2. What might lead the cartoonist to depict the federal government in this manner?

Analyzing Primary Sources

The federal system gives states the power to enact state constitutions. Read the following excerpt of South Carolina's constitution, written in 1895, then answer the questions.

"Any person who shall apply for registration [to vote] after January 1st, 1898, if otherwise qualified, shall be registered: Provided, That he can both read and write any section of the Constitution submitted to him by the registration officer or can show that he owns, and has paid all taxes collectible during the previous year on property in this State assessed at three hundred dollars ($300) or more.

Managers of election shall require of every elector offering to vote at any election, before allowing him to vote, proof of the payment of all taxes, including poll tax, assessed against him and collectible during the previous year."

3. Which of the following best describes the purpose of the provisions in this constitution?

   a. to make sure all taxes are paid on time

   b. to restrict the right to vote to a certain

Alternative Assessment

Building Your Portfolio

A More Perfect Union

Research one of the 37 states that was admitted to the United States after the Constitution was ratified. Then choose a state and imagine you are a politician there at the beginning of the admission process. Write a speech advocating admission or criticizing it. Be sure to include your reasons and be persuasive.

📶 internet connect

Internet Activity
KEYWORD: XXX Trusts
Topic: McCullough v. Maryland
GO TO: go.hrw.com
KEYWORD: SV3 GV4

Access the Internet through the HRW Go site to research the background of the Supreme Court decision in *McCullough v. Maryland*. Then imagine you are a newspaper reporter covering the case at

go.hrw.com

ACCESS ONLINE RUBRICS
FOR GRADING PROJECTS AND
PORTFOLIO ASSIGNMENTS

RETEACHING ACTIVITIES

These activities help you gear material toward students who need information presented in alternative ways. The activities focus on section objectives while presenting chapter content and reviewing chapter material.

Reteaching Activities

HOLT
AMERICAN
GOVERNMENT

HRW ONLINE RESOURCES
GO TO: go.hrw.com
TYPE IN: SD3 Teacher
SS Rubrics
SS Current Events

HOLT, RINEHART AND WINSTON

Additional Print and Technology Assessment Resources

- **Chapter Tests**
- **Daily Quizzes**
- **English Study Guides**
- **Spanish Study Guides**
- **Unit Tests and Unit Lab Activities**
- **Alternative Assessment Handbook**
- **Test Generator (located on the *One-Stop Planner CD-ROM with Test Generator*)**

HOLT AMERICAN GOVERNMENT

CONTENTS

UNIT 1 — FOUNDATIONS OF GOVERNMENT — XXXVIII

Chapter 2

ORIGINS OF U.S. GOVERNMENT 20

Chapter 3

THE U.S. CONSTITUTION 46

UNIT 2   **THE LEGISLATIVE BRANCH**   **90**

Chapter 6

CONGRESS AT WORK **112**

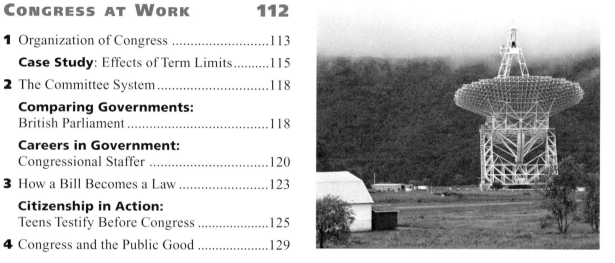

UNIT 3 ▸ THE EXECUTIVE BRANCH **140**

Chapter 7

THE PRESIDENCY **142**

Chapter 8

EXECUTIVE BRANCH AT WORK   168

Executive Branch Organization

PRESIDENT

EXECUTIVE OFFICE OF THE PRESIDENT

- White House Office
- Office of the Vice President
- Office of Management and Budget
- Council of Economic Advisers
- Office of National Drug Control Policy
- Office of the U. S. Trade Representative

- Council on Environmental Quality
- Office of Science and Technology Policy
- Office of Administration
- National Security Council
- Office of Policy Development
- National Economic Council

VICE PRESIDENT

CABINET DEPARTMENTS

Department of Agriculture	Department of the Interior
Department of Commerce	Department of Justice
Department of Defense	Department of Labor
Department of Education	Department of State
Department of Energy	Department of Transportation
Department of Health and Human Services	Department of the Treasury
Department of Housing and Urban Development	Department of Veterans Affairs

Chapter 9

ECONOMIC POLICY   190

Chapter 10

FOREIGN POLICY AND NATIONAL SECURITY   216

UNIT 4   THE JUDICIAL BRANCH   246

Chapter 11

THE FEDERAL COURT SYSTEM   248

Chapter *14*

ASSURING INDIVIDUAL RIGHTS   318

Chapter *15*

PROTECTING CIVIL RIGHTS   338

The Granger Collection, New York

Chapter *18*

POLITICAL PARTIES   404

Chapter *19*

THE ELECTORAL
PROCESS   428

FEATURES

Careers in Government

Citizenship in Action

Comparing Governments

Linking Government to Other Curricula

GOVERNMENT IN THE NEWS

CHARTS AND GRAPHS

Consumer Price Indexes, 1986–1996

Source: *Bureau of Labor Statistics, U.S. Department of Labor*

Major Events of the Cold War

1947	• President Truman issues a declaration known as the Truman Doctrine, establishing containment as the primary goal of U.S. foreign policy.
1949	• The Soviet Union takes complete control of Eastern Europe. • The Soviet Union explodes an atomic bomb. • Chinese Communists led by Mao Zedong win control of China.
1950	• The Korean War begins when North Korea invades South Korea.
1959	• Rebels led by Fidel Castro gain control of Cuba and seek help from the Soviet Union.
1961–73	• U.S. troops fight in the Vietnam War in an effort to support the noncommunist South Vietnamese government.
1962	• The Soviet Union secretly installs nuclear weapons in Cuba.
1972	• Nixon becomes the first U.S. president to visit China. • Nixon and Brezhnev negotiate the first Strategic Arms Limitation Talks (SALT I) agreement.
1987	• Mikhail Gorbachev initiates a series of reforms known as glasnost and perestroika.
1989	• East Germany announces it will dismantle the Berlin Wall.

![M]APS

Gerrymandering

ARKANSAS

Shreveport • Monroe •

LOUISIANA

Mississippi River

MISSISSIPPI

Alexandria •

TEXAS

Baton Rouge ★
Lafayette •

New Orleans •

■ Fourth Congressional District
□ Other Congressional Districts

0   25   50 Miles
0 25 50 Kilometers
Albers Equal-Area Projection

HOW TO USE YOUR TEXTBOOK

Use these built-in tools to read for understanding.

Why It Matters Today is an exciting way for you to make connections between what you are reading in your government book and the world around you. In each section, you will be invited to explore a topic that is relevant to our lives today by using CNNfyi.com connections.

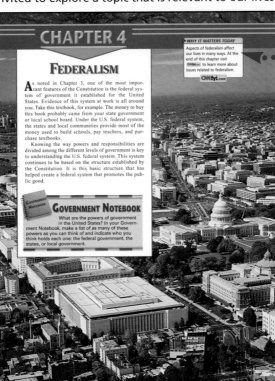

Read to Discover questions begin each section of Holt American Government. These questions serve as your guide as you read the section. Keep them in mind as you explore the section content.

Government Notebook activities invite you to explore how government concepts relate to your own life, while at the same time honing your writing skills.

Political Dictionary terms are introduced at the beginning of each section. The terms will be defined in context and are also defined on the Holt Researcher CD–ROM.

Interactive Captions accompany most of the book's rich images. Pictures are one of the most important primary sources social scientists can use to help analyze important issues. These features invite you to examine the images and make predictions about their content.

Use these review tools to pull together all the information you have learned.

Graphic Organizers will help you pull together important information from the section. You can complete the graphic organizer as a study tool to prepare for a test or writing assignment.

Homework Practice Online lets you log on to the HRW Go site to complete an interactive self-check of the material covered in the section.

Writing and Critical Thinking activities allow you to explore a section topic in greater depth and build your skills.

Building Social Studies Skills is a way for you to build your skills at analyzing information and gain practice in answering standardized-test questions.

Thinking Critically questions ask you to use the information you have learned in the chapter to extend your knowledge. You will be asked to analyze information by using your critical thinking skills.

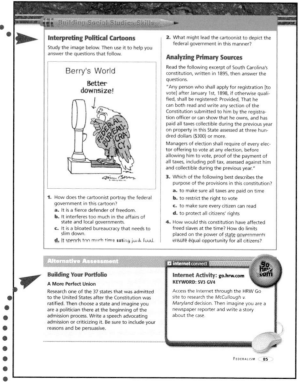

Building Your Portfolio is an exciting and creative way to demonstrate your understanding of government.

Use these online tools to review and complete online activities.

Internet Activity: go.hrw.com
KEYWORD: SV3 HP4

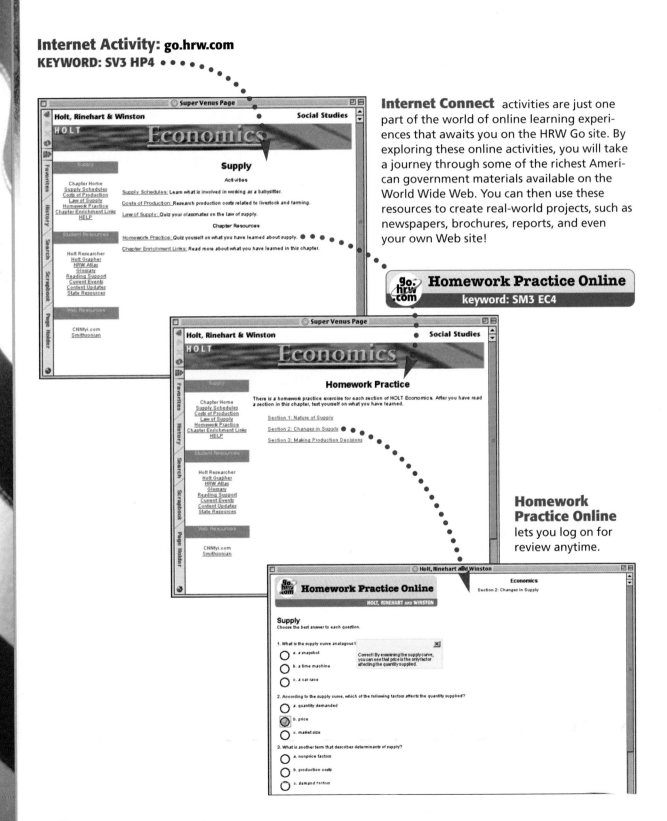

Internet Connect activities are just one part of the world of online learning experiences that awaits you on the HRW Go site. By exploring these online activities, you will take a journey through some of the richest American government materials available on the World Wide Web. You can then use these resources to create real-world projects, such as newspapers, brochures, reports, and even your own Web site!

Homework Practice Online
keyword: SM3 EC4

Homework Practice Online lets you log on for review anytime.

THEMES IN AMERICAN GOVERNMENT

Holt American Government examines the way in which government in the United States is organized and the impact that many aspects of government have on the lives of citizens. From this study of government emerges a series of themes: Political Foundations, Principles of Democracy, Constitutional Government, Political Processes, World Affairs, Citizenship, and Public Good. These themes provide a basis for defining and analyzing the U.S. political system and its effectiveness in fulfilling the needs of the public.

Political Foundations In understanding how the U.S. political system is structured, it is important to understand the connection between historical events and the framing of the Constitution. Many factors influenced the values and beliefs of the framers of the Constitution. These values and beliefs have an enduring influence through the key documents on which the U.S. political system is based.

Principles of Democracy Democratic systems of government are established to serve all of the people and to protect such democratic values as individual liberty, political representation, freedom of speech, and freedom of religion. Throughout the nation's history, changing political, economic, and social conditions have, in turn, led Americans to new interpretations of these basic democratic values. Furthermore, because of the overlapping nature of these principles, citizens, legislators, and the courts have struggled with the issue of how best to legislate for the protection of these rights. Government plays an important role in attempting to resolve conflicts over these principles.

Constitutional Government A constitution establishes regulations that strive to benefit all people in a society and to ensure that government promotes the good of society as a whole rather than that of a few individuals. In order to prevent one person or group from becoming too powerful, a constitution outlines the division of powers and responsibilities among several branches of government. A constitution also limits the power of the government and the people so that all can live in an orderly, secure environment, where basic freedoms and liberties are protected.

Political Processes The needs and desires of the citizens of the United States change. The political system must be flexible enough to meet the country's changing needs. Institutions such as political parties, elections, and public and private associations allow citizens to monitor and influence laws and the officials who write the laws.

World Affairs Thousands of governments exist around the world. The world, however, has no political system to establish relationships and to regulate interactions between countries. Throughout history, governments have used a variety of different methods to build relationships and to solve conflicts. With the development of technology that makes long-distance communication easier, international relations have become an essential role of government. Governments must choose how best to maintain foreign relationships.

Citizenship Citizens play a vital role in democratic systems of government. They are members of a self-governing community that depends upon the participation of the public to provide security and necessary services. Citizens are responsible for ensuring that government serves its purpose of protecting the fundamental rights of all people and promoting the shared good of the public.

Public Good Democratic government systems are organized to serve the needs of the people of the nation as a whole. What is good for one person or a small group may not serve the interests of the entire nation. Promoting the public good, however, also requires that government protect the rights of the minority and thus balance the needs of all people.

Sometimes, however, government does not promote the good of the people as a whole. Inefficiency, corruption, poor organization, lack of money, and changes in the needs of the people are all elements that contribute to governments' inability do what is best for the country as a whole.

Skills ★ Handbook

CRITICAL THINKING AND THE STUDY OF GOVERNMENT

Throughout *Holt American Government*, you are asked to think critically about the events and issues that have both shaped the U.S. political system and affected its place in the global community. Critical thinking is the reasoned judgment of information and ideas. People who think critically study information to determine its accuracy. They evaluate arguments and analyze conclusions before accepting their validity. Critical thinkers are able to recognize and define problems and develop strategies for resolving them.

The development of critical thinking skills is essential to effective citizenship. Such skills empower you to exercise your civic rights and responsibilities. For example, critical thinking skills enable you to judge the messages of candidates for political office and to evaluate news reports.

Helping you develop critical thinking skills is an important goal of *Holt American Government*. Using the following 14 critical thinking skills will help you better understand the forces behind political development. Additional skills strategies are in the Interactive Skill-Builder, which begins on page S16.

1 **Identifying points of view** involves identifying the factors that color the outlook of a person or group. Someone's point of view includes beliefs and attitudes that are shaped by factors such as age, sex, religion, race, and economic status. This critical thinking skill helps us examine why people see things as they do and reinforces the realization that people's views may change over time, or with a change in circumstances. A point of view that is highly personal or based on unreasoned judgment is said to be *biased*.

2 **Comparing and contrasting** involves examining events, situations, or points of view for their similarities and differences. *Comparing* focuses on both similarities and differences. Contrasting focuses only on differences. For example, by comparing democratic and nondemocratic political systems you might note that although both systems maintain different power structures, they are each established to keep order in society. By contrasting, you might note that in a democratic system the citizens are the ultimate authority in determining how the government is run. In a nondemocratic system, royal or military leaders may hold all governing power.

3 **Analyzing information** is the process of breaking something down into its parts and examining the relationships among them. By analyzing the parts, you can better understand the whole. For example, to analyze the U.S. judicial system, you might list all the levels of courts and the responsibilities of each type.

4 **Sequencing** is the process of placing events in correct chronological order to better understand the relationships among these events. You can sequence events in

U.S. presidential campaign buttons.

William Gropper's Senate Hearing *is a dramatic example of U.S. political art.*

two basic ways: according to *absolute* or *relative* chronology. Absolute chronology means that you pay close attention to the actual dates events took place. Placing events on a time line would be an example of absolute chronology. Relative chronology refers to the way events relate to one another. To put events in relative order, you need to know which one happened first, which came next, and so forth. You would only need to know enough about the dates of events to place them in order.

5 **Categorizing** is the process by which you group things together by the characteristics they have in common. By putting things or events into categories, it is easier to make comparisons and see differences among them.

6 **Summarizing** is the process of taking a large amount of information and boiling it down into a short and clear statement. Summarizing is useful when you need to give a brief account of a longer story or event. For example, it would be much more useful to summarize the events of the Great Depression than to try and reconstruct the whole story in detail.

7 **Making Generalization and Predictions** is the process of interpreting information to form more general statements and guess about what will happen next. A *generaliza-*

tion is a broad statement that holds true for a variety of events or situations. Making generalizations can help you see the "big picture" of events, rather than just focusing on details. It is very important, however, that when making generalizations you try not to include situations that do not fit the statement. When this occurs, you risk creating a stereotype, or overgeneralization. A *prediction* is an educated guess about an outcome. When you read, you should always be asking yourself questions like, "What will happen next? If this person does this, what will that mean for . . . ?", and so on. These types of questions help you draw on information you already know to see patterns in government.

8 **Drawing Inferences and Conclusions** is forming explanations for an event, a situation, or a problem. When you make an *inference,* you take information you know to be true and make an educated guess about what else you think is true about that situation. A *conclusion* is a prediction about the outcome of a situation based on what you already know. Often, you must be prepared to test your inferences and conclusions against new evidence or arguments.

9 **Problem Solving** is the process by which you pose workable solutions to difficult situations. The first step in the process is to identify a problem. Next you will need to gather information about the problem, such as its history and the various factors that contribute to it. After you have gathered information, you should list and consider the options for solving the problem. For each of the possible solutions, weigh their advantages and disadvantages and, based on your evaluation, choose and implement a solution. Once the solution is in place, go back and evaluate the effectiveness of the solution that you selected.

10 Decision Making is the process of reviewing a situation and then making decisions or recommendations for the best possible outcome. To complete the process, first identify a situation that requires a solution. Next, gather information that will help you reach a decision. You may need to do some background research to study the situation, or carefully consider the points of view of the individuals involved. Once you have done your research, identify options that might resolve the situation. For each option, predict what the possible consequences might be if that option were followed. After you have identified the best option, take action by making a recommendation and following through on any tasks that option requires.

11 Evaluating involves assessing the significance or overall importance of something, such as the success of a foreign policy or the influence of a president on society. You should base your judgment on standards that others will understand and are likely to think are important. To evaluate trade relations after the adoption of the North American Free Trade Agreement (NAFTA), for example, you might examine attitudes toward the condition of the U.S., Canadian, and Mexican economies. You also would assess the improvement, or lack of substantive improvement, in the economies of and political relationships among these countries.

12 Supporting a point of view means identifying an issue, deciding what you think about it, and persuasively expressing your position on it. Your stand should be based on specific information. In supporting a point of view, state your position clearly and give reasons to support it.

13 Studying contemporary issues and problems involves identifying a current topic frequently discussed in the media, reading several sources of information on the topic, and evaluating that information. Finding space for all the trash people create, for example, is a contemporary problem with which you may be familiar. You might feel the effects of it through recycling programs in your community or school. By studying this issue, you will be able to understand the cause of excess waste and evaluate solutions others have developed to ease the problem.

14 Applying a model involves depicting something in its ideal state and evaluating how well a specific example matches the ideal. A model of an ideal democratic system, for example, might be applied to the political system of Mexico. By evaluating how well each element of Mexico's political system matches each element of your model, you can determine whether Mexico has a democratic system of government or how closely it matches an ideal system.

Newspapers are an excellent source of information about contemporary issues in government and politics.

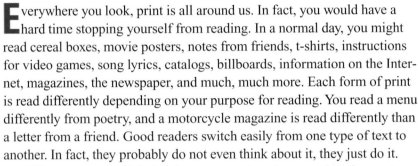

READING STRATEGIES

Becoming a Strategic Reader

by Dr. Judith Irvin

Everywhere you look, print is all around us. In fact, you would have a hard time stopping yourself from reading. In a normal day, you might read cereal boxes, movie posters, notes from friends, t-shirts, instructions for video games, song lyrics, catalogs, billboards, information on the Internet, magazines, the newspaper, and much, much more. Each form of print is read differently depending on your purpose for reading. You read a menu differently from poetry, and a motorcycle magazine is read differently than a letter from a friend. Good readers switch easily from one type of text to another. In fact, they probably do not even think about it, they just do it.

When you read, it is helpful to use a strategy to remember the most important ideas. You can use a strategy before you read to help connect information you already know to the new information you will encounter. Before you read, you can also predict what a text will be about by using a previewing strategy. During the reading you can use a strategy to help you focus on main ideas, and after reading you can use a strategy to help you organize what you learned so that you can remember it later. *Holt American Government* was designed to help you more easily understand the ideas you read. Important reading strategies employed in *Holt American Government* include:

A Tools to help you **preview and predict** what the text will be about

B Ways to help you **use and analyze visual information**

C Ideas to help you **organize the information** you have learned

A. Previewing and Predicting

How can I figure out what the text is about before I even start reading a section?

Previewing and **predicting** are good methods to help you understand the text. If you take the time to preview and predict before you read, the text will make more sense to you during your reading.

1 Usually, your teacher will set the purpose for reading. After reading some new information, you may be asked to write a summary, take a test, or complete some other type of activity.

"After reading about Congress, you will work with a partner to create a schedule and . . ."

Previewing and Predicting

step 1 Identify your purpose for reading. Ask yourself what you will do with this information once you have finished reading.

▼

step 2 Ask yourself what is the main idea of the text and what are the key vocabulary words you need to know.

▼

step 3 Use signal words to help identify the structure of the text.

▼

step 4 Connect the information to what you already know.

2 As you preview the text, use **graphic signals** such as headings, subheadings, and boldface type to help you determine what is important in the text. Each section of *Holt American Government* opens by giving you important clues to help you preview the material.

Looking at the section's **main heading** and sub-headings can give you an idea of what is to come.

Read to Discover questions give you clues as to the section's main ideas.

Political Dictionary terms let you know the key vocabulary you will encounter in the section.

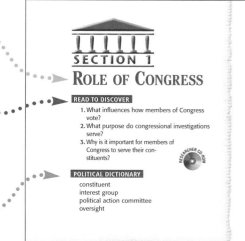

SECTION 1
ROLE OF CONGRESS

READ TO DISCOVER
1. What influences how members of Congress vote?
2. What purpose do congressional investigations serve?
3. Why is it important for members of Congress to serve their constituents?

POLITICAL DICTIONARY
constituent
interest group
political action committee
oversight

older people have contributed a lot of money to the member's campaign fund. The leadership of the member's political party supports the legislation. Thus, the decision to support increases in Social Security benefits is easy.

Many times, however, the decisions facing members of Congress are not so easy because the forces influencing a member's vote can conflict. How do members make decisions in these more difficult situations? They must weigh the conflicting influences—in particular, their personal beliefs, constituents' interests, interest groups' concerns, and political party loyalty. The power of these influences varies from issue to issue and from member to member.

Personal Beliefs Studies show that a congressperson's personal beliefs about what promotes the public good significantly influence his or her voting decisions. Members sometimes follow their personal beliefs even when those beliefs go against the wishes of voters back home.

In 1990 many members of Congress voted against a constitutional amendment that would

3 Other tools that can help you in previewing are **signal words**. These words prepare you to think in a certain way. For example, when you see words such as *similar to*, *same as*, or *different from*, you know that the text will probably compare and contrast two or more ideas. Signal words indicate how the ideas in the text relate to each other. Look at the list below for some of the most common signal words grouped by the type of text structures they include.

SIGNAL WORDS

Cause and Effect	Compare and Contrast	Description	Problem and Solution	Sequence or Chronological Order
because since consequently this led to...so if...then nevertheless accordingly because of as a result of in order to may be due to for this reason not only...but	different from same as similar to as opposed to instead of although however compared with as well as either...or but on the other hand unless	for instance for example such as to illustrate in addition most importantly another furthermore first, second ...	the question is a solution one answer is	not long after next then initially before after finally preceding following on (date) over the years today when

4 Learning something new requires that you connect it in some way with something you already know. This means you have to think before you read and while you read. You may want to use a chart like this one to remind yourself of the information already familiar to you and to come up with questions you want answered in your reading. The chart will also help you organize your ideas after you have finished reading.

What I know	What I want to know	What I learned

B. Use and Analyze Visual Information

How can all the pictures, maps, graphs, and political cartoons with the text help me be a stronger reader?

Using visual information can help you understand and remember the information presented in *Holt American Government*. Good readers make a picture in their mind when they read. The pictures, charts, graphs, political cartoons, and diagrams that occur throughout *Holt American Government* are placed strategically to increase your understanding.

1 You might ask yourself questions like these:

> Why did the writer include this image with the text?
>
> What details about this image are mentioned in the text?

2 After you have read the text, see if you can answer your own questions.

Analyzing Visual Information

step 1 As you preview the text, ask yourself how the visual information relates to the text.
▼
step 2 Generate questions based on the visual information.
▼
step 3 After reading the text, go back and review the visual information again.
▼
step 4 Connect the information to what you already know.

→ What are the people in this picture doing?

→ When was this picture likely taken?

→ What does this image tell me about American Government?

2 Maps, graphs, and charts help you organize information about a place. You might ask questions like these:

→ What is this a chart of?

→ What information was used to create the graph?

→ Why do some curves dip down on the right side of the graph?

Top 10 Countries in Military Spending

Country	Billions of U.S. Dollars
1. United States	$265.9
2. Russia	$53.9
3. France	$39.8
4. Japan	$37.0
5. China	$36.7
6. United Kingdom	$36.6
7. Germany	$32.4
8. Italy	$22.6
9. Brazil	$18.1
10. Taiwan	$13.9

(Figures are for 1998.)

Source: *World Almanac:* 2001

How do this graph and table support what I have read in the text?

What is the significance of each graph and table?

Number of Political Action Committees, 1975–2001

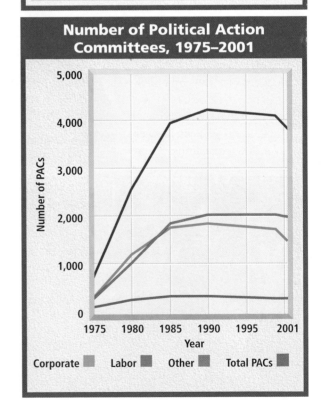

Corporate ■   Labor ■   Other ■   Total PACs ■

3 After reading the text, go back and review the visual information again.

4 Connect the information to what you already know.

C. Organize Information

Once I learn new information, how do I keep it all straight so that I will remember it?

To help you remember what you have read, you need to find a way of **organizing information**. Two good ways of doing this are by using graphic organizers and concept maps. **Graphic organizers** help you understand important relationships—such as cause-and-effect, compare/contrast, sequence of events, and problem/solution—within the text. **Concept maps** provide a useful tool to help you focus on the text's main ideas and organize supporting details.

Identifying Relationships

Using graphic organizers will help you recall important ideas from the section and give you a study tool you can use to prepare for a quiz or test or to help with a writing assignment. Some of the most common types of graphic organizers are shown below.

▶ Cause and Effect

Economic events cause people to react in a certain way. Cause-and-effect patterns show the relationship between results and the ideas or events that made the results occur. You may want to represent cause-and-effect relationships as one cause leading to multiple effects,

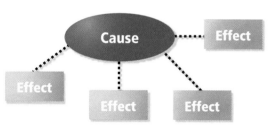

or as a chain of cause-and-effect relationships.

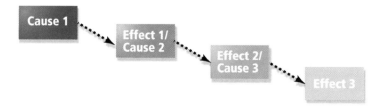

Constructing Graphic Organizers

step 1 Preview the text, looking for signal words and the main idea.

▼

step 2 Form a hypothesis as to which type of graphic organizer would work best to display the information presented.

▼

step 3 Work individually or with your classmates to create a visual representation of what you read.

◗ Comparing and Contrasting

Graphic Organizers are often useful when you are comparing or contrasting information. Compare-and-contrast diagrams point out similarities and differences between two concepts or ideas.

Characteristics | Shared Characteristics | Characteristics

◗ Sequencing

Keeping track of dates and the order in which events took place is essential to understanding end results. Sequence or chronological-order diagrams show events or ideas in the order in which they happened.

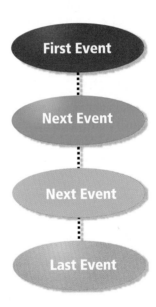

First Event

Next Event

Next Event

Last Event

◗ Problem and Solution

Problem-solution patterns identify at least one problem, offer one or more solutions to the problem, and explain or predict outcomes of the solutions.

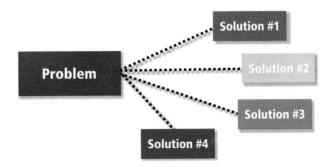

Problem

Solution #1

Solution #2

Solution #3

Solution #4

Identifying Main Ideas and Supporting Details

One special type of graphic organizer is the concept map. A concept map, sometimes called a semantic map, allows you to zero in on the most important points of the text. The map is made up of lines, boxes, circles, and/or arrows. It can be as simple or as complex as you need it to be to accurately represent the text.

Here are a few examples of concept maps you might use.

Constructing Concept Maps

step 1 Preview the text, looking at what type of structure might be appropriate to display on a concept map.
▼
step 2 Taking note of the headings, bold-faced type, and text structure, sketch a concept map you think could best illustrate the text.
▼
step 3 Using boxes, lines, arrows, circles, or any shapes you like, display the ideas of the text in the concept map.

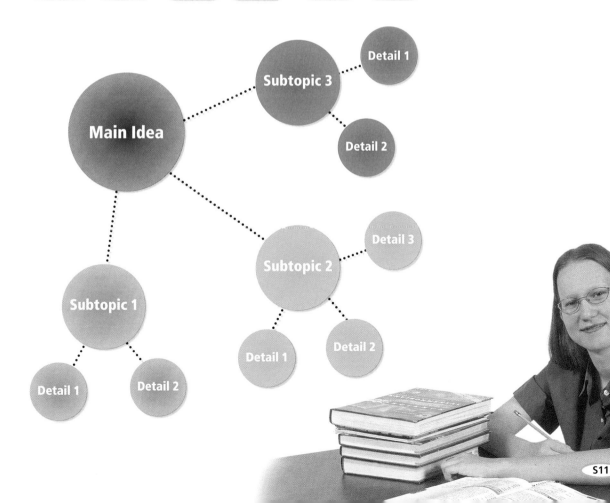

Standardized Test-Taking Strategies

A number of times throughout your school career, you may be asked to take standardized tests. These tests are designed to demonstrate the content and skills you have learned. It is important to keep in mind that in most cases the best way to prepare for these tests is to pay close attention in class and take every opportunity to improve your general social studies, reading, writing, and mathematical skills.

Tips for Taking the Test

1. Be sure that you are well rested.
2. Be on time, and be sure that you have the necessary materials.
3. Listen to the teacher's instructions.
4. Read directions and questions carefully.
5. **DON'T STRESS!** Just remember what you have learned in class, and you should do well.

Practice the strategies at go.hrw.com ·······

Tackling Social Studies

The social studies portions of many standardized tests are designed to test your knowledge of the content and skills that you have been studying in one or more of your social studies classes. Specific objectives for the test vary, but some of the most common include the following:

1. demonstrate an understanding of issues and events in history;
2. demonstrate an understanding of geographic influences on historical issues and events;
3. demonstrate an understanding of economic and social influences on historical issues and events;
4. demonstrate an understanding of political influences on historical issues and events;
5. use critical thinking skills to analyze social studies information.

Standardized tests usually contain multiple-choice and, sometimes, open-ended questions. The multiple-choice items will often be based on maps, tables, charts, graphs, pictures, cartoons, and/or reading passages and documents.

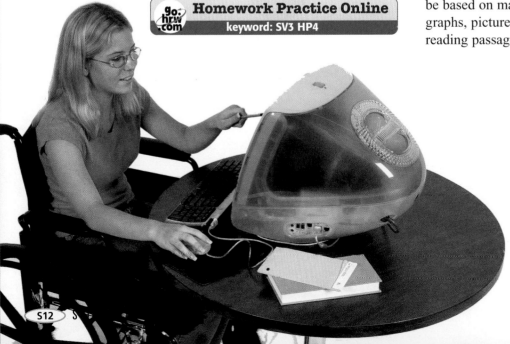

go.hrw.com **Homework Practice Online**
keyword: SV3 HP4

Tips for Answering Multiple-Choice Questions

1. If there is a written or visual piece accompanying the multiple-choice question, pay careful attention to the title, author, and date.

2. Then read through or glance over the content of the written or visual piece accompanying the question to familiarize yourself with it.

3. Next, read the multiple-choice question first for its general intent. Then reread it carefully, looking for words that give clues or can limit possible answers to the question. For example, words such as *most* or *best* tell you that there may be several correct answers to a question, but you should look for the most appropriate answer.

4. Read through the answer choices. Always read all of the possible answer choices even if the first one seems like the correct answer. There may be a better choice farther down in the list.

5. Reread the accompanying information (if any is included) carefully to determine the answer to the question. Again, note the title, author, and date of primary-source selections. The answer will rarely be stated exactly as it appears in the primary source, so you will need to use your critical thinking skills to read between the lines.

6. Think of what you already know about the time in history or person involved and use that to help limit the answer choices.

7. Finally, reread the question and selected answer to be sure that you made the best choice and that you marked it correctly on the answer sheet.

Strategies for Success

There are a variety of strategies you can prepare ahead of time to help you feel more confident about answering questions on social studies standardized tests. Here are a few suggestions:

1. Adopt an acronym—a word formed from the first letters of other words—that you will use for analyzing a document or visual piece that accompanies a question.

Helpful Acronyms

For a document, use SOAPS, which stands for

S Subject
O Overview
A Audience
P Purpose
S Speaker/author

For a picture, cartoon, map, or other visual piece of information, use OPTIC, which stands for

O Occasion (or time)
P Parts (labels or details of the visual)
T Title
I Interrelations (how the different parts of the visual work together)
C Conclusion (what the visual means)

2. Form visual images of maps and try to draw them from memory. Standardized tests will most likely include maps showing many features, such as states, countries, continents, and oceans. Those maps may also show patterns in settlement and the size and distribution of cities. For example, in studying the United States, be able to see in your mind's eye such things as where the states and major cities are located. Know major physical features, such as the Mississippi River, the Appalachian and Rocky Mountains, the Great Plains, and the various regions of the United States, and be able to place them on a map. Such features may help you understand patterns in the distribution of population and the size of settlements.

3. When you have finished studying a geographic region or period in history, try to think of who or what might be important enough for a standardized test. You may want to keep your ideas in a notebook to refer to when it is almost time for the test.

4. Standardized tests will likely test your understanding of the political, economic, and social processes that shape a region's history, culture, and geography. Questions may also

ask you to understand the impact of geographic factors on major events. For example, some may ask about the effects of migration and immigration on various societies and population change. In addition, questions may test your understanding of the ways humans interact with their environment.

5. For the skills area of the tests, practice putting major events and personalities in order in your mind. Sequencing people and events by dates can become a game you play with a friend who also has to take the test. Always ask yourself "why" this event is important.

6. Follow the tips under "Ready for Reading" below when you encounter a reading passage in social studies, but remember that what you have learned about government can help you in answering reading-comprehension questions.

Ready for Reading

The main goal of the reading sections of most standardized tests is to determine your understanding of different aspects of a piece of writing. Basically, if you can grasp the main idea and the writer's purpose and then pay attention to the details and vocabulary so that you are able to draw inferences and conclusions, you will do well on the test.

Tips for Answering Multiple-Choice Questions

1. Read the passage as if you were not taking a test.

2. Look at the big picture. Ask yourself questions like, "What is the title?", "What do the illustrations or pictures tell me?", and "What is the writer's purpose?"

3. Read the questions. This will help you know what information to look for.

4. Reread the passage, underlining information related to the questions.

5. Go back to the questions and try to answer each one in your mind before looking at the answers.

6. Read all the answer choices and eliminate the ones that are obviously incorrect.

Types of Multiple-Choice Questions

1. **Main Idea** This is the most important point of the passage. After reading the passage, locate and underline the main idea.

2. **Significant Details** You will often be asked to recall details from the passage. Read the question and underline the details as you read, but remember that the correct answers do not always match the wording of the passage precisely.

3. **Vocabulary** You will often need to define a word within the context of the passage. Read the answer choices and plug them into the sentence to see what fits best.

4. **Conclusion and Inference** There are often important ideas in the passage that the writer does not state directly. Sometimes you must consider multiple parts of the passage to answer the question. If answers refer to only one or two sentences or details in the passage, they are probably incorrect.

Tips for Answering Short-Answer Questions

1. Read the passage in its entirety, paying close attention to the main events and characters. Jot down information you think is important.

2. If you cannot answer a question, skip it and come back later.

3. Words such as *compare, contrast, interpret, discuss,* and *summarize* appear often in short-answer questions. Be sure you have a complete understanding of each of these words.

4. To help support your answer, return to the passage and skim the parts you underlined.

5. Organize your thoughts on a separate sheet of paper. Write a general statement with which to begin. This will be your topic statement.

6. When writing your answer, be precise but brief. Be sure to refer to details in the passage in your answer.

Targeting Writing

On many standardized tests, you will occasionally be asked to write an essay. In order to write a concise essay, you must learn to organize your thoughts before you begin writing the actual composition. This keeps you from straying too far from the essay's topic.

Tips for Answering Composition Questions

1. Read the question carefully.

2. Decide what kind of essay you are being asked to write. Essays usually fall into one of the following types: persuasive, classificatory, compare/contrast, or "how to." To determine the type of essay, ask yourself questions like, "Am I trying to persuade my audience?", "Am I comparing or contrasting ideas?", or "Am I trying to show the reader how to do something?"

3. Pay attention to keywords, such as *compare, contrast, describe, advantages, disadvantages, classify,* or *speculate.* They will give you clues as to the structure that your essay should follow.

4. Organize your thoughts on a separate sheet of paper. You will want to come up with a general topic sentence that expresses your main idea. Make sure this sentence addresses the question. You should then create an outline or some type of graphic organizers to help you organize the points that support your topic sentence.

5. Write your composition using complete sentences. Also, be sure to use correct grammar, spelling, punctuation, and sentence structure.

6. Be sure to proofread your essay once you have finished writing.

Gearing Up for Math

On most standardized tests you will be asked to solve a variety of mathematical problems that draw on the skills and information you have learned in class. If math problems sometimes give you difficulty, have a look at the tips below to help you work through the problems.

Tips for Solving Math Problems

1. Decide what is the goal of the question. Read or study the problem carefully and determine what information must be found.

2. Locate the factual information. Decide what information represents key facts—the ones you must have to solve the problem. You may also find facts you do not need to reach your solution. In some cases, you may determine that more information is needed to solve the problem. If so, ask yourself, "What assumptions can I make about this problem?" or "Do I need a formula to help solve this problem?"

3. Decide what strategies you might use to solve the problem, how you might use them, and what form your solution will be in. For example, will you need to create a graph or chart? Will you need to solve an equation? Will your answer be in words or numbers? By knowing what type of solution you should reach, you may be able to eliminate some of the choices.

4. Apply your strategy to solve the problem and compare your answer to the choices.

5. If the answer is still not clear, read the problem again. If you had to make calculations to reach your answer, use estimation to see if your answer makes sense.

Government is entwined in almost every aspect of our daily lives. To grasp this relationship, you will need to understand the forces that shape government. The skills covered in this handbook will enable you to analyze government systems and policies. The handbook will also introduce you to key sources of government information, which can be presented in a variety of forms. Your understanding and appreciation of government will grow as your study skills improve. Your study of government will also provide you with opportunities to sharpen your research, writing, and test-taking abilities.

1 FINDING THE MAIN IDEA

In the study of government, significant events and concepts sometimes get lost among surrounding issues. A key to understanding any complex issue is the ability to identify its central elements. This book is designed to help you focus on the most important concepts in government. The objectives at the beginning of each section are intended to guide your reading, and the chapter summary reinforces the main ideas presented.

How to Identify the Main Idea

Read introductory material. Read the title and the introduction, if there is one, which may point out the material's main ideas.

Have questions in mind. Formulate questions that you think might be answered by the material. Having such questions in mind will focus your reading.

Note the outline of ideas. Pay attention to any headings or subheadings, which may provide a basic outline of the major ideas.

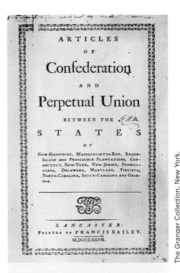

The Granger Collection, New York.

Identifying the main idea is critical to understanding the meaning of documents such as the Articles of Confederation.

Distinguish supporting details. As you read, distinguish sentences providing additional details from the general statements they support. A trail of facts, for instance, may lead to a conclusion that expresses a main idea.

Applying Your Skill

Read the paragraph below, from the Chapter 13 subsection titled "Balancing Rights and Interests to Promote the Public Good" to identify its main idea.

❝ Although the Constitution guarantees civil liberties, it does not guarantee absolute freedom to do as one wishes. The freedom to assemble with others in pursuit of a goal, for example, does not give people the freedom to riot or to destroy property, which would violate other people's right to safety and protection of their property. Recognizing the responsibilities that come with freedom is part of being a good citizen. ❞

As the lead sentence indicates, the paragraph focuses on limits to the personal freedoms guaranteed in the Constitution. Details are included to illustrate this concept—for example, the fact that the constitutional freedom of a group of people to assemble does not give them the right to riot, to harm others or their property, or to violate other people's right to safety. The main idea—that people who are good citizens generally respect the rights of others while exercising their constitutional freedoms—is most clearly stated in the concluding sentence—recognizing the responsibilities that come with freedom is part of being a citizen.

Practicing Your Skill

Read the first paragraph of the subsection "Assembly and Private Property" on page 313 of Chapter 13, and answer the following questions.

1. What is the paragraph's main idea? How does the writer support that idea?
2. What is the relationship between the main ideas in this paragraph and the one excerpted on the previous page? Combine the main ideas of both paragraphs into one statement that summarizes both of them.

② IDENTIFYING CAUSE AND EFFECT

Identifying and understanding cause-and-effect relationships is fundamental to interpreting government concepts. A *cause* is any action that leads to an event; the outcome of that action is an *effect*. To investigate both why an event took place and what happened as a result of it, political scientists ask questions such as What is the immediate activity that triggered the event? and What is the event? Your task is simpler than political scientists': to trace what he or she has already determined or theorized about the web of actions and results.

How to Identify Cause and Effect

Look for clues. Certain words and phrases are immediate clues to the existence of a cause-and-effect relationship.

Identify the relationship. Read carefully to identify how events are related. Writers do not always directly state the link between cause and effect. Sometimes a reader has to infer the cause or the effect.

Check for complex connections. Beyond the superficial, or immediate, cause and effect, check for other, more complex connections. Note, for example, whether (1) there were additional causes leading to a given effect; (2) a cause had multiple effects; and (3) the effects in turn caused any additional effects.

Applying Your Skill

The diagram below presents a cause-and-effect relationship in the problems surrounding U.S. and Soviet actions during the Cuban missile crisis. Note how an effect becomes a cause.

Cause and Effect Clues	
CAUSE	**EFFECT**
as a result of	aftermath
because	as a consequence
brought about	depended on
inspired	gave rise to
led to	originated from
provoked	outcome
produced	outgrowth
spurred	proceeded from
the reason	resulting in

CAUSE
The Soviet Union began secretly installing nuclear weapons in Cuba.

⬇

EFFECT/CAUSE
President Kennedy announced a naval blockade to stop ships carrying missiles to Cuba.

⬇

EFFECT
The Soviets agreed to withdraw the missiles.

Practicing Your Skill Answers

1. The main idea is that the First Amendment's right of assembly does not give people the right to use other people's property. The writer supports this by pointing out the Supreme Court's ruling on the issue in *Lloyd* v. *Tanner*.

2. The ideas are related because the one on the previous page points out that in general people must respect others' rights while exercising their constitutional freedoms, while the one on page 313 gives an example of a specific limitation being placed on a constitutional freedom. Combinations of sentences will vary but students should successfully combine both ideas into one sentence. Students should display an understanding of both paragraphs and should combine them in a sentence.

Practicing Your Skill
Answers

Charts and paragraphs will vary but students should clearly identify a process that has a cause-and-effect relationship and show the relationship between the actions and the outcomes.

Practicing Your Skill
Answers

1. Yes, the first and last statements can be proven to be true.

2. The sentence uses the word "unreasonable."

3. Yes, it points out that she voted in favor of 20 bills to increase funding for public education.

Practicing Your Skill

From your knowledge of the U.S. government, choose a political process that you believe to be shaped by cause-and-effect relationships. Draw a chart showing the relationships between the actions and the outcomes. Then write a paragraph explaining the connections.

❸ DISTINGUISHING FACT FROM OPINION

The ability to distinguish facts from opinions is essential in judging the soundness of an argument or the reliability of a political analysis. A fact can be proven or observed; an opinion, on the other hand, is a personal belief or conclusion. Thus, in an argument, opinions do not carry as much weight as facts, although some opinions can be supported by facts. One often hears facts and opinions mixed in everyday conversation as well as in advertising, political debate, and government policy statements.

How to Distinguish Fact from Opinion

Identify the facts. Begin by asking yourself whether the statement at hand can be verified. Determine whether it can be checked for accuracy in a source such as an almanac or encyclopedia. If so, it is probably factual. If not, it probably contains an opinion.

Identify the opinions. Look for clues that signal statements of opinion—for example, phrases such as *I think* or *I believe*. Comparative words like *greatest* or *more important* and value-laden words like *extremely* or *ridiculous* imply a judgment, and thus an opinion.

Applying Your Skill

Assessments of a document like the Constitution often mix fact and opinion. For example, read the following description of the Constitution, taken from a speech by Franklin D. Roosevelt:

❝ Our Constitution is so simple and practical that it is possible always to meet extraordinary needs by changes in emphasis and arrangement without loss of essential form. That is why our constitutional system has proved itself the most superbly enduring political mechanism the modern world has produced. It has met every stress of vast expansion of territory, of foreign wars, of bitter internal strife, of world relations. ❞

Roosevelt's assessment—that the U.S. Constitution is nearly perfect and superior to other devices for organizing a government system—is an opinion. Note Roosevelt's use of value-laden words and phrasing: *so simple, practical, possible always, extraordinary, most superbly, met every stress.*

Practicing Your Skill

Read the campaign advertisement and answer the questions below.

1. Can any of the statements in the advertisement be proved true?

2. What word does this advertisement use to describe the type of tax increases that Smart has voted against?

3. Does the advertisement provide any facts about Smart's voting record?

Teresa Smart
for U.S. Senate

According to recent studies, the public considers experience and a consistent voting record to be the most important qualifications of a senator.

- Smart has served in the U.S. Senate for eight years.
- Smart has voted against all legislation that calls for unreasonable tax increases.
- Smart voted in favor of 20 bills to increase funding for public education.

Elect Teresa Smart
She Is the Voice of Experience

4 BUILDING VOCABULARY

Studying government may challenge your reading comprehension as you encounter many new words. However, you can master new words and expand your vocabulary. Following the steps outlined below will assist you in this endeavor.

How to Build Vocabulary

Identify unusual words. As you read, be aware of words that you cannot pronounce or define. Keep a list of these words. Words that are somewhat familiar are the easiest to learn.

Study context clues. Study the sentence and paragraph where you find each new term. This *context*, or setting, may give you clues to the word's meaning. The word may be defined by either an example or another more familiar word that has the same or similar meaning.

Use the dictionary. Use a dictionary to help you pronounce and define the words on your list.

Review new vocabulary. Look for ways to use the new words—in homework assignments, conversation, or classroom discussions. The best way to master a new word is to use it.

Practicing Your Skill

1. What is context? How can it provide clues to a word's meaning?
2. As you read a chapter, list any unusual words that you find. Write down what you think each word means, and then check the definitions you wrote against those in a dictionary.
3. Use each of the words in your list at least one time. Try to think of ways in which you can use each word in everyday conversation.

5 CONDUCTING RESEARCH

To complete research papers or special projects, you may need to use resources beyond this textbook. For example, you may want to research specific subjects or government organizations not discussed here, or to learn additional information about a certain topic. Doing such research typically involves using the resources available in a library.

How to Find Information

To find a particular book, you need to know how libraries organize their materials. Books of fiction are alphabetized according to the last name of the author. To classify nonfiction books, libraries use the Dewey decimal system and the Library of Congress system. Both systems assign each book a *call number* that indicates where it is shelved.

To find a particular book's call number, look in the library's card catalog. The catalog lists books by author, title, and subject. If you know the author or title of the book, finding it is an easy task. If you do not know this information, or if you just want to find any book about a general subject, look under an applicable subject heading. Many libraries have computerized card catalogs. These catalogs generally contain the same information as a traditional card catalog, but

The general theory of employment, interest, and money
  by *John Maynard Keynes.*
  San Diego : Harcourt, Brace, Jovanovich, 1964 [1991 printing]
  xii, 403 p. : ill. ; 21 cm.
  Originally published: 1953.
  "A Harvest/HBJ book."
  Includes bibliographical references and index.
Subjects:
  Economics.
  Money.
  Monetary policy.
  Interest.
Search for other works by:
  Keynes, John Maynard, 1883-1946.

Language	Call Number	LCCN	Dewey Decimal	ISBN/ISSN
English (eng)	HB99.7 .K378 1964	91006533 //r91	330.15/6	0156347113 : $8.95

take up less space and are easier to update and to access.

Librarians can assist you in using the card catalog and direct you to a book's location. They also can suggest additional resources. Many libraries now rely on computerized resources and have access to the Internet. Specialized sources such as the *Holt Researcher Online: Economy and Government* also provide access to statistics and other government information.

Many research projects require the use of library resources.

How to Use Resources

In a library's reference section, you will find encyclopedias, specialized dictionaries, atlases, almanacs, and indexes to recent material in magazines and newspapers. Encyclopedias often will be the most readily available resource. Encyclopedias include economic, political, and geographical data on individual nations, states, and cities, as well as biographical sketches of important historical figures. Entries in these books often include cross-references to related articles.

To find up-to-date facts about a subject, you can use almanacs, yearbooks, and periodical indexes. References like *The World Almanac and Book of Facts* include government information and a variety of statistics. Encyclopedia yearbooks keep up with recent, significant developments not fully covered in encyclopedia articles.

Periodical indexes, such as the *Readers' Guide to Periodical Literature*, can help you locate current articles published in magazines. *The New York Times Index* catalogs the articles published in the *Times,* the U.S. daily newspaper with perhaps the most in-depth coverage of U.S. and world events.

Practicing Your Skill

1. In what two ways are nonfiction books classified?
2. What kinds of references contain information about government?
3. Where would you look to find the most recent coverage of a political or social issue?

⑥ ANALYZING PRIMARY SOURCES

There are many sources of firsthand political information, including editorials, policy statements, and legal documents. All of these are primary sources. Newspaper reports and editorial cartoons also are considered to be primary sources, although they are generally written after the fact. Because they permit a close-up look at the past—a chance to get inside people's minds—primary sources are valuable historical tools.

Secondary sources are descriptions or interpretations of events written after the events have

occurred by persons who did not participate in the events they describe. Government books such as *Holt American Government,* biographies, encyclopedias, and other reference works are examples of secondary sources.

How to Analyze Primary Sources

Study the material carefully. Consider the nature of the material. Is it verbal or visual? Is it based on firsthand information or on the accounts of others? Note the major ideas and supporting details.

Consider the audience. Ask yourself: For whom was this message originally intended? Whether a message was intended, for instance, for the general public or for a specific, private audience may have shaped its style or content.

Check for bias. Watch for words or phrases that present a one-sided view of a person or situation.

When possible, compare sources. Study more than one source on a topic. Comparing sources gives you a more complete, balanced account.

Practicing Your Skill

1. What distinguishes secondary sources from primary sources?
2. What advantage do primary sources have over secondary sources?
3. Of the following, identify which are primary sources and which are secondary sources: a newspaper, a biography, an editorial cartoon, a deed to property, a snapshot of a family vacation, a magazine article about the government system of Brazil. Think about the distinctions between primary and secondary sources. How might some of these sources prove to be both primary and secondary sources?

7 WRITING ABOUT GOVERNMENT

The Section Reviews, Chapter Reviews, and Unit Labs in *Holt American Government* present several writing opportunities. Following the guidelines below will improve your writing about government as well as other subjects.

How to Write with a Purpose

Always keep your purpose for writing in mind. That purpose might be to analyze, evaluate, synthesize, inform, persuade, hypothesize, or take a stand. As you begin your assignment, your purpose will determine the most appropriate approach to take, and when you are finished, it will help you evaluate your success.

Each purpose for writing requires its own form, tone, and content. The point of view you are adopting will shape what you write, as will your intended audience—whoever will be reading what you write.

Some writing assignments in *Holt American Government* ask you to write in a specific manner. For example, you might be required to create a brochure, a newspaper editorial, or an advertisement.

★ A **brochure** is a booklet containing descriptive, educational, or advertising material. Its purpose is to inform people or to promote an idea, a product, a service, or an event.

★ A newspaper **editorial** is a public statement of an opinion or a viewpoint. It takes a stand on an issue and gives reasons for that stand.
★ An **advertisement** is an announcement to promote a product or an event. Effective ads are direct and to the point, and use memorable language, such as jingles and slogans, to highlight important features.

How to Write a Paper or an Essay

Each writing opportunity will have specific directions about what and how to write. Regardless of the particular topic you choose, you should follow certain basic steps.

There are five major stages to writing a paper or essay: prewriting, creating an outline, writing a first draft, evaluating and revising the draft, and proofreading and producing the final paper. Each stage can be further organized into more specific steps and tasks. The guidelines outlined below can help improve your writing abilities.

Prewriting

Choose a topic. Select a topic for your paper. Take care to narrow your subject so that you will be able to develop and support a clear argument.

Identify your purpose for writing the essay or paper. Read the directions for the assignment carefully to identify the purpose for your writing. Keep that purpose in mind as you plan and write your paper.

Determine your audience. When writing for a specific audience, choose the tone and style that will best communicate your message.

Collect information. Write down your ideas and the information you already know about your topic, and do additional research if necessary. Your writing will be more effective if you have many details at hand.

Creating an Outline

Make a plan before you begin writing your first draft. Organize themes, main ideas, and supporting details into an outline. Review your purpose for writing and evaluate whether your outline accomplishes these goals.

Order your material. Decide what you want to emphasize. Order your material with that in mind. Determine what type of information belongs in an introduction, what belongs in the body of your paper, and what to leave for the conclusion.

The President's Roles

I. Chief Executive
   A. Head of the executive branch
   B. Responsible for carrying out the nation's laws
II. Commander in Chief
   A. Head of the U.S. armed forces
      1. Commands all military officers
      2. Not responsible for leading troops into battle
   B. Has final say in wartime decisions
III. Chief Agenda Setter
   A. Delivers several messages a year to Congress
   B. Delivers a State of the Union Address annually
   C. Sends Congress a budget plan
      1. Recommends how Congress should raise money
      2. Recommends how money should be spent
IV. Representative of the Nation
   A. Lobbies Congress on behalf of all Americans
   B. Gives support during times of crisis

Identify main ideas. Identify the main ideas to be highlighted in each section. Make these the main headings of your outline.

List supporting details. Determine the important details or facts that support each main idea. Rank and list them as subheadings, using additional levels of subheadings as necessary. Never break a category into subheadings unless there are at least two: no *A*s without *B*s, no *1*s without *2*s.

Put your outline to use. Structure your paper or essay according to your outline. Each main heading, for instance, might form the basis for a topic sentence to begin a paragraph. Subheadings would then make up the content of the paragraph. In a more lengthy paper, each subheading might be the main idea of a paragraph.

Writing the Draft

In your first draft, remember to use your outline as a guide. Each paragraph should express one main idea or set of related ideas, with details added for support. Be careful to show the relationships between ideas and to use proper *transitions*—sentences that build connections between paragraphs.

Evaluating and Revising the Draft

Review and edit. Revise and reorganize the draft as needed. Improve sentences by adding appropriate adjectives and adverbs. Omit words, sentences, or paragraphs that are unnecessary or unrelated to the main idea.

Evaluate your writing style. Make your writing clearer by varying the sentence length and rephrasing awkward sentences. Replace inexact wording with more precise word choices.

Proofreading and Publishing

Proofread carefully. Check for proper spelling, punctuation, and grammar. Then prepare a neat and clean final version. Appearance is important. It can affect the way your writing is perceived and understood.

Practicing Your Skill

1. What factor—more than any other—should affect how and what you write? Why?
2. Why is it important to consider the audience for your writing?
3. What is involved in the evaluating and revising of a first draft?
4. How can you make your writing clearer? In what ways might varying sentence length improve the quality of writing in your paper or essay?

8 LEARNING FROM VISUALS

Visuals are graphic images that can provide information about culture and society. These clues are available in a broad range of formats, including photographs, paintings, television, Web sites, and political cartoons. Visual images record diverse data. To extract this data, you must carefully examine the details in the image.

How to Study Visuals

Identify the subject. Look at the content of the picture. What is the main focus? For example, is it a group of people, a building, or a particular event? Who is the intended audience? What do you think the creator of the image is trying to convey? Read the title or captions or listen to the dialogue to pick up clues to its subject matter.

Examine the details. Gather subtle information from the image. Are there clues about time or place? Look at details such as clothing style, architecture, and the arrangement of the image's components to further evaluate its effect and meaning.

Identify the tone. Most people think that visuals present only facts. A visual image, however, also exposes feelings about a subject. What do the images reveal about people's feelings? How do you feel when you look at the picture? Does it make you laugh or feel sad or angry? Try to identify what specific elements in the image evoke your response.

Put the data to use. Combine the information you gather from the visual images and written or spoken words to analyze a particular subject.

Images such as political cartoons provide valuable clues about U.S. culture and society's perception of government.

Practicing Your Skill

1. What is the subject of this cartoon?
2. What are the clues that help you identify the place and the person illustrated in the cartoon?
3. What is the cartoonist's opinion of the Clinton administration's foreign policy? Do you agree with this opinion? Why or why not?

Practicing Your Skill Answers

1. The purpose for writing most affects how and what one writes because different purposes for writing require different forms, tones, and content.

2. The intended audience shapes the content and style of writing.

3. reorganizing, improving sentences, omitting words, sentences, or paragraphs

4. by varying sentence lengths and replacing inexact wording with more exact wording choices; a variety of sentence lengths keeps your paper or essay from sounding choppy and makes it easier for the reader to follow the information presented in the paper or essay.

Practicing Your Skill Answers

1. The cartoon depicts President Clinton experimenting in a tank to learn about foreign policy.

2. The place is identified by the White House in the background. The person is identified through caricature and the "C" on the helmet.

3. The cartoonist seems to imply that foreign policy decisions are being made by people who are not prepared to make them. Answers will vary, but students should state their opinion and offer an explanation for their reasoning.

⑨ UNDERSTANDING MEASUREMENT CONCEPTS AND METHODS

Measurements can give us information about the magnitude, amount, or size of a particular item. Measurements usually are presented in the form of numbers. Finding the information you need from these numbers, however, may be difficult unless you know what you hope to find. Understanding measurement methods and learning to read the results is key to learning about government and many other subjects.

Many measurements in *Holt American Government* are *statistics*. These are facts presented in the form of numbers and are typically arranged to show applicable information about a subject. Statistics often are presented in the form of *percentages* or *ratios*.

Measurements can provide a wide variety of information. For instance, you might read measurements that tell you how many people in your state agree with higher speed limits or what the rate of inflation was over the past year.

How to Read Measurements

Look for clues. Use the information presented with measurements to help you understand their significance. If the measurements appear in a chart or graph, read the title or labels to find clues. If the numbers appear in the text, read the paragraph surrounding them to gain more information.

Identify form. In what form is the measurement? Is it expressed as a percentage? a ratio?

Evaluate the method and purpose of the measurement. How was the data collected—through a poll, government census, or price analysis? Why was this information collected, and who will use it?

Put the data to use. Use the information in the measurements to build a mental picture of the data or group described. Draw conclusions from the information presented.

Practicing Your Skill

1. What is the subject of the first graph? the second graph?

2. Why do you think the data is presented in the form of percentages?

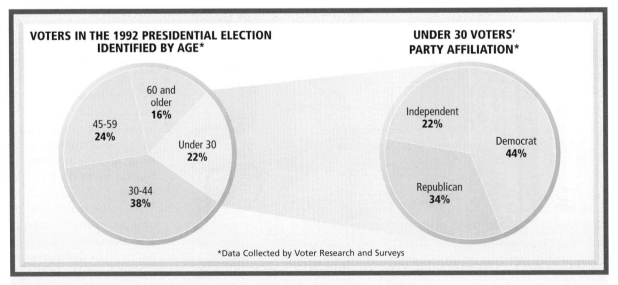

VOTERS IN THE 1992 PRESIDENTIAL ELECTION IDENTIFIED BY AGE*

- 60 and older **16%**
- 45-59 **24%**
- Under 30 **22%**
- 30-44 **38%**

UNDER 30 VOTERS' PARTY AFFILIATION*

- Independent **22%**
- Democrat **44%**
- Republican **34%**

*Data Collected by Voter Research and Surveys

Understanding measurements, such as this graphic illustration of statistics, is key to learning facts about government.

3. Which age group made up the smallest percentage of voters? Which political party won the votes of the largest percentage of voters under 30 years old?

4. How was the data collected? What groups, organizations, and individuals would be interested in using this data?

🔟 UNDERSTANDING CHARTS AND GRAPHS

Charts and graphs are means of organizing and presenting information visually. They categorize and display data in a variety of ways, depending on their subject. Several types of charts and graphs are used in this textbook.

Charts

Charts commonly used in government include tables, flowcharts, and organizational charts. A *table* lists and categorizes information. A *flowchart* shows a sequence of events or the steps in a process. Cause-and-effect relationships are often shown by flowcharts. An *organizational chart* displays the structure of an organization, indicating the ranking or function of its internal positions or departments and the relationships among them. For example, see the Federal Court System chart to the right.

How to Read a Chart

Read the title. Read the title to identify the focus or purpose of the chart.

Study the chart's elements. Read the chart's headings, subheadings, and labels to identify the categories used and the specific data given for each one.

Analyze the details. When reading quantities, note any increases or decreases in amounts. When reading dates, note intervals of time. When viewing an organizational chart, follow directional arrows or lines.

Put the data to use. Form generalizations or draw conclusions based on the data.

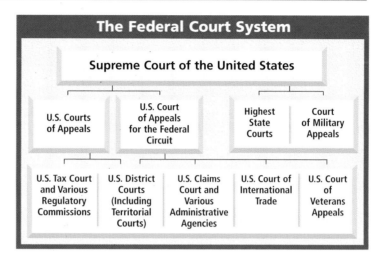

Organizational charts show the relationship among different components of an organization.

Graphs

There are several types of graphs, each of which is well-suited for a particular purpose. A *bar graph* displays amounts or quantities in a way that makes comparisons easy—for example, see the Biggest Recipients of U.S. Foreign Aid, 1993 bar graph on the next page. A *line graph* plots information by dots connected with a line. This line is sometimes called a *curve.* A line graph such as the one on the next page—Net Budget Receipts, 1990–1995—shows changes or trends over time. A *pie graph,* or *circle graph,* displays proportions by showing sections of a whole as if they were slices of a pie.

How to Read a Graph

Read the title. Read the title to identify the subject and purpose of the graph. Note the kind of graph it is, remembering what each kind is designed to emphasize.

S26

Practicing Your Skill Answers

1. The data collected is the amount of net budget receipts for 1990 to 1995. The vertical axis is broken down in intervals of $100 million. The horizontal axis is broken down by year.

2. The net budget receipts have been rising steadily from 1990 to 1995, increasing by just under $400 million during that period.

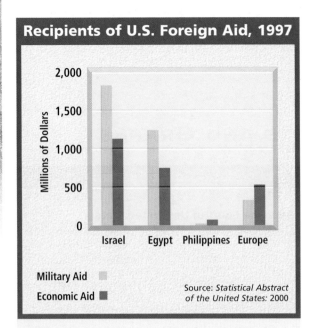

Recipients of U.S. Foreign Aid, 1997

Military Aid
Economic Aid

Source: *Statistical Abstract of the United States: 2000*

Bar graphs make it easy to compare related sets of data.

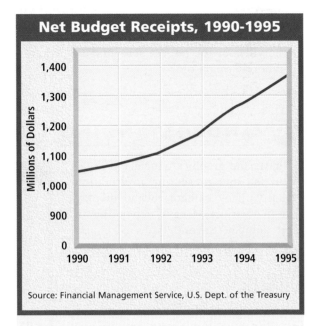

Net Budget Receipts, 1990-1995

Source: Financial Management Service, U.S. Dept. of the Treasury

Line graphs illustrate changes or trends over time.

Study the labels. To identify the type of information presented in the graph, read the label for each axis. The *horizontal axis* runs from left to right, generally at the bottom of the graph, while the *vertical axis* runs up and down, generally along the left-hand side. In addition, note the intervals of any dates or amounts that are listed. Study the labels for each axis in the Recipients of U.S. Foreign Aid, 1997 chart on this page.

Analyze the data. Note increases or decreases in quantities. Look for trends, relationships, and changes in the data.

Put the data to use. Use the results of your analysis to form generalizations and to draw conclusions about the subject matter of the chart or graph.

Practicing Your Skill

Use the Net Budget Receipts, 1990–1995 line graph on this page to answer the following questions.

1. Describe the type of data illustrated and the intervals used for the horizontal axis and the vertical axis.

2. What generalizations or conclusions can you draw from the information in this graph?

11 READING MAPS

The study of government and geography often are related. Government describes the political institutions and laws that regulate a group of people. Geography describes how physical environments affect human events and how people influence the environment around them. Geographers have developed six essential elements—the world in spatial terms, places and regions, physical systems, human systems, environment and society, and the uses of geography—to organize this information.

Geographic information for all six elements can be presented in text or represented visually in maps. Maps convey a wealth of varied information through colors, lines, symbols, and labels. To read and interpret maps, you must be able to understand their language and symbols.

Types of Maps

A map is an illustration drawn to scale of all or part of the earth's surface. Types of maps include physical maps, political maps, and special-purpose maps. *Physical maps* illustrate the natural landscape of an area. Physical maps often use shading to show relief—the rises and falls in the surface of the land—and colors to show elevation, or height above sea level.

Political maps illustrate political units such as states and nations by employing color variations, lines to mark boundaries, dots for major cities, and stars, or stars within circles, for capitals. Political maps show information such as territorial changes or military alliances. The Hazardous Waste Sites in the United States, 1996 map on this page is a political map.

Special-purpose maps present specific information such as explorers' routes, the outcome of an election, regional economic activity, or population density. The U.S. Boundaries, 1853 map on page S28 is a special-purpose map.

Many maps combine various features of the types of maps listed above. For example, a map may combine information from a political and a special-purpose map by showing boundaries between nations as well as trade routes from one region to another region.

Map Features

Most maps have a number of features in common. Familiarity with these basic elements makes reading any map easier.

Titles, legends, and labels. A map's *title* tells you what the map is about, what area is shown, and frequently the time period represented. The *legend,* or key, explains any special symbols, colors, or shading used on the map. *Labels* designate political and geographic place-names as well as physical features like mountain ranges, oceans, and rivers.

The global grid. The *absolute location* of any place on the earth is given in terms of *latitude* (degrees north or south of the equator) and *longitude* (degrees east or west of the prime meridian). The symbol for a degree is °. Degrees are divided into 60 equal parts called minutes, which are represented by the symbol '. The *global grid* is created by the intersection of lines of latitude *(parallels)* and lines of longitude *(meridians)*. Lines of latitude and longitude may sometimes be indicated by tick marks near the edge of the map or by lines across an entire map. Many maps also have *locator maps,* which show the subject area's location in relation to a larger area, such as a continent or hemisphere.

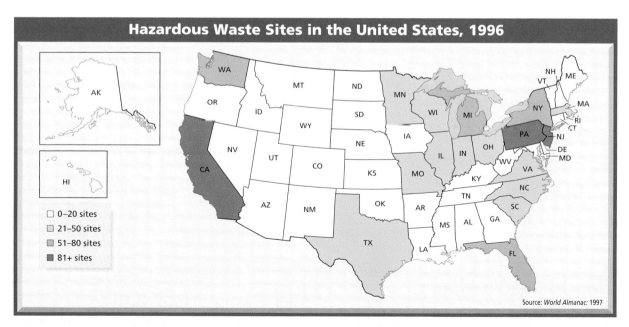

Maps present geographic information in a visual form.

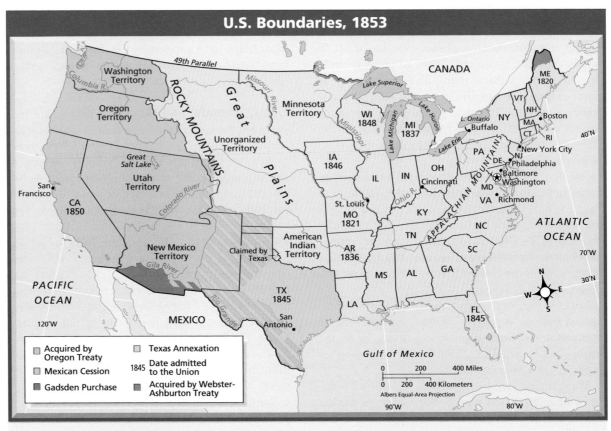

U.S. Boundaries, 1853

Legend:
- Acquired by Oregon Treaty
- Mexican Cession
- Gadsden Purchase
- Texas Annexation
- 1845 Date admitted to the Union
- Acquired by Webster-Ashburton Treaty

0   200   400 Miles
0   200   400 Kilometers
Albers Equal-Area Projection

Special-purpose maps illustrate a particular topic and may include features of physical and political maps.

Directions and distances. Most maps in this textbook have a *compass rose,* or *directional indicator*. The compass rose indicates the four cardinal points—N for north, S for south, E for east, and W for west. You can also determine intermediate directions—northeast, southeast, southwest, and northwest—using the compass rose. These directions are helpful in describing the relative location of a place. (If a map has no compass rose, assume that north is at the top, east is to the right, and so on.)

Many maps include a *scale*, showing both miles and kilometers, to help you relate distances on the map to actual distances on the earth's surface. You can use the scale to find the true distance between any two points on the map.

How to Read a Map

Determine the focus of the map. Read the map's title and labels to determine the map's focus—its subject and the geographic area it represents.

Study the map legend. Read the legend and become familiar with any special symbols, lines, colors, and shadings used in the map.

Check directions and distances. Use the directional indicator and scale as needed to determine direction, location, and distance.

Check the grid lines. Refer to lines of latitude and longitude, or to a locator map, to fix the locations in relation to a larger area.

Study the map. Study the map's basic features and details, keeping its purpose in mind. If it is a special-purpose map, study the specific information being presented.

Practicing Your Skill

For each of the maps in this lesson, answer the questions on the next page.

1. What is the special focus of each map in this lesson?
2. How is a map helpful in presenting this information?

3. What standard symbols, if any, are used in the map?
4. What do the color variations and different lines indicate?

12 TAKING A TEST

When it comes to taking a test, for government or any other subject, nothing can take the place of preparation. A good night's sleep added to consistent study habits give you a much better chance for success than hours of late-night, last-minute cramming. By preparing well, you will be better able to ignore distractions during the test.

But keeping your mind focused on the test and free from distractions is not all you can do to improve your test scores. Mastering some basic test-taking skills also can help. Keeping up with daily reading assignments and taking careful notes as you read can turn preparing for a test into a mere matter of review. Reviewing material that you already know takes less time—and causes less stress—than trying to learn something new under pressure.

You will face several basic types of questions on government tests—for example, fill-in-the-blank, short answer, multiple choice, matching, and essay. In answering multiple-choice questions, eliminate any answers that you know are wrong, in order to narrow your field of choice. When completing a matching exercise, first go through the entire list, matching only those items whose connection is clear. Then study any that remain.

Good preparation is essential for successful test-taking.

Read essay questions carefully so that you know exactly what you are being asked to write. Make an outline of the main ideas and supporting details that you plan to include in your essay. Keep your answer clear and brief, but cover all necessary points.

How to Take a Test

Prepare beforehand. This all-important step involves more than just studying and reviewing the material prior to the test. It also means being physically rested and mentally focused on the day of the test.

Follow directions. Read all instructions carefully. Listen closely if the directions are oral rather than written.

Preview the test. Skim through the entire test to determine how much time you have for each section. Try to anticipate which areas will be the most difficult for you.

Concentrate on the test. Do not watch the clock, but be aware of the time. If you do not know an answer, move on to the next question.

Review your answers. If you have time, return to questions that you skipped or were unsure of, and work on them. Review your essays to catch and correct any mistakes in spelling, punctuation, or grammar.

Practicing Your Skill

1. How can you improve your chances on multiple-choice questions?
2. Why is it important to skim through an entire test before you begin?
3. Name three things that can help you in taking a test.

Practicing Your Skill Answers

1. The first map identifies hazardous waste sites in the United States in 1996. The second map identifies U.S. boundaries in 1853.

2. The first map helps the reader by color-coding the states based on how many waste sites each state has. The second map helps the reader by using different colors to identify which land was owned by the United States during 1853.

3. The second map uses the compass rose, gives the scale, and identifies the capital with a star.

4. In the first map the color variations indicate the differences in the number of hazardous waste sites in a state, and the lines indicate the boundaries between states. In the second map the colors indicate how the United States acquired each section of land, and the lines indicate the boundaries of the states and the territories.

Practicing Your Skill Answers

1. You can improve your chances on multiple-choice questions by eliminating answers that you know are false.

2. Skimming through a test allows you to determine how much time to spend on each section and to see if any sections of the test appear problematic.

3. Answers will vary but may include preparing beforehand, following directions, previewing the test, concentrating while taking the test, and reviewing your answers.

PACIFIC
OCEAN

Strait of
Juan de Fuca

Puget Sound

Franklin D.
Roosevelt Lake

Seattle
Olympia ★ Tacoma
Spokane
WASHINGTON

Pend
Oreille
Lake

Flathead
Lake

Fort Peck
Lake

Missouri River

River

Lake
Sakakawea

Portland

Columbia River

Salem

Helena ★ **MONTANA**

Yellowstone

River

NORTH DAKOTA Fargo
★ Bismarck

Eugene **OREGON**

IDAHO

Billings

Yellowstone
Lake

Lake
Oahe

SOUTH DAKOTA
★ Pierre

★ Boise

Snake

River

WYOMING

Sioux Falls

Cape
Mendocino

Goose
Lake

Shasta
Lake

Sacramento River

Pyramid
Lake

Lake
Tahoe

Reno
Carson City ★

NEVADA

Great
Salt
Lake

★ Salt Lake City

Utah
Lake ● Provo

Casper

Cheyenne
★

NEBRASKA

Platte River

Om
Lincoln

Berkeley
Oakland
San Francisco
San Francisco Bay
San Jose

★ Sacramento
● Stockton
● Modesto

San Joaquin R.

UTAH

Green River

COLORADO

★ Denver

● Colorado
Springs

KANSAS

To

Monterey
Bay

● Fresno

CALIFORNIA

Las
Vegas

Lake
Powell

Arkansas

River

Wic

● Bakersfield

Lake
Mead

Colorado

River

Santa Fe
★

Keystone Lake

River

Canadian

River

OKLAHOM

Los Angeles
Long Beach
Channel
Islands

● Anaheim
● Santa Ana

Salton
Sea

ARIZONA

● San Diego

Phoenix ★

Gila

River

Albuquerque

NEW MEXICO

● Amarillo

Oklahoma City ★

Eu

Lubbock

Fort
Worth

Abilene ●

Tucson

El Paso

Gulf of
California

● Odessa

Pecos River

TEXAS

Colorado River

Brazos

To understand the relative locations of Alaska and Hawaii
as well as the vast distances separating them from the rest
of the United States, see the world map.

Rio

Amistad
Reservoir

Austin

San Antonio

MEXICO

Kauai

Oahu
Niihau Honolulu
Molokai
Lanai Maui
Kahoolawe

PACIFIC
OCEAN

N
W E
S

SCALE

HAWAII

Hawaii

ARCTIC OCEAN

Arctic Circle

RUSSIA

Bering Strait

St. Lawrence
Island
St. Matthew
Island

Nome ●

Yukon River

Fairbanks

CANADA

0   75   150 Miles

0   75   150 Kilometers

BERING SEA

N
W E
S

SCALE

Attu Island

Aleutian

Nunivak
Island

ALASKA

● Anchorage

0   250   500 Miles

0   250   500 Kilometers

Projection: Albers Equal Area

Islands

PACIFIC
OCEAN

Kodiak
Island

GULF OF
ALASKA

Juneau ★

Alexander
Archipelago

Corpus
Christi

Laredo

Padre
Island

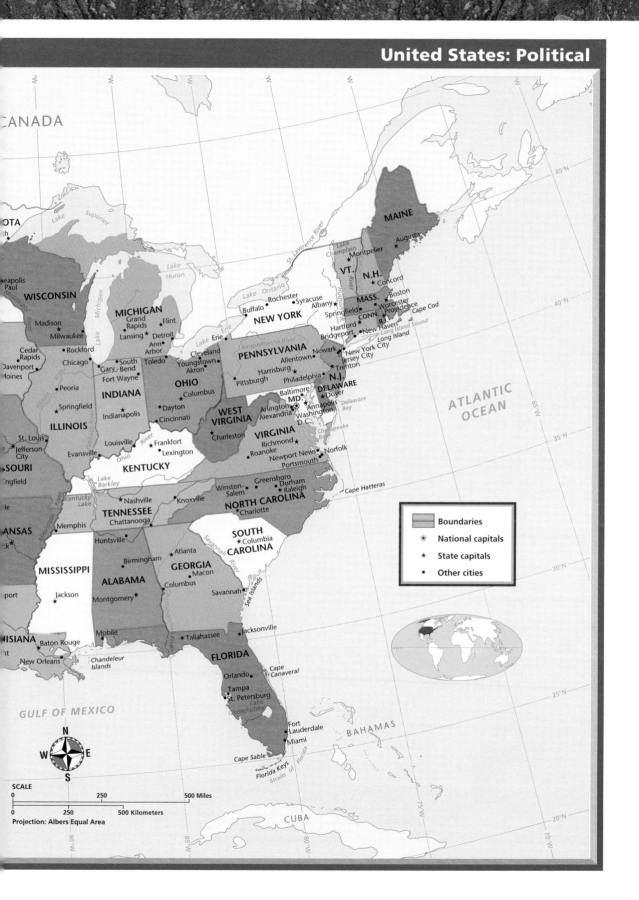

United States: Political

CANADA

MAINE
Augusta ★

VT.
Montpelier ★
N.H.
Concord ★

WISCONSIN

MICHIGAN
Grand Rapids
Flint
Lansing ★ Detroit
Ann Arbor

MASS.
Boston ★
Worcester
Springfield
CONN. Providence
Hartford ★ R.I. Cape Cod
New Haven
Bridgeport
Long Island Sound
Long Island

Lake Ontario
Rochester Syracuse
Buffalo Albany ★

NEW YORK

Cleveland
Youngstown
Akron
PENNSYLVANIA
Allentown
Harrisburg ★
Pittsburgh
Philadelphia

Newark
New York City
Jersey City
Trenton ★
N.J.
DELAWARE
Dover ★

Madison
Milwaukee
Cedar Rapids
Rockford
Chicago
Gary South Bend Toledo
Fort Wayne
OHIO
Columbus ★

INDIANA
Dayton
Cincinnati
Indianapolis ★

Peoria
Springfield ★

ILLINOIS

St. Louis
Jefferson City ★
Evansville

Louisville
Frankfort ★
Lexington

KENTUCKY

WEST VIRGINIA
Charleston ★

Baltimore
MD. Annapolis ★
Arlington Washington, D.C.
Alexandria
Delaware Bay

VIRGINIA
Richmond ★
Roanoke
Newport News
Portsmouth
Norfolk
Chesapeake Bay

ATLANTIC OCEAN

Lake Barkley
Nashville ★
Knoxville
TENNESSEE
Chattanooga
Memphis

Winston-Salem
Greensboro
Durham
Raleigh ★
NORTH CAROLINA
Charlotte
Cape Hatteras

SOUTH CAROLINA
Columbia ★

Huntsville

MISSISSIPPI
Jackson ★

Birmingham
ALABAMA
Montgomery ★

Atlanta ★
GEORGIA
Macon
Columbus
Savannah

Jacksonville

Mobile
Baton Rouge ★
New Orleans
Chandeleur Islands

Tallahassee ★
FLORIDA
Orlando
Cape Canaveral
Tampa
St. Petersburg
Lake Okeechobee

GULF OF MEXICO

Fort Lauderdale
Miami
Cape Sable
Florida Keys
Straits of Florida

BAHAMAS

CUBA

Lake Superior
Lake Michigan
Lake Huron
Lake Erie

St. Lawrence River
Lake Champlain

Legend
- Boundaries
- ⊛ National capitals
- ★ State capitals
- • Other cities

SCALE
0   250   500 Miles
0   250   500 Kilometers
Projection: Albers Equal Area

N
W E
S

45°N
40°N
35°N
30°N
25°N
20°N

65°W
75°W
70°W
80°W
85°W
90°W

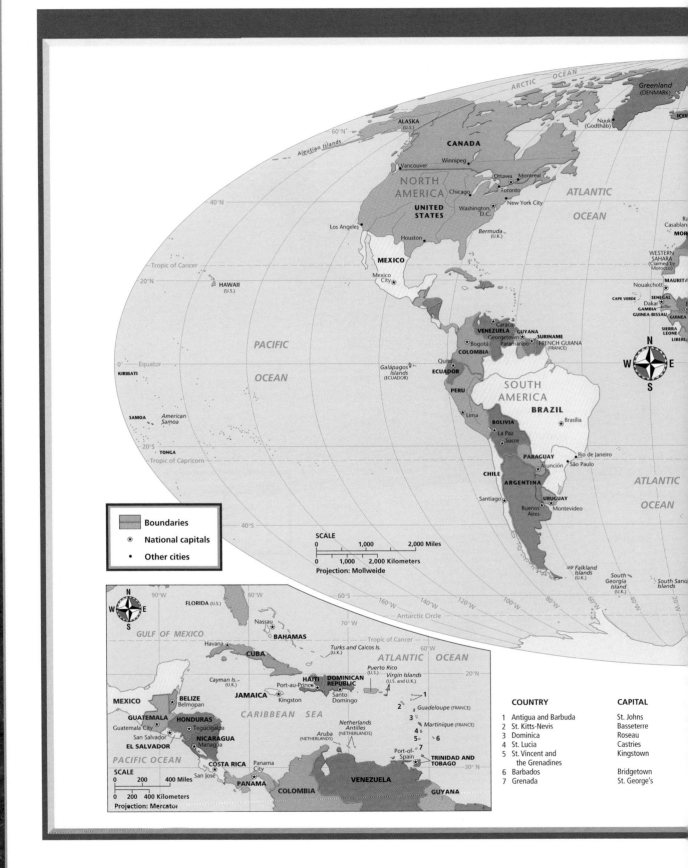

Boundaries

⊛ National capitals

• Other cities

SCALE
0 — 1,000 — 2,000 Miles
0 — 1,000 — 2,000 Kilometers
Projection: Mollweide

COUNTRY	CAPITAL
1 Antigua and Barbuda	St. Johns
2 St. Kitts-Nevis	Basseterre
3 Dominica	Roseau
4 St. Lucia	Castries
5 St. Vincent and the Grenadines	Kingstown
6 Barbados	Bridgetown
7 Grenada	St. George's

SCALE
0 — 200 — 400 Miles
0 — 200 — 400 Kilometers
Projection: Mercator

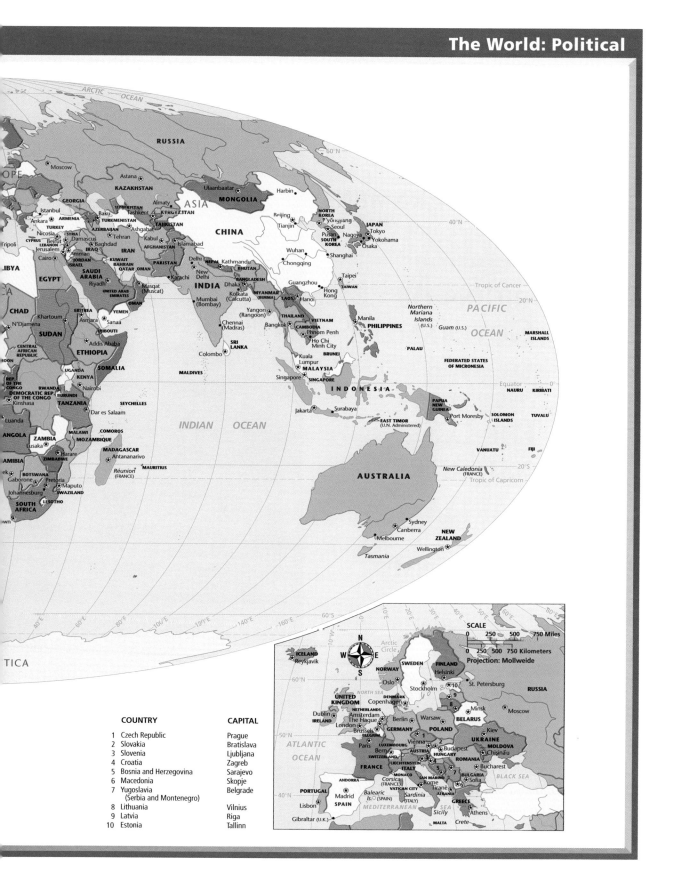

COUNTRY	CAPITAL
1 Czech Republic	Prague
2 Slovakia	Bratislava
3 Slovenia	Ljubljana
4 Croatia	Zagreb
5 Bosnia and Herzegovina	Sarajevo
6 Macedonia	Skopje
7 Yugoslavia (Serbia and Montenegro)	Belgrade
8 Lithuania	Vilnius
9 Latvia	Riga
10 Estonia	Tallinn

SCALE

0   250   500   750 Miles

0   250   500   750 Kilometers

Projection: Mollweide

UNIT 1

Lesson Options

Suggestions for customizing the material in Unit 1 to fit the specific schedule and curriculum of your classroom are located at the beginning of each chapter.

Main Ideas

Ask each student to read the Main Ideas and briefly answer each question in writing. Later, when you have finished Unit 1, ask students to return to their original answers and revise them using what they learned in the unit.

PUBLIC POLICY LAB

The Unit 1 Public Policy Lab appears on pages 86–89. This project is a real-world assignment in which students will work in groups to prepare a proposal for a bill of rights to be added to their school's constitution. Support materials for the lab appear in *Unit Tests and Unit Lab Activities with Answer Key.*

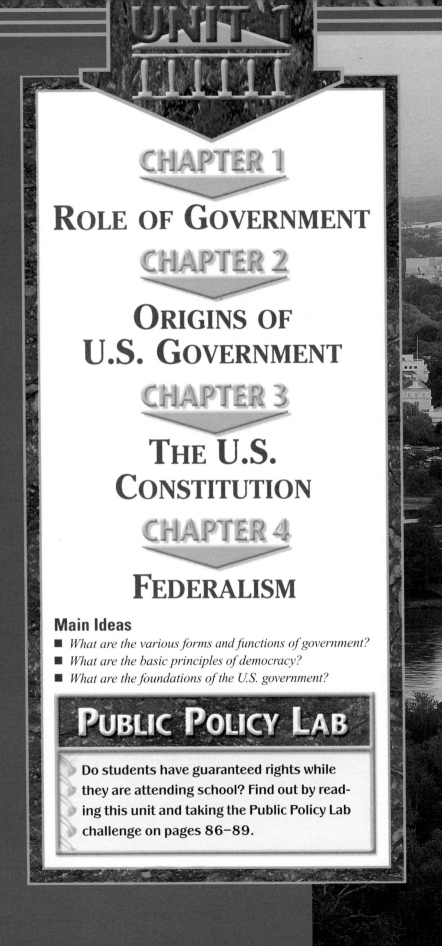

UNIT 1

CHAPTER 1
ROLE OF GOVERNMENT

CHAPTER 2
ORIGINS OF U.S. GOVERNMENT

CHAPTER 3
THE U.S. CONSTITUTION

CHAPTER 4
FEDERALISM

Main Ideas

- *What are the various forms and functions of government?*
- *What are the basic principles of democracy?*
- *What are the foundations of the U.S. government?*

PUBLIC POLICY LAB

Do students have guaranteed rights while they are attending school? Find out by reading this unit and taking the Public Policy Lab challenge on pages 86–89.

FOUNDATIONS OF GOVERNMENT

Unit 1 presents the basic concepts necessary to introduce students to American Government, including the origins, functions, and various forms of government; the principles and foundations of democracy; the historical background of U.S. government; the rights and responsibilities afforded by the U.S. Constitution; and the basis for a federal system of government.

Teaching with Photographs

Construction of a monument to honor George Washington began in an elaborate ceremony on July 4, 1848. Work continued successfully until 1854, when, in the midst of political turmoil over the tensions that eventually caused the Civil War, construction was halted. The monument remained unfinished at around 155 feet tall for 25 years while the United States recovered, both economically and physically, from the Civil War.

When construction resumed in 1880, the marble was taken from a different stratum. Thus, the top 400 feet of the 555-foot memorial are a slightly different color than the bottom 155 feet.

CHAPTER 1 ROLE OF GOVERNMENT

	OBJECTIVES	PACING GUIDE	REPRODUCIBLE RESOURCES
SECTION 1 **GOVERNMENT AND THE PUBLIC GOOD** (pp. 3–7)	▸ What is government, and why is it important? ▸ How have some philosophers described the nature and purpose of the state? ▸ What functions does government perform? ▸ How does government promote the public good?	**Regular** 1 day **Block Scheduling** .5 day	**ELL** Spanish Study Guide 1.1 **ELL** English Study Guide 1.1 **PS** Reading 48: *Second Treatise on Civil Government* **PS** Reading 49: *The Social Contract*
SECTION 2 **FORMS OF GOVERNMENT** (pp. 8–11)	▸ In what ways are monarchies, republics, and dictatorships different from one another? ▸ What are the advantages and disadvantages of unitary, federal, and confederal systems of government? ▸ What are the major advantages and disadvantages of presidential and parliamentary forms of government?	**Regular** 1.5 days **Block Scheduling** .75 day	**ELL** Spanish Study Guide 1.2 **ELL** English Study Guide 1.2
SECTION 3 **FOUNDATIONS OF DEMOCRACY** (pp. 12–16)	▸ What are the major principles of democracy? ▸ What is the difference between direct democracy and representative democracy?	**Regular** 1 day **Block Scheduling** .5 day	**ELL** Spanish Study Guide 1.3 **ELL** English Study Guide 1.3 **S** Simulations and Strategies for Teaching American Government, Activity 1 **E** Challenge and Enrichment Activity 1

Chapter Resource Key

PS	Primary Sources	**A**	Assessment	📼	Video
RS	Reading Support	**REV**	Review	💿	Videodisc
E	Enrichment	**ELL**	Reinforcement and English Language Learners	🌐	Internet
S	Simulations	🖱	Transparencies	💻	Holt Presentation Maker Using
SM	Skills Mastery	💿	CD-ROM		Microsoft ® PowerPoint ®

TECHNOLOGY RESOURCES	REINFORCEMENT, REVIEW, AND ASSESSMENT
• One-Stop Planner: Lesson 1.1 • Holt Researcher Online • Homework Practice Online	**REV** Section 1 Review, p. 7 **A** Daily Quiz 1.1
• Holt Researcher Online • Transparencies 1 and 2 • Global Skill Builder CD-ROM • Homework Practice Online	**REV** Section 2 Review, p. 11 **A** Daily Quiz 1.2
• Holt Researcher Online • Homework Practice Online	**REV** Section 3 Review, p. 16 **A** Daily Quiz 1.3

Chapter Review and Assessment

SM Global Skill Builder CD-ROM
• HRW Go site
REV Chapter 1 Tutorial for Students, Parents, and Peers
REV Chapter 1 Review, pp. 18–19
• Chapter 1 Test Generator (on the One-Stop Planner)
A Chapter 1 Test
A Alternative Assessment Handbook

One-Stop Planner CD–ROM

It's easy to plan lessons, select resources, and print out materials for your students when you use the *One-Stop Planner CD-ROM with Test Generator.*

🖅 internet connect

HRW ONLINE RESOURCES
Go To: go.hrw.com
Then type in a keyword.

TEACHER HOME PAGE
KEYWORD: SV3 Teacher

CHAPTER INTERNET ACTIVITIES
KEYWORD: SV3 GV1
Choose an activity on the foundations of government to:
▸ understand the ideas of John Locke and Thomas Hobbes.
▸ learn about different types of governments.
▸ research the election process.

CHAPTER ENRICHMENT LINKS
KEYWORD: SV3 CH1

HOLT RESEARCHER ONLINE
KEYWORD: Holt Researcher

ONLINE ASSESSMENT
Homework Practice
KEYWORD: SV3 HP1
Standardized Test Prep
KEYWORD: SV3 STP1
Rubrics
KEYWORD: SS Rubrics

ONLINE MAPS, CHARTS, AND GRAPHS
KEYWORD: SV3 MCG
▸ Sources of Authority
▸ How Power is distributed

CONTENT UPDATES
KEYWORD: SS Content Updates

HOLT PRESENTATION MAKER
KEYWORD: SV3 PPT1

ONLINE READING SUPPORT
KEYWORD: SS Strategies

CURRENT EVENTS
KEYWORD: S3 Current Events

HOLT PRESENTATION MAKER
Access Illustrated LECTURE
NOTES using Microsoft®
PowerPoint® on the
One-Stop Planner CD-ROM

OBJECTIVES

▶ Define government and explain its importance.
▶ Identify how some philosophers have described the nature and purpose of the state.
▶ List the functions that government performs.
▶ Describe how government promotes the public good.

MOTIVATE

Before introducing students to Chapter 1, set up stations in three or four corners of the classroom. At each station, have one large piece of butcher paper, a marker, and some objects or pictures that represent U.S. government, such as the flag, pictures of past or current presidents, the Constitution, and a voting ballot. Organize students into groups and assign one group to each station. Allow students about five minutes to generate words describing the importance or symbolism of the items at their station. Have each group write these words on the butcher paper with the marker and then read their list to the class. Tell students that in Chapter 1 they will learn about different types of government, what government is, why it is important, and what functions it serves. Explain that symbols of government, such as those at the stations, are everywhere and serve as reminders of the importance and the role of the U.S. government.

TEACH

Building a Vocabulary

 In spiral notebooks, have students create a Political Dictionary to be used throughout the course. The dictionary may be used as an activity at the start of each new section; it may also be used as a modification device for students having difficulty or sheltered English students during tests and homework assignments. List words the students will be expected to know for this section on the board. Have students list, define, and give an example of each of the terms using information provided in the text or on the *Researcher CD-ROM.*

Applying Information

 In small groups have students identify a law or rule that they must follow in their daily lives. Have students brainstorm what life would be like without that law or rule. Be sure to have students consider both the positive and negative results. Ask groups to share their thoughts. Lead students, through discussion, to the idea that without laws and rules, life would be chaotic and/or dangerous. Explain that governments serve the people they govern, but it is the people's responsibility to see to it that they do. Lead into the next activity by asking students to hypothesize how governments do this.

Debating Ideas

 Organize the class into two groups, assigning one group to the philosophy of Thomas Hobbes and the other to that of John Locke. Ask students to read the section of the text that pertains to their assigned philosopher. Students assigned to John Locke should also refer to Reading 48 in *From the Source: Readings in Economics and Government with Answer Key.* Ask students to identify ways in which this philosophy is evident in the U.S. Constitution, paying particular attention to the purpose of government or state according to their philosopher. Lead a class debate between the two groups regarding the legitimacy of each philosopher's claim arguing the purpose of government. Tell students that in the next activity they will be learning about the functions that the government serves in order to promote the public good.

Classifying Ideas

In columns on the board, list the following headings: *Maintaining Order, Providing Services, Resolving Conflict,* and *Promoting Values.* Using their texts as a reference, ask students to identify ways in which the U.S. government provides each of these functions to its citizens. List answers in the proper column as the students name them. Discuss how these functions relate to the previous debate regarding the philosophies of Thomas Hobbes and John Locke. Lead students to draw the conclusion that these functions are needed to promote the public good.

CLOSE

Have students return to their stations from the Motivate activity. Ask groups to discuss ways in which the item at their station represents one or more of the functions of government listed on the board (from the previous activity). Ask students to identify how the item may relate to the importance and purpose of government as well. Have groups brainstorm on other objects or pictures that represent the functions of the U.S. government. Encourage students to bring these objects and pictures to class. Allow time for each group to share their objects and pictures and their thoughts with the rest of the class.

OPTIONS

Visual-Spatial Learners

 Have students create a board game that focuses on the functions of government. Students should create situations that would require the government to react by fulfilling one of its functions: maintaining order, providing services, resolving conflict, or promoting values. Color-coded cards should be created for each function of government and should contain the government's reaction. For example, if a player lands on a square that says "violated curfew," he or she could draw a Maintaining Order Card that states what the government's reaction will be. Give students an opportunity to play the game and to offer their opinions about how well it represents the functions of government.

Gifted Learners

 Discuss with the class major political ideas in history such as natural law, natural rights, the divine rights of kings, and the social contract theory. Have students work in groups to create encyclopedia entries for each of these topics. Encourage students to include historic examples of countries that have followed these concepts.

Students Having Difficulty/ Sheltered English Students

 Have students examine current newspapers and magazines for examples of the functions of government—maintaining order, providing services, resolving conflict, and promoting values. Randomly assign each of these topics to individual students to research. Students should read articles pertaining to their topic and then write a brief summary explaining how the government accomplished its function. Encourage students to cut out these articles and share them with the class, make a collage, or add them to their Government Notebook. Have students share their work with the class to see if the class can identify the function being served.

REVIEW

Have students complete the Section 1 Review on page 7. Use the answers in the Annotated Teacher's Edition to assess student mastery of this section.

ASSESS

To assess student mastery of this section, have students complete Daily Quiz 1.1 in *Daily Quizzes with Answer Key*. For additional assessment options, see *Alternative Assessment Handbook* on the *One-Stop Planner CD-ROM*.

ADDITIONAL RESOURCES

Dionne, E.J. *The War Against Public Life: Why Americans Hate Politics.* 1991. Simon and Schuster.

Huckfeldt, Robert, and John Sprague. "Networks in Context: The Social Flow of Political Information." *The American Political Science Review.* December 1987.

LESSON 1.2 FORMS OF GOVERNMENT

TEXTBOOK PAGES 8-11

HOLT PRESENTATION MAKER
Access Illustrated LECTURE NOTES using Microsoft® PowerPoint® on the One-Stop Planner CD-ROM

OBJECTIVES

▶ Describe the differences between monarchies, republics, and dictatorships.

▶ Identify the advantages and disadvantages of features of unitary, federal, and confederal systems of government.

▶ List the major advantages and disadvantages of presidential and parliamentary forms of government.

MOTIVATE

On the board and/or around the room place maps, flags, or photos of various countries such as Australia, Cuba, France, Germany, Japan, and Great Britain. Ask students to choose one or two countries that they would like to visit or live in. Call on a variety of students to share their reasons for wanting to go there. Explain that these countries have different forms of government and that in this section students will learn about those forms. Have each student examine the Country Profiles section on the *Holt Researcher Online* to find out more information about the country he or she selected. Encourage students to share the information that they gathered and to discuss the similarities and differences between these countries.

TEACH

Building a Vocabulary

In their spiral notebooks, have students continue working on their Political Dictionary. List words the students will be expected to know for this section on the board. Have students list, define, and give an example of each of the terms, using information provided in the text or on the *Researcher CD-ROM*.

Role-Playing

Organize students into four groups and assign each group to be either an absolute monarchy, an authoritarian government, a classical republic, a despotism, a feudal country, a liberal democracy, or a totalitarian state. Have each group prepare a script and/or actions to portray the aspects of their assigned form of rule. Have students use the text and outside resources to acquire information about the form of government they have been assigned. Play a game similar to charades in which each group acts out their form of government and the other groups guess which one is being portrayed. Point out missing aspects in students' portrayals to the class. Organize the class into eight groups with each form of rule being role-played twice. Discuss the differences in control of authority among each of the forms of rule. Lead into the next exercise by discussing with students that governments vary not only based on who has authority but also on what authority each level of government exerts.

Comparing and Contrasting

Have students work in pairs to create a table comparing and contrasting the features of governments. Use the headings *federal, confederal,* and *unitary* for the various systems of government. Students should then use the Country Profiles section on the *Holt Researcher Online* to investigate countries that exemplify each of these forms of government and include them in the table. Have each group include at least 10 countries on their table. Then have students identify the advantages and disadvantages of each of these systems of government. Tell students that they will learn about the differences in having the executive branch run a government rather than the legislative branch.

Hypothesizing

Lead a class discussion exploring the differences between presidential and parliamentary forms of government. Then, challenge students to build on what they learned to identify the advantages and disadvantages of presidential and parliamentary forms of government. As a class or in small groups ask students to hypothesize ways in which their lives would be different if the United States was parliamentary instead of presidential; unitary or confederal instead of federal; monarchical or dictatorial instead of republican. Have each student choose one of these changes and write a few paragraphs describing what could happen as a result of this change. If time permits, have students share their ideas with the class.

CLOSE

Ask students to write down and then share with the class the form of rule and level of government of the country they chose to research in the Motivate activity. Based on the information in this section, have students discuss whether they would still want to live in this country. Have students explain their reasoning. If students do not want to live in the country they researched, have them choose a new country and identify its form of rule and level of government.

OPTIONS

Visual-Spatial Learners

   Have students develop a key and then color-code a world map identifying the various forms of rule and levels of government in different countries. Organize students into groups representing each of the populated continents of the world. Have each group work together in the Country Profiles section on the *Holt Researcher Online* to research countries not listed in the text. Have each group add their countries to the map.

Gifted Learners

 Have students use the Internet or other sources of world news to locate current governmental issues in countries under the various forms of rule and levels of government discussed in this section. Have students compare and contrast the types of issues that are occurring under each type of government. Students should attempt to draw conclusions about whether certain types of government have similar problems. Encourage students to display this information on a poster and to create an oral report to share with classmates.

Intrapersonal Learners

 Have students conduct research on dictatorships of the 1900s. Each student should write a paper about a dictator that discusses what country was under the dictator's rule, how the dictator obtained power, abuses that occurred under the dictator, and what happened to the dictator. Also have students write their feelings about the actions of the dictator and whether or not they feel that a dictatorship can ever promote the public good. Encourage students to share the information they researched with the rest of the class and have the class reach a conclusion about dictators.

REVIEW

Have students complete the Section 2 Review on page 11. Use the answers in the Annotated Teacher's Edition to assess student mastery of this section.

ASSESS

To assess student mastery of this section, have students complete Daily Quiz 1.2 in *Daily Quizzes with Answer Key.* For additional assessment options, see *Alternative Assessment Handbook* on the *One-Stop Planner CD-ROM.*

ADDITIONAL RESOURCES

Greider, William. *Who Will Tell the People: The Betrayal of American Democracy.* 1992. Simon and Schuster.

Steiner, David. "Political Theory, Educational Practice." *PS.* September 1994.

LESSON 1.3 FOUNDATIONS OF DEMOCRACY

TEXTBOOK PAGES 12–16

OBJECTIVES

▶ List the major principles of democracy.
▶ Identify the difference between direct democracy and representative democracy.

MOTIVATE

Organize students into six groups. Ask each group to imagine that Congress is trying to pass laws that will take away their right to vote at age 18, prevent women from holding public office, prevent immigrants in this country from attending public schools, eliminate jail sentences for theft, forbid guide dogs for visually-impaired people on airplanes, or take the money that would have been spent on education and use it to build golf courses. Have students brainstorm ways that they might inform Congress of their concerns or protest the proposed laws. Encourage groups to write letters voicing their opinions and to explain why they hold this opinion. Explain that in this section they will learn that the chance to voice concerns to lawmakers is a right of U.S. citizens because the United States is a representative democracy.

TEACH

Building a Vocabulary

 In their spiral notebooks, have students continue working on their Political Dictionary. List on the board words the students will be expected to know for this section. Have students list, define, and give an example of each of the terms, using information provided in the text or on the *Researcher CD-ROM*.

Acquiring Information

 List the six principles of democracy on the board or have students copy them on paper from the text. Tell students that they are to go on a "treasure hunt" around the campus or the community to locate examples of each of these principles. Organize students into groups to complete the task, and set a time limit. Students may want to take photographs, cassettes, or videotapes to show the class, if the equipment is available. Remind students to respect the privacy of others.

Have them write down what they find and explain why it is representative of one or more of the principles of democracy. Have each group explain what principle of democracy each of their examples show. As an introduction to the next activity, explain to students that in the next activity they will be conducting further research on one of the six principles of democracy.

Writing About Government

Have each student choose one of the six principles of democracy that he or she would like to research further. Have students use newspapers, magazines, and other outside resources to find examples of governments that follow the principle being researched and the resulting effect on society. Students should also find examples of governments ignoring the principle being researched and the resulting effect on society. Students should write a short paper describing the differences in the resulting societies. Discuss with students the differences that they have researched. Explain to students that they will learn about other differences in democracies in the next activity.

Role Playing

Organize students into two groups, one a representative democracy and the other a direct democracy. Ask students to act out an example of the lawmaking process in their form of democracy. Afterward, have students compare and contrast the differences between the forms of democracy and develop an opinion regarding which form of democracy is used in the United States. Have students brainstorm pitfalls and benefits that may be associated with a direct democracy for a country such as the United States.

CLOSE

Refer students to the hypothetical laws being proposed by Congress in the Motivate activity. Ask students to identify each of these laws in terms of the principle of democracy that it violates and explain why it would not be representative of that principle. Have students share their thoughts about these laws with the entire class.

Gifted Learners

 Using the Supreme Court Docket section on the *Holt Researcher Online,* have students choose and examine a Supreme Court decision dealing with one of the six principles of democracy in the United States. Encourage students to summarize the case and explain how it relates to the principle of democracy they identified. Examples of cases from which they may choose include *Brown* v. *Board of Education, NAACP* v. *Alabama,* and *Miranda* v. *Arizona.*

Students Having Difficulty/
Musical-Rhythmic Learners

 Have students review the chapter to identify ways that individuals can affect public policy and to identify examples of each method. Then have students conduct additional research to identify other ways individuals affect the public good. Have students discuss their research.

Visual-Spatial Learners

 Have students create an advertisement promoting one of the six principles of democracy. The advertisement should clearly promote the principle it is describing and should include some sort of visual. Have each student discuss his or her advertisement with the rest of the class and display the advertisements throughout the classroom.

REVIEW

Have students complete the Section 3 Review on page 16. Use the answers in the Annotated Teacher's Edition to assess student mastery of this section.

ASSESS

To assess student mastery of this section, have students complete Daily Quiz 1.3 in *Daily Quizzes with Answer Key.* For additional assessment options, see *Alternative Assessment Handbook* on the *One-Stop Planner CD-ROM.*

RETEACH

For students having difficulty with the lesson, have them complete Reteaching Activity 1. This activity is located in *Reteaching Activities with Answer Key* on the *Teaching Resources CD-ROM.*

ADDITIONAL RESOURCES

Gunderson, Joan. "Independence, Citizenship, and the American Revolution." *Signs.* Fall 1987.

Kadish, Mortimer. "Practice and Paradox A Comment of Social Choice Theory." *Ethics.* July 1983.

TOPICS INCLUDE

★ public policy
★ social contract
★ natural rights
★ function of government
★ public good
★ constitutional monarchy
★ republic
★ sources of government authority
★ distribution of power
★ majority rule
★ minority rights
★ direct democracy
★ representative democracy

 **GOVERNMENT NOTEBOOK**

The Government Notebook is a journal activity that encourages students to consider basic concepts of government that relate to their lives. A follow-up notebook activity appears on page 18.

▶ **WHY IT MATTERS TODAY**

To find additional lesson plans dealing with the role of government, visit CNNfyi.com or have students complete the GOVERNMENT IN THE NEWS activity on page 17.

CNNfyi.com

▶**WHY IT MATTERS TODAY**

The role of government continues to change as society evolves. At the end of this chapter visit CNNfyi.com or other resources to learn more about how the role of government is changing.

CNNfyi.com

ROLE OF GOVERNMENT

What prevents someone from placing a garbage dump next to your house or apartment? What makes sure you have the proper training to drive a car and determines when you can get your license? What ensures that the hamburger you buy at a local restaurant has been cooked safely? Who makes rules about whether or not school officials can search your locker?

The answer to these questions is government. You might think that government does not affect your everyday life or that it affects you only in negative ways. For example, some people complain about the taxes they have to pay. However, government actions, including collecting taxes, are intended to serve a vital purpose— promoting the well-being of a country's people. This chapter takes a close look at the role of government and how it affects the lives of the people it governs.

GOVERNMENT NOTEBOOK

In your Government Notebook, write a paragraph about the purpose of government. What role does government play in your life?

SECTION 1

GOVERNMENT AND THE PUBLIC GOOD

READ TO DISCOVER

1. What is government, and why is it important?
2. How have some philosophers described the nature and purpose of the state?
3. What functions does government perform?
4. How does government promote the public good?

POLITICAL DICTIONARY

government
state
citizen
sovereignty
law
natural law
public policy
divine right of kings
legitimacy
social contract
natural right
politics
value
public good

Imagine what things would be like if there were no traffic rules. For example, what if no one had to stop at a stop sign? Consider a busy highway with no posted speed limits or warnings for drivers to obey. Driving a car under these conditions would be very dangerous.

Government—an institution with the power to make and enforce rules for a group of people—posts the signs that help make roads safer for travelers. Setting traffic rules—as well as enforcing those rules—is just one way government works to make people's lives safer and more secure. In the words of English philosopher Thomas Hobbes (1588–1679), life without such security would be "nasty, brutish, and short."

What Is Government?

Signs of government at work are everywhere—a postal service logo on a mailbox or a badge worn by a police officer. Government may also appear in less obvious ways—a bridge over a highway or a curfew for young people.

Government, however, is more than just a collection of these symbols and services. It establishes the rules and regulations that govern everyday life. Of course, other institutions also establish rules such as religions, social clubs, and professional associations. It is government, however, that has the authority to set rules for all the people living in a political unit, or **state**.

This absolute authority that a government has over its **citizens**, or members of the state, is called **sovereignty**. The United States, France, Japan, Russia, Mexico, China, and Nigeria are a few of the nearly 200 sovereign states in the world.

How do the governments of these and other sovereign states establish rules for their societies? They do so by making law. **Law** is a set of rules, made and enforced by government, that is binding on society. **Natural law** is the system of justice derived from nature rather than from the rules of society. It would apply if government or laws did not exist.

POLITICAL FOUNDATIONS *City snowplows clear the streets during a blizzard in New York City.* **What signs of government do you see every day in your community?**

SECTION 1

GOVERNMENT AND THE PUBLIC GOOD

Lesson Plans

For teaching strategies, see Lesson 1.1 located at the beginning of this chapter or on the One-Stop Planner.

Political Dictionary

To reinforce the section's vocabulary terms, refer students to the Electronic Glossary on the *Researcher CD-ROM.*

Section Assessment

To assess students' mastery of this section, have them complete Daily Quiz 1.1 in *Daily Quizzes with Answer Key.*

Caption Answer

Answers will vary, but students may discuss traffic signals and signs, police officers, government buildings, or any other logical sign of government.

HISTORY Throughout the centuries, philosophers have taken a variety of approaches to the role of government in people's lives. English philosopher John Stuart Mill (1806–1873), in his essay *On Liberty,* explores government's and society's proper relationships to individuals. Mill argues that people should be free to pursue their own goals in their own ways, as long as they do not try to deprive others or keep others from doing the same. The reason that government might exert power over a person is to prevent harm to another. Indeed, everyone is better off, Mill says, when individuals are allowed to live as they see fit rather than as others think they should. Mill stresses that the main duty of government is to protect people from harm and secure their freedom to pursue their own good. ■

Caption Answer

Answers will vary, but students should point to actions that the government takes to fulfill the social contract.

There are laws covering everything from punishment for crimes, from murder and theft to littering, to programs for building highways, granting college loans, and providing job training. Laws also govern the ways in which such rules are enforced, such as by determining the punishment for breaking a rule.

Most societies have thousands of laws. These are part of **public policies,** or the plans and decisions that a government makes in a particular area of public concern. The public policy on traffic safety, for example, includes laws that set speed limits, require the use of seat belts, and establish rules for issuing driver's licenses. Regardless of their focus, all laws and policies have two things in common—they deal with a public problem and they are enforceable.

Origins of Government

Scholars have long debated the origins of the state and government. In the past, philosophers argued that rulers—typically kings and queens—received their authority to govern from God. This is known as the **divine right of kings.** The rightful authority any government has over its citizens is known as **legitimacy**.

In the 1600s Thomas Hobbes argued that people create the state by entering into a **social contract**. Under this contract, the people give up their individual sovereignty to the state. In exchange, the state provides peace and order.

English philosopher John Locke (1632–1704) developed his own ideas about the social contract. Locke argued that the contract creates a limited government that relies entirely on the consent of the governed. In other words, the government has legitimacy because the people, not God or anyone else, give it authority to govern.

Locke also believed that government's proper job is to secure people's natural rights. **Natural rights** are those that people have simply because they are human beings. The U.S. Declaration of Independence lists some of these natural rights: life, liberty, and the pursuit of happiness. Locke argued that the people may throw out governments that do not secure these rights. In *Of Civil Government,* from *Two Treatises on Government,* Locke stated,

> 66 Whosoever in authority exceeds the power given him by the law . . . may be opposed as any other man who by force invades the right of another. 99

Functions of Government

A government should secure citizens' natural rights and fulfill its part of the social contract by performing a variety of functions. In the United States you can see government working toward these goals all around you—the police officer walking a beat, the soldier coming home on leave, the health inspector checking a restaurant, officials debating ideas at a public meeting. These actions are examples of the critical functions of government—to maintain order, provide services, resolve conflicts, and promote society's shared values. How many of these functions a government actually serves varies from country to country.

Maintaining Order Government maintains order in society by enforcing laws that protect

PUBLIC GOOD *To enforce laws that prohibit littering, the government fines those who do not properly dispose of trash.* **In what other ways does government fulfill its part of the social contract?**

Political Scientist

Answer the following questions.

TRUE or FALSE

- ■ I enjoy watching political debates on television.
- ■ I keep up with current events and political issues.
- ■ During an election year, I try to stay informed about the candidates.
- ■ I have my own opinions when it comes to our government.

Like most people, you probably think of scientists as specialists who study the life sciences, such as biology. Some scientists, however, are social scientists. The role of a social scientist is to study the structure of a society and the activities of its members.

A social scientist who studies the structure and role of government is called a political scientist. Political scientists explore how government and political institutions function. They answer questions about government as well as seek solutions to its problems. They also offer theories on

Many political scientists teach at universities. **How do you become a political scientist?**

how to make government function better. For example, a political scientist might study a presidential campaign and election, analyzing the election's outcome and the public's response. He or she then might present the findings in a report or an article. Such an election analysis might be useful in future elections, or it might help gauge the nation's attitudes toward government and politics in general.

Most political scientists are employed as teachers or researchers at universities. Many others work in government agencies, conducting research and analyzing data. Still others work as members of "think tanks" for corporations and private institutes to research and study political issues and problems.

How do you become a political scientist? Education is key. Most jobs for political scientists require an advanced college degree. A budding political scientist must also have a keen interest in government and the political process. Review your answers to the True/False questions above. Perhaps you are already on your way.

the safety and security of the people and property. For example, police officers help protect society from those who murder, steal from, or harm other people.

In addition, government works to protect people from unfair or harmful business practices. It establishes laws that promote respect for individual rights in the workplace and in society. For example, government attempts to ensure that employers do not discriminate against workers because of race, ethnicity, gender, or religion. Government also protects and promotes businesses through such means as regulating commerce and protecting national industries. This protection allows businesses to perform functions essential to the community—building houses, transporting people, and creating new jobs, for example.

Government also maintains order by protecting the country from foreign invasion. National

---

Careers in Government

To help students learn about other careers in government, refer them to the Careers section on the *Holt Researcher Online.*

> **Caption Answer**
>
> usually an advanced college degree is required

THEMES IN GOVERNMENT

PUBLIC GOOD Where does the United States stand on health care? Medical costs became a controversial political issue in the 1980s, when technological advances resulted in sophisticated new equipment and procedures.

The United States spends more than any other country on medical care, but it is the only industrialized nation that does not have a national health insurance program. Instead, some employers provide group medical insurance to their employees. Some people have said this system is inadequate, arguing that more and more companies are unable or unwilling to pay the rising premiums and therefore fail to offer any health insurance to their employees. Others point out that millions of poor families have no coverage. According to some economists, the nation's prosperity will be threatened until health costs are brought under control. ■

POLITICAL FOUNDATIONS

Urging a class of graduating seniors from a Texas high school to involve themselves with the public good, a commencement speaker explained the phrase "No taxation without representation." The speaker pointed out that the phrase was not a complaint that taxes would deprive individuals of their money; instead, it was meant as a protest because without representation, colonists would not be heard in public discussions.

Political scientists note that when people discuss issues, they reflect on various points of view, compare values, work toward compromise, and even change their minds. In the course of exchanging ideas, people may see beyond their private interests to the common good.

Does talk stand in the way of action? Through discussion, people draw informed opinions on various issues and develop the skills needed to participate in government.

Therefore, the foundation of U.S. politics is an active, involved citizenry. Public discussion is the ground on which citizens arrive at a course of action. ■

Caption Answer
through its laws and policies

security is important for all governments because it helps protect citizens' lives, rights, and property.

Providing Services Government provides many needed services that people cannot easily provide on their own. It builds roads that carry people and goods. It inspects and approves food and medicines to make sure they are safe. Government also delivers mail across the country, provides assistance to people with low incomes, and builds schools.

Some people argue that other institutions, such as private businesses, could provide many of these services. In fact, private industry and other institutions do provide some important services. For example, people often send packages using a private delivery company instead of using the U.S. postal service. Private charities, churches, and other volunteer organizations also provide assistance

PUBLIC GOOD *As in other countries, people in the United States value quality health care for older people.* **How does U.S. government promote the values of U.S. citizens?**

to people with low incomes or no insurance. In general, however, government provides important services that private industry alone would not make available to all citizens. Because most government services do address issues of widespread concern, the benefits are shared by everyone.

Resolving Conflict Government helps resolve conflict by bringing people together to reach common goals through compromise. A compromise is a resolution of conflict in which each side gives in to some of the other side's demands.

Government brings about compromise through **politics**, the process by which people participating in government express opinions about what government should or should not do. Government then makes decisions according to those opinions.

The court system—part of government—has the authority to enforce the decisions reached in these compromises. Courts also act as a neutral party working to peacefully resolve disputes between people.

Promoting Values Maintaining order, providing services, and resolving conflict help government fulfill a fourth function, promoting common values. **Values** are basic principles by which people act and live their lives. These values include safety and willingness to compromise. Society in the United States also values equality of opportunity, respect for individual rights, a good education, health care for older people and those with low incomes, and personal responsibility. Because people find it difficult to promote common values by themselves, government helps by passing laws and setting policies.

The Public Good

These functions of government all share a fundamental purpose, to serve the public good. The **public good** is another term for the public interest or the well-being of society as a whole. Good government tries to pursue policies that serve the public interest.

How do governments determine what policies serve the public good? After all, people disagree about which public policies are best. Should government spend money on public schools, or should it provide grants to parents who want to send their children to private schools? Should

PUBLIC GOOD *Passengers in San Luis Obispo, California, board a federally funded Amtrak train.* **What other types of services does government provide?**

Caption Answer
Answers will vary, but students may discuss any of a wide range of services provided by the government.

government spend money building more roads, or should it increase funding for public transportation? Deciding which of these options makes good public policy is a vital responsibility of government.

One way to determine if a policy serves the public good is to ask if it reflects the narrow interests of a few or the broad concerns of many. Policies that fulfill only narrow interests usually do not serve the public good, while policies that address a wide range of concerns tend to promote the public good.

Throughout this textbook you will have the opportunity to consider whether various government policies serve the public good. You will investigate not only the structure and workings of government but also the results of government policies. Thus, you will not only study how government works, you also will have the opportunity to decide whether it works well.

SECTION 1 REVIEW

1. Identify and explain:
* government
* state
* citizen
* sovereignty
* law
* natural law
* public policy
* divine right of kings
* legitimacy
* social contract
* natural rights
* politics
* value
* public good

2. Identifying Concepts: Copy the diagram below. Use it to identify and describe the various functions of government.

```
Functions of Government
```

3. Finding the Main Idea

a. What is the difference between natural law and laws made by governments?
b. What is the social contract?

4. Writing and Critical Thinking

Comparing: Examine the ideas of John Locke and Thomas Hobbes and explain how they influenced the nature of governments.
Consider:
* Hobbes's view of the relationship between the people and the state
* Locke's view of government's responsibility to the people

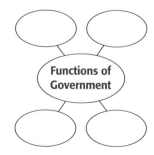

Homework Practice Online
keyword: SV3 HP1

SECTION 2

FORMS OF GOVERNMENT

READ TO DISCOVER

1. What are the differences between monarchies, republics, and dictatorships?
2. What are the advantages and disadvantages of unitary, federal, and confederal systems?
3. What are the major advantages and disadvantages of presidential and parliamentary forms of government?

POLITICAL DICTIONARY

monarchy
feudalism
absolute monarchy
constitutional monarchy
republic
classical republic
democracy
dictatorship
autocracy
oligarchy

authoritarian
totalitarian
despotism
unitary system
federal system
confederal system
presidential system
parliamentary
 system

Many kinds of government exist around the world. Governments differ in their sources of authority and in how power is shared among and within their national, regional, and local levels.

Sources of Authority

Whatever form a government takes, a key consideration is the source of the government's power. The basis of a government's power determines whether narrow interests or the public good is served.

Monarchies In some countries, the office of the head of state is a hereditary position. In most of these countries, which are called **monarchies**, the head of state is a king or a queen. **Feudalism** is a political system based on the rule of local lords bound to a monarch by ties of loyalty. Some monarchs reduced the power of nobles. This led to an

absolute monarchy, in which the king or queen had almost complete power. Until the early part of the 1900s, most countries were ruled by monarchs. Today roughly 30 countries have monarchs.

Many of these countries are **constitutional monarchies** in which the monarch is primarily a ceremonial head of state. The real power lies in another part of government. Constitutional monarchies include the United Kingdom and Japan. Monarchs have substantial power in only a few countries, such as Saudi Arabia, and Kuwait.

Republics Most countries today are republics. In its true form, a **republic** is a country in which the government's authority comes only from the people. Ancient Greek city-states allowed all adults to participate in government decisions. This is known as a **classical republic**. The government in a republic is made up of representatives elected by the people. How the people are represented differs, but all true republics are based on some form of representation. The United States is a republic, as are France, Mexico, and India. Constitutional monarchies also have representative systems of government.

The terms *republic* and *democracy* often are used interchangeably. **Democracy** comes from two Greek words that together mean "rule by the people." Democracy recognizes the authority of citizens to control their government—by voting, expressing their views, and forming or joining

CONSTITUTIONAL GOVERNMENT *Here, Queen Elizabeth of Great Britain leaves Buckingham Palace in a parade. **What is the role of a king or queen in a constitutional monarchy?***

Comparing Governments

Japan's Constitutional Monarchy

After Japan's defeat in World War II, its military-dominated government was abolished. Under the terms of the war's peace treaty, Japan was required to establish a peaceful government. In 1947 a new constitution was enacted, creating a system of government based on a European civil law system and heavily influenced by the British and the U.S. systems of government.

For this reason, there are several similarities among the governments of Japan, the United States, and Great Britain. For example, Japan's executive head of government is an elected prime minister, who is chosen by the Japanese legislature, the Diet. Like the U.S. Congress, the Diet is elected by the people. It is made up of two houses—a 511-member House of Representatives and a 252-member House of Councillors.

Japan is organized into 47 prefectures, which are similar to states or provinces. Like the elected governors of the United States, an elected governor administers each of Japan's prefectures.

Unlike the United States, however, Japan is a constitutional monarchy. Like Great Britain, which has a king or queen, Japan has a ceremonial head of state, the emperor. The reigning emperor is a symbol of the nation and holds no executive power.

political groups. Constitutional monarchies may also have a democratic form of government.

Dictatorships Some countries that call themselves republics have governments over which the people have little, if any, control. In some cases, government officials are not elected by the people. In others, elections are unfair or manipulated by those in control. These countries are not truly republics. They are dictatorships.

Power in a **dictatorship** is concentrated in the hands of a single person or a small group of people. If a single person holds the power, the government is an **autocracy**, which means "rule by one." (Note that a monarchy can be autocratic if

the monarch—one person—holds all the power.) If a small group of people holds the power, the government is an **oligarchy**, which means "rule by few."

A dictatorship's authority may rest on a combination of its leader's political power, military power, wealth, and/or social position. Dictators achieve and maintain power through force. Some dictators claim they truly represent the will of the people. In truth, however, dictatorships are **authoritarian** because rulers answer only to themselves, not to the people.

Sometimes dictatorships are so extreme that they become totalitarian. **Totalitarian** rulers

Sources of Authority

MONARCHY

- Head of state is a hereditary position.

Constitutional Monarchy
- King or queen is only the ceremonial head of state.
- Real power lies in another branch of government.

REPUBLIC (DEMOCRATIC)

BALLOT
- People are the source of authority.
- Government is made up of representatives elected by the people.

DICTATORSHIP

- Political and/or military power, wealth and/or social position are the source of leaders' authority.
- Power is achieved and maintained through force.

*One of the differences between types of government systems is the source of authority. **What is the source of authority in the U.S. government?***

The creation of the European Union (EU), which is a confederation made up of 15 independent nations, has created questions regarding the balance of power between the EU and its member states. Two conditions limit its power. The first condition is that the EU can legislate only in areas in which the member nations have granted it the right to be involved. Some of these areas are agriculture, industry, the environment, and monetary affairs. The second condition is the adoption of subsidiarity, a principle that limits the Union's authority to covering only areas that it is better equipped to handle than the individual members' governments. The national governments of the member states remain responsible for all other areas of government. ■

Transparency

An overhead transparency of the chart on this page is available in *Transparency Resources.* See Transparency 2: How Power Is Distributed.

Caption Answer

Power is divided among national, state, and local levels.

Caption Answer

(for page 11)

independently of the legislature

---

seek complete control over all aspects of citizens' lives, including political, religious, social, cultural, and even personal activities. This type of rule is known as **despotism**. There are several totalitarian states in the world today, including Burma (Myanmar) in South Asia.

Totalitarian governments often employ vast security networks and secret police to control citizens' actions. In addition, they try to influence people's beliefs through controlling the everyday aspects of life such as what news organizations report and what schools teach. Free speech is greatly limited, and political organizations that oppose the government are banned. Opponents of the government are imprisoned and sometimes killed.

Power Among Levels of Government

Governments also differ in how power is distributed among the national, regional, and local levels. Ways of distributing power fall into three types of systems: unitary, federal, and confederal.

Unitary Systems In a **unitary system**, all legal power is held by the national, or central, government. Local governments, such as those for provinces and cities, have no independent powers and are simply local representatives of the national government. Their job is to carry out decisions made by the national government. The United Kingdom, Israel, and Japan are examples of unitary systems.

Federal Systems Some countries have **federal systems** in which powers are divided among national, state, and local governments. In this system, some powers belong only to the national government, others only to state and local governments, and still others are shared by all three. The United States has a federal system of government, as do Germany, India, Australia, and Malaysia.

Confederal Systems In a **confederal system**, independent states join together to accomplish common goals. There may be no central government, but the members of the confederation may set up an organization to carry out agreed-upon policies.

The United States was a confederation from 1781 to 1789. In 1789 the Articles of Confederation were replaced with the U.S. Constitution and a federal system of government. Today, Canada, Russia, and the United Arab Emirates are examples of confederations. The European Union (EU) is a confederation of nations made up of 15 European countries that joined together to promote economic and political cooperation.

Power Within Levels of Government

Just as power may be distributed among levels of government, power within a single level of government also may be divided. In other words, different powers are given to the different branches of a government. The relationship between the

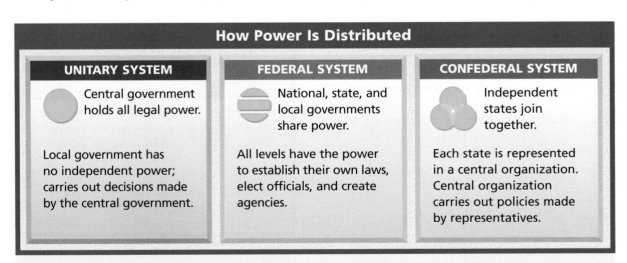

How Power Is Distributed

UNITARY SYSTEM	FEDERAL SYSTEM	CONFEDERAL SYSTEM
Central government holds all legal power.	National, state, and local governments share power.	Independent states join together.
Local government has no independent power; carries out decisions made by the central government.	All levels have the power to establish their own laws, elect officials, and create agencies.	Each state is represented in a central organization. Central organization carries out policies made by representatives.

Power among levels of government may be classified according to three types of systems. **How is power distributed in the U.S. government?**

branches of government may take two basic forms: presidential systems and parliamentary systems.

Presidential Systems The legislative branch, which makes the law, and the executive branch, which carries out the law, are separate and independent of each other in a **presidential system** of government. The executive branch usually is headed by a president, who is chosen independently of the legislature. This chief executive serves a set term in office and has powers separate from those of the legislature. Members of the executive branch cannot be members of the legislative branch. In addition to serving as head of the executive branch, the president also represents the country as head of state.

The United States has a presidential system of government. Each branch of government acts as a check on the others' powers. In some presidential systems, however, one branch of government may have much more power than the other(s). In France, for example, the president can dissolve part of the national legislature and call new elections.

Parliamentary Systems The chief executive, often called a prime minister or premier, is chosen by the parliament, or legislature, in a **parliamentary system** of government. The prime minister or premier and other officials appointed from the parliament make up the executive. If the

PRINCIPLES OF DEMOCRACY *Egypt has a parliamentary system of government. The head of state, President Hosni Mubarak, was elected by the national legislature.* **How is the head of state chosen in a presidential system?**

executive loses the parliament's support, a new government must be formed or a new legislative election held.

In parliamentary systems the chief executive of the government and the head of state are separate offices. In some parliamentary systems, such as in the United Kingdom, the head of state is a monarch. In others, such as in Israel, the head of state is a president.

SECTION 2 REVIEW

1. Identify and explain: monarchy, feudalism, absolute monarchy, constitutional monarchy, republic, classical republic, democracy, dictatorship, autocracy, oligarchy, authoritarian, totalitarian, despotism, unitary system, federal system, confederal system, presidential system, parliamentary system

2. Identifying Concepts: Copy the diagram below. Use it to compare the advantages and disadvantages of a federal, confederal, and unitary system of government.

	Advantages	Disadvantages
Federal		
Confederal		
Unitary		

Homework Practice Online
keyword: SV3 HP1

3. **Finding the Main Idea**

a. What is the difference between a republic and a classical republic? between a monarchy and an absolute monarchy?

b. What are the characteristics of authoritarianism? of totalitarianism? of despotism?

4. **Writing and Critical Thinking**

Analyzing: Compare the characteristics of a presidential and a parliamentary system. Write an analysis of the strengths and weaknesses of each.
Consider:
• the way each system divides power among its branches
• the way leaders of each system are selected

SECTION 3
FOUNDATIONS OF DEMOCRACY

READ TO DISCOVER

1. What are the major principles of democracy?
2. What is the difference between direct democracy and representative democracy?

POLITICAL DICTIONARY

anarchy
majority rule
liberal democracy
minority rights
direct democracy
representative democracy

During the 1900s, democracy was the one form of government that did not see a decline. Totalitarian dictatorships in Nazi Germany and Italy were defeated in World War II, and few countries today are ruled by absolute monarchs. The dictatorships that ruled Russia, as well as many countries in Eastern Europe and the rest of the world, have been replaced for the most part by democratic governments. Some authoritarian and totalitarian dictatorships do exist, but many countries have turned to democracy.

Why does democracy endure? Does it provide things that other forms of government do not?

Benefits of Democracy

In its ideal form, democracy is based on five broad principles that foster its success. It should

★ give people the opportunity to make choices,
★ recognize the dignity and worth of each person,
★ promote respect for the law,
★ protect the rights of the minority, and
★ produce policies that promote the public good.

Allowing Choice Imagine a restaurant in which the waiter selects your dinner for you. Even if you enjoy the food, you might feel you have missed something by having the waiter choose your meal. After all, deciding what to eat is a valued exercise of choice for most people. Many people want the same right to choose when it comes to more important matters, such as who governs their community and country. Most people want their government's decisions to reflect citizens' wishes.

In democracies, people have the opportunity to make their own choices. Some people have argued that ordinary people are not wise enough to govern themselves. Even though people sometimes make mistakes, the opportunity to choose is important because it allows people to take responsibility for their own lives.

People living in a democratic society make their own choices in free and fair elections. For example, voters in the United States elect a president every four years and representatives every two years. Voters also freely choose their state and local leaders and representatives.

Ideally, people in a democracy also have the right to make their own choices regarding other areas of their lives. No one can be forced to join or reject a particular religion or to worship in a particular way. People are free to declare their opinions publicly, to decide what kind of jobs they

PRINCIPLES OF DEMOCRACY *Democracies give people the opportunity to choose their own jobs. Citizens of the United States are free to choose jobs that suit their interests and abilities.* ***What other benefits does a democracy provide?***

Citizenship in Action

Teenage Volunteers Lend a Helping Hand

Teenage volunteers help to repair the roof of a church in Alabama.

The spirit of volunteerism in the United States—neighbors helping neighbors—is as old as the nation itself. In the early 1800s, for example, volunteer societies established by Christian groups supported educational activities and other concerns.

Today many of the nation's volunteers are young people. According to Denny Barnett of Volunteers of America, one of the country's oldest human-service agencies, people "are . . . getting involved at an earlier age." A recent study showed that more than 60 percent of kids between the ages of 12 and 17 on average volunteer more than three hours per week to a special cause.

No matter where you live or what your talents are, there is a nearby organization, group, or individual in need who could benefit from your efforts. For some volunteers, a favorite cause, such as the environment, is the best motivator for becoming involved. For example, in St. Louis a group of young people called the Earth Defenders scours vacant lots and other dumping sites, collecting and recycling thousands of pounds of discarded household items. The Earth Defenders clean these sites frequently, because within days of a cleanup project the lots are covered with trash again. Although the Earth Defenders may tire of picking up the trash, they are rewarded with the knowledge that their efforts have greatly benefited the environment.

Through their hard work and dedication, the Earth Defenders have converted six vacant lots into habitats for wildlife. The group has also been able to support its efforts with money raised through recycling, wise investment, and other activities. The members donate some of what they raise to other environmental causes, such as the National Wildlife Federation.

Involvement brings many rewards, not only to the community but to the volunteer as well. "I can say volunteering has helped me grow as a person," a young New Jersey volunteer said. In 1996 a report from the National Association of Secondary School Principals recommended that high school students receive academic credit for community service. Some people have even suggested that volunteer work be required for high school graduation.

Like Anne in Florida who helped the American Red Cross deliver aid to hurricane victims, or Ramiro in San Francisco who organized the planting of a vegetable garden to aid a homeless shelter, you too can make a difference by volunteering your time.

Start small—visit a nursing home, help clean up a beach or park, run a race for your favorite cause, or campaign for a political candidate. You might spend time volunteering for a few hours during the weekend, or over your summer vacation. These are some of the many ways that you can put your citizenship into action.

What Do You Think?

1. Why do you think many of the country's young people volunteer their time to a special cause?
2. Do you think that high school students should receive academic credit for their volunteer work? Why or why not?

What Do You Think? Answers

1. Answers will vary, but students may point to a sense of belonging to a group, a positive feeling gained from helping others, or serving the public good.
2. Answers will vary, but students may point out that by offering credit, schools may increase volunteerism, or that by offering credit, schools may be degrading the spirit of volunteerism. Students should defend their position.

would like to have, whether to pursue higher education, to live where they like, and to associate with others as they please.

The right to make one's own choices also carries responsibilities. One of the most important responsibilities is learning about candidates and issues in order to make educated voting decisions. People also have a responsibility to respect the rights and freedoms of others.

Ideally, participation in government teaches people to adopt a broader point of view and consider more than just their own concerns. By applying these lessons to the tasks of self-government, people will hopefully make decisions that promote the public good. Besides, in a democracy, government decisions will require the agreement of others. Political arguments that reflect only the self-interests of a small group generally will not succeed unless they appeal to the interests of people outside the group.

Thus, an organization whose goals ignore the needs and wants of others will probably have a hard time getting votes for its proposals. For example, a group that backs a policy allowing developers to build houses in the Grand Canyon would probably not gain much support. People who enjoy the beauty of the canyon would oppose such development.

Recognizing Individual Worth By allowing all citizens to participate in governing, democracy promotes the value of every human being. In a democracy, the views of each person—regardless of wealth, race, gender, or position in life—should be considered and valued.

Ideally, democracy promotes equality by giving all citizens the chance to participate fully in society. Equality of opportunity, however, does not mean equality of results. Rather, in a democracy all people are allowed equal opportunity to take risks and to succeed or fail on their own merits. Democracy thus allows people to take personal responsibility for their successes and failures.

Promoting Respect for Law If citizens participate in government, they are generally more likely to respect its laws than if the laws are simply forced upon them. How can citizens participate in making the laws that govern them? In the United States, citizens can speak at city council and other local government meetings. They can write to their representatives. You can participate in making rules that govern you by attending meetings of the student council and the school board, for example.

Ideally, democracy also gives people the right to challenge the fairness of a law. A citizen who happens to disagree with a law may organize other citizens to try to change it. All people in a democracy, however, have a responsibility to obey the laws that are established by government. If citizens ignored laws they did not like, or if government simply did not establish laws to maintain order in society, the result would be **anarchy**—a state of political disorder resulting from the absence of rules or government.

Protecting Minority Rights Most decisions in a democracy are made by majority rule.

CITIZENSHIP *The Internet is an excellent resource for keeping informed about political candidates and issues.* **What are some other ways that citizens can remain informed about their government?**

Majority rule occurs when decisions are based on the desire of more than half of the membership of a group. One of the ways that citizens in a democracy express what they want from government is by voting. Decisions are then based on the desires of the majority of voters.

A **liberal democracy** is a form of democracy that protects the rights of the minority. **Minority rights** are political rights that cannot be abolished in a democracy even though they are held by less than half of the population. These rights include freedom to attend a particular place of worship even if most people attend another. In addition, all citizens have the right to express their opinions even if their views are not popular.

Those in the majority have a responsibility to respect the views of the minority, even if they do not agree with them. Democracy encourages a respect for individual worth that makes it more likely this responsibility will be recognized.

Promoting the Public Good If all citizens participate in government, decisions likely will better promote the public good than if decisions are left to just a few people. Why? Remember that the public good is best served through policies that address a wide variety of society's concerns rather than just a few. Because democracy allows citizens to participate in the political processes that lead to decisions, more ideas and points of view are considered. Democracy thus serves the public good because it allows citizens to make informed decisions about which public policies are best for them.

Forms of Democracy

Although all democracies are based on these principles, not all democracies work the same way. There are two types of democracy—direct and representative.

Direct Democracy Systems in which laws may be made directly by all citizens are called **direct democracies**. Town hall meetings held in some parts of the United States, in which citizens of a town gather to vote on community matters, are an example of direct democracy.

You might be part of a direct democracy. Are you a member of a club? Perhaps you and all the other students in your school voted on the theme for a dance or the destination for a field trip. If so, you have participated in a direct democracy.

POLITICAL FOUNDATIONS *The Acropolis is a hilltop in Athens, Greece, upon which Athenians built their main religious and government buildings during the 400s B.C.* **How is the political system of ancient Greece reflected in the U.S. political system?**

C A S E   S T U D Y

The Greek Polis

POLITICAL FOUNDATIONS The roots of direct democracy reach back for centuries to ancient Greece. Ancient Greece had a well-developed political system that, by the 700s B.C., was centered around the polis. The polis, commonly translated as "city-state," was made up of a town or city and its surrounding countryside. Athens and Sparta were among the most important of the ancient Greek city-states.

The polis typically was ruled by an oligarchy of wealthy citizens. However, all citizens, which included only free (nonenslaved) males, were expected to participate actively in the government of the polis.

THEMES IN GOVERNMENT

CITIZENSHIP The experience of student leadership used to be its own reward, but some colleges across the country are beginning to pay student leaders for their services. Student leaders are being asked to take on more work than they used to. Some run night-safety escort services or day-care centers for students' children, and on one campus the student government supervises a $2-million budget, which is the same size as the budgets of some small businesses.

Critics contend that learning what it means to be a volunteer should be a part of the educational process. The editor of *Student Leader* magazine, however, points out that schools seeking competent student leaders will have to pay for them. ■

SECTION 3
REVIEW ANSWERS

Caption Answer

the people themselves

Caption Answer

the people themselves

1. Refer to the following pages: anarchy (14), majority rule (15), liberal democracy (15), minority rights (15), direct democracy (15), representative democracy (16).

2. Webs should include allowing choice, recognizing individual worth, promoting respect for the law, protecting minority rights, and promoting the public good.

3a. In town hall meetings all citizens may vote on community matters. In the United States, citizens elect representatives who vote on national policies that affect them.

3b. People can vote in local, state, and national elections, speak at local government meetings, and write to their representatives.

4. Students answers should reflect an understanding of the principles of democracy, including majority rule and minority rights.

By the 500s B.C. some city-states had begun to move away from rule by oligarchies. Despite the fact that free males were still the only group to be considered citizens, important democratic changes began to take place.

Athenian direct democracy reached its height in the 400s B.C. All Athenian citizens formed the popular assembly. A Council of Five Hundred, chosen by a drawing from a pool of all citizens, ran the daily business of government. The assembly, however, in which all citizens had the right to vote, had the real power to decide domestic and foreign matters.

PRINCIPLES OF DEMOCRACY *In a representative democracy, people elect leaders to make public policies. Here, citizens vote in a presidential election.* ***Who makes public policies in a direct democracy?***

Representative Democracy It is not always practical for public policies to be made directly by the people. This is particularly true in countries with millions—or, as in the case of the United States, hundreds of millions—of citizens. Most people agree that direct voting on every single law would be difficult if not impossible. Thus, in **representative democracies** such as the United States, the people elect representatives to conduct the business of government for them.

In contrast to dictatorships and other authoritarian forms of government, in representative democracies, government officials answer to the voters. If voters believe that government officials have not acted to promote the public good, they may vote those officials out of office and replace them with other representatives.

1. Identify and explain: anarchy, majority rule, liberal democracy, minority rights, direct democracy, representative democracy

2. Identifying Concepts: Copy the diagram below. Use it to identify and describe the five principles on which democracy is based.

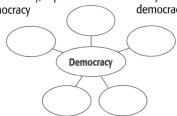

Democracy

Homework Practice Online

keyword: SV3 HP1

3. **Finding the Main Idea**

a. How are town hall meetings an example of direct democracy? How is the national government of the United States an example of representative democracy?

b. How can an individual influence government actions and policies?

4. **Writing and Critical Thinking**

Taking a Stand: Consider the basic principles of democracy and decide which you think is most important.
Consider:
• the role of majority rule in a democracy
• the need to protect the rights of individuals

IN THE NEWS

Shaping Political History

Many scholars have studied the origins of the state and of different types of government. One type is a monarchy, a classical form of government where sovereignty is vested in a single person, a monarch, whose right to rule is generally hereditary. The monarch is empowered to remain in office for life. A popular example of a monarchy today is Great Britain, whose monarch is Queen Elizabeth II. While the Queen is primarily a figurehead today, the classical form of a monarchy was much different.

During the Renaissance and for a time after, there emerged new monarchs who broke the power of nobility and centralized the state under their own rigid rule. Examples are Henry VII and Henry VIII of England and Louis XIV of France. Jacques-Benigne Bossuet (1627–1704) observed these monarchs and formulated the notion of "the divine right of kings." This concept held that monarchs ruled because they were chosen by God. This belief led to an absolute monarchy, or despotism, where one ruler had absolute authority.

Under powerful monarchs, the feudal society arose. Using this system, called feudalism, the ownership of all land was vested in the king. The nobles attained land from the king, and then they provided land to the seigneur who held a single manor. This produced a manorial system, where serfs—laborers tied to their land—worked from a seigneur, who granted them use of the land and protection in return for personal services.

After winning independence from Great Britain, the founders of the United States had the opportunity to create a different form of government—a democracy. From the beginning, Enlightenment philosophies shaped this new government. One especially influential English philosopher was John Locke (1632–1704). Locke believed there existed

Britain's Queen Elizabeth II tours the British Isles in July, 2001.

a social contract that created a limited government that is dependent on the will of the governed. He emphasized that natural law derived from nature, not the power of the state.

Locke also believed the government should secure the natural rights of its citizens. In Britain, the belief in natural law and the support of natural rights led to Magna Carta and the Glorious Revolution. Thomas Jefferson expressed these ideas in the Declaration of Independence as the right to life, liberty, and the pursuit of happiness. These concepts led the founders of the United States to develop a democratic system where political leaders received their authority from the people.

What Do You Think?

1. What are the differences between the ideas of the divine right of kings and natural law?

2. How does classical monarchy differ from democracy?

> **WHY IT MATTERS TODAY**
>
> The United States is one of the few countries never to have changed its system of government. Use **CNNfyi.com** or other **current events** sources to conduct research on a country that has recently undergone a change of its political system.
>
>
> CNNfyi.com

CHAPTER 1

Review Answers

Writing a Summary

Summaries should focus on the main points of each section. These may be found in the Read to Discover questions at the start of each section. Summaries should also use standard grammar, spelling, sentence structure, and punctuation.

Identifying Ideas

Refer to the following pages: natual law (3), divine right of kings (4), natural rights (4), feudalism (8), absolute monarchy (8), classical republic (8), authoritarian (9), totalitarian (9), despotism (10), liberal democracy (15).

Understanding Main Ideas

1. unitary—authority concentrated in national government; confederal—independent countries join together to accomplish goals,

(Continued on page 18)

Review

(Continued from page 17)
may delegate authority to central organization; federal—authority distributed among national, state, and local governments

2. Legitimacy is the rightful authority a government has over its citizens. It comes from the divine right of kings or from a social contract.

3. hereditary basis of power; people choose their representatives, single person or small group takes control

4. feudalism: based on the rule of local lords bound to a monarch by ties of loyalty; absolute monarchy: king or queen had nearly complete power; constitutional monarchy: king or queen is only a ceremonial leader

5. direct—citizens make and vote on laws; representative—citizens elect representatives to make laws and run the government

6. Choice allows people to take responsibility for their own lives. No, equal opportunity allows individuals to fail or succeed according to their own efforts and ability.

Reviewing Themes

1. Hobbes and Locke developed the theory of a social contract. Locke also believed that a government should secure peoples' natural rights.

2. Presidential system: legislature and executive are separate, executive serves a set term, chief executive and head of state are same person; Parliamentary system: executive is chosen by the legislature, executive serves until loses parliament's support, chief executive and head of state are different.

(Continued on page 19)

Writing a Summary

Using standard grammar, spelling, sentence structure, and punctuation, write a summary of the information in this chapter.

Identifying Ideas

Identify the following terms and explain their significance.

1. natural law

2. divine right of kings

3. natural rights

4. feudalism

5. absolute monarchy

6. classical republic

7. authoritarian

8. totalitarian

9. despotism

10. liberal democracy

Understanding Main Ideas

SECTION 1 *(pp. 3–7)*

1. How is government authority distributed in unitary, federal, and confederal systems?

2. What is legitimacy and where does a government get it?

SECTION 2 *(pp. 8–11)*

3. What is the source of authority in a monarchy? in a democratic republic? in a dictatorship?

4. How does feudalism differ from an absolute monarchy? from a constitutional monarchy?

SECTION 3 *(pp. 12–16)*

5. What is the difference between direct democracy and representative democracy?

6. Why is it important that democracy gives people the opportunity to make choices? Does equality of opportunity mean the same thing as equality of results? Why or why not?

Reviewing Themes

1. Political Foundations What ideas did Thomas Hobbes and John Locke develop about the nature of government?

2. Constitutional Government How does a presidential system differ from a parliamentary system?

3. Political Processes What processes can an individual citizen use to affect public policy?

Thinking Critically

1. Analyzing Read the U.S. Declaration of Independence on page 572. In what ways does the Declaration of Independence reflect John Locke's argument of a social contract between government and the people? Provide specific examples from the Declaration to support your position.

2. Comparing and contrasting Recall the differences between the presidential and parliamentary systems. In which system does the legislative branch choose the chief executive of government? How is the chief executive (the president) chosen in the United States? Do you think the influence of voters is stronger in one system compared to the other? Explain your answer.

3. Taking a stand In your own words, explain what the term public good means. How do you think government can promote the public good?

Writing About Government

Review what you wrote in your Government Notebook at the beginning of this chapter about the purpose of government. Now that you have studied the chapter, how would you revise your answer? How well do you think government in the United States carries out its functions? Record your answers in your Notebook.

Interpreting the Chart

Study the chart below. Then use it to help you answer the questions that follow.

1. How does the chart portray a confederal system?
   a. as a box
   b. as a pyramid
   c. as a Venn diagram
   d. as a sphere

2. How does the image for a federal system represent the division of power?

Analyzing Primary Sources

Leviathan

English Philosopher Thomas Hobbes (1588-1679) developed theories on the necessity and purpose of government. In *Leviathan* (1651), he describes a world without government (the "condition" mentioned below). Read the excerpt from *Leviathan* and answer the questions that follow.

"In such condition there is no place for industry, because the fruit thereof is uncertain; and consequently no culture of the earth; no navigation nor use of the commodities that may be imported by sea; no commodious [comfortable] building; no instruments of moving and removing such things as require much force; no knowledge of the face of the earth; no account of time; no arts; no letters [literature]; no society; and, which is worst of all, continual fear and danger of violent death; and the life of man solitary, poor, nasty, brutish, and short. . . ."

3. According to Hobbes, what does organized society provide? How do these provisions benefit the people in society?

4. Would a world without government be as Hobbes describes it? Explain.

How Power Is Distributed

UNITARY SYSTEM	FEDERAL SYSTEM	CONFEDERAL SYSTEM
Central government holds all legal power.	National, state, and local governments share power.	Independent states join together.
Local government has no independent power; carries out decisions made by the central government.	All levels have the power to establish their own laws, elect officials, and create agencies.	Each state is represented in a central organization. Central organization carries out policies made by representatives.

Building Your Portfolio

Imagine that you are U.S. ambassador to a country whose people only recently have over-thrown an authoritarian government. You have been invited to give a speech to representatives of the new government. Prepare a five-minute speech describing the benefits and challenges of democracy.

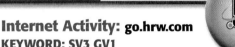
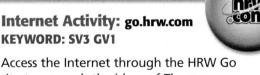

internet connect

Internet Activity: go.hrw.com
KEYWORD: SV3 GV1

Access the Internet through the HRW Go site to research the ideas of Thomas Hobbes and John Locke, two influential political philosophers that shaped democracy. Then create a chart in which you summarize, compare, and contrast their ideas on government and authority.

(Continued from page 18)

3. People can vote in local, state, and national elections, speak at local government meetings, and write to their representatives.

Thinking Critically

1. Answers will vary but should display an understanding of right to rule and government's responsibility to protect people's rights.

2. parliamentary; U.S. president is chosen independently of the legislature; students should note that in a presidential system citizens elect both the executive and legislative officials, but only legislative representatives are elected by citizens in a parliamentary system.

3. Answers will vary but students should give a definition and explain it; answers should show an understanding of the public good.

Writing About Government

The Government Notebook is a follow-up activity to the notebook activity that appears on page 2.

Building Social Studies Skills

1. a Venn diagram

2. divided into three levels to represent the three levels of a federal system: local, state, and national

3. Organized society provides the opportunity for secure businesses, common culture and knowledge, access to the arts, and personal safety.

4. Answers will vary, but students may argue that Hobbes is too extreme or too mild.

CHAPTER 2 ORIGINS OF U.S. GOVERNMENT

	OBJECTIVES	PACING GUIDE	REPRODUCIBLE RESOURCES
SECTION 1 **EARLY INFLUENCES** (pp. 21–24)	▶ What political ideals did English colonists bring with them to North America? ▶ What major documents limited the power of English monarchs? ▶ How were the ideals of limited and representative government evident in colonial governments?	**Regular** 2 days **Block Scheduling** 1 day	**ELL** Spanish Study Guide 2.1 **ELL** English Study Guide 2.1 **PS** Reading 1: *Magna Carta* **PS** Reading 2: *Mayflower Compact* **PS** Reading 4: *First Charter of Massachusetts* **PS** Reading 51: *Common Sense*
SECTION 2 **INDEPENDENCE** (pp. 25–30)	▶ What were two early attempts at unity among the colonies? ▶ What British policies pushed the colonies to cooperate with one another? ▶ What were some of the ideals that influenced the writing of the Declaration of Independence? ▶ How were the governments of the newly independent states similar?	**Regular** 1.5 days **Block Scheduling** .75 day	**ELL** Spanish Study Guide 2.2 **ELL** English Study Guide 2.2
SECTION 3 **THE FIRST NATIONAL GOVERNMENT** (pp. 31–34)	▶ What were the powers of the national government under the Articles of Confederation? ▶ How did limits on its power weaken the national government under the Articles? ▶ How did the states continue to struggle with unity after independence? ▶ How did Shays's Rebellion highlight the need for a stronger national government?	**Regular** 1.5 days **Block Scheduling** .5 day	**ELL** Spanish Study Guide 2.3 **ELL** English Study Guide 2.3 **PS** Reading 7: *Articles of Confederation* **E** Challenge and Enrichment Activity 2
SECTION 4 **THE CONSTITUTIONAL CONVENTION** (pp. 35–39)	▶ Who were the delegates to the Constitutional Convention? ▶ What major competing plans of government did the convention delegates debate? ▶ What were some of the compromises reached by the delegates?	**Regular** 1.5 days **Block Scheduling** .5 day	**ELL** Spanish Study Guide 2.4 **ELL** English Study Guide 2.4 **E** Simulations and Strategies for Teaching Government: Activity 2
SECTION 5 **RATIFYING THE CONSTITUTION** (pp. 40–42)	▶ What were the main arguments in the debate over ratification of the Constitution? ▶ What role did a bill of rights play in the debate? ▶ Which key states were among the last to ratify the Constitution?	**Regular** 1 days **Block Scheduling** .5 day	**ELL** Spanish Study Guide 2.5 **ELL** English Study Guide 2.5 **PS** Reading 19: *Patrick Henry's Speech* **PS** Reading 52: *The Federalist* "No. 10"

Chapter Resource Key

PS	Primary Sources	**A**	Assessment		Video
RS	Reading Support	**REV**	Review		Videodisc
E	Enrichment	**ELL**	Reinforcement and English Language Learners		Internet
S	Simulations		Transparencies		Holt Presentation Maker Using
SM	Skills Mastery		CD-ROM		Microsoft ® PowerPoint ®

TECHNOLOGY RESOURCES	REINFORCEMENT, REVIEW, AND ASSESSMENT
One-Stop Planner: Lesson 2.1 Holt Researcher Online Homework Practice Online Global Skill Builder CD-ROM CNN Presents American Government	**REV** Section 1 Review, p. 24 **A** Daily Quiz 2.1
One-Stop Planner: Lesson 2.2 Holt Researcher Online Homework Practice Online Global Skill Builder CD-ROM	**REV** Section 2 Review, p. 30 **A** Daily Quiz 2.2
One-Stop Planner: Lesson 2.3 Holt Researcher Online Homework Practice Online Transparency 3—Limits on Power of the National Government Global Skill Builder CD-ROM	**REV** Section 3 Review, p. 34 **A** Daily Quiz 2.3
One-Stop Planner: Lesson 2.4 Holt Researcher Online Homework Practice Online Cartoon Transparency 1—Constitutional Convention, Transparency 3—Limits on Power of the National Government Global Skill Builder CD-ROM	**REV** Section 4 Review, p. 39 **A** Daily Quiz 2.4
One-Stop Planner: Lesson 2.5 Holt Researcher Online Homework Practice Online Global Skill Builder CD-ROM	**REV** Section 5 Review, p. 42 **A** Daily Quiz 2.5

One-Stop Planner CD-ROM

It's easy to plan lessons, select resources, and print out materials for your students when you use the *One-Stop Planner CD-ROM with Test Generator.*

Chapter Review and Assessment

SM Global Skill Builder CD-ROM
HRW Go site
REV Chapter 2 Tutorial for Students, Parents, and Peers
REV Chapter 2 Review, pp. 44–45
Chapter 2 Test Generator (on the One-Stop Planner)
A Chapter 2 Test
A Alternative Assessment Handbook

HOLT PRESENTATION MAKER
Access Illustrated LECTURE NOTES using Microsoft® PowerPoint® on the One-Stop Planner CD-ROM

OBJECTIVES

▶ Identify the political ideals that the English colonists brought with them to North America.

▶ Explain the importance of a written constitution.

▶ Describe the major documents that limited the power of the English monarchs.

▶ Explain how the ideals of limited and representative government were evident in colonial governments.

MOTIVATE

Ask students to imagine that (as a class) they are stranded on a deserted island. In addition to finding food sources, building shelter, and identifying potential hazards, ask students to consider what sort of government they would have on their island. Give them several minutes to come to some agreement. Suggest that they consider elements of the U.S. government that they would include and elements that they would change. Ask students why it might be important to have a written constitution that outlined their ideas. After students have had the opportunity to discuss how to form a new government, allow them to explain their experience of trying to arrive at an agreement. Explain to students that in this section they will learn how the British colonists in North America created a new form of government.

TEACH

Building a Vocabulary

 In spiral notebooks, have students create a Political Dictionary to be used throughout the course. This dictionary may be used as an activity at the start of each new section; it may also be used as a modification device for students having difficulty or sheltered English students during tests and homework assignments. List words the students will be expected to know for this section on the board. Have students list, define, and give an example of each of the terms, using information provided in the text or on the *Researcher CD-ROM*.

Classifying Ideas

Write the terms *Limited Government* and *Representative Government* on the chalkboard. Ask students to describe what these terms mean. Explain to students that both were British ideals that influenced the U.S. government. Discuss the meaning of each term with the class and point out which concepts of limited and representative government students correctly listed earlier in the activity. Explain to students the ideals that were evident in early colonial governments. Have students attempt to categorize segments of the U.S. government into the categories listed on the chalkboard. Discuss with students the appropriate categorization.

Drawing Conclusions

 Organize students into groups of no more than five or six. Give a deck of cards to one person in each group, assigning him or her to be the "leader." Give each leader a note card that instructs him or her to make up a game as he or she goes along. The game should allow some students to win more cards or more points and should limit the ability of other students in the group to win cards or points. Encourage the leader to change the rules in the middle of the game to give some group members an advantage. Tell the whole class that they are to spend five minutes playing the game that their leader wants to play. After several minutes ask the group members to identify problems with the game they played. Now give the leaders a note card that instructs them to have their members decide on a game that everybody knows how to play and to play by the rules. After three to five more minutes, ask students to identify differences between this game and the previous one. Explain that the second game represented limited government. Tell students that in the next activity they will also learn about another form of government known as representative government.

Synthesizing Information

  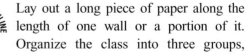 Lay out a long piece of paper along the length of one wall or a portion of it. Organize the class into three groups, assigning two or more students as researchers, one or two as the writers, and one or two as information coordinators. Tell students that they will be making a "Time Line to Unity." Using their text and the *Holt*

Researcher Online as resources, have each group identify important information regarding one of the following major documents: Magna Carta, the Petition of Right, or the English Bill of Rights. Have students write the information they obtain on the paper. Encourage students to leave space between events to allow for other events to be added in later sections. Afterward, have each group explain to the other groups how the document they studied limited the power of the English monarchs. Tell students that later in this section they will use this information to complete an activity.

CLOSE

Ask students once again to imagine that they are stranded on a deserted island. Have them form a system of government using the experience of the colonists and the ideals of limited and representative government, and have them write a constitution that outlines their government. Ask students to share their opinions regarding the difference between forming a government this time and the first time they tried to do this.

OPTIONS

Gifted Learners

 Encourage students to learn more about one or more of the monarchs discussed in this section (Charles I, Charles II, James II, and/or William and Mary). Students may need to utilize the library or the Internet for additional information. Encourage students to write a report profiling their person(s) and to share it with the rest of the class. Have students consider any contributions to the ideals of limited and representative government the person they researched may have made.

Students Having Difficulty/ Sheltered English Students

 Encourage students to fill in the time line they began in the second activity with additional information provided in this section, such as the beheading of Charles I, the crowning of Charles II and James II, and the Glorious Revolution. Have students work with a partner if they are having difficulty. Display students' time lines throughout the classroom.

Students Having Difficulty/ Sheltered English Students

 Discuss with students the concept of a bicameral legislature. Tell students that the British Parliament had a bicameral legislature, which probably influenced the United States to create such a legislature. Tell students that this concept was also adopted by most of the states. Have students use the State Profiles section on the *Holt Researcher Online* to review the types of state legislatures. Have students identify any state that does not have a bicameral legislature. Ask students to suggest reasons why so many state governments have bicameral legislatures.

Musical-Rhythmic Learners

 Organize the class into small groups. Each group should have at least one student who plays a musical instrument, if possible. Have each group write a song praising limited government. Students' songs should include ideas that served to shape early colonial governments and the modern U.S. government. After writing the song have students put it to music and perform their song for the rest of the class.

REVIEW

Have students complete the Section 1 Review on page 24. Use the answers in the Annotated Teacher's Edition to assess student mastery of this section.

ASSESS

To assess student mastery of this section, have students complete Daily Quiz 2.1 in *Daily Quizzes with Answer Key*. For additional assessment options, see *Alternative Assessment Handbook* on the *One-Stop Planner CD-ROM*.

ADDITIONAL RESOURCES

Howard, Dick. *Magna Carta:* Text and commentary. 1997. The University Press of Virginia.
Peters, William. *A More Perfect Union*. 1987. Crown Publishers, Inc.
A More Perfect Union. Brigham Young University. (video)

HOLT PRESENTATION MAKER
Access Illustrated LECTURE NOTES using Microsoft® PowerPoint® on the One-Stop Planner CD-ROM

OBJECTIVES

▸ Name two early attempts at unity in the colonies.
▸ Identify the British policies that pushed the colonies to cooperate with one another.
▸ List some of the ideals that influenced the writing of the Declaration of Independence.
▸ Explain the similarities among the newly independent states.

MOTIVATE

Ask students to write on a piece of paper one goal that they have achieved that means a lot to them. Then ask them to list any unsuccessful efforts at reaching the same goal and the obstacles that they overcame to achieve that goal. Ask for volunteers to share their goal and obstacles. Teachers may wish to model by sharing with the class their own goals, unsuccessful efforts, and obstacles. Explain to the class that in this section they will learn some of the unsuccessful efforts of the colonists and the obstacles that they had to overcome in order to reach their goal of independence.

TEACH

Building a Vocabulary

 In their spiral notebooks, have each student continue working on their Political Dictionary. List words the students will be expected to know for this section on the board. Have students list, define, and give an example of each of the terms using information provided in the text or on the *Researcher CD-ROM.*

Acquiring Information

 Organize students into pairs or groups of four. Explain that they are to write four newspaper articles describing the original colonies' early attempts at unity. They may choose headlines for their articles and add information from such sources as the Internet or the library. Students must write two articles about each of the attempts: one as if it were written at the start of the attempt, outlining the plan and the reasons for it; and one as if it were after the plan had failed,

explaining the reasons that the plan was unsuccessful. Have other newspaper articles available for students to get ideas from if necessary. Students may also debate reasons why each plan failed in order to practice debating skills for the next activity.

Debating Ideas

 Organize students into two teams, one representing the British government and the other representing the colonies. Have students debate the merits and negative effects of the Stamp Act and other policies that the colonists thought of as unfair. Encourage all students to participate. Explain to students that it was in part because of these unfair policies that the colonies wanted to declare independence. Tell students that the colonists feared creating a government that was too powerful and unrepresentative of the people, and that the colonists took this into consideration when adopting the Declaration of Independence.

Synthesizing Information

Ask students to make two columns on a piece of paper with the headings *Limited* and *Representative.* Ask students to recall the earlier lesson in which these ideals were discussed. In pairs or independently, have students go through the Declaration of Independence and list sentences or phrases that represent each of the ideals and write them under the appropriate heading. Ask students to share what they have written with the rest of the class. Discuss with students how these ideals still guide the U.S. government. Explain to students that in the next activity they will learn about how these principles guided the newly created states to grow in similar ways.

Comparing and Contrasting

 Pass out two or more newspapers from different cities such as the *New York Times,* the *Dallas Morning News,* or your local paper. In pairs or groups of three, ask students to identify similarities between the types of news covered in each of these newspapers at the national, state, and local levels. Explain to students that in a similar way, although the newly independent states were separate, they shared similar governmental practices. Have the class discuss the similar structures of and rights protected by the state governments. Have students create a list that covers the similarities and differences.

CLOSE

Have students return to the piece of paper on which they identified their personal goal and obstacles in the Motivate activity. Have students turn over that piece of paper and list some of the unsuccessful efforts and the obstacles that the colonies went through to reach their eventual goal of independence. Encourage students to include influences that led to the signing of the Declaration of Independence.

OPTIONS

Gifted Learners

 Using the Biographies section located on the *Holt Researcher Online*, have students look up more information on the Boston Tea Party or Samuel Adams and write a brief report that describes the contribution of the person or event to the independence movement. Be sure to have students consider the consequences on British authority and on the colonists' feelings of unity. Encourage students to share this information with the class.

Visual-Spatial Learners/Linguistic Learners

 Encourage students to do one of the following: (a) act out the Boston Tea Party as a small group, (b) draw or paint a picture depicting the Boston Tea Party, (c) conduct a dramatic reading of the events leading up to and during the Boston Tea Party, or (d) act out a comedic parody of the Boston Tea Party. Guide students to maintain historical accuracy, and have students consider the feelings of the colonists when portraying the situation.

Intrapersonal Learners

 Discuss with students the purpose of the Declaration of Independence and its significance. Encourage students to write an essay from the point of view of one of the contributing writers of the Declaration of Independence or of a person who signed the Declaration. Have students discuss the reasons for wanting to declare independence along with the fears that contributors had about signing their names to a document that declared the colonies' independence from Britain. Encourage students to share their essays.

Visual-Spatial Learners

 Give students a list of famous events that were important steps leading to the colonies' declaring independence, such as the Boston Massacre and the First Continental Congress. Have students create a map that identifies the location and the date(s) that each event took place. Have students color-code the events to indicate whether the action was carried out by the British or the colonists. Have students share their maps with the class. Display the finished products throughout the classroom.

REVIEW

Have students complete the Section 2 Review on page 30. Use the answers in the Annotated Teacher's Edition to assess student mastery of this section.

ASSESS

To assess student mastery of this section, have students complete Daily Quiz 2.2 in *Daily Quizzes with Answer Key*. For additional assessment options, see *Alternative Assessment Handbook* on the *One-Stop Planner CD-ROM*.

ADDITIONAL RESOURCES

Rhodehamel, John. *The American Revolution: Writings from the War of Independence*. 2001. Library of America.

McCaughey, Elizabeth. *Government by Choice: Inventing the United States Constitution*. 1987. Basic Books.

HOLT PRESENTATION MAKER Access Illustrated LECTURE NOTES using Microsoft® PowerPoint® on the One-Stop Planner CD-ROM

OBJECTIVES

▶ Describe the powers of the national government under the Articles of Confederation.

▶ Explain how limits on its power weakened the national government under the Articles.

▶ Describe the struggle for unity after independence.

▶ Explain how Shays's Rebellion highlighted the need for a stronger national government.

MOTIVATE

Organize the class into groups of four to five students. Give each group several pieces of a puzzle so that each group can fit together a partial image of the whole puzzle. Ask students to problem-solve any difficulties they encounter in completing their puzzle. When students begin to realize that they only have part of the whole puzzle, suggest that they work with another group or groups to complete the puzzle. Once the class has united to complete the whole puzzle, explain that in this section they will learn that the newly independent states had to problem-solve and unite to accomplish their goals. Explain to students that in this section they will be learning about problems with early attempts at government.

TEACH

Building a Vocabulary

In their spiral notebooks, have each student continue working on their Political Dictionary. List words the students will be expected to know for this section on the board. Have students list, define, and give an example of each of the terms using information provided in the text or on the *Researcher CD-ROM*.

Drawing Conclusions

Randomly choose 13 students to act as "Congress" and ask them to sit at the front of the room. Ask students in the class how they would feel if these 13 students alone had the power to decide such issues as what was studied, how homework and tests were graded, and who sat in which seats. Discuss problems with this system.

Explain that this was the type of power given to Congress by the Articles of Confederation. Referring to Reading 7: Articles of Confederation, discuss the strengths and weaknesses of Congress under the Articles. Discuss with students how the powers given to Congress led to problems with the government. Tell students that in the next activity they will be learning about some of the weaknesses of the national government under the Articles.

Applying Ideas/Information

Using the scenario from the previous activity, ask students to imagine that (a) these 13 students could make the laws but had no one to carry out the laws; (b) they had little means of obtaining materials for the class and could not prevent students from using their own, (c) they could not prevent students in the class from working as a group on projects and sharing answers; and (d) the 13 students could decide what would happen in the classroom, but they would not be able to enforce their decisions. Have students brainstorm what type of classroom would result from this type of system (i.e., Would it be consistent? Would there be respect for those 13 students making decisions? Would there be uniformity?). Have students refer to Reading 7: Articles of Confederation and consider the limits placed on government power by the Articles. Discuss the similarities between the problems with the limits in the classroom and those of the independent states. Afterward, have students try the following activity that highlights the difficulties that states faced as they tried to unify.

Analyzing Ideas/Information

On separate index cards, list the cultural beliefs, the economic interests, and a geographic description of the location of the 13 original states. Make several copies of each card. Pass a card to each student. Ask students to move around the classroom and try to find others who have their state. Teachers may wish to have students then identify the state to which their card refers. As a class, discuss the difficulties that may have arisen as a result of these differences between states. Point out that the colonies developed different types of economies based on different agricultural products and that each colony wanted to make sure that its interests were represented in the national government. Discuss how these differences would have made it difficult to unify. After completing this activity, tell students that in the next activity they will learn about the need for unity.

Identifying Cause and Effect

Have students identify events leading up to Shays's Rebellion. Ask students to discuss the point of view of the farmers. On one side of the board, list the problems with government that led to the rebellion. Ask students to identify the impact the rebellion had on government. List these results on the other side of the board. Ask students to hypothesize what might have happened had Shays's Rebellion not taken place and write a short essay describing what they think may have taken place. Have students discuss why Shays's Rebellion was an important event in the further unification of the states.

CLOSE

Ask students to recall the Motivate activity. Have them identify problems they had as groups and any frustrations they may have experienced while trying to complete the puzzle. Have students discuss how these problems and frustrations may have been similar to those faced by citizens of the states in the late 1700s. Have students create a list of the problems that were experienced under the Articles of Confederation and discuss them as a class. Lead students to realize the importance of a unified and strong national government.

OPTIONS

Gifted Learners/Linguistic Learners

Encourage students to read the actual Articles of Confederation, Reading 7 in *From the Source: Readings in Economics and Government with Answer Key*. Each student should create a list of important phrases contained in the document. Have students share some of its wording and meaning with the class during a dramatic reading.

Visual-Spatial Learners

Ask students to create a poster depicting the events that were discussed in this section. Encourage students to be as creative as possible. Examples might include making a pyramid showing the powers of Congress, limits on powers, problems among the states, Shays's Rebellion, and the May 1787 meeting to revise the Articles of Confederation. Encourage students to work together to create their posters if they so choose and to discuss their posters with the entire class.

Gifted Learners

Ask students to locate the text of the Northwest Ordinance online. Have students write a report on the Northwest Ordinance's significance regarding westward expansion, the addition of new states, and the importance of the Northwest Territory to commerce. Refer students to the State Profiles section on the *Holt Researcher Online* to obtain information on the states that made up the Northwest Territory and have students use additional resources. Encourage students to share the results of their research with the class.

REVIEW

Have students complete the Section 3 Review on page 34. Use the answers in the Annotated Teacher's Edition to assess student mastery of this section.

ASSESS

To assess student mastery of this section, have students complete Daily Quiz 2.3 in *Daily Quizzes with Answer Key*. For additional assessment options, see *Alternative Assessment Handbook* on the *One-Stop Planner CD-ROM*.

ADDITIONAL RESOURCES

Jillson, Calvin. *Constitution Making: Conflict and Consensus in the Federal Convention of 1787.* 1988. Agathon Press.

Phelan, Mary Kay. *Our United States Constitution: Created in Convention.* 1987. The Perfection Form Company.

A View from a Mountain. Virginia Bureau of Tourism. (videotape on Thomas Jefferson)

Hull, Mary E. *Shays' Rebellion and the Constitution in American History.* 2000. Enslow Publishers.

Burns, Ken. *Thomas Jefferson.* 1996. PBS Home Video.

OBJECTIVES

▸ List influential delegates to the Constitutional Convention.
▸ Identify the major competing plans of government that the delegates debated.
▸ Explain why the delegates compromised on a federal system of government.

MOTIVATE

Place a sign outside the classroom, on the door, or at the front of the room that says, "Welcome to Philadelphia." As students enter the room, shake their hands and welcome them to the Constitutional Convention. Give students color-coded tags that identify them as delegates of a particular state and give students a handout that describes the population and economy of that state. Have four tags that include the names George Washington, Benjamin Franklin, Alexander Hamilton, and James Madison. Ask students to meet in groups with other delegates from their states to discuss their state's wishes for the new government. Tell the class that today they are going to go back in time and live through the Constitutional Convention, which began on May 25, 1787.

TEACH

Building a Vocabulary

In their spiral notebooks, have each student continue working on their Political Dictionary. List words the students will be expected to know for this section on the board. Have students list, define, and give an example of each of the terms using information provided in the text or on the *Researcher CD-ROM*.

Developing Life Skills

Organize students into four groups. Using information found in the text, the library, and the Biographies section on the *Holt Researcher Online*, have students create résumés for the four delegates to the Constitutional

Convention discussed in the Motivate activity: George Washington, Benjamin Franklin, Alexander Hamilton, and James Madison. Have students consider the backgrounds of these delegates, including their education, their wealth, previous experience in government, and what state they are representing. Ask students to share the completed résumés. Discuss with students how it was difficult to get the delegates to the Constitutional Convention to agree on one plan of government that would please all the states. Tell students that in the next activity they will be learning about some of the different plans.

Debating Ideas

Have students organize themselves by state, using the same groups as in the Motivate activity. Place Virginia and New Jersey on opposite sides of the classroom. Divide the rest of the states up evenly between the two sides, sending the larger states to the Virginia side and the smaller states to the New Jersey side. Provide each group with a chalkboard or a large piece of paper on which to write their wishes for the new Constitution. Lead the class in a mock debate between supporters of the Virginia Plan and supporters of the New Jersey Plan. Be sure to include in the debate the differences in the executive branch, the legislative branch, the judicial branch, and the powers of the national government between the two plans. Have students complete the debate by agreeing to the terms of the Great Compromise. Tell students that in the next activity they will be learning about even more compromises that had to be made at the Constitutional Convention.

Role-Playing

Organize the class into groups, assigning them one of the following five topics to research and discuss: the House of Representatives, the Senate, slavery, trade, or the presidency. Once each group has had time to discuss their topic, ask them to role-play for the rest of the class the compromises that were made at the Constitutional Convention that pertain to their topic. Encourage students to use visual aides to demonstrate their ideas and any compromises made. Be sure to have each group identify which states were involved in each compromise.

CLOSE

Give a short speech thanking the delegates for all of their hard work during the Convention. Ask students to write a short letter to the constituents in their home state, telling them that they are on their way home and summarizing what happened at the Convention. Have students include an outline of the newly created government and describe any compromises that were made. Have students explain why they compromised on a federal rather than unitary system of government. On their way out of the classroom, have students sign a mock Constitution.

OPTIONS

Gifted Learners

In groups, have students create a Philadelphia newspaper with the date May 25, 1787. Encourage students to include such features as advertisements, weather reports, news about the Convention, and local news. Students may wish to use information from the Internet, the library, the Biographies section and the State Profiles section on the *Holt Researcher Online*, or other sources to find information about what happened at the Constitutional Convention.

Students Having Difficulty

Have students create a political cartoon to be published in the school newspaper. The cartoon should represent the differing opinions on the new government and compromise plans discussed at the Constitutional Convention. Students should attempt to show the compromises that settled these differences of opinion.

Linguistic Learners

Have students create a poem or a dramatic reading to greet the delegates to the Constitutional Convention. It should discuss the importance of the meeting and should attempt to identify the issues that will be debated at the Convention. Students should use the language of that time period in their poems or readings. Students may also wish to include requests from specific segments of the population designed to encourage delegates to address important issues. Encourage students to share their poems with the class and discuss their meanings.

Intrapersonal Learners

 Based on the state that students were assigned to represent during the Motivate activity, have students write a descriptive essay declaring whether they would have supported the Virginia Plan or the New Jersey Plan. Students should support their opinion by stating how this plan would benefit their state more than the other plan and how this plan would be better than the Articles of Confederation. Encourage students to share their ideas with the rest of the class.

REVIEW

Have students complete the Section 4 Review on page 39. Use the answers in the Annotated Teacher's Edition to assess student mastery of this section.

ASSESS

To assess student mastery of this section, have students complete Daily Quiz 2.4 in *Daily Quizzes with Answer Key*. For additional assessment options, see *Alternative Assessment Handbook* on the *One-Stop Planner CD-ROM*.

ADDITIONAL RESOURCES

Cronkite, Walter, reader. *All You Want to Know: The Constitutional Convention and the Ratification Debates*. 2000. Simon and Schuster. (audio)

Peltason, J.W. et al. *Corwin & Peltason's Understanding the Constitution*. 2000. HBJ College and School Division.

The Biography of James Madison. A&E Biography series. (video)

OBJECTIVES

▸ Identify the main arguments in the debate over ratification of the Constitution.
▸ Discuss the role of a bill of rights in the debate.
▸ Understand how the *Federalist Papers* explain the principles of the American constitutional form of government.

MOTIVATE

To help students synthesize the events that led to the signing of the Constitution, have them complete the "Time Line to Unity" started in Lesson 2.1. Place the date May 29, 1790, on the time line. Ask students to include as many events as they can from the last three sections. Remind students that the signing of the Constitution did not mean the end of debate. Tell students that people still mostly considered themselves New Yorkers or Virginians first, and Americans second. Explain that in this section students will learn what events took place between September 17, 1787, and May 29, 1790.

TEACH

Building a Vocabulary

 In their spiral notebooks, have each student continue working on their Political Dictionary. List words the students will be expected to know for this section on the board. Have students list, define, and give an example of each of the terms using information provided in the text or on the *Researcher CD-ROM*.

Classifying Information

 Organize students into two teams: Federalists and Antifederalists. Have students discuss the arguments made by each group for or against ratifying the Constitution that are presented in the text. Ask one student from each team to list each of their team's issues on a separate index card as they are discussed. Collect and shuffle these cards. Ask all students to stand next to their desks or tables. In each round, select one student from each team to play from their desk.

Read an issue from one of the cards. Have the student who believes that the idea on the card represents his or her team sit down. If the student who sat down is correct, he or she may remain seated; if not, he or she must stand up again and the player from the opposite team may sit down. The game is over when all students on one team are seated. Discuss with students that the debate between the Federalists and the Antifederalists did not end easily, and two large states—New York and Virginia—were two of the key states to finally ratify the Constitution. Lead a discussion about how James Madison, Alexander Hamilton, and John Jay wrote essays, which became the *Federalist Papers,* to explain how the new government would work. Tell students that these essays are still respected as analyses of the foundations of U.S. government.

Debating Ideas

 While students are still organized into Federalists and Antifederalists, have them hold a mock debate over the issue of a bill of rights. Tell students that conventions in some states recommended that the Constitution contain a bill of rights. Be sure that students include arguments such as the government only has the powers specifically listed in the Constitution, that all powers not given to the federal government belong to the states, and that the separation of powers between the three branches prevents any one branch from becoming too powerful. As a whole class, ask students to discuss their personal feelings regarding the need for a bill of rights. Encourage students to support their arguments with information from the chapter. Tell students that in the next activity they will learn about the order of ratification.

Acquiring Information

Remind students that all the states did not ratify the Constitution at the same time. Have students write several paragraphs describing the order of states to sign the Constitution and the importance of each state in influencing the others to sign. Have students utilize information in the State Profiles section on the *Holt Researcher Online* and other resources to help them. Discuss with students the importance of specific states in ratifying the Constitution.

CLOSE

Have students finish filling in the time line that they worked on in the Motivate activity. Lead a class discussion regarding the importance of the period of time between September 17, 1787, and May 29, 1790, as well as the significance of the major events on the time line. Be sure to have students include the dates that each state ratified the Constitution.

OPTIONS

Gifted Learners

Have students read *Federalist Paper* "No. 10," which can be found as Reading 52 in *From the Source: Readings in Economics and Government with Answer Key*. Have students write a paper describing the contribution that this reading and its author, James Madison, had on the ratification of the U.S. Constitution. Ask students if they can identify other significant figures who may have been influenced by this essay.

Students Having Difficulty/ Sheltered English Students

Have students make a bill of rights for the classroom. It should only contain rights that are based on those found in the Constitution. Students should be allowed to debate points that they wish to include in their bill of rights and should vote on either each proposed right or the final list of rights before adopting their bill of rights. Remind students that a two-thirds majority in each house of Congress was needed before the bill of rights could be submitted for states' approval. Encourage students to type their work or make a poster to display it.

Intrapersonal Learners

Explain to students that under the Articles of Confederation, approval from all 13 states was needed to pass an amendment to the Articles, but at the Constitutional Convention it was decided that only 9 states were needed to ratify the U.S. Constitution. Tell students that the Constitution went into effect after New Hampshire became the ninth state to ratify the document. Have students write an essay describing their feelings surrounding the legitimacy the Constitution would have had if the rest of the states had never ratified it. Encourage students to offer examples of what may have happened to the United States had the other four states never ratified the document. Encourage students to share their opinions.

REVIEW

Have students complete the Section 5 Review on page 42. Use the answers in the Annotated Teacher's Edition to assess student mastery of this section.

ASSESS

To assess student mastery of this section, have students complete Daily Quiz 2.5 in *Daily Quizzes with Answer Key*. For additional assessment options, see *Alternative Assessment Handbook* on the *One-Stop Planner CD-ROM*.

RETEACH

For students having difficulty with the lessons, have them complete Reteaching Activity 2. This activity is located in *Reteaching Activities with Answer Key*.

ADDITIONAL RESOURCES

Levy, Leonard Williams. *Origins of the Bill of Rights*. 2001. Yale University Press.

McCoy, Drew. *The Elusive Republic: Political Economy in Jeffersonian America*. 1980. W.W. Norton & Company.

Morgan, Edmund. *American Slavery, American Freedom: The Ordeal of Colonial Virginia*. 1975. W.W. Norton.

GOVERNMENT NOTEBOOK

The Government Notebook is a journal activity that encourages students to consider basic concepts of government that relate to their lives. A follow-up notebook activity appears on page 44.

▶ WHY IT MATTERS TODAY

To find additional lesson plans dealing with constitutional government or other forms of government, visit **CNNfyi**.com or have students complete the **GOVERNMENT** IN THE NEWS Activity on page 43.

CNNfyi.com

CHAPTER 2

ORIGINS OF U.S. GOVERNMENT

You are part of one of the most important experiments in the world—the U.S. government. As you can imagine, the task of forging one nation out of 13 independent states was no small achievement. When the framers of the Constitution transformed a loose confederation of states into a federal union, they created a new form of government that has survived, and succeeded, for more than 200 years.

GOVERNMENT NOTEBOOK

In your Government Notebook, create a list of the rights and freedoms you have as a U.S. citizen. Where do you think these rights and freedoms originated?

▶ WHY IT MATTERS TODAY

The Constitution affects the lives of Americans every day. At the end of this chapter visit **CNNfyi**.com to learn more about how the Constitution affects your life.

CNNfyi.com

SECTION 1
EARLY INFLUENCES

READ TO DISCOVER

1. What political ideals did English colonists bring with them to North America?
2. What major documents limited the power of English monarchs?
3. How were the ideals of limited and representative government evident in colonial governments?

POLITICAL DICTIONARY

constitution
Magna Carta
rule of law
bicameral
Petition of Right
English Bill of Rights
charter

When English colonists came to North America, they brought with them more than just tools needed to survive, such as axes and hoes for building homes and farms. They also brought the tools for creating a government—important ideals that had formed the basis of government in England.

An English Heritage

The ideals the English colonists brought to North America can still be found in British government today. Although Great Britain does not have a written **constitution**—a basic set of laws and principles establishing the nation's government—it has laws, historical documents, and judicial decisions dating back hundreds of years.

Two important British ideals strongly influenced the colonists in North America: limited government and representative government. These ideals helped shape government in the colonies—and later in the United States—in a way that serves the public good.

Limited Government Before the 1200s there were few limits on government in England. For example, without a written constitution monarchs could tax people or seize property at will, as well as give land to people who were loyal to them.

Consider what it would be like if student-body presidents had such power. They might reserve part of the gym for use only by their close friends. They might even decide to charge students a fee to pay for student government.

Of course, student-body presidents do not have such power. A president must act within the rules set by the school administration and an elected student council. In short, these forces limit what student government can do without the consent of the governed—the students.

The English nobles—the weathy landowners who enjoyed certain social and legal privileges—were no happier with their monarch's unlimited power than you would be with an all-powerful student-body president. In 1215 these nobles forced King John to sign **Magna Carta**, or "Great Charter." This

The Granger Collection, New York

POLITICAL FOUNDATIONS *This engraving from the 1800s shows King John signing Magna Carta.* **What important principle did Magna Carta represent that later influenced the U.S. Constitution?**

SECTION 1
EARLY INFLUENCES

Lesson Plans
For teaching strategies, see Lesson 2.1 located at the beginning of this chapter or the One-Stop Planner Strategy 2.1.

Political Dictionary

To reinforce the section's vocabulary terms, refer students to the Electronic Glossary on the *Researcher CD-ROM*.

Section Assessment
To assess students' mastery of this section, have them complete Daily Quiz 2.1 in *Daily Quizzes with Answer Key*.

Caption Answer

It established the rule of law, which limited the power of a government's leaders and meant that rulers must act according to set laws.

document limited the monarchy's power by helping establish the **rule of law**, under which government leaders, even monarchs, must act according to set laws. For example, monarchs could no longer levy taxes without the nobles' approval. The charter also gave people accused of crimes the right to a trial by their peers, or equals. This right prevented a monarch from imprisoning people or taking away their property on his or her sole authority. Although Magna Carta was meant only for the nobility, in time its protections applied to all English citizens.

By requiring English monarchs to consider how their decisions would affect the people they governed, Magna Carta laid the foundation for government that promotes the public good. As noted in Chapter 1, government promotes the public good when it reflects the interests of society as a whole instead of the narrow interests of the few or of one individual, such as a monarch.

Representative Government The English ideal of representative government is even older than the ideal of limited government. Representative government has its roots in a council of nobles and high religious officials that advised monarchs even before the signing of Magna Carta. This council gradually grew in importance. Eventually, representatives of local towns and villages became part of the council.

Over time the advisory council evolved into a **bicameral**, or two-chamber, legislature called Parliament. Nobles composed the upper house, or the House of Lords. The lower house, or the House of Commons, included lesser officials and local representatives. As representatives of the people, members of Parliament worked to limit the power of English monarchs. Two important documents—the Petition of Right and the English Bill of Rights—helped Parliament do this.

PRINCIPLES OF DEMOCRACY *England's bicameral Parliament is illustrated in these drawings of the House of Lords (left) and the House of Commons (right).* **Which house was made up of lesser officials and local representatives?**

Parliament forced Charles I to sign the **Petition of Right** in 1628. Like Magna Carta, the Petition of Right limited the ability of the monarch to act on his or her sole authority. The Petition of Right said that monarchs could not imprison people illegally, force citizens to house soldiers in their homes, or establish military rule during times of peace. It also required monarchs to obtain Parliament's approval, rather than simply the nobles' approval, before levying taxes.

Like Magna Carta, the Petition of Right was crucial to the development of government that promotes the public good. In forcing Charles to sign the Petition of Right, a representative body had placed restrictions on the monarch's power. It gave the people, through their representatives, a voice in government and made sure that the many opinions in a society would be heard.

The Petition of Right was part of an extended conflict between Charles and Parliament. That conflict eventually erupted into a civil war in which the army of Parliament defeated Charles's supporters. Charles was beheaded in 1649, and England did not have another king until 1660, when Charles II assumed the throne. James II, Charles's brother, succeeded him in 1685.

Parliamentary leaders who disagreed with James and his policies forced him from the throne by encouraging William of Orange, the husband of James's daughter, Mary, to invade England. In the Glorious Revolution of 1688, William arrived with his troops, and James fled the country. Parliament then asked William and Mary to serve as king and queen of England. Before they took the throne, however, Parliament forced them to accept the English Bill of Rights.

The **English Bill of Rights** clearly established that the monarchy could not rule without consent of Parliament. The document included many protections, such as the right to petition the king without fear of punishment and free parliamentary elections. It also forbade the monarch from maintaining an army without parliamentary consent and said that Parliament should operate without royal interference.

Along with Magna Carta and the Petition of Right, the English Bill of Rights helped protect English citizens' rights from being violated. The government could not violate or deny these rights and could rule only with the consent of the people it governed. This idea remains fundamental to ensuring that government serves and protects the public's best interests.

Colonial Development

By the time the Petition of Right and the English Bill of Rights were passed, English colonists had begun to settle parts of North America. The first permanent English colony was established at Jamestown, Virginia, in 1607. The organization of Jamestown and of later settlements clearly showed the influence of the basic principles of English government.

Charters The Jamestown colony was the first of several permanent colonies established by charter. A **charter** was an agreement whereby the English monarch gave settlers the right to establish a colony.

The efforts to limit government in the colonies were evident in most charters. The Massachusetts charter, for example, guaranteed elections.

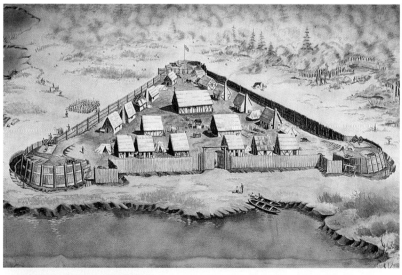

POLITICAL FOUNDATIONS *This painting of Jamestown, Virginia, by Francis Dayton illustrates the first permanent English colony in North America.* **What was the purpose of charters during English colonization?**

GLOBAL CONNECTIONS

The individual rights and privileges guaranteed to citizens through colonial charters served another purpose in addition to protecting those already living in North America. Colonial charters also contained explicit guarantees that served to encourage more immigrants to come to the colonies.

For example, in addition to guaranteeing the basic English rights to Virginia colonists, the Virginia Charter of 1606 included a very liberal landowning policy that gave colonists who owned land more control over their land than they would have had in England.

By using their charters to make the colonies more attractive both politically and economically, colonial promoters hoped to recruit more settlers to English North America. ■

Caption Answer

Charters gave settlers the right to establish a colony and were usually aimed at limiting government in the colonies.

Caption Answer
(for p. 24)

Colonial governments had councils and representative assemblies that helped limit governors' powers.

PRINCIPLES OF DEMOCRACY *This portrait of the trustees of Georgia, the ruling body of the colony of Georgia, is believed to have been painted in the 1700s.* **How did colonial governments reflect the ideals of limited and representative government?**

Officers were chosen from among the male settlers who were given the charter. The charter also gave these men the power and authority to establish an assembly that would make laws, elect officers, and govern the colony.

Governments With the addition of Georgia in 1733, the number of colonies grew to 13. Each colony had a system that reflected the ideals of limited and representative government. For example, each colony's governor served as the government's executive. Some governors were appointed and others were elected. Most governors, however, were advised by a council, which also served as the highest court in the colony and, in some cases, had as much power as the governor. The councils generally were made up of 12 male property owners who acted as advisers to the governor. In some colonies the council served as the upper house of the colony's assembly. Most colonies also had an assembly made up of the colonists' elected representatives. These councils and representative assemblies served to limit the governors' power.

There were three types of colonies—royal, proprietary, and corporate. Royal colonies—the most common type—belonged directly to the crown. Virginia was a royal colony. Proprietary colonies were those whose territory was granted by the king to an individual (or small group of individuals), called a proprietor, and put under the proprietor's personal control. Pennsylvania and Maryland were proprietary colonies. Corporate colonies were founded without any direct authorization from the English government. Although England controlled military affairs and trade in the corporate colonies, the Crown exercised such control on an irregular basis. Connecticut and Rhode Island were corporate colonies.

SECTION 1 REVIEW

1. **Identify and explain:**
   - constitution
   - Magna Carta
   - rule of law
   - bicameral
   - Petition of Right
   - English Bill of Rights
   - charter

2. **Analyzing:** Use the chart below to describe two British ideals that influenced North American colonists as they began to set up their governments.

Limited Government	Representative Government

3. **Finding the Main Idea**

   a. What were the three types of colonies in colonial North America and how did they differ?

   b. How was the power of Colonial governors limited?

4. **Writing and Critical Thinking**

   Drawing Conclusions: Write a paragraph explaining why it would be important for a country to have a written constitution.

   Consider the following:
   - the function of a constitution
   - what problems British subjects faced because they did not have a written constitution
   - how those problems could have been solved with a written constitution

Homework Practice Online
keyword: SV3 HP2

SECTION 2
INDEPENDENCE

READ TO DISCOVER

1. What were two early attempts at unity among the colonies?
2. What British policies pushed the colonies to cooperate with one another?
3. What were some of the ideals that influenced the writing of the Declaration of Independence?
4. How were the governments of the newly independent states similar?

POLITICAL DICTIONARY

New England Confederation
Albany Plan of Union
Stamp Act
tyranny
boycott
delegate
unicameral

When the first English colonists arrived in North America, they found that the land presented them with dangers as well as opportunities. These common dangers pushed the 13 colonies toward unity. Although early attempts at unity failed, the British government's actions eventually united the colonists in a common cause: independence.

Searching for Unity

Uniting the 13 colonies was a difficult task that presented several obstacles. What were the sources of differences among the colonies?

Obstacles One obstacle to colonial unity stemmed from the colonists' having come to North America for different reasons. Early colonists who settled in Virginia, for example, were sent by a company that wanted to make money from the region's natural resources. In contrast, the Puritans of the Massachusetts Bay Colony came to estab-

lish an ideal society in which they could freely practice their religion. The colony of Georgia, meanwhile, was created as a refuge for debtors who would otherwise have been put in jail. It also attracted people fleeing from religious persecution.

Varying economies and geography also led to differences among the colonies. The New England colonies developed fishing, lumber, and crafts industries. In contrast, South Carolina's colonists grew crops that thrived in a warm, moist climate. (See "Linking Government and Geography," page 27.)

Attempts at Unity Despite their differences, the English colonists did face some of the same dangers, such as the possibility of conflict with neighboring American Indians and non-English colonists. The need for defense produced two important, though unsuccessful, attempts at unity.

The first attempt was the **New England Confederation** of 1643. The four colonies in this confederation agreed to work together to defend against attacks by American Indians or by settlers of nearby Dutch colonies. The confederation had few powers, however. The objection of just one colony could keep the confederation from taking

The Metropolitan Museum of Art, Bequest of Jacob Rupert, 1939 (39.65.53)

POLITICAL FOUNDATIONS *The bronze statue* The Puritan, *made by American artist Augustus Saint-Gaudens in the 1800s, symbolically portrays Puritan life.* **Why did many Puritans leave England to live in North America?**

action. As a result, disagreements often prevented cooperation. The lack of cooperation, as well as the annulment of Massachusetts' charter, led to the end of the confederation in 1684.

Conflict between Britain and France brought a new effort at unity 70 years later. France controlled a part of present-day Canada and other land to the west of the British colonies. To plan for a defense against possible attacks by the French and their American Indian allies, the British government called a meeting of colonial representatives in 1754. Representatives of seven British colonies met with the Iroquois in Albany, New York, to form an alliance and develop a plan of action.

At the meeting, colonial representatives adopted the **Albany Plan of Union**, proposed by Benjamin Franklin. The plan called for a council of colonial representatives that could levy taxes and raise an army. The council also would regulate trade with American Indians. The individual colonial and British governments rejected the plan, however, so it was never put into effect.

An Ocean Apart

Although the need for common defense did not unify the colonies, other developments brought the

POLITICAL FOUNDATIONS *Benjamin Franklin, shown in this portrait painted by Joseph Wright, proposed the Albany Plan of Union.* **What did the plan propose?**

colonies closer together. At the same time, however, these developments strained the relationship between the colonies and Great Britain.

Political Distance Most of the colonies shared a growing political distance from Britain. The colonists had long been allowed to handle many of their internal affairs. In the more than 150 years since the first permanent settlement was established, elected assemblies in the colonies had gradually increased their authority.

In turn, the power of governors and their advisory councils had begun to weaken. Governors often felt more pressure from local colonial interests than from the faraway British government. In addition, the governors' salaries were controlled by the elected colonial assemblies.

British Policies The political distance between the colonies and Britain widened further after 1760, when the British throne passed to George III. There was a growing attitude among members of Parliament that the colonies had become too independent. The real spark to tensions, however, was the Seven Years' War, a global struggle that involved several European countries, including Britain and France.

The Seven Years' War had plunged Britain deep into debt. Because part of the conflict—known as the French and Indian War—had been fought on North American soil, the British government believed the colonists should help pay off the debt. Many members of Parliament also thought that it was time for the colonists to help pay for their own future defense against hostile forces.

To help raise money, the government under George III began to enforce a number of trade restrictions and taxes. In 1765, for example, Parliament passed the **Stamp Act**, which required colonists to pay a tax on many paper goods. A tax stamp on a newspaper, contract, or deck of playing cards showed that the tax had been paid.

In addition to raising money, the Stamp Act and other policies also served to protect British businesses. By forcing colonists to pay taxes on goods purchased from other countries, the government gave British businesses an advantage—the taxes made non-British foreign goods more expensive than those from Britain. The high prices caused by the policies angered colonial businesspeople who made money by importing non-British goods to sell in the colonies.

Linking

Government and Geography

Geographic Differences Among the Colonies

Before the colonists declared their independence from Great Britain, few economic ties unified the American colonies. The colonies had been founded at different times and for different reasons. In addition, geographic factors such as climate and soil quality caused the northern, middle, and southern colonies to develop economies that were distinct from one another. These factors also created political divisions among colonies, particularly the northern and southern colonies.

In the northern colonies, short growing seasons; thin, rocky soil; and frigid, hostile winters made farming difficult. Land was divided into small farms owned by individual families. Each of these farms usually produced only enough crops to feed the family that operated it. Poor agricultural conditions led many New Englanders to find work in other occupations. Many colonists fished full-time to earn their living, which helped spur economic growth in coastal port cities.

The settlement of the middle colonies was similar to that of the northern colonies, with land divided into individual family farms. However, the region's geography—rich soil, good water resources, and a moderate climate—made agriculture more profitable in this region. Farmers were able to raise crops for export to domestic and foreign markets.

In contrast, the warm, wet climate and an extended growing season of the southern colonies allowed southern planters to raise more crops in a year than farmers in the middle and northern colonies. Property in this region was divided into large plantations that produced export crops. Plantations were often built along large rivers and had their own docks, so ships could load crops and head directly for major trade destinations. This reduced the need for coastal port cities in the South.

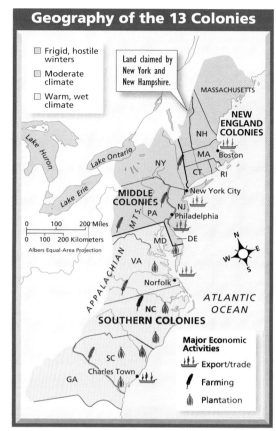

Geography of the 13 Colonies

- ☐ Frigid, hostile winters
- ☐ Moderate climate
- ☐ Warm, wet climate

Land claimed by New York and New Hampshire.

MASSACHUSETTS
NEW ENGLAND COLONIES
NH
MA • Boston
NY
CT
RI
• New York City
MIDDLE COLONIES
PA
NJ
• Philadelphia
MD — DE
VA
Norfolk •
ATLANTIC OCEAN
NC
SOUTHERN COLONIES
SC
Charles Town •
GA

Lake Huron
Lake Ontario
Lake Erie

0   100   200 Miles
0   100   200 Kilometers
Albers Equal-Area Projection

APPALACHIAN MTS

Major Economic Activities
- Export/trade
- Farming
- Plantation

Early colonists produced a variety of goods and services. Each region's geographic features helped to shape its economy.

Although the northern, middle, and southern colonists lived in different geographic regions, they all faced the challenges of settling and clearing land. Transporting goods to colonial markets also was difficult for farmers and planters throughout the colonies.

Eventually, the colonies achieved the unity needed to launch a new nation. Common goals, such as the desire for independence from Great Britain, led them to unite in spite of geographic and economic differences.

What Do You Think?

1. Do you think that citizens of the United States still identify with the geographic regions in which they live?
2. How has technology eliminated some of the physical barriers that existed among the colonies?

Colonial Reaction

Many colonists were outraged. They not only saw the policies as unfair to colonial businesses but also objected to being taxed when the British Parliament had no colonial representatives. Colonists argued that such taxation without representation was **tyranny**—absolute rule by a government that ignores the rights and welfare of the people.

Protests In October 1765, representatives from nine colonies met in New York at the Stamp Act Congress. They wrote a Declaration of Rights and Grievances to protest the Stamp Act and other British policies. Colonists also boycotted some British goods. A **boycott** is an agreement to stop buying or using a good or service.

Although Parliament eventually repealed the Stamp Act, it passed additional taxes and laws. Protests against such actions continued in the colonies. In 1770 these tensions erupted when British soldiers fired into a crowd of angry colonial protesters in Boston. Five people were killed in what became known as the Boston Massacre.

PRINCIPLES OF DEMOCRACY *The Boston Massacre of 1770 is portrayed in this engraving of a painting by Alonzo Chappel.* **How did the British government spark the rebellion that erupted into the Boston Massacre?**

In 1772 colonial activist Samuel Adams formed a group in Boston to help with the growing colonial resistance. The group developed as part of a network of patriotic groups called the Committees of Correspondence, which had been established in 1763. The network allowed colonists to communicate with each other about British policies.

In 1773 violence again broke out when Adams and other angry colonists, dressed as American Indians, boarded ships in Boston Harbor and dumped British tea overboard. This event, known as the Boston Tea Party, was a protest against a decision by Parliament to give a British company all rights to the tea trade in the North American colonies.

In response to the Boston Tea Party, the British government passed another set of laws in 1774. Called the Intolerable Acts by the colonists, the new laws tightened British control over the colonies even further and inspired the colonists to greater action.

Continental Congresses In 1774 delegates from all the colonies except Georgia met in Philadelphia at the First Continental Congress. A **delegate** is someone who officially represents the interests of other people or of a government. The Congress protested British policies and sent George III the Declaration and Resolves of the First Continental Congress. It also called for a boycott of British goods until British colonial policies were changed. The delegates planned for a second congress to meet the following May if need arose.

Officials in the British government responded by passing even stricter measures to tighten control over the colonies. The growing tensions finally led to battles between British troops and Massachusetts colonial militia at Lexington and Concord, on April 19, 1775.

Less than a month after the battles at Lexington and Concord, the Second Continental

Canada's Independence from Great Britain

When the 13 American colonies declared their independence from Great Britain in 1776, a new, completely independent nation was born. In 1867 Canada also gained independence from Britain. However, by signing the British North America Act, Canada did not make a complete break with Britain. Instead, the new Dominion of Canada became a self-governing nation with control over only its domestic policies. Britain continued to govern Canada's foreign affairs until 1931. Eventually, Canada gained complete independence with the passage of the Constitution Act in 1982.

Today Canada is a confederation with a parliamentary democracy. It is a member of the Commonwealth of Nations, an association of nations and territories that were once part of the former British Empire. The Canadian prime minister is the nation's leader, while the British monarch functions as Canada's symbolic head of government. The national parliament features a 104-member Senate and a 301-member House of Commons. Each of Canada's 10 provinces—which are similar to U.S. states—and 3 territories has a parliament headed by a provincial prime minister.

Congress met in Philadelphia. Again, representatives from 12 of the 13 colonies attended. This time, however, they met to discuss a plan of action, for the war had already begun. The road to independence lay ahead.

Declaration of Independence

By June 1776 nearly all delegates to the Second Continental Congress favored independence. They appointed several people to a committee to write a document explaining why they believed that independence was necessary. The Second Continental Congress adopted the Declaration of Independence on July 4, 1776. (See pages 562–64.)

The Declaration of Independence was written by a committee of five men: John Adams, Benjamin Franklin, Thomas Jefferson, Robert Livingston, and Roger Sherman. Jefferson, however, wrote most of the document.

Jefferson wrote about the "unalienable rights" of human beings—rights that cannot be taken away—including "life, liberty, and the pursuit of happiness." Recalling the arguments of philosopher John Locke, Jefferson also wrote that governments receive "their just powers from the consent of the governed." When a government fails to protect citizens' natural rights, the people have the right "to alter or to abolish it, and to institute new government." The Declaration also criticized George III's refusal to support actions that were "wholesome and necessary for the public good."

In many ways the Declaration of Independence mapped out the kind of government that Jefferson and his fellow delegates wanted for the colonies.

POLITICAL FOUNDATIONS *This painting by American artist Jean Leon Gerome Ferris shows Thomas Jefferson, John Adams, and Benjamin Franklin drafting the Declaration of Independence.* ***How did the ideas of John Locke influence the Declaration?***

Caption Answer

Jefferson was recalling Locke's ideas when he wrote in the Declaration that governments owe their power to "the consent of the governed."

SECTION 2 REVIEW ANSWERS

1. Refer to the following pages: New England Confederation (25), Albany Plan of Union (26), Stamp Act (26), tyranny (28), boycott (28), delegate (28), unicameral (30)

2. Colonists publicly denounced the new policies, organized boycotts, and participated in violent protests.

3a. From Locke, Jefferson got the idea that governments get their power to rule from "the consent of the governed."

b. They thought that British policies failed to protect colonists' natural rights and did not allow colonial representation in the policy-making process.

c. Most colonists feared that strong executives might abuse their powers much as British kings had done.

4. They were intended to give colonial governments the power to defend the colonies and levy taxes. The New England Confederation failed because one colony could stop the confederation from taking action. The Albany Plan of Union was rejected by the colonial and British governments.

Such a government was one that would include protections for basic rights and liberties. It also was one that would rely on the consent of the governed for authority and consider their broader interests. In short, this government would be more likely than other forms of government to act in ways that promote the public good.

State Governments

The individual governments of the colonies changed with independence. In early 1776, even before independence, some colonies had adopted new constitutions. Following the Declaration of Independence, the other colonies also adopted new constitutions. The new constitutions were similar in a number of ways.

Structure Not surprisingly, the new state constitutions reflected a desire for limited government. Legislatures elected by the people dominated the state governments, and legislative elections were held each year in all but one state. Americans' belief in the importance of regular elections was expressed by John Adams: "When annual elections end, there slavery [of the people] begins."

All the legislatures were bicameral with the exception of Pennsylvania's **unicameral**, or one-chamber, legislature. (In their first constitutions,

Georgia and Vermont also had unicameral legislatures. Later, they adopted bicameral legislatures, as did Pennsylvania.) Most new state constitutions gave few powers to the states' governors, because people associated a strong executive with the abuses of monarchy. They feared that a strong executive might eventually destroy representative government. Nine of the constitutions even limited a governor's term to one year.

Rights The new state constitutions also showed the influence of earlier efforts to protect individual rights. For example, most constitutions listed the rights that belonged to the people. Many of these rights were the same as those outlined in the English Bill of Rights and in colonial charters.

In addition, some states expanded voting rights. Although the colonial assemblies were elected bodies, not everyone had been able to vote in the elections. Depending on the colony, as much as 50 percent of free males could not vote, because many of the colonies had property qualifications for voting. In the new state constitutions, some of these restrictions were removed or lessened. By 1790 five states allowed all adult white male taxpayers to vote. Restrictions based on race and gender generally prohibited most American Indians, free and enslaved blacks, and women from voting, however.

SECTION 2 REVIEW

1. Identify and explain:
- New England Confederation
- Albany Plan of Union
- Stamp Act
- tyranny
- boycott
- delegate
- unicameral

2. Cause and Effect: Use the chart below to analyze the effects of changes in British colonial policy after 1760. Offer at least two ways in which colonists reacted.

Cause		Effect
British Policies:	⟶	**Colonial Reactions:**
Increased Trade Restrictions	⟶	_____
Higher Taxes	⟶	_____

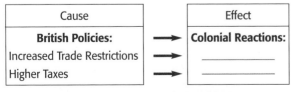

Homework Practice Online
keyword: SV3 HP2

3. **Finding the Main Idea**

a. What idea in the Declaration of Independence did Thomas Jefferson draw from John Locke?

b. Why did the authors of the Declaration of Independence believe that British policies violated the ideals of representative government?

c. Why did early state governments have weak governors?

4. **Writing and Critical Thinking**

Summarizing: Write a paragraph describing the purposes of the New England Confederation and the Albany Plan of Union. Be sure to explain why the two plans were unsuccessful.

Consider the following:
- the complaints against British rule
- the structure of each plan

SECTION 3
THE FIRST NATIONAL GOVERNMENT

READ TO DISCOVER

1. What were the powers of the national government under the Articles of Confederation?
2. How did limits on its power weaken the national government under the Articles?
3. How did the states continue to struggle with unity after independence?
4. How did Shays's Rebellion highlight the need for a stronger national government?

POLITICAL DICTIONARY

Articles of Confederation
ratification
Northwest Ordinance

Most of the fighting in the Revolutionary War ended with a U.S. victory at the Battle of Yorktown in 1781. A challenge now lay before the 13 independent states—that of forming a national government. In the same year the war ended, the states created a confederation, or what they called a "league of friendship." The weaknesses of this confederation, however, made unity among the states difficult and created pressure for a stronger national government.

Articles of Confederation

The Second Continental Congress had held the 13 states together during the war. It had run the affairs of the new nation during much of the fighting and had appointed George Washington as commander in chief of the army in 1775. The Congress also had negotiated treaties with foreign powers, created a national currency, borrowed money, and established

a postal service. There was, however, no constitution or other legal document giving Congress the authority to take these actions.

To remedy this, in 1777 the Second Continental Congress created a document to form a single national government. This document, the **Articles of Confederation**, loosely tied together the 13 independent states and gave a new national Congress the authority to act that the Second Continental Congress had lacked. Before it could go into effect, however, the Articles required the **ratification**, or formal approval, of all 13 states. Maryland, the last state to ratify the Articles, did so in 1781.

Many leaders in the former British colonies wanted a loose confederation of states. They feared that creating a strong national government would threaten the power of the states and the freedoms of the people. Therefore, the Articles of Confederation limited the powers of the national government.

Powers The powers of the new government lay in a unicameral legislature: the Congress. Delegates to the Congress were chosen by each state's legislature. Each state delegation had one vote. Majority approval was required to pass most decisions, while nine votes were necessary to make major decisions, such as whether to wage war or to sign a particular treaty. Any amendment to the Articles required the approval

POLITICAL FOUNDATIONS *The Articles of Confederation were ratified by the colonies in 1781.* **Why did many leaders want the loose confederation of states that was created under the Articles?**

SECTION 3
THE FIRST NATIONAL GOVERNMENT

Lesson Plans
For teaching strategies, see Lesson 2.3 located at the beginning of this chapter or the One-Stop Planner Strategy 2.3.

Political Dictionary
To reinforce the section's vocabulary terms, refer students to the Electronic Glossary on the *Researcher CD-ROM*.

Section Assessment
To assess students' mastery of this section, have them complete Daily Quiz 2.3 in *Daily Quizzes with Answer Key*.

Caption Answer
They feared that creating a strong national government would threaten the states' power and the freedoms of the people.

PUBLIC GOOD The issue of promoting and regulating trade was very important to the new nation. Not only was strong international commerce vital to the country's economy, but some people believed that it was necessary to maintain a virtuous American character.

Free trade in global markets, they argued, would give farmers and manufacturers the incentive to produce more goods than were required for subsistence. This would require discipline and thus keep Americans industrious and virtuous. Under the Articles of Confederation, however, the national government had no authority to promote global trade. ■

Caption Answer

The Northwest Ordinance banned slavery in the territory, allowed new states to enter the Union as equal partners, and contained a bill of rights for the new territory.

Transparency

An overhead transparency of the chart on the next page is available in *Transparency Resources.* See Transparency 3: Limits on the Power of the National Government Under the Articles of Confederation (1781).

---

of all 13 states. There was no national executive or judicial branch.

Only Congress, not the individual states, had the power to declare war and to conduct foreign policy. Congress appointed Benjamin Franklin and John Adams as U.S. representatives to France, for example. The Articles also gave Congress the authority to borrow money, establish military forces, settle arguments between states, and manage relations with American Indians.

CASE STUDY

The Northwest Ordinance

POLITICAL FOUNDATIONS The Articles of Confederation also gave Congress the power to admit new states to the Union. This power proved to be critical to the future of the United States.

Through a peace agreement signed after the Revolutionary War, the United States acquired

Northwest Territory

■ Northwest Territory
□ Original 13 colonies
□ Disputed territory

The Northwest Ordinance was passed by Congress in 1787 to manage the development of the newly acquired Northwest Territory. **What were some of the main points of the Northwest Ordinance?**

---

from Great Britain a large area between the 13 states and the Mississippi River. To manage development of this area, Congress passed the **Northwest Ordinance** of 1787, which set procedures for granting statehood to territories within the region.

The ordinance was one of the most important bills passed by the national government under the Articles of Confederation. Of particular importance was its ban on slavery within the Northwest Territory. The ordinance also served as the model for admitting all other states to the Union. It allowed new states to join the Union as equal partners with the original 13 states. This condition showed the desire of the country's leaders to prevent new states from being unfairly ruled by the original states. They did not want to replace British tyranny with a new tyranny of the original 13 states.

In addition to its rules on statehood, the ordinance included a bill of rights for the territories. These rights guaranteed representative government, religious freedom, and trial by jury, among other freedoms. These rights ensured that new states would have governments whose authority came from the consent of the people.

Limits on Power The Articles gave Congress several powers. To keep the national government from becoming stronger than the states, however, those powers were limited. For example, the exclusion of a president and an executive branch meant that there were no officials to carry out Congress's laws.

Congress also had no power to tax. It could ask member states for voluntary contributions, but it could not require that they pay. This meant that it was difficult to raise money for a national army or to repay money that the country had borrowed. In addition, Congress could not prevent the states from issuing their own money.

Furthermore, Congress had no power to regulate trade among states or with foreign countries. The states therefore could tax products coming from other states. For example, Virginia passed a tax law stating that any ship at its ports that failed

Limits on the Power of the National Government Under the Articles of Confederation (1781)

- No president or executive branch
- No national court system
- No officials to enforce laws
- No power to tax
- No power to regulate trade
- No power to establish national armed forces (each state raised its own troops under the direction of Congress)
- Major laws required approval of 9 out of 13 states to pass

The Articles of Confederation, ratified in 1781, limited the power of the national government. **How did these limits create obstacles for the national government?**

to pay duty could have its cargo legally seized. This law was intended to keep Maryland, Pennsylvania, and Massachusetts businesses from competing with those in Virginia. Such barriers to trade created major obstacles to economic development in the young country.

The absence of a national court system also added to the weakness of the national government. The lack of national courts meant that the government was forced to rely on state courts to enforce national laws. In addition, Congress had no powers to force states to obey the laws it passed.

Efforts to strengthen Congress's powers to deal with important problems often failed because amendments to the Articles required the approval of all the states. In other words, just one state could block approval of an amendment.

Obstacles to Unity Resurface

The weaknesses of the Articles made unity among the states difficult. As noted in Section 2, differences among the colonies had been obstacles to unity before the Revolutionary War. Although the colonies had temporarily put aside many of their

differences to unite against Great Britain, these cultural, economic, and geographic obstacles resurfaced after the war.

Cultural Differences Although many citizens of the new nation had a common language and ancestry, their beliefs—particularly religious ones—and ways of life often varied from state to state. Domination by a particular religious group varied from colony to colony. For example, while the Baptist Church was strongest in Rhode Island and North Carolina, the Presbyterian Church had the most members in New Jersey and Delaware. In addition, although around 48 percent of the colonists were from England, settlers had also come from Germany, France, and Sweden. Cultural differences raised concerns about a union that tied states too closely together. Many people feared that a strong unified government might force some groups to give up their beliefs.

Economic Differences Important economic differences from colonial years also were evident in the new nation. States feared that the economic interests of certain regions would win unfair advantages under a strong national government.

Slavery was a divisive economic as well as cultural issue. Southern plantation owners used slaves to work their fields. Many people, particularly in the states where slavery was illegal, opposed this practice. They believed that slavery violated the principles on which the nation was founded, especially the need to protect the natural rights of all

POLITICAL FOUNDATIONS *This painting from the 1700s shows slaves bringing indigo in from the fields. Colonists had conflicting views on the practice of slavery.* **What principle did many people believe slavery violated?**

CULTURAL PERSPECTIVES

Americans were separated by both geographic and cultural distances. Because of bad roads and unreliable transportation, mail and other sources of news could take an entire month to travel the 300 miles from Philadelphia to Pittsburgh.

People had difficulty communicating because in some areas English, German, Polish, and French were all spoken. New England fishers could not always relate to the needs of southern farmers. Reconciling such differences would prove difficult when state leaders forged a new national government. ■

human beings. Southern states thus feared that if a strong national government were to oppose slavery, their economic livelihood would suffer.

Geographic Isolation The size of the new nation also made it difficult to form ties among the states. Transportation between northern and southern states was not easy or quick. (See "Linking Government and Geography," page 27.)

Pressure for Stronger Government

The relative independence of the various states posed many problems for the young nation. Some states refused to help fund the national government, obey laws passed by Congress, and respect terms of foreign treaties. In fact, some states negotiated directly with foreign powers. Some states even formed their own armed services. These problems led many people to believe that a strong national government posed far less of a threat to the public good than did a weak government that could not unify the country or enforce the law.

In September 1786, representatives from Virginia organized a convention in Annapolis, Maryland, to try to resolve some of the differences among the states. Only five states—Delaware, New Jersey, New York, Pennsylvania, and Virginia—

attended the Annapolis Convention, but the delegates determined that a future meeting should be called to consider changes to the Articles. The convention called for all of the states to send representatives to Philadelphia in May 1787.

An armed rebellion in Massachusetts later in 1786 was further proof that a stronger national government was needed to maintain order and to protect and promote the public good of citizens in all states. The incident involved groups of armed farmers trying to prevent the state from seizing the property of people who could not pay their debts. (The Revolutionary War and economic problems afterward had left many farmers burdened by heavy debt.) The fighting came to be known as Shays's Rebellion, named after its leader, Daniel Shays. The rebellion eventually was put down by force, but it caused some people, including George Washington, to express frustration that the new nation could win a difficult war but could not keep order in peacetime.

As a result, by early 1787 several states had already chosen delegates for the May meeting. Shays's Rebellion also had forced the national Congress to officially recognize the need for a meeting among the states. Officials declared, however, that the meeting in Philadelphia was "for the sole and express purpose of revising the Articles of Confederation." No mention was made of writing a new constitution.

SECTION 3 REVIEW

1. Identify and explain:
- Articles of Confederation
- ratification
- Northwest Ordinance

2. Categorizing: What powers did the Articles of Confederation give the national government? List four of the powers in the web organizer below.

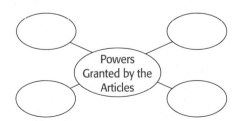

Powers Granted by the Articles

Homework Practice Online
keyword: SV3 HP2

3. Finding the Main Idea

a. Why were farmers in Massachusetts angry enough to join Shays's Rebellion?

b. How did leaders like George Washington react to Shays's Rebellion?

c. What was the eventual outcome of the rebellion and how did it affect the national Congress?

4. Writing and Critical Thinking

Analyzing: Write a paragraph describing how the acquisition of the Northwest Territory changed the physical characteristics of the United States, and explaining how the Northwest Ordinance affected the human characteristics of the region.

SECTION 4

THE CONSTITUTIONAL CONVENTION

READ TO DISCOVER

1. Who were the delegates to the Constitutional Convention?
2. What major competing plans of government did the convention delegates debate?
3. What were some of the compromises reached by the delegates?

POLITICAL DICTIONARY

Virginia Plan
New Jersey Plan
Great Compromise

On May 25, 1787, delegates met in Philadelphia to consider establishing a stronger national government for the 13 states. As the delegates arrived in the city, Philadelphia newspapers trumpeted their arrival, printing their names and political honors. Many in the city were proud that Philadelphia had been chosen as the site for the meeting, instead of New York City, where Congress met.

At the time, the delegates' home states did not attribute as much significance to the Convention as people would later. For example, the states provided limited financial support. Many delegates ran into debt at the boardinghouses where they were staying. At one difficult point during the Convention, a delegate suggested that his colleagues begin each day with a prayer. Another delegate responded that the Convention lacked the money to pay a minister.

Nonetheless, the Convention proceeded through the hottest Philadelphia summer in 30 years. The windows were kept closed, shutting out swarms of flies and shutting in the Convention's discussions. Delegates worked in secrecy, hoping to ensure free and open debate without interference from outsiders.

The delegates worked for four months, considering different plans of government. Who were these delegates? How did they finally piece together a plan for a new, stronger national government?

The Delegates

The delegates to the Constitutional Convention included many of the country's most distinguished leaders and political thinkers. Of the 55 delegates, 8 had signed the Declaration of Independence, 7 had been in the First Continental Congress, and 7 had been state governors. Most were wealthy and college-educated. Many would go on to become officials in the national government.

Among the best-known delegates were George Washington, Benjamin Franklin, and Alexander Hamilton. Washington was unanimously named chairman of the convention. His participation added a great deal of distinction to the gathering. Franklin was a respected scientist and philosopher. Hamilton had fought in the Revolution and served as a delegate in the Continental Congress.

Some other well-known leaders were absent. Thomas Jefferson was in Europe as a U.S. representative to France. Others, such as Patrick Henry from Virginia, declined to attend the Convention. They were suspicious that the delegates were plotting to create a powerful central government. Henry, for one, said that he "smelt a rat."

"Let's leave out 'NO TAXATION' 'WITHOUT REPRESENTATION'! What congress would vote taxes without consulting the people?"

CONSTITUTIONAL GOVERNMENT *The decisions made by the framers of the Constitution have had a lasting influence on the role of government in this country.* **What might have happened if they had left out of the Constitution some of the key limits on government?**

SECTION 4

THE CONSTITUTIONAL CONVENTION

Lesson Plans

For teaching strategies, see Lesson 2.4 located at the beginning of this chapter or the One-Stop Planner Strategy 2.4.

Political Dictionary

To reinforce the section's vocabulary terms, refer students to the Electronic Glossary on the *Researcher CD-ROM.*

Section Assessment

To assess students' mastery of this section, have them complete Daily Quiz 2.4 in *Daily Quizzes with Answer Key.*

Caption Answer

Students may suggest that the omission may have created a harsh, unrepresentative government.

Transparency

An overhead transparency of the cartoon on this page is available in *Transparency Resources.* See Cartoon Transparency 1: Constitutional Convention.

Transparency

An overhead transparency of the chart on this page is available in *Transparency Resources.* See Transparency 4: Rival Constitutional Plans.

Caption Answer

New Jersey Plan supporters feared states losing power so they favored a weak executive and a unicameral legislature. The Virginia Plan reflected a belief in a strong executive and a bicameral legislature.

Perhaps the most important delegate to the convention was James Madison of Virginia. Madison is sometimes called the "father of the Constitution." The notes he took during the Convention became the main record of what went on during the gathering. Madison prepared himself for the Convention by studying books about history and politics. Jefferson even sent him hundreds of books from Paris.

Rival Plans

Almost as soon as the Convention began, debate moved beyond the original goal of strengthening the Articles of Confederation to one of creating a new government. Indeed, the Convention adopted a resolution calling for a national government "to consist of a supreme legislative, executive, and judiciary." Debate centered around two competing plans for the government.

Virginia Plan Madison and his fellow Virginians proposed what became known as the **Virginia Plan**. This plan called for a strong government with a bicameral legislature, a strong executive, and a judiciary, a significant change from the Articles of Confederation. Membership in the legislature would be based on a state's population. The largest states, such as Virginia, Pennsylvania, North Carolina, Massachusetts, and Maryland, would have a greater number of representatives than the smaller states.

The people would directly elect one legislative house. States would nominate candidates for the second house. The first house would then elect members to the second house from among the state nominees.

Members of both the executive and judicial branches would be chosen by the legislature. The executive would carry out the laws passed by the legislature. The judiciary would include a

---

Rival Constitutional Plans

VIRGINIA PLAN		NEW JERSEY PLAN
• Strong executive who is chosen by legislature and carries out laws made by legislature	**EXECUTIVE BRANCH**	• Weak executive controlled by legislature
• Bicameral legislature • Membership based on state's population • First house elected by the people • Second house elected by first house from among candidates nominated by states	**LEGISLATIVE BRANCH**	• Strong unicameral legislature • Each state represented equally with one vote apiece • Representatives chosen by state legislatures
• A judiciary that includes a supreme court and lower courts and is elected by legislature	**JUDICIAL BRANCH**	• A supreme court with justices named by legislature
• To levy taxes • To make national laws • To regulate trade	**POWERS OF NATIONAL GOVERNMENT**	• To levy taxes • To regulate trade

Two competing plans for a national government emerged from the Constitutional Convention.
How did the structure of each proposal represent the concerns of the plans' supporters?

Careers in Government

National Park Ranger

When you think of park rangers, you probably envision uniformed men and women patrolling the nation's forests, canyons, and mountainsides and protecting its natural resources. Indeed, this is the role of many park rangers across the country. The National Park System, however, also includes sites of historical importance. National parks are a key part of the effort to preserve the natural and cultural heritage of the United States.

For example, at Philadelphia's Independence National Historical Park, where "the shrines of American liberty" are preserved and showcased, park rangers guide visitors through 24 historic sites daily. The park's centerpiece and most popular attraction is Independence Hall, where the Declaration of Independence was signed in 1776 and the Constitution was written in 1787. Park rangers at Independence National Historical Park are responsible for providing visitors with information about the historical significance of the site as well as for keeping visitors safe and preserving the national treasures in the park.

At Independence National Historical Park, approximately 75 park rangers are employed in the area of "interpretive work." Their job is interpreting

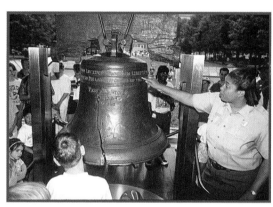

A park ranger at the Independence National Historical Park reads the inscription on the Liberty Bell to tourists.

history, primarily by giving historical tours. These rangers usually bring with them an interest in U.S. history, a college degree in a field such as history, and several years of experience working as a seasonal park employee or a museum guide. Another 25 rangers are responsible for law enforcement in the park. Their job is to protect the park's resources and manage the public's use of the park.

There is a great deal of competition for park ranger jobs. Having knowledge of several different subjects—such as U.S. history, behavioral sciences, botany, geology, and forestry—is a great advantage. Park rangers employed in the area of historical interpretation must have good communication skills, because they spend much of their time providing information.

Rangers must be willing to relocate often and to work at several different parks in order to move to higher-level positions in prime locations. Entry-level positions may involve keeping the park clean, working at an information desk, giving tours, and collecting entrance fees. Higher-level jobs often require giving lectures, setting up exhibits, and managing park resources. If you think this is the career for you, the best way to start is to volunteer at a historic site in your area.

Careers in Government

To help students learn about other careers in government, refer them to the Careers section on the *Holt Researcher Online.*

THEMES IN GOVERNMENT

POLITICAL FOUNDATIONS

Alexander Hamilton distrusted the judgment of the ordinary American more than James Madison did. Wanting a government that controlled the passions of the public, Hamilton argued that the federal government should be given almost unlimited powers with a minimum of checks and balances. Furthermore, he proposed that the president and senators be elected for life.

Most other delegates complained that Hamilton's plan was too similar to the British system of government and that Americans would never accept the plan. Consequently, it was not even debated at the Constitutional Convention. ■

national court system. Both branches would check the power of the legislative branch.

The national government would have the power to levy taxes, to make laws for the whole nation, and to regulate trade. The national government could reject state laws that violated national laws. And, in contrast to Congress under the Articles, the national government could force states to obey national laws.

New Jersey Plan Some delegates who feared that the states would lose too much power under the Virginia Plan presented a counterproposal, the **New Jersey Plan** (although not all its authors were from New Jersey). This plan also called for a national government with legislative, executive, and judicial branches. (See the chart on page 36.) Also like the Virginia Plan, the New Jersey Plan gave the national government the power to tax and the power to regulate trade across state lines.

The New Jersey Plan, however, called for the states to have a stronger role in the national government. In contrast to the Virginia Plan, the New Jersey Plan called for a unicameral legislature in which each state would be represented equally with one vote apiece. This was similar to the structure of the Congress under the Articles of Confederation. Representatives to the national legislature would be chosen by the state legislatures. There would be no house in which members were elected directly by the people.

On June 19, after only three days of debate over which of the two proposals should serve as the basis for further discussion, the delegates took a vote. Votes were by state delegation, not by individual delegates. Seven state delegations voted for the Virginia Plan, while only three voted for the New Jersey Plan. The other delegations were either split or did not vote.

The Great Compromise

Despite the strong vote for the Virginia Plan, the question of state representation in the new national legislature was not yet resolved. Small states wanted a government that gave them power equal to the large states. Success of the prospective new government depended on reaching a compromise. The delegates therefore debated the issue for another long, hot, and difficult month.

Finally, the delegates hammered out an agreement that borrowed elements from both the Virginia and New Jersey Plans. The agreement, first called the Connecticut Plan, came to be known as the **Great Compromise**. Adopted on July 16, 1787, this compromise called for a bicameral legislature. Representation in one chamber of the legislature, the House of Representatives, would be based on population. States with larger populations would have more representatives than states with smaller populations. Members would be elected directly by the peo-

ple. This part of the compromise was borrowed from the Virginia Plan.

The structure of the second chamber, the Senate, was adapted from the New Jersey Plan. Each state would have two representatives in the Senate. Thus, the small states would have equal footing with the large states in one half of the legislature. Senators were to be elected by state legislatures. Both the House of Representatives and the Senate would have to approve legislation by majority votes for it to become law.

Settling Other Issues

The Great Compromise resolved the major issues dividing the Convention. The delegates then turned to other difficult issues. What emerged from their efforts has been called a "bundle of compromises."

Slavery Slavery continued to be a divisive issue. Although slavery was banned in some northern states, slaves made up a considerable part of the southern states' populations. Southern delegates wanted slaves to be counted as part of each state's population, because doing so would increase their state's representation in the new House of Representatives.

Some delegates, mostly from the North, believed that slavery was evil and violated the natural rights of human beings. Many of these delegates argued that because slaves had no legal rights, they

CONSTITUTIONAL GOVERNMENT *The signing of the Constitution took place after almost four months of discussion and debate among the delegates.* ***What were the major issues on which delegates agreed to compromise?***

should not be counted in a state's population. In addition, many of the northern delegates hoped to limit the size of the South's representation.

Although some other delegates opposed slavery, they realized compromise was necessary to win support of southern states for the new Constitution. In fact, some southern delegates made it clear that the resolution of the issue on whether to include slaves in a state's population would be critical in their states' decisions to join the new Union.

The delegates finally agreed to count—for the purpose of determining a state's representation in Congress—three fifths of the total slave population. This compromise quieted the debate over slavery—for a time. Over the next several decades, however, the issue of slavery would again challenge the young country's unity and test its citizens' belief in the natural rights of human beings.

Trade Slavery also was part of the debate over trade issues. Southerners feared that Congress would use its legislative powers to make importing slaves into the United States illegal. In addition, southern delegates wanted to prohibit Congress from passing taxes on exports. The agricultural economies of southern states depended heavily on exported goods.

The Convention compromised on the issue of slavery by deciding that Congress could not ban the importation of slaves before 1808. In addition, Congress could not tax goods that were exported to other countries.

The Presidency The delegates also were split over the issue of the nation's chief executive. Some delegates believed that the president should be elected directly by the people. Other delegates wanted the president to be chosen by the states or by the national legislature.

The delegates decided on a system in which the president would be chosen by state electors. The number of a state's electors would match the number of its representatives in both houses of Congress. Many delegates assumed that state legislatures would choose the electors, but they permitted states to choose electors by popular vote. If no presidential candidate received a majority of electoral votes from the states, the House of Representatives would choose the president.

Finalizing the Constitution

The Convention delegates finished their work on the Constitution in August 1787. On September 17, most of the delegates signed the document. Those who did not sign either had already gone home or else opposed the proposed national government. In his closing remarks to the Convention, Benjamin Franklin noted that George Washington's chair had a sun on its back. Franklin had wondered frequently whether this was a rising or a setting sun. Having seen the Convention's work, he was now convinced it was a rising sun.

SECTION 4 REVIEW

1. Identify and explain:
- Virginia Plan
- New Jersey Plan
- Great Compromise

2. Contrasting: Use the Venn diagram below to explain the differences between the Virginia Plan and the New Jersey Plan. In the overlapping circle show how delegates compromised.

Virginia Plan | Compromises Reached | New Jersey Plan

Homework Practice Online
keyword: SV3 HP2

3. Finding the Main Idea

a. Why was George Washington's presence important to the Constitutional Convention?
b. What was James Madison's role in the Convention?
c. Why did delegates settle on a federal form of government instead of a system in which power was not divided between state and national governments?

4. Writing and Critical Thinking

Drawing Conclusions: Write a paragraph explaining whether you think delegates to the Constitutional Convention should have compromised on the issue of slavery.
Consider the following:
- how delegates compromised
- what might have happened without a compromise

SECTION 5

RATIFYING THE CONSTITUTION

READ TO DISCOVER

1. What were the main arguments in the debate over ratification of the Constitution?
2. What role did a bill of rights play in the debate?
3. Which key states were among the last to ratify the Constitution?

POLITICAL DICTIONARY

Federalist
Antifederalist

The battle to create a new government did not end with the signing of the Constitution. First, nine states had to ratify the document in special constitutional conventions, and the outcome of the ratification process was by no means certain. Both supporters and opponents of the Constitution prepared for ratification battles in each state.

Federalists and Antifederalists

Supporters of the new Constitution were called **Federalists** because they supported a stronger, federal form of government. Opponents were called **Antifederalists**. The Antifederalists were particularly strong in New York and Virginia. Without the support of these two key states, the battle for ratification would be more difficult.

Antifederalists Patrick Henry of Virginia was among the most famous Antifederalists. He and other Antifederalists argued that if the Constitution were ratified the national government would become too powerful. They believed that a popular government could exist only in a small territory. Popular government in a larger territory, such as the United States, would be too difficult because of the many competing interests. A large territory

with a popular government would have to be held together by force, which would restrict people's freedom. In addition, Antifederalists were concerned that a strong executive would be too similar to a monarch. Such a strong executive, they argued, would be a danger to representative government and to individual rights.

One of the Antifederalists' strongest criticisms was that the Constitution lacked something that every state constitution adopted after independence—a bill of rights that proclaimed individual rights that government could not ignore or deny. Antifederalists argued that the absence of a bill of rights from the new Constitution was dangerous. They believed that without such a bill, the document would create a powerful national government that could easily become unjust. Some also stated that adopting the Constitution without a bill of rights would cancel any previously held laws or customs that protected individual rights. As influential Antifederalist Richard Henry Lee wrote:

CONSTITUTIONAL GOVERNMENT *Patrick Henry, a famous Antifederalist from Virginia, thought the Constitution would create a national government that was too powerful.* **Why did the Antifederalists argue against a strong executive?**

The Granger Collection, New York

> " There are certain rights which we have always held sacred in the United States, and recognized in all our constitutions, and which, by the adoption of the new Constitution in its present form, will be left unsecured. . . . It is to be observed that when the people shall adopt the proposed Constitution, it will be their last and supreme act; . . . and wherever this Constitution, or any part of it, shall be incompatible with their ancient customs, rights, the laws or the constitutions heretofore established in the United States, it will entirely abolish them and do them away. "

Federalists The Federalists responded to these charges by arguing that the separate powers belonging to each branch of government would check those of the other branches. In this way, no single part of the government, such as the national legislature, could become too powerful and threaten the rights of the states or of the people.

As for a bill of rights, Federalists also argued that the Constitution limited the powers of the national government to those it listed. Any powers not listed were guaranteed to the states or to the people. For example, the Constitution did not give government the power to restrict freedom of speech. Federalists believed that the people have the right to free speech and that the Constitution did not need to specifically state this.

Ratification

Many opponents to ratification argued that the Constitution favored large states, but a small state was first to ratify it. On December 7, 1787, those attending Delaware's convention voted unanimously to ratify the Constitution. Many in Delaware and other small states believed that the Constitution and its call for equal state representation in the Senate would protect their interests against those of larger states.

Virginia and New York, however, were deeply split over ratification. Many people in each state thought that the Constitution gave the national government too much power. Virginia and New York were important because of their size, location, and population.

Patrick Henry and James Madison, both well-respected leaders, led opposite sides of the debate in Virginia. During the heated ratification process in

New York, Alexander Hamilton, Madison, and John Jay wrote 85 newspaper articles supporting the Constitution. The series of articles came to be called the *Federalist Papers.* While it is unclear how influential the essays were at the time, the *Federalist Papers* continue to be respected as an analysis of the Constitution and of the foundations of U.S. government.

To gain time to win supporters, Federalists repeatedly delayed a vote in the New York convention. The strategy worked. Opposition to ratification in New York gradually weakened as other state conventions ratified the Constitution. Virginia and New York finally ratified the Constitution, but only after New Hampshire on June 21, 1788, became the ninth state to do so.

Although they ratified the Constitution, conventions in a number of states made strong recommendations that a bill of rights be added to it. These recommendations came from some of the

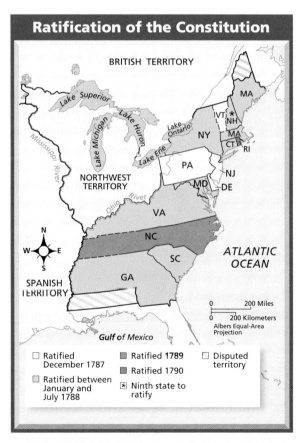

Ratification of the Constitution

☐ Ratified December 1787
☐ Ratified between January and July 1788
■ Ratified **1789**
■ Ratified 1790
☐ Disputed territory
✱ Ninth state to ratify

Rhode Island was the last state to ratify the Constitution. **How many states had to ratify the Constitution before it could be adopted?**

Profiles in American Government

For biographies of Alexander Hamilton, James Madison, John Jay, and other noted people in government, refer students to the Biographies section on the *Holt Researcher Online.*

Caption Answer
Nine

Caption Answer
New York

SECTION 5 REVIEW ANSWERS

1. Refer to the following pages: Federalist (40), Antifederalist (40)

2. Several states that had been closely divided over ratification strongly recommended a bill of rights. To ensure ratification, Federalists promised that the first Congress would pass a bill of rights.

3a. Based on earlier problems with powerful colonial governors, Antifederalists feared a strong executive would be a danger to representative government and to individual rights.

b. Federalists argued that the separation of powers within the federal government would restrict the power of the executive and prevent such abuses.

c. They were a collection of essays written by Madison, Hamilton, and Jay in which the authors explained the principles underlying the Constitution and tried to persuade states to ratify it.

4. Delaware was the first state to ratify the new Constitution. Under the Constitution, each state has equal representation in the Senate. The separation of powers prevented any one branch of government from becoming too pwerful or abusing the rights of individuals or states.

CONSTITUTIONAL GOVERNMENT *In this nineteenth-century engraving, New York celebrates the ratification of the Constitution with a parade. New York was an important state in the ratification of the Constitution because of its size and location.* **Which city became the first national capital?**

first Congress a bill of rights would be passed that covered the concerns of the states.

North Carolina ratified the Constitution in November 1789, while Rhode Island held out until May 1790. Their actions came long after the new government had settled in at the temporary national capital of New York City. The first Congress under the new U.S. Constitution had met in New York on March 4, 1789. George Washington had been sworn in as the nation's first president on April 30, 1789.

Philadelphia celebrated the new Constitution on July 4, 1788. A ship called the *Rising Sun* fired its cannon to salute the occasion. After parading through the city, huge crowds heard convention delegate James Wilson lead 10 toasts. The crowd toasted "the people of the United States" and "the whole family of mankind." After observing the festivities, Philadelphian Dr. Benjamin Rush wrote, "'Tis done. We have become a nation."

larger states—Massachusetts, North Carolina, and Virginia—which had been closely divided over whether to ratify. To secure the passage of the Constitution, the Federalists promised that in the

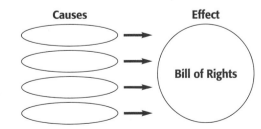

SECTION 5 REVIEW

1. Identify and explain:
• Federalist
• Antifederalist

2. Cause and Effect: Use the diagram below to explain what caused Federalists to promise that the first Congress would pass a bill of rights.

Causes → **Effect**

Bill of Rights

Homework Practice Online
go.hrw.com
keyword: SV3 HP2

3. **Finding the Main Idea**

a. Why did Antifederalists fear a strong executive in the new government?

b. How did Federalists answer the arguments against the new Constitution?

c. What were the *Federalist Papers* and what role did they play?

4. **Writing and Critical Thinking**

Analyzing: Write a paragraph explaining what advantages the Constitution provided to the smaller states.
Consider the following:
• what was the first state to ratify the Constitution?
• how was each state represented in the national government?
• what prevented the abuse of power by one state or branch over another?

GOVERNMENT IN THE NEWS

Building the Republic of Georgia

The republic of Georgia in southwest Asia was part of the Soviet Union from 1922 until 1991, when the Soviet state collapsed. Despite its newfound independence, Georgia continues to be economically and politically tied to Russia, the former heart of the Soviet Union. Internal dissent also threatens the young republic.

In 1994 in an effort to gain strength as a country, Georgia joined the Commonwealth of Independent States (CIS). The CIS was conceived as a successor state to the Soviet Union in its role of coordinating the foreign and economic policy of its member nations. The CIS treaty honored current borders and recognized each republic's independence, sovereignty, and equality. It established a free-market ruble zone, embracing the interdependent economies of the member republics, and authorized a joint defense force.

The transition to independence has been anything but easy for Georgia. Continued ethnic and political unrest has forced Georgia to depend on Russia for the security of its borders and the stability of its economy. Russian troops remain garrisoned at military bases in Georgia and serve as peacekeepers in the separatist regions of Abkhazia and South Ossetia. Georgia's president, Eduard Shevardnadze, has survived two assassination attempts since taking office in 1992.

The Georgian government has had continued problems with its military. In 1998 some 200 soldiers mutinied in protest of President Shevardnadze. Poor conditions in the military incited another mutiny in May 2001 outside of Tbilisi, Georgia's capital. About 900 National Guardsmen, armed with tanks and guns, occupied a military base, claiming that many soldiers lacked proper equipment. Some soldiers also reported it

At Vaziani military base near Tbilisi, Georgia, Russian tanks await transport out of Georgia.

had been more than a year since they had been paid. The mutiny ended when Shevardnadze met with the leaders of the mutiny, promising to investigate their complaints.

Suffering from a lack of natural energy sources, Georgia has become dependent on Russia for natural gas. This economic relationship has been complicated, however, by political and military tensions. An energy crisis constantly looms over Georgia. In 2001 Georgian officials asserted that Russia threatened to end the natural gas exchange unless Russian troops were allowed to remain in the country. Russian leaders are also angered by an alleged connection between Georgia and Chechnya, a neighboring Russian province currently in rebellion.

What Do You Think?

1. What challenges of independence are demonstrated by the experiences of the republic of Georgia?
2. Do you think that the difficulties of independence outweigh the benefits?

> **WHY IT MATTERS TODAY**
>
> The transition to independence is often a long and difficult process. Use **CNNfyi.com** or other **current events** sources to find additional information about Georgia or other countries that have declared independence in the past 20 years.
>
> **CNNfyi.com**

Government in the News Answers

1. Students might suggest that Georgia has faced internal dissent, a shortage of natural resources, and dependence on Russia.

2. Answers will vary, but students might suggest that independence inevitably involves some hardships.

CHAPTER 2

Review Answers

Writing a Summary

Summaries should focus on the main points of each section. These may be found in the Read to Discover questions at the start of each section. Summaries should also use standard grammar, spelling, sentence structure, and punctuation.

Identifying People and Ideas

For significance, refer to the following pages: constitution (21), rule of law (22), Benjamin Franklin (26), John Locke (29), Thomas Jefferson (29), Articles of Confederation (31), George Washington (35), James Madison (36), *Federalist Papers* (41).

Understanding Main Ideas

1. A written constitution outlines the laws that a government must follow. Without one, rulers can levy taxes or seize property without regard to the people.

2. The Magna Carta helped establish the rule of law; the
(Continued on page 44)

Petition of Right forced monarchs to consult Parliament and banned illegal imprisonment, and the English Bill of Rights denied the monarch the right to rule without the consent of Parliament.

3. Franklin proposed the Albany Plan of Union, which called for a council of representatives that could levy taxes and raise an army.

4. the rights that cannot be taken away, including "life, liberty, and the pursuit of happiness"

5. allowed Congress to regulate trade, print a national currency, and raise taxes to support a military

6. Compromise allowed the delegates to reach agreements on the structure of and representation in the legislature, slavery, trade, and the election of the executive.

7. The bicameral structure gave each state an equal number of senators and a number of representatives based on population. This satisfied smaller states that were afraid they would not be appropriately represented.

8. They wrote a series of essays eventually called the *Federalist Papers.*

Reviewing Themes
1. With a written constitution to outline the powers of government, a ruler cannot arbitrarily make laws that infringe on individual rights.
2. Those who owned slaves did not want other states or the national government

(Continued on page 45)

Review

Writing a Summary

Using standard grammar, spelling, sentence structure, and punctuation, write a summary of the information in this chapter.

Identifying People and Ideas

Identify the following terms or individuals and explain their significance.

1. constitution

2. rule of law

3. Benjamin Franklin

4. John Locke

5. Thomas Jefferson

6. Articles of Confederation

7. George Washington

8. Alexander Hamilton

9. James Madison

10. *Federalist Papers*

Understanding Main Ideas

SECTION 1 *(pp. 21–24)*

1. Explain the importance of a written constitution.

2. Which key documents limited the power of English monarchs and how did they do it?

SECTION 2 *(pp. 25–30)*

3. How did Benjamin Franklin try to bring unity to the country during the conflict between Britain and France?

4. In the Declaration of Independence, what rights did Thomas Jefferson consider "unalienable"?

SECTION 3 *(pp. 31–34)*

5. How did the Constitution address the weaknesses of the Articles?

SECTION 4 *(pp. 35–39)*

6. What role did compromise play in the Constitutional Convention?

7. Why did delegates compromise on a bicameral Congress?

SECTION 5 *(pp. 40–42)*

8. During the ratification battle in New York, how did the Federalists explain the principals of American constitutional government and try to win supporters?

Reviewing Themes

1. Public Good How does a written constitution protect individual rights?

2. Political Foundations How did slavery form an obstacle to unity among the states?

3. Constitutional Government Why did the promise of a bill of rights help the Constitution get ratified?

Thinking Critically

1. Analyzing What kind of government do you think best protects citizens' natural rights: a system based on federalism such as the one outlined in the Constitution, or a unitary system in which all authority rests with the central government? Explain your answer.

2. Synthesizing What English ideals did the delegates draw on during the Constitutional Convention as they hammered out the Constitution?

Writing about Government

Review the list of rights and freedoms that you created in your Government Notebook at the beginning of the chapter. Using what you have learned, add to your list the origin or source of each right or freedom. For assistance, refer to the Constitution on p. 572 and the Declaration of Independence on page 574 of your textbook.

Interpreting the Painting

Study the image below. Then use it to help you answer the questions that follow.

1. How does the artist portray the Constitutional Convention in this painting?
   a. It was accomplished by a very few men and was worthy of joyous public celebration.
   b. It consisted of months of private deliberations and debates among many men.
   c. It caused much dismay among those who feared that states would lose power.
   d. It was the spark that ignited the revolution for American independence.

2. How accurate is the artist's depiction?

Analyzing Primary Sources

Read the following excerpt of essay "No. 51" from the *Federalist Papers*, written by James Madison, then answer the questions.

"If men were angels, no government would be necessary. If angels were to govern men, neither external nor internal controls on government would be necessary. . . .

In republican government, the legislative authority necessarily predominates [has the most power]. The remedy for this inconveniency is to divide the legislature into different branches; and to render them, by different modes [methods] of election and different principles of action, as little connected with each other as the nature of their common functions and their common dependence on the society will admit."

3. Which of the following statements best describes the the author's point of view?
   a. People are so naturally good that they don't need to submit to government.
   b. The legislature should function under a unicameral system to strengthen state power.
   c. No controls are necessary to check power in government.
   d. To balance power, the legislature should be divided into two branches that function as independently as possible.

4. How was Madison in a unique position to explain and defend the new Constitution?

Alternative Assessment

Building Your Portfolio

The Great Debate

Create a program for a debate on ratification of the Constitution. Select three key leaders from the Constitutional Convention and include a biography of each in your program. Make sure to include a brief description of the participants' positions on the issues, their professions, and their life accomplishments.

internet connect

Internet Activity: go.hrw.com
KEYWORD: SV3 GV2

Access the Internet through the HRW Go site to research key events and concepts influencing United States government. Then create a poster, flyer, or handout for a town meeting. The meeting could concern the power of kings, colonial unification, the role of government, or Federalists and Antifederalists.

(Continued from page 44) telling them they could not. Those who disagreed with slavery argued that it contradicted the idea of natural rights upon which the nation was founded.

3. Many states ratified the Constitution with the strong recommendation that it include a bill of rights, and to secure passage Federalists promised to pass one in the first Congress.

Thinking Critically

1. Students may support a government based on federalism, arguing that rights are best protected by a balance of power between the states and the federal government; or they may argue that states themselves function as unitary governments and are able to protect individual rights.

2. They drew on the ideals of limited and representative government.

Building Social Studies Skills

1. a

2. Students may respond that while the convention involved a small number of delegates, the artist focuses on only three, which is misleading. The painting shows only the imagined aftermath of the Convention and doesn't depict the days of debate, nor the arguments that occurred while debating ratification.

3. d

4. Madison took notes that became the primary record of the Convention, and he sponsored the Virginia Plan, which proposed many of the provisions that eventually became part of the Constitution.

CHAPTER 3 THE U.S. CONSTITUTION

	OBJECTIVES	PACING GUIDE	REPRODUCIBLE RESOURCES
SECTION 1 **BASIC PRINCIPLES** (pp. 47–50)	▶ What are the five basic principles on which the U.S. Constitution is based? ▶ How does the Constitution ensure the people's authority over government? ▶ How does the Constitution provide for a system of limited government? ▶ In what way does the Constitution protect the rights of the states?	**Regular** 1.5 days **Block Scheduling** .75 day	**ELL** Spanish Study Guide 3.1 **ELL** English Study Guide 3.1 **PS** Reading 6: *English Bill of Rights* **PS** Reading 7: *Articles of Confederation* **PS** Reading 8: *Declaration of the Rights of Man and Citizen*
SECTION 2 **AMENDING THE CONSTITUTION** (pp. 51–55)	▶ Why did the framers establish ways to amend the Constitution? ▶ What are the methods for amending the Constitution? ▶ What is the purpose of the Bill of Rights?	**Regular** 1.5 days **Block Scheduling** 1 day	**ELL** Spanish Study Guide 3.2 **ELL** English Study Guide 3.2
SECTION 3 **A FLEXIBLE DOCUMENT** (pp. 56–59)	▶ How does the Constitution give the three branches of government flexibility in using their powers? ▶ How have political parties changed the way government operates? ▶ How does the Constitution allow custom and tradition to help shape government?	**Regular** 1 day **Block Scheduling** .5 day	**ELL** Spanish Study Guide 3.3 **ELL** English Study Guide 3.3
SECTION 4 **THE CONSTITUTION AND THE PUBLIC GOOD** (pp. 60–62)	▶ What were some of James Madison's contributions to the development of the U.S. government? ▶ How does the Constitution ensure that government makes laws that promote the public good? ▶ Why do critics claim that the Constitution sometimes makes government less effective?	**Regular** .5 day **Block Scheduling** .25 day	**ELL** Spanish Study Guide 3.4 **ELL** English Study Guide 3.4 **PS** Reading 52: *The Federalist Papers* "No. 10" **E** Challenge and Enrichment: Activity 3 **E** Simulations and Strategies for Teaching American Government: Activity 3

Chapter Resource Key

PS	Primary Sources	**A**	Assessment	📼	Video
RS	Reading Support	**REV**	Review	💿	Videodisc
E	Enrichment	**ELL**	Reinforcement and English Language Learners	🌐	Internet
S	Simulations	📠	Transparencies	💥	Holt Presentation Maker Using
SM	Skills Mastery	💿	CD-ROM		Microsoft ® PowerPoint ®

TECHNOLOGY RESOURCES	REINFORCEMENT, REVIEW, AND ASSESSMENT
One-Stop Planner: Lesson 3.1 Holt Researcher Online Homework Practice Online Transparencies 5 and 6 Global Skill Builder CD-ROM	**REV** Section 1 Review, p. 50 **A** Daily Quiz 3.1
One-Stop Planner: Lesson 3.2 Holt Researcher Online Homework Practice Online Transparency 7 Global Skill Builder CD-ROM	**REV** Section 2 Review, p. 55 **A** Daily Quiz 3.2
One-Stop Planner: Lesson 3.2 Holt Researcher Online Homework Practice Online	**REV** Section 3 Review, p. 59 **A** Daily Quiz 3.3
One-Stop Planner: Lesson 3.4 Holt Researcher Online Homework Practice Online Global Skill Builder CD-ROM CNN Presents American Government	**REV** Section 4 Review, p. 62 **A** Daily Quiz 3.4

Chapter Review and Assessment

SM Global Skill Builder CD-ROM
HRW Go site

REV Chapter 3 Tutorial for Students, Parents, and Peers

REV Chapter 3 Review, pp. 64–65

A Chapter 3 Test Generator (on the One-Stop Planner)

A Chapter 3 Test Alternative Assessment Handbook

One-Stop Planner CD–ROM

It's easy to plan lessons, select resources, and print out materials for your students when you use the **One-Stop Planner CD–ROM with Test Generator.**

---

internet connect

HRW ONLINE RESOURCES
Go To: go.hrw.com
Then type in a keyword.

TEACHER HOME PAGE
KEYWORD: SV3 Teacher

CHAPTER INTERNET ACTIVITIES
KEYWORD: SV3 GV3
Choose an activity on the U.S. Constitution to:
▶ write an essay on the Bill of Rights.
▶ propose a new amendment to the Constitution.
▶ create an oral presentation on the Cabinet.

CHAPTER ENRICHMENT LINKS
KEYWORD: SV3 CH3

ONLINE ASSESSMENT
Homework Practice
KEYWORD: SV3 HP3
Standardized Test Prep
KEYWORD: SV3 STP3

RUBRICS
KEYWORD: SS Rubrics

ONLINE MAPS, CHARTS, AND GRAPHS
KEYWORD: SV3 MCG
▶ Principles of the Constitution
▶ Checks and Balances in the Federal Government
▶ Rights and Powers granted by the Bill of Rights

CONTENT UPDATES
KEYWORD: SS Content Updates

HOLT PRESENTATION MAKER
KEYWORD: SV3 PPT3

ONLINE READING SUPPORT
KEYWORD: SS Strategies

CURRENT EVENTS
KEYWORD: S3 Current Events

OBJECTIVES

- List and define the five basic principles on which the U.S. Constitution is based.
- Discuss and give examples of how the Constitution ensures the people's authority over government.
- Provide examples of how the Constitution provides a system of limited government.
- Describe how the Constitution protects the rights of states.

MOTIVATE

Ask one student to read the Preamble of the Constitution to the class. Follow this with a dramatic reading of Benjamin Franklin's address to the Constitutional Convention on June 28, 1787. Ask students to share with the class situations in their lives that involved compromising to reach a solution. Have students describe how they compromised. Explain to students that this is how it was at the Constitutional Convention. Discuss the fact that not all of the delegates at the Convention agreed with the proposed constitution, but the representatives of each state were willing to put their differences aside and sign the document. Tell students that in this section they will be learning about the principles that shaped the Constitution and how the Constitution ensures that the people have authority over government.

TEACH

Building a Vocabulary

In spiral notebooks, have students create a Political Dictionary to be used throughout the course. This dictionary may be used as an activity at the start of each new section; it may also be used as a modification device for students having difficulty or sheltered English students during tests and homework assignments. List words the students will be expected to know for this section on the board. Have students list, define, and give an example of each of the terms, using information provided in the text or on the *Researcher CD-ROM.*

Identifying the Main Idea

Organize the class into five small groups. Assign to each group one of the five basic principles on which the Constitution is based: popular sovereignty, limited government, separation of powers, checks and balances, and federalism. Next, ask students to brainstorm how the particular principle assigned to their group ensures the people's authority over government. Have each group write either a song or a poem that includes the definition of their assigned principle and an example of how the people's authority is ensured based on the principle they are discussing. Have each group sing their song or read their poem to the rest of the class. After students have finished doing this, discuss the definition and significance of each of the five principles of U.S. government. Have students consider these principles when completing the following activity.

Taking a Stand

Ask students to identify the difference between how kings and queens rise to power and how the president of the United States takes office. Explain to students that one of the principles the U.S. Constitution is based on is popular sovereignty. Tell students that this principle means that the government's authority comes from the people and that officials in the United States are elected by the people. Have students write a descriptive essay explaining the benefits of having a government based on popular sovereignty. Students may wish to use actual examples or create fictional examples to support their arguments. Have students share their essays with the class.

Learning from Visuals

Have students provide examples of the government's system of checks and balances. Then have students create a visual model of the balance of powers between the three branches to share with the class. Students may use their textbooks and the library to gather information. Display the students' model in the classroom so it can be used as a reference. Tell students that in their next assignment, they will learn about the balance of power between the state and federal governments.

Comparing and Contrasting

Have students read segments of the Constitution and discuss the ways that states' rights are protected. Organize the class into small groups and assign to each group a research project consisting of an investigation of the constitutions of countries such as Canada or Mexico. Instruct groups to find out how these constitutions are similar to and different from the U.S. Constitution regarding the balance of power and the protection of states' rights for each government. Students should create a chart showing the similarities and differences. Encourage students to share their findings with the rest of the class.

CLOSE

Organize the class into four groups, assigning each group one of the following topics: (a) principles of the U.S. Constitution; (b) ways that the Constitution ensures the people's authority over government; (c) ways the Constitution provides checks and balances; and (d) ways the Constitution protects states' rights. Each group will have the responsibility of creating a study guide for their assigned topic. Once all of the groups are done, have each group distribute photocopies of their study guides to the entire class. Then, as a class, review the study guides to make sure that students understand the topics included in the study guides.

OPTIONS

Gifted Learners

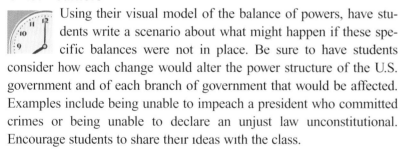

Using their visual model of the balance of powers, have students write a scenario about what might happen if these specific balances were not in place. Be sure to have students consider how each change would alter the power structure of the U.S. government and of each branch of government that would be affected. Examples include being unable to impeach a president who committed crimes or being unable to declare an unjust law unconstitutional. Encourage students to share their ideas with the class.

Students Having Difficulty

Have students create a list of ways that school rules protect their rights and the rights of other students. Examples might include not being able to hit people or call people names. Relate students' lists to the ways in which the Constitution protects states' rights. Encourage students to share their ideas with the class.

Logical-Mathematical Learners/Gifted Learners

Refer students to the Elections section on the *Holt Researcher Online* to find information on presidential elections. Have students analyze five different elections comparing the percentage of the popular vote for each candidate to the electoral vote each candidate received. Have students write a summary of their findings that discusses whether the principle of popular sovereignty is being followed in electing the president. Be sure to have students discuss the issue of representing the overall popular vote as compared to the overall popular vote of individual states.

Gifted Learners

Discuss with students the importance of the Supreme Court decision in *Marbury* v. *Madison.* Tell students that without the process of judicial review, the United States would be very different today. Assign each student a Supreme Court decision from the Supreme Court Docket section on the *Holt Researcher Online* that involves the overturning of an earlier decision. Have students write a few paragraphs hypothesizing what the United States would be like today if the decision had never been overturned. Encourage students to share their ideas with the class and to discuss the significance of the decision.

REVIEW

Have students complete the Section 1 Review on page 50. Use the answers in the Annotated Teacher's Edition to assess student mastery of this section.

ASSESS

To assess student mastery of this section, have students complete Daily Quiz 3.1 in *Daily Quizzes with Answer Key.* For additional assessment options, see *Alternative Assessment Handbook* on the *One-Stop Planner CD-ROM.*

ADDITIONAL RESOURCES

Adler, Mortimer. *We Hold These Truths: Understanding the Ideas and Ideals of the Constitution.* 1987. Collier MacMillan.

Barber, Sotiros. *On What the Constitution Means.* 1984. Johns Hopkins University Press.

OBJECTIVES

- Discuss the reasons framers established ways to amend the Constitution.
- Describe the methods for amending the Constitution.
- Explain the purpose of the Bill of Rights.

MOTIVATE

Provide students with a copy of your classroom rules and a copy of rules from a kindergarten class. Ask students to brainstorm and come up with at least five ways in which the rules have changed and the expectations have been altered between kindergarten and high school. Then have students discuss the reasons why the framers of the Constitution planned for ways to amend the document they had created. Have students explain why this amendment process was necessary for the new country. Ask students to give examples of technologies the framers could not have considered when they wrote the Constitution.

TEACH

Building a Vocabulary

In their spiral notebooks, have students continue working on their Political Dictionary. List words the students will be expected to know for this section on the board. Have students list, define, and give an example of each of the terms, using information provided in the text or on the *Researcher CD-ROM.*

Conducting Research

Assign each student one of the 27 amendments to research and summarize for the class. Instruct each student to prepare a short presentation to explain the amendment. Students in larger classes may need to work in pairs on one amendment. In small classes, students will need to cover more than one amendment. Ask students to define any new vocabulary terms encountered in the amendment. Instruct students to prepare an outline to explain each amendment to the class. Explain to students that in the next activity, they will learn about how amendments are proposed and ratified.

Debating Ideas

With the class, discuss the methods for proposing and ratifying amendments to the Constitution. Next, assign one student as the moderator and two other students as judges. Then organize the class into two groups. Instruct one group to research the pros of the Equal Rights Amendment and the other group to research the cons. Finally, conduct a debate on the Equal Rights Amendment, allowing the students assigned earlier to act as moderator and judges. Ask students to offer their opinions about whether the method of proposing or the method used to gain ratification may have influenced the fate of the Equal Rights Amendment. As a lead-in to the next activity, ask students if they know how amendments to their state constitution are proposed.

Acquiring Information

Have students research the constitution of a U.S. state. Ask students to develop a short report examining the ways in which the U.S. Constitution differs from the state constitution that they researched. Have students include any information that they find about the methods used to amend the state documents. Students may use their textbooks, the library, or the State Profiles section on the *Holt Researcher Online* to collect information. After students have completed this activity, have them further examine the U.S. Constitution in the following activity.

Classifying Information

Instruct students to read and discuss the Bill of Rights and then devise a plan to categorize these rights. For example, some amendments deal with the rights of the accused. After students have developed a classification plan, guide them in categorizing the remaining 17 amendments using the plan they have created. Have students illustrate their plan on large sheets of butcher paper.

CLOSE

As a concluding activity, have each student write an article about the amendment they were assigned during the Conducting Research activity. The article should include the written amendment, an explanation of how it was proposed and ratified, what category it fell under in the Classifying Information activity, and any current controversy surrounding this particular amendment. Students may choose to illustrate the reported amendment with a freehand drawing or a photograph. Have students share the information about the amendment with the rest of the class.

OPTIONS

Interpersonal Learners

Have students interview several adults or members of the local government about their knowledge of the Constitution and the Bill of Rights. Be sure to ask the people being interviewed if their rights have ever been violated or if they had experiences where constitutional safeguards have worked to protect their rights. Students might want to report this information in a journal or play portions of a tape-recorded interview to the class. Discuss the results of the interviews in each class. Keep a total count of the number of people who viewed the Bill of Rights with an overall positive attitude and those who had an overall negative attitude. Also keep track of which rights people felt have been violated in the past. Have a group of students translate this data into a chart and display it in the classroom. Discuss the overall results with each class.

Musical-Rhythmic Learners

Have students present a song or a poem that highlights the freedoms guaranteed in the Bill of Rights and the other 17 amendments. Encourage students to include what freedom the amendment protects, when it was passed, how it was passed, and what it means to them.

Gifted Learners

Encourage students to further examine the issue of ratification deadlines by conducting research and writing a paper. Students should examine the consequences that having or not having a ratification deadline may have had on proposed amendments. Students should be sure to identify the proposed amendment, the time period it was from, whether it had a ratification deadline, and, if so, how that deadline may have affected the proposed amendment. Students should also discuss whether or not they feel a ratification deadline should become standard procedure for all proposed amendments and offer reasons to support their opinions. Have students discuss their ideas with the class and see if the class can come up with a consensus regarding the issue. If students cannot reach a consensus, organize the class into groups based on the side students support and have them debate the issue.

Gifted Learners

Have students research the life of Barbara Jordan and report on it to the class. Students may wish to use the Biographies section on the *Holt Researcher Online* and other resources to gather information. Students should include the reasons that Ms. Jordan was labeled a constitutionalist and should mention her significant life achievements. Have students share their ideas with the class.

REVIEW

Have students complete the Section 2 Review on page 55. Use the answers in the Annotated Teacher's Edition to assess student mastery of this section.

ASSESS

To assess student mastery of this section, have students complete Daily Quiz 3.2 in *Daily Quizzes with Answer Key.* For additional assessment options, see *Alternative Assessment Handbook* on the *One-Stop Planner CD-ROM.*

ADDITIONAL RESOURCES

Berns, Walter. *Taking the Constitution Seriously.* 1987. Simon and Schuster.

Friendly, Fred, and Martha Elliot. *The Constitution: That Delicate Balance.* 1984. Random House.

Constitutional Papers. Reflective Arts International. (CD-ROM).

HOLT PRESENTATION MAKER
Access Illustrated LECTURE NOTES using Microsoft® PowerPoint® on the One-Stop Planner CD-ROM

OBJECTIVES

▶ Explain how the Constitution gives each of the three branches of government flexibility in using their powers.
▶ Discuss how political parties changed the way government operates.
▶ Describe the ways in which the Constitution allows custom and tradition to help shape government.

MOTIVATE

Organize the class into four groups. Give each group a card that lists an event showing the flexibility of the powers granted by the U.S. Constitution, such as the case of *Marbury* v. *Madison,* the Louisiana Purchase, or the executive order used to send troops to Vietnam. After students have discussed the importance of their assigned event, have the class decide what these events have in common. Discuss how they show that the Constitution is both a flexible and living document. Ask students what would happen if the government could only follow what was specifically written in the Constitution. Have students come up with issues that the framers of the Constitution could not have foreseen, but that may eventually be regulated by the government, such as Internet use.

TEACH

Building a Vocabulary

In their spiral notebooks, have students continue working on their Political Dictionary. List words the students will be expected to know for this section on the board. Have students list, define, and give an example of each of the terms, using information provided in the text or on the *Researcher CD-ROM.*

Navigating the Internet

Have students choose one branch of government and using the Internet research one action taken by that branch that illustrates the function of interpretation or reinterpretation of the Constitution. Have students consider the following topics: campaign spending, the budget, interpretation of an amendment, school prayer, executive immunity, and executive orders. Once students complete their research, have volunteers present their information to the class.

Conducting Research

Discuss with students how the Constitution gives each of the three branches of government flexible powers. Then organize students into groups of three assigning each student one of the branches of government. Have students use the library and other resources to document examples of their assigned branch of government using its flexible powers. When students have completed their research, have them get together with their partners and discuss the examples they researched. Then ask students to discuss whether this flexibility in the powers of each branch serves the public good. Finally, discuss why such flexible powers were built into the Constitution.

Role-Playing/Taking a Stand

As a class, discuss why political parties were formed and how they have shaped the operation of government. Organize students into two groups, each of which will represent a political party. Tell students that their group will have to create a party platform. Have each group complete the following steps:

1. Name their party.
2. Elect a party chief.
3. Describe a set of three to five principles for the party to promote (e.g., specific legislation to be proposed in Congress). This will serve as the party's platform.
4. Make a list of the ways that the party can promote their specified platform (e.g., political action committees, majority elected to Congress).
5. List the ways that the party plans to win national elections.
6. Have students discuss their platforms with the class.

After completing this activity have groups return to their desks. Explain to them the similarities between how they just created a political platform and how modern political parties adopt their political platforms. Have students discuss any difficulties they had with the steps. As a lead-in to the next activity explain to students that they will be learning about common political practices, such as the president naming his or her cabinet, that have evolved out of custom or tradition.

Conducting Research/Creating Charts

Write the names of the president's cabinet positions on small pieces of paper and place them in a hat. (You may have to use each position more than once.) Then have students pick the name of a cabinet position out of the hat and locate the person(s) who shares this position. Partners (or groups) will then conduct research in order to fill in one thirteenth of a large chart to be set up in the classroom. The chart will list the current cabinet member's name, his or her job description, and the departments under his or her control. After students have completed the chart, have each group explain the cabinet position they researched. Have students discuss how the cabinet members might influence changes in the Constitution or decisions made by the president.

CLOSE

Conduct a panel discussion in which several students are assigned roles as Supreme Court judges, legislators, and members of the executive branch of government. Give various students in the class review questions reflecting the content discussed in the Motivate activity and stated in the Objectives. After essential, teacher-written questions have been asked and answered, instruct students to ask a series of their own questions tailored to each group's functions in the U.S. government. Have each group answer questions about the department that they researched in the Conducting Research/Creating Charts activity.

OPTIONS

Students Having Difficulty

Have students work with peer tutors to create a study guide for Section 3. Make sure the following elements are included: objectives, vocabulary, overview of the section, and review questions. After each pair has finished their study guide, have pairs exchange their guides with one another. Have each pair complete the study guide they were given, and then have both pairs work together to review their answers. Discuss possible improvements to the study guides with each group.

Linguistic Learners

Allow several students to function as newspaper reporters at the next city council meeting. Encourage them to read a local paper prior to attending the meeting so they can know about what is going on in the community. Have them take notes at the meeting and ask questions when appropriate. Have students focus on any flexibility in the use of authority or the following of political customs that occur during the meeting. Have students compare what they have seen to what actually occurs in the U.S. government. Have these reporters discuss any differences and similarities with the class. Tell students that their written product will be part of the class newsletter and/or their own written portfolios.

REVIEW

Have students complete the Section 3 Review on page 59. Use the answers in the Annotated Teacher's Edition to assess student mastery of this section.

ASSESS

To assess student mastery of this section, have students complete Daily Quiz 3.3 in *Daily Quizzes with Answer Key.* For additional assessment options, see *Alternative Assessment Handbook* on the *One-Stop Planner CD-ROM.*

ADDITIONAL RESOURCES

Kirk, Russel. *The Conservative Constitution.* 1990. Regenery Gateway.
Rediscovering the Constitution. 1987. Congressional Quarterly.
Style and the Intellectual Origins of the Constitution. Films for the Humanities and Sciences. (video)

THE CONSTITUTION
LESSON 3.4 AND THE PUBLIC GOOD

TEXTBOOK PAGES 60-62

OBJECTIVES

▶ Discuss James Madison's contribution to the development of the U.S. Government.
▶ List ways the Constitution ensures that government makes laws that promote the public good.
▶ Discuss critics' claims that the Constitution sometimes makes government less effective.

MOTIVATE

Read aloud *Federalist Paper* "No. 10" (November 23, 1787) by James Madison in which he addresses the people of the state of New York on the issue of factions. Have students "translate" James Madison's eighteenth-century language into today's language. Have a few students share their translations with the class. Point out any inconsistencies that their translations may have. Explain to students that in this section, they will be learning how the Constitution promotes the public good.

TEACH

Building a Vocabulary

In their spiral notebooks, have students continue working on their Political Dictionary. List words the students will be expected to know for this section on the board. Have students list, define, and give an example of each of the terms, using information provided in the text or on the *Researcher CD-ROM.*

Recognizing Point of View

Discuss Madison's point of view on factions based on *Federalist Paper* "No. 10." Compare his views with those of Alexander Hamilton and Thomas Jefferson. Students will need to research Hamilton and Jefferson using the text, the Biographies section on the *Holt Researcher Online,* and other resources. Randomly assign each student one of these three leaders. Then have students create a speech, from their assigned person's point of view, concerning the advantage (or disadvantage) of the size of the United States in controlling factions and the Constitution's system of checks and balances. Have volunteers read their speeches. If possible, you may wish to videotape these presentations for later use. Discuss the accuracy of students' speeches. To help transition to the next activity tell students that they will be learning about how the Constitution ensures that laws serve the public good.

Solving Problems

Discuss how leaders such as James Madison, Alexander Hamilton, and Thomas Jefferson might have solved some of today's problems in government. Have students bring to class examples of local community problems, such as property tax issues, construction programs, or proposed government programs. Describe how the Constitution provides for solutions to these issues in ways that promote the public good. Have small groups come up with viable solutions to the problems presented in the articles and share them with the class. Explain to students that they will learn about how the Constitution sometimes acts as a check on government action.

Applying Ideas

Organize the class into four groups. Drawing on solutions presented in the previous activity, have one group of students create political cartoons, a second group write an editorial, a third group write a news article, and a fourth group find current events to illustrate gridlock (e.g., ineffective government). The focus of students' work should be to interpret effective and ineffective government approaches to problems. Have each group share their work with the rest of the class, then discuss actual instances in which the U.S. government has reached gridlock. Have students offer suggestions for preventing government gridlock and discuss the plausibility of their ideas.

CLOSE

Have students view the videotaped speeches from the Recognizing Point of View activity. Then have students collect information and materials from the rest of the section's activities in order to create *The Constitution and The Public Good Newsletter* for other current government classes or next year's government classes to view. Be sure to have the class include ways that the Constitution prevents factions, ways the Constitution ensures that laws promote the public good, and ways that the Constitution sometimes leads to less effective government. Make copies of the newsletter for students to use when reviewing the chapter.

OPTIONS

Sheltered English Students

 Have sheltered English students create captions for the political cartoons created by other students earlier in this section. Have them work with a peer tutor to ensure the accuracy of their captions. Students may also wish to create captions that have a different meaning than the ones that were previously written.

Intrapersonal Learners

 Have students create journal entries for James Madison, Alexander Hamilton, or Thomas Jefferson in which they express their fears of factions in the new government. Students may wish to consult the Biographies section on the *Holt Researcher Online* to obtain information on the person they have selected. Then have students write a self-reflective journal entry expressing their feelings about government gridlock today and the various factions seeking representation and power. Students may wish to share these with the rest of the class.

Gifted Learners

Have students examine newspapers and magazines to locate articles that focus on inefficiency in government, such as paying too much for specific pieces of equipment. Students may either write a paper or give an oral presentation describing the types of inefficiency in government that they found. Ask students to attempt to create solutions to these problems.

Interpersonal Learners

Encourage students to write their representatives in the U.S. Congress addressing the issues of inefficiency in government and avoiding responsibility for failed policies. Have students list problems that have been identified earlier in this lesson that pertain to these issues. Students should describe for their representatives how these issues are affecting the public good. Have students include suggestions for correcting these problems and have them request a response from their representatives. Encourage students to share any responses they receive with the rest of the class. Finally, discuss any suggestions their representatives made and whether they might work.

REVIEW

Have students complete the Section 4 Review on page 62. Use the answers in the Annotated Teacher's Edition to assess student mastery of this section.

ASSESS

To assess student mastery of this section, have students complete Daily Quiz 3.4 in *Daily Quizzes with Answer Key.* For additional assessment options, see *Alternative Assessment Handbook* on the *One-Stop Planner CD-ROM.*

RETEACH

For students having difficulty with the lessons, have them complete Reteaching Activity 3. This activity is located in *Reteaching Activities with Answer Key.*

ADDITIONAL RESOURCES

Jordan, Larry. *The U.S. Constitution: And Fascinating Facts About It.* 1999. Oak Hill Publishing Company.

Peck, Robert. *We the People: The Constitution in American Life.* 1987. Harry N. Abrams Inc. in cooperation with the American Bar Association.

Sexton, John, and Nat Brandt. *How Free Are We?: What the Constitution Says We Can and Cannot Do.* 1986. M. Evans Publishers.

GOVERNMENT NOTEBOOK

The Government Notebook is a journal activity that encourages students to consider basic concepts of government that relate to their lives. A follow-up notebook activity appears on page 64.

WHY IT MATTERS TODAY

To find additional lesson plans dealing with the U.S. Constitution, visit **CNNfyi.com** or have students complete the **GOVERNMENT IN THE NEWS** activity on page 63.

CNNfyi.com

CHAPTER 3

THE U.S. CONSTITUTION

The Constitution is the foundation on which the U.S. government and American society are based. It is a document that affects your life every day. It protects your freedom to write an article for the school newspaper. It also determines the scope of all laws in your community.

The Constitution has such far-reaching effects on society partly because it reflects certain basic principles of government. Two of these principles—limited and representative government—were discussed in Chapter 2. The framers of the Constitution incorporated these and other basic principles into the structures and responsibilities of the national government.

The framers also provided ways in which the Constitution could change with the times to help the country face new challenges. By doing these things, the framers not only designed a government that promotes the public good, they also crafted a system of government that has endured for more than two centuries.

GOVERNMENT NOTEBOOK

In your Government Notebook, write a paragraph about why you think that the plan of government provided by the U.S. Constitution has been successful for more than 200 years.

WHY IT MATTERS TODAY

The U.S. Constitution is a flexible document that still provides the foundation for our government. At the end of this chapter visit **CNNfyi.com** to learn more about how the Constitution continues to guide our nation.

CNNfyi.com

SECTION 1

BASIC PRINCIPLES

READ TO DISCOVER

1. What are the five basic principles on which the U.S. Constitution is based?
2. How does the Constitution ensure the people's authority over government?
3. How does the Constitution provide for a system of limited government?
4. In what way does the Constitution protect the rights of the states?

POLITICAL DICTIONARY

republicanism
popular sovereignty
separation of powers
checks and balances
veto
judicial review
unconstitutional

The concept of republicanism strongly influenced the framers of the constitution. **Republicanism** is the belief that the citizens of a state have political authority, they are bound by a social contract to obey laws, and their rights are guaranteed by a constitution.

The Constitution establishes rules that the U.S. government must observe. Five main principles form the basis of these rules: popular sovereignty, limited government, separation of powers, checks and balances, and federalism.

Popular Sovereignty

For a government truly to serve the people, it must be based on popular sovereignty. As noted in Chapter 1, sovereignty is the absolute authority that a government has over the citizens of that nation. **Popular sovereignty** means that the government's authority comes from the people. The principle of popular sovereignty can be found throughout the U.S. Constitution. For example, the Preamble, or introduction, to the Constitution begins, "We the People of the United States . . . do ordain [order] and establish this Constitution for the United States of America." The preamble also states that the new government should "establish justice, insure domestic tranquility, provide for the common defense, [and] promote the general Welfare."

The Constitution further establishes the people's authority by setting rules for the election of government officials. No one reaches government office by virtue of his or her birth, as in a monarchy. Rather, the U.S. Constitution established a republic in which citizens elect others to represent them.

Comparing Governments

A New Constitution for South Africa

Perhaps the greatest sign that democracy was coming to apartheid-free South Africa appeared in 1995, when the government invited the people to help write a new constitution. Citizens were allowed to voice their opinions by calling a "constitutional talk-line." More than 1.7 million people called in, wrote letters, and sent messages over the Internet with their suggestions for the new constitution.

After months of debate over citizens' and lawmakers' ideas, the drafters of the constitution completed the document. The Constitutional Assembly ratified the new constitution with a 420-to-1 vote on May 8, 1996.

The constitution—described by one government official as the country's "birth certificate"—makes the Republic of South Africa a democratic nation with a federal system and a strong central government. A president holds executive power with two deputy presidents—one from the majority party and one from the largest opposition party. The new two-house Parliament features a Senate, whose 90 members are elected by the legislatures of the country's nine provinces, and a National Assembly, whose 400 members are elected by the voters.

SECTION 1

BASIC PRINCIPLES

Lesson Plans

For teaching strategies, see Lesson 3.1 located at the beginning of this chapter or the One-Stop Planner strategy 3.1

Political Dictionary

To reinforce the section's vocabulary terms, refer students to the Electronic Glossary on the *Researcher CD-ROM.*

Section Assessment

To assess students' mastery of this section, have them complete Daily Quiz 3.1 in *Daily Quizzes with Answer Key.*

Enhancing the Lesson

For information about the government of South Africa and other nations throughout the world, see the Country Profiles section on the *Holt Researcher Online.*

HISTORY The desire to strictly define and limit the powers of the federal government caused a dilemma for President Thomas Jefferson, who firmly believed that the government possessed only those powers expressly granted in the Constitution. In 1803 Jefferson had the opportunity to purchase the Louisiana Territory from France. He believed, however, that the government did not have the power to hold foreign territory and had even less power to incorporate foreign territories into the United States.

Although Jefferson wanted a constitutional amendment that would give him the authority to make the Louisiana Territory part of the United States, he and other U.S. leaders wanted to ratify the treaty before Napoleon changed his mind.

In the end, Jefferson decided to violate his belief in the limited powers of government and to "rely on the nation to sanction an act done for its great good, without its previous authority." ■

Caption Answer

They prevent abuses of power.

Transparency

An overhead transparency of the chart on this page is available in *Transparency Resources*. See Transparency 5: Principles of the Constitution.

Limited Government

A government also cannot truly serve the people if it has unlimited power. Therefore, the Constitution established a limited government. As noted in Chapter 2, the English colonists brought the ideal of limited government with them to North America.

The Constitution limits government by establishing guidelines for how the government may act. Section 9 of Article I, for example, lists powers that the national government does not have, such as the power to grant titles of nobility. Other parts of the Constitution keep the government from violating citizens' individual liberties, such as the freedom of speech. Each of these restrictions upholds the principle of limited government.

Separation of Powers

Although the framers wanted to give the national government the power it needed to govern, they also wanted to prevent the concentration and abuse of power. They designed the Constitution to divide the responsibilities of government among three branches. This **separation of powers** makes sure that no one branch has too much power. The framers listed the responsibilities and powers of the three branches in the first three articles of the Constitution.

Article I lists the responsibilities of the legislative branch. Congress, a bicameral legislature, makes the nation's laws. Although the House of Representatives and the Senate share responsibility for passing legislation, each chamber has its own special powers. For example, legislation to fund the government must begin in the House of Representatives. Only the Senate, however, can approve presidential appointments and treaties with foreign countries.

Article II establishes the duties of the executive branch, which is made up of the president, vice president, and various executive departments. The executive branch executes, or carries out, the laws established by the legislative branch. In addition, the president serves as the commander in chief of the nation's armed forces and has the power to direct U.S. relations with foreign countries.

Article III sets out the role of the judicial branch of government. The Constitution establishes a Supreme Court as the nation's highest court and gives Congress the authority to establish courts below the Supreme Court.

Checks and Balances

The Constitution also prevents the concentration and abuse of power by giving each branch of government the authority to check, or restrain, the powers of the other two branches. This system of **checks and balances** divides power within the government. (See the chart on page 49.)

Executive and Legislative Checks The system of checks and balances forces each branch of government to consider the opinions and actions of the other branches. This is particularly true for the executive and legislative branches. For example, if Congress does not consider the wishes of the president when it writes legislation, the president may **veto**, or reject, that legislation. This veto power often encourages congressional leaders to meet with members of the executive branch to reach an agreement about controversial legislation before it is passed in Congress. For example, congressional leaders meet regularly with the president to discuss the federal budget. In some cases, however, the negotiations on legislation are difficult.

The president's power to affect legislation is limited, however. Congress is able to override a

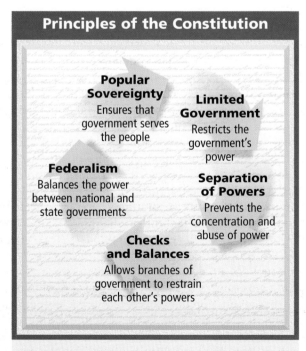

Principles of the Constitution

Popular Sovereignty
Ensures that government serves the people

Limited Government
Restricts the government's power

Federalism
Balances the power between national and state governments

Separation of Powers
Prevents the concentration and abuse of power

Checks and Balances
Allows branches of government to restrain each other's powers

The U.S. government must follow five basic principles established by the Constitution. **Why are these principles important to a democratic government?**

Checks and Balances in the Federal Government

POWERS		CHECKS ON POWERS
• Passes bills into law • Can pass laws over the president's veto by a two-thirds vote of Congress • Approves appointments to top government jobs • Holds the "power of the purse"	**LEGISLATIVE BRANCH**	• President's power to veto legislation passed by Congress • Supreme Court's power to rule that laws are unconstitutional
• Approves or vetoes laws • Carries out laws • Appoints federal court judges, ambassadors, and other high-level officials • Negotiates treaties	**EXECUTIVE BRANCH**	• Congress's ability to override the president's veto by a two-thirds vote • Congress's power to approve spending by the federal government • Senate's power to approve presidential appointments to top government jobs • Senate's authority to approve all treaties • Congress's power to impeach the president
• Interprets the meaning of laws • Rules on the constitutionality of laws passed by Congress and actions taken by the executive branch	**JUDICIAL BRANCH**	• Congress's (or the states') power to propose an amendment to the Constitution if the Supreme Court rules that a law is unconstitutional • Senate's authority to refuse to approve the appointments to federal court • Congress's power to impeach a federal judge

Each branch of the federal government has its powers checked by the other branches.
What are the checks on the legislative branch?

veto if at least two thirds of the members in both houses of Congress vote to do so. Congress also checks the executive branch through its "power of the purse," for only Congress can approve spending by the federal government. Congress can, for example, limit or refuse to approve money for programs that the president wants.

Congress also has checks on other presidential powers. The Senate, for example, can reject any presidential appointments to top government jobs. In addition, the Constitution states that international treaties negotiated by the president do not become law unless approved by a two-thirds vote in the Senate. These checks on executive power mean that the president must consider the wishes of Congress when proposing legislation, making appointments, and negotiating treaties.

Judicial Review The judicial branch also has an important role in the system of checks and balances. Although federal judges are nominated by the president and must be approved by the Senate, federal courts can check the powers of the legislative and executive branches through judicial review. **Judicial review** is the power of the courts to decide if laws and other government actions are valid under the U.S. Constitution.

A law or government action that is found to violate any part of the Constitution is said to be **unconstitutional**. Because the Constitution is the nation's highest law, an unconstitutional law or act is illegal and cannot be enforced by the government. (Keep in mind, however, that laws are reviewed only if their constitutionality is in question.)

Transparency
An overhead transparency of the chart on this page is available in *Transparency Resources.* See Transparency 6: Checks and Balances in the Federal Government.

Caption Answer

The legislative branch may be checked by a presidential veto or by the Supreme Court declaring a law unconstitutional.

GLOBAL CONNECTIONS

The system of checks and balances of the Constitution allows the president to veto legislation that he or she opposes. The parliamentary system of Great Britain, after which many aspects of the U.S. government were modeled, does not include a veto power. Legislation in Great Britain is usually advanced by the government currently in power, which would not have any reason to veto it.

Once the House of Commons and the House of Lords agree on the provisions of a bill, that bill must receive Royal Assent—or the monarch's approval—which is a formality and not a veto power. The last time that a piece of legislation did not receive Royal Assent was in 1707. There is no judicial review of legislation in Great Britain. ■

1. Refer to the following pages: republicanism (47), popular sovereignty (47), separation of powers (48), checks and balances (48), veto (48), judicial review (49), unconstitutional (49).

2. Charts will vary but should show an understanding of the purpose of government as outlined in the Preamble.

3a. popular sovereignty, limited government, separation of powers, checks and balances, federalism

3b. republicanism, checks and balances, federalism, separation of powers, popular sovereignty, and individual rights

4. Students' answers will vary but should reflect an understanding of the principles of the Constitution and the Preamble.

Judicial review is not specifically mentioned in the Constitution. Section 2 of Article III, however, implies that the courts have such power. The principle of judicial review was firmly established by the Supreme Court in the landmark case *Marbury* v. *Madison* in 1803.

In 1801 William Marbury and others were appointed to judicial posts by the outgoing president, John Adams. The commissions, or documents, that formally gave them their posts were not delivered before Adams left office, however. Thomas Jefferson, who had defeated Adams in the presidential election, ordered Secretary of State James Madison not to deliver the commissions. Without them, the appointees could not legally take their posts.

Marbury asked the Supreme Court to order Madison to deliver the commissions. Marbury based his case on the Federal Judiciary Act of 1789, part of which stated that cases like his must be taken directly before the Supreme Court. The Court ruled, however, that the Federal Judiciary Act violated the Constitution, which specifically listed the types of cases that the Court could consider without a lower court hearing them first.

Although the ruling meant that the Supreme Court could not force Madison to deliver the commissions, it established the broader power of the courts to decide the constitutionality of congressional actions. This power of judicial review allows the courts to check the power of other branches of government.

Federalism

The Constitution is designed to protect the rights of the states by establishing a federal system of government. As noted in Chapter 1, a federal system is one in which powers are divided among national, state, and local governments. In the U.S. federalist system, some powers belong to the national government, others to state governments, and still others are shared by both.

Although the framers of the Constitution wanted to protect states' rights, they also wanted a national government that had sufficient powers to maintain order and keep the country united. This is why the framers adopted a federal system instead of a unitary system. In the process, they created a distinct form of federalism. They had learned that a weak government, like the one formed under the Articles of Confederation, could not force states to obey national laws.

The Constitution specifically prohibits states from exercising certain powers that belong to the national government, such as negotiating treaties, coining money, or engaging in war, unless the state is facing imminent danger or invasion. In addition, Article VI of the Constitution states that the power of the national government is superior to that of the state governments. This "supremacy clause" declares that the Constitution—together with U.S. laws passed under the Constitution and treaties made by the national government—is "the supreme law of the land."

SECTION 1 REVIEW

1. Identify and Explain:
- republicanism
- popular sovereignty
- separation of powers
- checks and balances
- veto
- judicial review
- unconstitutional

2. Identifying Concepts: Copy the chart below. Use it to evaluate how the federal government serves the purposes set forth in the preamble of the Constitution.

Purpose	Example
Establish Justice	
Insure Domestic Tranquility	
Provide for the Common Defense	
Promote the General Welfare	

Homework Practice Online
keyword: SV3 HP3

3. **Finding the Main Idea**
- **a.** What are the basic principles on which the Constitution is based?
- **b.** How does the Constitution create a limited government?

4. **Writing and Critical Thinking**

Analyzing: How have the beliefs and principles contained in the Constitution shaped our national identity?

Consider the following:
- the limits the Constitution places on the power of government
- the framers' goals as described in the Preamble

I magine a house that was built 200 years ago. Since its construction, the house has been worked on several times. A second story, electricity, and indoor plumbing have been added. The exterior has been painted and repainted, and damaged boards have been replaced. The owners proudly say that they live in a "200-year-old house," and despite all the changes that have been made to the house, they are right. For 200 years that same house has provided shelter for generations of people.

In many ways the Constitution is like that old house. It has provided shelter for the people of the United States for more than 200 years. Also like the old house, the Constitution has changed a great deal during that time.

How and why did it change? The framers knew that they could not anticipate what challenges the government and people would face as the United States grew. Thus, just as an architect plans changes and additions to an old house, the framers developed methods for revising the Constitution.

Changes made to the Constitution are called **amendments**. All amendments must be proposed and ratified through a formal process. The ability to amend the Constitution has allowed the government to meet new needs and challenges.

Methods of Amending the Constitution

The procedures for amending the U.S. Constitution are found in Article V of the Constitution itself. The basic premise behind these procedures is that amending the Constitution should be more difficult than passing an ordinary law. Passing an ordinary law requires a majority vote, but passing an amendment requires more than a simple majority. By making it difficult to pass a constitutional amendment, the framers helped ensure that amendments would not be frivolous and would not represent only passing interests.

The Constitution sets out two ways to propose an amendment. There also are two ways to ratify a proposed amendment.

CONSTITUTIONAL GOVERNMENT *The ratification of the Twenty-sixth Amendment in 1971 lowered the voting age from 21 to 18.* **How does the Constitution enable the government to meet the changing needs of the people?**

Proposing Amendments One way amendments may be proposed is by a vote in Congress. In fact, all amendments to the Constitution so far have been proposed by Congress. At least two thirds of both the House (290 votes) and the Senate (67 votes) must approve an amendment before it can be sent to the states for ratification.

An amendment also may be proposed by a national convention that is called by Congress at the request of at least two thirds (34) of the state legislatures. No convention has ever been called to propose an amendment, however. Many people have pointed to the wording of Article V of the Constitution for an explanation. Article V does not say whether a convention can be limited to proposing only the amendment it was called to consider. As a result, some people have worried that a convention might decide to open up the entire Constitution for revision. Then amendments that the states had no intention of considering in the first place might be proposed.

Ratifying Amendments All but one of the Constitution's amendments have been ratified by votes in state legislatures. Under this method, legislatures in at least three fourths (38) of the states must approve an amendment before it becomes part of the Constitution.

The second method for ratifying an amendment requires the approval of special conventions in at least three fourths of the states. The Twenty-first Amendment was ratified in this way. This amendment **repealed**—or reversed by legislative act— the Eighteenth Amendment, which had outlawed the production, transportation, and sale of alcoholic beverages. With its repeal, the Eighteenth Amendment was no longer a formal part of the Constitution.

CASE STUDY

The Equal Rights Amendment

CONSTITUTIONAL GOVERNMENT The struggle to ratify the Equal Rights Amendment (ERA) is a good example of just how hard it is to amend the Constitution. The ERA aimed to bar discrimination based on a person's sex. Supporters first introduced such an amendment in Congress in 1923. Finally, after increased efforts to win support for

CONSTITUTIONAL GOVERNMENT *Women in Raleigh, North Carolina, participate in a rally for the ratification of the Equal Rights Amendment.* **Why is it important for people to have the freedom to participate in political demonstrations?**

the amendment, the 1972 Congress overwhelmingly voted to send the ERA to the states. However, as with most other amendments, Congress set a deadline for ratification.

In less than a year, 30 states had ratified the ERA. At that point, it appeared that the necessary 38 states would ratify the amendment. The process, however, bogged down soon after that. Opponents criticized the ERA on a number of grounds. Many saw the amendment as an attack on traditional family values. Others believed that the Constitution and the Civil Rights Act of 1964 already guaranteed equal rights for women. (The Civil Rights Act of 1964 is more fully explained in Chapter 13.) Yet others argued that the amendment would mean difficult changes in social standards, such as requiring women to be sent into military combat.

In 1978, to give supporters more time to win approval for the amendment, Congress moved the original deadline for ratification to 1982. This effort failed, however, as only 35 states had voted to ratify the amendment by that date. In addition, 5 of the 35 states voted to rescind, or take back, their ratification.

The 27 Amendments

Because of the difficult amendment process, only 27 amendments have been added to the Constitution. The importance of these amendments cannot be overstated. They have protected individual freedoms, expanded voting and other rights, and extended the government's powers.

Protecting Individual Freedoms The first 10 amendments, the **Bill of Rights**, were designed as a protection for individual freedoms. (See the chart below.) They were adopted only two years after the Constitution went into effect. As noted in Chapter 2, many states, upon ratifying the Constitution, made strong recommendations that a bill of rights be added.

The Bill of Rights protects citizens' freedom of speech, religion, and assembly, and it guarantees a free press and the rights of people accused of crimes. In addition to protecting individual freedoms, the Bill of Rights also acknowledges the rights and powers of the states and the people. The Ninth Amendment says that people hold additional rights not specifically mentioned in the Constitution. The Tenth Amendment says that the states and the people retain all the powers not specifically given to the national government and that the Constitution does not forbid them to have. These amendments were included in the Bill of Rights to ensure that the national government would not unjustly dominate the states and the people.

Expanding Voting and Other Rights In the more than 200 years since the Bill of Rights was ratified, other amendments have been adopted in clusters during periods of great social and political change. The Thirteenth, Fourteenth, and Fif-teenth Amendments, for example, were adopted just after the Civil War. These amendments banned slavery in the United States, recognized African Americans as U.S. citizens, and gave various rights, including the right to vote, to African American males.

In another era of social change—the first decades of the 1900s—four key amendments were passed. Two of these, the Seventeenth and Nineteenth Amendments, extended the reach of democracy by providing for the popular election of senators and by granting women the right to

Rights and Powers Granted by the Bill of Rights

FIRST AMENDMENT	Provides for freedom of religion, speech, press, and assembly
SECOND AMENDMENT	Asserts the need for a militia and protects the right to keep and bear arms
THIRD AMENDMENT	Prevents soldiers from taking over private homes during peacetime or war unless authorized to do so by law
FOURTH AMENDMENT	Prohibits unreasonable searches and seizures
FIFTH AMENDMENT	Protects the rights of accused persons
SIXTH AMENDMENT	Provides the right to a speedy, fair trial
SEVENTH AMENDMENT	Provides the right to a trial by a jury in civil suits
EIGHTH AMENDMENT	Prohibits excessive bail and fines, prohibits cruel and unusual punishment
NINTH AMENDMENT	Protects people's rights that are not specifically listed in the Constitution
TENTH AMENDMENT	Grants to the states and to the people powers that are not specifically listed in the Constitution

*The Bill of Rights protects the basic freedoms of all U.S. citizens. **What rights are guaranteed by the First Amendment?***

Citizenship in Action

Gregory Watson successfully campaigned for the ratification of the Twenty-seventh Amendment, which restricts the power of Congress to give itself a midterm pay raise.

Passing the Twenty-Seventh Amendment

Texan Gregory Watson accomplished what framer James Madison could not more than 200 years earlier. Largely because of Watson's efforts, the Twenty-seventh Amendment to the Constitution became law in May 1992. According to the amendment, "No law varying the compensation for the services of the Senators and Representatives, shall take effect, until an election of Representatives shall have intervened." In other words, Congress cannot give itself a pay raise in the middle of a term of office.

The amendment was introduced originally by James Madison in 1789 as part of a package of 12 amendments, 10 of which became the Bill of Rights. Maryland was the first state to ratify the amendment in 1789, and five other states soon followed. The amendment failed to be ratified by three fourths of the states, however. Because the amendment was sent to the states without a deadline, it was still considered "proposed" even though it had never been approved.

Watson believed that the passage of two centuries had not "robbed the amendment of its relevance." In 1982, when he was a student at the University of Texas in Austin, he launched a decade-long battle to ratify the dusty amendment. The project started out as a term paper and evolved into a one-man campaign.

Watson's battle began after he received a C on a research paper in which he argued in favor of ratifying the proposal that had become known as the "Madison amendment." His skeptical professor called the proposed amendment a "legal dead letter." Convinced of the amendment's timeliness despite the passage of nearly two centuries, Watson began his relentless quest to "show the American people what can be done if they just put forth a little elbow grease." Most of Watson's "elbow grease" was in the form of mail—letter after letter to legislators in the states that had not yet passed the proposed amendment.

Watson's efforts increased in 1991, when controversy arose after the U.S. Senate voted to give itself a "midnight pay raise." As many citizens shook their heads and pointed fingers at what they perceived as the greed of lawmakers, Watson became convinced that ratification of the Twenty-seventh Amendment was near.

Watson's efforts paid off on May 7, 1992, when Michigan became the thirty-eighth state—the final state needed—to pass Madison's centuries-old amendment. Justifiably proud to call his mission a success and no doubt wiser about the workings of the U.S. government, Watson stated, "You can wield (exercise) a great deal of power, and one person can still make a difference in this country."

What Do You Think?

1. What were the effects of the changes brought about by Gregory Watson?
2. What are some of the ways you can bring about change in your government?

vote. Before passage of the Seventeenth Amendment, state legislatures chose senators. Women did not have the right to vote in every state until the passage of the Nineteenth Amendment.

Extending Government Powers Two other important amendments were passed during the early 1900s, both of which expanded the reach of the government. First, the Sixteenth Amendment authorized a national income tax. This tax increased the amount of money the government could collect to pay for its programs and to pay other national expenses. Then the Eighteenth Amendment made Prohibition the law of the land. This amendment expanded the national government's powers by allowing it to regulate the manufacture, sale, and transportation of "intoxicating liquors" throughout the country.

Ratification Deadlines The last amendment to the Constitution, the Twenty-seventh, was ratified by the states in 1992. (See "Citizenship in Action" on page 54.) This amendment, which was originally proposed in 1789, says that no vote to increase congressmembers' salaries may take effect until after the next regularly scheduled congressional election. The 1789 Congress had not set a deadline for ratification. Almost 200 years later, efforts were made to revive the amendment. Some people argued that the process of ratifying the Twenty-seventh Amendment had already taken too long. Since 1919, Congress usually has set deadlines—generally around seven years—for

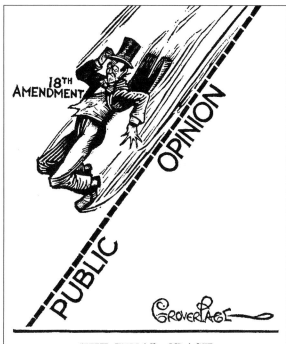

THE FINAL CRASH
—Page in the Louisville *Courier-Journal*

CONSTITUTIONAL GOVERNMENT *This historical cartoon depicts public reaction to the Eighteenth Amendment.* ***According to the cartoonist, what was the response to the amendment establishing Prohibition?***

ratifying amendments. Nonetheless, supporters of the Twenty-seventh Amendment were able to secure its ratification.

SECTION 2 REVIEW

1. Identify and Explain:
  • amendment
  • repeal
  • Bill of Rights
2. Identifying Concepts:
  Copy the chart to the right. Use it to identify the rights guaranteed by the Bill of Rights.

Rights Guaranteed by the Bill of Rights	
1.	6.
2.	7.
3.	8.
4.	9.
5.	10.

3. Finding the Main Idea
  a. What are the methods for proposing and ratifying constitutional amendments?
  b. What is the purpose of the Bill of Rights?

4. Writing and Critical Thinking
  Evaluating: The framers of the Constitution considered it important to allow for changes to be made to the Constitution. Do you think the methods they created are effective?
  Consider the following:
  • the process of amending the constitution
  • the amendments that have been passed so far
  • amendments that failed to pass or have been repealed

Homework Practice Online
keyword: SV3 HP3

Caption Answer
The cartoon shows public support rapidly declining.

SECTION 2 REVIEW ANSWERS

1. Refer to the following pages: amendment (51), repeal (52), Bill of Rights (53).

2. First: freedom of religion, speech, press, and assembly; Second: need for a militia and right to keep and bear arms; Third: prevents soldiers from taking over private homes without legal authorization; Fourth: prohibits unreasonable searches and seizures; Fifth: protects the rights of the accused; Sixth: right to a speed, fair trial; Seventh: right to a jury trial in civil suits; Eighth: prohibits excessive bail and fines, prohibits cruel and unusual punishment; Ninth: protects rights not listed in Constitution; Tenth: grants to states and people rights not listed in Constitution.

3a. proposed by a two-thirds vote in both houses of Congress or by a national convention called by two thirds of the states; ratified by receiving the approval of three fourths of the state legislatures or by approval of special conventions in three fourths of the states.

3b. It protects individual liberties and acknowledges the powers of the states and the people.

4. Answers will vary but should show knowledge of the methods of amending the Constitution and the existing amendments.

SECTION 3

A FLEXIBLE DOCUMENT

READ TO DISCOVER

1. How does the Constitution give the three branches of government flexibility in using their powers?
2. How have political parties changed the way government operates?
3. How does the Constitution allow custom and tradition to help shape government?

POLITICAL DICTIONARY

executive agreement
political party
cabinet

The Constitution has been called a "living document," which means that it is flexible and allows government to adapt to changing times. One way it does this, as noted in Section 2, is through the amendment process. The Constitution, however, has also allowed government to change in less formal ways. Government actions, political parties, and custom and tradition all have helped shape government under the Constitution.

Government Actions

The judicial, legislative, and executive branches have reinterpreted their constitutional powers many times. This process has allowed the government to meet new circumstances.

Court Decisions As noted in Section 1, the 1803 Supreme Court case of *Marbury* v. *Madison* established the federal courts' power to determine if a law or other government action is constitutional. Because the wording is vague in some places, the courts have been able to apply the Constitution to circumstances that the eighteenth-century framers could not have anticipated.

For example, the Fourth Amendment forbids "unreasonable searches and seizures." The authors of the amendment probably never imagined how new technologies, such as telephones, might change the concepts of "searching" and "seizing." Yet the courts have interpreted the amendment to include these new technologies. For example, they have been able to forbid law enforcement officials from recording private telephone conversations—a form of searching and seizing—without following certain procedures set by law.

Congressional Legislation Like the judicial branch, Congress has a great deal of flexibility in adapting to changing times. It decides how best to carry out its responsibilities and passes legislation that responds to new situations. To do this, Congress has created structures and taken on duties that are allowed by—but not specifically mentioned in—the Constitution.

For example, Section 1 of Article III gives Congress the power to establish federal courts below the Supreme Court. The Constitution does not specifically say how those courts should be

CONSTITUTIONAL GOVERNMENT *John Marshall, the third chief justice of the United States, established the Supreme Court's power of judicial review. **When and in what Supreme Court case was judicial review established?***

The Granger Collection, New York

Archivist

Perhaps you are one of the more than 1 million people who visited the National Archives in Washington, D.C., last year. The original copies of the Declaration of Independence, the U.S. Constitution, and the Bill of Rights are permanently displayed in this building, the country's storehouse for valuable historical documents.

Who is in charge of repairing, preserving, and overseeing these historical documents and other important public records? This is the job of an archivist. Archivists analyze documents, direct efforts to catalog them, and often educate researchers and government agencies about the documents, their histories, and the time periods in which they were created.

Archivists at the Library of Congress examine a manuscript to determine its condition.

Behind the scenes at the National Archives, for example, archivists oversee the safekeeping, preservation, and display of treasured U.S. artifacts. Permanently sealed in airtight bronze-and-glass cases, the Declaration of Independence, the Constitution, and the Bill of Rights are protected from curious onlookers as well as exposure to pollutants and other damaging elements. Each night, the entire display is lowered into a "fireproof, shockproof, and bombproof" vault 22 feet beneath the floor of the exhibition hall. A special archivist, called a preservationist, gauges the documents' deterioration, or decay, with the aid of a sophisticated camera and computers.

Archivists also help make thousands of government and historical documents available to the public by compiling reference information in the form of indexes, guides, bibliographies, and microfilmed documents. Administrative duties such as preparing budgets, attending scientific and association conferences, and taking care of fund-raising activities often are part of the job as well. Because the job entails extensive research and preparation of reference materials, most archivists spend much of their time working alone with little supervision. An enthusiasm for their work, however, helps prevent most archivists from being bothered by this isolation.

A career as an archivist usually requires some experience working in a museum or library, as well as a master's degree in history or a related field. Many archivists also have an additional degree in library science.

Many people compete for archivist jobs. Numerous volunteer opportunities are available to people interested in learning more about a career in this field. A part-time or volunteer position at a local library can provide valuable experience. Museums and cultural groups in your community may train volunteers to give guided tours for their organizations. Studying history and literature is also an excellent way to prepare for a career as an archivist.

Careers in Government

To help students learn about other careers in government, refer them to the Careers section on the *Holt Researcher Online*.

CULTURAL PERSPECTIVES

The flexibility of the Constitution allows the judicial branch to protect the rights and beliefs of minority groups in American society. In one such case, an Amish farmer named Jonas Yoder removed his daughter from the public school system after she reached the eighth grade. Yoder contended that higher education conflicted with his family's religious beliefs, which emphasized a simple and virtuous life.

The school district, however, charged Yoder with violating the mandatory school attendance laws of the state of Wisconsin. In 1972 the U.S. Supreme Court ruled that the application of the compulsory education law violated Yoder's First Amendment right to freedom of religion. The Court's decision illustrates the manner in which the Constitution can be interpreted to protect the many different cultural values held by the citizens of the United States. ■

structured. Rather, it gives Congress the flexibility to carry out this responsibility as needed over time. In fact, as the country has grown, Congress has passed legislation expanding and changing the system of lower-level federal courts to help the court system adapt to the new needs of the population.

Congress, like the courts, also interprets vague wording in the Constitution. For example, as labor issues have become increasingly important, Congress has passed laws concerning working conditions. These laws have included workplace safety rules and minimum wages that employers must pay workers. The power to pass such laws is not specifically mentioned in the Constitution. Because the products that workers make often travel across state lines, however, Congress has interpreted its constitutional power to control commerce among the states to include the authority to pass laws concerning working conditions.

Executive Actions The Constitution also gives the executive branch flexibility in interpreting its powers to take action. One example is the president's power to make **executive agreements**— arrangements that presidents establish with foreign governments that, unlike formal treaties, do not require Senate approval. This power has grown in ways not specifically mentioned in the Constitution.

At times, executive agreements have helped the government meet challenges that might have been more difficult to address using formal constitutional processes. In 1940, for example, President Franklin Roosevelt made an executive agreement with Great Britain to exchange old U.S. warships for the right to use British naval bases in and near North America. Roosevelt made the executive agreement because he feared that a formal treaty approving the same action would take too long. The agreement helped the United States react quickly to the challenge of improving its defense—while also helping a friend, Great Britain—during World War II.

Political Parties

Just as it does not specifically state every possible power and action of the three branches, the Constitution does not try to outline every detail of how the government should be run on a day-to-day basis. This flexibility allows officials to reorganize government to meet new challenges or react to new situations.

For example, political parties have long been an important part of U.S. elections even though they are not mentioned in the Constitution. A **political party** is an organized group that seeks to win elections in order to influence the activities of government. Many of the framers wanted to discourage political parties, fearing that they would divide rather than unite the nation. As is more fully explained in Chapter 18, however, political parties have played important roles in electing presidents and other government officials and in organizing the day-to-day operation of Congress. The Constitution's flexibility has allowed the political system to develop in this manner.

Custom and Tradition

Finally, the Constitution allows custom and tradition to help shape government. Customs and traditions are informal, long-established ways of doing things. They are not mentioned in the Constitution, but customs and traditions strongly influence how government carries out its functions.

For example, even though the Constitution does not provide for a formal body of leaders in the executive branch, President George Washington brought the heads of the executive departments together to act as his advisers. This group of department heads is called the **cabinet**. Cabinet meetings have since become an important

CONSTITUTIONAL GOVERNMENT *President George W. Bush meets with Canadian prime minister Jean Chretien and Chilean president Ricardo Lagos at the Summit of the Americas.* **Why is it important for the president to have the power to make executive agreements?**

POLITICAL PROCESSES *Franklin D. Roosevelt speaks to a crowd at a Bridgeport, Connecticut, train station while campaigning for a fourth term as president.* **Which amendment limits the number of terms a president can serve today?**

part of the federal government, with every president having had a cabinet to help accomplish the work of the executive branch.

Sometimes custom and tradition can bring pressure to make formal changes to the Constitution. For example, for more than 150 years no president served more than two terms in office. This custom dated back to George Washington, who did not seek re-election at the end of his second term in 1796. Franklin Roosevelt, however, was re-elected to a third presidential term in 1940 and a fourth in 1944. Many people opposed the idea of one person serving as president for so long. As a

result, Congress passed the Twenty-second Amendment, which limited presidents to two terms and thus formalized the custom that began with Washington. The amendment states that

66 No person shall be elected to the office of the President more than twice, and no person who has held the office of President, or acted as President, for more than two years of a term to which some other person was elected President shall be elected to the office of the President more than once. 99

SECTION 3 REVIEW ANSWERS

1. Refer to the following pages: executive agreement (58), political party (58), cabinet (58).

2. Judicial: determining if laws are unconstitutional; Legislative: creating structures and taking on duties not specifically mentioned in the Constitution; Executive: signing executive agreements

3a. Long-held informal customs and traditions shape how government is run, and they often bring pressure to make formal changes to the Constitution.

3b. The Constitution is vague in its wording and not specific about how certain powers are to be carried out.

4. Answers will vary but should reflect an understanding of federalism and knowledge of the goals of the framers of the Constitution.

SECTION 3 REVIEW

1. Identify and Explain:
- executive agreement
- political party
- cabinet

2. Identifying Concepts:
Copy the chart to the right. Use it to list examples of how the branches of government have interpreted their constitutional powers.

Chart: Interpreting Constitutional Powers — Executive, Judicial, Legislative

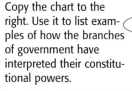

Homework Practice Online
keyword: SV3 HP3

3. **Finding the Main Idea**

a. How have custom and tradition affected how government functions?
b. How does the Constitution's wording allow the three branches of government to adapt to new circumstances?

4. **Writing and Critical Thinking**

Hypothesizing: The framers of the constitution adopted a distinct version of federalism. Why do you think they did so?

Consider the following:
- How power is shared between the levels of government
- Why the framers did not adopt a unitary system of government

SECTION 4

THE CONSTITUTION AND THE PUBLIC GOOD

READ TO DISCOVER

1. What were some of James Madison's contributions to the development of the U.S. government?
2. How does the Constitution ensure that government makes laws that promote the public good?
3. Why do critics claim that the Constitution sometimes makes government less effective?

POLITICAL DICTIONARY

faction

At the time of the Constitutional Convention, many delegates, such as James Madison, worried about whether popular government would be able to control the interests of **factions**—groups of people usually motivated by self-interest. A faction can consist of either a minority or a majority of the population. Majority factions, Madison argued, were more dangerous than minority factions. In a republican government, a minority faction can easily be defeated by a majority. A self-interested majority, however, can threaten the public good because a government that is run by such a group cannot be easily defeated.

Despite his concerns, Madison believed that the republic created by the Constitution could resist control by such a faction. At the same time, he argued that the Constitution provides a way to make sure that the government has sufficient authority to rule effectively and that it enacts policies that promote the public good. Was Madison right? This section explores how well the Constitution has accomplished these goals and how effective the U.S. government has been under the Constitution.

Preventing Control by Factions

Madison argued that the Constitution prevents control by factions in two ways. It takes advantage of the large size of the United States and it uses a system of checks and balances.

Size Madison was familiar with the arguments of his day that small republics were more likely to last than large republics. The citizens of small republics, it was argued, would be more likely to share interests, desires, and beliefs. Large republics, on the other hand, would have too many competing interests. Their governments would become arenas in which these interests would battle for control. The result would be tyranny by any faction that won control of government.

Madison, on the other hand, believed that having so many interests in a large republic like the United States was an *advantage*. The Constitution, with the rights and freedoms it promises, ensures that all interests have an equal chance to be represented. Madison said that with such a large number of interests competing for power, forming a faction that could completely dominate government would be difficult. In other words, a faction

James Madison believed that the large size of the United States would give all interests an equal chance to be represented. **Why did Madison believe that majority factions were more dangerous than minority factions?**

that did not consider other groups' interests would be unlikely to control government.

Checks and Balances Madison also argued that the Constitution prevents control by factions through a system of checks and balances. As noted in Section 1, the Constitution provides each of the branches of government with ways to check the powers of the other branches. The checks and balances system gives each branch of government what Alexander Hamilton called "constitutional arms for its own defense" against the other branches.

The framers of the Constitution believed that each branch would use its powers to check the powers of those heading the other branches. If a faction took control of one of the branches of government, for example, its power could be limited by the other branches.

Enacting Good Policies

According to Madison, the Constitution does more than just keep factions from using government for selfish, narrow interests. He also believed that the Constitution formed a republic in which it is *likely* that government will pass laws that serve the broader interests of society, or the public good.

Madison again based his beliefs on the large size of the United States. Because power under the Constitution lies with U.S. citizens, he argued that the government must pursue policies that address the interests of many people. Policies that serve only narrow, selfish interests—or that do not promote the public good—cannot win majority support in a large republic with many different interests. Policies based on the principles of "justice and the general good," however, are more likely to gain enough support to become law.

You can see Madison's ideas at work in your own community. Community debates over such issues as building a new convention center often revolve around how the community as a whole will benefit. Supporters of a new convention center might say that visitors to the center will spend money in the local community, thereby generating more tax revenue. If enough voters believe this argument and value the services that tax revenue helps provide, the convention center proposal will likely win majority approval. In contrast, a proposal that benefits only the narrow interests of one group, such as local construction companies, probably would not.

POLITICAL PROCESSES *Citizens protest a government shutdown caused by political gridlock during the preparation of the federal budget in 1995 and 1996. The shutdown led to the temporary closing of many federal buildings.* **Do you think that the Constitution's design promotes gridlock? Explain your answer.**

Effective Government

More than 200 years have passed since Madison made his arguments that the Constitution would help government promote the public good. Has the government fulfilled Madison's hopes?

The fact that representative government in the United States has thrived for more than two centuries is evidence that the Constitution has worked well. It has proved successful in protecting the individual rights of U.S. citizens. Although the country still faces many challenges, it has grown stronger and more prosperous.

Some critics, however, charge that the Constitution sometimes makes it difficult for government to promote the public good and function effectively. They argue that forming a majority from among the republic's many diverse opinions in pursuit of *any* policy, even a policy that promotes the public good, is too difficult. Even when such a majority exists, the Constitution limits the majority's ability to work effectively. These critics point to two major problems that can make effective government difficult under the Constitution: gridlock and avoiding responsibility.

Gridlock Some people believe that the Constitution's design promotes gridlock, a term that usually refers to a traffic jam in which cars

THEMES IN GOVERNMENT

PUBLIC GOOD The concern over government gridlock in the 1980s and 1990s prompted some scholars to re-examine the effectiveness of the government established by the Constitution. One feature that received criticism was the balance between population and representation in the Senate. Critics argued that because every state has two Senate seats regardless of population, the people who live in states with smaller populations have a greater share of power than they deserve in a democracy.

One observer noted that in 1996 it was possible to have a Senate majority (26 states) that represented less than 20 percent of the country's population. A proposed constitutional amendment, which would require 67 Senate votes for ratification, could be stopped by senators representing less than 5 percent of the nation's citizens. Though this imbalance raises serious questions about representative democracy, any changes to the system would require a constitutional amendment, which would be unlikely to pass the Senate. ■

SECTION 4 REVIEW ANSWERS

1. Refer to page 60.

2. Charts will vary but should accurately reflect the constitutional provisions that provide for checks and balances between the branches of government.

3a. Madison believed that the Constitution takes advantage of the large size of the United States and uses a system of checks and balances to keep any faction from dominating the government.

3b. Because some responsibilities are shared by more than one branch of government, leaders can blame others for problems and thus avoid responsibility.

4. Answers will vary but should demonstrate an understanding of Madison's ideas.

and other vehicles cannot move. Political gridlock occurs when the legislative process comes to a standstill because political opponents block each other's efforts.

In 1995 and 1996, for example, a Republican-led Congress and Democratic president Bill Clinton hit gridlock over the federal budget. They disagreed over tax cuts, how and when to balance the federal budget, and the funding of programs for health, education, and the environment.

After weeks of debate over the budget, Congress and the president still could not resolve their differences. Eventually, lacking funds ordinarily provided by the budget, the federal government partially shut down twice, for a total of 27 days. Thousands of federal workers—770,000 during the first shutdown and 280,000 during the second—were told not to report to work. Many people around the country began to criticize both the president and Congress, saying that their disagreements should not have led to a paralysis of the government.

Avoiding Responsibility Other critics say that the Constitution makes it too easy for government leaders to avoid responsibility for failed policies and other problems. In a democracy, elected officials should be held responsible for how effective they have been during their term in office. In a system with checks and balances, however, voters often cannot decide whom to hold responsible.

Think about the debate over federal spending. Many people believe the federal government spends too much money or spends it the wrong way. Whom should they hold responsible for that spending? The Constitution gives Congress the responsibility of passing laws that provide funds for federal government projects. But a president may sign or veto such laws. So both Congress and the president are responsible to varying degrees for government spending. This shared responsibility makes it hard to pinpoint where the blame for excessive or unnecessary spending rests and what action should be taken to avoid similar problems in the future.

Avoiding responsibility can make government less effective. Rather than make difficult but needed spending cuts, for example, some leaders might prefer to blame others for government's failure to bring spending under control. Voters, however, have the power to question the actions of their elected officials. If the president argues that Congress spends too much money or spends it irresponsibly, or if Congress charges that the president has created costly and unnecessary programs, voters can ask each side to explain why it did not take steps to block the other's actions.

After examining the issue, voters may determine that neither the president nor members of Congress are acting responsibly. The voters then can elect other people whom they believe will act more responsibly. In the end, it is the citizens in a democracy who must decide whether the government they have chosen is serving the public good and then take action accordingly.

SECTION 4 REVIEW

1. Identify and Explain:
   • factions

2. Identifying Concepts:
   Copy the chart below. Use it to show which provisions of the Constitution provide for checks and balances between the branches of government.

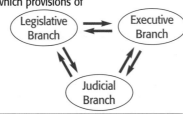

Homework Practice Online
keyword: SV3 HP3

3. ### Finding the Main Idea

   a. Why did James Madison believe the Constitution would prevent government form being controlled by factions?

   b. How can leaders use the system of checks and balances to try to avoid taking action?

4. ### Writing and Critical Thinking

   Hypothesizing: James Madison believed that the Constitution would produce effective government and good policies. Would he still think so if he saw how the government runs today?
   Consider the following:
   • the problem of gridlock
   • the increase in the size of the United States

GOVERNMENT
IN THE NEWS

Crimes, Commerce, and the Constitution

The Preamble to the U.S. Constitution pledges the federal government to "insure domestic Tranquility" and "promote the general Welfare." The role of the Bill of Rights in carrying out these aims is well known. Surprisingly, however, an important constitutional factor that also helps protect Americans is the power of Congress to regulate interstate commerce.

When the federal government wishes to enact legislation that outlaws a certain action, Congress must first determine either that the practice violates an existing federal law or that it falls under the jurisdiction of Congress. During the civil rights movement of the 1950s and 1960s, Americans demanded an end to segregation in public places, such as restaurants and bus stations. Congress determined that segregation interfered with interstate commerce. According to Article I, Section 8, of the Constitution, interstate commerce falls under the jurisdiction of Congress. Congress then enacted the Civil Rights Act of 1964, which outlawed discrimination in the United States.

In recent years the diversity of the U.S. population has increased. Most Americans have celebrated this change. At the same time, however, crimes have continued to be committed against people because of the victim's race, ethnicity, religion, sexual orientation, or disability. In 1998 James Byrd Jr., an African American, was brutally murdered by white men. Crimes such as this one, which have occurred throughout U.S. history, have recently been termed "hate crimes."

Many state governments have begun to pass stricter hate crime legislation. In 2001 the state of Texas, where Byrd was murdered, passed a law addressing hate crimes. The James Byrd Jr. Hate Crimes Act created tougher penalties for crimes motivated by the victim's race, gender, religion,

Governor of Texas Rich Perry signs into law The James Byrd Jr. Hate Crimes Act. To the left sits Byrd's mother, Stella.

disability, age, national origin, or sexual orientation. Supporters of the law argue that hate crimes are in essence more destructive than other crimes.

Recent hate crimes have also inspired calls for federal legislation. In order for such a law to be considered constitutional, however, its sponsors must establish that Congress indeed has authority in this area. The Hate Crimes Prevention Bill of 2001 argues that hate crimes do fall under federal jurisdiction. Section 2 of the bill describes hate crimes as "a serious national problem," a problem that "is sufficiently serious, widespread, and interstate in scope to warrant Federal intervention." Because "perpetrators cross State lines to commit such violence," and "such violence affects interstate commerce in many ways," the sponsors of the bill believe that the power of Congress to regulate matters of interstate commerce allows Congress to enact laws against hate crimes.

What Do You Think?

1. How might the power of Congress to regulate interstate commerce relate to its ability to make laws regarding hate crimes?

2. Do you think that hate crimes are different from other types of crimes?

> **WHY IT MATTERS TODAY**
>
> Both houses of Congress are always considering new pieces of legislation. Use CNNfyi.com or other **current events** sources to conduct research on new laws that have been proposed in either the House of Representatives or the Senate.
>
> CNNfyi.com

Government in the News Answers

1. If hate crimes involve or disrupt interstate commerce, the power of Congress to regulate interstate commerce could give it the power to make laws against hate crimes.

2. Answers will vary, but students should demonstrate informed reasoning in their opinions.

CHAPTER 3

Review Answers

Writing a Summary

Summaries should focus on the main points of each section. These may be found in the Read to Discover questions at the start of each section. Summaries should also use standard grammar, spelling, sentence structure, and punctuation.

Identifying Ideas

Refer to the following pages for significance: republicanism (47), popular sovreignty (47), separation of powers (48), checks and balances (48), judicial review (49), unconstitutional (49), amendment (51), repeal (52), Bill of Rights (53), political party (58).

Understanding Main Ideas

1. The Constitution lists the powers denied to government, protects citizens' individual liberties, and states

(Continued on page 64)

Review

(Continued from page 63)
that the government receives its authority from the consent of the people. 8D, 21A

2. The framers wanted to protect states' rights but still create a national government strong enough to maintain order.

3. The Bill of Rights lists the individual rights protected by the Constitution.

4. The procedure for proposing an amendment and the number of votes required for adoption make ratification difficult.

5. The diversity of interests in the large republic would make it difficult to form majority groups that could dominate government. This would ensure that selfish interests could not gain the majority needed to pass laws.

6. Each branch of government can restrict the power of the other two; therefore, no one branch can seize complete control.

Reviewing Themes

1. Answers will vary but should mention popular sovereignty, limited government, separation of powers, checks and balances, and federalism, and their effect on society.

2. The framers' belief in republicanism contributed to popular sovereignty and a constitution that guarantees individual rights.

3. It is a section of the Constitution stating that the power of the national government is superior

(Continued on page 65)

Writing a Summary

Using standard grammar, spelling, sentence structure, and punctuation, write a summary of the information in this chapter.

Identifying Ideas

1. republicanism
2. popular sovereignty
3. separation of powers
4. checks and balances
5. judicial review
6. unconstitutional
7. amendment
8. repeal
9. Bill of Rights
10. political party

Understanding Main Ideas

SECTION 1 (pp. 47–50)

1. In what ways does the Constitution reflect the principles of popular sovereignty and limited government?

2. Why did the framers' of the Constitution create a distinct form of federalism instead of adopting a unitary system of government?

SECTION 2 (pp. 51–55)

3. How does the Bill of Rights work to protect individual rights?

4. Why has the Constitution been amended only 27 times in more than 200 years?

SECTION 3 (pp. 56–59)

5. Why did James Madison believe that the U.S. republic's large size would help government serve the public good?

SECTION 4 (pp. 60–62)

6. How does the system of checks and balances help prevent one branch of government from becoming too powerful?

Reviewing Themes

1. Constitutional Government How have the basic principles of the Constitution shaped our nation?

2. Political Foundations How did the concept of republicanism influence the shape of the U.S. government?

3. Principles of Democracy What is the "supremacy clause"? How is it related to the principle of federalism?

Thinking Critically

1. Identifying Points of View In the Preamble to the Constitution the framers listed what their new government was intended to do. What values are reflected in the Preamble? How well has the U.S. government served its intended purpose?

2. Supporting a Point of View How does the Constitution affect your life today? Write a letter to the editor explaining how the Constitution continues to shape our national identity.

3. Analyzing Information Do you think that political parties are an important part of a democratic government? Do you think that political parties divide the nation, as the framers feared they might? Explain your answer.

Writing About Government

Review what you wrote in your Government Notebook at the beginning of the chapter about why you think the plan of government provided by the Constitution has been successful for more than 200 years. Now that you have finished studying this chapter, how would you revise your answer? Record your answers in your Notebook.

Interpreting the Graph

Study the bar graph below. Then use it to help you answer the questions that follow.

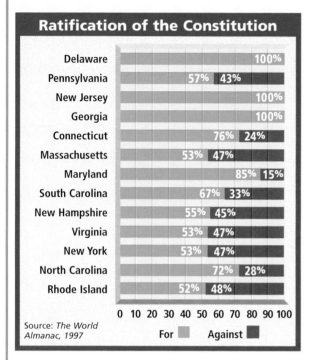

Ratification of the Constitution

State	For	Against
Delaware	100%	
Pennsylvania	57%	43%
New Jersey	100%	
Georgia	100%	
Connecticut	76%	24%
Massachusetts	53%	47%
Maryland	85%	15%
South Carolina	67%	33%
New Hampshire	55%	45%
Virginia	53%	47%
New York	53%	47%
North Carolina	72%	28%
Rhode Island	52%	48%

0 10 20 30 40 50 60 70 80 90 100

Source: *The World Almanac, 1997*

For ■ Against ■

1. How many states unanimously ratified the Constitution?
  a. 13   **c.** 3
  b. 0   **d.** 9

2. If there had been a 10 percent swing in votes in Pennsylvania, Massachusetts, Virginia, New York, and Rhode Island would the Constitution have been ratified? Explain.

Analyzing Primary Sources

Marbury v. *Madison*

Marbury v. *Madison* established the principle of judicial review. Read the following excerpt from the Court's majority opinion—which was written by Chief Justice John Marshall—and answer the questions that follow. "The powers of the legislature are defined and limited; and that those limits may not be mistaken or forgotten, the Constitution is written. To what purpose are powers limited, and to what purpose is that limitation committed to writing, if these limits may, at any time, be passed by those intended to be restrained? The distinction between a government with limited and unlimited powers is abolished if those limits do not confine the persons on whom they are imposed. . . .

If two laws conflict with each other, the courts must decide on the operation of each. So if a law be in opposition to the Constitution, if both the law and the Constitution apply to a particular case, so that the court must either decide that case conformably to [in agreement with] the law, disregarding the Constitution, or conformably to the Constitution, disregarding the law, the court must determine which of these conflicting rules governs the case"

3. Which of the following statements best describes Marshall's point of view?
  a. Congress has absolute power
  b. The Constitution is never wrong
  c. The Court decides what is Constitutional
  d. There are no limits on government

4. Do you think the principle of judicial review protects the public good? Why or why not?

(Continued from page 64)
to that of state governments. Federalism provides for a strong national government.

Thinking Critically

1. Answers will vary but should reflect a clear understanding of ideals reflected in the Preamble.

2. Answers will vary but should demonstrate an understanding of the affect of the Constitution on the nature of society.

3. Answers will vary but students should include examples of the role of political parties in government and examples of how parties have contributed to gridlock.

Writing About Government

The Government Notebook is a follow-up activity to the notebook activity that appears on page 46.

Building Social Studies Skills

1. c

2. It would not have been ratified because a 10 percent swing in votes in those states would have only left eight states in favor of it.

3. c

4. Answers will vary but students should exhibit knowledge of judicial review and *Marbury* v. *Madison*.

Alternative Assessment

To assess this activity see Writing to Describe in *Alternative Assssessment Handbook*.

Alternative Assessment

Building Your Portfolio

With a group, create a handbook for student-government officers at your school. Include a description of the responsibilities and powers of each office. Your handbook should be clearly written and easy to follow.

⬛ **Internet** connect

go.hrw.com

Internet Activity: go.hrw.com
KEYWORD: SV3 GV3

Access the Internet through the HRW Go site to research the Bill of Rights. Then write a persuasive essay in which you explain which amendment is the most important of the Bill of Rights. Support your explanation with at least three reasons. Use standard grammar, spelling, sentence structure and punctuation.

CHAPTER 4 FEDERALISM

	OBJECTIVES	PACING GUIDE	REPRODUCIBLE RESOURCES
SECTION 1 **POWERS AND RESPONSIBILITIES** (pp. 67–71)	▸ Which powers does the Constitution grant to the federal government, and which does it reserve for the states? ▸ Which powers are denied to the federal government, and which are denied to the states? ▸ What responsibilities do the federal and state governments have to each other? ▸ What role do the courts play in the U.S. federal system?	**Regular** 1.5 days **Block Scheduling** 1 day	**ELL** Spanish Study Guide 4.1 **ELL** English Study Guide 4.1 **PS** Reading 20: *Debate on the Proposed Constitution* **S** Simulations and Strategies for Teaching Government: Activity 4 **E** Challenge and Enrichment Activity 4
SECTION 2 **GROWTH OF FEDERALISM** (pp. 72–75)	▸ How has the federal government's involvement in states' affairs grown? ▸ How have grants-in-aid affected the growth of federalism? ▸ What role do federal mandates play in federalism?	**Regular** .5 day **Block Scheduling** .5 day	**ELL** Spanish Study Guide 4.2 **ELL** English Study Guide 4.2 **SM** Government Activities: Activity 4
SECTION 3 **RELATIONS AMONG THE STATES** (pp. 76–79)	▸ How are states admitted to the United States? ▸ In what ways do the states work together in the federal system?	**Regular** 1 day **Block Scheduling** .5 day	**ELL** Spanish Study Guide 4.3 **ELL** English Study Guide 4.3
SECTION 4 **FEDERALISM AND THE PUBLIC GOOD** (pp. 80–82)	▸ How does the national government in a federal system promote the public good? ▸ In what ways does dividing power in a federal system help government serve the public good? ▸ How has balancing federal and state interests helped to promote the public good?	**Regular** 1 day **Block Scheduling** .5 day	**ELL** Spanish Study Guide 4.4 **ELL** English Study Guide 4.4

Chapter Resource Key

PS	Primary Sources	**A**	Assessment		Video
RS	Reading Support	**REV**	Review		Videodisc
E	Enrichment	**ELL**	Reinforcement and English Language Learners		Internet
S	Simulations		Transparencies		Holt Presentation Maker Using
SM	Skills Mastery		CD-ROM		Microsoft ® PowerPoint ®

TECHNOLOGY RESOURCES	REINFORCEMENT, REVIEW, AND ASSESSMENT
One-Stop Planner: Lesson 4.1 Researcher Online Homework Practice Online CNN Presents American Government Transparency 8 Global Skill Builder CD-ROM	**REV** Section 1 Review, p. 71 **A** Daily Quiz 4.1
One-Stop Planner: Lesson 4.2 Researcher Online Homework Practice Online Holt American Government Videodisc: Federal Mandates: Whistle Bans and Public Safety Global Skill Builder CD-ROM	**REV** Section 2 Review, p. 75 **A** Daily Quiz 4.2
One-Stop Planner: Lesson 4.3 Researcher Online Homework Practice Online Global Skill Builder CD-ROM	**REV** Section 3 Review, p. 79 **A** Daily Quiz 4.3
One-Stop Planner: Lesson 4.4 Researcher Online Homework Practice Online Cartoon Transparency 3, Transparency 9 Global Skill Builder CD-ROM	**REV** Section 1 Review, p. 82 **A** Daily Quiz 4.4

Chapter Review and Assessment

SM Global Skill Builder CD-ROM
HRW Go site
REV Chapter 4 Tutorial for Students, Parents, and Peers
REV Chapter 4 Review, pp. 84–85
Chapter 4 Test Generator (on the One-Stop Planner)
A Chapter 4 Test
A Alternative Assessment Handbook

One-Stop Planner CD-ROM

It's easy to plan lessons, select resources, and print out materials for your students when you use the **One-Stop Planner CD-ROM with Test Generator**.

OBJECTIVES

▶ List the powers given to the federal government and to the state governments by the Constitution.

▶ List the powers denied to the federal government and to the state governments by the Constitution.

▶ Identify the responsibilities that the federal and state governments have to each other.

▶ Describe the courts' role in the federal system.

MOTIVATE

Organize students into small groups. Give each group a large piece of butcher paper and three different colored markers. Have each group define the terms *expressed, implied,* and *inherent.* Ask groups to identify examples in their own lives in which they have had either expressed permission, implied permission, or inherent ability to do something. Have students write their ideas on the butcher paper using a different color for each of the three examples. Let each group read from its paper and discuss the reasons for placing each example under the category that it chose. Explain that in this section students will learn what powers and responsibilities the federal and state governments are given or denied by the Constitution.

TEACH

Building a Vocabulary

In spiral notebooks, have students create a Political Dictionary to be used throughout the course. This dictionary may be used as an activity at the start of each new section; it may also be used as a modification device for students having difficulty or Sheltered English Students during tests and homework assignments. List words from this section that students will be expected to know on the board. Have students list, define, and give an example of each of the terms, using information provided in the text or on the *Researcher CD-ROM.*

Learning from Visuals

Organize students into six groups. Assign each of the words *expressed, implied,* and *inherent* to two groups. For each pair of groups with the same topic have one group cover the federal role and the other cover the states' role. Have students make a poster depicting the powers given to the level of government they were assigned. Encourage students to use such tools as newspapers, magazines, and computers. Have each group display and discuss the powers listed on its poster. Tell students that in the next activity they will learn about the powers denied the government.

Hypothesizing

List the powers denied to the federal government on one side of the chalkboard and those denied to the states on the other. Ask students to brainstorm what might happen if federal and state governments held the powers that are denied to them by the Constitution. Use examples from the Articles of Confederation to show what could happen when powers are poorly distributed. Have students share their examples with the class. Discuss the importance of denying certain powers to each level of the government. Tell students that in the next activity they will learn about the responsibilities that come with these powers.

Comparing and Contrasting

Write the headings *Powers* and *Responsibilities* on the board. Ask students to debate the difference between power and responsibility in their own lives. Guide them in distinguishing between the two and list examples of each on the board. Lead a discussion about the responsibilities of the federal and state governments. Ask students to brainstorm why they believe these are responsibilities and not powers. Have students choose one of the three main responsibilities the federal government has toward the states. Have students write an essay explaining the importance of these federal responsibilities and offering suggestions of what could happen if the federal government did not uphold its responsibility. Encourage students to share their ideas. As a lead-in to the next assignment tell students that they will learn about the courts' responsibility for interpreting the law.

Drawing Conclusions

 Organize students into groups of three. Tell students that two members of the group are to play games of tic-tac-toe and the third member should act as the referee. Explain that the rules of the game are standard but that certain special rules apply, such as no touching of the table or desk when it is not a player's turn, no saying words with more than one syllable, no looking at other teams, and no touching one's own face. Have the referees watch for any violations and record occurrences on a piece of paper. After students have had the opportunity to play a few rounds, have them discuss the similarities between the referees in their games and the role of the courts in the federal system. Try to point out that both the game and the courts are based on interpreting certain rules.

CLOSE

Ask students to consider the example they wrote during the Motivate activity. Have them brainstorm why it is important for the government to have expressed, implied, and inherent powers. Ask students to identify powers that are denied to the federal government. Lead a discussion regarding how the balance of powers in their own lives is similar to those in the federal and state governments.

OPTIONS

Gifted Learners

  Encourage students to learn more about federalism in other countries using the Country Profiles section on the *Holt Researcher Online* and other resources. Students may write papers or complete projects for extra credit in which they compare the division of powers in other countries to the division of power in the United States.

Students Having Difficulty/ Sheltered English Students

 Have students examine current newspapers and magazines for examples of powers exerted by one level of government that are denied to the other levels, such as the federal government printing new dollar bills. Encourage students to share these articles with the class by making a collage for each type of power or have students create a list of these powers in their Government Notebook.

Gifted Learners

  Have students write a short paper describing a Supreme Court case that involves a conflict of interest between a state government and the federal government. Students should include the state involved, what the conflict was, the decision in the case, and what effect the decision had. Encourage students to use the Supreme Court Docket section on the *Holt Researcher Online* and other resources to gather information.

Logical-Mathematical Learners

 Discuss with students that sometimes concurrent powers are used to manage large projects, such as highway construction and running public universities. Have students research projects that the federal government and state governments are working on together. Have students write a short paper describing a project. Be sure to have students discuss the amount of money being spent by both the federal and state governments. They should also describe any other commitments that either level of government has made to the project.

REVIEW

Have students complete the Section 1 Review on page 71. Use the answers in the Annotated Teacher's Edition to assess student mastery of this section.

ASSESS

To assess student mastery of this section, have students complete Daily Quiz 4.1 in *Daily Quizzes with Answer Key.* For additional assessment options, see *Alternative Assessment Handbook* on the *One-Stop Planner CD-ROM.*

ADDITIONAL RESOURCES

Cornell, Saul. *The Other Founders: Anti-Federalism and the Dissenting Tradition in America, 1788-1828.* 1999. University of North Carolina Press.

Durland, William. *William Penn, James Madison and the Historical Crisis in American Federalism (Studies in American History, Vol 28).* 2000. Edwin Mellen Press.

Wills, Gary. *Explaining America: The Federalist.* 2001. Penguin USA.

OBJECTIVES

▶ Explain how the federal government's involvement in states' affairs has grown.
▶ Describe how grants-in-aid have affected the growth of federalism.
▶ Identify the role of federal mandates in federalism.

MOTIVATE

Have students brainstorm ways in which the federal government has become more influential in their lives as they have gotten older (e.g., getting paid a minimum wage, registering for Selective Service, registering to vote). Explain that in the same way, the federal government has also become increasingly influential in the affairs of the states as the country has grown older. Tell students that in this section they will learn about the ways that the federal government has increased its influence over state governments.

TEACH

Building a Vocabulary

In their spiral notebooks, have students continue working on their Political Dictionary. List words students will be expected to know on the board. Have students list, define, and give an example of each term, using information provided in the text or on the *Researcher CD-ROM*.

Demonstrating Understanding

Organize students into six groups. Assign two groups each to play the roles of the FBI, the National Guard, or federal financial officials. Playing charades, have each group act out the ways in which the federal government has become increasingly involved in states' affairs. For example, students may act out the FBI assisting local authorities on a case. Discuss with students the actual ways that the federal government has expanded its authority in the areas

discussed. Tell students that in the next activity they will learn about additional ways that the federal government has extended its control over state governments.

Applying Information/Debating Ideas

Organize students in two groups: categorical grants and block grants. In pairs have students write or type a letter to the federal government requesting a grant (either categorical or block, based on the group to which they have been assigned). Have students explain why there is a need for the money, how it will be spent, and whom it will help. Lead a debate over which type of grant would best accommodate each proposal. Discuss with students the growing debate over whether money should be granted in the form of categorical grants or block grants. As a lead-in to the next activity tell students that they will be learning about federal mandates and increasing federal control over state governments.

Debating Ideas

Discuss the concept of federal mandates and the debate over them with the class. Then organize the class into two groups, one in favor of federal mandates and the other against them. Allow students time to consider the uses of mandates and how they affect states' rights to handle their own affairs. Have the group in favor of mandates create a proposed mandate to govern the other group. Then have the group against mandates respond regarding the effects of the mandate. Afterward, see if students have the same feelings about mandates.

CLOSE

Ask students to consider what might happen if each state could make its own decisions regarding such issues as minimum wage, registration for Selective Service, and the age at which a person may vote. Lead a discussion about the importance of having these issues decided by the federal government. Have students consider the topics discussed in this section when considering which, if any, of the methods of increasing control over state governments should be allowed.

OPTIONS

Gifted Learners

 Encourage students to learn more about the increased federal use of the FBI or the National Guard in states' affairs. Allow students to use outside resources such as newspapers, magazines, and the Internet. Have students present the information they obtain in an oral or a written report and offer them extra credit. Have student volunteers give their opinions on any controversial use of these organizations in states' affairs.

Interpersonal Learners

Have students interview people outside the classroom (parents, employers, teachers) on their opinions regarding federal mandates. Ask students to share the information with the class. Identify the majority view from the sample interviewed by all of the students. Discuss how this majority view is similar to or different from the view of students in the class.

Students Having Difficulty

Have students work with a peer tutor to investigate the use of federal mandates in their state or local area. Students should describe the action the mandate is trying to regulate and the result of following or not following the law. Students should also include their opinions on whether they think the mandate is fair to the state or local government.

REVIEW

Have students complete the Section 2 Review on page 75. Use the answers in the Annotated Teacher's Edition to assess student mastery of this section.

ASSESS

To assess student mastery of this section, have students complete Daily Quiz 4.2 in *Daily Quizzes with Answer Key.* For additional assessment options, see *Alternative Assessment Handbook* on the *One-Stop Planner CD-ROM.*

ADDITIONAL RESOURCES

Dye, Thomas. *American Federalism: Competition Among Governments.* 1996. Lexington Books.

Bauer, David. *The How-to Grants Manual: Successful Grantseeking Techniques for Obtaining Public and Private Grants.* 1999. Oryx Press.

Jennings, Jr., Edward T., Alex Pattakos, B. J. Reed, and Dale Krane (Editors). *From Nation to States: The Small Cities Community Development Block Grant Program.* 1986. State University of New York Press.

Peterson, Paul E., and Barry G. Rabe, Kenneth K. Wong. *When Federalism Works.* 2000. Brookings Institution Press.

OBJECTIVES

▶ Describe how states are admitted to the United States.
▶ List ways in which states work together in the federal system.

MOTIVATE

Acquire as many of the following items as possible and have them displayed when students enter the room: state flags, state flowers, lyrics to state songs, pictures of state birds, and state constitutions. Allow students to examine the items. Have students discuss the similarities and differences among these items. Explain that in this section they will learn how states are admitted to the United States as well as how the states work together in the federal system.

TEACH

Building a Vocabulary

In their spiral notebooks, have students continue working on their Political Dictionary. List words from this section that students will be expected to know on the board. Have students list, define, and give an example of each term, using information provided in the text or on the *Researcher CD-ROM*.

Applying Information

Have the class attempt to create a new fictional state. Go through the procedures for state admission for a territory, such as creating a petition asking for statehood. Ask students to decide on a state name, flag, song, flower, and bird. Encourage students to use the Internet or the State Profiles section on the *Researcher Online* for examples of what other states have done while deciding on these items. Allow some students to ask permission to create another state from the existing one if they wish. Have them choose state symbols as well. Explain to students that creating a petition for statehood and choosing state symbols may be the easy part of the admittance process, that states need to adopt a state constitution that is in line with the principles of the U.S. Constitution. Ask stu-

dents to remember discussions about the Constitutional Convention from Chapter 2. Tell students that some of these types of compromises were also common in deciding on state constitutions. Lead into the next activity by telling students that they will be learning about constitutional principles that guide interactions between states.

Role-Playing

Have students break up into groups of four or five students each. After examining the issues related to how states work together, have students role-play in their groups what might happen if states did not cooperate with one another through the Full Faith and Credit, Privileges and Immunities, and Extradition Clauses in the Constitution. Have groups share their ideas with the entire class. Lead a class discussion on the importance of these clauses. Tell students that they will learn more about interactions between the states in the next activity.

Acquiring Information

Discuss with the class the recent increase in interstate compacts and the types of issues that these agreements usually control. Organize the class into small groups. Have groups examine newspapers and magazines in search of articles dealing with interstate compacts. Remind students that it may be easier to find this information in newspapers for metropolitan areas that are close to the border of another state. Each group should report on any news of interstate compacts that it finds and should include any positive or negative outcomes of the agreements.

CLOSE

Ask if any students were born or have ever lived out of state. Allow those who have to use the State Profiles section on the *Researcher CD-ROM* and other resources to learn about their former state (e.g., year of admission, flag). Allow other students to choose any state they wish and do the same. Have students create a chart depicting when and how each state became part of the United States. Allow students to work in groups if they wish. Display the charts for the rest of the class to view.

OPTIONS

Gifted Learners

 Have students create situations where one state's actions could have a negative effect on another state, such as one state's pollution contaminating another state's water supply. Then have students create interstate compacts to deal with the problem. Have students share their compacts with the rest of the class.

Students Having Difficulty/ Sheltered English Students

 Encourage students to find out the difference in tuition costs for students living in state and those from out of state at a nearby public college or university or one that they are interested in attending. Have students find out how long it takes for a student to establish in-state residency at the school they are researching. Ask them to share this information with the rest of the class.

Acquiring Information

Have students create a map that identifies areas that have interstate compacts. Students can refer back to the Acquiring Information activity earlier in this section for a list of various interstate compacts. Have students identify the states involved in each compact and create a color-coded map to identify areas that currently have interstate compacts. Display this map in the classroom.

Logical-Mathematical Learners

Discuss the change in the federal mandate that has allowed states to set their own speed limits. Assign each student several states to research. Have students research changes in the speed limits and changes in the number of highway deaths for their assigned states. Then have students form a hypothesis about how the change in the speed limit affected the public good of each state.

REVIEW

Have students complete the Section 3 Review on page 79. Use the answers in the Annotated Teacher's Edition to assess student mastery of this section.

ASSESS

To assess student mastery of this section, have students complete Daily Quiz 4.3 in *Daily Quizzes with Answer Key.* For additional assessment options, see *Alternative Assessment Handbook* on the *One-Stop Planner CD-ROM.*

ADDITIONAL RESOURCES

Drake, Frederick D., and Lynn R. Nelson (Editors). *States Rights and American Federalism: A Documentary History (Primary Documents in American History and Contemporary Issues).* 1999. Greenwood Publishing Group.

Kenyon, Daphne A., and John Kincaid. *Competition Among States and Local Governments: Efficiency and Equity in American Federalism.* 1991. Urban Institute Press.

FEDERALISM AND THE PUBLIC GOOD

HOLT PRESENTATION MAKER
Access Illustrated LECTURE
NOTES using Microsoft®
PowerPoint® on the
One-Stop Planner CD-ROM

OBJECTIVES

▸ Describe how the national government in a federal system promotes the public good.

▸ Explain how the division of power in a federal system helps government promote the public good.

▸ List ways in which balancing federal and state interests has helped promote the public good.

MOTIVATE

Review with students ways in which government promotes the public good (see textbook section 1.1). Ask students to brainstorm difficulties the government would have in promoting the public good if there was no central authority or if all the power rested with the federal government. Explain to students that by providing a central authority while still distributing power among the three levels of government, the U.S. government promotes the public good. Tell students that throughout this section they will be learning about ways that federalism promotes the public good.

TEACH

Classifying Information

Discuss ways that federalism promotes the public good with the class. Then write the following headings on the chalkboard: *Providing Central Authority* and *Distributing Power.* Have students give examples of policies or actions of the federal government that fall into one of these categories. Discuss with students possible reasons the federal government followed this course of action. As a lead-in to the next activity, tell students that they will be examining ways that the school system promotes the public good.

Applying Information

 Ask students to identify ways in which their school system is similar to the federal government with regards to promoting the public good. Lead students to identify the school board and administration as the central authority and to understand that power is distributed among school districts, schools, principals, and teachers. Have students discuss the balance between the interests of the school district's administration and those of the schools. Discuss with students the public good that schools promote. Tell students that in the next exercise they will learn about distributing power.

Conducting Research

 In small groups, have students research ways of distributing power. Assign each group one of the following methods: encouraging alternate solutions to government problems, checking power, and promoting citizen participation within one's own state. Encourage students to use newspapers, magazines, and the Internet to locate specific examples of these ways of distributing power. Ask students to share the information and examples they find with the rest of the class. Finally, have students discuss the similarities and differences between these three methods of distributing power.

Developing Life Skills

Organize the class into two groups. One group will serve as the federal government, and the other as a state government. Choose a current news topic that deals with the federal government trying to extend its authority over state governments, such as proposals that would require all states to develop and administer standardized tests that meet federal guidelines. Have students form a compromise committee to reach an acceptable deal for both the state and federal governments. Have students consider the goal the federal government is trying to accomplish and the effect this may have on the state involved when making the compromise.

CLOSE

Remind students of the difficulties they discovered during the Motivate activity that showed the need for a central authority and a distribution of power. Lead a discussion regarding the importance of these issues as well as the importance of balancing federal and state interests. Then have students write a short paper weighing the need for central authority against the importance of states' rights. Have students consider examples from the section when writing their papers.

OPTIONS

Students Having Difficulty/ Sheltered English Students

 Have students create a cartoon depicting one of the ways that government promotes the public good that have been discussed in this section. Have each student share his or her cartoon with another student to see if it is clear how the cartoon shows the government promoting the public good. Then display the cartoons for other students to see.

Visual-Spatial Learners

  Individually or in pairs, have students create three-dimensional models representing the three ways of serving the public good discussed in this section. Encourage students to be as creative as possible. Have students discuss their models and then display the models for the class.

REVIEW

Have students complete the Section 4 Review on page 82. Use the answers in the Annotated Teacher's Edition to assess student mastery of this section.

ASSESS

To assess student mastery of this section, have students complete Daily Quiz 4.4 in *Daily Quizzes with Answer Key.* For additional assessment options, see *Alternative Assessment Handbook* on the *One-Stop Planner CD-ROM.*

RETEACH

For students having difficulty with the lessons, have them complete Reteaching Activity 4. This activity is located in *Reteaching Activities with Answer Key.*

ADDITIONAL RESOURCES

Kane, Francis. *Neither Beasts Nor Gods: Civic Life and the Public Good.* 1998. Southern Methodist University Press.

Shannon, John. "The Return to Fend-for-Yourself Federalism." Paper presented to the American Political Science Association. 1987.

Zimmerman, Joseph F. *Interstate Relations.* 1996. Praeger Publishers.

CHAPTER 4

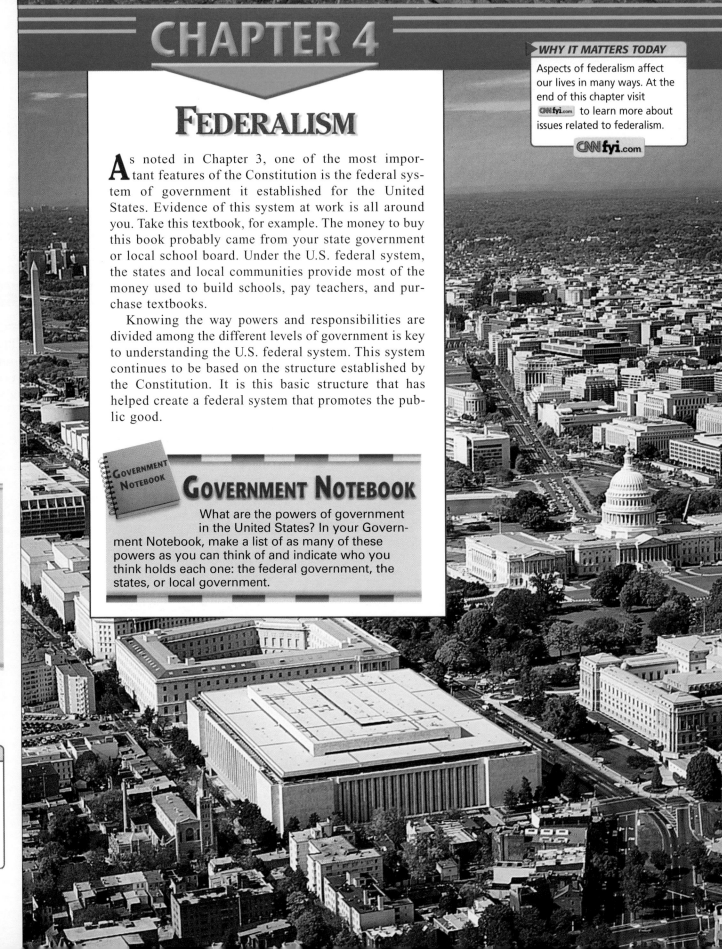

FEDERALISM

As noted in Chapter 3, one of the most important features of the Constitution is the federal system of government it established for the United States. Evidence of this system at work is all around you. Take this textbook, for example. The money to buy this book probably came from your state government or local school board. Under the U.S. federal system, the states and local communities provide most of the money used to build schools, pay teachers, and purchase textbooks.

Knowing the way powers and responsibilities are divided among the different levels of government is key to understanding the U.S. federal system. This system continues to be based on the structure established by the Constitution. It is this basic structure that has helped create a federal system that promotes the public good.

TOPICS INCLUDE

★ expressed power
★ implied power
★ inherent power
★ reserved power
★ concurrent power
★ categorical grant
★ block grant
★ federal mandate
★ act of admission
★ civil law
★ criminal law
★ extradition
★ interstate compact
★ distributing power
★ checking power

GOVERNMENT NOTEBOOK

The Government Notebook is a journal activity that encourages students to consider basic concepts of government that relate to their lives. A follow-up notebook activity appears on page 84.

GOVERNMENT NOTEBOOK

What are the powers of government in the United States? In your Government Notebook, make a list of as many of these powers as you can think of and indicate who you think holds each one: the federal government, the states, or local government.

WHY IT MATTERS TODAY

Aspects of federalism affect our lives in many ways. At the end of this chapter visit **CNNfyi.com** to learn more about issues related to federalism.

CNNfyi.com

WHY IT MATTERS TODAY

To find additional lesson plans dealing with federalism, visit **CNNfyi.com** or have students complete the **GOVERNMENT IN THE NEWS** Activity on page 83.

CNNfyi.com

SECTION 1

POWERS AND RESPONSIBILITIES

READ TO DISCOVER

1. Which powers does the Constitution grant to the federal government, and which does it reserve for the states?
2. Which powers are denied to the federal government, and which are denied to the states?
3. What responsibilities do the federal and state governments have to each other?
4. What role do the courts play in the U.S. federal system?

POLITICAL DICTIONARY

expressed powers
implied powers
Elastic Clause
inherent powers
reserved powers
concurrent powers

The Constitution outlines the powers and responsibilities of both the federal government and the states. In addition, the Constitution assigns the federal courts an important role in resolving conflicts among the different levels of government.

Powers of the Federal Government

The U.S. federal government holds three types of powers: expressed, implied, and inherent. These powers generally involve matters that affect all people in the United States and that are impractical for the states to handle. Some of these powers come from the Constitution, while others are simply those that are exercised by any government of a sovereign country.

Expressed Powers The powers that the Constitution expressly, or specifically, grants to the federal government are called **expressed powers**. For example, Article I, Section 8, lists the expressed powers of the legislative branch. These powers include issuing money, collecting national taxes, borrowing money, paying government debts, regulating trade among the states and with foreign governments, declaring war, and raising and maintaining armed forces.

Articles II and III list the expressed powers of the other two branches. Article II gives the president the power to command the armed forces and to direct relations with governments of other countries. Article III gives the judicial branch the power to decide several kinds of cases, including those concerning the Constitution, federal laws, and treaties. Federal courts may also rule on cases involving the U.S. government, certain foreign officials in the United States, and disputes among the states.

CONSTITUTIONAL GOVERNMENT *The federal government prints and issues the national currency. Here, a U.S. mint quality-control worker inspects currency-printing plates.* **Why is it more practical to have a national currency than to have each state print its own?**

SECTION 1

POWERS AND RESPONSIBILITIES

Lesson Plans

For teaching strategies, see Lesson 4.1 located at the beginning of this chapter or the One-Stop Planner Strategy 4.1.

Political Dictionary

To reinforce the section's vocabulary terms, refer students to the Electronic Glossary on the *Researcher CD-ROM.*

Section Assessment

To assess students' mastery of this section, have them complete Daily Quiz 4.1 in *Daily Quizzes with Answer Key.*

Caption Answer

If each state had its own currency, a person would have to use a different currency each time he or she crossed a state line.

ACROSS THE CURRICULUM

HISTORY Article I, Section 10, of the U.S. Constitution was the basis for the Supreme Court's decision in the 1819 case *Dartmouth College* v. *Woodward*. Dissatisfied with college president John Wheelock, the board of trustees limited his powers. Wheelock sent New Hampshire state legislations a pamphlet outlining the injustices he perceived. They responded with an act to withdraw the college's charter, which had been granted by King George III. Wheelock was given control of a new school—Dartmouth University—with a new charter.

The result was that Dartmouth College kept the students but Dartmouth University received the buildings. The college appealed to the Supreme Court, which ruled that a charter was a contract, and since the Court interpreted the U.S. Constitution to declare that no state can impair the obligations of contracts, the New Hampshire act was ruled unconstitutional. Dartmouth College regained its original charter.

The case has served to guarantee charter rights of all private colleges and to protect business corporations. ■

Implied Powers Not all powers of the federal government are expressly listed in the Constitution. The federal government also has **implied powers**, or powers that are suggested by the expressed powers.

The constitutional source of Congress's implied powers is Article I, Section 8. This section gives Congress the power "to make all laws which shall be necessary and proper" to exercise its other powers. This "necessary and proper" clause has been called the **Elastic Clause**, because it allows Congress to stretch its authority in ways not specifically granted nor denied to it by the Constitution.

For example, the Sixteenth Amendment to the Constitution expressly gives Congress the power to establish and collect taxes on incomes. Using its implied powers, Congress has established the Internal Revenue Service (IRS) to do the actual tax collecting.

Inherent Powers The federal government also has **inherent powers**, or powers that naturally belong to any government of a sovereign country. Governments of sovereign countries have used these powers throughout history. Like implied powers, inherent powers are not mentioned in the Constitution. Many of these inherent powers relate to foreign affairs, such as the making of international agreements, including acquiring new territory.

POLITICAL FOUNDATIONS *The U.S. government's decision to purchase Alaska was seen as foolish by some people, who thought Alaska was just a large block of ice, as noted in the above cartoon. (See the Linking Government and Economics feature on page 77.)* **What type of power allows governments to acquire new land?**

Powers of State Governments

In the U.S. federal system, some powers are reserved for the states. These **reserved powers** are not specifically mentioned in the Constitution. According to the Tenth Amendment, however, the powers that the Constitution does not give to the federal government nor specifically forbid to the states "are reserved to the states . . . or to the people."

Among the states' reserved powers are the authority to establish local governments, create public school systems, and enact criminal and civil laws. States may also pass laws promoting public health and safety, regulating business within their borders, and requiring licenses to work in various professional occupations. Professionals required to have licenses may include doctors, lawyers, accountants, and even the person you pay to cut your hair.

Concurrent Powers

The federal and state governments also hold some **concurrent powers**—those that the Constitution neither grants exclusively to the federal government nor denies to the states. For example, both the federal government and the states may establish court systems, make and enforce laws, collect taxes to pay the costs of governing, and borrow and spend money.

Limits on Federal and State Powers

The Constitution also limits the powers of the different levels of government. Some powers are denied only to the federal government, some only to the states, and some to both levels of government.

Government Power

FEDERAL GOVERNMENT POWERS
(Expressed Powers)

- To regulate interstate and foreign trade
- To coin and print money
- To establish post offices and construct post roads
- To raise and support armed forces
- To declare war and make peace
- To govern U.S. territories and admit new states
- To pass laws regulating immigration
- To make all laws "necessary and proper" to carry out its powers

SHARED POWERS
(Concurrent Powers)

- To collect taxes
- To borrow money
- To establish courts
- To charter banks
- To make and enforce laws
- To provide for the health and welfare of the people

STATE GOVERNMENT POWERS
(Reserved Powers)

- To regulate trade within the state
- To establish local governments
- To conduct elections
- To determine qualifications of voters
- To establish and support public schools
- To pass laws regulating businesses within state borders
- To make civil and criminal laws
- To pass license requirements for professionals

Some government powers are given only to states and others are given only to the federal government. A few are shared by both. **Are the powers reserved for the states specifically stated in the Constitution?**

Powers Denied to the Federal Government

Article I, Section 9, lists the powers that are denied to the federal government. For example, the federal government may not tax exports, pass laws favoring the trade of one state over another, or spend money unless authorized to do so by federal law.

As you know, the federal government also may not exercise powers that are not mentioned or implied in the Constitution or inherent to the governments of all countries. For example, it may not enact laws that establish a monarchy. In addition, the federal government may not exercise the powers that are reserved for the states, and it may not pass laws that threaten the federal system established by the Constitution.

Powers Denied to the States Article I, Section 10, explicitly lists powers that are denied to the states. For example, a state may not issue its own money, make a treaty with a foreign government, or go to war unless invaded or authorized to do so by the federal government. In addition, states cannot manage trade with other states or foreign countries without Congressional approval.

Powers Denied to Both Levels The Constitution denies some powers to both the federal government and the states. Neither level of government, for example, may deny people accused of crimes the right to trial by jury. In addition, the Constitution forbids the federal government and the states from granting titles of nobility.

Responsibilities

The federal system created by the Constitution includes more than a division of powers among the levels of government. The Constitution also notes the responsibilities that the federal government and the states have to each other.

Federal Responsibilities The federal government has three main responsibilities regarding the states. These include making sure that the states have republican governments, protecting the states from violent actions, and respecting the states' territories.

First, the federal government must ensure that all states have republican governments. Although the term *republican* is not defined in the Constitution, it has been interpreted to mean

PUBLIC GOOD The federal government plays an important role in providing relief to disaster victims. However, the government is helped in this role by organizations such as the American Red Cross.

During the spring of 1997, flooding damaged a large area near the North Dakota–Minnesota border. The American Red Cross helped bring relief to residents of the area. It opened 26 shelters to house more than 6,000 people and provided more than 200,000 meals to the flood victims. The Red Cross also opened 17 service centers where flood victims met with caseworkers to seek aid for essential items. The cost of these services was not cheap. The nonprofit agency received $18 million to help the victims. The major flood relief, however, came from the federal government. ■

Caption Answer
(for page 71)
use of the National Guard and financial assistance

SECTION 1
REVIEW ANSWERS

1. Refer to the following pages: expressed powers (67), implied powers (68), Elastic Clause(68), inherent powers (68), reserved
(Continued on page 71)

---

representative government. By allowing a state's representatives and senators to be seated in Congress, the federal government recognizes that a state's government is legitimate.

A second responsibility of the federal government is protecting the states from violent actions, such as foreign invasions. The framers made the federal government responsible for protecting all the states, which means that an attack against any one of the states is an attack against the United States as a whole.

Comparing Governments

Federalism in Mexico and Germany

The United States is just one of many countries with a federal system of government. Both Mexico and Germany, for example, are federal republics operating under a centralized government.

As in the United States, the citizens in Mexico elect a president to head the federal government. Mexico's legislature consists of a 128-member Senate and a 500-member Federal Chamber of Deputies—a legislative house similar to the U.S. House of Representatives. Distrito Federal—a federal district similar to Washington, D.C.—houses the major federal offices. State governors, who are elected by the citizens of the country's 31 states, direct the state governments and make decisions and policies on local matters.

Germany's government is organized somewhat differently from the U.S. and Mexican governments. Its president is elected by federal and state legislators and holds a largely ceremonial position. The country's chancellor, who is elected by the lower house of the legislature rather than by the people, is the head of the government. Like the United States and Mexico, however, Germany has a two-chamber legislature, consisting of the 69-member Bundesrat, or upper house, and the 656-member Bundestag, or lower house. In addition, citizens in each of Germany's 16 states elect members of a state legislature to govern state matters.

Although each state has the power to make and enforce laws within its boundaries, the federal government may intervene to help maintain order. In 1992, for example, federal troops helped stop violent rioting in Los Angeles. Such federal involvement has not happened often and usually has come at the request of state governors and local authorities.

In addition to protecting the states from violent actions, the federal government also helps states after natural disasters, such as earthquakes, fires, hurricanes, and floods. In 1996, for example, Congress authorized the distribution of $1.3 billion in natural disaster relief funds to states in the Northeast that had been damaged by blizzards the previous winter and to those in the Northwest that had been greatly damaged by flooding.

A third responsibility of the federal government is to guard the states' territorial rights. For example, Article IV, Section 3, of the Constitution says that no new states may be formed from the territory of other states without the approval of both the states concerned and Congress.

State Responsibilities The states also have responsibilities to the federal government. They must establish, for example, the boundaries for districts from which members of the House of Representatives are elected. States also set the rules for electing members of Congress and choosing presidential electors and pay the costs of running elections—for example, printing ballots and setting up voting locations.

States also maintain National Guard units that may be called into action by the governor or the federal government during emergencies. National Guard units served to augment security at U.S. airports after the September 11, 2001, terrorist attacks.

The Courts and the Federal System

The framers knew that the system of government they created might lead to conflicts between the federal and state governments. They knew, for example, that states might pass laws that conflicted with those passed by the federal government. How did the framers solve this problem?

Article III of the Constitution gives the judicial branch the authority to hear cases involving the Constitution, U.S. laws, and disputes among states. Thus, the judicial branch has the authority to act as referee between the federal government and the states. In most team sports, a referee makes decisions based on rules that the participants have agreed to follow. In the federal system, the courts—and particularly the Supreme Court—make decisions based on the rules listed in the Constitution.

By agreeing to follow its rules, the states acknowledge that the Constitution is the highest authority in disputes with the federal government. As noted in Chapter 3, the framers made it clear in Article VI that the power of the federal government is superior to the power of state governments. This article of the Constitution includes the Supremacy Clause, which declares that the Constitution, federal laws, and treaties made by the federal government are "the supreme law of the land."

The Supremacy Clause guides the federal courts in solving conflicts between state and federal laws. In 1819, for example, the Supreme

PUBLIC GOOD *National Guard units provide assistance to Iowa residents after a flood in 1993.* **What type of assistance does the federal government provide to states during times of crisis?**

Court ruled in *McCulloch* v. *Maryland* that the state of Maryland could not tax the Bank of the United States. The Supreme Court ruled that if the states had the power to tax any part of the federal government, they would be superior to it, which would be unconstitutional.

SECTION 1 REVIEW

1. Identify and explain:
- expressed powers
- implied powers
- Elastic Clause
- inherent powers
- reserved powers
- concurrent powers

2. Categorizing: The states derive their reserved powers from the Tenth Amendment. In the chart below, list the states' reserved powers.

States' Reserved Powers

3. Finding the Main Idea

a. What powers are denied to the federal government?
b. What powers are denied to state governments?
c. How do the federal courts serve as the federal system's referee?

4. Writing and Critical Thinking

Drawing Conclusions: Write a paragraph explaining why it is important that powers be divided between the federal government and the states.

Consider the following:
- the document establishing the division of powers.
- why states cannot negotiate trade agreements with foreign nations.
- the ways state and federal governments resolve conflicts.

Homework Practice Online
keyword: SV3 HP4

(Continued from page 70)

powers (68), concurrent powers (68)

2. Reserved Powers: see chart on p. 69.

3a. The federal government cannot tax exports, pass laws favoring the trade of one state over another, or spend money unless federally authorized.

3b. States cannot issue their own money, make a treaty with a foreign power, or go to war unless invaded or federally authorized.

3c. The courts, particularly the Supreme Court, make decisions and resolve disputes based on the rules listed in the Constitution.

4. Answers will vary, but students should mention that the Constitution established the structure that divides power between state and federal governments. The division of power is important for both efficiency of government and protection of individual rights. If states pass laws that conflict with national laws, those conflicts are resolved by the judicial branch.

SECTION 2

GROWTH OF FEDERALISM

READ TO DISCOVER

1. How has the federal government's involvement in states' affairs grown?
2. How have grants-in-aid affected the growth of federalism?
3. What role do federal mandates play in federalism?

POLITICAL DICTIONARY

revenue sharing
grant-in-aid
categorical grant
block grant
federal mandate

Debates about the federal system have long been part of U.S. politics. At various times since the founding of the republic, some states have argued that they had the right to nullify, or cancel, federal laws that they opposed. In the mid-1800s, eleven southern states even claimed the right to secede from, or leave, the United States. Many of the people in these states believed that under President Abraham Lincoln's administration, the federal government would threaten southern institutions, including the system of slavery, and hence their way of life.

The Civil War defeat of the 11 southern states that seceded from the Union in 1860 and 1861 firmly established the federal government's supreme authority. In addition, the Supreme Court has ruled that the Constitution's Supremacy Clause does not allow states to reject federal laws as long as those laws are constitutional.

The debate over the power of the state and federal governments continues today. Some of the fuel for that debate has come from the ways in which the federal government has increased its involvement in states' affairs.

Increasing Federal Involvement

In the 1900s the federal government has become increasingly involved in areas previously handled by state and local governments. In law enforcement, for example, the Federal Bureau of Investigation (FBI) often helps state and local officials solve major crimes. The federal government also helps fund the states' National Guard units.

The growth of federal involvement is particularly evident in the money that the national government has given to state and local governments. During the 1970s and early 1980s, for example, federal tax dollars were shared with state and local governments. Under this system of **revenue sharing**, states had a great deal of freedom in spending their share of federal money. Revenue sharing ended in the mid-1980s under pressure to cut federal spending.

In spite of such pressure, federal aid to the states has continued and, in some ways, even grown. Today, federal grants are major sources of income for state and local governments. To receive this aid, however, states often must follow rules and requirements set by the federal government.

The Grant System

One way that the role of the federal government has grown is through grants-in-aid. **Grants-in-aid** are money or other resources that the federal government provides to pay for state and local activities. Unlike money from revenue sharing, grants-in-aid are used for specific projects and programs authorized by the federal government.

The number and value of grants-in-aid have grown a great deal during the 1900s, but the roots of these grants reach back much further. The Land Ordinance of 1785 under the Articles of Confederation, for example, set aside land for public schools in the territories won from Great Britain during the Revolutionary War.

After the Constitution was ratified, the federal government continued to give aid to states. The Morrill Act of 1862, for example, gave grants of federally owned land to the states. The states used the money they earned from selling the land to establish colleges. Seventy state universities, including Texas A&M and Ohio State, have their origins in the Morrill Act.

Today grants to the states support not only education but also transportation systems, housing projects, and programs for people in need. How a grant-in-aid can be used depends on its form: categorical or block.

Categorical Grants Payments by the federal government to carry out specific activities are called **categorical grants**. Categorical grant programs include those for building airports and other public facilities, unemployment compensation, fighting crime, and providing relief after natural disasters such as floods and earthquakes.

Categorical grants often base the amount of aid that a state or local government receives on certain conditions, such as population. These grants also typically require that state or local governments contribute their own funds, in an amount determined by Congress. In this way, state and local governments show their commitment to the program.

Block Grants Another form of grant-in-aid is a **block grant**. These federal funds can be used by a state or locality in a broadly defined area such as welfare, community development, health, or education. Block grant projects include developing public transportation systems, anticrime programs, and community youth activities.

State and local governments usually prefer block grants to categorical grants because, as with revenue sharing, block grants give them more freedom to decide how to spend federal money. Some critics believe, however, that this flexibility allows states to ignore the needs of those for whom the aid was intended. Supporters of block grants, on the other hand, argue that state and local governments can better determine their citizens' needs than can the federal government.

Since the 1980s, block grants have become increasingly common. Some categorical grants to support libraries, aid science education, and teach students about the metric system, for example, became a part of the broader education block grants. In 1995 and 1996, many members

POLITICAL PROCESSES *Many state universities, including the Champaign-Urbana campus of the University of Illinois, were established as a result of federal aid provided by the Morrill Act of 1862.* **What other types of programs do grants-in-aid support?**

of Congress supported proposals for turning categorical grants into block grants. Rather than determining how much money should go to every program, the federal government would allow states to decide which priorities should be pursued with available funds. Under the 1996 welfare law, for example, all federal contributions to states for welfare are in the form of block grants.

Federal Mandates

The federal government also has become more involved in the affairs of the states through **federal mandates**—requirements that the federal government imposes on state and local governments. The federal government passes mandates to address issues that affect people in many or all of the states. For example, some federal mandates have established protections for the environment and measures to protect the health and safety of workers.

Forms of Mandates Federal mandates come in three basic forms. One form is a law directing state or local governments to take action on a particular issue. For example, the Asbestos Hazard Emergency Response Act of 1986 required public schools to take certain steps to protect children from exposure to asbestos, a fireproof mineral that

internet connect

TOPIC: Federal Block Grants
GO TO: go.hrw.com
KEYWORD: SV3 GV4

Have students access the Internet through the HRW Go site to research federal spending and block grants. Then ask students to imagine they have been hired by the city in which they live to write a grant proposal. Remind them to get a federal block grant to do something positive for their community. Ask them what they would write the grant for and how they would go about getting the grant funded. Then have them write a proposal and present it to the class.

can cause health problems and that was formerly used in insulation. In buildings using this insulation, tiny asbestos fibers travel through the air, causing lung damage in people who inhale them. Supporters of the 1986 law wanted to protect children's health in the country's public schools.

Another form of federal mandate gives states the choice between undertaking an activity themselves or having the federal government do it. For example, in 1970 the federal government passed the Clean Air Act to lower pollution levels. States were given money and were allowed to make their own rules to follow this law, on the condition that they met federal air quality levels. States that did not do so would have to accept federal enforcement of the law. State leaders often prefer to administer programs themselves because they can adapt government rules to local conditions, whereas the federal government often makes broad rules that all areas must follow.

Finally, federal mandates may come in the form of strings attached to federal aid. To receive this aid, a state or local government must follow certain requirements. For example, in 1986 Congress declared that states whose minimum age for drinking alcoholic beverages was 20 or less would lose

POLITICAL PROCESSES *EPA workers clean up a toxic waste dump in Houston. Federal environmental mandates often include aid to help states follow these rules.* **Why do some people argue that the federal government should provide funds for mandates?**

a percentage of their federal aid for constructing and maintaining highways if they did not raise the age to 21. Establishing a legal drinking age is a state responsibility, but by the end of 1988 all states had raised the minimum legal drinking age to 21 to keep from losing full federal highway funding.

Debate over Mandates People who do not think that the federal government should issue mandates argue that federal rules violate the rights of states to handle their own affairs. For example, some people argue that environmental laws passed by Congress interfere with state and local authority. Others declare, however, that such regulation is necessary because one state's environmental pollution often affects the residents of other states.

Critics also argue that the federal government should provide the funds to pay for its mandates. For example, Congress passed a law in 1993 requiring states to adopt certain rules making it easier for people to register to vote. Supporters argued that the law would increase voter registration. Some opponents, however, argued that the law would unfairly force state governments to pay for a program that they had not created.

States have fought against such unfunded mandates—with some success. In 1995, for example, Congress passed and President Clinton signed into law a bill that required that the Congressional Budget Office (CBO) submit a report on the costs a new bill would impose on state and local governments before that bill could be considered by Congress. If the CBO determined that the legislation would require expenditures of more than $50 million, and Congress refused to provide the funds to state governments for enforcement of the new law, then that bill could not be considered by Congress unless a special "point of order" vote was taken that would allow consideration of the legislation. The debate over balancing federal and state interests continues.

C A S E   S T U D Y

Drive 55?

CONSTITUTIONAL GOVERNMENT Changing times play an important role in the establishment and repeal of federal mandates. Consider, for example, federal mandates about speed limits on the country's highways.

In 1973 and 1974 a major rise in the price of oil caused fuel prices to skyrocket. The economic shock over the higher prices encouraged efforts to conserve energy. In one such effort, Congress passed a law that required any state receiving federal highway aid to lower its maximum speed limit to 55 miles per hour.

Setting speed limits is a state responsibility, but as with the federal mandate regarding a minimum drinking age, every state quickly lowered its maximum speed limit to 55 miles per hour in order to keep from losing federal funding. By the late 1980s, however, fuel prices had fallen, the fuel efficiency of cars had improved, and support for conserving energy was less common. In 1987 pressure from some states, notably large western states whose population centers are often far apart, led Congress to allow states to raise the speed limit to 65 miles per hour in rural areas.

In 1995 the federal mandate on speed limits changed again. Under growing pressure to roll back

POLITICAL PROCESSES *Some states increased their maximum speed limits to 75 miles per hour after the passage of the 1995 law that allowed states to set their own speed limits.* **Why did states lower their maximum speed limits to 55 miles per hour during the 1970s?**

federal rules, Congress passed a law allowing states to set their own speed limits on all roads. Opponents had argued that the higher speed limits would waste fuel and cause more deaths from traffic accidents. Others argued that the states could better determine safe speed limits inside their own borders. Most states set higher speed limits shortly after the law passed. The full result of these higher limits may not be known for several years.

SECTION 2 REVIEW ANSWERS

1. Refer to the following pages: revenue sharing (72), grant-in-aid (72), categorical grant (73), block grant (73), federal mandate (73)

2. law enforcement assistance, money for National Guard, revenue sharing, federal grants

3a. laws directing a state to take action on an issue; state permission to act on an issue that the federal government normally covers; and requirements to receive federal assistance

b. categorical grants: money the federal government gives to states to carry out specific activities such as building public facilities; block grants: federal money given to states for more broadly defined activities, such as community youth activities

4. Students may argue that federal involvement violates the rights of states to manage their own affairs, or they may say that the federal government protects individual rights with rules that dictate how states can spend federal money.

SECTION 2 REVIEW

1. Identify and explain:
- revenue sharing
- grant-in-aid
- categorical grant
- block grant
- federal mandate

2. Categorizing: The federal government is increasingly involved in states' affairs. In the web diagram below, list four examples, past and present, of increased federal involvement.

Increasing Federal Involvement

3. **Finding the Main Idea**
a. What are the forms of federal mandates?
b. What are the two kinds of grants-in-aid, and what do they fund?

4. **Writing and Critical Thinking**

Drawing Conclusions: Write a paragraph explaining your opinion of the federal role in states' affairs. Does the federal government have too much control? Too little?
Consider the following:
- how the role of the federal government in states' affairs has expanded.
- the benefits states derive from the federal government.
- the drawbacks to federal involvement.

Homework Practice Online
keyword: SV3 HP4

SECTION 3
RELATIONS AMONG THE STATES

Lesson Plans

For teaching strategies, see Lesson 4.3 located at the beginning of this chapter or the One-Stop Planner Strategy 4.3.

Political Dictionary

To reinforce the section's vocabulary terms, refer students to the Electronic Glossary on the *Researcher CD-ROM*.

Section Assessment

To assess students' mastery of this section, have them complete Daily Quiz 4.3 in *Daily Quizzes with Answer Key.*

> **Caption Answer**
>
> Besides driver's licenses, states must honor all other official records such as car registrations and wills.

SECTION 3
RELATIONS AMONG THE STATES

READ TO DISCOVER

1. How are states admitted to the United States?
2. In what ways do the states work together in the federal system?

POLITICAL DICTIONARY

enabling act
act of admission
civil law
criminal law
extradition
interstate compact

Part of the federal system involves how the states deal with one another. The Constitution not only establishes guidelines for state interaction, it also provides for the admission of new states. In addition, it ensures that any state, regardless of when it is admitted, has the same status and rights as all the other states.

Admitting New States

Not all states have been admitted in the same way. Of the 37 states admitted to the Union since the Constitution was ratified, 30 were admitted after often lengthy periods as U.S. territories. To become a state, a territory usually petitions, or asks, Congress to be allowed into the Union. If the petition is approved, Congress then passes an **enabling act**—legislation that directs the territory to draft a state constitution establishing a representative government.

Next, the territory elects delegates to draft a constitution. If approved by the residents of the territory, the document is submitted to Congress for approval. Once approved, Congress then passes an **act of admission**—legislation that makes the territory a state with status equal to that of all the other states.

Some states were admitted without long periods as territories. California became a state within two years of Mexico's turning it over to the United States after losing the Mexican War. When Texas was admitted, it had been an independent republic for nine years.

Some states were formed from existing states. As noted in Section 2, a new state may not be formed from the territory of an existing state without that existing state's permission. Vermont, Kentucky, Tennessee, and Maine were formed from existing states. West Virginia was also formed from an existing state—Virginia. Because Virginia had suceded from the Union during the Civil War, however, opponents of secession formed the Restored Government of Virginia and granted themselves permission to create the state of West Virginia.

States in the Federal System

Even though the Constitution gives states the right to manage their own affairs within their borders, it also encourages cooperation among them. How do the states cooperate with one another?

Full Faith and Credit One way that states cooperate is by recognizing one another's official acts. As Article IV, Section 1, of the Constitution states,

CONSTITUTIONAL GOVERNMENT *The Full Faith and Credit Clause in the Constitution requires states to honor other states' driver's licenses.* **What other official records must states honor?**

Linking

Government and Economics

Alaska: The Last Frontier

Soon after the United States was founded, Americans began moving west into the vast frontier lands. As Americans and new immigrants settled along the western border of the frontier, they began to push the frontier farther west. By the end of the 1800s, the country's western frontier had disappeared. Soon, U.S. explorers began to look northward, to a territory known as Alaska, which was to become America's new frontier. Now, this frigid land is one of the United States's most sparsely populated, yet economically prosperous, states. Even today, Alaska's license plates declare it to be "The Last Frontier."

U.S. secretary of state William H. Seward negotiated the $7.2 million purchase of Alaska with Russia in 1867. Many people in the United States, viewing Alaska as a national liability rather than an asset, criticized the purchase. Skeptics demanded to know the usefulness of this frozen land. Seward, however, knew of Alaska's valuable natural resources—Russians had been trapping furs in the region's vast forests for more than 100 years. In addition, Seward believed that Alaska's geographic location made it vital to U.S. military interests. Owning Alaska would strengthen U.S.

influence in the North Pacific and weaken Russia's power. Still, critics called the purchase Seward's Folly and made their opinions known by describing the region as Frigidia and President Andrew Johnson's Polar Bear Garden.

The Alaskan Purchase, however, was soon recognized as the United States's "biggest bargain" since Thomas Jefferson's 1803 Louisiana Purchase. For less than two cents an acre, the United States gained about 600,000 square miles of resource-rich land—expanding its territory by almost 20 percent. In 1896 the Klondike Gold Rush in Alaska silenced Seward's critics forever.

Alaska's natural resources include immense mineral deposits, dense forests, and plentiful fish and wildlife, in addition to petroleum reserves that have added to the economic wealth of the state and the country. Oil revenue generates about four fifths of the state's income. All Alaskan residents share in the wealth—just for living in the state they receive close to $1,000 per year from a state oil fund. In 1995 per capita income in Alaska exceeded $24,000 per year, among the highest in the United States.

The state's largest oil reserves lie beneath the North Slope near Prudhoe Bay, on the Arctic coast. These reserves are slowly being depleted, however, spurring controversial efforts to drill in Alaska's Arctic National Wildlife Refuge, a haven for caribou. Geologists maintain that this northern coastal plain of Alaska is potentially one of the top oil-producing regions in the world. Environmentalists, however, argue that drilling in the refuge would destroy the only untouched Arctic ecosystem in the world. Although the interpretation has shifted over the years, the nickname "The Last Frontier" still applies to Alaska.

What Do You Think?

1. Once Alaska's petroleum reserves in oil-rich Prudhoe Bay begin to run out, should oil companies be allowed to drill in the Arctic National Wildlife Refuge? Explain your answer.
2. Do you think that admitting Alaska into the Union was more important to the country's economy or to its foreign-policy aims? Explain your answer.

Although purchasing Alaska was initially criticized by some people, the territory was soon seen as a wise investment because of its plentiful wildlife, oil deposits, and dense forests.

Careers in Government

FBI Agent

When federal laws are broken in the United States, the Federal Bureau of Investigation (FBI) steps in to investigate. An agency of the U.S. Department of Justice, the FBI employs more than 10,000 agents in field offices across the country.

Approximately 280 types of crimes, such as car-jacking, kidnapping, bank robbery, the selling of military and political information to foreign countries—even failure to pay child support—fall under the FBI's jurisdiction. With so many different types of cases to investigate, the FBI must employ agents with experience in all areas of law enforcement. For example, agents with prior computer training are needed for computer fraud investigations, while agents who are fluent in a foreign language may be assigned to investigate international espionage cases.

FBI investigators conduct a search outside the Pentagon on Wednesday, September 12, 2001.

To gather information for a case, an FBI agent must interview people, research official records, and observe suspects. Often, as in the case of the 1995 bombing of a federal office building in Oklahoma City, the FBI works with local and state law enforcement officials to capture suspects. Once enough evidence is gathered, agents make arrests. Sometimes they participate in raids—the sudden seizure of illegal operations and organizations. After a case goes to court, agents often testify about the evidence gathered during the investigation.

How does someone become an FBI agent? The FBI employs people in many professions, including accountants, lawyers, and scientists. A college degree is required, and being able to speak one or more foreign languages is an advantage.

Potential candidates, who must be between 23 and 37 years old, go through a rigorous application process that includes written tests, interviews, a thorough background check, drug testing, and a physical examination. Those who successfully complete this process must then train for 16 weeks at the FBI Academy. During training, potential agents study academic and investigative subject matter, physical fitness, proper use of firearms, and self-defense. College students interested in a career as an FBI agent can apply to internship programs to gain an insider's look at the role of an FBI agent.

"Full faith and credit shall be given in each state to the public acts, records, and judicial proceedings of every other state." The term *public acts* refers to a state's **civil laws**—laws that govern relationships among individual parties and that define people's legal rights.

Thus, the Full Faith and Credit Clause declares that states must recognize other states' civil laws. These laws include contracts between individuals and businesses. A state also must recognize, for example, a person's legal ownership of property in another state.

States also honor the convictions, settlements, and other decisions of courts in other states. States do not have to enforce other states' **criminal laws**, which forbid certain actions and provide punishment for violations. Criminal laws cover such things as theft and murder.

Finally, the Full Faith and Credit Clause requires states to honor other states' official records, such as driver's licenses, car registrations, and wills. For example, anyone licensed to drive in Texas can legally drive in the other 49 states.

Privileges and Immunities States also cooperate with one another by respecting the rights of citizens of other states. As Article IV, Section 2, of the Constitution states, "The citizens of each state shall be entitled to all privileges and immunities of citizens in the several states." This means that a resident of one state cannot be unreasonably discriminated against by another state. Each state must offer all U.S. citizens full protection of the laws. In addition, all citizens must be allowed to pursue lawful occupations, have access to the courts, and conduct legal business with others.

A state can, however, make reasonable distinctions between its citizens and those who are residents of another state. It can require that a person become a resident of the state before being allowed to vote in local elections or serve on juries. To become a resident, a person usually must live in a state for a certain amount of time. States also may charge people who are not residents higher fees for some services that are supported by the state's taxpayers.

Extradition A third area in which states cooperate involves people who commit a crime and try to escape the authorities by fleeing to another state. Although one state cannot enforce another state's criminal laws, Article IV, Section 2, of the Constitution provides for the extradition of people who are suspected or convicted of having committed crimes. **Extradition** is the process of sending a suspect or criminal back to the state from which he or she has fled. Criminals and suspects are usu-

CONSTITUTIONAL GOVERNMENT *Governors may request that a suspected criminal be extradited to the state where the crime was committed.* **Why might governors make such a request?**

ally extradited at the request of the governor of the state in which the crime was committed.

In 1987 the Supreme Court ruled that governors must honor extradition requests from other states. Before that time, governors occasionally refused to extradite suspects for several reasons, such as fears that a suspect would not receive a fair trial or concerns about another state's prison conditions.

Interstate Compacts States also may make **interstate compacts**, or agreements with other states, if Congress approves. These agreements cover issues such as flood control, protection of natural resources, and pollution.

SECTION 3 REVIEW

1. **Identify and explain:**
   • enabling act
   • act of admission
   • civil law
   • criminal law
   • extradition
   • interstate compact

1. _____	4. _____
2. _____	5. _____
3. _____	6. _____

Homework Practice Online
keyword: SV3 HP4

2. **Sequencing:** The Constitution provides for the admission of new states to the Union. Use the chart below to list the steps that are usually taken by territories that want to become states.

3. **Finding the Main Idea**

   a. How do states cooperate with each other?
   b. What document authorizes states to seek extradition of suspects?

4. **Writing and Critical Thinking**

   Making Predictions: Write a paragraph explaining why it is important that the Constitution provides ways for states to cooperate with one another.
   Consider the following:
   • What might happen if one state regularly refused to extradite suspects?
   • What might happen if states did not recognize the rights of other states' citizens?

Lesson Plans

For teaching strategies, see Lesson 4.4 located at the beginning of this chapter or the One-Stop Planner Strategy 4.4.

Section Assessment

To assess students' mastery of this section, have them complete Daily Quiz 4.4 in *Daily Quizzes with Answer Key.*

Caption Answer

The protections might lead businesses to move to other states where protections are less stringent and costly.

SECTION 4
FEDERALISM AND THE PUBLIC GOOD

READ TO DISCOVER

1. How does the national government in a federal system promote the public good?
2. In what ways does dividing power in a federal system help government serve the public good?
3. How has balancing federal and state interests helped to promote the public good?

A federal system of government has been vital to the growth and success of the United States. It has also kept the republic united while allowing people at state and local levels to manage their own affairs. By providing a central authority, distributing power, and balancing federal and state interests, the U.S. federal system promotes the public good.

Providing Central Authority

One way that the federal system promotes the public good is by providing a central authority: the federal government. The federal government acts on issues that are important to all of the states. Consider, for example, efforts to protect the environment. A state might hesitate to enact certain environmental protections that, although popular with the state's citizens, might lead businesses to move to states with rules that are less costly to follow. In addition, businesspeople might be frustrated by a tangle of environmental rules that differ from state to state, making it more difficult and costly for businesses to operate. Such rules might make it more difficult to operate a business effectively.

It therefore promotes the public good if the federal government adopts a national environmental policy that all states must follow. Such a policy standardizes environmental rules so that citizens and businesses can plan their actions. It also addresses the concerns of interests such as businesses, private citizens, and the states. If the policy did not address all of these concerns, it would probably not be passed.

As a central authority, the federal government can also protect the rights of all citizens, no matter where they live. A citizen in Delaware, for example, has the same constitutional rights as another citizen living in Hawaii. The federal courts can ensure that constitutional rights and federal laws are applied equally throughout all 50 states. By making sure that the rights of all citizens are protected, the federal government again promotes the public good.

Distributing Power

The federal system also promotes the public good by making sure that power is distributed among the states and not concentrated solely in the federal government. How does this distribution of power help government promote the public good?

Encouraging Alternate Solutions One way the federal system promotes the public good is by allowing the states to search for alternate strategies

CONSTITUTIONAL GOVERNMENT *In 1994 the federal government designated a portion of the Mojave Desert as a protected wilderness area.* **Why might a state be hesitant to enact strict environmental protection laws?**

in addressing common challenges. In short, the states can act as "laboratories of democracy," conducting experiments with new policies and solutions from which other states and communities can learn.

Consider the debate over how to help people in need. Some people have argued that the federal government has a responsibility to provide for people in need. Others have argued that the states should be allowed to try different ways of providing such assistance. In fact, under the welfare reform passed by Congress in 1996, states make their own rules for helping people who are poor. Supporters of the idea that more responsibility should be given to the states argue that with state governments experimenting with their own plans, more successful methods will probably be developed.

Checking Power Distributing power among the states also makes majority tyranny and an abuse of power more difficult. Should a self-interested majority somehow gain control of the federal government, the states may act in ways that check its power. One way that states can do this is by refusing to ratify constitutional amendments proposed by Congress. States' reserved powers also prevent the federal government from acting in areas over which it has no constitutional authority. It works both ways, however. As Alexander Hamilton wrote in his essay "No. 28" in the *Federalist Papers,* "The national government will at all times stand ready to check the usurpations [wrongful seizures of

power] of the state governments, and these [the state governments] will have the same disposition [role] towards the [national] government." Federalism may thus be seen as an additional check and balance in the constitutional framework.

Promoting Participation Finally, distributing power in a federal system allows more decisions to be made at a local level, which means that more people can be involved in decisions that most affect their lives. For example, because the United States has a federal system, educational funding differs widely from state to state. In addition to public education, such services as fire protection, car registration, road construction, and libraries are provided by state and local government. As a matter of fact, the laws and government policies with the greatest effect on your daily life are generally state and local, not federal. By allowing decisions to be made locally and by involving more people in the decision-making process, the federal system promotes democracy and encourages government to consider citizens' concerns before making its policies. Both of these actions promote the public good.

Balancing Federal and State Interests

Creating a central authority and distributing power among the states are just two ways in which

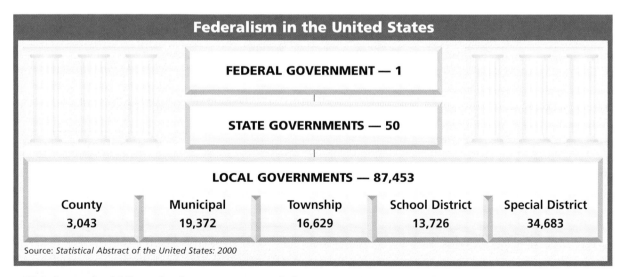

Federalism in the United States

FEDERAL GOVERNMENT — 1

STATE GOVERNMENTS — 50

LOCAL GOVERNMENTS — 87,453

County	Municipal	Township	School District	Special District
3,043	19,372	16,629	13,726	34,683

Source: *Statistical Abstract of the United States: 2000*

With thousands of different local governments, people have many opportunities to participate in the decision-making process. **How can you participate in your local government?**

SECTION 4 REVIEW ANSWERS

1. The federal system provides a central authority, distributes power, and balances federal and state interests.

2. The distribution of power to the states encourages alternate solutions, checks the power of federal and state governments, and promotes participation.

3a. States can experiment with new policies and solutions, and other states can learn from those experiments.

3b. Hamilton argued that the distribution of power formed a check on the powers of both state and federal governments.

4. Answers will vary, but students should point out that some say federal mandates violate states' rights while others point out that federal laws and courts protect citizens equally and that this protection serves the public good.

a federal system of government promotes the public good. In addition, good government needs to balance federal and state interests. There is debate, however, about where to find that balance.

The development of federalism in the United States has sometimes resembled a tug-of-war between supporters and opponents of the federal government's growing influence in states' affairs. Some people have strongly protested that federal mandates, for example, violate states' rights. As noted in Section 2, supporters of states' rights pushed Congress to stop passing unfunded mandates. Some people also have argued that some federal laws, such as those meant to protect the environment, violate the rights of states and local government authorities to control their own affairs.

Others, however, have pointed to the advantages of federal action. Federal laws, for example, have succeeded in extending voting rights to all eligible U.S. citizens, even in states that have tried to restrict those rights. Federal laws protecting individual rights such as voting are the best way to ensure that all citizens are treated fairly. In addition, federal courts have worked to protect the rights of citizens in all of the states. Supporters argue that such actions are necessary to ensure that the public good is served. In the end, of course, it is the responsibility of all citizens to determine the proper balance between state and federal interests and to work to secure that balance.

Berry's World

Better downsize!

BERRY'S WORLD reprinted by permission of Newspaper Enterprise Association, Inc.

© 1993 by NEA, Inc.

CONSTITUTIONAL GOVERNMENT *Some people believe that the federal government's influence over states' affairs is too great.* **How does this cartoon illustrate the debate about the power and size of the federal government?**

SECTION 4 REVIEW

1. List and explain: List and explain some of the ways in which the federal system serves the public good.

2. Cause and Effect: The federal system distributes power among the states. Use the chart below to describe three effects of this distribution of power that promote the public good.

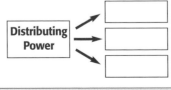

3. Finding the Main Idea

a. How are states "laboratories of democracy"?
b. What did Alexander Hamilton argue was the point of distributing power between states and the federal government?

4. Writing and Critical Thinking

Summarizing: Write a paragraph discussing the debate about the balance of power between the states and the federal government.
Consider the following:
• Why do some people oppose the federal government's growing involvement in state affairs?
• What are the advantages of federal involvement?
• What balance of power best serves the public good?

Homework Practice Online
keyword: SV3 HP4

IN THE NEWS

George W. Bush and Federalism

The past decade has seen the federal government return the powers of problem solving to the states. As a result of the welfare reform movement of the 1990s, states assumed greater responsibility for carrying out public assistance programs. The trend of letting states control social services continued when George W. Bush unveiled a new White House office for faith-based initiatives in January 2001, just days after becoming president.

Bush proposed that religious charities should have equal access to federal dollars without having to alter or mute the religious content of their work. In the past, religious groups had to create a secular (nonreligious) organization in order to receive federal funding, or simply relied on donations from the general public. Bush stated that religious organizations often do a better job of combating social problems such as poverty, addiction, and homelessness than federal agencies do. Supporters also argued that religious and community organizations know best how to spend money to solve problems.

Under Bush's plan Centers for Faith-Based and Community Initiatives were created in each of the Departments of Education, Justice, Labor, Health and Human Services, and Housing and Urban Development. Each state would also establish an agency to coordinate federal funding programs with local religious and community organizations. This arrangement would allow state and local officials to determine how best to spend social services dollars.

Legislation to enact the faith-based initiative has sparked several controversies. Some have charged that the proposal threatens the traditional separation of church and state. Other objections are rooted in views of federalism. The Salvation Army offered to support Bush's initiative in exchange for an exemption from certain state laws—those that prohibit discrimination against people of certain sexual orientation. As there is no federal law regarding such discrimination, and since the faith-based initiative involved federal dollars, the Salvation Army hoped to bypass state laws. In July 2001 the Bush administration refused this offer.

Some supporters of states' rights have voiced opposition to the plan as well. They contend that the Constitution does not provide the federal government with the authority to provide funding for welfare and charity programs. Instead, they argue, only the states have the authority and discretion to oversee social welfare programs.

The House of Representatives passed Bush's bill in July 2001. The bill moved on to the Senate for consideration. There it faced greater opposition from Democrats.

What Do You Think?

1. How does the faith-based initiative relate to the system of federalism in the United States?

2. Do you think charitable religious organizations should receive federal funding for their social-service programs?

> **WHY IT MATTERS TODAY**
>
> The United States continues to seek new ways of solving problems such as poverty and illiteracy. Use **CNNfyi.com** or other **current events** sources to investigate ways in which the federal government, local and state governments, and religious and community organizations are working to solve social problems.
>
> **CNNfyi.com**

Government in the News Answers

1. Students might suggest that the initiative would allow state and local authorities and organizations to allocate federal funding.

2. Answers will vary, but students should demonstrate an understanding of the benefits of and possible problems with the faith-based initiative.

CHAPTER 4

Review Answers

Writing a Summary

Summaries should focus on the main points of each section. These may be found in the Read to Discover questions at the start of each section. Summaries should also use standard grammar, spelling, sentence structure, and punctuation.

Identifying Ideas

Refer to the following pages: expressed power (67), implied power (68), inherent power (68), categorical grant (73), block grant (73), federal mandate (73), enabling act (76), act of admission (76), extradition (79), interstate compact (79).

Understanding Main Ideas

1. The Constitution gives the federal government three kinds of powers: expressed, implied, and inherent. The states' powers include authority to establish local

Continued on page 84)

Review

(Continued from page 83)

governments and school systems, and enact criminal and civil laws.

2. States cannot issue their own money, make treaties, or go to war unless attacked or authorized by the federal government. The federal government cannot tax exports, pass laws favoring the trade of one state over another, or spend money unless authorized by Congress.

3. The federal government has become more involved, especially through increased grants-in-aid.

4. They provide money for education, transportation systems, housing, and programs for people in need.

5. Laws directing state or local governments to take action; laws that give states a choice between allowing the federal government to administer them or carrying them out at the state level; and laws where federal aid comes with conditions that must be met.

6. A territory petitions Congress. If Congress approves the petition, it passes an enabling act and the territory drafts a constitution. If Congress and territory residents approve the constitution, then Congress passes an act of admission.

7. They cooperate by recognizing official acts of other states, respecting the rights of citizens from other states, forming interstate compacts, and honoring requests for extradition.

8. by providing a central authority, distributing power, and balancing federal and state interests

9. It makes tyranny and abuse more difficult by providing

(Continued on page 85)

Writing a Summary

Using standard grammar, spelling, sentence structure, and punctuation, write a summary of the information in this chapter.

Identifying People and Ideas

Identify the following terms and explain their significance.

1. expressed power
2. implied power
3. inherent power
4. categorical grant
5. block grant
6. federal mandate
7. enabling act
8. act of admission
9. extradition
10. interstate compact

Understanding Main Ideas

SECTION 1 *(pp. 67–71)*

1. What powers does the Constitution reserve to state governments and what powers does it grant to the federal government?

2. What powers does the Constitution deny state and federal governments?

SECTION 2 *(pp. 72–75)*

3. How has federal involvement in states' affairs changed?

4. How do federal grants-in-aid support state and local governments?

5. What three basic forms do federal mandates take?

SECTION 3 *(pp. 76–79)*

6. How are states admitted into the Union?

7. How do states work together in the federal system?

SECTION 4 *(pp. 80–82)*

8. How does federalism promote the public good?

9. How does the distribution of power between state and federal governments promote the public good?

Reviewing Themes

1. Constitutional Government The concept of limited government is an important principle of the U.S. political system. In what ways does the federal system limit government?

2. Political Processes Not everyone agrees on the role of the federal government. What arguments do opponents of federal mandates use to support their position?

Thinking Critically

1. Supporting a Point of View Some people argue that the federal government has become too involved in state and local affairs. Do you agree with that assessment? Why or why not?

2. Drawing Conclusions What do you think would have happened if the Constitution had not given the courts the authority to hear cases involving the Constitution, U.S. laws, and disputes among the states?

3. Analyzing Information What responsibilities do the states have to the federal government?

4. Drawing Conclusions What do you think would happen if states no longer had to obey the Full Faith and Credit Clause?

Writing About Government

Review the list of government powers that you wrote in your Government Notebook at the beginning of the chapter. Given what you have learned, how would you revise your list? Do you need to switch some of the powers you listed to other levels of government? Record your revisions in your Notebook.

Interpreting Political Cartoons

Study the image below. Then use it to help you answer the questions that follow.

Berry's World

Better downsize!

FEDERAL BUREAU-CRA-CY

© 1993 by NEA, Inc.

1. How does the cartoonist portray the federal government in this cartoon?
  a. It is a fierce defender of freedom.
  b. It interferes too much in the affairs of state and local governments.
  c. It is a bloated bureaucracy that needs to slim down.
  d. It spends too much time eating junk food.

2. What might lead the cartoonist to depict the federal government in this manner?

Analyzing Primary Sources

Read the following excerpt of South Carolina's constitution, written in 1895, then answer the questions.

"Any person who shall apply for registration [to vote] after January 1st, 1898, if otherwise qualified, shall be registered: Provided, That he can both read and write any section of the Constitution submitted to him by the registration officer or can show that he owns, and has paid all taxes collectible during the previous year on property in this State assessed at three hundred dollars ($300) or more.

Managers of election shall require of every elector offering to vote at any election, before allowing him to vote, proof of the payment of all taxes, including poll tax, assessed against him and collectible during the previous year."

3. Which of the following best describes the purpose of the provisions in this constitution?
  a. to make sure all taxes are paid on time
  b. to restrict the right to vote
  c. to make sure every citizen can read
  d. to protect all citizens' rights

4. How would this constitution have affected freed slaves at the time? How do limits placed on the power of state governments ensure equal opportunity for all citizens?

Building Your Portfolio

A More Perfect Union

Research one of the 37 states that was admitted to the United States after the Constitution was ratified. Then choose a state and imagine you are a politician there at the beginning of the admission process. Write a speech advocating admission or criticizing it. Be sure to include your reasons and be persuasive.

🖉 internet connect

Internet Activity: go.hrw.com
KEYWORD: SV3 GV4

Access the Internet through the HRW Go site to research the *McCullough v. Maryland* decision. Then imagine you are a newspaper reporter and write a story about the case.

(Continued from page 84)
a check on the power of each level of government.

Reviewing Themes

1. By distributing power, the federal system prevents any one branch or level of government from becoming too powerful.

2. Some critics say federal mandates violate states' rights, and others argue that the federal government should provide funding for any mandates.

Thinking Critically

1. Students may argue that federal interference violates states' rights, or they may say federal involvement promotes the public good.

2. Students may say that conflicts between states and between state and federal governments would have no opportunity for resolution.

3. They must establish boundaries for House districts, set rules for electing members to Congress and for choosing presidential electors, pay the cost of running elections, and maintain National Guard units.

4. States would no longer have to recognize other states' civil laws. Students should offer examples.

Building Social Studies Skills

1. c.

2. Students may say that the artist seems to be criticizing the federal government for expanding.

3. b.

4. Many freed slaves would not have been able to vote because they could not read. As long as the federal government supports equal opportunity, limits that keep federal authority supreme prevent state governments from violating that principle.

LAB OBJECTIVES

The Unit 1 Public Policy Lab incorporates the following objectives:
- investigate issues relating to students' rights.
- compare other schools constitutions to students' own school constitutions.
- use a decision-making process to create a bill of rights for students' own school constitution.

Using the Lab

Before beginning the lab, organize students into groups and distribute copies of the Public Policy Lab Unit 1 Activity found in *Unit Tests and Unit Lab Activities with Answer Key.* Then have students read the assignment on this page. Discuss the assignment with students and point out the documents on pages 87–89 that students will use during the lab.

The What Do You Think? questions will help guide students during the project. In addition, the lab worksheet includes a step-by-step checklist for students to monitor their progress. For assessment guidelines, see the Group Activity rubric in the *Alternative Assessment Handbook.*

PUBLIC POLICY LAB

You Make the Decision

Drafting a Bill of Rights

You are a member of your school's student council. Your principal has asked the council to prepare a proposal for a bill of rights to be adopted as an amendment to your school's constitution. Next month, your principal will present the proposal at a school-board meeting open to all parents, students, and members of the community.

The school administration has received numerous phone calls and letters from students, parents, and community organizations concerned about the rights of students. Your principal has provided a copy of the following documents: your school's constitution, a bill of rights recently adopted by another high school in your city, and two of the letters she has received.

Government Notebook Assignment

Record your decision-making process in your Government Notebook.

1. Review the documents and answer the WHAT DO YOU THINK? questions.
2. You and the other members of the council (your group) should identify key issues that need to be addressed in your proposed bill of rights.
3. Once you have identified the key issues, the council needs to gather additional information. You may want to study articles on student rights issues and search for policies established by other student councils.
4. As a council, discuss the results of your research. Identify which key issues you would like to address in your proposed bill. Predict the consequences that addressing certain key issues could have on your proposed bill being accepted and on your fellow students.
5. Implement your decision by drafting your proposed bill of rights. Make sure your proposed bill clearly states the rights guaranteed to students.

Highland High School
Federal Heights, CO 80221

Office of Kate Stevenson

Memorandum
Date: February 10
To: Highland High School Student Council
From: Principal Stevenson

I would like the Student Council to prepare a proposal for a school bill of rights to be presented in an open meeting of the Board of Education on the second Thursday of next month. If the suggested bill of rights meets the approval of the Board of Education, it will be proposed as an amendment to the school constitution at the next Student Council meeting. Study the Highland High School Constitution, taking note of the purpose of the constitution and the duties of the Student Council.

I have provided a copy of the bill of rights adopted by Eastside High School Student Council, which you may want to use as a model. I also have provided copies of two letters on student rights issues. After reviewing these documents, the council will need to conduct some outside research. The council should form small research groups, and each group should research the answer to one of the following questions:

- In the last 10 years, has the Supreme Court ruled on any cases concerning the violation of student rights? What were the rights in question? What was the Court's final ruling?
- What are some examples of negative and positive impacts of a student bill of rights at other high schools?
- What resources are needed to enforce a school bill of rights?
- What methods have other high schools used to reach a compromise between students and faculty members on issues of student rights?
- What are the safety and health issues associated with student rights?

There may be other questions that you will need to address as you conduct your research and analyze the constitution, model bill of rights, and letters. Below is a list of resources that might aid you in your research.

- relevant articles in the Readers' Guide to Periodical Literature
- interviews with school administrators or student council members at other high schools
- Internet sites on student issues

Thank you for your help. I look forward to reading your proposal.

STUDENT COUNCIL MEETING

When:
Wednesday, February 10, at 1 p.m.

Where:
Student Council Office, Room 112

We will be working on an important assignment from Principal Stevenson.

DON'T MISS THIS MEETING!

THE CONSTITUTION OF HIGHLAND HIGH SCHOOL

The Constitution of Highland High School is created in order that the elected members of the Student Council may establish better interaction among the students, faculty, and administration, as well as promote the well-being of the school and community.

Article I. Powers of the Student Council
All powers of the student government shall be vested in the Highland High School Student Council.

Article II. Membership of the Council
A. The council shall consist of no more than 40 members.
  1. The council membership shall include 10 elected representatives from each grade.
    (a) Council members from all grades except 9 shall be elected by their respective grades before May 30 of each year.
    (b) Council members from grade 9 shall be elected by their respective grade before October 31 of each year.
B. A vacancy on the Student Council shall be filled by the student who was next in line in the election results or through appointment by the faculty adviser.
C. Any Student Council member who is suspended from school will be removed from the Student Council.

Article III. Meetings of the Council
A. The Student Council shall meet after school once a week from the beginning of September through May 30.
B. The Student Council shall meet once a month during the school day. This meeting shall take place on the second Wednesday of each month.
C. The president or adviser may call special meetings as needed.
D. Meetings will not commence without a quorum, or one half of the present Student Council membership plus the faculty adviser.

Article IV. Duties of the Council
The duties of the Student Council shall be:
A. To represent student opinion.
B. To discuss any concerns of the student body and to initiate action.
C. To act as a liaison between the students and faculty.
D. To promote involvement in school-sponsored activities or events.
E. To organize and promote student government elections.

Article V. Amending the Constitution
The constitution may be amended by a two-thirds vote of the entire membership of the Student Council. Any proposed amendment to the Constitution must be typed in its entirety and proposed before the Student Council in the meeting during which the vote is taken. All Student Council members will have the opportunity to present arguments for or against the proposed amendment during this meeting.

Ratified January 22, 2002

What Do You Think?

Answers

1. Answers will vary, but students should explain any reasons this bill of rights would or would not be appropriate for their school. Students should identify important issues that were not addressed.

2. Answers will vary, but students should demonstrate a thorough analysis of the organizations and people involved in their school.

What Do You Think?

Answers

1. She thinks that Mr. Lee should not have been allowed to censor the type of articles that the newspaper is allowed to publish.

2. the students' views

3. It would give students the right to express their opinions and also give them the means to make those opinions available to the students for whom the paper is intended.

PUBLIC POLICY LAB *continued*

EASTSIDE HIGH SCHOOL
BILL OF RIGHTS

Amendment I
Students have the right to publish school newspapers, yearbooks, newsletters, and literary magazines expressing their opinions. Students have the right to express their opinions openly and participate in speech demonstrations as long as they do not commit violent acts, break laws, or disturb others.

Amendment II
Students have the right to present complaints and concerns to school officials through the Student Concerns Committee.

Amendment III
Student representatives and school administrators shall together create a code of conduct for acceptable student behavior.

Amendment IV
Students' grades shall reflect academic performance. Students' opinions or conduct in matters unrelated to established academic standards shall not be evaluated in the grading process.

Amendment V
Students shall have the right to participate in curriculum development through the student and faculty committees established by the school administration and the Student Council.

Amendment VI
School administrators may not restrict students' right to dress or appear as they choose unless it can be determined that a student's dress or appearance may present health or safety hazards.

◄ WHAT DO YOU THINK?

1. Do the rights guaranteed in this document address the needs of the students at your school? What issues or concerns are not addressed in this bill of rights?

2. Does your school have the necessary organizations and people to ensure protection of these rights?

Principal Kate Stevenson
Highland High School
Federal Heights, CO 80221

Dear Principal Stevenson:

I am the editor in chief of the *Highland Star*. Last month, a fellow student submitted a letter to the editor criticizing the school administration for its new policy that bans all nonschool-sponsored clubs or groups from holding meetings on school property.

Our newspaper adviser, Paul Lee, would not allow this letter to be printed in the school newspaper. He felt that because the letter criticized you and other school administrators, it should not be published. Mr. Lee does not want the newspaper to become an outlet for student complaints and criticism of school administrators.

Although I do not completely agree with what was written in this particular letter, I feel that the *Highland Star* should be accessible to all students no matter what their opinions of school faculty and administration might be. Teachers and administrators should not limit students' right to express their opinions in their own newspaper. I hope that the school administrators will consider creating some policies to protect students' right to free speech.

Sincerely,

Elizabeth Reynolds

Elizabeth Reynolds
Editor in Chief
Highland Star

WHAT DO YOU THINK? ►

1. Why does Elizabeth Reynolds think that Mr. Lee's decision violated students' right to free speech?

2. Whose views does Elizabeth Reynolds think the school newspaper should represent?

3. How would an amendment protecting freedom of speech make the Highland Star more accessible to students?

P·Q·E   Parents for Quality Education
2270 Deer Creek Drive, Suite 714 • Federal Heights, CO 80221

Principal Kate Stevenson
Highland High School
Federal Heights, CO 80221

Dear Principal Stevenson:

As an organization of concerned parents and community members, Parents for Quality Education (PQE) is disturbed by a growing problem in local junior high and high schools. We have noticed an increasing popularity in extreme and unkempt dress and hairstyles among students. PQE feels that inappropriate extremes in the dress styles of students disrupt the learning environment and can lead to disorder in the classroom.

We hope that the Highland High School administration will more carefully regulate the appearance of its students by adopting a school dress code. By establishing a dress code, the disruptive influence that inappropriate dress styles have on students will be eliminated, making the teachers' jobs easier and the school environment more conducive to learning.

Please do not hesitate to contact our organization with any comments or questions. We would be pleased to meet with members of the school administration to discuss policy changes in this area. PQE is concerned about the education of the community's youth, and we want to help make our schools the best that they can be.

Sincerely,

George Hernandez

George Hernandez
Chairman
Parents for Quality Education

◄WHAT DO YOU THINK?

1. What policy does PQE think school administrators should adopt?

2. Would this type of policy violate students' rights?

3. What reasons does PQE give to support the adoption of this policy?

internet connect

Internet Activity go.hrw.com
KEYWORD: SV3 GVPL

Access the Internet through the HRW Go site to employ a decision-making process to draft a student bill of rights. Use the research links and the decision-making tutorial that are provided to your group to complete the Government Notebook Assignment.

What Do You Think?
Answers
1. a dress code policy

2. According to Amendment VI, unless a student's dress is presenting health or safety hazards, the school administration does not have the right to restrict his or her appearance.

3. PQE argues that the unkempt appearance of many students leads to disruptive behavior in the classroom and thus infringes on the teacher's ability to adequately instruct his or her class.

Lesson Options

Suggestions for customizing the material in Unit 2 to fit the specific schedule and curriculum of your classroom are located at the beginning of each chapter.

Main Idea

Ask each student to read the Main Ideas and briefly answer each question in writing. Later, when you have finished Unit 2, ask students to return to their original answers and revise them using what they learned in the unit.

PUBLIC POLICY LAB

The Unit 2 Public Policy Lab appears on pages 136–39. This project is a real-world assignment in which students will work in groups to prepare a written recommendation on a proposed amendment to the U.S. Constitution.

Support materials for the lab appear in *Unit Tests and Unit Lab Activities with Answer Key.*

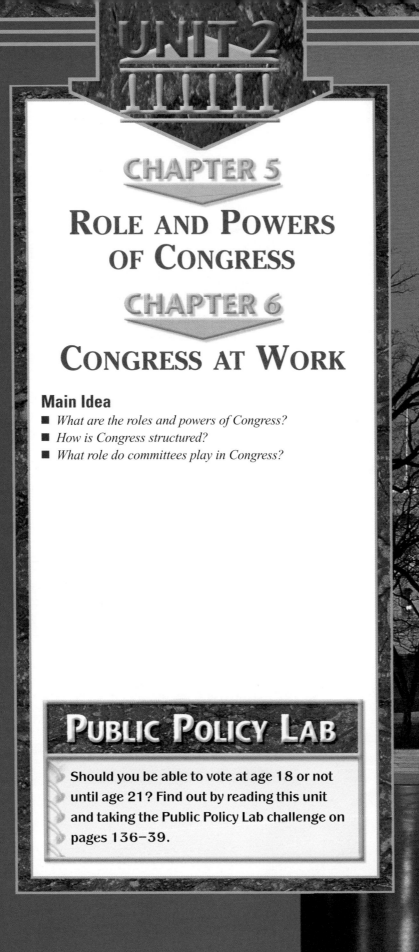

UNIT 2

CHAPTER 5

ROLE AND POWERS OF CONGRESS

CHAPTER 6

CONGRESS AT WORK

Main Idea

- *What are the roles and powers of Congress?*
- *How is Congress structured?*
- *What role do committees play in Congress?*

PUBLIC POLICY LAB

Should you be able to vote at age 18 or not until age 21? Find out by reading this unit and taking the Public Policy Lab challenge on pages 136–39.

LEGISLATIVE BRANCH

Unit 2 introduces students to various concepts involving the legislative branch, including how Congress makes laws, oversees agencies, and helps constituents; the makeup of and the qualifications for both the House of Representatives and the Senate; the expressed, special, implied, and denied powers of Congress; the terms, sessions, and rules of Congress; the kinds of committees in and the resources of Congress; how a bill becomes a law; and how Congress promotes the public good.

Teaching with Photographs

The Capitol Building was originally designed by Dr. William Thornton. His 1793 plan was one of many submitted for the building. It won him $500 and a plot of land within the city. The south wing, also known as the House wing, was completed in 1807 under Benjamin H. Latrobe's leadership. The modern-day Senate and House wings were built by Thomas U. Walter during the 1850s and 1860s.

The Capitol is topped by a cast-iron dome, which is topped with the Statue of Freedom. The bronze statue is more than 19 feet tall and weighs close to 15,000 pounds.

CHAPTER 5 ROLE AND POWERS OF CONGRESS

	OBJECTIVES	PACING GUIDE	REPRODUCIBLE RESOURCES
SECTION 1 **ROLE OF CONGRESS** (pp. 93–97)	▶ What influences how members of Congress vote? ▶ What purpose do congressional investigations serve? ▶ Why is it important for members of Congress to serve their constituents?	**Regular** 1 day **Block Scheduling** .5 day	**ELL** Spanish Study Guide 5.1 **ELL** English Study Guide 5.1 **PS** Reading 66: *Profiles in Courage*
SECTION 2 **HOUSES AND MEMBERS OF CONGRESS** (pp. 98–104)	▶ How do the houses of Congress differ in their structure and membership? ▶ How are congressional districts drawn? ▶ What is the typical profile of a U.S. congressmember?	**Regular** 1.5 days **Block Scheduling** .75 day	**ELL** Spanish Study Guide 5.2 **ELL** English Study Guide 5.2
SECTION 3 **POWERS OF CONGRESS** (pp. 105–108)	▶ To what main areas of governing do Congress's expressed powers apply? ▶ What special powers does Congress hold? ▶ What are the implied powers of Congress? ▶ What constitutional limits exist on congressional powers?	**Regular** 1 day **Block Scheduling** .5 day	**ELL** Spanish Study Guide 5.3 **ELL** English Study Guide 5.3 **E** Challenge and Enrichment Activity 5 **E** Simulations and Strategies for Teaching American Government: Activity 5

Chapter Resource Key

PS	Primary Sources	**A**	Assessment		Video
RS	Reading Support	**REV**	Review		Videodisc
E	Enrichment	**ELL**	Reinforcement and English Language Learners		Internet
S	Simulations		Transparencies		Holt Presentation Maker Using
SM	Skills Mastery		CD-ROM		Microsoft ® PowerPoint ®

TECHNOLOGY RESOURCES	REINFORCEMENT, REVIEW, AND ASSESSMENT
💿 One-Stop Planner: Lesson 5.1 🌐 Researcher Online 🌐 Homework Practice Online 📽 Transparency 4 💿 Global Skill Builder CD-ROM	**REV** Section 1 Review, p. 97 **A** Daily Quiz 5.1
💿 One-Stop Planner: Lesson 5.2 🌐 Researcher Online 🌐 Homework Practice Online 💿 Holt American Government Videodisc: *Gerrymandering: Drawing the Line* 📽 Transparency 10 💿 Global Skill Builder CD-ROM	**REV** Section 2 Review, p. 104 **A** Daily Quiz 5.2
💿 One-Stop Planner: Lesson 5.3 🌐 Researcher Online 🌐 Homework Practice Online 📽 Transparency 11 📼 CNN Presents American Government	**REV** Section 3 Review, p. 108 **A** Daily Quiz 5.3

Chapter Review and Assessment

SM Global Skill Builder CD-ROM
🌐 HRW Go site
REV Chapter 5 Tutorial for Students, Parents, and Peers
REV Chapter 5 Review, pp. 110–111
💿 Chapter 5 Test Generator (on the One-Stop Planner)
A Chapter 5 Test Alternative Assessment Handbook

One-Stop Planner CD–ROM

It's easy to plan lessons, select resources, and print out materials for your students when you use the *One-Stop Planner CD-ROM with Test Generator.*

📶 internet connect

HRW ONLINE RESOURCES
Go to: **go.hrw.com**
Then type in a keyword.

TEACHER HOME PAGE
KEYWORD: SV3 Teacher

CHAPTER INTERNET ACTIVITIES
KEYWORD: SV3 GV5
Choose an activity on Congress to:
▶ compare and contrast the roles, requirements, and powers of both houses of Congress
▶ create a campaign poster for a congressional campaign
▶ create a pamphlet on the Watergate scandal

CHAPTER ENRICHMENT LINKS
KEYWORD: SV3 CH5

HOLT RESEACHER ONLINE
KEYWORD: Holt Reseacher

ONLINE ASSESSMENT
Homework Practice
KEYWORD: SV3 HP5
Standardized Test Prep
KEYWORD: SV3 STP5
Rubrics
KEYWORD: SS Rubrics

ONLINE MAPS, CHARTS, AND GRAPHS
KEYWORD: SV3 MCG
▶ Sizes of Legislatures
▶ U.S. House Representation after the 2000 Census
▶ Gerrymandering
▶ The Congress of the United States
▶ Expressed Powers of Congress
▶ Powers Denied to Congress

CONTENT UPDATES
KEYWORD: SS Content Updates

HOLT PRESENTATION MAKER
KEYWORD: SV3 PPT5

CURRENT EVENTS
KEYWORD: S3 Current Events

OBJECTIVES

▶ List influences that cause members of Congress to vote in certain ways.

▶ Discuss the purpose of congressional investigations.

▶ Discuss the importance of members of Congress serving their constituents.

MOTIVATE

Tell students to imagine that they have each been elected to represent their state in Congress. Instruct students to prepare an outline of a speech to be given to constituents describing how they plan to vote and serve in the upcoming congressional session. Have volunteers share the issues that they feel should be addressed. Discuss the similarities and differences in the outlines with the entire class. Ask students if they think that congressional delegates actually accomplish what they pledge. As a lead-in to this section, tell students that they will be learning about the actual role of Congress.

TEACH

Building a Vocabulary

In spiral notebooks, have students create a Political Dictionary to be used throughout the course. The dictionary may be used as an activity at the start of each new section; it may also be used as a modification device for students having difficulty or sheltered English students during tests and homework assignments. List words the students will be expected to know for this section on the board. Have students list, define, and give an example of each of the terms, using information provided in the text or on the *Researcher CD-ROM*.

Practicing Skills

Discuss with students the factors that influence how a member of Congress votes. Ask students to expand on the outlines they created in the Motivate activity by including current issues in their speech. Have students use newspapers or magazines to research current issues to form an opinion on each issue. Students should also list groups that may want to influence the congressmember's vote on each decision. Have volunteers give their speeches to the class and discuss the

participants identified as seeking to influence each issue. As a transition to the next activity, tell students that they will be learning more about these influences.

Recognizing Point of View

Assign a topic to each of four or five cooperative learning groups. Topics could include a range of current issues relevant to students' states of residence, such as tobacco regulation, logging and habitat protection, insect control, and airport security measures. Instruct students to work together to write a letter to constituents from the point of view of a congressional staff member regarding an upcoming vote in Congress. (Students may want to peruse newspapers for current topics before beginning this activity.) Students should relate their congressmember's point of view on an issue important to the region he or she has been elected to represent. Tell students that at least one of the four voting influences should be addressed in the letter to show awareness and understanding of influences on voting. As a transition to the next activity, tell students that they will learn about the purposes of congressional investigations.

Conducting Research

Give students the option of researching the purposes of congressional investigations or the ways that congressmembers respond to constituents. Have them prepare a short report to present to the class. Topics could include examples and explanations of recent congressional investigations or examples of political action committees and how these committees influence Congress. Tell students that they will use their reports in the Close activity.

Developing Life Skills

Ask students to contact various community members or persons in their families and find out whether these individuals have ever written or wanted to write to a congressperson. Then have students write a letter to their representative on behalf of a person (or group of individuals) who is experiencing a problem that calls for government action or who would like to urge support for a particular government action or bill in Congress. If a student cannot locate a person(s) needing help, have them write on their own behalf or gather ideas from recent newspapers or magazines. Students might also choose to interview school personnel to find a topic.

CLOSE

Conduct a discussion with the class on the purposes of congressional investigations and the ways that congressmembers respond to constituents. Have students cite examples from their reports created in the Conducting Research activity. Discuss with students the significance of congressional investigations into improper conduct and of constituents attempting to influence members of Congress. Encourage students to write to their representatives regularly to offer their opinion on issues.

Students Having Difficulty/ Sheltered English Students

 First, have students tape-record a letter to a congressperson in their district about a topic of interest to them or community members. Then have students exchange their recording with another student. Finally, have each student transcribe the recording they have received into a letter to be sent to a congressional representative. Encourage students to use vocabulary from the chapter in their letters.

Visual-Spatial Learners/Gifted Learners

Have students devise a survey that addresses at least 10 serious community concerns, such as spending on education and public transportation. Then instruct students to have at least 10 community members complete the survey. Encourage students to interview as wide a variety of people as possible. Have students create a chart that summarizes the findings of their survey. Discuss the results of individual charts to identify examples of bias, propaganda, point of view, or frame of reference discovered by students' research.

Gifted Learners

 Discuss with students the significance of congressional oversight of government agencies. Explain to students that oversight may include reviewing an agency's overall operation or may investigate one specific aspect of an agency. Have students use newspapers, magazines, and the Internet to investigate congressional oversight. Students should then write a report that discusses the agency being investigated, the reason for the investigation, the extent of the investigation, and the decision made by Congress. Encourage students to discuss their findings with the class.

REVIEW

Have students complete the Section 1 Review on page 97. Use the answers in the Annotated Teacher's Edition to assess student mastery of this section.

ASSESS

To assess student mastery of this section, have students complete Daily Quiz 5.1 in *Daily Quizzes with Answer Key*. For additional assessment options, see *Alternative Assessment Handbook* on the *One-Stop Planner CD-ROM*.

ADDITIONAL RESOURCES

Rosenthal, Alan. *The Third House: Lobbyists and Lobbying in the States.* 1993. CQ Press.

Herrnson, Paul; Clyde Wilcox, and Ronald Shaiko, eds. *The Interest Group Connection.* 1998. Seven Bridges Press.

Crotty, William, and Mildred Schwartz. *Representing Interests and Interest Group Representation.* 1994. University Press of America.

Rothenberg, Lawrence. *Linking Citizens to Government: Interest Group Politics at Common Cause.* 1992. Cambridge University Press.

HOUSES AND MEMBERS OF CONGRESS

TEXTBOOK PAGES 98–104

HOLT PRESENTATION MAKER
Access Illustrated LECTURE
NOTES using Microsoft®
PowerPoint® on the
One-Stop Planner CD-ROM

OBJECTIVES

▸ Explain how the houses of Congress differ in their structure and membership.

▸ Provide a description of how congressional districts are drawn.

▸ Discuss the typical congressperson's profile.

MOTIVATE

Count off all students in class by ones and twos. Inform the ones that they are campaign managers/speechwriters and the twos that they are congressional candidates. Direct ones to pair off with twos or pair students off ahead of time. Give students time to devise a campaign strategy, slogan, and short speech to announce their candidacies for Congress. Videotape the campaign managers' introductions and the candidates' speeches. Show the videotaped speeches and ask students to identify the personality type that candidates are trying to portray in their speeches. Discuss these characteristics with the class and ask the class if they feel it is important for members of Congress to fit a specific personality type. Afterward, tell students that in this section they will be learning about the makeup of Congress and of its members.

TEACH

Building a Vocabulary

In their spiral notebooks, have students continue working on their Political Dictionary. List words the students will be expected to know for this section on the board. Have students list, define, and give an example of each of the terms, using information provided in the text or on the *Researcher CD-ROM*

Comparing and Contrasting

Divide the class into three groups. Assign different groups to research the structure and membership of their state legislature, the House of Representatives, and the Senate. The final group product should include a written report along with a visual to represent the contrasting information. Have the groups compare the varying legislative branches. Tell students that in the next activity they will learn about how congressional districts are determined.

Understanding Maps/Creating Maps

Obtain current voting district maps from several states using the Internet or by contacting local politicians. Assign pairs of students a specific state to research. Information to be gathered should include the state's population, land area, population density, and the number of representatives in the U.S. Congress. Students may use the State Profiles section on the *Holt Researcher Online* to gather this information. Instruct students to draw voting districts based on their research. After pairs have completed their maps, give them the current official voting district map from their state to compare. Finally, discuss with students the actual ways that districts are drawn. Ask students to give their opinions about whether racial or ethnic backgrounds should be considered when creating district boundaries. Discuss the controversy surrounding this issue with the class. Tell students that in the next activity they will learn about the profile of a typical congressmember.

Role-Playing

Have students work in pairs. One member of each team will be responsible for writing a job description for a senator or a representative and preparing interview questions for each candidate. The other team member will be responsible for preparing a résumé as if she or he is "applying" for the position of senator or representative. Have team members role-play as interviewer/interviewee. Discuss with students the profile of a typical congressmember.

CLOSE

Have students write to one of their congressmembers and express their views on a number of issues discussed in class, such as voting influences, congressional investigations, and qualifications for office. Have students state what they have learned about these issues and share their suggestions for changes. Ask students to request feedback about their opinions. Let students share replies to their letters with the rest of the class over the course of the semester.

OPTIONS

Logical-Mathematical Learners

 Students may research and present findings concerning changing demographics in their state and one other state. Based on current and past census findings, have students prepare pie charts to illustrate percentages of major ethnic groups in each state currently and ten years ago. Then instruct students to research and prepare pie charts to illustrate percentages of representatives in Congress from each major ethnic group currently and ten years ago in both states. Have students compare the similarities or differences between the data they gathered on the ethnic makeup of the state populations with the ethnic backgrounds of the members of Congress from those states.

Visual-Spatial Learners

 Have students work in pairs to create Venn diagrams to illustrate the requirements of membership in the House of Representatives and in the Senate. Encourage students to use their imaginations to create icons to represent the individual requirements for serving in either house.

REVIEW

Have students complete the Section 2 Review on page 104. Use the answers in the Annotated Teacher's Edition to assess student mastery of this section.

ASSESS

To assess student mastery of this section, have students complete Daily Quiz 5.2 in *Daily Quizzes with Answer Key.* For additional assessment options, see *Alternative Assessment Handbook* on the *One-Stop Planner CD-ROM.*

ADDITIONAL RESOURCES

Gertzog, Irwin. *Congressional Women: Their Recruitment, Treatment, and Behavior.* 1984. Praeger.

Monmonier, Mark. *Bushmanders and Bullwinkles: How Politicians Manipulate Electronic Maps and Census Data to Win Elections.* 2001. University of Chicago Press.

Rush, Mark. *Does Redistricting Make a Difference?: Partisan Representation and Electoral Behavior.* 2001. Lexington Books.

Shannon, W. Wayne. *Party, Constituency, and Congressional Voting: A Study of Legislative Behavior in the United States House of Representatives.* 1981. Greenwood Press.

LESSON 5.3 POWERS OF CONGRESS

TEXTBOOK PAGES 105–108

OBJECTIVES

▶ List the main areas of governing contained in Congress's expressed powers.
▶ Describe special powers granted to Congress by the Constitution.
▶ Describe Congress's implied powers.
▶ Explain constitutional limits on congressional powers.

MOTIVATE

Read to the class an imaginary message from the president asking Congress to declare war on an imaginary country. Then tell students that this is a typical way that a president would seek support for declaring war, but that this is not a real situation. Ask students to classify which type of power—expressed, special, or implied—Congress would be called on to exercise after such a speech. Facilitate a discussion of the three types of powers and have students brainstorm examples of each. Tell students that in this section they will be learning about the powers of Congress.

MOTIVATE

Building a Vocabulary

In their spiral notebooks, have students continue working on their Political Dictionary. List words the students will be expected to know for this section on the board. Have students list, define, and give an example of each of the terms, using information provided in the text or on the *Researcher CD-ROM.*

Organizing Ideas/Information

Instruct students to first organize the expressed powers of Congress into five main areas using the Expressed Powers of Congress chart on page 105, class notes, or library research. Next, have each group choose one of the five main areas and create a game show or board game to help fellow students remember the expressed powers. The games can be elaborate or simple, depending on block scheduling and/or teacher preference. Discuss each of the types of powers that Congress possesses and offer

examples of each. As a transition to the next activity, tell students that they will be learning more about the special powers of Congress.

Conducting Research

Instruct students to investigate one of these topics dealing with the special powers of Congress: (a) Richard M. Nixon's 1974 threatened impeachment; (b) Bill Clinton's impeachment trial; (c) the North American Free Trade Agreement (NAFTA) approval background; (d) the electoral college process in the 2000 presidential election; or (e) the confirmation process of Supreme Court appointees during the last 10 years. Have each student prepare a report to be presented to the class that discusses the use of one of the above-mentioned special powers. Tell students that in the next activity they will be learning about the implied powers of Congress.

Debating Ideas/Role-Playing

Have students investigate Supreme Court cases that involve the implied powers of Congress, such as the case of *McCulloch* v. *Maryland,* which can be found in the Supreme Court Docket section on the *Holt Researcher Online.* Divide the class into three groups—the Supreme Court, the state of Maryland, and McCulloch. Instruct each group to organize its points and elect one or several group members to present arguments. Finally, have the students in the Supreme Court group discuss the case, then render a decision based on their research.

Evaluating Ideas/Information

Have students write an analysis of ways that the powers of Congress have been limited, such as the Tenth Amendment to the U.S. Constitution. First, have students discuss the meaning of the imposed limit, then have them give examples of rights held by individual states. Next, tell students they have been asked to testify before Congress regarding the constitutionality of an existing law (e.g., the Americans with Disabilities Act). Tell students that their papers should either support or oppose the limit imposed on Congress and indicate whether or not Congress overstepped its bounds when it passed the law in question.

CLOSE

Ask students to make a list of the powers of the national government and a list of powers that reside with the individual states. Note that the Tenth Amendment does not specifically list the powers of the states. Have students pretend to become time travelers and travel to the future or to the past, then choose one or two powers granted to the states for discussion. After group discussion have individual members write an editorial for a past or present newspaper, commenting on the results of the use or misuse of these powers. Students may choose either to "rewrite" history (e.g., Illinois decides to print its own currency) or write the results of future events (e.g., Maine secedes from the United States).

OPTIONS

Students Having Difficulty/Sheltered English Students

  Ask students to pair with classmates and swap editorials from the Close activity. Have students read their editorials aloud as if they were giving commentary on television. Then instruct the other student to write out the main points and discuss each of them with their partner.

Body-Kinesthetic Learners

  Have students form groups of four to five. Instruct students that they will be writing an advertising campaign for the game they created in the Organizing Ideas/Information activity earlier in this section. Have groups focus on highlighting the expressed powers of Congress in their advertisements. Encourage each group to create a different type of advertisement such as print ads, radio ads, or television ads.

REVIEW

Have students complete the Section 3 Review on page 108. Use the answers in the Annotated Teacher's Edition to assess student mastery of this section.

ASSESS

To assess student mastery of this section, have students complete Daily Quiz 5.3 in *Daily Quizzes with Answer Key*. For additional assessment options, see *Alternative Assessment Handbook* on the *One-Stop Planner CD-ROM*.

RETEACH

For students having difficulty with the lessons, have them complete Reteaching Activity 5. This activity is located in *Reteaching Activities with Answer Key*.

ADDITIONAL RESOURCES

Granstaff, Bill. *Losing Our Democratic Spirit: Congressional Deliberation and the Dictatorship of Propaganda*. 1999. Praeger.

Reedy, George. *The U.S. Senate: Paralysis or a Search for Consensus?* 1986. Crown Publishers.

One Woman, One Vote. 1995. Educational Film Center. (video)

Charge and Countercharge: A Film of the Era of Senator Joseph R. McCarthy. 1981. Document Associates. (video)

CHAPTER 5

GOVERNMENT NOTEBOOK

The Government Notebook is a journal activity that encourages students to consider basic concepts of government that relate to their lives. A follow-up notebook activity appears on page 110.

WHY IT MATTERS TODAY

To find additional lesson plans dealing with the U.S. Congress, visit **CNNfyi.com** or have students complete the **GOVERNMENT IN THE NEWS** activity on page 109.

CNNfyi.com

ROLE AND POWERS OF CONGRESS

Unlike the capitals of Europe—which had grown as important cities for hundreds of years before becoming centers of government—Washington, D.C., was a planned city. It was designed in 1791 by French architect Pierre Charles L'Enfant, with the help of Benjamin Banneker and other surveyors.

The city was located on an area of flat and marshy land carved from Maryland. L'Enfant described a hill in the area as a "pedestal waiting for a monument." On that pedestal, he placed the home of Congress. This was a deliberate statement about the importance that the framers gave to the national legislature.

Although it has changed greatly since L'Enfant chose its location, Congress remains a vital part of the federal government. This chapter looks at the roles, houses, members, and powers of this important legislative body.

GOVERNMENT NOTEBOOK

In your Government Notebook, describe what characteristics and qualifications you think members of Congress should have in order to carry out their work.

WHY IT MATTERS TODAY

The U.S. Congress serves as the people's voice in government. At the end of this chapter visit **CNNfyi.com** to learn more about how Congress works for all Americans.

CNNfyi.com

SECTION 1

ROLE OF CONGRESS

READ TO DISCOVER

1. What influences how members of Congress vote?
2. What purpose do congressional investigations serve?
3. Why is it important for members of Congress to serve their constituents?

POLITICAL DICTIONARY

constituent
interest group
political action committee
oversight

Congress—the legislative branch of the federal government—was so important to the framers of the Constitution that it was the first branch of government they discussed in the Constitution. In addition, Congress's structure and powers are outlined in much more detail than are those of the executive and judicial branches.

Congress has three key roles. Its main role is to legislate, or to make laws. However, it also oversees the performance of government agencies and provides services to the people its members represent.

Making Laws

Congress is responsible for making the nation's laws. How do members of Congress make these policy decisions? What influences how they vote?

Some of the choices that members of Congress face are easy to make. For example, suppose that a member votes for increasing Social Security benefits for older people. This decision reflects the member's personal beliefs. The member's district also has a large number of retirees that support such a policy. Interest groups representing older people have contributed a lot of money to the member's campaign fund. The leadership of the member's political party supports the legislation. Thus, the decision to support increases in Social Security benefits is easy.

Many times, however, the decisions facing members of Congress are not so easy because the forces influencing a member's vote can conflict. How do members make decisions in these more difficult situations? They must weigh the conflicting influences—in particular, their personal beliefs, constituents' interests, interest groups' concerns, and political party loyalty. The power of these influences varies from issue to issue and from member to member.

Personal Beliefs Studies show that a congressperson's personal beliefs about what promotes the public good significantly influence his or her voting decisions. Members sometimes follow their personal beliefs even when those beliefs go against the wishes of voters back home.

In 1990 many members of Congress voted against a constitutional amendment that would have banned flag burning, even though the proposed amendment had a high level of support in

PUBLIC GOOD *Representative Richard Gephardt of Missouri addresses a crowd.* **Do you think members of Congress should support local interests over general national interests?**

SECTION 1

ROLE OF CONGRESS

Lesson Plans

For teaching strategies, see Lesson 5.1 located at the beginning of this chapter or the One-Stop Planner Strategy 5.1.

Political Dictionary

To reinforce the section's vocabulary terms, refer students to the Electronic Glossary on the *Researcher CD-ROM.*

Section Assessment

To assess students' mastery of this section, have them complete Daily Quiz 5.1 in *Daily Quizzes with Answer Key.*

Caption Answer

Answers will vary, but students should discuss the responsibility of representing local interests while promoting the public good of the nation.

Transparency

An overhead transparency of the cartoon on this page is available in *Transparency Resources*. See Cartoon Transparency 4: Constituent Interests.

Caption Answer

Answers will vary, but students should discuss the influence that contributions from interest groups may have, and should offer support for their opinion.

---

their districts. Some of these members believed that such an amendment would limit citizens' right of free speech. Others thought that the matter could be handled in a standard piece of legislation rather than in a constitutional amendment. In this case, the members' own views about what best serves the public outweighed concerns about going against the wishes of voters in their district.

Constituents' Interests Congressmembers' voting decisions also are influenced by the wishes of the people they represent. Members of Congress are elected to serve as representatives of the people. Unlike the president, who is elected by all voting U.S. citizens, members of Congress are elected by people who live in one locality (a district or a state). This means that even though Congress makes laws for the whole country, members answer only to the people of their locality.

A grasp of this situation is crucial to understanding how members of Congress behave in making laws. A member represents his or her **constituents**—the residents of his or her district or state—and must consider how policy decisions will affect them, not just the country as a whole. For example, when members from farming areas debate new agricultural policies, they must consider the effects of those policies on farmers in their districts.

The public is divided over whether members of Congress should support local interests (their district or state) over general national interests (the nation). Polls do show that most people think

members should consider the public good over local interests, and many people will even criticize members for not doing so. Polls also show, however, that most people expect their congressmembers to take care of their local interests.

Interest Groups A third force influencing congressional voting is **interest groups**—people acting together to achieve shared political goals. Interest groups provide information on issues, suggest legislation to congressmembers, and promote legislation that is favorable to their groups. They also contribute to members' campaigns through **political action committees** (PACs). PACs are separate political branches of interest groups formed for the purpose of participating in politics and giving money to candidates. (The role of interest groups in the political system is more fully explained in Chapters 6 and 17.)

How do such contributions influence members' voting behavior? Some evidence shows that congressmembers who vote for a bill favored by a certain interest group have received on average far larger campaign contributions from that group than have members voting against the bill. This finding may be misleading, however. No conflict might exist between the members' personal views and those of the interest group. Besides, interest groups often contribute to a campaign to help elect someone who already is sympathetic to their goal, not because they are trying to sway that person to their point of view.

PRINCIPLES OF DEMOCRACY *Interest groups are sometimes criticized for using campaign contributions to try to influence congressional candidates and get them to see their group's point of view.* **Do you think that interest groups have the power to influence how a member of Congress votes on a bill?**

Careers in Government

Congressmember

Investigative hearings and debates on the floors of the House and Senate are familiar images of Congress. Much of a congressmember's work, however, takes place behind the scenes, away from the news media. Members of Congress have unpredictable schedules full of meetings and appointments. A congressmember usually works around 60 hours a week, and he or she is constantly on call for emergency meetings on pressing matters.

Members of Congress spend an average of three hours a day in the office. The rest of their time is spent meeting with constituents and interest groups, attending committee meetings, traveling to and from their home districts, and presenting, preparing, and voting on bills. An effective congressmember must have excellent communication skills, an awareness of his or her constituents' interests, and plenty of energy to maintain a fast-paced, hectic schedule.

Two of a congressmember's most important jobs, the researching and writing of bills, take place through committee meetings. The committee system allows work to be divided among members and adds to Congress's efficiency. Representatives are assigned to serve on at least one committee, and senators sit on at least two. (The committee system is discussed in Chapter 6.)

Statistically, the typical member of Congress is a college-educated, white male around 52 years old. Anyone, however, can be elected to Congress, regardless of color, sex, profession, or economic status. In 1917, for example, Jeannette Rankin defied statistics to become the first congresswoman. Then in 1969, Shirley Chisholm became the first African American woman in Congress.

Members of Congress, such as Senator Olympia Snowe of Maine, work long hours attending meetings, working on legislation, and traveling to their home districts.

Many members of Congress are experienced state and local politicians. Congress, however, is made up of people from all walks of life and a diversity of experience and training. For example, Representative Steve Largent was a professional football player, and Representative Lynn Woolsey ran a consulting business for 12 years.

How do you become a member of Congress? Learning about the political process is the first step. One way to do that is by entering a congressional internship program offered through a university. Internships provide an opportunity to get an inside look at Congress in action.

Political Party Loyalty Party loyalty also affects how members of Congress vote. In fact, party loyalty on key votes in Congress has increased over the past 20 years. In 1994, for example, nearly every Republican running for the House of Representatives signed the Contract with America, a set of proposed legislative reforms. Then, in early 1995, almost every House Republican voted for most of the Contract's provisions.

Reasons for increased party loyalty include strong party leadership in Congress and in congressional election campaigns. In addition, members of the same party have increasingly shared more of the same political beliefs and values.

PRINCIPLES OF DEMOCRACY *Senator Barbara Boxer of California speaks to constituents at a luncheon.* **Why do you think that more people do not request help from members of Congress?**

Overseeing Agencies

Congress also is responsible for overseeing the performance of government agencies. It does this through congressional **oversight**, which involves conducting investigations of agency actions and programs.

Congress oversees every aspect of agency behavior and investigates such matters as why an agency has been slow in regulating the use of a toxic chemical, whether discrimination has taken place in an agency, or why an agency's expensive new computer system is not working. Many congressional investigations involve discovering how an agency operates from day to day. Often, though, such investigations focus on abuses and scandals in government programs.

Traditionally, Congress had put little energy into congressional oversight, inspiring political scientists to label it Congress's "neglected function." Many said that members of Congress conducted so few investigations because passing new programs was more dramatic than finding out how well existing ones were working.

In recent years, however, congressional investigations have increased greatly. One reason for this is that tighter budgets have reduced the amount of money available for new programs, leading to greater scrutiny of both old and new programs.

In addition, past scandals and abuses have led many citizens to become dissatisfied with the government. The public, therefore, usually supports investgations that uncover shortcomings in government agencies. Members of Congress, in turn, find that there are political incentives, such as favorable publicity, for being involved in such investigations.

Helping Constituents

Members of Congress receive more than 200 million pieces of mail and e-mail each year. Much of this mail involves specific constituent requests, which can range from birthday greetings for a relative to major policy changes. Responding to such requests is an important part of a congressperson's job and is one way that members represent their constituents' interests.

One survey has revealed that roughly 17 percent of Americans report that they, or a member of their family, have at some time requested help from a member of Congress.

Individual Requests Most constituent mail involves issues such as obtaining information or expressing views about legislation, requesting help with finding a government job, or asking for assistance with government services, such as Social Security. Some mail, however, deals with more unusual, personal requests. As you can imagine, some of these requests cannot be fulfilled. For example, congressional offices have received requests to change a student's grade in a course at a state university. One constituent even requested assistance from a congressperson in moving a train track that he felt was too close to the fence in his backyard. As one observer says, there is often a

66 Monday morning ritual wherein the congressman returns to the Washington office from a visit to the district and empties his pockets of dozens of scraps of paper, each of which contains the name and address of

a constituent along with hastily scribbled notes about some difficulty the person is experiencing with a federal agency. **"**

Detecting Patterns Constituent service does more than merely help individual citizens. Congressional staffs look for changes and patterns in constituent requests. Such patterns may signal a problem with a government program or a change in constituents' general attitudes. For example, an increase in complaints about student loan applications being denied might send a signal to a congressional office that some change in the law is having an unwanted effect on students who are seeking loans. Members of Congress can use this information to change the system.

Handling Requests The majority of constituent service involves ordinary citizens with ordinary requests. These requests usually are handled by congressional staff members.

Occasionally, however, a constituent whom the congressmember particularly values—a close friend, generous campaign contributor, or large employer in the locality—has a problem with a government agency. After receiving this person's request for personal assistance, the member might approach the government agency directly. Of course, government agencies respond with greater urgency to requests by members of Congress than they do to similar requests from

office staff. For this reason, members of Congress must avoid using the power of their office unethically to influence agencies on behalf of a particularly valued constituent.

CONSTITUTIONAL GOVERNMENT *Congressperson Constance Morella of Maryland meets with staff in her office. What types of constituent requests might a congressional staff member handle?*

SECTION 1 REVIEW ANSWERS

1. Refer to the following pages: constituent (94), interest group (94), political action committee (94), oversight (96).

2. personal beliefs, constituents' interests, interest groups' concerns, and political party loyalty.

3a. constituents—voice approval or disapproval, may vote against a member based on policy; interest groups—provide information, organize constituents, raise money; political parties—provide assistance, publicity, and funding for party members

3b. Issues include scandals or problems involving government programs. Budget restraints require closer scrutiny of government programs, and elected officials often benefit from their involvement in such investigations.

4. Answers will vary, but students should address an issue, provide an account of the problem, and present an argument for their position.

SECTION 1 REVIEW

1. Identify and explain:
• constituent
• interest group
• political action committee
• oversight

2. Identifying Concepts: Copy the chart below. Use it to identify the various factors that influence how a member of Congress votes on legislation.

Factors that Influence how Members of Congress Vote on Legislation

Homework Practice Online
keyword: SV3 HP5

3. **Finding the Main Idea**

a. How do constituents, interest groups, and political parties influence how members of Congress vote on legislation?

b. On what types of issues do congressional investigations tend to focus? Why has the number of such investigations risen in recent years?

4. **Writing and Critical Thinking**

Problem Solving: Think about a law or regulation that affects you and that you might like to see changed. Compose a letter to your congressperson asking for assistance.

Consider the following:
• what agency enforces the law in question
• how other laws might be affected

SECTION 2

HOUSES AND MEMBERS OF CONGRESS

Lesson Plans

For teaching strategies, see Lesson 5.2 located at the beginning of this chapter or the One-Stop Planner Strategy 5.2.

Political Dictionary

To reinforce the section's vocabulary terms, refer students to the Electronic Glossary on the *Researcher CD-ROM.*

Section Assessment

To assess students' mastery of this section, have them complete Daily Quiz 5.2 in *Daily Quizzes with Answer Key.*

THEMES IN GOVERNMENT

POLITICAL PROCESSES

Because there are many more representatives than senators and because House terms last only two years, Capitol Police sometimes fail to recognize new House members. As a result, House members wear lapel pins to distinguish themselves from visitors to Capitol Hill.

SECTION 2

HOUSES AND MEMBERS OF CONGRESS

READ TO DISCOVER

1. How do the houses of Congress differ in their structure and membership?
2. How are congressional districts drawn?
3. What is the typical profile of a U.S. congressmember?

POLITICAL DICTIONARY

census
apportion
gerrymandering
franking privilege
immunity

The House of Representatives and the Senate share many responsibilities. The two houses, however, are quite different in their structure and membership.

House of Representatives

The Constitution's framers intended the House to be closer to the people than would be the Senate. Their expectation was that the House would attract ordinary citizens serving for a brief period.

Size The size of the House of Representatives is set by Congress itself, not by the Constitution. The Constitution simply states that all House seats, whatever their number, must be distributed among the states according to their population. A national **census**, or official population count, is taken every 10 years and serves as the basis for determining this distribution.

For its first meeting in 1789, the House had just 65 members. As the nation's population grew, the House added more members to represent the greater number of citizens. After the 1910 census the number of seats was raised to the current number of 435. To prevent the House from growing too large and unmanageable, this number was set as the limit. (Since 1900, four nonvoting delegates have been added to the House from the District of Columbia, Guam, the U.S. Virgin Islands, and American Samoa. In addition, Puerto Rico is represented by a resident commissioner in the House.)

Although the number of seats has ceased to grow, the nation's population has not. This means that as

Comparing Governments

Legislatures Come in All Sizes

There is no magic number when it comes to deciding the size of a country's legislature. The actual number of legislators is determined by each country's constitution, laws, or customs.

Consider the United Kingdom and Thailand, for example. Although both countries have a population of around 60 million, their legislatures vary greatly. In 1997, U.K. voters elected 659 representatives to the House of Commons, the elected chamber of the legislature. That same year, Thai voters elected 500 people to their House of Representatives. This means that there was one U.K. representative for every 91,000 people living in the United Kingdom and one Thai representative for every 124,000 Thais.

The table below compares various countries' populations and their number of elected representatives.

Country	Population	Representatives	Persons per Representative
India	1,030 million	545	1.9 million
South Korea	48 million	273	176,000
Venezuela	24 million	165	145,000
United Kingdom	60 million	659	91,000
Thailand	62 million	500	124,000

Source: *The World Factbook 2001*

PRINCIPLES OF DEMOCRACY *Members of the 107th Congress gather in the House chamber for a joint session.* **Why is it impractical for the number of seats in Congress to grow as the size of the population increases?**

time passes and the population grows, each member of Congress represents an increasing number of citizens. For example, the population of all the states in 1910 was roughly 91 million, so each of the 435 House members represented an average of 209,000 people. In comparison, the population of all the states in 2000 was roughly 281 million, so each member represented an average of 646,000 people.

Terms Representatives serve two-year terms. If a representative dies or resigns before the end of a term, the governor of the representative's state must call a special election to fill the seat.

Congressional Districts As noted in Chapter 2, the framers of the Constitution agreed in the Great Compromise that representation in the House would be determined by population. The larger a state's population, the greater its representation in the House. After each census, Congress uses the new population count to **apportion**, or distribute, the 435 seats among the states.

States with significant population growth may acquire seats from those that lose residents or grow less rapidly. Every state, however, is entitled to at least one representative, no matter how small its population. Over the past 20 years, the western and southern regions of the country have gained seats, largely because of the population growth of states such as California, Florida, and Texas. At the same time, the northeastern and midwestern regions have lost seats as population has decreased or growth has slowed in states such as New York and Illinois.

Once the House seats are apportioned, each state legislature usually determines the boundaries of the congressional districts in its state. Thus, the legislature of a state that holds nine seats in the House must divide the state into nine congressional districts. How such divisions are drawn has been a source of controversy since the nation's beginnings.

One Person, One Vote In the past, critics charged that the system of determining boundaries for congressional districts was unfair because districts within a state varied in population size. Because of this variation, citizens living in smaller districts had greater representation in the House than did those living in larger districts.

Residents of a district with 200,000 people, for example, would be disproportionately represented in the House compared to residents of a district with 600,000 people. At one time, some congressional districts had eight times as many residents as other districts in the same state.

The Supreme Court addressed this issue in the 1964 case *Wesberry* v. *Sanders*. In its decision the Court established the "one-person, one-vote" principle by banning districts that had grossly unequal populations. The ruling means that each person's "vote," or representation in the House, should be roughly equal to every other person's. This decision led to the redrawing of many districts. Although there always will be differences in population among districts, huge variations no longer exist.

Some critics charge, moreover, that the system of apportioning seats *among* the states is unfair. For example, the state of Wyoming, which

CULTURAL PERSPECTIVES

The system of apportionment and redistricting has been controversial for a variety of reasons. Demographic changes—such as the dramatic post–World War II population migration from the so-called Rust Belt of the Northeast and Midwest to the Sunbelt—may reduce a region's congressional representation at precisely the time when its constituents need federal attention the most.

Concerns over attempts to create district boundaries that have a majority of particular ethnic groups may be overstated. Despite concerns that redistricting can be manipulated for partisan purposes, some studies indicate that most voters do not necessarily respond in a predictable partisan fashion based on their racial or ethnic background. ■

Enhancing the Lesson

For more information on *Wesberry* v. *Sanders* and other Supreme Court decisions, see the Supreme Court Docket section on the *Holt Researcher Online.*

ACROSS THE CURRICULUM

TECHNOLOGY Computers may prove worthwhile in helping to reapportion congressional seats as equitably as possible. While human beings might consciously, or subconsciously, redraw congressional districts for partisan purposes, computers, if programmed impartially, could provide fast and completely objective outlines for congressional redistricting.

Computers could establish districts based on a preset method and could even allow for situations in which gerrymandering was deemed appropriate. Of course, since computers operate strictly on information provided to them by humans, human input would continue to have a significant impact on successful computerized reapportionment. ∎

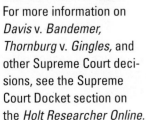

Enhancing the Lesson

For more information on *Davis* v. *Bandemer, Thornburg* v. *Gingles,* and other Supreme Court decisions, see the Supreme Court Docket section on the *Holt Researcher Online.*

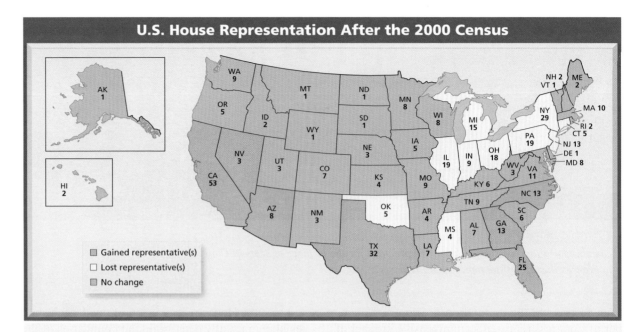

U.S. House Representation After the 2000 Census

WA 9, AK 1, OR 5, ID 2, MT 1, ND 1, MN 8, WI 8, MI 15, NH 2, VT 1, ME 2, NY 29, MA 10, RI 2, CT 5, NJ 13, DE 1, MD 8, SD 1, WY 1, NE 3, IA 5, IL 19, IN 9, OH 18, PA 19, WV 3, VA 11, NV 3, UT 3, CO 7, KS 4, MO 9, KY 6, NC 13, CA 53, HI 2, AZ 8, NM 3, OK 5, AR 4, TN 9, SC 6, MS 4, AL 7, GA 13, TX 32, LA 7, FL 25

- ▇ Gained representative(s)
- ☐ Lost representative(s)
- ▇ No change

After each census, the seats in Congress are reapportioned among the States.
How are seats apportioned among the states? Why do some people think this is unfair?

has a population of around 495,000, has one representative. Montana, which has a population of 905,000, also has one representative. Because every state is entitled to at least one representative, regardless of population, Wyoming has the same representation in the House as Montana. Many people say that this is unfair because Montana's member of the House is representing almost twice as many people as is Wyoming's.

Gerrymandering Another criticism of the apportionment process is that districts sometimes are drawn for political reasons. The practice of establishing district lines that favor one political party over another is called **gerrymandering**. The term dates to 1812, when Massachusetts governor Elbridge Gerry carved a district specifically to benefit the Republican Party. Some observers noted that the oddly shaped new district looked like a salamander. Soon it became known as a "gerrymander."

Gerrymandering by political parties takes place in one of two ways. Parties may draw district lines that concentrate their strength in a number of districts. This builds a solid base for the party and ensures it will win a certain number of seats. Parties also may draw district lines that weaken an opposition party's support by splitting

it across several districts. In the 1986 case *Davis* v. *Bandemer,* the Supreme Court issued a decision against extreme cases of political gerrymandering, saying that if the practice existed for a long time and was truly harmful to a political minority, it violated the Constitution.

C A S E   S T U D Y

Racial Gerrymandering

PRINCIPLES OF DEMOCRACY In recent years, race often has been a central issue in debates about apportionment. Over the years, many critics have charged that some district lines were drawn to purposely keep minority candidates from winning elections. This type of discrimination was addressed in 1982 by amendments to the Voting Rights Act of 1965. The amendment forbids various unfair election practices, including gerrymandering, that discriminate against minorities. Moreover, in the 1986 case *Thornburg* v. *Gingles,* the Supreme Court ruled that it is illegal to divide areas into several districts in order to weaken the political strength of minority groups living in those areas.

In response to this decision, a number of states tried to make up for past discrimination by redrawing congressional district lines. By concentrating as many minority voters into one district as possible, these new lines made it easier for members of minority groups to be elected. The result was a number of districts that were as strangely shaped as those they replaced. These districts were challenged in court for using "racial gerrymandering" to help minorities win congressional elections. Critics charged that this was a form of discrimination against nonminority candidates.

In response, the Supreme Court ruled that there would be strict examination of any district boundaries drawn with race as a leading factor. The Court did not rule out the use of race as one consideration, however. Some House districts today continue to be challenged based on charges of racial gerrymandering, and the boundaries of some districts have been redrawn as a result of court rulings.

Qualifications The Constitution establishes certain requirements for members of the House of Representatives. Members must be

★ at least 25 years old,
★ U.S. citizens for at least seven years, and
★ legal residents of the state they represent.

By custom, representatives also live in the district they represent, but this is not required by the Constitution.

Salary and Benefits Representatives receive an annual salary of $145,100—an amount determined by Congress itself. Concern over the possible abuse of Congress's power to set its own compensation led to the passage of the Twenty-seventh Amendment. Ratified in 1992, this amendment states that congressional pay increases cannot take effect until after the next congressional election. As a result, a congressmember would only get the pay increase if he or she were re-elected.

Members receive many other benefits in addition to their salaries. They are provided with office space in congressional buildings near the Capitol. They receive allowances to hire staff, to travel toand maintain offices in their home districts, and

Gerrymandering

ARKANSAS

Shreveport • Monroe •

LOUISIANA
Mississippi River
MISSISSIPPI

Alexandria •

TEXAS

Baton Rouge ★
Lafayette •
New Orleans •

■ Fourth Congressional District
□ Other Congressional Districts

0 25 50 Miles
0 25 50 Kilometers
Albers Equal-Area Projection

POLITICAL PROCESSES *During redistricting in the early 1990s, Louisiana's Fourth Congressional District was drawn so that African Americans made up a majority of the district's population.* **What consequences might this redistricting have on the residents of the Fourth District?**

for stationery, newsletters, and other supplies. They also have the **franking privilege**, which allows them to send official mail for free. In addition, members can take advantage of generous pensions, life insurance, special tax deductions, medical services, free parking, free health club memberships, library research facilities, and many other programs and services.

The Constitution also gives members of Congress a form of **immunity**, or legal protection. To protect their freedom of speech, members cannot be sued for anything they say while performing congressional business. They also cannot be arrested in or on their way to or from a meeting in Congress unless they are accused of a serious crime. These laws ensure that congressmembers are not unnecessarily prevented from performing their duties.

Senate

The framers of the Constitution intended for the Senate to differ from the House. They thought that the Senate should attract an older, more experienced

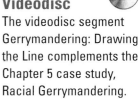

Holt American Government Videodisc

The videodisc segment Gerrymandering: Drawing the Line complements the Chapter 5 case study, Racial Gerrymandering. Barcodes for the Spanish version of the video are available in *Holt American Government Videodisc Teacher's Guide.*

PLAY SEGMENT

PAUSE

RESUME PLAY

PLAY OPTION A

PLAY OPTION B

PLAY OPTION C

PLAY EPILOGUE

ACROSS THE CURRICULUM

HISTORY Although minimum ages are established by the Constitution for serving in both the House and the Senate, there have been cases of people being too young who have actually served in office. The youngest senator ever was John H. Eaton, who was sworn into office in 1818 when he was only 28 years old. To be a senator, one is required to be 30 years old. William Charles Coles Clairborne entered the House of Representatives in 1797 at the age of 22, although the minimum requirement is 25 years of age. ◼

group of people who would serve longer terms as the nation's senior leaders. These senior leaders would be somewhat more removed from the voters than representatives. Until the Seventeenth Amendment, which passed in 1913, senators were chosen by the state legislatures, not by the people.

Today the Senate does indeed have a more dignified atmosphere than the House. For example, when moving from the House to the Senate, Dan Quayle—who later became vice president—noted that there are no basketball games organized among the senators, as there are in the House. The Senate's stately atmosphere stems partly from its legacy as the more privileged body and partly from the fact that senators are older on average than are members of the House.

The difference in prominence between the two bodies also is evident in the fact that members of the House often run for the Senate later in their careers, but senators rarely go on to run for the House. Senators also are generally better known. As one congressman said, "You'd be someone who was 34 years in the House and call somebody downtown and they would say, 'What was your name, again?' . . . But when you were a senator, it was a whole different ball game."

Size The Constitution sets the Senate's size at two members from each state. The first Senate had 26 members representing the 13 original states. Today the Senate has 100 members representing the 50 states. Each senator represents his or her entire state.

Terms Senators serve six-year terms. Senatorial elections, however, are held every two years. This rotating system means that only one third of the Senate's members are up for election at one time, thus ensuring that the Senate has continuity and experience in its membership. If a senator dies or resigns before the end of a term, the governor of the senator's state may appoint someone to fill the seat until a special election or the next regular election is held.

The Congress of the United States

HOUSE OF REPRESENTATIVES		SENATE
435 Representatives (Based on state populations)		100 Senators (2 from each state)

REPRESENTATIVES		SENATORS
2 years	LENGTH OF TERM	6 years
Entire House elected every 2 years	WHEN ELECTED	One third of Senate elected every 2 years
At least 25 years old	REQUIRED AGE	At least 30 years old
U.S. citizen at least 7 years	CITIZENSHIP	U.S. citizen at least 9 years
Resident of the state where elected	LEGAL RESIDENCE	Resident of the state where elected
$ 145,100	SALARY	$145,100

As you can see in this chart, the requirements for membership in the House of Representatives differ from those for membership in the Senate. **What is the salary of members of the House and the Senate?**

Linking

Government and History

The Roman Senate

In writing the U.S. Constitution, the framers looked to the experiences and ideas of various peoples throughout history. The government of the ancient Roman Republic, for example, influenced how the framers structured the new U.S. government. To help keep its leaders from gaining too much power, the republic had divided authority among different members and parts of the government. Similarly, the U.S. framers assigned independent powers to three distinct branches of government.

The framers also recalled the composition of the Roman Senate. This body was composed mainly of experienced, older leaders who had held high-level government positions. In fact, the word *senate* comes from the Latin *senex,* meaning "old, old man." The framers hoped that the U.S. Senate also would be composed of older, wiser leaders.

The Roman Senate was partly an advisory body, but it also controlled public finances and set foreign policy. The Senate grew in authority throughout the years of the republic and remained a part of Roman government even after the founding of the Roman Empire.

In support of the U.S. Constitution, James Madison argued that the Senate was an important part of Roman government. Of course, Madison recognized that the Roman Republic was not a true democracy. But he saw in the Roman Senate an example of the value of mature, experienced leadership. "History informs us of no long-lived republic which had not a senate," Madison wrote.

There were, of course, differences between the Senate of ancient Rome and the Senate created by the U.S. framers. For example, Roman senators served for life. U.S. senators, on the other hand, serve only six-year terms. They can, however, be re-elected.

In addition, although there is an age requirement for the U.S. Senate, there was none for the Roman Senate. There were age requirements, however, for many other positions in Roman government. Because Romans could not be appointed to the Senate without first having held a government position, they generally were not eligible for the Senate until sometime in their 30s.

The ranks of the Roman Senate were dominated by wealthy, established families. Citizens holding jobs that the Romans considered beneath the dignity of the office—for example, gladiators and actors—were not eligible for appointment. In addition, citizens whose private businesses might have distracted them from their senatorial duties also were ineligible. Over time, however, citizens from a variety of backgrounds were appointed to the Senate.

The number of U.S. Senate seats is 100, while during most years of the Republic, the Roman Senate had about 300 seats. The actual number varied, depending on political conditions at the time. During times of civil war or other crises, for example, many seats in the Senate might become vacant. Some Roman leaders, particularly during the empire, expanded the size of the Senate so they could appoint more of their supporters. The number of senators rose to about 2,000 in the late stages of the Roman Empire, in the A.D. 300s.

What Do You Think?

1. Should candidates running for the U.S. Senate be required to have previous government experience? Why or why not?
2. In what ways can running a private business help or hurt a government official in the performance of his or her duties?

The Curia Julia *was the main meeting place of the Senate during the years of the Roman Empire. The* Curia *was built during the dictatorship of Julius Caesar (100 B.C.–44 B.C.).*

(Continued on page 104)

What Do You Think? Answers

1. Answers will vary, but students should mention the pros and cons of previous government experience.

2. Answers will vary, but students should acknowledge the positive and negative effects of business ownership on job performance.

SECTION 2 REVIEW ANSWERS

1. Refer to the following pages: census (98), apportion (99), gerrymandering (100), franking privilege (101), immunity (101).

2. House: 435 members; $145,100 plus office space, allowances for staff, travel, home district office, and supplies, franking privilege, immunity; two-year term; at least 25, U.S. citizen for seven years, legal resident of state represented. Senate: 100 members; same salary and benefits as House members; six-year term; at least 30, U.S. citizen for nine years, legal resident of state represented.

(Continued from page 103)

3a. House seats are redistributed every 10 years according to the population of the states. Each state is guaranteed one representative. Each state gets two senators.

3b. The framers intended the House to be closer to the people and to attract ordinary citizens serving for brief periods of time. They intended the Senate to be somewhat more removed from the people and to attract older people who would serve longer terms.

4. Answers will vary, but students should demonstrate an understanding of the system of apportionment and the impact it has on citizens' representation in Congress.

Qualifications The Constitution also establishes certain requirements for senators. They must be

★ at least 30 years old,
★ U.S. citizens for at least nine years, and
★ legal residents of the state they represent.

Salary and Benefits Like representatives, senators receive an annual salary of $145,100. They also receive the same benefits and legal protections as House members.

Members of Congress

Who are the members of Congress? Most are businesspeople or lawyers. Almost every member of Congress has a college degree, and most have advanced degrees. Most members also are white, male, and more than 40 years old. Minority groups and women generally are not represented in Congress in proportion to their numbers in the U.S. population. For example, some 12.3 percent of the U.S. population was African American in 2000. In 2001, however, only 7 percent of congressmembers were African American. In addition, more than half of the population is female, and only 14 percent of all seats in Congress were held by women in 2001.

Although these groups, as well as Asian Americans and Hispanic Americans, are still underrepresented in relation to their numbers in the population, the disproportionately low representation of minority groups and women in Congress has been gradually changing. The 1992 elections pro-

PRINCIPLES OF DEMOCRACY *In 2001 Senator Ben Nighthorse Campbell was the only American Indian in Congress.* **Does the membership of Congress represent the diversity of the U.S. population?**

duced increases in the numbers of African Americans, Hispanic Americans, and particularly women in Congress. The number of female senators increased from two to six, one of whom was Carol Moseley-Braun, the only African American then serving in the Senate. The number of women in the House increased from 28 to 47.

In addition, Ben Nighthorse Campbell was elected to the Senate in 1992—the first American Indian to serve in the Senate in 60 years. By 2001 the number of women in the House had risen to 62, and the number of women in the Senate had risen to 13. There were 21 Hispanic American, 8 Asian American, and 3 native American representatives in Congress. However, there were no Hispanic Americans or African Americans in the Senate.

SECTION 2 REVIEW

1. Identify and explain:
• census
• apportion
• gerrymandering
• franking privilege
• immunity

2. Identifying Concepts: Copy the chart below. Use it to describe the two houses of Congress.

House of Representatives	Items to Consider	Senate
	Size	
	Salary and Benefits	
	Length of Term	
	Qualifications	

Homework Practice Online
go.hrw.com
keyword: SV3 HP5

3. **Finding the Main Idea**

a. How are seats in the House and Senate distributed among the states?

b. What were the intentions of the framers of the Constitution for the House and the Senate?

4. **Writing and Critical Thinking**

Evaluating: Is the current system of apportionment fair? What would be your solution to the problem of apportioning congressional districts?

Consider the following:
• the "one-person, one-vote" principle established by the Supreme Court
• the intent of the framers of the Constitution

SECTION 3
POWERS OF CONGRESS

READ TO DISCOVER

1. To what main areas of governing do Congress's expressed powers apply?
2. What special powers does Congress hold?
3. What are the implied powers of Congress?
4. What constitutional limits exist on congressional powers?

POLITICAL DICTIONARY

impeach
ex post facto law
bill of attainder
writ of *habeas corpus*

Most of the powers assumed by Congress are specifically listed in the Constitution. As you will learn, Congress has also assumed some powers that are *not* mentioned in the Constitution. The Constitution does, however, outline several specific limits on what actions Congress may take.

Expressed Powers

As noted in Chapter 4, the powers specifically granted to the federal government are called expressed powers because they are specifically expressed, or listed, in the Constitution. Expressed powers give Congress the right to make laws in five main areas: government finance, regulation of commerce, national defense, law enforcement, and national sovereignty.

The majority of these powers can be found in Article 1, Section 8, of the Constitution—for example, the power to raise and collect taxes, regulate foreign and interstate commerce, coin and print money, and provide and maintain military forces. (See the chart on this page.) Other articles within the Constitution list additional powers.

For example, Section 3 of Article 4 gives Congress the power to admit new states into the Union. Article 3, Section 3, gives it the right to determine the punishment for treason.

Special Powers

In addition to the expressed powers, the Constitution gives Congress several special powers. Some of these are held by the Senate, some by the House, and some by both.

Expressed Powers of Congress

- To lay and collect taxes, to pay the nation's debts, and to provide for the common defense and general welfare of the United States
- To borrow money
- To regulate foreign and interstate commerce
- To establish uniform rules for becoming a citizen
- To coin money and set a uniform standard of weights and measures
- To punish counterfeiters
- To establish post offices and post roads
- To make copyright and patent laws
- To establish a system of national courts
- To punish piracy and other offenses against the law of nations
- To declare war
- To raise and maintain armies
- To raise and maintain a navy
- To establish military laws
- To call up a national militia
- To organize, arm, and discipline the militia
- To govern the District of Columbia
- To make all laws that shall be necessary and proper for carrying into execution previously mentioned powers

---

The chart above lists powers specifically granted to Congress in the Constitution. **Which expressed powers give Congress the right to make laws concerning government finances?**

SECTION 3
POWERS OF CONGRESS

Lesson Plans

For teaching strategies, see Lesson 5.3 located at the beginning of this chapter or the One-Stop Planner Strategy 5.3.

Political Dictionary

To reinforce the section's vocabulary terms, refer students to the Electronic Glossary on the *Researcher CD-ROM.*

Section Assessment

To assess students' mastery of this section, have them complete Daily Quiz 5.3 in *Daily Quizzes with Answer Key.*

Transparency

An overhead transparency of the chart on this page is available in *Transparency Resources.* See Transparency 11: Expressed Powers of Congress.

Caption Answer

collect taxes, borrow money, and coin money

Impeaching Officials Congress holds the power to formally accuse and bring federal officials to trial. The most important officials in the government, including the president and vice president, may be removed from office if they are found guilty of serious crimes against the nation.

The charges against an accused official must be drawn up in the House of Representatives. If a majority of representatives votes to pursue the charges, the official is **impeached**, or formally accused. The procedure of drawing up and passing the charges against the accused in the House is called impeachment.

Trials on impeachment charges are held in the Senate, with the vice president acting as the judge. If the president is being impeached, however, the chief justice of the United States presides instead. In this case the vice president cannot preside because of a conflict of interest—if the president were found guilty, the vice president would become president. The members of the Senate act as the jury. If two thirds of the Senate find the official guilty, he or she can be dismissed from office.

The impeachment process has been used rarely, with only 16 federal officials having been impeached. Two were presidents—Andrew Johnson and Bill Clinton. At his impeachment trial in 1868, President Johnson was found not guilty of the charges against him by one vote. In 1974 the threat of impeachment caused President Richard M. Nixon to resign from office. In 1999 the Senate acquitted President Clinton on two charges by votes of 55–45 and 50–50.

Approving Treaties The Senate has the power to reject any treaty, or written agreement, between the United States and other countries. A treaty that is not approved by a two-thirds vote in the Senate does not become law. This congressional right can be a powerful tool in foreign policy. Several treaties signed by U.S. presidents have never been enacted because the Senate refused to approve them.

Approving Appointments The Senate also must approve or reject all major appointments made by the president, including Supreme Court justices, ambassadors, and cabinet members. Appointments require a majority vote for approval.

Deciding Elections The House of Representatives holds the power to decide presidential elections under certain circumstances. If no can-

POLITICAL PROCESS *President Clinton's 1999 impeachment trial.* **What role does impeachment play in the system of checks and balances?**

didate for president receives a majority of electoral votes—ballots cast by members of the Electoral College—the House of Representatives must choose the winner from among the three candidates receiving the most votes. (The Electoral College is more fully explained in Chapter 7.) The representatives of each state collectively have one vote to cast, for a total of 50 votes. The candidate who receives a majority of the total House votes (at least 26) becomes president.

Similarly, if no candidate for vice president were to receive a majority of electoral votes, the Senate would choose the vice president. In this case, however, each senator has one vote, for a total of 100. Again, the candidate who receives a majority of the Senate votes (51) is elected.

The House has used its electoral power twice. It chose Thomas Jefferson as president in 1801 and John Quincy Adams in 1825. The Senate has used its electoral power only once—to choose Richard M. Johnson as vice president in 1837.

Implied Powers

As noted in the Expressed Powers of Congress chart on page 105, the last power listed is the most general and far-reaching. The Constitution states that Congress has the power "to make all laws which shall be necessary and proper for carrying into execution the foregoing [previously mentioned] powers" specifically granted to it. As noted in Chapter 4, the additional powers implied by this Necessary and Proper, or Elastic, Clause have allowed Congress to stretch its expressed powers. Congress has thus been able to create legislation addressing situations that were unforeseen by the framers of the Constitution.

The debate over the Elastic Clause and Congress's implied powers has gone on almost as long as the Constitution has existed. One of the key disputes regarding this issue arose in 1819 in the Supreme Court case *McCulloch* v. *Maryland.*

The subject of the case, as noted in Chapter 4, was the Bank of the United States.

The Bank of the United States was originally established in 1791. The bank's charter ended in 1811, and a bill to establish a new charter met with opposition and was vetoed by President Madison in 1816. Eventually, however, a new charter passed, and a Second Bank of the United States began operation in 1817. The bank had been a source of controversy since the time of its creation. Many people, including Thomas Jefferson, had stated that the Constitution did not give Congress the right to set up a national bank and that its creation was a violation of states' rights. Indeed, this argument was the basis of the state of Maryland's case in *McCulloch* v. *Maryland.*

The Supreme Court, however, decided the case in Congress's favor. In a unanimous decision, the Court declared that Congress had the right to determine what was "necessary and proper" to fulfill its constitutional duties. Creating a national bank fell into this category.

Another of Congress's implied powers involves its establishment of the nation's military academies. Although not specifically given the power to do so in the Constitution, Congress set up military academies to train army, navy, air force, coast guard, and merchant marine officers. Congress justified its actions by saying that the academies are "necessary and proper" for it to carry out its constitutional right to raise and maintain an army and a navy. Thus, the Elastic Clause implies, or suggests, that Congress has the right to establish military academies.

The Elastic Clause has allowed Congress to expand its powers significantly. In fact, Congress has used this clause to justify much of the federal law passed during the 1900s. The clause aroused very little debate at the Constitutional Convention, however. The framers probably did not anticipate that Congress would use its implied powers so extensively, for the clause does not seem to grant any authority beyond that already contained in Section 8 of Article 1.

CONSTITUTIONAL GOVERNMENT *The Second Bank of the United States stands in Independence National Park in Philadelphia, Pennsylvania.* **Why was the bank a source of controversy?**

Enhancing the Lesson

RESEARCHER ONLINE
go.hrw.com

For more information on *McCulloch* v. *Maryland* and other Supreme Court decisions, refer students to the Supreme Court Docket section on the *Holt Researcher Online.*

Caption Answer

Some people claimed that Congress did not have the authority to establish a bank.

⚡ **internet** connect

TOPIC: Watergate and Congressional Investigation
GO TO: go.hrw.com
KEYWORD: SV3 GV5

Have students access the Internet through the HRW Go site to research the resignation of Richard Nixon and the threat of impeachment that led to his resignation. Then create a pamphlet that explains the Watergate scandal and presents the issues surrounding Nixon's resignation.

SECTION 3 REVIEW ANSWERS

1. Refer to the following pages: impeach (106), *ex post facto* law (108), bill of attainder (108), writ of *habeas corpus* (108).

2. Expressed powers: raise and collect taxes, regulate foreign and interstate trade, coin and print money, provide and maintain military forces, and borrow money. Special powers: impeach officials, approve treaties and appointments, and decide elections. Implied powers: the Elastic clause allows Congress to pass legislation addressing situations not addressed in the Constitution, such as creating a national bank and establishing military academies.

3a. Limits include judicial review, the Tenth Amendment, and Article 1, Section 9, of the Constitution.

3b. Expressed powers are specifically granted by the Constitution, Implied powers are not specifically listed but are considered "necessary and proper."

4. Answers will vary but should reflect knowledge of the limits of Congress's powers and an understanding of the need for those limits.

Limits on Powers

The powers of Congress are limited in several important ways. As noted in Chapter 3, the Supreme Court can use the power of judicial review to determine when Congress has reached beyond the powers granted to it by the Constitution. Any law that the Court rules unconstitutional has no force.

Another limit on Congress's powers is the Tenth Amendment to the Constitution. It declares that the states or the people shall keep all the powers not specifically granted to the national government. These powers, as noted in Chapter 4, are called reserved powers.

Article 1, Section 9, of the Constitution further restricts the powers of Congress. For example, it keeps Congress from taxing exports and from favoring the trade of a particular state. It also prevents Congress from passing an **ex post facto law**—a law that applies to an action that took place before the law was passed—or a **bill of attainder**—a law that punishes a person who has not been convicted in a court of law. In addition, Congress cannot suspend the **writ of habeas corpus**—a court order requiring police

Powers Denied to Congress

- To pass *ex post facto* laws
- To pass bills of attainder
- To suspend the writ of *habeas corpus*
- To tax exports
- To pass laws violating the Constitution
- To pass laws giving a state or group of states an unfair trade advantage
- To grant titles of nobility
- To engage in spending that has not been authorized by legislation

The chart above lists the powers denied to Congress in the Constitution.
Why do you think that the framers of the Constitution denied Congress the power to grant titles of nobility?

to bring all persons accused of a crime to court and to show sufficient reason to keep them in jail—except "when in cases of rebellion or invasion the public safety may require it." (*Ex post facto* laws, bills of attainder, and the writ of *habeas corpus* are more fully explained in Chapter 14.) See the chart on this page for additional restrictions that Article 1, Section 9, places on Congress.

SECTION 3 REVIEW

1. **Identify and explain:**
   - impeach
   - *ex post facto* law
   - bill of attainder
   - writ of *habeas corpus*

2. **Identifying Concepts:** Copy the chart below. Use it to identify the powers of Congress as expressed, special, or implied.

   Powers of Congress

Expressed	Special	Implied

3. **Finding the Main Idea**

   a. What limits does the Constitution place on Congress's powers?

   b. What is the difference between expressed powers and implied powers?

4. **Writing and Critical Thinking**

   Decision Making: Imagine that you have been asked to write a new constitution for a foreign country. What limitations would you place on the legislative branch of government?

   Consider the following:
   - the powers denied to Congress by the U.S. Constitution
   - the dangers of unlimited legislative power

go. hrw. com **Homework Practice Online**
keyword: SV3 HP5

IN THE NEWS

Personal Beliefs and How They Affect Policy

On August 9, 2001, in a speech to the nation, President George W. Bush announced limits on federal funding for research on stem cells already extracted from human embryos left over from in vitro fertilization. He based his decision on two factors:

- 60 stem cell lines must already exist.
- The "life and death decision" has already been made not to let them become human beings.

What is the significance of this decision? The government policy could provide a perspective for deciding many ethical issues posed by science, such as those rising from cloning or euthanasia.

What This Decision Means

President Bush will allow federal funding for research on 60 lines of embryonic stem cells. These lines of cells have the ability to regenerate themselves indefinitely, but not all have been approved by the National Institutes of Health, which sets federal standards for research.

Embryonic stem cells have the potential to turn into any other kind of cell in the body, and have been looked to as possibly leading to treatments for Alzheimer's disease, Type I diabetes, and Parkinson's disease.

Why This Decision Was Difficult

Elected officials are torn between serving the larger public interests and the interests of their constituents. Because Bush is supported by groups who oppose abortion, he may risk losing re-election in the future.

On the other hand, many people applaud his decision, which helps his presidential future.

Karen Hughes, an adviser to President Bush, gives a press conference on stem cell research.

Emotionally Charged Decisions

Stem cell research is an emotionally charged issue. Some scientists were satisfied with the decision, while others were not. Scientists who were critical of the decision thought that working with only 60 stem cell lines was like "operating with one hand tied behind your back."

Some conservative politicians have lambasted the president, stating that killing human embryos for research is wrong. They feel this research is leading the country into moral decay. Because of the complexity of this issue, President Bush moved to the center. But how do the people feel? In a recent Gallup poll, 55 percent of the respondents said they would support use of "extra" embryos that were going to be destroyed anyway.

What Do You Think?

1. How do you feel about stem cell research?
2. Who might benefit from stem cell research?

> **WHY IT MATTERS TODAY**
>
> Controversy surrounds stem cell research. Use CNNfyi.com or other **current events** sources to find additional information concerning this research.
>
> CNNfyi.com

Government in the News Answers

1. Answers will vary, but should reflect an understanding of the controversy surrounding the issue.

2. Among the people who might benefit are those with Alzheimer's disease, Type I diabetes, and Parkinson's disease.

CHAPTER 5

Review Answers

Writing a Summary

Summaries should focus on the main points of each section. These may be found in the Read to Discover questions at the start of each section. Summaries should also use standard grammar, spelling, sentence structure, and punctuation.

Identifying Ideas

Refer to the following pages: constituent (94), interest group (94), political action committee (94), census (98), apportion (99), gerrymandering (100), immunity (101), impeach (106), *ex post facto* law (108), write of *habeas corpus* (108).

Understanding Main Ideas

1. Each can influence how a member of Congress votes: constituents voice their opinions or vote; interest

(Continued on page 110)

Review

(Continued from page 109)

groups provide information, organize constituents, and raise money; political parties provide assistance, publicity, and funding.

2. to legislate, oversee government agencies, and provide constituent services

3. by the population distribution as indicated by each official census

4. Representatives: at least 25 years old, U.S. citizens for at least seven years, and legal residents of the state they represent. Senators: at least 30 years old, U.S. citizens for at least nine years, and legal residents of the state they represent.

5. expressed—raising and collecting taxes, regulating foreign and interstate commerce, coining money, declaring war, maintaining a military; special— impeach federal officials, approve treaties and presidential appointments; implied—whatever is " necessary and proper" to carry out its expressed powers.

6. tax exports, favor any particular state in matters of trade, pass *ex post facto* laws or bills of attainder, suspend the writ of *habeas corpus*

Reviewing Themes

1. The framers wanted the House to attract ordinary citizens serving for short periods of time and the Senate to attract an older, more experienced group of people who would serve the country for longer periods.

(Continued on page 111)

Writing a Summary

Using standard grammar, spelling, sentence structure, and punctuation, write a summary of the information in this chapter.

Identifying Ideas

Identify the following terms and explain their significance.

1. constituent

2. interest group

3. political action committee

4. census

5. apportion

6. gerrymandering

7. immunity

8. impeach

9. *ex post facto* law

10. writ of *habeas corpus*

Understanding Main Ideas

SECTION 1 *(pp. 93–97)*

1. What role do constituents, interest groups, and political parties play in the policies made by Congress?

2. What are Congress's three main roles?

SECTION 2 *(pp. 98–104)*

3. How are congressional districts for the House of Representatives determined?

4. What qualifications does the Constitution set for senators and representatives?

SECTION 3 *(pp. 105–108)*

5. What types of powers does Congress hold?

6. What powers are denied to Congress by the Constitution?

Reviewing Themes

1. Political Foundations Why did the framers specify terms of different length for represtatives and senators?

2. Political Processes How do constituents' requests help members of Congress perform their jobs?

3. Public Good How is the public good promoted by having congressional powers defined in the Constitution? What might happen if there were no limitations on Congress's powers?

Thinking Critically

1. Making Predictions The nation's growing population threatens the principle of "one person, one vote." How would you change the apportionment of seats in the House to fix the problem? Write a paragraph explaining your solution.

2. Supporting a Point of View The Constitution establishes few qualifications for members of Congress. Should there be additional qualifications, such as a set number of years' experience in state government? Write a paragraph that supports your opinion on this issue.

3. Decision Making Should members of Congress vote according to their personal beliefs or their constituents' interests? Explain your answer.

Writing About Government

Review what you wrote in your Government Notebook at the beginning of this chapter about what you think are the qualifications and characteristics of a good congressperson. Now that you have studied the chapter, how would you revise your answer? Should the qualifications for members of Congress be expanded? Record your answers in your Notebook.

Interpreting the Map

Study the map below. Then use it to help you answer the questions that follow.

Gerrymandering

ARKANSAS

Shreveport • Monroe •

LOUISIANA

MISSISSIPPI

Alexandria •

TEXAS

Baton Rouge ★

Lafayette •

New Orleans •

■ Fourth Congressional District
□ Other Congressional Districts

0   25   50 Miles
0 25 50 Kilometers
Albers Equal-Area Projection

1. Approximately how many miles is it from the northeasternmost point in Louisiana's Fourth District to the southernmost?
   a. 10
   b. 50
   c. 175
   d. 500

2. What does this map reveal about the African American population of Louisiana?

Analyzing Primary Sources

Wesberry v. *Sanders*
The 1964 Supreme Court case of *Wesberry* v. *Sanders* banned congressional districts with grossly unequal populations. Read the excerpt from the Court's majority opinion, which was written by Justice Hugo L. Black, and answer the questions that follow.

> "We agree . . . that the 1931 Georgia apportionment grossly discriminates against voters in the Fifth Congressional District. A single Congressman represents from two to three times as many Fifth District voters as are represented by each of the congressmen from the other Georgia congressional districts. The apportionment statute thus contracts the value of some votes and expands that of others.
>
> We hold that, construed [interpreted] in its historical context, the command of Article I, Section 2, that Representatives be chosen "by the People of the several States" means that as nearly as is practicable one man's vote in a congressional election is to be worth as much as another's."

3. Which of the following statements best describes Justice Black's point of view?
   a. Georgia's apportionment was fair.
   b. One vote is worth as much as another.
   c. Some votes are worth more than others.
   d. The Constitution does not address this issue.

4. Some House members represent far more people than other members. How do you think Justice Black would have felt about this situation? Explain your answer.

(Continued from page 110)

2. Patterns of requests may alert representatives to problems.

3. Limits ensure the people retain control over government. A lack of defined limitations could lead to abuses or social instability.

Thinking Critically

1. Answers will vary, but students should explain their answer.

2. Answers will vary, but students should provide support for their opinion.

3. Answers will vary, but students should explain their answers.

Writing About History

The Government Notebook is a follow-up activity to the notebook activity that appears on page 92.

Building Social Studies Skills

1. c
2. Students should note that African Americans appear to be concentrated in urban areas and along the Mississippi River.
3. b
4. Answers will vary, but students should explain their answer.

Alternative Assessment

To assess this activity see Rubric 1: Acquiring Information I *Portfolio and Performance Assessment for Social Studies.*

Building Your Portfolio

With a group, create a Serving in Congress handbook for potential congressional candidates describing the structure and functions of Congress. Include a chart illustrating the benefits of serving in Congress, the terms of office, and the constitutional qualifications for members of Congress. Also include statistical information about the makeup of the current Congress.

☐ internet connect

Internet Activity: go.hrw.com
KEYWORD: SV3 GV5

Access the Internet through the HRW Go site to compare and contrast the roles, requirements, and powers of both houses of Congress. Then create an illustrated diagram to present your information. Focus on issues such as term lengths, number of members, and any other information that is unique to either the House or Senate.

go. hrw .com

CHAPTER 6 CONGRESS AT WORK

	OBJECTIVES	PACING GUIDE	REPRODUCIBLE RESOURCES
SECTION 1 **ORGANIZATION OF CONGRESS** (pp. 113–117)	▶ What are the terms and sessions of Congress? ▶ How is congressional leadership organized? ▶ What are the rules of conduct in Congress?	**Regular** 1 day **Block Scheduling** .5 day	**ELL** Spanish Study Guide 6.1 **ELL** English Study Guide 6.1 **PS** Reading 73: *Contract with America*
SECTION 2 **THE COMMITTEE SYSTEM** (pp. 118–122)	▶ What kinds of committees are there in Congress? ▶ How are committee assignments made? ▶ What kinds of staff help congressmembers and committees perform their work?	**Regular** 1.5 days **Block Scheduling** .5 day	**ELL** Spanish Study Guide 6.2 **ELL** English Study Guide 6.2 **PS** Reading 29: *Excerpt from a Filibuster*
SECTION 3 **HOW A BILL BECOMES A LAW** (pp. 123–128)	▶ What was the relationship between the U.S. government and business before the 1880s? ▶ What was the purpose of early antitrust legislation? ▶ How has the government enforced antitrust legislation?	**Regular** 1 day **Block Scheduling** .5 day	**ELL** Spanish Study Guide 6.3 **ELL** English Study Guide 6.3
SECTION 4 **CONGRESS AND THE PUBLIC GOOD** (pp. 129–132)	▶ Do special interests obstruct Congress in promoting the public good? ▶ What is the main criticism of the committee system, and how does it affect the public good? ▶ What role does Congress play in promoting the public good?	**Regular** .5 day **Block Scheduling** .25 day	**ELL** Spanish Study Guide 6.4 **ELL** English Study Guide 6.4 **E** Challenge and Enrichment: Activity 6

Chapter Resource Key

PS	Primary Sources	**A**	Assessment	📼	Video
RS	Reading Support	**REV**	Review	💿	Videodisc
E	Enrichment	**ELL**	Reinforcement and English Language Learners	🌐	Internet
S	Simulations		Transparencies	💻	Holt Presentation Maker Using
SM	Skills Mastery	💿	CD-ROM		Microsoft ® PowerPoint ®

TECHNOLOGY RESOURCES	REINFORCEMENT, REVIEW, AND ASSESSMENT
⊚ One-Stop Planner: Lesson 6.1 ⊞ Holt Researcher Online ⊞ Homework Practice Online ⬚ Transparency 12: Congressional Leadership ⊚ Global Skill Builder CD-ROM	**REV** Section 1 Review, p. 117 **A** Daily Quiz 6.1
⊚ One-Stop Planner: Lesson 6.2 ⊞ Holt Researcher Online ⊞ Homework Practice Online ⬚ Transparency 13: Congressional Standing Committees ⊚ Global Skill Builder CD-ROM	**REV** Section 2 Review, p. 122 **A** Daily Quiz 6.2
⊚ One-Stop Planner: Lesson 6.3 ⊞ Holt Researcher Online ⊞ Homework Practice Online ⊚ Global Skill Builder CD-ROM	**REV** Section 3 Review, p. 128 **A** Daily Quiz 6.3
⊚ One-Stop Planner: Lesson 6.4 ⊞ Homework Practice Online	**REV** Section 4 Review, p. 132 **A** Daily Quiz 6.4

Chapter Review and Assessment

SM Global Skill Builder CD-ROM
⊞ HRW Go site
REV Chapter 6 Tutorial for Students, Parents, and Peers
REV Chapter 6 Review, pp. 134–135
⊚ Chapter 6 Test Generator (on the One-Stop Planner)
A   Chapter 6 Test
A   Chapter 6 Test Alternative Assessment Handbook

☼ One-Stop Planner CD-ROM

It's easy to plan lessons, select resources, and print out materials for your students when you use the *One-Stop Planner CD-ROM with Test Generator.*

☑ internet connect

HRW ONLINE RESOURCES
Go To: go.hrw.com
Then type in a keyword.

TEACHER HOME PAGE
KEYWORD: SV3 Teacher

CHAPTER INTERNET ACTIVITIES
KEYWORD: SV3 GV6
Choose an activity on the Congress at work to:
▶ create a flow chart showing how a bill becomes a law.
▶ write a letter expressing your opinion on term limits.
▶ create a radio broadcast on pork barrel spending.

CHAPTER ENRICHMENT LINKS
KEYWORD: SV3 CH6

HOLT RESEARCHER ONLINE
KEYWORD: Holt Researcher

ONLINE ASSESSMENT
Homework Practice
KEYWORD: SV3 HP6
Standardized Test Prep
KEYWORD: SV3 STP6
Rubrics
KEYWORD: SS Rubrics

ONLINE MAPS, CHARTS, AND GRAPHS
KEYWORD: SV3 MCG
▶ Years Served in the House
▶ Congressional Leadership
▶ Congressional Standing Committees

CONTENT UPDATES
KEYWORD: SS Content Updates

HOLT PRESENTATION MAKER
KEYWORD: SV3 PPT6

ONLINE READING SUPPORT
KEYWORD: SS Strategies

CURRENT EVENTS
KEYWORD: S3 Current Events

LESSON 6.1 | ORGANIZATION OF CONGRESS

TEXTBOOK PAGES 113–117

OBJECTIVES

- List the terms and sessions of Congress.
- Describe the organization of congressional leadership.
- Identify the rules of conduct in Congress.

MOTIVATE

For Sections 6.1 through 6.3 have students participate in a "mock congress." Ask students to brainstorm a bill, or proposed law, that they would like to see go into effect in the classroom. Have students decide on the one rule that they would most like to pass and that they feel the teacher would be willing to enact. Explain to students that for the next three lessons they will participate in a mock congress that will try to get this rule established as a class law. Tell students that they will learn about the organization of Congress in this section.

TEACH

Building a Vocabulary

In spiral notebooks, have students create a Political Dictionary to be used throughout the course. The dictionary may be used as an activity at the start of each new section; it may also be used as a modification device for students having difficulty or sheltered English students during tests and homework assignments. List words the students will be expected to know for this section on the board. Have students list, define, and give an example of each of the terms, using information provided in the text or on the *Researcher CD-ROM.*

Acquiring Information/Role-Playing

Discuss with students the terms and sessions of Congress. Although all students will serve in the mock congress, ask for two volunteers or nominations for students to participate in a mock congressional election. Have one student act as the incumbent and the other as the challenger. Have each student give a campaign speech. Lead a class discussion on which candidate they would vote for and why. Discuss the criticisms of and supports for term limits and electing incumbents over challengers. Tell students that they will structure their mock congress in the next activity.

Mastering Concepts

Organize the students so that approximately three fourths of them are in one group and the other one fourth are in another. The larger group will represent the House and the smaller the Senate. Students may either decide which political party they will belong to, or the teacher may randomly assign parties. Once party affiliation of each student has been determined, lead the class in determining the majority party. Have that majority party choose a Speaker of the House to lead the House of Representatives and a president *pro tempore* to lead the Senate. The teacher, acting as the president, should assign a vice president. Also, have students choose majority and minority floor leaders and majority and minority whips. Discuss the roles of each of these positions. Tell students that in the next activity they will learn about rules for Congress.

Taking a Stand

Lead students in a discussion on the importance of rules of conduct for Congress. Discuss the rules regarding financial matters. Allow students to discover, through discussion, why taking money from campaigns and using it for personal expenses would cause problems. Ask students to talk about any campaign-finance controversies they may be aware of. Allow students to decide if rules of conduct are needed in their mock congress. If students decide that rules are necessary, put these rules of conduct into effect.

CLOSE

Have students consider the bill they chose to attempt to get passed into law during the Motivate activity and the sequence they have followed to attempt to pass it. Ask students to consider why it is important to have such structure in Congress and why they could not just vote without establishing structure and rules. Have students create a list of the steps that they have taken so far in order to establish leadership and order for their congress. Compare these steps with the actual process used by Congress. Guide students to draw the conclusion that making laws is a great responsibility and that strict guidelines are important for maintaining an orderly government.

OPTIONS

Gifted Learners

 Encourage students to learn more about Dick Armey, Tom Daschle, or other congressional leaders by using the Internet, magazines, newspapers, and the Biographies section on the *Holt Researcher Online.* Have them share some articles, pictures, or political cartoons with the class, and lead a class discussion or debate about them.

Visual-Spatial Learners/Students Having Difficulty

 Have students create a Congressional Leadership diagram for the class, similar to the one on textbook page 116, that includes how each position is obtained. Ask students to fill in the names of the students in the class in each position as well as who currently holds that position in Congress. Encourage students having difficulty with the lesson to utilize this chart to help them study for Daily Quiz 6.1 and the Chapter 6 Test.

Students Having Difficulty/ Sheltered English Students

 Encourage students to make party affiliation badges for members of the mock congress in the classroom. Ask them to distinguish between members of the House and the Senate and to include leadership titles where appropriate. Teachers may wish to allow students access to a computer to make the badges and access to a laminator to laminate them.

Gifted Learners

 Encourage students to conduct research on rules of conduct violations committed by members of the House and Senate. Have students write a report discussing the violation that was committed and what sort of reprimand was issued. Students should include their opinion regarding whether the reprimand received was appropriate.

REVIEW

Have students complete the Section 1 Review on page 117. Use the answers in the Annotated Teacher's Edition to assess student mastery of this section.

ASSESS

To assess student mastery of this section, have students complete Daily Quiz 6.1 in *Daily Quizzes with Answer Key.* For additional assessment options, see *Alternative Assessment Handbook* on the *One-Stop Planner CD-ROM.*

ADDITIONAL RESOURCES

Baker, Ross. *House and Senate.* Third edition. 2000. W. W. Norton and Company.

Greenberg, Ellen. *The House and Senate Explained.* 1996. W. W. Norton and Company.

A Day in the Life of a Representative. Films for the Humanities and Sciences. (video)

For an overview of the legislative process and for information on finding legislative information, see: http://www.library.yale.edu/govdocs/legislat.html

HOLT PRESENTATION MAKER
Access Illustrated LECTURE
NOTES using Microsoft®
PowerPoint® on the
One-Stop Planner CD-ROM

OBJECTIVES

▶ Discuss the types of committees in Congress.
▶ Explain how committee assignments are made.
▶ Describe the kinds of staff that help congressmembers and committees perform their work.

MOTIVATE

Have both the mock house and the mock senate write up their proposed rule or bill. Explain that although this is the only bill they will be considering as a mock congress, the actual Congress must examine hundreds of bills. Lead students to the conclusion that if they had hundreds of bills to consider, they would not have time to consider all of them and some committees would have to be formed. Explain that in this lesson they will form committees in the class congress and learn about the committee system in the actual Congress.

TEACH

Building a Vocabulary

In their spiral notebooks, have students continue working on their Political Dictionary. List words the students will be expected to know for this section on the board. Have students list, define, and give an example of each of the terms, using information provided in the text or on the *Researcher CD-ROM*.

Demonstrating Understanding

Lead students in a discussion on the different congressional committees and the importance of each. Allow students to decide which standing committees, one of which must be a rules committee in each house, they will need for their mock congress. Next, have students determine which committees and subcommittees will be needed in each of the houses of congress. Have students select the joint and conference committees they wish to have. Lead students in a discussion of the need for each of these in their mock congress, and tell them that in the next activity they will learn more about select committees.

Applying Information

Discuss committee chairpersons and committee membership with students. Have students in the majority party of each house select someone to act as the chairperson for each of the committees they chose in the previous activity. Teachers may wish to designate several students as having seniority prior to the activity in order to simulate the way these selections are actually made by the U.S. Congress. Next, have students choose committees on which they wish to serve. If too many wish to serve on the same committee, have students campaign for a spot on the committee.

Drawing Conclusions

As a way of emphasizing the importance of membership on particular committees, have students conduct research using outside resources to find out if any of their state representatives serve on standing committees. Then have students use newspapers or other outside resources to track legislation that originated in that committee. Have students examine the legislation to see if it brings any particular benefit to their state or community. Ask students to draw conclusions about whether their representatives used their committee membership to influence legislation that benefited their state. Tell students that in the next activity they will learn about congressional staffs.

Writing About Government

Lead the class in a discussion regarding the three kinds of congressional staff. Have students decide which type of staff person he or she would consider being for the U.S. Congress. Ask students to identify a congressmember from their state and use the Internet to obtain his or her address. Have students write a letter to the congressmember asking for information about the job responsibilities of his or her staffers, the education and experience required to be a staffer, and how a person can apply to be a staffer. It will probably take several weeks or months to receive any feedback regarding students' questions, so have students refer to the Careers section on the *Holt Researcher Online* to find out more information about congressional staffers. When students receive a response to their letters, allow them to share the information with the class.

CLOSE

Have students identify bills currently under consideration in the U.S. Congress. Encourage students to choose bills that they will be able to consider in their committees in the mock congress. Have students discuss these bills in their committees and determine what information they would need for their committee to be able to act on the bill. Lead a discussion on the importance of committees and staffers in helping Congress to carry out its duties.

OPTIONS

Students Having Difficulty/ Sheltered English Students

  Encourage students to learn more about the job of a congressional staffer using the information available in the Biographies section on the *Holt Researcher Online*. As an extra credit project, have students write/type either the information they find or their ideas about how they would feel about having such a job.

Gifted Learners

 Have students write a paper about the role of one or more committees in Congress. Have different students write about different committees. Students should gather information for their papers from the Internet or library. Information about each committee should include the type of legislation considered by each committee, the size of the committee, key legislation that was approved by the committee, who chairs the committee, and any other pertinent information about the committee. Students should share the information they gather with the rest of the class. As a class, students should compile a chart summarizing the information.

Intrapersonal Learners/Gifted Learners

 Discuss with the class the increasing importance of congressional staffers. Tell students that for the first 100 years of Congress only committee chairs had staffs, but now there are thousands of staff members who not only serve representatives but committees and congressional agencies as well. Have students conduct research using the library and the Internet to describe the changes in the role and the importance of congressional staffs. Remind students that one of the principles that guides the U.S. government is that officials who represent the people should be elected by the people. Have students write an essay stating their opinion regarding the increased importance of congressional staffers and how their increased importance relates to the principle of representative government. Have students share their ideas with the rest of the class and allow time for class discussion on the topic.

REVIEW

Have students complete the Section 2 Review on page 122. Use the answers in the Annotated Teacher's Edition to assess student mastery of this section.

ASSESS

To assess student mastery of this section, have students complete Daily Quiz 6.2 in *Daily Quizzes with Answer Key*. For additional assessment options, see *Alternative Assessment Handbook* on the *One-Stop Planner CD-ROM*.

ADDITIONAL RESOURCES

Bisnow, Mark. *In the Shadow of the Dome: Chronicles of a Capitol Hill Aide.* 1990. Morrow.

Porter, Christopher. *How to Get a Job in Congress (Without Winning an Election).* 2000. Blutarsky Media.

Price, David. *The Congressional Experience.* 2000. Westview Press.

OBJECTIVES

- Describe how bills get referred to a committee.
- Explain the purpose of committee hearings and markup sessions.
- Discuss what happens to a bill when it reaches the full House or Senate floor.
- List the courses of action that can be taken by the president on a bill passed by Congress.

MOTIVATE

On a large piece of butcher paper or on the chalkboard, write the word *bill* on the far left side and the word *law* on the far right. Draw a dotted line between them. Ask students to brainstorm what they think happens to a bill that is being considered as law. Write down their ideas under the headings. Explain to students that in this section they will discover what actually happens to a bill under consideration and that they will experience the process using the bill they wrote in the Motivate activity of the previous lesson.

TEACH

Building a Vocabulary

In their spiral notebooks, have students continue working on their Political Dictionary. List words the students will be expected to know for this section on the board. Have students list, define, and give an example of each of the terms, using information provided in the text or on the *Researcher CD-ROM*.

Debating Ideas

Lead a discussion regarding the referral process of a bill. In their committees have students explore such resources as current newspapers and magazines to identify bills under consideration in the House and Senate. Have students determine how these bills were referred to the committee or subcommittee that referred them to the full House or Senate. Allow students time to debate these bills in their subcommittees, committees, or the entire mock house and senate. Tell students that in the next activity they will learn about committee hearings.

Role-Playing

Using the bill the students chose in Lesson 6.1 to make into law and wrote out in the Motivate activity in Lesson 6.2, have students hold mock hearings in their committees. Then have a mock Senate committee go through the process of markup. Have these students present an oral committee report to the rest of the class explaining any changes they have made to the bill. Write the wording from the original bill and from the new version that has gone through the markup process on the chalkboard or overhead projector for the entire class to examine. Ask students to identify if there are any changes in the bill's original intent or meaning that have resulted from the markup process. Explain to students that it is during the markup process that interest groups and others seeking to sway legislation can influence the wording of or terms of a bill, which sometimes creates opposition to the bill. Tell students that in the next activity they will learn about rules for the House and Senate.

Mastering Concepts/Role-Playing

Discuss with students the floor rules in the House and in the Senate. Allow time for the rules committee to decide on the rules for the bill they are considering. Encourage the party whips to go about their job of determining party vote as these decisions are being made. Once the bill has made it to the floor of both the mock house and the mock senate, allow students to hold a floor debate and then vote on the bill. If needed, students may also choose to have a conference committee to resolve differences in wording.

Synthesizing Information

Lead a discussion on the action a president can take on a bill passed by Congress. Acting as the president, the teacher then can choose to act in a way that is appropriate for the bill the students have presented. If the bill becomes law, discuss the significance of this new classroom rule and the importance of following the procedures used by Congress to ensure fairness. If the bill is vetoed by the teacher, lead a discussion on things that could have been done differently in order to get the bill passed.

CLOSE

List the steps the class bill took above the heading on the chalkboard or paper used in the Motivate activity. Discuss the similarities and differences between the students' thoughts at the beginning of the lesson and during the actual process regarding how a bill becomes law. Discuss the importance of the process and the reasons there are so many steps.

OPTIONS

Gifted Learners

 Encourage students to identify one bill currently under consideration either by committees or subcommittees. Have students keep a log following the progress of the bill until it is defeated or signed into law. Encourage them to cut out or copy articles regarding the bill they are tracking and include them in their log. Have students keep track of the bill's significant developments.

Students Having Difficulty/
Visual-Spatial Learners/Sheltered English Students

 Have students create a visual model of the process a bill goes through in becoming law. Have students start from subcommittees or committees and chart the process all the way to becoming a law. Instruct students to include what will happen if a bill is defeated at any of the stages. Students should also include all of the options the president has regarding acting on a bill and the override of a veto by Congress. Have students use different colors for the steps that are always necessary and for those that are not. Display the final product in the classroom to assist students in remembering the process of a bill becoming law.

Gifted Learners

 Discuss with students the use of filibusters to delay the final vote on a bill. Explain to them that the Senate has adopted a two-thirds majority vote in enacting cloture. Instruct students to consult the library and the Internet to research instances in which filibusters were used to delay a vote. Have students write a short paper describing who was trying to delay the vote and why, what topic the vote covered, the length of the filibuster, and the final outcome of the vote once the filibuster was ended.

REVIEW

Have students complete the Section 3 Review on page 128. Use the answers in the Annotated Teacher's Edition to assess student mastery of this section.

ASSESS

To assess student mastery of this section, have students complete Daily Quiz 6.3 in *Daily Quizzes with Answer Key*. For additional assessment options, see *Alternative Assessment Handbook* on the *One-Stop Planner CD-ROM*.

ADDITIONAL RESOURCES

Dekieffer, Donald. *The Citizens Guide to Lobbying Congress.* 1997. Chicago Review Press.

Redman, Eric. *The Dance of Legislation.* 2001. University of Washington Press.

Congress Stack. Highlighted Data, Inc. (CD-ROM)

OBJECTIVES

▶ Identify whether special interest groups obstruct Congress in promoting the public good.

▶ Explain the main criticism of the committee system and how it affects the public good.

▶ Describe the role Congress plays in promoting the public good.

MOTIVATE

Review with students ways in which government promotes the public good, as discussed in Chapter 1, Section 1. Ask students to consider the public good in the classroom and how they, as the mock congress, acted to promote it. Discuss which category of promoting the public good that the students' bill or law falls into. Have students justify their reasoning. As a lead-in to the next activity, tell students that in this section they will be learning about various ways that Congress promotes the public good. List these ideas on the board.

TEACH

Building a Vocabulary

In their spiral notebooks, have students continue working on their Political Dictionary. List words the students will be expected to know for this section on the board. Have students list, define, and give an example of each of the terms, using information provided in the text or on the *Researcher CD-ROM*.

Judging Information/Writing About Government

Lead a discussion about special interest groups and their influence on Congress. Have students consider the examples of possible pork-barrel spending on textbook page 130 and discuss examples of pork-barrel spending that they are aware of. Ask students to write a brief essay supporting or defending the issue of pork-barrel spending. Lead a class discussion on the different opinions. Also discuss how the examples would either aid or obstruct Congress in promoting the public good. Tell students that critics charge that special interest groups may obstruct Congress's ability to promote the public good and that there are also complaints that the committee system affects the public good.

Tell students that in the next activity they will be learning about these issues.

Debating Ideas

Lead a discussion on the criticisms of Congress being unrepresentative of the people it represents. Identify specific ways that Congress has been unrepresentative and encourage students to debate these complaints among themselves. Instruct students to consider examples from their mock committees to hypothesize how a committee system affects the public good. Tell students that in the next exercise they will learn about the role Congress performs in promoting the public good.

Drawing Conclusions

Have students determine how Congress promotes the public good. Ask them to hypothesize what would happen to the public good if Congress did not exist. Discuss these effects, both positive and negative, as a class. Next, lead a class discussion weighing the effect of special interests on congressional policy decisions. Then have students attempt to develop a plan to reduce the role of special interests in influencing congressional policies dealing with the public good. Tell students that in the next activity they will be examining conflicts between interest groups.

Recognizing Point of View/Taking a Stand

Provide students with literature that describes a controversy that can or will be settled through legislation. For example, a news magazine article on the ongoing argument between logging interests and environmental interests. Be sure that sources describe both sides of the argument. Have each student write a few paragraphs describing the issues involved in the controversy and how these issues relate to the public good. Students should take a stand on the issue. After students have turned in their essays, create two columns on the chalkboard, one representing each side of the chosen controversy. Then, make a mark under the column that each essay supports. (You should get a mixture of support for both sides.) Explain to students that determining which interests promote the public good is not always easy and that this makes weighing the concerns of interest groups an important job.

CLOSE

Refer students to the ideas they came up with in the Motivate activity on how their mock congress promoted the public good of the classroom. Ask students to compare their ideas to the ways in which the U.S. Congress promotes the public good. Allow students to discuss the similarities and differences between the two. Explain to students that it is important for citizens to be informed in order to ensure that Congress promotes the public good.

OPTIONS

Students Having Difficulty/ Sheltered English Students

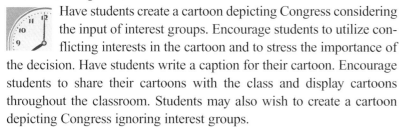 Have students create a cartoon depicting Congress considering the input of interest groups. Encourage students to utilize conflicting interests in the cartoon and to stress the importance of the decision. Have students write a caption for their cartoon. Encourage students to share their cartoons with the class and display cartoons throughout the classroom. Students may also wish to create a cartoon depicting Congress ignoring interest groups.

Gifted Learners

Using magazines and newspapers, have students identify special interest groups currently attempting to influence Congress. Have students identify the issues that they read about and either take a stand on the issue or hypothesize how they think Congress will act regarding it. Encourage students to follow the issue to see if what they wished to happen does or if they were correct in their hypothesis. Allow students to share information with the class.

Intrapersonal Learners/Gifted Learners

 Organize the class into several small groups. Each group will represent a state or region of the country. Have each group use the library and other resources to research examples of pork-barrel spending for the area they have been assigned or bring in articles for groups to use. Each group should identify what the money was spent on, how it aided the area, which representatives pushed for this federal money, and whether they agree with this appropriation of federal money. Have each group discuss its findings with the rest of the class.

REVIEW

Have students complete the Section 4 Review on page 132. Use the answers in the Annotated Teacher's Edition to assess student mastery of this section.

ASSESS

To assess student mastery of this section, have students complete Daily Quiz 6.4 in *Daily Quizzes with Answer Key.* For additional assessment options, see *Alternative Assessment Handbook* on the *One-Stop Planner CD-ROM.*

RETEACH

For students having difficulty with the lessons, have them complete Reteaching Activity 6. This activity is located in *Reteaching Activities with Answer Key.*

ADDITIONAL RESOURCES

Elving, Ronald D. *Conflict and Compromise: How Congress Makes the Law.* 1996. Touchstone Books.

Goldstein, Kenneth M. *Interest Groups, Lobbying, and Participation in America.* 1999. Cambridge University Press.

Political Partisanship vs. Serving the People. Films for the Humanities and Sciences. (video)

GOVERNMENT NOTEBOOK

The Government Notebook is a journal activity that encourages students to consider basic concepts of government that relate to their lives. A follow-up notebook activity appears on page 134.

WHY IT MATTERS TODAY

To find additional lesson plans dealing with the U.S. Congress at work, visit **CNNfyi**.com or have students complete the GOVERNMENT IN THE NEWS activity on page 133.

CNNfyi.com

CHAPTER 6

CONGRESS AT WORK

Some people might praise Congress by saying that no other institution in the world operates quite like it. Others might utter these words as an insult, criticizing Congress for being slow and for operating under complicated, mazelike rules.

Still, Congress has developed a remarkable system for tackling the enormous task of making the nation's laws. To fully appreciate this system, you must begin by examining the organization of Congress as well as the legislative process. This chapter also considers the impact of Congress on the well-being of the citizens it serves.

GOVERNMENT NOTEBOOK

In your Government Notebook, write a paragraph describing the process you think Congress goes through in considering and voting on legislation.

WHY IT MATTERS TODAY

Your representatives in Congress try to pass legislation that promotes the public good. At the end of this chapter visit **CNNfyi**.com to learn more about how Congress works for all Americans.

CNNfyi.com

READ TO DISCOVER

1. What are the terms and sessions of Congress?
2. How is congressional leadership organized?
3. What are the rules of conduct in Congress?

POLITICAL DICTIONARY

quorum
term limits
incumbent
majority party
minority party
Speaker
floor leader
party whip
president *pro tempore*
censure
expulsion

Making laws that govern a nation of millions of people is a great responsibility. As noted in Chapter 5, Congress operates under a set of rules that determines how to carry out this responsibility. Some of these rules are outlined in the Constitution. Others have been made by Congress itself. These rules dictate how long Congress is in session, who leads Congress, and how sessions are conducted.

Terms and Sessions

Congressional elections take place every even-numbered year in November. All of the members of the House and one third of the members of the Senate are elected in any congressional election year. Each new term of Congress begins on January 3 following the November election and lasts two years. Each Congress is numbered, from the 1st Congress in 1789 and 1790 to the 107th Congress in 2001 and 2002, and so on.

Each congressional term is divided into two 1-year sessions. Prior to the adoption of the Twentieth Amendment, which states that each new congressional term will begin on January 3, congressional terms began in December, 13 months after congressional elections had taken place. The amendment was passed to prevent congresspeople from serving an entire year as "lame ducks"— members who had not been re-elected.

After the passage of the amendment, sessions lasted from January until August or September. During the last few decades, however, Congress has remained in session almost continuously. Members take recesses, or breaks, of various lengths during the summer, before elections, and around holidays. When Congress is in session, a **quorum**, or majority of members, must be present to conduct business.

Sometimes problems that require congressional action arise while Congress is in recess. If necessary, the president can recall congressmembers to Washington for a special session. This rarely happens, however.

Term Limits

Today there are no **term limits**—legal limits on the number of terms a person can serve—for members of Congress. Term limits have been the subject of much debate in recent years, however. Those in favor of term limits criticize Congress, saying that it is an institution in which career politicians dominate the lawmaking process. These critics believe that a person who is new to Congress might be more in touch with citizens' concerns.

Political observers have noted a curious fact. Although Congress as an institution may be unpopular, voters generally are satisfied with their own representatives and senators. Therefore, **incumbents**, or officeholders, tend to have a good chance of being re-elected. This may be because of name recognition or because incumbents have had the opportunity to help constituents and to get projects and pass favorable legislation for their districts or states. They also have a record of performance in Congress that voters can evaluate. Challengers cannot be similarly evaluated because they have not been in office. Voters often remember what the incumbent has

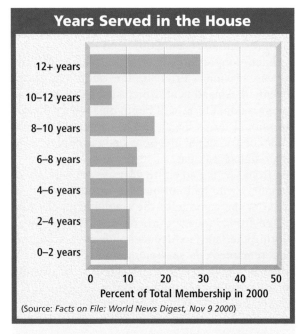

Years Served in the House

	Percent of Total Membership in 2000
12+ years	(about 29)
10–12 years	(about 5)
8–10 years	(about 16)
6–8 years	(about 12)
4–6 years	(about 14)
2–4 years	(about 10)
0–2 years	(about 13)

(Source: *Facts on File: World News Digest, Nov 9 2000*)

*In both the House and Senate a large percentage of Congress members are incumbents. A large percentage of incumbents, however, serves for more than 12 years. **What percentage of representatives has served for more than 12 years?***

done for their state or community and view challengers as untried and inexperienced.

The Permanent Congress Since the 1950s the incumbent advantage has helped keep congressional turnover low—around 8 percent. In 1988 congressional turnover figures were particularly low—with 97 percent of the incumbents running for re-election winning their races. Such statistics fed a growing concern over lengthy periods of congressional service. Many people charged that these incumbent leaders had become entrenched in a "permanent Congress." These critics believed that Congress had become unresponsive to the people and resistant to change.

The congressional elections in 1992 marked a downturn, for a time at least, in the permanent Congress. An unusually large number of House members retired. In addition, the number of incumbents who ran for re-election and were defeated rose from 7 in 1988 to 43 in 1992. Thus, the House saw its biggest change since 1948, with 110 representatives—more than one fourth of its membership—newly elected. In the elections of 1994 the trend continued, with 87 new members elected—35 of whom had defeated incumbents and 52 of whom had taken seats for which incumbents did not seek re-election. In 1996 and 2000, incumbents made a much stronger showing, with close to 90 percent of them gaining re-election.

Support for Term Limits Criticism of the permanent Congress has sparked a grassroots movement at the state level for term limits. In 1990 Colorado passed a law establishing term limits for its congressmembers. In 1992 thirteen more proposed laws establishing term limits made it onto state ballots, and all of them passed.

In 1995, however, the Supreme Court ruled that neither the states nor Congress may impose term limits on members of Congress without a constitutional amendment. Many citizens' groups and some legislators are working to pass an amendment for Congress similar to the Twenty-second Amendment, which limits the president to two terms.

POLITICAL PROCESSES *Grassroots movements for term limits were sparked by critics of politicians who serve in Congress for long periods.* ***What are some of the criticisms of a permanent Congress?***

Effects of Term Limits

PRINCIPLES OF DEMOCRACY What effects would term limits have on the work of Congress? Critics of term limits argue that government is complicated and that it often takes several terms to understand it. Short-term members have little experience in the running of Congress and must depend more on well-informed nonelected groups, including interest groups. As a result, a Congress of only short-term members might be less likely to reach independent decisions.

Critics of term limits also argue that the chance for re-election gives politicians a reason to do a good job. A congressmember who could not run again for office would be less likely to work hard to address the concerns of voters. In addition, say critics, when voters are unhappy with the performance of an incumbent, they can remove that person from office simply by electing someone else.

Supporters of term limits reply that one or two terms is enough time to learn the job and that the current system encourages unnecessary spending. To gain re-election, they say, some representatives try to win the favor of voters by securing nonessential projects for their districts. Supporters believe that members whose terms are limited by law will do what is right rather than merely what will get them re-elected.

Congressional Leaders

Congressional leadership is organized strictly by party. In each house of Congress the political party that holds the most seats is called the **majority party**. The political party with fewer seats is called the **minority party**. Presiding officers and committee chairs always come from the majority party. Members also receive their committee assignments based on their party membership.

The House operates under stronger leadership than does the Senate and is controlled by stricter

POLITICAL PROCESSES *Speaker of the House Dennis Hastert, right, speaks to the press after the attacks of September 11, 2001, as Senate Majority Leader Tom Daschle, left, and House Minority Leader Richard Gephardt, center, look on.* **What makes a party the majority party?**

rules. Having more than four times as many members as the Senate, the House requires more structure to keep it functioning smoothly.

House Leaders The most influential position in the House of Representatives is that of **Speaker**. Although the Constitution mentions the position of the Speaker, it says nothing about the powers accompanying the office. In practice, as the presiding officer of the House, the Speaker officially gives the floor to members who wish to speak. The Speaker also controls floor debates and has a powerful hand in controlling the flow of legislation. The Speaker not only assigns legislation to committees but also helps appoint committee members and other House leaders from his or her party.

The visibility of the Speaker's office has increased dramatically in the past two decades. This has been particularly true at times when one party has controlled Congress while the other party has held the presidency. In such cases the Speaker has

Caption Answer
The majority party is the party that holds the most seats.

GLOBAL CONNECTIONS

The House of Commons in the British Parliament also has a Speaker, but the responsibilities of that position are far different from those of the Speaker in the U.S. House of Representatives. Instead of acting as a party leader who supports legislation as the U.S. Speaker does, the British Speaker acts much more like an umpire. The British Speaker acts as an impartial observer whose duties include maintaining order, presiding over deliberations, and ensuring that the rules of the House of Commons are obeyed. ■

internet connect

TOPIC: Term Limits
GO TO: go.hrw.com
KEYWORD: SV3 GV6

Have students access the Internet through the HRW Go site to research the pros and cons of term limits. Then ask students to write a letter to the editor in which they express their opinions on this subject. Remind students to include at least three main reasons for their opinion, to include facts from their research in their letters, and to use standard grammar, punctuation, spelling, and sentence structure.

Caption Answer

The vice president serves as the presiding officer of the Senate and breaks tie votes.

SECTION 1 REVIEW ANSWERS

1. Refer to the following pages: quorum (113), term limits (113), incumbent (113), majority party (115), minority party (115), Speaker (115), floor leader (116), party whip (116), president *pro tempore* (116), censure (117), expulsion (117).

2. For censure, students should point out that it only takes a majority vote of either house and usually

(Continued on page 117)

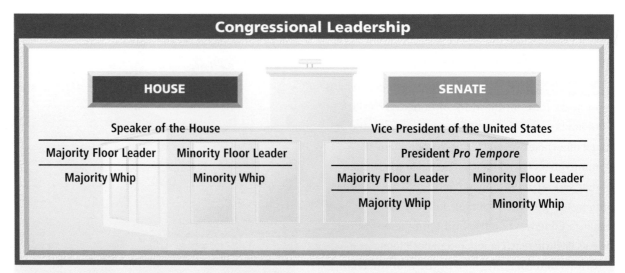

Congressional Leadership

HOUSE	SENATE
Speaker of the House	Vice President of the United States
Majority Floor Leader Minority Floor Leader	President *Pro Tempore*
Majority Whip Minority Whip	Majority Floor Leader Minority Floor Leader
	Majority Whip Minority Whip

This chart illustrates the organization of leadership in Congress. There are only small differences between the organization of the leadership in the House and the Senate.
What is the vice president's role in the Senate?

emerged as a leader of the opposition to the president and his party's policies. In the mid-1990s, for example, when President Clinton and the Democratic Party held the White House and the Republicans were the majority party in Congress, Speaker Newt Gingrich became well known as a strong voice in government.

House members of each party also choose their own **floor leader**. The majority floor leader serves as an assistant to the Speaker and is the second-most-influential member of the House. The minority floor leader is the minority party's chief spokesperson. These two people are commonly referred to as the majority leader and the minority leader.

In addition, each party chooses its own **party whips**. The main function of a party whip is to monitor and influence how his or her party's members vote on legislation. Today many members are involved in each party's whip organization. For example, almost half of all House Democrats belonged to their party's whip organization during a recent congressional session. Whips act as an intelligence network for the party leadership. By discovering members' opinions on particular legislation, whips enable leaders to more efficiently drum up support for the party's official stance.

Senate Leaders The presiding officer in the Senate is the vice president of the United States.

Unlike the Speaker of the House, the vice president's only substantial role in Congress is to break tie votes. In the absence of the vice president, the **president *pro tempore*** is the formal head of the Senate. The president *pro tempore* is the person in the majority party who has been in the Senate the longest.

The general organization of the Senate parallels that of the House—and the leaders of both houses are selected in a similar manner. The most powerful Senate leader, however, is the majority leader. He or she is the main strategist for the majority party and serves as the party's chief spokesperson.

Rules of Conduct

The Constitution gives Congress the power to judge its members' qualifications. When the House or the Senate questions the constitutional qualifications of a newly elected member, it may refuse to seat the member unless its concerns are resolved. Such challenges are rarely made and may be reviewed by the Supreme Court.

Both houses also have the right to judge their members' behavior. The House and the Senate have each set strict rules of conduct for their members, including in financial matters. For example, members may not use campaign contributions for personal expenses. In addition, they must disclose their financial holdings. This helps

POLITICAL PROCESSES *Former senator David Durenberger listens to the proceedings during a Senate Ethics Committee hearing investigating charges that he improperly reported his personal finances.* **What types of punishment may congressmembers receive for violating rules of conduct?**

prevent or uncover any conflicts of interest between members' potential financial gain and the legislation they consider.

Either house may vote by a simple majority to discipline one of its members because of poor conduct. Such discipline might be in the form of a reprimand—or scolding—or it might be a stronger disciplinary measure called a **censure**.

In January 1997 the House officially reprimanded Speaker Newt Gingrich—the first formal punishment the House had ever imposed on a Speaker. Gingrich was charged with bringing discredit upon the House after it was discovered that he had used tax-exempt donations for political purposes and then submitted false information about his actions to the House Ethics Committee that was investigating him. The report submitted by the investigative subcommittee did not conclude whether Gingrich's actions were "intentional" or merely "reckless," but it did say that Gingrich had failed to seek adequate legal advice regarding the donations. In addition to the reprimand, the committee fined Gingrich $300,000. The penalty was approved by a 395-to-28 vote.

For more serious or criminal conduct, the House or the Senate may vote to expel a member. **Expulsion** requires a two-thirds vote and formally removes a member from office. Only 4 representatives and 15 senators have been expelled in the history of Congress. Of the 15 senators, 14 were expelled during the Civil War for supporting the southern states' secession. Other members, however, have resigned under threat of expulsion. Senator Bob Packwood, for example, resigned in 1995 after lengthy hearings on charges that he had engaged in sexual and official misconduct while in office.

SECTION 1 REVIEW

1. Identify and explain:
- quorum
- term limits
- incumbent
- majority party
- minority party
- Speaker
- floor leader
- party whip

- president *pro tempore*
- censure
- expulsion

2. Comparing and Contrasting: Copy the Venn diagram below. Use it to identify the similarities and differences between censure and expulsion.

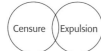

Censure   Expulsion

Homework Practice Online
keyword: SV3 HP6

3. | **Finding the Main Idea**

    a. What is the leadership structure in Congress and what is the role of each leader?

    b. When are members of Congress elected, and when do they take office? How long do their terms last?

4. | **Writing and Critical Thinking**

    Taking a Stand: Do you support term limits for members of Congress, or do you believe that they should be able to serve an unlimited number of terms? Why?

    Consider:
- how term limits would affect the structure of Congress
- the advantages and disadvantages of term limits

(Continued from page 116)

only involves a strong reprimand or a fine. For expulsion, students should point out that it requires a two-thirds vote of either house, is only used in cases of serious or criminal misconduct, and actually removes the representative from office.

3a. The House leader is the Speaker, who assigns legislation to committees and controls floor debates. Both the House and Senate have a floor leader for each party who serves as spokesperson for his or her party and has party whips who monitor how their party votes on legislation. The vice president presides over the Senate and breaks tie votes; in the absence of the vice president, the president *pro tempore* formally leads the Senate.

3b. November of even-numbered years; winners take office on January 3 after the election; House members serve two years; Senators serve six years.

4. Answers will vary, but students' opinions should include a discussion of the advantages and disadvantages of term limits. A possible advantage is that newer members of Congress are more in touch with citizens' concerns. A possible disadvantage is that Congress members would not be able to benefit from many years of experience.

SECTION 2
THE COMMITTEE SYSTEM

READ TO DISCOVER
1. What kinds of committees are there in Congress?
2. How are committee assignments made?
3. What kinds of staff help congressmembers and committees perform their work?

POLITICAL DICTIONARY

bill
appropriations
standing committee
subcommittee
select committee
joint committee
conference committee
seniority system

As you can imagine, Congress faces a huge and complex task in making the nation's laws. No member of Congress could possibly examine all proposed legislation in detail. Thus, congressional committees were formed to allow legislation to be examined by smaller bodies that are more expert in the subject than the House or the Senate as a whole. In this way, Congress can give more in-depth consideration to proposed legislation.

Each congressional committee deals with a specific area of public policy, such as defense, education, or health. Committees pore over **bills**, or proposed legislation, before they are submitted to the House or the Senate as a whole. Committees also oversee the performance of the executive branch agencies in their policy area.

Committees have existed since the first Congress. In the beginning, however, members resisted giving much power to committees. They feared that committees might develop into powerful groups that could force legislation through the rest of Congress. By the 1820s, however, committees began to play a role similar to the one they have today.

Types of Committees

There are two basic types of committees: authorizing and appropriations. Authorizing committees establish government policies. They propose solutions to public problems, such as crime, and determine how much funding is needed to put them into effect. The actual **appropriations**—funds set aside for specific purposes—for these solutions are made by appropriations committees.

Each house has many authorizing committees but only one appropriations committee. No authorized government program can become law unless it receives funding from the appropriations committee.

Comparing Governments

British Parliament

Britain, like the United States, has a bicameral legislature, though the structure of the British Parliament is very different from that of Congress. Parliament is made up of both a lower house—the House of Commons—and an upper house—the House of Lords. The monarch holds the largely ceremonial position of chief of state. The king or queen does, however, have the power to reject legislation passed by the houses of Parliament, although no monarch has exercised this power since the early 1700s.

The 659 members of the House of Commons are elected by the people. The House of Commons is considered the primary governing body of Britain because nearly all legislation is made in this house. In addition, the House of Commons has the power to pass bills into law without the approval of the House of Lords, most of whose more than 1,200 members inherit their seats. Although the House of Lords has no veto power, it may suggest revisions to bills passed by the House of Commons.

Congressional Standing Committees

HOUSE STANDING COMMITTEES

- Agriculture, Nutrition, and Forestry
- Appropriations
- Armed Services
- Banking, Housing, and Urban Affairs
- Budget
- Commerce, Science, and Transportation
- Energy and Natural Resources
- Environment and Public Works
- Finance
- Foreign Relations
- Governmental Affairs
- Judiciary
- Health, Education, Labor, and Pensions
- Rules and Administration
- Small Business and Entrepreneurship
- Veterans' Affairs

SENATE STANDING COMMITTEES

- Agriculture
- Appropriations
- Armed Services
- Budget
- Education and the Workforce
- Energy and Commerce
- Financial Services
- Government Reform
- House Adminstration
- International Relations

The chart above includes a list of House and Senate standing committees.
Why do you think that the House and Senate have many similar committees?

Congressional committees can also be divided into five other categories. These are standing committees, subcommittees, select committees, joint committees, and conference committees.

Standing Committees The permanent committees in each house of Congress are called **standing committees**. There are currently 19 standing committees in the House and 16 in the Senate. (See the chart above.) Standing committees deal with broad areas of legislation, such as trade, foreign policy, or finance.

Subcommittees Standing committees are further divided into smaller, more specialized bodies called **subcommittees**. There are about 215 subcommittees in Congress.

Traditionally, the chairs of the standing committees were able to dominate the subcommittees by appointing the subcommittee chairs. This changed, however, with reforms in the 1970s. These reforms allowed more less-experienced members to head subcommittees, which gave these members more power in the committees themselves. In addition, many new subcommittees were formed in the House. Soon, more than 50 percent of the House majority members were chairing subcommittees. In the Senate, more than 80 percent chaired subcommittees.

Select Committees Committees created to deal with special issues not covered by standing committees are known as **select committees**. These committees usually focus on investigations rather than legislation and usually are temporary. A select committee in the Senate investigated the Whitewater case in the mid-1990s.

Joint Committees Committees made up of members from both the House and the Senate are called **joint committees**. These committees deal with matters that are best handled by the two houses working together. Some joint committees, such as the Joint Economic Committee, study and advise Congress in key policy areas. This is more efficient than having two committees—one in the House and one in the Senate—study broad policy issues.

Conference Committees Members of both houses of Congress also meet together in **conference committees**—temporary bodies appointed to work out a compromise between House and Senate versions of a bill passed by both houses. Conference committees are explained more fully in Section 3.

An overhead transparency of the chart on this page is available in *Transparency Resources*. See Transparency 13: Congressional Standing Committees.

Caption Answer

Answers will vary, but students should mention the similar roles of the House and the Senate.

THEMES IN GOVERNMENT

CONSTITUTIONAL GOVERNMENT

In 1965 Congress established the Joint Committee on the Organization of Congress to investigate the congressional committee system. The group held hearings and recommended reform.

Five years passed, however, before Congress completed the bill that contained some of the Joint Committee's suggestions. The Legislative Reorganization Act of 1970 responded to the dissatisfaction of junior members who claimed that committee chairs held too much power. By requiring committees to hold public meetings and by allowing a majority of members to convene a committee, the act undermined the chairs' authority and provided opportunities for other committee members to influence decisions. ■

Careers in Government

Congressional Staffer

Have you ever wanted to work on Capitol Hill? The opportunity to work with lawmakers and to influence public policy attracts armies of young people seeking congressional staff jobs.

Congressional staffers generally are young, with most of them using the position as a stepping-stone to another career. Some go on to work for interest groups and government agencies. Some even run for office, occasionally winning the seat of their retiring boss.

One route to staff jobs is through summer internships. Each summer, thousands of young people take these apprentice positions, often for little or no pay. Most congressmembers hire interns only from their state or district, and most interns are college undergraduates. Students typically find summer internships with the help of a college placement office, through personal connections with the member, or through persistent letter writing.

Internship jobs usually involve clerical work, such as sorting mail, running errands, and filing papers. Interns, however, also experience the atmosphere of Congress, learn its procedures, and make contacts with staffers who can help them secure permanent jobs later.

Here, an intern works in the office of Representative Henry Bonilla. An internship can provide valuable experience for later jobs.

Competition for entry-level staff jobs is fierce. Many job-seekers move to Washington, D.C., and support themselves by working odd jobs. They submit hundreds of resumés, often going door-to-door looking for openings. Frequently, members of Congress will reward people who worked actively on their campaigns by giving them staff positions. Most people who land entry-level jobs have enthusiasm, a high energy level, good communications skills, and related job experience.

Committee Assignments

By dividing its labor into committees, Congress is better able to examine important issues and make effective decisions. At the same time, committee assignments give members a visible role for which they can claim credit in their district or state. For these reasons, committee assignments are critical to members of Congress.

Committee Chairs Given the importance of committees, committee chairs hold a great deal of power. They always belong to the majority party and traditionally were selected using the **seniority system**, or by the length of time they served on the committee in question. Today, although chairs are not always the most senior member, seniority still plays an important role in chair assignments.

There is a case to be made for the seniority principle. Members who serve on the same committee for a long time can gain great skill in dealing with specific policy areas. The seniority principle also gives chairs considerable independence because they do not have to rely on the party leadership or on other members to keep their jobs.

As a result of the seniority system, by the 1960s some longtime congressmembers had chaired the same committees for more than 10 years. This locked out many younger members of Congress from powerful committee chair positions. Critics of the system believed that it prevented the introduction of new leadership and new ideas.

POLITICAL PROCESSES *Senator Patrick Leahy and Senator Charles Schumer, members of the Senate Judiciary Committee, discuss the appointment of federal judges with Martha Barnett, president of the American Bar Association. **What role does seniority play in the selection of committee chairs?***

In response, Congress in the 1970s changed the way committee chairs are selected. Today they are elected by members of the majority party. Although the most senior members still are most often elected, some younger members with fewer years of service have been made chairpersons.

In 1995 members of the 104th Congress changed the committee structure further. The Republican majority in the House cut overall committee staff by one third, limited the number of terms a person could serve as a committee chair, and eliminated three standing committees. These changes were part of a larger effort to reduce the size of government.

Committee Membership The most critical factor in determining committee membership is the members' own wishes. A member is most likely to join a committee on which he or she has asked to serve. Members ask to serve on particular committees for various reasons. Some seek special benefits for their districts or states. Members can accomplish this by influencing policy in areas important to their constituents; forest policy, for example, might be highly important to people in a logging district. A member also can help constituents by obtaining government money for projects in their locality. As one committee member said, "As far as I can see, there is really only one basic reason to be on [this] committee. . . . Most of all, I want to be able to bring home projects to my district."

Other members seek committee assignments to influence broad public policy issues of national concern, even though such assignments often give the member no particular advantages with constituents. For example, a representative might seek an appointment on the International Relations Committee even though the committee's work does not relate directly to his or her district.

The more powerful committees typically receive more applications than there are seats available. As a result, members often have to "run" for seats on committees such as the House's Appropriations, Budget, Rules, and Ways and Means Committees, and the Senate's Armed Services, Foreign Relations, Finance, and Appropriations Committees. Selections are based on the political needs of the member, how long the member has been in Congress, his or her loyalty to the party leadership, and whether or not the member's state already has representatives on the committee.

Once members have been named to a committee, they may stay as long as they wish (except for appointees to the House Budget Committee, which limits membership to six years). Many members remain on a committee to increase their seniority. The member with the most seniority often becomes the committee chair and holds great influence in directing the committee's work.

Congressional Resources

Performing all the work of Congress requires extensive resources. For this reason, congressmembers and committees have large staffs to assist them. In addition, congressional agencies conduct valuable research that helps members of Congress and their staffs do their jobs.

Personal Staff For the first 100 years of Congress, only committee chairs had staffs. The other members' offices were simply their desks on the House and Senate floors. By 1827 the House was hiring young boys as "pages," or messengers. Pages often were orphans or the children of members' friends. Members had started hiring personal staff by the 1890s.

Caption Answer

Seniority plays an important role in determining committee chairs, although the chair is not always the most senior member of a committee.

GLOBAL CONNECTIONS

The support staffs for congressmembers in the United States are quite large when compared to those of other nations. The U.S. legislative staff numbers more than 23,000 employees, which is more than that of any other country. ■

SECTION 2 REVIEW ANSWERS

1. Refer to the following pages: bill (118), appropriations (118), standing committee (119), subcommittee (119), select committee (119), joint committee (119), conference committee (119), seniority system (120).

2. Standing committees deal with broad areas of legislation, such as foreign policy or finance; subcommittees further divide standing committees into more specialized bodies; select committees are set up to deal with special issues not covered by standing committees; joint committees deal with matters that require the attention of both houses; conference committees work out compromises

(Continued on page 122)

(Continued from page 121)

on legislation between the House and the Senate.

3a. Congressional committees were formed to allow legislation to be examined by smaller bodies than the House or Senate. The members of these committees are usually more expert in their subject matter than members of Congress in general. This allows Congress to give more in-depth consideration of proposed legislation.

3b. Members request specific committee assignments. Assignments to popular committees are determined by seniority and other factors. Members seek assignments in order to influence national policy or to please constituents by obtaining government projects for their districts.

4. Answers will vary, but students should discuss the total number of people that members of Congress represent and the amount of legislation that goes through each house. Having resources fills the need for Congress to be fully informed in order to make important decisions; students may suggest a lack of communication and preparation.

CONSTITUTIONAL GOVERNMENT *Representative Solomon Ortiz discusses legislative issues with a member of his staff.* **In what ways do congressional staff members help Congress fulfill its responsibilities?**

Today the number of congressional staffers is in the thousands. These people work directly for the members and play a key role in their work. They suggest policies to members, draft bills, and negotiate with other staff about the language of proposed legislation. Before committee hearings, they write questions for members to ask witnesses.

Stories abound of staffers who are powerful players in making public policy. Members have even complained at times about the power of their own staffers. "Senators, I fear, are becoming annoying constitutional impediments [stumbling blocks] to the staff," a senator once said. "Someday we may just allow the staff to vote and skip the middle man."

These concerns should be kept in perspective, however. Staffers make many suggestions, but they seldom act against the wishes of their employer.

Committee Staff Committee members have staffs as well. These people formally work for, and are on the payroll of, the committee. However, each member of a committee typically hires one or more committee staffers who work primarily for him or her, so they actually function much like personal staff. Because they deal with a single policy area, though, committee staffers tend to know more about the issues they work on than do personal staff.

Congressional Agencies In addition to congressional staffs, there are several agencies that help Congress carry out its work. The Library of Congress provides research facilities, and the Congressional Budget Office (CBO) helps deal with the enormous budget process each year. In addition, the General Accounting Office (GAO) watches over the spending of funds appropriated by Congress, and the Government Printing Office (GPO) prints thousands of publications that provide members and the public with information on the U.S. government.

SECTION 2 REVIEW

1. Identify and explain:
- bill
- appropriations
- standing committee
- subcommittee
- select committee
- joint committee
- conference committee
- seniority systems

2. Evaluating: Copy the chart below. Use it to identify the role of each type of committee listed.

Type	Role
Standing	
Subcommittee	
Select	
Joint	
Conference	

Homework Practice Online

keyword: SV3 HP6

3. **Finding the Main Idea**

a. What role do congressional committees fill?

b. How are committee assignments made, and why are particular committee assignments sought?

4. **Writing and Critical Thinking**

Taking a Stand: Why is it important for members of Congress to have many resources to help them do their jobs? What might happen if they had only one or two staff members?

Consider:
- the number of people members of Congress represent
- the amount of legislation that members of Congress must consider

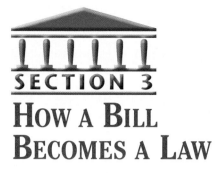

SECTION 3

HOW A BILL BECOMES A LAW

READ TO DISCOVER

1. How are bills referred to a committee?
2. What is the purpose of committee hearings and markup sessions?
3. What happens to a bill when it reaches the full House or Senate floor?
4. What courses of action can the president take on a bill passed by Congress?

POLITICAL DICTIONARY

filibuster
cloture
roll-call vote
pocket veto
line-item veto

The Constitution states that each house of Congress may set its own procedures. Thus, the House and the Senate set the specific rules for considering legislation, except for the procedures dealing with presidential vetoes, which are established in the Constitution.

The legislative process developed by the House and the Senate is slow and includes many steps. This careful process ensures that legislation is thoroughly considered before being passed or rejected. It also means that only a very small percentage of the bills introduced are passed. For example, only 610 of the 10,513 bills introduced in the 102nd Congress were passed into law.

Although citizens, interest groups, the president, and others may suggest ideas for a bill, only members of Congress may introduce legislation. A bill may be introduced first in the House or in the Senate, except for tax bills, which must begin in the House. By custom, appropriations bills also begin in the House. After being introduced, a bill generally goes through six main steps before becoming a law:

★ referral to committee,
★ hearings,
★ markup,
★ floor consideration,
★ conference committee, and
★ presidential action.

Referral to Committee

In most cases a bill that is introduced in Congress is referred to a committee, which may send it to a subcommittee for consideration. Committee consideration is crucial. A bill rarely reaches the full House or Senate floor without committee approval.

In the House, referral decisions are made by the Speaker, and in the Senate by the presiding officer. Most referrals are routine. In the Senate, for example, a bill about price supports for peanuts goes to the Agriculture, Nutrition, and Forestry Committee, and a bill about weapons development goes to the Armed Services Committee.

In cases where the referral is not so straightforward, however, the referral power gives the

---

II

107TH CONGRESS
1ST SESSION
S. 355

To require the Secretary of the Treasury to mint coins in commemoration of the contributions of Dr. Martin Luther King, Jr., to the United States.

IN THE SENATE OF THE UNITED STATES

FEBRUARY 15, 2001

Ms. LANDRIEU (for herself, Mr. SANTORUM, Mr. BREAUX, Mr. CLELAND, Mr. DODD, Mr. DURBIN, Mr. FEINGOLD, Mrs. FEINSTEIN, Mr. HARKIN, Mr. JOHNSON, Mr. LEVIN, Mr. LIEBERMAN, Mr. NELSON of Florida, Mr. REID, Ms. STABENOW, Mr. TORRICELLI, Mr. BROWNBACK, Mr. CHAFEE, Mr. COCHRAN, Ms. COLLINS, Mr. CORZINE, Mr. SPECTER, Mr. VOINOVICH, Mr. MILLER, and Mrs. CARNAHAN) introduced the following bill; which was read twice and referred to the Committee on Banking, Housing, and Urban Affairs

---

A BILL

To require the Secretary of the Treasury to mint coins in commemoration of the contributions of Dr. Martin Luther King, Jr., to the United States.

1   Be it enacted by the Senate and House of Representa-
2 tives of the United States of America in Congress assembled,
3 **SECTION 1. SHORT TITLE.**
4   This Act may be cited as the "Dr. Martin Luther
5 King, Jr., Commemorative Coin Act of 2001".
6 **SEC. 2. FINDINGS.**
7   Congress finds that—

POLITICAL PROCESSES *All House and Senate bills are labeled and numbered to make identification easier.* **Who is responsible for suggesting bills?**

SECTION 3

HOW A BILL BECOMES A LAW

Lesson Plans

For teaching strategies, see Lesson 6.3 located at the beginning of this chapter.

Political Dictionary

To reinforce the section's vocabulary terms, refer students to the Electronic Glossary on the *Researcher CD-ROM*.

Section Assessment

To assess students' mastery of this section, have them complete Daily Quiz 6.3 in *Daily Quizzes with Answer Key*.

Caption Answer

Bills may be suggested by citizens, interest groups, the president, and others.

PUBLIC GOOD *Committee hearings usually are open to the public, enabling many journalists and camera crews to attend.* **Why is it important for the public to have access to information presented in these hearings?**

majority party a powerful tool in controlling legislation. Which committee considers a bill greatly affects its fate because committees often have a predetermined position on issues coming before them. For example, it makes a world of difference whether a bill dealing with the control of pesticides is referred to an agricultural or an environmental committee. The agricultural committee will tend to limit such control, while the environmental committee will tend to strengthen it. Drafters of legislation often write bills in ways that encourage their referral to the committees most likely to favor their passage.

Hearings

Many bills have committee or subcommittee hearings, which usually are open to the public. Journalists, television camera crews, interest group representatives, and tourists crowd into hearings. Not all committee members attend, however. With busy schedules and hearing times that often conflict, all members of a subcommittee are seldom present at any but the most important hearings. Staffers often sit in for those who are absent.

Supporters and opponents of a bill testify at its hearing. Typically, testimony comes from the bill's sponsors and from federal and public officials.

Representatives of interest groups also testify. Many times, ordinary citizens who are affected by the problem the bill addresses—for example, competition from foreign products—have testified. Celebrities also have appeared. In 2000, for example, Michael J. Fox, who has Parkinson's disease, testified during a Senate committee hearing on the need for stem cell research.

Committee chairs often use hearings and the accompanying media coverage to build support for, or increase opposition to, a bill. Chairs also have some freedom in deciding who testifies and in what order. Again, this freedom enables chairs to affect how committee members, the media, and the public view the bill.

Markup

In the Senate, after a subcommittee approves a bill, the exact phrasing is decided, line by line, at the full committee level. This process is called markup. In the House, markup typically takes place at both the subcommittee and full committee levels.

In markup sessions, crucial decisions are made about what specific features a bill will have. For example, for coal miners to qualify for government benefits, how much proof must there be that their lung disease was caused by mining? Should employers who hire illegal immigrants be jailed or

Citizenship in Action

Teens Testify Before Congress

It is not everyday that a teen gets to testify before Congress, but it happens more than you may think. Members of the public are asked to testify on a regular basis, and young people who have taken a stand on policies or have a story to share are asked to present their point of view. Sometimes members of Congress also request that teens testify to share their perspectives on issues that affect them.

Take 17-year-old Doug Gorton. In 2000, he and his classmates were asked to appear before the Congressional Commission on Web-based Learning to discuss how they integrate technology into their regular school day. The Commission asked the students and their teacher certain questions in an effort to report to Congress and the president on the Internet and education.

To the teens, testifying in front of a congressional commission was both nerve-wracking and exhilarating. At first the students were intimated by their surroundings, but once they got used to it, they began to share their thoughts freely.

Members of the commission patiently listened to each teen, taking notes as they spoke. When the students observed the seasoned politicians and their aides in action, they realized that the politicians could be discussing anything—the fate of the free world, a message from a colleague, or when they would break for lunch. Whatever their message, it was thrilling for the students not only to testify, but to be a part of the Washington scene, even for a short time. It proved that Washington was business as usual. But what a fascinating business it was!

Another teen who testified before Congress was Elisa Svensson, an intern at the Institute for Youth Development. In March of 1999, she testified before the House Commerce Subcommittee on Health and the Environment about youth tobacco use and other risky behaviors. She reported that in her senior year in high school she found it alarming to see kids hide behind cars in the parking lot to sneak a smoke. It proved that tobacco was controlling their lives. She admitted that many of her peers were apathetic about the dangers of tobacco and other drugs. She then related a story of seeing a teenage girl smoking a cigarette sitting next to her mother. Instead of reacting, her mother was also smoking a cigarette. She said that teens desperately need not only education but strong models of behavior, namely from their parents.

Some young people are asked to testify before congressional committees to share their views on issues that have affected their lives.

What Do You Think?
1. Why are young people sometimes asked to testify before a congressional committee?
2. Why might Elisa Svensson's testimony have been relevant to the House Commerce Subcommittee on Health and the Environment?

only fined? Markup is time-consuming, precise work that involves mountains of details.

Traditionally, markup sessions were held in secret. Since the 1970s, however, most have been open, though not televised. Some people suggest that the openness has increased the influence of interest groups because they can closely observe a committee's actions and possibly pressure its members. Still, markup sessions are the most likely place in Congress for genuine debate rather than speech-making and posturing for the media.

After markup, a bill must be approved by the full committee before it can move to the House or Senate floor. A bill that fails to be approved dies in committee, and no further action is taken. If a bill is approved, however, committee staff members write a committee report. This report explains the changes that the bill would bring about and presents major arguments on the bill's behalf. The report helps members who are not on the committee to make their voting decisions.

Floor Consideration

For both the House and the Senate, there are standard operating rules that guide procedures for the passage of a bill. Some rules set procedures for voting, admission to the floor, and how business is conducted. In addition, before reaching the House or Senate floor for consideration and voting, most major bills are given strict, specific floor rules that limit floor debate and the changes that can be made to a bill. Strict floor rules thus increase the influence of committees because their work cannot be changed much by the full House or Senate. In contrast, the less strict the floor rules are, the more likely it is that a committee's bill will be changed by the full House or Senate.

Floor Rules in the House The House Rules Committee devises the set of rules that determines the conditions for debate and amendment of a House bill. Although rules can vary a great deal from bill to bill, there are traditionally three main types of rules—open, closed, and modified. An open rule allows representatives to propose any amendments that relate to the subject of the bill at hand. A closed rule prohibits amendments altogether. A modified rule determines that some parts of the bill may be amended, but not others.

House rules are not easily changed because of tight control by the House leadership. In some cases, however, the Rules Committee may allow what is called a waiver, or an abandoning, of point of order. This waiver allows a technical violation of House standard operating procedures—such as those for voting, orders of business, and duties of officers—so that the bill will make it to the House floor more quickly.

Although the Rules Committee acts on most bills, some actually bypass the rules process altogether. For example, some minor bills go to the floor on a set day and pass with little debate. In addition, bills that are considered noncontroversial may proceed under a suspension-of-the-rules procedure, which is set by the Speaker and dictates that only 40 minutes of debate will be allowed, no amendments will be heard, and a two-thirds vote is required for passage. The Speaker may enact this procedure only if the bill calls for expenditures of less than $100 million. Yet other bills—known as "privileged" bills—may be sent to the floor at any time and do not go through the Rules Committee. These generally are major bills such as budget or appropriations bills.

POLITICAL PROCESSES *This photo shows the electronic tally of floor votes in the House as broadcast on C–Span.* **How do committee reports help members of Congress make their voting decisions?**

POLITICAL PROCESSES *This 1965 photo shows Senate leader Everett Dirksen as he prepares materials to read in a filibuster against a bill to strike down right-to-work laws.* **How can a senator use a filibuster to block legislation?**

Filibusters Sometimes it is impossible to negotiate a unanimous consent agreement. In such cases, a bill may fall prey to a notorious congressional procedure known as a **filibuster**—an effort by one or more senators to hold up the final vote on a bill through delaying tactics. These tactics range from nonstop speechmaking to the offering of endless amendments. The Senate may sit for hours during a filibuster. A filibuster allows an intense minority to block the actions of the majority.

Over the years the Senate has moved to limit filibusters. In 1917 the Senate adopted a rule allowing a two-thirds, or 67-vote, majority to call for **cloture**, which stops a filibuster by setting a time limit on debate. This majority was lowered to three fifths, or 60 votes, in 1975.

Floor Rules in the Senate

The Senate does not follow a strict set of rules, as in the House. Standard Senate floor rules, for example, place no limit on how much time may be spent debating a bill nor on the number and kind of amendments that may be offered.

The Senate's standard rules, however, often are set aside if the members of the Senate unanimously agree to do so. A unanimous consent agreement can change many procedures—for example, it can set the length of time a bill can be debated or determine whether amendments can be submitted and if so, how many. Thus, if one senator objects to the Senate's standard debate rules, he or she can ask that a special rule be set for the bill.

The requirement for unanimous consent on changing a bill's particular debate rules gives senators a great deal of power. By withholding consent to the debate rule of a bill he or she dislikes, any member can tie the Senate in knots. In effect, every senator has veto power over the rules of each bill that comes to the floor. As one former representative observed, "If you just want to be unpleasant and have a temper tantrum . . . , you can have a field day in the Senate. You can break all the toys in the sandbox if that's what you want in order to get your way and you can pout with very great effect." Senate leadership must often negotiate to achieve a unanimous consent agreement.

Voting After all floor debate, congressmembers vote on the bill and any amendments made to it. Critical bills usually receive a **roll-call vote**, in which each member is called on individually to declare his or her vote.

Conference Committees

A bill that has been passed in one house is then sent to the other house for consideration. In most cases, a similar or identical bill is already being considered in the other house. The other house may pass a somewhat different bill. House and Senate versions of a bill may then be sent to a joint conference committee. As noted in Section 2, conference committees consist of both House and Senate members, who almost always come from the committees that drafted the initial versions of the bill.

Because conference committee members usually are chosen from among supporters of the bill, they have strong reasons to compromise rather than let the bill die in conference. In addition, the bills that are sent to conference committees generally are some of the most important or controversial pieces of legislation. After differences are resolved, the committee prepares a conference report. It is rare for the House or the Senate to reject a conference committee's recommendation.

THEMES IN GOVERNMENT

POLITICAL PROCESSES The longest Senate filibuster on record took place on August 28 and 29, 1957 during Senate debate on the Civil Rights Act of 1957. Strom Thurmond, then a democratic Senator from South Carolina, vigorously opposed civil rights legislation. He held the Senate floor for 24 hours and 18 minutes. The entire debate on the bill lasted 121 hours and 31 minutes. Despite Thurmond's efforts, the bill passed. ■

internet connect

TOPIC: Pork-Barrel Spending
GO TO: go.hrw.com
KEYWORD: SV3 GV6

Have students access the Internet through the HRW Go site to research the uses and abuses of congressional pork barrel spending. Then ask them to create a talk radio broadcast in which they assume the roles of a host, a congressmember, and an irate taxpayer discussing congressional spending. Remind them to define pork barrel spending and when it ceases to be spending for the public good and becomes "pork." Students should include specific examples of what they consider to be "pork" in their broadcast.

Presidential Action

A bill that has been passed by both houses is sent to the president, who may do one of four things:

★ sign the bill, which makes it law;
★ veto the bill;
★ keep the bill for 10 days without signing it. If Congress is in session during this time, the bill becomes law without the president's signature. This option is rarely used and is reserved for bills that the president dislikes but not enough to veto; or
★ **pocket veto** the bill. If the president receives a bill within 10 days of Congress's adjournment, he or she may hold the bill without signing it, and the bill does not become a law.

Vetoes are relatively rare. While Congress can pass a bill over a presidential veto, it is difficult to obtain the required two-thirds vote in both houses. Therefore, to ensure a bill's approval, Congress often works to answer presidential concerns about a bill before it is sent to the White House.

POLITICAL PROCESSES *President George W. Bush signs his tax relief bill, turning it into a law.* **What role does the president play after both houses of Congress have passed a bill?**

In 1996 Congress passed, and the president approved, a bill establishing a **line-item veto**, which gives the president the additional authority to veto certain parts of a spending bill without vetoing the entire measure. Once President Clinton used the line-item veto in 1997, congressmembers filed a lawsuit against the line-item veto, saying it was unconstitutional. In 1998 the Supreme Court ruled against the law because it allowed the president to change laws enacted through proper procedures.

SECTION 3 REVIEW

1. Identify and explain:
- filibuster
- cloture
- roll-call vote
- pocket veto
- line-item veto

2. Analyzing: Copy the chart below. Use it to identify and explain the steps involved in enacting a law.

Stages of Enacting a Law	
1. Referral to Committee	4. Floor Consideration
2. Hearings	5. Conference Committees
3. Markup	6. Presidential Action

3. **Finding the Main Idea**

a. How are bills assigned to a committee, and how can referring a bill to a particular committee affect its fate?
b. What can the president do with a bill after receiving it?

4. **Writing and Critical Thinking**

Analyzing: Why might it be important for Congress to follow particular steps each time a bill is introduced?
Consider:
- the process of how a bill becomes a law
- the overall variety of legislation that is considered by Congress

Homework Practice Online
keyword: SV3 HP6

SECTION 4

CONGRESS AND THE PUBLIC GOOD

READ TO DISCOVER
1. Do special interests obstruct Congress in promoting the public good?
2. What is the main criticism of the committee system, and how does it affect the public good?
3. What role does Congress play in promoting the public good?

POLITICAL DICTIONARY
interest groups
pork-barrel spending
home district

There is no doubt that Congress affects the well-being of the citizens it serves. The question is whether that effect is good or bad. Criticisms of Congress arose even before the 1st Congress met. One newspaper stated almost 100 years ago that "if God had made Congress, He would not boast of it." Are such criticisms justified? Or do Congress and its members work for the public good?

Influence of Special Interests

One major criticism of Congress is that it promotes special interests at the expense of the public good. In other words, congressmembers give too much weight to the narrow concerns of interest groups and of their home districts or states.

Interest Groups Critics charge that **interest groups** use campaign donations and other tactics to control members of Congress. As noted in Chapter 5, there is some connection between interest group support and congressmembers' voting behavior. However, this connection often stems from the fact that interest groups contribute to the campaigns of members who already

share the groups' views. (The connection between interest groups and members of Congress is explained more fully in Chapter 17.)

In fact, members often vote *against* the views of interest groups that support them. They do so because they are influenced more by their own beliefs, their constituents' views, and the position of their political party than they are by interest groups.

Home Districts Congress also has been criticized for the role that constituents' interests play in the lawmaking process. By representing their constituents, members of Congress give U.S. citizens a voice in government. Sometimes, however, members represent their constituents' interests by acquiring funds for unnecessary projects. This **pork-barrel spending** awards projects and grants, or "pork," from the government "barrel" to a member's **home district** or state. Projects include the construction of government buildings, roads, bridges, and other transportation projects. While these projects might be helpful to the community that receives them, they often are not the best use of taxpayers' money.

PUBLIC GOOD *High school student Nicole Gurule interviews Senator Pete Domenici of New Mexico.* **Why is it important for Congress to listen to the concerns of the public?**

SECTION 4

CONGRESS AND THE PUBLIC GOOD

Lesson Plans
For teaching strategies, see Lesson 6.4 located at the beginning of this chapter.

Political Dictionary
To reinforce the section's vocabulary terms, refer students to the Electronic Glossary on the *Researcher CD-ROM.*

Section Assessment
To assess students' mastery of this section, have them complete Daily Quiz 6.4 in *Daily Quizzes with Answer Key.*

Caption Answer
Answers will vary, but students should point out that it is a major way for representatives to find out their constituents' concerns.

PUBLIC GOOD What constitutes "pork" is often in the eye of the beholder. For example, in 1981 Representative George Goodling of Pennsylvania refused to support President Ronald Reagan's budget and tax programs until he received projects for his home district. Goodling wanted assurance that a military base in his district would remain open. He also wanted $37 million appropriated for the cleanup of Three Mile Island, a nuclear power plant located in his district.

Goodling received what he wanted and in return supported the Reagan programs. Critics might charge that Goodling was practicing pork-barrel politics, but his constituents would argue that he protected jobs and the environment in his district.

Some recent examples of pork include funding studies on the Japanese quail's mating habits, why people fall in love, a replica of the Pyramid of Cheops, and how long it takes eggs to cook. ■

Caption Answer

Answers will vary depending on students' opinons about what constitutes pork.

Opinions about what constitutes pork differ, however. It has been said that one person's "pork is another's good investment." For example, are there any government construction projects, such as a new highway, under way where you live? Does this seem like pork-barrel spending to you, or is it a good investment in the growth of business and jobs in your community? This may be a difficult question to answer because the response often varies depending on whom one asks.

Nonetheless, because many members work hard to bring federal money to their district or state, it is easy to find examples of what most observers would view as pork. For example, the following might qualify by most people's standards:

★ $500,000 to renovate the boyhood farm of Lawrence Welk, a television orchestra leader, so it could become a tourist attraction in Strasburg, North Dakota. The money was part of an agriculture appropriations bill.
★ $320,000 to buy the home of President William McKinley's in-laws in Canton, Ohio (McKinley's own home is no longer standing), for donation to the state of Ohio as a museum.
★ $10 million to build a ramp to Milwaukee's County Stadium parking lot.

PUBLIC GOOD *Senator Robert Byrd of West Virginia worked hard to bring this high powered telescope, named in his honor, to his state.* **Do you feel this is an example of pork-barrel spending or not?**

Others might not be so easy to identify. For example, Senator Robert Byrd of West Virginia, for many years the chair of the Senate Appropriations Committee, was particularly aggressive in seeking federal money for his state. As a result, a number of government offices moved to West Virginia, including the Federal Bureau of Investigation (FBI) Identification Center and an Internal Revenue Service (IRS) processing center. This helped bring additional money and jobs to West Virginia.

Some people defend pork-barrel spending as an appropriate way to address and represent local concerns. A problem arises, however, because not every district shares equally in such spending. Members of certain committees, such as the House Agriculture Committee and the Senate Environment and Public Works Committee, bring their constituents a much larger share of pork-barrel spending than is received by people in other areas.

What if all constituents received an equal share of pork-barrel spending? Would this promote the public good? To answer this question, you must understand how legislators pay for pork-barrel spending. Like all government spending, pork-barrel projects are paid for by taxes. Thus, if everyone's local concerns were rewarded with pork-barrel projects, high taxes would result. Pork-barrel spending, whether it is equally or unequally distributed, has a price.

The evidence suggests, however, that the granting of projects to meet district needs, like the granting of interest groups' contributions, is a problem but is not out of control. In fact, pork-barrel spending is a rather small slice of government spending, about 1 percent according to one budget expert's estimate.

With the Balanced Budget Act, only 1,664 pork-barrel projects were approved in 1997. However, since 1997, the number of pork-barrel projects has increased. During Bill Clinton's last budget, 6,454 pork-barrel projects were approved costing taxpayers nearly $16 billion. Thus far under President George W. Bush it looks like pork-barrel costs will continue to increase. By mid-May of 2001, the House Appropriations committee considered 18,898 projects worth an estimated $279 billion. Of course, only a small percentage of these projects will be approved, but the overall number proposed shows how many lawmakers are trying to bring money to their states.

CITIZENSHIP *Concerned citizens in Sacramento, California, rally against pork-barrel spending.* **Why have some members of Congress campaigned against pork-barrel projects benefiting their state?**

This increase in pork-barrel spending has occurred in spite of efforts to fight it in the mid-1990s when a number of candidates even campaigned against pork-barrel projects benefiting their own districts or states. According to one observer,

❝ People seem to feel that you're not doing them any favors by recycling their tax dollars through Washington and bringing home a few pennies. ❞

During the mid-1990s, Greg Ganske, an Iowa Republican, campaigned against several projects the incumbent Democrat had brought to the district. During the campaign, Ganske said that the projects were "like shipping a nice lean Iowa pig to Washington and getting back two thin strips of bacon."

Power of the Committee System

Another criticism of Congress is that it sets up unrepresentative committees. In other words, critics believe that current congressional committees do not properly represent the concerns of Congress or the country as a whole.

What is the basis of this charge? As you have learned, members often serve on a committee because their constituents have a strong interest in programs in that committee's policy area. For example, a House member from a rural farming district might seek assignment to the Agriculture Committee. Critics thus charge that most committee members represent a few strong local concerns instead of the interests of the country as a whole. Many people worry that unrepresentative committees often use their powerful influence to push harmful legislation through Congress and to control congressional investigations.

There are, however, several forces that weaken committees' ability to force narrow, locally oriented policies on Congress as a whole. First, members with many different viewpoints are assigned to the key committees. As a result, committees are generally not dominated by one viewpoint. In addition, most committee assignments are based more or less proportionally on a party's representation in Congress. (The majority party controls a slightly larger percentage of committee seats than its percentage of seats in Congress as a whole.) This helps to keep committees representative.

Also, committees' recommendations are not always followed by the full House or Senate. Committee members know that they can be overruled if they stray too far from what most members and their constituents want. Finally, the opening of committee hearings to the public and to the media makes it more difficult to pass narrow legislation that does not represent the interests of the country or the wishes of a majority of congressmembers.

Voice of the People

When judging Congress's role in promoting the public good, keep in mind that Congress is only one part of the larger system of the U.S. government. The federal government is also made up of the president, all the government agencies, and the federal courts.

THEMES IN GOVERNMENT

POLITICAL PROCESSES
Some political scientists argue that the committee system has weakened in recent decades. They point to three trends that appeared in the 1960s, 1970s, and 1980s that reduced committee power.

First, new concerns arose, such as conserving energy and protecting the environment, that did not fit into the traditional committee system. These issues forced many committees to interact in order to achieve policy goals, and this process of interaction eroded the dominance of any one committee.

Second, the growing concern over the size of the federal budget and the deficit affected all congressional business. Committee members were forced to pay attention to how their proposals would be perceived in an era of financial belt-tightening.

Finally, the growing emphasis on party loyalty in the 1980s and 1990s increased partisan voting, which limited the effectiveness of the committees. ■

SECTION 4 REVIEW ANSWERS

CONSTITUTIONAL GOVERNMENT *Members of the Senate Judiciary Committee hold hearings on the nomination of John Ashcroft for the position of attorney general.* **What types of issues do you think this committee would commonly discuss?**

Indeed, the local concerns represented in Congress are checked and balanced as they should be by the executive and judicial branches. In contrast to Congress, the president and the rest of the executive branch represent the national concerns of the majority of U.S. citizens as a whole. The judicial branch defends the minority's concerns by protecting citizens' constitutional rights.

It would be inefficient and even harmful if all institutions of the national government were as locally oriented as Congress. It is essential, however, to have one branch of government that directly provides a place that represents the local concerns of the people, whether they live in the congressperson's district or are part of an interest group.

SECTION 4 REVIEW

1. Identify and explain:
- interest groups
- home districts
- pork-barrel spending

2. Evaluating: Copy the chart below. Use it to explain the influence of special interests.

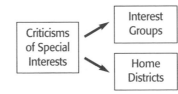

3. **Finding the Main Idea**

a. Whom does Congress represent that no other branch of government represents?

b. How does Congressional representation differ from other branches of government?

c. Why is Congressional representation essential to the public good?

4. **Writing and Critical Thinking**

Analyzing: Why do you think that some congressional reformers spend much of their time attacking instances of pork-barrel spending even though it accounts for only a tiny percentage of the federal budget?

Consider the following:
- public opinion of pork-barrel spending
- benefits and harms of pork-barrel spending

go.hrw.com **Homework Practice Online**
keyword: SV3 HP6

GOVERNMENT IN THE NEWS

The Pros and Cons of Pork Barrel Politics

When the Republican Party took over the White House from the Democrats in 2001, Washington politics as usual was in for a big change, right? In theory, yes, but in reality, politics as usual in Washington does not change all that much, no matter which party is in the White House.

As an example, let us take a look at the time-honored political tactic used by both parties called pork-barrel spending. That is when congressional lawmakers push pet projects for their district or state by inserting extra expenditures into spending bills coming up for a vote. This tactic bypasses the normal process for budget authorization. If and when the bill passes, the pork rides right along with it.

Of course, one legislator's pork, is another's necessity, like the construction of a new government building in California, or roads in Georgia, or bridges in Michigan, and other projects. However, some pork is a pure perk through and through that legislators hope the voters in their home states will remember at re-election time.

Pork-barrel spending hit a record $18.5 billion in 2000, according to the latest annual report by the watchdog organization Citizens Against Government Waste (CAGW). Since 1991, CAGW has catalogued over 23,000 pork-barrel projects in its Congressional "Pig Book." According to their 2001 report, the number of individual pork projects has nearly tripled in the last three years, from 2,143 to an incredible 6,333.

Examples of gross government waste cited in the report include: $550,000 for a Dr. Seuss memorial, $12 million for research on wood, $400,000 for a parking lot in a town of 300 people, and $460 million for an assault ship the Navy did not request. Is this spending ridiculous?

"Your constant cries to cut the pork sadden me, Senator."

This cartoon presents a humorous look at the politics of pork-barrel spending.

Well, it depends on whom you ask. A lot of lawmakers in Congress will not apologize for pushing their pet projects. They'll tell you that it's the grease that makes the legislative engine run smoothly. They maintain the attitude that if you approve my pork-barrel project, I will approve yours. Other lawmakers criticize pork-barrel spending because it promotes special interests at the expense of the public good.

What Do You Think?

1. Is pork-barrel spending fair? Explain your reasoning.

2. Why is pork-barrel spending likely to continue?

> **WHY IT MATTERS TODAY**
>
> While pork-barrel spending can help certain areas receive much needed government dollars, it adds to today's government costs Use **CNNfyi.com** or other **current events** sources to find additional information on government spending. Report on any instances of pork-barrel spending that you find.
>
> **CNNfyi.com**

Government in the News Answers

1. Students arguing in favor of pork-barrel spending may point out that it brings essential dollars to communities. Those arguing against it may point out that the money could be put to a better use.

2. Students should point out that pork-barrel spending is likely to continue because it is one way that representatives can clearly show they are helping their districts.

CHAPTER 6

Review Answers

Writing a Summary

Summaries should focus on the main points of each section. These may be found in the Read to Discover questions at the start of each section. Summaries should also use standard grammar, spelling, sentence structure, and punctuation.

Identifying Ideas

See the following pages; quorum (113), incumbent (113), censure (117), expulsion (117), bill (118), standing committee (119), joint committee (119), filibuster (127), role-call vote (127), pork-barrel spending (129)

Understanding Main Ideas

1. standing, select, joint, and conference committees; these committees exist so that specialized groups can

(Continued on page 134)

Review

(Continued from page 133)

consider legislation pertaining to their expertise so that consider legislation pertaining to their expertise so that Congress can handle the overwhelming amount of proposed legislation it must consider.

2. Speaker—selected from the majority party; floor leaders and party whips—selected from within each party; Senate leader—vice president; if the vice president is absent, president *pro tempore*.

3. based on member requests, although popular committees require "running" for an assignment

4. personal, committee, and agency staffs

5. referral to committee, hearings, markup, floor consideration, conference committee, presidential action

6. Special interests have too much influence; constituent interests play too big a role; committees are unrepresentative.

Reviewing Themes

1. sign it into law; veto it; keep it more than 10 days without signing so bill becomes a law; pocket veto

2. They can censure or expel a legislator.

3. It can promote the public good by providing valuable resources for an area but hurt the public good because those funds might have been better used elsewhere.

(Continued on page 135)

Writing a Summary

Using standard grammar, spelling, sentence structure, and punctuation, write a summary of the information in this chapter.

Identifying Ideas

Identify the following terms or individuals and explain their significance.

1. quorum

2. incumbent

3. censure

4. expulsion

5. bill

6. standing committee

7. joint committee

8. filibuster

9. role-call vote

10. pork-barrel spending

Understanding Main Ideas

SECTION 1 *(pp. 113–117)*

1. What types of committees are in Congress, and why do they exist?

2. How are leaders in each house of Congress selected?

SECTION 2 *(pp. 118–122)*

3. How are committee assignments made?

4. Who assists members of Congress with their work?

SECTION 3 *(pp. 123–128)*

5. What are the six steps in the legislative process after a bill is introduced?

SECTION 4 *(pp. 129–132)*

6. What are some major criticisms of Congress?

Reviewing Themes

1. Government What are the courses of action that a President can take on a bill passed by Congress?

2. Government What official actions may Congress take against a member who breaks the rules of Congress?

3. Economics How can money brought to an area both promote and hurt the public good?

Thinking Critically

1. Political Processes Does requiring unanimous consent on a bill's rules give individual senators too much power? Explain your reasoning.

2. Principles of Democracy Leaders of congressional committees are selected from the majority party. Do you feel that this system gives one party too much control in the legislative process? Explain your answer.

3. Public Good Do you agree with the practice of allowing journalists to attend subcommittee hearings? How might media coverage of these hearings promote the public good?

Writing about Government

GOVERNMENT NOTEBOOK

Review the process that you outlined in your Government Notebook at the beginning of the chapter. Now that you have studied the chapter compare that process with the real legislative process in Congress. Is the real process more complicated than you originally imagined? Write your answer in your notebook.

(Continued from page 134)

Interpreting the Graph

Study the graph below. Then use it to help you answer the questions that follow.

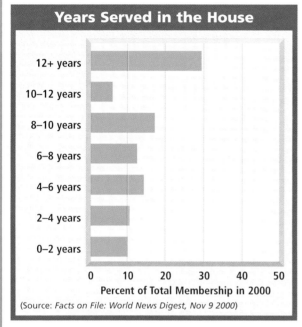

Years Served in the House

- 12+ years
- 10–12 years
- 8–10 years
- 6–8 years
- 4–6 years
- 2–4 years
- 0–2 years

Percent of Total Membership in 2000
(0   10   20   30   40   50)

(Source: *Facts on File: World News Digest, Nov 9 2000*)

1. What does the graph show about the number of years served by typical members of Congress?
   a. Most members have served from 0 to 2 years.
   b. Most members have served from 2–4 years.
   c. Most members have served from 8 to 10 years.
   d. Most members have served for more than 12 years.

2. Based on this data, should term limits be enforced?

Analyzing Primary Sources

Read the excerpt below in which Representative Earl Pomeroy speaks on the difficulties of passing the Balanced Budget Amendment. Then answer the questions that follow.

"The agreement before us represents at least procedurally the hardest thing this body ever tries to do, compromise differences, accept less than what each party wants, and tolerate aspects of the agreement each party would not include if it were simply a matter of writing its own package. Throughout the history of this place, this Chamber is mostly a matter of winner-take-all, the party of the majority passes the bills they want. . . . That often means a Presidential veto and the legislative initiative dies in the partisan standoff. . . . but the American people deserve better and the President and the leaders of Congress, both House and Senate, both majority and minority, have worked to give them better. This budget agreement accomplishes that difficult task."

3. Which of the following statements best describes the author's point of view regarding the need for compromise between political parties?
   a. The party in control of Congress should pass the legislation it wants to pass.
   b. If the President does not agree with proposed legislation he or she should veto it.
   c. Compromise should never be made between political parties.
   d. Compromise should be expected between both houses of Congress.

4. How does the structure of the legislative branch make compromise difficult?

Building Your Portfolio

Imagine that you head a citizen's group that has submitted a proposal to your representative to set aside part of your district as a national park. How can you and fellow citizens help influence the bill's process through Congress. Consider the steps that you should take and devise a plan to help secure the passage of the bill. If your plan is viable, consider sending it to your actual representative for consideration.

◢ internet connect

Internet Activity: go.hrw.com
KEYWORD: SV3 GV6

Access the Internet through the HRW Go site to conduct research on how a bill becomes a law. Then construct a flow chart or diagram to show how a bill moves back and forth from the House to the Senate and then to the president. Use different colors to show the different routes to final approval. Make sure you include committees in your diagram.

Thinking Critically

1. Students should explain their reasoning and discuss the power that the unanimous consent agreement gives one senator.

2. Those supporting too much influence may say that the system allows the party in the majority to control major committees. Those that do not find a problem with it may point out that the system allows the majority party to exercise the powers that voters wanted them to have.

3. Students should state their opinions about whether television crews should be allowed and whether they support the public good.

Social Studies Skills

1. d

2. Students may state yes because the data shows that legislators stay in office for a long time and are therefore not responsive to voters, or they may state no because citizens can benefit from the experience of legislators.

3. d

4. The winner-take-all tradition in Congress makes it compromise difficult, especially when parties have different views.

Alternative Assessment

To assess this activity see Group Project in the *Portfolio and Performance Assessment for Social Studies.*

LAB OBJECTIVES

The Unit 2 Public Policy Lab incorporates the following objectives:

▶ review letters and editorials to determine the point of view of the author.

▶ conduct research on support for changing the minimum voting age.

▶ use a decision-making process to create a written recommendation regarding changing the voting age.

Using the Lab

Before beginning the lab, organize students into groups and distribute copies of the Public Policy Lab Unit 2 Activity found in *Unit Tests and Unit Lab Activities with Answer Key*. Then have students read the directions for the assignment on this page. Discuss the assignment with students and point out the documents on pages 137–39 that students will use during the lab.

The What Do You Think? questions on pages 138–39 will help guide students during the project. In addition, the lab worksheet includes a step-by-step checklist for students to monitor their progress. For assessment guidelines, see the Group Activity rubric in the *Alternative Assessment Handbook*.

PUBLIC POLICY LAB

You Make the Decision

Congressional Staffer for a Day

*I*magine that you are part of a group of staff members who work in the office of Representative Joan Campbell. The congresswoman needs your group to develop a recommendation on whether she should support a proposed amendment to the U.S. Constitution to raise the minimum legal voting age to 21.

The issue has created a great deal of controversy, and Campbell has received a number of letters from constituents on the issue. To help you make your recommendation, your boss, the chief of staff, has given you the following documents: two of the letters Campbell has received, a newspaper editorial for you to review, and a fact sheet about the issue.

Government Notebook Assignment

Record your decision-making process in your Government Notebook.

1. Review the documents and answer the WHAT DO YOU THINK? questions.
2. As a group, identify the issues your recommendation should address.
3. Once you have identified the key issues, your group needs to gather additional information. You may want to examine recent voter-turnout statistics and review the history behind the Twenty-sixth Amendment.
4. As a group, you should discuss the results of your research. Identify the options you have for your recommendation. Predict the consequences each option could have on the political process in the United States.
5. Implement your decision by developing a recommendation for Campbell. Make sure the recommendation is written neatly or typed. In your recommendation make sure you support your decision with clear arguments based on your research and document analysis and a discussion of how the letters and newspaper editorial influenced your decision.

Office of U.S. Representative
Joan Campbell

To: Staff Researchers

From: Harold Box, Chief of Staff

Representative Campbell is looking forward to hearing your recommendation on the proposed amendment to raise the minimum legal voting age to 21. Please review the fact sheet that follows. It will provide applicable background information. I also have provided two letters and a newspaper editorial on the issue.

After you read those documents, your group will need to conduct some outside research, with each member uncovering the answer to one of the following questions:

- Has the United States ever repealed an amendment? If so, explain the circumstances.
- How have amendments and other laws to extend voting rights affected voter turnout?
- What attempts have been made to increase voter turnout, particularly among young people?
- How high is voter turnout in other democratic countries? What is the minimum legal voting age in several of them?

Other research questions may cross your mind as you read the letters and the newspaper editorial. Below is a list of some sources you might find useful in doing your research. You might need to find other sources as well.

- library almanacs and encyclopedias
- *Statistical Abstract of the United States* (volumes by years)
- applicable articles listed in the *Readers' Guide to Periodical Literature*
- interviews seeking the opinions and experiences of people in the local congressional district

Good luck!

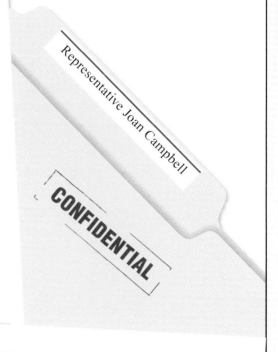

Representative Joan Campbell

CONFIDENTIAL

Office of U.S. Representative
Joan Campbell

FACT SHEET

Proposed Amendment to Raise the Minimum Legal Voting Age to 21

- The Twenty-sixth Amendment was ratified in 1971. It lowered the minimum legal voting age from 21 to 18 in all federal, state, and local elections.

- Some observers have said that making people aged 18 to 20 eligible to vote has been one cause for a decline in voter turnout. About 61 percent of eligible voters cast ballots in the 1968 presidential election. Just over 55 percent voted in 1972. Turnout has been even lower since then.

- Surveys have shown that far less than half of people aged 18 to 20 even bother to register to vote. Only 31.2 percent of people in that category said they voted in the 1996 presidential election. In comparison, 54.2 percent of all eligible voters said they voted.

- The proposed amendment would make anyone under the age of 21 ineligible to vote. Sponsors say the amendment would help ensure that eligible voters are mature enough to take their right to vote seriously.

What Do You Think?
Answers

1. The goal of CRV is to help in the development of mature and educated voters.

2. CRV believes that raising the minimum voting age would help restore responsible voting.

3. CRV provided campaign volunteers and financial contributions to Representative Campbell's re-election campaign.

What Do You Think?
Answers

1. The proposed amendment would stop Anthony Washington from being able to vote in the next federal election.

2. Anthony Washington points out that he is a responsible citizen by stating that he has worked to register voters and has volunteered to work on political campaigns. These examples help his case by demonstrating that some voters under 21 are responsible and active.

3. He points out that he is old enough to serve in the military and have other adult responsibilities.

PUBLIC POLICY LAB *continued*

CITIZENS FOR RESPONSIBLE VOTING
1111 Main Street
Chicago, IL 60607

Representative Joan Campbell
U.S. House of Representatives
The Capitol
Washington, DC 20515

Dear Representative Campbell:

As president of Citizens for Responsible Voting (CRV), I am writing to you in support of the proposed amendment to raise the minimum legal voting age back to 21. The goal of CRV is the development of educated and mature voters. We believe that your support for the amendment will help restore responsibility to the voting booth.

As you are aware, just over half of eligible voters have cast ballots in recent presidential elections. We believe the low level of voter turnout is partly because the minimum legal voting age was lowered to 18 by the Twenty-sixth Amendment.

Many of our young people today are fine, well-educated citizens. On the other hand, too many 18- to 20-year-olds do not take the time to study the election issues and candidates. In addition, many young people have not exercised their right to vote. We believe that this failure to vote reflects a lack of the maturity that is needed to make important decisions about our government.

We believe that raising the minimum legal voting age back to 21 would give young people more time to mature and learn about our election system. When older, they will be better able to research and understand the issues and the stands taken by candidates for public office.

As you will recall, we supported your re-election last year by providing campaign volunteers and donating to your campaign fund. We did those things because of your past support for efforts to promote responsible voting. We hope you will continue to be a strong supporter of our efforts.

Sincerely,

Sheila Goldstone

Sheila Goldstone
President
Citizens for Responsible Voting

◀ WHAT DO YOU THINK?

1. What is the goal of CRV?

2. What does CRV believe raising the minimum legal voting age would do?

3. What have been CRV's connections with Representative Campbell in the past?

Representative Joan Campbell
U.S. House of Representatives
The Capitol
Washington, DC 20515

Dear Representative Campbell:

I am a senior at Central High School, and I have heard that there is a proposed amendment to the Constitution that would change the minimum legal voting age back to 21. I hope you will vote against this amendment.

I have worked to register eligible voters, and I have volunteered to work on political campaigns. If the law does not change, I will vote when I turn 18.

I think raising the minimum voting age would unfairly penalize me. I know that some people my age do not vote. But no one is proposing that older people be penalized because not everyone older than 20 votes.

I will be old enough to serve my country in the military and will have other responsibilities as an adult when I turn 18. I believe I should also have the right to vote.

Please vote no on the amendment.

Sincerely,

Anthony Washington

Anthony Washington
Central High School
Chicago Ridge, IL 60415

WHAT DO YOU THINK? ▶

1. How would the proposed amendment affect Anthony Washington?

2. How does Washington demonstrate that he is responsible in his role as a citizen? Does that help his argument that the amendment should be defeated? Explain.

3. What other reasons does Washington give to support his argument that the amendment should be defeated?

Congress Should Reject Attempt to Raise Voting Age

Congress is considering an amendment to the U.S. Constitution that would repeal the Twenty-sixth Amendment and raise the minimum legal voting age back to 21. The amendment should be defeated because it is the wrong solution to the problems its supporters have identified.

Supporters of the amendment believe a higher minimum legal voting age would increase voter turnout. They also argue that older voters are more likely to have the maturity and sense of responsibility to educate themselves about issues and candidates for public office. Supporters of the amendment are right when they say that low voter turnout among young people is evidence that many do not take their right to vote seriously enough.

Opponents of the proposed amendment point to the Fifteenth and Nineteenth Amendments. Those amendments extended voting rights to former slaves and to women. Not all African Americans and women vote, but no one proposes repealing those important amendments.

In addition, we believe that taking away the right to vote is no way to teach maturity and responsibility. One way to become mature and responsible is by accepting the challenges that society provides. One of the biggest challenges democracy presents citizens is choosing the best people to serve in government.

Many adults under the age of 21 have accepted the challenge and responsibility of voting. They should not be penalized because others their age have chosen to ignore that same challenge.

A better solution to the problem of low voter turnout would include ways to get more voters, from the age of 18 up, to educate themselves about the issues and candidates and actually go to the polls. We should not instead be proposing laws that would prevent some people from voting. The proposed amendment should not be passed.

▲ WHAT DO YOU THINK?

1. What did the Fifteenth and Nineteenth Amendments do? Are the results of these amendments applicable to the debate over raising the voting age?

2. What does the editorial writer suggest is a better solution to the problem of low voter turnout?

☑ internet connect

Internet Activity go.hrw.com
KEYWORD: SV3 GVPL

Access the Internet through the HRW Go site to employ a problem solving process to advise Representative Campbell whether she should support the proposed amendment. Your process should include these steps: identification of the problem, gathering background information, listing and considering options, considering advantages as well as disadvantages, choosing a solution, and implementing and evaluating your solution. Research links and a problem solving tutorial are provided.

What Do You Think? Answers

1. The Fifteenth and Nineteenth Amendments extended voting rights to former slaves and women. Students' answers may vary regarding the significance of this data to the debate over raising the voting age.

2. The author suggests that a better solution would involve finding ways to get people over 18 to educate themselves about issues and candidates and thus be motivated to go to the polls.

UNIT 3

Lesson Options

Suggestions for customizing the material in Unit 3 to fit the specific schedule and curriculum of your classroom are located at the beginning of each chapter.

Main Idea

Ask each student to read the Main Ideas and briefly answer each question in writing. Later, when you have finished Unit 3, ask students to return to their original answers and revise them using what they learned in the unit.

PUBLIC POLICY LAB

The Unit 3 Public Policy Lab appears on pages 242–45. This project is a real-world assignment in which students will work in groups to prepare a speech for the president to increase support for a trade summit.

Support materials for the lab appear in *Unit Tests and Unit Lab Activities with Answer Key.*

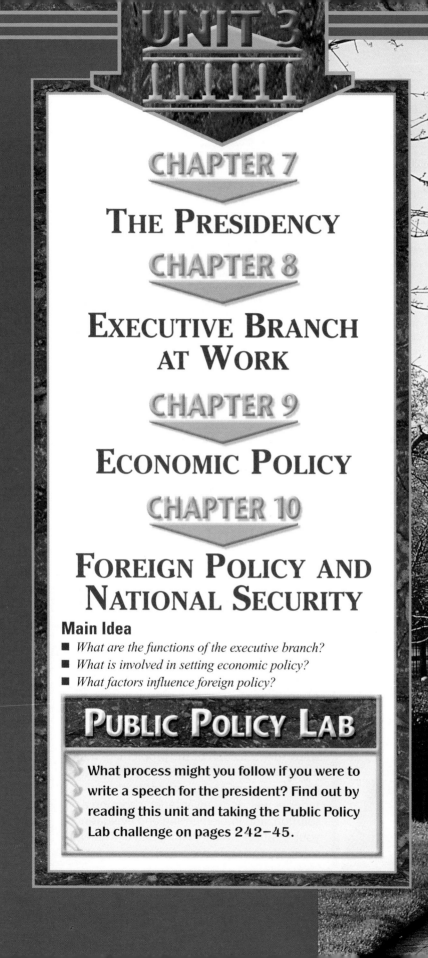

UNIT 3

CHAPTER 7
THE PRESIDENCY

CHAPTER 8
EXECUTIVE BRANCH AT WORK

CHAPTER 9
ECONOMIC POLICY

CHAPTER 10
FOREIGN POLICY AND NATIONAL SECURITY

Main Idea

■ *What are the functions of the executive branch?*
■ *What is involved in setting economic policy?*
■ *What factors influence foreign policy?*

PUBLIC POLICY LAB

What process might you follow if you were to write a speech for the president? Find out by reading this unit and taking the Public Policy Lab challenge on pages 242–45.

THE EXECUTIVE BRANCH

UNIT 3 OVERVIEW

Unit 3 presents the basic concepts necessary to introduce students to the executive branch, including the nomination and election process, presidential powers, and the organization of the executive office. The unit also discusses various aspects of national policy making, such as raising revenue and influencing economic policy and the making of U.S. foreign policy and national security strategies.

Teaching with Photographs

The White House is located in Washington, D.C., at 1600 Pennsylvania Avenue. It was designed by Irish-born architect James Hoban and received its name after its exterior walls were painted white. The original structure was burned by British troops on August 24, 1814. Its rebuilding began in October 1817 under Hoban's leadership.

Aside from being the residence of the U.S. president and family, the building serves a variety of functions, including hosting meetings that help determine foreign and international policy, the signing of legislation, and receptions for guests. Public tours of the building are also given.

CHAPTER 7 THE PRESIDENCY

	OBJECTIVES	PACING GUIDE	REPRODUCIBLE RESOURCES
SECTION 1 THE PRESIDENTIAL OFFICE (pp. 143–147)	▶ What are the roles of the president? ▶ What are the qualifications and terms of the office of the presidency? ▶ What is the order of presidential succession?	**Regular** .5 day **Block Scheduling** .5 day	ELL Spanish Study Guide 7.1 ELL English Study Guide 7.1 PS Reading 17: *The U.S. Presidential Oath of Office* PS Reading 31: *John F. Kennedy's Inaugural Address*
SECTION 2 PRESIDENTIAL POWERS (pp. 148–156)	▶ What are the president's executive and foreign-policy powers? ▶ What judicial and legislative powers does the president have? ▶ How has presidential power grown over the years?	**Regular** 1.5 days **Block Scheduling** 1 day	ELL Spanish Study Guide 7.2 ELL English Study Guide 7.2
SECTION 3 PRESIDENTIAL NOMINATION AND ELECTION (pp. 157–164)	▶ What is the electoral college? ▶ How are presidential candidates chosen? ▶ How are convention delegates chosen? ▶ What is the format for national conventions?	**Regular** 1.5 days **Block Scheduling** 1 day	ELL Spanish Study Guide 7.3 ELL English Study Guide 7.3 E Challenge and Enrichment Activity 7 E Simulations and Strategies for Teaching American Government: Activity 7

Chapter Resource Key

PS	Primary Sources	A	Assessment		Video
RS	Reading Support	REV	Review		Videodisc
E	Enrichment	ELL	Reinforcement and English Language Learners		Internet
S	Simulations		Transparencies		Holt Presentation Maker Using Microsoft ® PowerPoint ®
SM	Skills Mastery		CD-ROM		

TECHNOLOGY RESOURCES	REINFORCEMENT, REVIEW, AND ASSESSMENT
One-Stop Planner: Lesson 7.1 Researcher Online Homework Practice Online Transparency 14 Global Skill Builder CD-ROM	**REV** Section 1 Review, p. 147 **A** Daily Quiz 7.1
One-Stop Planner: Lesson 7.2 Researcher Online Homework Practice Online Transparency 5 Global Skill Builder CD-ROM	**REV** Section 2 Review, p. 156 **A** Daily Quiz 7.2
One-Stop Planner: Lesson 7.3 Researcher Online Homework Practice Online Transparency 15 CNN Presents American Government	**REV** Section 3 Review, p. 164 **A** Daily Quiz 7.3

Chapter Review and Assessment

SM Global Skill Builder CD-ROM
HRW Go site
REV Chapter 7 Tutorial for Students, Parents, and Peers
REV Chapter 7 Review, pp. 166–167
A Chapter 7 Test Generator (on the One-Stop Planner)
A Chapter 7 Test

One-Stop Planner CD–ROM

It's easy to plan lessons, select resources, and print out materials for your students when you use the *One-Stop Planner CD–ROM with Test Generator.*

OBJECTIVES

▶ Describe the roles of the president.
▶ List the qualifications and terms of the president.
▶ Identify the order of presidential succession.

MOTIVATE

Ask students what types of jobs or careers they would like to have when they are out of school. Have students write down several examples of these jobs and have them list what they think the qualifications are. Allow several students to answer and explain why they think these qualifications are necessary. Ask students to brainstorm what qualities it takes to be the president of the United States. As a class, create a list of qualifications that students would require for and the salary they would pay the president. Tell students that they may be surprised by the actual qualifications. Explain that in this section they will find out specific information about the presidency.

TEACH

Building a Vocabulary

In spiral notebooks, have students create a Political Dictionary to be used throughout the course. The dictionary may be used as an activity at the start of each section; it may also be used as a modification device for students having difficulty or Sheltered English Students during tests and homework assignments. List words that students will be expected to know for this section on the board. Have students list, define, and give an example of each term, using information provided in the text or on the *Researcher CD-ROM.*

Role-Playing

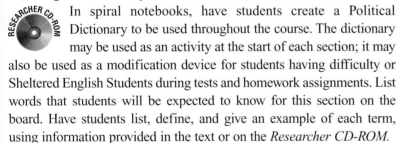

Organize the class into seven groups. Assign each group one of the president's roles: chief executive, commander in chief, chief legislator, representative of the nation, chief of state, foreign-policy leader, or party leader. Explain to students that they will be presenting information to the rest of the class about their assigned role. Encourage students to be as creative as they can and to use whatever resources are necessary. Presentations may include role-playing, songs, debates, or speeches. Students may wish to make hats or signs depicting their presidential role. Discuss with the class the accuracy of students' portrayal of the president's roles. If there are any inconsistencies, be sure to point them out. Tell students that with this many different roles, you would expect there to be many qualifications to be president. Let students know that in the next activity they will be learning about the surprisingly few qualifications required to become president.

Developing Life Skills/Acquiring Information

Using the classified advertisements of your local newspaper, identify several local job openings and obtain job applications for a few of these jobs. Pass the advertisements and applications around for students to see. Point out to students the wide range of qualifications that these jobs require. Have students work in small groups to create a classified advertisement seeking a qualified candidate for the presidency of the United States and an appropriate job application. Ask students to consider the president's seven roles and the importance of the position to determine what qualifications they believe the president should possess. Have groups share their classified ads and applications with the class. Then discuss the actual presidential qualifications. Tell students that although these qualifications are not very strict, presidents have tended to be well educated with impressive professional and political backgrounds. Explain to students that occasionally a president may not be able to fulfill the duties of the office and that in the next activity students will learn about what happens when this occurs.

Hypothesizing

Have students read about the order of presidential succession found in this section of the text. Lead a discussion on the order of succession. Place Transparency 14: Presidential Succession on the overhead projector or refer students to the chart on textbook page 147 to assist with explaining the process of replacing a president. Ask students to hypothesize what would happen if the succession continued all the way to the secretary of veterans affairs. Have them consider whether the people in each of these positions would be qualified for the job. Ask the class how having the secretary of veterans affairs become president would affect the citizens of the United States. What impact would it have on each of the president's seven roles? Would he or she be as respected as an elected president?

CLOSE

Refer students to the discussion about their career choices that took place during the Motivate activity. Have students compare their list of presidential qualifications and salary to the actual qualifications and salary of the president of the United States. Ask students to discuss reasons for the discrepancies between what they thought the qualifications and salary should be and what they actually are. Ask students if they feel that the qualifications should be changed through an amendment and if so, what the new ones should be.

OPTIONS

Gifted Learners

  Have students learn more about one or more former U.S. presidents. Encourage them to use the Biographies section on the *Holt Researcher Online* and other resources. Students should research information about election(s), including campaign slogans and biographical information on the candidates. Students should also investigate each president's background to see if they would meet any changes that students felt were necessary in the qualifications for president. Students may produce written or oral reports and should discuss their findings with the class.

Students Having Difficulty/ Sheltered English Students

  Have students use the Careers section on the *Holt Researcher Online* and other career resources to learn more about one or more of the careers that they listed in the Motivate activity. Have students compare the actual qualifications for these positions to the ones they had hypothesized to see if they would still like to pursue those careers.

Intrapersonal Learners/Gifted Learners

 Discuss the importance of the president's State of the Union address with the class. Divide the class into four groups. Give each group photocopies of a State of the Union address or a section of one, making sure to give each group a speech from a different president. Have each group read the address and identify the main policies that the president is seeking to enact. Then have each group conduct research to see if the president was successful in enacting those policies and how that was accomplished. Have groups share their information with the class.

REVIEW

Have students complete the Section 1 Review on page 147. Use the answers in the Annotated Teacher's Edition to assess student mastery of this section.

ASSESS

To assess student mastery of this section, have students complete Daily Quiz 7.1 in *Daily Quizzes with Answer Key.* For additional assessment options, see *Alternative Assessment Handbook* on the *One-Stop Planner CD-ROM.*

ADDITIONAL RESOURCES

Richardson, James D., ed. *A Compilation of the Messages and Papers of the Presidents, 1789–1897.* 1897. Government Printing Office.

Podwell, Janet, and Steven Anzovin. *Speeches of the American Presidents.* 2001. H. W. Wilson Co.

Flexner, James. *George Washington and the New Nation, 1783–1793.* 1970. Little, Brown Publishing.

Shull, Steven A. *American Civil Rights Policy From Truman to Clinton: The Role of Presidential Leadership.* 1999. M.E. Sharpe. inc.

HOLT PRESENTATION MAKER
Access Illustrated LECTURE NOTES using Microsoft® PowerPoint® on the One-Stop Planner CD-ROM

OBJECTIVES

▶ List the president's executive and foreign-policy powers.
▶ Describe the judicial and legislative powers of the president.
▶ Discuss how presidential power has grown over the years.

MOTIVATE

Lead a discussion on the powers and responsibilities of executives, focusing on presidents of student councils, companies, or school clubs rather than on presidents of countries. As a class create a list of a president's responsibilities. Ask students how similar they think the powers of these executives are to those of the U.S. president. Explain to students that in this section they will learn about the far-reaching powers of the president of the United States.

TEACH

Building a Vocabulary

In their spiral notebooks, have students continue working on their Political Dictionary. List words the students will be expected to know for this section on the board. Have students list, define, and give an example of each of the terms, using information provided in the text or on the *Researcher CD-ROM*.

Learning from Visuals

Organize students into small groups. Assign each group one of the executive, diplomatic, or military powers of the president. Have students use outside resources such as newspapers and magazines to make a visual representation of their assigned powers. Students may create a 3-D model, a collage, or a cartoon. Have students present their visual to the class and describe the powers it shows. Discuss any discrepancies between how students' representations of the president's executive and foreign-policy powers depict those powers and the actual powers held by the president. Tell students that the president also has duties that pertain to judicial matters that will be discussed in the next activity.

Analyzing Information

Lead a discussion about the judicial and legislative powers of the president. Have students brainstorm the effects of a president being able to appoint conservative or liberal justices and discuss these effects as a class. Have students discuss the importance of reprieves, pardons, and commutation and how they affect the decisions of the courts. Discuss with students the president's roles in the legislative process such as recommending, vetoing, and lobbying for legislation.

Mastering Concepts

To help expand students' knowledge of presidential powers, bring in several articles dealing with occasions when presidents have pardoned an individual or individuals. (Examples may include the pardoning of those who avoided the draft by fleeing the United States during the Vietnam War, or President Ford's pardon of Richard Nixon for his involvement in Watergate.) Have students work in groups to analyze the special circumstances surrounding the presidential pardons discussed in the articles. Point out to students that presidential pardons are seldom granted and that special circumstances are usually considered before granting a pardon. Allow time for groups to share their articles with the rest of the class so that students are exposed to each particular instance of presidents' use of the pardon. Tell students that in the next activity they will learn about the changes in the extent of presidential powers.

Hypothesizing

Discuss different ways that the power of the president has changed over the years. Include Thomas Jefferson's use of presidential war powers, the Louisiana Purchase, the establishment of the Bank of the United States, and Franklin D. Roosevelt's use of the media to push legislation through Congress. Have small groups develop a "What-If" newspaper that discusses what the United States might be like had these powers not been included in the president's role.

CLOSE

Have students compare the list of presidential powers that they created in the Motivate activity and the actual powers of the U.S. president. Ask students to identify ways in which these are similar and different. Encourage students to think about reasons why presidential powers have limits placed on them and any problems that could cause. Then have students hypothesize how the powers of the student council president could emulate those of the president.

OPTIONS

Students Having Difficulty/ Sheltered English Students

  Have students use the Biographies section on the *Holt Researcher Online* and other resources about the U.S. presidents to create a study guide dealing with the use of presidential powers by a specific president. Be sure to have students include examples of the executive, foreign-policy, judicial, and legislative powers used by that president. Students should also include any contributions to the growth of presidential power accomplished by that president. Encourage students to share the information they have learned with other students who are having difficulty with the topic. Students may wish to make a chart that shows the growth of presidential power from George Washington's presidency to today.

Gifted Learners/Interpersonal Learners

Encourage students to learn more about the growth of presidential power by having them interview adults who have witnessed changes in the president's roles. Some possible topics to ask people about are Franklin D. Roosevelt's pushing through New Deal legislation, John F. Kennedy's role in increasing the president's war powers, or Bill Clinton's use of the line-item veto, which temporarily expanded the president's legislative powers. Students should be encouraged to tape their interviews and share them with the class or to write an interview on the topic for the school paper.

Students Having Difficulty

 Have students examine the cartoons in this chapter on textbook pages 149, 154, and 156. Then ask students to write a few paragraphs to describe what the cartoons say about presidents' use or misuse of their position and of its power. Encourage students to identify the uses of symbolism in each of the cartoons and then describe the political events that inspired each of these cartoons. Allow students time to discuss their interpretations of the cartoons. Be sure that students correctly describe what each cartoon depicts or discuss the actual meaning with them.

Intrapersonal Learners/Gifted Learners

 Have students conduct research using the Internet and other outside resources about the claim of executive privilege. Have students write about five instances in which presidents have claimed the privilege. Have students describe the circumstances in each case and say whether they think the claim of executive privilege in these circumstances compromised the president's authority as the leader of the country or the authority of one of the other branches of government. Encourage students to share their findings with the rest of the class.

REVIEW

Have students complete the Section 2 Review on page 156. Use the answers in the Annotated Teacher's Edition to assess student mastery of this section.

ASSESS

To assess student mastery of this section, have students complete Daily Quiz 7.2 in *Daily Quizzes with Answer Key*. For additional assessment options, see *Alternative Assessment Handbook* on the *One-Stop Planner CD-ROM*.

ADDITIONAL RESOURCES

Schlesinger, Arthur. *The Imperial Presidency.* 1998. Replica Books.
Schlesinger, Arthur. *The Age of Jackson.* 1972. Little Brown Publishing.
Hersman, Rebecca K.C. *Friends and Foes: How Congress and the President Really Make Foreign Policy.* 2000. Brookings Institution Press.

PRESIDENTIAL NOMINATION AND ELECTION

HOLT PRESENTATION MAKER
Access Illustrated LECTURE NOTES using Microsoft® PowerPoint® on the One-Stop Planner CD-ROM

OBJECTIVES

▶ Describe the electoral college.
▶ Explain how presidential candidates are chosen.
▶ Discuss how convention delegates are chosen.
▶ Describe the format for national conventions.

MOTIVATE

As a lead-in to this section, tell students that it has become necessary to elect a president that will serve all of the school's government classes. Tell students that during the course of this section each class will: be organized into two groups, one representing the Democratic Party, the other the Republican Party; hold nominations for presidential candidates; hold state primaries; hold a national convention; cast the popular vote; cast the electoral vote; and count the votes to decide who will be the next president and vice president. Students will probably have questions about how this process will work; answer a few of them but then encourage them to wait until each stage occurs throughout the course of the lesson to ask their questions. Divide each class into the two political parties that will take part in the mock presidential election. Allow each political party to choose a name or assign one to be the Democrats and the other the Republicans. Have the students in each party choose a few students (from any government class) to be nominated for the presidency. Tell students to focus on qualities other than popularity when selecting candidates because the president will be responsible for communication between students and teachers.

TEACH

Building a Vocabulary

In their spiral notebooks, have students continue working on their Political Dictionary. List words the students will be expected to know for this section on the board. Have students list, define, and give an example of each of the terms, using information provided in the text or on the *Researcher CD-ROM.*

Role-Playing

Discuss the process of state primaries with students. Have students break into the political party groups formed in the Motivate activity. Tell students in each group that they will now be holding a primary election to see which nominee carries the preference of their group, which will represent one state. Allow students a few minutes to discuss the pros and cons of each nominee. Have students vote by secret ballot to determine which of the nominees their group would like to support at the national convention. Have each group then decide on a few of its own members to serve as delegates at the national convention. These students must be willing to attend the national convention, which will have to be held after school or during lunch.

Role-Playing

Hold mock national conventions for each of the political parties either after school or during lunch. Videotape the conventions so that students in each class may watch them. Allow the top three candidates from the mock primaries to address the delegates at the mock national convention. Candidates may choose to make advertisements for their candidacy to give to their delegates at the convention. After all of the speeches have been made, have students cast secret ballots to see which candidate their party will support for the presidency. Have students watch the videotape of the mock national convention to see how the process works and to see which candidate their party will support in the general election.

Role-Playing

Discuss with students the role of the electoral college. Choose a random number of students from each class to serve as electors in the electoral college. Have students cast secret ballots to simulate the popular vote in the election. Remind students that although they can vote for anyone they want, they should choose from the candidates that were chosen from each political party at the mock national conventions. After the popular vote has been counted, have the electors cast their votes for the candidate who received the most votes from their classroom. After all classes have voted, tabulate the votes.

Acquiring Information/Mastering Concepts

  Discuss with students the various steps taken in their mock election. Organize the class into four groups. Each group will be responsible for researching and analyzing one step of the election process for the last presidential election. The first group should examine the nomination process and discuss the major candidates that were nominated and the background of each one. The second group should research the primaries and caucuses to determine which candidate won in each state and if there were primaries that changed the outcome of the nomination. The third group should research each party's national convention and report on the major events that occurred there and any party platform decisions that were made. The fourth group should investigate the actual voting in the election for both the popular vote and the electoral vote and explain any discrepancies between the two. Students may wish to use the Biographies and the Elections sections on the *Holt Researcher Online* to help them with their research. Once students have finished, encourage them to share the information they gathered with the rest of the class.

CLOSE

Tell students which candidate won the mock election for president. Have students share their ideas about the steps they took in electing a president. Discuss the similarities and differences between the actual process and the steps that students followed to elect a president. Have the class create a graphic organizer on butcher paper that shows the steps in the actual presidential election process.

OPTIONS

Visual-Spatial Learners

 Ask students to research the delegates from their state at the most recent national conventions, or in the event of an election year, the current delegates. Ask students to provide the class with a model or a time line depicting the events of the national conventions and highlighting contributions from delegates of their own state. Have students include party platforms on important issues, campaign slogans, and other important campaign components.

Gifted Learners/Musical-Rhythmic Learners

  Have students read the U.S. Presidential Oath of Office, which is Reading 17 in *From the Source: Readings in Economics and Government with Answer Key.* Working individually or in small groups, students should put the oath of office to music or make it into a rap song. Have students share their songs with the rest of the class.

REVIEW

Have students complete the Section 3 Review on page 164. Use the answers in the Annotated Teacher's Edition to assess student mastery of this section.

ASSESS

To assess student mastery of this section, have students complete Daily Quiz 7.3 in *Daily Quizzes with Answer Key.* For additional assessment options, see *Alternative Assessment Handbook* on the *One-Stop Planner CD-ROM.*

RETEACH

For students having difficulty with the lessons, have them complete Reteaching Activity 3. This activity is located in *Reteaching Activities with Answer Key.*

ADDITIONAL RESOURCES

Reichley, A. James. *Elections American Style.* 1987. Brookings Institution.

Thurber, James, and Candice Nelson, eds. *Campaigns and Elections American Style.* 1995. Westview Press.

TOPICS INCLUDE

GOVERNMENT NOTEBOOK

The Government Notebook is a journal activity that encourages students to consider basic concepts of government that relate to their lives. A follow-up notebook activity appears on page 166.

▶ WHY IT MATTERS TODAY

To find additional lesson plans dealing with the presidency, visit **CNNfyi.com** or have students complete the **GOVERNMENT IN THE NEWS** activity on page 165.

CNNfyi.com

CHAPTER 7

THE PRESIDENCY

If you have heard of only one address in Washington, D.C., it is likely to be 1600 Pennsylvania Avenue—the address of the White House, home and office of the president of the United States. The White House attracts more visitors each year than any other building in the country. This is not surprising, as the presidency is the major focus of attention in the U.S. political system.

Although presidents do not and cannot "run" the country single-handedly, most modern presidents have had decisive influence over U.S. foreign policy and have set much of the agenda for economic and domestic policy. This chapter looks at the many roles, qualifications, and powers of the president, as well as the presidential nomination and election processes.

GOVERNMENT NOTEBOOK

In your Government Notebook, list all of the presidents who have served since you entered the first grade. What do you remember about these presidents and their terms in office?

▶ WHY IT MATTERS TODAY

The president of the United States is widely considered to be the most powerful person in the world. At the end of this chapter visit **CNNfyi.com** to learn more about the presidency.

CNNfyi.com

READ TO DISCOVER

1. What are the roles of the president?
2. What are the qualifications and terms of the office of the presidency?
3. What is the order of presidential succession?

POLITICAL DICTIONARY

State of the Union address
diplomacy
foreign policy
presidential succession

Lesson Plans

For teaching strategies, see Lesson 7.1 located at the beginning of this chapter or the One-Stop Lesson Planner Strategy 7.1.

Political Dictionary

To reinforce the section's vocabulary terms, refer students to the Electronic Glossary on the *Researcher CD-ROM*.

Section Assessment

To assess students' mastery of this section, have them complete Daily Quiz 7.1 in *Daily Quizzes with Answer Key*.

> **Caption Answer**
>
> The president commands all military officers by keeping in touch with them and having the final say in wartime decisions.

Since 1789 many children in America have proudly exclaimed, "I'm going to grow up to be president." However, speaking as a present-day high school student, would you like to apply for the job? Before you answer, read on to learn about the president's roles in the U.S. government as well as the position's qualifications and terms of office.

The President's Roles

The president plays many vital roles in U.S. government. Some of these roles are outlined in the Constitution. Others have been assumed and expanded by those who have held the office.

Chief Executive Article II, Section 1, of the Constitution states that "the executive power shall be vested in [given to] a President of the United States of America." This means that as head of the executive branch, the president is responsible for executing, or carrying out, the nation's laws.

Commander in Chief Article II, Section 2, of the Constitution states that "the President shall be Commander in Chief of the army and navy of the United States." As head of the U.S. armed forces, the president commands all military officers in both wartime and peacetime. This does not mean that he or she actually leads U.S. troops into battle. The president does, however, stay in frequent contact with the nation's military leaders and has the final say in wartime decisions.

Chief Agenda Setter The Constitution requires that the president "shall from time to time give to the Congress information of [about] the state of the Union, and recommend to their [Congress's] consideration such measures as he shall judge necessary." To carry out this provision, each year the president delivers at least two messages to Congress. In January the president delivers a **State of the Union address**, which sets forth the programs, policies, and legislation that the president wants Congress to enact. The president also sends Congress a budget proposal, recommending how the federal government should raise and spend its money.

Representative of the Nation As one of two nationally elected officials in the government, the president represents—in a way that no member of

CONSTITUTIONAL GOVERNMENT *On September 14, 2001, President George W. Bush meets with New York City firefighters.* ***What are the president's responsibilities as commander in chief?***

Enhancing the Lesson

To learn more about France or other countries of the world, refer students to the Country Profiles section on the *Holt Researcher Online.*

Congress can—*all* of the people. As President Woodrow Wilson wrote, "He [the president] is the representative of no constituency, but of the whole people. When he speaks in his true character, he speaks for no special interest." President Harry Truman stated a similar idea: "The president is the only lobbyist that 150 million Americans have. The other 20 million are able to employ people to represent them . . . but someone has to look out after the interests of the 150 million that are left." (The population of the United States at the time was around 170 million.)

As the people's main elected representative, the president is often the focus of political attention. This becomes most apparent during crises. For example, the president often travels to the site of a natural disaster—such as a hurricane in Florida or

Comparing Governments

The French Prime Minister

In most countries with a parliamentary system of government, the prime minister—rather than a monarch or a president—is the chief executive. Prime ministers generally are involved in both domestic and foreign policy. The French parliamentary system, however, is organized somewhat differently. In France, the president, who is elected by the people, and the prime minister, who is appointed by the president but is responsible to the Parliament, share executive powers. The president largely manages foreign affairs, while the prime minister takes responsibility for the daily operations of the government.

Another unusual characteristic of the French parliamentary system is that the prime minister is allowed to hold other government positions while helping run the nation. For example, several French politicians have served as mayor of a city while also serving the nation as prime minister. Many people in France believe that such combinations are a good way for their leader to stay in touch with the public while serving as the nation's executive.

CITIZENSHIP *President George W. Bush awards John Brown, a Navajo Code Talker during World War II, the Congressional Gold Medal.* **What duties must the president assume as the country's chief of state?**

an earthquake in California—to show the nation's concern. "In times of crisis," one observer has noted, "citizens expect their president to be personally on duty and in charge."

Chief of State As chief of state the president symbolizes the United States and its people. This means that the president represents the nation when meeting with foreign leaders both at home and abroad. In this role, the president engages in **diplomacy**, or the art of conducting negotiations with foreign countries. Such diplomacy builds international ties that further U.S. economic and security interests.

In the role of chief of state, the president also performs many ceremonial duties. These include awarding medals to citizens who have made notable contributions to society, lighting the nation's Christmas tree, and opening the professional baseball season by throwing the first pitch.

WORLD AFFAIRS *President George W. Bush and First Lady Laura Bush with British Prime Minister Tony Blair and his wife, Cherie, at Camp David.* **Why is it important for the president to establish friendships with foreign leaders?**

Foreign-Policy Leader Related to the role of chief of state is that of foreign-policy leader. As the head of one of the most powerful countries in the world, the president must give constant attention to the nation's **foreign policy**—its plans for dealing with other countries. The goals of U.S. foreign policy are to promote trade and friendship with other countries while maintaining the security of the United States. (The goals and principles of U.S. foreign policy are more fully explained in Chapter 10.) The president's special role in foreign affairs is suggested in the Constitution by the role as commander in chief and the power to negotiate treaties with foreign nations. Also, the Constitution states that the president must take an oath to "preserve, protect and defend the Constitution of the United States." Congressmembers are not required to take an oath, suggesting that the president has a special responsibility for national security.

Party Leader As the leader of his or her political party, the president makes speeches to help other party members who are running for public office. The president also helps the party raise money for its political campaigns, candidates, and programs.

Qualifications and Terms of Office

You now know the roles that the president must play once in office. What qualifications, though, must a person have to reach the presidency, and what are the terms of office?

Formal Qualifications Article II, Section 1, of the Constitution states that the president must

★ be a native-born U.S. citizen,
★ be at least 35 years of age, and
★ have been a U.S. resident for at least 14 years.

The Constitution contains no other formal qualifications for the presidency.

Presidential Background In addition to fulfilling the above formal qualifications, the people who have become president also have shared similar personal backgrounds. For example, to date all presidents have been white, male Christians. This pattern shows signs of changing, however. In 1984 Geraldine Ferraro was the Democratic nominee for vice president. Also in 1984 and again in 1988, Jesse Jackson, an African American, made a strong bid for the presidency. In fact, recent polls sug-

Profiles in American Government

For a biography of all former U.S. presidents and other noted people in American government, refer students to the Biographies section on the *Holt Researcher Online.*

CULTURAL PERSPECTIVES

Recently Brazilians argued over the number of terms that their president may serve. Brazil's constitution allowed a president to serve only one term, but some Brazilians contended that Brazilian voters deserved the right to decide how many terms their presidents should serve.

Brazilians who opposed a second term were wary of dictatorship. According to some political analysts, Brazilians tend to put their faith in individuals rather than the constitution. These analysts believe that faith in a single person spawns dictatorship.

A 1997 amendment allowed Cardoso to run for a second term. In the October 1998 election Cardoso was reelected with 53 percent of the vote. ■

THEMES IN GOVERNMENT

PUBLIC GOOD Being president of the United States is often considered to be the most powerful position in the world, but it may also be the most underpaid, especially when compared to professional baseball players.

The president's salary is $400,000 per year. For the 2000 Major League Baseball season, the team with the lowest payroll per player was the Minnesota Twins. Their players' salaries averaged $601,680 per year. The team with the highest payroll in the big leagues was the New York Yankees. Their players' salaries averaged $3,656,542 per year, almost 10 times as much as the president's 2001 salary. The highest paid player in baseball in 2001 was Alex Rodriquez of the Texas Rangers who made roughly $25,200,000, which is over 63 times as much as the president of the United States makes. Some people question whether this disparity has any impact on the overall public good. ■

Transparency

An overhead transparency of the chart on the next page is available in *Transparency Resources.* See Transparency 14: Presidential Succession.

CONSTITUTIONAL GOVERNMENT *President Franklin D. Roosevelt was the only U.S. president to serve more than two terms in office. Here, an interest group advertises its support of Roosevelt's campaign for his third term.* **Which amendment to the Constitution established a two-term limit for the presidency?**

gest that almost all Americans would vote for a qualified woman, African American, or Jewish American for president.

In addition, most of the nation's 43 presidents have been highly educated. Of the 24 presidents who served during the 1700s and 1800s, when few people went to college, 15 were college graduates. All twentieth-century presidents except for Harry S Truman attended college, and several earned advanced degrees. (President Truman earned a law degree—law schools did not require an undergraduate degree at the time.)

Terms The Constitution sets the president's term of office at four years. Originally, however, the *number* of terms a president could serve was not

specified. After serving two terms, George Washington stated that he did not wish to be considered for a third term and stepped down. All presidents afterward followed this two-term tradition until Franklin D. Roosevelt, who was elected to a third term in 1940 and a fourth in 1944.

To keep one person from holding the nation's highest office for such a long time, Congress in 1947 proposed the Twenty-second Amendment, which the states ratified in 1951. This amendment set forth a constitutional two-term limit for the presidency.

Salary and Benefits Currently the president earns $400,000 a year, plus $50,000 for official expenses and additional allowances for travel and entertainment. Congress sets the president's salary. However, to prevent Congress from using this power to influence the president, a change in salary cannot take place until the beginning of the next presidential term.

The presidency carries several benefits in addition to salary. The president and his or her family live in the White House, a stately mansion that features both offices for White House staff and private living quarters for the presidential family. For special meetings and vacations, the president may use Camp David, a mountain retreat in Maryland.

To travel to Camp David and anywhere else in the world, the president has a fleet of cars, helicopters, and airplanes, including the presidential jet, *Air Force One.* One story has it that when President Lyndon B. Johnson began boarding one of two helicopters and an aide informed him that his was the other one, Johnson replied, "They're *all* mine."

Presidential Succession The Constitution states that if the president dies, resigns, or is removed from office, the vice president becomes president. This provision has been invoked nine times—eight times when the president died in office and once following a resignation.

What would happen if both the president and the vice president should die or resign? The

Presidential Succession

1. Vice President
2. Speaker of the House
3. President *Pro Tempore* of the Senate
4. Secretary of State
5. Secretary of the Treasury
6. Secretary of Defense
7. Attorney General
8. Secretary of the Interior
9. Secretary of Agriculture
10. Secretary of Commerce
11. Secretary of Labor
12. Secretary of Health and Human Services
13. Secretary of Housing and Urban Development
14. Secretary of Transportation
15. Secretary of Energy
16. Secretary of Education
17. Secretary of Veterans Affairs

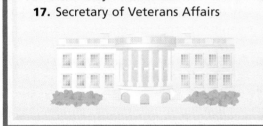

The chart above lists the order of succession for the presidency if the president should die or resign. **Which cabinet member is fourth in line for the presidency?**

Constitution gives Congress the right to decide **presidential succession**, or who should fill the presidency and in what order. According to a law passed by Congress in 1947, presidential succession after the vice president is as follows: Speaker of the House of Representatives, president *pro tempore* of the Senate, and the members of the cabinet—in the order in which their departments were created.

If the president is succeeded by the vice president, who becomes the new vice president? Until 1967 no one did—the office remained empty until the next presidential election. In 1965, however, Congress proposed the Twenty-fifth Amendment, which the states ratified two years later. The amendment provided for the president to nominate a new vice president.

The new law was tested in 1973, when Vice President Spiro Agnew was forced to resign after he pled no contest to income tax evasion. It was later determined that he also had received illegal payoffs from construction company executives while he was governor of Maryland and vice president. President Richard Nixon nominated Gerald Ford to fill the office. When Nixon resigned in 1974 as a result of Watergate, Ford became president. Ford nominated Nelson Rockefeller as his vice president, creating a situation in which neither the president nor the vice president was elected by the people. The nominee takes office only if approved by a majority vote of both houses of Congress. The Twenty-fifth Amendment also provides that the vice president should serve as acting president if the president is too ill to serve.

Caption Answer

the secretary of state

SECTION 2 REVIEW ANSWERS

1. Refer to the following pages: State of the Union address (143), diplomacy (144), foreign policy (145), presidential succession (147).

2. chief executive: carries out the nation's laws; commander in chief: commands all military leader; chief agenda setter: delivers State of the Union address and submits budget to Congress; representative of the nation: speaks for all people; chief of state: engages in diplomacy, performs ceremonial duties; foreign-policy leader: promotes U.S. goals when dealing with other nations; party leader: supports other political party members running for office, helps raise money

3a. Washington established a tradition of serving only two terms.

3b. be a native-born U.S. citizen, be at least 35 years old, have been a U.S. resident for at least 14 years

4. Answers will vary but should demonstrate knowledge of the duties of the president and the need for a clearly defined, orderly succession.

SECTION 1 REVIEW

1. Identify and explain:
- State of the Union address
- diplomacy
- foreign policy
- presidential succession

2. Identifying Concepts: Copy the chart to the right. Use it to list the roles of the president and the duties of each role.

Role	Duties

Homework Practice Online
keyword: SV3 HP7

3. **Finding the Main Idea**

   a. What tradition did George Washington establish for the president's terms of office?
   b. What formal qualifications must a person fulfill to be president?

4. **Writing and Critical Thinking**

   Decision Making: Do you agree with the current order of presidential succession? Create a chart showing how you would change the order and explaining your reasons.

   Consider the following:
   - the responsibilites and roles of the president
   - the right of the voters to choose their leaders

Lesson Plans

For teaching strategies, see Lesson 7.2 located at the beginning of this chapter or the One-Stop Lesson Planner Strategy 7.2.

Political Dictionary

To reinforce the section's vocabulary terms, refer students to the Electronic Glossary on the *Researcher CD-ROM.*

Section Assessment

To assess students' mastery of this section, have them complete Daily Quiz 7.2 in *Daily Quizzes with Answer Key.*

Caption Answer

The Senate has the power to approve or reject the president's cabinet appointments.

SECTION 2
PRESIDENTIAL POWERS

READ TO DISCOVER

1. What are the president's executive and foreign-policy powers?
2. What judicial and legislative powers does the president have?
3. How has presidential power grown over the years?

POLITICAL DICTIONARY

executive order
executive privilege
alliance
executive agreement
diplomatic recognition
reprieve
pardon
commutation

Many people believe that the president has the power to "run" the nation. This impression, however, is not shared by presidents themselves. Contemplating the transition of his successor, Dwight Eisenhower, from the military to the White House, President Truman said, "He'll sit here, and he'll say, 'Do this! Do that!' *And nothing will happen.* Poor Ike—it won't be a bit like the Army." President John F. Kennedy liked to quote William Shakespeare's play *Henry IV,* in which one character boasts, "I can call spirits from the vasty deep," to which another replies, "Why so can I, or so can any man; But will they come when you do call them?"

Presidents may have felt so limited partly because it is Congress that makes the laws. The president's role regarding domestic policy is often merely to try to influence the legislature. As you will learn, however, the president does have decisive and far-reaching foreign-policy powers, and presidential power has grown over the years. In addition, as Chapter 9 explains, the president has the power to influence U.S. economic policy through his or her recommendations regarding the nation's budget.

Executive Powers

The president's executive powers are simple and yet far-reaching. They include carrying out laws and appointing officials. Presidents also have claimed an additional power, executive privilege.

Executing Laws Article II, Section 3, of the Constitution states that the president "shall take care that the laws be faithfully executed." This simple phrase gives the president great powers. Because laws passed by Congress are generally quite broad, the president has a great deal of freedom in interpreting how to carry out and enforce them.

One way that the president exercises this power is by issuing **executive orders**—detailed instructions, regulations, and rules that have the force of law. Executive orders have been used to state how legislation is to be carried out and enforced.

Appointing Officials The president's executive powers also include appointing officials. As the

CONSTITUTIONAL GOVERNMENT *President George W. Bush nominated Gale Norton, seen here, for Secretary of the Interior.* **What constitutional power does Congress have over the president's cabinet appointments?**

Constitution states, the president "shall nominate, and by and with the Advice and Consent of the Senate, shall appoint Ambassadors, other public Ministers, and Consuls, Judges of the supreme Court, and all other Officers of the United States, whose Appointments are not herein otherwise provided for." By appointing people to fill key positions in government, the president can influence the government's priorities and policies.

The president's appointment power is limited to key officials, such as the heads of the major executive departments and agencies and other policy-making officials. Most federal employees are hired under a civil service merit system, which is more fully explained in Chapter 8. Their jobs are out of reach of the president.

The president's appointment power is checked by the Senate, which confirms or rejects appointments of many high-level government officials. The Senate has used its power to refuse presidential appointments only rarely.

Executive Privilege Perhaps the most controversial executive power is the president's occasional refusal to give Congress information that it has requested. Although the term was first used in 1955, presidents since George Washington have based such refusals on the idea of **executive privilege**, or the president's right not to hand over documents or to testify regarding matters that are believed by the president to be the executive branch's confidential business.

One of the most dramatic cases of executive privilege happened during the Watergate investigation in 1973. When the Senate began investigating the case, President Richard Nixon resisted, announcing that none of his aides would be allowed to testify before the Senate Watergate Committee. Afterward, when the Senate learned of the existence of tape recordings of White House meetings, Nixon again claimed executive privilege and refused to hand over the tapes. After a nearly one-year struggle, the Supreme Court ruled that executive privilege did not apply in the case and that Nixon must hand over the tapes.

The debate over executive privilege continues. Some argue that certain matters, such as delicate negotiations with foreign countries, often must be kept secret. Others, however, believe that Congress must have access to all the material it needs to oversee agencies and to write legislation.

From *Herblock Special Report* (W.W. Norton, 1974). Reprinted by permission

March 27, 1973

POLITICAL FOUNDATIONS *This cartoon illustrates President Richard Nixon's attempt to use the power of executive privilege to prevent White House aides from testifying during the Watergate investigations.* **How did the Supreme Court rule on executive privilege in the Watergate investigation?**

Diplomatic Powers

Although many officials in the Department of State and other agencies help conduct U.S. foreign policy, the president is the main person responsible for the nation's foreign policy. The president has assumed this leading role partly because of the speed with which foreign-policy decisions must be made, particularly during crises. A large body such as Congress, by requiring debate and majority agreement, would on the other hand move too slowly to handle many foreign-policy situations.

Making Treaties With the advice and consent of the Senate, the president has the power to make treaties, or agreements, between the United States and other countries. Treaties include peace agreements to end wars and trade agreements that set up economic ties and terms of trade. Another kind

THEMES IN GOVERNMENT

POLITICAL PROCESSES The claim of executive privilege was made on numerous occasions during the Clinton administration. In 1996 Bill Clinton's lawyer refused to turn over several documents requested by Republican members of the House Government Reform and Oversight Committee.

The documents were sought in an attempt to investigate President Clinton's policies toward immigration and drug abuse. They included a memo from President Clinton to FBI Director Louis Freeh dealing with Clinton's drug policy and a memo from Vice President Al Gore to President Clinton regarding naturalization of citizens. ■

Linking
Government and Journalism

Reporters swarm around President George W. Bush. Media coverage of the president of the United States is unyielding.

The President and the Media

Few photographs exist of President Franklin D. Roosevelt in a wheelchair. Yet the president, who contracted polio when he was 39 years old, relied on a wheelchair to move around. Roosevelt disliked being photographed in his wheelchair, and the press respected his wishes. "There was an unspoken code of honor" among members of the press, writes historian Doris Kearns Goodwin.

At the time, most Americans did not know that their president was in a wheelchair. Why did the press hold to this "unspoken code"? Roosevelt had a good working relationship with the press, in part because he held frequent press conferences. Members of the press respected his wishes, and he provided them with information for their stories.

The news media today play a far different role than they did during the Roosevelt administration. The actions and personal lives of more recent presidents have been examined much more closely than earlier administrations. What changed? The Watergate break-in, which led to President Richard M. Nixon's resignation, was perhaps the single event that changed the relationship between the media and the president. Investigative journalism, a technique popularized by reporters who exposed the Watergate scandal, often focuses on uncovering negative stories about the lives of high-level officials.

Is this justified? How much does the public have the right to know about the private life of the nation's president? These are highly debated questions in today's media-focused world. Television news and newspaper headlines are the public's foremost sources of knowledge about the president. This information helps shape the public's view of the president and opinions on issues. During his administrations, President Bill Clinton was plagued by stories on Whitewater, Travelgate, and his use of the White House for campaign fund-raising. These stories often portrayed the president in less than favorable ways. Some people say that the media focus too much attention on the personal lives of presidents when providing this information. Others argue that the job of the media is to act as a watchdog over political leaders.

As the public has gained greater access to information about the activities of the president, the relationship between the president and the media has become less friendly and respectful. Presidents have argued that the media's coverage is too critical, and the media claim that the public has a right to know what the president is doing.

In spite of these criticisms, the president does receive many benefits from media coverage. Increased access to media has allowed recent presidents to influence public support for their policy agendas, for example. In addition, major television coverage of the presidential speeches allows the president to publicly announce his or her legislative agenda for the year. During times of crisis, the president can use the media as a tool to rally the public's support. In essence, the media enable the president to establish a relationship with the public.

What Do You Think?

1. Do you think that the media place too much emphasis on negative stories? Why?
2. Do you think the public has a right to know information about the president's personal life? Explain your answer.

Military Powers

The Constitution states that only Congress can declare war. As commander in chief of the armed forces, however, the president may send U.S. forces anywhere in the world that there is danger to the United States. In this role the president may order troops, warships, and fighter planes to faraway places. The president also makes recommendations to Congress about the military's size and equipment needs. In the 1990s, for example, President Clinton recommended to Congress that the numbers of U.S. soldiers, naval vessels, and long-range bombers be reduced.

WORLD AFFAIRS *President Richard Nixon and Soviet leader Leonid Brezhnev signed the antiballistic missile (ABM) treaty in 1972.* **For what reasons might a president sign a treaty with another country?**

of treaty forms **alliances**—agreements between two or more countries to help each other for defense, economic, scientific, or other reasons.

Making Executive Agreements Not all issues among countries need be worked out through treaties, however. The president and the leader of a foreign government may arrange a more informal understanding, or **executive agreement**. These agreements cover a variety of areas such as educational and scientific exchange programs, joint economic ventures, and economic assistance. In 1995, for example, through an executive agreement with Mexican president Ernesto Zedillo, President Clinton arranged for a loan of $20 billion to Mexico.

The use of executive agreements has grown in recent years in part because they allow presidents to make foreign policy without going through the Senate's slow-moving treaty approval process. Congress needs only to be officially notified of the agreement within 60 days.

Recognizing Governments The president also has the right to establish **diplomatic recognition**, or to determine whether the United States officially recognizes a government as the proper representative of its country's people. To recognize a foreign country means to set up official relations with that nation's government.

Committing Troops Presidents have committed U.S. soldiers to foreign duty for many reasons. In 1992 President George Bush sent U.S. troops to Somalia to help keep the peace and pass out food to starving people. In 1994 President Clinton sent soldiers to Haiti to help restore democracy in that country. These situations involved little in the way of conventional warfare.

War Powers Act Presidents have, however, sent U.S. troops into battle—in Korea, Vietnam, and many smaller conflicts. Though they were not declared wars, these conflicts involved all of the costs of a declared war, including sending soldiers into combat. As a result, Congress has sometimes challenged presidential power to commit U.S. soldiers to battle. Presidents have responded by asserting that authority to do so stems from their constitutional powers as commander in chief.

In 1973 Congress passed the War Powers Act which requires that soldiers sent abroad by the president be brought back within 60 days unless Congress approves the action. This time may be extended to 90 days if needed to ensure the safe removal of U.S. troops. Some critics of the act argue that it gives the president a power not stated in nor intended by the Constitution—the power to conduct undeclared war for 60 to 90 days without congressional approval. Others believe that the act was necessary, however, to limit the president's

Careers in Government

The Military

Many young people—men and women alike—find a rewarding career in the military. In 1775, when George Washington took command of the country's first army, soldiers learned to load muskets and fire cannons. In contrast, today's military is one of computer-operated tanks and sophisticated jet fighters. Although combat preparedness is still a major aspect of military training, today's military jobs also include those requiring technical expertise in fields such as communications, electronics, and medicine. The role of the military—to defend the nation—remains unchanged, however.

The U.S. armed forces is made up of five branches: the Army, Navy, Air Force, Marine Corps, and Coast Guard. Each branch employs personnel in occupations that range from meteorology to equipment maintenance. Military employees are provided with specialized, complex training, and each branch has its own training programs.

An enlistee is trained in one of the many military occupation specialties, which include such jobs as rocket specialist, air traffic controller, emergency medical technician, illustrator, and computer programmer. Enlistees enter the armed forces by enrolling in a branch of the military. Many enlisted men and women enter the military after graduating from high school.

Military officers, however, are usually college educated. Officers in all branches of the military except the Coast Guard can train in the Reserve Officer Training Corps (ROTC), which is offered at colleges and universities. Graduates completing the four-year ROTC program leave college as officers. Officers in all branches are trained to perform functions such as combat leadership, technical support in electronics and computers, and military intelligence.

Military officers also may train at one of the country's four service academies, which include the U.S. Military Academy, the U.S. Air Force Academy, the U.S. Naval Academy, and the U.S. Coast Guard Academy. All of the academies are now open to women. In addition, Officer Candidate School (OCS) and state-controlled military schools, such as the Citadel and Virginia Military Institute, provide officer training.

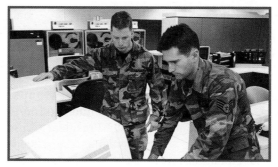

Military personnel at the Satellite Operation Center near Denver, Colorado, keep an eye on missiles around the world.

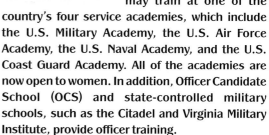

powers as commander in chief.

In fact, the act did not end the debate over committing U.S. troops. President George Bush sent U.S. soldiers to the Persian Gulf to lead a ground and air attack on Iraq, which had invaded its neighbor Kuwait in 1990. American troops, along with forces from several other countries, defeated Iraq in 1991 and won back Kuwait's independence. Some people criticized the Persian Gulf operation because it took place without Congress's having issued a declaration of war. Others pointed out, however, that Bush did meet with Congress about sending U.S. troops to the area and that Congress issued a statement supporting the operation.

Judicial Powers

As you know, the Constitution gives the president the power to appoint Supreme Court justices with the approval of the Senate. How much influence does this power give presidents over the Court? Conservative presidents do tend to appoint justices with conservative ideals, just as liberal presidents tend to appoint justices with liberal ideals. Once on the Court bench, however, justices often demonstrate intellectual independence. Several presidents have been dismayed when one of their Court appointees handed down a decision that ran counter to what they expected. Supreme Court justices, unlike other presidential appointees, cannot be removed from office by the president once they are seated. Thus, the appointment power does not place Supreme Court justices under presidential control.

The president's judicial powers also include the appointment of all other federal judges, and the granting of reprieves, pardons, and commutations. A **reprieve** postpones the carrying out of a person's sentence for humanitarian reasons or to allow a convicted person to present new evidence. Reprieves are sometimes granted in death penalty cases. A **pardon** grants a release from punishment to a convicted criminal and frees the person from serving out his or her sentence. A **commutation** lessens the severity of a convicted person's sentence.

Legislative Powers

In addition to the preceding executive and judicial powers, the president holds several legislative powers. A president can influence congressional action by recommending legislation, vetoing legislation, and lobbying members of congress.

Recommending Legislation According to the Constitution, only members of Congress may actually introduce bills. Congress and the public, however, have come to expect the president to play a key role in setting the legislative agenda. For example, President Woodrow Wilson presented to Congress a legislative reform program that he called the "New Freedom." Among the proposed reforms were the lowering of a high protective tariff and the creation of the Federal Reserve system.

The State of the Union address has become the

POLITICAL PROCESSES *President George Bush meets with U.S. soldiers during Operation Desert Storm in 1990.* **What restrictions does the War Powers Act place on the president's power to send soldiers abroad?**

president's major opportunity for proposing a legislative program. This speech tends to outline the president's priorities in broad terms. The details of the legislative program usually are contained in the president's annual budget, which proposes how much money government will spend and on what programs. (The president's role in the budget process is more fully explained in Chapter 9.)

Vetoing Legislation The veto power is largely a preventive measure. It does not enable the president to produce legislation, but it can block laws with which he or she disagrees. Because vetoes are difficult to override, the president can sometimes use the threat of a veto to pressure Congress into modifying a bill. In addition, as noted in Chapter 6, the line-item veto would increase the president's power by allowing the president to veto certain parts of a spending bill without vetoing the entire measure. As noted in Chapter 6, however, the line-item veto was declared unconstitutional by the Supreme Court in 1998.

Lobbying Presidents lobby members of Congress on behalf of certain bills by making personal telephone calls and by inviting members of Congress to the White House. Presidential lobbying typically

Caption Answer

Troops must be brought back within 60 days, or 90 days if there is danger in removing them.

THEMES IN GOVERNMENT

POLITICAL PROCESSES

Several recent presidents, including President Clinton, have lobbied for the line-item veto, which can be used by governors in 43 states. Bill Clinton used the power nine times in his 10 years as governor of Arkansas.

In April of 1996 a federal judge struck down the law that established the line-item veto. The court ruled that the law was unconstitutional because it changed the balance of power between the executive branch and Congress and because Congress did not have the authority to make such a change.

The case was appealed to the Supreme Court, which did not rule on the constitutionality of the law, but rather dismissed the challenge because the president had not yet actually used the law and therefore had not brought personal harm to those bringing the challenge. In August 1997 President Clinton exercised the power, which set the stage for further challenges to the bill's constitutionality. The following year the Supreme Court found the line-item veto to be unconstitutional. ■

POLITICAL PROCESSES *President George W. Bush meets with his advisers to discuss the federal budget.* **How does the president work to gain the support of members of Congress for certain programs and policies?**

takes place just before final floor consideration—particularly if the count is so close that a handful of votes could make the difference. Of course, some presidents have used this power more than others. President Lyndon Johnson, for example, called members frequently. In fact, he once called to lobby a senator at 2:30 A.M. Johnson began the conversation by asking how the member was doing. "I was just lying here waiting for you to call me, Mr. President," came the sarcastic reply.

Sometimes a president will offer support or threaten to withhold support for a project that is crucial to a member's district in order to pressure the person into backing a particular bill. More often, however, presidential lobbying involves wooing, not threatening. For example, Donald Regan, a close adviser to President Ronald Reagan, described the president's lobbying efforts by saying that "the President never bullied, never threatened, never cajoled [sweet-talked]. It was always: Let me explain why I'm for this bill, and I hope that we can count on your vote."

Growth of Presidential Power

As noted in Chapter 3, many of the delegates to the Constitutional Convention believed that executive power was necessary for effective government, but they feared creating an executive that

was too strong. As a result, they placed several checks on presidental powers. Nonetheless, the power of the presidency has grown—in large part because of the individuals who have held the office.

Early Presidents President George Washington, determined to establish the new government's role as representative of the American people, set out to make the president a symbol of federal authority. During 1794's Whiskey Rebellion, when a ragtag band of farmers in western Pennsylvania rose up to oppose a federal tax on liquor, Washington himself accompanied more than 12,000 militia partway to the scene of the rebellion. This display of military might was meant to show how much force the president could summon to ensure that people obey federal laws.

CONSTITUTIONAL GOVERNMENT *Some presidents have pushed their power to the limits of what the Constitution allows. In this cartoon, published in 1832, President Andrew Jackson is portrayed as a royal leader with little respect for the Constitution.* **Why is it important that Congress and the Supreme Court check the president's power?**

The third president, Thomas Jefferson, was the model of the president as a strong executive. This was unexpected of a man who had earlier expressed concerns about the power of the office. One way that Jefferson increased presidential power was through foreign affairs. In 1801, he sent U.S. naval ships to the Mediterranean Sea to take action against the Barbary pirates, who were demanding that U.S. commercial vessels pay increasing amounts of money to sail along northern Africa without being attacked. Some historians regard his action as the first example of an undeclared presidential war.

In addition, Jefferson acted beyond the expressed powers of government when he purchased Louisiana from France in 1803. The Constitution does not mention any power to purchase foreign lands. Moreover, Jefferson signed an agreement to buy the territory before he got congressional approval to make the purchase. Jefferson defended his action by arguing that if he had not acted swiftly, France might have retracted its offer to sell the territory.

President Andrew Jackson cast himself as a champion of the common citizen in his fight against the second Bank of the United States. Declaring the bank a symbol of economic privilege, he vetoed congressional legislation intended to renew the bank's charter and made the bank an issue in the 1832 presidential campaign. "Never before," wrote two political analysts, "had a chief executive gone to the people over the heads of their elected legislators." This image of the president as representative of the people has become a defining aspect of the presidency today.

The Modern Presidency Modern presidents have used frequent speeches and media attention to try to reach the people. One of the earliest presidents to do so was Theodore Roosevelt. Roosevelt took advantage of these tools, traveling around the country making direct appeals to the public on legislation. The press covered his

POLITICAL PROCESSES *President Theodore Roosevelt frequently made speeches and used the press during his presidency.* **How have the media helped shape the image of modern presidents?**

speeches, thus further drawing the public's attention to Roosevelt's ideas. Presidents ever since have followed Roosevelt's path.

Woodrow Wilson might be considered the first president to act the way that someone living today expects a president to act. For the most part, Wilson merely extended techniques Roosevelt had used. He lobbied Congress directly, installing a telephone line between the White House and Congress, and held regular press conferences. In addition, as you read earlier, Wilson proposed an entire legislative program to Congress.

President Franklin D. Roosevelt went on to refine the techniques that were used by Theodore Roosevelt and Woodrow Wilson. He took advantage of the technology of radio by broadcasting "fireside chats" to Americans. In addition, Roosevelt proposed the most thorough legislative agenda in U.S. history to try to bring the country out of the Great Depression. One result of Roosevelt's actions was a tremendous increase in public interest in the president and his ideas. This increased public response shows that the president was becoming the focus of attention in the American political system.

SECTION 2
REVIEW ANSWERS

1. Refer to the following pages: executive order (148), executive privilege (149), alliance (151), executive agreement (151), diplomatic recognition (151), reprieve (153), pardon (153), commutation (153).

2. Executive: executing laws, appointing officials, executive privilege; Diplomatic: making treaties, making executive agreements, recognizing governments; Military: committing troops, War Powers Act; Judicial: appoint Supreme Court justices and federal judges, grant reprieves, pardons, and commutations; Legislative: recommend legislation, veto legislation, lobbying.

3a. The possible need for secrecy in delicate situations conflicts with Congress's need to know.

3b. Wilson lobbied Congress directly, installed a phone line between the White House and the Capitol, held regular press conferences, and proposed an entire legislative program. Roosevelt used radio and proposed the most thorough legislative agenda in U.S. history.

4. Answers may vary, but students should state their opinion on the presidency and support their position.

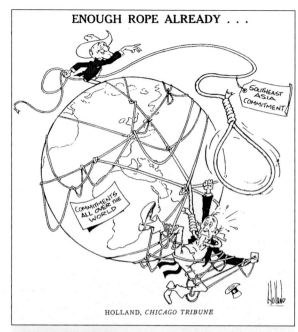

ENOUGH ROPE ALREADY . . .

SOUTHEAST ASIA COMMITMENT

COMMITMENTS ALL OVER THE WORLD

HOLLAND, *CHICAGO TRIBUNE*

WORLD AFFAIRS *The cartoon above comments on President Lyndon B. Johnson's decision to commit U.S. troops abroad.* **What does this cartoon say about the consequences of that decision?**

The Imperial Presidency Many people began to fear that presidential power was expanding dangerously during the presidencies of Lyndon Johnson and Richard Nixon in the 1960s and early 1970s. Both of these presidents, for example, committed hundreds of thousands of U.S. soldiers in an undeclared war in Vietnam. (Congress did, however, approve the funds for the war.) The use of such seemingly unrestrained power led many Americans to claim that the office had become "the imperial presidency."

Concerns over presidential power peaked with the Watergate case, in which President Nixon helped cover up the illegal break-in of Democratic Party headquarters by members of his own re-election committee. Nixon resigned to avoid facing impeachment charges for abusing the powers of the presidency.

The Presidency Today Distrust of the president and of government in general has remained high long after the events of the 1960s and 1970s. This distrust is reflected in an increase in the number of investigations of government actions. Investigations such as the Iran-Contra affair, Whitewater, and the Clinton impeachment regularly splash across newspaper headlines.

Some people argue that the search for acts of government wrongdoing has become a thin disguise for political witch-hunts, distracting both the president and Congress from their duties. Still, congressional investigations act as a vital check on presidential power. Despite the many accusations and investigations that have tarnished its image, the presidency is still the focus of the U.S. political system and the most powerful office in the world.

SECTION 2 REVIEW

1. Identify and explain:
- executive order
- executive privilege
- alliance
- executive agreement
- diplomatic recognition
- reprieve
- pardon
- commutation

2. Identifying Concepts: Copy the chart below. Use it to list the types of powers the president has and give examples of each.

Powers	Examples

3. Finding the Main Idea

a. Why is executive privilege a source of controversy?
b. How did Woodrow Wilson and Franklin Roosevelt help establish the modern presidency?

4. Writing and Critical Thinking

Supporting a Point of View: Do you think the presidency has become too powerful an office? Write a paragraph defending your position.
Consider the following:
- the growth in presidential power over the years
- the checks on presidential power

Homework Practice Online
keyword: SV3 HP7

SECTION 3

PRESIDENTIAL NOMINATION AND ELECTION

READ TO DISCOVER

1. What is the electoral college?
2. How are presidential candidates chosen?
3. How are convention delegates chosen?
4. What is the format for national conventions?

POLITICAL DICTIONARY

nominate
electoral college
elector
caucus
convention
primary election
general election
party platform
plank
popular vote
plurality

Have you made up your mind about running for president? Even if you fulfill the formal qualifications listed in Section 1, you must leap one more hurdle to become an official candidate—securing your party's nomination.

The first step in the process of choosing the president is to **nominate** candidates—that is, to propose people to run for an elective office. The Constitution makes no mention of how presidential candidates should be nominated. While the framers did design a system for choosing the nation's president and vice president, they did not anticipate how the U.S. political system would develop.

Electoral College

When first discussing how the president would be selected, the framers found themselves in disagreement. Some believed that the president should be selected by popular vote, while others thought that Congress should choose the president. The system finally agreed upon was the **electoral college**—a special body made up of people selected by each of the states—which votes for the president and vice president. (See the chart below for a description of how the framers intended the electoral college to work.)

In the Constitution, the framers planned for each **elector**—or electoral college member—to cast two ballots. One ballot, or electoral vote, had to be cast for a person who was not a resident of the elector's state. The person who received the majority (more than half) of the votes was president, and the person who received the next-highest number of votes

The Original Plan of the Electoral College

1. Each state has the same number of electors as it has senators and representatives.

2. In their respective states, electors vote for two candidates— one of whom may not be a resident of the electors' home state.

3. A list of these candidates is presented to Congress, and the number of votes for each candidate is counted.

4. The person who wins the majority of electoral votes becomes president.

5. The person having the second-greatest number of electoral votes becomes the vice president.

6. If two candidates tie for first place in the electoral vote, or if no candidate wins a majority of the votes, the president is chosen by the House of Representatives, with each state having one vote.

7. If a tie occurs for second place, the Senate chooses the vice president.

CONSTITUTIONAL GOVERNMENT *The framers' original plan for the electoral college was changed by the Twelfth Amendment.* **What were the flaws of the original plan?**

Lesson Plans

For teaching strategies, see Lesson 7.3 located at the beginning of this chapter or the One-Stop Lesson Planner Strategy 7.3.

Political Dictionary

To reinforce the section's vocabulary terms, refer students to the Electronic Glossary on the *Researcher CD-ROM*.

Section Assessment

To assess students' mastery of this section, have them complete Daily Quiz 7.3 in *Daily Quizzes with Answer Key*.

Caption Answer

Answers will vary, but students should suggest the lack of consideration given to the president and vice president having been opponents.

---

would be the vice president. Each state had as many electoral votes as it had members of Congress.

The first two elections under the plan worked smoothly—George Washington was unanimously elected twice. As political parties developed during the 1790s, however, the system began to show flaws.

Instead of electors each selecting the person they considered to be best for the job, they began voting only for members of their own political party. The rules governing the electoral college did not account for this change, which led to some difficult situations. During the election of 1796, for example, Thomas Jefferson lost to John Adams by only three electoral votes. He thus became Adams's vice president, despite the fact that they were members of rival parties.

By the election of 1800 the lines between political parties were firmly drawn in the electoral college. Thus, the electors, who were chosen according to their party affiliation, voted exclusively for their own party's candidates in the election.

During the election of 1800, a majority of the electors chosen were members of the Democratic-Republican Party. When they voted, they chose, per electoral college rules, two people—Thomas Jefferson and Aaron Burr. Jefferson was the party's choice for president, and Burr the party's choice for vice president.

Because each elector cast one ballot for Jefferson and one for Burr, however, Burr and Jefferson were tied. Following the Constitution, the election was thus thrown to the House of Representatives, which tied 35 times before its members finally chose Jefferson as president and Burr as vice president. To prevent such a situation in the future, Congress passed and the states ratified the Twelfth Amendment in 1803–04. The amendment stated that the president and vice president would be elected with separate ballots. It did not, however, change any other part of the electoral college.

Nomination Procedures

As you have read, the framers did not establish a system for nominating the presidential and vice presidential candidates, only for electing them once nominated. For this reason, the process for nominating candidates has changed a great deal throughout U.S. history.

The Granger Collection, New York

POLITICAL PROCESSES *In 1800 Thomas Jefferson (right) was chosen as president, and Aaron Burr (left) as vice president, after 35 tie votes in the House of Representatives.*
What major change did the Twelfth Amendment make to the original plan?

POLITICAL PROCESSES *George W. Bush, with his wife Laura, and Dick Cheney, with his wife Lynne, accepted the Republican nominations for president and vice president at the 2000 Republican National Convention.* **What role do national conventions play in the nominating process?**

Early Nominating Procedures During the early 1800s, the parties chose presidential candidates in congressional caucuses. A **caucus** is a meeting of people, such as members of a political party, who gather to make decisions on political courses of action. These meetings, which went on behind closed doors, were criticized by many voters, who believed them to be unrepresentative. For this reason, most states replaced the congressional caucus as a means of nominating presidential candidates by the 1820s. (Caucuses are more fully explained in Chapter 19.)

Conventions The death of the caucus led to the rise of another means of nominating presidential candidates—**conventions**. These party gatherings are held to nominate candidates, determine rules that govern the party, and make decisions about the party's stance on issues of the day. The first one held—a National Republican Convention—nominated John Quincy Adams in 1828. In the election of 1832, all three parties in the running used a national convention to nominate presidential and vice presidential candidates. The procedure is still used today.

Conventions are attended by delegates—people elected or appointed to select a party's candidates. Delegates generally are selected through one of two means—presidential primaries or state caucuses.

Presidential Primaries

As you have read, conventions are now used for nominating presidential candidates. Before the national conventions are held, however, most states hold presidential primary elections to determine who will be the convention delegates. **Primary elections** are state elections held before the national conventions that determine the candidates for each party. After the conventions, voters nationwide actually choose officials in a **general election**.

Presidential primaries generally serve two functions: to select delegates to the convention, as mentioned above, and to show voters' preferences for presidential candidates. In some states the primaries serve only one of these functions; in others they serve both. It is important for candidates to know what kind of primary a state holds, as it may affect how they spend their campaign time and resources.

In some states' presidential primaries, party members vote for their choice of presidential candidates only. Delegates to the national convention are awarded to the candidates, based on the results of the primary. This system is called a "binding presidential preference" system. In states with "beauty-contest" primaries, voters choose their favorite candidate, but actual selection of the delegates to represent each candidate takes place independently. In yet other states with "delegate selection" systems, voters choose only the delegates to the convention, without indicating which candidate the delegates will support.

Finally, in some states voters express a preference for a presidential candidate and vote for a slate of delegates. These states include New Jersey, Pennsylvania, Vermont, West Virginia, and Illinois.

In some states delegates are awarded to candidates based on the percentage of votes the candidates receive in the primary. For example, in Kentucky, the top four candidates who have at least 15 percent of the vote are awarded a certain percentage of the delegates.

In just a few states—West Virginia, Illinois, Pennsylvania, and New Jersey—the candidate who receives the greatest percentage of votes receives all of that state's delegates at the party's national convention. In these "winner-take-all" states, a candidate can actually win less than half of the votes and still win all of the delegates for that state. For example, if there are three top candidates, and one receives 40 percent of the vote, another 35 percent of the vote, and the third 25 percent, the top candidate still gets all of that state's delegates at the party convention.

Caucuses

Party caucuses are held in some states instead of or in addition to presidential primaries. (Some states also hold local or state conventions.) Caucuses usually originate at the local level. These meetings are held on the same day at places around the state and are open to any party supporter. Many states, however, have systems that hold additional caucuses at the county, congressional district, and state level before making final decisions on candidates. The party caucuses also elect delegates to the national convention.

Turnout in caucuses is lower than in primaries because people often need to stay an entire evening to participate in a caucus meeting but only a few minutes to vote in a primary. State law, not convenience, however, determines whether the parties choose presidential convention delegates by primary or by caucus.

The Nominating Season

The presidential nominating season usually starts with caucuses in early February of each presidential election year and ends with the last primaries in early June. Some states begin their nomination process earlier than others do, and the order is important. The decisions of voters and financial contributors in states with primaries later in the year may be affected by the results of earlier primaries. The "front-loading" of primaries—the scheduling of primaries early in the year—can therefore have a great effect on the outcome of the nomination process. The momentum gained in winning or making a strong showing in early primaries—even in small states with few electoral votes—can boost a candidate to the front of the pack. Likewise, a poor showing weeds out many candidates early in the process.

Over time, front-loading has become increasingly significant. States such as California, once proud because their June primaries gave the candidates the last chances to face off against one another, began to see their primaries become less important because front-loading had already determined a winner. As a result, in 1996 California and several other states moved up their presidential primary dates to March.

POLITICAL PROCESSES *Citizens of Runnells, Iowa, meet at the local fire station to vote in a caucus for the presidential election.* **Why is there generally better participation in primaries than in caucuses?**

Indeed, understanding the importance of early momentum, presidential candidates have been looking for increasingly earlier chances to gain victories. Some people, hoping to shorten presidential nomination contests, have proposed holding a national primary on a single day.

National Conventions

Though the candidates for each political party may already be determined after the primaries, it is at the national party conventions where the candidates are officially chosen. Party conventions are gigantic, boisterous events filled with tradition. The formal business of a convention is nominating presidential and vice presidential candidates and agreeing on the party's views on issues of the day. Conventions also try to unify the party for the upcoming campaign through informal events and party-oriented rallies. As a result, many conventions take on a carnival-like atmosphere. Delegates and other attendees wear festive, multicolored hats and carry signs; members of the party make rousing speeches; and music and balloons fill the air.

Still, the conventions do have official party business to conduct. The format of the convention includes opening speeches, the adoption of a party platform, floor demonstrations by delegates, and a state-by-state roll call for the presidential and vice presidential nominations.

Speeches Conventions at times can seem like one long speech. Influential figures in the party give speeches about the party and about the broad themes that the party supports. The most important speech is that of the keynote speaker, who presents the themes that the party will feature in the forthcoming presidential campaign.

Party Platform The biggest controversy at conventions generally centers around approving the **party platform**, or the party's positions on issues of the day. The platform is made up of several **planks**—each of which represents the party's position on a particular issue.

Platforms often lead to bitter disagreement among groups within a party—as the abortion issue has among conservatives and moderates in the Republican Party. Party leaders generally attempt to settle disagreements before the

POLITICAL PROCESSES *Harold Ford Jr., a congressman from Tennessee, made a keynote speech at the 2000 Democratic National Convention.* **How do political parties use national conventions to promote party unity?**

convention, to keep delegates from bickering on prime-time TV and thus to keep the party from appearing splintered. Sometimes, however, the conflicts make their way into the convention. Finally, delegates vote on whether to adopt the party platform.

Floor Demonstrations At one time, conventioneers held spontaneous demonstrations on behalf of their candidates. Now, however, these demonstrations are carefully planned, with exuberant music and a display of floating balloons. Party leaders strictly control the length of floor demonstrations to keep them from interfering with other events the party wants to have broadcast on prime-time television.

State-by-State Roll Call Though the balloting for the nomination of presidential and vice presidential candidates could be done much more quickly by computer, the state-by-state roll call of the delegates is one tradition that has lasted. Each state's party leader is called upon, at which point he or she announces how the state's vote will be distributed.

ACROSS THE CURRICULUM

HISTORY For the Republican National Convention of 1860, one of Abraham Lincoln's supporters recommended, with a straight face, that Chicago might be a good neutral site, since Illinois would have no candidate. Of course, when the delegates got to the city, they found that Illinois did indeed have a candidate.

In Chicago, Lincoln's supporters established headquarters and worked behind the scenes, making promises and deals in attempts to obtain the party's nomination for Lincoln. When Lincoln learned of this, he sent a wire from Springfield forbidding any bargaining. His cohorts continued anyway, reasoning that because Lincoln was not there he did not know what they were up against. They went on haggling, promising cabinet positions, and giving out phony admission tickets in order to pack the building on nomination day. ■

As noted earlier, some states require that the state's primary winner receive all of its delegates. Others allow their delegates to be split among two or more candidates. In any case, a candidate must receive over 50 percent of the convention's votes to become the party's nominee. If no candidate receives this high a percentage on the first ballot, additional ballots are taken until a majority candidate emerges.

C A S E   S T U D Y

Conventions: From Proving Ground to Media Event

POLITICAL PROCESSES National conventions were once a place where several of a party's candidates could present themselves and explain their positions before the convention delegates. In fact, for most of the history of conventions, the nomination of the party's presidential candidate was undetermined at the convention's start—except in the case of an incumbent president running for re-election, who was usually renominated. For many years, most delegates were more loyal to local party leaders than to a certain candidate. In that

POLITICAL PROCESSSES *The Florida delegation cheers loudly as it announces its support for Al Gore at the 2000 Democratic National Convention.* **What percentage of votes must a candidate receive to become a party's nominee?**

era leaders had little contact with one another before the convention. Thus, it was at the conventions that these leaders would work out compromises to gain a majority for one candidate.

It often took numerous ballots before a majority of delegates could agree on a candidate. Have you ever heard of Champ Clark? He was the front-runner entering the Democratic National Convention of 1912. On the 46th ballot, however, he lost to Woodrow Wilson. At the Democratic convention of 1924, it took 103 ballots to nominate John Davis. It generally took the Democrats more ballots than it did Republicans because until 1936 the Democrats required a two-thirds convention majority for nomination.

Since 1952, however, neither party has taken more than one ballot to nominate a candidate. Airplane travel and inexpensive long-distance telephone service have made it easier for local party leaders to discuss the possible nominees before reaching the convention floor. In addition, today the vast majority of delegates are elected in primaries that determine their votes. No longer true nominating bodies, conventions thus have become "coronations" of the candidate who led in the primaries and caucuses, as well as a launching pad for the general election campaign. They are designed to give favorable media exposure to the candidate and to the party's platform.

The Election

Once the candidates are chosen, they campaign for several months until the election, which is held on the first Tuesday after the first Monday in November. This period is filled with speechmaking, personal appearances, and other campaigning by the

Comparing Popular and Electoral Votes

WINNER DID NOT RECEIVE THE MOST POPULAR VOTES

Year	Candidate	Popular Vote	Electoral Vote
1824	* John Quincy Adams	105,321	84
	Andrew Jackson	155,872	99
	Other Candidates	90,869	78
1876	* Rutherford B. Hayes	4,033,950	185
	Samuel Tilden	4,284,757	184
1888	Benjamin Harrison	5,444,337	233
	Grover Cleveland	5,540,050	168
2000	George W. Bush	50,455,156	271
	Albert Gore Jr.	50,997,335	266

CLOSE POPULAR VOTE

Year	Candidate	Popular Vote	Electoral Vote
1884	Grover Cleveland	4,911,017	219
	James G. Blaine	4,848,334	182
1960	John F. Kennedy	34,227,096	303
	Richard M. Nixon	34,108,546	219
	* Harry F. Byrd		15
1968	Richard M. Nixon	31,785,480	301
	Hubert H. Humphrey	31,275,166	191
	George C. Wallace	9,906,473	46
1976	Jimmy Carter	40,828,929	297
	Gerald R. Ford	39,148,940	240

* 1824—Elected by the House of Representatives because no candidate won a majority

1876—An electoral commission set up to rule on contested election results in three states gave Hayes the presidency.

1960—Received electoral votes but no popular votes

Source: *The World Almanac. David Leip's Atlas of U.S. Presidential Elections (http://www.uselectionatlas.org/)*

According to the rules of the electoral college, a presidential candidate can win without the most popular votes. The popular vote in several presidential races has been very close. **Does the electoral vote always reflect the popular vote?**

Caption Answer
The electoral vote does not always reflect the popular vote.

THEMES IN GOVERNMENT

POLITICAL PROCESSES
When John Quincy Adams ran for president in 1824, he had already distinguished himself as secretary of state for President James Monroe. However, Adams lacked popular appeal. The other candidates were Treasury Secretary William Crawford, Speaker of the House Henry Clay, and military hero Andrew Jackson.

On election day Jackson received a plurality but not a majority of popular or electoral votes. As prescribed in the Twelfth Amendment, the House of Representatives was to choose by ballot from among the three candidates with the highest number of electoral votes. Clay was out of the running, but he could and did sway the House vote. Clay was skeptical as to whether Jackson could be counted on to advocate Clay's legislative plans. Crawford, paralyzed by a serious illness, was taken out of consideration. That left Adams, whose political ideals were similar to Clay's. Clay supported Adams, and the House elected him president. ■

candidates. (The process of political campaigning is more fully explained in Chapter 19.) Finally, on election day, citizens go to the polls to vote for the candidate of their choice—or do they?

Electoral College and the Popular Vote As you have learned, U.S. voters do not cast their votes directly for the president and vice president. Instead, the **popular votes**—votes cast by the general public—are actually cast for slates of electors who are pledged to the candidates for whom people wish to vote. In all but two states, candidates who receive a **plurality**—or most—of the popular votes statewide receive all of that state's electoral votes. For this reason, a close national popular vote may still result in one candidate's winning a large majority of the electoral votes.

Criticisms of the Electoral College The winner of the national popular vote has almost always been elected president. The fact that the electoral college system allows a candidate

SECTION 3 REVIEW ANSWERS

1. Refer to the following pages: nominate (157), electoral college (157), elector (157), caucus (159), convention (159), primary election (159), general election (159), party platform (161), plank (161), popular vote (163), plurality (163).

2. Charts should include caucuses, primary elections, national conventions, and general elections.

3a. to settle a disagreement over whether the president should be elected by popular vote or chosen by Congress; each elector would vote for two candidates, one of whom could not be from the elector's home state, and whoever received the most votes would be president and the runner-up would be vice president.

3b. At first, candidates were chosen by party members in congressional caucuses; now delegates attend conventions to nominate candidates.

4. Answers will vary but should demonstrate knowledge of the structure of the electoral college and the potential for a winner of the popular vote to lose the presidential election.

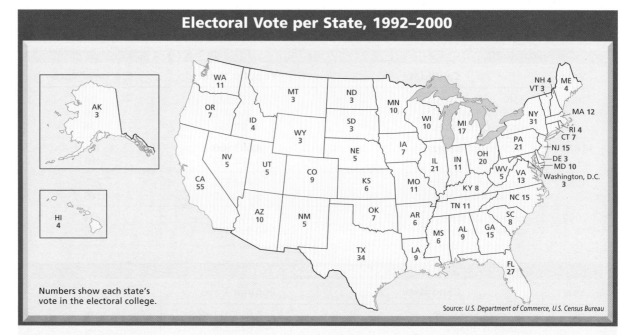

Electoral Vote per State, 1992–2000

Numbers show each state's vote in the electoral college.

Source: U.S. Department of Commerce, U.S. Census Bureau

States get the same number of electoral votes as their representation in Congress. **Which state has the greatest number of electral votes?**

who did not receive the most popular votes to win an election, however, has caused many people to criticize the electoral college.

Some people are wary of the fact that the electors are not required to vote for the candidate to whom they are pledged, making it possible for the electoral college to disregard the popular vote.

Other people feel that the electoral college system is weak because a strong bid by a third-party or an independent candidate might prevent either major-party candidate from winning a majority. In such a case, the House of Representatives—instead of the people through their electors—would decide the election.

SECTION 3 REVIEW

1. Identify and explain:
- nominate
- electoral college
- elector
- caucus
- convention
- primary election
- general election
- party platform
- plank
- popular vote
- plurality

2. Identifying Concepts: Copy the chart below. Use it to list the steps involved in electing a president.

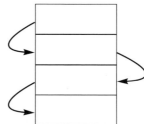

3. Finding the Main Idea

a. Why did the framers create the electoral college, and how did they expect it to work?

b. How have the nomination procedures for presidential and vice presidential candidates changed over time?

4. Writing and Critical Thinking

Decision Making: How do you think the president and vice president should be selected?

Consider the following:
- the framers' reasons for creating the electoral college
- the goal of elections that reflect the majority's wishes

Homework Practice Online

keyword: SV3 HP7

GOVERNMENT IN THE NEWS

The 2000 U.S. Election: The Long Wait

On November 7, 2000, Americans went to the polls to vote in the presidential election, after an eight-year run by the Democratic administration of Bill Clinton and Al Gore. The Republican ticket of Texas governor George W. Bush and Dick Cheney was challenging the Democratic ticket of Vice President Al Gore and Senator Joseph Lieberman for the right to claim the White House.

When the polls closed that night, Americans waited for the results of one of the closest elections in U.S. history. Gore won the battleground states of Pennsylvania, Illinois, and Michigan, while Bush claimed Ohio, Tennessee, and Missouri. In other states, Gore and Bush were still neck and neck. So they waited to see who won.

They waited while the TV networks predicted a winner. They waited while the TV networks withdraw their predictions—the vote was too close to call in the pivotal state of Florida. As the night wore on, it became clear that whoever won Florida would win the election.

In the early morning hours of November 8, the major networks declared a victory, calling Florida and the election for Bush. Having heard that he had lost Florida by about 50,000 votes, Gore called Bush and conceded. But 45 minutes later, Gore received news that Bush's lead in Florida had shriveled to a few thousand votes. Gore then called back to retract his concession.

The presidential contenders waited as both sides waged court battles to have certain Florida ballots either thrown out or recounted. They waited while bleary-eyed counters inspected "chads," referring to the small pieces of paper punched out of punch card ballots. To complicate matters, the simple, straightforward chad was soon followed by

the "hanging chad," the "dimpled chad," and the "pregnant chad."

Lawsuits, countersuits, appeals, and court hearings followed. The long wait for the final presidential vote count finally ended 36 days later. On December 13, George W. Bush and the Republicans declared victory, one day after the U.S. Supreme Court ruled against Al Gore's call for another hand recount of votes in Florida. The 2000 election was finally over.

To this day, though, the debate goes on. Who really won the 2000 presidential election? Al Gore received around 540,000 more popular votes nationwide than did George W. Bush. However, with Florida going to Bush, Bush officially won the White House, with a higher electoral vote.

What Do You Think?

1. Did you know that if Gore had won his home state of Tennessee, he would have won the election? Why is this true?

2. If you were in office, what would you do to improve the current voting system?

> **WHY IT MATTERS TODAY**
>
> Elections can become very complicated. Use CNNfyi.com or other current events sources to find additional information about other elections in our federal, state, or local governments. Also, you may look at international elections to find similar occurrences.
>
> CNNfyi.com

Government in the News Answers

1. Tennessee's 11 electoral votes would have given Gore enough to win the presidency.

2. Answers will vary but may address the conflict between the popular vote and the electoral vote.

CHAPTER 7

Review Answers

Writing a Summary

Summaries should focus on the main points of each section. These may be found in the Read to Discover questions at the start of each section. Summaries should also use standard grammar, spelling, sentence structure, and punctuation.

Identifying Ideas

For significance see the following pages: State of the Union address (143), foreign policy (145), presidential succession (147), executive order (148), executive privilege (149), executive agreement (151), electoral college (157), conventions (159), primary elections (159), general elections (159)

Understanding Main Ideas

1. salary and expense account, White House, Camp David, cars, airplanes, and helicopters

2. Chief executive carries out laws; commander in chief heads the armed forces; chief legislator

(Continued on page 166)

(Continued from page 165)

informs Congress about the state of the union and presents budget proposals; representative of the nation represents all of the people; chief of state represents the country when meeting with foreign leaders; foreign-policy leader promotes trade and friendship with other countries while maintaining U.S. security; party leader makes speeches in support of other party members; answers will vary.

3. executive, diplomatic, military, judicial, and legislative powers; Examples will vary.

4. Examples will vary.

5. Parties hold national conventions, where delegates nominate candidates.

6. a body of electors chosen by the states to vote for president and vice president; because it does not always truly reflect the popular vote

Reviewing Themes
1. Answers may vary, but students should address the point that the Senate may check presidential appointments.
2. Answers will vary, but students should offer an explanation and give support for it.
3. Answers will vary, but students should offer support for their reasoning.

Thinking Critically
1. Answers will vary, but should reflect an understanding of the current system and offer support for the changes made.

(Continued on page 167)

CHAPTER 7
Review

Writing a Summary

Using standard grammar, spelling, sentence structure, and punctuation, write a summary of the information in this chapter.

Identifying Ideas

1. State of the Union address
2. foreign policy
3. presidential succession
4. executive order
5. executive privilege
6. executive agreement
7. electoral college
8. convention
9. primary election
10. general election

Understanding Main Ideas

SECTION 1 (pp. 143–147)

1. What are the benefits of being president?

2. Describe the roles of the president. Do you think any are more important than the others?

SECTION 2 (pp. 148–156)

3. What are the president's five main powers? Give an example of each.

4. What are some examples of how presidential power has grown over the years?

SECTION 3 (pp. 157–164)

5. How are presidential and vice presidential candidates nominated?

6. What is the electoral college, and why has it sometimes been criticized?

Reviewing Themes

1. Constitutional Government The Constitution gives the president the power to appoint government officials, with Senate approval. Do you think that this power gives the president too much influence on the government? Why or why not?

2. Political Processes Why do you think the framers of the Constitution did not establish guidelines for nominating presidential candidates? Explain your answer.

3. Public Good What system of electing the president would better serve the public good: the electoral college system or a direct popular vote? Why?

Thinking Critically

1. Decision Making Imagine that you have been asked to revise the order of presidential succession. Review the current system and write a paragraph outlining your new system.

2. Making Predictions The power of the presidency has grown over the years. What changes do you foresee in the future?

3. Problem Solving In the 2000 presidential election, the electoral vote did not reflect the popular vote. How would you change this situation?

Writing About Government

GOVERNMENT NOTEBOOK

Review what you wrote in your Government Notebook at the beginning of the chapter about the presidents you remember. Now that you have studied this chapter, can you find within your recollections any examples of the president's roles and powers? Record your answers in your Notebook.

Interpreting the Graph

Study the graph below. Then use it to help you answer the questions that follow.

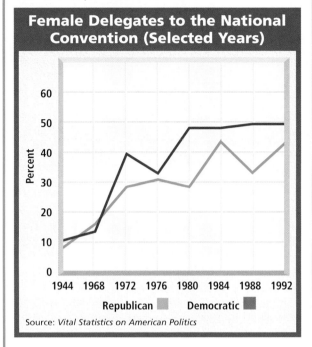

Female Delegates to the National Convention (Selected Years)

Percent — 1944 1968 1972 1976 1980 1984 1988 1992

Republican ■ Democratic ■

Source: *Vital Statistics on American Politics*

1. In what year did the Republican Party have a higher percentage of female convention delegates than the Democratic Party?
a. 1944 **c.** 1976
b. 1968 **d.** 1984

2. What was the percentage of male delegates to the national conventions in 1944? in 1988?

Analyzing Primary Sources

President Dwight D. Eisenhower's Farewell Address

On January 17, 1961, President Eisenhower gave a Farewell Address in which he described his hopes for the future of the country. Read the following excerpt and answer the questions that follow.

"As we peer into society's future, we—you and I, and our government—must avoid the impulse to live only for today. . . . We cannot mortgage the material assets of our grandchildren without risking the loss also of their political and spiritual heritage. . . .

. . . As one who has witnessed the horror and the lingering sadness of war—as one who knows that another war could utterly destroy this civilization which has been so slowly and painfully built over thousands of years—I wish I could say tonight that a lasting peace is in sight.

Happily, I can say that war has been avoided. Steady progress toward our ultimate goal has been made. But, so much remains to be done. As a private citizen, I shall never cease to do what little I can to help the world advance along that road."

3. Which of the following statements best reflects Eisenhower's point of view?
a. Things are getting worse.
b. There is reason for cautious hope.
c. There is nothing to fear.
d. War would be good for the country.

4. What experiences has Eisenhower had that might bias his perspective?

(Continued from page 166)

2. Answers will vary, but should demonstrate knowledge of how presidential power has grown.

3. Answers will vary, but students should offer support for proposed changes.

Writing About History
The Government Notebook is a follow-up activity to the notebook activity that appears on page 142.

Building Social Studies Skills
1. b
2. Republican: 1944—92%; 1988—65% Democratic: 1944—89%; 1988—51%
3. b
4. His experiences in war

Alternative Assessment
To assess this activity see *Rubric 1: Acquiring Information I Portfolio and Performance Assessment for Social Studies.*

Alternative Assessment

Building Your Portfolio

Imagine that you are an adviser to the top officials of a country that is planning to hold its first presidential election. You have been asked to brief key government leaders on the role of the president in the U.S. political system. Write a report describing the roles and duties of the president. You may want to include examples of activities associated with each role.

⏻ internet connect

Internet Activity: go.hrw.com
KEYWORD: SV3 GV7

Access the Internet through the HRW Go site to conduct research on the qualifications, daily job requirements, and personal qualities needed in a successful president. Then write a newspaper classified advertisement for the president of the United States. Be sure to include qualifications, a brief job description, salary, and benefits. Make it as realistic as possible by looking in a local newspaper for examples of what the ad might look like.

CHAPTER 8 EXECUTIVE BRANCH AT WORK

	OBJECTIVES	PACING GUIDE	REPRODUCIBLE RESOURCES
SECTION 1 **EXECUTIVE OFFICE OF THE PRESIDENT AND THE CABINET** (pp. 169–175)	▶ Explain how the Executive Office of the President is organized. ▶ Describe the role of the vice president. ▶ Discuss how the cabinet helps carry out the work of the executive branch.	**Regular** 1.5 days **Block Scheduling** .5 day	**ELL** Spanish Study Guide 8.1 **ELL** English Study Guide 8.1 **E** Simulations and Strategies for Teaching Government: Activity 8 **E** Challenge and Enrichment Activity 8
SECTION 2 **THE FEDERAL BUREAUCRACY** (pp. 176–181)	▶ Explain why Congress sets up independent agencies. ▶ Describe how independent agencies help carry out the work of the executive branch. ▶ Discuss how government positions are filled.	**Regular** 1 day **Block Scheduling** .5 day	**ELL** Spanish Study Guide 8.2 **ELL** English Study Guide 8.2 **SM** Government Activities: Activity 8
SECTION 3 **THE EXECUTIVE BRANCH AND THE PUBLIC GOOD** (pp. 182–186)	▶ Describe the power of the presidency. ▶ Discuss some common criticisms of government agencies.	**Regular** .5 day **Block Scheduling** .25 day	**ELL** Spanish Study Guide 8.3 **ELL** English Study Guide 8.3

Chapter Resource Key

PS	Primary Sources	**A**	Assessment		Video
RS	Reading Support	**REV**	Review		Videodisc
E	Enrichment	**ELL**	Reinforcement and English Language Learners		Internet
S	Simulations		Transparencies		Holt Presentation Maker Using
SM	Skills Mastery		CD-ROM		Microsoft ® PowerPoint ®

TECHNOLOGY RESOURCES	REINFORCEMENT, REVIEW, AND ASSESSMENT
One-Stop Planner: Lesson 8.1 Holt Researcher Online Homework Practice Online CNN Presents American Government Transparency 16 and 17: White House Staff and Executive Branch Organization Global Skill Builder CD-ROM	**REV** Section 1 Review, p. 175 **A** Daily Quiz 8.1
One-Stop Planner: Lesson 8.2 Holt Researcher Online Homework Practice Online Global Skill Builder CD-ROM	**REV** Section 2 Review, p. 181 **A** Daily Quiz 8.2
One-Stop Planner: Lesson 8.3 Holt Researcher Online Homework Practice Online Cartoon Transparency 6: Inefficiency in Government Global Skill Builder CD-ROM	**REV** Section 3 Review, p. 186 **A** Daily Quiz 8.3

Chapter Review and Assessment

SM Global Skill Builder CD-ROM
HRW Go site
REV Chapter 8 English Study Guide
REV Chapter 8 Review, pp. 188–189
Chapter 8 Test Generator (on the One-Stop Planner)
A Chapter 8 Test
A Alternative Assessment Handbook

One-Stop Planner CD-ROM

It's easy to plan lessons, select resources, and print out materials for your students when you use the *One-Stop Planner CD-ROM with Test Generator.*

internet connect

HRW ONLINE RESOURCES
Go To: go.hrw.com
Then type in a keyword.

TEACHER HOME PAGE
KEYWORD: SV3 Teacher

CHAPTER INTERNET ACTIVITIES
KEYWORD: SV3 GV8
Choose an activity on the executive branch to:
▶ research how the role of the vice president has changed
▶ research and debate topics related to the executive branch and the public good
▶ apply for a government job.

CHAPTER ENRICHMENT LINKS
KEYWORD: SV3 CH8

HOLT RESEARCHER ONLINE
KEYWORD: Holt Researcher

ONLINE ASSESSMENT
Homework Practice
KEYWORD: SV3 HP8
Standardized Test Prep
KEYWORD: SV3 STP8
Rubrics
KEYWORD: SS Rubrics

ONLINE MAPS, CHARTS, AND GRAPHS
KEYWORD: SV3 MCG
▶ White House Staff
▶ Executive Branch Organization
▶ Federal Civilian Employment

CONTENT UPDATES
KEYWORD: SS Content Updates

HOLT PRESENTATION MAKER
KEYWORD: SV3 PPT8

ONLINE READING SUPPORT
KEYWORD: SS Strategies

CURRENT EVENTS
KEYWORD: S3 Current Events

go.hrw.com

OBJECTIVES

▶ Explain how the Executive Office of the President is organized.
▶ Describe the role of the vice president.
▶ Discuss how the cabinet helps carry out the work of the executive branch.

MOTIVATE

Give students a task they will need the assistance of others in the room to complete, such as moving the teacher's desk and file cabinet across the room. Allow students to discover on their own that they need help from classmates to accomplish the task. When the work is completed, ask students what made the job difficult or easy and why help from others was needed. Explain to students that in this section they will learn about groups who assist the president in fulfilling his or her job.

TEACH

Building a Vocabulary

In spiral notebooks, have students create a Political Dictionary to be used throughout the course. The dictionary may be used as an activity at the start of each new section; it may also be used as a modification device for students having difficulty or Sheltered English Students during tests and homework assignments. List words the students will be expected to know for this section on the board. Have students list, define, and give an example of each of the terms, using the text or the *Researcher CD-ROM*.

Learning From Visuals/Navigating the Internet

Organize the class into small groups. Have each group make a presentation about one of the various organizations that make up the Executive Office of the President. Each presentation should describe what each group does to assist the president and should describe the size of the organization and tell how much it has grown over the years. Encourage students to create visual aids for their presentations and to give each group member a part. Students may wish to use the Internet, the text, or current magazine and newspaper articles to obtain information about the current activities of the organizations. Have students describe when the organization was formed, how it assists the president, and other ways the organization helps to promote the public good. Tell students that in the next activity they will learn about the role of the vice president.

Writing About Government

On the board or an overhead projector, list the name of the current vice president and several former ones. Ask students to identify what all of these people have in common. Tell students that they are or have been vice presidents. Discuss with students the roles that vice presidents serve. Be sure to include their roles of breaking tie votes in the Senate, performing ceremonial tasks, representing the president, and focusing on specific policy areas. Then have each student choose one of these vice presidents to research. Ask students to use resources such as the Biographies section on the *Holt Researcher Online,* the Internet, and the library to find out all that they can for their reports. Students should include the vice presidents' term of office, the presidents under whom they served, and any important actions they may have taken as vice president. Encourage students to present their findings to the rest of the class. Tell students that in the next activity they will learn about cabinet departments.

Acquiring Information

Ask students to work in small groups or pairs to find out more about what each of the cabinet departments does. Have students use the Executive Departments section on the *Holt Researcher Online* to find information about these departments. Encourage students to identify current activities of each department as well as former activities and how they may or may not be important to the students' personal lives as U.S. citizens. Students may wish to create a collage or display that shows newspaper and magazine clippings and other pertinent information they have found. Encourage students to share this information with the rest of the class. Allow time for discussion on the importance of these departments.

CLOSE

Ask students to consider the task they were asked to complete during the Motivate activity. Lead a discussion on other tasks that need to be done that cannot be accomplished without assistance from others. Encourage students to consider any occupations, besides the presidency, that include tasks that cannot be completed effectively without the help of others. Organize the class into three groups. Have each group create a study guide that describes help the president receives in fulfilling the duties of the office. Have one group cover the vice president's role, another the cabinet's role, and another the role of the rest of the Executive Office. Photocopy each group's study guide and distribute them to other students.

OPTIONS

Gifted Learners

 Have students read one or more of the presidential speeches located in *From the Source: Readings in Economics and Government with Answer Key*. Have students analyze the speech or speeches to categorize which, if any, of the departments or organizations discussed in this section could have helped the president fulfill each of the claims made during the speech. Have students write a summary that describes the promises made in each speech and which departments or organizations could have helped each president fulfill each promise.

Students Having Difficulty/ Sheltered English Students

 Encourage students to obtain more information on past or current first ladies of the United States. Teachers may wish to create a worksheet with spaces for students to fill in information such as birthplace, education, and activities as first lady, or teachers may allow students to determine which information they would like to include. Students may wish to share their findings with the rest of the class or compare earlier first ladies' actions with the actions of more recent first ladies. Information on some first ladies can be found in the Biographies section on the *Holt Researcher Online*.

REVIEW

Have students complete the Section 1 Review on page 175. Use the answers in the Annotated Teacher's Edition to assess student mastery of this section.

ASSESS

To assess student mastery of this section, have students complete Daily Quiz 8.1 in *Daily Quizzes with Answer Key*. For additional assessment options, see *Alternative Assessment Handbook* on the *One-Stop Planner CD-ROM*.

ADDITIONAL RESOURCES

Patterson, Jr., Bradley H. *The Ring of Power: The White House Staff and Its Expanding Role in Government.* 1988. Basic Books.

Relyea, Harold C., ed. *Executive Office of the President.* 1997. Greenwood Press.

The Role of the First Lady. 1997. Films for the Humanities & Sciences. (video)

HOLT PRESENTATION MAKER
Access Illustrated LECTURE NOTES using Microsoft® PowerPoint® on the One-Stop Planner CD-ROM

OBJECTIVES

▶ Explain why Congress sets up independent agencies.
▶ Describe how independent agencies help carry out the work of the executive branch.
▶ Discuss how government positions are filled.

MOTIVATE

List the following agencies on the board: Equal Employment Opportunity Commission, Environmental Protection Agency, National Aeronautics and Space Administration, Central Intelligence Agency, and Peace Corps. Ask students to describe what they know about the function of each of these agencies. Have students brainstorm on the importance of each of them. Ask students if they would like to work for any of these agencies or if they know anyone who is employed by one of these organizations. Explain to students that in this section they will learn about independent agencies and how they work with the executive branch to promote the public good.

TEACH

Building a Vocabulary

In their spiral notebooks, have students continue working on their Political Dictionary. List words the students will be expected to know for this section on the board. Have students list, define, and give an example of each of the terms, using information provided in the text or on the *Researcher CD-ROM*.

Synthesizing Information

Discuss with students the reasons for establishing independent agencies. Have students or pairs of students obtain information from the Executive Department section on the *Holt Researcher Online* and other resources about why specific independent agencies have been set up and how they help the executive branch perform its duties. Have each student or each group research a different independent agency. It may be helpful to give students a handout on the information they should gather or have students agree upon what information to research. Have additional resources ready to complement the information that is available on the *Holt Researcher Online.* Allow students approximately 20 minutes to gather all of the information they need. Students may also wish to include information on how one of these agencies has affected their own lives. Have each student or a representative from each group orally summarize information on the agency they researched.

Debating Ideas

Organize students into two groups. Have one group compare the similarities between regulatory commissions and government corporations and the other group contrast the differences. Ask students to debate these similarities and differences in terms of the effectiveness of these organizations and the way in which they are organized. Tell students that they will be learning about the civil service system in the next activity.

Hypothesizing

Have students write an editorial on the way in which government positions have been filled throughout history. Have students hypothesize how things would be different today if the U.S. government still operated under the spoils system or if all government employees were simply appointed. In addition, have students consider the effects of the changes made by the Bush administration regarding government appointees. Have volunteers share their ideas with the rest of the class.

Mastering Concepts

To help students further understand the concept of independent agencies, have them create collages of the work accomplished by these agencies. Encourage students to use the Internet, magazines, and newspapers to find pictures of projects or actions pertaining to these organizations. Examples include the space shuttle, certain dams, and environmental cleanup projects. Have students identify which agency each picture represents. Display completed collages throughout the classroom.

CLOSE

Using the Executive Departments section on the *Holt Researcher Online,* newspapers, magazines, and other outside resources, students should find out more about the agencies listed on the board during the Motivate activity. Ask students to give a brief report to the class on their findings, including activities of the agencies, whether the agencies are regulatory commissions or government corporations, and how agency positions are filled. Students may also want to include what qualifications are needed to become employed by the agencies, and where the agencies are headquartered.

OPTIONS

Students Having Difficulty/ Sheltered English Students

 Have students interview civil service workers about their jobs. Students should ask about the application, hiring process, training process, job responsibilities, salary, and benefits. Encourage students to prepare interview questions in advance, tape the interview, and transcribe the interview into a question-and-answer format. Have students share this information with the rest of the class. The class may wish to create a chart summarizing all of the types of jobs interviewed.

Intrapersonal/Gifted Learners

 Discuss with students how President Bush's administration reflects the population of the United States. Encourage students to consider the issue of diversity in society and the importance of representing all segments of the population. Students may wish to research the issue of diversity in government on the Internet and at the library, or by conducting interviews with adults. Encourage students to present their findings to the class.

Gifted Learners

 Encourage students to learn more about abuses of the spoils system by conducting research on scandals in the system during the 1800s. Be sure to have students identify what the scandal was over, what politicians were involved in the scandal, who uncovered the scandal, and the final result of the scandal. Have students write a short paper on the scandal that discusses these topics. Encourage students to share the results of their findings with the rest of the class and to discuss the consequences of such scandals.

REVIEW

Have students complete the Section 2 Review on page 181. Use the answers in the Annotated Teacher's Edition to assess student mastery of this section.

ASSESS

To assess student mastery of this section, have students complete Daily Quiz 8.2 in *Daily Quizzes with Answer Key.* For additional assessment options, see *Alternative Assessment Handbook* on the *One-Stop Planner CD-ROM.*

ADDITIONAL RESOURCES

Aberbach, Joel D., and Bert A. Rockman. *In the Web of Politics: Three Decades of the U.S. Federal Executive.* 2000. Brookings Institution Press.

Birnbaum, Jeffrey. *Madhouse: The Private Turmoil of Working for the President.* 1996. Times Books.

Wilson, James. *Bureaucracy: What Government Agencies Do and Why They Do It.* 1989. Basic Books.

Powers of the President: Bureaucracy, Court, and Media. 1997. Films for the Humanities & Sciences. (video)

HOLT PRESENTATION MAKER
Access Illustrated LECTURE NOTES using Microsoft® PowerPoint® on the One-Stop Planner CD-ROM

OBJECTIVES

▶ Describe the power of the presidency.
▶ Discuss some common criticisms of government agencies.

MOTIVATE

Ask students to read the first paragraph of Section 8.3 in their textbook. Pass out pieces of white paper to each student. Ask students to draw a cartoon depicting criticisms of the executive branch, as suggested by the paragraph and discussed throughout the section. Have students describe to the rest of the class their cartoon's message. Tell students that in this section they will be learning about how the executive branch affects the public good.

TEACH

Building a Vocabulary

 In their spiral notebooks have students continue working on their Political Dictionary. List the word students will be expected to know for this section on the board. Have students list, define, and give an example of the term, using information provided in the text or on the *Researcher CD-ROM*.

Taking a Stand

 Ask students to consider the question "Is the presidency too powerful?" Allow volunteers to speak on the issue one at a time, as in a public forum. Encourage students to cite examples to support their position and to suggest ways of controlling presidential power if they think it is necessary. Discuss with students ways that the United States has attempted to limit presidential power and explain the reasons why these limits were put into place. Tell students that in the next activity they will learn more about criticisms of government agencies.

Drawing Conclusions

 Have students use newspapers and magazines to research criticisms of government agencies and how they influence the public good. Have all groups write an essay comparing the information they found in their research to the ideas discussed in the text. Encourage students to consider the point of view of the civil service worker and the feasibility of electing that many people to office. Tell students that in the next activity they will learn about improving government agencies.

Debating Ideas

 Have students consider the solutions for improving government agencies set forth in Section 8.3, such as performance-based evaluations, contracting out work, and privatization of government functions. Give students articles to read that discuss both sides of these issues or allow students to bring in articles discussing these topics. Encourage students to consider the arguments made in these articles when they debate the issues as they relate to the public good. Have students consider how the issues relate to their own lives as they take a stand.

Mastering Concepts

 Discuss with the class the concept of performance-based evaluations. Tell them that one way that federal agencies are attempting to improve employees' accountability is by using these on-the-job evaluations. Explain to students that the usefulness of performance-based evaluations also depends on an employee's understanding of what he or she is expected to do on the job. This has led to the creation of results-oriented performance standards, which establish job targets for individuals. Organize the class into several small groups. Instruct each group to choose a different task (e.g., washing a car, making a pizza, writing a term paper). Have them brainstorm questions that can be asked to evaluate a person's performance of that task (e.g., Did the person rinse all of the soap off the car? Was sauce evenly distributed on the entire pizza? Did the paper clearly state its objectives?). Then have each group write results-oriented performance standards for the task that clearly show how the task will be evaluated (e.g., rinse the car thoroughly, distribute sauce evenly, clearly state the paper's objectives). Once all the groups have finished, have them describe for the class the task they want to evaluate, the questions they asked to see if a task was performed correctly, and the standard objectives they established for the task. Allow other groups to make suggestions regarding steps in the process that each of the groups might have missed (e.g., Did they clean the inside of the car as well? Was there enough pepperoni on the pizza? Were the stated objectives of the paper thoroughly explained).

CLOSE

Ask students to trade their cartoons from the Motivate activity with another student in the class. Allow time for each student to identify the problem being addressed by his or her partner's cartoon. Ask students to discuss with their partner the criticisms of presidential power and of government agencies that their cartoons identified and to discuss other problems that were previously mentioned in this section. Encourage students to suggest solutions for these problems.

OPTIONS

Students Having Difficulty/ Sheltered English Students

 Have students examine the political cartoons made during the Motivate activity. Then have students write captions for other students' cartoons, attempting to incorporate vocabulary terms from the text into the new captions. Sheltered English Students who speak a foreign language may wish to write a caption for their cartoon in their native language, then exchange it with another student who speaks the same language. Both students should then translate the other student's caption into English.

Interpersonal Learners

 Have students make up a questionnaire relating to one or more of the issues discussed in this section. Ask students to interview parents, teachers, employers, and other important people in their lives for their opinions on presidential power and the inefficiency of government agencies. Encourage students to compile their results and demonstrate them to the rest of the class in graph form.

Gifted Learners

 Encourage students to investigate ways in which U.S. presidents seek the public support that they rely on. Organize the class into several groups and assign a president to each group. Have students use the Biographies section on the *Holt Researcher Online* to determine major policies that required public support in order to become law. Then have students use outside resources to see how the president attempted to gain the needed support (for example, did the president address Congress, or address the nation on television?). Have each group present its report orally.

REVIEW

Have students complete the Section 3 Review on page 186. Use the answers in the Annotated Teacher's Edition to assess student mastery of this section.

ASSESS

To assess student mastery of this section, have students complete Daily Quiz 8.3 in *Daily Quizzes with Answer Key*. For additional assessment options, see *Alternative Assessment Handbook* on the *One-Stop Planner CD-ROM*.

RETEACH

For students having difficulty with the lessons, have them complete Reteaching Activity 8. This activity is located in *Reteaching Activities with Answer Key*.

ADDITIONAL RESOURCES

Kernell, Samuel. *Going Public: New Strategies of Presidential Leadership.* 1993. Congressional Quarterly.

Powers of the President: The Constitution and Congress. 1997. Films for the Humanities & Sciences. (Video)

Wilson, Robert A., ed. *Power and the Presidency.* 1999. Public Affairs.

CHAPTER 8

TOPICS INCLUDE

GOVERNMENT NOTEBOOK

The Government Notebook is a journal activity that encourages students to consider basic concepts of government that relate to their lives. A follow-up notebook activity appears on page 188.

▶ WHY IT MATTERS TODAY

To find additional lesson plans dealing with the executive branch, visit CNNfyi.com or have students complete the GOVERNMENT IN THE NEWS Activity on page 187.

CNNfyi.com

▶ WHY IT MATTERS TODAY

The executive branch of the U.S. government touches our lives in many ways. At the end of this chapter visit CNNfyi.com to learn more about how the executive branch affects your life.

CNNfyi.com

EXECUTIVE BRANCH AT WORK

Is the orange juice in your refrigerator really orange juice? Thanks to the Food and Drug Administration (FDA), an agency in the executive branch, you can be sure that if a carton says it contains 100 percent orange juice, the product inside is indeed pure orange juice. If the product is less than 100 percent orange juice, the FDA requires that the total percentage of juice in the beverage be declared on the container.

Regulations like this affect almost every part of your life. Among other things, regulations make sure that products are safe, that you are not discriminated against at work, and that your savings are insured. This chapter looks at how the executive branch is organized to meet these and other goals set by Congress.

GOVERNMENT NOTEBOOK

Look around your home tonight, and list in your Government Notebook all of the products you think are affected by federal regulations.

SECTION 1

EXECUTIVE OFFICE OF THE PRESIDENT AND THE CABINET

READ TO DISCOVER

1. How is the Executive Office of the President organized?
2. What is the role of the vice president?
3. How does the cabinet help carry out the work of the executive branch?

POLITICAL DICTIONARY
secretary
attorney general

To learn how the executive branch carries out its duties, you first need to know how it is organized. Two key parts of the executive branch are the Executive Office of the President and the cabinet.

Executive Office of the President

The Executive Office of the President is made up of several separate organizations, including the White House staff, the National Security Council, the Office of Management and Budget, the Council of Economic Advisers, and the National Economic Council. In addition, the vice president has taken on a key role in helping the Executive Office carry out its work.

White House Staff A striking feature of the modern presidency is the growth of the White House office staff. George Washington's staff consisted only of personal assistants, including nephews, whom he paid out of his own pocket. As one political observer noted of early presidents, they lacked "even so much as a receptionist or a personal guard to control access to [their] person."

As a result, early presidents spent much of their day meeting with visitors who came in off the street—"vendors, wayfarers, curiosity-seekers, and bearers of grievances of every conceivable [imaginable] sort." Not until after the Civil War did Congress appropriate funds for the president to hire White House personal staff and groundskeepers. Until then, he had to pay for them out of his own salary.

Today the White House staff serves as the president's personal staff and close advisers. They are appointed by the president without Senate confirmation. A chief of staff manages all of the White House staff and controls access to the president.

The people under the chief of staff are organized into groups that each handle a separate area, including national security issues, domestic policy, speechwriting, relations with Congress, and dealings with the press and the public. Given the influence of the media today, the White House press office is critical to a president's success. The press secretary, who heads the office and often presents televised briefings to the press, is one of the most visible members of the White House staff.

Speechwriting also is crucial to a president's success, particularly since speeches are a major means by which the president reaches the general public. President Warren Harding hired the first

POLITICAL PROCESSES *The White House chief of staff has many assistants, such as the two shown here, to help manage the White House.* **What are some of the responsibilities of the people who work under the chief of staff?**

THEMES IN GOVERNMENT

POLITICAL PROCESSES The office of Communications, Speechwriting, and Media Affairs is responsible for writing all of the president's official communications. Once a presidential appearance has been scheduled, a speechwriter prepares a draft, which is then fact-checked for errors by a researcher. The president is usually only involved in writing the most important speeches, such as the annual State of the Union address. Such a speech might go through many revisions. Richard M. Nixon's 1971 State of the Union address went through 14 drafts before it was considered ready to be delivered to the nation. ■

Enhancing the Lesson

For more information on the Central Intelligence Agency, see the National Organizations section on the *Holt Researcher Online.*

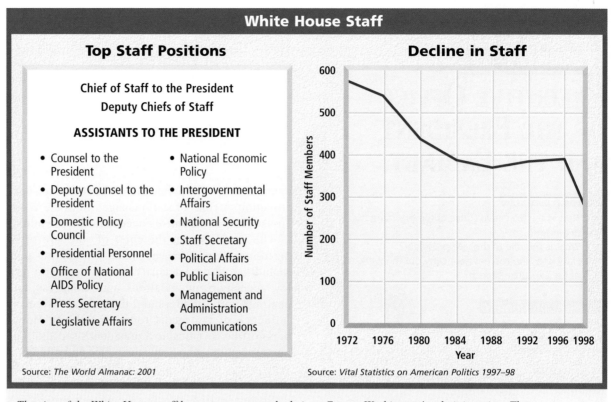

White House Staff

Top Staff Positions

Chief of Staff to the President
Deputy Chiefs of Staff

ASSISTANTS TO THE PRESIDENT

- Counsel to the President
- Deputy Counsel to the President
- Domestic Policy Council
- Presidential Personnel
- Office of National AIDS Policy
- Press Secretary
- Legislative Affairs

- National Economic Policy
- Intergovernmental Affairs
- National Security
- Staff Secretary
- Political Affairs
- Public Liaison
- Management and Administration
- Communications

Source: *The World Almanac: 2001*

Decline in Staff

(line graph: Number of Staff Members (y-axis, 0 to 600) vs. Year (x-axis: 1972, 1976, 1980, 1984, 1988, 1992, 1996, 1998). The line starts near 575 in 1972, declines to about 390 by 1984, levels near 370, rises slightly to about 390 in 1996, then drops to about 280 in 1998.)

Source: *Vital Statistics on American Politics 1997–98*

The size of the White House staff has grown a great deal since George Washington's administration. The chart on the left shows some of the chief assistants the president relies on for support. The chart on the right shows how White House staff numbers began to decline in the 1970s as presidents' staffing priorities changed. **Which member of the White House staff might handle the president's media relations?**

---

presidential speechwriter, called a literary clerk, in 1921. Prior to that, presidents generally wrote their own speeches.

Through President Lyndon Johnson's administration, important speeches were usually written by a senior adviser to the president, not by someone with the title "speechwriter." The task of speechwriting has now become a separate and distinct staff function. Speechwriters work on the Inaugural Address, as well as the annual State of the Union message and the greetings that presidents give to people—ranging from returning astronauts to college baseball champions—who are invited to meet the president at the Rose Garden, which is located outside the Oval Office.

An important part of the White House staff's work deals with the complicated day-to-day operation of the presidency. The Scheduling and Advance Office, for example, plans presidential trips. Once a site is selected, this office handles

a mountain of details—from the exact timing and route of the president's motorcade through city streets to the location of television cameras at speaking engagements.

Answering telephones and mail also are major jobs in the White House. In 1998 under President Bill Clinton, for example, the White House received some 43,000 letters a week. That does not even include the electronic mail sent to the White House. In 1998 the White House averaged some 20,000 e-mail messages per week.

National Security Council The National Security Council (NSC) was set up in 1947 to improve coordination among the government departments that deal with national security issues—particularly the Central Intelligence Agency (CIA) and the Departments of State and Defense. At first the NSC was made up of representatives from the various agencies as well as a permanent council staff. In 1949, however, the

Citizenship in Action

Presidential Recognition

On April 24, 2001, President George W. Bush honored 300 young people, ages 14 to 21, for their contributions to the environment. From a nature trail in Tennessee, to a recycling program in New Jersey, to a fish habitat in Alaska, to ponds in Utah, students of all ages and backgrounds joined together for one reason: to show their creativity, commitment, and concern for improving the environment.

The President's Environmental Youth Awards program encourages individuals, school classes, schools, summer camps, public interest groups, and youth organizations to promote local environmental awareness and to channel this awareness into positive community involvement. Young people in all 50 states and the U.S. territories are invited to participate in the program, which offers young citizens an opportunity to become an environmental force within their communities.

At the ceremony, President Bush offered a warm welcome to the winners and shared his feeling about living off the land, describing his experience on his ranch in Central Texas. He expressed the belief that "if you own your own land, every day is Earth Day because you work with your land on a daily basis." He said that the proper role of the federal government is to set high standards and goals, but stressed that it is the people who must work together to achieve these goals.

As an example of his environmental policy, Bush explained plans to fully fund the federal Land and Water Conservation Fund, and promised that regulatory policy would be based on "sound science." The purpose of his environmental policy, Bush said, is to ensure that both

President Bush recognizes Environmental Youth award winners at a White House ceremony.

economic growth and environmental protection go hand in hand.

During his campaign for president, Bush sent a strong moral message to teens, encouraging them to avoid "wrong choices in life," and urged teens to be strong role models for others. While standing before the winners of the President's Environmental Youth Awards, he congratulated the group on being an inspiration to the youth of America. The president encouraged the students, their parents, and sponsors to continue to lead their communities with sound environmental education to ensure that the world of the future will be a safer, cleaner place.

What Do You Think?

1. Why is supporting programs that recognize the contributions of outstanding individuals part of the president's role?
2. What do you think should be the role of the federal government in environmental issues? Express and defend your point of view.

> **WHY IT MATTERS TODAY**
>
> What are environmentalists concerned about today? Research environmentalists' goals for energy and the Earth on CNNfyi.com .

Profiles in American Government

For more information about John Adams and George W. Bush, see the Biographies section on the *Holt Researcher Online.*

WORLD AFFAIRS *Vice President Dick Cheney (right) greets Mexican President Vicente Fox before Fox addresses the U.S. Congress. **Why do you think that vice presidents have become more involved as public spokespersons for the president in recent years?***

council was reorganized and placed in the Executive Office of the President. A national security adviser, who is appointed by the president, heads the NSC staff.

With this change, the NSC staff became part of the president's staff, and the national security adviser assumed a prominent role in making national security decisions. For example, when U.S. soldiers were sent in to stop a revolt in 1965 in the Dominican Republic, President Lyndon Johnson sent his national security adviser to hold talks with local political groups. This was the first time a national security adviser traveled to another country to take part in negotiations.

Office of Management and Budget Because executive branch agencies must submit their budget requests to the Office of Management and Budget (OMB), this office is one of the president's key tools for influencing these agencies. For example, OMB could potentially withhold funding for a program that the president considers ineffective. The OMB staff also helps prepare the president's annual budget recommendations to Congress.

Council of Economic Advisers The Council of Economic Advisers was set up in 1946 to give expert economic advice to the president. It is made up of three members and a staff of about 40. The council participates with many other groups—such as the White House staff, the Treasury Department, the National Security Council, and the OMB—in advising the president on economic policy.

National Economic Council In January 1993 President Bill Clinton signed an executive order establishing another executive branch advisory body—the National Economic Council—to provide guidance on economic policy. The main goal of the council is to coordinate economic policy in the same way that the National Security Council coordinates advice on U.S. foreign policy. At the top of the council's list of duties is to monitor and advise the president on U.S. trade and industrial technology.

The Vice President The Constitution states that the vice president is to preside over the Senate and to be first in line of succession to the presidency. As head of the Senate, the vice president can vote on legislation only when the senators' votes are tied, which does not happen often.

For many years the vice president's role in government did not amount to much more than the above two functions. The first vice president, John Adams, said of the position:

❝ My country has in its wisdom contrived [invented] for me the most insignificant office that ever the invention of man contrived or his imagination conceived. ❞

Usually asked to perform ceremonial tasks, such as representing the president at the funerals of foreign leaders, past vice presidents were seen rarely and heard even less.

Today, however, presidents often give their vice presidents an active role in and responsibility for a specific policy area. President Bush, for example, had Vice President Dick Cheney run the transition team and fashion the new administration's energy policy. Vice presidents also have become more involved as public spokespersons for the president. Given these developments, the office is often seen as a path to the presidency itself. In fact, many vice presidents later run for president, with 15 out of 46 having received their party's nomination as of 2000. Some vice presidents,

Executive Branch Organization

PRESIDENT

EXECUTIVE OFFICE OF THE PRESIDENT

- Domestic Policy Council
- Office of National AIDS Policy
- President's Foreign Intelligence Advisory Board
- Office of Management and Budget
- Council of Economic Advisers
- Office of National Drug Control Policy

- U. S. Trade Representative
- Council on Environmental Quality
- Office of Science and Technology Policy
- Office of Administration
- National Security Council
- Office of Homeland Security

VICE PRESIDENT

CABINET DEPARTMENTS

Department of Agriculture	Department of the Interior
Department of Commerce	Department of Justice
Department of Defense	Department of Labor
Department of Education	Department of State
Department of Energy	Department of Transportation
Department of Health and Human Services	Department of the Treasury
Department of Housing and Urban Development	Department of Veterans Affairs

Executive offices and cabinet departments were organized to help the president make policy and enforce the law in all areas of government. **Which executive offices and cabinet departments advise the president on economic policy?**

including Al Gore, have even run for president before becoming vice president.

CASE STUDY

Role of the First Lady

POLITICAL PROCESSES The role of the first lady is difficult to define. Some first ladies have taken an active role in the country's policy making. Others have promoted social causes. But each first lady has had to determine for herself how to define her role.

While current first lady Laura Bush does not often express her political opinions, no one doubts her passion for education. Motivated by her background as a teacher and librarian as well as her lifelong passion for reading, she has become an active supporter of literacy programs. She stresses the importance of recruiting teachers to meet current classroom shortages, and she often visits schools, where she sits in a circle, surrounded by upturned faces, expressively reading from a book.

Many first ladies have used their visibility to advance social causes. For example, Lady Bird Johnson embraced conservation issues and the beautification of the nation's highways. Rosalyn Carter promoted mental health programs. Nancy Reagan established the Just Say No campaign against drug use, and Barbara Bush, like her daughter-in-law, promoted literacy programs.

While working with charities is considered an acceptable role for the president's spouse, some people object to first ladies helping establish national policy because she has not been approved by the Senate, as most high-level policy makers are. It was in this role that former first lady Hillary Rodham Clinton often drew both praise and criticism.

In her White House years, her voice was rarely silent. President Clinton gave his wife a key role in domestic policy making, naming her to head the Task Force on National Health Care Reform, perhaps the most influential position ever awarded a first lady. In this position, she sought to reorganize the

Enhancing the Lesson

For more information about the Department of Commerce, the Department of Labor, the Department of the Treasury, and the Occupational Safety and Health Administration, see the Executive Departments section on the *Holt Researcher Online*. Also, for more information about Alexander Hamilton and Thomas Jefferson, see the Biographies section on the *Holt Researcher Online*.

Caption Answer

(for page 175)
It would make little sense to meet with all of them together, because they all specialize in different areas.

SECTION 1 REVIEW ANSWERS

1. Refer to the following pages: secretary (174), attorney general (174).

2. White House Office—made up of the president's personal staff and close advisers, organized into groups that handle different areas such as national security issues, domestic policy, speechwriting, and dealings with Congress, the press, and the public; National Security Council—coordinates activities between government agencies involved in national security issues; Office of Management and Budget—

(Continued on page 175)

---

nation's healthcare system. Near the end of her husband's term in the White House, Hillary Clinton campaigned for and won a Senate seat. In her first 100 days as junior senator from New York, Mrs. Clinton introduced 10 bills and cosponsored 66 more.

Hillary Clinton was not the first presidential spouse to take an active role in politics, however. Eleanor Roosevelt paved the way by serving as President Franklin D. Roosevelt's "eyes and ears." Her activities brought her further into the public eye than any previous first lady had been.

In the future, the role of the president's spouse will vary, depending on the experience, background, and interests of the person who performs the role.

The Cabinet

In addition to the Executive Office of the President, there are 14 cabinet departments that assist the president in carrying out the work of the executive branch. The heads of cabinet departments are called **secretaries**, the one exception being the **attorney general**, who is the head of the Department of Justice.

Cabinet departments are divided into units that perform the actual work of the government. These units may be called bureaus, administrations, offices, agencies, or services. Examples include the Occupational Safety and Health Administration (OSHA) in the Department of Labor, the Internal Revenue Service (IRS) in the Department of the Treasury, and the Patent and Trademark Office and the Minority Business Development Agency in the Department of Commerce.

Before the tremendous growth of the Executive Office of the President, the cabinet was the president's main advisory body. As the Constitution states, the president might "require the opinion, in writing, of the principal officer in each of the executive departments, upon any subject relating to the duties of their . . . offices." George Washington relied heavily on his cabinet as a body of advisers. He even requested that some of the members of his cabinet—Henry Knox, Alexander Hamilton, and Thomas Jefferson—meet with one another if important matters arose when he was traveling.

More than 200 years later, however, the cabinet's role as an advisory body is much less significant. Cabinet meetings are now infrequent, and those that do occur are mainly ceremonial. Some secretaries, however, are still frequently consulted by the president—in particular, the attorney general and the secretaries of state, defense, and the treasury. The president relies more on these cabinet members' advice because their departments deal with areas of key

Comparing Governments

Homeland Security

The increase in terrorist activities around the world has spurred nations to try new methods of countering this menace. On September 11, 2001, terrorists attacked the United States. Soon after, President George W. Bush issued an executive order creating the Office of Homeland Security. The new office holds cabinet-level status. Tom Ridge, formerly the governor of Pennsylvania, was appointed to head the Office of Homeland Security.

In the past, counterterrorism efforts were handled by many different agencies at all levels of government. Ridge is charged with creating a comprehensive national strategy to prevent terrorist attacks in the United States. As the director of homeland security, Ridge leads the Homeland Security Council, which includes the attorney general, the director of the FBI, and the secretaries of agriculture, defense, health and human services, and the treasury, and other top officials. The new office faced its first challenge when in October 2001 a number of letters in Washington, D.C., and other East Coast cities were found to contain deadly anthrax bacteria. Terrorists were believed to be behind the anthrax attacks.

Unlike the United States, the state of Israel has had to live with terrorism as a daily threat for decades. Instead of a separate government office to coordinate antiterrorist efforts, the Israeli military—the Israel Defense Forces (IDF)—oversees Israel's fight against terrorism. The IDF is responsible for arresting terrorists and preventing terrorist attacks, which has often involved the use of military force.

Here President Bush meets with members of his cabinet.
Why does the president rarely meet with all cabinet members at the same time?

national concern, including crime, foreign affairs, the military, and economic concerns.

Why do current presidents rely so little on the cabinet for advice? One reason is that they rely heavily on the advice of members of the White House staff, as you have read. Another is that cabinet meetings are both impractical and time-consuming. If the president needs advice on what position to take in trade negotiations with Japan, for example, he or she might consult with the secretary of commerce individually. However, a meeting including the secretary of veterans affairs and other cabinet members who may have limited knowledge of the issue at hand would make little sense.

In addition, cabinet departments, like many other organizations, tend to be territorial. To protect their budgets and areas of influence, cabinet secretaries and their staffs may offer advice that is more beneficial to their specific areas of concern than to achieving the president's goals or to serving the public good. For example, officials in the Department of Health and Human Services might recommend improvements in health coverage programs without considering their costs, which is the concern of the Treasury Department and the OMB.

SECTION 1 REVIEW

1. Identify and explain:
  • secretary
  • attorney general

2. Identifying Concepts:
Copy the web on the right onto a separate sheet of paper. Use the web to identify and describe the six main divisions of the Executive Office of the President.

Executive Office of the President

3. Finding the Main Idea
  a. How has the role of the vice president changed?
  b. How is the cabinet organized?
  c. Why do presidents rely less on cabinet meetings for advice?

4. Writing and Critical Thinking
  Summarizing: Write a paragraph describing how the roles of the president's cabinet and the Executive Office of the President have changed over time.
  Consider the following:
  • the role of George Washington's cabinet compared to the current cabinet's role
  • the role modern executive departments play

(Continued from page 174)

oversees the budgets of executive branch agencies and prepares the president's annual budget recommendations to Congress; Council of Economic Advisers—advises the president on economic issues; National Economic Council—coordinates economic policy; vice president—presides over the Senate and is first in line of succession to the presidency; National Economic Council

3a. Originally a largely ceremonial position, in recent years vice presidents have become involved in policy issues and have served as public spokespersons for the White House.

3b. The cabinet is organized into 14 departments, which are further divided into agencies, bureaus, administrations, offices, and services.

3c. Presidents now rely more on the White House staff because cabinet meetings are impractical and time-consuming.

4. Students should describe a decrease in the significance of the president's cabinet in relation to an increase in the importance of the Executive Office of the President. Students should provide specific examples from the text to support their reasoning.

SECTION 2

THE FEDERAL BUREAUCRACY

READ TO DISCOVER

1. How do government agencies help carry out the work of the executive branch?
2. Why does Congress set up independent agencies?
3. How are government positions filled?

POLITICAL DICTIONARY

bureaucracy
bureaucrat
public comment
independent agency
regulatory commission
government corporation
civil servant
spoils system
merit system

The many agencies of the executive branch are important to the running of the government. In other words, these agencies perform much of the actual work of government. Most of the federal government consists of the cabinet departments. In addition, there are a number of independent agencies. Together these organizations make up the federal **bureaucracy**—a highly organized system of people and their work. People who work in a bureaucracy are called **bureaucrats**.

Government Agencies' Work

How do government agencies help the executive branch carry out its duties? They do so by advising the president and Congress on policy decisions and by making and carrying out the rules and regulations needed to enforce the law.

Advising Government Officials Most of the government's expert knowledge is found in the executive branch agencies. Why is this so? Many mid- to lower-level employees in these agencies stay in their jobs until they retire. As a result, the agencies have a deep pool of experience and continuity that is needed for studying and managing the huge, complex programs of the federal government. These agencies share their knowledge by generating reports and statistics that the president and Congress need in order to make policy and legislative decisions.

Making Rules The rules made by executive branch agencies have the force of law, though they usually carry only civil, not criminal, penalties for any violations. Over the years, agencies have passed a tremendous number of rules, which appear in the Code of Federal Regulations. As of 2000 this publication ran to some 200 volumes.

Agencies must follow set procedures for issuing a rule. For example, an agency cannot issue a rule without first giving notice and allowing a period for **public comment**, during which

POLITICAL PROCESSES *Here a member of the Peace Corps, an executive branch agency, talks to children in Ecuador.* **What functions do other executive branch agencies perform?**

interested parties can give their opinions on the proposed rule. After notification, the public has at least 30 days to submit written comments. For key proposals, however, agencies almost always hold public hearings as well, at which experts and other witnesses testify and deliver research reports.

The publication of a final rule must be accompanied by a "statement of reasons" explaining why each provision was adopted, as well as the evidence supporting those decisions. In addition, rules may be challenged in court. By allowing outside forces to examine the rule-making process, government provides a check on agency power.

The process from proposal to completion may take a long time and involve as much as 5,000 pages of recorded notes. Rule-making proceedings usually last a year or more. It is easy to see how citizens who want government to act quickly might become upset at what they see as the grinding—or spinning—of wheels. It is also understandable that the businesses, workers, and consumers whose lives are directly affected by a particular rule insist on its being thoroughly considered.

Implementing Rules Even after laws are passed and rules are written, government agencies still have a great deal of work to do. They must implement, or carry out, the rules they have created. This can be a difficult task. The Social Security Administration must provide checks to more than 45 million people each month. The armed forces must organize a fighting force of thousands of vehicles, weapons, and soldiers. The National Institutes of Health must decide who receives grants for medical research. The Immigration and Naturalization Service must patrol the nation's borders. To accomplish these enormous tasks, agencies employ a multitude of people.

Independent Agencies

The executive branch agencies outside the cabinet departments are called **independent agencies**. Congress creates these agencies to help the president carry out the work of the executive branch. They are independent in the sense that they are separate from the cabinet departments—often because they perform duties that do not fall under the scope of a cabinet department or because they serve the interest of several depart-

ments. Thus, they function best as separate organizations.

Today there are more than 40 independent agencies. They include the Social Security Administration, which runs the Social Security system; the Equal Employment Opportunity Commission (EEOC), which hears job discrimination claims; the Environmental Protection Agency (EPA), which monitors air, water, and ground pollution; the Federal Communications Commission (FCC); and the National Aeronautics and Space Administration (NASA), which runs the nation's space program. Other examples include the Central Intelligence Agency (CIA) and the Peace Corps.

Regulatory Commissions Some independent agencies have a greater degree of autonomy, or self-rule, than others. The agencies that act with the least direction from the White House are called **regulatory commissions**—independent agencies that have the power to establish and enforce regulations.

Regulatory commissions maintain so much independence because of their leadership. They

POLITICAL PROCESSES *Family members of victims of a plane crash attend a hearing held by the National Transportation Safety Board.* **What are the functions of independent regulatory commissions?**

HISTORY The New York customhouse was one of the most important sources of federal government revenue in the 1800s. Because the Customhouse was so large and important, its offices were an important part of the political spoils system of the era.

In 1871 Chester A. Arthur was appointed collector of the Customhouse. In that position, Arthur made more money than the president of the United States did at that time. The customhouse was so corrupt that President Rutherford B. Hayes finally suspended Arthur from the position of collector. Ironically, Arthur became president in 1881 and was a strong supporter of civil service reform, lending his support to the Pendleton Act. ■

Enhancing the Lesson

For more information about the regulatory commissions on this page, see the Executive Departments section on the *Holt Researcher Online.*

Caption Answer

Answers will vary, but students may suggest that it could decrease the number of people abusing drugs or prevent people from accidentally taking medicine that could hurt them.

---

are usually headed by a set number of commissioners from each party who are appointed by the president for fixed terms and confirmed by the Senate. In fact, many commissioners serve longer than do the presidents who appoint them. Regulatory commissions are more strongly influenced by Congress than the White House but, on the whole, act independently of both.

Why is it particularly important that regulatory commissions be free of political pressure? The commissions monitor and police key areas of national interest. Members of these commissions thus must be free from political pressures so they can make unbiased and well-reasoned decisions.

There are around a dozen regulatory commissions, including the Securities and Exchange Commission (SEC), which regulates the stock market; the Federal Trade Commission (FTC), which oversees business practices; and the National Labor Relations Board (NLRB), which

PUBLIC GOOD *The Food and Drug Administration requires pharmacies to provide customers with prescription-drug information sheets.* **How does this regulation promote the public good?**

puts a stop to unfair labor practices. Other examples include the Nuclear Regulatory Commission (NRC) and the Consumer Product Safety Commission (CPSC).

Government Corporations Some of these independent agencies—called **government corporations**—are run as nonprofit businesses. By far the largest of these corporations is the U.S. Postal Service. Others include the Federal Deposit Insurance Corporation (FDIC), which guarantees people's bank deposits, and the Tennessee Valley Authority (TVA), which provides affordable electricity to many rural areas in the South. Believing that these corporations run more efficiently than most other government agencies, many people argue that new government corporations should be set up to take over agency functions such as the nation's air traffic control system. Government corporations generally are set up when an agency's business is mostly commercial, when an agency generates its own income, and when the agency's work requires more flexibility than government agencies usually have.

Government Employees

The question of how the federal government fills government jobs has long been a source of controversy. Will effective government best be achieved by lifetime employees or by political appointees who share the views of each newly and democratically elected administration? Will a government run by people owing their jobs to the party in power lead to corruption?

These questions have been answered differently at different times. As you will see, government positions today are filled with both politically appointed and nonappointed **civil servants**—people employed by the federal government.

The Spoils System Between 1789 and 1828 the number of federal employees was extremely small. Positions were primarily filled by wealthy citizens who stayed at their jobs despite changes in presidential administrations.

In 1829, however, when Andrew Jackson took office as president, a new system emerged. Jackson passed out a large number of government jobs to his political supporters. He believed that people who held office permanently might

PRINCIPLES OF DEMOCRACY *Many people criticized the way in which federal employees were selected under President Andrew Jackson.* **What was this cartoonist's opinion of the spoils system?**

turn their public offices into private property and become a type of aristocracy. Believing in the abilities of ordinary citizens, Jackson stated that the government jobs were "so plain and simple that men of intelligence may readily qualify themselves for their performance." Jackson decided that the policy of keeping agency officials in their jobs permanently should be replaced by a policy of rotation in office. He believed that democratically elected officials should bring into office with them people who share the ideas for which a majority of the electorate voted.

This policy, of course, benefited Jackson by giving him more power and influence over government policies. As one senator stated it, Jackson's doctrine was like the doctrine of governing the behavior of victorious armies—"to the victor belong the spoils of the enemy." Soon,

Jackson's system came to be known as the **spoils system**.

Pressure for Reform After the Civil War, critics of the spoils system began a movement for reform. They pointed out that the quality of government service dropped as inexperienced and even incompetent people were appointed to jobs just because they had worked for the winning candidate. The spoils system, reformers argued, led to a government driven by personal benefit rather than public spirit. Furthermore, the spoils system symbolized a decline in moral standards and a rise in the worship of money, which they believed had gotten out of hand during the business expansion that took place after the Civil War. Ending the spoils system was crucial, in their view, to raising the nation's moral well-being.

The reform movement grew during the 1870s, particularly after several corruption cases. One of the most damaging was the discovery of the Whiskey Ring, a group of officials—including President Ulysses S. Grant's personal secretary—who took bribes from distillers wanting to avoid paying an alcohol tax. Even with these cases, however, reform might have failed had it not been for the assassination of President James

PUBLIC GOOD *Federal employees such as air traffic controllers often are required to pass an examination before they are hired for a government job.* **How has the merit system ensured that all applicants for federal jobs have an equal opportunity to be hired?**

CULTURAL PERSPECTIVES

The examinations given for federal jobs vary dramatically. Some are written while others are oral. Some are performance-based while others focus on general skills. This variety brings into question the validity of the tests being administered.

Some people have raised concerns about the ability of these exams to test the skills needed in the positions that people are seeking. Others have claimed that these tests discriminate against women and minorities. ■

Profiles in American Government

For more information about Andrew Jackson and Ulysses S. Grant, see the Biographies section on the *Holt Researcher Online*.

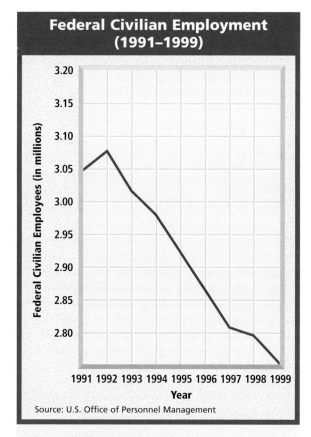

Federal Civilian Employment (1991–1999)

Y-axis: Federal Civilian Employees (in millions)

Source: U.S. Office of Personnel Management

*This graph illustrates the changes in federal civilian employment. The number of civilians employed by the federal government has decreased since 1992. **What was one of the reasons for the downsizing of the federal work force in the 1990s?***

Garfield in 1881. He was killed by a an unstable man who had tried unsuccessfully to get a job in the new administration.

The Pendleton Act The reform movement led to the Pendleton Civil Service Act of 1883, which gradually replaced the spoils system with a more rational one. Under the **merit system**, federal employees secure jobs through competitive exams and then stay on the job even after new presidents take office.

At first, the Pendleton Act applied the merit system to only about 10 percent of government employees, but it was slowly expanded to cover most of the government workforce. In 1897 President William McKinley strengthened the goals of the Pendleton Act with an order prohibiting the dismissal of employees hired through the merit system, except for good cause. Even so,

a large number of officials continued to be appointed politically in the United States.

Political Appointees Merit system civil servants make up the bulk of the executive branch agencies' workforce. A small portion—about 3,000—of top agency officials are political appointees. Of these, some 1,100—cabinet secretaries, deputy secretaries, undersecretaries, assistant secretaries, and various agency heads—are appointed by the president. Around 700 must be confirmed by the Senate. The remaining 2,000 are named by the presidential appointees themselves, without the Senate's approval.

It is no longer true, if it ever was, that most political appointees are unqualified and receive their jobs only as a reward for work in a presidential campaign or because they belong to a powerful interest group. A few political appointees may fit that description, but they are the exception rather than the rule. Political appointees, especially those in top positions, are generally well educated. Many have had prior government experience as well.

Civil Service Today The number of federal employees has been fairly constant for about 25 years, though efforts at downsizing have steadily decreased this number in recent years. In addition, given steady population growth, the percentage of federal employees as part of the population as a whole has dropped.

As of 2000 there were 2.8 million federal employees, including political appointees and the military, making the federal government the single largest employer in the country. Many people believe that the majority of these employees work shuffling papers at a desk in Washington, D.C.

Actually, government jobs are as diverse as are the government's tasks. Federal workers include soldiers, police officers, drug agents, accountants, engineers, firefighters, rescue workers, park rangers, biologists, chemists, physicists, and doctors. Also, less than 16 percent of civil servants work in the Washington, D.C., area.

Most cabinet departments and many individual agencies have offices in federal buildings in 10 regional centers that the federal government runs across the United States: in Boston, New York City, Philadelphia, Atlanta, Chicago, Dallas/Fort Worth, Kansas City, Denver, San Francisco, and Seattle. (Some agencies put their regional offices in other cities, however.)

In addition, many government agencies have small local offices. For example, the Social Security Administration has more than 1,300 local offices that receive applications for Social Security cards and benefits, as well as answer questions from citizens. If you live in a city or large town, you might look in your telephone directory (under *U.S. government*) to find out what federal agencies have offices located in your city.

Downsizing of the Federal Government

With rising pressure for smaller, more efficient government, President Clinton announced in 1993 that the federal government would shed 272,900 workers by 1999, the first major downsizing of the federal workforce in decades. In 1994 Congress approved a proposal to offer selected federal employees "buyouts"—cash payments for voluntary retirement—similar to those that many private companies have used to reduce the size of their workforces.

The results of these efforts were significant. By 1998 the federal workforce numbered around 2,765,000, down from around 2,999,000 in 1993. While most of these were civilian positions in the Department of Defense, the nondefense workforce also was cut significantly. All but one of the exec-

POLITICAL PROCESSES *The federal government employs people in many different professions. These federal workers are scientists who inspect fruit trees and other crops.* **Do most federal employees work in Washington, D.C.?**

utive branch departments saw cuts in their staffs. The Agriculture Department, for example, was cut 15 percent, or by 17,136 workers, and the Department of the Interior also was cut 15 percent, or by 11,522 workers.

SECTION 2 REVIEW

1. Define and explain:
- bureaucracy
- bureaucrat
- public comment
- independent agency
- regulatory commission
- government corporation
- civil servant
- spoils system
- merit system

2. Identifying Concepts: In the chart below, summarize the three main tasks of government agencies.

Tasks of Government Agencies

1.
2.
3.

3. Finding the Main Idea

a. Who sets up the independent agencies of the executive branch and what activities do the agencies oversee?

b. How has the civil service system changed over time?

4. Writing and Critical Thinking

Problem Solving: Write a paragraph describing how you think most government positions should be filled. Should jobs go to career civil servants who take exams to qualify, or should they go to political appointees? Before you begin to write, use a problem-solving process to gather information about the issue, consider a solution, and evaluate the effectiveness of that solution.

Homework Practice Online
keyword: SV3 HP8

SECTION 3

THE EXECUTIVE BRANCH AND THE PUBLIC GOOD

READ TO DISCOVER

1. Is the presidency too powerful?
2. What are some common criticisms of government agencies?

POLITICAL DICTIONARY
privatization

Just as Congress has its critics, so does the executive branch. The principal criticisms of the executive branch center around the power of the presidency and the size, complexity, and maze-like procedures of the executive branch agencies.

The Presidency and the Public Good

One of the most powerful offices in the world, the presidency holds a great potential for abuse of power. For many years people have debated whether the president has too much power and what are appropriate ways of maintaining or reducing it.

Growth of Presidential Power
Some critics charge that the president today is exactly what the framers wished to avoid—a sort of elected monarch. These people believe that the growth of presidential power has upset the checks and balances set up by the Constitution. Is this the case?

The president holds far-reaching foreign-policy powers, though they can be checked by Congress.

However, Congress has the power to decide domestic matters by passing laws, though the president can affect domestic policy by influencing and creating public pressure on Congress.

As noted in Chapters 5 and 6, the locally elected members of Congress provide a special voice for local concerns. The president, as a nationally elected official, balances this viewpoint by representing all of the nation's people. Thus, just as it is vital that Congress represent local concerns, it is crucial that the president have a strong enough voice and powers of office to represent the concerns of the country as a whole. This balance of power promotes the public good.

Reliance on Public Support Another criticism of the presidency is that in trying to act effectively as a representative of the nation, the president must work to gain majority support for policies. As noted in Chapter 7, Andrew Jackson was the first president to appeal directly to the public for support of his policies. Modern presidents have sharpened Jackson's technique by using more sophisticated and influential tools to help them reach the public.

Why do critics believe that such actions might harm the public good? While trying to gain public support, the president can spend a great deal of time on media relations—becoming more concerned with image than with the substance of

POLITICAL PROCESSES *Ronald Reagan, like other modern presidents, carefully prepared for public appearances.* **How much time do you think presidents should spend on media relations? Why?**

Careers in Government

Presidential Aide

Long days and a lot of responsibility—that is how one might describe the job of a presidential aide, whose role is to make the president's job easier. Though each president determines how heavily to rely on aides for assistance, high-level aides, such as the White House chief of staff, usually play a powerful role in assisting the president. The chief of staff often meets with the president several times a day; sets the president's daily schedule; arranges all of the president's trips; screens telephone calls, memos, and letters; and supervises the writing of speeches.

Presidential aides assist the president in almost every area of the job, from formulating policy to dealing with the media. Aides often work an average of 12 hours a day and six or seven days a week. Although presidential aides

A presidential aide works in the White House News Office.

work difficult hours, they do receive significant benefits. High-ranking aides have a great deal of power and prestige. They also enjoy other fringe benefits, such as large offices, the use of a chauffeur-driven car, and gourmet meals prepared by White House chefs.

Only a small percentage of the president's aides hold high-profile positions that bring "celebrity" status. Most of the president's staff work behind the scenes, assisting high-level aides with their responsibilities. Lower-level aides answer phones, write letters, help prepare speeches, research legislation, and answer questions from the media. All presidential aides are appointed by the president and generally are well educated and civic minded. While some aspire to political careers, others simply enjoy the experience of working for the nation's most important leader.

Careers in Government

To help students learn about other careers in government, refer them to the Careers section on the *Holt Researcher Online*.

---

internet connect

TOPIC: Presidential Power
GO TO: go.hrw.com
KEYWORD: SV3 GV8

Have students access the Internet through the HRW Go site to research issues regarding the executive branch and the public good. Then conduct a debate of the following topics in your classroom: What are the checks and balances that control presidential power? Does delegation of presidential power serve the public good or is it unavoidable because of a president's schedule? What checks and balances are in place to manage the various agencies of the executive branch? Does the president have too much power? Have students take notes on both sides for their arguments.

governing. In other words, as a president spends more time trying to present one side of an issue to the public, the facts and the importance of the issue can easily get lost in a battle of images. As Donald Regan's memoir of the Reagan presidency states,

> " Every moment of every public appearance was scheduled, every word was scripted, every place where Reagan was expected to stand was chalked with toe marks. The President was always being prepared for a performance. "

The amount of time that a president spends presenting a certain image varies, and determining the degree to which such efforts affect the public good is difficult. No matter what the effect, however, the media will continue to play a large role in presidential politics.

Government Agencies and the Public Good

The executive branch agencies perform much of the day-to-day work of the government. As a result, they also receive the lion's share of criticism. Two major criticisms of these agencies are that they are staffed with nonelected officials and that they are inefficient.

Nonelected Officials Most of the millions of federal employees are civil servants. This means that much of the work of the government is carried out by nonelected officials. As critics point out, this situation contradicts a basic democratic idea: that government rules should be made by representatives of the people. Unless the people elect the rule makers, they cannot make sure that the government's rules promote the public good.

PRINCIPLES OF DEMOCRACY *The cartoon above criticizes the wastefulness and inefficiency of federal agencies. **According to this cartoonist, what is one cause of government inefficiency?***

Many critics of government agencies even believe them to be armies of arrogant bureaucrats who issue endless commands and trample civil liberties without having to answer to the people. Is this an accurate assessment?

In reality, delegating power to nonelected officials in government agencies is a democratic choice made by elected officials. Consider the many people who visit a certain doctor for an illness and instead see a physician's assistant who was hired by the doctor. This assistant is not the person whom the patients have "elected" to see. However, these patients may trust their doctor to hire only competent assistants, just as many voters trust Congress to make sure that the agencies to which it assigns rule-making powers will promote the public good.

One still may ask, however, whether this delegation of power promotes the public good or is simply unavoidable, given the high number of government activities and the time limits on members of Congress. There are in fact positive reasons for giving decision-making powers to agencies. Most elected officials are generalists concerned with a variety of issues. Agency officials, however, often devote their careers to just a few policy issues. Sensibly, these employees are given responsibility for areas in which they are experts.

Keep in mind also that government agencies do not work unchecked. Congress creates, oversees—and can dissolve—agencies. In addition, the Office of Management and Budget (OMB),

guided by the elected president, has control over the administration of the agency budgets. These checks ensure that agencies do not run wild in making and implementing rules.

Inefficiency People sometimes criticize government agency officials not for making too many rules, but for accomplishing too little. Say, for example, a hurricane slams into the Atlantic coast, and the Federal Emergency Management Agency (FEMA) does not send relief quickly enough. In this case "the bureaucracy" might be denounced as being wasteful and inefficient.

However, most large organizations, public or private, are in some ways inefficient. Some civil servants are arrogant, some incompetent, and some wasteful. To paint all government officials in this image, however, is unfair.

Many government agencies in fact operate effectively. The Environmental Protection Agency (EPA) has secured much cleaner air than the country had just 15 years ago. The Customs Service rapidly processes piles of paperwork on imports. Remember also that government agencies often tackle the hardest problems—if it were easy and

PUBLIC GOOD *The federal government funds programs to clean up pollution in the Florida Everglades. **Do you think that government has found effective solutions to problems such as air pollution?***

profitable to deal with poverty and crime, the private sector would likely have done so long ago.

Improving Agency Management

While often successful, not all government agencies are managed as well as they could be and therefore do not promote the public good as well as they might. How can agency management be improved? Some people believe that the government should use performance measures, contract out some government functions, and turn others over to private companies.

Performance Measures One suggestion for improving agencies is to increase their accountability for their performance while giving them greater discretion in how best to do their job. In 1993 Congress attempted to implement this solution by passing the Government Performance and Results Act, which required agencies to set strategic goals, measure performance, and report on their progress in meeting those goals.

For many programs, measuring these accomplishments is a simple matter. People who call a Social Security hot line can be surveyed to find out how satisfied they are with the way their questions were answered. The amount of time it takes to process a veteran's benefit application can be measured. These sorts of standards can be used to rate agencies' performance and pinpoint areas needing improvement.

What about cases in which performance measures are more complicated? For example, how should a school's performance be measured? A survey of student satisfaction might show only a dislike for homework. Looking at scores from the Scholastic Aptitude Test (SAT) would show only how well prepared some students were for admission into college. To fully evaluate a school, the Department of Education can develop a bundle of performance measures that take into account student, parent, and teacher satisfaction; SAT scores; graduation rates; and so on. Using performance measures becomes even more complicated when people disagree about what feature of performance is most important—should the government look first at how well a school prepares the brightest students or at whether it minimizes the dropout rate?

Some of the changes that performance measures require can be difficult for government agencies to make, but these changes may present opportunities for the people working in the agencies. Results-oriented performance standards give people clearer goals for which to strive and greater freedom in deciding how to do their jobs.

Contracting Out Many people argue that government agencies are incapable of operating efficiently enough. The solution, they say, is to contract out as many government functions as possible. When government contracts out work, it hires a private company to produce a good or perform a service. For example, a city government might contract out its garbage collection to a private company, Acme Trash. Acme collects the garbage, and the city pays Acme with tax dollars. Thus, although a private company performs the service, the government retains the right to oversee the company's work.

Government in fact already contracts out many responsibilities. Private companies develop weapons systems for the Department of Defense, and the government buys services such as building management and debt collection from private firms. This practice is similar to that of private companies that contract out some functions to other private companies. Many companies, for example, hire advertising agencies to prepare marketing materials, and law firms to provide legal services.

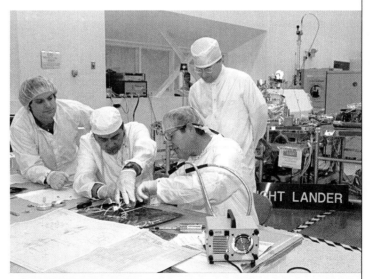

POLITICAL PROCESSES *NASA's Jet Propulsion Laboratory, located near Pasadena, California, is managed by the California Institute of Technology.* **Why do some people think that contracting out government work is a good solution to inefficiency?**

Caption Answer

Answers will vary, but students may point out that many people think that government agencies are incapable of operating efficiently.

SECTION 3 REVIEW ANSWERS

1. Refer to page 186.

2. Contracting out allows the government to hire private companies to perform a service while maintaining the right to oversee it. Privatization means that a company takes complete control over a government function.

3a. Critics contend that the growth of presidential power has upset the system of checks and balances.

3b. The need for public support can lead the president to spend too much time cultivating an image for the public and the media instead of working on important policy issues.

4. Students may choose any functions or none, but they should support their opinions with information they have gathered.

PUBLIC GOOD *In many states, trash collection and recycling services are provided by private companies.* **What government services in your community do you think could be better provided by a private company?**

In addition, contracting out also presents its own problems. For example, the government has had great difficulties in dealing with defense contractors. On occasion, weapons systems created by these companies have not performed up to expectation. Because so few companies can make submarines and fighter planes, the government often has little leverage over the companies. In turn, as private companies, the defense contractors have conflicting goals—promoting the public good and trying to make as much profit as possible.

Contracting out, however, is unlikely to work in all instances. There are several government activities—such as diplomacy and the arrest of criminals—that are undertaken in the name of the people of the United States as a whole and should not be handled by private parties. Do citizens, for example, want the U.S. Embassy in Tokyo staffed by employees of Diplomacy, Inc.? Would these employees represent the U.S. public or their company? In other cases, the performance of a job by U.S. government employees has symbolic value. By hiring its own rangers, the National Park Service shows that the national parks are the property of all U.S. citizens.

Privatization Another possible solution to problems in agency management is **privatization**—the turning of an entire government function over to a private company. In the case of city garbage collection, privatization would mean the government would no longer collect taxes to pay for garbage collection. Instead, Acme Trash would not only collect the garbage but also charge customers directly.

What services might be privatized? Rather than having the Forest Service manage the national forests, the Department of the Interior could sell them to private owners. Rather than having a national space program, space exploration could be left to private companies. In these cases, though, the forests might be cut down for timber, and space exploration might be stopped because of its enormous costs. By removing agencies from their role as overseer, some people argue that privatization takes away a major motivation for the companies to promote the public good.

SECTION 3 REVIEW

1. Define and explain:
- privatization

2. Identifying Concepts: What are the differences between contracting out a government service and privatizing it? Use the chart below to contrast the two options.

Contracting Out Government Service	Privatizing Government Service

Homework Practice Online
keyword: SV3 HP8

3. **Finding the Main Idea**

a. Why do some people say that the presidency is too powerful?

b. What is a possible effect of the president's reliance on public support?

4. **Writing and Critical Thinking**

Problem Solving: Write a paragraph describing what kinds of government functions, if any, you think should be privatized. How would privatizing these functions promote—or threaten—the public good? Before you begin to write, use a problem-solving process to gather information about the issue, consider a solution, and evaluate the effectiveness of that solution.

GOVERNMENT IN THE NEWS

Privacy and the Population Count

Once every 10 years the U.S. Department of Commerce's Bureau of the Census takes a head count of the U.S. population. The census does much more than just count people, however. It also gathers information about them, including their age, occupation, ethnic origin, and whether they live in a city or rural area. In this way, the census provides an update on the ever-changing face of American society. The primary use of census information, however, is to determine the distribution of congressional representation among the states.

The census process begins when the Bureau of the Census mails surveys to U.S. households. The Census Bureau then sends out about 500,000 census takers to count those who do not have a permanent address. Census takers visit nursing homes, prisons, and college dormitories. They go to shelters and soup kitchens in order to count homeless Americans. Census takers also visit households that did not respond to the initial survey.

Each household receives a set of questions called the short form. These questions ask for the number of occupants of each household as well as for their age, sex, and race. These results are then used to determine the total population of the United States. The 2000 census found 285,926,083 people living in the United States.

Along with the short form, approximately 700,000 people also receive an additional survey of more than 50 questions, known as the long form. The long form asks for more personal details, such as the housing conditions and education level of the members of the household, for example. In 2000 the long form made headlines when some of those who received it objected to its questions. These people felt uneasy about answering what they felt were intrusive personal questions.

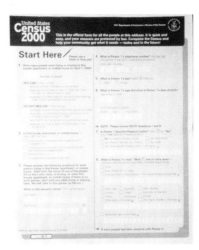

The census short form, seen here, enables the Census Bureau to take an accurate population count.

While some long-form questions bring up sensitive issues, each question supplies information essential for government programs. Without information about housing conditions, people's education level, or race and ethnicity, the government would be hard-pressed to supply adequate funding to housing, education, or civil rights programs. Nevertheless, some politicians, including then-governor George W. Bush of Texas, commented that if people found the questions too intrusive, then they might consider not responding to them. Although 67 percent of households returned their short form in 2000—a 2 percent increase from 1990—the rate of response to the long form was 56 percent, down significantly from 1990.

What Do You Think?

1. What are the results of the census used for?
2. Do you think that people should be required to respond to the census long form?

WHY IT MATTERS TODAY

How do census results affect our daily lives? Use CNNfyi.com or other **current events** sources to find additional information about the census.

CNNfyi.com

Government in the News Answers

1. Students might suggest that census results are used to learn the total population of the United States, to determine the distribution of congressional representation, and to provide critical information for government services.

2. Answers will vary, but students should demonstrate an understanding of what the results of the long form are used for and what objections some people have to the long form.

CHAPTER 8

Review Answers

Writing a Summary

Summaries should focus on the main points of each section. These may be found in the Read to Discover questions at the start of each section. Summaries should also use standard grammar, spelling, sentence structure, and punctuation.

Identifying Ideas

secretary (174), attorney general (174), bureaucracy (176), bureaucrat (176), independent agency (177), regulatory commission (177), government corporation (178), spoils system (179), merit system (180), privatization (186)

Understanding Main Ideas

1. The vice president now handles policy issues and
(Continued on page 188)

Review

(Continued from page 187)

serves as spokesperson for the White House.

2. the White House Office, the National Security Council, the Office of Management and Budget, the Council of Economic Advisers, the National Economic Council, and the vice president.

3. helps carry out the work of the executive branch.

4. They advise government officials, make and enforce rules, and provide information to other agencies and branches of government.

5. Answers may include the Social Security Administration, the Equal Employment Opportunity Commission, the National Aeronautics and Space Administration, or the Central Intelligence Agency.

6. civil servant—a career government employee who relies on merit to get the job; appointee—chosen by the president or another appointee based on political reasons.

7. Students may choose increasing power or the tendency to rely on image to gain public support.

8. Congress and the judiciary.

9. It takes away from time a president could use on policy issues.

10. Use performance measures, contract out some government functions, and privatize some functions.

Reviewing Themes

1. Students should support their opinions with examples from the text.

(Continued on page 189)

Writing a Summary

Using standard grammar, spelling, sentence structure, and punctuation, write a summary of the information in this chapter.

Identifying Ideas

Identify the following terms and explain their significance.

1. secretary

2. attorney general

3. bureaucracy

4. bureaucrat

5. independent agency

6. regulatory commission

7. government corporation

8. spoils system

9. merit system

10. privatization

Understanding Main Ideas

SECTION 1 *(pp. 169–175)*

1. How has the role of the vice president changed in recent years?

2. Of what elements does the Executive Office of the President consist?

3. What is the role of the cabinet?

SECTION 2 *(pp. 176–181)*

4. What functions do independent agencies serve?

5. List three independent agencies.

6. What is the difference between a civil servant and a political appointee?

SECTION 3 *(pp. 182–186)*

7. List one major criticism of the presidency.

8. What government body checks the power of the president?

9. Why do some people worry about the time a president spends gaining public support?

10. What are three common suggestions for improving agency management?

Reviewing Themes

1. Political Processes Do you think the privatization and contracting out of government functions, such as developing weapons systems, is a good solution to inefficiency in the federal government? Explain your answer.

2. Political Processes Should the president rely on the advice of the White House staff rather than the executive branch agencies in the policy-making process? Why or why not?

3. Public Good Why is it important for regulatory commissions to be free from political pressures? Could political influence over regulatory agencies jeopardize the public good?

Thinking Critically

1. Supporting a Point of View Some people argue that the presidency has grown too powerful. Do you agree? Why or why not? What mechanisms exist to check the power of the president? Are they effective?

2. Identifying Cause and Effect What caused the Pendleton Act and what was its effect?

3. Making Predictions How do you think the federal government would be different if all jobs were awarded using the spoils system instead of the merit system?

Writing about Government

Review what you wrote in your Government Notebook at the beginning of the chapter about federally regulated products. Given what you have learned, do you need to revise your list? Research which agency in the executive branch is responsible for regulating each product you have listed. Record your findings in your Notebook.

Interpreting the Table

Study the table below. Then use it to help you answer the questions that follow.

	Almost Every Day	At Least Once a Week	Once or Twice a Month	A Few Times a Year	Never
1984	2.6	7.4	14.1	44.9	31.0
1986	1.7	8.4	14.0	44.9	31.0
1988	2.6	6.3	13.4	45.4	32.3
1990	1.8	6.9	13.0	43.3	35.1
1991	2.4	5.9	14.6	44.6	32.4
1992	2.8	7.4	16.5	41.7	31.6
1993	2.7	8.0	15.0	44.0	30.3
1994	3.2	7.6	17.2	44.8	27.2

Percentage of High School Seniors Participating in Volunteer or Community Service Work: 1984–1994

Source: University of Michigan Institute for Social Research

1. According to these statistics, in which year did the smallest percentage of high school seniors perform volunteer work?
   - **a.** 1984
   - **b.** 1988
   - **c.** 1990
   - **d.** 1994

2. Between 1990 and 1994, did the amount of volunteer work and participation in community affairs by high school seniors increase or decrease?

Analyzing Primary Sources

In 1997 Madeleine Albright became the first female secretary of state. Read the following excerpt from a press briefing at which Albright presented the U.S. Department of State's annual human rights report, then answer the questions.

"When human rights standards are observed, sustainable economic progress is more likely; violent conflicts are easier to prevent; terrorists and criminals find it harder to operate, and societies are more fully able to benefit from the skills and energy of their citizens.

In such an environment, Americans are safer, and we are more likely to find good partners with whom to pursue shared economic, diplomatic, and security goals. That is why human rights are and will remain a key element in our foreign policy."

3. Which of the following best summarizes Albright's point of view?
   - **a.** Human rights are important and the United States is in a position to help safeguard them.
   - **b.** Economic progress is not linked to human rights.
   - **c.** The United States has no stake in supporting human rights standards abroad.
   - **d.** Terrorists and criminals must benefit from human rights standards.

4. What does this excerpt indicate about that administration's foreign-policy goals?

(Continued from page 188)

2. Students may say it is more efficient to rely on White House staff, or that executive branch agencies should have more influence. Students should support their opinions.

3. Answers will vary but might note that undue political influence could lead regulatory agencies to ignore certain violations for political purposes.

Thinking Critically

1. Answers will vary but should discuss the potential for abuse of power, the far-reaching foreign-policy powers of the president, and that Congress provides a check on presidential power.

2. Corruption cases sparked a reform movement that culminated in the Pendleton Act, which was responsible for the merit system in federal employment.

3. Students may argue that bureaucracy would be less efficient or that political appointees have the potential to be as effective as career civil servants.

Building Social Studies Skills

1. c.

2. increase

3. a.

4. The Clinton administration considered human rights a high priority.

Alternative Assessment

To assess this activity see Writing to Describe in Alternative Assessment Handbook.

Alternative Assessment

Building Your Portfolio

Regulatory Handbook

With a group of students, create a handbook on federal regulatory commissions. List three or four commissions that oversee business and labor issues, describe the function of each, and include examples of regulations that each commission has implemented. Your handbook should be clearly written, well designed, and easy to follow.

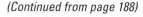

Internet connect

Internet Activity: go.hrw.com
KEYWORD: SV3 GV8

Access the Internet through the HRW Go site to research the different agencies that are a part of the Executive Branch. Write a letter to the White House Personnel Office explaining why you would like to work for an agency and what qualifies you for the job. Look at the online application so you know which qualifications to address.

CHAPTER 9 ECONOMIC POLICY

	OBJECTIVES	PACING GUIDE	REPRODUCIBLE RESOURCES
SECTION 1 **RAISING REVENUE** (pp. 191–195)	▶ What are the major types of federal taxes? ▶ How does the federal government collect taxes? ▶ What sources of revenue, other than taxes, does the federal government have? ▶ What factors have affected the political debate over tax policy in recent decades?	**Regular** 1 day **Block Scheduling** .5 day	**ELL** Spanish Study Guide 9.1 **ELL** English Study Guide 9.1 **PS** Reading 39: Interstate Commerce Act of 1887
SECTION 2 **INFLUENCING THE ECONOMY** (pp. 196–203)	▶ How is the U.S. economy organized? ▶ What are the goals of economic stabilization policy? ▶ What tools does the U.S. government use to stabilize the economy?	**Regular** 1.5 days **Block Scheduling** 1 day	**ELL** Spanish Study Guide 9.2 **ELL** English Study Guide 9.2 **PS** Reading 41: Federal Reserve Act of 1913
SECTION 3 **THE FEDERAL BUDGET** (pp. 204–207)	▶ How has the federal budget-making process changed over the years? ▶ What role does the president play in planning the budget? ▶ Why are attempts at reducing the budget politically controversial?	**Regular** 1 day **Block Scheduling** .25 day	**ELL** Spanish Study Guide 9.3 **ELL** English Study Guide 9.3 **PS** Reading 40: Sherman Antitrust Act of 1890
SECTION 4 **DEFICIT SPENDING AND THE ECONOMY** (pp. 208–212)	▶ What factors can cause the federal government to operate at a deficit? ▶ How does the national debt influence the U.S. economy? ▶ In what ways do the national debt and the federal deficit influence each other?	**Regular** 1 day **Block Scheduling** .5 day	**ELL** Spanish Study Guide 9.4 **ELL** English Study Guide 9.4

Chapter Resource Key

PS	Primary Sources	**A**	Assessment		Video
RS	Reading Support	**REV**	Review		Videodisc
E	Enrichment	**ELL**	Reinforcement and English Language Learners		Internet
S	Simulations		Transparencies		Holt Presentation Maker Using
SM	Skills Mastery		CD-ROM		Microsoft ® PowerPoint ®

TECHNOLOGY RESOURCES	REINFORCEMENT, REVIEW, AND ASSESSMENT
One-Stop Planner: Lesson 9.1 Holt Researcher Online Homework Practice Online Transparency 18 Global Skill Builder CD-ROM	**REV** Section 1 Review, p. 195 **A** Daily Quiz 9.1
One-Stop Planner: Lesson 9.2 Holt Researcher Online Homework Practice Online Transparency 19 Global Skill Builder CD-ROM	**REV** Section 2 Review, p. 203 **A** Daily Quiz 9.2
One-Stop Planner: Lesson 9.3 Holt Researcher Online Homework Practice Online Cartoon Transparency 7 Transparency 20 Global Skill Builder CD-ROM	**REV** Section 3 Review, p. 207 **A** Daily Quiz 9.3
One-Stop Planner: Lesson 9.4 Holt Researcher Online Homework Practice Online *Holt American Government Videodisc:* Land Use: Oil Exploration in Alaska Cartoon Transparency 8 Global Skill Builder CD-ROM **E** Challenge and Enrichment: Activity 9 **E** Simulations and Strategies for Teaching American Government: Activity 9 CNN Presents American Government	**REV** Section 4 Review, p. 212 **A** Daily Quiz 9.4

Chapter Review and Assessment

- Global Skill Builder CD-ROM
- HRW Go site
- **REV** Chapter 9 Tutorial for Students, Parents, and Peers
- **REV** Chapter 9 Review, pp. 214–15
- Chapter 9 Test Generator (on the One-Stop Planner)
- **A** Chapter 9 Test
- **A** Alternative Assessment Handbook

One-Stop Planner CD–ROM

It's easy to plan lessons, select resources, and print out materials for your students when you use the *One-Stop Planner CD-ROM with Test Generator.*

---

internet connect

HRW ONLINE RESOURCES
Go To: go.hrw.com
Then type in a keyword.

TEACHER HOME PAGE
KEYWORD: SV3 Teacher

CHAPTER INTERNET ACTIVITIES
KEYWORD: SV3 GV9
Choose an activity on economic policy to:
- conduct an interview with John Maynard Keynes or Milton Friedman.
- create a poster about the Federal Reserve system.
- make an oral presentation on deficit spending.

CHAPTER ENRICHMENT LINKS
KEYWORD: SV3 CH9

HOLT RESEARCHER ONLINE
KEYWORD: Holt Researcher

ONLINE ASSESSMENT
Homework Practice
KEYWORD: SV3 HP9
Standardized Test Prep
KEYWORD: SV3 STP9
Rubrics
KEYWORD: SS Rubrics

ONLINE MAPS, CHARTS, AND GRAPHS
KEYWORD: SV3 MCG
- Federal Reserve Districts
- Organization of the Fed
- The Budget Process

CONTENT UPDATES
KEYWORD: SS Content Updates

HOLT PRESENTATION MAKER
KEYWORD: SV3 PPT9

ONLINE READING SUPPORT
KEYWORD: SS Strategies

CURRENT EVENTS
KEYWORD: S3 Current Events

HOLT PRESENTATION MAKER
Access Illustrated LECTURE NOTES using Microsoft® PowerPoint® on the One-Stop Planner CD-ROM

OBJECTIVES

▶ List the major types of federal taxes.

▶ Explain how the federal government collects taxes.

▶ Describe the sources of revenue, other than taxes, of the federal government.

▶ Discuss the factors that have affected the political debate over tax policy in recent decades.

MOTIVATE

Organize the class into groups, assigning each group a different five-year interval from 1945 to 1995. Have each group create a pie chart depicting the amount of money collected from each type of tax for their interval. Have students create their group's chart using the Graphing Tool on the *Holt Researcher Online* or using butcher paper. Students may use information from the Federal Budgets section on the *Holt Researcher Online* or other resources to gather the information needed. Ask students to compare pie charts and to discuss the changes in tax revenue from 1945 to 1995. Be sure to have students identify the areas of tax revenue that have grown the most, the least, or remained relatively the same during that time period. Explain to students that in this section they will learn more about taxes and other revenue raised by the federal government.

TEACH

Building a Vocabulary

In spiral notebooks, have students create a Political Dictionary to be used throughout the course. The dictionary may be used as an activity at the start of each new section; it may also be used as a modification device for students having difficulty or for Sheltered English Students during tests and homework assignments. List words the students will be expected to know for this section on the board. Have students list, define, and give an example of each of the terms, using information provided in the text or on the *Researcher CD-ROM*.

Learning From Visuals

Organize students into six groups, each representing a different type of federal tax. Have each group develop a presentation explaining it's type of tax to the rest of the class. In their presentations, students should include what each tax covers and how it is collected. Each group should create a visual to help explain its tax. Explain to the class that the income tax is the largest source of revenue for the U.S. government and tell them that in the next activity they will learn how this tax is collected.

Developing Life Skills

Bring to class blank and completed copies of tax forms such as the 1040, the 1040EZ, and your state's simplest tax form, if applicable. Discuss how income taxes are filed and how the federal government collects other taxes. Have students organize into groups and fill out both a federal and state tax form using the information on a sample W2. Have students calculate the percentage of tax paid at each level. Discuss the differences between the ways taxes are collected by the federal government and the state government and any differences in filling out federal and state forms. Explain to students that in the next activity they will be learning about types of nontax revenue collected by the national government.

Creating Charts and Graphs

Reassemble students into the groups they were in during the Motivate activity. Have students use the library, the Internet, and the Graphing Tool on the *Holt Researcher Online* to create a chart depicting the nontax revenue that the federal government received for their assigned interval. Ask students to share their charts with the class and to discuss changes in nontax revenue that have occurred from 1945 to 1995. Tell students that in the next activity they will learn about the factors that influence the political debate over tax policy.

Debating Ideas

Discuss with students some of the various debates regarding tax policy that are found in this section of the chapter. Provide students with a few articles that contain information about the benefits of programs that redistribute wealth. Then organize students into two groups. Have students debate the issue of how much tax revenue should be used for programs that redistribute wealth. Encourage students to include factors affecting the debate, such as the national deficit, abuse of the welfare system, citizens' objections to paying more in taxes, and the role of government.

CLOSE

Have students compare and contrast the charts and graphs that they created dealing with tax and nontax revenue collected by the federal government. Discuss with students the changes in both forms of revenue that have occurred over the years. Have students offer suggestions regarding changing trends in revenue collection, and encourage them to draw conclusions regarding why these trends have occurred. Encourage students to share their conclusions with the class.

OPTIONS

Gifted Learners

Have students write a paper that discusses their beliefs about how much federal money should be used to aid economically disadvantaged people. Papers should include suggested options for federal spending and predicted consequences for each option. Students should state which political party's philosophy (as discussed in this section), if any, they support. Students should offer explanations for their reasoning, and should use information about the federal government to support their choice. Students who do not agree with the philosophies should explain their own philosophy or choose another philosophy to support. Encourage students to share their ideas with the class.

Students Having Difficulty/Sheltered English Students/Logical-Mathematical Learners

Have students review several examples of completed 1040EZ tax forms, including some that contain purposely made mathematical errors. Try to create various kinds of mistakes, such as adding or subtracting incorrectly, using the wrong deduction amount, or entering the wrong amount of tax from the tax table. Be sure to give students copies of the W2 forms that correspond with the 1040EZ forms that they are reviewing and a copy of a tax booklet. Have students identify and correct the mistakes that they find.

Body-Kinesthetic Learners

Have students work in groups to create the *Raising Revenue Board Game.* Encourage students to be as creative as possible in creating a board game that simulates the collection of revenue by the U.S. government. Students should allot each player a certain amount of money, then create a variety of tax situations that participants will encounter. Have students include positive situations, such as exemptions and deductions, and negative situations, such as increases in personal income tax or decreases in personal deductions. Encourage students to attempt to use all of the tax situations mentioned in this section of the text in their game. The winner of the game should be the participant who finishes with the most money. Once students have finished creating the game, allow them time to play and then discuss the impact of the situations they created on participants in the game. Tell students that changes in the U.S. government's tax policies similarly affect U.S. citizens and businesses.

REVIEW

Have students complete the Section 1 Review on page 195. Use the answers in the Annotated Teacher's Edition to assess student mastery of this section.

ASSESS

To assess student mastery of this section, have students complete Daily Quiz 9.1 in *Daily Quizzes with Answer Key.* For additional assessment options, see *Alternative Assessment Handbook* on the *One-Stop Planner CD-ROM.*

ADDITIONAL RESOURCES

Adams, Charles. *Those Dirty Rotten Taxes.* 1998. Simon and Schuster.
Edsall, Thomas Byrne, with Mary D. Edsall. *Chain Reaction.* 1992. W. W. Norton and Company.

HOLT PRESENTATION MAKER
Access Illustrated LECTURE NOTES using Microsoft® PowerPoint® on the One-Stop Planner CD-ROM

OBJECTIVES

▶ Explain how the U.S. economy is organized.
▶ List the goals of economic stabilization policy.
▶ Describe the tools used by the U.S. government to stabilize the economy.

MOTIVATE

Organize students into groups of two or three. Provide each group with a newspaper or have students bring in their own. Ask students to place articles and advertisements from the newspaper into these categories: *goods offered, services offered,* and *economic indicators of the U.S. economy.* Ask students to discuss reasons for placing each article or advertisement in specific categories. Tell students what category an item should fall under if students are incorrect. Explain to students that the U.S. economy has many different aspects and many factors that influence it and that in this section they will be learning more about the U.S. economy.

TEACH

Building a Vocabulary

In their spiral notebooks, have students continue working on their Political Dictionary. List words the students will be expected to know for this section on the board. Have students list, define, and give an example of each of the terms, using information provided in the text or on the *Researcher CD-ROM.*

Developing Life Skills

Organize students into small groups. Have each group create a list of products that are in demand by consumers their age (e.g., trendy clothes, the newest soft drink, celebrity-endorsed basketball shoes). Have each group decide on one of these items that it would like to manufacture. Then have each group create a list of factors to be considered when selling a product, such as a selling price, advertising costs, production costs, and the market to which the product is directed. Have each group create an advertisement for its product. Advertisements can be designed for print, radio, or television. Ask groups to share their ads with the rest of the class and to explain the factors that they considered when creating the ad. Display the print ads throughout the classroom and save copies of radio and television ads to play as samples for next semester's classes. After students have finished sharing their ads, discuss with them the five main rights of the free-enterprise system in the United States. Tell students that in the next activity they will learn about the goals of government stabilization of the economy.

Synthesizing Information

Explain to students the two main goals of stabilization: full employment and low inflation. Ask students to use a classified section of a recent newspaper to find a job that they might enjoy and to identify that job's monthly salary. (Have students account for taxes when figuring this amount.) Then use the classifieds to have students find housing that they would like and could afford. Discuss other expenses such as utilities, gas, auto payments, and food with the class. Ask students to create a rough budget and to compare it to the amount they were expecting to earn from the job. Create imaginary situations that could alter the amount of money that students would have available, such as a 20 percent increase in housing costs or becoming unemployed, and have students discuss how this would affect their budget. Point out to students that these negative consequences are some of the reasons that the government works to create a stable economy with low inflation and full employment. Tell students that in the next activity they will be learning how the government stabilizes the economy.

Debating Ideas

Organize students into two groups, one concerned with fiscal policy and the other with monetary policy. Have each group identify why their policy is better than the other in terms of stabilizing the economy. Ask students to debate their reasons with the other group. Have students utilize material in this section to support their reasoning. Discuss the benefits of both policies.

CLOSE

Ask students to examine the advertisements they categorized in the Motivate activity and to consider the consequences of the following on one or more of the advertised items: increased/decreased demand, increased inflation, a recession, lower/higher employment, or increased taxation. Using information presented in this section of the text, have students write a short essay predicting the consequences these changes would have on the products in their ads.

OPTIONS

Students Having Difficulty/ Sheltered English Students

  Have students examine a newspaper on microfilm from the year in which they were born or use information from the Economic Indicators section on the *Holt Researcher Online* to create a poster showing the differences between current prices of several popular items and prices in the year they were born. Have students calculate the total percentage increase in the cost of each item. Students may wish to project on the poster the differences between the present price and possible prices a number of years in the future as well. Encourage students to offer explanations, including government policies, for significant differences in the percentage increase for the items.

Intrapersonal/Gifted Learners

  Ask students to conduct interviews with people of different ages regarding the minimum wage at the time when they had their first job. Students should try to include people who would have started working in the 1930s. Have students create a line graph showing the increase in minimum wage indicated by the people they interviewed. Students should then create a line graph showing the actual increase in the minimum wage using information found in the Economic Indicators section on the *Holt*

Researcher Online. Have students compare their results with other students and discuss possible reasons for any differences between the actual minimum wage and what people remember.

Gifted Learners

  Have students examine information about the prime and discount lending rates in the Banking and Finance section and information about unemployment rates in the Economic Indicators section of the *Holt Researcher Online.* Ask students to determine if there appears to be a correlation between changes in either of the lending rates and increases or decreases in the unemployment rate. Have students write a short essay discussing their findings and offering possible explanations for the changes. Encourge students to share their ideas with the rest of the class.

REVIEW

Have students complete the Section 2 Review on page 203. Use the answers in the Annotated Teacher's Edition to assess student mastery of this section.

ASSESS

To assess student mastery of this section, have students complete Daily Quiz 9.2 in *Daily Quizzes with Answer Key.* For additional assessment options, see *Alternative Assessment Handbook* on the *One-Stop Planner CD-ROM.*

ADDITIONAL RESOURCES

Blank, Rebecca. "Are Part-time Jobs Bad Jobs?" *The Changing Structure of U.S. Wages.* 1990. Brookings Institution.

Pearlstein, Steven. "Recovery's Weak Spot Is Wages." *Washington Post.* March 9, 1994.

LESSON 9.3 THE FEDERAL BUDGET

TEXTBOOK PAGES 204–207

OBJECTIVES

- Discuss how the federal budget-making process has changed over the years.
- Describe the role the president plays in planning the budget.
- Explain why attempts at reducing the budget are politically controversial.

MOTIVATE

Organize students into small groups and give each group a large piece of paper and a marker. Ask students to look at the cartoon on textbook page 204 or display Cartoon Transparency 7: Preparing the Budget, which is located in *Transparency Resources,* on the overhead projector. Have students write on the paper words that describe the cartoon, their impressions of it, or their interpretation of what the cartoonist is trying to say. Allow groups to share their descriptions with the rest of the class. Tell students that in this section they will learn more about the federal budget and the budget-making process.

TEACH

Building a Vocabulary

In their spiral notebooks, have students continue working on their Political Dictionary. List words the students will be expected to know for this section on the board. Have students list, define, and give an example of each of the terms, using information provided in the text or on the *Researcher CD-ROM.*

Drawing Conclusions

Organize students into four groups. Assign each group one of these sets of years: before 1921, 1921 to 1939, 1940 to 1974, and 1974 to present. Have students conduct research on the changes in the budget process discussed in this section. On poster board, have students create a pro-and-con chart of the different changes to the budget process during each of these periods. Have students share the information they have included on their posters with the rest of the class,

and then have students discuss their ideas about which is the best process and how it could be improved. Discuss with students that the budget process will most likely continue changing as time goes by and tell them that in the next activity they will learn about the president's role in creating the budget.

Hypothesizing

Lead a discussion on the president's role in the budget process. Discuss the differences between the agendas of the last few presidents. Have students hypothesize how a president's platform, political party affiliation, and priorities may influence the budget. Have students find articles that discuss a presidential stand on a particular budget issue. Then as a class discuss whether students feel that the president's stand on the issue supports the overall public good or is designed to follow a party platform or aid a specific interest group. Have students consider the impact the president's role in the budget process may have on their own lives. Tell students that in the next activity they will learn about some of the arguments against reducing the budget.

Role-Playing

Organize students into groups representing each of the different participants in the budget-making process. Ask students to go through the process of preparing a new budget using the budget of a school club, a community group, or a sample U.S. budget from a recent year as an example. Students should follow the same steps and procedures as the actual federal government, complete with the presidential veto power at the end of the process. To familiarize students with these steps, display Transparency 20: The Budget Process, which is located in *Transparency Resources,* or have students refer to The Budget Process chart on textbook page 207. Once students have completed revising the budget have them discuss their feelings on the adequacy of the system. Ask the class if there are any parts of the new budget that they do not agree with. Encourage students to offer their opinions about what should be changed in the budget. Point out that there are many differences in opinion regarding the federal budget and that it may be impossible to get everyone to agree on what constitutes an appropriate budget. Ask students to bring in articles about the federal budget throughout the semester.

CLOSE

Once again display Cartoon Transparency 7: Preparing the Budget, which is located in *Transparency Resources,* or refer students to the cartoon on page 204. Have students consider what they now know about the budget process and ask them to comment on the accuracy of their descriptive words from the Motivate activity. Allow students to create their own cartoons or posters, individually or in small groups, depicting what they have learned about the federal budget. Discuss the accuracy of students' work.

OPTIONS

Gifted Learners

 Have students write a report about the job of government economist. Students can refer to the Careers section on the *Holt Researcher Online* or other resources to get general information about the position. Students should also discuss the impact of particular economists on U.S. economic policy, using information from the Biographies section on the *Holt Researcher Online* and other resources to gather information on economists. Encourage students to share their information with the class.

Gifted Learners

 Ask students to write a proposal asking for federal money for a project in which they are interested, such as improving the roads in their neighborhood. Students may wish to view actual proposals as examples. Encourage students to keep in mind the budget process and the role of politics. Have students share their proposals with the class. Encourage students to contest the merit of proposals that do not seem necessary.

Interpersonal/Visual-Spatial Learners

 Encourage students to interview an economist or a professor of economics from a nearby college or university. Students should focus the interview on the steps of the federal budget-making process and attempt to get the interviewee's opinion on what factors are most influential. Students should also attempt to find out the interviewee's opinion regarding changes that have occurred in the budget-making process over the years, changes in the president's role in the process, and why attempts at decreasing the budget have been controversial. Encourage students to videotape the interviews and to edit the videotapes so that they contain only pertinent information. Have students share their final products with the rest of the class. Finally, have students compare the interviews to attempt to determine if the interviewee believes in Keynesianism or monetarism and to see if they can identify his or her political affiliation. Have students discuss these issues as a class.

REVIEW

Have students complete the Section 3 Review on page 207. Use the answers in the Annotated Teacher's Edition to assess student mastery of this section.

ASSESS

To assess student mastery of this section, have students complete Daily Quiz 9.3 in *Daily Quizzes with Answer Key.* For additional assessment options, see *Alternative Assessment Handbook* on the *One-Stop Planner CD-ROM.*

ADDITIONAL RESOURCES

Mishel, Lawrence, and David Frankel. *The State of Working America.* 1991. M. E. Sharpe.

Steeper, Fred. *The Swing Is Different.* 1995. Strategies Inc.

DEFICIT SPENDING AND THE ECONOMY

TEXTBOOK PAGES 208–212

HOLT PRESENTATION MAKER
Access Illustrated LECTURE
NOTES using Microsoft®
PowerPoint® on the
One-Stop Planner CD-ROM

OBJECTIVES

▶ Discuss the factors that can cause the federal government to operate at a deficit.

▶ Explain how the national debt influences the U.S. economy.

▶ Describe how the national debt and the federal deficit influence each other.

MOTIVATE

Ask students to examine the sample budgets that they created in Lesson 9.3. Have students consider what would happen if they did not make enough money to cover the expenses listed in their budget. Allow them time to discuss the consequences of spending that exceeds revenues. Explain that a similar situation occurs in the federal government when it spends more money than it takes in and that this situation has created problems with the economy and in creating a budget. Tell students that in this activity they will learn more about the impact of the U.S. government spending more than it takes in.

TEACH

Building a Vocabulary

In their spiral notebooks, have students continue working on their Political Dictionary. List words the students will be expected to know for this section on the board. Have students list, define, and give an example of each of the terms, using information provided in the text or on the *Researcher CD-ROM*.

Taking a Stand/Navigating the Internet

Discuss with students factors that contribute to a federal deficit, such as disagreements between political parties, uncontrollable spending based on prior commitments, and the public's reluctance to pay higher taxes. Then ask students to debate the issue of cutting back on or eliminating entitlement programs. Encourage students to use the Internet and recent issues of newspapers and magazines to support their stand. Students may wish to share their own experiences with entitlements, or those of family members, to comment on

the merit of these programs. Encourage students to discuss alternatives to cutting these programs and the pros and cons of these alternatives. Explain to students that the issue of deciding which groups or programs receive federal money, and how much money these groups or programs should get, has made it difficult to pass a budget bill. Point out that these differences led to efforts like the Gramm-Rudman-Hollings Act to force the president and Congress to work together to reduce deficits. Tell students that in the next activity they will learn about how the national debt influences the U.S. economy.

Synthesizing Information

Ask students to consider the growth of inflation over the past decade and other factors that can contribute to budget deficits. Have students hypothesize how inflation may be related to the growth of the national debt over time. Have students write a short essay on the consequences of an increasing national debt on both national and local economies. Encourage students to include predictions in their essays about what might happen to the U.S. economy in the next 10 years if the current debt is not checked at the current rate. Have students include the factors influencing their predictions. Tell students that in the next activity they will learn about ways that the national debt and the federal deficit influence each other.

Developing Life Skills

Have students investigate current interest rates for bank loans, new home mortgages, or school tuition loans. (Information may be available on the Internet, in newspapers, or in the library.) In small groups, have students work out a payment plan on a loan for the specific amount assigned to each group, including the interest. Then, using the same process, students can investigate the impact of the national debt on the federal budget. Groups can refer to the Federal Budgets section on the *Holt Researcher Online* to find information on the most recent national debt figures. Have students attempt to figure out the yearly interest paid on that amount, using figures on the discount lending rate from the Banking and Finance section on the *Holt Researcher Online*. Discuss with students how this amount of deficit affects each new budget and the overall functioning of the economy.

CLOSE

In small groups, have students try to come up with a way to balance the budget, considering the factors contributing to the deficit that they learned about in this section. Ask them to write up a proposal using graphs and pictures as necessary. Allow each group to present their ideas to the class. Discuss and debate the plausibility of each idea and try to vote to see if the class can agree upon one idea.

OPTIONS

Gifted/Intrapersonal Learners

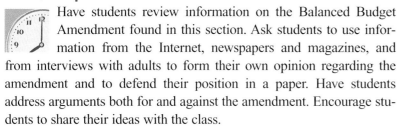 Have students review information on the Balanced Budget Amendment found in this section. Ask students to use information from the Internet, newspapers and magazines, and from interviews with adults to form their own opinion regarding the amendment and to defend their position in a paper. Have students address arguments both for and against the amendment. Encourage students to share their ideas with the class.

Students Having Difficulty/
Sheltered English Students

Using the information from this section about comparing governments and additional information about the budget, students should create pie graphs showing the percentage of the gross domestic product that is made up of the deficit. Have students create graphs for each 10-year period starting in 1950 and compare the percentages of the gross domestic product made up of the deficit for each of these years. Have students analyze these figures to see how the percentage has changed over the years. Students should write a few paragraphs describing their findings.

Intrapersonal Learners

Have students consider the need to find ways to limit government spending. Students should write a two-page paper that states their opinion about how such goals can be achieved and about the wisdom of trying to achieve them. Students should discuss both positive and negative consequences that particular proposals may have on the U.S. economy and society. Encourage students to share their opinions with the class and to debate differences in their opinions on the topic. See if students can agree on one plan.

REVIEW

Have students complete the Section 4 Review on page 212. Use the answers in the Annotated Teacher's Edition to assess student mastery of this section.

ASSESS

To assess student mastery of this section, have students complete Daily Quiz 9.4 in *Daily Quizzes with Answer Key*. For additional assessment options, see *Alternative Assessment Handbook* on the *One-Stop Planner CD-ROM*.

RETEACH

For students having difficulty with the lessons, have them complete Reteaching Activity 9. This activity is located in *Reteaching Activities with Answer Key*.

ADDITIONAL RESOURCES

After the Cold War: Living With Lower Defense Spending. 1992. Office of Technology Assessment.

Morris, Stephen. *Deficits and the Dollar Revisited.* 1987. Institute of International Economics.

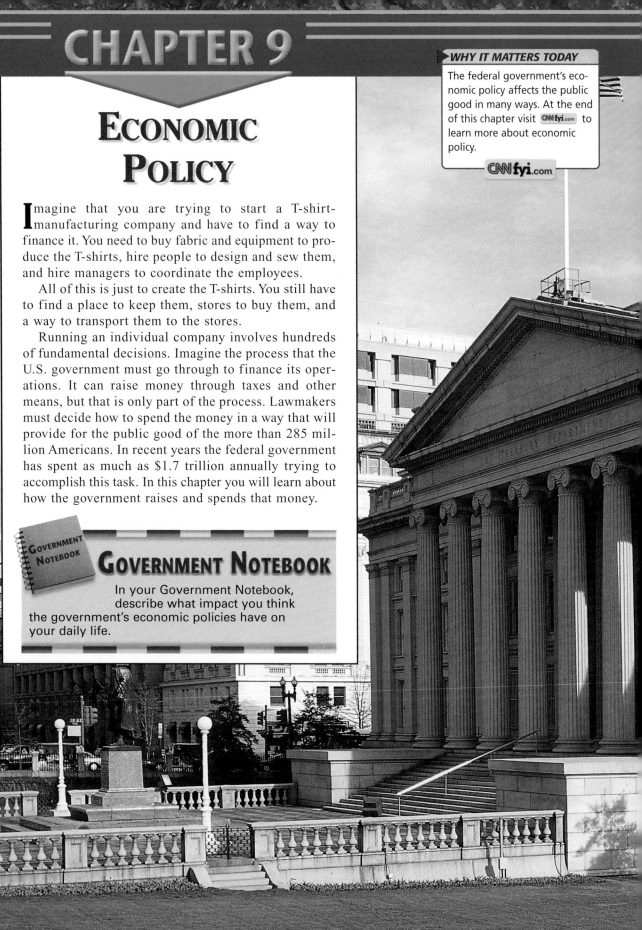

TOPICS INCLUDE

GOVERNMENT NOTEBOOK

The Government Notebook is a journal activity that encourages students to consider basic concepts of government that relate to their lives. A follow-up notebook activity appears on page 214.

▶WHY IT MATTERS TODAY

To find additional lesson plans dealing with economic policy, visit **CNNfyi**.com or have students complete the **GOVERNMENT IN THE NEWS** activity on page 213.

CNNfyi.com

190

CHAPTER 9

ECONOMIC POLICY

Imagine that you are trying to start a T-shirt-manufacturing company and have to find a way to finance it. You need to buy fabric and equipment to produce the T-shirts, hire people to design and sew them, and hire managers to coordinate the employees.

All of this is just to create the T-shirts. You still have to find a place to keep them, stores to buy them, and a way to transport them to the stores.

Running an individual company involves hundreds of fundamental decisions. Imagine the process that the U.S. government must go through to finance its operations. It can raise money through taxes and other means, but that is only part of the process. Lawmakers must decide how to spend the money in a way that will provide for the public good of the more than 285 million Americans. In recent years the federal government has spent as much as $1.7 trillion annually trying to accomplish this task. In this chapter you will learn about how the government raises and spends that money.

GOVERNMENT NOTEBOOK

In your Government Notebook, describe what impact you think the government's economic policies have on your daily life.

▶WHY IT MATTERS TODAY

The federal government's economic policy affects the public good in many ways. At the end of this chapter visit **CNNfyi**.com to learn more about economic policy.

CNNfyi.com

SECTION 1

RAISING REVENUE

READ TO DISCOVER

1. What are the major types of federal taxes?
2. How does the federal government collect taxes?
3. What sources of revenue, other than taxes, does the federal government have?
4. What factors have affected the political debate over tax policy in recent decades?

POLITICAL DICTIONARY

revenue
tax
exemption
deduction
excise tax
estate tax
gift tax
customs duty
standard of living

As you can imagine, the federal government cannot develop and sustain its programs without **revenue**—the income it collects. Today, **taxes**—charges laid on individuals and businesses by a government—are the federal government's primary source of revenue.

Federal Taxes

For fiscal year 2000, federal taxes totaled just under $2 trillion. (A fiscal year is a 12-month financial period that might or might not follow the regular calendar year. The federal government's fiscal year begins on October 1 and ends on September 30.) The federal government relies on several types of taxes for revenue. The graph on this page shows the percentage of revenue that each tax generates.

Individual Income Tax The individual income tax makes up the federal government's largest

source of revenue. In 2000 around half of all federal revenue came from this tax. The individual income tax is levied on a person's taxable income, including wages or salaries, business profits, tips, interest, and dividends (payments received as a return on an investment). It is a progressive tax, which means that it takes a larger percentage from a high-income person than from a low-income person.

The income tax is not assessed on a person's entire yearly income. Rather, taxable income is the sum of all sources of a person's income minus certain deductions and exemptions. Each taxpayer is allowed a standard **exemption**—an amount of income upon which the government does not levy a tax. Plus, other exemptions exist for each dependent—or additional person reliant on the taxpayer's income such as a child.

Deductions are amounts that the government allows taxpayers to subtract from their taxable income. For example, the government allows people who have borrowed money to pay for a home to deduct interest payments on the loan from their taxable income. If a person has an income of

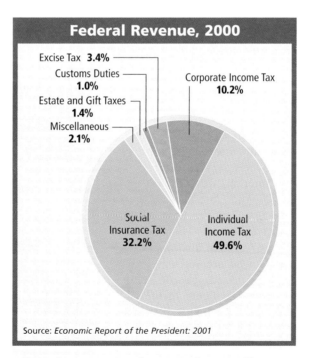

Federal Revenue, 2000

Excise Tax **3.4%**
Customs Duties **1.0%**
Estate and Gift Taxes **1.4%**
Miscellaneous **2.1%**
Corporate Income Tax **10.2%**
Social Insurance Tax **32.2%**
Individual Income Tax **49.6%**

Source: *Economic Report of the President: 2001*

Federal revenue comes from several sources. The social insurance tax and the individual income tax make up more than four fifths of this revenue. **What type of tax makes up the smallest percentage of federal revenue?**

SECTION 1

RAISING REVENUE

Lesson Plans

For teaching strategies, see Lesson 9.1 located at the beginning of this chapter or the One-Stop Lesson Planner Strategy 9.1.

Political Dictionary

To reinforce the section's vocabulary terms, refer students to the Electronic Glossary on the *Researcher CD-ROM.*

Section Assessment

To assess students' mastery of this section, have them complete Daily Quiz 9.1 in *Daily Quizzes with Answer Key.*

Transparency

An overhead transparency of the chart on this page is available in *Transparency Resources.* See Transparency 18: Federal Revenue, 2000.

> **Caption Answer**
>
> Customs duties make up the smallest percentage of federal tax revenue.

CITIZENSHIP *People who have borrowed money to pay for a home are allowed to deduct interest payments on their loan from their taxable income.* **What other types of income tax deductions does the government allow individuals?**

$50,000, interest payments totaling $5,000 would reduce taxable income to $45,000. A person may also deduct certain charitable donations. In addition, certain kinds of income are nontaxable; for instance, interest income that is earned on money that has been borrowed by a state or local government is not taxable.

Most employees pay individual income taxes through a payroll deduction system. Under this system, employers withhold a certain percentage of an employee's pay and forward it to the Internal Revenue Service (IRS)—the branch of the Treasury Department in charge of tax collection. This "pay-as-you-go" system also applies to people who are self-employed. Self-employed people make quarterly payments to the IRS based on the amount of income they expect to earn over the calendar year. Overpayments are typically refunded in the next calendar year.

Do you recognize the date April 15? This day—Tax Day—inspires dread in many people around the country. On or before April 15, all U.S. residents who earned taxable income in the preceding year must file their tax returns with the IRS. Tax returns list all sources of a person's income, any exemptions and deductions the person can legally claim, and the amount of money that he or she owes to or is owed by the IRS.

Corporate Income Tax A corporation—a form of business organization—also must pay a federal income tax. The corporate income tax is based on a corporation's net income—that is, all income earned above the cost of maintaining the business.

The corporate income tax is the most complicated federal tax because of the numerous deductions that the government allows a corporation to take. Many of these tax breaks are granted to help achieve certain national goals. For example, to promote industrial growth, the government may allow a corporation to deduct the costs of expansion and modernization. In addition, corporations may deduct a certain percentage of their charitable donations.

Corporate income taxes are the federal government's third-largest source of revenue. In 2000, for example, corporate income taxes accounted for about 10 percent of all federal revenue.

PUBLIC GOOD *Corporations may be allowed to take tax deductions for modernizing their equipment and facilities.* **What other types of deductions can corporations take?**

Social Insurance Taxes In addition to the revenue it receives from income taxes, the federal government collects huge sums of money each year to finance two social welfare programs:

★ Old-Age, Survivors, and Disability Insurance (OASDI)—or Social Security—and
★ Medicare, which provides health care to the elderly, regardless of their income level.

These social programs are funded through taxes collected under the Federal Insurance Contributions Act (FICA). FICA taxes are paid by both the employee and the employer. As with individual income taxes, FICA taxes are withheld from workers' pay. The employer matches the amount paid by the employee and sends the full payment to the government. Self-employed people must pay the entire FICA tax themselves, although they can deduct 50 percent of the money paid in such taxes from their taxable income.

Excise Taxes The government also receives revenue from **excise taxes**, which are levied on the manufacture, sale, or consumption of certain goods or services. The federal government places excise taxes on such goods and services as tobacco, gasoline, alcohol, and telephone systems. In 2000, excise taxes accounted for 3.4 percent of federal revenue.

An excise tax is a regressive tax, for it charges all taxpayers the same rate. Because the excise tax imposes the same tax on everyone purchasing a certain good or service, it takes a larger percentage of a lower income than it does of a higher income.

Estate and Gift Taxes The federal government also generates revenue through estate and gift taxes. An **estate tax** is a tax placed on a deceased person's assets when they are transferred to someone else. Federal estate taxes are levied on all such assets worth more than $675,000 (to be increased to $1 million in 2002 and $3.5 million by 2009). A **gift tax** is a tax placed on the transfer of certain gifts of value to individuals. Gift taxes are paid by anyone giving gifts the total value of which exceeds a certain amount in a given year. Federal estate and gift taxes account for only 1.4 percent of total federal revenue.

Customs Duties Also known as tariffs or import duties, **customs duties** are taxes levied by the federal government on goods brought into the United States from abroad. The United States collects these duties not only to raise revenue but also to protect U.S. business, agriculture, and industry from harmful foreign competition.

The Constitution gives Congress the power to levy customs duties. Congress has, in turn, authorized the president to raise or lower these duties by certain percentages, as well as to make agreements with foreign countries to help reduce trade barriers. The president's decisions generally are based on the recommendations of the U.S. International Trade Commission (ITC). If the president does not follow the recommendations of the ITC, Congress can override presidential decisions by a two-thirds vote.

Before the introduction of the federal income tax, customs

CONSTITUTIONAL GOVERNMENT *Consumers must pay an excise tax each time they purchase goods such as gasoline, tobacco, and alcohol. What type of a tax is an excise tax?*

THEMES IN GOVERNMENT

PUBLIC GOOD In 1994 the Advisory Council on Social Security was created to investigate problems with the Social Security system. Economists working for the council concluded that, if left in its current form, the system would run out of funds by the year 2029. In addition, there will only be enough payroll taxes to pay 75 percent of the Social Security benefits. A major contributing factor to this problem will be paying benefits to baby boomers, who make up one third of the U.S. population.

Although the council has not been able to agree on one plan to remedy the situation, it has recommended some changes. For example, some Social Security funds should be invested in the stock market, rather than just in government bonds. Other recommendations include increasing taxes on benefits that exceed a person's lifetime contribution to the system. Further, government workers who previously were exempt from the tax should also be required to start paying into the system. ■

Caption Answer
regressive tax

THEMES IN GOVERNMENT

PUBLIC GOOD The Tax Reform Act of 1986 was "revenue-neutral" in that the total amount of taxes raised did not change. The tax burden was simply shifted. The shift occurred because liberal Democrats, who wanted to close loopholes enjoyed by the wealthy, allied themselves with supply-side Republicans, who wanted lower rates and therefore agreed with such reforms as exempting low-income workers from the federal tax roll.

The result was indeed lower tax rates, but itemized deductions, investment interest deductions, and personal exemptions were phased out for high-income taxpayers. Middle-class taxpayers also lost some tax deductions. In five years the act closed $300 billion in loopholes, but this was offset by lower tax rates. ■

Profiles in American Government

For a biography of Presidents Ronald Reagan and George Bush and of other noted people in government, refer students to the Biographies section on the *Holt Researcher Online*.

POLITICAL FOUNDATIONS *Customs duties are placed on goods brought into the United States from abroad. Congress has the power to levy customs duties. **Why does the U.S. government collect customs duties?***

duties were the most important source of revenue for the United States. Today, however, customs duties amount to only about 1 percent of federal revenue.

Nontax Revenue

Taxes are not the only source of revenue for the federal government. In fact, in 2000 the net federal receipts—the total amount of money raised by the federal government—included more than $42 billion in nontax revenue.

This money comes from several sources. The main source of nontax revenue is composed of earnings by Federal Reserve banks. (The Federal Reserve system and its role in the U.S. economy are more fully explained in Section 2.) Fees and fines collected by various government agencies also provide revenue for the federal government.

Do you have a passport? Whenever you pay the processing fee for a federal service such as a passport, you are contributing to federal revenue. Other nontax revenue includes fees paid for patents, trademarks, or copyrights; fines imposed by the federal courts; and money earned from the sale or lease of federal lands.

Politics of Making Tax Policy

When lawmakers create tax policy, they must address two questions: How high should taxes be, and what tax advantages should be offered? In recent decades, Democrats—motivated in part by the desire to fund government programs to aid less-advantaged citizens—generally have favored higher and more progressive taxes. Many Democrats also have opposed tax advantages for the wealthy. Republicans generally have favored lower taxes.

A significant feature of the tax debate since the 1970s has been growing public opposition to taxes. By the late 1970s, disillusionment with government led people to question the usefulness of much government spending. Around the same time, supply-side economics was gaining support among Republicans. Supply-side economists argue that taxes should be cut to stimulate economic growth. According to this view, if income were taxed less, people would produce more because they would get to keep more of their earnings.

In 1980 presidential candidate Ronald Reagan made a cut in income taxes one of the major themes of his campaign. Reagan won the election, and in 1981 he got Congress to accept a 25 percent cut over three years. The tax cut of 1981 was one of two major changes in tax law during Reagan's presidency. The other change was the Tax Reform Act of 1986. Income tax rates were slashed again and made less progressive. Many tax advantages enjoyed by the wealthy also were repealed.

In 1990, huge budget shortfalls inspired compromise on a tax increase, which Congress passed and President George Bush signed. In 1993 President Bill Clinton and Congress took action and passed a sharp increase in the top income tax rate, affecting about 1.2 percent of all taxpayers. After the congressional elections of 1994, Congress and the president reached an agreement on modest tax cuts within the framework of a plan to balance the budget by the year 2002.

In 2001 President George W. Bush signed into law a $1.35 trillion tax cut. The immediate effect was a tax refund of between $300 and $600 for nearly all taxpayers. The plan's remaining tax relief is slated to occur gradually over the following 10 years. This includes an across-the-board reduction in all tax rates and the creation of a new 10 percent bottom tax rate. Democratic critics charge that the tax cut favors the wealthiest Americans and that it leaves the government unable to spend money on other priorities, including education and a Medicare prescription drug program.

Tax Policy and the Public Good

Tax policy decisions affect both the U.S. **standard of living**—that is, how well people in general are doing—and the distribution of economic benefits. People disagree about whether or not government should use taxation to redistribute wealth. Supporters of redistribution argue that the natural distribution of the income and wealth produced by the U.S. economy is unfair. Unequal opportunities and sometimes sheer luck have too big an impact on economic success, they say. Therefore, the government should equalize wealth through income redistribution.

Opponents of income redistribution make several counterarguments. First, they hold that the uneven distribution of income broadly reflects important differences in people's efforts to earn a living as well as in their contributions to soci-

ety. They also argue that redistribution schemes hurt economic growth and hence tend to reduce people's overall standard of living. High taxes on wealthy individuals take away some of the personal benefit from their economic endeavors and thus discourage them from making larger contributions to society.

Courtesy of David Horsey, Seattle Post-Intelligencer.

PUBLIC GOOD *Some people believe that government should use taxation to redistribute wealth.* **What criticism does this cartoon make of government tax policy?**

SECTION 1 REVIEW ANSWERS

1. Refer to the following pages: revenue (191), tax (191), exemption (191), deduction (191), excise tax (193), estate tax (193), gift tax (193), customs duty (193), standard of living (195).

2. individual income tax, social insurance tax, corporate income tax, excise tax, estate and gift taxes, custom duties, nontax revenue

3a. individual income tax

3b. income earned by the Federal Reserve system and fees and fines collected by government agencies

4. Answers will vary but students should clearly express and defend a point of view on the issue of tax policy.

SECTION 1 REVIEW

1. Identify and Explain:
- revenue
- tax
- exemption
- deduction
- excise tax
- estate tax
- gift tax
- customs duty
- standard of living

2. Identifying Concepts: Copy the chart below. Use it to identify the sources of revenue for the federal government.

Federal Reserve

3. Finding the Main Idea

a. What type of tax generates the most revenue for the U.S. government?

b. What are the primary sources of the federal government's nontax revenue?

4. Writing and Critical Thinking

Supporting a Point of View: Review the debate on tax policy and choose a side. Explain and defend your point of view.

Consider the following:
- the effects of raising or lowering taxes
- the need to fund the federal government

Homework Practice Online
keyword: SV3 HP9

SECTION 2

INFLUENCING THE ECONOMY

Lesson Plans

For teaching strategies, see Lesson 9.2 located at the beginning of this chapter or the One-Stop Lesson Planner Strategy 9.2.

Political Dictionary

To reinforce the section's vocabulary terms, refer students to the Electronic Glossary on the *Researcher CD-ROM.*

Section Assessment

To assess students' mastery of this section, have them complete Daily Quiz 9.2 in *Daily Quizzes with Answer Key.*

Caption Answer

Answers will vary, but students may point out that private ownership and free markets allow the manufacture of products most in demand, thus improving sales and economic growth.

SECTION 2

INFLUENCING THE ECONOMY

READ TO DISCOVER

1. How is the U.S. economy organized?
2. What are the goals of economic stabilization policy?
3. What tools does the U.S. government use to stabilize the economy?

POLITICAL DICTIONARY

free enterprise
recession
inflation
fiscal policy
monetary policy
disposable income
Federal Reserve system
reserve requirements
discount rate
open-market operations
bond
Keynesianism
deficit
monetarism

The ways in which the U.S. government chooses to spend $1.8 trillion a year directly affect the overall national economy. There is more to economic policy, however, than just raising money and spending it on government programs. The government also attempts to stabilize the economy and promote economic growth.

The two main goals in economic stabilization are full employment and low inflation. The government uses two tools to achieve these goals: fiscal policy and monetary policy. It also uses industrial policy to promote growth in the economy. This chapter will explain just what each of these terms means. To understand how government economic policies work, however, you must first understand how the U.S. economy is organized.

Organization of the U.S. Economy

The United States has what is known as a **free-enterprise** economy—one in which business can be conducted freely, with little government intervention. A free-enterprise system is dependent on a market in which goods and services are exchanged openly and freely.

Free-Enterprise System The free-enterprise system of the United States is based on five main individual rights:

★ to own private property and enter into contracts,
★ to make individual choices,
★ to engage in economic competition,
★ to make decisions based on self-interest, and
★ to participate in the economy with limited government involvement and regulation.

A major benefit of the free-enterprise system is that it produces what consumers want. If consumer demand for blue jeans is higher than that for formal gowns, for instance, more jeans

POLITICAL FOUNDATIONS *In a free-enterprise system, individuals can choose which goods and services they want to buy.* **Why do some people believe that private ownership and free markets provide the best environment for economic growth?**

will be produced than gowns. In addition, producers who offer lower-quality jeans at the same price as their competitors' higher-quality jeans will likely sell little merchandise or even go out of business. Supporters of free enterprise believe that private ownership and free markets will provide the best environment for economic growth, because businesspeople motivated to make money are constantly driven to look for new things to produce or better ways to produce them.

Government and the Economy Economic policy in the U.S. free-enterprise system often has been a source of political controversy. The basic political disputes involve the extent to which government should intervene in the operation of the free market (such as when consumer demands shift from American-made products to goods made abroad).The free market leaves some people unemployed or with low-paying jobs. Some people believe that government should address this problem by making the distribution of income and wealth more even. Others believe that government should reduce the pain when economic disruptions occur.

In addition, although the free market usually works well to achieve economic growth, many people think that there are situations in which government intervention can produce stronger economic growth than the free market would if left alone. Similarly, some argue that the government should play a role in stabilizing the economy by taking steps to lessen the cycles of boom and **recession**—economic downturns— that historically have been characteristic of a free-market system.

Democrats have traditionally favored greater government intervention in the economy. In general, they support greater equality in income and do not believe as strongly that the free market will solve all economic problems. These ideas gain greater electoral support from lower-income voters, who are more likely to suffer from economic disruption or instability. Republicans have been inclined toward minimizing government involvement, a policy often called laissez-faire (French for "let [the people] do [as they will]"). Laissez-faire policy reflects a greater faith in the ability of the market to create high overall standards of living, as well as a worry that government intervention tends to hurt rather than help the economy. Support for laissez-faire

policy often comes from higher-income voters, who have more of a cushion against economic disruption or instability.

Stabilization Goals

The terms *economic growth* and *economic stabilization* mean different things for the U.S. economy. Economic growth determines a country's long-term standard of living. It determines whether a country will achieve more wealth or remain poverty-ridden. Economic stability involves changes in unemployment and **inflation**—the general rise in prices that often accompanies economic booms. Economic growth rates determine how high the economic airplane is flying; economic stability determines how bumpy the ride is. It is possible for a growing economy to be unstable. Likewise, it is possible for a poor country to have low rates of inflation and unemployment.

The government attempts to fulfill two main goals with a stabilization policy. These are full employment and low inflation.

Full Employment Full employment is an obvious goal for government because people need income to survive. During economic downturns, employment levels drop, sometimes dramatically. Loss of a job can cause serious problems even for two-income households, which can have difficulty paying all of their monthly bills—such as payments on a home loan—on a single income. In addition, unemployment hurts the general public because it lowers the total output of the economy.

Low Inflation During economic upswings, harmful inflationary pressures can develop. Thus, stabilization policy is designed to temper major growth booms in the economy, as well as recessions.

Inflation creates significant problems such as hindering economic growth. It pushes up interest rates beyond the level justified by the current rate of inflation, as banks cushion themselves against the risk of even higher inflation in the future when the borrowed money will be paid back. Because higher interest rates mean an increased cost of borrowing money, they discourage investment in new plants and equipment.

Inflation also can have significant negative psychological effects. When prices go up rapidly, people feel insecure, as if an earthquake were shaking

PUBLIC GOOD In 1996 President Bill Clinton signed the Telecommunications Act, which deregulated the telephone industry. Until the bill was passed, Bell Atlantic, which provided phone service in the mid-Atlantic region, was a regulated monopoly. While the company was not very efficient, it was a good corporate citizen, offering stable employment for many Americans.

Critics of the legislation contend that the deregulation of the industry essentially downplayed Bell Atlantic's efforts to be a good corporate citizen providing secure jobs and to cut waste and become a competitive business. Critics also contend that in becoming a competitive business, Bell Atlantic may have to cut back some of the niceties of its services, which may translate to a loss of jobs.

Proponents of deregulation contend that such changes, even when they involve laying off workers, is good. Stabilization, they argue, means stagnation. Competition, they say, will create new jobs and foster long-term economic growth. ■

Enhancing the Lesson

For more information on unemployment rates, see the Economic Indicators section on the *Holt Researcher Online.*

Caption Answer

Increased taxes reduce people's disposable income and corporations' net profits. This causes decreased spending and business activity and drives prices down.

under them. In a famous line many people think was a key element in his landslide victory in the 1980 presidential election, Ronald Reagan asked the viewers during a televised debate with President Jimmy Carter, "Are you better off today than you were four years ago?" In fact, the numbers showed that many people *were* better off: real per capita spendable income in 1980 was nearly 7.5 percent higher than when Carter entered office in 1976, and the unemployment rate was lower. A lot of people *felt* worse, however. The biggest reason was that for two years inflation had been running at a rate of more than 12 percent.

Tools for Economic Stabilization

Government may use both fiscal and monetary policies to deal with unemployment and inflation. **Fiscal policy** is a set of government spending, taxing, and borrowing policies used to achieve desired levels of economic performance. **Monetary policy** is a set of procedures designed to regulate the economy by controlling the amount of money in circulation as well as the level of interest rates.

Fiscal Policy The federal government uses the budget to develop fiscal policy through its taxing and spending plans. By increasing spending or by lowering taxes, the government can increase the overall level of demand for goods and services in the economy, thereby putting more money into a slow-moving economy and stimulating growth. On the other hand, the government may decide to decrease spending if a rapidly growing economy is producing inflation.

In addition to adjusting spending, the federal government also uses taxation as a tool for stabilizing the economy. If unemployment is very high, for example, the government may respond by cutting taxes. A tax cut will increase people's **disposable income**—the amount they have to spend after accounting for financial obligations such as taxes—and allows businesses to keep more of their profits. When people have more money, demand for goods and services rises. When businesses have more, they are able to invest money and hire more workers, thus decreasing unemployment.

If inflation is high, however, policy makers may raise taxes. Higher taxes reduce a person's disposable income and a corporation's net profits. This reduces the amount of money people spend and slows business activity, which, in turn, tends to lower prices.

Monetary Policy The second way in which the federal government tries to influence the economy is through its monetary policy. Monetary

How the Government May Use Fiscal Policy

TO ENCOURAGE GROWTH	TO ENCOURAGE STABILIZATION
Increased Spending, Lower Taxes	**Increased Taxes, Lower Spending**
• The government spends more money to stimulate growth in the economy.	• The government increases taxes to slow a rapidly growing economy and widespread price increases.
• The government cuts taxes to increase individual spending and business output.	• Individuals spend less, and businesses make smaller profits.
• Businesses expand and create jobs.	• Slower business activity and decreased spending lead to lower prices.
Result increased growth in the economy and higher employment	**Result** low inflation rates and stable growth in the economy

The government's taxing and spending plans may be used to achieve different results.
What results may be achieved if the government increases taxes?

Government and Economics

Raising the Minimum Wage

In 1996 about 13 million Americans worked in minimum-wage jobs in the service, retail, and agricultural industries. President Bill Clinton backed a congressional effort to raise the minimum wage.

1996 also was a presidential election year, however, and the proposal to raise the minimum wage became entangled in politics. Politicians, business owners, economists, and the public at large aired differing views about the government's role in helping workers and the possible economic impact of the legislation.

Many restaurant owners predicted that raising the minimum wage would make earning a profit extremely difficult. "I would probably end up out of business," concluded Nevada pizzeria owner Sandra Murphy. The National Restaurant Association warned that raising the minimum wage would mean that many minimum-wage workers would lose their jobs, because these workers did not produce enough to justify a higher wage. Economists warned that because employers would have to pay more to employees, fewer new jobs would be created.

Some politicians agreed with restaurant own-

ers and strongly opposed the wage hike. Senator Don Nickles criticized it as the response of a heavy-handed federal government interfering in the free market. Bob Dole, the Republican presidential candidate in 1996, accused the Democrats, most of whom supported the increase, of caving in to pressure from labor unions.

The American Federation of Labor and Congress of Industrial Organizations (AFL-CIO)—the nation's largest labor union—did endorse the wage increase. The union noted that the minimum wage had not increased since 1991. Union leaders argued that minimum-wage workers' pay, when adjusted for inflation, was near a 40-year low. They predicted that raising the minimum wage would ease poverty and help lower taxes by enabling people to rely less on food stamps and other public assistance.

Both sides of the debate used economists' studies to support their position. Supporters of a minimum-wage increase pointed to research showing that the 1990 and 1991 minimum-wage increases caused little if any job loss. Critics of the wage hike countered by citing studies that predicted the increase would reduce the number of minimum-wage jobs by 20 percent.

With 80 percent of Americans favoring an increase in the minimum wage Republicans and Democrats eventually joined forces to pass the measure. In August 1996 Clinton signed into law a two-step increase, which brought the minimum wage to $5.15 per hour in September 1997. A new effort to further increase the minimum wage failed in December 2000.

In early 2001 President George W. Bush said that he would support a minimum-wage increase if states were allowed to opt out of it, but Democrats rejected that proposal.

Many workers received an increase in their wages after Congress passed a bill to raise the minimum wage.

What Do You Think?

1. What are some of the possible positive and negative ways a minimum-wage increase could affect the U.S. economy?
2. Do you support an increase in the minimum wage? Explain your point of view and provide examples to support your answer.

What Do You Think? Answers

1. Answers will vary. Positives may include reducing poverty and lowering taxes. Negatives may include fewer jobs being created and driving some employers out of business.

2. Answers will vary, but students should use information from the text to support their answers.

THEMES IN GOVERNMENT

PUBLIC GOOD Minimum-wage increases may not represent an increase in real income if prices are rising more rapidly than wages. In 1991 the minimum wage was $4.25 per hour; the next time it was increased was in 1996, when it was raised to $4.75 per hour—a 12 percent increase. In 1991 the consumer price index for all items was 136.2. At the end of 1996, it had risen to 156.9. This 15 percent increase reflected the fact that during those years the actual buying power of minimum-wage workers decreased 3 percent, even though wages were increased 50 cents per hour.

People who make economic decisions based on a wage increase without thinking about concurrent price changes are said to be operating under "money illusion." Money illusion is fairly common because some people are not informed about the relation of wage increases to price changes. ■

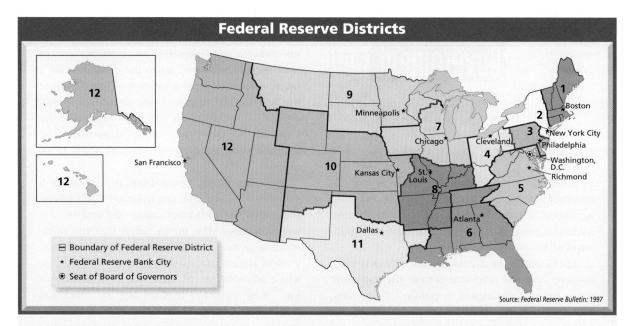

Federal Reserve Districts

- Boundary of Federal Reserve District
- ★ Federal Reserve Bank City
- ⊗ Seat of Board of Governors

Source: *Federal Reserve Bulletin: 1997*

The Federal Reserve system is divided into 12 districts. Each district has its own Federal Reserve bank, which is owned by other banks in the district. **In which Federal Reserve district is your state located?**

policy is controlled through the **Federal Reserve system**—or the "Fed"—which is the central banking system of the United States. The Fed, created by the Federal Reserve Act of 1913, is an independent government agency.

The Fed is not a bank like your neighborhood bank. You cannot set up an account there. It gives out no automated teller cards, and it will not lend you money. Rather, the Fed is a "central bank" that controls how much money is in circulation. The Fed is organized unlike any other government agency. It is made up of 12 regional Federal Reserve banks and more than 13,000 of privately owned member banks.

The Fed's two main decision-making bodies are the Board of Governors and the Federal Open Market Committee (FOMC). The Board of Governors, located in Washington, D.C., heads the Federal Reserve system. It is made up of seven members who are appointed by the president and confirmed by the Senate for 14-year terms. The chair of the Board of Governors is also appointed by the president. The board supervises the Fed's banking services and issues policies that regulate the U.S. money supply. It also oversees the activities of the district and member banks and approves the appointments of their presidents. The FOMC steers the strategy of the Fed's monetary

policy. The seven members of the Board of Governors and the president of the Federal Reserve Bank of New York are permanent members of the FOMC. The remaining four members are presidents of district Federal Reserve banks who serve one-year terms on a rotating basis.

The Federal Reserve system is divided into 12 geographic districts, each of which houses one Federal Reserve bank. The 12 district banks, which are not operated for profit, perform regulatory functions for banks in their district. After subtracting their operating costs, the district banks send their yearly income to the U.S. Treasury.

Each Federal Reserve bank is owned by other banks in the district, which buy stock in the district bank. These banks are called member banks. There are around 8,500 commercial banks in the United States. Of these, more than 3,300 are members of the Federal Reserve system.

Making Monetary Policy

The Federal Reserve uses three tools to implement monetary policy. These are:

★ reserve requirements,
★ the discount rate, and
★ open-market operations.

Reserve Requirements The first tool the Fed uses to implement monetary policy involves rules for banks. These **reserve requirements** determine the minimum amount of money that a bank must keep on hand at all times and thus not lend out to its patrons. By raising reserve requirements, the Fed lowers the amount of money that banks can lend, thereby decreasing the money supply in the economy. A lowering of reserve requirements has the opposite effect.

The Fed rarely changes reserve requirements, for to do so creates uncertainty in the banking system. Changes may also make it more difficult for banks to make long-term loans and investments.

Discount Rate A second tool that the Federal Reserve uses is the **discount rate**—the interest rate that it charges to banks. Remember that the Fed is a banker's bank. If a bank wants to borrow money so that it can, in turn, lend the money to a person or business, it can do so by borrowing from the Fed. The lower the discount rate, the more inclined banks are to borrow from the Fed; the higher the rate, the less inclined they are. Thus, because the overall money supply in the U.S. economy increases when banks lend more money to customers, the Fed can influence the economy by adjusting the discount rate.

The Fed also sets the federal funds rate—the interest rate at which banks can borrow funds from each other. Raising or lowering the federal funds rate can encourage or discourage banks from borrowing from each other. Although it does not affect the money supply directly, raising or lowering the federal funds rate does have an impact on banking and the economy in general.

Open Market Operations The most common way the Federal Reserve influences the economy is through **open-market operations**—the purchase or sale of bonds in order to finance the operations of government. **Bonds**, or securities, are certificates issued by a government to a lender from whom it has borrowed money. By buying or selling these bonds, the Fed is able to increase or decrease the money supply in the economy.

When the Federal Reserve buys government bonds from private investors, the money supply increases because the Fed pays by adding funds to the general economy. In contrast, when the Fed sells bonds, it tightens the money supply by accepting funds that had been in circulation.

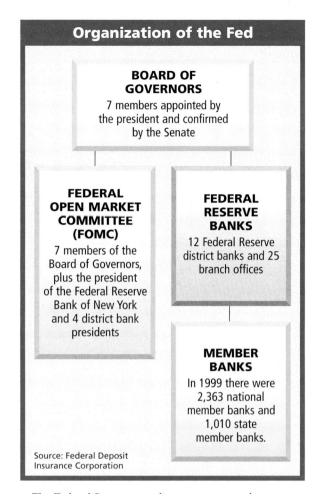

Organization of the Fed

BOARD OF GOVERNORS

7 members appointed by the president and confirmed by the Senate

FEDERAL OPEN MARKET COMMITTEE (FOMC)

7 members of the Board of Governors, plus the president of the Federal Reserve Bank of New York and 4 district bank presidents

FEDERAL RESERVE BANKS

12 Federal Reserve district banks and 25 branch offices

MEMBER BANKS

In 1999 there were 2,363 national member banks and 1,010 state member banks.

Source: Federal Deposit Insurance Corporation

The Federal Reserve supplies money to member banks across the country. Member banks must follow the rules and regulations established by the Fed.
Which branch of the Fed steers overall monetary strategy?

Monetary versus Fiscal Policy

Monetary policy can work much faster than fiscal policy. Fiscal policy is tied to annual budgets and involves a lag between when an economic problem occurs and when shifts in fiscal policy are actually felt. A change in monetary policy, on the other hand, works much more quickly, since a change in policy is effective immediately.

Remember that fiscal policy is made entirely by the president and Congress. They decide how much to tax and how much to spend. Monetary policy, however, is controlled by an independent agency that is not elected by the people. For this reason, some people believe that the Fed's role in making economic policy is too great. Others,

THEMES IN GOVERNMENT

POLITICAL PROCESSES

Before deciding whether to raise interest rates, the Federal Reserve chair heeds a number of signals. A few of them are listed here:

★ U.S. auto sales, which supply billions of dollars annually to the economy,

★ commodity prices, which help set the prices of finished goods,

★ factory overtime, which strains the ability to produce and increases pressure for higher wages when it reaches high levels,

★ stock value increases, which may cause people to spend more, thus pushing up prices, and

★ supplier performance, which might push up prices when suppliers fail to keep up with retailers' demands. ■

PUBLIC GOOD *The Federal Reserve influences the economy by buying and selling bonds.* **What happens to the money supply when the Fed sells government bonds?**

however, say that the lack of political pressure ensures that the Fed will do what is best for the economy, not what is best for a political party.

The country can be guided most effectively when fiscal and monetary policy are used together. For example, if inflation is the most important economic problem, monetary and fiscal policies should work together to curb demand and thus reduce prices. The Fed would need to reduce the money supply and the availability of credit, while Congress and the president would need to agree on a fiscal policy that involves decreased federal spending, increased taxes, or both.

Economic Policy and the Public Good

Between the 1930s and the 1960s the most important economic policy debates involved stabilization policy. During the last two decades, stabilization policy debates have become less important as political leaders have turned their attention to issues of long-term economic growth.

The economic doctrine supporting active government stabilization is most often called **Keynesianism** (KAYN-zee-uh-ni-zuhm), after John

Maynard Keynes. Keynes was a British economist who called for the government to stimulate the economy during the Great Depression. Keynesians argue that active government stabilization policies can counteract instability in the normal operation of a free-market economy. In response to an economic slowdown, Keynesian fiscal policy calls for the government to run a budget **deficit**—or to let expenses exceed revenue—and to use its monetary policy to provide low interest rates to stimulate the economy. An example of this is the GI Bill, which helped keep the economy stable after World War II. The GI Bill provided U.S. soldiers with assistance for education; loans for home, business, and farm ownership; and financial support during times of unemployment.

The high point for Keynesianism came during the 1960s. In 1963 President John Kennedy proposed a tax cut, hoping that consumers would respond by spending more money and thus stimulating the economy. The proposed tax cut was not to be offset by government spending cuts, however, and would therefore result in a budget deficit. Kennedy hoped that the deficit would eventually disappear as the economy improved.

The tax cut, which was passed during President Lyndon Johnson's administration, contributed to increased economic growth and seemed to support Keynesian ideas. Loosened restrictions on government spending made possible an expansion of spending on public aid while running budget deficits.

During the 1970s Keynesian doctrine faced growing intellectual and political challenges. The benefits of the economic boom of the late 1960s were increasingly undercut by inflation. Then in late 1973 an increase in oil prices following an embargo by oil-producing nations resulted in a mixture of high inflation and lower economic growth. In this climate, Milton Friedman, a University of Chicago professor and leading economic conservative, popularized the principle of **monetarism**.

Monetarists argue that a market economy, working properly and left alone, most likely will operate at full employment and low inflation.

They believe that economic downturns—including the Great Depression—have occurred not because of economic instability, but because government policies have intervened in the economy's operation and drastically cut the supply of money. Monetarists believe that government's only role in economic stabilization should be to keep the money supply expanding at a steady pace to accommodate economic growth.

Industrial Policy and Economic Growth

Stabilization policy aims to even out the bumps in the business cycle. In addition, over the past 15 years there have been debates about whether government aid (often called industrial policy) can increase overall economic growth.

When the phrase *industrial policy* was introduced in the early 1980s, it frequently referred to attempts to prop up declining industries. Arguments on behalf of aid to such industries involve maintaining the current number of jobs in these inefficient industries rather than improving the overall economy. In recent years, however, the phrase has been used almost exclusively to refer to aiding "industries of the future." These industries—particularly high-tech ones such as computer technology, semiconductors, telecommunications, and biotechnology—hold promise for future economic growth. Supporters suggest that aiding

such industries would improve overall economic growth by allowing these new industries to move forward more quickly.

Supporters of industrial policy have argued that Japan successfully followed a bold policy to target important industrial sectors, particularly those involving high-tech consumer goods. They also point to various internationally successful sectors of the U.S. economy, such as agriculture, computer technology, biotechnology, and aviation, which have benefited both from significant government research money and from government purchases (particularly for defense). Industrial policy supporters argue that if such industries are not supported by the government, they will lag behind their global competitors in basic scientific research and development, for current market forces alone will not support such future-oriented endeavors.

Opponents of industrial policy have expressed skepticism about the ability of government to improve on the free market. They hold that the government cannot do a better job than private investors in picking the economic winners of the future and should thus stay on the sidelines.

The most insistent criticism of industrial policy has to do with the way the U.S. political system works. Even if a good case might be made for industrial policy in theory, opponents argue that pork-barrel politics and interest group influence are likely to result in the wrong industries being chosen for government help.

SECTION 2 REVIEW ANSWERS

1. Refer to the following pages: free enterprise (196), recession (197), inflation (197), fiscal policy (198), monetary policy (198), disposable income (198), Federal Reserve system (200), reserve requirements (201), discount rate (201), open-market operations (201), bond (201), Keynesianism (202), deficit (202), monetarism (202).

2. Increased spending: Effect—spending stimulates growth in the economy, businesses expand and create jobs; Result—increased growth in the economy and higher employment. Higher taxes: Effect—higher taxes lead people to spend less, businesses make smaller profits; Result—lower prices and stable growth.

3a. monetary policy—procedures designed to control the amount of money in circulation and the level of interest rates; fiscal policy—set of government spending, taxing, and borrowing policies used to achieve desired levels of economic performance.

3b. The goal is to increase economic growth. Industries that have benefited include computer technology, semiconductors, telecommunications, and biotechnology.

4. Answers will vary but students should demonstrate an understanding of the effects of government spending and the impact of the GI Bill.

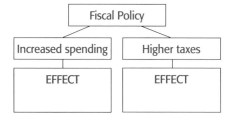

SECTION 2 REVIEW

1. Identify and Explain:
- free enterprise
- recession
- inflation
- fiscal policy
- monetary policy
- disposable income
- Federal Reserve system
- reserve requirements
- discount rate
- open-market

2. Identifying Concepts: Copy the chart below. Use it to show the impact on the economy of a fiscal policy of increased spending and a policy of increased taxes

Fiscal Policy	
Increased spending	Higher taxes
EFFECT	EFFECT

3. Finding the Main Idea
- **a.** What is the difference between monetary policy and fiscal policy?
- **b.** What is the goal of industrial policy, and what industries have benefited from it?

4. Writing and Critical Thinking

Drawing Conclusions: How do you think programs such as the GI Bill affect American society?
Consider the following:
- the cost of the program
- the benefits people receive from the program

Homework Practice Online
go.hrw.com
keyword: SV3 HP9

SECTION 3

THE FEDERAL BUDGET

READ TO DISCOVER

1. How has the federal budget-making process changed over the years?
2. What role does the president play in planning the budget?
3. Why are attempts at reducing the budget politically controversial?

POLITICAL DICTIONARY

federal budget
Office of Management and Budget
Congressional Budget Office
resolution
reconciliation

In 1789 Congress created the Treasury Department as one of the original executive departments. Alexander Hamilton, the first secretary of the treasury, established the role of the federal government in the economy by promoting a form of national economic planning. Hamilton believed that the country required a national spending program based on the priorities and needs of the nation as a whole. The executive branch would submit departmental estimates of funding to Congress, asking for the money needed to carry out the programs. Today, the U.S. national spending program is known as the **federal budget**.

Changes in the Budget Process

Though the idea of preparing a federal spending plan came from Alexander Hamilton, the means by which the budget is prepared has changed dramatically over the past two centuries. In fact, the budgetary process as it now stands is fairly new. Before the early 1900s the United States had no formal system for planning how to spend the revenues that it collected. Each federal department simply issued requests for funds as the money was needed. By the early 1900s many people in government, including President William Howard Taft, were calling for a more orderly budget process.

Budget and Accounting Act of 1921 A significant step in reforming the national budget process was made in 1921 with the passage of the Budget and Accounting Act. This legislation gave a newly established Bureau of the Budget the power to raise or lower agencies' spending requests before they were sent to Congress.

Office of Management and Budget In 1939 the Bureau of the Budget was moved from the Treasury Department to the Executive Office of the President. This made it easier for the president to influence the budget and thus increased the president's role in making economic policy. The position of director of the **Office of Management and Budget** (OMB)—as the bureau was renamed in 1971—has high-level status.

Congressional Budget and Impoundment Control Act of 1974 The process by which Congress examines the president's budget proposal has changed considerably over the last two decades. For nearly 200 years, there was no process by which Congress could consider the budget as a whole. Congress never voted on overall

"...Comes unassembled. Does not include batteries or instructions...."

ETTA HULME reprinted by permission of Newspaper Enterprise Association, Inc.

POLITICAL PROCESSES *The budget process has undergone numerous changes over the past 100 years, yet it is still a complex procedure that does not always run smoothly.* **What does this cartoon imply about Congress's ability to prepare the budget?**

One of President Bill Clinton's campaign promises was to provide funding to public schools for Internet access. Here, President Clinton and Vice President Al Gore visit a computer facility at a public school. **What is the president's role in the preparation of the budget?**

spending levels but rather on a series of separate appropriations bills for different agencies over several months. This made it difficult to compare one appropriation with another. In theory, a member could vote in favor of every proposal to spend money and against every proposal to levy taxes.

To amend this situation, Congress passed the Congressional Budget and Impoundment Control Act of 1974, which limited presidential impoundments and set ceilings for the budgets each year. (An impoundment is a refusal by the president to spend funds that Congress has authorized and appropriated.)

The 1974 Budget Act created budget committees in the House and Senate to allow Congress to review the president's budget proposal more systematically. The law also created the **Congressional Budget Office** (CBO) to provide economic data, information, and analysis to both houses of Congress.

Preparing the Budget Today

When preparing a budget, agencies do not begin with a blank slate. Rather, they—and the president and members of Congress—look over the previous

year's budget to determine which areas of government should receive more, or less, funding than last year. That is, if an agency received an appropriation of $1 billion last year and is asking for $1.1 billion this year, examination typically will not center on the $1 billion, but on whether the additional $100 million is justified.

President's Role The budget process begins with the Office of Management and Budget's guidelines about the overall fiscal situation that detail the kinds of programs the president wants to support or reduce. Each agency then uses those guidelines to develop a spending proposal, which is considered by OMB. Two considerations tend to drive OMB's evaluation of a proposal: keeping spending in line and remaining loyal to the president's priorities.

Members of the OMB staff review the agencies' requests and present their overall recommendations to the president. Over the next several months, each federal agency, OMB, and the president review and negotiate a working budget proposal. Upon completion, the budget proposal is submitted to Congress before the established deadline, which is January 1.

Appropriations Process According to the U.S. Constitution, "No money shall be drawn from the Treasury, but in consequence of appropriations made by law." Once the president's proposed budget has been submitted, Congress takes the lead in the budgetary process. It must draft and approve spending and revenue bills for the coming fiscal year. As noted in Chapter 6, spending for a program must first be authorized, and then funds are appropriated for it. Authorizations and appropriations are arrived at after a long process of review, debate, and compromise.

The Budget Committees of both the House and Senate set overall spending targets and revenue goals, based at least partly on the president's proposal. Congress then must pass a resolution setting

Caption Answer

The president works with federal agencies and the OMB to review and negotiate a working budget proposal.

THEMES IN GOVERNMENT

PUBLIC GOOD President George W. Bush listed his priorities in his 2001 State of the Union address. Some of his goals were to:

★ spend $5.7 billion for increased military salaries, health care, and housing,

★ begin testing students on basic reading and math skills every year between the third and eighth grades,

★ spend $238 billion on Medicare funding in 2002 and to begin a new prescription drug program for low-income seniors, and

★ help Americans who do not have health care to buy their own insurance with tax credits. ■

Profiles in American Government

For a biography of Alexander Hamilton and other noted people in government, refer students to the Biographies section on the *Holt Researcher Online.*

Careers in Government

On a given day, economists at the Congressional Budget Office might be called on by Congress to analyze the potential economic impact of a major bill or prepare a report on how the economy will fare in the next five years. At the General Accounting Office, economists might examine the budget of a government agency, looking for ways to cut costs.

Aside from colleges and universities, the federal government is the largest employer of economists. State and local governments also employ economists to work in areas such as welfare and urban economics, monetary and fiscal policy, and industrial organization. Other economists work at universities as teachers and researchers. In addition, economists work for businesses and industries in areas such as finance and marketing.

Lawrence Lindsey, the chairman of President Bush's National Economic Council, has made a career out of studying economics.

Students who find that they are skilled at crunching numbers may find a position as an economist fulfilling. Lawrence Lindsey, the chairman of President George W. Bush's National Economic Council, took his love for economics into the realm of public policy. His study of economics taught him some basic principles, which he now applies to economic policymaking. There is, he explained, "a method to economic science, which is to look at the data and follow the direction the numbers point to, telling you where the truth is, and never be ashamed to admit that your first idea was wrong. . . . I don't know if that's a particular economic concept, but it is a very good way of doing research and pursuing policy. If you're wrong, then say you're wrong and try a new approach."

Lindsey served on the Council of Economic Advisers during the Reagan administration, and as a special assistant during the administration of George Bush. From 1991 to 1997 Lindsey was a member of the Federal Reserve's Board of Governors.

During the 2000 presidential campaign, Lindsey served as George W. Bush's economic adviser, and was the main architect of Bush's tax cut plan. As chairman of the National Economic Council, Lindsey essentially oversees the entire economic policymaking process. On his shoulders rests the responsibility of making sure that U.S. economic policy accurately reflects the president's agenda. This involves keeping an eye on the national and global economy and personally advising the president on a daily basis.

---

forth these goals. A **resolution** is a formal declaration or statement that does not require the signature of the president and does not have the force of law. In the case of the budget, Congress passes a concurrent resolution—a formal declaration by both houses. This resolution details the complete federal spending and tax plan for the upcoming fiscal year. Congress must complete the concurrent resolution for the next fiscal year by April 15,

although it may later revise the resolution. Congressional review of the budget continues with extensive hearings by the committees and subcommittees that have jurisdiction over the programs or agencies to be funded. Legislators examine agencies' requests and hear testimony from administration officials.

The various congressional committees, overseen by the House and Senate Appropriations

The Budget Process

EXECUTIVE ROLE

1. OMB sends guidance for spending proposals to federal agencies.
2. Each federal agency develops a spending proposal.
3. OMB considers agency spending proposals and presents recommendations to the president.
4. The president reviews and develops a working budget with OMB.
5. OMB submits a final budget proposal to the president.
6. The president approves the proposal and submits it to Congress.

CONGRESSIONAL ROLE

7. Appropriations and Budget Committees review the president's budget proposal in committee hearings.
8. Appropriations and Budget Committees draft a concurrent resolution detailing the overall taxing and spending plan.
9. Appropriations and Budget Committees complete the reconciliation process to come up with a reconciliation bill representing final spending limits.
10. Congress passes a reconciliation bill.
11. Congress passes appropriations bills.
12. Congress sends the appropriations bills to the president for approval or veto.

Preparing the budget is a major responsibility of the executive and legislative branches. **What is the role of the OMB in this process?**

Committees, then prepare detailed spending and tax legislation but must keep within the limits set in the resolution. This process is called **reconciliation**, because the bills must be reconciled not only with the plan set forth in the concurrent resolution but also with already authorized spending for existing programs. Reconciliation thus is a two-step process. First, Budget Committees receive instructions on how much revenue needs to be generated or how much spending needs to be cut in order to meet goals set out in the resolution. Second, the committee recommendations are combined in a reconciliation bill that represents the final spending limits for all appropriations.

Congress passes 13 major appropriations bills each year. The funding for the Departments of Commerce, Justice, and State, for example, may be grouped together into one bill. The U.S. Department of Defense, on the other hand, receives a large portion of the budget and has its funding addressed in a separate appropriations bill. After passing both houses, the appropriations bills go to the president for final approval or veto.

SECTION 3 REVIEW

1. Identify and Explain:
- federal budget
- Office of Management and Budget
- Congressional Budget Office
- resolution
- reconciliation

2. Identifying Concepts: Copy the chart to the right.

Use it to illustrate the roles of the executive and legislative branches in preparing the federal budget.

Executive Branch	Legislative Branch

3. Finding the Main Idea

a. What changes have been made to the budget-making process since the early 1900s?

b. What factors influence Congress's decisions in the appropriations process?

4. Writing and Critical Thinking

Drawing Conclusions: What happens if Congress and the president are unable to reach an agreement on a budget?

Consider the following:
- the budget-making process
- the constitutional powers of the president and Congress

Homework Practice Online
go.hrw.com
keyword: SV3 HP9

SECTION 4

DEFICIT SPENDING AND THE ECONOMY

READ TO DISCOVER

1. What factors cause the federal government to operate at a deficit?
2. How does the national debt influence the U.S. economy?
3. In what ways do the national debt and the federal deficit influence each other?

POLITICAL DICTIONARY

gross domestic product
entitlements
national debt
Gramm-Rudman-Hollings Act

In this chapter, you have learned how the government takes in money and how decisions are made on how to spend it. At times the government has spent a lot more money than it raised, leading to the accumulation of a huge national debt.

Federal Deficit

If the government spends more than it takes in, in both tax and nontax revenue, the budget is in deficit. Between 1789 and 1932, two thirds of federal budgets showed a surplus, meaning the government raised more revenue than it spent. Between 1932 and 1997, however, the budget has shown a surplus only eight times. In 1998 the budget showed a surplus of $69 billion, the first surplus since 1969.

As noted in Section 1, at the beginning of Ronald Reagan's first presidential term in 1981, individual income taxes were cut 25 percent. Overall government spending continued to rise, however. As a result, between 1981 and 1982 the deficit increased by about 62 percent. By 1983 the deficit was around 6 percent of the **gross domestic product** (GDP)—the total dollar value,

or price, of all finished goods and services produced within a country during one year.

Budget Deficit and Politics

The budget deficit became a major political issue in the 1990s. Deficit reduction, however, proved difficult initially for three main reasons: political disagreements over which programs to cut, uncontrollable spending, and a reluctance of the general public to accept either tax increases or major spending cuts in programs.

Political Disagreements Budget cutting involves making tough choices about which programs to cut and by how much. Almost everyone involved in politics can come up with a plan to reduce the deficit significantly by producing a budget in line with their own political views. For example, Democrats may propose cutting defense spending and raising taxes, particularly on the wealthy. Republicans may propose cutting domestic social spending. The problem lies in obtaining a political majority for a plan that fairly distributes the pain of deficit reduction to all groups.

Uncontrollable Spending Much of the budget consists of so-called uncontrollable spending—a term that refers to spending based on the government's prior legal commitments. This type

POLITICAL PROCESSES *Many citizens are concerned about the size of the deficit yet are opposed to spending cuts.* **What point of view is illustrated in this cartoon?**

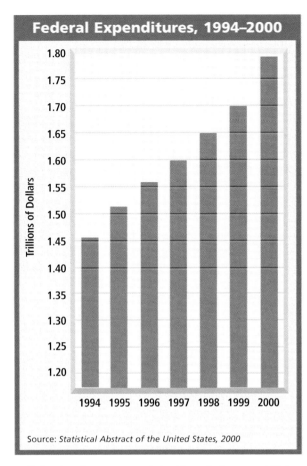

Federal Expenditures, 1994–2000

Trillions of Dollars

1994	1.455
1995	1.515
1996	1.56
1997	1.60
1998	1.65
1999	1.70
2000	1.79

Source: *Statistical Abstract of the United States, 2000*

Federal outlays increased significantly between 1994 and 2000. Uncontrollable spending often makes budget cutbacks difficult. **How much did federal outlays increase between 1997 and 2000?**

of spending occurs each year without specific appropriation.

Major examples of uncontrollable spending include (1) payments on the national debt; (2) current payments under contracts the government has signed in the past (for example, the government must pay rent on any buildings it leases); and (3) **entitlements**, or benefits that federal law requires be given to all persons who legally qualify for them (for example, benefits from Social Security and Medicare, as noted in Section 1).

In 1995 about 58 percent of federal outlays consisted of entitlements. The largest entitlements are Social Security (mostly pensions for elderly people), Medicare (health-care benefits for elderly people), and Medicaid (health-care benefits for the poor). Other important entitlement programs are veterans' benefits, crop support payments to farmers, food stamps, civilian and military retirement, unemployment insurance, and government-backed loans for college students.

Many budget debates of recent years have been over entitlement programs, particularly Social Security, Medicare, and Medicaid. Senior citizens have been well organized in opposing entitlement cutbacks. They have argued that such cuts not only would break the government's promise to provide the entitlements but also would hurt the disadvantaged. Supporters of entitlement cutbacks have argued that the nation simply can no longer afford to spend as much on Medicare and other programs as it has in the past. Many deficit-reduction proposals have involved lowering entitlement benefit levels (as with college student loans and medicare) or ending a program's entitlement status entirely (as with welfare).

Comparing Governments

Budget Deficits Around the World

At about $107 billion, the 1996 U.S. budget deficit dwarfed the budget shortfalls of many other industrial nations. Yet by another measure the 1996 deficit seems rather small, having made up only 1.4 percent of the nation's gross domestic product (GDP). Even Japan, which in recent years had boasted budget surpluses, racked up a budget deficit in 1995 that was 3.9 percent of its GDP.

In the early 1990s widening budget deficits in Europe caused so much concern that leaders of the 15 European Union member nations agreed to a common economic goal. The 1993 Maastricht Treaty—which established a common currency within the European Union—required members to reduce their 1997 budget deficit to no more than 3 percent of their GDP. In 1996, experts predicted that more than half of the European nations would overshoot this deficit mark.

Many nations' deficits have similar causes—higher spending on social programs, growing unemployment, a stubborn economic recession. To address these concerns and to balance their books, governments around the world will have to make difficult choices.

PUBLIC GOOD *Students planning to attend college may apply for government-backed student loans. Student loans are just one form of entitlement program funded by the federal government.* **What is one group that has opposed entitlement cutbacks in recent years?**

Reluctant Public People usually oppose higher taxes and are generally unhappy that the government spends such huge amounts of money overall. However, at the same time, widespread public support for costly government programs has been consistent. Part of the reason that politicians have had difficulty cutting spending is the public's reluctance to allow favored programs to be scaled back or eliminated.

The National Debt

When the government's expenditures are higher than its revenue, it must borrow money to make up the difference, thus increasing the debt. The **national debt** is the sum of all money the U.S. government owes as a result of borrowing.

The Size of the National Debt The national debt has skyrocketed from about $908 billion in 1980 to $5.7 trillion in 2001. Just how much money is $5.7 trillion? If you wanted to pay off the national debt by paying $1 million a day, it would take you more than 15,000 years—and that does not even include interest payments.

Interest Payments on the Debt If you were to borrow money from the bank, you would have to pay back the amount you borrowed, plus any interest that had accumulated. The federal government also must pay interest on the money it borrows. About 11 percent of current federal expenditures consists of interest payments on the national debt.

The Debt and the Economy As you can imagine, a national debt of some $5 trillion has serious implications for the U.S. economy. Huge budget deficits can cause foreign investors to lose faith in the U.S. dollar. If foreign investors believe that U.S. deficit spending is out of control, they may exchange their dollars for a currency that appears to be more stable. This action, in turn, would cause the U.S. dollar to lose some of its value in relation to other currencies.

In recent years, as deficits were brought under control and reduced, the value of the dollar has increased. When the government borrows billions of dollars to finance deficit spending, the investment funds that are available for the economy in general decrease substantially. In other words, there is a limited amount of money available to be borrowed. When the government borrows huge amounts of money, the competition for the remaining available funds causes interest rates to rise, which in turn slows down the economy.

Balancing the Budget

The issue of how to address budget deficits has long been a matter of debate. In 1997, however, the president and Congress agreed on a plan to balance the budget. As the history outlined below shows, such attempts had been made before.

Gramm-Rudman-Hollings Act In response to the huge budget deficits of the 1980s, Congress passed the Balanced Budget and Emergency Deficit Control Act of 1985, known as the **Gramm-Rudman-Hollings Act** (GRH). The legislation was designed to force Congress and the president to work together to reduce the mounting budget deficits.

The GRH required the president's budget staff and the Congressional Budget Office to produce a joint report on the budget. This report would include estimates on how much the proposed budget would exceed expected revenue and how much

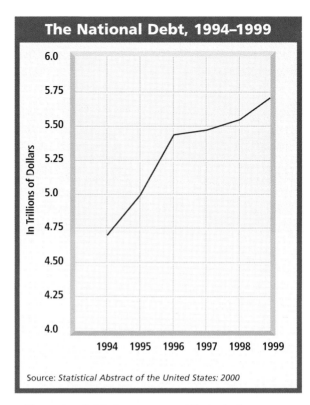

The National Debt, 1994–1999

In Trillions of Dollars

6.0	
5.75	
5.50	
5.25	
5.0	
4.75	
4.50	
4.25	
4.0	

1994 1995 1996 1997 1998 1999

Source: *Statistical Abstract of the United States: 2000*

The national debt has grown rapidly in the last several years. **How can a debt of this size affect economic growth?**

the budget would need to be cut to meet deficit-reduction targets. An official in the General Accounting Office (GAO), called the comptroller general, would then be allowed to make budget cuts if the president and Congress could not agree on how to do so. In 1986, however, the U.S. Supreme Court ruled that this method of cutting spending was unconstitutional. In response, Congress amended the procedures and moved the dates for achieving a balanced budget from 1991 to 1993.

C A S E   S T U D Y

Budget Enforcement Act

POLITICAL PROCESSES Balancing the budget is not easy. In 1990, the Gramm-Rudman-Hollings (GRH) Act had come under attack in Congress. Critics of the balanced budget law charged that it just was not working because budget makers were getting around the law with clever accounting tricks.

Members of Congress worked out new legislation to reform the budget process. In November 1990 President George Bush signed the Budget Enforcement Act (BEA) into law.

The BEA changed the budget process in many ways. Instead of focusing on just one year, budget makers are now required to predict what will be included in the budgets of the next five years. The act also established what are known as "pay-as-you-go" (PAYGO) restrictions, requiring that any increase in spending be paid for by an increase in taxes and that any decrease in taxes be offset by spending cuts. The law set specific limits on spending for defense, social programs, and foreign aid. That way, money saved in one area cannot be spent in another. The BEA also established a ceiling for the deficit for each year.

Balanced Budget Amendment Some lawmakers believed that a constitutional amendment requiring a balanced budget was ultimately the only way to solve the deficit problem. In March 1997, however, the Senate rejected a proposed constitutional amendment that would have required the federal government to maintain a balanced budget each year. (The House had previously passed a similar measure.) Many lawmakers, as well as President Clinton, who called the balanced budget amendment "both unnecessary and unwise," were against the amendment. They argued that a balanced budget should come by reaching a mutually agreed-upon budget proposal, not by amending the Constitution.

The 1993 Clinton Plan The budget deficit began a steady decline in 1993. An important step in the turnaround was an economic package proposed during President Clinton's first year in office and adopted despite some Republican opposition in Congress. The plan increased taxes on wealthier Americans and decreased spending on some programs.

In 1996 the budget deficit stood at just 1.4 percent of GDP, the lowest percentage in almost 20 years. Low inflation (which reduces interest rates and thus interest payments on the national debt) and strong economic growth (which increases tax revenues) helped lower the deficit.

Holt American Government Videodisc

The video segment Land Use: Oil Exploration in Alaska complements the Chapter 9 case study, Budget Enforcement Act. Barcodes for the Spanish version of the video segment are available in *Holt American Government Videodisc Teacher's Guide.*

PLAY SEGMENT

PAUSE

RESUME PLAY

PLAY OPTION A

PLAY OPTION B

PLAY OPTION C

PLAY EPILOGUE

POLITICAL PROCESSES *In the 1990s House Budget Committee Chairman John Kasich led the fight for a balanced budget.* **What act helped produce the first federal budget surplus in nearly 30 years?**

Balanced Budget Act of 1997

Lawmakers continued to work on means to eliminate the deficit entirely. In August 1997, President Clinton signed into law the Balanced Budget Act of 1997. The act was intended to finally eliminate budget deficits. Clinton said of the act that it "prepares Americans to enter the next century, stronger than ever. By large, bipartisan majorities in both Houses, we have risen to that challenge." These efforts at eliminating deficits have been successful. In 1998 the federal budget showed a surplus for the first time in nearly 30 years. Following years continued to show surpluses. Furthermore, the government predicts that the budget will be in surplus through the year 2011 and beyond. If the projections hold true, the national debt will be largely retired in just over 10 years. These optimistic numbers must be tempered with the knowledge that a slowing economy and increased government spending could bring a return of budget deficits.

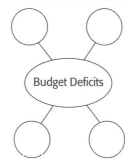

SECTION 4 REVIEW

1. Identify and Explain:
- gross domestic product
- entitlements
- national debt
- Gramm-Rudman-Hollings Act

2. Identifying Concepts:
Copy the chart at right. Use it to illustrate the factors that contributed to budget deficits.

Budget Deficits

Homework Practice Online
keyword: SV3 HP9

3. Finding the Main Idea

a. What is uncontrollable spending? What are some examples of entitlements?

b. How did the accumulation of debt contribute to budget deficits?

4. Writing and Critical Thinking

Decision Making: Should the federal government use the budget surplus to pay down the national debt, or to fund new or existing programs?

Consider the following:
- the effects of the national debt on the economy
- the benefits of programs such as the GI Bill

IN THE NEWS

The Effects of Genetic Engineering

Many people believe that genetic engineering holds great promise for the future of society. Through this technology, scientists can take the attributes of one living thing and transfer them to another living thing. This process involves DNA, a chemical found in every organism. DNA contains codes that determine everything from a human's eye color to the shape of a tree's leaves. Scientists are now able to "cut" DNA out of one organism and place it into the DNA of another—a process called splicing.

Once the stuff of science fiction, genetic engineering has become a reality, particularly in the agriculture industry. By cutting and splicing DNA, agriculturists can select characteristics they feel are suitable for a certain crop or livestock. In 2000, for example, scientists were able to genetically engineer a type of rice to include a higher amount of the vitamin beta-carotene. Because the body uses beta-carotene to produce vitamin A, scientists predict that this new rice will help fight malnutrition around the world.

Some feel, however, that genetic engineering could have consequences that do more harm than good. Many scientists argue that altering the DNA of food should be halted until researchers have had the chance to study the long-term effects of genetically engineered foods.

Even if genetically engineered foods prove to be harmless, or even healthy, many consumers simply do not feel comfortable eating such food. In 2000 a genetically engineered type of corn, called StarLink, accidentally found its way into a number of human foods. StarLink had not been approved for human consumption. After the "outbreak" of StarLink, more than 50 people reported

The potential effect of genetically altered foods, such as this corn, have caused controversy in recent years..

having had allergic reactions caused by StarLink's presence in their food.

In June 2001 the Centers of Disease Control and Prevention found no link between StarLink and the reported allergic reactions. Researchers suspected that the reactions were caused not by StarLink but were actually natural allergies caused by the foods themselves.

What Do You Think?

1. How does genetic engineering affect society?
2. What role do you think the government should play regarding genetic engineering of food? Explain your answer.

> **WHY IT MATTERS TODAY**
>
> Identify examples of genetic engineering in today's society. What organizations are protesting genetic engineering in an effort to institute government regulations? Use **CNNfyi.com** or other **current events** sources to find additional information on this subject.
>
> **CNNfyi.com**

Government in the News Answers

1. Students might suggest that some foods now have increased nutritional value but that the long-term consequences are as yet unknown.

2. Answers will vary. Some students might suggest that the government should regulate genetic engineering, and others might suggest that the new technology should be unregulated.

CHAPTER 9

Review Answers

Writing a Summary

Summaries should focus on the main points of each section. These may be found in the Read to Discover questions at the start of each section. Summaries should also use standard grammar, spelling, sentence structure, and punctuation.

Identifying Ideas

Refer to the following pages: revenue (191), tax (191), free enterprise (196), fiscal policy (198), monetary policy (198), deficit (202), federal budget (204), gross domestic product (208), entitlements (209), national debt (210).

Understanding Main Ideas

1. individual income tax, social insurance tax, corporate income tax, and earnings by the Federal Reserve banks

(Continued on page 214)

(Continued from page 213)

2. It can raise taxes to slow growth and encourage stabilization, and lower taxes to promote growth and higher employment.

3. Short-term costs were increased spending contributing to a budget deficit. Long-term benefits included more people attending college, buying homes, and starting businesses.

4. The government has provided aid to specific industries, particularly high-tech industries, to encourage faster growth, which in turn has led to new discoveries and products.

5. It created budget committees in Congress to allow a more systematic review of the president's budget proposal.

6. spending based on prior legal commitments by the government; payments on the national debt, payments under contracts the government has signed in the past, entitlements

Reviewing Themes

1. to own private property and enter into contracts, to make individual choices, to engage in economic competition, to make decisions based on self-interest, and to participate in the economy with limited government involvement and regulation

2. fiscal policy—government spending, taxing, and borrowing policies; monetary policy—procedures designed to control the amount of money in circulation

(Continued on page 215)

CHAPTER 9
Review

Writing a Summary

Using standard grammar, spelling, sentence structure, and punctuation, write a summary of the information in this chapter.

Identifying Ideas

Identify the following terms and explain their significance.

1. revenue	**6.** deficit
2. tax	**7.** federal budget
3. free enterprise	**8.** gross domestic product
4. fiscal policy	**9.** entitlements
5. monetary policy	**10.** national debt

Understanding Main Ideas

SECTION 1 *(pp. 191–195)*

1. What are the federal government's main sources of revenue?

SECTION 2 *(pp. 196–203)*

2. How can the federal government use tax policy to influence the economy?

3. What were the short-term costs and long-term benefits of the GI Bill?

4. How has government policy contributed to scientific discoveries and improved consumer products?

SECTION 3 *(pp. 204–207)*

5. How did the Congressional Budget and Impoundment Control Act change the way the president's budget proposal is considered?

SECTION 4 *(pp. 208–212)*

6. Define uncontrollable spending and list three examples.

Reviewing Themes

1. Principles of Democracy On what five main rights is the U.S. free-enterprise system based?

2. Political Processes Name and describe the main policies that the federal government uses to stabilize the economy and promote economic growth.

3. Public Good Why do you think the public has been reluctant to support cuts in government spending?

Thinking Critically

1. Supporting a Point of View Should government redistribute wealth through taxes? Write a paragraph that states and supports your opinion on the issue. Be sure to consider how tax policy decisions affect the standard of living in the United States.

2. Drawing Conclusions Why do you think that individual rights are a key element of the free-enterprise system?

3. Identifying Cause and Effect How has the creation of the Office of Management and Budget helped increase the president's role in making economic policy?

Writing about Government

Review what you wrote in your Government Notebook at the beginning of the chapter. After reading the chapter, do you believe the government is more, or less, involved in the economy than you originally thought? Record your answer in your notebook.

Interpreting the Visual Record

Study the political cartoon below. Then use it to help you answer the questions that follow.

"...Comes unassembled. Does not include batteries or instructions...."

1. How does the cartoon portray the budget?
a. as a living thing
b. as a complex machine
c. as a group of people
d. as a collection of odds and ends

2. How do you think the artist feels about Congress and the budget?

Analyzing Primary Sources

In 1934 British economist John Maynard Keynes visited President Franklin D. Roosevelt and recorded his thoughts on the New Deal, Roosevelt's plan for helping the United States cope with the Great Depression. Read this excerpt from Keynes's notes and answer the questions that follow.

"In many parts of the world the old order has passed away. But, of all the experiments to evolve a new order, it is the experiment of young America which most attracts my own deepest sympathy. For they are occupied with the task of trying to make the economic order work tolerably well, while preserving freedom of individual initiative and liberty of thought and criticism.

The older generation of living Americans accomplished the great task of solving the technical problem of how to produce economic goods on a scale adequate to human needs. It is the task of the younger generation to bring to actual realization the potential blessings of having solved the technical side of the problem of poverty. The central control which the latter requires involves an essentially changed method and outlook."

3. Which of the following statements best describes Keynes's point of view?
a. The New Deal is a big mistake.
b. Government should not be involved in the economy.
c. New ideas will be needed to recover from the Great Depression.
d. Very few changes have occurred.

4. According to Keynes, why is it hard "to make the economic order work tolerably well, while preserving freedom of individual initiative"?

(Continued from page 214)

3. Answers will vary but students should provide support for their opinion.

Thinking Critically

1. Answers will vary but students should state their opinion and offer support for it and address the impact of redistribution on the standard of living.

2. Answers will vary, but students should state their opinions and explain their reasoning.

3. The OMB works directly with the president and agencies to create a budget.

Writing about Government

The Government Notebook is a follow-up activity to the notebook activity that appears on page 190.

Building Social Studies Skills

1. b
2. Congress is poorly equipped to handle budgetary matters.
3. c
4. The problem of poverty requires central controls.

Alternative Assessment

To assess this activity see Writing to Describe in *Alternative Assessment Handbook*.

Alternative Assessment

Building Your Portfolio

Imagine that you are an economic adviser to the president of the United States. You have been asked to analyze the government's industrial policy. Prepare a plan for how the government can support research to develop new products. Include your analysis of the potential impact of some recent technological developments and suggestions on how the government should react to future scientific discoveries.

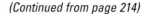

internet connect

Internet Activity: go.hrw.com
KEYWORD: SV3 GV9

Access the Internet through the HRW Go site to research the differences between fiscal and monetary policy. Then imagine you are the host of "Political Economy Today" and conduct an interview with John Maynard Keynes and Milton Friedman in which they interpret current issues from a fiscal and monetary perspective.

CHAPTER 10 FOREIGN POLICY AND NATIONAL SECURITY

	OBJECTIVES	PACING GUIDE	REPRODUCIBLE RESOURCES
SECTION 1 **GOALS AND PRINCIPLES OF U.S. FOREIGN POLICY** (pp. 217–221)	▸ What are the primary goals of U.S. foreign policy? ▸ How have factors such as location and geographic characteristics influenced U.S. policies toward a nation? ▸ What are the principles that have historically guided U.S. foreign policy?	**Regular** 1 day **Block Scheduling** .5 day	**ELL** Spanish Study Guide 10.1 **ELL** English Study Guide 10.1 **PS** Reading 21: George Washington's Farewell Address
SECTION 2 **MAKING FOREIGN POLICY** (pp. 222–227)	▸ Why does the executive branch have the greatest influence over foreign policy? ▸ How does the U.S. Department of State affect foreign policy decisions? ▸ How is the U.S. Department of Defense organized? ▸ What are the roles of the Central Intelligence Agency and Congress in making foreign policy?	**Regular** 1 day **Block Scheduling** .5 day	**ELL** Spanish Study Guide 10.2 **ELL** English Study Guide 10.2 **PS** Reading 30: "Four Freedoms"
SECTION 3 **HISTORY OF U.S. FOREIGN POLICY** (pp. 228–233)	▸ What are the principles that shaped U.S. leaders' foreign policy decision in the early years of the nation? ▸ What was the policy of containment? ▸ What was the significance of the expansion of communism for U.S. foreign policy?	**Regular** 1.5 days **Block Scheduling** .75 day	**ELL** Spanish Study Guide 10.3 **ELL** English Study Guide 10.3 **PS** Reading 10: Monroe Doctrine **PS** Reading 15: Truman Doctrine **PS** Reading 28: "Fourteen Points"
SECTION 4 **FOREIGN AID AND ALLIANCES** (pp. 234–238)	▸ How does providing aid to other nations help the United States? ▸ What are the defense alliances that the United States maintains today? ▸ How do alliances and foreign-aid programs promote the public good?	**Regular** 1 day **Block Scheduling** .5 day	**ELL** Spanish Study Guide 10.4 **ELL** English Study Guide 10.4

Chapter Resource Key

PS	Primary Sources	**A**	Assessment		Video
RS	Reading Support	**REV**	Review		Videodisc
E	Enrichment	**ELL**	Reinforcement and English Language Learners		Internet
S	Simulations		Transparencies		Holt Presentation Maker Using
SM	Skills Mastery		CD-ROM		Microsoft ® PowerPoint ®

One-Stop Planner: Lesson 10.1
Holt Researcher Online
Homework Practice Online
Global Skill Builder CD-ROM

REV Section 1 Review, p. 221
A Daily Quiz 10.1

One-Stop Planner: Lesson 10.2
Holt Researcher Online
Homework Practice Online
Cartoon Transparency 9

REV Section 2 Review, p. 227
A Daily Quiz 10.2

One-Stop Planner: Lesson 10.3
Holt Researcher Online
Homework Practice Online
E Simulations and Strategies for Teaching American Government: Activity 10
Transparency 21
CNN Presents American Government

REV Section 3 Review, p. 233
A Daily Quiz 10.3

One-Stop Planner: Lesson 10.4
Holt Researcher Online
Homework Practice Online
E Challenge and Enrichment: Activity 11
Transparency 22

REV Section 4 Review, p. 238
A Daily Quiz 10.4

Chapter Review and Assessment

SM Global Skill Builder CD-ROM
HRW Go site
REV Chapter 10 Tutorial for Students, Parents, and Peers
REV Chapter 10 Review, pp. 240–241
REV Test Generator, Chapter 10
Chapter 10 Test Generator (on the One-Stop Planner)
A Chapter 10 Test
A Chapter 10 Test Alternative Assessment Handbook

One-Stop Planner CD-ROM

It's easy to plan lessons, select resources, and print out materials for your students when you use the *One-Stop Planner CD-ROM with Test Generator.*

internet connect

HRW ONLINE RESOURCES
Go To: go.hrw.com
Then type in a keyword.

TEACHER HOME PAGE
KEYWORD: SV3 Teacher

CHAPTER INTERNET ACTIVITIES
KEYWORD: SV3 GV10

Choose an activity on foreign policy and national security to:

▸ conduct a class poll on foreign policy doctrines.
▸ create a graph on foreign aid.
▸ create a pamphlet on détente.

CHAPTER ENRICHMENT LINKS
KEYWORD: SV3 CH10

HOLT RESEARCHER ONLINE
KEYWORD: Holt Researcher

ONLINE ASSESSMENT
Homework Practice
KEYWORD: SV3 HP10
Standardized Test Prep
KEYWORD: SV3 STP10
Rubrics
KEYWORD: SS Rubrics

ONLINE MAPS, CHARTS, AND GRAPHS
KEYWORD: SV3 MCG
▸ Major Events of the Cold War
▸ Members of NATO

CONTENT UPDATES
KEYWORD: SS Content Updates

HOLT PRESENTATION MAKER
KEYWORD: SV3 PPT10

ONLINE READING SUPPORT
KEYWORD: SS Strategies

CURRENT EVENTS
KEYWORD: S3 Current Events

GOALS AND PRINCIPLES OF U.S. FOREIGN POLICY

TEXTBOOK PAGES 217–221

HOLT PRESENTATION MAKER
Access Illustrated LECTURE NOTES using Microsoft® PowerPoint® on the One-Stop Planner CD-ROM

OBJECTIVES

- Identify the primary goals of U.S. foreign policy.
- Examine how factors such as location or geographic characteristics influence U.S. policy toward a nation.
- Explain the principles that have historically guided U.S. foreign policy.

MOTIVATE

On the board list the five basic goals of U.S. foreign policy as described in this section: preserving national security, supporting democracies, promoting world peace, providing aid to people in need, and establishing free and open trade. Ask students to work individually to list as many examples of U.S. actions as possible that could fit under each category. After students have completed the task, list some of their ideas on the chalkboard and conduct a discussion about how many of these actions could be placed under different categories. Tell students that formulating U.S. foreign policy is a difficult task and that there are many factors to consider. Discuss some of these factors with students. Explain to students that in this section they will study the necessity of having a thoughtful foreign policy that incorporates each of these categories.

TEACH

Building a Vocabulary

In spiral notebooks, have students create a Political Dictionary to be used throughout the course. The dictionary may be used as an activity at the start of each new section; it may also be used as a modification device for students having difficulty or English Language Learners during tests and homework assignments. List words the students will be expected to know for this section on the board. Have students list, define, and give an example of each of the terms, using information provided in the text or on the *Researcher CD-ROM*.

Debating Ideas

Discuss with students the primary goals of U.S. foreign policy, and the four basic approaches to foreign policy mentioned during the Motivate activity. Then, organize the class into groups of four. Assign each student the position of one of the four basic approaches to U.S. foreign policy: America First, realism, neoisolationism, and idealism. Have students debate whether the United States should have entered World War I based on the reasoning of their assigned foreign policy argument. On a piece of paper, students should list the positions and supporting arguments for each group. After returning to a full class, students should debate the various positions for involvement and the pros and cons of each position. Finally, lead students in a discussion of the actual outcome of the debate over entry into World War I and the relative strengths and weaknesses the actual groups held in the debate. Identify the foreign-policy goals that were met by the decision to enter World War I and which approaches to U.S. foreign policy were followed. Tell students that in the next activity they will learn about the principles that have historically guided U.S. foreign policy.

Comparing and Contrasting/
Navigating the Internet/Identifying the Main Idea

List the primary goals of U.S. foreign policy, mentioned in the Motivate activity, on the chalkboard. Tell students to look on either the Democratic or Republican National Committee's Web site or conduct library research to find out the president's position on current foreign-policy issues. After researching the party's position, have students make a list of the president's key ideas and foreign-policy objectives. Lead students in a discussion about how the current administration's objectives match with the long-term goals of U.S. foreign policy as mentioned in this section. Have all students create a chart that depicts the current U.S. foreign-policy goals on the top and the long-term goals in the left column. Have students place an X in the squares that have coinciding goals.

Acquiring Information/Classifying Information

  Assign each student a president or various presidents to research. In their research, have students identify their president's main foreign policy goals, whether these goals were met during the president's term, and which of the U.S. foreign policy approaches were being followed. Students may wish to use the Biographies section on the *Holt Researcher Online* as they research. After students have finished, have them use a large sheet of paper to construct a grid identifying the foreign policy goals and approaches of each president. Display the finished chart in the classroom.

CLOSE

Ask students to look again at the foreign-policy goals they studied earlier in this section. Discuss how their view of these goals has changed and whether they feel that the goals are as valid now as they felt they were in the beginning of their study. Ask students to support their answers based on material from this section.

OPTIONS

Gifted/Intrapersonal Learners

 Assign students Reading 21: George Washington's Farewell Address that is found in *From the Source: Readings in Economics and Government with Answer Key.* Have them use standard grammar, spelling, sentence structure, and punctuation to write a paper about how U.S. foreign policy has adhered to or varied from the two main ideas of the address: as little political connection with other nations as possible and avoidance of permanent alliances. Have students write a paragraph stating specific instances in which foreign policy has met or varied from George Washington's expectations. Encourage students to identify specific factors, such as an increased dependence upon international trade, that they feel have altered U.S. foreign policy for better or for worse.

Students Having Difficulty/Sheltered English Students

 Have students make a chart with the top horizontal labels being the various U.S. foreign-policy goals and the left vertical labels the various principles of U.S. foreign policy. Ask students to place an X in each box where the goals and principles seem to match. Have students explain why they chose to place an X in each of these boxes.

REVIEW

Have students complete the Section 1 Review on page 221. Use the answers in the Annotated Teacher's Edition to assess student mastery of this section.

ASSESS

To assess student mastery of this section, have students complete Daily Quiz 10.1 in *Daily Quizzes with Answer Key.* For additional assessment options, see *Alternative Assessment Handbook* on the *One-Stop Planner CD-ROM.*

ADDITIONAL RESOURCES

Sellers, Mortimer, ed. *The New World Order: Sovereignty, Human Rights and the Self-Determination of Peoples.* 1996. Oxford Press.

The Development of U.S. Foreign Policy: World War I to Kennedy. Clearvue. (CD-ROM)

For more information about national security, see:
http://www.nsa.gov

LESSON 10.2 MAKING FOREIGN POLICY

TEXTBOOK PAGES 222–227

OBJECTIVES

▶ Explain why the executive branch has greater influence over foreign policy than does any other branch of government.

▶ Explain how the U.S. Department of State affects foreign policy decisions.

▶ Describe how the U.S. Department of Defense is organized according to the U.S. Constitution.

▶ Explain the roles of the Central Intelligence Agency and Congress in making foreign policy.

MOTIVATE

Organize the class into groups of four. Assign each student the role of either president, secretary of state, secretary of defense, or CIA director. Tell students to imagine that the president is seeking advice on how to conduct foreign policy toward a particular country that the United States may be having problems with. For example, students may choose China and may recreate the incident when the Chinese detained the crew of an American spy plane which was downed in China. Acting within their assigned role and within their groups, each student will present the president with the specifics of the foreign policy they are seeking in their situations. The president will decide what foreign-policy option to pursue and explain what arguments—made by advisers from the group—helped to shape the policy. Have the class reunite, and then explain to students that in this section they will study the need to balance various interests in foreign policy.

TEACH

Building a Vocabulary

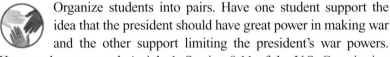

In their spiral notebooks, have students continue working on their Political Dictionary. List words the students will be expected to know for this section on the chalkboard. Have students list, define, and give an example of each of the terms, using information provided in the text or on the *Researcher CD-ROM.*

Evaluating Information/Navigating the Internet/Conducting Research

Organize the class into groups of three and assign a former U.S. president to each group. Tell students that their groups will assess their assigned president's involvement in foreign policy. Have each group chart the major events that occurred outside of the United States during their president's term. Encourage students to check out "The American Presidency" home page (http://www.grolier.com/presidents/preshome.html). Be sure students include events in which the United States was directly involved, and the president's reaction to the event. After creating their chart, students should briefly explain the foreign policy that the presidents followed and how it affected the events. Tell students that in the next activity they will be learning why the executive department has a greater influence on foreign policy than the legislative and judicial branches.

Analyzing Ideas/Debating Ideas

Organize students into pairs. Have one student support the idea that the president should have great power in making war and the other support limiting the president's war powers. Have students research Article 1, Section 8.11 of the U.S. Constitution and the War Powers Act of 1973 to gain some insight into the topic. Then have students debate the value of each position. Explain to students that the president's role as commander in chief of the armed forces and as representative of the nation (discussed in Chapter 7, section 1) has served to make the executive department the most influential branch in terms of creating foreign policy. Tell students that in the next activity they will be learning about the U.S. Department of State's role in foreign policy.

Role-Playing/Navigating the Internet

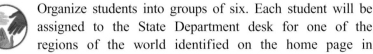

Organize students into groups of six. Each student will be assigned to the State Department desk for one of the regions of the world identified on the home page in (http://www.state.gov). Have students investigate the travel warnings in each region and what actions, if any, are currently being pursued by the

United States. Have each student argue for increasing the United States's role in their region, based on the events currently taking place there. Return to full class to discuss the travel warnings identified by the Department of State and whether the positions seem to be in line with the primary goals of U.S. foreign policy discussed in Section 1. Discuss with students the role of the State Department in determining foreign policy. Tell students that in the next activity they will be learning about the foreign-policy roles of the Department of Defense and the Central Intelligence Agency (CIA).

Creating Charts and Graphs/Navigating the Internet

 Ask half of the class to sign on to the Department of Defense Web site (http://www.defenselink.mil/sites/o.html organization) and then create a chart showing the various divisions of the department. Under each division, students should write a description of its function. Have the other half of the class do the same activity with the CIA Web site (http://www.cia.gov). Have each group explain their charts to the rest of the class; then discuss the role of these agencies with the class.

CLOSE

Ask students to recall the Motivate activity at the beginning of the section. Discuss whether the advice the presidents received from each participant seemed to be of equal importance at that time. Then ask students to apply the knowledge of foreign policy that they acquired during the study of this section to decide if the same participant was equally, less, or more important in the actual development of U.S. foreign policy. Have students write a few paragraphs explaining how each of the participants in the Motivate activity actually influence foreign policy.

OPTIONS

Gifted Learners

 Have students use standard grammar, spelling, sentence structure, and punctuation to write a paper about how Articles 1 and 2 of the U.S. Constitution deal with foreign policy. Students should discuss why the founders took the approach they did and why it is or is not effective today. Encourage students to share their opinions with the rest of the class.

Students Having Difficulty/Sheltered English Learners

 Have students use Articles 1 and 2 of the U.S. Constitution to make a chart showing what each branch of government can and cannot do in relation to foreign policy. Students should identify any current practices that seem to contradict the powers that the Articles give each branch in terms of foreign policy.

Linguistic Learners

Discuss with students the importance of having numerous officials work toward determining foreign policy. Encourage students to write a poem expressing their feelings about the importance of the United States maintaining peaceful relations with other countries. Poems should take into account the consequences of going to war with another country, the benefits of maintaining peaceful relations with other countries, and the importance of limiting one official's power when creating foreign policy. Allow time for volunteers to read their poems to the class and for the class to discuss the poems.

REVIEW

Have students complete the Section 2 Review on page 227. Use the answers in the Annotated Teacher's Edition to assess student mastery of this section.

ASSESS

To assess student mastery of this section, have students complete Daily Quiz 10.2 in *Daily Quizzes with Answer Key*. For additional assessment options, see *Alternative Assessment Handbook* on the *One-Stop Planner CD-ROM*.

ADDITIONAL RESOURCES

Dender, David, and Bruno Leone. *American Foreign Policy in Opposing Viewpoints Series*. 1993. Greenhaven Press.

Peterson, Paul E., ed. *The President, the Congress, and the Making of Foreign Policy*. 1994. University of Oklahoma Press.

LESSON 10.3 HISTORY OF U.S. FOREIGN POLICY

TEXTBOOK PAGES 228-233

HOLT PRESENTATION MAKER
Access Illustrated LECTURE
NOTES using Microsoft®
PowerPoint® on the
One-Stop Planner CD-ROM

OBJECTIVES

▶ Identify the principles that shaped U.S. leaders' foreign-policy decisions in the early years of the nation.
▶ Explain the policy of containment.
▶ Explain the significance of the expansion of communism on U.S. foreign policy.

MOTIVATE

Have students create a timeline on paper or on the board, noting the various historical events described in this section. Organize students into groups of four and ask each group to make a list of reasons why events influence other events. When the class is reassembled, discuss how events influence not only the time in which they occur but also events that occur later. Tell students that in this section they will study the historic development of U.S. foreign policy.

TEACH

Building a Vocabulary

In their spiral notebooks, have students continue working on their Political Dictionary. List words the students will be expected to know for this section on the board. Have students list, define, and give an example of each of the terms, using information provided in the text or on the *Researcher CD-ROM.*

Analyzing Ideas

Organize students into three groups. Assign each group one of the following: Reading 10: The Monroe Doctrine; Reading 15: the Truman Doctrine; or Reading 28: Woodrow Wilson's "Fourteen Points" speech, which are located in *From the Source: Readings in Economics and Government with Answer Key.* Have students as a group identify the principles of U.S. foreign policy that are discussed in these readings. Have each group form a consensus about how these doctrines have influenced later foreign policies. Encourage students to identify examples of U.S. actions that supported the princi-

ples of foreign policy addressed in these readings. Have each group share its ideas with the rest of the class. Tell students that in the next activity they will be introduced to the concept of the Cold War.

Identifying Cause and Effect/ Role-Playing/Navigating the Internet

Explain to students the rise of the Cold War and the growing fear of communism after World War II. Tell students that much of U.S. foreign policy was focused on the containment of communism. Have students identify various crises in Europe following World War II and write them on note cards. Organize students into groups of four. Two students should be assigned as diplomats from the United States and two from the former Soviet Union. Have students use the library and the Internet to gather information about the crises listed on the note cards. After identifying the cause of the major events they listed, each group should propose a solution based on the principles of U.S. foreign policy discussed in this section. Then groups should attempt to negotiate a settlement relying on their assigned positions for guidance. Following the negotiations, students should compare their solution to the actual outcome of the event. Each group should share its solutions with the class. Tell students that in the next activity they will be learning about the influence of Cold War events on U.S. foreign policy.

Hypothesizing/Predicting Outcome/ Acquiring Information

Have each student create a two-column chart. On one side of the chart, students should write in a major event of the Cold War (you may wish to give students a list of events to include), and on the other side students should write in the date or dates the event occurred. Have students study the chart to draw conclusions about why they think each event preceded the next event. Then have students as a class suggest what might have been the next event had the previous event's outcome been different. (For example, the Berlin airlift failed to provide West Berlin with enough supplies, and the city fell to the Soviet Union.) Afterward, discuss with the class the significance of the expansion of communism on U.S. foreign policy and how it led to containment.

CLOSE

Ask students to think about the various historical events that they studied in this section. Ask them to decide which of the events they believe was the most significant as a turning point in U.S. foreign relations. Then have students write a brief essay supporting their view. Be sure to have students support their reasoning with information presented in this chapter. Encourage students to share their opinions with the rest of the class. Stress to students that these events show the influence that the fear of communism had on U.S. foreign policy.

OPTIONS

Gifted Learners

Have students read about the Tonkin Gulf Resolution. Then have students discuss how it changed the president's powers in relation to those specified in the U.S. Constitution. After the discussion, have students use standard grammar, spelling, sentence structure, and punctuation to write a paper arguing for or against the powers allotted to the president in the resolution. Encourge students to list other presidential orders for the use of the military, issued without the consent of Congress, that have occurred since the Tonkin Gulf Resolution and to explain their point of view regarding whether these actions were justified.

Intrapersonal/Linguistic Learners

Encourage students to investigate the fear that filled the United States during the Cuban missile crisis. Encourage students to review newspaper articles from that time period or to interview adults who lived through the crisis to obtain information on the subject. Have students write a poem describing the national reaction to the Cuban missile crisis. Encourage students to share their poems with the rest of the class.

Students Having Difficulty

Ask students to review the material on World War I, World War II, the Korean War, and the Vietnam War in their textbook. Then have them make a chart listing the causes and results of each war. Ask them to identify what principles of U.S. foreign policy discussed throughout the chapter were involved in the U.S. leaders' decision to enter each of these wars.

REVIEW

Have students complete the Section 3 Review on page 233. Use the answers in the Annotated Teacher's Edition to assess student mastery of this section.

ASSESS

To assess student mastery of this section, have students complete Daily Quiz 10.3 in *Daily Quizzes with Answer Key*. For additional assessment options, see *Alternative Assessment Handbook* on the *One-Stop Planner CD-ROM*.

ADDITIONAL RESOURCES

Gaddis, John Lewis. *We Now Know: Rethinking Cold War History.* 1997. Oxford Press.

Lynch, Allen. *The Soviet Breakup and U.S. Foreign Policy. 1992.* Foreign Policy Association.

The History of U.S. Foreign Relations. U.S. Department of State. (video)

For documents relating to U.S. foreign policy before 1898, see: http://www.mtholyoke.edu/acad/intrel/pre1898.htm

OBJECTIVES

▶ Explain how providing foreign aid to other nations helps the United States.

▶ Identify the defense alliances that the United States maintains today.

▶ Explain how alliances and foreign-aid programs promote the public good.

MOTIVATE

Organize the class into groups of four. Have students produce a list of reasons why the United States would send military aid and economic support to industrialized nations, developing nations, and underdeveloped nations. Have students as a class look at the chart on textbook page 234 and discuss which category each of these nations falls into and the importance of each of these countries to the interests of the United States. Students may wish to use the Country Profiles section on the *Holt Researcher Online* to acquire information about each country's economic and political background. Tell students that in this section they will learn about the need to support other nations and why the United States forms alliances.

TEACH

Building a Vocabulary

In their spiral notebooks, have students continue working on their Political Dictionary. List words the students will be expected to know for this section on the board. Have students list, define, and give an example of each of the terms, using information provided in the text or on the *Researcher CD-ROM*.

Evaluating Ideas/Evaluating Information/ Identifying the Main Idea

Encourage students to sign on to the Cato Institute site (http://www.cato.org/) and other appropriate Web sites or use library resources about different views on foreign-aid policies of the United States. Students should create a list of the key arguments for and against

foreign policy. Once the list is complete, have students write a brief summary of the main arguments. Students should consider how they feel about foreign aid; if they would change U.S. foreign-aid policies; and if the current policies meet the goals of U.S. foreign policy discussed in the first section of this chapter. Discuss arguments for and against the use of foreign aid with the class. Explain to students that sometimes involvement with one nation can lead to conflicts with other nations. Tell students that in the next activity they will learn about the United States's defense alliances.

Understanding Maps/Using Maps/ Drawing Conclusions

Have students conduct research to identify countries that are currently allied with the United States. Have students label these countries on a world map, using a labeling scheme that identifies the member countries of the North Atlantic Treaty Organization and those of the Organization of American States. Students may wish to refer to the International Organizations section on the *Holt Researcher Online* to find out information about the purpose of both of these organizations. Discuss with students the reasons that the United States becomes involved in defense alliances and the potential problems associated with belonging to these alliances. Tell students that in the next activity they will examine alliances' affect on the public good.

Drawing Conclusions/Taking a Stand

Have students use information presented in this section to write a paper that discusses how alliances and foreign-aid promote the public good. Students may choose to support or reject the use of one or both of these foreign aid policies by the United States. Students can research additional events to offer support for their opinion. Once students have finished, create a table that identifies the number of students per classroom that are for and against each of these policies. Display this table for students and attempt to identify reasons for the differences in the number of students in each class who support and oppose each of them.

CLOSE

Organize students into the same groups of four as in the Motivate activity. Organize them to compare the reasons they listed at the beginning of the section for sending foreign aid to the countries that they have learned about in the study of this section. Have students identify and explain the differences in the reasons for granting foreign aid. Encourage students to discuss whether they feel the United States should be granting aid to the countries identified.

OPTIONS

Gifted Learners

 Have students use outside resources to create a list of the top 20 countries receiving U.S. foreign aid and the type of aid that each country receives. Have students use the Country Profiles section on the *Holt Researcher Online* to evaluate the importance of each nation to the United States and address the relationship between the amount of aid given and their importance to the United States.

Students Having Difficulty/ Sheltered English Students

 Give students a list of several examples of the United States providing foreign aid. The list should identify the problems the country receiving aid was having at the time. Have students identify which foreign policy goal(s) of the U.S. Agency for International Development the aid was meant to accomplish. Discuss these goals with the class. Encourage students to examine magazine and newspaper articles dealing with these countries to see if the aid being given is helping each country achieve the desired goal. Discuss these results as a class.

Logical-Mathematical Learners

 Discuss with students the concept of ranking foreign-aid contributions made by various countries based on the percentage of gross national product spent on foreign aid. This is discussed in the Comparing Governments feature in this section of the textbook. Encourage students to use the Country Profiles section on *Holt Researcher Online* and other resources to determine the percentage of several countries' gross national product spent on foreign aid. Assign a different country to each student. Then have the class create a list ranking all of the countries researched.

Gifted Learners

 Discuss Amnesty International and its attempts to ensure the fair treatment of people throughout the world. Have students access Amnesty International's Web site at (www. amnesty. org) to read about possible human rights violations that the organization has investigated. Organize the class into several groups and have each group read about a few of these instances. Then have each group report back to the class about the possible human rights violations. Encourage students to discuss whether these reports or others from similar types of organizations should influence the conduct of U.S. foreign policy, and if so, how.

REVIEW

Have students complete the Section 4 Review on page 238. Use the answers in the Annotated Teacher's Edition to assess student mastery of this section.

ASSESS

To assess student mastery of this section, have students complete Daily Quiz 10.4 in *Daily Quizzes with Answer Key*. For additional assessment options, see *Alternative Assessment Handbook* on the *One-Stop Planner CD-ROM*.

RETEACH

For students having difficulty with the lessons, have them complete Reteaching Activity 3. This activity is located in *Reteaching Activities with Answer Key*.

ADDITIONAL RESOURCES

Dender, David, and Bruno Leone. *Opposing Viewpoints Series: The New World Order.* 1991. Greenhaven Press.

Thompson, Kenneth, ed. *NATO and the Changing World Order: An Appraisal by Scholars and Policymakers.* 1996. University Press of America.

For information about NATO, see:
http://www.nato.int

GOVERNMENT NOTEBOOK

The Government Notebook is a journal activity that encourages students to consider basic concepts of government that relate to their lives. A follow-up notebook activity appears on page 240.

WHY IT MATTERS TODAY

To find additional lesson plans dealing with U.S. foreign policy today, visit CNNfyi.com or have students complete the GOVERNMENT IN THE NEWS activity on page 239.

CNNfyi.com

CHAPTER 10

FOREIGN POLICY AND NATIONAL SECURITY

The way the United States interacts with the rest of the world affects more of your daily life than you probably imagine. For example, the odds are very good that you have purchased products that were made in foreign countries. You were able to do so because the U.S. government's foreign-policy decisions help to maintain free and open trade with other nations. Are you hoping to visit a foreign country someday? Once again, your ability to do so hinges upon U.S. foreign policy. The goals and history of U.S. foreign policy, and what it means to you, are the focus of this chapter.

GOVERNMENT NOTEBOOK

In your Government Notebook, list as many ways in which countries interact as you can. How do you think the government goes about monitoring this interaction?

WHY IT MATTERS TODAY

The nation's economy and security both depend on a sound foreign policy. At the end of this chapter visit CNNfyi.com to learn more about American foreign policy.

CNNfyi.com

SECTION 1

GOALS AND PRINCIPLES OF U.S. FOREIGN POLICY

READ TO DISCOVER

1. What are the goals of U.S. foreign policy?
2. How do such factors as location or geographic characteristics affect U.S. policy toward a place?
3. What principles have historically guided U.S. foreign policy?

POLITICAL DICTIONARY

national security
trade embargo
isolationist
realism
internationalist
neoisolationist
idealism

The United States currently recognizes and maintains relations with more than 180 countries throughout the world. The U.S. government determines its interactions with these nations through foreign-policy decisions. As noted in Chapter 7, a nation's foreign policy is its plan for shaping economic, diplomatic, military, and political relationships with other countries. Historically, several basic goals and principles have guided U.S. foreign-policy decisions.

Foreign-Policy Goals

While the actual policies for maintaining foreign relations have changed dramatically, the fundamental goals of U.S. foreign policy have remained somewhat constant. These goals include maintaining national security, supporting democracy, promoting world peace, and providing aid to people in need. Since the mid-1930s, establishing free and open trade has become another goal of U.S.

foreign policy—as the United States trades goods and services with many of the world's nations.

Maintaining National Security The most important goal of U.S. foreign policy is to preserve **national security**—that is, to protect the rights, freedoms, and property of the United States and its people. The United States must consider national security foremost in foreign affairs.

Supporting Democracy As you know, since its creation the United States has been a democratic country. A strong belief in democracy often has led the United States to aid other democratic nations as well as those moving toward democracy.

Promoting World Peace U.S. foreign policy also is based on the goal of promoting and maintaining world peace. The more nations are at peace, the less likely the United States will be drawn into an existing conflict. To advance this goal, the United States sometimes becomes actively involved in resolving disputes between other countries.

Providing Aid to People in Need As a world leader, the United States often has assumed the responsibility of providing humanitarian and other relief to foreign countries. This aid might come in the form of money, food, or military assistance.

WORLD AFFAIRS *U.S. Secretary of State Colin Powell.* **Why is ensuring that other nations are at peace important to U.S. foreign-policy goals?**

SECTION 1

GOALS AND PRINCIPLES OF U.S. FOREIGN POLICY

Lesson Plans

For teaching strategies, see Lesson 10.1 located at the beginning of this chapter or the One-Stop Planner Strategy 10.1.

Political Dictionary

To reinforce the section's vocabulary terms, refer students to the Electronic Glossary on the *Researcher CD-ROM*

Section Assessment

To assess students' mastery of this section, have them complete Daily Quiz 10.1 in *Daily Quizzes with Answer Key.*

Caption Answer

The United States is less likely to become involved in conflicts if the world's nations are at peace.

WORLD AFFAIRS *In 1928 U.S. secretary of state Frank Kellogg signed the Kellogg-Briand Pact. All countries entering into this agreement officially renounced war as a foreign-policy tool.* **Why do you think that many countries signed this pact?**

In 1992, for example, the United States sent soldiers to Somalia to keep the food sent there by international relief organizations from being stolen by warlords. This type of support aids people in need and helps maintain stability in foreign countries.

Location has also played a prominent role in U.S. foreign policy. In the late 1800s U.S. interests in Cuba—90 miles off the coast of Florida—drew it into the Spanish-American war. Cuba's location again brought the United States into an international conflict during the Cuban missile crisis in 1962.

Establishing Free and Open Trade The nation's leaders have attempted to establish and maintain strong global economic ties through free trade—the exchange of goods and services across national borders without restrictions. For example, diplomatic relationships have been established in the Middle East to secure access to the rich oil reserves there.

Free trade's greatest economic benefits include increasing the size of the market to which domestic businesses can sell their goods and giving U.S. consumers a chance to buy goods from around the world. Politically, trade can also be a powerful tool. For example, from 1985 to 1991, the U.S. government used a **trade embargo**—a stoppage of commerce and trade—against South Africa to pressure that nation to end its practice of apartheid, a racially motivated political and economic segregation designed to ensure white minority rule.

Principles of Foreign Policy

The question of which basic principles should guide U.S. foreign policy has been controversial throughout the nation's history. In making foreign policy, two basic questions must be answered:

★ How active should the United States be in world affairs?
★ What guidelines should be used to evaluate U.S. activities abroad?

These questions have been answered in different ways at various points in U.S. history. In general, the United States has followed four basic approaches to foreign policy: isolationism, realism, neoisolationism, and idealism.

Isolationism The **isolationist** doctrine reflects the view that a nation should tend to its domestic affairs rather than to international affairs. Supporters of isolationism believe:

★ the United States has many domestic problems, and U.S. policy makers should focus on those exclusively;
★ most countries think primarily about their own interests, so the United States should too;
★ being in a militarily defensible location, the United States does not need to become involved in other nations' affairs; and

★ staying out of other countries' affairs will keep the United States out of war.

Isolationism was the main philosophy behind U.S. foreign policy during many periods of U.S. history, particularly during the 1800s and the 20 years between World War I and World War II. Since World War II, isolationism has had very little support among foreign-policy scholars or policy makers in Washington, as it became less practical in the post–World War II world.

Realism Some of the most serious criticisms of isolationism have come from backers of **realism**, which has been probably the most dominant U.S. foreign-policy doctrine since World War II. Realists and isolationists both believe that U.S. foreign policy should be evaluated by how well it promotes U.S. national interests. However, realists believe that the U.S. national interest is best promoted by an **internationalist** approach—the taking of an active role in international affairs. Realists believe that this approach should include military intervention when necessary. U.S. interests include national security as well as international trade relations.

Realists believe that isolationism ignores the reality of world affairs. They say that many countries are dangerous and are ruled by aggressive leaders trying to dominate other countries. In addition, realists say that because no world government exists to resolve international disputes satisfactorily, a nation's only tool for stopping an aggressive country is action—alone or in alliance with like-minded nations.

Thus, realists conclude that by avoiding participation in world affairs, the United States could become a victim of another nation's aggression. They argue that the United States must be strong and prepared for war, thereby achieving peace by scaring off aggressors.

Finally, some realists argue that the United States must

sometimes use force simply to show that it is militarily strong. A refusal to act in a certain situation might cause potential aggressors to believe that the United States is unable to defend itself. At the same time, realists hold that for the most part the United States should not use force unless vital national interests—such as national security or opportunities to trade with other countries—are at stake.

In the view of realists, vital interests matter more than similar belief systems when it comes to choosing alliances with other nations. The United States's primary goal should be to gain allies that are militarily strong and strategically located and that can help in preventing the expansion of hostile countries. According to this view, the United States should not hesitate to ally itself with countries whose values may differ from U.S. values or to oppose countries, if necessary, whose values it shares. For this reason, realism is sometimes called power politics or realpolitik, which means "realist politics."

Neoisolationism People who adhere to the **neoisolationist** doctrine think that the United

WORLD AFFAIRS *Secretary of State Cordell Hull (third from left) led the U.S. delegation to the 1933 Pan American Conference in Uruguay. At the conference, U.S. leaders declared that the United States would not intervene in South American politics.* **Why do some people argue that the United States should stay out of other countries' affairs?**

CULTURAL PERSPECTIVES

The German word *Realpolitik* is often used in discussing the principle of realism in foreign policy. The term was first used in 1853 by a German writer critical of liberal policies, and it gained prominence during the unification of Germany in the nineteenth century. Europeans and Americans, however, use the word with different meanings. In Europe, *Realpolitik* means a foreign policy based on the use of power. In the United States it refers to a very practical foreign policy based on vital interests and does not necessarily refer to the use of pressure and military might to achieve policy goals. ■

Caption Answer

Students might suggest either isolationist arguments covered in this section or an explanation of their own reasoning.

Enhancing the Lesson

For more information about isolationism, see George Washington's Farewell Address, located in *From the Source: Readings in Economics and Government with Answer Key.*

HISTORY During his administration, President Jimmy Carter included the idealistic goal of improving human rights in his foreign-policy agenda. Carter's policies drew international attention to human rights violations in many countries, most notably the Soviet Union, South Africa, Cambodia, and certain countries in Latin America. These countries could no longer abuse people's rights without fear of negative publicity and international consequences. ∎

Caption Answer

They object to tyranny and injustice and believe that the United States should support democratic values everywhere.

Caption Answer

(for page 221) Answers will vary but students should exhibit knowledge of each of these views.

SECTION 1
REVIEW ANSWERS

1. Refer to the following pages: national security (217), trade embargo (218), isolationist (218), realism (219), internationalist (219), neoisolationist (219), idealism (220).

(Continued on page 221)

States should keep its foreign involvement to a minimum, not only for the good of the United States but also because such involvement is likely to be bad for other nations in whose affairs the United States would intervene. The prefix *neo,* or new, serves to distinguish this doctrine from traditional isolationism, which focuses only on the interests of the United States.

In support of their view, neoisolationists cite several U.S.-backed governments in the 1960s and 1970s, saying that they did not have popular support. Even when the motives behind the support were good, neoisolationists argue, it failed to help most people in those countries. Neoisolationists believe that the United States should not interfere in other countries' internal affairs—a principle called noninterference. They argue that even people being kept down by oppressors should be left to attempt to overthrow their rulers without outside help. They warn that the people of a small country may resent a strong foreign government's intervention in their affairs, even if it is acting against the domestic oppressor.

Finally, neoisolationists believe that it is ethically necessary to avoid war. In their view, to engage in involvement in another nation's affairs not only violates the rights of that nation's people but also may lead to war.

Idealism Supporters of the doctrine of **idealism** argue for an internationalist foreign policy, but unlike realists, their internationalist motivations are based on what is good for other countries as well as for the United States. They believe that decision makers should take into account the interests and rights of people both inside and outside the United States. Idealists oppose injustice and tyranny around the world and believe that the U.S. government should support democratic values everywhere. Although to a lesser extent than realism, idealism has heavily influenced U.S. foreign policy. For example, the United States has acted many times to put a stop to violations of human rights, as in Haiti in 1994.

Idealists tend to work for international cooperation as well as for economic and humanitarian assistance to less-fortunate foreign countries. They also support efforts to promote friendship and cooperation across borders, particularly among nations sharing democratic values.

Like neoisolationists, but unlike realists, idealists believe that supporting tyrannical governments is wrong—even when doing so might protect the nation's vital interests. Idealists argue that support for tyrannical governments in a world where many people strongly believe in humanitarian ideals is likely to both make enemies abroad and reduce support for an active foreign policy within the United States.

Finally, idealists believe that U.S. foreign policy should protect American ideals. In particular, the actions of the United States should be associated with defense of human rights.

Some idealists are less inclined to support the use of force than are realists, instead preferring nonmilitary international action, such as economic boycotts or the withholding of economic aid from nations with tyrannical governments. Other idealists support U.S.

PUBLIC GOOD *Protesters in Hartford, Connecticut, demonstrate against U.S. military action in Afghanistan in October, 2001. **Why do idealists believe that foreign-policy makers should take into account the interests of people both inside and outside of the United States?***

military action in foreign countries, perhaps even more readily than realists, because they are willing to use force to stop injustice and not just to protect vital national interests.

During the 1990s the United States was involved in Somalia, Bosnia, and Haiti. All of these countries were of little military or economic importance to the United States but their people were suffering. Isolationists, neoisolationists, and most realists opposed the U.S. actions there, but idealists supported them.

U.S. Foreign Policy and the Public Good

Although there are plenty of exceptions, Republicans today are generally either realists or isolationists, while Democrats generally are either neoisolationists or idealists. Each of these foreign-policy principles has a limited scope, so the public good is often best promoted by making trade-offs among them. Idealism tends to focus on ethics in U.S. foreign policy, but it could be argued that it would be foolish not to support a strategically located foreign government—even if its values were not the same as Americans' values— if this would stop a worse aggressor from taking

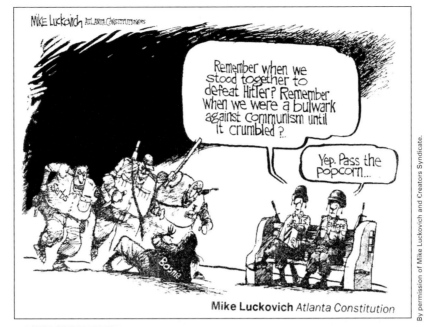

Mike Luckovich *Atlanta Constitution*

By permission of Mike Luckovich and Creators Syndicate.

WORLD AFFAIRS *The cartoon above portrays the United States and Europe as uninterested bystanders rather than as a bulwark, or strong protection, against the abuse of people's rights in other countries.* **Why do you think U.S. involvement in Bosnia was opposed by isolationists, neoisolationists, and most realists?**

over other nations. Such an argument would, however, violate strict idealist principles.

Similarly, isolationists and neoisolationists stress the cost and horror of war, but many people believe that the United States could pay a heavy price for allowing others to dominate the world. On the other hand, some foreign-policy analysts suggest that force should be used only when it would serve a vital national interest *and* a moral cause.

(Continued from page 220)

2. Students should mention: maintaining national security, supporting democracy, promoting world peace, providing aid to people in need, and establishing free and open trade.

3a. Realism promotes the belief that the United States must be strong and active in world affairs to protect itself. Idealism promotes the belief that the United States must be cooperative and benevolent in world affairs. Both principles argue for an internationalist approach to foreign policy.

3b. Answers will vary. Students might suggest that location and geographical characteristics can influence U.S. foreign policy toward a nation.

4. Answers will vary, but should reflect an understanding of the various principles that have influenced U.S. foreign policy.

SECTION 1 REVIEW

1. Identify and Explain:
- national security
- trade embargo
- isolationist
- realism
- internationalist
- neoisolationist
- idealism

Homework Practice Online
keyword: SV3 HP10

2. Identifying Concepts: Copy the graphic organizer below. Use it to list the goals of U.S. foreign policy.

U.S. Foreign Policy →

Goals
1.
2.
3.
4.
5.

3. **Finding the Main Idea**

a. What is the principle of realism? How does it differ from idealism? How is it similar?

b. What are some factors that can influence U.S. policy toward a nation?

4. **Writing and Critical Thinking**

Drawing Conclusions: What should be the guiding principle of U.S. foreign policy?
Consider the following:
- the goals of U.S. foreign policy
- the role of public opinion in foreign policy

SECTION 2

MAKING FOREIGN POLICY

READ TO DISCOVER

1. Why does the executive branch have the greatest influence over foreign policy?
2. How does the U.S. Department of State affect foreign policy?
3. How is the U.S. Department of Defense organized?
4. What are the roles of the Central Intelligence Agency and Congress in making foreign policy?

POLITICAL DICTIONARY

presidential doctrine
summit conference
embassy
consulate
ambassador
consul
Foreign Service
passport
visa

The executive branch generally takes the most influential role in foreign-policy decision making. The main figures within the executive branch that have influential foreign-policy roles are the president, the Departments of State and Defense, and the Central Intelligence Agency. In addition, the National Security Council plays an important role in coordinating activities that involve national security.

Role of the President

The president generally is considered the nation's most influential foreign-policy decision maker. This influence comes from several sources.

Influence Through General Acceptance
Much of the president's control over foreign policy comes from the general acceptance that presidential influence in this area is appropriate. That is, both the people of the United States and the U.S. Congress generally have accepted that the president should assume the leading role in matters of foreign policy. This has happened for various reasons.

As noted in Chapter 7, the primary reason that the people and Congress have allowed the president to assume this authority is that dealing with foreign governments and international crises often requires decisiveness and speed. A president can respond more quickly than can a large body such as Congress.

Even when urgency is not an issue, Congress generally has accepted presidential influence over foreign policy. For example, of the five declarations of war in U.S. history, only two (War of 1812 and the Spanish-American War) were initiated by Congress. The others (the Mexican War, World War I, and World War II) were initially requested by the president. As the country's top nationally-elected official, the president is typically regarded as the most appropriate national spokesperson in foreign affairs.

Presidents also have asserted their leadership in foreign policy by issuing foreign-policy statements. These **presidential doctrines** do not pass

WORLD AFFAIRS *President George W. Bush attends the first working session of the 2001 G8 summit in Genoa, Italy.* **Why has the president assumed the leading role in matters regarding foreign policy?**

through the legislative process and are intended to set the direction of foreign policy. Such doctrines do not have the force of law, so specific steps to carry them out must be taken through legislation or budgetary appropriations. Presidential doctrines do set a strong guideline for future decisions, however. Similarly, presidents may hold **summit conferences**—meetings between the heads of state of two or more nations. The statements made or understandings reached at these meetings do not have the force of law, but they do strongly influence public debate.

Influence As Commander in Chief As commander in chief, the president can make important foreign-policy decisions. In this capacity, presidents also can undertake military action in times of crisis without seeking congressional approval.

Presidents have used this power not only in ordering short-term military strikes but also in committing military forces to serve in what have been called undeclared wars. Undeclared wars, such as the Korean War and the Vietnam War, are longer military actions that are undertaken without an official congressional declaration of war. In addition to these two longer actions, the United States has engaged in more than 100 limited military actions.

Influence Through Executive Agreements As noted in Chapter 7, presidents also can negotiate executive agreements—formal understandings with foreign governments. These agreements do not require ratification by the Senate. Generally, such agreements have been minor, often involving implementation details on already signed treaties. However, there have been significant exceptions. Examples from the 1900s include President Franklin Roosevelt's trading 50 aging destroyers to British prime minister Winston Churchill for 50 air bases in British territory in the Western Hemisphere in 1940, before U.S. entry into World War II. Another example is the General Agreement on Tariffs and Trade (GATT)—trade agreements among most of the world's nations—which began in 1947.

Role of the U.S. Department of State

The U.S. Constitution gives the president the authority, with the advice and consent of the Senate, to make treaties, appoint diplomatic officials, and receive foreign delegates. To help the president execute these duties, Congress established the U.S. Department of State in 1789. The head of the State Department, the secretary of state, is the highest-ranking member of the cabinet and fourth in line for presidential succession.

The mission of the State Department is to promote good relations between the United States and other countries. The State Department generally opposes the use of force to solve serious conflicts, preferring to make every possible effort at diplomacy. The department is responsible for maintaining diplomatic relations with approximately 180 countries throughout the world. Included in its duties are establishing and maintaining **embassies,** or diplomatic centers, and **consulates,** which deal with U.S. commercial interests. The department also issues passports and visas.

Organization and Structure The State Department is organized into bureaus dealing with U.S. relations with specific regions of the world (Europe and Canada, East Asia and the Pacific, the Middle East and South Asia, Africa, and Latin America) and bureaus dealing with foreign-policy issues including human rights, drug trafficking,

WORLD AFFAIRS *This building of unusual design is the U.S. embassy in Lima, Peru.* **Why does the United States maintain embassies in other countries?**

THEMES IN GOVERNMENT

WORLD AFFAIRS The Department of State—the executive branch department concerned with foreign policy—is organized into a number of bureaus and agencies. The Bureau of Oceans and International Environmental and Scientific Affairs coordinates policies on issues such as marine conservation and cooperation of commercial interests in space. The Bureau of Population, Refugees, and Migration helps develop reproductive health service programs and assists refugees who relocate to the United States. The Bureau for International Narcotics and Law Enforcement Affairs works to stop the illegal international drug trade. These bureaus and others like them reflect the many foreign-policy issues that are the responsibility of the State Department. ■

Caption Answer

The United States maintains embassies to inform the U.S. government of events in each country, explain U.S. laws to the host country, transmit official communications, and negotiate agreements with the host country.

Foreign-Service Officer

In her long career in the Foreign Service, Ruth Davis—the former principal deputy assistant for consular affairs and a former U.S. ambassador to the African nation of Benin—has met with major international figures and seen the world. Not only has she chatted with King Juan Carlos of Spain and dined with opera singer Luciano Pavarotti, she has also traveled to Tokyo to help make the final bid for holding the 1996 Olympic Games in Atlanta, Georgia. Foreign-service officers (FSOs) like Davis get an insider's look at other governments and cultures while helping to shape and carry out U.S. foreign policy.

Applicants to the foreign service must pass a series of difficult tests to become officers. The written portion of the foreign-service examination tests the applicant's knowledge of U.S. and world history, government, economics, and English grammar. An all-day oral exam, a thorough background check, and a medical examination also are required.

Though a college education is not mandatory, most FSOs have a bachelor's degree, and more than half have earned advanced degrees. College courses in economics, history, government, geography, literature, business, environmental studies, and foreign languages are recommended for potential officers.

Those accepted into the Foreign Service go through orientation and months of training, including language courses, before their first two- to four-year tour overseas. To advance in the service, officers must work at a consulate or embassy and show fluency in at least one foreign language. Officers later choose to specialize in administrative, consular, economic, or political areas. FSOs usually alternate tours of duty overseas with short-term assignments in Washington, D.C.

Once overseas, the main duties of FSOs include collecting data, writing reports, and meeting with key officials. Embassy staffers develop and maintain close contacts with government officials, educators, the media, and business and community leaders in their host countries. These contacts help the officers collect reliable information and gain cultural insights inaccessible to most other Americans.

Officers in the Foreign Service go through extensive training to gain the skills necessary to be diplomatic representatives of the United States.

international economic and business affairs, and environmental and scientific matters.

Maintaining Embassies and Consulates One main duty of the State Department is to organize and maintain offices abroad. The United States maintains embassies in about 130 foreign countries. An **ambassador** is the chief diplomatic official at each embassy. He or she acts as a personal representative of the U.S. president. Ambassadors usually are appointed based on their foreign-service records. In many cases, however, they are political appointees, receiving their posts as a reward for supporting the president or a particular political party.

The embassy staffs assist the ambassadors in executing their duties. These duties include keeping the United States informed of events in, and explaining U.S. laws and policies to, the host country, as well as transmitting official communications and negotiating diplomatic agreements between the two countries.

To protect U.S. commercial interests in foreign countries, the United States maintains consulates in many of the world's major commercial centers.

Each consulate is headed by a **consul**, who also is appointed by the president and confirmed by the Senate. Consuls' primary goals are to promote U.S. trade and commerce and assist American citizens with travel-related matters or other problems. They also issue immigration and tourist visas to travelers to the United States.

The State Department maintains a staff of nearly 28,000 employees. Of those, more than 17,000 work at U.S. embassies and consulates around the world. The men and women of the State Department who serve abroad form what is called the **Foreign Service**.

POLITICAL PROCESSES *Controlling and coordinating all the branches of the armed forces of the United States is a complex task. To facilitate this process, the National Security Amendments of 1949 delegated authority over the armed forces to the Department of Defense. Secretary of Defense Donald Rumsfeld, seen here, organizes the efforts of the Army, Navy, and Air Force, and supervises all U.S. military activities around the world.* **Where are the Department of Defense's headquarters located?**

Issuing Passports and Visas A **passport** is a formal document issued by a government to one of its citizens for travel to other countries. The State Department is responsible for issuing passports to U.S. citizens. No citizen may legally leave the United States—except for trips to Mexico, Canada, and some other nearby nations—without a passport. In addition, most countries will not allow travellers to enter without displaying a valid passport. A passport entitles a person to all of the privileges established by international laws and treaties.

Another responsibility belonging to the State Department is issuing **visas**—seals that are placed on foreign passports and that entitle their holder to enter the United States. The U.S. government requires that all visitors to the United States obtain a visa. Many other countries around the world, however, require only a passport.

Role of the U.S. Department of Defense

The State Department supervises all of the diplomatic activities of the United States. The supervision of U.S. military activities, however, is handled by the Department of Defense.

To maintain the U.S. military, Congress established the War Department as one of the three original executive departments during George Washington's first term as president. In 1797 the Navy Department was established, and national defense functions were divided between the War Department and the Navy Department until the 1940s. The National Security Act amendments of 1949 placed all branches of the armed forces under the authority of one government office, called the U.S. Department of Defense (DOD). The DOD is headed by a secretary of defense, with individual secretaries supervising the Army, Navy, and Air Force.

Organization of the DOD The DOD is a huge establishment with global responsibilities. Its headquarters are in the Pentagon, a massive building that covers around 34 acres outside of Washington, D.C. It employs almost 700,000 civilians and nearly 1.4 million members of the armed forces.

The DOD is not only larger than any other department, but it also must follow the strictest

Caption Answer

The Department of Defense is housed in the Pentagon.

Enhancing the Lesson

For more information about the Department of Defense, see the Executive Departments section on the *Holt Researcher Online.*

The Constitution requires Congress to oversee the activities of the executive branch. In the case of the Central Intelligence Agency (CIA), however, oversight can become a complicated issue. Members of Congress have to balance the needs of a democracy against national security issues. Because many CIA activities are secret, congressional reviews of agency activities might reveal secrets that are vital to national security. On the other hand, the failure to conduct thorough oversight of CIA activities might lead to the overlooking of abuses, including violations of U.S. law. This creates special problems for investigating the CIA. ∎

Caption Answer

Framers of the Constitution feared a military state and thus made the military subject to civilian authority.

Transparency

An overhead transparency of the cartoon on the next page is available in *Transparency Resources*. See Cartoon Transparency 9: Commander in Chief.

guidelines. This is because the framers of the Constitution were well aware of the dangers that could result from a military state. That is, if the military were to take control of the government, the ideals of democracy might be jeopardized. To prevent the nation's military from interfering with free government, the framers determined that the military would be under civilian control.

As you know, the Constitution states that the president is the commander in chief of all U.S. armed forces. The secretary of defense, the deputy secretary, and the secretaries of the three armed services are all civilians, as are most of their staff. Thus, the military is at all times subject to civilian authority.

Joint Chiefs of Staff Although the DOD is headed by civilian leaders, recommendations about military actions come from military advisers. The most influential military advisers in the United States are the members of the Joint Chiefs of Staff. The president, the vice president, and the secretaries of defense and state seek consultation on military matters from this group on a regular basis.

The group includes only five people: the chair, the Army chief of staff, the chief of naval operations, the Air Force chief of staff, and the Marine

PUBLIC GOOD *The Joint Chiefs of Staff, shown here in 2000, frequently consult with the president and other executive officials on military matters.* **Why is the Department of Defense not headed by a military leader?**

Corps commandant, who is present only when Marine Corps matters are at issue. The chair is selected by the president and serves as the nation's top military officer.

Role of the Central Intelligence Agency

Foreign-policy decisions are sometimes made with the aid of information gathered by the Central Intelligence Agency (CIA), which Congress created by the National Security Act of 1947. Congress's goal was to create a single organization responsible for providing the president with foreign intelligence—information about the activities of other governments. Broadly speaking, the CIA, which is an independent government agency within the executive branch, undertakes three kinds of activities: gathering information related to national security, analyzing that information, and briefing the president and the National Security Council (NSC) on its findings. In addition, the CIA sometimes engages in covert, or secret, operations. Covert operations are efforts to promote U.S. foreign-policy goals through sometimes unconventional means, such as by supporting political parties or rebel factions in other countries. Covert actions are controversial and are often supported by realists but opposed by idealists and neoisolationists.

One major task of the CIA is to predict for policy makers how foreign governments will behave and what their defense capabilities are. For example, the CIA might attempt to predict whether Russia's government will remain stable and friendly, or to determine if North Korea has nuclear weapons. To analyze these situations, the CIA uses both open sources (including foreign newspapers and consultations with academic experts) and secret intelligence operations.

National Security Council

As noted in Chapter 8, the National Security Council (NSC) was set up in 1947 to improve coordination among the government departments that deal with national security issues—in particular the CIA and the Departments of State and Defense. A national security adviser, who is appointed by the president, heads the NSC staff, which is part of the Executive Office of the President.

WILSON PULLS LAGGARD CONGRESS INTO PREPAREDNESS
Kirby in the New York *World*, 1916

POLITICAL PROCESSES *In 1917 President Woodrow Wilson asked Congress for a declaration of war against Germany. The cartoon above illustrates the reluctance of Congress to organize for and declare war.* **How has Congress's power to declare war been undercut in the past?**

Role of Congress

As you have read, the executive branch assumes the greatest responsibility for foreign policy. The Constitution, however, grants crucial foreign-policy powers to Congress. These powers include the power to declare war, appropriate money for national defense, and ratify treaties.

Declaring War The U.S. Constitution balances the president's power as commander in chief with Congress's power "to declare war," "to raise and support armies," and "to provide and maintain a navy." However, as noted, the United States has had two major undeclared wars and more than 100 limited military engagements that were not declared by Congress. Thus, Congress's constitutional power to declare war has in many ways been undercut.

Appropriating Money Congress's greatest source of influence in foreign-policy making lies in its constitutional authority to appropriate government funds. Congress has the final authority over the funding of government services—including national defense. Likewise, Congress is responsible for any appropriations related to financial aid to foreign countries.

Ratifying Treaties According to the Constitution, the president must seek the "advice and consent" of the Senate in making treaties with foreign countries. Altough the president often negotiates treaties without the benefit of congressional advice, treaties only become official with Senate approval by at least a two-thirds vote.

Confirming Appointments The final constitutional foreign-policy power granted to Congress involves the confirmation of the president's diplomatic appointments. Article II of the Constitution states that presidential foreign-affairs appointments, such as those for consuls and ambassadors, must be approved by the Senate. This power is another check on the actions of the president.

SECTION 2 REVIEW

1. Identify and Explain:
- presidential doctrine
- summit conference
- embassy
- consulate
- ambassador
- consul
- Foreign Service
- passport
- visa

2. Identifying Concepts: Copy the graphic organizer below. Use it to show how the president gains influence over foreign policy.

general acceptance	→	
role as Commander in Chief	→	
executive agreements	→	

Homework Practice Online
keyword: SV3 HP10

3. Finding the Main Idea

a. Why does the Constitution place the Department of Defense under non-military control?
b. How do the U.S Department of State and the CIA influence foreign policy?

4. Writing and Critical Thinking

Supporting a Point of View: Who should have the most influence over foreign policy?
Consider the following:
- reasons the executive branch has the most influence over foreign policy
- influences Congress can have on foreign policy

SECTION 2 REVIEW ANSWERS

1. Refer to the following pages: presidential doctrine (222), summit conference (223), embassy (223), consulate (223), ambassador (224), consul (225), Foreign Service (225), passport (225), visa (225).

2. General acceptance—the people and Congress believe that the president should take the lead in foreign policy; role as Commander in Chief—the president controls the military, an important aspect of foreign policy; executive agreements—presidents can negotiate with foreign governments without Congressional approval.

3a. The framers of the Constitution placed the DOD under civilian control because they feared a military state.

3h. The State Department aims to maintain good relations with other countries through diplomacy. The CIA gathers information on foreign governments.

4. Answers will vary. Some students might mention that the executive's influence over foreign policy is justified. Other students might mention that other branches of government should have more input.

SECTION 3

HISTORY OF U.S. FOREIGN POLICY

Lesson Plans

For teaching strategies, see Lesson 10.3 located at the beginning of this chapter.

Political Dictionary

To reinforce the section's vocabulary terms, refer students to the Electronic Glossary on the *Researcher CD-ROM.*

Section Assessment

To assess students' mastery of this section, have them complete Daily Quiz 10.3 in *Daily Quizzes with Answer Key.*

Enhancing the Lesson

For more information about the Monroe Doctrine, see the Monroe Doctrine Reading in *From the Source: Readings in Economics and Government with Answer Key.*

Caption Answer

The United States gained overseas territory and emerged as a world power.

SECTION 3

HISTORY OF U.S. FOREIGN POLICY

READ TO DISCOVER

1. What principle shaped leaders' foreign-policy decisions in the early years of the United States?
2. What is containment?
3. What significance did the expansion of communism have on U.S. foreign policy?

POLITICAL DICTIONARY

Monroe Doctrine
Truman Doctrine
containment
détente
glasnost
perestroika

As noted in Section 1, U.S. foreign policy historically has been based on four basic approaches—isolationism, realism, neoisolationism, and idealism. How the United States turns these principles into policy, however, has changed dramatically over the past 200 years, as has its role in the world.

Isolationist Policies

During the 1800s the United States was a minor participant in world affairs. Foreign policy during this period was based on neutrality in European wars, a principle that was formally established by President Washington in his Farewell Address in 1796.

In 1823 the **Monroe Doctrine** turned this principle of neutrality into an official foreign-policy agenda. The doctrine also stated, however, that the United States would not tolerate European interference in the Americas:

❝ The American continents, by the free and independent condition which they have assumed and maintain, are henceforth not to be considered as subjects for future colonization by any European powers. . . . We should consider any attempt on their part to extend their system to any portion of this hemisphere as dangerous to our peace and safety. ❞

Rise to World Power

By the late 1800s the United States had become one of the most important industrialized nations in the world. As companies produced increasing numbers of goods, the desire for global markets and international relationships became evident. The United States began pulling away from its isolationist policies and embracing the principles of internationalism. As the rest of the world became more important to the United States, Americans became interested in preserving stability in other nations. This shift to international involvement began with the Spanish-American War, which redefined the United State's role in the world.

POLITICAL FOUNDATIONS *The Spanish-American War, fought in the Philippines and Cuba, marked a turning point in foreign affairs.* **How did the Spanish-American War change U.S. foreign policy?**

Spanish-American War of 1898 Although it lasted a mere four months, the Spanish-American War of 1898 was a turning point in U.S. history. Cubans, discontented with Spanish rule, were in rebellion. Stories of Spain's brutal treatment of Cuban civilians, together with the sinking of the *Maine*—a U.S. ship that had been based in Cuba to protect U.S. interests—led the United States to declare war on Spain in April 1898. U.S. involvement in the war reflected both idealist principles—American sympathy with the struggle for Cuban independence—and realist principles—growing support for U.S. expansion in other areas of the world.

The U.S. victory was decisive, winning independence for Cuba and possession of Guam, Puerto Rico, and the Philippines for the United States. Having gained control of overseas territories, the United States emerged from the war as a world power.

World War I After the Spanish-American War, the United States attempted to return to its isolationist policies in its dealings with Europe. The outbreak of war in Europe in 1914, however, threatened all U.S. foreign-policy goals, particularly that of promoting democracy. President Woodrow Wilson, an idealist, saw the European war as a struggle between the democracy of Britain and the monarchy of Germany. In his words, it was a war to make the world "safe for democracy." He argued that a peace settlement should be followed by the creation of a League of Nations, an international organization dedicated to stopping further aggression. President Wilson hoped that the establishment of the league would make World War I the last of its kind.

Leaders of America's European allies had a different idea. They used victory to claim territory and repayment from the defeated nations, rather than making the world democratic or ending war. The League of Nations was created, but the U.S. Senate rejected U.S. membership in it in an effort to return the country to an isolationist era. The United States then returned to practicing isolationist principles—at least until until December 1941.

World War II Realists and idealists supported U.S. involvement in World War II from the beginning. Germany and Japan were militarily aggressive and posed a possible threat to U.S. security. In addition, both nations had oppressive governments. Some isolationists, however, remembering the brutality of World War I, denounced U.S. involvement. Attempting to respect these sentiments, President Franklin Roosevelt announced U.S. neutrality at the war's outbreak but in fact supported the Allied cause in many ways.

When Japanese planes attacked the U.S. naval base at Pearl Harbor, in the Hawaiian Islands, on December 7, 1941, President Roosevelt called for a declaration of war on Japan, and Congress issued it. The United States and the other Allies won the war in 1945. The war left Europe in ruins, while no fighting took place on the U.S. mainland, leaving the United States the most powerful nation in the world. This position was enhanced by the development of the atomic bomb by American scientists, giving the nation unmatched military technology.

Cold War

As noted in Section 1, one goal of U.S. foreign policy is to promote democracy. Another goal is national security, which may be jeopardized by powers opposing U.S. interests. At the end of World War II, the Soviet Union threatened the realization of these goals. As a result, U.S.-Soviet relations became so strained that one speechwriter coined the term *Cold War* to describe the hostility between the two nations.

Origins of the Cold War At the end of World War II, the Soviet Union, in part because it feared the emergence of a strong postwar Germany, used its troops to establish control over Eastern Europe and the eastern part of Germany. To consolidate their control, the Soviets set up governments based on communism—a political and economic philosophy that puts government in control over a nation's industries and farms, as well as over most aspects of citizens' lives. (The ideas of communism are more fully explained in Chapter 22.)

In March 1947 President Harry Truman issued a "declaration" of the Cold War. In a speech that set forth what came to be known as the **Truman Doctrine**, Truman announced a basic U.S. foreign-policy strategy that would remain in place for the next 40 years—**containment**. Containment reflected idealist and realist principles and was based on the view that communism threatened democratic values and that Soviet expansion must be stopped.

Caption Answer

Answers will vary, but students should point out that the U.S. goal of stopping the spread of communism required action on many fronts.

ACROSS THE CURRICULUM

HISTORY President Dwight D. Eisenhower faced a Cold War crisis with China that began in 1954 and continued into 1955. Communist Chinese forces had begun shelling the tiny islands of Quemay and Matsu, which are off the coast of China and were under the control of Taiwan, a U.S. ally. The president and his secretary of state both publicly stated that the United States might use nuclear weapons if the Communists attacked in the Taiwan Strait, which is located between China and Taiwan. Worried about this threat, the Communists began talks with U.S. diplomats and stopped shelling the islands. President Eisenhower had used his position as commander in chief to ease tensions that otherwise might have led to war. ■

Major Events of the Cold War

1947	• President Truman issues a declaration known as the Truman Doctrine, establishing containment as the primary goal of U.S. foreign policy.
1949	• The Soviet Union takes complete control of Eastern Europe. • The Soviet Union explodes an atomic bomb. • Chinese Communists led by Mao Zedong win control of China.
1950	• The Korean War begins when North Korea invades South Korea.
1959	• Rebels led by Fidel Castro gain control of Cuba and seek help from the Soviet Union.
1961–73	• U.S. troops fight in the Vietnam War in an effort to support the noncommunist South Vietnamese government.
1962	• The Soviet Union secretly installs nuclear weapons in Cuba.
1972	• Nixon becomes the first U.S. president to visit China. • Nixon and Brezhnev negotiate the first Strategic Arms Limitation Talks (SALT I) agreement.
1987	• Mikhail Gorbachev initiates a series of reforms known as glasnost and perestroika.
1989	• East Germany announces it will dismantle the Berlin Wall.
1991	• The Soviet Union dissolves.

Many critical events occurred during the period of hostility between the United States and the Soviet Union known as the Cold War. **Why was the United States involved in military conflicts in several foreign countries during the Cold War?**

The primary goal of containment was to keep the Soviet Union from setting up communist governments outside of Eastern Europe. Containment was based on the theory that if Soviet expansion could be stopped, communism might eventually collapse.

By 1949 the Soviet Union had taken control of Eastern Europe. Previously, U.S. leaders had taken some comfort in knowing that the United States was the only nation possessing nuclear weapons. This feeling of security was not to last. In September 1949 President Truman announced that the Soviet Union had exploded an atomic bomb. The two most powerful nations in the world had now joined an atomic arms race that would lead to fears of global nuclear war. Preventing such a war became the primary concern of foreign-policy makers.

In addition, the focus of the Cold War had expanded to areas outside of Europe. In 1949, Communists led by Mao Zedong seized control of China. Communist governments in North Korea, Cuba, and Vietnam soon threatened U.S. containment efforts as well.

Korean War After World War II, Korea, a country on a peninsula adjacent to China, had been divided into two parts: a communist north and a noncommunist south. In 1950 North Korea invaded South Korea in an attempt to bring the south under communist rule. In response, troops from the United States and other nations were sent by the United Nations to help defend South Korea. Within a few months these troops had not only repelled the attack but moved into North Korea. Communist China, worried by the approach of U.S. troops near its border, sent its own soldiers. The bloody war continued for three years, with neither side gaining a lasting advantage. On July 27, 1953, an armistice was finally signed; in 2000, North and South Korea began to work toward reconciliation.

Cuban Missile Crisis The event that came closest to sparking a nuclear confrontation during the Cold War took place in Cuba. By the late 1950s many Cubans resented their neighbor, the United States, which had dominated their island-nation for decades. In 1959 Cuba's pro-American dictator was overthrown by a group of rebels led by Fidel Castro, who appealed to Cubans' widespread anti-Americanism. Opposed by the United States, Castro turned to the Soviet Union for help.

WORLD AFFAIRS *President John F. Kennedy met with Russian leaders in October 1963. At the time of this meeting, the Soviets had already placed nuclear weapons in Cuba.* **What actions did President Kennedy take when he found out about the weapons?**

In 1962 the Soviet Union began secretly installing nuclear weapons in Cuba. When this operation was discovered, President John F. Kennedy announced a naval blockade to stop ships carrying missiles to Cuba. If the Soviet Union were able to install nuclear weapons in Cuba, it could easily threaten the United States with nuclear destruction. For the first time, a direct confrontation occurred between nuclear-armed powers. Six tense days after Kennedy announced the blockade, the Soviets agreed to withdraw the missiles. The incident was known as the Cuban missile crisis.

CASE STUDY

U.S. Foreign Policy Toward Cuba

WORLD AFFAIRS The United States played a dominant role in Cuban affairs until Fidel Castro gained power in 1959. These close ties originated with U.S. support of Cuba during the Spanish-American War of 1898. After the war, U.S. soldiers occupied Cuba, and the United States retains a base in Guantánamo Bay to this day.

The United States continued to be involved in the island's affairs. By the 1950s Americans owned most of Cuba's mines and cattle ranches and controlled half of its sugar production. The United States bought much of Cuba's sugar, and Cubans purchased American-made manufactured goods. Cuba's casinos and resorts attracted American tourists.

Soon after Cuban army colonel Fulgencio Batista (fool-hayn-syoh bah-TEE-stah) took control of the government by force in 1952, the United States granted his government formal diplomatic recognition. U.S. business leaders supported the dictator, who prevented a rebellion in March 1952 from disrupting business operations.

Fidel Castro's 1959 revolution strained relations between the United States and Cuba. Castro's government took over American-owned land and businesses, and the two countries broke off diplomatic relations when Castro established communist rule in Cuba. In 1961 the United States organized a group of Cuban exiles to invade Cuba at the Bay of Pigs and remove Castro from office. The Bay of Pigs invasion was an embarrassing failure for the United States when the rebels were captured and the Cuban people failed to rise against Castro as was expected.

In the decades after the Bay of Pigs invasion and the Cuban missile crisis, the United States continued its efforts to weaken Castro's regime through an economic blockade. Under President Clinton, the United States continued to enforce an economic embargo on Cuba. In July 2001, President George W. Bush ordered stricter enforcement of the trade embargo against communist Cuba and pledged his support for democratic opposition. Despite the efforts of 10 U.S. presidents, Fidel Castro, at over 75 years of age, has retained power and remains a continuing challenge for U.S. foreign policy.

Caption Answer

President Kennedy announced a naval blockade of Cuba to stop the flow of nuclear missiles to Cuba, and threatened nuclear retaliation against the Soviet Union if missiles were launched from Cuba.

GLOBAL CONNECTIONS

The Cuban Liberty and Democratic Solidarity Act (Helms-Burton Act) has resulted in a backlash against the United States from countries such as Canada, Mexico, France, Germany, Britain, and Italy. The protest is in response to one particular section of the act. This section allows U.S. nationals who have had property confiscated on or after January 1, 1959, by the Cuban government to bring legal action against people or businesses that subsequently use or benefit from that property. These countries—generally considered friendly to the United States—disagree with the act because it prescribes that legal actions be brought against foreign investors in Cuban businesses. ∎

Enhancing the Lesson

For more information about the governments of Cuba and Russia, see the Country Profiles section on the *Holt Researcher Online.*

CITIZENSHIP *The Vietnam War Memorial honors the men and women who served in the military during the Vietnam War.* **How did the Vietnam War and the continual fear of communist expansion influence U.S. foreign policy?**

☑ internet connect

TOPIC: Nixon, Kissinger, and the Cold War
GO TO: go.hrw.com
KEYWORD: SV3 GV10

Have students access the Internet through the HRW Go site to conduct research on Richard Nixon's foreign policy. Then ask students to create a pamphlet on Nixon's Vietnam policy, his trip to China, and Henry Kissinger's policy of détente. Students should take the point of view of a reporter writing about the events as they happen, and their pamphlet should reflect what it was like to live during the Cold War.

Vietnam War The Cold War left many scars on the United States. None, however, are more visible than those left by the Vietnam War. U.S. troops fought in Vietnam from 1961 to 1973—making it the longest war in U.S. history.

In the years that followed World War II, a nationalist movement arose in Vietnam, then a colony of France. The Vietnamese nationalists, made up primarily of communist forces, fought the French and won their independence. In the truce agreement that followed, Vietnam was divided, creating the communist North and the noncommunist South.

In 1959 Communists helped begin a rebellion in South Vietnam. President Dwight Eisenhower responded by providing military and economic assistance to the anticommunist government. This assistance increased under President John Kennedy's administration. In 1965 President Lyndon Johnson further escalated U.S. involvement in the conflict by committing large numbers of combat troops to support South Vietnam and by ordering the bombing of North Vietnam.

In 1969, in response to mounting public opposition to the conflict, President Richard Nixon began scaling back the number of U.S. troops in Vietnam. Nixon tried to win the war through increased bombing against North Vietnam and by mining and blockading North Vietnamese ports. U.S. troops left Vietnam in 1973, and in 1975 the U.S.-backed South Vietnamese government surrendered. By that time more than 58,000 Americans had been killed or were missing in action, and many who returned home suffered tremendous emotional, physical, and psychological scars from the war.

Détente The horrors of Vietnam and the continual fear of further communist expansion dominated U.S. thinking about foreign policy for more than a decade. President Nixon and his foreign-policy adviser Henry Kissinger took a realist approach. Believing that the war had weakened the United States, Kissinger wanted to decrease tensions with communist nations. The resulting policy was known as **détente**, a French word meaning "relaxation." The policy was targeted at the Soviet Union but applied to China and other communist nations as well.

The key elements of this strategy were the Strategic Arms Limitation Talks (SALT) and Nixon's 1972 visit to China. His visit, the first by a U.S. president, was a dramatic event for two reasons. First, the United States had not established diplomatic relations with China's communist government since it had come to power in 1949. Second, the United States had spent two decades trying to isolate China from the rest of the world. The purpose of his visit, President Nixon said, was "to seek normalization of relations between the two countries."

Later in 1972, Nixon met in Moscow with Soviet premier Leonid Brezhnev. They signed the first SALT agreement. SALT was a treaty in which both sides agreed to limit the production of certain nuclear weapons. The arms race dragged on, however, and the Soviet Union continued its aggressive policies. Détente was followed by a return to containment and a massive military buildup during the 1980s.

The Collapse of Communism The late 1980s marked perhaps the most dramatic shift in global relations in modern history—the collapse of communism. Events leading up to this collapse began in the Soviet Union when new leaders tried unsuccessfully to modernize their nation's decaying political and economic system through a series of political reforms.

Relations between the United States and the Soviet Union improved dramatically after Mikhail Gorbachev became the general secretary of the Communist Party's Central Committee in 1985 and the Soviet president in 1988. At that time, the Soviet Union had been suffering from economic and political problems for years. Gorbachev, believing that his country needed massive change, initiated a program of reforms in 1987 that expanded freedoms and reformed the political process. These programs called for greater openness (**glasnost**) and economic restructuring (**perestroika**). In 1989 Gorbachev decided not to block anticommunist movements in Eastern Europe. As a result, all the communist governments there soon collapsed.

Perhaps the period's most dramatic moment occurred on November 9, 1989, when East Germany declared that it would open its border with the West. This action led to the destruction of the most notorious symbol of the split between Eastern and Western Europe—the Berlin Wall. (The wall had been built in 1961 to separate communist East Berlin, the capital of East Germany, from democratic West Berlin, which was politically part of West Germany.) Armed police had patrolled the border between the halves of the city, as well as that between East and West Germany, for

WORLD AFFAIRS *President Richard Nixon and China's premier Zhou Enlai review troops of China's Red Army during Nixon's famous trip to China in 1972.* **What message did Nixon hope to send to Chinese leaders by visiting their country?**

decades. After the dismantling of the wall, the two countries agreed to unify, re-forming the nation of Germany in October 1990.

In response to the dramatic turn of events, a group of Soviet generals and old-line Communists tried to overthrow Gorbachev in August 1991. The revolt collapsed after several days of a pro-Gorbachev strike led by Boris Yeltsin, president of Russia, the largest republic in the Soviet Union. Within months, the Soviet Union had dissolved.

By the 1990s China and Vietnam, while retaining their communist political structure, were adopting market-oriented economic policies, and even Vietnam was seeking friendship with the United States. The only traditional communist countries left in the world were Cuba and North Korea.

SECTION 3 REVIEW

1. Identify and Explain:
- Monroe Doctrine
- Truman Doctrine
- containment
- détente
- glasnost
- perestroika

2. Identifying Concepts: Copy the chart below. Use it to list the foreign policy approaches taken during different eras in U.S. history.

Historical Era	Type of Policy
Late 1800s	
1920–1941	
Cold War	

3. **Finding the Main Idea**

a. How did the Monroe Doctrine shape foreign policy?

b. How have relations between the United States and Cuba changed over time? What is the political significance to the United States of Cuba?

4. **Writing and Critical Thinking**

Decision Making: What should be the new aims of U.S. foreign-policy now that the Cold War is over?
Consider the following:
- the past goals of U.S. foreign-policy
- the new challenges of the post Cold War era

Homework Practice Online
keyword: SV3 HP10

Caption Answer

Nixon hoped to send the message that it was time to seek normal relations between the United States and China.

SECTION 3 REVIEW ANSWERS

1. Refer to the following pages: Monroe Doctrine (228), Truman Doctrine (229), containment (229), détente (232), glasnost (233), perestroika (233).

2. Late 1800s—internationalist; 1920–1941—isolationist; Cold War—realist and idealist.

3a. The Monroe Doctrine declared a policy of neutrality and stated that the United States would not tolerate European interference in the Americas.

3b. Relations: Until the late 1950s, the United States had a dominant economic and military presence in Cuba. Since Castro's revolution, relations have been tense. Significance: Some students might mention that a communist nation so close to the United States has been a symbolic and actual threat during the past 50 years. Other students might mention the large, anti-Castro population in the United States.

4. Some students might suggest that the United States should return to isolationist policies. Other students might suggest that the post Cold War era demands that the United States maintain an internationalist approach.

SECTION 4

FOREIGN AID AND ALLIANCES

READ TO DISCOVER

1. How does providing foreign aid to other nations help the United States?
2. What defense alliances does the United States maintain today? What factors determine alliance selections?
3. How do alliances and foreign-aid programs promote the public good?

POLITICAL DICTIONARY

foreign aid
Marshall Plan
U.S. Agency for International Development
defense alliance
collective security
North Atlantic Treaty Organization
multilateral treaty
bilateral alliance

The foreign policy of the United States changed dramatically after communism ceased to pose a significant threat to U.S. national security. Promoting foreign-aid programs and maintaining defense alliances, however, remain critical factors in U.S. foreign policy.

Foreign Aid

Every president since World War II has supported **foreign aid**—economic and military assistance to foreign countries. U.S. foreign aid began in the early 1940s with the Lend-Lease program, which supplied money and military supplies to U.S. allies during World War II. Since then, the United States has spent about $500 billion in foreign economic and military aid—an impressive amount but only a very small portion of total U.S. expenditures over the last 50 years.

Critics of foreign aid, particularly isolationists, argue that U.S. tax dollars should be used exclusively to help people at home. Others add that much foreign aid is wasted on inefficient government projects and often provides money to corrupt rulers, rather than contributing to the development of strong market-based economies.

By contrast, supporters of foreign-aid programs contend that by providing economic assistance to foreign nations, the United States is actually promoting the public good not only of other countries but of the United States as well. This argument is based on the idea that some friendly countries need and deserve our help.

Furthermore, the governments of countries with weak economies might fall to forces hostile to the United States; whereas, if strengthened by foreign aid, such countries can eventually become good markets for U.S. goods. Germany, for example, a former recipient of U.S. foreign aid, has imported more than $20 billion of U.S. goods annually in recent years.

The Marshall Plan The most significant U.S. effort at providing financial assistance to foreign nations occurred through an aid program that was proposed by George Marshall, the secretary

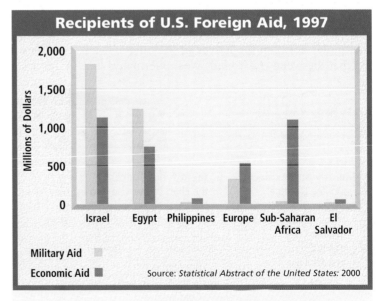

Recipients of U.S. Foreign Aid, 1997

Military Aid
Economic Aid

Source: *Statistical Abstract of the United States: 2000*

This graph shows how much economic and military aid some countries received from the United States in 1997. **Does the United States give more in military aid or economic aid to these countries?**

Workers in Haiti stack food sent by the United States as humanitarian aid. **How does USAID help the United States achieve its foreign-policy goals?**

of state under President Harry Truman. The **Marshall Plan** was an economic assistance program that poured around $13 billion into the 16 nations of Western Europe between 1948 and 1952. During this period these nations were suffering because of the financial burdens of World War II. The Marshall Plan restored them to economic health.

USAID Prior to the 1960s, foreign-aid programs were implemented individually. That is, no central institution existed for assessing the need for, and the possible benefits of, providing aid to foreign nations. Since 1961, however, the **U.S. Agency for International Development** (USAID), part of the State Department, has been responsible for implementing most U.S. foreign-aid programs. The agency works to help achieve U.S. foreign-policy goals in five principal areas—promoting economic growth, advancing democracy, delivering humanitarian support to victims of disasters, promoting public health, and protecting the environment.

Alliances and Pacts

In addition to providing aid to foreign countries, the United States pursues its foreign-policy goals by establishing alliances and pacts with foreign nations. **Defense alliances** are agreements in which nations pledge to come to each other's aid in case of attack. A primary goal of these alliances is **collective security**, the ensuring of

Comparing Governments

Ranking the United States in Global Giving

In the early 1960s the United States was spending more than any other industrial nation on aid to developing countries. By 1995, however, the United States had cut these expenditures. Moreover, the United States ranked last among the leading industrial nations in the amount of foreign aid it gave as a percentage of gross national product (GNP)—the total dollar value of all final goods and services produced during one year by the residents of a nation.

The size of the U.S. economy, however, allows the nation to contribute a much higher *amount* than most countries. Countries with relatively small economies—such as Portugal, Ireland, and New Zealand—cannot possibly contribute as much as the United States, even though they might give a more generous portion of their GNP. In 1996 the United States contributed .12 percent of its GNP to poor countries, compared to the .42 percent average among the rest of the world's 21 high-income countries.

The United States is not the only country to cut its foreign-aid expenditures. Many other industrialized countries, including Japan, Italy, and Germany, have been forced to reduce foreign aid because of severe budget restrictions. As the largest contributors of foreign aid tighten their belts, major recipients feel the loss. It has been estimated that if the rate of decline continues, aid will end by 2015.

THEMES IN GOVERNMENT

POLITICAL PROCESSES In an era of federal budget cutting, agencies such as the U.S. Agency for International Development (USAID) have engaged in political efforts to gain public support for their programs. Some polls indicate that U.S. citizens believe that foreign aid makes up a substantial portion of the federal budget, perhaps as high as 20 percent. In fact, in 2000 foreign aid constituted less than one percent of the entire budget. USAID pointed to the success of several of its humanitarian programs, including AIDS education and famine relief, as justification for the relatively small expense of foreign-aid programs. ■

internet connect

TOPIC: Graphing Foreign Aid
GO TO: go.hrw.com
KEYWORD: SV3 GV10

Have students access the Internet through the HRW Go site to find current information on foreign aid. Then ask students to use the Holt Grapher to create a graph that illustrates changes in foreign aid over the last decade. Students should choose either military or economic aid as categories for their graphs.

Citizenship in Action

Amnesty International's Power to Liberate

Since 1948 the United Nations Universal Declaration of Human Rights has been the international standard for fair treatment of people. Many countries have incorporated the standards proclaimed in this document into their national laws. Although the declaration has prompted worldwide efforts to protect human rights, some countries continue to abuse these rights.

Amnesty International, an organization established in 1961, works to bring human rights abuses to light. Part of Amnesty International's efforts include massive letter-writing campaigns to pressure governments to end the abuse, torture, and unfair imprisonment of their citizens. In the process, Amnesty International volunteers have discovered that sometimes a simple letter can have the power to liberate.

Amnesty International volunteers in Boston, Massachusetts, decorate T-shirts as part of a project to inform the public of human rights abuses.

Amnesty International has about 200,000 members around the world, including more than 30,000 U.S. high school and college students. These students sponsor lectures, discussions, and even art exhibits to educate fellow students about human rights. In Minneapolis, Minnesota, for example, a group of middle and high school students studied poems, songs, and pictures illustrating the worldwide struggle for human rights. Then they created a large outdoor sculpture of four figures with interlocking arms and covered it with statements appealing for tolerance, respect, peace, and human rights.

College students in the organization have drawn on the many resources on their campuses to promote human rights. At Mary Baldwin College in Virginia, Kate Shunney knew that her fellow students had the energy and abilities to further Amnesty's mission.

During an orientation to educate students about the group's worldwide efforts, Shunney explained the letter-writing campaigns and told the stories of Asian refugees, exiled Soviet political objectors, and Holocaust survivors. Her speech attracted many new members to the local chapter of Amnesty International. In one year, the energetic group sent some 300 letters to political leaders around the globe, helping to free nearly a dozen prisoners.

These simple hand-written letters from students and other Amnesty members of all ages communicate several powerful messages. They not only draw attention to human rights abuses; they also show that people working together can make a difference in the lives of prisoners in seemingly hopeless conditions. The success of the letter campaigns shows that communication and education are a key to protecting human rights around the world.

What Do You Think?

1. Why do you think Amnesty International depends on thousands of volunteers around the world to promote its efforts to free people who are unfairly imprisoned?

2. In what ways are letter-writing campaigns an effective tool in fighting human rights abuses?

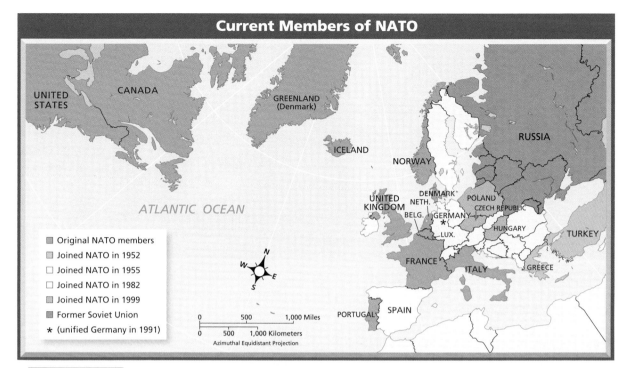

Current Members of NATO

UNITED STATES
CANADA
GREENLAND (Denmark)
ICELAND
NORWAY
ATLANTIC OCEAN
RUSSIA
UNITED KINGDOM
DENMARK
NETH.
BELG.
LUX.
GERMANY *
POLAND
CZECH REPUBLIC
HUNGARY
TURKEY
FRANCE
ITALY
GREECE
PORTUGAL
SPAIN

Legend:
- Original NATO members
- Joined NATO in 1952
- Joined NATO in 1955
- Joined NATO in 1982
- Joined NATO in 1999
- Former Soviet Union
- * (unified Germany in 1991)

0   500   1,000 Miles
0   500   1,000 Kilometers
Azimuthal Equidistant Projection

WORLD AFFAIRS *NATO was formed in 1949 when several countries signed a treaty to create a unified defense of Western Europe and North America.* **Which three countries joined NATO in 1999?**

peace through the guarantee of mutual defense. Treaties that the United States and other nations have signed to achieve this goal include the North Atlantic Treaty Organization, the Rio Pact, and the Organization of American States. In addition the United States is a member of the United Nations, a worldwide forum with more than 180 member countries, that was designed to resolve disputes and achieve other important international goals. (The United Nations is more fully explained in Chapter 23.)

North Atlantic Treaty Organization
In 1949, four years into the Cold War, the Western nations formed the **North Atlantic Treaty Organization** (NATO). NATO was only the second alliance that the United States had ever joined in peacetime. The goal of NATO was to create a unified defense of the North Atlantic area, composed of Western Europe and North America. All member countries agreed that "an armed attack against one or more of them in Europe or North America shall be considered an attack against them all."

NATO is an example of a **multilateral treaty**—an agreement signed by several countries.

Today NATO includes the original 12 members— the United States, Canada, the United Kingdom, France, Italy, Portugal, the Netherlands, Belgium, Luxembourg, Denmark, Norway, and Iceland— plus Greece and Turkey, which joined in 1952; Spain, which joined in 1982; Germany, which joined in 1990 (replacing West Germany), and Poland, the Czech Republic, and Hungary, which all joined in 1999.

For more than 40 years the focus of this alliance was mutual defense against Soviet aggression. In the post-Cold War era, however, NATO's focus has shifted to expanding cooperation with new partners in Central and Eastern Europe and in the former Soviet Union. Three Eastern European countries—Poland, the Czech Republic, and Hungary—in 1999 joined NATO in 1999.

Rio Pact
The Inter-American Treaty of Reciprocal Assistance of 1947, known as the Rio Pact, is a defense agreement signed by 22 republics in the Americas. The agreement states that "an armed attack by any State shall be considered as an attack against all American States."

GLOBAL CONNECTIONS

The changing political climate in Europe has created some debate over expanding membership in the North Atlantic Treaty Organization (NATO). Now, the more prosperous former communist countries that have made sufficient democratic and economic reforms, such as Poland, Hungary, and the Czech Republic, joined NATO in 1999. Several NATO members—including France, Spain, Italy, and Greece— have also pushed to have Romania added to this list of nations to be invited to join. This move has created debate regarding why new countries are asked to join. The countries that would like Romania to join NATO point out that it has importance for its strategic location, while the United States has argued that enlargement of NATO should not be based just on a country's strategic position. ■

Enhancing the Lesson

For more information about the North Atlantic Treaty Organization and the Organization of American States, see the International Organizations section on the *Holt Researcher Online.*

SECTION 4 REVIEW ANSWERS

1. Refer to the following pages: foreign aid (234), Marshall Plan (235), U.S. Agency for International Development (235), defense alliance (235), collective security (235), North Atlantic Treaty Organization (237), multilateral treaty (237), bilateral alliance (238).

2. Defense alliances—NATO, Rio Pact, OAS, U.S.—Japan Mutual Security Treaty; multilateral treaties—NATO, Rio Pact, OAS; bilateral treaty—U.S.—Japan Mutual Security Treaty.

3a. Students might suggest aid creates markets for U.S. goods; improves the quality of life abroad and ensures peace and stability; or that tax money could be better spent at home, or that aid money is spent inefficiently.

3b. Defense alliances can prevent war from breaking out by opposing a would-be aggressor.

4. Speeches will vary. Some students might suggest that friendly countries deserve foreign aid, and that aid ensures favorable markets for the United States. Other students might suggest that U.S. tax dollars should be spent on promoting the public good at home.

 **WORLD AFFAIRS** *Philippine president Elpidio Quirino (left) and U.S. president Harry Truman (right) watch as Secretary of State Dean Acheson signs a mutual defense pact in 1951.* **What is the purpose of bilateral alliances?**

Organization of American States Like the Rio Pact, the Organization of American States (OAS) is a mutual agreement among the republics in the Americas. OAS, however, is concerned with resolving economic—rather than military—disputes. It also is responsible for implementing the Rio Pact's terms for safeguarding the Americas against attack.

Bilateral Treaties of Alliance The United States is an active partner in various **bilateral alliances**—security agreements between two nations. For example, the United States still adheres to the 1951 U.S.-Japan Mutual Security Treaty—which allows it to maintain land, sea, and air forces in Japan, in return for agreeing to protect Japan in a time of crisis. In addition, the bilateral alliance supports the foreign-policy goal of open and free trade. The United States also maintains bilateral treaties with the Philippines, signed in 1951 as well, and South Korea, approved in 1954.

Since the signing of these treaties, the issues that most affect U.S. foreign-policy decisions have changed dramatically, particularly with the end of the Cold War during the late 1980s and 1990s. Even so, these and other treaties remain vital to the realization of U.S. foreign-policy goals.

SECTION 4 REVIEW

1. Identify and Explain:
- foreign aid
- Marshall Plan
- U.S. Agency for International Development
- defense alliance
- collective security
- North Atlantic Treaty Organization
- multilateral treaty
- bilateral alliance

2. Identifying Concepts: Copy the graphic organizer below. Use it to list examples of the types of alliances the United States maintains today.

Alliances and Pacts
Defense Alliance:
Multilateral Treaty:
Bilateral Alliance:

3. Finding the Main Idea

a. What are the benefits and drawbacks, both domestic and foreign, of providing foreign aid?

b. Why does the United States maintain defense alliances during times of peace?

4. Writing and Critical Thinking

Supporting a Point of View: Imagine you are a Senator who must vote on a foreign aid bill. Write a speech supporting or opposing foreign aid. **Consider the following:**
- the benefits and drawbacks of providing aid
- public opinion of foreign aid

go. hrw .com **Homework Practice Online**
keyword: SV3 HP10

The Oil Fields in the Middle East: Boom or Bust?

During World War II, six billion of the seven billion barrels of petroleum used by the Allied Powers came from the United States. After World War II, policymakers increasingly focused their attention on the Middle East and particularly the Persian Gulf region, which they believed would become the center of post-war oil production.

In the 1970s foreign oil producers were in a position to raise world oil prices. When the price of oil doubled during the oil embargo of 1973 and 1974, it became obvious how vulnerable the nation was to the demands of foreign oil producers.

The oil crises of the 1970s had an unanticipated effect. Rising oil prices stimulated conservation efforts as well as exploration of new oil sources. As a result, oil prices fell. The sharp decline in world oil prices was one of the factors that led Iraq to invade Kuwait in 1990 in a bid to gain control over 40 percent of the Middle East's oil reserves.

Taiwan: Between the Giants

In 1949 when Communists led by Mao Zedong took over China, some 2 million Nationalist Chinese fled to the island of Taiwan, which lies just 100 miles off the coast of mainland China. For more than 50 years Taiwan has staunchly opposed the government of the People's Republic of China, while Communist China has maintained that Taiwan is merely a province in rebellion. Taiwan's opposition to communism has made it a crucial ally of the United States.

In 1979 the United States promised to continue providing Taiwan with military aid in order to protect it against a Chinese invasion. Relations with Taiwan have proven complex, however. Because China is a potential superpower and an increasingly important trade partner, U.S. foreign-

Since 1949, Taiwan has played a crucial role in U.S.-Chinese relations.

policy makers have worked to maintain good relations with China as well as with Taiwan.

In April 2001 the George W. Bush administration agreed to sell an unprecedented amount of arms and military vehicles to Taiwan, including helicopters, missiles, submarines, and torpedoes. President Bush also pledged substantial U.S. military support to defend Taiwan if China should attack. Although Bush's comments did not signal a significant change in U.S. policy toward Taiwan, some Chinese and U.S. officials felt they contributed to increased tensions between the two countries. Whatever course relations between the United States and China may take, Taiwan will undoubtedly play a critical role.

What Do You Think?

1. What is the economic significance to the United States of the oil fields in the Middle East?

2. Why is Taiwan politically significant to the United States?

> **WHY IT MATTERS TODAY**
>
> Look up ways in which the United States is increasing its oil productivity. Identify other measures the United States is exploring outside of the Middle East. Use **CNNfyi.com** and other **current events** sources to find the answers.
>
> **CNNfyi.com**

(Continued on page 240)

Review

(Continued from page 239)

cant factor in U.S. foreign relations. The natural resources of the Middle East have driven U.S. policy-makers to devote attention to that area of the world.

2. isolationism, realism, neoisolationism, and idealism

3. In general, people feel that the president should have the most influence over foreign policy. As commander in chief, the president wields considerable influence in areas of foreign policy involving the military. Through executive agreements, the president can make foreign policy without the approval of Congress.

4. The CIA provides information about other governments to the president. Congress has the power to declare war, approve funding for defense and foreign aid, ratify treaties, and confirm the president's diplomatic appointments.

5. For over 40 years, U.S. foreign policy was aimed at halting the expansion of communism.

6. NATO, the Rio Pact, and the OAS

Reviewing Themes

1. Students might suggest that Vietnam led to détente with communist countries. Since Vietnam, U.S. presidents have been reluctant to send U.S. troops into combat.

2. The president has gained greater influence over foreign policy. Many feel that the president should control foreign policy because the executive branch can take quicker action. The president's role as commander in

(Continued on page 241)

Writing a Summary

Using standard grammar, spelling, sentence structure, and punctuation, write a summary of the information in this chapter.

Identifying Ideas

Identify the following terms and explain their significance.

1. national security

2. isolationist

3. internationalist

4. neoisolationist

5. idealism

6. containment

7. glasnost

8. Marshall Plan

9. defense alliance

10. collective security

Understanding Main Ideas

SECTION 1 *(pp. 217–221)*

1. Describe how factors such as location and geographic characteristics have guided U.S. foreign policies toward certain nations.

2. What principles have guided U.S. foreign policy throughout American history?

SECTION 2 *(pp. 222–227)*

3. Explain why the executive branch has a greater influence over foreign policy than any of the other branches of government.

4. What are the roles of the Central Intelligence Agency and Congress in making foreign policy?

SECTION 3 *(pp. 228–233)*

5. How did the expansion of communism affect U.S. foreign policy?

SECTION 4 *(pp. 234–238)*

6. What defense alliances does the United States maintain today?

Reviewing Themes

1. Political Processes How do you think the Vietnam War changed the way the United States conducts foreign policy?

2. Political Processes How has the role of the president in foreign policy changed over time? Has Congress's influence in foreign policy increased or decreased over time?

3. Public Good How do the U.S. government's efforts to build good relations with other countries promote the public good? Do you think U.S. foreign policy in general has promoted the public good?

Thinking Critically

1. Making Predictions What will be the most important foreign policy issue facing the United States during the next decade? Write a paragraph explaining your answer, and include the foreign policy approach you think the United States should take to this issue.

2. Finding the Main Idea Review the section describing how foreign policy is made. Which branch of government is primarily responsible for making foreign policy? Do you think this is appropriate?

3. Drawing Inferences Do you think the end of the Cold War marked a major turning point in the history of U.S. foreign policy?

Writing about Government

Review what you wrote in your Government Notebook at the beginning of this chapter about how the government might monitor the interactions between countries. Now that you have studied this chapter, how would you revise your response? Explain your answer in your notebook.

Interpreting the Chart

Study the chart below. Then use it to help you answer the questions that follow.

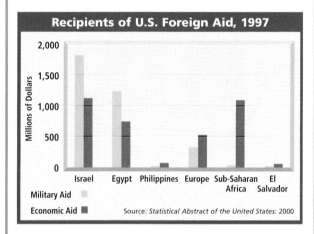

Recipients of U.S. Foreign Aid, 1997

Millions of Dollars

Israel Egypt Philippines Europe Sub-Saharan El
Africa Salvador

Military Aid
Economic Aid

Source: *Statistical Abstract of the United States: 2000*

1. Which country receives the most military aid from the United States? the second most?
 a. Egypt; Europe
 b. Israel; Egypt
 c. Israel; Europe
 d. Philippines; Egypt

2. Why might Israel and Egypt receive more military aid than economic aid?

Analyzing Primary Sources

The Truman Doctrine, announced by President Harry S Truman in 1947, set forth containment as the basic U.S. foreign-policy strategy. Read the following excerpt, and answer the accompanying questions.

"At the present moment in world history nearly every nation must choose between alternative ways of life. The choice is too often not a free one.

One way of life is based upon the will of the majority, and is distinguished by free institutions, representative government, free elections, guarantees of individual liberty, freedom of speech and religion, and freedom from political oppression [persecution]. The second way of life is based upon the will of a minority forcibly imposed upon the majority. It relies upon terror and op-pression, a controlled press and radio, fixed elections, and the suppression [limiting] of personal freedoms.

I believe that it must be the policy of the United States to support free peoples who are resisting attempted subjugation [conquering] by armed minorities or by outside pressures."

3. Which of the following statements best summarizes the Truman Doctrine?
 a. the United States must aid oppression
 b. the suppression of personal freedoms, while unfortunate, are unavoidable
 c. the United States must take an active role in opposing totalitarianism
 d. the United States does not differ greatly from communist nations

4. Do you think that the goals of U.S. foreign policy are the same today as in 1947?

(Continued from page 240)

chief has undercut Congress's ability to declare wars.

3. Students might suggest that when nations receive American aid they become stronger allies.

Thinking Critically

1. Answers will vary but should demonstrate knowledge of the foreign-policy approaches the United States has taken in the past.

2. Answers will vary. Students should mention that the executive dominates foreign-policymaking. Some students might suggest that only the executive can handle the pace and demands of foreign policy. Others might suggest that the executive wields too much influence.

3. Answers will vary but should discuss how the Cold War shaped U.S. foreign policy and how the end of the Cold War might influence foreign policy.

Writing About Government

The Government Notebook is a follow-up activity to the notebook activity that appears on page 216.

Building Social Studies Skills

1. b
2. Students might suggest that political and geographic factors influence the type of aid received.
3. c
4. Answers will vary. Students might suggest that spreading democracy remains a goal of U.S. foreign policy but U.S. foreign policy is not directly aimed at fighting communism.

Alternative Assessment

To assess this activity see Rubric 1: Acquiring Information I *Alternative Assessment Handbook.*

Building Your Portfolio

With a group, create a notebook of newspaper and magazine articles about issues in U.S. foreign policy. Divide the notebook into five sections: North America, South America, Europe, Africa, and Asia/Australia. Organize the articles according to the geographical location to which they relate. Assign to group members the task of writing summaries for each article. Label each article according to the issue it addresses, including economic, military, diplomatic, or any other category.

internet connect

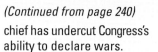

Internet Activity: go.hrw.com
KEYWORD: SV3 GV10

Access the Internet through the HRW Go site to conduct research on isolationism, neoisolationism, realism, and idealism in foreign policy. Write a definition of each term, and ask a random sample of your classmates which doctrine they most agree with. Publish the results of your sample as a class poll.

LAB OBJECTIVES

The Unit 3 Public Policy Lab incorporates the following objectives:

▶ review documents to determine the agenda and policy recommendations for a foreign trade summit with Libertaria.

▶ conduct research on successful economic and trade agreements.

▶ use a problem-solving process to write a speech to gain public support for a summit with Libertaria.

Using the Lab

Before beginning the lab organize students into groups and distribute copies of the Public Policy Lab Unit 3 Activity found in *Unit Tests and Unit Lab Activities with Answer Key*. Then have students read the directions for the assignment on this page. Discuss the assignment with students and point out the documents on pages 243–45 that students will use during the lab.

The What Do You Think? questions on pages 244–45 will help guide students during the project. In addition, the lab worksheet includes a step-by-step checklist for students to monitor their progress. For assessment guidelines, see the Solving Problems rubric in the *Alternative Assessment Handbook*.

PUBLIC POLICY LAB

You Solve the problem

Writing Presidential Speeches

*I*magine that you and your classmates are speechwriters for the president of the United States. The president's chief of staff has asked your group to write a speech for a press conference about an upcoming foreign-trade summit with Prime Minister Kaya Nikano of Libertaria. The purpose of the summit is to negotiate an agreement to establish a free-trade zone between the two countries. The president wants to use this press conference to gain public support for the summit and the trade agreement. The president's chief of staff has sent you the following documents: a memo describing the goals for the speech, copies of the summit agenda, policy recommendations from advisers, and a letter from Prime Minister Nikano.

Government Notebook Assignment

Record your problem-solving process in your Government Notebook.

1. Review the documents and answer the WHAT DO YOU THINK? questions.
2. Identify the problem you are trying to solve with this speech.
3. Conduct outside research to gather information on factors that contribute to successful economic and trade agreements between the United States and other countries. Compare past economic and trade agreements with the proposed agreement between the United States and Libertaria.
4. List and consider the options your group has with writing this speech. Consider the advantages and disadvantages associated with each of these options.
5. Choose and implement a solution by writing a speech for the president to give at the press conference. Present the speech to the rest of your class.
6. As a class, evaluate the effectiveness of each group's speech at gaining public support for the summit and the trade agreement.

OFFICE OF THE PRESIDENT OF THE UNITED STATES

STAFF MEMORANDUM

To: Staff Speechwriters
From: Chief of Staff

DK

The president will be attending a press conference on April 15 where he will be speaking to the press and the public about the upcoming free-trade summit with Prime Minister Kaya Nikano in Paris. This press conference is crucial for setting the tone for the summit. The speech must clearly establish the president's goals and agenda for the summit and show how accomplishing them will increase domestic prosperity.

The broad goals of the Paris Free-Trade Summit are to
- open new markets,
- create a free-trade area, and
- improve the quality of life for the people of both countries.

The president's speech must emphasize that a free-trade treaty will enable the United States to increase its gross domestic product by
- expanding the export of domestic goods and services and
- creating more high-wage jobs.

Please carefully review the policy recommendations of Secretary of Commerce James Lin and U.S. Trade Representative Alice Brooks before preparing this speech. Both recommendations include statistics that clearly show the projected economic growth that would result from a free-trade treaty with Libertaria. Please examine the summit agenda for a more detailed description of the summit goals.

The speech should stress the importance of this treaty in the future growth and development of the U.S. economy. This speech will be an important tool of the president in generating broad public support for the free-trade agreement. Public support for the agreement may be key to gaining congressional approval. I appreciate your assistance and look forward to reading this speech.

Thank you.

The President's Paris Free-Trade Summit Agenda

The focus of the Paris Free-Trade Summit agenda is to build on the good political and trade relations that already exist between Libertaria and the United States. We aim to seek a higher level of openness and cooperation and to address current trade restrictions maintained by both countries. We are committed to creating a trade agreement that is mutually supportive. In pursuit of these goals, we will construct a long-term plan for further negotiations and agreements. Priority at this summit will be given to
- promoting high-tech U.S. exports;
- supporting high-growth U.S. export industries, particularly those requiring highly skilled labor;
- eliminating barriers that adversely affect the creation of new jobs and the maintaining of existing—particularly high-wage and high-skill—jobs;
- opening markets for Libertarian exports; and
- creating an agenda for further trade negotiations with Libertaria over the next 10 years.

What Do You Think?
Answers

1. The growth of the U.S. economy relies on increasing consumption of U.S. exports.

2. Answers will vary, but students may discuss that such an agreement would increase trade with Libertaria.

3. It is expected that by the year 2013 the United States will trade more with Libertaria than with Europe or Japan.

What Do You Think?
Answers

1. Answers will vary, but students may discuss the public wanting more jobs with higher pay.

2. Opening new markets for high-tech goods could create 150,000 new jobs.

3. These specialists may want to focus on the creation of high-skilled jobs because they pay about 16 percent more than other manufacturing jobs.

PUBLIC POLICY LAB *continued*

SECRETARY OF COMMERCE
James Lin

The goals of the free-trade summit must reflect the interdependence of the U.S. and Libertarian economies in a global market. The long-term economic prosperity of the United States will be significantly affected by the economic development and stability of the countries with which we establish strong trade relations.

Identifying the major foreign consumers of American goods is crucial to U.S. economic policy. The growth of the U.S. economy relies on increased consumption of U.S. exports. Consider the following statistics on Libertarian consumption of American goods. For every dollar Libertaria spends on imports, 47 cents goes toward goods made in the United States. Libertaria maintains trade barriers that are approximately two times higher than ours, yet the United States sold almost $100 billion worth of goods in Libertaria last year. If current trends in trade between the United States and Libertaria are maintained, by the year 2013 the United States will sell more to Libertaria than to Europe or Japan.

I strongly recommend that the president concentrate significant efforts on building strong trade relations with the major consumers of American goods. This can only be done by negotiating mutually beneficial trade agreements with those countries, one of which is Libertaria. By working to ensure the economic growth and development of our trade partners, we secure our own country's future economic growth.

WHAT DO YOU THINK? ▶

1. Do you think that the public is concerned about how trade agreements will affect employment in the United States? Explain your answer.

2. Why does Alice Brooks think that opening new markets for high-tech goods is essential to the growth of the U.S. economy?

3. Why might foreign-policy specialists recommend a focus on the creation of more high-skilled jobs?

◀ WHAT DO YOU THINK?

1. What role do exports play in the growth of the U.S. economy?

2. How may a free-trade agreement affect the future consumption of U.S. exports?

3. Why is it particularly important for the health of the U.S. economy that the United States have good relations with Libertaria?

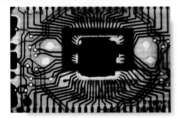

★ | U.S. TRADE REPRESENTATIVE
Alice Broo

Policy Recommendation

The major goal of the upcoming Paris Free-Trade Summit is economic growth. This goal can be accomplished only through creating economic opportunity, particularly through new jobs. The creation of high-wage, high-quality jobs is essential to improving Americans' standard of living.

Libertaria is a major consumer of American computers and electronics. An increased effort to build strong trade relations with foreign consumers of such goods is essential to the growth of American industry. By making the rules fair and breaking down trade barriers, the United States will be able to export more of its goods to this market. By the year 2010, given appropriate diplomatic efforts, U.S. exports could increase 35 percent. By concentrating on opening up the market for high-tech goods, the United States could create 150,000 new jobs in the high-tech industry. High-skilled jobs such as these pay about 16 percent more than do other manufacturing jobs in our economy.

Economic stability and growth—not only for the United States but also for our trading partners—depends on the diligent efforts of government leaders to create and move forward with a strategy that is based on creating high-wage, high-skilled jobs through opening markets and reducing barriers. The successful outcome of this summit relies on the ability of the president and Prime Minister Nikano to negotiate an agreement that will stimulate both countries' economies.

FROM THE DESK OF KAYA NIKANO

Dear Mr. President:

In response to your most recent correspondence, I wish to ensure that you and I have a clear understanding of the central matters concerning trade relations between the United States and Libertaria.

Countries entering into a free-trade agreement must be willing to accept foreign products into their markets. If the consumers in Libertaria are going to be able to buy American goods, they must be able to generate income by the sale of goods and services in the United States. To increase economic integration and free trade, we must work together with private industries and financial institutions to promote productive investment and trade. We must move toward lifting trade barriers.

Libertaria has made monumental progress in economic development and stability over the last 10 years. The debt burden has been reduced to a manageable level, and we have the fastest-growing economy in the Western Hemisphere. The United States has played a key role in helping Libertaria reach its current level of prosperity through investment and other economic aid. Our aim in the next several years is to open our markets to American goods and services, as well as establish markets in the United States for our exports.

Creating a mutually beneficial trade environment should be given careful attention, encouragement, and support. I look forward to our meeting as a vital step toward achieving this goal.

Sincerely Yours,

Kaya Nikano

Kaya Nikano

◀WHAT DO YOU THINK?

1. Why do you think Prime Minister Kaya Nikano believes that removing trade regulations is key to developing better trade relations?

2. How might the United States benefit from establishing strong trade relations with one of the world's fastest-growing economies? What would Libertaria gain from a free-trade agreement with the United States?

🔗 **internet** connect

Internet Activity: go.hrw.com
KEYWORD: SV3 GVPL

Access the Internet through the HRW Go site to use a problem-solving process to prepare a presidential speech explaining why the free-trade summit is important to the U.S. economy. Research links and a problem-solving tutorial are provided.

What Do You Think?
Answers

1. Answers will vary, but students may suggest that removing trade regulations would help Libertaria to generate income by selling goods abroad.

2. Answers will vary, but students should suggest that it would increase trade and create jobs for the United States. Libertaria would gain a chance to generate income by trading in the United States.

UNIT 4

Lesson Options

Suggestions for customizing the material in Unit 4 to fit the specific schedule and curriculum of your classroom are located at the beginning of each chapter.

Main Ideas

Ask each student to read the Main Ideas and briefly answer each question in writing. Later, when you have finished Unit 4, ask students to return to their original answers and revise them using what they learned in the unit.

PUBLIC POLICY LAB

The Unit 4 Public Policy Lab appears on pages 290–93. This project is a real-world assignment in which students will work in groups to review documents pertaining to a court case to determine if the case should be sent back to the district court. Support materials for the lab appear in *Unit Tests and Unit Lab Activities with Answer Key*.

CHAPTER 11

THE FEDERAL COURT SYSTEM

CHAPTER 12

THE U.S. LEGAL SYSTEM

Main Ideas

- *What is the role of the courts in the United States?*
- *What are the basic types of laws?*
- *How is the U.S. legal system structured?*

PUBLIC POLICY LAB

Do police officers have the right to search people's homes without a search warrant? Find out by reading this unit and taking the Public Policy Lab challenge on pages 290-93.

JUDICIAL BRANCH

Unit 4 presents the basic concepts necessary to introduce students to the judicial branch, including the role of the courts, limits on court authority, court organization, the Supreme Court, and the appointment process. The unit also discusses the U.S. legal system, including the different types of U.S. law, the role of the police and the courts in the criminal justice system, and the corrections system.

Teaching with Photographs

The Supreme Court has not always been housed in the stately building pictured here. Although the original design of the capital city included a building for the Supreme Court, the building's construction was put off for many years. As a result, the Supreme Court was frequently forced to move its headquarters until 1935, when the Supreme Court Building was finally completed. Some of the locations the Supreme Court has held include the Royal Exchange Building in New York City; the State House in Philadelphia; the Capitol Building in Washington, D.C.; a tavern in Washington, D.C.; and a rented house on Capitol Hill.

CHAPTER 11 — THE FEDERAL COURT SYSTEM

	OBJECTIVES	PACING GUIDE	REPRODUCIBLE RESOURCES
SECTION 1 THE LOWER COURTS (pp. 249–54)	▸ What are the role and the authority of the lower courts? ▸ How are the lower courts organized? ▸ How are lower-court judges selected?	**Regular** 1.5 days **Block Scheduling** .75 day	ELL Spanish Study Guide 11.1 ELL English Study Guide 11.1 PS Reading 37: Judiciary Act of 1789
SECTION 2 THE SUPREME COURT (pp. 255–62)	▸ How has the role of the Supreme Court changed over time? ▸ How are Supreme Court justices appointed, and what are their terms of office? ▸ How does the Supreme Court operate?	**Regular** 1.5 days **Block Scheduling** .75 day	ELL Spanish Study Guide 11.2 ELL English Study Guide 11.2
SECTION 3 THE COURTS AND THE PUBLIC GOOD (pp. 263–66)	▸ What are the main criticisms of the judiciary? ▸ How can the courts' power be checked?	**Regular** 1 day **Block Scheduling** .5 day	ELL Spanish Study Guide 11.3 ELL English Study Guide 11.3

Chapter Resource Key

PS	Primary Sources	A	Assessment		Video
RS	Reading Support	REV	Review		Videodisc
E	Enrichment	ELL	Reinforcement and English Language Learners		Internet
S	Simulations		Transparencies		Holt Presentation Maker Using
SM	Skills Mastery		CD-ROM		Microsoft ® PowerPoint ®

TECHNOLOGY RESOURCES	REINFORCEMENT, REVIEW, AND ASSESSMENT
💿 One-Stop Planner: Lesson 11.1 🌐 Holt Researcher Online 🌐 Homework Practice Online 💾 Transparencies 23, and 24 Cartoon Transparency 10 💿 Global Skill Builder CD-ROM	**REV** Section 1 Review, p. 254 **A** Daily Quiz 11.1
💿 One-Stop Planner: Lesson 11.2 🌐 Holt Researcher Online 🌐 Homework Practice Online	**REV** Section 2 Review, p. 262 **A** Daily Quiz 11.2
💿 One-Stop Planner: Lesson 11.3 🌐 Holt Researcher Online 🌐 Homework Practice Online **E** Challenge and Enrichment: Activity 11 **E** Simulations and Strategies for Teaching American Government: Activity 11 📼 CNN Presents American Government	**REV** Section 3 Review, p. 266 **A** Daily Quiz 11.3

Chapter Review and Assessment

SM Global Skill Builder CD-ROM
🌐 HRW Go site
REV Chapter 11 Tutorial for Students, Parents, and Peers
REV Chapter 11 Review, pp. 268–69
💿 Chapter 11 Test Generator (on the One-Stop Planner)
A Chapter 11 Test
A Chapter 11 Test Alternative Assessment Handbook

 One-Stop Planner CD-ROM

It's easy to plan lessons, select resources, and print out materials for your students when you use the *One-Stop Planner CD-ROM with Test Generator.*

HOLT PRESENTATION MAKER
Access Illustrated LECTURE
NOTES using Microsoft®
PowerPoint® on the
One-Stop Planner CD-ROM

OBJECTIVES

- Identify the role of the lower courts and describe their authority.
- Explain how the lower courts are organized.
- Describe the process by which lower-court judges are selected.

MOTIVATE

Organize students into small groups. Ask each group to define the word *justice.* Have each group present its definition to the rest of the class. Then read a dictionary definition of the word *justice* to the class. Ask students to provide examples of individuals or groups who help establish justice in our society. Lead the class in a discussion of what society would be like without laws and the court system. Explain that in this section students will learn how the lower courts of the federal judiciary are set up and about the authority these courts have to interpret the law.

TEACH

Building a Vocabulary

In spiral notebooks, have students create a Political Dictionary to be used throughout the course. This dictionary may be used as an activity at the start of each new section; it may also be used as a modification device for students having difficulty or Sheltered English Students during tests and homework assignments. List words the students will be expected to know for this section on the chalkboard. Have students list, define, and give an example of each of the terms, using information provided in the text or on the *Researcher CD-ROM.*

Classifying Information

Organize the class into small groups (preferably four groups). Assign each group two of the specific instances in which federal courts have original jurisdiction. (See the chart on textbook page 250.) Have students cut a large piece of paper in half. Have them write the instances at the top of each of the pages. Then ask them to investigate specific examples of court cases that fall under each category. Refer students to the Supreme Court Docket section on the *Holt Researcher Online* to assist them with their research. After each group has finished, it should share its examples with the class. Have students display their papers in the room so the entire class may use them as references during study of the chapter. Tell students that they will be learning about lower-court organization in the next activity.

Comparing and Contrasting

In three separate columns on the chalkboard, list the following headings: *district courts, courts of appeals,* and *special courts.* In order to describe each type of lower court as accurately as possible, have the class create a list of three to five characteristics of all courts to discuss. Each descriptive category should be listed on the left-hand side of the chalkboard. Then lead the class in filling in the correct information under the first two column headings—district courts and courts of appeals. After the first two columns are completed, ask students to list the appropriate courts that fall under the third heading—special courts. (Refer students to the chart on textbook page 253 if necessary.) Assign each student the task of researching one of the special courts listed to find out the same descriptive information that was provided in the first two columns. Students may collaborate with classmates and should present their research to the class. Students will learn about the process of appointing federal judges in the following activity.

Role-Playing/Debating Ideas

Explain that because of a recent string of (fictitious) classroom thefts, it is imperative for the class to appoint a judge in order to restore order and carry out justice. Before anyone can be appointed, however, the class must first decide on two things: the process of appointing the judge and the length of term the judge will serve. Organize the class into four groups. Two groups will debate the issue of the appointment process: one group will argue in favor of appointment by the teacher, and the other group will argue for appointment by the teacher with student approval. The other two groups will debate the issue of the length of term served: one group will argue for the judge to serve the entire year, and the other group will argue that the judgeship should change each quarter. After groups have debated the assigned topics, discuss the actual process of appointment and the length of terms for federal judges. Point out similarities between the process that students just used and the actual appointment process. Encourage students to follow the news for coverage of judicial appointments.

CLOSE

Have students return to the same groups they were in during the Motivate activity. Remind them of the examples they gave of groups or individuals who help establish justice in our society. Lead a discussion on how things would be different if the way these people receive their positions, the length of time they serve, and the duties they perform changed depending on who was president. Remind students that the terms, the way judges receive their positions, and their duties remain the same under each president. Discuss with students the importance of maintaining a stable, well-organized judiciary.

OPTIONS

Gifted Learners

Have students research the history of the U.S. penal system to analyze the ways in which the contemporary judicial system might reflect an earlier view of justice. (Remember the ancient law of justice found in the Code of Hammurabi—"an eye for an eye.") Students may complete an oral or written report for extra credit. Have students share their findings with the class.

Students Having Difficulty/ Sheltered English Students

Encourage students to gain a further understanding of the difference between loose constructionists and strict constructionists. Refer students to the Supreme Court Docket section on the *Holt Researcher Online* and other resources, and then have students classify each decision as being based on a strict constructionist or loose constructionist view. Students should explain their reasoning either orally or in writing, using information from this section and their research to justify their answers. Have students share their findings with the class.

Gifted Learners

Have students conduct research on the number of cases being heard at each level of the federal court system. Have each student write a paper that provides information on the number of cases heard and offers his or her opinion regarding whether the federal court system can handle this number of cases. Be sure to have the students consider the original role of the federal courts and the limited role originally assigned to the Supreme Court. Have students suggest alternatives to the current system. Encourage students to share their ideas with the class.

Visual-Spatial Learners

Organize the class into several small groups. Allow each group to select a country. Have students use the library and the Internet to research the court system of their selected country. Students should examine that country's court system to identify if it is broken down into different levels, as the U.S. system is, and should also examine how judges obtain their positions. Have students create a chart that compares the court system of their selected country to that of the United States. Have each group share its findings with the class.

REVIEW

Have students complete the Section 1 Review on page 254. Use the answers in the Annotated Teacher's Edition to assess student mastery of this section.

ASSESS

To assess student mastery of this section, have students complete Daily Quiz 11.1 in *Daily Quizzes with Answer Key.* For additional assessment options, see *Alternative Assessment Handbook* on the *One-Stop Planner CD-ROM.*

ADDITIONAL RESOURCES

Garraty, John, ed. *Quarrels That Have Shaped the Constitution.* 1987. Harper & Row.

Kramnick, Isaac, and R. Laurence Moore. *The Godless Constitution.* 1997. W. W. Norton.

OBJECTIVES

▶ Describe how the role of the Supreme Court has changed over time.
▶ Discuss how Supreme Court justices are appointed and explain what their terms of office are.
▶ Explain how the Supreme Court operates.

MOTIVATE

Ask student volunteers to express their opinion on the following issues: capital punishment, abortion, affirmative action, and the welfare system. Lead a group discussion in which students debate both sides of these issues. Encourage students to appreciate the difficulty of making laws and decisions about these issues that satisfy all people. Tell students that it is the Supreme Court's responsibility to rule on the constitutionality of controversial laws. Explain that in this section students will learn about the Supreme Court and its role in the judicial system.

TEACH

Building a Vocabulary

In their spiral notebooks, have students continue working on their Political Dictionary. List words the students will be expected to know for this section on the chalkboard. Have students list, define, and give an example of each of the terms, using information provided in the text or on the *Researcher CD-ROM*.

Acquiring Information/Analyzing Information

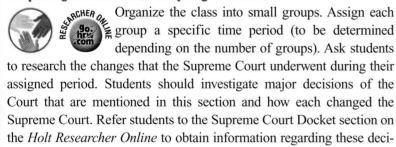

Organize the class into small groups. Assign each group a specific time period (to be determined depending on the number of groups). Ask students to research the changes that the Supreme Court underwent during their assigned period. Students should investigate major decisions of the Court that are mentioned in this section and how each changed the Supreme Court. Refer students to the Supreme Court Docket section on the *Holt Researcher Online* to obtain information regarding these deci-

sions. Encourage groups to share their findings with the class. Be sure to highlight important changes that students may have missed. Tell students that in the next activity they will learn about the appointment process for Supreme Court justices.

Predicting Outcomes

Organize the class into small groups. Have students make a list of personality characteristics that they feel a Supreme Court justice should possess. Each group should also list any educational and professional achievements that group members think Supreme Court justices should have attained. After brainstorming, each group should share with the class its opinions about the personal and professional qualifications of justices. Discuss with the class the actual way that Supreme Court justices are appointed and the actual term they serve. Tell students that in the next activity they will learn about the way the Court operates.

Acquiring Information/Mastering Concepts

Discuss with students the scrutiny that nominees to the Supreme Court must undergo before obtaining the Senate's approval. Explain to students that sometimes the Senate does not give approval to a nominee. Have students use the Internet and the library to research instances in which the Senate did not approve a presidential nominee to the Supreme Court. Have students attempt to identify the issue or issues that contributed to the nominee's rejection. Have students write an essay describing the issues surrounding the nominee and the student's opinion about whether the Senate was justified in rejecting the nominee. Ask students to share their findings with the class. Have the class attempt to draw conclusions about what types of issues can lead the Senate to reject a nominee and which issues it is willing to overlook.

Synthesizing Information

Lead a discussion on the process that the Supreme Court uses to decide which cases to hear. Organize the class into three groups. Have each group research examples of one of the three different kinds of opinions—majority, concurrent, and dissenting—that the Supreme Court may have issued in a landmark decision. Each group should present its example to the class and discuss the reasons why this type of opinion was written. Discuss the importance of the different kinds of opinions and the role they may play in establishing or overruling precedents.

CLOSE

To help students better understand the role of the Supreme Court, have them role-play a Supreme Court case on one of the topics introduced in the Motivate activity. Organize the class into three groups, one to support the topic chosen, one to oppose it, and the rest to act as Supreme Court justices. Have the first two groups prepare a brief that outlines the arguments for their topic. Assign one student from the two groups the role of the lawyer presenting the arguments on each side. Instruct the third group—the Supreme Court justices—to listen to the arguments and then to discuss the cases as though they were meeting in private conference. Ask two volunteers to present the majority and dissenting opinions.

OPTIONS

Gifted Learners

 Encourage students to discover more about the individuals serving on the Supreme Court. Using magazines, newspapers, and other resources, students should choose one of the current justices and prepare a one- or two-page biography. Each biography should include information about that justice's education, positions held prior to appointment, the year appointed to the Supreme Court, and any other relevant information. Students should be prepared to share their reports in class.

Students Having Difficulty/ Sheltered English Students

 Have students create a poster or a political cartoon that illustrates and explains the role of the Supreme Court in the U.S. system of government. The poster or cartoon should include such concepts as conferences, opinions, and the changing role of the Supreme Court. Have students explain their cartoons to the rest of the class. Display cartoons throughout the classroom.

Gifted Learners

  Discuss the importance of the Marshall Court with the class. Have students research the Marshall Court using the Biographies and Supreme Court sections on the *Holt Researcher Online* and other resources. Have students write a short essay that hypothesizes what the role of the Supreme Court would be today if the Marshall Court had not established the principle of judicial review. Encourage students to share their ideas about the Marshall Court and its decisions with the class.

Intrapersonal Learners

Have students read about the case of *Plessy* v. *Ferguson,* which can be found in the Supreme Court Docket section on the *Holt Researcher Online.* Have students write a dissenting opinion to the Court's decision that argues against the ruling. Have students use emotion and logic from later Supreme Court decisions to justify their answers. Ask students to share their reasoning with the class.

REVIEW

Have students complete the Section 2 Review on page 262. Use the answers in the Annotated Teacher's Edition to assess student mastery of this section.

ASSESS

To assess student mastery of this section, have students complete Daily Quiz 11.2 in *Daily Quizzes with Answer Key.* For additional assessment options, see *Alternative Assessment Handbook* on the *One-Stop Planner CD-ROM.*

ADDITIONAL RESOURCES

Baum, Lawrence. *The Supreme Court.* 1995. CQ Press.
Storing, Herbert. *The Complete Anti-Federalist.* 1981. University of Chicago Press.
May It Please the Court. 1994. David E. Kelley Productions. (video)

OBJECTIVES

▶ List and describe the issues raised by judicial activism and judicial restraint.
▶ Explain how the courts' power can be checked by the other branches of government.

MOTIVATE

Lead a discussion about the role of the courts and ask students how often they feel the judicial branch acts in the best interest of the people. Have students provide examples of events in which they feel the courts served the public good and when they believe the courts overstepped their bounds. Explain that in this section students will learn about some of the major criticisms of the judiciary and ways that its power is checked by the other branches of government.

TEACH

Building a Vocabulary

In their spiral notebooks, have students continue working on their Political Dictionary. List words the students will be expected to know for this section on the chalkboard. Have students list, define, and give an example of each of the terms, using information provided in the text or on the *Researcher CD-ROM*.

Acquiring Information/Creating Charts and Graphs

Organize students into groups. Have them define *judicial activism* and *judicial restraint* and give an example of each. Then have students conduct a public-opinion poll by interviewing teachers, relatives, or neighbors to find out whether people are advocates of judicial activism or judicial restraint. Remind students that they should provide a brief explanation of the difference between the two terms. Students should present the results of their survey in the form of a bar graph and should compare their graphs with other students' graphs. Tell students that in the next

activity they will learn about arguments for and against the popular election of federal judges.

Debating Ideas

Organize the class into three groups. Hold a debate on the issue of whether federal judges should be popularly elected or appointed. Choose one group to argue for popular election and another group to argue for appointment. Have students use information in this section of the text to support their arguments. Assign the third group the task of evaluating each team's presentation and voting to determine the winning side. Tell students that in the next activity they will learn about checks on the judicial branch.

Applying a Model/Learning from Visuals

Organize the class into two groups, with one group representing the legislative branch and the other the executive branch. Have each group make a list of the different ways its branch of government checks the power of the judicial branch. Have a volunteer from each group share his or her ideas with the class. Have a small group of volunteers use the information from the group presentations to create a diagram showing how the system of checks and balances works to limit the power of the judicial branch. Display the model in the classroom for students to use as a reference.

Conducting Research/Mastering Concepts

Discuss the use of judicial activism that requires specific actions in order to bring about change in society. Ask students whether the courts have overstepped their authority or whether they are within the bounds of their authority in the cases discussed in this section. Have students conduct research using newspapers, magazines, and the Internet to find more examples of judicial activism. Have students discuss these examples as a class. Once again, ask students to offer their opinions regarding the appropriateness of the courts' decision in these cases.

CLOSE

Have students create a bulletin board about criticisms of the judicial branch and its activities. Ask each student to bring in newspaper or magazine articles, political cartoons, or other materials that illustrate a criticism of the judicial branch. Special categories should be created for the Supreme Court, special courts, and lower courts. Display the bulletin board in the classroom, and encourage students to continually add new information to it.

OPTIONS

Students Having Difficulty/Sheltered English Students/Intrapersonal Learners

Emphasize the importance of limiting the power of the judicial branch of government. Ask students to recall a situation in their own life when they have witnessed an individual or a group misuse power. Have students write a journal entry about how people were affected by this misuse of power and how they think this particular situation could have been avoided. Help students make the connection between their personal situation and the constitutional limitations placed upon the federal courts in the U.S. system of government. Encourage students to share their ideas with the class.

Gifted/Linguistic Learners

Ask students to imagine that they are columnists for the local newspaper. They must write this week's column on the societal changes they believe will happen as a result of the recent ratification of a constitutional amendment that eliminated the old system of checks and balances among the three branches of government. Tell students that it is crucial to sway public opinion in favor of restoring the old system in order to avoid a major disruption in the balance of power in government. Encourage students to share their ideas with the rest of the class.

Intrapersonal/Gifted Learners

Have students conduct research on instances in which the United States used federal troops to support a Supreme Court decision. Have students write a short essay describing the circumstances surrounding the case, the decision made by the Court, and the reason for the use of troops to enforce the decision. Students should also include their personal opinion on whether troops were needed to enforce the decision. Have students discuss their essays with the class.

Gifted Learners

 Discuss with students some of the methods used to check the Supreme Court's power. Tell students that three constitutional amendments have been ratified in direct response to Supreme Court decisions. Organize the class into three groups. Each will research either the Eleventh Amendment, the Sixteenth Amendment, or the Twenty-sixth Amendment. Encourage students to search the Internet and access the Supreme Court Web site or other appropriate resource to read about how the amendments check the Court's power. Have each group share their findings with the rest of the class.

REVIEW

Have students complete the Section 3 Review on page 262. Use the answers in the Annotated Teacher's Edition to assess student mastery of this section.

ASSESS

To assess student mastery of this section, have students complete Daily Quiz 11.3 in *Daily Quizzes with Answer Key.* For additional assessment options, see *Alternative Assessment Handbook* on the *One-Stop Planner CD-ROM.*

RETEACH

For students having difficulty with the lessons, have them complete Reteaching Activity 11. This activity is located in *Reteaching Activities with Answer Key.*

ADDITIONAL RESOURCES

Burke, Edmund. *Reflections on the Revolution in France.* edited by J. C. D. Clark. 2001. Standard University Press.

GOVERNMENT NOTEBOOK

The Government Notebook is a journal activity that encourages students to consider basic concepts of government that relate to their lives. A follow-up notebook activity appears on page 268.

WHY IT MATTERS TODAY

To find additional lesson plans dealing with the federal court system, visit CNNfyi.com or have students complete GOVERNMENT IN THE NEWS activity on page 267.

CNNfyi.com

THE FEDERAL COURT SYSTEM

In *The Federalist* "No. 78," Alexander Hamilton stated that "the judiciary is beyond comparison the weakest of the three departments of power." The legislature controls lawmaking and spending, and the executive "holds the sword of the community." In contrast, courts have "no influence over either the sword or the purse; no direction either of the strength or of the wealth of the society." Courts cannot even enforce their own decisions, but must depend on "the aid of the executive."

Hamilton's opinion might be different were he to see the judiciary at work today. Both the lower federal courts and the Supreme Court have expanded their power significantly since the 1700s. This increased power has sparked a debate over the judicial branch's role in promoting the public good.

GOVERNMENT NOTEBOOK

In your Government Notebook, make a list of the things in your daily life that you think might be affected by Supreme Court decisions.

WHY IT MATTERS TODAY

The courts interpret laws to ensure that they are being fairly applied. At the end of this chapter, visit CNNfyi.com to learn more about the federal courts.

CNNfyi.com

SECTION 1
THE LOWER COURTS

READ TO DISCOVER

1. What are the role and the authority of the lower courts?
2. How are the lower courts organized?
3. How are lower-court judges selected?

POLITICAL DICTIONARY

precedent
strict constructionist
loose constructionist
jurisdiction
original jurisdiction
district court
court of appeals
circuit
appellate jurisdiction
brief
senatorial courtesy

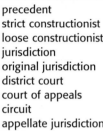

The federal court system consists of the lower courts and the Supreme Court. The Supreme Court is more fully explained in Section 2. This section discusses the lower courts—their role, authority, organization, and judges.

Role of the Courts

The lower federal courts perform the day-to-day work of the judicial branch. That is, they hear and decide thousands of cases that are brought to the federal court system each year. In performing this duty, the courts resolve disputes, interpret the law, and set precedents.

Resolving Disputes The lower courts hear "cases and controversies," reviewing and resolving specific disputes between specific parties. For example, suppose you apply for a job at Acme, Inc., but are not hired because the company has an illegal, discriminatory hiring policy. You, as a job applicant of Acme, may contest the company's policy in court. If you had not applied to Acme, however, and only had heard about its policy from a friend, you could not sue Acme merely on general principles as a concerned citizen. Rather, the law allows only people who have suffered a specific injury to bring suit.

Setting Precedents Although the courts rule only on specific cases, their decisions can have much broader and more far-reaching consequences. This is because in addition to announcing their specific decisions, the courts also provide the legal grounds, or reasoning, for these decisions. These grounds serve as **precedents**, or guiding principles, for determining what is legal in future situations that involve similar issues. Judges, lawmakers, government officials, companies, and citizens look to these precedents to guide their actions.

Interpreting the Law What philosophy should judges apply when resolving disputes and setting precedents? Some people are **strict constructionists**. They believe that laws and the Constitution should be interpreted strictly according to the wording they contain. If any wording is vague, the courts should examine the historical record to determine the authors' intended meaning. These records might include transcriptions of debates over bills and proposed amendments, discussions and debates at the

"Maybe I'm in the minority here, but aren't we becoming obsessed with constitutionality?"

CONSTITUTIONAL GOVERNMENT *Some judges hold that the Constitution should be interpreted strictly according to the words and phrases it contains.* **What tools do the courts use to interpret the meaning of any vague wording in the Constitution?**

SECTION 1
THE LOWER COURTS

Lesson Plans

For teaching strategies, see Lesson 11.1 located at the beginning of this chapter or the One-Stop Lesson Planner Strategy 11.1.

Political Dictionary

To reinforce the section's vocabulary terms, refer students to the Electronic Glossary on the *Researcher CD-ROM*.

Section Assessment

To assess students' mastery of this section, have them complete Daily Quiz 11.1 in *Daily Quizzes with Answer Key*.

Transparency

An overhead transparency of the cartoon on this page is available in *Transparency Resources*. See Cartoon Transparency 10: Strict Constructionist vs. Loose Constructionist.

> **Caption Answer**
>
> historical records, to determine the authors' intended meaning

Constitution Convention, and documents such as the *Federalist Papers*.

For example, Article I of the Constitution gives Congress the power "to regulate commerce . . . among the several states." A review of historical records shows that the framers wanted to prevent states from setting their own rules regarding trade and business with other states. Such practices had damaged the national economy under the Articles of Confederation. Strict constructionists argue that the framers did not mean for Congress to use this power to design other business regulations, such as minimum-wage laws. They instead believe that the proper way to address changing circumstances is not by reinterpreting the Constitution and the laws passed by Congress but by passing constitutional amendments or new laws.

Other people prefer a "living Constitution." These **loose constructionists** believe that the Constitution and other laws must be interpreted in light of current political and social conditions. In other words, judges should consider *current* standards in applying to specific cases the general intentions of the documents' authors.

For example, the Eighth Amendment to the Constitution prohibits "cruel and unusual punishment." A punishment is considered cruel if it inflicts more pain or humiliation than the lawbreaker deserves, given the nature of the crime. When the framers wrote these words, public beatings were in common practice. Examples of what society considers cruel have changed over the years, however, and today most people would consider public beatings to be cruel and unusual. Loose constructionists thus argue that the courts should now interpret the Eighth Amendment to mean that public beatings are unconstitutional.

Authority of the Courts

Article III of the Constitution states that "the judicial power of the United States shall be vested in one supreme Court, and in such inferior courts as the Congress may . . . establish." The First Congress used this constitutional power to set up a system of federal courts under the Judiciary Act of 1789. Congress was given the power to establish the lower federal courts, but the courts receive their **jurisdiction**, or authority to interpret and administer the law, from the Constitution.

Lower federal courts have **original jurisdiction**—the authority to hear a case's

---

Extent of the Jurisdiction of Lower Courts

The lower courts hear cases in which

- a person is accused of disobeying the U.S. Constitution,
- a person is accused of violating a U.S. treaty,
- a person is accused of breaking federal laws passed by Congress,
- the U.S. government or a U.S. citizen is charged with an offense by a foreign nation,
- a person is accused of committing a crime on a U.S. ship at sea,
- a U.S. ambassador or other foreign-service official is accused of breaking the laws of the country in which he or she is stationed,
- a person is accused of committing a crime on certain types of federal property, and
- a citizen of one state brings a lawsuit against a citizen of another state.

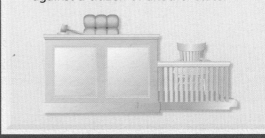

The Constitution outlines the jurisdiction of the nation's courts. Federal courts administer the law for many types of federal crimes. **Why do you think that the federal courts hear cases in which a citizen from one state sues a citizen of another state?**

---

initial trial—only over cases arising under the Constitution and other federal laws and over those involving diplomats, treaties, state governments, the U.S. government, and citizens of other countries or of more than one state. (See the chart on this page for the extent of lower courts' jurisdiction.)

In addition, a few special types of disputes, which are discussed in Section 2, fall under the original jurisdiction of the Supreme Court. All other disputes are left to state, county, or municipal courts, which are discussed in Unit 7.

Linking

Government and Philosophy

Philosophy and the U.S. Court System

"You and I, my dear friend," wrote Constitutional Convention delegate John Adams to a fellow delegate, "have been sent into life at a time when the greatest lawgivers of antiquity (ancient times) would have wished to live." Few people, he concluded, had the chance to create their own laws. To write these laws and—just as importantly—build the court system to uphold them, the delegates at the Constitutional Convention drew on the writings of political philosophers dating back to the ancient Greeks.

The writings of Aristotle, a Greek who lived from 384 to 322 B.C., provided the basic ideas on the functions and purpose of government. Aristotle argued that the main goal of government should be to promote the public good, a novel idea for his time. He believed that law and justice helped people achieve a good life. "For man, when perfected, is the best of animals," he argued, "but when separated from law and justice, he is the worst of all."

Later philosophers echoed Aristotle's belief in the connection between the law and the public good. In his *Two Treatises of Government* (1690),

The Granger Collection, New York

In 1748 Baron Charles de Montesquieu published Spirit of the Laws, *in which he argued for the separation of government powers.*

English philosopher John Locke agreed that people formed governments to preserve the public good. In exchange for giving up some of their liberties, people accepted their government's "right of making laws . . . and of employing the force of the community in execution of such laws." Courts and laws protected individual rights and property, rather than threatening citizens' liberty.

Baron Charles de Montesquieu, a French philosopher, believed that the main aim of government should be to promote liberty. He argued that government could most effectively achieve this goal by dividing its authority among executive, legislative, and judicial branches.

In *Spirit of the Laws*, published in 1748, Montesquieu called for this bold concept of the separation of powers to defend people's freedom from a too-powerful government. He argued that a combined executive and legislative branch would abuse its power and destroy liberty. He also stated that the judiciary would become too powerful if joined with the legislative branch, which was a common practice at the time.

The writings of Locke and Montesquieu particularly influenced the framers of the Constitution. In the *Federalist Papers*, James Madison praised Montesquieu's separation of powers as an "invaluable precept (precious principle) in the science of politics." Thomas Jefferson, advising a friend who wanted to study law, also "generally recommended" Montesquieu's *Spirit of the Laws* and cited Locke's "little book of Government" as "perfect as far as it goes."

Drawing on these philosophers, the framers of the Constitution created a separate court system that sought to protect liberty as it enforced the Constitution. As a separate body, the judiciary could check the power of the legislative branch, which the framers saw as the greatest threat to liberty. Judges could make sure that legislators did not create new laws that violated the Constitution.

What Do You Think?

1. How did Montesquieu build upon Aristotle's belief that the main goal of government should be to promote the public good?
2. How did the ideas of Locke and Montesquieu influence the framers of the Constitution?

What Do You Think? Answers

1. Montesquieu called for separation of powers among branches of government as a way to promote liberty.

2. They led the framers to create a separate court system that could check the power of the legislature.

GLOBAL CONNECTIONS

How have countries dealt with prosecuting people accused of committing genocide during World War II? The answer varies based on how each country deals with the issue of retroactivity—which allows for the prosecution of specific crimes even though these acts were not illegal at the time they were committed.

France has now built this concept into its legal system and has successfully prosecuted people for crimes against humanity that were committed during World War II.

Italy, however, operates under the principle of nonretroactivity—which does not allow prosecuting people for crimes that were not illegal when the acts were committed. The policy of nonretroactivity has led to difficulties in prosecuting people who were responsible for genocide during World War II because there were no laws against genocide in Italy's criminal code during the World War II period. ■

Caption Answer
Answers will vary.

Lower Court Organization

The lower courts are divided into district courts and courts of appeals. These two types of courts play different roles in the legal system. The lower court system also includes several specialized courts.

District Courts The trial courts of the federal system are called **district courts**. These courts are assigned to specific geographic areas and have original jurisdiction over federal cases that arise there. The District of Columbia has one district court, and each state has from one to four, generally depending on the size of its population.

District courts engage in the oldest and most fundamental judicial activity—making a decision in a dispute. Any trial decision is based on the *facts* of the case (the specifics of what happened) as well as the *law* (the general, established rules of society). The basic task of district courts is to determine the facts and then reach a verdict by applying the law to them.

Cases are tried before a district court judge and a jury, though the defendant can waive, or give up, the right to a jury. Both sides support their position by providing evidence, some of which may be supplied by witnesses. In criminal cases a U.S. attorney from the Justice Department serves as the prosecutor. In civil cases the opposing parties are represented by their own attorneys. Some district court civil cases are tried before a jury as well as a judge, though the right to a jury is typically waived in such cases.

Courts of Appeals Appeals of cases from the U.S. district courts are heard by the **courts of appeals**. Although about one third of district court decisions are appealed, only around one fifth of them are actually reviewed. The remainder are settled out of court.

There are 13 U.S. courts of appeals, each of which covers a large judicial district called a **circuit**. The 50 states are divided into 11 circuits. There is also a circuit for the District of Columbia and a Federal Circuit, which hears certain kinds of cases involving federal agencies. The Federal Circuit has jurisdiction over all states and territories. Each court of appeals has a total of 6 to 28 judges. There are no juries in a court of appeals, so cases are heard by the judges alone. Usually, a panel of only three of a circuit's judges hear any one case, although some important cases may be decided by the entire court.

Appeals courts were established to give individuals who have received an unfavorable decision another chance to be heard. This opportunity

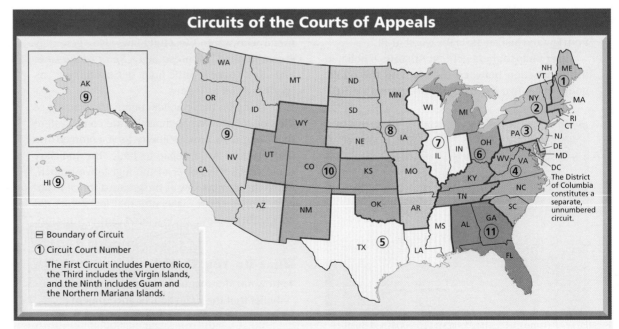

Circuits of the Courts of Appeals

Boundary of Circuit
① Circuit Court Number

The First Circuit includes Puerto Rico, the Third includes the Virgin Islands, and the Ninth includes Guam and the Northern Mariana Islands.

The District of Columbia constitutes a separate, unnumbered circuit.

*The U.S. federal court system is divided into 13 circuits, including one for the District of Columbia and A Federal Circuit. **In which circuit is your state located?***

is rooted in the U.S. legal and cultural tradition. The appeals courts' **appellate jurisdiction** means they have the power to review cases previously decided by a lower court.

Appeals courts are limited in the scope of their examination. They may not review a trial's determinations of the *facts*, such as whether a defendant robbed a store. Therefore, no new facts are presented to a court of appeals. Rather, courts of appeals may review only issues of *law*, such as whether a defendant's confession to a robbery was legally obtained. They only determine whether the person appealing the case received his or her full rights under the law during the district court trial.

Thus, courts of appeals do not hold another trial of the cases they review. Judges make their decisions based on two types of information: the written record from the district court trial and **briefs**, or written legal arguments, submitted by both sides in the case. Thus, whereas a district court trial is basically an oral proceeding, an appeal is basically a written one, although oral arguments are often allowed.

There are a variety of decisions that the judges may make in an appealed case, including reversing the decision, affirming it, or sending the case back to district court for a retrial if the appeals court finds that an individual's legal rights were not fully protected. If the court of appeals finds that the individual's rights were observed and the law was properly applied to the facts, it upholds, or affirms, the district court's decision. If it finds that the law was not properly applied, the court of appeals reverses the lower court's decision.

Other Courts In addition to the district courts and courts of appeals, Congress has set up several special courts to handle specific types of cases. For example, the U.S. Court of Claims hears cases involving money claims against the federal government. (See the chart on this page for a list of special courts.)

Federal Judges

Most federal judges, not including those who preside over special courts, serve for life, although Congress can impeach and convict them for serious crimes. The framers established life terms for these judges so that they could remain independent of political pressure.

Delegates at the Constitutional Convention discussed various methods for choosing federal

Comparing Governments

Russian Courts

After more than 70 years of communist rule, the Soviet Union disbanded in 1991, and Russia, a former Soviet republic, became independent. Russia is currently struggling to build a democratic system. Yet many judicial practices, especially jury trials, fall far short of the democratic ideal.

In 1994, after jury trials were introduced, more and more acquittals resulted as independent-minded jurors rejected questionable evidence. As a result, the legal establishment, intent on resisting change, successfully lobbied against the expansion of jury trials.

The jury-trial experiment in Russia has been halted. In 1999, more than 99 percent of non-jury trials ended in convictions. Liberal Russian law experts state that judges are absolute in their attempt to convict the accused, jeopardizing a measured decision.

The cause of this problem lies with Russian law, which assigns the responsibility for ensuring that evidence gets presented to the judge, rather than the prosecutor. This removes the judge's objectivity, making the judge more of an ally of the prosecution.

SECTION 1 REVIEW ANSWERS

1. Refer to the following pages: precedent (249), strict constructionist (249), loose constructionist (250), jurisdiction (250), original jurisdiction (250), district court (252), court of appeals (252), circuit (252), appellate jurisdiction (253), brief (253), senatorial courtesy (254).

2. District courts—make decisions in disputes by determining the facts of the case and applying law to them; Courts of Appeals—review issues of law, but not findings of fact, in decisions by lower courts; Special courts—handle specific types of cases.

3a. District courts decide disputes; courts of appeals hear appeals of cases from district courts.

3b. resolve disputes—decide on specific cases brought by injured parties; interpret the law—decide how laws and the Constitution should be applied to disputes, set precedents—announce decisions that provide legal ground for similar issues

4. Answers will vary but students should give their opinions and defend them.

POLITICAL PROCESSES *Burnita Shelton Matthews was the first woman to be appointed U.S. district court judge. President Harry Truman appointed her to the District of Columbia federal district court in 1949.* **Who handles most of the nominations for district court judges?**

judges. Some favored a system in which the president would have independent appointment powers, while others feared that this would give the president too much power. The resulting compromise established the same system as that used for appointing top officials of the executive branch: nomination by the president and approval or rejection by a simple majority of the Senate. Today this selection process varies somewhat, depending on the position being filled.

District Court Appointments By far the largest number of judicial appointments are those to the district courts. Because there are so many district court positions, the nominations of district court judges are handled mostly by the Department of Justice and by White House staffers, not by the president.

The traditional principle in making district court nominations has been **senatorial courtesy**. That is, the executive branch allows senators in the president's party to approve or disapprove each potential nominee for a position in a district in their state before the official nominations are made. The other senators then almost always follow the lead of those senators and approve the nominee. In return for this courtesy, the Senate confirms almost all of the president's nominations for the district courts.

Courts of Appeals Appointments Individual senators have less influence over appeals court nominations. Appeals court appointments involve several states, so senatorial courtesy does not play a role.

On the other hand, because of the vital role of courts of appeals in interpreting the law and setting precedents, the Senate examines appeals court nominations far more carefully than those for district courts. Another reason for this closer examination is that appeals court judges are more likely to wind up later serving on the Supreme Court. For example, seven of the nine current Supreme Court justices formerly served as judges in the U.S. courts of appeals.

SECTION 1 REVIEW

1. Identify and Explain:
- precedent
- strict constructionist
- loose constructionist
- jurisdiction
- original jurisdiction
- district court
- court of appeals
- circuit
- appellate jurisdiction
- brief
- senatorial courtesy

2. Identifying Concepts: Copy the chart below. Use it to describe the organization and functions of the lower federal courts.

Type of Court	Function

Homework Practice Online
keyword: SV3 HP11

3. Finding the Main Idea
a. What are the functions of the district courts and the courts of appeals?
b. How do the lower courts resolve disputes, interpret the law, and set precedents?

4. Writing and Critical Thinking
Drawing Conclusions: Do you think that loose constructionist interpretations endanger the integrity of the Constitution? Explain your answer.
Consider the following:
- the intentions of the framers of the Constitution
- changes that have occurred since the Constitution was written

SECTION 2
THE SUPREME COURT

1. How has the role of the Supreme Court changed over time?
2. How are Supreme Court justices appointed, and what are their terms of office?
3. How does the Supreme Court operate?

POLITICAL DICTIONARY

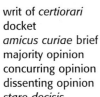

writ of *certiorari*
docket
amicus curiae brief
majority opinion
concurring opinion
dissenting opinion
stare decisis

As noted in Chapter 5, Pierre Charles L'Enfant designed the capital of Washington, D.C., in 1791. L'Enfant's original plans for the city did not include a building for the Supreme Court. In a revised plan, though, L'Enfant did include a home for the Court—in marshland about halfway between the Capitol Building and the president's mansion. This building was never constructed, however, because of the high cost of draining the marsh. Such an expense was viewed as unjustified due to the Court's small size and small caseload.

Lacking other quarters, the Supreme Court met in chambers in the Capitol Building. (During one year, while the Capitol was under construction, the Court met in a tavern.) In 1824 a newspaper reporter described the Court's quarters in the Capitol as "not in a style which comports [is consistent] with the dignity" of the Supreme Court, complaining that "the room is on the basement story in an obscure [unnoticeable] part of the north wing. . . . A stranger might traverse [cross] the dark avenues of the Capitol for a week, without finding the remote

corner in which Justice is administered to the American Republic." The Supreme Court did not gain its own building until 1935.

This modest position of the Supreme Court has changed considerably. Today the Court is held in higher esteem, with a far-reaching impact on the public policies that influence people's day-to-day lives. For example, the Supreme Court's decisions affect where you go to school, the conditions where you work, the laws protecting your environment, and where and when you may vote.

Development of the Supreme Court

Initially, the Supreme Court was part of the weakest branch of government. Over time, however, the Supreme Court has become in some respects the most powerful institution in the country.

The Early Years Much of the first session of Congress was taken up with discussion of the organization of the judicial branch. The result was the Judiciary Act of 1789. This law established the three-level structure of the federal court system, which is made up of district courts, courts of appeals, and the Supreme Court.

CONSTITUTIONAL GOVERNMENT *The construction of the Supreme Court building was completed in 1935.* **Where was the Supreme Court housed before its permanent quarters were finished?**

Enhancing the Lesson

For more information on *Marbury* v. *Madison* and other Supreme Court decisions, see the Supreme Court Docket section on the *Holt Researcher Online.*

Widely considered to be the greatest Supreme Court justice in U.S. history, John Marshall is said to have given power to the piece of paper that was the Constitution.

Marshall argued that in order to build a nation invested with essential governmental powers, the Court should be a vigorous arm of the Constitution. Marshall helped to secure fundamental powers for the federal government with his most significant decisions—*Marbury* v. *Madison*, which established the process of judicial review; *McCulloch* v. *Maryland*, which expanded federal powers beyond those listed in the Constitution; and *Gibbons* v. *Ogden*, which broadly interpreted the central government's power to manage commerce. ∎

CONSTITUTIONAL GOVERNMENT *John Jay (1745–1829) was the first chief justice of the United States. This portrait of him was begun by artist Gilbert Stuart and is believed to have been finished by John Trumbull.* **What is the role of the chief justice?**

President George Washington appointed a number of distinguished people, many of whom had been present at the Constitutional Convention, to serve on the Court. The first chief justice—the justice who presides over the Court—was John Jay, a coauthor of the *Federalist Papers* and a leader in New York's battle over ratification of the Constitution.

During its early years the Supreme Court was considered a fairly insignificant institution. Antifederalist views against the judiciary were still strong, and many people felt that Jay's Court lacked the right to serve as the nation's highest judicial body. During the first decade the Court heard only around 50 cases. Unsurprisingly, given the lack of Court activity, Jay's position was a part-time job. In fact, in 1794 Jay took off to lead a U.S. diplomatic mission to Britain, and he was a candidate for governor of New York while sitting on the bench. After winning that election in 1795, Jay resigned from the Court. Asked to return as chief justice in 1800, Jay declined, stating his belief that the Court could never "obtain the energy, weight, and dignity which were essential to its affording due support for the National Government."

The Marshall Court The modest role of the Court changed abruptly with John Marshall's 1801 appointment as chief justice. The Court handed down several landmark decisions during the time that Marshall served as its chief (1801–35), including *Marbury* v. *Madison,* which established the principle of judicial review. As noted in Chapter 3, judicial review gives the Court the final voice in deciding the constitutionality of government laws and policies.

Through this and other decisions, Marshall made the Supreme Court a significant force in government. These decisions gave the Court the power to influence whether and how Congress and the president may pursue specific public policies.

The Justices

Who are the Supreme Court justices who make these far-reaching decisions? How long do they serve and how are they appointed?

Supreme Court justices do not have to meet any constitutional age or professional requirements, such as having had experience serving as a lawyer or a judge. However, all Supreme Court justices have had legal training, and today most are graduates of top law schools and have previously served as federal judges.

The Constitution does not state the size of the Supreme Court. Rather, the number of justices is set by Congress. The Judiciary Act of 1789 set the number of justices at six. The current number of nine justices was set in 1869. The chief justice of the United States, who presides over the group, is the nation's highest judicial officer.

Like other federal judges, Supreme Court justices serve for life, although they, too, may be impeached by Congress for serious crimes. Typically, justices have chosen to stay on the Court up to an advanced age—often into their seventies and eighties. During the 1800s a majority died in office. More recent justices almost always have retired. The average age of justices retiring from the Court since 1970 is 78.

Several justices have continued serving despite serious illnesses, often because they did not want a president with political views that were different from their own to nominate their successor. For example, Justice Harry Blackmun retired in 1994 at age 85, purposely staying in office long enough to give a president closer to his political ideology—Democrat Bill Clinton, as it turned out—the chance to make an appointment to replace him. About the prospect that he might be replaced by a conservative appointee if he retired, Justice Thurgood Marshall once told his clerks, "If I die, prop me up and keep on voting."

Justices of the Supreme Court

	Year Appointed	President by Whom Appointed
Chief Justice		
William H. Rehnquist	1972*	Nixon
Associate Justices		
John Paul Stevens	1975	Ford
Sandra Day O'Connor	1981	Reagan
Antonin Scalia	1986	Reagan
Anthony M. Kennedy	1988	Reagan
David H. Souter	1990	Bush
Clarence Thomas	1991	Bush
Ruth Bader Ginsburg	1993	Clinton
Stephen G. Breyer	1994	Clinton

*Appointed as chief justice in 1986 by President Reagan

*The president has the power to appoint justices to the Supreme Court. **Which of the justices was appointed most recently?***

Terms The Supreme Court's regular annual term begins on the first Monday in October. Justices hear cases throughout the year until summer recess, usually the last week in June.

Court Appointments Supreme Court justices, including the chief justice, are appointed by the president with the approval of the Senate. In view of their importance, and contrary to the previously mentioned procedure of appointing lower court judges, these nominations have the president's personal attention. Unlike cabinet appointments, though, the opportunity to appoint justices to the Supreme Court is not guaranteed to every president. Such appointments depend on a vacancy occurring in the Court. All but four presidents, however, have had the chance to make at least one appointment. These appointments have become among the most important decisions that presidents make. After all, because justices usually serve very long terms, judicial appointments can thus influence national politics for years after the president who made them leaves office.

Presidential nominations to the Supreme Court have never been approved automatically by the Senate. In fact, since 1789 the Senate refused to confirm or took no action on 28 of 148 Supreme Court nominees. Such negative reactions were more common in the last century than in this one, however. For example, five of the six justices nominated by President John Tyler and three of the four nominated by President Millard Fillmore were either rejected or not acted upon. In contrast, only 7 of the 63 nominations since 1900 met this fate.

Although the number of rejections has decreased significantly in this century, the degree of care with which the Senate examines appointments has increased. Since 1939 the Senate Judiciary Committee has subjected nominees to intense background investigations and lengthy public hearings to examine their personal lives and legal views. As a result, several nominations have produced bruising political battles that ended with dramatic final votes broadcast on television. As recently as 1991, for example, hearings for the appointment of Clarence Thomas, who faced charges of sexual harassment by a former co-worker, were broadcast on television for days and received front-page newspaper coverage.

CASE STUDY

Packing the Court

CONSTITUTIONAL GOVERNMENT In 1935 and 1936 the Supreme Court declared unconstitutional about a half dozen pieces of federal legislation regulating business. These laws had been passed under President Franklin D. Roosevelt's New Deal program to fight the depression of the 1930s.

Frustrated by the Court's overturning of key legislation, Roosevelt proposed at the beginning of his second term in 1937 to change the Court fundamentally by raising the number of justices up to 15. His proposal would have allowed presidents to nominate an additional justice to the Court each time a justice who had served at least 10 years reached the age of 70. It was no coincidence that between 1933 and 1937 four of the justices—each around 70 years old—had formed a voting block that declared much of Roosevelt's New Deal legislation unconstitutional.

Opponents denounced the idea, saying that it would give the president the power to "pack" the

THEMES IN GOVERNMENT

POLITICAL PROCESSES
According to some experts, cronyism prompted President Harry Truman to appoint Fred M. Vinson as chief justice of the United States. Truman hoped that his old friend's geniality would bring peace to the fragmented Supreme Court. Vinson failed, however, because of what some people perceived to be his inability to lead and his superficial approach to the various cases the Court heard.

The Court, which remained divided, is known as one of the most divided Supreme Courts in U.S. history. During Vinson's last annual term the Court reached a unanimous decision in only 19 percent of the cases. Vinson himself seemed to contribute to this division by averaging 13 dissents per term, among the highest of any chief justice. ■

Profiles in American Government

For biographies of Bill Clinton, Thurgood Marshall, John Tyler, Millard Fillmore, and other noted people in government, refer students to the Biographies section on the *Holt Researcher Online*.

Court with justices who were friendly to him. The new plan was never tested, however. Within three months of Roosevelt's presenting his proposal, but before it was considered in congressional committees, the Court upheld the constitutionality of two key pieces of New Deal legislation—on labor and the minimum wage. As a result, Roosevelt backed off from pushing his court-packing plan, which Congress later rejected decisively. The verdicts were the result of one justice—Owen Roberts—shifting his opinion to support Roosevelt's legislation. "A switch in time," as a contemporary saying put it, had "saved nine."

Roosevelt eventually achieved his goal of influencing the Court's composition, however. During the next few years, all of Roosevelt's judicial opponents on the Court either died or resigned. This allowed Roosevelt to appoint a total of nine justices with ideals closer to his own.

CONSTITUTIONAL GOVERNMENT *Here, the U.S. Supreme Court justices assemble for a portrait. Standing (left to right): Ruth Bader Ginsburg, David Souter, Clarence Thomas, and Stephen Breyer. Sitting (left to right): Antonin Scalia, John Paul Stevens, William Rehnquist, Sandra Day O'Connor, and Anthony Kennedy.* **How are Supreme Court justices selected?**

The Supreme Court at Work

How does the Supreme Court decide which cases to hear, and how are cases argued before the Court? Once a case is selected, it goes through five stages: briefs, oral argument, conference, preparation of opinions, and announcement of decisions.

Choosing Cases The Supreme Court serves chiefly as an appeals court, reviewing cases that have been tried and appealed in the lower federal courts and decisions of the highest state courts that involve alleged violations of the Constitution or other federal laws. Of the cases heard by the Supreme Court, 12 percent have come from the state courts. The Supreme Court does, however, have original jurisdiction in cases that involve these listed situations:

★ diplomatic representatives of other nations,
★ disputes between two or more states, and
★ disputes between a state and the federal government.

Compared to the president and Congress, the Supreme Court might seem to have little control over what it considers. The president and members of Congress may pursue public policies addressing any number of possible issues—from job growth and civil rights to health-care reform and protection of the environment. In contrast, the Supreme Court may not take such initiative. It may act on only the "cases and controversies" that are appealed to it by others.

The Supreme Court is not merely a cork bobbing in the currents, however. On closer inspection, it has considerable control over which issues it considers. Each year thousands of cases on many public policy issues are appealed to the Court. The Court can choose to hear—or, more often, not to hear—any case from among this vast pool. Thus, the Court has the freedom to set its agenda by addressing cases that involve the public policy issues it believes are most pressing. Similarly, the Court also can shape public policy by refusing to hear a case, thus quietly supporting the lower court's decision.

Who May Appeal Anyone may appeal a high state court or federal appeals case to the Supreme Court if a violation of the U.S. Constitution is

Careers in Government

Law Clerk

Like the Supreme Court, the lower federal courts employ law clerks. These lawyers gain an insider's view of judicial decision making as they work with federal judges on important legal issues.

Law clerks in the federal district courts help judges try a wide range of civil and criminal cases, involving everything from civil rights violations to drug smuggling. Law clerks in the appeals courts research cases decided in the district courts. Special federal courts such as the U.S. Tax Court and U.S. Court of Veterans Appeals also employ law clerks who assist judges with cases.

Before judges make a decision, law clerks put in countless hours summarizing the case or appeal at hand, researching the legal issues involved, and writing down their conclusions. They often prepare the judge's final written draft of the decision, review and proofread the argu-

Law clerks spend much of their time in law libraries, researching legal issues.

ment, and check the accuracy of the document.

The application process for federal clerkships is extremely competitive. Judges require that clerks have a law degree, and often they must have passed the appropriate state bar exam. In choosing whom to hire, judges weigh the applicants' grades, writing ability, work experience, recommendations from professors, and extracurricular activities.

According to former Supreme Court clerk Julia Shelton, "Clerkships are a great way to make the transition from law student to lawyer." Clerks get direct experience in the major areas of the law and learn from experienced judges.

Many lawyers go on to use the experience they gain during their one- or two-year clerkships to further their law careers. Private law firms heavily recruit lawyers who have had experience as federal clerks. Other former clerks go on to distinguished careers in government service or teaching.

charged. Unlike the lower courts of appeals, however, the Supreme Court is not required to hear an appeal.

Most petitioners who appeal to the Supreme Court do so by requesting a **writ of *certiorari*** (suhr-shuh-RAR-ee). In legal terms the Supreme Court "grants *cert*" if it agrees to hear the appeal and "denies *cert*" if it refuses. Four of the nine justices must agree to grant *cert* for an appeal to be heard by the Court. If such an agreement is reached, the case is placed on the Court's **docket**, or schedule. If, however, the Supreme Court denies *cert,* the lower court decision is left standing. The Court does not have to provide a reason for denying *cert.*

Although the number of appeals has grown dramatically over the years, the number of cases the Court has agreed to hear has steadily declined—from an average of around 180 argued cases a year between 1981 and 1987 to only 90 in 1996. Even at its highest, however, this number is far below the number of decisions made by Congress, let alone the number made by executive agencies.

Most participants in a case are represented by a lawyer who is a member of the Supreme Court bar. To be admitted into this group, a lawyer must have been a member of a state bar for at least three years and must be known to be of good moral and professional character.

Filing Briefs The lawyer for each party in the case generally files a written brief. When the federal government is a party, its brief is filed by

Careers in Government

To help students learn about other careers in government, refer them to the Careers section on the *Holt Researcher Online.*

⚡ internet connect

TOPIC: Rules of the Supreme Court
GO TO: go.hrw.com
KEYWORD: SV3 GV11

Have students access the Internet through the HRW Go site to research how the Supreme Court functions, when it accepts cases for hearing, and who the justices are. Then ask them to create a map that illustrates how a case gets through the Supreme Court. The map should be annotated and should reflect the current Supreme Court rules.

THEMES IN GOVERNMENT

PUBLIC GOOD The Supreme Court's choice in 1953 to postpone its ruling in the *Brown* v. *Board of Education* case until reargument the following year may have affected the outcome of perhaps the most important decision in modern U.S. history. During initial hearings, Chief Justice Fred Vinson encouraged the justices to uphold segregation, and it is claimed that the vote would have been 5 to 4 in favor of maintaining segregation. During the postponement, however, Vinson died and Earl Warren was named chief justice.

During reargument of the case, Chief Justice Warren appealed to the justices to vote against segregation. He presented the issue in terms of morality. Warren told the judges that only a belief in the inferiority of African Americans could justify segregation, and if the Court were to uphold segregation, it must do so on that basis.

The justices may have taken Warren's comments to heart. The final vote in the case was 9 to 0 to end segregation. ∎

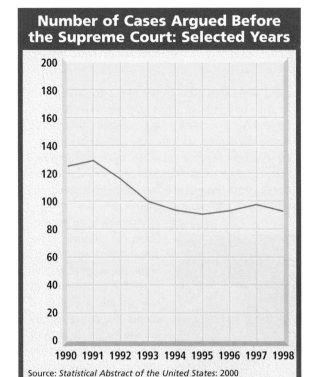

Number of Cases Argued Before the Supreme Court: Selected Years

Source: *Statistical Abstract of the United States: 2000*

The Supreme Court hears many cases each year. **Why do you think that the number of cases the Court agrees to hear has declined since 1988?**

the solicitor general of the United States, an official of the Department of Justice.

Groups that are greatly affected by a case but are not one of the parties involved may be granted the Court's permission to file *amicus curiae* (uh-MEE-kuhs KYOOR-ee-eye) **briefs**. (*Amicus curiae* means "friend of the court" in Latin.) These briefs state the group's concerns and arguments regarding the case. For example, the federal government may be allowed to file an *amicus curiae* brief in a water rights disagreement between two states, as this issue involves the nation's water supply.

These briefs usually make arguments relating the case to precedents and to provisions in the Constitution, other federal laws, and state laws. Sometimes, however, briefs make an argument about why a certain decision would make good public policy. For example, in *Brown* v. *Board of Education of Topeka,* a brief presented psychological data about the harmful effects of segregation on the social development of African American children. This information contributed significantly to the Court's reasoning in outlawing segregation in public schools.

Oral Argument The most dramatic stage of a Supreme Court case is the oral argument that lawyers make before the justices. In the early years of the Supreme Court, there were no written briefs, only oral argument. Because no time limits existed on oral arguments, some went on for days. In 1848 the Court imposed its first limit on the length of oral argument—eight hours per case. Limits have since been tightened further and now stand at 30 minutes per side, except in rare cases of extreme importance.

The Court uses an official timer to time lawyers' arguments. When a red light goes on, the chief justice notifies the lawyer that his or her time is up. Chief Justice Charles Evans Hughes supposedly stopped lawyers in midword when their time expired. A later chief justice, Warren Burger, referred to this practice by stating that the Court is "more liberal now. We allow a lawyer to finish the sentence . . . provided, of course, the sentence is not too long."

During oral argument, lawyers seldom have the chance to make prepared speeches. Rather, justices often interrupt them to ask questions about the case. The public may witness this process, but because the number of seats in the courtroom is extremely small, only a few people may witness the entire argument, while others are allowed to listen

CONSTITUTIONAL GOVERNMENT *The photo above shows the timer used in the Supreme Court to time lawyers' oral arguments.* **How many minutes does each side have to present its argument?**

for only about three minutes before being ushered out to make way for the next group. People are seated to view Supreme Court proceedings on a "first-come, first-served" basis.

Conference The justices meet in private conference twice a week to review petitions for new cases, debate current cases, and conduct other Court business. The chief justice presides at this conference and is first to speak, offering his or her views. The remaining justices then present their views, in order of seniority on the Court. The atmosphere of the conferences varies from case to case, but discussion of cases is limited to some degree. Controversial cases typically involve greater dialogue among the justices. After the newest member of the Court has spoken, a tally of the votes is generally taken (unless the justices have all made their votes clear during their initial comments). The decision reached during this conference can change, however, as the justices prepare the Court's official opinion, or decision, on the case.

Preparing Opinions When the chief justice votes with the majority of the justices, he or she decides who will draft the Court's opinion. Otherwise, the most senior justice voting with the majority makes the assignment. The assignment of a justice to an opinion can have a decisive effect on the Court's ruling in a case. An opinion that is drafted by a liberal justice will be much different from one drafted by a conservative justice. Thus, the chief justice or senior justice assigning the case must take such considerations into account, particularly if the preliminary vote on a case is close. An opinion written by a moderate justice may have a better chance of keeping—and maybe increasing—majority support for the ruling.

The chosen justice writes a draft opinion and circulates it among the other justices for comment. During this process, justices often discuss the content of the opinion, negotiating about whether the grounds, or reasoning given for the opinion, should be changed.

The eight justices reviewing the draft opinion can endorse—or refuse to endorse—the draft depending on whether certain changes are made. Through such negotiations, votes on the case's outcome may shift from what they had been in conference, affecting the size of the majority supporting the Court's decision or changing the decision itself.

CONSTITUTIONAL GOVERNMENT *The room shown in the photo above is the Supreme Court justices' conference room. Justices meet here to review petitions for new cases.* **What role does seniority play in the Supreme Court justices' procedure for reviewing petitions?**

There are three main kinds of opinions that the Court may issue in a case. Most cases include a **majority opinion** that reflects the views of the majority of the Court—both on the outcome of the case and on the grounds for deciding it. A justice may also issue a **concurring opinion** that agrees with the majority *outcome* but disagrees with all or part of the *grounds* stated in the majority opinion. A concurring opinion instead offers other grounds for the decision. A justice also may issue a **dissenting opinion** that disagrees with the one reached by the majority and explains the grounds for the dissent. In addition, in some cases the Court will issue a plurality decision, in which the justices agree on a certain result but disagree on the grounds for the decision. In such instances the Court will issue no majority opinion, only a series of separate opinions in which justices explain the reasons for their votes.

Dissenting opinions often are addressed more to Supreme Courts of the future than to the present court. One study shows that about three fourths of Supreme Court decisions that overrule earlier Court precedents are based on previous cases' dissenting opinions.

The Supreme Court rarely reverses its decisions, however. Most justices place great weight on **stare decisis** (STER-ee di-SY-suhs), or upholding precedents set by earlier courts. (*Stare decisis* is a Latin

ACROSS THE CURRICULUM

LITERATURE The Illinois Supreme Court issued a 25-page ruling on a case that began because of a fictional story. In 1991 *Seventeen* magazine published Lucy Logsdon's "Bryson," a story describing the title character as a loud bully. Logsdon had attended an Illinois high school where she had run-ins with another student whose last name was Bryson.

The real Bryson, who says she suffered stress as a result of the publication, filed a libel suit. Logsdon argued that she meant the name Bryson to sound like Tyson after famed boxer Mike Tyson.

Lower courts dismissed the case, but the Supreme Court upheld Bryson's right to sue, stating that people could conclude that the story was about Bryson even though her first name and the name of the town are not given. ∎

Caption Answer

Responsibilities vary depending on the justice for whom the clerk works. Most clerks read cases, make recommendations about which cases the Court should hear, and help draft opinions.

SECTION 2 REVIEW ANSWERS

1. Refer to the following pages: writ of *certiorari* (259), docket (259), *amicus curiae* brief (260), majority opinion (261), concurring opinion (261), dissenting opinion (261), *stare decisis* (261).

2. briefs, oral argument, conference, preparation of opinions, announcement of decision

3a. There are eight associate justices and one chief justice. Candidates are nominated by the president and approved by the Senate.

3b. cases involving diplomatic representatives of other nations, disputes between two or more states, and disputes between a state and the federal government.

4. Answers will vary but students should clearly state and explain their point of view. Students might mention that appointing rather than electing a justice eliminates influence from political matters and public opinion.

CONSTITUTIONAL GOVERNMENT *Clerks for the Supreme Court justices often use the reading room in the Court library.* **What are the primary responsibilities of law clerks in the Supreme Court?**

term meaning "let the decision stand.") For example, some experts believe that some of the more conservative justices on the current Court disagree with the *Roe* v. *Wade* decision, which supports women's right to an abortion. However, say the experts, these justices have refused to vote to revisit and overturn the decision because their support of *stare decisis* has outweighed their views on the constitutionality of the right to an abortion.

Justices' Staffs

Writing and rewriting opinions is a time-consuming, lengthy process. To help in this enormous task, justices employ a personal staff of clerks. Compared to congressional and presidential staffs, each justice's staff is tiny. At its largest, a justice's staff generally consists of four law clerks, two secretaries, and one messenger.

Justice Horace Gray began the practice of hiring law clerks in the Supreme Court in 1882. Each year, he hired at his own expense a new law school graduate to assist him. Gradually, the practice spread. Usually, clerks serve one year, although this has not always been so. A clerk to Justice Pierce Butler served for 16 years in the 1920s and 1930s.

Clerks generally read the cases that are appealed to the Court and make recommendations about which ones the Court should hear. Clerks also help draft the justices' opinions. A clerk's role in this task depends on the justice for whom he or she works. A clerk to Justice Louis Brandeis said of their division of labor, "He wrote the opinion; I wrote the footnotes." Other clerks write almost all of an opinion, with the justices making editorial changes.

Announcing Decisions

Although justices once read lengthy parts of their opinions in public sessions, they no longer do so. Also, before 1965, Court decisions were announced only on Mondays. Today they are announced on other days as well, to allow more media coverage. Decisions also are now announced earlier in the day to make it easier for reporters to meet press deadlines. The Supreme Court does not hold press conferences, however, to explain its rulings or to answer questions about them.

SECTION 2 REVIEW

1. **Identify and Explain:**
   - writ of *certiorari*
   - docket
   - *amicus curiae* brief
   - majority opinion
   - concurring opinion
   - dissenting opinion
   - *stare decisis*

2. **Identifying Concepts:** Copy the chart below. Use it to illustrate the stages a case goes through after being selected for hearing by the Supreme Court.

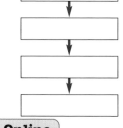
Homework Practice Online
keyword: SV3 HP11

3. **Finding the Main Idea**
   a. How many Supreme Court justices are there, and how are they appointed?
   b. In what types of cases does the Supreme Court have original jurisdiction?

4. **Writing and Critical Thinking**

   Decision Making: Should Supreme Court justices be appointed for life? Write a paragraph explaining your point of view.
   Consider the following:
   - how responsive the Court should be to the public
   - the effects politics can have on legal matters

SECTION 3

THE COURTS AND THE PUBLIC GOOD

READ TO DISCOVER

1. What are the issues raised by judicial activism and judicial restraint?
2. How can the courts' power be checked?

POLITICAL DICTIONARY

judicial restraint
judicial activism

The judiciary, like the other branches of the federal government, has its share of critics. The two main criticisms of the courts are that federal justices are appointed rather than elected and that the courts often overstep their powers. Are these criticisms valid? How is the courts' power checked?

Appointment versus Election

As you have learned, Supreme Court justices and other federal judges serve for life. Although they may be impeached by Congress for serious crimes, once on the bench they are largely immune from the actions of the president, Congress, and other outside influences. Interest groups do submit briefs in some court cases, but they neither contribute money to judges and justices nor target them in lobbying campaigns as they do in the case of presidential and congressional candidates.

Critics charge that a system in which justices can make unpopular decisions and still keep their positions for life invites the abuse of judicial power. Instead of putting power into the hands of elected officials who must answer to the people, the current system of judicial appointment results in an enormously powerful judiciary that, critics say, answers to no one.

Are the critics right? Are the courts capable of ignoring many of the outside influences that affect other institutions of U.S. government? In fact, when interest groups have tried to lobby the courts through demonstrations and letter-writing campaigns, the courts have criticized these attempts to influence their decisions and have refused to submit to political pressure. In addition, judges do not participate in party politics. Justice Sandra Day O'Connor, for example, declined an invitation to appear as a guest of honor of the National Federation of Republican Women at that party's 1984 convention.

Few people would agree, however, that this independence of the courts has resulted in the abuse of judicial power. The framers of the Constitution set up a free judiciary so that judges could make decisions based on the public good, including protecting minority rights, rather than simply bowing to the wishes of the majority. Elected justices would undoubtedly fear handing down unpopular decisions that might prevent them from being re-elected. As one observer notes, "Few American politicians would care to run on a platform of desegregation, pornography, abortion, and the 'coddling' of criminals." (In this context "pornography" refers to expansive court decisions regarding free speech, and "coddling of criminals" refers to expansive decisions regarding the constitutional rights of accused persons.)

POLITICAL PROCESSES *In 1981 Sandra Day O'Connor, the first female Supreme Court justice, was sworn into office. She is shown here on the day of her swearing-in with President Ronald Reagan and (left) Chief Justice Warren Burger.* **Why are Supreme Court justices appointed rather than elected?**

SECTION 3

THE COURTS AND THE PUBLIC GOOD

Lesson Plans
For teaching strategies, see Lesson 11.3 located at the beginning of this chapter or the One-Stop Lesson Planner Strategy 11.3.

Political Dictionary
To reinforce the section's vocabulary terms, refer students to the Electronic Glossary on the *Researcher CD-ROM.*

Section Assessment
To assess students' mastery of this section, have them complete Daily Quiz 11.3 in *Daily Quizzes with Answer Key.*

Caption Answer
Supreme Court justices are appointed rather than elected so that they are independent of from political pressures.

President Ronald Reagan appointed three conservative justices to the Supreme Court. The Senate refused to confirm federal judge Robert Bork, however, when Reagan nominated him. Bork, an opponent of judicial activism, was seen as a threat to individual rights.

In his book *Slouching to Gomorrah* Bork suggested that Congress should be able to overrule Court decisions. Some others who support judicial restraint go so far as to argue that Congress and the president should simply ignore those Court decisions that they consider to be wrong. ■

Caption Answer

Answers will vary, but students may discuss government intervention in the administration of prisons and mental health facilities.

⧉ internet connect

TOPIC: Landmark Cases
GO TO: go.hrw.com
KEYWORD: SV3 GV11

Have students access the Internet through the HRW Go site to conduct research on landmark cases decided by the Supreme Court. Then ask students to create a pamphlet with which to present their information. Students should include the issues, outcomes, and importance of the cases they include in their pamphlet.

In addition, although the courts do maintain much independence, they are not wholly unresponsive to the public. Long-term changes in the Supreme Court's opinions generally follow long-term public opinion trends. Many of those changes are determined by new personnel on the Court. That is, as public opinion shifts on issues, voters elect new presidents with contemporary views who in turn appoint justices with similar views. As a result, the Court's opinions also shift, although with a bit of a lag, as justices serve much longer terms than presidents and generally value continuity with previous Court decisions.

The combination of changes in opinion and new justices on the Court therefore is critical to how strictly the Court will adhere to precedent. This is why the courts have reversed themselves on some issues, such as segregation. By reflecting the change in public opinion on certain issues, the courts show some responsiveness to the needs and wishes of the majority.

Judicial Restraint Versus Judicial Activism

Another criticism of the courts is that they have overstepped their constitutional powers. It is true that since the 1960s the intervention of the federal courts in the administration of government programs, for example, has grown dramatically. The courts have become involved in the management of state prisons, schools, mental health facilities, and many other institutions. Consider the following examples.

In 1969 a federal judge ruled that an Arkansas prison's officials did not fulfill their constitutional duties to protect inmates. Prisoners had filed numerous petitions, saying that they were housed in overcrowded dormitories, clothing was inadequate, and the food was insufficient. Agreeing with many of their complaints, the federal district court ordered the state to improve conditions.

In school desegregation cases, judges often have issued detailed orders telling school districts how to run their school system. In one 1986 case a judge ordered Kansas City, Missouri, to scrap its existing school system and to spend millions of dollars for various school improvements. The city's taxpayers funded much of the improvements.

In Alabama in 1971, Judge Frank Johnson ruled that the state's mental health system in effect unconstitutionally denied adequate treatment to patients. In his ruling, Johnson issued orders, developed in cooperation with mental health experts, for specific actions that the state was to undertake. In addition, Johnson ordered that state funds necessary to carry out his court order were to have priority over nonessential state functions in the state's budget and said that he himself would ensure that the funds were provided if the legislature failed to appropriate them.

Not surprisingly, rulings such as these have been controversial, sparking a debate over the judiciary's role. Critics argue that courts should not establish priorities for a state's budget because this is a legislative responsibility and because the courts are inexperienced in the running of government agencies. Critics also fear that such intervention prevents states and communities from pursuing the policies that best meet the specific needs of their citizens. In general, these critics support **judicial restraint**,

POLITICAL PROCESSES *The courts have ruled that school districts must provide bilingual education to students whose first language is not English.* ***What are other examples of federal courts' intervention in the administration of government programs?***

or a limited use of judicial power.

In contrast, those who support judicial intervention, or **judicial activism**, believe that judges should intervene when unacceptable conditions have been ignored or constitutional rights have been violated. Judicial activism can take many forms, however. In the early 1900s, for example, judges taking an activist role struck down legislation designed to protect children from harsh labor conditions. In recent years, conservative judges have held some federal laws unconstitutional for violating the principles of federalism.

As noted in previous chapters, Congress tends to represent the concerns of localities and organized groups, while the president advances the concerns of the nation as a whole. Like Congress, the federal courts sometimes give special weight to intense concerns of a minority of the population. Unlike Congress, however, the courts allow people to have their voices heard even if they are not well funded or well organized like the interest groups that lobby members of Congress. As a result, many people believe that judicial activism is sometimes necessary to ensure that the views and rights of the minority are heard and protected.

Checking Judicial Power

The Constitution provides important checks on the judiciary's power just as it does for the other branches of government. Among the more important of these checks are the president's and Senate's power to appoint and confirm justices. In addition, Congress can check court decisions by amending the Constitution and sometimes by simply passing suitable laws. States and individuals sometimes have even attempted to check the courts' power illegally by refusing to obey judicial decisions.

Passing Amendments If the Supreme Court rules that a certain policy violates the Constitution, Congress could legalize the policy by passing a constitutional amendment to allow

CONSTITUTIONAL GOVERNMENT *The Sixteenth Amendment overturned a Supreme Court ruling that declared the federal income tax unconstitutional.* ***How can Congress check the Supreme Court's power?***

it. At least 3 of the 27 amendments to the Constitution have been passed in direct response to Supreme Court decisions:

★ the Eleventh Amendment, which deals with lawsuits against a state, overturned an early Supreme Court decision;
★ the Sixteenth Amendment, which authorizes a federal income tax, overturned a Supreme Court ruling that declared such a tax to be unconstitutional;
★ the Twenty-sixth Amendment, which lowers the voting age to 18 in national elections, overturned a Court decision stating that Congress had no constitutional power to set the voting age.

Refusing to Obey Court Decisions As you recall from the beginning of the chapter, Alexander Hamilton noted in the *Federalist Papers* that the courts have no "sword" with which to enforce their decisions. Rather, they must rely on the executive branch for enforcement.

As a result, court rulings sometimes have been resisted, gotten around, or ignored. President Andrew Jackson, for example, when balking at a Supreme Court decision that would have protected American Indians' lands in the state of Georgia, supposedly remarked, "[Chief Justice] John Marshall has made his decision; now let him enforce it."

More recent examples include resistance by some state governments in the 1950s and 1960s to Supreme

CULTURAL PERSPECTIVES

Sometimes the Supreme Court checks itself by making decisions that supersede its previous rulings. During World War II, the U.S. military carried out an order forcing people of Japanese ancestry to leave the western part of the United States for relocation centers. When Toyosaburo Korematsu, a U.S. citizen of Japanese descent, remained in a military area, he was charged with defying the order. In the 1944 case *Korematsu* v. *United States,* the Supreme Court upheld the relocation of the Japanese Americans. Critics called the decision the country's greatest wartime error. Those who were forced to move to the relocation centers lost their liberties simply because of the circumstances of their birth.

While the Court has not specifically overruled the decision, its racist bias has been set aside by the body of law since *Brown* v. *Board of Education.* The Court's most recent rulings have tended not to allow distinctions made solely on race or ethnicity. ■

SECTION 3 REVIEW ANSWERS

1. Refer to the following pages: judicial restraint (264), judicial activism (265).

2. the president's power to appoint and the Senate's to confirm justices, passing amendments or laws, refusing to obey court decisions; examples will vary.

3a. Those who favor judicial restraint argue that courts should not issue orders that ought to be left to legislators, while supporters of judicial activism contend that courts issue detailed orders only after more general orders have been ignored.

3b. advantages—removed from political pressures of running for office; disadvantages—may abuse power without fear of losing their jobs

4. Answers will vary but students should explain their reasoning and exhibit knowledge of the issue. Some students might suggest that judicial activism is often used to support the individual rights of minorities. Other students might suggest that judicial restraint is often used to uphold the will of the majority.

CONSTITUTIONAL GOVERNMENT *U.S. Army troops escort African American students from Central High School in Little Rock, Arkansas, in 1957. In some states, federal troops had to enforce the Supreme Court's decision to integrate public schools.* **Why do you think there have been so few challenges to Supreme Court decisions?**

Court decisions calling for the integration of public schools. In some of these instances, the president called out federal troops to enforce the Supreme Court's decisions.

What is surprising, however, is not that some court decisions have been resisted but just how few challenges there have been. Even powerful groups and individuals have acknowledged the courts' authority over them. No president, for example, has ever defied a Supreme Court decision regarding him personally. The most dramatic court order to a president was the unanimous 1974 Supreme Court decision ordering President Richard M. Nixon to turn over tape recordings of White House conversations about the Watergate cover-up. Nixon accepted the decision and delivered the tapes, which revealed his part in the cover-up of the Watergate break-in and led to his resignation a few weeks later.

SECTION 3 REVIEW

1. Identify and Explain:
- judicial restraint
- judicial activism

2. Identifying Concepts:
Copy the chart below. Use it to list the checks on the power of the courts and examples of each check.

Check on Courts' Power	Example

3. **Finding the Main Idea**

a. Describe the argument over judicial restraint and judicial activism.

b. What are the advantages and disadvantages of the appointment system for federal judges?

4. **Writing and Critical Thinking**

Supporting a Point of View: Do you support judicial restraint or judicial activism? Clearly state your opinion and offer support for your decision.
Consider the following:
- the need to check the power of the judiciary
- the need to interpret laws for changing times

Homework Practice Online
keyword: SV3 HP11

GOVERNMENT IN THE NEWS

Freelancers Battle for Rights

On June 25, 2001, the Supreme Court ruled seven to two that newspaper and magazine publishers could not sell freelance contributions to electronic databases without the permission of the writers.

In 1993 Jonathan Tasini, president of the National Writers Union, and five other writers filed suit against three major publishers—the New York Times Company, Newsday, and Time Inc. The suit alleged that the publishers sold the authors' articles to electronic databases, such as LEXIS/NEXIS, without the authors' permission and without any additional compensation. Tasini charged that this was an infringement of the authors' copyright.

Publishers argued that the use of the articles in databases constituted "revision" of the writers' original work, stating that the placement of articles into a database was no different than issuing a microfilm or microfiche copy of the newspaper. The authors claimed that because no formal contracts existed between themselves and the publishers, they had not sold any electronic rights, to newspapers. In short, the authors believed that they, not the publishers, retained rights after the article was published for the first time.

In 1997, a U.S. district court ruled in favor of the publishers, saying that they were legally exercising their right to reproduce and distribute a revision of an author's contribution. In 1999, however, a U.S. appeals court overturned the 1997 decision, and in 2001 the case went to the Supreme Court. The Court upheld the 1999 decision. The Court ruled that a database was not simply a revision of the author's work, but that each article stands alone. It also declared that in the absence of a formal contract, the owner of the

New technologies such as the Internet and e-books, pictured here, have dramatically changed the publishing industry.

copyright is presumed to own the privilege of reproducing and distributing the work.

In principle, the Supreme Court decision in 2001 is a victory for writers. However, publishers are now urging writers to agree to contracts in which they sign away all their rights. This term is called "all-rights" or "work-for-hire." When a publisher retains all rights to a writer's work, then he or she can use the work at will without any further compensation for the writer. This may lead to a situation where publishers pay writers the same or even lower rates for their work.

What Do You Think?

1. Who do you think should control the reproduction of written works, the author or the publisher? Explain your answer.

2. How do you feel about the effect of new technologies such as the Internet? What sorts of new challenges do they pose for the legal system? Explain your answer.

> **WHY IT MATTERS TODAY**
>
> Look up other Supreme Court cases that protect individual rights. Use **CNNfyi.com** or other **current events** sources for information.
>
> **CNNfyi.com**

Government in the News Answers

1. Answers will vary. Some students might suggest that the author should retain the rights to their own creations. Other students might suggest that without publishers, the authors' works would go largely unread. Students should clearly explain their reasoning.

2. Answers will vary, but students should clearly explain their reasoning.

CHAPTER 11

Review Answers

Writing a Summary

Summaries should focus on the main points of each section. These may be found in the Read to Discover questions at the start of each section. Summaries should also use standard grammar, spelling, sentence structure, and punctuation.

Identifying Ideas

Refer to the following pages: precedent (249), strict constructionist (249), loose constructionist (250), jurisdiction (250), district court (252), court of appeals (252), majority opinion (261), dissenting opinion (261), judicial restraint (264), judicial activism (265).

Understanding Main Ideas

1. District courts are the trial courts, and courts of appeals hear appeals of district court decisions.

(Continued on page 268)

Review

(Continued from page 267)

2. Department of Justice or White House staffers select presidential appointees; Senate approves or rejects them.

3. Power has increased to include judicial review and judicial activism.

4. Lawyers file a written brief, and then justices hear oral arguments, have conferences to discuss the case, prepare opinions, and announce their decision.

5. appoint and approve or reject justices, pass amendments, refuse to obey decisions

6. Federal judges are appointed, not elected; they overstep their power.

Reviewing Themes

1. Answers will vary but students should support their opinions.

2. restraint—courts should not have legislative responsibilities, intervention stops states from running their own programs; activism—judges should intervene when necessary; answers will vary.

3. Answers will vary but students should discuss the need for balance among the branches of government.

Thinking Critically

1. Answers will vary but students should discuss the Court's independence from political pressures and the importance of judges being impartial. Students should offer support for their predictions.

(Continued on page 269)

Writing a Summary

Using standard grammar, spelling, sentence structure, and punctuation, write a summary of the information in this chapter.

Identifying Ideas

Identify the following terms and explain their significance.

1. precedent

2. strict constructionist

3. loose constructionist

4. jurisdiction

5. district court

6. court of appeals

7. majority opinion

8. dissenting opinion

9. judicial restraint

10. judicial activism

Understanding Main Ideas

SECTION 1 *(pp. 249–254)*

1. Describe the organization of the lower federal courts.

2. What is the selection process for lower-court judges?

SECTION 2 *(pp. 255–262)*

3. How has the Supreme Court's power changed since the late 1700s?

4. Describe the process a case goes through in the Supreme Court.

SECTION 3 *(pp. 263–266)*

5. How do the executive and legislative branches check the Supreme Court's power?

6. What are some common criticisms of the judiciary?

Reviewing Themes

1. **Political Processes** Do you think that the principle of senatorial courtesy is an efficient method for nominating and appointing district court judges? Explain you answer.

2. **Political Processes** What are the arguments for both judicial restraint and judicial activism? If you were a federal judge, which would you practice, and why?

3. **Public Good** The president appoints federal judges and the Senate confirms them. How does this sharing of power promote the public good?

Thinking Critically

1. **Making Predictions** Why is it important that presidents are unable to pack the Supreme Court? Write a paragraph predicting what would happen if each president were allowed to add to or change the Court's membership at will.

2. **Finding the Main Idea** Review the arguments for and against judicial activism. How do they compare to the ideas of strict constructionists and loose constructionists?

3. **Drawing Inferences** Why do you think the Supreme Court has jurisdiction on disputes between states?

Writing About Government

Review what you wrote in your Government Notebook at the beginning of this chapter about the areas of your daily life that are affected by Supreme Court decisions. Now that you have studied this chapter, how would you revise your list? Are there any additional areas that you would include? Explain your answer in your notebook.

Interpreting the Chart

Study the chart below. Then use it to help you answer the questions that follow.

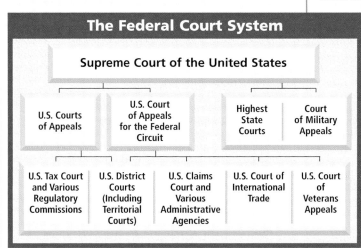

The Federal Court System

Supreme Court of the United States

- U.S. Courts of Appeals
- U.S. Court of Appeals for the Federal Circuit
- Highest State Courts
- Court of Military Appeals

- U.S. Tax Court and Various Regulatory Commissions
- U.S. District Courts (Including Territorial Courts)
- U.S. Claims Court and Various Administrative Agencies
- U.S. Court of International Trade
- U.S. Court of Veterans Appeals

1. Which court reviews cases appealed from the highest state courts?

 a. U.S. Courts of Appeals
 b. Court of Military Appeals
 c. U.S. District Courts
 d. the Supreme Court

2. The U.S. Court of Appeals for the Federal Circuit hears cases from which four courts?

Analyzing Primary Sources

The Supreme Court ruled against public school segregation in the 1954 case *Brown* v. *Board of Education of Topeka*. Read the excerpt from the Court's majority opinion, and answer the questions that follow.

In each of the cases, minors of the Negro race . . . seek the aid of the courts in obtaining admission to the public schools of their community on a nonsegregated basis. In each instance, they had been denied admission . . . under laws requiring or permitting segregation according to race. This segregation was alleged [claimed] to deprive the plaintiffs of the equal protection of the laws under the Fourteenth Amendment. In each of the cases other than the Delaware case, a . . . federal District Court denied relief to the plaintiffs on the so-called "separate but equal" doctrine. . . .

We come then to the question presented: Does segregation of children in public schools . . . , even though the physical facilities and other tangible [material] factors may be equal, deprive the children of the minority group of equal educational opportunities? We believe that it does. . . .

3. Which of the following statements best reflects majority opinion the point of views?

 a. The lower court's ruling should stand.
 b. The "separate but equal" doctrine is valid.
 c. Segregated schools are acceptable.
 d. Segregated schools are unacceptable.

4. Do you think this opinion reflects judicial restraint or judicial activism?

(Continued from page 268)

2. Answers will vary but students should note similarities between strict construction and judicial restraint and between loose construction and judicial activism.

3. Answers may vary, but students should note that a state's courts might be inclined to rule in the interest of its own state.

Writing About Government

The Government Notebook is a follow-up activity to the notebook activity that appears on page 248.

Building Social Studies Skills

1. d

2. U.S. District Courts, U.S. Court of Claims, U.S. Court of International Trade, U.S. Court of Veterans Appeals

3. d

4. Students might suggest judicial activism, as the decision overturned a previous Court decision.

Alternative Assessment

To assess this activity see Group Activity and Judging Information *Alternative Assessment Handbook*.

Alternative Assessment

Building Your Portfolio

With a group, create a notebook of newspaper articles on Supreme Court cases. Organize the articles according to the court from which each case was appealed. Divide the notebook into three sections: Highest State Courts, U.S. Courts of Appeals, and U.S. Courts of Appeals for the Federal Circuit. Write summaries for each article, describing the issues being examined and the Court's final decision.

internet connect

Internet Activity: go.hrw.com
KEYWORD: SV3 GV11

Access the Internet through the HRW Go site to research the structure of the federal court system. Then create a mobile that displays your information. Focus on the jurisdictions of various courts and the cases that each court handles.

CHAPTER 12 THE U.S. LEGAL SYSTEM

	OBJECTIVES	PACING GUIDE	REPRODUCIBLE RESOURCES
SECTION 1 **U.S. LAW** (pp. 271–274)	▸ What is common law, and where did it originate? ▸ What is statutory law? ▸ Whom does administrative law govern? ▸ What is the difference between civil law and criminal law?	**Regular** 1 day **Block Scheduling** .5 day	**ELL** Spanish Study Guide 12.1 **ELL** English Study Guide 12.1 **PS** Reading 69: *Opinion in re Gault* **E** Simulations and Strategies for Teaching Government: Activity 12 **E** Challenge and Enrichment Activity 12
SECTION 2 **THE CRIMINAL JUSTICE SYSTEM** (pp. 275–280)	▸ Who enforces criminal laws? ▸ What process does an accused person go through after his or her arrest? ▸ What is a plea bargain?	**Regular** 1.5 days **Block Scheduling** .5 day	**ELL** Spanish Study Guide 12.2 **ELL** English Study Guide 12.2 **SM** Government Activities: Activity 12
SECTION 3 **CORRECTIONS** (pp. 281–286)	▸ What are the various sentencing options in the criminal justice system? ▸ What is parole? ▸ Why is capital punishment controversial? ▸ What happens to juvenile offenders after their arrest?	**Regular** .5 day **Block Scheduling** .25 day	**ELL** Spanish Study Guide 12.3 **ELL** English Study Guide 12.3

Chapter Resource Key

PS	Primary Sources	**A**	Assessment		Video
RS	Reading Support	**REV**	Review		Videodisc
E	Enrichment	**ELL**	Reinforcement and English Language Learners		Internet
S	Simulations		Transparencies		Holt Presentation Maker Using
SM	Skills Mastery		CD-ROM		Microsoft ® PowerPoint ®

TECHNOLOGY RESOURCES	REINFORCEMENT, REVIEW, AND ASSESSMENT
💿 One-Stop Planner: Lesson 12.1 🔳 Holt Researcher Online 🔳 Homework Practice Online 💿 CNN Presents American Government 💿 Global Skill Builder CD-ROM	**REV** Section 1 Review, p. 274 **A**　Daily Quiz 12.1
💿 One-Stop Planner: Lesson 12.2 🔳 Holt Researcher Online 🔳 Homework Practice Online 💾 Transparency 25 💿 Global Skill Builder CD-ROM	**REV** Section 2 Review, p. 280 **A**　Daily Quiz 12.2
💿 One-Stop Planner: Lesson 12.3 🔳 Holt Researcher Online 🔳 Homework Practice Online 💾 Transparency 26 💿 Holt American Government Videodisc: Juvenile Crime: Sentencing in Ohio 💿 Global Skill Builder CD-ROM	

Chapter Review and Assessment

SM Global Skill Builder CD-ROM
🔳 HRW Go site
REV Chapter 12 Tutorial for Students, Parents, and Peers
REV Chapter 12 Review, pp. 288–289
💿　Chapter 12 Test Generator (on the One-Stop Planner)
A　Chapter 12 Test
A　Alternative Assessment Handbook

One-Stop Planner CD-ROM

It's easy to plan lessons, select resources, and print out materials for your students when you use the *One-Stop Planner CD-ROM with Test Generator.*

🔳 internet connect

HRW ONLINE RESOURCES
Go to: go.hrw.com
Then type in a keyword.

TEACHER HOME PAGE
KEYWORD: SV3 Teacher

CHAPTER INTERNET ACTIVITIES
KEYWORD: SV3 GV12
Choose an activity on the legal system to:
▶ learn about the legal process.
▶ compare and contrast legal systems.
▶ write a report on the private corrections industry.

CHAPTER ENRICHMENT LINKS
KEYWORD: SV3 CH12

HOLT RESEARCHER ONLINE
KEYWORD: Holt Researcher

ONLINE ASSESSMENT
Homework Practice
KEYWORD: SV3 HP12
Standardized Test Prep
KEYWORD: SV3 STP12
Rubrics
KEYWORD: SS Rubrics

ONLINE MAPS, CHARTS, AND GRAPHS
KEYWORD: SV3 MCG
▶ The Legal Process
▶ Largest U.S. Prison Inmate Populations

CONTENT UPDATES
KEYWORD: SS Content Updates

HOLT PRESENTATION MAKER
KEYWORD: SV3 PPT12

ONLINE READING SUPPORT
KEYWORD: SS Strategies

CURRENT EVENTS
KEYWORD: S3 Current Events

OBJECTIVES

▶ Define common law and describe its origin.
▶ Define statutory law.
▶ Explain whom administrative law governs.
▶ Discuss the difference between civil law and criminal law.

MOTIVATE

Ask students to identify some of the laws governing their lives, such as those concerning speeding, parking, and curfew. List their responses on the board or on the overhead projector. Ask students to rank the laws from least severe to most severe in terms of the penalties for breaking them. Discuss with students that some laws carry more severe penalties than others and that there are several different types of laws that they will learn about in this section.

TEACH

Building a Vocabulary

In spiral notebooks, have students create a Political Dictionary to be used throughout the course. The dictionary may be used as an activity at the start of each new section; it may also be used as a modification device for Sheltered English Students or by students having difficulty during tests and homework assignments. List words the students will be expected to know for this section on the board. Have students list, define, and give an example of each term, using information provided in the text or on the *Researcher CD-ROM*.

Navigating the Internet/Conducting Research

Discuss the concept of common law with students. Organize students into groups and have them use the Internet and the Supreme Court Docket section located on the *Holt Researcher Online* to identify examples of historical court cases involving common law in the United States. Some students may wish to research current newspapers, magazines, and legal journals for cases in which common law plays a role. Have students present their findings to the class. Explain to students that there is another type of law called statutory law that they will learn about in the next activity.

Navigating the Internet/Conducting Research

Discuss statutory laws with students. Ask students to identify types of statutes or laws that affect their lives and to explain the difference between common law and statutory law. Organize students into groups and have them use the Internet and the Supreme Court Docket section on the *Holt Researcher Online* to identify examples of court cases involving statutory laws in the United States. Some students may wish to research current newspapers, magazines, and legal journals for current cases in which a violation of statute plays a role. Have students present their findings to the class. Explain to students that in the next section they will learn about laws that govern independent agencies.

Debating Ideas

Explain to students why administrative agencies are necessary and why people create and follow administrative laws. Discuss arguments for and against these agencies' having such authority. Give students copies of articles about administrative agencies. Have students decide whether they think that independent agencies have too much power. Lead students in a debate over this issue. Tell students that there are still further divisions of law—those covering the criminal code and those dealing with private disputes—which will be discussed in the next section.

Creating Charts

Organize students into two groups: one studying criminal law and the other civil law. Students should use the Internet, newspapers, and magazines to research the difference in the two types of law. Have students work together to create large posters showing examples of their assigned type of law and ones with different types of punishments given for violating the laws students have pictured. Ask students to identify the differences in the types of punishments given for violating each type of law. Have each group present their posters to the other and then display the posters in the classroom.

CLOSE

Using butcher paper, the chalkboard, or the overhead, make a chart with *common, statutory, constitutional,* and *administrative* as the column headings and *civil* and *criminal* as the row headings. Students should use the list generated in the Motivate activity and research from other activities in this section to fill in the chart, placing the laws they identified in the appropriate row and column. Encourage students to think of additional laws and to fill in the entire chart with at least one example of each. Discuss students' reasons for placing each law in the location they chose.

OPTIONS

Gifted Learners

  Ask students to select one or more of the court cases listed in the Supreme Court Docket section on the *Holt Researcher Online*. Ask students to write a report on the case they chose and to include important details of the case and relevant information learned from this section, such as the type of law that was violated. In the instance of sensational cases students may wish to locate an old newspaper or a magazine clipping and include it with the report. Encourage students to share their reports with the class.

Body-Kinesthetic Learners

Have students create a board game describing various positive situations that involve the community, such as receiving a good citizenship award, and various negative situations that involve the violation of laws. Students should create different color-coded cards representing criminal and civil laws. Each card should contain a penalty, appropriate to the violation, for landing on certain spaces. Have students play the game. Once students have finished, have them discuss the game's similarities to real life.

Students Having Difficulty/ Sheltered English Students

 Explain to the class the concept of criminal law. Tell students that there are two types of criminal law: misdemeanors and felonies. Encourage students to think about violations of law that they may have committed or about violations of the law that they have heard about others committing. Ask students to write these violations on small pieces of paper and to place them in a box. Write the specific types of offenses that the students have identified on the board. Try to classify these offenses into categories of misdemeanors and felonies. Invite a police officer, lawyer, or judge to the class to discuss the possible penalties for each of these crimes. Allow students to ask questions regarding the differences between felonies and misdemeanors.

REVIEW

Have students complete the Section 1 Review on page 274. Use the answers in the Annotated Teacher's Edition to assess student mastery of this section.

ASSESS

To assess student mastery of this section, have students complete Daily Quiz 12.1 in *Daily Quizzes with Answer Key*. For additional assessment options, see *Alternative Assessment Handbook* on the *One-Stop Planner CD-ROM*.

ADDITIONAL RESOURCES

Gest, Ted. *Crime & Politics: Big Government's Erratic Campaign for Law and Order.* 2001. Oxford University Press.

Hill, Gerald and Kathleen Thompson Hill. *Real Life Dictionary of the Law: Taking the Mystery Out of Legal Language.* 1995. General Publishing Group.

Johnson, John W. Editor. *Historic U.S. Cases: An Encyclopedia.* 2001. Routledge.

269D

HOLT PRESENTATION MAKER
Access Illustrated LECTURE NOTES using Microsoft® PowerPoint® on the One-Stop Planner CD-ROM

OBJECTIVES

▶ Identify who enforces criminal laws.
▶ Describe the process an accused person goes through after an arrest.
▶ Describe a plea bargain.

MOTIVATE

Introduce students to the roles of the police, lawyers, and judges by having students read about these careers in the Careers section located on the *Holt Researcher Online*. Have students describe what they believe to be the extent of each profession's role in the legal process. Discuss with students the various roles and how each is important to maintaining an efficient criminal justice system. Ask students to share with the class examples of interactions they have had with any of the above professionals. Tell students that they will be learning more about the criminal justice system in this section.

TEACH

Building a Vocabulary

In their spiral notebooks, have students continue working on their Political Dictionary. List words the students will be expected to know for this section on the chalkboard. Have students list, define, and give an example of each of the terms, using information provided in the text or on the *Researcher CD-ROM*.

Systhesizing Information

Divide students into three groups. Ask the first group to create a visual diagram on butcher paper that shows the organization of the police throughout the country. They should place national police organizations at the top of the diagram and work downward, labeling state and local police. Students should describe the role of each police organization. The second group should create a flowchart to describe the process of making arrests, starting with the investigation crimes. The third group should create a chart describing the process of becoming a police officer at each of the different levels of government: national, state, and local. Groups may use outside resources and should be encouraged to contact law enforcement agencies to help gather information for the assignment. After all groups have finished creating their visuals, groups should present their information to the rest of the class. Tell students that in the next activity they will learn what an accused person goes through after his or her arrest.

Role-Playing

Organize students into eight groups, with each group representing one step of the legal process described in this section of the textbook. Each group should research what takes place during its step of the process. Then have students act out a hypothetical criminal case. The class may make up the case as a group or the teacher may wish to use an actual case found in the Supreme Court Docket section on the *Holt Researcher Online*. The teacher should guide the role-play to ensure that it represents what actually happens during each step portrayed. Afterward, discuss with students any inaccuracies and describe the correct version. Tell students that in the following activity they will learn about a process that keeps many cases from reaching court.

Debating Ideas

Discuss with students the process of plea bargaining. Have students identify reasons why a person would want to accept a plea bargain and reasons why a prosecutor would want to offer one to the accused. Divide students into two groups—one that supports plea bargaining and one that opposes it. Have the groups debate their positions on plea bargaining, keeping in mind the effect of the crime on the victim(s) and the changes in sentencing that would occur as a result of the offender accepting the plea bargain. Students may wish to examine newspapers, magazines, or public records of court cases to find support for their positions. Lead the debate, and have students write the reasons for supporting and opposing plea bargaining on the chalkboard. After the debate, discuss with students the legitimacy of the arguments they made.

CLOSE

Have students write a summary of the duties that the police, lawyers, and judges perform in the legal process, based on what they have learned in this section. Be sure to have students discuss each group's role, from investigating a crime to sentencing. Have students compare what they learned to what they thought during the Motivate activity. Ask students if the duties these professionals fulfill are any more or less important than they had originally thought. Ask students to offer support for their reasoning.

OPTIONS

Students Having Difficulty/ Sheltered English Students

 Have students watch a video of a popular movie or television program in which the main plot concerns the criminal justice system. Some students may need to utilize a school video player, or the teacher may need to provide the tape for the students. Parent permission may be needed for some movies, depending on the content. Have students write or verbally present a review of the movie for the rest of the class that describes the accuracy of the portrayal of the role of police, lawyers, and judges in the legal system.

Intrapersonal Learners/Gifted Learners

Have students learn more about what occurs when someone is accused of a crime, is arrested, and must go to court. Encourage students to do one or more of the following: ride in a squad car during one or more police shifts; interview attorneys for the defense and the state prosecutor's office; sit in a courtroom and watch initial court appearances, preliminary hearings, indictments, arraignments, jury selections, trials, or verdicts and sentencing hearings; follow one case from arrest through the entire legal process; or interview someone who has been accused of a crime and was found not guilty, accepted a plea bargain, or was found guilty and is serving time in jail. Encourage students to take all the time that they need to obtain the information and to write a report and present it to the rest of the class. Some students may wish to use audio or video equipment in their presentations.

Visual-Spatial Learners

  Review the steps of the legal process with the class. Then organize the class into several small groups. Have each group create a flowchart depicting the role of one of the following occupations in the legal process: police officer, lawyer, and judge. Remind students to start with the process of investigating the crime and conclude with the court determining a verdict. Students may wish to review the diagrams created during the Synthesizing Information activity found earlier in this lesson. Once each group has completed its diagram, allow members to discuss the information it contains with the class. To ensure accuracy, compare diagrams by groups that have been assigned similar occupations. Display the completed diagrams throughout the classroom.

REVIEW

Have students complete the Section 2 Review on page 280. Use the answers in the Annotated Teacher's Edition to assess student mastery of this section.

ASSESS

To assess student mastery of this section, have students complete Daily Quiz 12.2 in *Daily Quizzes with Answer Key*. For additional assessment options, see *Alternative Assessment Handbook* on the *One-Stop Planner CD-ROM*.

ADDITIONAL RESOURCES

Adamson, Charles F. *The Toughest Cop in America.* 2001. Dilettante Press.

Schmalleger, Frank, and Gordon M. Armstrong. Editors. *Crime and the Justice System in America.* 1997. Greenwood Publishing Group.

Grand Jury: An Institution Under Fire. 1980. Pacific Street Films. (video)

Trial of a Criminal Case. 1982. American Bar Association. (video)

LESSON 12.3 CORRECTIONS

TEXTBOOK PAGES 281–286

OBJECTIVES

- List the various sentencing options in the criminal justice system.
- Describe parole.
- Discuss the capital punishment controversy.
- Describe what happens to juvenile offenders after their arrest.

MOTIVATE

Have students use current newspapers, magazines, or public court records to locate information on recent sentences that have been issued for various crimes. Ask students to investigate some situations in which different rulings were handed down for the same offense. Ask students to discuss the difference in the sentences issued to these individuals and to attempt to explain the reasons behind these different sentences.

MOTIVATE

Building a Vocabulary

In their spiral notebooks, have students continue working on their Political Dictionary. List words the students will be expected to know for this section on the chalkboard. Have students list, define, and give an example of each of the terms, using information provided in the text or on the *Researcher CD-ROM*.

Comparing and Contrasting

Discuss with students the four types of sentencing options presented in this section: probation, imprisonment, parole, and capital punishment. Have students write a short paper comparing and contrasting the various forms of sentencing options, based on information from the text. Students should consider reasons why judges would choose a particular option. Afterward, discuss with the students the pros and cons of sentencing an individual to probation rather than imprisonment, letting a convicted individual out of jail early

on parole, and invoking capital punishment. Tell students that in the next activity they will learn more about the sentencing option of parole.

Role-Playing

Organize students into two groups. Assign one group the role of the parole board and have the other group create hypothetical situations to present to the board for consideration. Once the group has made its decisions regarding the hypothetical situations, reverse the roles of the groups and repeat the activity. Lead a discussion on the importance of the board and what crimes and situations preclude parole. Discuss with students the factors that are considered when deciding if a person should be eligible for parole. Tell students that in the next activity they will learn about the controversial topic of capital punishment.

Taking a Stand/Debating Ideas

Ask students to read about capital punishment in their textbook. After they read the text, have the class organize itself into two groups: students for and students against capital punishment. Groups may want to utilize newspapers and magazines to find support for their positions. Give each group a piece of butcher paper on which their reasons for their stand can be written with markers. Have groups form an argument that will then be presented to the other side. Encourage students to debate their positions. If either group is undecided, encourage it to make a decision based on the arguments presented by the other group. Some students may wish to switch sides during the discussion. Point out to students that people frequently change their opinions on capital punishment because it is such a controversial issue.

Learning From Visuals

Divide students into three groups to represent juvenile crime, the juvenile court system, and the juvenile corrections system. Ask students to think of a creative way to visually depict the topic they have been assigned. Students may need to conduct research to find statistics that will support their topic. After completing their research, students should present their visuals to the class.

CLOSE

Have small groups create study guides containing questions about the important aspects of the corrections system discussed in this section of the text. Be sure to have students include probation, imprisonment, parole, capital punishment, and juvenile crime in their guides. Have groups exchange study guides, and then have each group answer the questions. When they finish, students should return the study guide to the group that created it to be graded. Groups should review their work together and should discuss any inconsistencies between the study guides.

OPTIONS

Students Having Difficulty/Sheltered English Students

 Have students create a chart depicting the corrections system. Students may need to use the library or the Internet in order to research the topic. Students should include statistics regarding the number of criminals being housed in the corrections system or examples of the various types of corrections options. Be sure to have students include information on probation, imprisonment, parole, and capital punishment and have them include information about the level of security of the different corrections options, such as maximum or minimum security. Encourage students to discuss their charts with the rest of the class.

Musical-Rhythmic Learners/Visual-Spatial Learners

  Individually or in small groups, students should create an advertisement that encourages juveniles not to commit crimes. Students may wish to write jingles or songs for their advertisements and record them on audiotape or videotape. These students should play their advertisement for the class. Other students may wish to create a print ad on butcher paper to be displayed in the classroom. The advertisements should include the types of sentences that may be given as well as statistics on crime. Encourage students to be creative in discouraging other teens from committing crimes. Have students share their ads with the rest of the class.

Intrapersonal Learners

 Discuss with students one of the most common arguments against capital punishment—that African Americans have been sentenced to death more often than other groups in society. Have students use yearly data to investigate the percentages of each race of people that have been sentenced to capital punishment. Students should consult historical abstracts in the library to obtain the information. Students should examine any trends revealed by the data and determine any changes in trends in recent years. Encourage students to form an opinion on the topic based on this data and information presented in the Taking a Stand/Debating Ideas activity found earlier in this section. Students may wish to write to their representatives to express their opinion on the death penalty.

REVIEW

Have students complete the Section 3 Review on page 286. Use the answers in the Annotated Teacher's Edition to assess student mastery of this section.

ASSESS

To assess student mastery of this section, have students complete Daily Quiz 12.3 in *Daily Quizzes with Answer Key.* For additional assessment options, see *Alternative Assessment Handbook* on the *One-Stop Planner CD-ROM.*

RETEACH

For students having difficulty with the lessons, have them complete Reteaching Activity 13. This activity is located in *Reteaching Activities with Answer Key.*

ADDITIONAL RESOURCES

Champion, Dean J. *The Juvenile Justice System: Delinquency, Processing, and the Law.* 2000. Prentice Hall.

Miller, Gerome G. *Search and Destroy: African-American Males in the Criminal Justice System.* 1997. Cambridge University Press.

Mitchell, Hayley R. Editor. *The Complete History of the Death Penalty.* 2001. Greenhaven Press.

Watterson, Kathryn. *Women in Prison: Inside the Concrete Web.* 1996. Northeastern University Press.

Death Row and the Death Penalty. 1984. United Press International. (video)

TOPICS INCLUDE

GOVERNMENT NOTEBOOK

The Government Notebook is a journal activity that encourages students to consider basic concepts of government that relate to their lives. A follow-up notebook activity appears on page 288.

WHY IT MATTERS TODAY

To find additional lesson plans dealing with the U.S. legal system, visit CNNfyi.com or have students complete the GOVERNMENT IN THE NEWS Activity on page 287.

CNNfyi.com

THE U.S. LEGAL SYSTEM

How do you regard the laws that govern your community and nation? Some people may see laws as restrictions of their freedom. Most believe that laws generally serve positive functions in U.S. society. For example, laws determine who receives certain benefits, laws create government programs and the organizations to administer them, and laws forbid certain behaviors that harm people or their property. Laws also make it difficult for government officials to make random decisions that may negatively affect people.

GOVERNMENT NOTEBOOK

In your Government Notebook, make a list of ways—both positive and negative—that laws affect your everyday life.

WHY IT MATTERS TODAY

The U.S. legal system affects our lives every day. At the end of this chapter, visit CNNfyi.com to learn more about how the legal system affects you.

CNNfyi.com

SECTION 1
U.S. LAW

READ TO DISCOVER

1. What is common law, and where did it originate?
2. What is statutory law?
3. Whom does administrative law govern?
4. What is the difference between civil law and criminal law?

POLITICAL DICTIONARY

common law
statutory law
statutory interpretation
constitutional interpretation
administrative law
felony
misdemeanor
plaintiff
defendant

A s you know, laws govern people's conduct. You may not realize, however, that there are several types of U.S. law, including common, statutory, constitutional, and administrative. Many of these laws can be further classified as criminal or civil laws. Together, these laws help ensure that both governmental actions and standards of social conduct promote the public good.

Common Law

Common law, also called judge-made law, is a body of law based on judicial rulings in earlier cases. The common-law system first developed in England during a period when very few written laws existed. When conflicts arose to which no law applied, judges had to make decisions based on their individual sense of fairness. Judges in other jurisdictions who recognized these rulings as fair then used them in similar cases. As noted in Chapter 11, this acceptance of earlier court decisions is known as *stare decisis*.

Today the U.S. legal system incorporates this common-law heritage. For example, common law includes much of the law applied to cases in which one person blames another for injury and sues for damages. To help decide these cases, judges developed the principle that a defendant must generally have acted negligently, or irresponsibly, before he or she could be required to pay damages to an injured party. Thus, someone whose non-negligent actions harmed another person would not have to pay damages.

The term *negligence* has been applied to many different types of cases, and there are different levels of negligence. For example, officers of federally chartered banks have been charged with negligence for approving large loans that were not repaid, causing the banks to fail. Other professionals, such as stockbrokers, can be charged with negligence if their apparent failure to perform according to the standards of their profession causes someone harm, such as an investor's losing large amounts of money.

POLITICAL FOUNDATIONS *English judges dressed in their traditional robes and wigs march in a procession.* **How does the U.S. legal system incorporate the English common-law tradition?**

SECTION 1
U.S. LAW

Lesson Plans
For teaching strategies, see Lesson 12.1 located at the beginning of this chapter or the One-Stop Planner Strategy 12.1.

Political Dictionary
To reinforce the section's vocabulary terms, refer students to the Electronic Glossary on the *Researcher CD-ROM.*

Section Assessment
To assess students' mastery of this section, have them complete Daily Quiz 12.1 in *Daily Quizzes with Answer Key.*

Caption Answer

The U.S. legal system has based its concept of negligence on common-law tradition.

THEMES IN GOVERNMENT

POLITICAL PROCESSES

Some critics charge that administrative laws can become so restrictive that they reduce businesses' profits without creating any benefits for the American people. The Occupational Safety and Health Administration (OSHA), which oversees workplace safety, is frequently used as an example of an agency whose administrative laws are sometimes unduly burdensome. To support their case, critics point out that a brick-making factory in Pennsylvania was cited for having railings that were only 40 inches high, although no accidents had ever occurred. (OSHA regulations dictate that railings must be 42 inches high.) Some business owners resent the enforcement of a multitude of OSHA regulations that they think have little effect on worker safety. ■

Caption Answer

Answers will vary, but students might mention the Federal Trade Commission, the Environmental Protection Agency, or the Food and Drug Administration.

Both judges and lawyers rely on precedents, or earlier rulings, in their interpretations of the law, thus ensuring stability and predictability in the legal system. Because they have been tested repeatedly in different court cases, rulings based on common-law precedents are given as much respect as rulings based on legislative statutes.

Statutory Law

Statutory law consists of laws (also called statutes) passed by city councils, state legislatures, and Congress—the lawmaking bodies of local, state, and national government. Statutory law serves a variety of purposes. For example, statutes may be passed to create or abolish government programs, increase or decrease the penalty for a crime, or change the salaries of government workers.

In making rulings, courts often must decide the meaning of laws that legislatures have passed, a process referred to as **statutory interpretation**, or statutory construction. Statutes are valid as long as they are not found to be in conflict with the Constitution.

PUBLIC GOOD *Administrative law applies to agencies such as the Occupational Safety and Health Administration (OSHA).* ***What other agencies operate under administrative law?***

Constitutional Law

Constitutional law has supreme standing over all other types of law. A court can invalidate any statutory or common law that contradicts a constitutional provision.

Ruling on the intended meaning of phrases in the Constitution is called **constitutional interpretation**. As noted in Chapter 11, judges often have to interpret the Constitution because its language is broad concerning many important points. This lack of clarity has allowed the Supreme Court to use its power of judicial review to reach expansive or narrow interpretations of the Constitution each time it hears a case.

Administrative Law

Administrative law includes the regulations made by executive departments and independent agencies and the laws that govern their actions. Examples of agencies that operate under administrative law include the Federal Trade Commission, the Environmental Protection Agency, and the Food and Drug Administration.

Agencies are part of the executive branch, and they also act as agents of Congress by helping to implement congressional legislation. Their power is limited in two ways, however. First, the Constitution places the same restrictions on agencies that it places on the president and Congress. Second, Congress determines the structure and powers of all agencies, and the president appoints their top leadership, with the advice and consent of the Senate.

The power that Congress delegates to these agencies comes in three forms. First, Congress authorizes agencies to make rules and regulations that fill in the details of legislation. For example, the Food and Drug Administration (FDA) determines which food additives are safe for human consumption and makes regulations regarding their use. Second, Congress authorizes agencies to enforce the rules they make. For example, the FDA can fine companies that use a food additive it has outlawed. Third, Congress authorizes agencies to attempt to resolve disputes that arise over their enforcement measures. The agencies can also represent the government in court cases that result from those disputes. A food company that believes it has been wrongly fined can demand an agency hearing on the matter. If dissatisfied with this ruling, the company can appeal to a federal court, which hears arguments from both the company and the agency.

Because agency officials are not elected, some people argue, these agencies have too much power, and as a result, they adopt many unfair regulations. Administrative law is intended to ensure that agencies do not abuse their power.

Criminal and Civil Law

Statutory laws can be further classified as either criminal or civil. As noted in Chapter 4, criminal law covers actions that are forbidden by a society's government and punishable by imprisonment, while civil law

POLITICAL PROCESSES *An FBI evidence response team outside the Pentagon in Washington, D.C., after the September 11, 2001, terrorist attacks.* **What other types of crimes might federal agents investigate?**

covers private disputes, such as ones involving personal injury or the breaking of a contract. People found to be at fault in civil law cases must pay fines or settle the dispute according to the law, but they are not subject to imprisonment.

Criminal Law Criminal law covers two main types of crime—felonies and misdemeanors. **Felonies** are serious crimes, such as murder, rape, or burglary. **Misdemeanors** are less serious crimes, such as resisting arrest.

Most felonies and misdemeanors are covered by state laws and deal with crimes against people and property. Some crimes, however, are covered by federal law. Crimes against the national government—evading income tax, counterfeiting U.S. currency, and threatening the life of the president, for example—are federal crimes. Other federal crimes include illegal actions that take place across state lines and offenses such as kidnapping, drug trafficking, bank fraud, the shooting of migratory birds out of season, drunken driving on government land, illegal possession of a firearm, and carjacking. Denial of a person's civil rights under the Constitution is also a federal crime.

Crimes are more than private disputes; they are considered an offense against society as well as against an individual victim. To find a person

Comparing Governments

The Power of the Courts

By establishing the power of judicial review in *Marbury* v. *Madison*, the Supreme Court created for itself a much more powerful tool than any held by high courts in other democratic nations at the time. Historically, national governments did not grant their highest courts the power to cancel a law made by the national legislature. Great Britain's High Court of England, for example, to this day has no power to cancel laws made by Parliament.

Since World War II, however, judicial review has been established in the constitutions of several countries other than the United States, such as Germany, Japan, and India. In addition, the French during this period established a Constitutional Council with the right to cancel Parliamentary laws that it found to be in conflict with the national constitution.

Caption Answer
kidnapping, drug trafficking, bank fraud, carjacking, and others

Enhancing the Lesson
For more information about *Marbury* v. *Madison* and other Supreme Court decisions, see the Supreme Court Docket section on the *Holt Researcher Online.*

THEMES IN GOVERNMENT

PUBLIC GOOD Is the United States becoming a safer place in which to live? Statistics say that it is. The number of serious crimes reported in the United States has been decreasing. Reported crimes declined in 2000 to 1,251,200 from 1,408,500 in 1999 and 2,218,500 in 1993. The 2000 total is the lowest since the Justice Department began its crime survey in 1972. ■

internet connect

TOPIC: Comparing Legal Systems
GO TO: go.hrw.com
KEYWORD. SV3 GV12

Have students access the Internet through the HRW Go site to compare and contrast legal systems across the world. Then ask students to create a poster that illustrates the differences between the federal court system and the justice system of another country. Ask students to illustrate their posters.

© 1999 by Sidney Harris.

PRINCIPLES OF DEMOCRACY *Civil law cases involve the settlement of disputes between two or more parties. The above cartoon gives a humorous look at how some of these cases might be considered extreme or unnecessary.* **What is the reason for lawsuits regarding contracts?**

another for causing some harm. A party generally files a suit to seek a remedy—money, property, or an action. In civil cases the party bringing the suit is known as the **plaintiff**, while the party against whom the suit is brought is known as the **defendant**. In a civil case a party does not have to prove beyond a reasonable doubt that a wrong was committed. Rather, civil cases are generally decided in favor of the party whose position is supported by most of the evidence that is presented.

Three major categories of civil law involve contracts, torts, and property law. Contracts are legal promises made between two or more parties. When one side breaks a contract, another side may sue, or bring a lawsuit against, the contract breaker. Torts are harms that one party causes another and for which the victim may receive damages. Tort lawsuits often involve accidents, such as car wrecks. Property law involves violations of the rights one has as an owner of land or other personal property.

guilty of a crime, guilt must be established beyond a reasonable doubt. This means that a person cannot be convicted of a crime unless very little doubt exists about his or her guilt.

Civil Law Civil law involves disputes in which one private party brings a lawsuit against

SECTION 1 REVIEW

1. Define and explain:
- common law
- statutory law
- statutory interpretation
- constitutional interpretation
- administrative law
- felony
- misdemeanor
- plaintiff
- defendant

2. Identifying Concepts: Use the web to identify four different types of U.S. law.

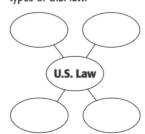

U.S. Law

3. **Finding the Main Idea**

a. What is the origin of U.S. common law?
b. Who makes statutory laws?
c. To whom do administrative laws apply?
d. What is the difference between civil and criminal law?

4. **Writing and Critical Thinking**

Summarizing: People can file lawsuits against those who cause them harm. Write a paragraph describing how this right protects people. How might this right be abused?

Homework Practice Online
keyword: SV3 HP12

SECTION 2

THE CRIMINAL JUSTICE SYSTEM

READ TO DISCOVER

1. Who enforces criminal laws?
2. What process does an accused person go through after his or her arrest?
3. What is a plea bargain?

POLITICAL DICTIONARY

county
bail
bond
indictment
grand jury
information
arraignment
no-contest plea
petit jury
voir dire
peremptory challenge
sequester
subpoena
hung jury
plea bargain

People sometimes violate the law. The job of the criminal justice system is to stop these violations and to punish lawbreakers. The criminal justice system of the United States consists of three parts: police, courts, and corrections. In this section you will learn about the role of the police and the courts in the criminal justice system. The corrections system will be discussed in Section 3.

Police

More than 725,000 police officers enforce the law across the country. They work at the local, state, and national levels, and their jobs involve many responsibilities. Not only do they protect highways and neighborhood streets

and maintain peace and order, they also investigate, arrest, and book people accused of crimes.

Organization The police system in the United States is highly decentralized. Though the system exists at the local, state, and federal levels, most law enforcement agencies are located in counties, cities, and towns. (**Counties**—divisions within a state that function as units of government over a particular area—are more fully discussed in Chapter 21.) At the county level, the county police or sheriff's department is the main law enforcement agency. Its duties include preserving order, enforcing court orders, and patrolling areas within the county. Town and city police perform a similar function within town and city limits. At the state level, police patrol state highways and have the responsibility of enforcing some state laws.

The United States, unlike some other countries, does not have a national police force. However, some national agencies, such as the Federal Bureau of Investigation, do help enforce federal laws and aid local authorities in detecting local crimes and catching offenders. Federal offenses in which these agencies would become involved include kidnapping, the attempted assassination

PUBLIC GOOD *Police officers patrol the streets of Austin, Texas, on bicycles.* **How do the duties of police officers employed by a city or county differ from the duties of a state police officer?**

SECTION 2
THE CRIMINAL JUSTICE SYSTEM

Lesson Plans

For teaching strategies, see Lesson 12.2 located at the beginning of this chapter or the One-Stop Planner Strategy 12.2.

Political Dictionary

To reinforce the section's vocabulary terms, refer students to the Electronic Glossary on the *Researcher CD-ROM.*

Section Assessment

To assess students' mastery of this section, have them complete Daily Quiz 12.2 in *Daily Quizzes with Answer Key.*

Caption Answer

State police officers focus on patrolling state highways and enforcing state laws, while others serve a variety of local functions.

of a president, mail fraud, bank robbery, and the hijacking of an aircraft.

Arresting Suspects After a criminal act has been committed, police officers must make decisions about a number of factors before making an arrest. First, they must investigate the crime and then decide whether there is enough evidence to arrest someone. If they did not witness the crime, they may need to obtain an arrest warrant—or court authorization—before an arrest can be made. Second, they must decide what level of control or force is necessary to make the arrest.

Police officers may use force sometimes, but not more than is necessary to do their job effectively, whether making an arrest, controlling a crowd, or fulfilling any other police function. In general, the use of lethal, or deadly, force is forbidden unless an officer or other person is threatened with serious bodily harm or death. In some states, however, an officer may use lethal force against a suspect who is fleeing after an arrest, even if the arrest was only for a misdemeanor offense.

Because of three significant Supreme Court cases, *Gideon* v. *Wainwright, Miranda* v. *Arizona,* and *Escobedo* v. *Illinois,* the police cannot question people without informing them of their constitutional rights to remain silent and to secure the services of an attorney. (The rights of the accused are more fully explained in Chapter 14.) After an arrest, the accused is "booked" at the police station, where his or her picture and fingerprints are taken. These are then used to check the person's identity and examine criminal records to determine whether he or she has been previously arrested or convicted.

Courts

Once the police arrest and book someone for a crime, he or she then awaits appearance in court. The accused person's first court proceeding after an arrest must be held as soon as possible, unless there is good cause for delay.

Appearance in Court At the initial hearing, a judge determines whether there is sufficient evidence to hold the person and, if so, whether to set **bail**—an amount that the accused must deposit with the court to be released from jail while awaiting trial. The bail money—called a **bond**—is held as security to ensure that the accused will not flee

The Legal Process

APPEARANCE IN COURT
Accused appears before a judge, who may set bail.

PRELIMINARY HEARING
Judge decides if there is enough evidence to have the accused bound over for formal charges.

INDICTMENT
Formal accusation is brought against the accused by a grand jury or an information [sworn statement].

ARRAIGNMENT
Accused is formally notified of charges and enters plea.

JURY SELECTION
Prosecution and defense attorneys choose panel of 6 to 12 people to decide accused person's guilt or innocence.

TRIAL
Prosecution and defense present evidence and question witnesses to prove guilt or establish innocence.

VERDICT
Jury decides guilt or innocence, usually by unanimous decision.

SENTENCING
Judge sets punishment for convicted defendant.

Each step in the legal process is necessary to guarantee that the rights of the accused are protected. **How many people are selected to serve on a jury?**

from the jurisdiction of the court. It is returned when the accused appears for the trial.

Even though people are presumed innocent until proved guilty and the Eighth Amendment prevents judges from setting "excessive bail," the Supreme Court has ruled that people do not have the *right* to be released on bail. To protect the community from people accused of serious crimes, judges may set high bail or refuse to set bail at all.

Preliminary Hearing Many states give accused people the right to appear at a preliminary hearing, though they may give up that right. At a preliminary hearing the judge will review a copy of the complaint, which is the written statement of the facts of the case. The judge will then determine whether there is reason to believe that an offense was committed and that the defendant is the one who committed it.

The preliminary hearing is largely one-sided, with the prosecutor trying to persuade the judge that there is sufficient reason for the case to go to trial. If the judge determines that there is enough evidence, the accused will then answer formal charges at the next stage of the process.

Indictment The **indictment**, or the formal accusation against the accused, is the next step in the process after the initial appearance in court or the preliminary hearing, depending on the jurisdiction. In the federal courts and in about half of the states, a person is indicted by a grand jury. A **grand jury** is made up of 12 to 23 people who decide if the government has enough evidence to try an accused person on formal charges.

Grand jury meetings are closed to the public, and only the prosecutor is allowed to present evidence. Grand juries almost always accept the prosecutor's recommendation to begin formal criminal proceedings. They can also act as powerful investigative tools because they can call any person to appear as a witness before them and can order any person to produce documents and papers related to the case. (The grand jury system is more fully explained in Chapter 14.)

States that do not use the grand jury system indict by an information. An **information** is an affidavit, or sworn statement, in which the state's prosecuting attorney declares that there is sufficient evidence against the accused to justify trying the case.

Arraignment At **arraignment** the accused is formally notified of the charges against him or her and is asked to enter a plea of guilty or not guilty. Most states also permit a **no-contest plea**, which comes from the term *nolo contendere,* or "I will not contest it." The major difference between a guilty plea and a no-contest plea is that with a no-contest plea, the accused does not deny committing the offense but does deny that the offense involved any moral wrongdoing.

In some instances a not-guilty plea can later be changed to a guilty plea, and a guilty plea can sometimes be withdrawn. If the accused pleads not guilty, a trial will be scheduled. Sometimes, however, he or she may accept a plea bargain, in which case there will be no trial. (You will learn more about plea bargains later in this section.)

Caption Answer

A grand jury decides if the government has enough evidence to try a case, while a petit jury decides a person's innocence or guilt.

CONSTITUTIONAL GOVERNMENT *The jury (seated, top left) and judge listen to the court proceedings of a trial.* **How is a grand jury different from a petit jury?**

Careers in Government

State Trial Judge

Every Friday, California state trial judge Peter Mirich takes a helicopter or ferry from San Pedro, California, to Santa Catalina, an island just off the California coast. There he presides over a small municipal court and hears cases typical of a popular resort town, ranging from falsifying a license to disturbing the peace. In the afternoon the judge may perform wedding ceremonies. In this small town there are few criminal cases. In fact Judge Mirich has presided over just one murder case on the island – the only one in almost 50 years.

Judge Mirich is one of 12,000 state, county and municipal trial court judges in the country. State courts handle around 27 million criminal and civil cases each year in the United

Judge Peter Mirich, flying to Santa Catalina in a private helicopter to preside over the city's municipal court

States. State court judges weigh the evidence that is presented, apply the appropriate laws, and decide penalties. In jury trials, judges must also instruct the jurors on how to apply the law to the evidence.

At municipal court level, judges try misdemeanor cases and civil cases involving minor monetary damages. Municipal court judges also hold preliminary hearings to decide if defendants charged with felonies should be tried in a superior court. Superior court judges handle felonies and

civil cases concerning higher monetary damages. They also run juvenile and family courts.

A judge must have a college education and a law degree. Many also have years of experience practicing law. Although any type of lawyer may become a judge, district attorneys – also known as prosecuting attorneys – are particularly likely to be selected as judges because of their courtroom experience.

The process of selecting judges varies from state to state, and sometimes this process takes time. Sometimes judges are elected, and sometimes state governors or legislatures appoint them. Once selected, judges may serve for fixed terms or until mandatory retirement. In some states, judges may serve many terms, and sometimes they move up from municipal courts to superior courts. Consider Richard Paez (who is Hispanic) and Marsha Berzon, two California judges. After waiting more than two years, they were finally confirmed in March, 2000, by the Senate. Why the long wait? Critics charge that in a Republican-controlled Senate, it is harder for women and minorities to be confirmed. Critics claim that in spite of the great need for judges, there are many other vacancies that have not been filled because of politics.

Jury Selection In the criminal justice system a defendant has the right to a trial by jury. A trial jury, sometimes called a **petit** (PEHT-ee) **jury**, is a panel of people who live in the community and are chosen to hear a case to determine a person's guilt or innocence. In the federal courts and in all but two states, a trial jury is made up of 12 people. Trial by jury is the defendant's right under the Sixth Amendment to the Constitution. However, the

defendant may choose to give up this right in favor of a "bench" trial—a trial held before a single judge.

If the defendant chooses a jury trial, the lawyers from both sides must agree on the people to serve on the jury, from a pool of citizens summoned for jury duty. To guide them in their selections, the lawyers engage in the process called ***voir dire*** (VWAHR DIR), meaning "to speak the truth," in which they question each potential juror and may ask the judge to dismiss anyone they believe holds a strong opinion about the case. For example, if the defendant is a stockbroker, any potential jurors who appear hostile to stockbrokers may be dismissed.

The defense lawyer or prosecuting attorney may dismiss a juror without giving a reason by issuing a **peremptory challenge**. Such challenges are used when a potential juror's presence on the jury might harm the defense's or prosecution's chances of winning, but no reason for dismissal would satisfy the judge. Usually each side is limited to about six peremptory challenges.

Once members of the jury are chosen, they are sworn in and the trial begins. In cases that receive a lot of publicity, the jury may be **sequestered**, or kept in isolation, in a hotel during the trial. In an attempt to keep their viewpoints from being influenced by outside information, sequestered jurors are allowed neither to speak about the case with family or friends nor to watch television, read newspapers, or observe other media.

Trial Both sides in a criminal trial have the right to call witnesses to testify about the case. If a witness will not come to the court voluntarily, he or she may receive a **subpoena**—a court order requiring the person's presence.

The lawyers ask their own witnesses questions in a process called direct examination, and they question the other side's witnesses in a process called cross-examination. The judge also may question the witnesses. Witnesses must respond to every question, unless answering the question will reveal their participation in a crime. The right not to answer such questions is protected by the Fifth Amendment. (The Fifth Amendment is more fully explained in Chapter 13.) Similarly, defendants in a criminal case are not required to testify, though they may choose to if they wish.

After the prosecution has presented its case, the defense routinely asks for a dismissal of the charges on the grounds that the evidence is insufficient to prove beyond a reasonable doubt that the defendant is guilty. If the judge sustains the motion, the defendant is acquitted—or freed from the charges. If the judge rejects the motion, the defense can take one of two actions. It can rest its case, hoping that its cross-examination of the prosecuting witnesses raised enough reasonable doubt to result in an acquittal. Or, if the defense feels the need to make a stronger case, it can present

CONSTITUTIONAL GOVERNMENT *Former football star O. J. Simpson was tried in both a criminal court case and a civil court case for the deaths of his former wife and her friend.* **Under what circumstances may a person be tried twice for the same charges?**

its own witnesses. In this case, however, the prosecution may call additional witnesses to rebut—or contradict—the defense's new witnesses.

Finally, the lawyers make their closing arguments to the jury. The defense also will renew its motion to dismiss the charges, giving the judge a final opportunity to acquit the defendant before the case is submitted to the jury.

The Verdict The judge tells the jury to decide on a verdict of guilty or not guilty. If the defendant is found guilty, he or she will face sentencing. The verdict may be appealed, however, by claiming that errors were made in the trial. If the verdict is overturned on appeal, the defendant may receive a new trial or the prosecution may drop the case.

In states requiring a unanimous verdict, the presence of one or more jurors who vote differently from the majority results in a **hung jury**—a jury that is unable to reach a verdict. In the event of a hung jury, the state may either retry the defendant on the same charge or else on a lesser charge. This is the only circumstance under which the government can try a defendant twice for the same offense. (Under the Fifth Amendment, it is illegal to retry someone for a crime of which he or she has been acquitted.) A person may, however,

Caption Answer

In the case of a hung jury a second trial may be needed; a person may be tried on a criminal charge by a state and then on a similar charge in a civil case.

THEMES IN GOVERNMENT

CONSTITUTIONAL GOVERNMENT

Though the number of peremptory challenges is typically limited to 6, in more serious crimes such as murder the number might be as high as 40. One of the few limits placed on peremptory challenges concerns race. In the case of *Batson* v. *Kentucky,* the U.S. Supreme Court ruled that a prosecutor's use of peremptory challenges to exclude members of a particular race from the jury violated the Fourteenth Amendment of the Constitution. In 1990 New York State reaffirmed this ban by prohibiting defense attorneys from using race as the only criterion for a peremptory challenge.

In a famous case involving Washington, D.C., mayor Marion Barry, the defense used 10 of 12 peremptory challenges to eliminate white jurors, while the prosecution used all 12 of its peremptory challenges to eliminate African Americans. ■

be tried on a criminal charge by a state and then be tried for a similar charge in a civil, rather than a criminal, case. As noted in Section 1, criminal laws deal with actions that are forbidden by society, while civil laws deal with disputes between private parties. Thus, a person accused of killing someone, for instance, can be charged in a criminal court for murder and in a civil court for causing pain and suffering to the victim's relatives.

Sentencing In state, local, and federal courts, after a person has been convicted of a crime, he or she receives a sentence. Sentencing statutes vary considerably from state to state. In recent years legislatures and sentencing commissions have moved toward establishing specific sentencing guidelines for each crime, rather than leaving judges to choose a sentence within broad, unspecified guidelines.

After a defendant in a criminal trial is found guilty, the prosecuting and defense attorneys suggest a sentence they consider appropriate. The defense lawyer is likely to emphasize the defendant's good record and chance to become a productive member of society, while the prosecution is likely to emphasize injuries to society or to the victim and the victim's family, as well as any prior criminal record the defendant might have. Then, considering information from a probation report if applicable, the judge makes a sentencing decision.

The judge does not need to explain how he or she decided on the sentence, and the sentence cannot be appealed as long as it falls under proper legal guidelines. Sentences for the same crime can vary greatly because the range of sentencing guidelines is generally very broad, and each judge has great leeway in determining the sentence for a crime.

Plea Bargaining Some defendants avoid going to trial by accepting a **plea bargain**—agreeing to plead guilty to a less serious charge, which generally results in a shorter sentence than he or she would receive if found guilty in a jury trial. In the U.S. criminal justice system today, more than 90 percent of convictions are obtained through a plea bargain. The Supreme Court upholds plea bargains so long as defendants understand the charges, know that they are giving up their rights to a jury trial, and realize that they are acknowledging guilt.

Those who support the use of plea bargaining argue that trials usually are costly and sometimes lengthy. Also, no matter how strong the case is against the accused, there is always a chance in a jury trial that the defendant may be found not guilty. With a plea bargain, finding the defendant guilty is a certainty. Opponents of plea bargaining argue that it allows those who are guilty to avoid adequate punishment.

SECTION 2 REVIEW

1. Define and explain:
- county
- bail
- bond
- indictment
- grand jury
- information
- arraignment
- no-contest plea
- petit jury
- *voir dire*
- peremptory challenge
- sequester
- subpoena
- hung jury
- plea bargain

2. Identifying Concepts: Copy the chart to the right onto a separate sheet of paper and use it to describe what happens after a person is arrested and booked.

The Legal Process

3. **Finding the Main Idea**

a. What role do police play in the criminal justice system?

b. What is a plea bargain and why do some people oppose them?

4. **Writing and Critical Thinking**

Problem Solving: Sentences for the same crime can vary greatly from person to person. Use a problem-solving process to gather information about sentencing inequality, consider a solution, and evaluate the effectiveness of that solution. Then write a paragraph explaining the problem, describing your solution to the problem, and explaining why you believe it would be effective.

 Homework Practice Online
keyword: SV3 HP12

SECTION 3
CORRECTIONS

READ TO DISCOVER

1. What are the various sentencing options in the criminal justice system?
2. What is parole?
3. Why is capital punishment controversial?
4. What happens to juvenile offenders after their arrest?

POLITICAL DICTIONARY

probation
parole
capital punishment
juvenile delinquent

Once a person has been convicted of a crime in the United States, various types of sentences may be imposed. In some instances, people who have not committed a serious crime may be placed on probation. More serious offenders generally are imprisoned. Some of the most serious offenders, however, may receive the death sentence.

Juvenile offenders are treated differently in the criminal justice system than are adults. Although juvenile offenders have some of the same rights and receive some of the same punishments as adults, their correction, or punishment, is often handled in a much different manner.

Probation

Around 60 percent of all persons convicted of crimes in state and federal courts are sentenced to probation. Under a sentence of **probation**, someone found guilty of an offense remains free but under supervision. In 2000 more than 3.8 million people were on probation in the United States. Supporters of probation argue that it benefits both the defendant and society. The probationer retains his or her freedom, and society does not have to pay the high cost of imprisonment.

When sentencing an offender to probation, a judge hopes that the person will use the freedom to become more responsible and avoid future crime. The defendant may be on probation for several years and may be required to participate in a drug treatment or other kind of program, maintain employment, or stay in school. The judge determines the length and terms of probation, as well as how closely the offender will be monitored by authorities. If the offender violates certain set conditions, a judge may revoke probation and instead impose a prison or jail sentence.

Imprisonment

More serious or repeat offenders usually are not placed on probation, but are imprisoned. In 2000 more than 1.9 million people were in U.S. prisons and jails. A prison is a state or federal correctional institution where inmates serve a sentence of a year or more (for felonies). A jail generally is a county or local institution where accused persons await trial, sentencing, or transfer to another correctional institution. A jail may also house convicted persons who are serving sentences of less than one year (for misdemeanors).

The organizations that run prisons at the state and federal levels usually are called departments of correction. These departments decide if offenders

CONSTITUTIONAL GOVERNMENT *Some offenders are required to perform community service as a part of their sentence.* **What are some of the conditions of probation that an offender might be required to follow?**

SECTION 3
CORRECTIONS

Lesson Plans

For teaching strategies, see Lesson 12.3 located at the beginning of this chapter or the One-Stop Planner Stategy 12.3.

Political Dictionary

To reinforce the section's vocabulary terms, refer students to the Electronic Glossary on the *Researcher CD-ROM.*

Section Assessment

To assess students' mastery of this section, have them complete Daily Quiz 12.3 in *Daily Quizzes with Answer Key.*

Caption Answer

may be required to attend drug treatment, stay employed, or attend school

Largest U.S. Prison Inmate Populations (end of 1999)

Prison System	Number of Inmates
Texas	163,190
California	163,067
Federal	135,246
New York	73,233
Florida	69,596
Ohio	46,842
Michigan	46,617
Illinois	44,660
Georgia	42,091
Pennsylvania	36,525

Source: *World Almanac: 2001*

Prison populations in many states are so large that officials are searching for solutions to the problem of overcrowded prison facilities. **What are some alternatives to imprisonment that may help address the problem of overcrowded prisons?**

should be sent to a maximum-, medium-, or minimum-security prison or jail. They base their decisions on the offenders' age, how dangerous they are, and how likely they are to attempt to escape. In theory, the jail or prison to which a person is sent depends on the crime committed. However, state prisons are so overcrowded today that many state prisoners are now housed in county or city jails.

Although most people agree that lawbreakers should be removed from society for a period of time, they often disagree on the reasoning behind imprisonment. There are usually four major arguments for putting people behind bars—it serves as a form of retribution, as rehabilitation, as a deterrent to other would-be criminals, and as a form of protection for society.

When people say that imprisonment is proper retribution for a crime, they mean that it is a deserved punishment for a crime committed against society. They argue that it would be wrong not to punish people who have significantly harmed others.

Some people believe that imprisonment is a deterrent to future crime. They argue that the threat of a prison term will keep people from committing illegal acts.

The third major argument for imprisonment is that it will rehabilitate a convicted criminal. People who believe that prison is a form of rehabilitation hold that the purpose of imprisonment is to reform criminals and then free them to become law-abiding members of society.

Finally, some people feel safer knowing that a convicted criminal is off the streets. They say that putting a criminal behind bars keeps him or her from committing other crimes, therefore serving to protect members of the community.

Parole

After serving part of their sentence, many prisoners are eligible for **parole**—early release from prison. The amount of time an offender must serve before being eligible for parole varies greatly from state to state. Every state, however, maintains a parole board to determine when and if a prisoner will be released. Each board's members are chosen by the governor of its state. Parole boards typically meet with a prospective parolee at the prison to determine if he or she is eligible for parole. This process also involves examining the prisoner's previous record and the facts of the crime for which he or she was imprisoned. If parole is denied, the prisoner remains in prison, but may be reviewed for parole at a later date set by law.

An inmate who is granted parole must fulfill his or her parole terms until the time remaining on the sentence is served (minus any time subtracted from the sentence for the good behavior of the inmate while in prison). The parole agency may require that the parolee receive counseling, be tested for illegal drug use, attend school, or avoid certain people or places. If the parolee violates the terms of his or her parole, the parole agency will re-evaluate the case to decide whether to cancel parole and send the offender back to prison.

Capital Punishment

The most serious offenders may receive **capital punishment**—the death penalty. Capital punishment is legal in 38 states and is usually reserved only for people convicted of murder.

PUBLIC GOOD *Camp Sandhill, located near Patrick, South Carolina, is a private juvenile correction facility that houses 32 boys.* **How has the treatment of juvenile offenders changed since the 1800s?**

Capital punishment sentences are delivered far more frequently than they are carried out. There were 98 people executed in 2000, and 3,500 inmates sat on death row. The sentence in many death penalty cases is eventually reversed or reduced.

Capital punishment is a highly controversial topic in the United States. Research, however, indicates that a majority of Americans support its use in at least some instances. Reflecting this sentiment, Congress—in the 1994 crime bill—increased the number of offenses subject to the death penalty.

Supporters of capital punishment frequently argue that people who commit the worst crimes deserve to die. They also suggest that would-be killers will be less likely to commit murder if they know that they might face death if caught. Supporters further argue that the death penalty is less expensive than life imprisonment.

Opponents of capital punishment argue that cost savings are offset by the fact that in the United States, offenders on death row spend years appealing their cases. These appeals are very expensive and may in some cases cost more than life imprisonment. Opponents also argue that the

death penalty has not worked in preventing people from committing horrible crimes, and most importantly has sentenced innocent people to death in some instances. But possibly the most controversial charge leveled by opponents is the claim that capital punishment is discriminatory. In support of this claim, they note that African Americans receive the death penalty in a much higher proportion than do whites in cases involving similar circumstances. (Capital punishment is further discussed in Chapter 15.)

Juvenile Crime

Young people are responsible for a large number of the nation's crimes. Each state has special laws that apply to **juvenile delinquents**—or young offenders. The legal definition of a juvenile varies across the country. It can range anywhere from under 16 to under 21 years of age, depending on the state. Separate criminal justice agencies designed to deal with juvenile offenders first emerged in the 1800s. Before that time, juveniles at least 14 years old were fully accountable for their crimes and could be tried in adult courts. They could be sentenced to adult prisons and even

Citizenship in Action

Teen Court

The 17-year-old defendant sat nervously in the witness chair. Facing the judge and jurors, the prosecuting attorney described the crime: vandalism to a vehicle. The jurors listened attentively to the facts and chose the maximum punishment: 25 hours of community service, payment for damage to the car, and four weeks of service as a juror.

Though this sounds like a scene from a regular courtroom, this particular court was different. The attorneys, jurors, and most of the key courtroom personnel were teenagers, just like the defendant. These peer courts, known as teen courts, allow young, first-time offenders and some second-time offenders to be heard by a jury of their peers.

Teen courts provide a legal alternative to the juvenile court system. In most teen courts the defendants—some as young as 7 years old and others as old as 19—have already pleaded guilty to misdemeanor charges in a juvenile court. These juveniles come before a teen court only because the judges who heard their initial trials sent them there.

The crimes with which the juveniles are charged include shoplifting, vandalism, violation of curfew, truancy, and possession of alcohol or drugs. Sentences might include hours of community service or repayment to the victim. Defendants also might be required to attend an alcohol, drug, or violence prevention workshop and to obey a curfew. Defendants may also have to write letters of apology to their victims or sometimes even a research paper. Many teen courts also require service on a teen court jury.

Teen courts often issue harsher sentences to their peers than regular juvenile courts do. For example, a Kentucky teen court sentenced a teenager to 90 hours of community service, four months of jury duty in teen court, and a one-month curfew for carrying a concealed weapon. The teenager appealed the sentence in a standard juvenile court and received only a $50 fine and two days of service on a teen court jury.

The success of teen courts stems from a number of factors. Teen court defendants must examine their actions and take into account the effect of their actions on others. Teen courts also give teenagers a second chance. Once the defendant completes his or her sentence, the court clears the charge from the defendant's criminal record.

Perhaps the most important factor, however, is positive peer pressure. In teen court, defendants receive punishment from teenagers just like themselves. "The kids who are the prosecuting and defense attorneys and the kids who sit on the jury take it very seriously," says Bill Ferchland, a lawyer who has served as a teen court judge. "And that means that the defendants take it seriously."

Teen courts allow young defendants the opportunity to have their cases heard by a jury of their peers.

What Do You Think?

1. Do you think that teen courts are an effective legal alternative to standard courts?

2. Why do you think many teens volunteer their time as attorneys, jurors, or personnel in teen courts?

to death. During the late 1800s, however, many people believed that the juvenile justice system needed to be reformed and that young people should be given special attention rather than receiving the same punishments as adults. Today's juvenile court is based on the idea that the government must assume the role of parent to juveniles accused of crimes.

Juvenile Court Treatment of juvenile offenders today varies depending on the offense, and some states even try juveniles as adults if they commit serious crimes such as murder. Juveniles who are arrested are taken to a juvenile detention center that is separate from the adult jail. Most states deny bail to juveniles, and judges must decide whether to release a juvenile based on the likelihood that he or she might flee or pose a threat to the community.

Although juveniles have the right to an attorney and are presumed innocent until proved guilty, in the past they have had no right to a trial by jury. In recent years, however, about one quarter of the states have passed legislation allowing trial by jury for many juvenile offenses.

Juvenile Corrections Juveniles who are found guilty beyond a reasonable doubt may be sentenced to probation, to community service, or to pay a fine. (See the Citizenship in Action feature, opposite page.) They also may be required to serve time in a juvenile detention center. The judge decides the length of the sentence, but the juvenile must be released when he or she reaches adulthood. Instead of giving juveniles probation or time in a detention center, some states are experimenting with juvenile "boot camps." These camps are designed like military boot camps and are intended to provide a structured environment where juvenile offenders can learn positive social values.

Possible Juvenile Court Penalties

- Warned and dismissed
- Required to attend appropriate counseling or youth assistance programs
- Required to pay for damages
- Placed on monitored probation
- Required to perform community service
- Sent to a youth corrections facility (Sentences range from 30 days to until the offender turns 21 years old.)
- Fined $15 to several hundred dollars plus court costs

Sentences for juvenile offenders vary depending on such factors as the severity of the crime and the offenders' juvenile record. **How does the treatment of juvenile offenders differ from the treatment of adult offenders?**

CASE STUDY

Boot Camps

PUBLIC GOOD The first boot camps for criminal offenders were established in 1983 in Georgia as an alternative to jail, prison, or juvenile detention centers. Often modeled after boot camps used to train military recruits, most of these programs have incorporated many typical military features, such as drill instructors, barracks-style housing, and military-style uniforms.

Boot camps vary widely in time spent per day on military drill, discipline, and physical labor. Camps in Pennsylvania require juveniles to spend only 10 percent of their day on these activities, while camps in South Carolina require 80 percent. Other activities that are emphasized include education, counseling, and physical fitness.

As of 2000 there were approximately 70 juvenile camps in 24 states. Boot-camp programs can last as few as 30 days or as long as 300 days. One study of such boot camps, including those for adults, found that between 3 and 42 percent of those attending either drop out or fail and that most of those do so in the first weeks of a program. Another study of boot camps discovered

---

Caption Answer
Juvenile offenders are taken to separate facilities, and most states deny them bail.

PUBLIC GOOD *Juvenile offenders sentenced to boot camp are often required to perform military drills such as marching.* **Why are boot camps less expensive than prisons?**

that between 7 and 52 percent of offenders are expelled from boot camps as a part of disciplinary action. The percentage varies so widely because different camps tolerate different levels of misconduct.

Boot camps have proven to be an effective alternative to incarceration in some ways, but not in others. The positive aspects include maintaining inmates' physical fitness and improving their education. Also, boot camps spend less money per inmate than do prisons. Unfor-

tunately, boot camps have not reduced the rate of people who revert to criminal behavior upon being released from custody. In addition, boot camps have only proved to be less expensive than prison because they keep offenders for shorter periods of time. In the long run, however, boot camps may be a better option than prisons if they succeed in improving educational performance, physical conditioning, and attitudes of offenders.

SECTION 3 REVIEW

1. Define and explain:
- probation
- parole
- capital punishment
- juvenile delinquent

2. Identifying Concepts: Use the chart at right to compare and contrast opposing opinions about the death penalty.

Death Penalty	
Supporters argue:	Opponents argue:

3. **Finding the Main Idea**

a. What are some of the advantages of probation?

b. How are juvenile offenders treated compared to adult offenders?

4. **Writing and Critical Thinking**

Problem Solving: What alternatives to imprisonment do you think might help solve prison crowding and prevent crime? Use a problem-solving process to gather information about alternatives. Then consider solutions and evaluate their effectiveness. Finally, write a paragraph describing and defending your ideas.
Consider the following:
- the role of education
- current sentencing laws

Homework Practice Online
keyword: SV3 HP12

GOVERNMENT IN THE NEWS

Prisons Are Big Business

Today, the U.S. prison population of almost two million inmates represents 25 percent of the total number of prisoners around the globe. It's not only a big statistic, it's big business.

The rise in the number of prisoners in the United States, and by extension, their housing, upkeep, care, and general economic impact, has led to a "prison economy" of far-reaching financial significance. For example, did you know that on the New York Stock Exchange you can now buy shares in a company that owns and rents prisons?

All across the United States the prison economy is making it's mark in dollars and cents. For example, states swap convicts back and forth, either to relieve overcrowded facilities or to fill up prisons that have vacancies. Prisoner swapping has become such big business that Dominion Management, Inc., of Kansas City was created to meet the growing demand.

In Texas, prisons have become such big business that they employ more people inside the state than Microsoft does worldwide. Corporate America has taken notice of the prison economy in a big way. Corporate giants like Chase bank have invested in prisons, and so have mutual funds like Fidelity.

Pure and simple, many of America's corporate icons have discovered that there is big money to be made from convicts. It is estimated that: Inmates now control more than $100 million in deposits at the nation's banks and other financial institutions; make long-distance calls worth over $1 billion annually; and spend about a half-billion dollars on everything from candy bars to TV sets.

Prisons have outgrown their old image as simply houses of detention. Instead, they can be thought of as public works projects. Like the massive road and bridge projects sponsored by the federal government during the depression era, prisons create

The California City Correctional Center, above, is a for-profit, maximum-security prison.

money and jobs. In fact, prisons create the kind of jobs that are rapidly disappearing in the U.S.—jobs requiring low skill, paying a decent wage.

Unskilled workers and those with little education can qualify for prison jobs because in many cases they require only on a GED and a clean record. Once on the job, these people can often rise in salary to $25,000 or more annually. In a small town, where most prisons are found, even a modest income can go a long way. Add the desperately needed benefits that go with a prison job and, for many people, the incentive to apply can be really big.

What Do You Think?

1. Do you think corporations should be allowed to make profits off prisoners? What kind of conflicts might arise from this arrangement?

2. One out of every four prisoners worldwide is incarcerated in the United States. Why might the percentage of Americans in prison be so high?

> ▶ **WHY IT MATTERS TODAY**
>
> How much money does it take to house a prisoner? How can a community benefit from this? Use **CNNfyi.com** or other **current events** sources to look up facts about the increasing U.S. prison population.
>
> **CNNfyi.com**

Government in the News Answers

1. Students may agree or disagree, but should note conflicts of interest, such as that corporations with a profit motive may be less likely to be concerned for the well-being of prisoners than for the cash they can make off of them.

2. Students answers will vary, but they may note that Americans are not more likely to commit crimes than citizens of other nations, but that the high prison population reflects tougher sentencing laws combined with political pressures to be tough on crime and prison corporations seeking ever-increasing profits.

CHAPTER 12

Review Answers

Writing a Summary
Summaries should focus on the main points of each section. These may be found in the Read to Discover questions at the start of each section. Summaries should also use standard grammar, spelling, sentence structure, and punctuation.

Identifying Ideas
Refer to the following pages: common law (271), statutory law (272), bail (276), bond (276), indictment (277), arraignment (277), subpoena (279), probation (281), parole (282), capital punishment (282)

Understanding Main Ideas
1. Civil laws apply to private disputes and are punishable

(Continued on page 288)

Review

(Continued from page 287)

by fines, while criminal laws cover actions prohibited by the government and are punishable by fines or imprisonment.

2. common, statutory, constitutional, and administrative

3. Misdemeanors include minor crimes such as petty larceny; felonies are serious crimes such as arson, robbery, and murder.

4. Refer to The Legal Process chart on page 276.

5. In all federal courts and about half of state courts, grand juries decide if the government has enough evidence to formally accuse people and bring them to trial.

6. The range of sentencing guidelines is very broad and each judge has much discretion when determining the sentence for a crime.

7. The probationer gets to remain free and taxpayers do not have to pay the high cost of imprisonment.

8. After serving part of their sentence, prisoners meet with a state parole board. Board members examine the prisoner's prior record and his or her behavior while incarcerated to determine whether to grant parole.

9. Juvenile offenders are housed separately from adults, cannot post bail, and are not allowed jury trials in some states.

10. pro: less expensive than life imprisonment, works as a deterrent, culprits deserve to die; con: appeals are costly, innocent people may die, it is cruel and unusual, it is discriminatory

(Continued on page 289)

Writing a Summary

Using standard grammar, spelling, sentence structure, and punctuation, write a summary of the information in this chapter.

Identifying Ideas

Identify the following terms and explain their significance.

1. common law   **6.** arraignment

2. statutory law   **7.** subpoena

3. bail   **8.** probation

4. bond   **9.** parole

5. indictment   **10.** capital punishment

Understanding Main Ideas

SECTION 1 *(pp. 271–274)*

1. How are criminal laws and civil laws different?

2. List the four main types of law.

3. What is the difference between a felony and a misdemeanor?

SECTION 2 *(pp. 275–280)*

4. List the steps that an accused person typically goes through after being booked by the police.

5. What part does the grand jury play in indicting someone who is accused of a crime?

6. Why can different people convicted of the same crime receive widely different sentences?

SECTION 3 *(pp. 281–286)*

7. What are two benefits of probation?

8. By what process is a prisoner granted parole?

9. In what ways are juvenile offenders treated differently from adults?

10. What are the major arguments for and against the death penalty?

Reviewing Themes

1. Political Processes Why do you think that some states require their juries to unanimously agree on a verdict?

2. Constitutional Government What are some of the reasons that constitutional law takes precedence over other types of law?

3. Principles of Democracy Do you think that all accused people should have the right to stay out of jail until their trial? Why or why not?

Thinking Critically

1. Taking a Stand Do you agree with the death penalty? Why or why not? What arguments from the opposing side make you question your position? Which of your own arguments do you think is weakest? Strongest?

2. Identifying Cause and Effect Why do you think juveniles are treated differently from adults? Do you think that the treatment of juveniles in the U.S. court system promotes the public good? Explain your answer.

3. Evaluating Why is it important for police officers to follow certain procedures, such as informing suspects of their constitutional rights, when they make arrests?

Writing about Government

Review the list you made in your Government Notebook about positive and negative ways that laws affect your everyday life. In what ways do you think the U.S. legal system works to protect most Americans? In what ways is it effective and what areas need improvement? Explain your answers in your Notebook.

Interpreting Political Cartoons

Study the political cartoon below. Then use it to help you answer the questions that follow.

© 1999 by Sidney Harris.

"Mrs. Melnik, from around the corner— she's been a customer for fifteen years— didn't like last week's pot roast, and she's suing us for breach of contract."

1. Which of the following best describes the cartoonist's point of view?
   a. People against whom lawsuits are filed should take the charges more seriously.
   b. Civil lawsuits often result in criminal charges.
   c. Some people file frivolous civil lawsuits to settle minor disputes.
   d. Contract law is one of the three main categories of civil law.

2. Why do you think the cartoonist drew this?

Analyzing Primary Sources

Read the following excerpt from the Supreme Court's opinion in *Lewis* v. *United States,* written by Justice Sandra Day O'Connor. Then answer the questions that follow.

"Petitioner argues that, where a defendant is charged with multiple petty offenses in a single prosecution, the Sixth Amendment requires that the aggregate potential penalty be the basis for determining whether a jury trial is required. . . .

We disagree. The Sixth Amendment reserves the jury trial right to defendants accused of serious crimes. . . . We determine whether an offense is serious by looking to the judgment of the legislature, primarily as expressed in the maximum authorized term of imprisonment. Here, by setting the maximum authorized prison term at six months, the legislature categorized the offense of obstructing the mail as petty. The fact that the petitioner was charged with two counts of a petty offense does not revise the legislative judgment as to the gravity of that particular offense, nor does it transform the offense into a serious one, to which the jury trial right would apply."

3. Which of the following best summarizes the Court's point of view?
   a. The defendant in this case should be charged with more serious crimes.
   b. Any defendant deserves a trial by jury.
   c. The maximum prison term for multiple petty offenses should be increased.
   d. Only defendants charged with serious crimes have the right to a trial by jury.

4. Where is the right to a jury trial established?

Building Your Portfolio

Biography

Research the career of a state or federal judge, and write a one-page biography of that person. Find out about the judge's education, previous jobs, and important rulings. You may want to begin your research in the library or on the Internet. If possible, include a photograph of the judge in your biography.

☑ internet connect

Internet Activity: go.hrw.com
KEYWORD: SV3 GV12

Access the Internet through the HRW Go site to research the legal process in the criminal justice system. Then write a skit that illustrates the legal process, jury selection, plea-bargaining, and sentencing. Your skit must account for all portions of the legal process.

(Continued from page 288)

Reviewing Themes

1. Answers will vary, but students may argue that the failure to reach a unanimous verdict indicates that it is reasonable to doubt the accused's guilt.
2. Answers will vary but students should recognize the Constitution as the foundation of the nation's political and legal system.
3. Answers will vary but students should offer and defend a position on the issue.

Thinking Critically

1. Students' opinions will vary, but they should note which of their own arguments is strongest and which is weakest, and they should discuss opposing arguments they find to be compelling.
2. Students should state their opinions on both subjects and explain their reasoning.
3. Students' answers will vary, but they should discuss the importance of protecting the rights of the accused.

Building Social Studies Skills

1. c.
2. Answers will vary, but the student may say the cartoonist was trying to point out that many lawsuits can be considered extreme or unnecessary.
3. d
4. the Sixth Amendment

LAB OBJECTIVES

The Unit 4 Public Policy Lab incorporates the following objectives:

▶ review documents from a lawyer to determine if they support her claim that a client was subjected to an illegal search.

▶ conduct outside research to find out information about the appeals process and how much evidence is needed to appeal a case.

▶ use a decision-making process to debate with other judges whether the evidence submitted warrants an appeal.

Using the Lab

Before beginning the lab, organize students into groups and distribute copies of the Public Policy Lab Unit 4 Activity found in *Unit Tests and Unit Lab Activities with Answer Key.* Then have students read the directions for the assignment on this page. Discuss the assignment with students and point out the documents on pages 291–93 that students will use during the lab.

The What Do You Think? questions on pages 291–93 will help guide students during the project. In addition, the lab activity includes a step-by-step checklist for students to monitor their progress. For assessment guidelines, see the Group Activity rubric in the *Alternative Assessment Handbook.*

PUBLIC POLICY LAB

You Make the Decision

Judging an Appeal

You are a sitting judge on a federal court of appeals. Your panel is hearing an appeal of a case in which the defendant, John Goode, has been convicted in a federal district court of participating in a crime ring. Goode's attorney, Mary Kelly, has challenged her client's conviction. She has submitted the following documents as evidence for your panel to examine: a Brief of Appellant stating her arguments in asking the court of appeals to send the case back to federal district court for retrial, copies of the applicable amendments, and a transcript of the arresting officer's testimony in Goode's trial. The prosecutor in Goode's trial, Will Gordon, has supplied a legal brief (Brief of Appellee) opposing Kelly's motion for a new trial.

Your panel needs to decide in favor of or against sending Goode's case back to district court. Prepare a written legal opinion that addresses the arguments made by the attorneys.

Government Notebook Assignment

Record your decision-making process in your Government Notebook.

1. Review the documents and answer the WHAT DO YOU THINK? questions.

2. As a group, identify the issues to be addressed in your legal opinion.

3. After identifying the key issues, gather additional information. You may want to examine past legal cases dealing with similar issues.

4. Discuss the results of your research. Identify the options you have for completing your legal opinion. Predict the consequences each option could have for this case.

5. As a panel, make a decision on Goode's appeal. Implement your decision by writing your legal opinion. You should address the arguments made by Kelly, as well as how they affected your decision.

EXHIBIT 1

Fourth Amendment to the U.S. Constitution

The right of the people to be secure in their persons, houses, papers, and effects, against unreasonable searches and seizures, shall not be violated, and no warrants shall issue but upon probable cause, supported by oath or affirmation, and particularly describing the place to be searched, and the persons or things to be seized.

EXHIBIT 2

Fifth Amendment to the U.S. Constitution

No person shall be held to answer for a capital or otherwise infamous crime, unless on a presentment or indictment of a grand jury . . . ; nor shall any person be subject for the same offense to be twice put in jeopardy of life or limb; nor shall be compelled in any criminal case to be a witness against himself, nor be deprived of life, liberty, or property, without due process of law; nor shall private property be taken for public use, without just compensation.

EXHIBIT 3

Eighth Amendment to the U.S. Constitution

Excessive bail shall not be required, nor excessive fines imposed, nor cruel and unusual punishments inflicted.

◀ WHAT DO YOU THINK?

1. Identify five things the Fifth Amendment specifically forbids. Why do you believe the protection against self-incrimination is important?

2. What does the Eighth Amendment guarantee? How has the Supreme Court ruled on the right of accused people to be released on bail? Do you agree with the Supreme Court's position?

WHAT DO YOU THINK? ▶

1. Do you believe that Lt. Theodore's search violated Goode's rights? Explain your answer.

2. Why did Lt. Theodore go to Goode's house?

FEDERAL DISTRICT COURT
TRANSCRIPT

Case:
The United States v. John Goode

EXHIBIT 4

Date:
May 31, 2002

Transcript:

EXCERPT FROM THE TESTIMONY OF LT. JOEL R. THEODORE, AN OFFICER IN THE CITY POLICE DEPARTMENT, UNDER CROSS-EXAMINATION BY DEFENDANT'S ATTORNEY:

KELLY: Lt. Theodore, why did you go to the home of the defendant, Mr. Goode, on February 2 of this year?

THEODORE: Well, I had been providing security at a Groundhog Day ceremony, and I got to thinking about the crime ring we had busted the year before. During a trial of one of the members of that crime ring last year, Mr. Goode had refused to testify about his connection to the defendant, claiming the Fifth Amendment right not to incriminate oneself. Well, that sounded to me like Mr. Goode was guilty of taking part in the ring's criminal activity and did not want to admit it. Second, one of his neighbors told me at the Groundhog Day ceremony that Mr. Goode had been selling a lot of new televisions from his home in the last two days. I decided that I needed to drive over to Mr. Goode's house and check it out.

KELLY: But you did not get a search warrant to do that, did you?

THEODORE: No, I did not. I thought that if I went to get a search warrant from a judge, Mr. Goode would have time to sell the last of the televisions I suspected had been stolen when he was part of the crime ring the year before. I thought I needed to go over to his house right away.

KELLY: You have testified that Mr. Goode would not let you in the door but that you could see five new televisions in his living room. And then you forced your way into the house without a search warrant. Is that right?

THEODORE: Well, yes. I thought I had reason enough to go in without a search warrant because I saw what I believed was evidence of a crime. After I checked the televisions out, I discovered that serial numbers on them matched those of stolen televisions from the year before. I then arrested Mr. Goode and took him to the police station.

What Do You Think?
Answers

1. The Fifth Amendment forbids trying someone for a crime without a grand jury indictment; trying someone twice for the same crime; forcing someone to testify against him- or herself; depriving someone of life, liberty, or property without due process of law; and forcing someone to give up private property without just compensation. Students should offer and explain their opinions about protection from self-incrimination.

2. The Eighth Amendment prohibits courts from requiring excessive bail or fines, and from inflicting cruel and unusual punishment. The Supreme Court has not ruled in favor of the guaranteed right to be released on bail. Answers will vary.

What Do You Think?
Answers

1. Answers will vary, but students should give their opinions about Lt. Theodore's search and should explain their reasoning.

2. Lt. Theodore thought that before he could get a warrant, Mr. Goode might sell the last of the TVs.

291

What Do You Think?
Answers

1. They appealed the conviction on the following grounds: the arresting officer did not obtain a search warrant before searching the defendant's home, the defendant's refusal to testify in a previous case was used against him in his trial, and the bail established for him was excessively high. Answers will vary, but students should explain if they feel these arguments warrant a retrial.

2. Answers will vary, but students should explain whether they feel it was used improperly and explain why they feel that way.

3. Goode was unable to secure his release from jail because he had only about $10,000 in the bank and his bail was set at $500,000. Answers will vary regarding whether the bail is excessive, but students should offer their opinions and explain their reasoning.

PUBLIC POLICY LAB *continued*

No. 12-789
In the Federal Court of Appeals

John Goode
v.
United States

BRIEF OF APPELLANT

My client, Mr. John Goode, is appealing in the federal court of appeals his conviction of participating in the transportation of stolen goods across state lines. We are appealing Mr. Goode's conviction on the following grounds.

First, the arresting police officer entered the appellant's home, searched the premises, and arrested him with neither a search warrant nor an arrest warrant. In doing so, the arresting officer violated Mr. Goode's rights as protected under the Fourth Amendment to the U.S. Constitution.

Please see Exhibit 4, which is an excerpt from the district court testimony of Lt. Joel Theodore. We believe that Mr. Theodore did not have sufficient evidence to justify a search warrant in the first place. In addition, if he did have such evidence, we believe he was required by the Constitution to request a search warrant from a judge before entering Mr. Goode's home.

Second, Mr. Goode's refusal to testify in an earlier trial of suspected members of the crime ring in question—a refusal that was based on his Fifth Amendment right not to incriminate himself—was used as evidence against him in his trial. For example, in his testimony, Lt. Theodore mentioned Mr. Goode's refusal to testify, saying that it revealed his guilt in a crime about which he wished to remain silent for fear of incriminating himself. In addition, in his summation the prosecuting attorney at Mr. Goode's trial also told jurors that they could assume that Mr. Goode's refusal to testify, either at his trial or at earlier trials, was basically an admission of guilt.

Finally, the presiding federal judge in Mr. Goode's trial ordered bail for the defendant set at $500,000. We believe the bail was excessive and therefore a violation of the Eighth Amendment to the U.S. Constitution. As a result of this excessive bail, Mr. Goode—whose bank accounts contain only about $10,000—was unable to secure his release from jail prior to his conviction.

Based on these arguments, we believe Mr. Goode's case should be sent back to federal district court for retrial. Thank you.

Respectfully submitted,

Mary Kelly

Mary Kelly
Attorney-at-Law

▲ WHAT DO YOU THINK?

1. On what grounds are John Goode and his lawyer appealing his conviction? Do you think Mary Kelly presents convincing arguments for why this case should be sent back for retrial?

2. Do you believe that Goode's use of the Fifth Amendment's protection against self-incrimination was improperly used to convict him of a crime? Why or why not?

3. Why was Goode unable to secure his release from jail? Do you think the bail was excessive or justified?

WHAT DO YOU THINK? ▼

1. Why does the government believe that searching John Goode's home and arresting him without a search warrant was justified?

2. Do you believe that refusing to testify in your own trial should be taken as an admission of guilt? Why or why not?

3. Why might the judge believe that Goode would flee the country if he were able to post bond? For what other reasons might the judge set a high bail?

No. 12-789
In the Federal Court of Appeals

John Goode
v.
United States

Brief of Appellee

The government believes that Mr. Goode's appeal of his conviction for participating in the transportation of stolen goods across state lines should be rejected by the court of appeals. The arguments presented by Mr. Goode's attorney, on examination, do not justify sending the case back for retrial in federal district court.

Mr. Goode's argument that his rights under the Fourth Amendment were violated when Lt. Theodore searched his home without a search warrant and arrested him without an arrest warrant are weak. Based on information provided by a neighborhood witness and on his own suspicions that Mr. Goode was involved in a crime ring, Lt. Theodore had every reason to believe that Mr. Goode might dispose of important evidence if the search were delayed. By waiting, Lt. Theodore would have allowed Mr. Goode to flee the scene and escape arrest.

Second, Mr. Goode's refusal to explain under oath his connections with the crime ring that was broken last year was a legitimate cause for suspicion that he was guilty of a crime. If Mr. Goode were not involved in a crime, what objection should he have to testifying in court? Our use in court of his refusal to testify in an earlier trial, then, was justified.

Finally, the $500,000 bail set for Mr. Goode prior to his trial was justified. The high bail was based on the judge's concern that Mr. Goode had the resources to leave the country and would try to do so if he were able to post bond.

We believe, then, that Ms. Kelly has failed to justify sending Mr. Goode's case back for retrial in federal district court.

Respectfully submitted,

Will Gordon
Federal Attorney

🔲 **internet** connect

Internet Activity: go.hrw.com
KEYWORD: SV3 GVPL

Access the Internet through the HRW Go site to employ a decision-making process to consider John Goode's appeal, to vote on its merits, and to write a decision. Research links and a decision-making tutorial are provided.

What Do You Think?
Answers

1. Will Gordon stated that Lt. Theodore's search was justified. Gordon had information from a neighborhood witness indicating possible wrongdoing, and he had reason to believe the evidence might be eliminated if he waited.

2. Answers will vary, but students should take into account the Fifth Amendment when forming an opinion and should offer support for their answers.

3. Students should point out that the judge might have believed that Goode, having sufficient resources, would flee the country. Answers will vary, but students should explain other reasons why the judge would set such a high bail based on information from the sources.

UNIT 5

Lesson Options

Suggestions for customizing the material in Unit 5 to fit the specific schedule and curriculum of your classroom are located at the beginning of each chapter.

Main Ideas

Ask each student to read the Main Ideas and briefly answer each question in writing. Later, when you have finished Unit 5, ask students to return to their original answers and revise them using what they learned in the unit.

PUBLIC POLICY LAB

The Unit 5 Public Policy Lab appears on pages 360–63. This project is a real-world assignment in which students will work in groups to review information about possible campaign violations by a local representative in order to write a story about the issue. Support materials for the lab appear in *Unit Tests and Unit Lab Activities with Answer Key.*

CHAPTER 13

FUNDAMENTAL FREEDOMS

CHAPTER 14

ASSURING INDIVIDUAL RIGHTS

CHAPTER 15

PROTECTING CIVIL RIGHTS

Main Ideas

- *What fundamental freedoms are guaranteed by the Bill of Rights?*
- *What steps does the government take to protect individual rights?*
- *What are civil rights and how are they protected?*

PUBLIC POLICY LAB

Do reporters have to follow certain procedures when writing news stories? Find out by reading this unit and taking the Policy Lab Challenge on pages 360–63.

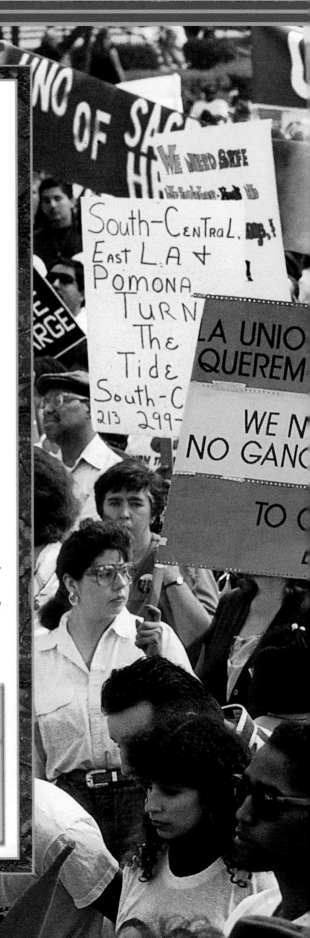

RIGHTS AND RESPONSIBILITIES

Unit 5 presents the basic concepts necessary to introduce students to ideas of individual freedoms and rights, including interpretations regarding freedom of religion, issues dealing with freedom of speech and the press, limitations placed on freedom of assembly and petition, protections of individual liberties, the rights of the accused, how to ensure fair trials and punishments, how a person becomes a citizen, the rights that aliens possess, equal protection under the law, and protection of civil rights.

Teaching with Photographs

The struggle for safer neighborhoods in Los Angeles, California, appears to have united a wide variety of the city's residents in protest. Protesters are pictured carrying signs that denounce gangs, drugs, and graffiti. Some grassroots organizations appear to be appealing to entire communities to act together for the common good. Ask students to identify other types of grassroots organizations and to explain their purpose.

CHAPTER 13 FUNDAMENTAL FREEDOMS

	OBJECTIVES	PACING GUIDE	REPRODUCIBLE RESOURCES
SECTION 1 **FREEDOM AND THE BILL OF RIGHTS** (pp. 297–299)	▶ How does the Constitution protect civil liberties? ▶ Whose civil liberties does the First Amendment guarantee? ▶ What is the role of laws and the courts in balancing individuals' civil liberties with the interests of the community?	**Regular** .5 day **Block Scheduling** .25 day	**ELL** Spanish Study Guide 13.1 **ELL** English Study Guide 13.1 **PS** Reading 11: *Seneca Falls Declaration of Women's Rights* **PS** Reading 16: *Universal Declaration of Human Rights*
SECTION 2 **FREEDOM OF RELIGION** (pp. 300–303)	▶ How has the Supreme Court interpreted the Establishment Clause to define the relationship between religion and public schools? ▶ How does the Supreme Court decide if government aid to religious groups is constitutional? ▶ How has the Free Exercise Clause been interpreted?	**Regular** 1 day **Block Scheduling** .5 day	**ELL** Spanish Study Guide 13.2 **ELL** English Study Guide 13.2 **PS** Reading 36: *Virginia Statute for Religious Freedom*
SECTION 3 **FREEDOM OF SPEECH AND OF THE PRESS** (pp. 304–311)	▶ What challenges exist in balancing individuals' freedom of speech with the need to protect national security? ▶ What boundaries exist on the media's freedom of expression? ▶ How does the First Amendment affect symbolic speech and hate speech?	**Regular** 2 days **Block Scheduling** 1 day	**ELL** Spanish Study Guide 13.3 **ELL** English Study Guide 13.3
SECTION 4 **FREEDOM OF ASSEMBLY AND PETITION** (pp. 312–314)	▶ How does the First Amendment protect the rights of assembly and petition on public property? ▶ How is the freedom to demonstrate restricted on private property? ▶ How does freedom of assembly support freedom of association?	**Regular** .5 day **Block Scheduling** .25 day	**ELL** Spanish Study Guide 13.4 **ELL** English Study Guide 13.4 **PS** Reading 57: *On Liberty*

Chapter Resource Key

PS	Primary Sources	**A**	Assessment		Video
RS	Reading Support	**REV**	Review		Videodisc
E	Enrichment	**ELL**	Reinforcement and English Language Learners		Internet
S	Simulations		Transparencies		Holt Presentation Maker Using
SM	Skills Mastery		CD-ROM		Microsoft ® PowerPoint ®

TECHNOLOGY RESOURCES	REINFORCEMENT, REVIEW, AND ASSESSMENT
One-Stop Planner: Lesson 13.1 Holt Researcher Online Homework Practice Online Cartoon Transparency 12 Global Skill Builder CD-ROM	**REV** Section 1 Review, p. 299 **A** Daily Quiz 13.1
One-Stop Planner: Lesson 13.2 Holt Researcher Online Homework Practice Online Holt American Government Videodisc: Church and State: *Rosenberger* v. *UVA* Cartoon Transparency 13 Global Skill Builder CD-ROM	**REV** Section 2 Review, p. 303 **A** Daily Quiz 13.2
One-Stop Planner: Lesson 13.3 Holt Researcher Online Homework Practice Online Transparency 28 Global Skill Builder CD-ROM	**REV** Section 3 Review, p. 311 **A** Daily Quiz 13.3
One-Stop Planner: Lesson 13.4 Holt Researcher Online Homework Practice Online Global Skill Builder CD-ROM E Challenge and Enrichment: Activity 13 F Simulations and Strategies for Teaching American Government: Activity 13 CNN Presents American Government	**REV** Section 4 Review, p. 314 **A** Daily Quiz 13.4

Chapter Review and Assessment

SM Global Skill Builder CD-ROM
HRW Go site
REV Chapter 13 Tutorial for Students, Parents, and Peers
REV Chapter 13 Review, pp. 316–317
Chapter 13 Test Generator (on the One-Stop Planner)
A Chapter 13 Test Alternative Assessment Handbook

One-Stop Planner CD-ROM

It's easy to plan lessons, select resources, and print out materials for your students when you use the *One-Stop Planner CD-ROM with Test Generator.*

internet connect

HRW ONLINE RESOURCES
Go To: go.hrw.com
Then type in a keyword.

TEACHER HOME PAGE
KEYWORD: SV3 Teacher

CHAPTER INTERNET ACTIVITIES
KEYWORD: SV3 GV13
Choose an activity on fundamental freedoms to:
▶ understand the importance of the First Amendment.
▶ write a letter to Congress regarding school prayer.
▶ create a political cartoon on symbolic speech

CHAPTER ENRICHMENT LINKS
KEYWORD: SV3 CH13

HOLT RESEARCHER ONLINE
KEYWORD: Holt Researcher

ONLINE ASSESSMENT
Homework Practice
KEYWORD: SV3 HP13
Standardized Test Prep
KEYWORD: SV3 STP13
Rubrics
KEYWORD: SS Rubrics

ONLINE MAPS, CHARTS, AND GRAPHS
KEYWORD: SV3 MCG
▶ Some Forms of Protected Symbolic Speech

CONTENT UPDATES
KEYWORD: SS Content Updates

HOLT PRESENTATION MAKER
KEYWORD: SV3 PPT13

ONLINE READING SUPPORT
KEYWORD: SS Strategies

CURRENT EVENTS
KEYWORD: S3 Current Events

HOLT PRESENTATION MAKER
Access Illustrated LECTURE NOTES using Microsoft® PowerPoint® on the One-Stop Planner CD-ROM

OBJECTIVES

▶ Describe how the Constitution protects individuals' civil liberties.

▶ Identify whose civil liberties the First Amendment guarantees.

▶ Describe the role of laws and the courts in balancing the civil liberties of individuals with conflicting interests in the community.

MOTIVATE

Ask students to list on a sheet of paper those things that they believe they have the right to do without interference from the government (e.g., choose their religion or whom they associate with). On the chalkboard, write the various items that students have listed. After briefly discussing whether each item is constitutionally protected, explain the basic principle that in the United States civil rights are guaranteed by the Constitution. Tell students that there are other countries that do not protect these civil rights. Ask students to give examples of countries that do not ensure the civil rights that students have listed. Encourage students to discuss civil rights violations in other countries that they have heard about in the news. As a lead-in to the next activity, tell students that they will be learning about how the Constitution protects their rights.

TEACH

Building a Vocabulary

In spiral notebooks, have students create a Political Dictionary to be used throughout the course. The dictionary may be used as an activity at the start of each new section; it may also be used as a modification device for Sheltered English Students or students having difficulty during tests and homework assignments. List words that students will be expected to know for this section on the board. Have students list, define, and give an example of each of the terms, using information provided in the text or on the *Researcher CD-ROM.*

Demonstrating Understanding/Debating Ideas

Have students read the First Amendment of the U.S. Constitution. Tell them that people in a democracy must be free to question the government, express themselves, and exchange information without fear of harm or arrest for what they say about the government. Organize students into groups of three or four and have each group list on sheets of paper reasons why citizens must have such freedoms. Return to the full class and have students hang their lists on one of the walls. Ask each group to explain its list. Tell students that although the Constitution protects the right to freedom of speech, some limits apply and that in the next activity they will learn about some of these limits.

Mastering Concepts

Write the word *fire* on the chalkboard and ask students to describe what would happen if someone screamed that word in a small room with only two or three people. Then ask students what would happen if someone screamed that word in a crowded theater. List on the chalkboard other words that the students think could cause panic or public harm if they were shouted simply for the thrill of it. Explain to students that freedom of speech needs to have some limits to ensure the public's safety. Explain to students that the time and situation involved may influence a person's freedom of speech. Refer students to the Supreme Court Docket section on the *Holt Researcher Online* to examine the decision of *Schenck* v. *United States,* in which the Supreme Court established the principle of "clear and present danger." Have students write a short essay explaining whether they agree with the decision. Have students offer examples of situations in which this principle could be applied. Tell the class that in the next activity they will learn about other challenges to free speech.

Identifying Cause and Effect/ Evaluating Information

Organize students into groups of four. Have each group read about the freedom of speech case *Hazelwood School District* v. *Kuhlmeier,* which is located in the Supreme Court Docket section on the *Holt Researcher Online.* Two students in each group should then answer the question "What arguments were used or could be used to support the case's argument for free expression?" Have the other two students in each group answer the question "What arguments were used or could be used to oppose the idea of free expression?" Then have students as a class make a chart for each viewpoint. Ask students to offer their opinions on the Supreme Court's decision. Finally, explain to students that the decision served to balance the rights of individuals with the interests of the community.

CLOSE

Have students use individual sheets of paper to list in one column as many freedoms as they can that they personally enjoy. In a second column have them list as many freedoms as they can that adults enjoy. In a third column ask students to identify those that both groups enjoy. Discuss with the class how the freedoms studied in this section apply to everyone and yet may have some limitations because of age or circumstances. Also discuss which items have been limited by court decisions, and have students offer reasons for this.

OPTIONS

Gifted Learners

 Using the *Holt Researcher Online,* students should summarize and compare the cases of *Hazelwood School District* v. *Kuhlmeier* and *Schenck* v. *United States.* Have students consider the special circumstances that affected the Court's decision in both cases. Then ask students to write a brief evaluation of how each of these cases impacted the concept of freedom of speech. Have students include any other relevant Supreme Court decisions affecting free speech.

Musical-Rhythmic Learners

 Have students create a song entitled "The Free Speech Blues." Students should include examples of times in U.S. history when the right to free speech has been limited and give the reasons for that restriction. Students may wish to include comedic examples of what could happen if limitations on free speech were carried to extremes. Encourage students to work with other students who have a musical skill and then present their song to the class.

Intrapersonal Learners

 Have students use the Internet and other resources to see if U.S. citizens are entitled to the same civil liberties when they are traveling in foreign countries that they enjoy when they are in the United States. Teachers may wish to give students copies of articles that discuss instances of U.S. citizens being tried in foreign lands. Once students have completed their research, have them write a descriptive essay expressing their feelings about civil liberties.

Visual-Spatial Learners

 Organize the class into three or four small groups. Have each group examine the contributions of at least one famous civil-rights lawyer. Students should create a flow chart that depicts the issues involved in the major cases defended by the lawyer, the strategy the lawyer used to win the case, and how the case upheld individuals' civil liberties.

REVIEW

Have students complete the Section 1 Review on page 299. Use the answers in the Annotated Teacher's Edition to assess student mastery of this section.

ASSESS

To assess student mastery of this section, have students complete Daily Quiz 13.1 in *Daily Quizzes with Answer Key.* For additional assessment options, see *Alternative Assessment Handbook* on the *One-Stop Planner CD-ROM.*

ADDITIONAL RESOURCES

The Civil Rights Movement. Opposing Viewpoints Series. 1996. Greenhaven Press.
Civil Rights: The Long Struggle. Issues in Focus Series. 1996. Enslow.
Eyes on the Prize. 1990. Public Broadcasting System. (video)

OBJECTIVES

▶ Discuss how the Supreme Court has interpreted the Establishment Clause to define the relationship between religion and public schools.

▶ Describe how the Supreme Court decides if government aid to religious groups is constitutional.

▶ List why the Supreme Court has allowed tax exemptions for religious groups.

▶ Describe how the Free Exercise Clause has been interpreted.

MOTIVATE

Ask students to name religious groups in their community, and list them on the chalkboard. Pick any one of those listed and tell students that henceforth that religion will be the official class religion and that everyone must practice it. Allow students to make arguments against adopting this religion as an official class religion; then discuss with the class why not everyone will want to give up his or her chosen religion and follow an official national religion. Explain to students that in this section they will study how the Constitution protects their right to choose what religion, if any, they practice.

TEACH

Building a Vocabulary

In their spiral notebooks, have students continue working on their Political Dictionary. List words the students will be expected to know for this section on the board. Have students list, define, and give an example of each of the terms, using information provided in the text or on the *Researcher CD-ROM*.

Identifying the Main Idea/Practicing Skills: Writing

Ask students to read the Court's decision in *Engel* v. *Vitale*, located in the Supreme Court Docket section on the *Holt Researcher Online*. Then have students write an essay that is either in support of or in opposition to the ruling. Students must use the

main ideas of the Court's decision to support their own contention. As a class, discuss the decision and list students' arguments for and against the ruling on the chalkboard. Tell students that in the next activity they will learn about the constitutionality of government aid to religious groups.

Analyzing Information/Applying Ideas/Judging Information

Organize students into groups of three. Have each group read the Court's decision *Lemon* v. *Kurtzman,* located in the Supreme Court Docket section on the *Holt Researcher Online,* which discusses aid to parochial schools. On the chalkboard, make a list of items that might be provided to schools. Students must decide if providing these items violates the *Lemon* test as outlined in the ruling. Discuss each item and why it is or is not in violation of the test. Some items to list for consideration might be buses, support for learning-disabled students, textbooks for use in religion class, textbooks for use in biology, funds to pay for heating and cooling the entire complex—church and school included—money for a new roof for the school, money to fill in potholes in the parking lot that the school and church share, and funds to assist in paying for school uniforms. Explain to students that they will soon be learning more about the separation of church and state.

Debating Ideas/Hypothesizing

Have the entire class read the court decision in *Walz* v. *Tax Commission,* located in the Supreme Court Docket section on the *Holt Researcher Online,* which deals with tax exemptions for religious groups. Divide the class in half, with one side supporting the decision and one side opposing it. Have students create a list of arguments that support their positions. Lead a class debate between the two groups regarding the validity of the decision. Draw the conclusion that the Court must walk a fine line—trying to balance the need to prevent discrimination while at the same time protecting religious freedom. Tell students that in the next activity they will learn about the Free Exercise Clause.

Recognizing Point of View/Taking a Stand

 Have students read the Religion and Saluting the Flag case study, which deals with the cases of *West Virginia State Board of Education* v. *Barnette* and *Minersville School District* v. *Gobitis.* On a sheet of paper have students make a chart with the headings *For* and *Against,* and for each case list the opposing and supporting ideas for the ruling. Ask students to write a five-paragraph essay in which they support or oppose the decisions. In addition to basing their decision on their own ideas, students should incorporate arguments from the court cases found in the Supreme Court Docket section on the *Holt Researcher Online.*

CLOSE

Ask students to think about the present society compared to that of their grandparents as well as that of the early American colonies. Discuss whether they believe there is a difference in how religion is viewed today compared to how people viewed it 50 or 250 years ago, and what these differences are and why. Explain to students that the time in which a case is considered often makes a difference in its outcome. Have students offer examples from this section that show changing policies dealing with the separation of church and state, and encourage students to explain how these decisions reflect the view of religion from that time period.

OPTIONS

Students Having Difficulty/ Sheltered English Students

 Ask students to make a time line of all of the court cases discussed in this section. For each case, students should write brief descriptions of what issue the case involved and what the Supreme Court decided. Students should also be encouraged to share their opinion about each case. Display the time lines throughout the room.

Gifted/Intrapersonal Learners

 Have each student interview three or more adults concerning their opinion of government support for private education. Students should ask what specific items or programs the interviewees think should or should not be funded. Students should then write a summary of their findings. For each opinion, students should decide—based on the cases studied in this section—if the items discussed with the interviewees are acceptable or unacceptable for funding and cite the case to which they think it applies.

Intrapersonal Learners

 Discuss with students the Supreme Court rulings from this section that deal with customs and religion. Have students write a descriptive essay addressing the Court's decisions regarding the use of "In God We Trust" on money and allowing religious displays on public property during specific holidays. Students should state whether they agree or disagree with these decisions. Encourage students to share their ideas with the rest of the class.

REVIEW

Have students complete the Section 2 Review on page 303. Use the answers in the Annotated Teacher's Edition to assess student mastery of this section.

ASSESS

To assess student mastery of this section, have students complete Daily Quiz 13.2 in *Daily Quizzes with Answer Key.* For additional assessment options, see *Alternative Assessment Handbook* on the *One-Stop Planner CD-ROM.*

ADDITIONAL RESOURCES

Gay, Kathlyn. *Church and State: Government and Religion in the United States.* 1992. Milbrook Publishers.

Haynes, Charles C., ed. *Finding Common Ground: A First Amendment Guide to Religion and Public Education.* 1995. Freedom Forum First Amendment Center at Vanderbilt University.

OBJECTIVES

▶ Describe the challenges that exist in balancing individuals' freedom of speech with the need to protect national security.

▶ Identify boundaries that exist regarding the media's freedom of expression.

▶ Evaluate how the First Amendment affects symbolic speech and hate speech.

MOTIVATE

Write the words *stupid* and *crook* on the chalkboard. Then ask the class if there would be a problem if a newspaper reporter used either of these words in a story about a local official. Explain that while we have freedom of speech, there are limitations, based on the capacity of words to harm. The word *stupid,* for example, is an opinion. The word *crook,* however, holds legal ramifications that should be backed up by facts. Tell students that in this section they will study what rights and limitations there are on various forms of speech.

TEACH

Building a Vocabulary

In their spiral notebooks, have students continue working on their Political Dictionary. List words the students will be expected to know for this section on the board. Have students list, define, and give an example of each of the terms, using information provided in the text or on the *Researcher CD-ROM.*

Organizing Ideas/Evaluating Ideas

After reading *Schenck* v. *United States* and *Brandenburg* v. *Ohio,* located in the Supreme Court Docket section on the *Holt Researcher Online,* students should write a definition of *treason* and *sedition* at the top of their paper. They should then write the ideas from each of these rulings that they think apply to each definition. Finally, students should decide if they think the defendant in either case

presented a "clear and present danger" to the United States and should give their reasons for their opinions. Discuss students' ideas with the class. Be sure to point out the significant impact that these cases had on regulating freedom of speech. Explain that not only can individuals' freedom of speech be limited, but the media can also have certain limits on their freedom of expression. Tell students that in the next activity they will learn about limits placed on the media.

Acquiring Information/Demonstrating Understanding/Drawing Conclusions

Prior to class, the teacher should obtain as many different tabloid newspapers as possible. Students should read the material on libel found in this section and the discussion of the court case *New York Times* v. *Sullivan,* located in the Supreme Court Docket section on the *Holt Researcher Online.* Organize students into groups of three and give several different tabloid newspapers to each group. For each paper, have students list those stories that they think could be potentially libelous and offer support for their reasoning. Each group should choose several examples from their tabloid newspapers and explain to the class their reasons for considering the article to be potentially libelous. Discuss whether the articles discussed actually are potentially libelous. Tell students that there are limits placed not only on written speech and spoken words, but also on symbolic speech. Tell students that in the next activity they will learn about some of the limits on symbolic speech.

Judging Information/Recognizing Point of View

After reading the discussion of symbolic speech in this section and the court cases *United States* v. *O'Brien* and *Tinker* v. *Des Moines School District,* located in the Supreme Court Docket section on the *Holt Researcher Online,* ask students to brainstorm as many examples as they can that might be considered symbolic speech. List students' ideas on the chalkboard and discuss each regarding whether it is considered symbolic and whether it would be allowed under the court cases studied. Encourage students to think of examples of symbolic speech that are restricted in school.

Most students have heard ethnic or racial slurs. Ask students if those epithets are protected by freedom of speech. Have students write a short paper defending their position on the issue. Students can refer to the court cases in this section and to other material discussed in class to support their answers. Have students consider the topics of libel, slander, and obscenity when writing their papers. Encourage students to discuss their papers. Finally, remind students of your school's policies concerning the use of such language.

OPTIONS

Gifted Learners

 Ask students to research freedom of speech in newspapers and magazines. Then have students report on several examples of how the issue has been covered in the media. Reports should summarize the arguments made in the articles concerning any tests to the issue of free speech and commenting on the outcome of the test as reported in the media. Encourage students to share their findings with the rest of the class. Be sure to allow time for the class to discuss their opinions on these issues.

Students Having Difficulty/ Sheltered English Students

 Ask students to pair with classmates that have worked on the Gifted activity above. Have students read the gifted learners' summaries of the articles they researched during the activity. Students should then discuss the summary with the student who wrote it to prepare for writing their own summary of the same article or of a related issue. If students choose to summarize the same article that their partner used, remind them to write it in their own words. Encourage students to consider the possible ramifications of each free speech issue being discussed.

Gifted Learners

 Explain to students the purpose of the Federal Communications Commission (FCC) and have them read the material discussing it in this section. Have students write a short paper discussing the role of the FCC in upholding standards regulating obscenity in public broadcasts. Encourage students to use the Executive Departments section on the *Holt Researcher Online* and other resources to find information about the FCC.

Intrapersonal Learners

 Discuss with students the concept of false advertising. Ask students to identify reasons why the government would want to regulate false or misleading advertising. Tell students that in 1942 the Supreme Court ruled that protections under the right to free expression did not apply to business advertising. Discuss examples of businesses that are not permitted to advertise on public television. Have students write a descriptive essay stating whether they agree with these limitations. Students should support their arguments, using material from this section, and by discussing their own beliefs about what contributes to the public good. Encourage students to share their ideas with the entire class.

REVIEW

Have students complete the Section 3 Review on page 311. Use the answers in the Annotated Teacher's Edition to assess student mastery of this section.

ASSESS

To assess student mastery of this section, have students complete Daily Quiz 13.3 in *Daily Quizzes with Answer Key*. For additional assessment options, see *Alternative Assessment Handbook* on the *One-Stop Planner CD-ROM*.

ADDITIONAL RESOURCES

Leahy, James E. *The First Amendment, 1791–1991: Two Hundred Years of Freedom*. 1991. McFarland and Co.

Marcus, Laurence. *Fighting Words: The Politics of Hateful Speech*. 1996. Praeger.

Wagman, Robert. *The First Amendment Book*. 1991. World Almanac.

FREEDOM OF ASSEMBLY AND PETITION

TEXTBOOK PAGES 312–314

HOLT PRESENTATION MAKER
Access Illustrated LECTURE NOTES using Microsoft® PowerPoint® on the One-Stop Planner CD-ROM

OBJECTIVES

▶ Describe how the First Amendment protects the rights of assembly and petition on public property.

▶ Discuss how the freedom to demonstrate is restricted on private property.

▶ Describe how freedom of assembly supports freedom of association.

MOTIVATE

Ask students to give examples of people they have seen demonstrating or handing out flyers in their community. Have students identify what types of issues these individuals were promoting. Discuss what these individuals were hoping to accomplish and if they were successful. Share with students examples of actual protests and describe factors that may have contributed to their success or failure. Encourage students to watch for protests that are covered on the news so that they can discuss them later in class. Explain to students that in this section they will learn how the Constitution protects our right to peaceful assembly and petition.

TEACH

Building a Vocabulary

In their spiral notebooks, have students continue working on their Political Dictionary. List words the students will be expected to know for this section on the board. Have students list, define, and give an example of each of the terms, using information provided in the text or on the *Researcher CD-ROM*.

Developing Life Skills/Solving Problems

Organize students into groups of four and ask them to discuss issues that are of importance to them or to the community but are not currently being addressed to their satisfaction. Each group should pick one issue and discuss its importance with the rest of

the class. The class as a whole should discuss reasons for and against holding a demonstration or circulating a petition to bring about a solution to the issues. If students feel that a particular issue is significant enough that they would like to act on it, encourage them to discuss which type of protest would best suit their goals. Assist students in reaching a decision on the issue. Tell students that they will learn about the differences in the right to assemble on public property as compared to private property in the following activity.

Acquiring Information/Draw Conclusions

Have students read about the Supreme Court's decision in *Lloyd Corporation* v. *Tanner,* located in the Supreme Court Docket section on the *Holt Researcher Online.* Discuss with students the differences between the constitutional protections given to demonstrators on public property as compared to demonstrators on private property. Have students research the issue, using the library and the Internet, and then write several paragraphs describing the differences in the constitutional protections provided for assembly on both public and private property. Have students describe any stipulations that must be met to ensure freedom of assembly. Discuss with students that the government has at times tried to limit freedom of association. Tell students that in the next activity they will learn about constitutional guarantees for freedom of association.

Demonstrating Understanding/Drawing Conclusions

Throughout the 1960s organizations such as the NAACP held marches, passed out literature, and picketed various locations in order to advance the cause of minority rights. Discuss the circumstances surrounding the case *National Association for the Advancement of Colored People* v. *Alabama.* Then have students read about the case, which is located in the Supreme Court Docket section on the *Holt Researcher Online.* Have students discuss the value of such groups in changing policies, and ask the class to discuss why the court reached the decision it did. Ask students if such activities are legal under the First Amendment. Ask students if they can name other such groups and actions, and discuss their answers in class.

CLOSE

Provide students with examples of groups, actions, and locations for protests (e.g., individuals handing out anti-pornography flyers at the local grocery store, union workers blocking the entrance to a factory, political groups marching in support of a political candidate, members of a women's group going door-to-door to get signatures on a petition). Discuss whether these actions are protected under the First Amendment. Have students base their reasoning on what they have learned in this section. For actions that are not protected by the First Amendment, have students suggest ways that these groups could alter their protests so that they would be protected.

OPTIONS

Gifted Learners

Have students research major protest movements that occurred in the United States during the twentieth century. They should make a time line indicating when and where the protests occurred and what they involved. For each of the items on their time line, students should summarize the outcome of the protest (i.e., did it accomplish its goal, and if so how?). Allow students to compare their time lines and have the class create a time line that includes all the significant events from the individual time lines. Display the class's time line for other classes to see.

Intrapersonal Learners

Discuss with students the Supreme Court's decision to require officials in Skokie, Illinois, to allow a neo-Nazi party to march through their community even though the population contained many Jewish citizens. Ask students to write a descriptive essay that considers why the Supreme Court has allowed controversial groups to assemble as long as they follow time, place, and manner regulations. Encourage students to support their reasoning with material discussed in this section and throughout the chapter.

Musical-Rhythmic Learners/ Students Having Difficulty

 Discuss with students the use of music as a form of political protest. Play samples of songs for students that protest against actions of the government. Have students write an explanation of what they think each song is protesting and what time period they believe the song is from. Encourage students to bring in other examples of appropriate songs that are based on political protest. Play these songs and discuss the similarities and differences between the songs the teacher brought in and the students' songs. Are there any significant changes in meaning? Are there any significant changes in tone? Ask students to hypothesize why each generation has its own versions of protest songs.

REVIEW

Have students complete the Section 4 Review on page 314. Use the answers in the Teacher's Edition to assess student mastery of this section.

ASSESS

To assess student mastery of this section, have students complete Daily Quiz 13.4 in *Daily Quizzes with Answer Key.* For additional assessment options, see *Alternative Assessment Handbook* on the *One-Stop Planner CD-ROM.*

RETEACH

For students having difficulty with the lessons, have them complete Reteaching Activity 13. This activity is located in *Reteaching Activities with Answer Key.*

ADDITIONAL RESOURCES

Schulke, Flip. *He Had a Dream: Martin Luther King, Jr., and the Civil Rights Movement.* 1995. W. W. Norton.

Cleary, Edward. *Beyond the Burning Cross: The First Amendment and the Landmark* R.A.V. *Case.* 1994. Random House.

Lomasky, Loren. *Persons, Rights, and the Moral Community.* 1987. Oxford University Press.

GOVERNMENT NOTEBOOK

The Government Notebook is a journal activity that encourages students to consider basic concepts of government that relate to their lives. A follow-up notebook activity appears on page 316.

WHY IT MATTERS TODAY

To find additional lesson plans dealing with our fundamental freedoms, visit CNNfyi.com or have students complete the GOVERNMENT IN THE NEWS activity on page 315.

CNNfyi.com

The Granger Collection, New York.

FUNDAMENTAL FREEDOMS

Do you read a newspaper or a magazine in your free time? Did you watch your favorite television show last night? Do you attend a place of worship? Have you ever written a letter to the editor of the local newspaper or to a government official about an issue?

What do all of these activities have in common? Each involves freedoms that are protected by the First Amendment. These and other protections found in the Bill of Rights guarantee fundamental freedoms to you and other residents of the United States.

GOVERNMENT NOTEBOOK

The First Amendment protects the freedoms of religion, speech, the press, assembly, and petition. Are these rights without limit? What restrictions do you think the government may place on these rights? Write your answer in your Government Notebook.

WHY IT MATTERS TODAY

Changing events require us to continually reexamine and redefine our rights and freedoms. At the end of this chapter visit CNNfyi.com to learn more about the fundamental freedoms all Americans enjoy.

CNNfyi.com

SECTION 1

FREEDOM AND THE BILL OF RIGHTS

READ TO DISCOVER

1. How does the Constitution protect civil liberties?
2. Whose civil liberties does the First Amendment guarantee?
3. What is the role of laws and the courts in balancing individuals' civil liberties with the interests of the community?

POLITICAL DICTIONARY

civil liberty
alien

As noted in Chapter 2, several states made strong recommendations that a bill of rights be added to the Constitution upon its ratification. President George Washington also supported adding a bill of rights to the Constitution. James Madison, although he had originally thought a bill of rights unnecessary, took the lead in the first session of the initial Congress in developing the amendments. Twelve amendments were originally proposed for ratification by the states. The two amendments that were not ratified at the time dealt with how members of the House of Representatives would be apportioned among the states and how congressmembers would be compensated for their service.

About 18 months passed before the necessary three quarters of the states agreed to ratify the Bill of Rights. Massachusetts, one of the states that originally had called for a bill of rights as a condition for ratifying the Constitution, was one of three states that did not ratify the Bill of Rights when it was proposed in Congress. Connecticut ratified it only in 1932, Georgia and Massachusetts in 1939. (Of course, because three quarters of the states had ratified the Bill of Rights, it applied to all states in the Union, even though it had not yet been ratified by all.)

Curiously, the adoption of the Bill of Rights was not seen as an earthshaking event at the time, as is indicated by the text of a letter Thomas Jefferson sent to the states on March 1, 1792, in his official capacity as secretary of state. The letter listed the adoption of the Bill of Rights after a law Congress had passed regulating fishing! Today, however, most people in the United States understand the profound impact the Bill of Rights has had on the rules of the U.S. political system and the content of U.S. public policies.

Civil Liberties

The Bill of Rights is designed to protect people's civil liberties. **Civil liberties** are basic individual rights and freedoms that are protected from government violation. When drawing up the Bill of Rights, members of the initial Congress specifically wanted to guarantee freedom of speech, assembly, and religion in order to protect individual rights and prevent a tyranny of the majority. These freedoms are considered to be among the most fundamental civil liberties. In listing these rights in the First Amendment, the framers conferred upon them a special place in the American consciousness. They believed that respecting these freedoms was among the most important duties of government and society.

POLITICAL FOUNDATIONS *President George Washington, shown here arriving for his second inauguration in 1793. It was during Washington's presidency that the first 10 amendments were added to the Constitution.* **Which civil liberties did the drafters of the Bill of Rights particularly wish to guarantee?**

SECTION 1

FREEDOM AND THE BILL OF RIGHTS

Lesson Plans

For teaching strategies, see Lesson 13.1 located at the beginning of this chapter or the One-Stop Lesson Planner Strategy 13.1.

Political Dictionary

To reinforce the section's vocabulary terms, refer students to the Electronic Glossary on the *Researcher CD-ROM.*

Section Assessment

To assess students' mastery of this section, have them complete Daily Quiz 13.1 in *Daily Quizzes with Answer Key.*

Caption Answer

freedom of speech, assembly, and religion

Careers in Government

Civil Rights Lawyer

In 1971, civil rights attorneys Morris Dees and Joseph Levin joined civil rights activist Julian Bond to found the Southern Poverty Law Center. The center is a nonprofit organization staffed by lawyers who provide legal assistance to vitims of civil rights violations and racially motivated crimes.

As well-known defenders of the civil rights of poor citizens, the center's lawyers battle to fulfill the promise of the Civil Rights Act of 1964. Their caseload involves everything from challenging segregation in recreational facilities to acquiring better medical care and social services for the poor. In one case, civil rights lawyers at the center helped gain financial compensation for a cotton mill worker who had contracted a lung disease as a result of an unsafe job environment. This case led to the passage of federal laws regulating working conditions in cotton mills.

Morris Dees, cofounder of the Southern Poverty Law Center, works to provide legal assistance to victims of civil rights violations.

Civil rights lawyers such as those employed by the Southern Poverty Law Center spend years studying and preparing for a career in law. Lawyers must earn a college degree and graduate from a law school approved by the American Bar Association. In addition, potential lawyers must pass the bar exam of the state in which they plan to practice law. Passing the bar exam generally requires months of preparation. After completing the necessary education and certification, some new lawyers work with well-established lawyers or law firms to gain experience.

Many people interested in a career in law turn to the federal government. Its departments and agencies employ attorneys who work in many fields of law, including civil rights. For example, the Equal Employment Opportunity Commission (EEOC), created by the 1964 Civil Rights Act, hires lawyers to defend people fighting discrimination in the workplace.

To whom do First Amendment freedoms and other constitutional protections belong? In several places, the Bill of Rights refers to "person" and to "the people," but nowhere does it define who the people are. In addressing this issue the Supreme Court has ruled that the protections of civil liberties granted by the Constitution are not limited to U.S. citizens. For the most part, these constitutional protections also guarantee the civil liberties of **aliens**, or resident noncitizens. The government may, however, limit some civil liberties of aliens who reside in the United States.

Balancing Rights and Interests to Promote the Public Good

Although the Constitution guarantees civil liberties, it does not guarantee absolute freedom to do as one wishes. The freedom to assemble with others in pursuit of a goal, for example, does not give people the freedom to riot, which would violate other people's right to safety. Recognizing the responsibilities that come with freedom is part of being a good citizen.

How are one person's civil liberties balanced with the rights of others and the interests of the majority? What happens, for example, when a person's religious beliefs necessitate behavior that is illegal? Who decides if the freedom of the press to report on a criminal investigation threatens the accused's right to a fair trial?

The government tries to answer questions such as these by passing laws that balance individual liberties with the rights and interests of society. The courts then use the power of judicial review to determine whether government actions and laws violate constitutional protections.

The Supreme Court's approach to cases involving civil liberties has been influenced by two views. One view holds that the liberties protected by the Bill of Rights, particularly those of the First Amendment, are absolute, or without limit. Those who subscribe to this point of view argue that the First Amendment's statement that "Congress shall make no law" restricting free speech means that *all* federal laws that restrict free speech in any way are unconstitutional.

However, the government often passes laws that set boundaries on an individual's rights so others' rights or interests are not threatened. This reflects a second view—that the Supreme Court's role is to decide whether the government has promoted the public good by properly restricting a civil liberty to protect others' rights, or majority interests.

The Supreme Court has often chosen this latter approach. Throughout this and the next two chapters, you will see how the Court and the rest of the federal government have tried to ensure a proper balance of liberties.

LIBERTY'S CROWN

Courtesy of Karl Hubenthal, Los Angeles Herald-Examiner.

CONSTITUTIONAL GOVERNMENT *This political cartoon illustrates the liberties protected by the Bill of Rights. Many of these rights are found in the First Amendment.* **Why do you think that the cartoonist placed these rights on the spikes of the Statue of Liberty's crown?**

Transparency
An overhead transparency of the cartoon on this page is available in *Transparency Resources.* See Cartoon Transparency 12: Liberty's Crown.

Caption Answer
Answers will vary but students should offer a logical explanation of why these rights make up Liberty's crown.

SECTION 1 REVIEW ANSWERS

1. Refer to the following pages: civil liberty (297), alien (298).

2. Lists should include freedom of religion, speech, the press, and assembly.

3a. Answers will vary, but students may suggest that this balance is necessary to promote the public good.

3b. The Bill of Rights

4. Answers will vary, but students should express their opinion and provide examples to support it.

SECTION 1 REVIEW

1. Identify and Explain:
- civil liberty
- alien

2. Identifying Concepts: Copy the chart below. Use it to list the freedoms found in the First Amendment.

First Amendment Freedoms

Homework Practice Online
keyword: SV3 HP13

3. **Finding the Main Idea**

a. Why is it important to balance individual liberties and majority interests?

b. What part of the Constitution protects the civil liberties of people in the United States?

4. **Writing and Critical Thinking**

Evaluating: Should the government have the power to limit individual rights to promote the public good? Give examples to support your opinion.

Consider the following:
- the freedoms guarenteed by the Bill of Rights
- the importance of promoting the public good
- the danger of limiting people's freedom

SECTION 2
FREEDOM OF RELIGION

READ TO DISCOVER

1. How has the Supreme Court interpreted the Establishment Clause to define the relationship between religion and public schools?
2. How does the Supreme Court decide if government aid to religious groups is constitutional?
3. Why has the Supreme Court allowed tax exemptions for religious groups?
4. How has the Free Exercise Clause been interpreted?

POLITICAL DICTIONARY

Establishment Clause
Engel v. *Vitale*
Free Exercise Clause

Religion is a part of many people's lives in the United States. For example, surveys conducted in 2000 showed that over 90 percent of people in this country were members of a church, synagogue, mosque, temples of various faiths, or other place of worship. The freedom to choose your religious beliefs, or to hold no religious belief, is a basic civil liberty guaranteed by the First Amendment.

The Establishment Clause

One way the Constitution protects the freedom of religion is through the First Amendment's **Establishment Clause**. This clause states that "Congress shall make no law respecting an establishment of religion." Under the Establishment Clause the government may not act in ways that establish an official religion, that favor one religion over another, or that favor religion generally.

At the time the Bill of Rights was written, most countries supported an official religion. Even many of the American states had official religions. After U.S. independence, support grew in the states to put an end to official religions. Many U.S. citizens thought that their young country was too diverse to allow religious beliefs to be imposed on people. As a result, religious freedom was included in the First Amendment. Later, Thomas Jefferson wrote in a personal letter that the First Amendment established "a wall of separation between church and State."

Whether the Establishment Clause does indeed build such a wall has been controversial. As cases about this subject have arisen, the Supreme Court has defined the relationship between government and religion. Many such establishment cases have involved prayer in public schools, government aid for religious organizations, and tax policies toward religious bodies.

Religion in Public Schools Religion in public schools has been a source of heated debate, and the Supreme Court's rulings have varied according to the case and the time period in which it was heard. Some states, for example, once allowed programs in which students could attend voluntary religion classes during school hours. However, in 1948 in *McCollum* v. *Board of Education,* the Court ruled

CONSTITUTIONAL GOVERNMENT *All citizens of the United States have the freedom to worship as they choose.* **Why is the U.S. government prohibited from establishing an official religion?**

that an Illinois religious-instruction program unconstitutionally established religion because it received official support. In a later case, the Court ruled in favor of a school that permitted students to leave campus to receive religious instruction outside the school grounds.

Some of the most controversial decisions about the Establishment Clause involve prayer in schools. Officially sponsored prayers once were common in U.S. public schools. In the 1962 case **Engel v. Vitale,** however, the Supreme Court ruled that this practice violated the Establishment Clause. The Court said that all officially sponsored prayer in public schools, even when participation was voluntary, represented unconstitutional official support for religion. Other Court decisions since 1962 have kept public schools from sponsoring religious activities, such as Bible readings and moments of silence for meditation or prayer.

The Court has not ruled, however, against students praying on their own in school. In fact, students are free to pray on their own at any time and in any place—in or out of school. Religious works also may be used in public schools as part of literature courses and other nonreligious studies.

Nevertheless, criticism of the Supreme Court's decisions on school prayer has been strong. Critics have argued that prayer and religious study are vital to teaching morals and values. Some have tried to pass constitutional amendments that would allow public schools to set aside time for voluntary prayer. In addition, Congress acted in 1984 to allow student religious groups to meet in public schools. Under the 1984 Equal Access Act, student religious groups have the same right as other student groups to use public school buildings for meetings. The Supreme Court ruled that the Equal Access Act was constitutional as long as the clubs are created and led by students.

Government Aid for Religion The Supreme Court also has heard establishment cases about government aid for religious organizations, such as parochial (puh-ROH-kee-uhl) schools. Parochial schools are elementary and high schools run by churches or other religious groups.

People who believe in giving government aid to parochial schools argue that the families of students in these schools are required to pay taxes to support the public education system and that these taxes should go to the schools that their children attend, parochial or public. By lowering tuition costs, government aid to parochial schools also would make it easier, they argue, for families to exercise their right to choose their children's schools. Currently, government aid does help parochial schools provide some services, such as buses.

Opponents of government aid argue that sending children to parochial schools is a financial burden that families freely choose and should handle on their own. They also argue that government aid would violate the Establishment Clause because it would support religious education.

SHOE

POLITICAL PROCESSES *Although the Constitution protects citizens' right to practice their religion by attending parochial school, the government does not provide financial assistance to families who send their children to private schools. Some people have proposed a school voucher program that would provide a certain amount of government assistance to these families.* ***Would you support legislation establishing this program?***

Drawing upon principles of past rulings, the Supreme Court in 1971 established in *Lemon* v. *Kurtzman* a three-part test for deciding if a government law aiding a religious body violates the Establishment Clause. Under the *Lemon* test a law must

★ have a secular, or nonreligious, purpose;
★ neither advance nor limit religion; and
★ not result in excessive government involvement with religion.

Instances of government aid that have passed the *Lemon* test include providing special education teachers and transportation to and from school. The Supreme Court has ruled that such aid, although perhaps indirectly supporting religion, promotes important nonreligious goals, including securing the welfare and safety of children.

Taxes and Religion The Establishment Clause has also affected the way tax laws are written. Federal, state, and local governments do not tax property owned by churches and other religious organizations if it is used for religious purposes. Supporters of this policy have argued that taxing churches and other religious properties would in effect allow the government to limit the freedom of religion.

Other people have argued, however, that tax exemptions for religious property violate the Establishment Clause. These people believe that tax exemptions provide official support for religion by giving it a privilege not enjoyed by other organizations. Some people also argue that such tax exemptions unfairly increase property tax rates by placing the entire tax burden on the nonexempt.

The Supreme Court consistently has sided with those who support tax exemptions for religious property. In 1970 the Court ruled in *Walz* v. *Tax Commission* that tax exemptions help the government take a neutral approach toward religion, neither supporting it nor restricting it. In other decisions, however, the Court has said that the government may refuse to grant a tax exemption to a religious organization practicing racial discrimination. In such cases the Supreme Court has tried to balance the need to prevent discrimination with the protection of religious freedom.

POLITICAL FOUNDATIONS *Many towns and cities in the United States decorate public buildings with religious and nonreligious displays during holidays.* **What has the Supreme Court said about this practice?**

Custom and Religion In spite of the separation of church and state, many official U.S. symbols and customs involve religion. The money you use, for example, bears the phrase *In God We Trust*. During certain holidays your local government may sponsor a religious display on publicly owned property. How do the courts apply the Establishment Clause to these situations?

The Supreme Court has ruled that these references to God and to religious beliefs do not support religion as much as they recognize many Americans' deeply held beliefs. The Court has used this reasoning to rule, for example, that chaplains may open sessions of Congress and of state legislatures with a prayer. In addition, holiday displays in which nonreligious figures such as Santa Claus share space with religious symbols like Nativity scenes are constitutional. In general, the Court has held that these long-practiced customs do not violate the Establishment Clause.

The Free Exercise Clause

In addition to the Establishment Clause, the First Amendment guarantees freedom of religion through its Free Exercise Clause. The **Free Exercise Clause** states that "Congress shall make no law . . . prohibiting the free exercise" of religion. This clause protects the right of a person to hold any religious beliefs he or she chooses. The right to *believe* as one wishes, however, is not the same as the right to *behave* as one wishes.

The Supreme Court has ruled that religious practices may be restricted if they threaten the health and safety of others or if they violate social standards and constitutional laws. For example, in 1879 the Court ruled in *Reynolds* v. *United States* that Mormons could not engage in bigamy—the act of marrying one person while legally married to another. The Court said that even though bigamy was (at the time) allowed by the Mormon faith, federal law prohibited the practice. The Court also has ruled that state governments may require vaccinations for children whose parents' religious beliefs forbid such medical practices. In this case, the Court valued protecting citizens' health over preserving the absolute free exercise of religion.

The Court has, however, supported some religious practices that violate the law but do not threaten the public interest. In a 1972 case, Wisconsin officials argued that requiring all children to attend school is a vital public interest. Amish families, who reject many modern practices for religious reasons, argued that schooling after the eighth grade threatens their beliefs. The Court, considering that few Amish children lived in the community, ruled that the state's requirement threatened Amish religious freedom more than an exemption for the Amish threatened the state's interest in educating its citizens.

CASE STUDY

Religion and Saluting the Flag

CONSTITUTIONAL GOVERNMENT Another issue concerning free exercise of religion involved pledging allegiance to the U.S. flag. In 1943 the Supreme Court ruled that people could not be forced to salute the flag if doing so would violate their religious beliefs. In *West Virginia State Board of Education* v. *Barnette*, Jehovah's Witnesses objected to their children's saluting the flag. The Witnesses argued that their religion did not allow them to pay homage to the U.S. flag, which they saw as an object of worship.

The Supreme Court had ruled against the Witnesses in a similar case just three years earlier. In *Minersville School District* v. *Gobitis*, the Court ruled that a community's interest in using the flag to encourage patriotism and national unity was more important than a person's religious beliefs.

In 1943, however, the Supreme Court decided that refusing to salute the flag posed no danger to patriotism and public order. What had changed? In part, the Court was reacting to the persecution of Jehovah's Witness children that had occurred as a result of the *Minersville* decision. In addition, forcing people to believe and act according to government rules had become a sensitive issue. At the time, the United States was at war with countries ruled by totalitarian dictatorships that controlled every aspect of their citizens' lives. The Court did not base its decision against forced saluting on the Free Exercise Clause, however. Rather, it determined that requiring people to say the Pledge of Allegiance violated their First Amendment guarantee of free speech.

SECTION 2 REVIEW ANSWERS

1. Refer to the following pages: Establishment Clause (300), *Engel* v. *Vitale* (301), Free Exercise Clause (302).

2. Webs should include: religion in public schools, government aid for religion, taxes and religion, custom and religion.

3a. If the aid passes the criteria established by the *Lemon* test, aid is allowed; otherwise it is not.

3b. no

4. Answers will vary but students should demonstrate an understanding of the issues raised by *Engel* v. *Vitale*.

SECTION 2 REVIEW

1. **Identify and Explain:**
   - Establishment Clause
   - *Engel* v. *Vitale*
   - Free Exercise Clause
2. **Identifying Concepts:** Copy the web to the right. Use it to describe the different types of cases the Supreme Court has heard involving the Establishment Clause.

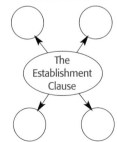

The Establishment Clause

3. **Finding the Main Idea**
   a. Under what circumstance does the Supreme Court allow government aid to religious groups?
   b. Does the Free Exercise Clause allow all religious practices?

4. **Writing and Critical Thinking**

   Decision Making: Do you agree or disagree with the ruling in *Engel* v. *Vitale*? Explain your answer.

   Consider the following:
   - government funding of public schools
   - the meaning of the Free Exercise Clause

go.hrw.com Homework Practice Online
keyword: SV3 HP13

SECTION 3

FREEDOM OF SPEECH AND OF THE PRESS

READ TO DISCOVER

1. What challenges exist in balancing individuals' freedom of speech with the need to protect national security?
2. What boundaries exist on the media's freedom of expression?
3. How does the First Amendment affect symbolic speech and hate speech?

POLITICAL DICTIONARY

treason
sedition
Schenck v. *United States*
prior restraint
shield law
libel
slander
obscenity
Federal Communications Commission
symbolic speech
draft
hate speech

In 1579 John Stubbs published a book in England criticizing a proposed marriage of Queen Elizabeth. Because criticizing the country's leaders was not allowed at the time, the government ordered that Stubbs's right hand be cut off at the wrist so that he could never write again.

Today such a book might be a tame addition to the shelves of your local bookstore. This is because the First Amendment guarantees freedom of speech and freedom of the press in the United States. These freedoms are among the most cherished liberties assured by the Bill of Rights. The freedom to express your opinions, popular or not, in speech or in print, is vital to a democracy.

As with freedom of religion, the Supreme Court has applied the First Amendment guarantees of free speech to government laws and actions. At times the Court has interpreted the First Amendment to strike down *any* laws that limit free expression. At other times the Court has tried to promote the public good by balancing free speech with other liberties. Although finding this balance sometimes has meant setting boundaries on expression, Americans still enjoy great freedom to speak out and express their ideas.

Freedom of Speech and National Security

National security is one area in which the Supreme Court has allowed the government to establish boundaries on free speech. As you know, the Constitution gives the government the authority to protect the nation against foreign powers and domestic threats. It is largely this latter responsibility that has sparked questions about balancing free speech with national security.

Treason and Sedition One form of domestic threat is treason. **Treason** is the act of aiding and comforting an enemy of the United States in a time of war—for example, spying on one's government for a foreign power. Article III, Section 3, of the

CONSTITUTIONAL GOVERNMENT *A group of young people protests the U.S. government's involvement in the Vietnam War.* **In what kinds of cases has the Supreme Court allowed government to limit free speech?**

Constitution gives Congress the authority to punish people found guilty of treason. What about acts committed during peacetime?

The government has answered this question differently over time. For example, Congress has passed laws restricting speech that criticizes government. Many of these laws specifically address **sedition**—the use of language that encourages people to rebel against lawful government. Several people in U.S. history have in fact been accused of endangering the nation's security through seditious language.

Whether a statement is seditious is debatable, of course. Some people might think that a particular criticism of the government encourages others to work against unfair government policies, but others might consider it seditious. In cases of sedition, then, the Supreme Court has had to decide how to balance the security interests of the nation with individuals' right to free speech.

Alien and Sedition Acts The first laws against sedition were passed by Congress in 1798, just seven years after the adoption of the Bill of Rights. Among other things, the Alien and Sedition Acts made it illegal to say anything "false, scandalous [disgraceful] and malicious [spiteful]" against the government or its officials. The acts were aimed at opponents of President John Adams and his Federalist supporters, and in fact, only opponents of the Federalists were ever convicted under the laws. One such opponent, a congressman, was jailed for four months and fined $1,000. Newspaper editors also were jailed or fined for their critical words.

Opposition to the Alien and Sedition Acts was strong from those who believed that the acts violated the First Amendment's freedoms of speech and the press. The Alien and Sedition Acts were never tested in the courts, however, and Congress allowed them to expire in 1801. In that same year President Thomas Jefferson pardoned all those who had been convicted under the acts, and Congress voted to refund the fines that had been paid.

Clear and Present Danger After the assassination of President William McKinley by an anarchist in 1901, public opinion began to favor legislation punishing seditious acts. Then in 1917 and 1918, after the United States had entered World War I, Congress again passed sedition laws forbidding verbal attacks on the government. By the end of World War I, 32 states had laws against

Comparing Governments

Freedom of Speech in Singapore

As you know, the First Amendment of the Constitution guarantees that "Congress shall make no law . . . abridging the freedom of speech, or of the press." Although laws in the United States restrict certain types of speech, people can legally express unfavorable comments about the U.S. government.

Not all nations share this freedom. In Singapore, criticism of the government in the press is forbidden. A federal statute in Singapore protects freedom of speech but restricts people from saying anything that the courts identify as disrespectful of judicial authority, harmful to someone's reputation, or an "incitement to any offense." In 1994, for example, the nation's Supreme Court found the *International Herald Tribune* and its distributors guilty of having criticized three of Singapore's high-ranking government officials in a newspaper article. Although the newspaper published letters of apology for the article, it was fined $678,000 for breaking the law.

sedition-related offenses. More than 1,900 people were prosecuted for such offenses, and more than 100 newspapers and periodicals were censored for publishing items considered seditious. Congress also passed laws against using language that might encourage someone to disobey military orders or to avoid required military service. In 1919 the Supreme Court upheld the conviction of a man who had been prosecuted under these laws. The man had been arrested for handing out documents urging others to avoid required military service. In this case, ***Schenck v. United States,*** the Court established a key rule for drawing the boundaries of constitutional protections for free expression: the clear-and-present-danger test.

Under the Court's clear-and-present-danger test, the First Amendment did not cover expressions that were closely connected to the committing of an illegal action. "The most stringent [strict] protection

Enhancing the Lesson

For more information on *Schenck* v. *United States* and other Supreme Court decisions, see the Supreme Court Docket section on the *Holt Researcher Online.*

CULTURAL PERSPECTIVES

Mohandas Gandhi was sentenced in 1922 to a six-year prison term for sedition. Gandhi led India's struggle for independence from the British Empire.

While supporting nonviolence, Gandhi led a boycott of government services. Furthermore, because India was used as an outlet for British goods, Gandhi led demonstrations in which imported textiles were burned. He opened shops that sold Indian-made fabrics and wore handmade loincloths to support Indian producers, symbolize a simple life, and identify with poor Indians.

In March 1922 Gandhi was found guilty of sedition for urging people to act against the British government. During sentencing the judge praised Gandhi's nonviolence and expressed his hope that events in India would lead to Gandhi's early release. Gandhi served two years of the sentence. ■

of free speech," wrote Justice Oliver Wendell Holmes in the Court's majority opinion, "would not protect a man in falsely shouting fire in a theatre and causing a panic." The danger posed in the *Schenck* case was that encouraging men to disobey orders or to refuse military service might harm the nation's ability to defend itself in war.

In the 1969 case *Brandenburg* v. *Ohio* the Supreme Court made the clear-and-present-danger test less restrictive by ruling that simply expressing a belief that the government should be overthrown or that violence might be necessary to achieve certain goals is protected by the First Amendment. To convict a person of sedition, the government must prove that a person's words are meant to encourage *actively* the violent overthrow of the government or are likely to *succeed* in encouraging others to commit violence.

Freedom of Speech and the Media

The government and the courts also have tried to find a balance between the media's freedom of expression and other rights and interests. Media, as you know, include newspapers, magazines, books, television, radio, motion pictures, and computer networks. How has the media's right to freedom of expression been defined?

Prior Restraint With few exceptions, the First Amendment has been interpreted to forbid the government from using **prior restraint**, or stopping someone from expressing an idea or providing information. The case that established this rule against prior restraint involved a Minnesota law designed to keep newspapers from publishing sensational articles about government corruption. In 1931 the Supreme Court ruled in *Near* v. *Minnesota* that the law was a form of censorship. As such, it violated the

First Amendment's free-press protections, which—according to the Supreme Court—extend to the states through the Fourteenth Amendment's Due Process Clause.

In other prior-restraint cases the courts have allowed the media to publish material that public officials considered secret. In 1971, for example, the Supreme Court ruled that the government could not prevent the *New York Times* and other newspapers from publishing the Pentagon Papers. These classified, top-secret government documents, secretly copied and given to the newspapers, discussed controversial and previously secret accounts of U.S. involvement in the Vietnam War. The Court did not accept the government's argument that publishing the papers would harm national security. In the Pentagon Papers case the justices did, however, state that the government could use prior restraint when it could give compelling reasons for doing so.

CONSTITUTIONAL GOVERNMENT *In 1971 the Supreme Court upheld the* New York Times's *right to publish the Pentagon Papers.* **Under what conditions can the government restrict a newspaper's right to publish top-secret documents?**

Trials There are also some boundaries on the rights of the press during court trials. News reporters often have used the First Amendment guarantee of a free press to avoid giving testimony about the identities of their news sources or about information they have discovered in their work. Reporters fear that sources would be less likely to give information if they might be publicly named in court.

Federal courts, however, have refused to accept the argument that the First Amendment protects reporters from naming their sources. In 1972 the Supreme Court ruled in *Branzburg* v. *Hayes* that the First Amendment did not excuse reporters from the responsibilities that all citizens have to testify about information applicable in a court proceeding.

Some states have passed **shield laws** that allow reporters to protect the identity of their sources from state courts. In addition, many reporters who have been summoned to federal courts or to state courts without shield laws have gone to jail rather than reveal information about their sources.

Libel The Supreme Court also has ruled that abusing the freedom of speech to harm the character and reputation of others unjustly is not protected by the First Amendment. **Libel** is a written statement or visual presentation that is defamatory, or unjustly harms another person's character and reputation. **Slander** is verbal defamation.

Libel cases most often involve the news media. The 1964 Supreme Court case *New York Times* v. *Sullivan* established guidelines for determining when a public figure has been libeled. In that case, the *New York Times* and a group of African American clergymen had published a newspaper advertisement that harshly criticized some Alabama state officials' reactions to protests against racial discrimination. Some of the statements in the advertisement were false, and the state officials sued for libel.

The Supreme Court, however, decided that the officials had not been libeled. In a landmark ruling, the Court established a standard for libel involving public officials. The Court ruled that to be libelous, a false statement about a public official must reflect "actual malice" on the part of the author. That is, such a statement cannot be found libelous unless someone proves that it was made "with knowledge that it was false or with reckless disregard of whether it was false or not." The Court later extended this standard to public figures who are not officials—for example, celebrities.

CONSTITUTIONAL GOVERNMENT *Many states have shield laws that allow reporters to protect the anonymity of their sources.* ***Do reporters have a responsibility to avoid libel?***

The argument for the *Sullivan* standard stems from the view that free expression in the media helps monitor possible government abuses. Making it easy to sue successfully for libel might make the media more hesitant to publish hard-hitting stories involving government officials. Nevertheless, courts have allowed the government to establish some boundaries on free expression through libel laws.

Obscenity The First Amendment does not protect obscenity. In general, an **obscenity** is something sexually indecent and highly offensive. In legal terms, however, defining obscenity is a difficult task for the courts because different people find different things offensive. Nevertheless, in the 1957 case *Roth* v. *United States* the Court ruled that obscenity was something "utterly without redeeming social value." In the 1973 case *Miller* v. *California* the Supreme Court redefined obscenity as material

★ in which the major theme would be judged to appeal to indecent sexual desires by the average person applying "contemporary [current] community standards";
★ that shows in a clearly offensive way sexual behavior not allowed by state laws; and

ACROSS THE CURRICULUM

LITERATURE In 1933 federal district judge John M. Woolsey made a landmark decision regarding obscenity in *United States* v. *One Book Called Ulysses.* The obscenity law was restrictive at the time: works were judged by isolated passages—offensive sections were marked in red, and decisions were based on them.

Woolsey argued that any text must be read in its entirety when obscenity laws are applied. He went on to say that, when applying this approach to James Joyce's *Ulysses,* he did not find it pornographic. Joyce was trying to portray characters' observations and shifting thoughts. This honest effort, noted Woolsey, required passages that some people might object to; however, no one had to read the book. Woolsey's decision was ultimately upheld by the Supreme Court. ■

PSYCHOLOGY During the 1950s subliminal messages inserted into movies telling people to eat or drink a specific product are estimated to have increased snack sales by 60 percent at movie theaters. In the 1970s the FCC outlawed subliminal messages when a television advertisement for a game called Husker Du contained messages telling children that they should buy it.

Now subliminal messages are back, this time on a software program that flashes messages to people as they work on their computers. The new program contains messages on a variety of topics. People with attention deficit disorder, for example, are told that they can sit still and concentrate. Experts say that the messages do not work, yet government agencies, including the National Security Agency, have ordered the software. ■

Transparency

An overhead transparency of the chart on this page is available in *Transparency Resources.* See Transparency 28: Television Ratings System.

Caption Answer

Answers will vary, but students should state their opinion and offer support for it.

★ that is "lacking serious literary, artistic, political, or scientific value."

Even with these factors, determining what is obscene is difficult because personal and community standards vary. In another case that same year the Supreme Court ruled that a Georgia community could not use its local standards to ban the motion picture *Carnal Knowledge*—which starred several well-known and respected actors—for obscenity. The ruling seemed to limit the extent to which a local community's standards could differ from what the Court thought of as "national" standards. In doing so, the ruling further complicated the question of whether something is obscene or protected speech.

The Supreme Court has ruled, however, that sexually explicit material involving children is not protected expression regardless of whether it meets the three-part test for obscenity. Congress and the states have passed laws against such material. In 1996 Congress also passed a law restricting obscenity on the Internet, the first major legislation affecting communication via computers. Critics challenged the law, and the Supreme Court ruled in 1997 that it was unconstitutional.

Licensing Radio and television stations generally have fewer First Amendment protections against government actions than do newspapers, magazines, and other print media. This is true in part because radio and television broadcast over airwaves owned by the public. To operate, radio and television stations must receive a license from the **Federal Communications Commission (FCC).**

In fact, in 1934 the FCC developed a set of rules that radio and television stations must follow in order to receive an FCC license. Even though the FCC could not censor broadcasters or restrict the First Amendment protections of broadcast news reporters, the FCC could subject the renewal of a station's license to the various rules that it or Congress set. For example, stations had to restrict the broadcast of violent or sexually explicit material during certain times of the day, particularly during "family hour," the first hour of prime-time programming. In addition, broadcasters had to operate under what was known as the equal-time doctrine. This policy required that opposing political candidates be given equal time on a station to state their views.

These restrictions were gradually cut back in the 1970s and 1980s, however, partially in response to the development of cable and satellite broadcasting and greater public access to the media. Interestingly, the courts have ruled that cable television stations have broader First Amendment protections than do other broadcasters. This is because cable programming is not broadcast over public airwaves. Many people, including some members of Congress, have petitioned broadcasters to reinstate family hour programming and to return to the original FCC standards.

False Advertising The courts take a more definite stand on limiting freedom of speech when it relates to commercial advertising. In particular, courts have ruled that the government may

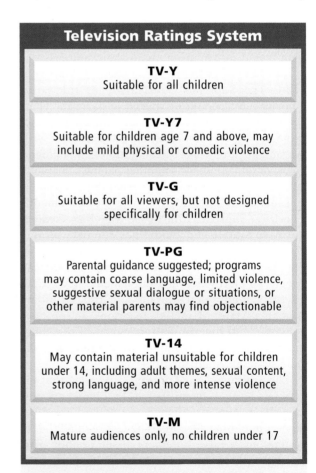

Television Ratings System

TV-Y
Suitable for all children

TV-Y7
Suitable for children age 7 and above, may include mild physical or comedic violence

TV-G
Suitable for all viewers, but not designed specifically for children

TV-PG
Parental guidance suggested; programs may contain coarse language, limited violence, suggestive sexual dialogue or situations, or other material parents may find objectionable

TV-14
May contain material unsuitable for children under 14, including adult themes, sexual content, strong language, and more intense violence

TV-M
Mature audiences only, no children under 17

Television broadcasters agreed to a ratings system that went into effect in 1997. Political officials and consumers pressed for the system as a way to shield children from inappropriate programming. **Why might some people criticize this rating system?**

Citizenship in Action

The Tinker's Silent Protest

In 1965 three students—13-year-old Mary Beth Tinker, 15-year-old John Tinker, and 16-year-old Christopher Eckhardt—made a choice that would bring them to the attention of the Supreme Court. These young people were part of a group that decided to silently protest the U.S. government's involvement in the Vietnam War by wearing black armbands during the holiday season. They took this action to mourn the deaths of soldiers killed in the war.

When Des Moines school district officials learned of the group's plan, they feared that the controversial nature of the protest would cause a disturbance in the schools. The school board adopted a policy banning the wearing of the armbands. Students who arrived at school wearing one of the symbols of protest would be asked to remove it. Any student who refused would be suspended from school until he or she agreed to return to school without the armband.

Mary Beth and John Tinker display the armbands they wore to protest the U.S. government's involvement in the Vietnam War.

In mid-December, Mary Beth, John, and Christopher came to school wearing black armbands. The students were sent home and suspended. They then refused to return to school without the armbands until after New Year's Day, the end of the group's planned period of protest.

Shortly after this incident the students' fathers filed a complaint in district court, asking that the school officials and school board be prohibited from disciplining the students for their actions. The court dismissed the complaint and supported the board's policy on the grounds that it was adopted to prevent disturbances in the classroom. The Tinkers appealed the case, but the court of appeals upheld the district court's ruling.

The Supreme Court agreed to hear the case in 1968. In *Tinker* v. *Des Moines Independent Community School District,* the Court ruled that wearing an armband is symbolic speech and as an expression of opinion is protected by the First Amendment. The Court found no evidence to support the school board's claim that it had acted to prevent disturbance in the schools. The board did not prove that the wearing of the armbands had interfered with school discipline.

Furthermore, the Court ruled that in order for school officials to ban an expression of opinion, they must show evidence that their actions were not based merely on fear of the expression of controversial or unpopular opinions. In the Court's majority opinion, Justice Abe Fortas stated, "Students in school as well as out of school are 'persons' under our Constitution. They are possessed of fundamental rights which the State must respect, just as they themselves must respect their obligations to the State." The Court, however, did not prohibit schools from limiting students' rights to express themselves, but merely required them to provide a constitutionally valid reason for restricting students' speech.

What Do You Think?

1. What limits should be placed on students' rights to express themselves in their schools?
2. Have you ever expressed your opinions in your school? What forms of expression did you use?

What Do You Think? Answers

1. Answers may vary, but students may discuss schools', colleges', and universities' responsibility to promote the public good and individuals' freedom to express their opinions.
2. Answers will vary, but students should list examples and explain under what categories they fall.

ACROSS THE CURRICULUM

TECHNOLOGY Northwestern University engineering professor Arthur Butz has used his free access to the Internet to spur a debate over the Holocaust. Butz contends that the extent of the tragedy has been greatly exaggerated and misrepresented.

Administrators tolerate Butz's comments because of the university's strong support for freedom of speech for professors and because Butz avoids the topic in class and provides a disclaimer on his Web page.

But the issue has raised old and new questions. How far does academic freedom extend? How far does it extend in cyberspace? The questions are vital because Web sites can be seen by millions, and as schools work to provide Internet access they must weigh academic freedom against freedom of speech. ∎

pass laws against false advertising. The courts have agreed that false or misleading advertising works against the public interest. For example, the First Amendment does not protect an ad that exaggerates the health benefits of a product or that makes claims about a product that may do nothing beneficial or may actually harm someone.

For many years federal courts ruled that the right to free expression did not apply to business advertising. The Supreme Court ruled in 1942, for example, that business advertising was commercial, as opposed to "pure," speech. As such, it was not protected by the First Amendment. In later years, however, the Court extended some protections to business advertising, such as ads for professional services. The government may still restrict false advertising and advertising that is not in the public interest—for example, cigarette ads on television.

Freedom of Speech and Individual Behavior

Debate over free speech is not limited to national security issues and the media. The Supreme Court also has applied First Amendment protections to cases that involve personal conduct and those that involve speech that expresses hatred.

Personal Conduct Some of the most difficult questions about what forms of expression are protected by the First Amendment involve personal conduct. The Supreme Court has ruled that some conduct is a form of symbolic speech that is protected by the First Amendment. **Symbolic speech** is an action meant to deliver a message.

Deciding which actions are examples of protected symbolic speech, however, has been difficult for the courts. In fact, the Supreme Court has ruled that not all conduct designed to communicate a message is protected by the First Amendment. In the 1968 case *United States* v. *O'Brien*, for example, the Court ruled that burning a draft card was not protected symbolic speech. The **draft** was a policy requiring men to serve in the military. Destroying a draft card was against the law. In the 1960s and early 1970s, a number of men around the country burned their draft cards to protest U.S. involvement in the Vietnam War. In the *O'Brien* decision the Court ruled that it could not accept "the view that an apparently limitless variety of conduct can be labeled 'speech.'"

CONSTITUTIONAL GOVERNMENT *Demonstrators in Baltimore, Maryland, burn draft files in protest of the Vietnam War.* **Why did the Court rule that burning draft cards is not protected by the Constitution?**

One year later, however, the Court ruled that students in an Iowa high school could wear black armbands to protest the Vietnam War. In the 1969 case *Tinker* v. *Des Moines Independent Community School District,* school officials argued that the issue was one of conduct, not the right to free expression. (See Citizenship in Action, page 309.) School officials claimed that the armbands would cause discipline problems. The Supreme Court ruled, however, that wearing the armbands sent a political message and was thus a form of symbolic speech protected by the First Amendment. The Court also determined that no disruption had actually occurred.

In addition to the *Tinker* case, the Supreme Court has also ruled that laws may not restrict other forms of symbolic speech. For example, in 1989 and 1990 the Court ruled that state and federal laws against burning the U.S. flag as a form of protest violated the right to free speech. The Court said that the First Amendment protected freedom of expression even when a vast majority of people disagreed with the particular form of expression—in this instance, flag burning.

Hate Speech In addition to symbolic speech issues, the Supreme Court in recent years has addressed cases involving rules to curb hate speech. Supporters of such rules define **hate speech** as the expression of hatred or bias against a person, based on characteristics such as race, sex, religion, or sexual orientation. During the late 1980s many colleges passed rules that prohibited hate speech.

Various federal courts have ruled that many hate speech rules are unconstitutional because they are so vague that a reasonable person could not know what speech the rules actually limit. Some students and teachers, for example, were reluctant to express their opinions for fear of punishment. The courts also have declared as unconstitutional some hate speech rules that banned certain language, such as racist opinions, simply because it offended some people.

Supporters of hate speech rules point to the 1942 case of *Chaplinsky* v. *New Hampshire,* in which the Supreme Court said that using "insulting or 'fighting' words" that are likely to cause a fight or other physical disturbance are not protected by the First Amendment. Some of these supporters propose that future hate speech rules should be limited to restricting these types of "fighting words." Colleges continue to struggle to uphold the sometimes conflicting values of the First Amendment and respect for the dignity of all groups of people.

Some Forms of Protected Symbolic Speech

Music Lyrics

Flag Desecration [spoiling]

Works of Art

Theatrical Performances

Political Buttons

Armbands

T-Shirt Slogans

Public Demonstrations

Sit In/Stand In

The forms of symbolic speech illustrated in this chart are protected by law. **Under what conditions might the Supreme Court restrict these forms of symbolic speech?**

Caption Answer

These forms of symbolic speech can be restricted if they are ruled obscene, are considered "fighting words," or threaten national security.

SECTION 3 REVIEW ANSWERS

1. Refer to the following pages: treason (304), sedition (305), *Schenck* v. *United States* (305), prior restraint (306), shield law (307), libel (307), slander (307), obscenity (307), Federal Communications Commission (308), symbolic speech (310), draft (310), hate speech (311).

2. Tables will vary but should provide examples of the benefits and dangers of free speech and a free press.

3a. It licenses radio and television stations and regulates broadcast content.

3b. It established the clear-and-present-danger test for limiting free expression.

3c. conduct meant to deliver a message, such as wearing armbands in protest

4. Answers will vary, but students should state their opinion and provide support.

SECTION 3 REVIEW

1. Identify and Explain:
- treason
- sedition
- *Schenck* v. *United States*
- prior restraint
- shield law
- libel
- slander
- obscenity
- Federal Communications Commission
- symbolic speech
- draft
- hate speech

2. Identifying Concepts: Copy the chart below. Use it to list examples of the benefits and dangers of the right to free speech and a free press.

	Free Speech	Free Press
Benefits		
Dangers		

3. **Finding the Main Idea**

a. What is the role of the FCC?
b. How did *Schenck* v. *United States* affect the freedom of speech?
c. What kinds of actions qualify as symbolic speech?

4. **Writing and Critical Thinking**

Evaluating: Do you think the FCC should regulate what radio and television stations can broadcast? Explain your answer.

Consider the following:
- the importance of a free press
- the need to promote the public good

Homework Practice Online
keyword: SV3 HP13

SECTION 4

FREEDOM OF ASSEMBLY AND PETITION

READ TO DISCOVER

1. How does the First Amendment protect the rights of assembly and petition on public property?
2. How is the freedom to demonstrate restricted on private property?
3. How does freedom of assembly support freedom of association?

POLITICAL DICTIONARY

picketing

Perhaps you have seen people demonstrating in your community for laws to protect the environment or seen them passing out flyers calling for lower taxes. Or maybe you have seen news reports of people addressing a meeting of your local government about traffic laws or zoning issues. You might know someone who has joined with others to march in front of a business to demand higher wages or better working conditions.

What gave these people the right to demonstrate and to address government officials about their concerns? The people in each of these examples exercised their rights of assembly and petition. Along with freedoms of religion and speech, the rights of assembly and petition are protected by the First Amendment. As with other First Amendment liberties, however, the government may act to promote the public good by balancing these freedoms with conflicting interests.

Demonstrations and Protests

Demonstrations and protests are among the most common examples of the rights of assembly and petition. Such gatherings include abortion protests, marches in support of equal rights, and parades honoring certain groups or causes. The purpose of many of these demonstrations is to persuade government officials and others to pursue certain goals.

As with other civil liberties guaranteed by the Bill of Rights, the freedom to demonstrate peacefully is protected from the actions of the federal government, as well as from state and local governments. In some cases, however, the courts have allowed governments to set boundaries on the freedom to assemble, in order to protect the rights of others.

Assembly and Public Property It has long been recognized that the freedom to demonstrate on public property may be regulated in the interest of keeping order and shielding people from loud noise, blocked streets, and other intrusions. Such restrictions are called time, place, and manner

POLITICAL PROCESSES *Picketing on public property such as a public sidewalk in front of a business is permitted.* ***Do businesses have the right to prohibit picketing on their private property?***

regulations. The courts have said that these rules must be applied fairly and that they may not be used as a means to restrict a specific group's freedom to demonstrate.

One example of a time, place, and manner regulation is a parade permit that local governments may require people to obtain before holding demonstrations on public streets. Such a permit identifies the location and route of the parade or demonstration, as well as the time it will occur. The permit process allows local authorities to develop procedures for managing traffic flow and to prepare for problems that might occur during the demonstration.

In some cases the courts also have allowed governments to regulate demonstrations for reasons of public safety. Police may halt demonstrations that turn violent, for example, and arrest those responsible for the violence. In doing so, the police are protecting the safety of others.

The Supreme Court also has allowed laws prohibiting demonstrations in jails and restricting demonstrations that would disrupt school activities. These laws are allowed because such demonstrations would interfere with critical activities, such as maintaining control of jails and educating children.

The courts have ruled against other restrictions on public assembly, however, even ones that attempted to prevent highly unpopular activities in a community. In 1978, for example, the Illinois Supreme Court ruled that officials in Skokie, Illinois—a largely Jewish suburb of Chicago—could not stop members of a neo-Nazi party—a U.S. version of the Nazi Party—from parading through the city. In the 1930s and 1940s the Nazi government in Germany was responsible for the murder of millions of Jews as well as others. Among Skokie's residents were Jews who had survived Nazi persecution, as well as relatives of the Nazis' victims. Before the ruling, local officials had attempted to stop the neo-Nazi parade for fear that it might lead to violence and to enforce several Skokie ordinances imposing criminal penalties on certain kinds of speech and assembly. The U.S. Supreme Court refused to review the state court's ruling, however, which had stated that the First Amendment protected the neo-Nazis' right to assemble. Therefore, they were allowed to march.

Assembly and Private Property Among the strongest boundaries on freedom of assembly are those involving demonstrations on private property. The First Amendment right of assembly does not give people the right to use others' private property, such as a business or residence. In 1972, for example, the Supreme Court ruled in *Lloyd Corporation* v. *Tanner* that a shopping mall could prevent people who were on its private property from passing out literature opposing U.S. involvement in the Vietnam War. Such activities, however, could take place on the public sidewalks and streets outside the mall.

In some circumstances, private businesses also may prevent picketing on their property. **Picketing**

PRINCIPLES OF DEMOCRACY *Any group of individuals that wants to demonstrate on public property must first obtain a permit. Government officials have occasionally attempted to prevent controversial groups from demonstrating, as was the case in Skokie, Illinois, during the 1970s.* **What are the restrictions that regulate public demonstrations called?**

ACROSS THE CURRICULUM

SOCIOLOGY Government reaction to demonstrations has occasionally yielded disastrous results. Student leaders organized a national strike in the spring of 1970 after President Nixon ordered troops into Cambodia. On May 4 at Kent State University near Cleveland, Ohio, members of the National Guard fired into a crowd gathered for a midday protest. Four people were killed, two of whom were not taking part in the rally but were simply walking to class. Shortly thereafter, at Jackson State University in Mississippi, two African American students were killed during a peaceful protest. As a result, students at more than 450 colleges and universities went on strike, and 80 percent of campuses experienced some form of protest. One university president called May 1970 the worst month in the history of higher education. ■

Enhancing the Lesson

For more information on *Lloyd Corporation* v. *Tanner* and other Supreme Court decisions, see the Supreme Court Docket section on the *Holt Researcher Online.*

Caption Answer

time, place, and manner restrictions

Enhancing the Lesson

For more information on *National Association for the Advancement of Colored People (NAACP)* v. *Alabama* and other Supreme Court decisions, see the Supreme Court Docket section on the *Holt Researcher Online.*

SECTION 4 REVIEW ANSWERS

1. Refer to the following page: picketing (313).

2. Tables will vary. Examples of restrictions allowed may include requiring permits, reasons of public safety, and prohibited in jails and schools; restrictions denied may include demonstrations expressing unpopular views.

3a. They are rules for governing the right to freely assemble.

3b. It has been interpreted to mean that people have a right to associate with groups without government interference.

4. Answers will vary but students should state their opinion and provided support.

is walking or standing in front of a place of business or other property, often holding signs urging others not to buy the company's products or asking others not to cross the picket line to work for the company. Although picketing may be prohibited on the company's property, it is allowed on the surrounding public property.

Peaceful Association

The First Amendment's guarantee of freedom of assembly has been used for more than protecting the right to demonstrate. The courts also have interpreted the freedom of assembly to mean that people have a right to associate with various groups without interference from the government.

A key Supreme Court ruling involving the right of free association was the 1958 decision in *National Association for the Advancement of Colored People (NAACP)* v. *Alabama.* The NAACP is an organization that was founded in 1909 to work for equal rights for African Americans. The 1958 case reached the Supreme Court after the state of Alabama fined the

PRINCIPLES OF DEMOCRACY *The First Amendment's guarantee of freedom of assembly has also been interpreted to mean that people have the right to associate with various groups without government interference. The above photograph shows a meeting of the NAACP.* **What did the Supreme Court rule in the NAACP v. Alabama case?**

NAACP for not providing government officials a list of its state members. The Court ruled that Alabama officials could not force the NAACP to provide the names of its members. Such a rule, the Court said, violated the right of people to associate and organize in pursuit of a lawful goal without interference from the government.

SECTION 4 REVIEW

1. Identify and Explain:
 • picketing

2. Identifying Concepts:
 Copy the chart to the right. Use it to describe the types of restrictions on the freedom to assemble that the Supreme Court has allowed and denied.

Restrictions allowed	Restrictions denied

Homework Practice Online
keyword: SV3 HP13

3. Finding the Main Idea

a. What are time, place, and manner regulations?

b. How is freedom of association protected by the First Amendment?

4. Writing and Critical Thinking

Identifying Points of View: Do you think courts should uphold the right to stage a public demonstration even for groups that whose views might be offensive to others in the community?

Consider the following:
 • the need to protect the public good
 • the First Amendment right of free assembly

GOVERNMENT IN THE NEWS

September 11, 2001, and Open Society

On September 11, 2001, terrorists unleashed a devastating attack against the United States. For weeks, Americans were glued to their televisions, radios, newspapers, and the Internet, hungry for news about the events.

Observers wondered whether the media would face restrictions after September 11. The terrorists were able to carry out their plan in part because the United States is an open society—civil liberties are protected and citizens are allowed to travel and communicate freely. Some feared that Americans—including the news media—would face greater scrutiny from government authorities.

On October 12, 2001, U.S. attorney general John Ashcroft issued a memorandum regarding the Freedom of Information Act (FOIA). FOIA, passed in 1966, allows all U.S. citizens access to governmental records except those that if released would threaten a person's privacy or national security. FOIA has allowed historians, for example, to view formerly top-secret presidential papers. Ashcroft's directive could make it more difficult to access government information. Ashcroft instructed government agencies to consult with the Justice Department on all matters involving FOIA, including lawsuits requesting information. Ashcroft also announced that the Justice Department would defend agencies that decide to withhold records.

The news media was crucial to informing Americans and the world about the September 11 attacks and their aftermath. When U.S. military action began in Afghanistan, however, many journalists found that their ability to report on the war was severely restricted by the Pentagon. Reporters were not allowed to accompany troops on their missions, nor were they allowed to interview troops after returning from their missions. When three U.S. sol-

New York City mayor Rudolph Giuliani speaks to the press. For many Americans, the news took on an increased importance after the terrorist attacks of September 11, 2001.

diers were killed by "friendly fire," military officials prevented reporters from getting near the scene.

Being denied access to the military, journalists argue, violates the First Amendment's guarantee of the freedom of the press. U.S. officials admit that there have been some limitations but that these are imposed in order to prevent leaks of information that would threaten the security of U.S. troops. The Pentagon's chief spokesperson Victoria Clarke commented on the restrictions facing journalists in the *Columbia Journalism Review*. "Providing for the common defense is in the Preamble to the Constitution, and the rights of the press are in the First Amendment," she said. "Those two things are so important that it is probably valuable that there is this healthy tension."

What Do You Think?

1. What role did the news media play following the events of September 11, 2001?

2. Do you think citizens and the media should have unlimited access to government information?

> **WHY IT MATTERS TODAY**
>
> Information and news about their government are important to U.S. citizens. Use **CNNfyi.com** or other **current events** sources to investigate issues regarding the government, the news media, and national security.
>
> **CNNfyi.com**

Government in the News Answers

1. Students might mention that people around the world watched the events unfold on television and relied on the news for information about the disasters.

2. Answers will vary but should demonstrate an understanding of the balance between the freedom of the press and the necessity to protect information that is vital to national security and the safety of U.S. armed services personnel.

CHAPTER 13

Review Answers

Writing a Summary

Summaries should focus on the main parts of each section. These may be found in the Read to Discover questions at the start of each section. Summaries should also use standard grammar, spelling, sentence structure, and punctuation.

Identifying Ideas

Refer to the following pages: civil liberty (297), Establishment Clause (300), *Engel* v. *Vitale* (301), Free Exercise Clause (302), treason (304), sedition (305), *Schenck* v. *United States* (305), symbolic speech (310), hate speech (311), picketing (313)

(Continued on page 316)

(Continued from page 315)

tections in support of the public good.

3. Government cannot establish or favor a religion or prohibit religious exercises.

4. determines whether the connection between the expression and committing an illegal act is close; may require journalists to reveal sources, require licensing for TV and radio, establish laws against libel, slander, obscenity, and false advertising

5. part of freedom of speech; hate speech—expresses bias based on such characteristics as gender; fighting words—likely to cause physical disturbance

6. People may associate with groups without government interference.

Reviewing Themes

1. Answers will vary, but students should give their opinion and support it.

2. Answers will vary, but students should state their opinion and explain their reasoning.

3. Answers will vary, but students should give their opinion, support it, and explain if they feel there are too many limits.

Thinking Critically

1. Answers will vary, but students may discuss citizens' rights to their own beliefs.

(Continued on page 317)

CHAPTER 13
Review

Writing a Summary

Using standard grammar, spelling, sentence structure, and punctuation, write a summary of the information in this chapter.

Identifying Ideas

Identify the following terms and explain their significance.

1. civil liberty
2. Establishment Clause
3. *Engel* v. *Vitale*
4. Free Exercise Clause
5. treason
6. sedition
7. *Schenck* v. *United States*
8. symbolic speech
9. hate speech
10. picketing

Understanding Main Ideas

SECTION 1 *(pp. 297–299)*

1. How are civil liberties guaranteed in the Bill of Rights? Do aliens have the same rights as citizens?

2. What is the role of the courts in finding a proper balance between individual's civil liberties and some wider public interest?

SECTION 2 *(pp. 300–303)*

3. What is the importance of the Establishment and Free Exercise Clauses of the First Amendment?

SECTION 3 *(pp. 304–311)*

4. How does the Supreme Court apply the clear-and-present-danger test to free-expression cases? In what ways may government set boundaries on free speech in the media?

5. How is symbolic speech protected by the First Amendment? What is the difference between the free expression that is restricted by many hate speech rules and that which the courts have called fighting words?

SECTION 4 *(pp. 312–314)*

6. How does the freedom of assembly protect the right of association?

Reviewing Themes

1. **Public Good** Do you think First Amendment rights should ever be restricted? In what kinds of situations should this occur?

2. Do you think that reporters should be required to testify in criminal cases about the identities of their sources? Explain your answer.

3. **Principles of Democracy** Why are the freedoms of speech and of the press important in a democracy? Do you think that the government places too many limits on these freedoms?

Thinking Critically

1. **Summarizing** Imagine that you are visiting a country where freedom of religion is not a right. Write a short newspaper editorial explaining why religious freedom is valued in the United States.

2. **Supporting a Point of View** Imagine that you were a Supreme Court justice on the case of *Schenck* v. *United States.* How would you have ruled? Explain your answer.

3. **Evaluating** Are there times when the rights of an individual must be restricted for the public good? Are there times when an individual's rights should be upheld even at the expense of the public good? Provide examples and explain your reasoning.

Writing about Government

Review what you wrote in your Government Notebook at the beginning of this chapter about the ways that government may restrict First Amendment rights. Now that you have studied this chapter, how would you revise your answer? Why is it important that these rights are not without limit? Record your answers in your Notebook.

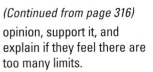

Interpreting the Visual Record

Study the political cartoon below. Then use it to help you answer the questions that follow.

LIBERTY'S CROWN

FREEDOM OF WORSHIP
RIGHT OF ASSEMBLY
TRIAL BY JURY
BILL OF RIGHTS
DUE PROCESS
RIGHT TO BEAR ARMS
FREE PRESS
FREE SPEECH

1. How many of the spikes on the Statue of Liberty's crown represent First Amendment rights?

a. two
c. five
b. four
d. seven

2. Why do you think the artist chose the statue's crown to represent the Bill of Rights?

Analyzing Primary Sources

In a letter to the Committee of the Danbury Baptist Association in Connecticut on January 1, 1802, Thomas Jefferson expressed his belief that the First Amendment created a wall separating church and state. Read the excerpt below and answer the questions that follow.

"Believing with you that religion is a matter which lies solely between man and his God, that the legislative powers of government reach actions only, and not opinions, I contemplate [think] with sovereign [greatest] reverence that act of the whole American people which de-clared that their legislature should 'make no law respecting an establishment of religion, or pro-hibiting the free exercise thereof,' thus building a wall of separation between church and State."

3. Which of the following statements best reflects Jefferson's point of view?

a. religion is a government matter

b. religion is a private matter

c. the law is unclear

d. Americans support a state religion

4. To what is Jefferson referring when he writes of "that act of the whole American people"?

Building Your Portfolio

Create a Free Press Handbook that student reporters might use as part of their training to become broadcast or print journalists. The hand-book should describe how the First Amendment affects various parts of the media, including information about the role of the FCC and the restrictions that the courts allow to be placed on free expression.

🖵 internet connect

Internet Activity: go.hrw.com
KEYWORD: SV3 GV13

go. hrw .com

Have students access the Internet through the HRW Go site to research first amend-ment rights. Assign students to research one of the rights guaranteed in the First Amendment. Have students research key court cases and interpretations of their spe-cific rights. Assign class reports on key issues related to that right.

(Continued from page 316)

opinion, support it, and explain if they feel there are too many limits.

Thinking Critically

1. Answers will vary, but students may discuss citi-zens' rights to their own beliefs.

2. Answers will vary, but students should demon-strate knowledge of the facts of the case and explain their reasoning.

3. Answers will vary, but students should provide examples and explain their reasoning.

Writing About History

The Government Notebook is a follow-up activity to the notebook activity that appears on page 296.

Building Social Studies Skills

1. b

2. Answers will vary, but students may suggest the crown symbolizes the importance of the Bill of Rights.

3. b

4. the First Amendment

Alternative Assessment

To assess this activity see Advertisements and Writing to Describe *Alternative Assessment Handbook*.

CHAPTER 14 ASSURING INDIVIDUAL RIGHTS

	OBJECTIVES	PACING GUIDE	REPRODUCIBLE RESOURCES
SECTION 1 **PROTECTING INDIVIDUAL LIBERTIES** (pp. 319–325)	▸ What does the term *due process* mean? ▸ How is procedural due process different from substantive due process? ▸ How do the Fourth Amendment and due process protect people's security against unreasonable state action? ▸ How does the Bill of Rights protect people's privacy?	**Regular** 2 days **Block Scheduling** .75 day	**ELL** Spanish Study Guide 14.1 **ELL** English Study Guide 14.1 **PS** Reading 70: A Theory of Justice
SECTION 2 **RIGHTS OF THE ACCUSED** (pp. 326–328)	▸ How does the Constitution protect the right of *habeas corpus* and protect against bills of attainder and *ex post facto* laws? ▸ How do requirements for bringing charges before grand juries protect the rights of people accused of crimes? ▸ How does the Fifth Amendment protect against self-incrimination?	**Regular** 1 day **Block Scheduling** .5 day	**ELL** Spanish Study Guide 14.2 **ELL** English Study Guide 14.2
SECTION 3 **ENSURING FAIR TRIALS AND PUNISHMENTS** (pp. 329–334)	▸ Which amendments of the Bill of Rights help guarantee the right to a fair trial? ▸ In what ways does the Bill of Rights protect convicted criminals from excessive punishments?	**Regular** 1.5 days **Block Scheduling** .75 day	**ELL** Spanish Study Guide 14.3 **ELL** English Study Guide 14.3

Chapter Resource Key

PS	Primary Sources	**A**	Assessment		Video
RS	Reading Support	**REV**	Review		Videodisc
E	Enrichment	**ELL**	Reinforcement and English Language Learners		Internet
S	Simulations		Transparencies		Holt Presentation Maker Using
SM	Skills Mastery		CD-ROM		Microsoft ® PowerPoint ®

TECHNOLOGY RESOURCES	REINFORCEMENT, REVIEW, AND ASSESSMENT
⊚ One-Stop Planner: Lesson 14.1 📇 Holt Researcher Online 📇 Homework Practice Online 🖱 Cartoon Transparency 14 ⊚ Global Skill Builder CD-ROM	**REV** Section 1 Review, p. 325 **A** Daily Quiz 14.1
⊚ One-Stop Planner: Lesson 14.2 📇 Holt Researcher Online 📇 Homework Practice Online 🖱 Transparencies 29 and 30	**REV** Section 2 Review, p. 328 **A** Daily Quiz 14.2
⊚ One-Stop Planner: Lesson 14.3 📇 Holt Researcher Online 📇 Homework Practice Online ⊚ Global Skill Builder CD-ROM	**REV** Section 3 Review, p. 334 **A** Daily Quiz 14.3

Chapter Review and Assessment

SM Global Skill Builder CD-ROM
📇 HRW Go site
REV Chapter 14 Tutorial for Students, Parents, and Peers
REV Chapter 14 Review, pp. 336–337
⊚ Chapter 14 Test Generator (on the One-Stop Planner)
A Chapter 14 Test
A Chapter 14 Test Alternative Assessment Handbook

One-Stop Planner CD-ROM

It's easy to plan lessons, select resources, and print out materials for your students when you use the **One-Stop Planner CD-ROM with Test Generator.**

📶 **internet** connect

HRW ONLINE RESOURCES
Go To: **go.hrw.com**
Then type in a keyword.

TEACHER HOME PAGE
KEYWORD: **SV3 Teacher**

CHAPTER INTERNET ACTIVITIES
KEYWORD: **SV3 GV14**
Choose an activity on assuring individual rights to:
▸ learn about due process and civil liberties.
▸ write an article on the grand jury system.
▸ understand the pros and cons of the death penalty.

CHAPTER ENRICHMENT LINKS
KEYWORD: **SV3 CH14**

HOLT RESEARCHER ONLINE
KEYWORD: **Holt Researcher**

ONLINE ASSESSMENT
Homework Practice
KEYWORD: **SV3 HP14**
Standardized Test Prep
KEYWORD: **SV3 STP14**
Rubrics
KEYWORD: **SS Rubrics**

ONLINE MAPS, CHARTS, AND GRAPHS
KEYWORD: **SV3 MCG**
▸ Constitutional Protections for Those Accused of Crimes
▸ Miranda Rights

CONTENT UPDATES
KEYWORD: **SS Content Updates**

HOLT PRESENTATION MAKER
KEYWORD: **SV3 PPT14**

ONLINE READING SUPPORT
KEYWORD: **SS Strategies**

CURRENT EVENTS
KEYWORD: **S3 Current Events**

HOLT PRESENTATION MAKER
Access Illustrated LECTURE
NOTES using Microsoft®
PowerPoint® on the
One-Stop Planner CD-ROM

OBJECTIVES

▶ Define the term *due process.*
▶ Explain the difference between procedural due process and substantive due process.
▶ Describe how due process and the Fourth Amendment protect people's security against unreasonable state action.
▶ Explain how the Bill of Rights protects the people's right to privacy.

MOTIVATE

Present the following scenario, and have students place themselves in the situation: You are driving home on a Saturday night and are pulled over for speeding. When questioned by the police officer, you say that you were not speeding. The officer disagrees and wants to revoke your license. Ask students how they think they would respond in a situation like this. Lead a discussion about what students believe are the correct procedures that should be followed before a license suspension could occur. Have students come up with as many rights as possible that they would have under the given situation. Explain to students that in this chapter they will learn about how the Constitution protects individual liberties, how it guarantees certain rights to people accused of crimes, and how it ensures an individual of a fair trial when determining guilt or innocence.

TEACH

Building a Vocabulary

In spiral notebooks, have students create a Political Dictionary to be used throughout the course. This dictionary may be used as an activity at the start of each new section; it may also be used as a modification device for students having difficulty or sheltered English students during tests and homework assignments. List words the students will be expected to know for this section on the board. Have students list, define, and give an example of each of the terms using information provided in the text or on the *Researcher CD-ROM.*

Classifying Information/ Demonstrating Understanding

Briefly review the concept of checks and balances in the U.S. system of government. Explain that one of the ways the judicial branch checks the legislative branch is by deciding whether the federal government has followed *due process.* Explain that the goal of the activity is to help clarify how governmental actions are limited in order to prevent individual liberties from being taken away unjustly. Write the term *due process* on the chalkboard. Organize the class into small groups. Have each group brainstorm ideas and share them with the other groups to create a single definition of the word. Compare the class definition with the one in the textbook or dictionary. Underneath the term *due process* on the chalkboard create two columns, with the term *procedural due process* heading the first column and the term *substantive due process* heading the second column. Have each group come up with two examples of laws that would violate each type of these due process guarantees. List each group's examples under the appropriate columns on the board, and lead a discussion to help clarify the role of government and the role of the courts in protecting people's civil liberties. Tell students that in the next activity they will learn about ways in which due process applies to states' actions.

Recognizing Point of View/Taking a Stand

Briefly describe the two-fold goal of both the federal and state governments—attempting to protect individual rights and liberties as well as providing for the public good. Ask students whether they believe both goals can be achieved at the same time or whether they feel the two are mutually exclusive, or incompatible. Organize the class in half, asking students to take either one viewpoint or the other. Have each side describe scenarios or cite past legislation that would help to defend their view. Allow 10 to 15 minutes for each side to express its point of view. Lead a discussion about whether there comes a point at which the general welfare of the people becomes more important than individual rights. If so, have students give examples of these situations. If not, have students justify their position. Have students read *Gitlow* v. *New York* and *Mapp* v. *Ohio,* located in the Supreme Court Docket section on the *Holt Researcher*

Online. Have students write a summary of how these cases shaped the meaning of due process for states. Tell students that in the next activity they will learn about how the Bill of Rights protects people's privacy.

Predicting Outcome/Debating Ideas

  Present a brief description or outline of the 1985 Supreme Court case of *New Jersey* v. *T.L.O.* Then pose the question: Should school officials have the right to search your property? Explain that the objective is to determine whether the constitutional protections against unreasonable searches apply to students. Organize the class into small groups. Have them identify the constitutional grounds upon which each side based its argument. Allow 10 to 15 minutes for groups to debate the opposing viewpoints. Have groups predict how they think the Supreme Court ruled in this case and give reasons why. Afterwards, have students read *New Jersey* v. *T.L.O.* located in the Supreme Court Docket section on the *Holt Researcher Online* to find out the Supreme Court's decision and the basis for their ruling. Ask students whether they agree with the final decision in this case. Ask whether their feelings may have been different had the case involved an employer and an employee instead of school officials and a student.

CLOSE

Refer students to the Supreme Court cases found in this section. Ask each student to write an essay reflecting their opinion on the outcome of these cases. Have students consider the effects these decisions have had on protecting due process, security rights, and the right to privacy. Encourage students to write the essay in terms of their feelings on the issue of individual rights and the responsibility of the government to protect the people. Ask volunteers whose essays express various viewpoints to share their essays with the rest of the class.

OPTIONS

Body-Kinesthetic Learners/Interpersonal Learners

  On small pieces of paper or note cards write important concepts discussed in this section, placing one term on each piece of paper. Some terms to include are *First Amendment, Fourth Amendment, Fifth Amendment, police power, exclusionary rule,* and *right to privacy*. Place the slips of paper in a hat. Organize the class into three to four small groups. One at a time each group should pick a piece of paper and attempt to act out the concept that they have chosen. Allow each group a few minutes to organize their performance before they are asked to go before the class. Have the rest of the class try to guess what terms or concepts are being acted out. Leave time at the end of the class for discussing the relevance of the terms presented as well as the difficulty students had enacting these terms.

Students Having Difficulty/ Sheltered English Students

 Give students sample situations involving a police officer and a teenager whom the officer has just pulled over. Have students write an appropriate dialogue between the two. Encourage students to include applicable questions that each individual could ask the other as well as appropriate responses. Have each student predict what the final outcome would most likely be in this situation based on the dialogue he or she presented. Students may earn extra credit for including an appropriate illustration of the scene described.

REVIEW

Have students complete the Section 1 Review on page 325. Use the answers in the Annotated Teacher's Edition to assess student mastery of this section.

ASSESS

To assess student mastery of this section, have students complete Daily Quiz 14.1 in *Daily Quizzes with Answer Key.* For additional assessment options, see *Alternative Assessment Handbook* on the *One-Stop Planner CD-ROM.*

ADDITIONAL RESOURCES

Epstein, Lee, and Walker, Thomas. *Constitutional Law for a Changing America: Rights, Liberties, and Justice.* 1992. Congressional Quarterly.

Keynes, Edward. *Liberty, Property, and Privacy: Toward a Jurisprudence of Substantive Due Process.* 1996. Pennsylvania State University Press.

OBJECTIVES

▶ Explain how the Constitution protects the right of *habeas corpus* and protects against bills of attainder and *ex post facto* laws.
▶ Describe how requirements for bringing charges before grand juries protect the rights of people accused of crimes.
▶ Describe how the Fifth Amendment protects against self-incrimination.

MOTIVATE

Begin the activity by writing the following statement on the board: *An individual is considered innocent until proven guilty.* Lead a discussion in which students share their feelings about this concept. Have students describe what this statement means to them, whether they believe in this principle, and whether they feel the American legal system supports this founding principle. Ask students to provide examples of situations in U.S. society that either support or refute this concept. Make a list of these examples on the board. Explain that in this section students will learn several of the measures the Constitution takes to protect individuals accused of crimes.

TEACH

Building a Vocabulary

In their spiral notebooks, have each student continue working on their Political Dictionary. List words the students will be expected to know for this section on the chalkboard. Have students list, define, and give an example of each of the terms, using information provided in the text or on the *Researcher CD-ROM.*

Organizing Ideas/Synthesizing Information

Organize the class into small groups. Explain that the objective of this activity is to devise an imaginary handbook about the rights of the accused that can be used by professionals in the field of law who are presently active in the field. Assign each group one of the rights of a person accused of a crime. The handbook should contain the five constitutional protections listed in the chart in this section of the text as well as the Miranda rights described in this section. Each group is responsible for explaining how each right is to be protected and to what extent that right is guaranteed by the Constitution. Each group should then share their information with the rest of the class. Extra credit may be awarded to students who volunteer to put together a final product summarizing all the groups' work for the class. The handbook should be displayed in class and used as a reference when needed. Tell students that in the next activity they will learn why people are read their rights before questioning.

Applying a Model

Draw a circle on the chalkboard. Inside the circle write the term *Miranda rights.* Draw six lines shooting out from the circle. At the end of each line draw a smaller circle. Explain to students that each of the six outer circles represents one of the rights outlined in the Miranda Rule. Review with students the Supreme Court decision in the 1966 case of *Miranda* v. *Arizona* located in the Supreme Court Docket section on the *Holt Researcher Online.* Have students describe each of the rights and list them in the circles until all of them are filled in. Students may wish to refer to the chart on page 328 in the text for help. Lead a discussion on the importance of police officers reading suspected criminals their Miranda rights before they answer any questions. Draw another circle on the chalkboard and write inside it the words *class rights.* Invite the class to participate in the same activity, this time coming up with appropriate rights for students as members of the class. Compare the similarities of the rights described in each of the two drawings. Tell students that they will learn about the requirements for bringing charges against a person in the following activity.

Hypothesizing

Discuss with students the constitutional protections against self-incrimination. Ask students to discuss reasons for having such protections built into the Constitution. Have students read about the *Brown* v. *Mississippi* Supreme Court decision and how it applies to the concept of self-incrimination. Ask students to write a short essay hypothesizing what would happen if police officers were allowed to torture suspects to gain confessions or if people did not have protection from self-incrimination. Encourage students to share their ideas with the rest of the class.

CLOSE

Have students reflect on comments that were made during the Motivate Activity discussing the issue of "innocent until proven guilty." Ask them to relate their views on that issue to the issue of the freeing of guilty people vs. the imprisoning of innocent people. Lead a discussion about student views on whether the current legal system places too much, not enough, or the right amount of emphasis on the constitutional rights of people accused of crimes. Have students cite examples of past situations or previous court cases that defend their position. Examine the costs and benefits to society of adhering to the principle that it is better that a guilty person go free than it is for an innocent person to be punished.

OPTIONS

Intrapersonal Learners

 Organize students into three or four groups to write and perform a skit based on the plight of an individual who is wrongly convicted of a crime. Each group should assign students to play the necessary roles. Some possible characters may include an arresting officer, a judge, attorneys, and the convicted person. Discussions following the performances should include such topics as rights of the accused, personal responsibility, and appropriate actions by those involved in the situation. Discuss with students the actual requirements for bringing a bill of indictment against a person accused of a crime.

Students Having Difficulty/ Sheltered English Students

Have students make flash cards to help them study the important concepts outlined in this section. These concepts may include: *Miranda rights, writ of habeas corpus, bills of attainder, ex post facto laws, grand jury proceeding,* and *self-incrimination.* If possible, pair students up so that they will have a partner with whom to review the material. Provide students with note cards and markers. The term or concept should be written on one side of the card. On the other side students should give a brief description of the term or concept and at least one example that illustrates it.

Gifted Learners

 Have students prepare a letter to be sent to a state's attorney expressing either their approval or their discontent with one of the founding principles of the American legal system—that a person is innocent until proven guilty. Students should support their position by citing past court cases in which they perceive the system has failed or by citing cases or events in which they believe the system worked and justice prevailed.

Gifted Learners

 Have students search for articles dealing with cases involving the rights of the accused. Organize the class into two groups. One group will search for articles dealing with the use of the rights of the accused, such as a defendant pleading the Fifth Amendment. The other group will search for violations of the rights of the accused, such as the torturing of a suspect until he or she confesses to a crime. Allow students time to discuss the articles they researched and to offer explanations why the participants in each instance chose the course of action that they did.

REVIEW

Have students complete the Section 2 Review on page 328. Use the answers in the Annotated Teacher's Edition to assess student mastery of this section.

ASSESS

To assess student mastery of this section, have students complete Daily Quiz 14.2 in *Daily Quizzes with Answer Key.* For additional assessment options, see *Alternative Assessment Handbook* on the *One-Stop Planner CD-ROM.*

ADDITIONAL RESOURCES

Linfield, Michael. *Freedom Under Fire: U.S. Civil Liberties in Times of War.* 1990. South End Press.

Baker, Liva. *Miranda: The Crime, the Law, the Politics.* 1983. Atheneum.

HOLT PRESENTATION MAKER
Access Illustrated LECTURE NOTES using Microsoft® PowerPoint® on the One-Stop Planner CD-ROM

OBJECTIVES

▶ Explain how the Bill of Rights helps to guarantee the right to a fair trial.

▶ List and describe the ways that the Bill of Rights protects convicted criminals from excessive punishments.

MOTIVATE

At the end of the class period previous to this one, explain to students that they will be starting a new section about the Bill of Rights, and as part of the preparation for an activity each student needs to bring in an item that they feel symbolizes the freedoms and rights that are outlined in the Bill of Rights. (This will be hard to do and many students will probably not do it.)

As class begins ask students to get out the items they brought with them. Make note of those students who did not bring anything to class. Explain to students who failed to complete the required task that they will not only receive a failing grade on this assignment, but they will also receive a failing grade for the entire unit. State that make-up work will not be allowed and that there will be no further discussion on the subject.

After a brief pause reassure students that your tirade was merely an act, a way of introducing the new section. Ask students to respond how they felt when they were being punished. Ask whether they felt the punishment was fair or excessive. Explain that in this section students will learn how the Bill of Rights protects people from being treated unfairly during a trial and from excessive punishment.

TEACH

Building a Vocabulary

In their spiral notebooks, have each student continue working on their Political Dictionary. List words the students will be expected to know for this section on the chalkboard. Have students list, define, and give an example of each of the terms, using information provided in the text or on the *Researcher CD-ROM*.

Classifying Ideas/Information

Explain to students that the objective of this activity is to list and describe the specific amendments that establish the right to a fair trial and prohibit cruel and unusual punishment. Organize the class into four groups. Place a large piece of paper across the chalkboard or a wall. Draw vertical and horizontal lines to create a grid with four rows and four columns. Write the following headings at the top of the four columns: *Fifth Amendment, Sixth Amendment, Seventh Amendment,* and *Eighth Amendment.* Each group is assigned to fill in the four boxes in the column underneath each amendment. Each column should contain the following information: 1) an explanation of what rights the amendment guarantees; 2) important reasons why the amendment was adopted; 3) any restrictions or exceptions to these constitutional rights; and 4) examples of violations of the rights guaranteed by each amendment. After the grid is filled in completely discuss with students the explanations under each amendment. Then find a place to display it throughout the rest of the unit so students may use it as a reference guide. Tell students that they will learn about protections against cruel and unusual punishments in the next activity.

Judging Information/Making Decisions

Explain to students that the Constitution not only guarantees rights to those accused of committing crimes but also guarantees rights to those convicted of crimes. Have a student read aloud the Eighth Amendment. Organize the class into small groups. Ask groups to create their own definition of "cruel and unusual punishment" and share their ideas with the other groups. Have students consider various types of crimes when coming up with their definition of what would be cruel and unusual punishment for each type of crime. Lead a discussion about the difficulty each group had in coming up with a clear definition of excessive punishments. Ask students to consider some forms of punishment that were accepted many years ago but no longer exist today. Ask students to make a judgment as to whether forms of punishment are more or less cruel today than they were one or two hundred years ago. Explain to students that they will discuss the topic of capital punishment in the next lesson.

Conducting Research

 Introduce the topic of capital punishment in relation to the Eighth Amendment's protection from cruel and unusual punishment. Lead a discussion in which students express their viewpoints on the issue. Divide the class into small groups. Assign each group the task of researching a previous capital punishment case (a case in which the defendant was found guilty and was sentenced to death). To conduct their research, students may wish to refer to *In re Kemmler, Furman* v. *Georgia,* or *Gregg* v. *Georgia* located in the Supreme Court Docket section on the *Holt Researcher Online* or they may use other library resources. Each group should prepare a summary of the proceedings, including details about the crime and any special circumstances about the case, and elect a spokesperson to make a brief presentation to the class. After each group has made its presentation lead another discussion about the issue of capital punishment to discover whether students' viewpoints changed after listening to the presentations of past court cases.

CLOSE

Ask students to remember how they felt when they were being treated unfairly during the Motivate activity. Lead a class discussion about what might be done to prevent such treatment. Relate the classroom incident to the societal safeguards in the Bill of Rights that protect individuals from being denied a fair trial and from being punished excessively. Organize the class into small groups to brainstorm ideas about creating a bill of rights for the class. Allow each group 10 to 15 minutes to organize their ideas. Have students consider concepts from this section when creating their bill of rights. Make a list on the board of all of the ideas from each of the groups. Hold a class vote to come up with the 10 best proposals that the students wish to include in their bill of rights. List these rights on a piece of butcher paper or poster board to display in the classroom.

OPTIONS

Students Having Difficulty/ Musical-Rhythmic Learners

 Have students write a poem or a song that expresses the importance of ensuring fair trials and imposing fair punishment for crimes. Encourage students to emphasize the importance of societal values such as fairness and justice. Encourage students to share their poems with the class and to discuss their meaning.

Gifted Learners

 Discuss with students the right to a trial by jury. Explain to them that sometimes people accused of crimes waive their right to a jury trial and choose to have a judge hear their case, in hopes that a judge may be more lenient. Have students hypothesize why a person would want to do this and then conduct research for information that would support their hypothesis. Have students share their ideas and the support for their hypothesis with the rest of the class. Refer to the Themes in Government: Political Processes annotation in section 12.2 of the text to see if students have drawn a valid conclusion.

REVIEW

Have students complete the Section 3 Review on page 334. Use the answers in the Annotated Teacher's Edition to assess student mastery of this section.

ASSESS

To assess student mastery of this section, have students complete Daily Quiz 14.3 in *Daily Quizzes with Answer Key.* For additional assessment options, see *Alternative Assessment Handbook* on the *One-Stop Planner CD-ROM.*

RETEACH

For students having difficulty with the lessons, have them complete Reteaching Activity 3. This activity is located in *Reteaching Activities with Answer Key.*

ADDITIONAL RESOURCES

Garcia, Alfredo. *The Sixth Amendment in Modern American Jurisprudence: A Critical Perspective.* 1992. Greenwood Press.

Lewis, Anthony. *Gideon's Trumpet.* 1989 (reissue). Vintage.

For statistics regarding corrections. see:

http://silcom.com/~paladin/corrfaq.html

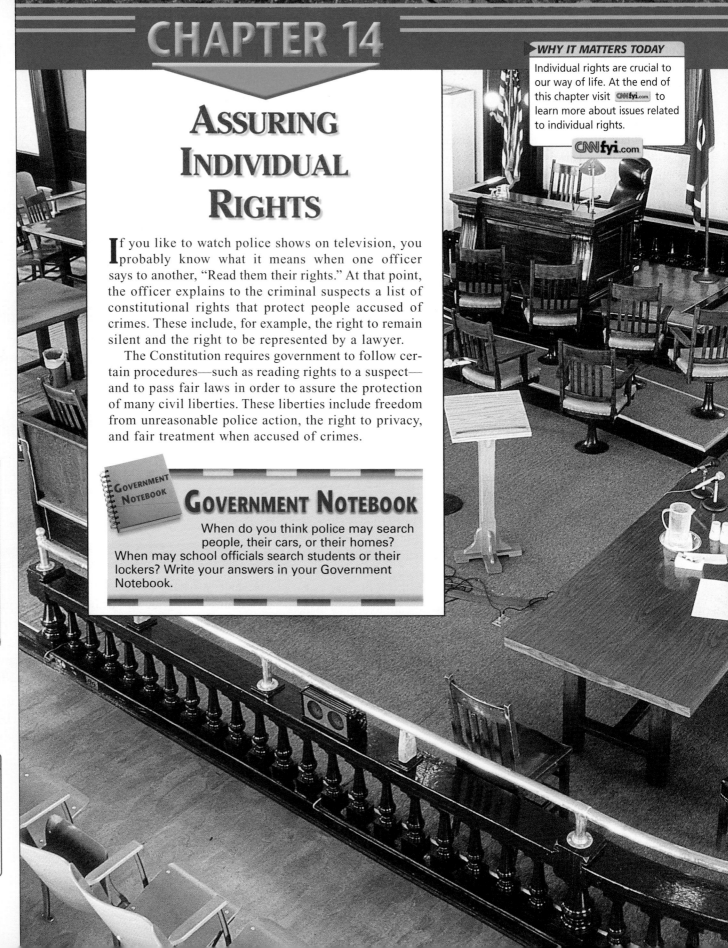

GOVERNMENT NOTEBOOK

The Government Notebook is a journal activity that encourages students to consider basic concepts of government that relate to their lives. A follow-up notebook activity appears on page 336.

WHY IT MATTERS TODAY

To find additional lesson plans dealing with individual rights, visit CNNfyi.com or have students complete the GOVERNMENT IN THE NEWS feature on page 335.

CNNfyi.com

ASSURING INDIVIDUAL RIGHTS

I f you like to watch police shows on television, you probably know what it means when one officer says to another, "Read them their rights." At that point, the officer explains to the criminal suspects a list of constitutional rights that protect people accused of crimes. These include, for example, the right to remain silent and the right to be represented by a lawyer.

The Constitution requires government to follow certain procedures—such as reading rights to a suspect—and to pass fair laws in order to assure the protection of many civil liberties. These liberties include freedom from unreasonable police action, the right to privacy, and fair treatment when accused of crimes.

GOVERNMENT NOTEBOOK

When do you think police may search people, their cars, or their homes? When may school officials search students or their lockers? Write your answers in your Government Notebook.

WHY IT MATTERS TODAY

Individual rights are crucial to our way of life. At the end of this chapter visit CNNfyi.com to learn more about issues related to individual rights.

CNNfyi.com

SECTION 1

PROTECTING INDIVIDUAL LIBERTIES

READ TO DISCOVER

1. What does the term due process mean?
2. How is procedural due process different from substantive due process?
3. How do the Fourth Amendment and due process protect people's security against unreasonable state action?
4. How does the Bill of Rights protect people's privacy?

POLITICAL DICTIONARY

due process
procedural due process
substantive due process
police power
search warrant
probable cause
exclusionary rule

As noted in Chapter 13, the First Amendment secures many of the fundamental freedoms that people living in the United States enjoy. Additional individual liberties are protected by other constitutional amendments. The Fifth Amendment, for example, is vital to securing citizens' basic liberties. It states that the federal government may not take away anyone's "life, liberty, or property, without due process of law." **Due process** refers to government's duty to follow fair procedures set by law when carrying out government functions.

Due Process of Law

How do the courts decide whether the government has acted with due process? The courts have recognized that the concept of due process can be broken down into two parts: procedural due process and substantive due process. The courts use both of these aspects of due process to determine whether government uses its police power reasonably.

Procedural Due Process According to the concept of **procedural due process**, government must apply a law fairly and act according to procedures and rules set by that law. As noted in Chapter 13, time, place, and manner regulations guide the holding of parades. These rules help government protect public safety and manage the use of public streets. A government that does not carry out these rules fairly and according to law has not acted with due process.

For example, suppose a group named Save Our City asks for a permit to hold a demonstration. The group wants to protest the city's lax pollution control laws. City officials, however, refuse to give the group a permit unless it agrees to hold its demonstration at 6:00 A.M. outside of the city limits—ensuring that few people will see the group's efforts. Save Our City responds by taking the city to court. The group argues that city

POLITICAL PROCESSES *Part of the responsibility of government is to carry out rules fairly and to keep the peace. Government must, however, practice procedural due process in performing these roles.* **How may government officials use their power to restrict people's freedom of speech and assembly?**

SECTION 1

PROTECTING INDIVIDUAL LIBERTIES

Lesson Plans
For teaching strategies, see Lesson 14.1 located at the beginning of this chapter.

Political Dictionary
To reinforce the section's vocabulary terms, refer students to the Electronic Glossary on the *Researcher CD-ROM.*

Section Assessment
To assess students' mastery of this section, have them complete Daily Quiz 14.1 in *Daily Quizzes with Answer Key.*

Caption Answer
They may impose time, place, and manner restrictions.

RESEARCHER ONLINE
go.
hrw.
.com

For more information
about *Gitlow* v. *New York*
and other Supreme Court
decisions, see the
Supreme Court Docket
section on the *Holt
Researcher Online.*

ACROSS THE CURRICULUM

HISTORY Substantive due
process has its origins in
English law. Magna Carta,
a document signed by
King John in 1215,
declared that no freeman
"shall be arrested, or
detained in prison, or
deprived of his freehold, or
outlawed, or banished, or
in any way molested . . .
unless by the lawful judgment of his peers and by
the law of the land."
Legal theorists argued
that this portion of Magna
Carta guaranteed the right
to fair treatment by the
government and created
substantive due process
because it limited the
authority of the Crown. In
1354 the phrase *law of the
land* was replaced in some
legal documents with the
term *due process*, which
became a standard part of
English law. ■

Caption Answer

Police may have to
restrict individual liberties in order to promote
and protect the health,
safety, and welfare of the
people.

---

officials have unfairly and unreasonably used their
authority to restrict the group members' freedom
of speech and assembly.

In this case, the court must determine whether
or not city officials have unfairly used the law's
procedures, perhaps to keep critics of the city's
pollution laws from being heard. If the city officials have unfairly administered the law, then they
have not acted with procedural due process.

Substantive Due Process The court also may
consider whether the city's time, place, and manner regulations are fair and reasonable in the first
place. In doing so, the court is applying a second
aspect of due process, referred to as **substantive
due process**. Applying substantive due process
involves considering whether or not a law is fair
and reasonable and whether or not it unjustly
restricts constitutional freedoms.

Applying substantive due process to the Save
Our City case means asking whether government
should be involved at all in deciding how groups
conduct demonstrations. As noted in Chapter 5,
government does have good reasons for establishing time, place, and manner regulations—for
example, the management of traffic flow and the
protection of public safety. Therefore, the court
would likely rule that the law on giving out parade permits has met the
standard of substantive due process.
Nevertheless, city officials still must
observe procedural due process by
applying the law fairly and reasonably.

Due Process
and the States

Originally, the Fifth Amendment's
Due Process Clause and the rest of
the Bill of Rights protected people
from federal government actions
only. The framers assumed that bills
of rights in state constitutions would
ensure that state governments did not
violate people's rights.

Just after the Civil War, however,
the Fifth Amendment's protections
were extended to state actions by
the Fourteenth Amendment. This
amendment sought to ensure the
rights of freed slaves by granting

---

them—as well as everyone else born or naturalized in the United States—U.S. citizenship and
hence the right of due process. Anticipating that
the southern states might refuse to recognize that
African Americans had the right to due process,
Congress added a provision declaring the states
may not "deprive any person of life, liberty, or
property, without due process of law."

In the 1925 case of *Gitlow* v. *New York,* the
Supreme Court issued the first in a series of rulings clearly stating that the freedoms in the Bill
of Rights are protected from the actions of both
the federal *and* state governments. The Court used
as its justification the Due Process Clause of the
Fourteenth Amendment.

Gitlow involved a man who had called for overthrowing the government. The Supreme Court
upheld New York State's right to punish the man
for breaking a law forbidding people from plotting such action. For the first time, however, the
Court also ruled that, in general, the First
Amendment does protect a person's right to free
speech from being violated by the states.
Following *Gitlow,* other Supreme Court rulings
firmly established that the states must respect the
fundamental freedoms guaranteed by the Bill
of Rights.

PUBLIC GOOD *Bailiffs of a superior court in Massachusetts escort
a prisoner into a courtroom for his trial.* **Why might the exercise of
police power restrict some individual liberties?**

Linking

Government and History

American Legal Traditions

You probably recall reading about certain court rulings in which judges helped justify their decisions by citing previous rulings. As noted in Chapter 12, judges often use this body of rulings to make decisions on situations for which no written laws exist. This so-called common law constitutes an important part of the legal systems not only in Great Britain but also in many of its former colonies, including Canada, Australia, and New Zealand. Common law also plays a significant role throughout all of the United States except Louisiana.

Because its early settlers were French, Louisiana's legal system developed from French civil law. The French civil law system, known as the Code Napoleon, developed during the early 1800s. At that time, French emperor Napoléon Bonaparte combined France's civil laws into one code that joined the traditional law of northern France, the Roman-influenced law of southern France, and newer ideas that had emerged during the French Revolution. By replacing France's regional statutes, the Code Napoleon became that country's first national body of law.

In England, common law evolved over centuries, beginning in the 1100s with the monarch's royal courts. Judges and lawyers recorded the cases at first in annual reports and later in ongoing records. New court decisions were then bound by those made previously. The decisions that were cited in new cases soon became known as common, because of their widespread impact. Thus, the English courts are called common-law courts.

Common-law courts were not the only source of justice available to citizens. English citizens also were able to petition the monarch for justice. If citizens felt that they would not receive a fair decision in a common-law court, for example, they might ask the monarch to intervene. He or she often assigned the job of hearing petitions to the lord chancellor, England's highest legal

The use of common law to determine rulings on cases for which no written law exists was adopted by many of Great Britain's former colonies, including the United States.

authority. Eventually, courts of equity were established in the 1300s to hear cases not addressed by common law. These courts, which chancellors administered, added flexibility to the common-law system.

Sometimes the two systems came into conflict, as when a chancellor declared a common-law ruling unfair or inappropriate and refused to enforce it. In an attempt to solve the problem, King James I declared that equity rule was superior to common law. However, equity and common law eventually merged in 1873 to form one legal system.

The system of common law was transported to the English colonies in America by the colonists and later spread to the individual states. Each state (except Louisiana) developed its own version of common law to deal with its own cases. Over time, however, much of what was once common law has been made into statutory law. Common law and equity law, which also came to America with the colonists, began to merge in most legal systems throughout the United States in 1848.

What Do You Think?

1. Imagine that you are a lawyer preparing a court case. Why is knowledge of common law important to your preparation?
2. Should judges always consider previous rulings in deciding a court case? Why or why not?

internet connect

TOPIC: Civil Liberties Chronology
GO TO: go.hrw.com
KEYWORD: SV3 GV14

Have students access the Internet through the HRW Go site to conduct research on Supreme Court cases involving civil liberties. Then have students create annotated time lines that show a chronology of legal decisions regarding due process, searches and seizure, the rights of the accused, and fair trials and punishments.

Enhancing
the Lesson

RESEARCHER ONLINE
go.
hrw
.com

For more information about *Mapp* v. *Ohio* and other Supreme Court decisions, see the Supreme Court Docket section on the *Holt Researcher Online.*

THEMES IN GOVERNMENT

PUBLIC GOOD Critics charge that the exclusionary rule allows criminals to go free merely because law enforcement officials make honest mistakes in their efforts to apprehend those who violate the law. A study in California, however, revealed that the number of suspects not prosecuted because of the exclusionary rule was quite small. Researchers concluded that less than 1 percent of felony prosecutions in California were dropped because of exclusionary rule violations. In violent crimes the number of cases dropped in California was 1 in 2,500, suggesting that the protection of constitutional rights provided by the exclusionary rule is not contributing to violent crime. ■

Caption Answer

because a car can be driven away, giving a person the chance to destroy evidence

In short, the due process clause limits the government's **police power**—or its authority to promote and to protect the health, safety, and welfare of the people. This power is exercised primarily by state and local governments.

Exercising police power, such as fighting crime, often restricts some individual liberties. To fight crime, police may, for example—if following proper procedures—enter homes or limit people's freedom by jailing them. To prevent abuse of police power, the Constitution requires government to act within the framework of the Bill of Rights.

Protecting People from Government Intrusion

The Constitution further protects individual liberties by protecting people from government intrusion. The Fourth Amendment guarantees "the right of people to be secure in their persons, houses, papers, and effects, against unreasonable searches and seizures." In other words, government cannot use its police power in ways that unjustly subject citizens to government interference.

PUBLIC GOOD *Police officers may search people's personal possessions, including their vehicles, if they have probable cause to do so.* **Why are police not required to obtain a warrant to search a car?**

Security at Home The Fourth Amendment requires authorities to respect the security of private homes. This means, for example, that police must follow set rules in entering and searching homes and in seizing any contents for use as evidence in a criminal trial. One of these rules states that, except under certain circumstances, police cannot search a home without first obtaining a written order from a judge. This **search warrant** allows police to enter a home or other private property to search for specific items.

Before a judge will issue a search warrant, police must show that they have reasonable grounds, or **probable cause**, for requesting one. If, for example, a police officer sees someone deal drugs and then enter a certain home, or has information from a reliable source that the home contains illegal drugs, that officer has probable cause to request a warrant to search for illegal drugs.

Authorities do sometimes enter a private home without a warrant and seize items as evidence for a criminal case. In such instances, however, judges typically rule that the evidence is tainted, or illegally obtained. Under what is referred to as the **exclusionary rule**, tainted evidence—no matter how strong—is barred from use in court. In the 1961 case *Mapp* v. *Ohio,* the Supreme Court extended the exclusionary rule to state trials.

Since the early 1970s, however, the Supreme Court has identified some exceptions to the exclusionary rule. Tainted evidence may be used in a trial if, for example, a police officer, acting in "good faith," obtained a search warrant that turns out to be invalid. The Court also has ruled that tainted evidence that could have been legally obtained anyway can be used in court.

In addition, the Court has ruled that police do not need to obtain search warrants in certain cases. For example, police do not need a warrant to search through garbage that people have placed outside their home for trash collection. Police also may seize evidence that is "in plain view" even if it is not listed in the search warrant used to enter the home.

CASE STUDY

Gun Control

CONSTITUTIONAL GOVERNMENT One of the most debated issues of constitutional interpretation comes from the Second Amendment, which states that "a well-regulated militia, being necessary to the security of a free state, the right of the people to keep and bear arms, shall not be infringed." Many Americans believe that the amendment supports their right to own firearms to protect their homes or engage in the sport of hunting. Many other Americans feel that firearms are dangerous and need to be restricted.

In 1993 Congress passed the fiercely debated Brady gun control law, which requires a five-day waiting period for buying handguns, and gives local authorities time to determine if a buyer has committed a felony and is thus prohibited from buying a gun. Recently, the Supreme Court ruled that gun legislation should be enforced by the states and not the federal courts, thereby modifying parts of the Brady bill.

Of special concern to most Americans are the threats that firearms pose to young people. In 1996, Missouri school officials discovered 341 students with guns at school. They were found in lockers, backpacks, or hidden in clothing. In order to curtail this problem, Jay Nixon, the attorney general of Missouri, proposed legislation to ban guns within 1000 feet of public schools. Nixon believed the ban would discourage guns in school, proving that guns would not be tolerated on school property.

Across the country in 1997, firearms took the lives of 8,657 young people between the ages of five and 24. The nation was horrified two years later when two students murdered 12 of their classmates and one teacher at Columbine High School in Littleton, Colorado. During the aftershocks of this event, debates over gun control raged amongst parents, politicians, and young people alike.

Many proposals for gun control were aimed at safety measures to ensure that firearms would only be used by responsible adults, while continuing to respect the rights of those who would use guns for sport and personal protection. Gun control advocacy has risen ever since John Hinckley's attempted assassination of President Reagan. James Brady, injured in the attempt, inspired and lobbied for the 1993 Brady bill. Overall, as of 1999, accidental deaths caused by firearms had declined every year since 1993.

CONSTITUTIONAL GOVERNMENT *State and federal laws regulate the sale and ownership of firearms. **How do some people use the Second Amendment to argue that government should not restrict citizens' right to own firearms?***

Personal Security The Fourth Amendment prevents police from conducting unreasonable searches of people and their possessions. The Supreme Court has ruled, for example, that police cannot stop people in public and search them unless the officers involved have reason to think that the suspects are armed or dangerous. On the other hand, the Court

Caption Answer
by pointing to the passage that says the people's right to "bear arms, shall not be infringed"

Enhancing the Lesson

For more information about *United States* v. *Miller* and other Supreme Court decisions, see the Supreme Court Docket section on the *Holt Researcher Online.*

GLOBAL CONNECTIONS

British gun control laws are much stricter than U.S. laws. Under the Criminal Justice Act of 1967, anyone wanting to purchase a shotgun must obtain a shotgun certificate from the local police certifying that the applicant has no criminal record or history of mental illness.

Gun purchasers must list on a firearms certificate a reason for owning a firearm. Certificates for rifle purchase often specify where a person can hunt. As a result of these strict laws, there are far fewer handguns in Great Britain than in the United States, and the use of handguns in crimes is also much lower there. Most British handgun owners use their weapons only in target-shooting clubs. ■

Enhancing the Lesson

For more information about *Olmstead* v. *United States, New Jersey* v. *T.L.O.,* and other Supreme Court decisions, see the Supreme Court Docket section on the *Holt Researcher Online.*

THEMES IN GOVERNMENT

POLITICAL PROCESSES

Prior to the Supreme Court ruling in *New Jersey* v. *T.L.O.,* the doctrine of *in loco parentis* was used to determine the legal authority of school officials in regard to students attending school. This doctrine recognized school officials as taking the place of students' parents while students were in school. Thus, school officials had the rights and responsibilities of parents, including the duty to protect the health and safety of the students.

In the case of *New Jersey* v. *T.L.O.,* the Supreme Court ruled that school officials acted as representatives of the state, not as parents. Nonetheless, the Court argued that students' Fourth Amendment protections are not clearly defined. ■

"There are indications that little Tommy is being naughty.
But not enough for me to authorize a wiretap."

PRINCIPLES OF DEMOCRACY *Protections outlined by the Fourth Amendment limit the way in which government can intrude on individual liberties. **What must police do in order to tap a telephone?***

has allowed employers to require workers to submit to drug testing, considering it a reasonable way to protect public health and safety.

The Supreme Court has allowed police greater leeway in conducting searches of people's personal possessions—including cars, boats, and other vehicles—than in searching homes. A police officer may, for example, search a car without a warrant if he or she has probable cause to believe it contains illegal drugs or weapons. The Court recognizes that because a car can be driven away, delaying a search until a warrant is obtained might give a suspect the opportunity to destroy or get rid of evidence.

Police also may stop drivers at random to check whether they are intoxicated. The Supreme Court has allowed such checkpoints because it considers their use a reasonable way to protect public safety from the dangers posed by drunk drivers.

Security and Private Communication Fourth
Amendment protections have been extended to private communications between people. Listening to private conversations is considered a form of search

and seizure. One way that police may "seize" private telephone conversations is through the use of electronic devices known as wiretaps. Are there circumstances under which the use of these devices violates Fourth Amendment rights?

In 1928 the Supreme Court ruled that law enforcement authorities could use wiretaps to listen to private telephone conversations without search warrants. In that case, *Olmstead* v. *United States,* the Court stated that wiretapping was not a form of illegal search and seizure because it did not involve breaking into a private home.

Later, the increased number and sophistication of such devices led the Supreme Court to change direction on this issue. In 1967 the Court ruled that authorities cannot listen to private telephone conversations without first obtaining a warrant. In addition, Congress has passed laws against using electronic devices to listen to private conversations without a warrant.

Student Rights Fewer restrictions apply to authorities searching students or their possessions. In 1985, for example, the Supreme Court ruled that school officials did not need a warrant to search students' possessions. The case of *New Jersey* v. *T.L.O.* involved a 14-year-old New Jersey student who school officials believed had broken school rules on smoking. An official searched the student's purse and found marijuana, along with evidence indicating that she had smoked and sold some of it.

The Supreme Court ruled that school officials had acted properly to guard students' health and safety and to keep order. To conduct searches of students or their possessions the Court said, school officials need only "reasonable" grounds to suspect a student has broken the law or school rules.

Protecting the Right to Privacy

The Constitution does not specifically address the issue of privacy. The courts, however, have deter-

CONSTITUTIONAL GOVERNMENT *Supreme Court justice Louis Brandeis argued that the Court should not allow the government to wiretap people's telephones without a warrant.* **What controversial 1973 Court decision centered around a woman's right to privacy?**

mined that the Bill of Rights provides a right of privacy against the government's police power. In 1928 Supreme Court justice Louis Brandeis, writing for the minority, argued that the Court was wrong to allow government to wiretap telephones without a

warrant. The framers, Brandeis wrote, "sought to protect Americans in their beliefs, their thoughts, their emotions and their sensations." In doing so, he said, the framers recognized the people's "right to be let alone—the most comprehensive of rights and the right most valued by civilized men."

Some 37 years later, in the *Griswold* v. *Connecticut* case, the Supreme Court agreed with Brandeis's view by ruling that the Constitution does guarantee a right of privacy. The 1965 case involved a state law that prohibited the use and promotion of birth control devices. The Court said that such laws violated a married couple's "zone of privacy created by several fundamental constitutional guarantees."

Some judges and constitutional scholars argue that the right to privacy does not exist because it is not specifically mentioned in the Constitution. These opposing views about the right to privacy have played a leading role in the bitter controversy over abortion. In 1973 the Supreme Court ruled in *Roe* v. *Wade* that laws restricting a woman's freedom to have an abortion in the first three months of pregnancy violate her right to privacy. Many people strongly oppose the Court's ruling in *Roe* and argue that government should ban abortion.

Over time the Court has revisited the abortion issue, and since 1989 has allowed state governments to place certain restrictions on the right to have an abortion. One such restriction prevents unmarried females under the age of 18 from having an abortion without the approval of their parents or a judge.

SECTION 1 REVIEW

1. Identify and Explain:
- due process
- procedural due process
- substantive due process
- police power
- search warrant
- probable cause
- exclusionary rule

2. Identifying Concepts: Copy the graphic organizer below. Use it to describe procedural and substantive due process.

Procedural — Due Process — Substantive

Homework Practice Online
keyword: SV3 HP14

3. **Finding the Main Idea**
- **a.** What protections does the Fourth Amendment guarantee?
- **b.** How did the 1965 Supreme Court case *Griswold* v. *Connecticut* affect the right to privacy?

4. **Writing and Critical Thinking**

Supporting a Point of View: The right to privacy is not specifically guaranteed in the Constitution. Do you think it should be? Explain your answer.
Consider the following:
- the intentions of the framers of the Constitution
- past and present political debates over privacy

SECTION 1 REVIEW ANSWERS

1. Refer to the following pages: due process (319), procedural due process (319), substantive due process (320), police power (322), search warrant (322), probable cause (322), exclusionary rule (322)

2. procedural due process: governments apply laws fairly; substantive due process: a law is formulated fairly

3a. by forcing authorities to show probable cause to obtain a search warrant, the Fourth Amendment protects citizens from unjust government interference

3b. It determined that the Constitution established a "zone of privacy."

4. Answers will vary. Students should take a position regarding a constitutional right to privacy and offer supporting arguments for it.

SECTION 2

RIGHTS OF
THE ACCUSED

Lesson Plans
For teaching strategies, see Lesson 14.2 located at the beginning of this chapter.

Political Dictionary

To reinforce the section's vocabulary terms, refer students to the Electronic Glossary on the *Researcher CD-ROM.*

Section Assessment
To assess students' mastery of this section, have them complete Daily Quiz 14.2 in *Daily Quizzes with Answer Key.*

Transparency
An overhead transparency of the chart on this page is available in *Transparency Resources.* See Transparency 29: Constitutional Protections for Those Accused of Crimes.

Caption Answer

It is important so that force cannot be used to gain a confession.

SECTION 2

RIGHTS OF
THE ACCUSED

READ TO DISCOVER

1. How does the Constitution protect the right of *habeas corpus* and protect against bills of attainder and *ex post facto* laws?
2. How do requirements for bringing charges before grand juries protect the rights of people accused of crimes?
3. How does the Fifth Amendment protect against self-incrimination?

POLITICAL DICTIONARY

presentment
Miranda Rule

As you have learned, the government uses its police power to prevent crime and to arrest people who break the law. Even though these actions are needed to protect the public, the use of police power must not violate the constitutional rights of people who are accused of crimes. Upholding accused people's rights may make it harder at times for government to bring about justice. These rights, however, reflect the framers' desire to protect innocent people from being wrongly convicted of crimes.

Writ of *Habeas Corpus*

The Constitution states that authorities cannot hold a person in jail without showing good reasons for doing so. Specifically, accused people have a right to a writ of *habeas corpus*. As noted in Chapter 5, this writ is a court order that requires police to bring a person accused of a crime to court and to show good reasons for keeping him or her in jail. (*Habeas corpus* is a Latin term meaning "you have the body.") The right to a writ of *habeas corpus* is guaranteed by Article I, Section 9, of the Constitution.

The Constitution allows the federal government to suspend the right to *habeas corpus* only "when in cases of rebellion or invasion the public safety may require it." President Abraham Lincoln believed such a case existed when he suspended the right during the Civil War. Lincoln took it upon himself to suspend *habeas corpus,* even though the Constitution lists that power in Article I, which deals with the powers of Congress. Despite some opposition to Lincoln's action, Congress approved it in an 1863 law. In 1866, however, the Supreme Court ruled in *Ex parte Milligan* that Lincoln and Congress had acted improperly and that neither had the power to suspend *habeas corpus* in areas that were not

Constitutional Protections for Those Accused of Crimes

1. **Writ of *habeas corpus*** Police must appear in court with the accused and show good reason to keep him or her in jail.

2. **Bill of attainder** The government may not pass laws directed at specific individuals.

3. ***Ex post facto* laws** The government may not pass laws that punish people for actions that were legal when they took place.

4. **Grand jury** A person accused of a federal crime must be brought before a panel of citizens who decide if the government has enough evidence to try him or her on formal charges.

5. **Self-incrimination** An accused person cannot be forced to provide evidence to support a criminal charge against himself or herself.

*The Constitution outlines specific protections for people accused of crimes. These protections make it more difficult for the government to wrongly convict innocent people. **Why is it important that accused people be protected against self-incrimination?***

in open rebellion and in which civilian courts still functioned.

Bills of Attainder

As noted in Chapter 5, the Constitution also states in Article I, Sections 9 and 10, that neither Congress nor a state government can pass bills of attainder, or laws that are directed against a specific person. The Supreme Court has ruled that a law can be considered a bill of attainder even if it prescribes a form of punishment other than imprisonment. In the 1946 case *United States* v. *Lovett,* the Court overturned a congressional act that prohibited three specified federal government employees from collecting a salary. The men had been suspected of having political beliefs that many people considered harmful to the United States. The Court ruled that the law punished the men by withholding their salaries even though they had not been found guilty of a crime. The law was thus found to be an unconstitutional bill of attainder.

Ex Post Facto Laws

The Constitution also prohibits authorities from punishing people for actions that were legal at the time they took place. As noted in Chapter 5, the Constitution states in Article I, Sections 9 and 10, that the federal and state governments cannot pass *ex post facto* laws, or laws that apply to actions that took place before those laws were passed. For example, government may not pass a law today that outlaws buying foreign automobiles and then punish people who bought a foreign car yesterday. The prohibition against *ex post facto* laws applies only to laws that may impose punishment or other penalties.

Grand Juries

The Fifth Amendment protects the rights of all people accused of federal crimes by requiring that their case be brought before a grand jury. As noted in Chapter 12, a grand jury is a panel of citizens who decide if the government has enough evidence to try an accused person.

In a grand jury proceeding the attorney for the government presents its case against the accused. If the grand jury agrees that the government has enough evidence to support its case, it may return

a "true bill of indictment" that calls for a trial. If the government's evidence does not satisfy the grand jury, the accused person is not sent to trial and can no longer be kept in police custody.

Less often, a grand jury will decide to conduct its own investigation rather than accept evidence from a government attorney. If the grand jury believes its own investigation has found sufficient information to send an accused person to trial, it may issue a **presentment**, or formal report authorizing a trial.

The Fifth Amendment's requirement for a grand jury applies only in federal cases, although some states do have their own grand juries to consider cases against people accused of state crimes. In other state cases, however, no grand jury is convened. Lawyers for the state simply bring formal charges in what is called an information. As noted in Chapter 12, an information is an affidavit, or sworn statement, in which the state's lawyer declares that there is sufficient evidence against the accused to justify trying the case.

Self-Incrimination

The Fifth Amendment also protects against self-incrimination, stating that people accused of crimes cannot be forced to provide evidence against themselves. Thus, accused people may legally refuse to testify at their own trials if such testimony might incriminate them. They also cannot be forced to incriminate themselves when being questioned by law enforcement officials. The 1936 case *Brown* v. *Mississippi,* for example, involved an incident in which police had tortured a suspect to force a confession. The Supreme Court ruling in the case stated that police may not physically force a criminal suspect to confess to a crime. Other cases have established that police may not threaten people or use other methods to force them to incriminate themselves.

The Supreme Court also has ruled that police must inform criminal suspects of their right to refuse to answer questions. This requirement—known as the **Miranda Rule**—stems from the 1966 case *Miranda* v. *Arizona.* The case involved Ernesto Miranda, who, after two hours of police questioning, confessed to kidnapping and raping a woman. The Court ruled that his confession could not be used in a trial because the police had not effectively advised him of his rights to remain silent and to consult with a lawyer. The Court also determined

Enhancing the Lesson

For more information about *United States* v. *Lovett, Brown* v. *Mississippi, Miranda* v. *Arizona,* and other Supreme Court decisions, see the Supreme Court Docket section on the *Holt Researcher Online.*

🖃 **internet** connect

TOPIC: Grand Juries
GO TO: go.hrw.com
KEYWORD: SV3 GV14

Have students access the Internet through the HRW Go site to find information on the grand jury system and how it functions. Ask students to use the information to create a multimedia display or 3D model that explains the process and function of grand juries.

SECTION 2 REVIEW ANSWERS

1. Refer to the following pages: presentment (327), Miranda Rule (327).

2. Students might suggest that the writ of *habeas corpus* demands that the United States show good reason for holding people in custody; the Miranda rights ensure that suspects will not be forced into false confessions.

3a. Refer to the chart on this page. The Miranda rights ensure that police inform criminal suspects of their right not to answer questions.

3b. that there is sufficient evidence to take the case to trial.

4. Answers will vary. Students might suggest that people are innocent until proven guilty, and that certain rights are necessary to ensure a fair trial.

Miranda Rights

Before asking you any questions, it is my duty to advise you of your rights:

1. You have the right to remain silent.

2. If you choose to speak, anything you say may be used against you in a court of law or other proceeding.

3. You have the right to speak with an attorney before answering any questions, and you may have an attorney present with you during questioning.

4. If you cannot afford an attorney and you want one, an attorney will be provided for you free of charge.

5. Do you understand what I have told you?

6. You may also waive the right to counsel and your right to remain silent, and you may answer any question or make any statement you wish. If you decide to answer questions, you may stop at any time to consult with an attorney.

PUBLIC GOOD *Criminal suspects who are arrested must be informed of their Miranda rights before police may question them.* **Why do you think the Supreme Court believed that suspects should be informed of their right to an attorney?**

that police should have informed Miranda that a lawyer would be provided for him if he could not afford one and that anything he said could be used against him in court.

Today police across the country inform criminal suspects of their "Miranda rights" before questioning them. Suspects, however, may decide to give up these rights and answer police questions. The statements that criminal suspects then freely make, even confessions, may be used against them in court.

Critics of the Miranda Rule have argued that the requirement ties the hands of police officers by making it harder for them to carry out their duties. These critics also argue that some people who are guilty of crimes are released from jail simply because a police officer did not properly inform the accused person of his or her rights to silence and to a lawyer.

Supporters of the Miranda Rule, however, say that it protects innocent people from being tricked or brutally forced into confessing to crimes they did not commit. Although over time the Supreme Court has allowed some exceptions to the Miranda Rule, the Court has generally supported the principle that accused people cannot be guaranteed their rights without being informed of them by police.

Note that protections against self-incrimination do not allow criminal suspects to refuse to be fingerprinted and photographed, to participate in a police lineup, or to submit to blood and other tests commonly used in an investigation. These are all considered proper parts of the evidence-gathering process.

SECTION 2 REVIEW

1. Identify and Explain:
- presentment
- Miranda Rule

2. Identifying Concepts: Copy the graphic organizer below. Use it to explain different ways the rights of the accused are protected.

Protecting the Rights of the Accused	

3. Finding the Main Idea

a. What are the Miranda rights? What do they ensure?

b. What must the government prove when taking a case before the grand jury?

4. Writing and Critical Thinking

Drawing Conclusions: Why is it important that certain rights be extended to people accused of crimes? Write an essay explaining your answer.
Consider the following:
- why the rights of the accused are protected
- the notion that people are innocent until proven guilty

Homework Practice Online
keyword: SV3 HP14

SECTION 3

ENSURING FAIR TRIALS AND PUNISHMENTS

READ TO DISCOVER

1. Which amendments of the Bill of Rights help guarantee the right to a fair trial?
2. In what ways does the Bill of Rights protect convicted criminals from excessive punishments?

POLITICAL DICTIONARY

change of venue
bench trial
double jeopardy

As noted in Section 2, the Constitution requires government to respect the rights of the accused during investigations. Similarly, government must respect a person's right to a fair trial and must act fairly when punishing people convicted of crimes.

The Right to a Fair Trial

What provisions of the Constitution regarding a fair trial must the government respect? The Fifth, Sixth, Seventh, and Eighth Amendments together establish the following: the right to a speedy and public trial, the right to trial by jury, the right to an adequate defense, and restrictions on trying a person twice for the same crime.

Speedy Trial The Sixth Amendment guarantees the right to a speedy trial. This means that the period of time between the filing of formal charges and the start of a trial must be reasonable. Starting a trial as soon as possible keeps an accused person who cannot or will not post bail from being held in jail for an unnecessarily long period of time. Speedy trials also reduce the

chance that evidence may be lost and that witnesses may forget what they saw or heard.

Sometimes long delays are unavoidable, however. In some cases the accused person's attorney may ask for a delay to prepare a more thorough defense. Sometimes a court already has a full docket, or schedule, which delays starting a trial.

As noted in Chapter 12, judges may allow an accused person to be released on bail while awaiting trial, and the Eighth Amendment keeps judges from setting excessive bails. Defining *excessive* is difficult. In general, the courts have said that an excessive bail is one greater than is necessary to assure the appearance of the accused person in court. After the trial begins, the bail money is returned.

Public Trial The Sixth Amendment also guarantees the right to a public trial. Public trials help prevent abuses of the law by allowing the public to witness, or check on, the proceedings. Even though judges may keep some people out of the courtroom to maintain order and to ensure that witnesses and the jury are not influenced unfairly, they may not keep members of the general public from attending the trial.

CONSTITUTIONAL GOVERNMENT *In accordance with the protections specified in the Sixth Amendment, members of the general public are allowed to attend trials.* ***How do public trials help prevent abuses of the law?***

SECTION 3

ENSURING FAIR TRIALS AND PUNISHMENTS

Lesson Plans

For teaching strategies, see Lesson 14.3 located at the beginning of this chapter.

Political Dictionary

To reinforce the section's vocabulary terms, refer students to the Electronic Glossary on the *Researcher CD-ROM.*

Section Assessment

To assess students' mastery of this section, have them complete Daily Quiz 14.3 in *Daily Quizzes with Answer Key.*

Caption Answer

They help to prevent abuses of the law by allowing the public to witness the proceedings.

Public trials also function as a kind of laboratory for citizens to see how the justice system works. Indeed, much of the media use this argument to justify their presence in the courtroom.

A current debate involving the media centers on whether or not the courts should allow trials to be televised. Federal court proceedings are not televised, but television cameras are allowed in courtrooms in 47 states. One of the most famous televised trials took place in 1995, when a California jury found former football star O. J. Simpson not guilty of murder charges. Millions of people watched the trial on cable and broadcast television.

The extensive and sensational media coverage of the Simpson trial spurred the debate over television cameras in the courtroom. Journalists argued that the public had a right to view the court proceedings. Opponents argued that allowing the media into the courtroom enabled reporters to sensationalize the case and influenced the conduct of the trial. To prevent the trial's massive media coverage from influencing members of the jury, the judge ordered that jury members be sequestered in a hotel when they were not in the courtroom. For these reasons, many people argued that television cameras should be kept out of courtrooms in the future.

PUBLIC GOOD *News media outside the Los Angeles courthouse await the verdict at the O. J. Simpson trial.* **How did the media coverage of the Simpson trial change the way that many people feel about having television cameras in a courtroom?**

Comparing Governments

The Right to a Speedy Trial

Imagine spending eight long months in prison while waiting to stand trial for a crime you did not commit. Fortunately, the U.S. Constitution is designed to protect people from such an ordeal. In France, however, where the right to a speedy trial is not constitutionally guaranteed, prisoners endure an average of nearly eight months behind bars while awaiting trial.

For serious crimes, officials can hold a suspect for an unlimited period if he or she is considered a flight risk or a threat of some kind. With 35 percent of its 51,000 prisoners currently awaiting trial, France has one of the highest rates of pretrial imprisonment in Europe.

Trial by Jury As you have learned, the Constitution prevents the government from finding someone guilty of a crime without due process of law. One element of due process is the right to a trial by an impartial jury. The Sixth Amendment and Seventh Amendment—as well as Article III, Section 2, of the Constitution—all guarantee the right to a trial by jury.

As noted in Chapter 12, a trial jury, or petit jury, usually is made up of 12 people. The trial must be held in the district in which the crime was committed, and the panel of jurors must represent a fair cross-section of the community. To make sure that juries are representative, jurors are chosen at random from lists of registered voters or other such official lists. The Supreme Court has ruled that people cannot be kept off a jury based on their race, sex, economic status, national origin, or religion.

Accused people who believe that they cannot receive a fair trial in the community where the crime took place may ask for a **change of venue**, or that their trial be moved to another location. For example, a trial might be moved if media coverage of the crime has biased potential local jurors against the defendant. Such an instance occurred with the trial of Timothy McVeigh, who was accused of bombing a government building in

Oklahoma City. McVeigh's trial was moved to Denver, Colorado.

Federal cases must be decided by unanimous verdicts. A few states, however, allow most criminal cases to be decided by less than a unanimous vote of jurors. In cases involving disputes over civil laws, many states allow jurors to reach a verdict with a less-than-unanimous vote, usually two thirds or three fourths.

An accused person may give up the right to a trial by jury in favor of a **bench trial**, in which a judge decides the case. Judges, however, may refuse to grant requests for a bench trial.

CONSTITUTIONAL GOVERNMENT *People accused of a crime have the right to be represented by a lawyer.* **What did the Supreme Court say in Gideon v. Wainwright about this right?**

Adequate Defense

The Sixth Amendment guarantees defendants the right to an adequate defense. This means that people accused of crimes have the right to

★ be informed of the charges against them,
★ question witnesses against them in court,
★ present their own witnesses in court, and
★ be represented by counsel—a lawyer.

In 1932 the Supreme Court ruled that the last right listed—the right to counsel—was so critical that in cases involving capital offenses, or crimes punishable by death, the government must appoint lawyers for people who cannot afford them. The Court said that without a lawyer, even an innocent person "faces the danger of conviction because he does not know how to establish his innocence." In 1938 the Supreme Court ruled that in all federal cases, the government must provide a lawyer for people who cannot afford to hire one.

Then, in the 1963 case *Gideon* v. *Wainwright,* the Supreme Court issued a landmark ruling regarding the right to counsel in state courts. The case involved a man named Clarence Gideon, who had been convicted in a Florida court of breaking into a pool hall with the intent to commit a misdemeanor. At his trial, Gideon claimed that he was too poor to afford an attorney and requested that one be provided. The judge refused, and Gideon was convicted.

While serving a five-year sentence in a Florida state prison, Gideon mailed a petition about his case, written on borrowed paper, to the Supreme Court. The Supreme Court agreed to hear his case, and there Gideon argued that the state of Florida had violated his Sixth Amendment right to counsel by not providing him with a lawyer.

The Supreme Court agreed. Speaking for the Court, Justice Hugo Black wrote that "any person [hauled] into court, who is too poor to hire a lawyer, cannot be assured a fair trial unless counsel is provided for him. This seems to us to be an obvious truth." The Court ruled that in federal and state criminal cases involving serious crimes, the court must appoint a lawyer to represent an accused person who cannot afford one. Gideon later was found not guilty in a new trial in which he was represented by a state-appointed lawyer.

In 1972 the Supreme Court extended the right to counsel even further. It ruled that an accused person cannot be sent to jail for any offense unless he or she has either been represented by counsel or voluntarily given up that right. This ruling covers all cases that could involve imprisonment, no matter how minor the crime.

Double Jeopardy

The Fifth Amendment provides protection against **double jeopardy**, or

Enhancing the Lesson

For more information on *Gideon* v. *Wainwright* and other Supreme Court decisions, see the Supreme Court Docket section on the *Holt Researcher Online.*

CULTURAL PERSPECTIVES

Although the right to adequate legal defense applies to American Indians who live on reservations, many tribes have instituted laws regarding who may serve as an attorney in a tribal court.

Some tribes contend that the adversarial behavior and attitudes that mark courtroom proceedings conflict with their tribal heritage. The Navajo require that any attorney appearing before one of their courts must be admitted to practice according to the tribe's regulations. Other tribes permit only their members to appear as attorneys in their courts. These restrictions have survived tests in federal court and serve as an example of differing perspectives regarding the practice of law in the United States. ■

To help students learn about other careers in government, refer them to the Careers section on the *Holt Researcher Online.*

POLITICAL PROCESSES

Double jeopardy does not prevent an accused person from being tried with the same evidence. In recent years a number of cases have been tried in federal courts after state courts have found the defendant not guilty. Using federal civil rights laws, prosecutors have charged the accused with violating the civil rights of the people they were alleged to have attacked. A recent example is that of O. J. Simpson, who was found not guilty of murder in a California court only to be found liable in a federal court for the deaths of Nicole Brown Simpson and Ron Goldman.

The case involved a total of three legal actions, a wrongful death suit (which was filed by the Goldmans and called for compensatory damages) and two survivorship suits (which were filed by the Goldmans and the Browns and which called for punitive damages). The jury awarded the Goldman family $8.5 million in compensatory damages and $12.5 million in punitive damages. The family of Nicole Brown Simpson was also awarded $12.5 million in punitive damages. ■

Careers in Government

Court Reporter

No television courtroom drama would be complete without the prominently placed court reporter, whose fast-paced typing provides a constant accompaniment to the court proceedings. In real life as well, the court reporter—like the judge and jury—is a standard fixture in the U.S. courtroom. The job of the court reporter, or court stenographer, is to record the court's proceedings word for word, usually using abbreviations and other shorthand techniques. As the court reporter types, the

Court reporters use abbreviations and other shorthand techniques to record court proceedings.

steno machine—which allows words to be typed with only one stroke rather than several—spits out a steady stream of symbol-covered paper that resembles cash register tape.

By the end of the much-publicized O. J. Simpson trial, two court reporters—now almost celebrities as well—typed an estimated 3 million words, or 30,000 pages, of court transcripts.

Today's court reporters take advantage of the latest technology. Keyboards are often linked to a computer system that gives judges and lawyers an immediate transcript of the proceedings, and allows the court reporter to communicate with them without interrupting the trial.

Simpson-trial court reporter Christine Olson became interested in court reporting as a high school senior. "I could type 100 words a minute on a manual typewriter," she says with pride. According to Olson, studying piano as a child helped give her the dexterity needed to become a master of the keyboard.

Those interested in a court-reporting career should investigate degree programs offered at business colleges or community colleges. While an interest in law might make the job more appealing, manual dexterity and knowing how to type are essential.

being tried more than once for the same crime. If a person is found not guilty of a crime in a state court, for example, the state cannot put him or her on trial again for the same crime. Similarly, if the person is found guilty, the state may not put him or her on trial again in order to win a harsher punishment.

Double jeopardy does not include, however, situations in which a person breaks both a state and a federal law with the same act. This might happen, for example, in cases involving federal and state laws made to control the possession and use of illegal drugs. In addition, if a person breaks several state or several federal laws when committing a crime, he or she may be tried separately on each charge. For example, a person who breaks

into a home to steal a computer and then sets fire to the house may be tried separately for illegally entering the home, for stealing the computer, and for setting fire to the house.

Protections against double jeopardy also do not apply to cases in which a jury fails to deliver a verdict in the first trial. A person may be tried again in a second trial that is considered a continuation of the first trial.

Providing for Fair Punishment

What happens to people who have been found guilty of crimes in fair trials? What protections does the Bill of Rights provide for convicted people? The Eighth Amendment protects people convicted of crimes from "cruel and unusual punishment." Defining what is cruel and unusual, however, is difficult. The debate over the death penalty, for instance, has been particularly fierce.

Cruel and Unusual Punishment

Deciding which punishments are cruel and unusual is difficult for many reasons. Different people have varying opinions about what is cruel. Also, societal standards change over time. For example, do you think that whipping a convicted criminal is cruel? The Massachusetts officials who put such punishments into law during the 1700s certainly believed at the time that they were appropriate. Proposing such punishments today, however, likely would prompt an outcry, for most present-day Americans would consider them unusually harsh.

Just as the Supreme Court has established guidelines for dealing with other civil liberties issues, it has also set guidelines for applying the Eighth Amendment's prohibition against cruel and unusual punishment. In the 1910 case *Weems* v. *United States,* for example, the Court ruled that a Coast Guard officer had been punished too harshly for stealing money. Using an old law, a lower court had sentenced the officer to 15 years of hard labor in chains and fined him nearly seven times the amount of money he had stolen.

In overturning the sailor's punishment, the Supreme Court argued that societal standards are critical in deciding what is cruel and unusual. The Eighth Amendment, the Court said, "is not fastened to the absolute but may acquire meaning as public opinion becomes enlightened by humane justice."

Federal courts also have applied the Eighth Amendment in cases involving living conditions and overcrowding in prisons. In 1969, for example, a federal court found that parts of the Arkansas prison system violated the Eighth Amendment because of poor living conditions, including inadequate clothing and food for prisoners. In addition, during the early 1990s the federal courts oversaw more than 80 percent of federal prisons, in order to ensure that prisons met adequate standards for cell space, food, and clothing.

Capital Punishment

As noted in Chapter 12, one of the most controversial issues involving the Eighth Amendment is capital punishment, or the

Caption Answer
Furman v. *Georgia*

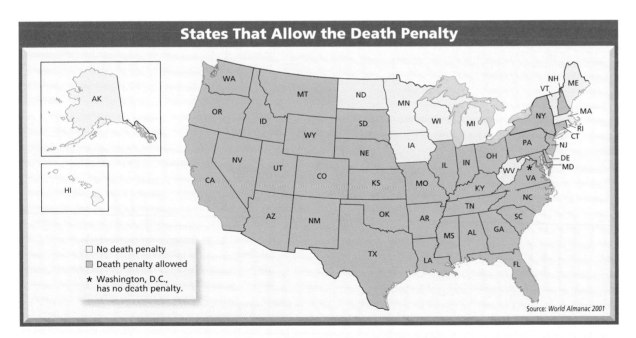

States That Allow the Death Penalty

- ☐ No death penalty
- ☐ Death penalty allowed
- ★ Washington, D.C., has no death penalty.

Source: World Almanac 2001

Since 1976 the Supreme Court has approved several laws that allow capital punishment. **What 1972 Supreme Court case ruled that capital punishment laws across the country violated the Eighth Amendment?**

SECTION 3 REVIEW ANSWERS

1. Refer to the following pages: change of venue (330), bench trial (331), double jeopardy (331).

2. The Fifth, Sixth, Seventh, and Eighth Amendments together establish: the right to a speedy trial, the right to a trial by jury, the right to an adequate defense, and restrictions on double jeopardy.

3a. People have different opinions regarding cruelty, and the standards of society change over time. The Supreme Court looks to societal standards to define cruel and unusual.

3b. It ensures that the accused does not have to wait in jail too long, reduces the chance that evidence may be lost or that witnesses will forget what happened, and prevents abuses of the law by allowing the public to witness the proceedings.

4. Answers will vary, but students should take a position regarding the death penalty and support it with evidence and by mentioning various Supreme Court cases.

death penalty. The Supreme Court has considered cases involving the death penalty since the 1800s. In the 1890 case *In re Kemmler,* for example, the Court ruled that the death penalty was not cruel and unusual punishment.

In general, until the early 1970s the Supreme Court refused to find any law unconstitutional that allowed government to hand out death sentences to people convicted of serious crimes. In the 1972 case *Furman* v. *Georgia,* however, a sharply divided Court ruled that the capital punishment laws enforced by states across the country violated the Eighth Amendment. In that case, several justices said that many death penalty decisions were influenced by racism and other factors that made such punishments inconsistent—and thus unfair—in their application.

Over the next few years, states changed their capital punishment laws to address the Supreme Court's concerns. In 1976 in *Gregg* v. *Georgia,* the Supreme Court ruled in favor of a new Georgia law allowing the death penalty. The law called for a two-step process in cases involving capital punishment. First, a jury decides whether the accused person is guilty or innocent. If the jury finds the

PRINCIPLES OF DEMOCRACY *Florida attorney general Robert Shevin argued in* Profitt v. Florida *that the death penalty may prevent some criminal behavior.* ***What 1890s Supreme Court decision ruled that some forms of the death penalty were not cruel and unusual punishment?***

accused person guilty, it then decides whether the death penalty should be imposed. The jury—or in a bench trial, the judge—also must consider whether any other circumstances involved in the case make the death penalty an inappropriate punishment. In addition, the state's highest court automatically reviews each death penalty case.

Since 1976 the Supreme Court has approved other laws allowing capital punishment. In addition, new state and federal laws passed in 1994 increased the number of crimes that are punishable by death.

SECTION 3 REVIEW

1. Identify and Explain:
- change of venue
- bench trial
- double jeopardy

2. Identifying Concepts:
Copy the chart below. Use it to list the ways the Bill of Rights ensures fair trials.

Fair Trials
•
•
•
•

Homework Practice Online
keyword: SV3 HP14

3. **Finding the Main Idea**

a. Why is defining "cruel and unusual punishment" difficult? How has the Supreme Court suggested it be defined?

b. Why is a speedy and public trial vital to protecting the rights of accused people?

4. **Writing and Critical Thinking**

Identifying Points of View: Do you think the death penalty is fair? Or is it cruel and unusual punishment? **Consider the following:**
- the two-step process in capital punishment cases
- the various Supreme Court cases involving capital

GOVERNMENT IN THE NEWS

Incorporation and the Legacy of Vigilance

Americans enjoy the benefits of both state and national citizenship. But this dual citizenship also requires them to follow the laws of two governments. While government at every level has expanded dramatically since the ratification of the U.S. Constitution, Americans have been vigilant in defending their civil liberties. The "incorporation" doctrine, which protects citizens against unconstitutional acts of state governments, has played a vital part in this legacy of vigilance.

The first 10 amendments to the Constitution—known as the Bill of Rights—guarantee the freedom to speak publicly and to practice one's religion, and freedom from "cruel and unusual punishments," among other important rights. For decades, courts agreed that the Bill of Rights protected citizens only from abuses by the *federal* government, not the *state* governments.

After the Civil War, Congress passed the Fourteenth Amendment, which prohibits the states from denying certain legal protections to their citizens. The Supreme Court ruled in the Slaughterhouse Cases (1873) that, despite this important amendment, citizens did not have the same protections from state government that they had from the federal government. Thus, for example, while the Fifth Amendment stated that defendants could not be forced to testify against themselves in federal court, they could be forced to do so in a state court.

Some Americans felt uneasy about this disparity and argued that the Fourteenth Amendment "incorporated" the Bill of Rights; that is, it gave citizens the same protections from the states that they had from the federal government. In *Adamson v. California* (1947), Supreme Court justice Hugo Black argued in dissent that all the protections the Bill of Rights should apply to the states. Although

In 1989, Johnny Paul Penry, seen here, received a death sentence. Because of the incorporation doctrine, the Supreme Court awarded Penry a new sentencing hearing in 2000.

they never fully incorporated the Bill of Rights, Supreme Court rulings had extended virtually all of its provisions to the states by the late 1960s.

In June 2001, the Supreme Court ruled that a Texas judge failed properly to instruct jurors that they must consider evidence of Johnny Paul Penry's mental retardation in deciding whether he deserved a death sentence. The Court decided that his death sentence, reached without the jury's full and proper deliberation, constituted "cruel and unusual" punishment under the incorporated Eighth Amendment. The Court has ordered a new sentencing hearing.

Today incorporation goes largely unnoticed because it is so fundamental to our concept of civil liberties, but its relevance cannot be overstated.

What Do You Think?

1. What has been the effect of the incorporation doctrine on individual rights?
2. How would individual rights in the United States be different without the incorporation doctrine?

> **WHY IT MATTERS TODAY**
>
> Americans continue to rely upon the incorporation doctrine as a safeguard of individual rights. Use CNNfyi.com or other **current events** sources to find recent state court cases involving the Bill of Rights.
>
> CNNfyi.com

Government in the News Answers

1. Students might suggest that the incorporation doctrine ensures that U.S. citizens enjoy the same rights under state law that they do under federal law.

2. Answers will vary, but students might suggest that without the incorporation doctrine, citizens might have fewer protections from state governments.

CHAPTER 14

Review Answers

Writing a Summary

Summaries should focus on the main points of each section. These may be found in the Read to Discover questions at the start of each section. Summaries should include standard grammar, spelling, sentence structure, and punctuation.

Identifying Ideas

Refer to the following pages:

due process (319), procedural due process (319), substantive due process (320), police power (322), search warrant (322), probable cause (322), presentment (327), Miranda Rule (327), bench trial (331), double jeopardy (331).

Understanding Main Ideas

1. Substantive due process determines if the government has the authority to

(Continued on page 336)

(Continued from page 335)

create and enforce regulations, while procedural due process ensures that the government applies such laws fairly and according to set procedures.

2. Due process protects privacy by providing set procedures for gathering evidence.

3. The writ of *habeas corpus* prevents an individual from being jailed without sufficient reason.

4. It requires police officers to inform suspects of their constitutional rights. It informs the accused of their right not to provide evidence against themselves.

5. the death penalty; used the Eighth Amendment to determine how and when the death penalty can be used.

6. a speedy and public trial with adequate defense for the accused and the right to a trial by jury.

Reviewing Themes

1. Students might suggest that the judicial branch ensures that the rights of individuals are protected, including those accused of crimes.

2. Critics argue that news coverage can influence the conduct of the trial. Journalists argue that the public has a right to see the workings of a trial and how the justice system works.

3. *Miranda v. Arizona* established rules for police aimed at protecting the rights of individuals suspected of crimes. Students might mention *Gideon v. Wainwright, Furman v. Georgia, Weems*
(Continued on page 337)

CHAPTER 14
Review

Writing a Summary

Using standard grammar, spelling, sentence structure, and punctuation, write a summary of the information in this chapter.

Identifying Ideas

Identify the following terms and explain their significance.

1. due process
2. procedural due process
3. substantive due process
4. police power
5. search warrant
6. probable cause
7. presentment
8. Miranda Rule
9. bench trial
10. double jeopardy

Understanding Main Ideas

SECTION 1 *(pp. 319–325)*

1. What is the difference between procedural due process and substantive due process?

2. What role does due process play in protecting the security and privacy of the people?

SECTION 2 *(pp. 326–328)*

3. How does the writ of *habeas corpus* protect the rights of the accused?

4. What is the Miranda Rule? In what way does this rule protect people's right not to incriminate themselves?

SECTION 3 *(pp. 329–334)*

5. What is capital punishment? How has the Supreme Court applied the Eighth Amendment to cases involving capital punishment?

6. What elements of a fair trial are protected by the Bill of Rights?

Reviewing Themes

1. Constitutional Government What is the role of the judicial branch of government in protecting the rights of individuals?

2. Public Good How might the newsmedia influence trials? What are some positive and negative aspects of news coverage of trials?

3. Constitutional Government What is the significance of *Miranda v. Arizona*? What other Supreme Court cases have been pivotal in protecting individual rights?

Thinking Critically

1. Drawing Inferences Why does the Bill of Rights emphasize the protection of the rights of those accused of crimes? Have certain punishments ever violated these rights?

2. Taking a Stand How important do you feel individual rights are in the United States? Are there times when individual rights are more important than the greater public good? Why or why not?

3. Comparing and Contrasting What are the rights of accused people in the United States? What might happen if these rights were ignored?

Writing about Government

Review what you wrote in your Government Notebook at the beginning of this chapter about when searches by police and school officials are appropriate. Now that you have studied this chapter, how would you revise your response? Explain your answer in your notebook.

Interpreting the Visual Record

Study the political cartoon below. Then use it to help you answer the questions that follow.

"There are indications that little Tommy is being naughty. But not enough for me to authorize a wiretap."

1. What is the cartoonist's point of view regarding wiretaps?
  a. Wiretapping is a serious act that should only be allowed under certain circumstances.
  b. Wiretapping should be permitted under any circumstance.
  c. Not much evidence is required in order to allow a wiretap.
  d. Wiretaps are not an invasion of privacy.

2. What are some advances in technology that might threaten people's privacy? How do you think the government should respond?

Analyzing Primary Sources

In 1792 Joel Barlow, a scholar of European political theory, wrote an essay on his views of government responsibility. In his essay he discusses the principles of equality and justice upon which the U.S. government was built. The following excerpt from his essay describes government's responsibility regarding laws. Read the excerpt and answer the questions that follow.

"It is not enough that the laws be rendered familiar to the people; but the tribunals [courts of justice] ought to be near at hand, easy of access, and equally open to the poor as to the rich. The means of coming at justice should be cheap, expeditious [quick and efficient], and certain; the mode of process should be simple and perfectly intelligible to the meanest [lowest] capacity, unclouded with mysteries and unperplexed [not confused] with forms. In short, justice should not familiarize itself as the well-known friend of every man; and the consequence seems natural, that every man would be a friend to justice."

3. Which of the following statements best reflects the beliefs of Joel Barlow?
  a. Justice in society is not the government's responsibility
  b. The government must ensure that laws and courts are fair, efficient, and accessible.
  c. It is inevitable that courts are slow and unfair.
  d. Courts in the United States should be run like courts in Europe.

4. Do you think that the Supreme Court and the Bill of Rights adequately protect the rights of individuals?

Building Your Portfolio

Imagine you are involved in founding a new organization, such as a union or a club. Create a pamphlet about due process that the new organization might use in developing rules for its members. The pamphlet should include explanations of procedural and substantive due process as well as suggest policies that the organization might use to ensure that its official actions follow due process. One policy, for example, might forbid secret trials of members accused of breaking a rule.

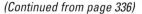

internet connect

Internet Activity: go.hrw.com
KEYWORD: SV3 GV14

Access the Internet through the HRW Go site to locate information on the use of the death penalty in the United States. Students should read pro and con arguments on the death penalty, as well as data from a number of sources regarding which states impose the death penalty, the imposition of death sentences in federal crimes, and how often it is imposed. Then have students prepare a legal brief on the issue.

(Continued from page 336)

v. United States, or *United States v. Lovett.*

Thinking Critically

1. Answers will vary. Students might suggest that because all people are innocent until proven guilty, those accused of crimes should have the same rights as all others. Past types of punishment have occasionally been found to be cruel and unusual. The Supreme Court ruled in 1972 that capital punishment laws were influenced by racism.
2. Answers will vary, but students should take a stand and support their answer with specific examples.
3. Students might mention the Miranda Rights, as well as the guarantees in the Bill of Rights.

Writing About Government

The Government Notebook is a follow-up activity to the notebook activity that appears on page 216.

Building Social Studies Skills

1. a
2. Students might mention the Internet, and the government should regulate the Internet. Others might suggest that the government should not get involved.
3. b
4. Students should support their opinion with specific examples.

Alternative Assessment

To assess this activity see Writing to Inform in *Alternative Assessment Handbook.*

CHAPTER 15 PROTECTING CIVIL RIGHTS

	OBJECTIVES	PACING GUIDE	REPRODUCIBLE RESOURCES
SECTION 1 **CITIZENSHIP AND IMMIGRATION** (pp. 339–341)	▸ What are the responsibilities of citizenship? ▸ In what two ways may a person become a U.S. citizen by birth? ▸ How does an immigrant become a U.S. citizen?	**Regular** 1 day **Block Scheduling** .5 day	**ELL** Spanish Study Guide 15.1 **ELL** English Study Guide 15.1
SECTION 2 **DIVERSITY AND EQUAL PROTECTION** (pp. 342–345)	▸ How has U.S. immigration policy changed over time? ▸ In what ways is the United States an ethnically diverse country? ▸ What are the benefits and challenges of diversity in the United States?	**Regular** 1 day **Block Scheduling** .5 day	**ELL** Spanish Study Guide 15.2 **ELL** English Study Guide 15.2
SECTION 3 **STRUGGLE FOR CIVIL RIGHTS** (pp. 346–349)	▸ What two tests do federal courts use to determine whether laws respect the Equal Protection Clause? ▸ How did the Equal Protection Clause help the civil rights movement fight government discrimination?	**Regular** 1 day **Block Scheduling** .5 day	**ELL** Spanish Study Guide 15.3 **ELL** English Study Guide 15.3
SECTION 4 **CIVIL RIGHTS LAWS** (pp. 350–356)	▸ How have civil rights laws protected the rights of African Americans? ▸ How have civil rights protections been extended to other minority groups?	**Regular** 1.5 days **Block Scheduling** .75 day	**ELL** Spanish Study Guide 15.4 **ELL** English Study Guide 15.4 **PS** Reading 32: "I Have a Dream" **PS** Reading 44: Civil Rights Act of 1964 **PS** Reading 47: Americans with Disabilities Act of 1990

Chapter Resource Key

PS	Primary Sources	**A**	Assessment	📼 Video
RS	Reading Support	**REV**	Review	💿 Videodisc
E	Enrichment	**ELL**	Reinforcement and English Language Learners	🖥 Internet
S	Simulations		Transparencies	💻 Holt Presentation Maker Using
SM	Skills Mastery		CD-ROM	Microsoft ® PowerPoint ®

TECHNOLOGY RESOURCES	REINFORCEMENT, REVIEW, AND ASSESSMENT
One-Stop Planner: Lesson 15.1 Holt Researcher Online Homework Practice Online Transparency 31 Global Skill Builder CD-ROM	**REV** Section 1 Review, p. 341 **A** Daily Quiz 15.1
One-Stop Planner: Lesson 15.2 Holt Researcher Online Homework Practice Online Transparency 32 Global Skill Builder CD-ROM	**REV** Section 2 Review, p. 345 **A** Daily Quiz 15.2
One-Stop Planner: Lesson 15.3 Holt Researcher Online Homework Practice Online Global Skill Builder CD-ROM	**REV** Section 3 Review, p. 349 **A** Daily Quiz 15.3
One-Stop Planner: Lesson 15.4 Holt Researcher Online Homework Practice Online Global Skill Builder CD-ROM **E** Challenge and Enrichment: Activity 15 **E** Simulations and Strategies for Teaching American Government: Activity 15 CNN Presents American Government	**REV** Section 4 Review, p. 356 **A** Daily Quiz 15.4

Chapter Review and Assessment

SM Global Skill Builder CD-ROM

HRW Go site

REV Chapter 15 English Study Guide

REV Chapter 15 Review, pp. 358–359

Chapter 15 Test Generator (on the One-Stop Planner)

A Chapter 15 Test

A Alternative Assessment Handbook

One-Stop Planner CD-ROM

It's easy to plan lessons, select resources, and print out materials for your students when you use the *One-Stop Planner CD-ROM with Test Generator.*

---

internet connect

HRW ONLINE RESOURCES
Go To: go.hrw.com
Then type in a keyword.

TEACHER HOME PAGE
KEYWORD: SV3 Teacher

CHAPTER INTERNET ACTIVITIES
KEYWORD: SV3 GV15
Choose an activity on protecting civil rights to:
▶ create a multimedia presentation on civil rights laws.
▶ review current immigration patterns and policy.
▶ study current affirmative action policies.

CHAPTER ENRICHMENT LINKS
KEYWORD: SV3 CH15

HOLT RESEARCHER ONLINE
KEYWORD: HOLT RESEARCHER

ONLINE ASSESSMENT
Homework Practice
KEYWORD: SV3 HP15
Standardized Test Prep
KEYWORD: SV3 STP15
Rubrics
KEYWORD: SS Rubrics

ONLINE MAPS, CHARTS, AND GRAPHS
KEYWORD: SV3 MCG
▶ How an Alien Becomes a Citizen
▶ Racial/Ethnic Population of the United States in 2000

CONTENT UPDATES
KEYWORD: SS Content Updates

HOLT PRESENTATION MAKER
KEYWORD: SV3 PPT15

ONLINE READING SUPPORT
KEYWORD: SS Strategies

CURRENT EVENTS
KEYWORD: S3 Current Events

HOLT PRESENTATION MAKER
Access Illustrated LECTURE NOTES using Microsoft® PowerPoint® on the One-Stop Planner CD-ROM

OBJECTIVES

▶ Describe the responsibilities of citizenship.
▶ List the two ways a person may become a U.S. citizen by birth.
▶ Describe how an immigrant can become a U.S. citizen.

MOTIVATE

On a large map of the United States or the world, students should place a colored thumbtack on the city in which they were born. Discuss with students the privileges and responsibilities of being a U.S. citizen. If there are any students in the class who were born in a different country, discuss whether they are U.S. citizens. Discuss the differences between the rights of foreign citizens in their home country and the rights of citizens of the United States. Explain to students that in this section they will learn how people can become U.S. citizens as well as how they can lose their citizenship.

TEACH

Building a Vocabulary

In spiral notebooks, have students create a Political Dictionary to be used throughout the course. The dictionary may be used as an activity at the start of each new section; it may also be used as a modification device for students having difficulty or sheltered English students during tests and homework assignments. List words the students will be expected to know for this section on the chalkboard. Have students list, define, and give an example of each of the terms, using information provided in the text or on the *Researcher CD-ROM*.

Creating Maps

First, remind students that all children born in the United States as well as in U.S. territories automatically become U.S. citizens even if their parents are not citizens. Have the class make a large world map and highlight the United States and its territories to show these areas. If there are any stu-dents who were born in another country and became citizens of the United States, have them place a thumbtack on the country in which they were born. Refer students to the Country Profiles section on the *Holt Researcher Online* to find out information about these countries. As a class students should discuss the variety of places where U.S. citizens can come from. Tell students that in the next activity they will learn how immigrants can become U.S. citizens.

Recognizing Point of View

Ask students to identify reasons the government might want to control immigration to the United States. Then discuss with students the ways an immigrant can become a U.S. citizen and the limitations placed on the number of immigrants allowed annually. Organize students into small groups. Ask students to imagine that they are starting their own country. Have students make up their own rules governing how an immigrant becomes a citizen. Would they include tests to become a citizen? Would there be a waiting period? Would they have restrictions on the number of immigrants allowed each year? Allow students to discuss their ideas and to explain their reasoning to the rest of the class. Tell students that in the next activity they will learn about the ways U.S. citizens can lose their citizenship.

Predicting Outcome

Tell students that sometimes the United States may denatural-ize a person (take away their citizenship). Ask students to identify reasons why the United States might want to do this. Tell students that very few people actually have their citizenship revoked, and identify some of the ways this happens. Tell students that people have renounced their U.S. citizenship and have students identify reasons why a person might wish to do so. Discuss with students the conse-quences of renouncing citizenship. Organize the class into small groups, giving each group a list of acts a person can commit against the United States government. Have each group attempt to identify whether or not a citizen could lose their citizenship for committing each of these acts. Discuss students' answers as a class. Have students write a short essay explaining why the United States has made the process of revoking citizenship a difficult one.

CLOSE

Ask students to imagine that they are to host a student from another country in their homes. Ask students to create a means of explaining U.S. citizenship to the foreign student, including the obligations of citizenship, how an immigrant can become a U.S. citizen, and how a person can lose their citizenship. Some students may write a report, and others may wish to make a visual, such as a chart. Encourage students to be creative and to discuss what they have learned with the rest of the class. Display their work for other classes to see.

OPTIONS

Gifted Learners

 Ask students to consider one or more of the issues discussed in connection with the material in this section on acquiring U.S. citizenship through naturalization or loss of citizenship. Have the students take a stand either for or against the issue(s) and defend their position in a written report. For example, some students may feel that the United States should take away a convicted murderer's citizenship or that there should not be any yearly limitations on the number of people allowed to immigrate and become naturalized citizens. Encourage students to discuss any changes they would make in the system.

Students Having Difficulty/ Sheltered English Students

 Have students examine newspapers and magazines from recent months or years looking for articles on U.S. citizenship. Have them write a review of the article(s) or create a poster with cutouts of the articles. Encourage students to give a verbal presentation of their findings to the rest of the class and, as a class, to debate any controversy over the issue.

Students Having Difficulty/ Sheltered English Students

 Discuss with students the many famous people who have immigrated from foreign countries and become U.S. citizens. Examples include Arnold Schwarzenegger and Madeline Albright. Have students choose a famous person who has become a U.S. citizen and then research his or her background. Students should develop an oral report that describes the country the person came from, his or her reasons for leaving and how he or she became well known in the United States. Students may want to use the Country Profiles section on the *Holt Researcher Online* and other resources to help them with their research. Once students have finished their research, they should present their reports to the rest of the class. Create a giant world map on butcher paper and have students pin a picture of their research subject on his or her country of origin.

Interpersonal Learners/Students Having Difficulty

 Encourage students to learn more about the process of becoming a naturalized citizen by writing to the U.S. Immigration and Naturalization Service or by visiting the agency's website. Students should research specific information, such as the process of naturalization, the service's responsibilities to those who want to become citizens, and what career opportunities are available with the agency. Have students share their research with the rest of the class.

REVIEW

Have students complete the Section 1 Review on page 341. Use the answers in the Annotated Teacher's Edition to assess student mastery of this section.

ASSESS

To assess student mastery of this section, have students complete Daily Quiz 15.1 in *Daily Quizzes with Answer Key*. For additional assessment options, see *Alternative Assessment Handbook* on the *One-Stop Planner CD-ROM*.

ADDITIONAL RESOURCES

Immigration and the American Identity: Selections from Chronicles, a Magazine of American Culture 1995, The Rockford Institute.

Bouvier, Leon. *Peaceful Invasions: Immigration and Changing America*. 1992. University Press of America.

Eberly, Don, ed. *Building a Community of Citizens: Civil Society in the 21st Century*. 1994. University Press of America.

HOLT PRESENTATION MAKER
Access Illustrated LECTURE NOTES using Microsoft® PowerPoint® on the One-Stop Planner CD-ROM

OBJECTIVES

▶ Describe how U.S. immigration policy has changed over time.
▶ Discuss the ways in which the United States is an ethnically diverse country.
▶ List the benefits and challenges of diversity in the United States.

MOTIVATE

Pass around the class examples of several types of applications, such as those for various colleges or universities and from a variety of businesses for jobs. Ask students to notice the similarities and differences in the applications. Ask students if any of them ask for information about the applicant's race or ethnicity. Ask students to hypothesize why some businesses and universities would want to know this information. Explain to students that in this section they will be learning more about diversity in the population of the United States.

TEACH

Building a Vocabulary

In their spiral notebooks, have students continue working on their Political Dictionary. List words the students will be expected to know for this section on the chalkboard. Have students list, define, and give an example of each of the terms using information provided in the text or on the *Researcher CD-ROM*.

Taking a Stand

Lead students in a discussion on the pros and cons of the various ways in which the United States has handled immigration in the past. Ask students to consider current immigration policy. Have students identify reasons the United States does not allow unlimited immigration. Then discuss the former policy of excluding Chinese immigrants and explain that the United States no longer excludes immigrants based on ethnicity. Have students debate the issue of a certain number of immigrants being allowed to emigrate from each

hemisphere. Students should also discuss the issue of denying certain rights, such as public education, to illegal aliens. Allow students to research their points of view and to present them in a logical and disciplined fashion. Tell students that they will be learning about the ethnic diversity of the United States in the next activity.

Navigating the Internet

Ask student volunteers to identify their own ethnicity and discuss familial, religious, or cultural traditions that they identify as relating to their ethnicity. If the class does not have a wide variety of ethnic backgrounds, have students identify some of the other ethnic groups found in the United States. Have students research the different cultures discussed in the class using the Internet or the school library. Have students create a visual, such as a poster or display, and discuss items from their own ethnic background. Students may wish to bring to class an ethnic dish or popular music, clothing, or other examples that represent their ethnic background for the class to see. Students from other countries may wish to bring a map of their country, pictures of their native land, or examples of the national dress. Allow students to make oral presentations to the rest of the class on information that they found that represents the diversity of the class. Discuss how the diversity of the classroom compares to that of the nation. Tell students that during the next activity, they will learn about some of the benefits and challenges of having such a diverse population.

Debating Ideas

Organize students into two groups. Have one group create a list of the benefits of having such a diverse population and have the other create a list of some of the problems associated with having such a diverse population. Then have students discuss the benefits and challenges of diversity in the United States. Ask students to consider the difference between "melting" many cultures together versus each culture maintaining its unique characteristics within mainstream society. Ask students to debate how these two theories may impact the issues of diversity, acculturation, prejudice, and discrimination.

CLOSE

Provide for students demographics from their school, district, city, and state regarding race and/or ethnicity. Organize students into groups and have them create a chart depicting these demographics. Have students compare their local and state ethnic diversity to that of the country. Then have each student write a short essay describing how the demographics from their community reflect current or past immigration policies and how the ethnic diversity can benefit their community. Ask students to share their ideas with the rest of the class.

OPTIONS

Sheltered English Students/Interpersonal Learners

 Have students who are from, or who have relatives from, other countries give a report to the class on their home country. Students may wish to read a story in their native language, describe the meaning of a few everyday words from their native language, or have a relative visit the class as a guest speaker to describe their native country or language. Encourage the class to make a chart comparing and contrasting the countries discussed.

Intrapersonal Learners/Visual-Spatial Learners

  Have students interview members of their family regarding their family history. Encourage students to obtain information regarding immigration (for students other than Native Americans), the variety of ethnic backgrounds represented in their family history, other languages spoken, family traditions associated with their cultural heritage, and the meaning of the family name. Students should be encouraged to present their findings in a creative manner, including making a family tree. Students may wish to use the Country Profiles section on the *Holt Researcher Online* to find information about the nations their countries emigrated from. Have students discuss the information they gather with the rest of the class.

Gifted Learners

 Have students study the effects of the migration of various ethnic groups to the United States. Each student should select a group and explore elements of its heritage that have become part of U.S. culture, such as foods, music, or art. Other students may wish to investigate such factors as what region of the United States a particular ethnic group tended to migrate to and how the group affected that area, such as by serving as a pool of less-skilled laborers or introducing a production process to a particular industry. Have students share their information with the rest of the class. Then have them write a paper discussing how the culture of the United States has come to incorporate such a wide variety of backgrounds.

Students Having Difficulty

  Have students use the Country Profiles section on the *Holt Researcher Online* to obtain information about the countries of their ethnic origin. Students should create a chart comparing the country or countries to the United States. Charts should include information such as the size of the country, the population, its type of government, and the major products it produces. Have students discuss their charts with the class. Ask students what conclusions they might draw from their charts about the ease with which immigrants from these countries would adapt to American culture.

REVIEW

Have students complete the Section 2 Review on page 345. Use the answers in the Annotated Teacher's Edition to assess student mastery of this section.

ASSESS

To assess student mastery of this section, have students complete Daily Quiz 15.2 in *Daily Quizzes with Answer Key*. For additional assessment options, see *Alternative Assessment Handbook* on the *One-Stop Planner CD-ROM*.

ADDITIONAL RESOURCES

Jackson, Donald. *Even the Children of Strangers: Equality Under the U.S. Constitution*. 1992. University Press of Kansas.

Wlodkowski, Raymond. *Diversity and Motivation: Culturally Responsive Teaching*. 1995. Jossey-Bass Publishers.

HOLT PRESENTATION MAKER
Access Illustrated LECTURE
NOTES using Microsoft®
PowerPoint® on the
One-Stop Planner CD-ROM

OBJECTIVES

▶ List the two tests used by the federal courts to determine whether laws uphold the Equal Protection Clause.

▶ Discuss how the Equal Protection Clause helped the civil rights movement fight government discrimination.

MOTIVATE

As each student enters the classroom, give him or her an index card with either a number or a letter on it. When all students are present, have them organize themselves according to their cards, numbers on one side of the room and letters on the other. Tell students that for the rest of the class they are not allowed to cross the invisible line separating the two groups nor should they communicate with the "other side." Randomly assign certain privileges to one of the groups that the other does not have, such as being able to speak without raising a hand, being called on first, or being able to leave their seat without permission. Encourage students to jot down their feelings on these differences as the class progresses. Tell students that one of the challenges of an ethnically diverse population is in maintaining the civil rights of all segments of the population. Tell students that they will be learning about how the courts deal with this challenge during this section. Encourage students to watch for articles or broadcasts that focus on the Equal Protection Clause. Have students write summaries about them to present to the class for discussion.

TEACH

Building a Vocabulary

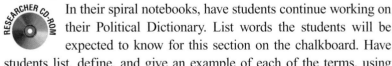

In their spiral notebooks, have students continue working on their Political Dictionary. List words the students will be expected to know for this section on the chalkboard. Have students list, define, and give an example of each of the terms, using information provided in the text or on the *Researcher CD-ROM*.

Acquiring Information

Discuss the use of the rational basis test and the strict scrutiny test by the courts to determine whether laws uphold the Equal Protection Clause. Have students identify reasons why the courts would use the rational basis test for determining such things as drinking age, driving age, voting age, and reasons why the courts would use the strict scrutiny test. Students should then conduct research using newspapers, magazines, and the library to find examples of other laws that would require the use of one of these tests to determine their constitutionality. Students should share their examples with the class. Have the entire class create a chart that identifies the type of law and the test it must pass. Tell students that in the next activity, they will be learning what the courts have said about equal protection.

Identifying the Main Idea

Explain to students that the Supreme Court's views about what can be considered discrimination have changed over time. Organize students into small groups and have each group examine one of the court cases listed in the section. Students should use the Supreme Court Docket section on the *Holt Researcher Online* to find additional information on the Court's decisions. Allow each group to discuss the Court's ruling in each of these cases and how the case applied the Equal Protection Clause to the issue of civil rights. Students may wish to identify additional cases that have had a significant impact on civil rights. Tell students that they will be learning more about civil rights in the next activity.

Hypothesizing

Write the word *minority* on the chalkboard. Have students attempt to define the term. Explain to students that the term does not just apply to racial or ethnic groups and that any group that does not make up the majority of a population is considered to be in the minority. Explain to students that although in a democracy the majority is supposed to determine policy, it is also the government's duty to protect the rights of minority groups. As a class discuss the difference between *de jure* and *de facto* segregation. Have students think of examples of *de facto* segregation and the effects that it may have. Ask students to use a problem-solving process to come up with ways in which this type of segregation could be eliminated.

CLOSE

Have students read from the notes they took during the Motivate activity. Ask students to identify the differences in the ways each group was treated and how that made each of them feel. Allow students to discuss how this type of treatment represents segregation. Have each group use information from this section to create a chart that lists each of the unfair actions taken against one group and explains why each action would be found unconstitutional based on the Equal Protection Clause. Have both groups share their reasoning with the rest of the class.

OPTIONS

Students Having Difficulty/ Sheltered English Students

 Have students create a cartoon or other drawing that depicts one or several types of segregation discussed in this section. Students might want to depict historical examples of segregation, such as on buses. Then each student should create a caption that tells why this type of segregation is illegal. Have students share their cartoons with the rest of the class or display the finished cartoons for other classes to see.

Musical-Rhythmic Learners/Visual-Spatial Learners

Ask students to imagine that they were living when the separate-but-equal doctrine was in use. Using information from this section students should create an advertisement making legal arguments against this doctrine. Students

may design print ads, radio ads, or television ads. Once students have finished have them share their ads with the rest of the class. Display or record ads for other classes to see.

Musical-Rhythmic Learners/Linguistic Learners

  Discuss with the class ways in which the civil rights movement benefited from the Equal Protection Clause. Organize the class into several small groups. Have each group work together to create a poem or song that discusses the significance of Supreme Court rulings on the civil rights movement. Groups should cite cases by name and should describe each case's impact. Once all groups are finished, have them present their poem or song to the rest of the class.

REVIEW

Have students complete the Section 3 Review on page 349. Use the answers in the Annotated Teacher's Edition to assess student mastery of this section.

ASSESS

To assess student mastery of this section, have students complete Daily Quiz 15.3 in *Daily Quizzes with Answer Key*. For additional assessment options, see *Alternative Assessment Handbook* on the *One-Stop Planner CD-ROM*.

ADDITIONAL RESOURCES

Branch, Taylor. *Pillar of Fire: America in the King Years, 1963–65.* 1998. Simon and Schuster.

Chestnut, J.L. *Black in Selma: The Uncommon Life of J.L. Chestnut, Jr.* 1990. Farrar, Straus, and Giroux.

OBJECTIVES

▸ Discuss how civil rights laws have protected the equal rights of African Americans.

▸ Describe how civil rights protections have been extended to other minority groups.

MOTIVATE

Have students list some of the things they like to do. Then have students imagine what it would feel like if such things as the color of their hair, where they lived, or whether they were left- or right-handed determined the places they could go and the things they could do. Lead a discussion asking students to discuss what their thoughts and feelings would be if they experienced such discrimination. Explain that in this section, students will learn how civil rights laws have helped protect African Americans and other minority groups from discrimination.

TEACH

Building a Vocabulary

In their spiral notebooks, have students continue working on their Political Dictionary. List words the students will be expected to know for this section on the chalkboard. Have students list, define, and give an example of each of the terms, using information provided in the text or on the *Researcher CD-ROM*.

Creating Maps

In small groups, have students write short summaries of the major events leading up to the Civil Rights Acts of 1964 and 1968 and the Voting Rights Act of 1965. Teachers may wish either to include a list of events or have students conduct research to determine what events to include. Use a large map of the United States and have students create a "trail of equal rights" by marking on the map places in which major events in the struggle for equal rights occurred. Connect the events with string or yarn in the order in which they hap-

pened. Students may hypothesize the placement of some of the events or consult the Internet for exact location. Discuss the significance of each event and of the civil rights movement. Tell students that during the next activity they will be identifying examples of civil rights laws in action.

Learning From Visuals

Discuss with students the ways in which equal rights laws have helped protect the rights of African Americans. Show pictures or films that identify various forms of discrimination that have occurred in the United States. Organize students into small groups. Send students on a "scavenger hunt" to locate or to take pictures of areas in their school and community where civil rights laws are at work, or have students report on examples of civil rights laws at work. Have students compare these examples with the various forms of discrimination discussed earlier. (For example, students may show a picture of a single water fountain and describe how this contrasts with the segregated drinking fountains of the past, or students may compare a photograph of an integrated classroom to that of segregated classrooms.) Encourage students to be as creative as possible in their depiction of civil rights laws in action. Have each group share their examples with the rest of the class. Tell students that in the next activity they will learn about ways that civil rights laws extend to other minority groups.

Acquiring Information

Have students read about and then discuss the issue of extending civil rights. Explain to students the importance of guaranteeing civil rights to minority groups. Discuss with students the use of affirmative action programs in schools and businesses. Explain to students that debate has surrounded the implementation of these programs in recent years. Have students search for information about the debate over affirmative action using newspapers, magazines, and the Internet, and encourage students to form their own opinion on the topic. Have students discuss and possibly debate the arguments for and against affirmative action programs. Afterwards, encourage students to write an essay describing their stance on affirmative action.

CLOSE

Ask students to predict what, if any, changes may be made in civil rights laws and segregation patterns in the next 10 years. Have students write a brief report on their hypotheses. Encourage students to identify trends discussed in this section to support their hypothesis. Some students may wish to share their reports with the class.

OPTIONS

Gifted Learners

  Have students write a short research paper on Martin Luther King Jr., or any other significant leader in the struggle for civil rights. Encourage students to include information about the person's background, his or her contributions to the civil rights struggle, and the challenges they faced during their struggle. Students may wish to refer to the Biographies section on the *Holt Researcher Online* to help with their research. Have students share the information they gathered with the rest of the class and encourage the class to create a poster depicting significant figures in the civil rights struggle.

Students Having Difficulty/Sheltered English Students

  Have students use the Internet or the National Organizations section on the *Holt Researcher Online* to find out more information about organizations designed to help minority groups. Have students write or present a brief report to the rest of the class on the organization they choose. Students should include the year the organization was formed, the number of members, its purpose, and its current activities. Encourage students to share the information they gather with the rest of the class.

Linguistic Learners

  Individually or in small groups, students should read Martin Luther King Jr.'s "I Have a Dream" speech, Reading 32, in *From the Source: Readings in Economics and Government with Answer Key*. Have students write a brief essay describing whether or not the ideas contained in his speech have come true. Have students support the reasons for their answers. Have students share their ideas with the rest of the class.

Gifted Learners

  Have students choose one Supreme Court decision from this section to investigate, using resources such as the Supreme Court Docket section on the *Holt Researcher Online* and the Internet. Students should research the subject that the case dealt with as well as find out the Court's decision and its impact on the civil rights movement. Students should then summarize their research in a brief essay and share their ideas with the rest of the class. In addition, have each student create a chart in his or her Government Notebook to summarize all of the cases discussed in class.

REVIEW

Have students complete the Section 4 Review on page 356. Use the answers in the Annotated Teacher's Edition to assess student mastery of this section.

ASSESS

To assess student mastery of this section, have students complete Daily Quiz 14.3 in *Daily Quizzes with Answer Key*. For additional assessment options, see *Alternative Assessment Handbook* on the *One-Stop Planner CD-ROM*.

RETEACH

For students having difficulty with the lessons, have them complete Reteaching Activity 15. This activity is located in *Reteaching Activities with Answer Key*.

ADDITIONAL RESOURCES

Roof, Judith, and Robyn Wiegman, eds. *Who Can Speak?: Authority and Critical Identity*. 1995. University of Illinois Press.

Waldron, Ann. *Hodding Carter: The Reconstruction of a Racist*. 1993. Algonquin.

CHAPTER 15

TOPICS INCLUDE

★ becoming a U.S. citizen
★ losing citizenship
★ immigration policies
★ diversity in the United States
★ equal protection under the law
★ civil rights and equal protection
★ segregation
★ protests to gain civil rights
★ civil rights laws
★ extending civil rights

GOVERNMENT NOTEBOOK

The Government Notebook is a journal activity that encourages students to consider basic concepts of government that relate to their lives. A follow-up notebook activity appears on page 358.

▶ WHY IT MATTERS TODAY

To find additional lesson plans dealing with the protection of civil rights, visit CNNfyi.com or have students complete the GOVERNMENT IN THE NEWS activity on page 357.

CNNfyi.com

PROTECTING CIVIL RIGHTS

Most Americans or their ancestors came to this country from other lands. Not all Americans have enjoyed equal opportunity or experienced equal justice. In fact, many of the diverse groups of people in the United States have experienced significant challenges. For many, the struggle to win equality is highlighted by the civil rights movement of the 1950s and 1960s. Efforts continue today to fulfill the promise of equal opportunity for everyone in the United States. These efforts are necessary because securing the rights and freedoms guaranteed to everyone by the Constitution is vital to promoting the public good.

GOVERNMENT NOTEBOOK

How should government work to prevent discrimination in the United States? Record your answer in your Government Notebook.

▶ WHY IT MATTERS TODAY

The protection of civil rights is an ongoing struggle. At the end of this chapter visit CNNfyi.com to learn more about civil rights.

CNNfyi.com

SECTION 1

CITIZENSHIP AND IMMIGRATION

READ TO DISCOVER

1. What are the responsibilities of citizenship?
2. In what two ways may a person become a U.S. citizen by birth?
3. How does an immigrant become a U.S. citizen?

POLITICAL DICTIONARY

civic responsibilities
jus sanguinis
jus soli
naturalization
denaturalization
expatriation

As noted in Chapter 13, the Constitution guarantees certain fundamental freedoms to all people in this country. Becoming a full participant in the U.S. democratic system, however, requires citizenship. Certain obligations come with citizenship. Some examples of these **civic responsibilities** are understanding and obeying the law, respecting the rights of others, paying taxes, voting, and participating in public service.

Becoming a U.S. Citizen

The framers did not define citizenship in the Constitution. They assumed that each state would establish rules for becoming state citizens and that those people would be considered U.S. citizens.

Today a person can become a U.S. citizen in three ways. In two of these, citizenship is determined by birth. The third is a legal process overseen by the U.S. Department of Justice.

By Birth Most Americans become citizens by birth. People can become citizens by birth in two ways: by being born to U.S. citizens or by being born in the United States or in a U.S. territory.

Congress has long allowed a person born in a foreign country to become a U.S. citizen if at least one of his or her parents is a U.S. citizen. This principle of citizenship by parentage is known as *jus sanguinis* (YOOS SAHNG-gwuh-nuhs), a Latin phrase meaning "law of the blood."

A child born in a foreign country whose parents are both U.S. citizens gains citizenship only if one of the parents has resided at some point in the United States or in a U.S. territory. A child who has one parent who is a U.S. citizen and one who is a citizen of another country becomes a citizen only if the parent who is a U.S. citizen has lived in the United States or in a U.S. territory for at least five years. Two of the five must have been after the parent was 14 years old. In addition, the child can only maintain citizenship by living in the United States for two continuous years sometime between his or her fourteenth and twenty-eighth birthdays.

A second way a person can become a citizen is by being born in the United States or in a U.S. territory. This principle of citizenship by birthplace is called *jus soli* (YOOS soh-LEE), a Latin phrase meaning "law of the soil." The principle was set into law by the Fourteenth Amendment, which was ratified in 1868 and made freed slaves U.S. citizens. The Fourteenth Amendment states that "all persons born . . . in the United States . . . are citizens of the United States and of the State wherein they reside."

What about children born in this country whose parents are citizens of a foreign country? Are they

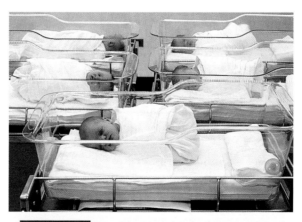

CITIZENSHIP *People can become citizens by being born in the United States or in a U.S. territory.* **In what other way may people become citizens by birth?**

SECTION 1

CITIZENSHIP AND IMMIGRATION

Lesson Plans

For teaching strategies, see Lesson 15.1 located at the beginning of this chapter or the One-Stop Lesson Planner Strategy 15.1.

Political Dictionary

To reinforce the section's vocabulary terms, refer students to the Electronic Glossary on the *Researcher CD-ROM*.

Section Assessment

To assess students' mastery of this section, have them complete Daily Quiz 15.1 in *Daily Quizzes with Answer Key*.

Caption Answer

by being born to U.S. citizens

U.S. citizens? In most cases they are, but only if their parents were under the authority of the United States at the time the children were born. A child born in the United States to parents officially representing a foreign country, for example, is not given citizenship.

Through Naturalization The third way to gain citizenship is through **naturalization**, a legal process by which immigrants become citizens. The naturalization method of becoming a citizen is authorized by the Fourteenth Amendment. Congress, however, passes the laws that outline the naturalization process.

The first part of the naturalization process usually involves entering the United States legally. To do so, foreigners must prove that they can support themselves financially and that they can read and write. They also must prove they do not have certain diseases, mental illnesses, a drug addiction, or a criminal past. Several other restrictions also bar people from entering the United States. One, for example, bars the entry of anarchists, or people who favor the violent overthrow of the government.

Generally, only aliens admitted as permanent residents may become U.S. citizens. Thus foreign visitors, people studying here from abroad, and others who do not plan to live out their lives in the United States do not receive citizenship. Although they are not required to do so, aliens may file a citizenship application and a "declaration of intention." A declaration of intention states that the applicant is over 18 years of age, is planning to give up citizenship in another country, and plans to become a U.S. citizen. Children under 8 automatically become citizens when both of their parents' naturalization has been officially completed. When only one parent has been naturalized, a petition may be filed for citizenship of the child as long as he or she is under 18 and lives with the naturalized parent.

After entering the country legally, an alien can complete the naturalization process only if he or she

★ has been a lawful resident of this country continuously for at least five years (three years if married to a U.S. citizen) and has been physically present in the country for at least half of this period;
★ is at least 18 years old;
★ completes a citizenship application;
★ is able to speak, read, and write English;

★ demonstrates good moral character, belief in the principles of the Constitution, and knowledge of U.S. history and government;
★ supports the order and happiness of the United States; and
★ takes an oath of allegiance to the United States at a swearing-in ceremony.

The U.S. government has occasionally given citizenship to a group of people all at once in a process called collective naturalization. The

How an Alien Becomes a Citizen

PETITION FOR NATURALIZATION
After an alien has lived in the United States at least five years (or three years if married to a U.S. citizen), he or she files an application called a petition for naturalization.

EXAMINATION
A naturalization examiner conducts an examination in which the applicant must show that he or she is a person of good moral character who believes in the principles of the Constitution and supports the order and happiness of the United States. The applicant also must prove that he or she can read, write, and speak English and is knowledgeable about the history and government of the United States. Examinations may be given at a private, designated testing center or at the interview by the immigration examiner.

FINAL HEARING
If the applicant meets all of the qualifications, he or she is granted citizenship at a final hearing. There, the alien swears an oath of allegiance and is given a certificate of naturalization.

Becoming a U.S. citizen involves a lengthy naturalization process. **How many years must someone reside in the United States before he or she can petition for naturalization?**

Constitution's Fourteenth Amendment, for example, collectively naturalized freed slaves and other African Americans. The most common reason for collective naturalization, however, is the acquisition of new territory. When Texas joined the nation in 1845, for example, Congress declared Texas residents naturalized U.S. citizens.

Losing Citizenship

The involuntary loss of U.S. citizenship has occurred only rarely. States may not take away someone's citizenship, though they may restrict some of the rights of a person convicted of a serious crime, usually a felony. A state may, for example, take away a felon's right to vote.

The Supreme Court has ruled that in most cases, the federal government also may not take away someone's citizenship. One Court decision, for example, declared that the federal government may not take away the citizenship of someone who deserts from the military in wartime. The removal of someone's citizenship for desertion, stated the Court, breaks the Constitution's prohibition against cruel and unusual punishment.

The Supreme Court also has limited the federal government's ability to take away citizenship in other situations. Citizens cannot lose their citizenship just by illegally avoiding military service during wartime, nor can naturalized citizens do so simply by returning to their original countries for a few years. Even voting in foreign elections does not automatically cause a loss of citizenship.

PRINCIPLES OF DEMOCRACY *U.S. citizens may vote in elections in a foreign country, such as Nigeria, without endangering their U.S. citizenship.* **What is it called when an individual voluntarily gives up his or her citizenship?**

A court may, however, take away the citizenship of a naturalized citizen who can be shown to have become a U.S. citizen by fraud. A person who lies, for example, about his or her background or provides other false information during the naturalization process may undergo **denaturalization**, or loss of citizenship.

Every citizen has the right to renounce, or give up voluntarily, his or her citizenship, an act known as **expatriation**. A person may give up his or her citizenship in several ways, such as by being naturalized as a citizen of or by pledging allegiance to another country.

SECTION 1 REVIEW ANSWERS

1. Refer to the following pages: civic responsibilities (339), *jus sanguinis* (339), *jus soli* (339), naturalization (340), denaturalization (341), expatriation (341).

2. Diagrams will vary but should reflect an understanding of personal and civic responsibilities.

3a. Foreigners must prove that they can support themselves, read and write, and do not favor violent overthrow of the government. They must also prove that they do not have certain diseases, mental illnesses, a drug addiction, or a criminal past.

3b. They are obligations that come with citizenship. Examples include understanding and obeying the law, respecting the rights of others, paying taxes, voting, and participating in public service.

4. Answers will vary, but students should state their opinion and provide support.

SECTION 1 REVIEW

1. Identify and Explain:
- civic responsibilities
- *jus sanguinis*
- *jus soli*
- naturalization
- denaturalization
- expatriation

2. Identifying Concepts: Copy the chart below. Use it to list examples of personal and civic responsibilities.

Personal responsibilities / Civic responsibilities

3. **Finding the Main Idea**
a. What are the requirements for naturalization?
b. What are civic responsibilities?

4. **Writing and Critical Thinking**
Analyzing Information: Are there times when an individual should set aside personal interests for the public good?
Consider the following:
- the obligations of citizenship
- individual freedoms

Homework Practice Online
keyword: SV3 HP15

SECTION 2

DIVERSITY AND EQUAL PROTECTION

Lesson Plans

For teaching strategies, see Lesson 15.2 located at the beginning of this chapter or the One-Stop Lesson Planner Strategy 15.2.

Political Dictionary

To reinforce the section's vocabulary terms, refer students to the Electronic Glossary on the *Researcher CD-ROM.*

Section Assessment

To assess students' mastery of this section, have them complete Daily Quiz 15.2 in *Daily Quizzes with Answer Key.*

Caption Answer

1882

SECTION 2

DIVERSITY AND EQUAL PROTECTION

READ TO DISCOVER

1. How has U.S. immigration policy changed over time?
2. In what ways is the United States an ethnically diverse country?
3. What are the benefits and challenges of diversity in the United States?

POLITICAL DICTIONARY

illegal alien
deportation
amnesty
ethnic group
prejudice
discrimination

At various times, concern over the number of newcomers arriving in this country has led to efforts to restrict immigration. The diversity brought by immigration has benefited U.S. society in numerous ways. On the other hand, diversity has presented significant challenges, including prejudice and discrimination.

Immigration Policies

You or your ancestors probably immigrated to this country under certain rules. These rules have changed greatly over time, however, with varying limits on the number of foreigners who may come to the United States to live.

Unrestricted Immigration For much of colonial and early U.S. history, there were few immigration rules. Indeed, before the late 1800s anyone who wanted to come to the United States could do so with few or no restrictions.

Why did people come? Throughout the 1800s many came for the land available in the country's vast interior and for jobs in rapidly growing U.S. industries. In fact, so many immigrants arrived during this period that by 1890 they made up nearly 15 percent of the U.S. population.

Over time, tensions developed between immigrants and people already living in the United States. These tensions were caused partly by competition for jobs between immigrant and native-born workers. Differences in cultural traditions, beliefs, and ways of life often caused conflict as well.

Irish immigrants, for example, faced hostility from native-born citizens as well as from other immigrants. The majority of Irish immigrants were Roman Catholics, while most other people in the United States were Protestants. In addition, Irish communities often kept themselves apart by operating their own hospitals, orphanages, and schools. As a result, some native-born citizens feared that Irish immigrants would not become part of U.S. society. Others feared that immigrants might lack respect for the rule of law and threaten the U.S. political system.

Immigration Restrictions Hostility toward immigrants led Congress over time to restrict

CITIZENSHIP *During the 1800s, people from around the world could come to the United States with few immigration restrictions. **When did the government first start placing restrictions on immigration from certain countries?***

Careers in Government

Immigration Officer

The Immigration and Naturalization Service (INS) consists of men and women who work as immigration officers. Their jobs titles include adjudication officer, immigration inspector, detention officer, criminal investigator-special agent and deportation officer.

A typical day for an immigration officer might include transporting aliens, checking medical records and visas, patrolling borders, or making arrests. The INS is responsible for handling hundreds of thousands of cases of legal and illegal immigration a year. As immigrants enter the nation, INS officials are faced with decisions concerning their placement, health, safety, and asylum.

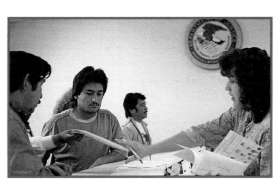

Each year, immigration officers help thousands of people file applications for citizenship. The INS is also responsible for enforcing immigration laws.

In respect to health standards, earlier attempts in the 1990s by INS officers to require that new immigrants have insurance were quashed by the INS administration. Thus, critics say, the cost of medical care of the uninsured immigrants is passed on to the taxpayer, straining the financial stability of the health care community.

President George W. Bush and President Vincente Fox of Mexico met in 2001 to discuss the possibility of legalizing the status of millions of immigrant Mexican laborers now in the United States. In a speech at the White House, President Fox challenged Bush to give "migrants and their communities their proper place in the history of our bilateral nations." Proponents feel it is time to recognize immigrants for the economic, political, and cultural energy they have poured into this country.

Other changes in immigration policy are also challenging INS officers. In June 2001, the U.S. Supreme Court ruled that the INS could not indefinitely detain immigrants convicted of crimes in the United States solely because their homeland would not take them back, a decision that could affect hundreds of people in the agency's custody. The ruling focused on immigrants who were legally admitted to the country but were later convicted of crimes in the United States. In all, INS officers ensure that the United States's heritage as a nation of immigrants continues today in an orderly, legal manner.

Careers in Government

To help students learn about other careers in government, refer them to the Careers section on the *Holt Researcher Online.*

THEMES IN GOVERNMENT

CITIZENSHIP Since the federal government only keeps records of foreigners who come into the country and not of American citizens who leave, no one knows exactly how many Americans are living abroad. One 1993 State Department survey estimates that 2.6 million U.S. citizens live in other countries, but this estimate excludes government employees and dependents of civilian and military employees. Thus, the number is no doubt higher. ∎

---

immigration. In 1882 Congress imposed a tax on those who entered the country and denied entry for convicted criminals, paupers, and people with mental illnesses. Some 20 years later, Congress banned anarchists from entering the United States.

Also in 1882, Congress for the first time banned all immigration from a particular country—in this case, China. Congress was moved to action partly by native-born workers in California who claimed that the low wages paid to Chinese workers lowered wages for everyone else. For similar reasons, Japan, because of pressure from the U.S. government, agreed to restrict emigration to the United States beginning in 1900.

Continuing pressures to restrict immigration led Congress to pass laws in 1921 and 1924 setting specific ceilings on the number of immigrants allowed from each European country. The ceilings were based on the national origins of the U.S. population. The largest group of U.S. citizens at that time—around 47 percent—had western and northern European ancestors. Correspondingly, Congress allowed more immigration from northern and western Europe than from eastern and southern Europe. In addition, the new laws effectively banned immigration from Asia and Africa. Latin Americans were allowed to immigrate to the United States, but they faced strict requirements for coming into the country.

Immigration Policy Today Following World War II, immigration restrictions generally were eased. In the 1950s small numbers of Asians—around 100 per country annually—were allowed to immigrate to the United States. Then in 1965 Congress passed the Immigration and Nationality Act. The new law allowed 290,000 immigrants annually, with 120,000 from the Western Hemisphere and 170,000 from the Eastern Hemisphere. The law was partly designed to reunite U.S. citizens and legal residents with their relatives in foreign countries.

The eased restrictions contributed to dramatic increases in immigration from Asia during the 1970s and 1980s. For example, Asian countries accounted for around 38 percent of all legal immigration to the United States in the 1980s. Many of these immigrants were Filipino. Others were Vietnamese, who began coming to the United States in large numbers during and after the Vietnam War in the 1970s.

Immigration from Latin America also has soared since 1965. By the 1970s more than 40 percent of the legal immigrants to the United States were coming from Latin America. Cuban immigration was highest during the 1960s and 1970s. Today, immigration from Latin America remains at around 50 percent of the total.

The level of legal immigration today is determined by the Immigration Act of 1990, which increased the legal immigration limit to 675,000 a year, not counting refugees. Adjusting this legal limit remains a subject of debate in Congress.

Illegal Immigration One of the most difficult immigration problems in recent years has involved keeping people from entering the United States illegally. In the mid-1990s, for example, about 4 million illegal immigrants were estimated to be living in the United States. Counts of the illegal immigrant population are unreliable, however, because these people must avoid being discovered if they are to remain in the country. These **illegal aliens** came to the United States without legal immigration papers and by law may not remain

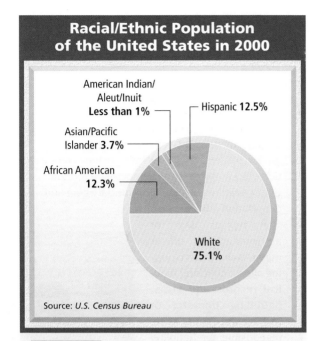

Racial/Ethnic Population of the United States in 2000

American Indian/Aleut/Inuit **Less than 1%**

Asian/Pacific Islander **3.7%**

African American **12.3%**

Hispanic **12.5%**

White **75.1%**

Source: *U.S. Census Bureau*

CITIZENSHIP *The United States contains a rich diversity of peoples and cultures.* **What percentage of the U.S. population in 2000 was African American?**

here. Any who are caught may be **deported**, or forcibly returned to their countries of origin.

In an attempt to control illegal immigration, Congress passed the Immigration Reform and Control Act of 1986. The law gave illegal aliens a one-time **amnesty**, or general pardon that government gives to people who have broken a law. The act allowed illegal aliens who could prove they had lived in the United States since before 1982 to apply to stay in the United States as legal residents. The act also outlawed the hiring of illegal aliens, a step designed to decrease the flow of illegal aliens by reducing job opportunities for them. In 1994, California voters approved a law that denied state benefits, including public education and medical benefits, to illegal aliens and their children. The Supreme Court, however, declared the measure unconstitutional.

In 1996 Congress passed additional measures designed to further restrict illegal immigration. This Illegal Immigration Reform and Immigrant Responsibility Act of 1996 increased border controls and provided stronger penalties for creating and using false identification papers. The act also placed additional restrictions on the use of public benefits by aliens, as well as stricter penalties for those who employ illegal aliens.

A Nation of Diversity

Immigration has led to a diverse U.S. population. People and cultures from around the world can be found in many places in the United States, particularly in large urban areas such as Los Angeles and New York City. This great diversity has brought many benefits, as well as some difficult challenges.

Benefits of Diversity The United States contains a rich mixture of peoples, cultures, and traditions from around the world. This diversity provides several advantages. First, the diversity of cultures makes many people's lives richer. Such diversity gives us the chance to enjoy the foods, music, literature, and celebrations of other cultures. Second, the mixture of different ideas and values in a diverse society encourages creativity in many areas, from literature and the arts to business.

The blending of many cultures and traditions has resulted in a unique U.S. culture. Within this tapestry, many distinct cultural traditions survive and flourish. Neighborhoods such as Chinatown in San Francisco, Polish Hamtramck in Detroit, and Little Italy in New York City are examples of the rich diversity that exists in the United States.

Each of these neighborhoods is populated largely by one **ethnic group**—a group of people within a country who share common characteristics such as race, nationality, religion, language, or cultural heritage. U.S. ethnic groups include American Indians, Irish Americans, Italian Americans, Korean Americans, and Jewish Americans. According to the 2000 census, the population of the United States was 281,421,906. More than 35 million Hispanics lived in the United States in 2000. More than 34 African Americans lived in the United States that same year. (See the chart on the opposite page.)

Challenges of Diversity Such significant diversity of peoples and cultures has presented challenges as well as benefits. Among these challenges are prejudice and discrimination. **Prejudice** is an opinion formed without careful and reasonable investigation of the facts. Suppose, for example, that a white business owner refuses to hire African Americans because he or she dislikes them. The owner's hiring decisions are not based on a reasonable judgment of each job candidate's skills. Instead, the owner partly bases the decisions on his or her personal prejudice against African Americans. Acts of prejudice like this are called **discrimination**.

Unfortunately, some people do harbor prejudices against people who are different from them, and discrimination too often is the result. In the past, government sometimes was used by powerful majorities to discriminate against people in the minority. Over time, however, various groups have struggled to overcome this discrimination. Particularly in this century, as you will see, much progress has been made in ending discrimination.

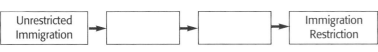

SECTION 2 REVIEW

1. Identify and Explain:
- illegal alien
- deportation
- amnesty
- ethnic group
- prejudice
- discrimination

2. Identifying Concepts: Copy the graphic organizer below. Use it to show how the effects of unrestricted immigration contributed to immigration restrictions.

Unrestricted Immigration → ☐ → ☐ → Immigration Restriction

3. Finding the Main Idea

a. Have immigration policies ever targeted a specific country?

b. What led Congress to restrict immigration?

4. Writing and Critical Thinking

Decision Making: Do you favor increasing or decreasing the number of immigrants allowed into the United States? Explain your answer.

Consider the following:
- the benefits of diversity
- the challenges of diversity

Homework Practice Online
keyword: SV3 HP15

SECTION 3

STRUGGLE FOR CIVIL RIGHTS

READ TO DISCOVER

1. What two tests do federal courts use to determine whether laws respect the Equal Protection Clause?
2. How did the Equal Protection Clause help the civil rights movement fight government discrimination?

POLITICAL DICTIONARY

civil rights
suspect classification
civil rights movement
segregation
Jim Crow law
de jure segregation
separate-but-equal doctrine
de facto segregation

Much of the progress against discrimination has been made in the courts. Judges have used the Fourteenth Amendment's Equal Protection Clause to prevent discrimination by federal and state governments. This clause has been key in securing all citizens' civil rights, particularly those of African Americans. **Civil rights** are those powers or privileges that governments grant to individuals to guarantee their equal treatment under the law.

Equal Protection of the Law

As you have learned, the Equal Protection Clause is part of the Fourteenth Amendment, which was added to the Constitution after the Civil War to protect the rights of the newly freed slaves. The amendment says that a state government may not "deny to any person within its jurisdiction the equal protection of the laws." In short, the Equal Protection Clause keeps state governments from classifying people *unfairly* and from making unreasonable distinctions between groups of people. Such classifications imply that government considers it acceptable to treat some people differently from others.

Reasonable Distinction Making sure that people are guaranteed equal protection under the law does not prohibit government from making some distinctions between classes of people. For example, many state governments charge state park visitor fees to pay for the maintenance of the parks. People who do not visit parks do not pay the fees. Thus, in this situation the government has reasonably discriminated, or distinguished, between two groups of people—park visitors and nonpark visitors.

When is discrimination considered reasonable? Today, federal courts generally use two guidelines to decide if government has made fair distinctions between classes of people in specific circumstances. These guidelines are the rational basis test and the strict scrutiny test.

Rational Basis Test The courts recognize that government sometimes has good reasons, or a rational basis, for treating some classes of people differently from others. Differences in treatment are considered valid under the rational basis test

PRINCIPLES OF DEMOCRACY *When the legal drinking age was set at 21, the rational basis test was used to determine that in this case discrimination was reasonable.* **What other guideline is used in determining if discrimination is reasonable?**

CONSTITUTIONAL GOVERNMENT *Some southern schools, such as the Moton School in Virginia, remained legally segregated into the mid-1950s despite the addition of the Thirteenth, Fourteenth, and Fifteenth Amendments.* **What term means segregation by law?**

THEMES IN GOVERNMENT

CITIZENSHIP The Fourteenth Amendment defined citizenship (all people born or naturalized in the United States and subject to its laws), and it prohibited laws depriving people of life, liberty, or property without due process. Thus, with this amendment, the idea of a national citizenship was introduced into the Constitution, realizing the Declaration of Independence's proposition that "all men are created equal." ■

if they are part of a law that establishes reasonable methods of accomplishing a legitimate goal of government.

The rational basis test can be used to judge many current laws with which you might be familiar. Think about the minimum legal age for drinking alcoholic beverages, for example. This law treats people under 21 differently by prohibiting them from drinking alcohol. Is this discrimination reasonable? Legislators believe that people under 21 have not gained enough life experience to make wise decisions about drinking alcohol. The courts have agreed, stating that these laws pursue a legitimate goal of discouraging irresponsible consumption of alcohol.

Strict Scrutiny Test In cases where government makes distinctions between people based on race or national origin, federal courts have adopted a much stricter standard than that used in the rational basis test. Because such distinctions often reflect prejudice, federal courts automatically presume that they are of suspect, or doubtful, legality. Called **suspect classifications**, these distinctions are immediately considered by the courts to be possible violations of the Equal Protection Clause. In such cases, the courts scrutinize the law strictly.

When courts apply the strict scrutiny test, government must show that a classification is more than just a reasonable method of achieving a legitimate goal. Instead, government must show

that there are compelling reasons that make such a law important to the public interest. The higher standard applied by the strict scrutiny test is much harder for government to meet than the standard under the rational basis test.

To understand the strict scrutiny test, suppose that a city government passed a law requiring a local high school to set up one cafeteria for white students and one for African American students. City officials might argue that such a law was a reasonable effort to minimize disagreements among students of different races. Under the strict scrutiny test, however, the government would have to show that keeping students separated by race served some compelling public interest. The courts in fact have ruled that no compelling reason exists in such a case and have struck down similar laws.

Civil Rights and Equal Protection

The Equal Protection Clause has played a key role in the **civil rights movement**—the struggle by minorities and women to gain in practice the rights guaranteed to all citizens by the Constitution. The movement has a long history and an enduring legacy.

***De Jure* Segregation** Among the most visible examples of government discrimination against

CONSTITUTIONAL GOVERNMENT *During the late 1800s many southern states enacted laws that segregated numerous public places.* **Which amendments passed after the Civil War freed slaves and gave constitutional liberties to African Americans?**

African Americans was **segregation**, or mandatory separation of the races. Southern states began enacting segregation policies under the so-called **Jim Crow laws** of the late 1800s.

Jim Crow laws covered nearly all areas of life, particularly in the South. The laws required, for example, separate schools for white students and African American students. Public transportation, public rest rooms, hotels, restaurants, places of entertainment, and other public places also were segregated by law. Even public drinking fountains carried signs reserving some of them for "Whites Only" and others for "Colored," or African Americans.

De jure (dee JOOHR-ee) **segregation**, or segregation by law, became policy in the South despite the existence of the Thirteenth, Fourteenth, and Fifteenth Amendments to the Constitution. These three amendments had been passed after the Civil War to free the slaves and to give constitutional liberties to African Americans. For many decades, however, federal courts refused to rule that segregation policies violated constitutional civil rights protections.

One landmark segregation case was *Plessy* v. *Ferguson* in 1896. In that case the Supreme Court upheld a Louisiana law requiring separate railway coaches for white and African American passengers. The *Plessy* decision enshrined the **separate-but-equal doctrine** in U.S. law for

decades afterward. This doctrine held that segregation laws did not violate the Equal Protection Clause so long as the facilities reserved for each race were equal to those for the other.

In reality, however, separate facilities often were anything but equal. African American students frequently had access only to older, broken-down schools that were far inferior to those reserved for whites. Efforts to show that the separate-but-equal doctrine was not, in fact, permitted by the Equal Protection Clause became the main goal in the struggle to secure African Americans' civil rights.

Rolling Back Segregation The fight against the separate-but-equal doctrine continued for many years. Eventually, the Supreme Court turned against Jim Crow laws. In *Sweatt* v. *Painter* in 1948, for example, the Court ruled that a segregated law school for African American students at the University of Texas could not provide students with equal educational opportunities and therefore violated the Equal Protection Clause.

In 1954, civil rights supporters won a major victory. That year, the Supreme Court ruled in *Brown* v. *Board of Education of Topeka* that the segregation of public schools necessarily made for unequal education. A racially segregated school, the Court said, "generates a feeling of inferiority" among African American students "that may affect their hearts and minds in a way unlikely ever to be undone." Therefore, the Court said, "separate educational facilities are inherently [by their very nature] unequal."

In 1955 the Supreme Court ordered states to act "with all deliberate speed" to integrate, or desegregate, their schools. The resistance of prosegregation whites, mostly in southern states, slowed the pace of integration, however. Federal law enforcement officials and federal troops occasionally were used to protect African American students enrolling in formerly all-white schools. Finally, in the 1971 case *Swann* v. *Charlotte-Mecklenburg* the Supreme Court upheld a lower federal court's power to impose busing plans and set racial admission levels to speed desegregation.

Over time the Supreme Court ruled against legally segregated public transportation, prisons, and other facilities. In fact, it extended its rulings to overturn every state law segregating a public place. In 1967 the Court ruled in *Loving* v. *Virginia* that state laws banning interracial marriages violated the Equal Protection Clause.

De Facto Segregation Even though *de jure* segregation ended by the early 1970s, the separation of the races has continued. Even today **de facto segregation** (literally "segregation in fact") exists in school systems around the country. In neighborhoods with mainly African American populations, for example, enrollment in local schools often is largely African American. Similarly, communities with largely white populations often have local schools in which enrollment is mainly white.

Efforts to eliminate *de facto* segregation often have been bitterly opposed. In the 1970s, for

CONSTITUTIONAL GOVERNMENT *To help eliminate* de facto *segregation the government used busing programs in the nation's schools.* **How did people react to many of these efforts?**

example, many whites reacted with hostility when courts ordered white students bused into black neighborhoods to integrate public schools. African Americans also were bused to schools in white neighborhoods. The strongest reactions occurred in northern cities such as Boston, where violence broke out between black and white students. Busing and other means to eliminate *de facto* segregation remain controversial.

SECTION 3 REVIEW ANSWERS

1. Refer to the following pages: civil rights (346), suspect classification (347), civil rights movement (347), segregation (348), Jim Crow law (348), *de jure* segregation (348), separate-but-equal doctrine (348), *de facto* segregation (349).

2. *Plessy*—established separate-but-equal doctrine; *Sweatt*—segregated law school violated Equal Protection Clause; *Brown*—struck down separate-but-equal doctrine; *Loving*—state laws banning interracial marriages violated Equal Protection Clause

3a. Examples may include requiring separate schools for blacks and whites and segregated facilities for public transportation, public rest rooms, hotels, restaurants, places of entertainment, and drinking fountains.

3b. It required public schools to be integrated.

4. Answers will vary, but students should state their opinion and provide support.

SECTION 3 REVIEW

1. Identify and Explain:
- civil rights
- suspect classification
- civil rights movement
- segregation
- Jim Crow law
- *de jure* segregation
- separate-but-equal doctrine
- *de facto* segregation

2. Identifying Concepts: Copy the chart below. Use it to explain how these court decisions effected African Americans.

Decision	Effect
Plessy v. *Ferguson*	
Sweatt v. *Painter*	
Brown v. *Board of Education of Topeka*	
Loving v. *Virginia*	

3. Finding the Main Idea

a. What are some examples of Jim Crow laws?

b. How did the Supreme Court's decision in the *Brown* case affect public schools?

4. Writing and Critical Thinking

Summarizing: Do you think the government should try to eliminate *de facto* segregation? Explain your answer.
Consider the following:
- the requirements of the Equal Protection Clause
- the importance of promoting the public good
- the constitutional right to free association

go.hrw.com **Homework Practice Online**
keyword: SV3 HP15

SECTION 4

CIVIL RIGHTS LAWS

READ TO DISCOVER

1. How have civil rights laws protected the rights of African Americans?
2. How have civil rights protections been extended to other minority groups?

POLITICAL DICTIONARY

affirmative action
quota

The struggle for civil rights did not end with court victories against segregation. Through marches, protests, and close work with lawmakers, civil rights supporters have gained the passage of key legislation protecting the civil rights of African Americans and other minority groups.

Civil Rights Laws

The first civil rights laws, which were passed in the late 1800s, were not strictly enforced by the courts and did little to protect against discrimination. The growing strength of the civil rights movement in the 1950s and 1960s, however, produced several effective civil rights laws.

Early Laws The first civil rights laws were passed in the 10 years following the Civil War. The Civil Rights Act of 1866 sought to protect African Americans' constitutional rights, such as the right to vote. In addition, an 1875 act outlawed racial discrimination in public places, such as theaters and hotels.

In general, however, these early civil rights laws made little progress in preventing racial discrimination. This failing resulted in large part from court rulings that not only weakened the effects of such laws but also declared many of their provisions unconstitutional.

Failure of Early Laws The federal and state governments' failure to protect African Americans' civil rights was clear by the late 1800s. African Americans accused of crimes, for example, often did not receive fair trials. In addition, many African Americans were lynched, or murdered by mobs acting outside the law. Such lynchings often went unpunished.

The severe discrimination experienced by African Americans gradually persuaded many people that the federal government needed to take a stronger role in protecting individual rights. In response, Congress passed civil rights laws in 1957 and 1960. However, these laws were of limited scope. The failure to pass strong civil rights laws led civil rights supporters to intensify their efforts. Through marches, demonstrations, and boycotts, civil rights supporters pressed Congress for stronger legislation.

Nonviolent Protests One of the earliest boycotts began in December 1955 when Rosa Parks—an African American seamstress in Montgomery, Alabama—was arrested for refusing to give up her seat to a white person on a public bus as required by city segregation laws. Alabama civil rights leaders responded to the arrest by asking African

PRINCIPLES OF DEMOCRACY *"Sit-ins" such as the one pictured here were used as a nonviolent method of protesting segregation.* **What were some other forms of nonviolent civil rights protest?**

PRINCIPLES OF DEMOCRACY *Martin Luther King, Jr., waves to a crowd of some 250,000 Americans who had gathered in Washington, D.C., to express their support for the civil rights movement.* **In what year did the March on Washington occur?**

American citizens to boycott the city buses until the city changed the laws. The bus company lost 65 percent of its normal income as a result. The boycott did not end until almost a year later, when the Supreme Court ruled that the segregation of buses was unconstitutional.

Most civil rights supporters conveyed their message through nonviolent protest. In February 1960 in Greensboro, North Carolina, for example, four African American college students staged a "sit-in" at a Woolworth store's lunch counter, which refused to serve black customers. The students entered the store, sat down at the lunch counter, and were refused service. They stayed for a few hours and then left. The next day, they returned to the store and sat for a few more hours. By the fourth day, some whites began participat-ing. During the first six months of the protest, police arrested more than 1,600 participants. The sit-ins, which were almost always led by high school or college students, spread to other south-ern cities.

Despite their use of nonviolent methods, the pro-testers often were the victims of violence from oth-ers. During 1961, for example, members of the Congress of Racial Equality organized the Freedom Rides—bus trips that both African Americans and white civil rights supporters took to various south-ern cities to challenge the segregation practices in bus terminals. The Freedom Riders rode through-out the South, intentionally ignoring the segrega-tion signs in terminals along the way. In Alabama, when buses and their riders were attacked by angry mobs, the local authorities offered little or no pro-tection. In Mississippi, riders were arrested and jailed. In spite of these incidents, the Freedom Riders continued their efforts.

In August 1963 more than 250,000 Americans gathered in Washington, D.C., to express their support for the civil rights movement. This March on Washington was led in part by Martin Luther King Jr.—a dynamic civil rights activist, Baptist minister, and president of the Southern Christian Leadership Conference—who was one of the guiding forces behind the principle of nonviolent protest. It was at this event that King made his famous "I Have a Dream" speech, in which he declared, "I have a dream that my four little children will one day live in a nation where they will not be judged by the color of their skin, but by the content of their character."

Change Takes Hold Such pressures finally led to the passage of the most important civil rights laws in a century. The 1964 Civil Rights Act forbade seg-regation of public places, such as restaurants, lunch counters, movie theaters, and hotels. The act also extended civil rights protections to minority groups other than just African Americans. It prohibited employers and administrators of any program receiving federal funding from discriminating based on race, national origin, religion, or sex.

Profiles in American Government

For a biography of Martin Luther King Jr., and other noted people in the civil rights movement, refer students to the Biographies section on the *Researcher CD-ROM.*

LITERATURE Writer Lewis Allan's "Strange Fruit," a reaction to lynching in the South, was set to music, and jazz singer Billie Holiday—despising the racism she experienced on the road—adopted it as a signature ballad. It was recorded in 1939 and became one of her best-sellers. She always closed her shows with it and would not return to the stage after she had sung it. ∎

In contrast to court decisions on civil rights laws in the 1800s, the Supreme Court ruled that the 1964 Civil Rights Act was constitutional. The Court decided that congressional authority to prevent discrimination in public places came from its constitutional power to regulate commerce among the states. Motels, for example, are considered part of interstate commerce partly because they receive many out-of-state customers. Similarly, restaurants serving out-of-state food are said to be involved in interstate commerce as well.

As a result of the 1964 law, facilities that had once been closed to African Americans opened their doors. Many public schools that had been slow to integrate were pushed into action, fearing that their state's attorney general would file lawsuits against them otherwise. Similarly, agencies that received federal grants for local projects, such as youth programs and public facilities, also were affected by the new law.

Another key civil rights law, the Voting Rights Act of 1965, helped African Americans secure equal opportunity at the ballot box. Among other things, the law prohibited the use of literacy and other tests to decide if a person could vote. These tests had been used to prevent many African Americans in the South from voting. The law also allowed federal agents to help African Americans register to vote in states where they faced discrimination. As a result, between 1964 and 1968 the percentage of registered African American voters in several states rose significantly—from 7 to 59 percent in Mississippi, for example. (Voting is more fully explained in Chapter 19.)

Congress has since passed other civil rights laws as well, including the Civil Rights Acts of 1968 and 1991. The 1968 act prohibited discrimination based on race, national origin, and religion in the advertising, financing, sale, and rental of housing. The 1991 law strengthened protections against discrimination in the workplace.

Extending Civil Rights

The progress made by African Americans has encouraged other groups that are working to end discrimination. These groups include Hispanic Americans, American Indians, Asian Americans, people with disabilities, and women.

Hispanic Americans Hispanic Americans compose a rapidly growing ethnic group in

Comparing Governments

Nonviolent Protests in Myanmar

As in the United States, nonviolent protest has been used by people around the world who demand fair treatment and civil rights. In 1988, for example, prodemocracy supporters in Myanmar (then called Burma) participated in nonviolent demonstrations against General Ne Win, who had ruled the South Asian country for more than 25 years. The military reacted by crushing the demonstrations and killing thousands of people, while military leaders took over the government.

In response, protester Daw Aung San Suu Kyi (daw awng suhn soo chee) cofounded a prodemocracy opposition party, the National League for Democracy. Suu Kyi bravely spoke out against the military government. As a result of her actions, she was placed under house arrest for six years, and the army arrested hundreds of her supporters. Suu Kyi's efforts drew world attention, however, and she received the Nobel Peace Prize in 1991 in recognition of her nonviolent campaign. Political pressure eventually forced the military government to release her. "We must have the courage to face the bully's challenge," Suu Kyi said, as she vowed to continue her party's nonviolent struggle for democracy. Myanmar's military, however, continues to exercise significant political and economic power.

the United States. Hispanic Americans are U.S. citizens or residents who are of Latin American or Spanish descent.

Hispanic Americans have faced discrimination in several areas, such as employment and housing. Progress has been made, however, in extending civil rights to Hispanic Americans. By 2000, 21 seats in the House of Representatives, and 197 Hispanic Americans in state legislatures as of 2001.

American Indians American Indians today make up around 1 percent of the U.S. population.

For most of U.S. history, the federal government considered American Indians to be conquered peoples with their own separate governments. As a result, they were long denied many civil rights. For example, some American Indians could not vote until 1924, when they were granted U.S. citizenship.

Since the 1960s American Indians have used protests, court cases, and lobbying efforts to secure their civil rights. In 1975, for example, Congress expanded protections of the Voting Rights Act to require that ballots be printed in American Indian languages in communities with large American Indian populations. (The same law required that ballots be printed in Spanish and other languages of large non-English-speaking minority populations where appropriate.)

Asian Americans Like Hispanic Americans, Asian Americans are a rapidly growing ethnic group in the United States. Increasing immigration from Asia, particularly since the 1970s, has fueled this growth.

At different points in U.S. history, racial prejudice has been a source of discrimination against Asian Americans. For example, Japanese Americans on the West Coast, many of them U.S. citizens, were held in detention centers while the United States and Japan were at war with each other during World War II. Like other ethnic minorities, however, Asian Americans today are protected by the civil rights acts of the 1950s and 1960s.

People with Disabilities Civil rights protections were extended again in 1990 with the passage of the Americans with Disabilities Act (ADA). The ADA forbids employers and the owners of public accommodations to discriminate against people with disabilities.

You can see the effects of the ADA in many places. Businesses have installed ramps, widened doors, and made other changes to provide access to people with disabilities. The ADA also mandated establishment of the Telecommunications Relay Service (TRS), which enables people with hearing and speech impairments to communicate by telephone with anyone in the country.

Women From early in the country's history, women did not have the same rights as men. Except for the Nineteenth Amendment, which

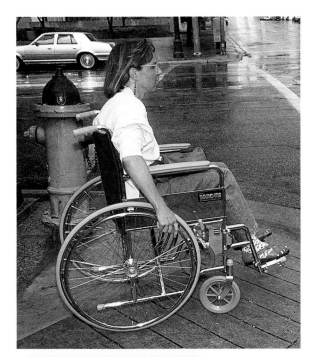

CONSTITUTIONAL GOVERNMENT *The Americans with Disabilities Act prohibits discrimination against people with disabilities.* **What effects of the ADA can you see in your school?**

gave women the right to vote in 1920, the Constitution contains no references to people's sex. Because of this lack of clearly stated constitutional protections, courts once regularly ruled against claims of sex discrimination in employment and other areas. Courts also refused to rule against the practice of excluding women from juries. In a 1961 case, for example, the Supreme Court ruled that such exclusions were proper in light of the place of women at "the center of home and family life."

Efforts to win equal rights for women have made significant progress, however. The civil rights acts of the 1960s, for example, included protections against sex discrimination. In addition, in the 1971 case *Reed* v. *Reed* the Supreme Court for the first time ruled against a law that discriminated against women. The case involved an Idaho law that gave fathers preference over mothers in deciding who should administer the estates of children who had died. In later cases the Court ruled that government must have strong reasons for making legal distinctions between men and women.

Progress toward equal rights for women has brought many changes to U.S. society. Since 1979,

THEMES IN GOVERNMENT

POLITICAL PROCESSES In 1992 Brown University, in an effort to downsize, stopped funding its women's volleyball and gymnastics. Men's golf and water polo were also cut, and women were still offered a variety of sports. Volleyball players and gymnasts still felt shunned, however, and filed a suit under a 1972 federal gender-equality statute.

The courts decided that Brown is in violation of Title IX, which establishes ratios based on numerical proportionality to determine how many athletic opportunities a school must provide to females. The first court to hear the case even went so far as to instruct Brown that it needed to fund four more women's athletic teams. Brown's appeal of the decision was heard by the U.S. Court of Appeals First Circuit. The court overruled the lower court's decision that Brown must fund four more teams, but upheld the court's decision that Brown, and other schools, still needed to comply with Title IX. ■

Enhancing the Lesson

For more information about *Reed* v. *Reed* and other Supreme Court decisions, see the Supreme Court Docket section on the *Holt Researcher Online.*

Citizenship in

Action

Many students from the University of California at Los Angeles protested the end of affirmative action in the state university system.

Speaking Out on Affirmative Action

Affirmative action programs at businesses and universities seek to provide special consideration for minority applicants during the making of hiring, admissions, or scholarship decisions. Supporters of affirmative action argue that these programs create a more diverse environment at school or in the workplace and help to compensate for social inequalities that have hindered minorities. Opponents, however, believe that such programs have served their purpose and are no longer necessary. As a result, many of these programs have recently been challenged as unfair or unconstitutional.

College students across the country have joined this heated debate. The 1995 decision by the University of California board of regents to end affirmative action in the state university system created an uproar. Thousands of students from the Los Angeles campus (UCLA) protested, demanding that the decision be repealed. Other students, such as African Student Union member Shauna Robinson, organized a public forum designed to educate students about the need for affirmative action.

Protests then spread to other California college campuses, where student organizations worked to influence opinion on affirmative action. Despite these efforts, the ban on affirmative action remains in effect.

California students also formed groups supporting the regents' decision. One such group was Students Against Affirmative Action and for Equality, which argued that admissions criteria involving race were unnecessary. This group suggested that alternative criteria such as financial hardship would be more impartial and would still help many minority students.

The controversy in California spurred many groups around the country to action. After attending a protest by UCLA students, civil rights leader Jesse Jackson urged young African Americans throughout the country to defend affirmative action policies. He accused young people of having become "much too comfortable" and called on them to protect hard-won civil rights.

High school students around the nation also joined the debate. *United Youth of Boston,* an independent high school student newspaper, published articles discussing affirmative action. Inspired by the reports, students at Boston's Madison Park High School organized forums on racism, poverty, and education.

The status of affirmative action is still uncertain. A 1997 poll taken by the Joint Center for Political and Economic Studies suggested that African Americans age 18 to 25 were more likely to support affirmative action than older African Americans or whites. More than 80 percent of the whites polled and about half of the African Americans and Hispanics were against preferential treatment for minorities. No matter what decisions local, state, and federal government make on affirmative action, the debate over the subject has encouraged many students to explore and discuss their rights and responsibilities as U.S. citizens.

What Do You Think?

1. What is your opinion of affirmative action programs at universities?
2. What were some of the ways in which college students worked to educate the public about affirmative action?

PRINCIPLES OF DEMOCRACY *Protesters march by the New York Public Library during a parade for women's suffrage in the early 1900s.* **In what year were women guaranteed the right to vote?**

for example, women have outnumbered men on college campuses. In addition, women now work in occupations that once were closed to them, including medicine, law, and engineering.

CASE STUDY

Affirmative Action

CONSTITUTIONAL GOVERNMENT **Affirmative action** refers to policies that are used to help end the effects of both historical and continuing discrimination, particularly in jobs and education. Some people believe that affirmative action guarantees freedom from racial and sexual discrimination. Opponents argue that establishing numerical goals—or **quotas**—based on race or sex is unfair, and can lead to "reverse discrimination." Debate over affirmative action seems to divide our nation rather than solve the problem.

Supporters argue that affirmative action measures are one of the best ways to ensure that minorities and women have the same opportunities that others have. Without such efforts, they argue, minorities and women would continue to earn less money as well as hold fewer high-level jobs in top companies and fewer positions in certain fields.

Recent criticism has been directed toward colleges and universities using an affirmative action quota system, saying that placement should occur through merit, not sex or racial status. Supporters of affirmative action feel that ending affirmative action in college admission would unfairly exclude entire minority groups from higher education.

Opponents of affirmative action expresses views of concern over favoring members of one group over another. Apparently, the Supreme Court agrees. The University of California school system ended affirmative action in the mid-1990s. California voters then abolished sex and racial preferences in a 1996 statewide initiative. The Supreme Court upheld the initiative's constitutionality. Public colleges in the states of Texas and Georgia also ended affirmative action. Since then, enrollment of African Americans and Hispanics has dropped.

SECTION 4 REVIEW ANSWERS

CONSTITUTIONAL GOVERNMENT *People disagree about affirmative action policies.* **What issue has been particularly controversial in policies surrounding affirmative action?**

The seesaw battle for and against affirmation action at educational institutions continues. In 2001 the University of Michigan found itself embroiled in lawsuits over its admissions policy and affirmative action. Supporters of the university's affirmative action policy feared that "reducing the diversity among the University of Michigan student body likely will deny significant communities within Michigan the ability to fully participate in the political and economic benefits of our society."

The latest supporter of an affirmative action issue is President George W. Bush. In August 2001, he filed a brief with the U.S. Supreme Court that supports a Department of Transportation (DOT) set-aside program for federal highway contracts.

The DOT's "disadvantaged business enterprises" program offers incentives to prime contractors who use businesses owned by women or people of color as subcontractors. But this measure based placement not on a person's race but their having "suffered discrimination on account of race, ethnicity or cultural bias."

As the battle for affirmative action wages on, supporters and opponents continue to argue over how much consideration race and sex should be given in making employment and admissions decisions.

SECTION 4 REVIEW

1. Identify and Explain:
- affirmative action
- quota

2. Identifying Concepts: Copy the chart to the right. Use it to identify the key civil rights laws of the 1960s and explain how each one helps protect the civil rights of African Americans.

Civil Rights Law	Protections provided

Homework Practice Online
keyword: SV3 HP15

3. **Finding the Main Idea**

a. How did the citizens of Montgomery, Alabama end segregation on buses?

b. How has the civil rights movement affected groups other than African Americans?

4. **Writing and Critical Thinking**

Drawing Conclusions: Do you think affirmative action is an appropriate tool for overcoming the effects of past discrimination? Explain your answer.
Consider the following:
- the right of all citizens to receive equal treatment
- the need to avoid additional discrimination

GOVERNMENT IN THE NEWS

Both Sides of the Border

In recent years, the vast majority of immigrants to the United States have come from Latin American countries, with immigrants from Mexico far outnumbering any other group. Many immigrants enter the country illegally. As of 2001 there were an estimated 6.5 million illegal immigrants in the United States. The issue of illegal immigration continues to vex officials on both sides of the U.S.-Mexico border.

Many immigrants have little choice but to leave their country. Two major earthquakes in El Salvador in 2001 caused many Salvadorans to flee to the United States and left Salvadorans already in the United States unable to return to their homeland.

Many immigrants seek economic opportunity. Researchers report that illegal immigrants in the United States send home billions of dollars each year to aid their families. Funds totaling more than $6 billion go to Mexico; only oil and tourism provide more money to Mexico's economy. Immigrants also benefit the United States, adding some $10 billion into the U.S. economy every year. The agricultural and food service industries depend heavily upon immigrant labor from Mexico.

Illegal immigration also has serious drawbacks for the United States and Latin America. More Mexican families emigrate from Mexico every year and fewer return, leaving some Mexican villages nearly abandoned. The U.S. border patrol has in recent years increased security at well-known border-crossing sites. Undeterred, many immigrants find other, more dangerous means of crossing. In Mexico, the smuggling of immigrants from Central America in trucks bound for the United States has become a billion-dollar industry. In May 2001 fourteen Mexican immigrants died in the sweltering heat of the southern Arizona desert after illegally crossing the border from Mexico.

Potential immigrants wait in line at the U.S. Immigration and Naturalization Services. Political and economic factors as well as foreign relations all affect immigration policy-making.

Fundamentally, entering the United States without permission is illegal. Illegal immigration is nevertheless a fact, and any change in U.S. immigration policy would have dramatic consequences on the country's economy and its foreign relations, particularly with Mexico. In 2001 the Bush administration considered a proposal to give legal status to some of the estimated 3 million Mexicans currently in the United States illegally.

Supporters of this proposal, both in the United States and Mexico, believe that since many illegal immigrants have jobs, they ought to be considered legal. Some critics argue, however, that the rate of illegal immigration is tied to the rate of legal immigration—those who have legal status in the United States are able to provide connections to those seeking to enter illegally.

What Do You Think?

1. How does immigration help and harm the United States and Latin America?

2. Do you think illegal immigrants with jobs should be granted legal status?

> **WHY IT MATTERS TODAY**
>
> Immigration is a crucial factor in the economic, social, and foreign policies of the United States. Use CNNfyi.com or other **current events** sources to find information on immigration policy and immigration statistics.
>
> **CNNfyi.com**

(Continued on page 358)

Review

(Continued from page 357)

very restrictive but has loosened up in recent years, allowing a 675,000 annual limit of immigrants.

3. benefits—rich experiences of various cultures; challenges—discrimination

4. the rational basis and strict scrutiny tests

5. prohibits distinction or classification by race

6. The courts weakened effects of early laws but declared present laws constitutional; civil rights laws protect other minority groups, people with disabilities, and women.

Reviewing Themes

1. Answers will vary. Students should list busing and other examples and describe whether they feel these programs work.

2. Answers will vary, but students should demonstrate an understanding of the obligations of citizenship.

3. Answers will vary, but students should support their opinions.

Thinking Critically

1. Such laws often reflect prejudice. Answers will vary but students may consider civil rights issues.

2. Answers will vary, but students should offer support for their answers

3. Answers will vary, but students should state their opinion and provide support.

(Continued on page 359)

Writing a Summary

Using standard grammar, spelling, sentence structure, and punctuation, write a summary of the information in this chapter.

Identifying Ideas

Identify the following terms and explain their significance.

1. civic responsibilities

2. naturalization

3. illegal alien

4. deportation

5. amnesty

6. civil rights movement

7. segregation

8. Jim Crow law

9. separate-but-equal doctrine

10. affirmative action

Understanding Main Ideas

SECTION 1 *(pp. 339–341)*

1. In what three ways may a person become a U.S. citizen? How can a person lose U.S. citizenship?

SECTION 2 *(pp. 342–345)*

2. Describe U.S. immigration policy during the United States's first 100 years as a nation. How has immigration policy changed since then?

3. What benefits and challenges does diversity present?

SECTION 3 *(pp. 346–349)*

4. What guidelines do courts use to determine whether government laws violate the Equal Protection Clause?

5. What role does the Equal Protection Clause play in protecting the civil rights of African Americans?

SECTION 4 *(pp. 350–356)*

6. Why were civil rights laws of the 1950s and 1960s more successful than earlier civil rights laws? What groups besides African Americans do civil rights laws protect?

Reviewing Themes

1. Constitutional Government Why do you think that *de facto* segregation is difficult to combat? What has the government done to eliminate this? Has this been effective?

2. Citizenship Under what circumstances would you sacrifice your personal interests for the public good? Would you go to war?

3. Public Good Imagine that it is the 1950s. Write a short newspaper editorial explaining why segregation should be outlawed in public places.

Thinking Critically

1. Drawing Conclusions Why must there be compelling reasons for passing a law that has suspect classifications? Why do you think the courts created the strict scrutiny test?

2. Summarizing How diverse is your community? In what ways has your community been shaped by various cultures?

3. Decision Making Would you support being bused to a different school in order to promote racial integration?

Writing about Government

Review what you wrote in your Government Notebook at the beginning of this chapter about the ways government should work to prevent unfair discrimination. Now that you have studied this chapter, would you revise your answer? Do actual government methods match those that you listed? Does the government do more or less than you believe it should? Record your answers in your Notebook.

Interpreting the Visual Record

Study the table below. Then use it to help you answer the questions that follow.

Foreign-Born Population in the United States		
Country of Origin	Estimated Population	Percentage of U.S. Foreign-Born Population
Mexico	7.2 million	27.2%
Phillippines	1.5 million	5.5%
China/ Hong Kong	985,000	3.7%
Vietnam	966,000	3.7%
Cuba	943,000	3.6%
India	839,000	3.2%
El Salvador	761,000	2.9%
Dominican Republic	679,000	2.6%
Great Britain	655,000	2.5%
Korea	611,000	2.3%
Elsewhere	11.4 million	42.9%

Source: Statistical Abstract of the United States: 2000

1. What percentage of the U.S. foreign-born population comes from China, Hong Kong, Korea, the Phillippines, and Vietnam combined?
- **a.** 12.5
- **b.** 10.5
- **c.** 15.2
- **d.** 10.2

2. Which country accounts for over 27 percent of the foreign-born population?

Analyzing Primary Sources

LETTER FROM BIRMINGHAM JAIL

Martin Luther King Jr., led the civil rights movement of the 1950s and 1960s. In 1963 King was jailed because he refused to obey a court order to put an end to civil rights demonstrations in Birmingham, Alabama. While in jail, he wrote this letter. Read the excerpt below and answer the questions that follow.

"We know through painful experience that freedom is never voluntarily given by the oppressor [persecutor]; it must be demanded by the oppressed [people who are persecuted]. Frankly I have never yet engaged in a direct action movement that was 'well timed,' according to the timetable of those who have not suffered unduly [excessively] from the disease of segregation. For years now I have heard the word 'Wait!' It rings in the ear of every Negro with a piercing familiarity. . . . We must come to see with the distinguished jurist of yesterday that 'justice too long delayed is justice denied.' We have waited for more than 340 years for our constitutional and God-given rights."

3. Which of the following statements best reflects King's point of view?
- **a.** Change is happening too fast
- **b.** African Americans should be patient
- **c.** The oppressor gives freedom willingly
- **d.** Justice has been delayed too long

4. Why did King believe that waiting for the right time to protest segregation was futile?

(Continued from page 358)

Writing About History

The Government Notebook is a follow-up activity to the notebook activity that appears on page 338.

Building Social Studies Skills

1. c
2. Mexico
3. d
4. The wait could be never ending.

Alternative Assessment

To assess this activity see Rubric 1: Acquiring Information I *Alternative Assessment Handbook.*

Alternative Assessment

Building Your Portfolio

Use the library and other resources to identify important individuals in the struggle for civil rights—for example, Martin Luther King Jr. Create a biographical sketch of one of these people, including his or her background, accomplishments, and role in the civil rights movement. In addition, include illustrations and a list of resources readers can use to learn more about the person.

internet connect

Internet Activity: go.hrw.com
KEYWORD: SV3 GV15

Access the Internet through the HRW Go site to find information on civil rights laws. Then create a multimedia presentation that illustrates the history of civil rights laws as well as the campaigns to end discrimination in schools, housing, hiring, sports participation, and public access.

LAB OBJECTIVES

The Unit 5 Public Policy Lab incorporates the following objectives:

▶ read documents, such as a newswriting guide, a list of facts from a reporter's research, and a letter from the state attorney general.

▶ review the documents to answer questions pertaining to them.

▶ use a decision-making process to synthesize information to write a story on it.

Using the Lab

Before beginning the lab, organize students into groups and distribute copies of the Public Policy Lab Unit 5 Activity found in *Unit Tests and Unit Lab Activities with Answer Key.* Then have students read the directions for the assignment on this page. Discuss the assignment with students and point out the documents on pages 361–63 that students will use during the lab.

The What Do You Think? questions on pages 361–63 will help guide students during the project. In addition, the lab worksheet includes a step-by-step checklist for students to monitor their progress. For assessment guidelines, see the Group Activity rubric in the *Alternative Assessment Handbook.*

PUBLIC POLICY LAB

You Make the Decision

Reporting the News

*I*magine that you are part of a team of newspaper reporters assigned to investigate a major story. Your team has uncovered important evidence concerning charges that a local representative to your state's legislature has broken state law by using campaign funds for personal purposes. Your team has gathered several documents to help you in deciding how to write the story. These documents include a newswriting guide that points out the important elements of a news story plus a sample newspaper article, a list of facts about the campaign-funds story, notes that two reporters have taken during interviews with sources, and a letter from the state attorney general listing her concerns about the newspaper's coverage of the case.

Your team needs to decide what information to include in your story. Write the story and include a memo to your editor explaining why you used some pieces of information in your story but not others.

Government Notebook Assignment

Record your decision-making process in your Government Notebook.

1. Review the documents and answer the WHAT DO YOU THINK? questions.
2. As a team, identify the issues to be decided before writing the story.
3. Gather additional information. You may want to examine other newspaper stories that have dealt with similar issues.
4. Identify the options you have for writing your story. Predict the consequences each option could have.
5. Decide which pieces of information you will use in your story. Implement your decision by writing the story. Prepare a memo to your editor explaining why you have chosen to use some pieces of information but not others.

The Daily Post

ELEMENTS OF A NEWS STORY

A news story is a factual explanation of details surrounding a noteworthy event. Unlike an editorial, a news story does not include the opinion of the reporter. In fact, the reporter must strive to write a balanced story that takes no position on the facts of the case.

A news story contains the following elements:

Headline
Every reporter writing for *The Daily Post* should suggest a headline for his or her story. Headlines are short titles that summarize the story's subject. Headlines should not be complete sentences.

Byline
The byline is the name of the reporter or reporters who have written the story.

Dateline
The dateline is the location of the news story: NEW YORK, ALBUQUERQUE, or our hometown, CHARLESTOWN.

Lead
The lead is the first sentence of a news article. In general, the lead tells the reader not only who did what and where, but also when and how it was done.

Body
The rest of the article, called the body, tells the reader the "why" behind the story. The body is made up of paragraphs and includes quotations from sources and applicable details about the story's subject. Paragraphs should be short—no more than two or three sentences.

Facts of the campaign-funds story:

- Darryl Stevens is serving his second term in the state House of Representatives.

- Stevens raised $500,000 for his last campaign. He is accused of using $300,000 of that money to purchase a new lakefront home.

- Stevens's trial is set to start on June 20, which is next week.

- Recent interviews with an anonymous source (code-named "Deep Pockets") and a former police officer (Sherry Tate) indicate that Stevens might be guilty but that police may have acted improperly in the investigation.

- Tate was dismissed from the force for conduct unbecoming a police officer.

- This state does not have a shield law.

Large Company to Hire More Workers

By Ruby Chang

CHARLESTOWN—The president of the largest employer in the Charlestown area announced Tuesday that the company will be adding more than 500 jobs over the next year.

Compurama will hire more workers because sales of the company's computers are increasing rapidly, said Juan Vasquez, the company's president. Compurama currently employs 2,000 people.

"It looks like our efforts to improve the design of our products are really paying off," Vasquez said.

The company began to improve its product line last year. Sales of the company's newest product, the CyberRama computer, have increased by 50 percent over the last year, Vasquez said.

"Customers really seem to like the faster speed and extra features we have put into the CyberRama computer," Vasquez said.

One source, who asked not to be identified, said that Vasquez still is interested in selling Compurama even though its sales have increased. Vasquez denies that he wants to sell the company.

◀ WHAT DO YOU THINK?

1. What new information have you collected from interviews that might interest readers? Why would such information make a good lead for your story?

2. The trial is set to start next week. How do you think publicity from your news story might affect potential jurors?

3. What is a shield law? Why is it important to know that your state has no such law?

What Do You Think? Answers

1. The important new information is that the police may have acted improperly in the investigation and that Tate was dismissed for her actions. Answers will vary, but students should state their opinions about why this would be a good lead.

2. Answers will vary, but students should state their opinions and explain their reasoning.

3. Shield laws are laws in some states that protect journalists from being forced to reveal their sources. It is important to know whether a state has such a law so that reporters can decide if they want to use a source that prefers to remain confidential.

1. Answers about credibility will vary based on students' opinions. The staff member does claim to have seen a check written to Stevens from his campaign's account.

2. Answers will vary based on students' opinions, but students may suggest that the staff member's details would supply a motive for Stevens to take the money and provide a lead for investigating what he may have done with the money.

3. The Supreme Court has ruled that wiretapping is considered the same as searching property and therefore requires a warrant. Yes, the chief should have obtained a warrant.

4. Tate does not seem very reliable because all of her information is second-hand. She did not personally witness the police chief order the wiretap.

5. Answers will vary, but students should explain their reasoning and should offer support for their explanations.

PUBLIC POLICY LAB *continued*

June 3 interview w/ "Deep Pockets" (staff member in Stevens's office; can't use name; fears losing job; Stevens won't comment)

Q: Is there evidence that Stevens used campaign money for personal use?

A: Just before last November's election, I saw a check for $300,000 that was made out to Representative Stevens personally. The check was drawn on his campaign's account.

Q: Do you know what the money was used for?

A: I remember that Stevens had earlier told various staff members that he needed a lot of money to buy a new house at the lake. Shortly after the election, he told the whole staff that he had purchased a lake house and would be moving in after Christmas.

Q: But do you know for sure that the $300,000 check from his campaign was used to buy the new house?

A: Well, no, I don't. But how else would he be able to come up with $300,000 so fast? And it's very suspicious that he got the check just a few weeks before buying the house.

June 4 interview with Sherry Tate, former Charlestown police officer (can't confirm this information with other sources; police chief says Tate is wrong)

Q: How did Charlestown police find out that Representative Stevens might have broken the law?

A: The police chief suspected that Stevens might have used campaign money for personal purposes. Another police officer told me that the chief ordered him to tap Stevens's phones. In phone conversations with a friend, Stevens mentioned that he had gotten $300,000 from his campaign to buy a house at the lake.

Q: Did the police get a search warrant to tap Stevens's phones?

A: The officer told me that no search warrant was issued.

Q: The police chief says that he did not order Stevens's phones to be wiretapped.

A: Then the chief is a liar.

Q: Will the recorded telephone conversation be used in court?

A: I doubt it. The recorded conversations helped the police discover other evidence indicating that Stevens had broken the law.

WHAT DO YOU THINK?

1. How believable is the anonymous staff member from Stevens's office? Did he or she personally see a check to Stevens from the campaign's account?

2. Do you think the staff member's suspicions about how the money was used are newsworthy? Why or why not?

3. What has the Supreme Court said about wiretapping telephones? Should the police chief have obtained a search warrant if he wanted to tap Stevens's phones?

4. How believable is Sherry Tate? Did she personally witness the police chief order Stevens's phones to be tapped?

5. Do you think that printing Tate's charge that the chief is a liar might be libelous? Why or why not?

STATE OFFICE OF THE ATTORNEY GENERAL

Editor
The Daily Post
2254 State Street
Charlestown, Rhode Island 02813

Dear Editor:

It has come to my attention that reporters from your newspaper are preparing to write a story on the upcoming trial of Representative Darryl Stevens. I have a number of concerns about this possible story.

First, there is the possibility that further publicity in your area on this topic will make it difficult for Representative Stevens to get a fair trial. If potential jurors read the story in your newspaper, they might form their own conclusions before the trial even begins. I insist that you withhold the publication of any other stories about the case until after the trial.

Second, I have learned that one source for the upcoming story has requested that he or she not be named. If the anonymous source has applicable information about the case, he or she should testify about it in open court rather than anonymously in your newspaper. Therefore, your reporter must supply the source's name and address to the proper authorities. I remind you that this state currently has no shield law.

Finally, information your reporter has gathered indicating that the police chief acted improperly in any way cannot be confirmed by us or other sources. If that information is used in the story, you probably can expect that the police chief will sue you for libel.

Sincerely,

Dwonna Jones

Dwonna Jones
State Attorney General

◀ WHAT DO YOU THINK?

1. What is prior restraint, and what has the Supreme Court ruled on it? Does the attorney general have the right to demand that the newspaper not publish the story?

2. Should you reveal the name of "Deep Pockets" so that he or she can be called to testify in court? What has the Supreme Court said about such cases? Would you be willing to go to jail for refusing to identify an anonymous source?

3. What has the Supreme Court said about libel? Is the police chief a public official? Do you think that publishing the improper wiretapping charge and the charge that he is a liar would show reckless disregard for the truth? Why or why not?

What Do You Think? Answers

1. The Supreme Court has ruled against prior restraint (stopping something from being published because it could threaten security) except in cases where the material to be published posed a serious threat to national security. No, because the article does not pose a threat to national security.

2. Answers will vary, but students should state their opinions and explain their reasoning. The Supreme Court has allowed lower courts to force reporters to reveal their sources in states without shield laws. Answers will vary based on students' beliefs.

3. The Supreme Court has made it difficult for public officials to sue for libel because of the nature of their positions. Students should explain their reasoning about a police chief being a public official. Answers will vary, but students should state their opinions about whether the article shows reckless disregard and should explain their reasoning.

UNIT 6

Lesson Options

Suggestions for customizing the material in Unit 6 to fit the specific schedule and curriculum of your classroom are located at the beginning of each chapter.

Main Ideas

Ask each student to read the Main Ideas and briefly answer each question in writing. Later, when you have finished Unit 6, ask students to return to their original answers and revise them using what they learned in the unit.

PUBLIC POLICY LAB

The Unit 6 Public Policy Lab appears on pages 454–57. This lab project is a real-world assignment in which students, working in groups, will take on the roles of campaign consultants for opposing presidential candidates preparing for a debate. *Unit Tests and Unit Lab Activities with Answer Key* provides support materials to help students complete the lab.

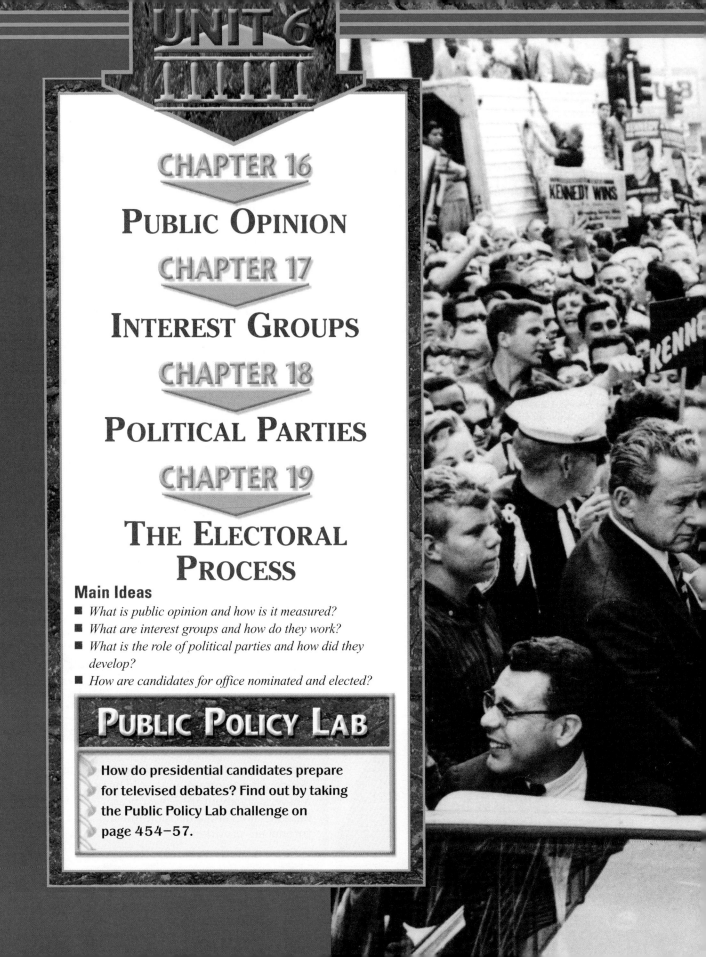

UNIT 6

CHAPTER 16
PUBLIC OPINION

CHAPTER 17
INTEREST GROUPS

CHAPTER 18
POLITICAL PARTIES

CHAPTER 19
THE ELECTORAL PROCESS

Main Ideas
- *What is public opinion and how is it measured?*
- *What are interest groups and how do they work?*
- *What is the role of political parties and how did they develop?*
- *How are candidates for office nominated and elected?*

PUBLIC POLICY LAB

How do presidential candidates prepare for televised debates? Find out by taking the Public Policy Lab challenge on page 454–57.

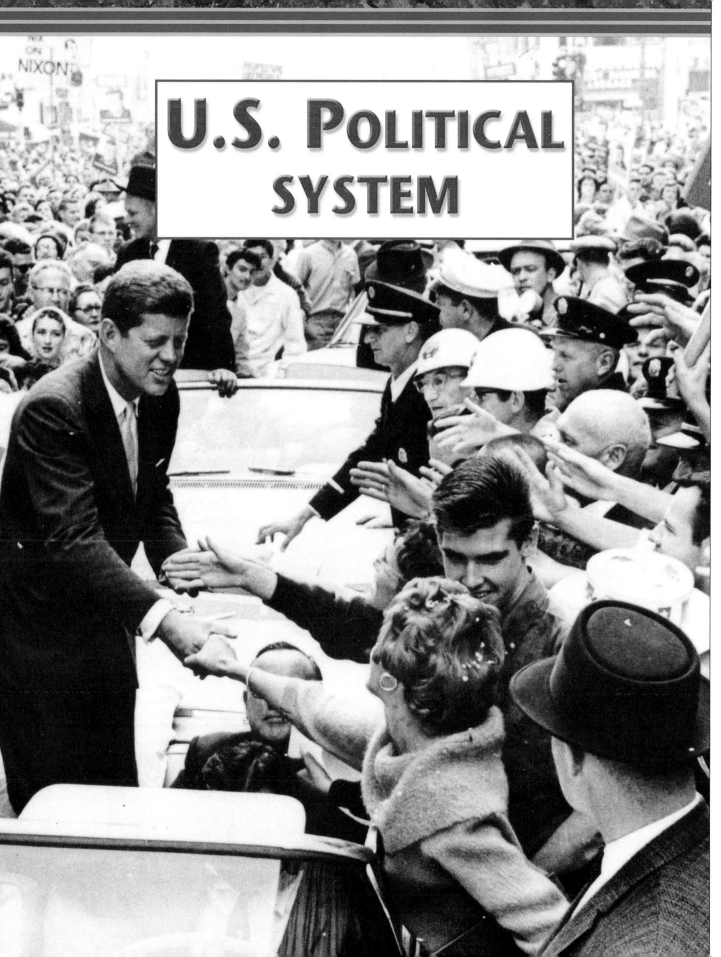

U.S. POLITICAL SYSTEM

Unit 6 presents the concepts necessary to introduce students to the U.S. political system including the influence of public opinion, interest groups, and political parties, as well as the electoral process.

In exploring the unit's concepts, students will find numerous examples relevant to their lives. In addition, they will have the opportunity to apply these concepts to events and issues around them.

Teaching with Photographs

On November 2, 1960, the streets around San Diego's Central District Plaza were crowded with an estimated 20,000 supporters of Democratic presidential nominee Senator John F. Kennedy.

Kennedy impressed voters with his charm, wit, good looks, and war record. Some voters were wary of the fact that Kennedy was a Roman Catholic, but he calmed their concerns by assuring the public that he believed strongly in the separation of church and state. A strong performance in a series of televised debates was apparently a deciding factor for many voters to support the young and charismatic Kennedy.

CHAPTER 16 PUBLIC OPINION

	OBJECTIVES	PACING GUIDE	REPRODUCIBLE RESOURCES
SECTION 1 **WHAT IS PUBLIC OPINION?** (pp. 367–371)	▶ What is public opinion and how does it shape political events? ▶ What factors influence public opinion? ▶ What is the media's role in influencing public opinion?	**Regular** 1.5 days **Block Scheduling** .75 day	**ELL** Spanish Study Guide 16.1 **SM** English Study Guide 16.1 **E** Simulations and Strategies for Teaching Government: Activity 16 **E** Challenge and Enrichment Activity 16
SECTION 2 **MEASURING PUBLIC OPINION** (pp. 372–376)	▶ What is polling, and how is it used to determine public opinion? ▶ What types of polls exist? ▶ What are some of the main concerns in conducting a poll?	**Regular** 1 day **Block Scheduling** .5 day	**ELL** Spanish Study Guide 16.2 **SM** English Study Guide 16.2 **SM** Government Activities: Activity 16
SECTION 3 **THE MEDIA AND THE PUBLIC GOOD** (pp. 377–380)	▶ What is the role of the media? ▶ What are some criticisms of the media? ▶ What are the checks on media influence?	**Regular** 1 day **Block Scheduling** .5 day	**ELL** Spanish Study Guide 16.3 **SM** English Study Guide 16.3

Chapter Resource Key

PS	Primary Sources	**A**	Assessment	📼	Video
RS	Reading Support	**REV**	Review	💿	Videodisc
E	Enrichment	**ELL**	Reinforcement and English Language Learners	🌐	Internet
S	Simulations	💻	Transparencies	⚡	Holt Presentation Maker Using
SM	Skills Mastery	💿	CD-ROM		Microsoft ® PowerPoint ®

TECHNOLOGY RESOURCES	REINFORCEMENT, REVIEW, AND ASSESSMENT
One-Stop Planner: Lesson 16.1 Holt Researcher Online Homework Practice Online CNN Presents Government Transparency 33 and Transparency 34 Global Skill Builder CD-ROM	**REV** Section 1 Review, p. 371 **A** Daily Quiz 16.1
One-Stop Planner: Lesson 16.2 Holt Researcher Online Homework Practice Online Cartoon Transparency 15 Global Skill Builder CD-ROM	**REV** Section 2 Review, p. 376 **A** Daily Quiz 16.2
One-Stop Planner: Lesson 16.3 Holt Researcher Online Homework Practice Online Cartoon Transparency 16 Global Skill Builder CD-ROM	**REV** Section 3 Review, p. 380 **A** Daily Quiz 16.3

Chapter Review and Assessment

SM Global Skill Builder CD-ROM
HRW Go site
REV Chapter 16 Tutorial for Students, Parents, and Peers
REV Chapter 16 Review, pp. 382–383
Chapter 16 Test Generator (on the One-Stop Planner)
A Chapter 16 Test
A Alternative Assessment Handbook

One-Stop Planner CD–ROM

It's easy to plan lessons, select resources, and print out materials for your students when you use the **One-Stop Planner CD-ROM with Test Generator.**

internet connect

HRW ONLINE RESOURCES
Go To: go.hrw.com
Then type in a keyword.

TEACHER HOME PAGE
KEYWORD: SV3 Teacher

CHAPTER INTERNET ACTIVITIES
KEYWORD: SV3 GV16
Choose an activity on public opinion to:
▸ examine the effect of word choice and question order in polls.
▸ create a brochure on the influence of polls in politics.
▸ learn about the role of the mass media in the political process.

CHAPTER ENRICHMENT LINKS
KEYWORD: SV3 CH16

HOLT RESEARCHER ONLINE
KEYWORD: Holt Researcher

ONLINE ASSESSMENT
Homework Practice
KEYWORD: SV3 HP16
Standardized Test Prep
KEYWORD: SV3 STP16
Rubrics
KEYWORD: SS Rubrics

ONLINE MAPS, CHARTS, AND GRAPHS
KEYWORD: SV3 MCG
▸ Citizens Registered and Voting in Presidential Elections, 1964–2000
▸ U.S. Households with Cable Television, 1981–1999

CONTENT UPDATES
KEYWORD: SS Content Updates

HOLT PRESENTATION MAKER
KEYWORD: SV3 PPT16

ONLINE READING SUPPORT
KEYWORD: SS Strategies

CURRENT EVENTS
KEYWORD: S3 Current Events

OBJECTIVES

▶ Define public opinion and explain how it shapes political events and public policy.
▶ Identify and describe the factors that influence public opinion.
▶ Define and describe the media's role in influencing public opinion.

MOTIVATE

On individual sheets of paper have students list things about which they have asked advice during the last week or two (e.g., buying a certain record, whether a particular clothing style looked good on them, whether they ought to see a certain popular movie). During class discussion list some of the items identified by students on the chalkboard. Ask students if they agreed with and followed the other person's advice. Some students probably chose not to follow the advice. Divide the class into two groups, one comprised of students who followed the advice and one comprised of students who did not. Have each group think about the reasons why they chose their course of action, and discuss their reasoning with the class. Tell students that in this section they will learn why we seek other's opinions, what public opinion is, and how it influences our lives.

TEACH

Building a Vocabulary

In spiral notebooks, have students create a Political Dictionary to be used throughout the course. The dictionary may be used as an activity at the start of each new section; it may also be used as a modification device for students having difficulty or Sheltered English Students during tests and homework assignments. List words that students will be expected to know for this section on the chalkboard. Have students list, define, and give an example of each of the terms, using information provided in the text or on the *Researcher CD-ROM.*

Conducting Research/Evaluating Information

Discuss with students the importance of public opinion in shaping political events, especially elections, and public policy. Organize the class into several small groups. Each group should then be assigned one or two federal elections to research in order to try to determine the impact of public opinion on the election(s). Results of several elections may be found in the Citizens Registered and Voting in Federal Elections, 1964–2000, chart in this section of the text. Students may also want to refer to the Elections section on the *Holt Researcher Online.* Each group should research the election(s) that they were assigned. On a sheet of paper students should make a list of the major issues or the major events during each campaign that may have influenced the public's opinion. Within each group, students should then discuss the results of the election(s) in relation to the candidates' stance on the major issues. For example, if the country was on the brink of war, did the candidate who supported war or the candidate who opposed war win the election. Each group should present their findings to the rest of the class. The class should then discuss how they think public opinion influenced the outcome of the election(s) and what other factors may have influenced the final election results as well. Tell students that in the next activity they will learn about the factors that influence public opinion.

Developing Life Skills/Distinguishing Fact from Opinion

Discuss with students the influence that the media have in shaping public opinion and the ways in which they do so. Tell students about the importance of distinguishing fact from opinion. Each student should bring to class an article from a newspaper or a magazine that they think represents the opinion of the writer rather than simply stating the facts. Each student should write an explanation about why he or she believes the article expresses opinion rather than fact. For example, students could identify the subjective words used in the article. Students should discuss their interpretation of their articles with the class and should identify how the article may influence the reader. Encourage students to attempt to identify common ways of trying to influence the reader.

CLOSE

On the chalkboard, list the factors that bring about political socialization that are discussed in this section of the textbook. Students should discuss how much they feel they are influenced by each of these factors and should offer explanations for their opinions. Tell students that everyone has a variety of influences in the development of their opinions and that an appreciation of those influences helps us to understand our own as well as others' positions.

OPTIONS

Gifted Learners

Ask students to watch the nightly news on one of the national networks. The teacher should choose the network or have students vote on which network to watch so that all students watch the same newscast on a particular night. Immediately following each broadcast, students should write a description of a few stories they saw and how they felt about each story. During class the next day students should discuss the stories and give their opinion of them. There will most likely be different interpretations and opinions. Lead a discussion of what factors led the students to interpret the stories differently (e.g., religion, heritage, language). Finally, using examples from the broadcast, students should write an essay on how and why individuals interpret the news differently. Discuss with students any general differences in opinion expressed in different class periods.

Students Having Difficulty/ Sheltered English Students

Bring to class two articles that discuss the controversy over an issue affecting the public good, such as timber interests versus environmental interests. Articles should be of approximately the same length and should be typed so that there are no visual differences in the articles. One article should be biased in support of one side of the argument (e.g., pro-timber interests), while the other should be biased in favor of the opposing viewpoint (e.g., pro-environmentalism). Give different articles to different rows, being careful not to tell students that their articles are different. After students have read the articles, have them cast a secret ballot to see which view of the issue the class supports. After all the ballots have been counted, tell students that they have read different articles, each containing bias. Have students discuss how the article they read influenced their personal opinion, how it may have influenced the overall voting, and how bias in the media can affect an election.

REVIEW

Have students complete the Section 1 Review on page 371. Use the answers in the Annotated Teacher's Edition to assess student mastery of this section.

ASSESS

To assess student mastery of this section, have students complete Daily Quiz 16.1 in *Daily Quizzes with Answer Key*. For additional assessment options, see *Alternative Assessment Handbook* on the *One-Stop Planner CD-ROM*.

ADDITIONAL RESOURCES

Lippmann, Walter. *Public Opinion.* 1997. Free Press.

Mutz, Diana C. *Impersonal Influence: How Perceptions of Mass Collectives Affect Political Attitudes.* 1998. Cambridge University Press.

Splichal, Slavko, ed. *Public Opinion and Democracy: Vox Populi-Vox Dei.* 2001. Hampton Press.

Wolfe, Alan. *One Nation After All.* 1999. Penguin USA.

Zaller, John R. *The Nature and Origins of Mass Opinion.* 1992. Cambridge University Press.

OBJECTIVES

▶ Define polling, and describe how is it used to determine public opinion.

▶ Describe the types of polls that currently exist.

▶ Describe some of the main concerns in conducting a poll.

MOTIVATE

The day prior to beginning this section write a question such as *Should uniforms be required of all students in public schools?* on the chalkboard. Students should be told to ask their parent(s) or other adults the question. On the next day of class, draw a line down the chalkboard. Label one side *students* and the other side *parents.* Ask each student how their parent(s) responded, and then ask students their opinions on the issue. Tabulate the totals. Discuss with students the results of the poll, and encourage students to identify reasons for any differences in each column's total. Tell students that they have just participated in an opinion poll. Tell them that in this section they will learn about polling techniques and their advantages and disadvantages.

TEACH

Building a Vocabulary

In their spiral notebooks, have students continue working on their Political Dictionary. List words the students will be expected to know for this section on the chalkboard. Have students list, define, and give an example of each of the terms, using information provided in the text or on the *Researcher CD-ROM.*

Classifying Ideas/Making Decisions

Tell students that you are interested in finding out about their beliefs and personal lives. Give students a list of general questions. Some should deal with politics, others with school, and still others with students' opinions on various topics. The list should also contain four boxes after each question. The boxes should be labeled *in person, by telephone, by*

mail, and *only after I've finished this class.* Have students check the box next to each question that describes the way that they would be most comfortable answering that question. After students have finished, calculate the number of responses in each category for each question, and write the results on the chalkboard. Tell students that what you have just done is a form of polling, and explain to them the reasons why people conduct polls. Discuss with students the different categories that they had to choose from, and explain to them that these categories represent the various types of polls that exist. Tell students that in the next activity they will learn about some of the problems associated with conducting polls.

Demonstrating Understanding

On sheets of paper students should make a chart analyzing the various influences on conducting polls (e.g., sampling, wording, order, timing). On one side they should list the type of influence and on the other side the various ways that altering the influence could affect the result of a survey. Ask students for examples that demonstrate how a particular influence could affect a participant's response. Ask students to then select a question from each of the categories in the previous exercise, and then have the entire class discuss the advantages or disadvantages of that particular wording of the question. Tell students that in the next activity they will conduct their own poll.

Applying a Model

Organize the class into several small groups. Each group will conduct a poll that takes into account each of the influences discussed in this section of the text. The teacher may assign topics (e.g., tax reform, school funding, violence on TV) or allow students to chose a topic. Each group should develop a questionnaire to use to interview people about the group's assigned topic. Each group should then share their questionnaire with another group, asking for comments about how they may be inadvertently influencing respondents' answers. After revising the questionnaire, each group should poll as many of their peers, teachers, parents, and community members as possible. Each group should report the results of their questionnaire to the entire class and discuss what problems, if any, they encountered while conducting the poll (e.g., reluctance to participate, misinterpretation or lack of understanding of questions, size of sample).

CLOSE

On the chalkboard write the question *Do you trust opinion polls?* Have students state their opinions and explain their answers based on information presented in this section of the chapter. Keep a tally on the chalkboard of students' answers. Explain to students that they must be careful in their reading of the results of polls to be sure that the poll is representative of the overall population and that the wording of the questions is not biased. Tell students that now that they have studied the limitations of such polls they are better capable of assessing polls' validity and usefulness.

OPTIONS

Gifted Learners/Logical-Mathematical Learners

Have students return to the groups they were in during the Applying a Model activity. Students should use the results obtained from their poll to analyze the poll based on a variety of factors (e.g., percentage of each gender participating in the poll, percentage of respondents by age, variance of responses by question). Have students use the percentages that they calculate to determine the validity of the poll. Results should be reported to the entire class, and other groups should be allowed to offer their opinions about the poll's validity.

Intrapersonal Learners

Discuss with students the controversy surrounding exit polls and the possible effects that showing them on television or announcing them on the radio could have on people who are still voting. Have students conduct research to find articles dealing with regulations on exit polls. Have students write a descriptive essay describing these regulations and take a stand regarding whether the actions taken will have the desired result. Encourage students to discuss their ideas with the rest of the class.

Students Having Difficulty/ Sheltered English Students

 Encourage students to visit the Web sites of various polling organizations. Have students use information from the sites to track changes in public opinion on a key issue or campaign. For instance, students can see how the current president's approval rating has changed throughout his or her presidency or how public opinion has changed regarding support for the death penalty. Have students create a graph showing the changes that occurred over a period of time. Encourage students to share the information they gather with the rest of the class.

REVIEW

Have students complete the Section 2 Review on page 376. Use the answers in the Annotated Teacher's Edition to assess student mastery of this section.

ASSESS

To assess student mastery of this section, have students complete Daily Quiz 16.2 in *Daily Quizzes with Answer Key*. For additional assessment options, see *Alternative Assessment Handbook* on the *One-Stop Planner CD-ROM*.

ADDITIONAL RESOURCES

Asher, Herbert. *Polling and the Public: What Every Citizen Should Know.* 1998. Congressional Quarterly.

Robinson, Matthew. *Mobocracy: How the Media's Obsession with Polling Twists the News, Alters Elections, and Undermines Democracy.* 2001. Prima Publishing.

Warren, Kenneth F. *In Defense of Public Opinion Polling.* 2001. Westview Press.

OBJECTIVES

▸ Define and discuss the role of the media.
▸ Identify and describe some of the criticisms of the media.
▸ List and describe the checks on the media's influence.

MOTIVATE

On the chalkboard list the following headings: *radio, TV, newspaper,* and *magazine.* Ask students to indicate which they have read, watched, or listened to during the past week. Then ask students to estimate how many hours they think they spent in each case. Finally, ask students to discuss how much influence they think each of these types of media have on their opinion of what is going on around them. Encourage students to discuss their opinions and to identify examples of controversy surrounding the media's influence that they have heard about. Tell students that in this section they will study the role of the media in influencing public opinion.

TEACH

Building a Vocabulary

In their spiral notebooks, have students continue working on their Political Dictionary. List words the students will be expected to know for this section on the chalkboard. Have students list, define, and give an example of each of the terms, using information provided in the text or on the *Researcher CD-ROM.*

Acquiring Information/Developing Life Skills

Discuss with students the media's roles of informing the public, acting as gatekeeper, and serving as a watchdog. On the chalkboard write the following words: *news, weather, sports, entertainment,* and *advertisement.* Organize students into three groups. Have each group track information about one of the major network's newscasts by watching a local television newscast and keeping track of the amount of time spent on each of the above activities during that newscast. In class, students should use this information to create a pie chart. Discuss with students how much time is actually spent on "news" in the newscast. Have each group share the information they researched with the rest of the class, and encourage groups to compare and contrast the amount of time spent on each category for each network. Ask students to write a brief essay analyzing the kind of "news" coverage available and how it influences our perception of events. Students should also address the problem of the lack of "depth" in news stories. Encourage students to share their opinions with the class. Tell students that in the next activity they will learn about some of the criticisms of the media.

Acquiring Information/Demonstrating Understanding

List on the chalkboard or overhead projector as headings the criticisms of the media discussed in this section: *lack of objectivity, maintaining a negative focus, relying too much on visual imagery,* and *providing "horse race coverage."* Have students return to the groups they were in during the previous activity. Have them once again take notes on the same network's newscast, but this time have students examine the broadcast looking for examples of the criticisms listed above. Have students discuss examples of these criticisms that were contained in the newscast they watched. Have students compare and contrast these criticisms to determine if the networks are similar in what they broadcast or if they take different approaches to covering the news. Tell students that in the next activity they will learn about checks on the media's influence.

Demonstrating Understanding

Using information provided in this section of the text, students should list checks that limit media's influence on the public. On the chalkboard or an overhead projector write the First Amendment and underline the words *freedom of the press.* Ask students to write a brief essay discussing how placing limits on the influence of the media may or may not be constitutional. Have students discuss their opinions with the rest of the class and then ask if legislation should ever limit media's influence. Discuss students' responses.

CLOSE

Have students ask their parents and grandparents the question posed in the Motivate activity. Encourage students to think about any similarities or differences between these answers and their own responses. Are there any major differences in the amount of time spent with the different types of media for different age groups? Have students discuss their parents' and grandparents' responses and whether or not they reinforce the influence of the media. Ask students to write a short paper describing why they feel there should or should not be checks on the media's influence. Encourage students to share their opinions with the rest of the class.

OPTIONS

Gifted Learners

 Ask students to read the first section of a newspaper and record what type of stories are on the front page, second page, and so forth. Have them write an essay analyzing the kind of stories that are placed on each page. Students should consider why each story might be placed on a specific page and the impact each story exerts based on its location in the newspaper. Encourage students to share their findings with the rest of the class.

Students Having Difficulty/ Sheltered English Students

 Ask students to look at the Table of Contents in a local newspaper. Have them record what the various sections of the paper cover. Ask them which sections are the largest and why they think that might be. Ask them to look at the front pages and tell what first draws their attention (probably a picture or a big headline). Discuss the importance of placement of a story and the impact of visuals on our perception of the news. Students should be encouraged to discuss how the visuals in the newspaper they reviewed complemented each story.

Linguistic Learners

 Have students bring in newspaper and magazine articles that use visuals to report on an issue. For example, an article dealing with the positive benefits of U.S. foreign aid might include a picture of food being delivered to malnourished people. Next, students should rewrite the article and think of a different visual that would change the meaning of the article. For example, students could rewrite the above article by discussing why foreign aid is a waste of taxpayers money and by including a table showing the amounts of foreign aid given to each country. Discuss with students the impact that media biases may have on public opinion.

REVIEW

Have students complete the Section 3 Review on page 380. Use the answers in the Annotated Teacher's Edition to assess student mastery of this section.

ASSESS

To assess student mastery of this section, have students complete Daily Quiz 16.3 in *Daily Quizzes with Answer Key*. For additional assessment options, see *Alternative Assessment Handbook* on the *One-Stop Planner CD-ROM*.

RETEACH

For students having difficulty with the lessons, have them complete Reteaching Activity 16. This activity is located in *Reteaching Activities with Answer Key*.

ADDITIONAL RESOURCES

Cook, Timothy E. *Governing with the News: The News Media as a Political Institution*. 1998. University of Chicago Press.

Jamieson, Kathleen Hall, and Karlyn Kohrs Campbell. *The Interplay of Influence: News, Advertising, Politics, and the Mass Media*. 2001. Wadsworth Publishing Company.

Mindich, David T. Z. *Just the Facts: How "Objectivity" Came to Define American Journalism*. 2000. New York University Press.

GOVERNMENT NOTEBOOK

The Government Notebook is a journal activity that encourages students to consider basic concepts of government that relate to their lives. A follow-up notebook activity appears on page 382.

▶ WHY IT MATTERS TODAY

To find additional lesson plans dealing with public opinion, polling, and the media, visit **CNNfyi**.com or have students complete the **GOVERNMENT IN THE NEWS** Activity on page 381.

CNNfyi.com

PUBLIC OPINION

How many times have you been asked the question "What do you think?" Consider all the times a teacher has called on you in class. Think about the hours you spend with your friends and family trying to decide what to do or what to wear. Your opinions—and those of other citizens—also matter to government officials. By making your opinions heard, you can influence not only government but also laws that affect you.

GOVERNMENT NOTEBOOK

In your Government Notebook, list all the times in one day that you express your opinion. What forms does your opinion take? Think not only about what you say and write but also about the choices you make in clothes, classes, and activities.

▶ WHY IT MATTERS TODAY

Public opinion, polling, and the media affect our lives in many ways. At the end of this chapter, visit **CNNfyi**.com to learn more about how they affect you.

CNNfyi.com

SECTION 1

WHAT IS PUBLIC OPINION?

READ TO DISCOVER

1. What is public opinion, and how does it shape political events?
2. What factors influence public opinion?
3. What is the media's role in influencing public opinion?

POLITICAL DICTIONARY

public opinion
ideology
political socialization

Consider the following scenario. Your friend comes to you during the day at school and tells you that he likes a certain girl and wants to ask her out on a date. He wants to know what you think he should do. You tell your friend that in your opinion the best idea is to walk up to her and casually ask her to go to a movie with him. Your friend takes your advice. He asks her out, she accepts, and they make plans. Because he valued your opinion, your friend took your advice. In other words, your opinion influenced your friend's actions.

Just as your friends, family, and teachers want to know your opinion about certain things, public officials want to know what you and the rest of the public think about important local and national issues. The collective opinion of large numbers of people is called **public opinion**.

Role of Public Opinion

In a democracy, government officials respect public opinion as the voice of the majority of the people. Thus, by making their opinions heard on specific issues, people can influence the government policies that affect them.

Consider the antiapartheid movement in South Africa. For many years, black South Africans were suppressed by apartheid, a government system of racial segregation that restricted where they could live and work and that denied them the right to vote. After years of often violent demonstrations against the government and strong actions by other nations, the leaders of South Africa began to allow multiracial elections in 1994. Nelson Mandela, black nationalist leader of the African National Congress Party, was elected president. The pressure of international public opinion had helped to force an end to apartheid.

As a citizen in your own community, you might agree or disagree with certain laws. Have officials in your community ever passed laws about which you had strong feelings? If so, did you express your opinion? In some communities, teens have expressed their opinions about laws by speaking before or writing letters to their city councils. If public opinion about an issue is strong enough, it may cause the law to be changed.

Forms of Public Opinion

How can government officials, researchers, and others concerned with public opinion tell what people's views are? One way is by examining people's

WORLD AFFAIRS *Nelson Mandela, South Africa's former president, led the antiapartheid movement in that country.* **How can people living in democratic countries influence government policies?**

SECTION 1

WHAT IS PUBLIC OPINION?

Lesson Plans

For teaching strategies, see Lesson 16.1 located at the beginning of this chapter or the One-Stop Planner Strategy 16.1.

Political Dictionary

To reinforce the section's vocabulary terms, refer students to the Electronic Glossary on the *Researcher CD-ROM.*

Section Assessment

To assess students' mastery of this section, have them complete Daily Quiz 16.1 in *Daily Quizzes with Answer Key.*

> **Caption Answer**
>
> Answers will vary, but students may mention voting and expressing opinions.

Transparency

An overhead transparency of the chart on this page is available in *Transparency Resources*. See Transparency 33: Citizens Registered and Voting in Presidential Elections, 1964–2000.

Caption Answer
1996

Citizens Registered and Voting in Presidential Elections, 1964–2000

Year	Voting Age Population	Registered	Voted	Percent of Voting Age Population Who Voted
1964	114,090,000	73,715,818	70,644,592	61.92%
1968	120,328,186	81,658,180	73,211,875	60.84%
1972	140,776,000	97,328,541	77,718,554	55.21%
1976	152,309,190	105,037,986	81,555,789	53.55%
1980	164,597,000	113,043,734	86,515,221	52.56%
1984	174,466,000	124,150,614	92,652,680	53.11%
1988	182,778,000	126,379,628	91,594,693	50.11%
1992	189,529,000	133,821,178	104,405,155	55.09%
1996	196,511,000	146,211,960	96,456,345	49.08%
2000	205,815,000	156,421,311	105,586,274	51.30%

Source: Federal Election Commission

In federal elections only around half of the eligible voters exercise their right to vote.
In what year did the percent of eligible voters who voted in federal elections drop below 50 percent?

participation in the political process. One obvious way people participate in politics is by voting. Citizens who are 18 or over, have not been convicted of a felony, and have taken the time to register are eligible to vote. Unfortunately, only around half of the eligible voters take the time to vote in presidential elections. In other elections, turnout is even lower.

People participate in the political process in ways other than voting, however. No matter what your age and even if you are not a citizen, you can speak out or write about political issues, demonstrate, sign a petition, write a letter to a public official, or join an interest group that has specific political goals. Some people donate money or time to political candidates and interest groups. Through all these forms of political participation, people make their views known.

Influences on Public Opinion

You now know how people express their political opinions, but what helps form those opinions in the first place? Ideology, family, school, and the media all influence how people form their opinions.

Ideology One factor affecting people's viewpoints on certain issues is their **ideology**—or basic set of political beliefs. By conducting interviews, political scientists have discovered that

many people do maintain a set of basic beliefs about freedom, opportunity, and equality, and that this ideology influences their political ideas about both issues and candidates.

You have probably heard relatives or friends speak of themselves as liberal, conservative, or moderate. These are different types of ideology. In general, a person with a conservative ideology believes that in order to promote the public good, government should be less involved in economic issues, while someone with a liberal ideology believes that government should actively protect and advance the general welfare of citizens. A moderate usually holds some liberal and some conservative beliefs.

Political Socialization Some of people's earliest influences, such as family and school, affect how they form their opinions. In fact, family beliefs, ideas learned in school, job experiences, and influences from income, education, age, gender, race, and geographic region all combine to produce a person's **political socialization**. This process helps determine how someone's political opinions will develop over his or her lifetime.

The political socialization process starts very early. Research by political scientists has shown that people develop some basic political preferences as children. Many children can name some countries

Linking

Government and Psychology

Politics and the Mind

Why would anyone want to know your emotions on election day? When considering how to vote, you base your decisions partly on personal factors, such as feelings, personality traits, and values. Political psychologists study these factors to help them determine how people make political decisions.

By scientifically studying the public's thoughts and behavior, political psychologists analyze how people form political beliefs and make decisions about political issues. One of the earliest political psychologists was Harold Laswell. In 1930 Laswell published a study arguing that people act according to personal motives when making political decisions. In particular, Laswell thought that many people who had feelings of inferiority sought political power to prove their own worth.

In 1960, Angus Campbell's book *The American Voter* presented the results of surveys in which voters were asked questions about their ability to influence politics. This study showed that people who felt they could bring about political changes were more likely to vote than those who did not feel that their efforts could result in change. This theory was supported by a 1963 study listing a number of other psychological factors that also encouraged voting. These factors included a strong sense of identification with a political party, interest in specific issues or candidates, and concern about the results of an election.

Political ideology has also been a focus of political psychology. During the 1940s a group of researchers studied the psychological influences on fascism and anti-Semitism. The study found that people who joined the Nazi Party had harsh, impulsive personalities, favored strict punishment, and tended to blame others—in that case, Jews—for their problems. Supporting these findings, a study in the United States during the 1960s showed that people who felt powerless, isolated, and dissatisfied were more likely to hold extreme views.

Political psychologists also study psychological socialization, or how people's emotions, opinions, and behavior make them part of a larger society. In 1971 psychologist Joseph Adelson studied the development of political thought in adolescents, based on a theory developed by psychologist Jean Piaget. Adelson noted that different stages in children's mental development coincided with changes in political attitudes. The most dramatic changes appeared in children between the ages of 12 and 16, with older adolescents better able to think abstractly about politics.

The political development that teens undergo often reflects their upbringing. Psychologist Judith Gallatin's 1980 study showed, for example, that parents play an important role in the formation of their children's political views. This role is more pronounced when both parents hold similar political beliefs and when political discussion is encouraged in the home. Gallatin's study also showed that teenagers raised in unusually strict or lenient families are less likely to be aware of political issues and tend not to be involved in politics.

Political psychologists analyze why some people participate more actively in the political process than others.

What Do You Think?

1. Why might voting be more common among people who believe that their actions can lead to political change?
2. What factors other than parental interest might influence a teen's political beliefs? Explain your answer.

What Do You Think?
Answers
1. Answers will vary, but students may suggest that people are more likely to take action if they think that doing so will make a difference.
2. Answers will vary, but students should state their opinion and offer support for it.

ACROSS THE CURRICULUM

SOCIOLOGY Voting behavior has attracted the attention of sociologists, who have attempted to gauge the impact of education, income, and occupation on voting habits. Studies have revealed that education is the greatest influence on a person's decision to vote. People with higher levels of education are more likely to vote than people with little education. Income made some difference—poor people were the least likely to vote, but rich people voted at the same levels as people in the middle class. Finally, the type of job a person has does not seem to indicate how often a person will vote. ■

CITIZENSHIP *Most U.S. citizens learn to say the Pledge of Allegiance in school at a young age. As adults many citizens continue to promise loyalty to their country by reciting the pledge.* **In what other ways does political socialization occur?**

they like and do not like by the age of six. Studies have shown that children as young as fourth grade frequently have political party preferences. In many cases these choices reflect the political beliefs of the children's parents or guardians.

School is also a significant part of the socialization process. In school you learn about your government, how it was founded, and why it is a good system. You also learn to say the Pledge of Allegiance, in which you promise loyalty to your country.

Other influences, such as those arising from regional background and income, also affect how people form their opinions. For example, people with low incomes are often more likely than those with high incomes to back government programs that provide health care, stimulate job growth, or redistribute income. Though regional opinion differences have lessened over the years, southerners do tend to be more conservative on moral and social issues than people in other regions of the country.

Recent research suggests that the key period in forming political beliefs is during the late teens or early twenties. At this time, people have new experiences, meet new people, and live more independently of their parents. People are open to new influences during that period, and therefore are more likely to be affected by major political events (such as wars or economic crises) and by popular ideas of the day.

Media Another major factor influencing public opinion is the media. Consider your daily activities. Do you spend time watching television or listening to the radio? If so, you may find that the media—magazines, newspapers, television, radio, and books—influence your opinions. The media provide people with much of the knowledge they use to form their opinions.

The media's influence on public opinion has grown over the years with the development of radio and television. Before television became popular, researchers in the 1930s and 1940s studied politicians ability to affect people's opinions through radio speeches. Radio was used often by the great political speakers of the age, such as President Franklin Roosevelt and British prime minister Winston Churchill. Adolf Hitler, dictator of Germany from 1933 to 1945, also used radio to rally support for his policies. Through radio, politicians had found a way to influence the way these people thought about the issues.

With the rise of television, media's ability to affect public opinion became even greater. One way television affects public opinion is by giving priority to certain issues. "The media do not affect *what* people think," it has been said, "but rather what they think *about*." In fact, some studies have shown that people tend to rank an issue as more important if it has received a high degree of evening news coverage.

In one study conducted in New Haven, Connecticut, for example, researchers had different groups of people watch television news broadcasts for a week. The broadcasts were the same as the actual national news shown each night, but with a few changes. One group of viewers saw a large number of stories on problems with U.S. defense capabilities, and a second saw a large number of stories about defense, inflation, and pollution. A third saw many stories about arms control, civil rights, and unemployment, and a fourth about unemployment only. (The stories, which were taken from earlier newscasts, were inserted into the newscasts without the viewers' knowledge.)

The researchers found that viewers who saw more stories on the targeted problems were more likely than the other groups to rate these problems as major national issues. As you can see from this study, the media play a considerable role in influencing people's opinions. You will learn more about the media, as well as how they affect the public good, in Section 3.

The Nature of Public Opinion

There are two key factors that influence the nature of public opinion. These are how strongly people feel about an issue and with which side of the issue people identify.

Strength of Opinion How strongly people feel about an issue is one factor that may determine the nature of public opinion. When answering a question such as "Are you for or against the death penalty?" people generally would say either, "I support it" or "I oppose it." The answer to such a question, however, would not reveal the *strength* of the opinion held. Because some issues matter a great deal more to some people than to others, determining the strength of people's opinions is important to understanding the nature of public opinion—strength of opinion can influence someone's vote, as well as how politically active the person will be regarding an issue.

Face of the Issue Which side of the issue a person identifies with is also an important factor when measuring public opinion. Just about every public policy the government might adopt has attractive and unattractive qualities. Environmental policies can preserve nature, for example, but by forcing factories to spend money on pollution control devices they can also make products more expensive. Not surprisingly, most people want both a clean environment and less expensive products. Nonetheless, people often take a stand on a particular side of an issue. Someone who hears about an environmental policy during a broadcast on air pollution would be more likely to support the legislation than someone who hears about it in connection with rising prices for consumer goods. Politicians, interest groups, and political parties frequently try to encourage people to see the "face" of the issue most favorable to their cause.

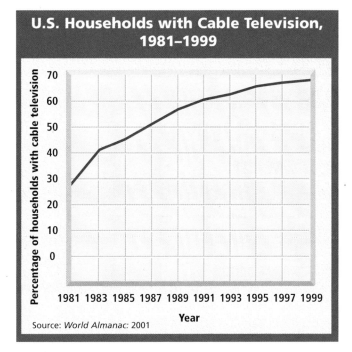

U.S. Households with Cable Television, 1981–1999

Percentage of households with cable television

Year

Source: *World Almanac:* 2001

With the rise of television's popularity, the media's influence has increased. **How do media affect people's opinions?**

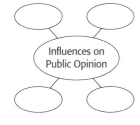

SECTION 1 REVIEW

1. Define and explain:
- public opinion
- ideology
- political socialization

2. Identifying Concepts: What helps to form Americans' political opinions? In the web on the right list four things that influence people's opinions.

Influences on Public Opinion

3. Finding the Main Idea

a. What factors shape the nature of public opinion?
b. How can public opinion affect politics?

4. Writing and Critical Thinking

Analyzing: How much does the media affect your opinions? Write a paragraph describing your opinions about re-cent political issues and how you came to form them.
Consider the following:
- the source or sources of your information about the issues
- whether your opinion agrees with those of your friends and family members

go. hrw .com Homework Practice Online
keyword: SV3 HP16

Transparency

An overhead transparency of the chart on this page is available in *Transparency Resources.* See Transparency 34: U.S. Households with Cable Television.

Caption Answer

Answers will vary, but students should support their opinions.

SECTION 1 REVIEW ANSWERS

1. Refer to the following pages: public opinion (367), ideology (368), political socialization (368).

2. ideology, family, school, and the media

3a. the strength of the opinion held and the side of an issue with which one identifies

3b. In a democracy, politicians who do not listen to the majority of the people may not be reelected.

4. Students' answers will vary, but they should discuss the sources of their information on the issues and consider the influence on their opinions of family, friends, and the media.

SECTION 2

MEASURING PUBLIC OPINION

READ TO DISCOVER

1. What is polling, and how is it used to determine public opinion?
2. What types of polls exist?
3. What are some of the main concerns in conducting a poll?

POLITICAL DICTIONARY

polling
exit poll
sampling
sampling error

Have you ever filled out a questionnaire on the food service in the school's cafeteria or on a theme for a school dance? If so, you were responding to a poll. **Polling**—surveying a population on an issue—is the most reliable way of determining what the public thinks. In this case the pollsters at your school hoped to find out what you and other students thought about the cafeteria food or the dance. In a similar way, pollsters around the country survey people about their opinions on such things as presidential candidates and government policies.

Polling

The history of polling stretches back to the last century, but modern polling started in the 1930s and is now a regular feature of political life in the United States. Pollsters have asked Americans questions about almost everything—not only about politics but also about whether they snore or believe in the predictions of fortune-tellers.

There are several kinds of polls in use today, and they have varying levels of reliability. The most reliable polling methods were pioneered in the 1930s by George Gallup.

Origins of Polling George Gallup is the founder of modern political polling. While working on his doctoral degree, Gallup became convinced that the survey method that newspapers and other organizations were using was inaccurate. Many of the polling questions being asked were open-ended, failing to probe residents for specific, detailed answers. For example, one poll might ask respondents which sections of the newspaper they read. Some people, embarrassed to admit that they read only the comics and not the editorial page, would answer falsely.

Gallup developed a polling method that involved, in this instance, going through each section of the newspaper to determine which sections interested the respondent. In this way the respondent could express interest in each section separately. (In response to an early Gallup poll revealing that not only children but also adults read the comics, the *Des Moines Register and Tribune* decided not to cut back, but to expand its comic section.)

Gallup gained fame in 1936 by attacking the presidential poll that a weekly magazine called the *Literary Digest* had conducted since 1916. The magazine polled voters by mailing out millions of ballots to people whose names had been gathered from lists of automobile and telephone owners. In 1936 the *Digest* predicted that Republican Alfred

POLITICAL PROCESSES *Pollsters often ask citizens about their political opinions.* **How can open-ended polling questions lead to inaccurate results?**

PUBLIC GOOD *Telephone interviews are a quick and inexpensive method for conducting polling surveys.* **What are other common types of polls?**

M. Landon would win over Democrat Franklin D. Roosevelt.

Gallup claimed that the methods used in the *Digest* poll were flawed and that the poll was unrepresentative of all voters. He made this determination because the lists on which the poll was based did not include low-income voters, who at that time were less likely to have cars or telephones. Gallup then declared that his own poll would produce more-accurate results. He backed his claim by declaring that if he were proved wrong, he would refund the money that newspapers had paid for the columns he had written. Gallup predicted that Roosevelt would win the election with 54 percent of the vote.

The *Literary Digest* poll was in fact flawed, and for just the reason that Gallup had mentioned. The *Digest*'s faulty prediction became perhaps the most famous polling blooper ever, for Roosevelt won the greatest landslide victory in U.S. history up to that point. (Actually, even Gallup's poll was off, underestimating Roosevelt's victory by 7 percent.)

With the success of his 1936 presidential poll, Gallup launched a career as the pioneer of modern polling. Gallup had better results than other pollsters because he used a more scientific method of polling. That is, he polled a group of people who better represented the U.S. population as a whole. Gallup's success firmly established statistical sampling methods in opinion polling. This kind of scientific polling has become increasingly complex and more accurate as pollsters have developed better techniques.

Types of Polls The most common types of polls are in-person interviews, telephone interviews, and mail questionnaires. In-person interviews were common in the early days of polling and are still used by a few polling organizations, such as the one founded by Gallup. Most polling organizations, however, have abandoned in-person interviews for telephone interviews, which are quicker and less expensive.

Mail questionnaires have also been popular for many years. Some early mail questionnaires used "straw ballots," which people could clip out of a newspaper, fill out, and drop in the mail. Mail polls are inexpensive and allow more questions, but generally fewer people respond to them. In some cases, however, researchers who have carefully selected the population they will be polling have used them with much success.

In 1967 the Columbia Broadcasting System (CBS) pioneered another technique—the exit poll. An **exit poll** surveys a fraction of voters in randomly selected voting precincts after they have cast their ballots. This allows pollsters to discover how people actually voted without waiting for the official votes to be counted.

The use of exit polls has been criticized. In 1980, a television network using exit poll results declared Ronald Reagan the winner of the presidential election while people on the West Coast were still voting. After that election, networks agreed not to release actual poll numbers for a state until voting ended in that state . However, networks still had access to the numbers before their release. Based on exit polls taken during the 2000 presidential election, networks incorrectly predicted who Florida voters would choose—twice. After the 2000 election, some in the media have predicted the demise of the exit poll.

Conducting Polls

If pollsters are to gain reliable results from a poll, they must follow certain guidelines. Getting accurate results depends on how people are chosen to participate in the poll, the type of poll that is used, proper question wording and order, and how familiar the public is with the issue.

CULTURAL PERSPECTIVES

Most polls, are conducted over the telephone, and most of the interviewers are middle-aged women with some college education. This fact reflects some of the realities of American society. Poll taking is typically a part-time job, and middle-aged women are more likely than men to take such positions; men and younger women more commonly desire full-time employment. Because a growing number of women in the United States have been seeking full-time work, however, the employee makeup of the poll-taking industry will probably change. ■

internet connect

TOPIC: Political Influence of Polling
GO TO: go.hrw.com
KEYWORD: SV3 GV16

Have students access the Internet through the HRW Go site to research ways in which public opinion is influenced and measured in American politics. Then ask students to create a brochure in which to display their research. Remind students to use standard grammar, punctuation, sentence structure, and spelling in their brochure.

Careers in Government

Pollster

Pollsters conduct surveys on public opinion for many kinds of clients, ranging from political groups to media organizations to business interests. The information they collect can help shape public policy, change corporate plans, and inform the public on important issues. They may conduct polls over the phone, through the mail, on the Internet, or in person.

Some pollsters work as independent consultants. For example, Frank Luntz is an independent pollster whose firm assists Republican candidates for public office. Luntz earned undergraduate and graduate degrees in political science before starting his own business in 1991. In 1994 he guided the polling work that helped Republicans prepare their Contract with America. He then became one of House Speaker Newt Gingrich's advisers on public opinion.

As his reputation grew, *TIME* magazine named Luntz among "50 of America's most promising leaders age 40 and under." *USA Today* labeled him one of the nine most influential minds in the GOP.

Other independent pollsters help businesses test public opinion before marketing new products.

Pollsters need to know how to listen and communicate well in order to gather acccurate information.

Some pollsters may be called upon to determine the best ways to conduct fund-raising drives.

Many pollsters work for companies that supply the news media with polling information. Others may work for nonprofit organizations, providing information on public views to politicians, journalists, scholars, and public interest organizations.

Pollsters must have strong writing and analytical skills to create unambiguous questionnaires and to interpret the results accurately. In addition, pollsters need a clear knowledge of current events so that they can ask questions on important subjects at the appropriate times. They also need to be good communicators and listeners to determine what their clients need to know.

What Do You Think?

1. What is a political pollster?
2. How valuable is a pollster to a political race?

▶ WHY IT MATTERS TODAY

Find information about other pollsters and how they measure public opinion. Use or other **current events** sources to find this information.

CNNfyi.com

Sampling Modern public opinion polls depend heavily on accurate **sampling**—or the choosing of a group of people to participate in a poll. To get a poll result that accurately reflects the total population's opinion, participants must be chosen at random.

Good polling relies on the randomness of the sample much more than its size. The 1936 *Literary Digest* poll, for example, had a sample of more than 2 million, but came up with inaccurate results because the sample was not random. Many national polls try to determine the opinions of over 200 million potential voters by questioning only 1,500 respondents. Some people doubt the validity of such polls. Indeed, when Americans once were polled about whether national polls with 1,500 respondents could be accurate, only 28 percent thought they could be, while 56 percent said they could not.

Hundreds of election polls have proved, however, that such a sample size can indeed give accurate results. As one political scientist points out, cooks test soups by sampling only one spoonful from a large pot, and doctors test blood by drawing a single drop from a whole body. Mathematical proofs have demonstrated that a small random sample can accurately represent the opinions of hundreds of millions of people.

A sample cannot, however, reveal with certainty what the *exact* distribution of opinion in response to a question would have been if everyone in the population had been surveyed, instead of just a sample. The uncertainty that sampling introduces is called **sampling error**. The likely size of the possible error, which can be determined through statistics, is expressed as a percent above and below a poll's result. For example, a poll might find that candidate A leads candidate B by 55 percent of the vote to 45 percent. If the sampling error were 5 points, however, candidate A might get between 50 to 60 percent of the vote while candidate B might get 40 to 50 percent.

Question Wording The wording of a poll's questions can lead to inaccurate results. Questions that make a one-sided statement and ask poll respondents to agree or disagree with it tend to get biased results.

For example, suppose someone in your school conducts a poll worded in this way: "All students should be allowed to go off campus for lunch. Do you agree or disagree?" Because of how the statement is phrased, most students being polled would probably agree. Now consider this wording: "Some students believe that the school day should start 30 minutes earlier so that there would be extra time to leave campus for lunch. Other students believe that the school should keep the shorter day and continue to hold lunch in the cafeteria. Which belief comes closer to your opinion?" Even though both questions are asking about the same situation, your answer to the second one might be different because it presents more information.

Certain words also can affect results. For example, in a poll about how to cut government

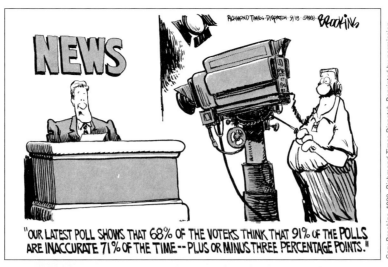

"OUR LATEST POLL SHOWS THAT 68% OF THE VOTERS THINK THAT 91% OF THE POLLS ARE INACCURATE 71% OF THE TIME -- PLUS OR MINUS THREE PERCENTAGE POINTS."

Gary Brookins, 1988, *Richmond Times-Dispatch*. Reprinted by permission.

PUBLIC GOOD *Television networks often broadcast the results of exit polls and public opinion polls.* **Why is randomness more important than sampling size in getting accurate polling results?**

budgets, only 8 percent of the respondents identified "aid to the needy" as an area for cuts. When the poll referred to this budget area as "public welfare programs," however, 39 percent supported cuts. Why the change? The two terms bring up very different images in respondents' minds. "Aid to the needy" calls up a picture of human suffering. In contrast, "public welfare" has become negatively associated with people who take advantage of government welfare programs.

Keep wording's effect on responses in mind when analyzing poll results. Those who wish to use poll results to advance a particular viewpoint can manipulate question wording to create inaccurate results.

Question Order Just as different ways of wording a question can affect a poll's response, so can the order in which questions are asked—even if the wording is unchanged. The earlier questions in a poll may lead people to see an issue in a certain way, thus possibly affecting how they answer later questions.

Think about the following situation. A pollster is conducting a poll during a presidential election year. The economy is in a slump. The order of the pollster's questions is as follows: 1) How well do you think the country is doing these days? 2) What do you think of President Pat Hartley's economic policies? 3) Are you going to vote for President Hartley in the election? The pollster's questions

Caption Answer
Answers will vary, but students should point out that polls have been accurate with small samples and that randomness seems to be more important. Students should explain their opinions on the subject.

THEMES IN GOVERNMENT

POLITICAL PROCESSES
Pollsters must take care to ensure that the wording and the order of poll questions do not create a bias. In some instances, however, there is no remedy for the influence of wording. In one 1988 poll Americans were asked if they preferred George Bush or Michael Dukakis in the upcoming presidential election. When Dukakis was named first in the question, he had a 12-point lead over Bush. When Bush was named first, however, Dukakis's lead fell to 4 points. Though pollsters recognized the influence that the word order of the question had, there was no "correct" way to rephrase the question. In any case, both results were inaccurate—Bush won by almost eight points. ■

Presidential Public Approval

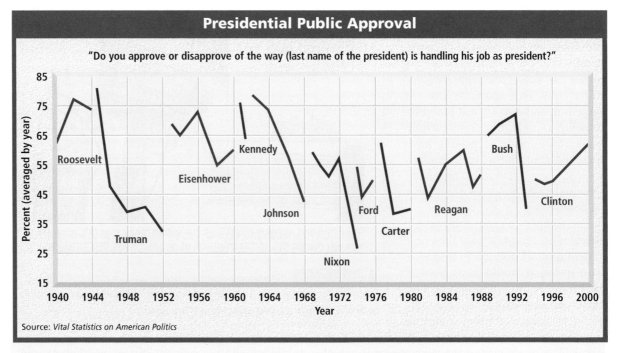

"Do you approve or disapprove of the way (last name of the president) is handling his job as president?"

Source: *Vital Statistics on American Politics*

For more than 50 years citizens have been polled about how well they feel the president is handling his job. **Which president experienced the most dramatic drop in his approval rating during his time in office?**

remind the respondent that the country is in an economic slump and suggest that President Hartley might be somehow responsible. The respondent thus is more likely to have a negative response to the question about voting for President Hartley.

Timing When a poll is held also can affect its results. Public opinion often can change dramatically, particularly on new issues. Early polls on such issues often are poor predictors because people have not yet developed strong opinions.

For example, polls sometimes are conducted very early during a presidential race. These polls may give a misleading impression of how people will actually vote. After all, as the events unfold and people find out more information, their opinions about candidates often change. As a result, you should be cautious about results of early polls.

SECTION 2 REVIEW

1. Define and explain:
- polling
- exit poll
- sampling
- sampling error

2. Identifying Concepts: Use the chart below to identify and describe the four main types of modern polls.

Four Types of Modern Polls	
1.	3.
2.	4.

Homework Practice Online

keyword: SV3 HP16

Finding the Main Idea

a. How is polling significant in determining public opinion?

b. How can a poll's sampling affect its results?

Writing and Critical Thinking

Taking a Stand: Do you think that polls promote the public good? Write a paragraph explaining your answers.

Consider the following:
- whether polls can be accurate enough to reflect public opinion
- whether polls influence voters

SECTION 3

THE MEDIA AND THE PUBLIC GOOD

READ TO DISCOVER

1. What is the role of the media?
2. What are some criticisms of the media?
3. What are the checks on media influence?

POLITICAL DICTIONARY

censorship
bias
objectivity

On what do you rely to gain information about what is going on in the world around you? If you want information about your school, you might read your student newspaper. If you are looking for news about the music world, you might read *Spin* magazine or watch MTV.

As you can see from these examples, one role of the media is to provide information. By fulfilling this and other roles, the media help promote the public good. The media are not, however, without their critics and limitations.

Role of the Media

As noted in Chapter 13, the First Amendment guarantees freedom of the press. The news media have constitutional protection from government **censorship**—the control of information or speech. This protection of the press, the framers believed, promotes the public good by allowing the media to provide information and to serve as a watchdog over government officials and policies. These are the most important roles of the media, whose freedom enables them to determine how much coverage to give to each story.

Informing the Public The media's role as a source of information is significant because they provide facts that people in a democracy need to make wise decisions about their government. "Were it left to me to decide whether we should have a government without newspapers, or newspapers without a government," wrote Thomas Jefferson in 1787, "I should not hesitate a moment to prefer the latter." By providing information to citizens, the media play a key role in promoting the public good.

C A S E   S T U D Y

"Rock the Vote" and "Choose or Lose"

POLITICAL PROCESSES One way that the media can promote the public good is by encouraging citizen participation in elections. In 1990, for example, MTV began airing public service announcements urging viewers to register to vote and head to the polls. Spots featured pop singer and actress Madonna, rapper Ice-T, and the members of the band R.E.M.

The ads were part of the music industry's Rock the Vote campaign. "The idea is to raise the political consciousness (awareness) of kids and to make voting hip," explained Jody Uttal, cofounder of the campaign. Rock the Vote also organized record stores to pass out voter registration materials.

In 1992 MTV also began a political awareness campaign called Choose or Lose. Journalist Tabitha

CONSTITUTIONAL GOVERNMENT *The Constitution guarantees freedom of the press. This freedom allows the media to provide information free from government control.* **Why are the media important in a democracy?**

SECTION 3

THE MEDIA AND THE PUBLIC GOOD

Lesson Plans

For teaching strategies, see Lesson 16.3 located at the beginning of this chapter or the One-Stop Planner Strategy 16.3.

Political Dictionary

To reinforce the section's vocabulary terms, refer students to the Electronic Glossary on the *Researcher CD-ROM*.

Section Assessment

To assess students' mastery of this section, have them complete Daily Quiz 16.3 in *Daily Quizzes with Answer Key*.

Caption Answer

The media provide information to and serve as a watchdog for the public.

PUBLIC GOOD The gate-keeping function of the media is sometimes more critically known as agenda setting. Because media selection determines which stories reach the public, the media wield tremendous influence over public opinion, and thus public policy.

During the early 1980s broadcasters had ignored the famine in Ethiopia, which remained unknown to most Americans. In October 1987 one news network aired a report on the tragedy. The news story sparked an interest in the fate of the Ethiopians and triggered relief efforts. While the decision to air the story resulted in aid for Ethiopians, thus probably saving many lives, the media's influence must still be questioned. What if the story had not been aired? Why was it not shown earlier?

In a democracy the gatekeeping or agenda-setting function can contribute to the public good, but it gives the media a power that should be closely monitored. ■

Soren hosted forums with Democratic candidate Bill Clinton and Republican president George Bush. In 1995 Rock the Vote produced a film series called *Out of Order: Rock the Vote Targets Health.* These films focused on health care issues. In 1996 Rock the Vote debuted the first program to register voters by phone, created the first Web site for online registration, and took to the road with the MTV Choose or Lose bus, registering 37,000 voters.

Each year since, Rock the Vote has created a series of events and promotions to increase political activism. In 2000, with its radio partners, volunteers, concert and bus tours, and Web site, Rock the Vote registered over 500,000 new voters.

Rock the Vote campaigns have had varying degrees of success, and many young Americans are still apathetic about politics. Still, anyone running for local, state, or federal offices who wants to appeal to young voters, particular those ages 18–24, will find a very large base from which to draw support.

Serving As a Watchdog In its watchdog role the media check the power of government and other institutions, such as business and sports. They do so by investigating and exposing abuses of power by people who are harming the public good to benefit themselves.

Defending the public against "special interests" is a critical part of this role. For example, suppose that the media run a story about how a company is trying to get the government's permission to build a pollution-generating factory near a community's water supply. Without the media's coverage of this story, the public might have been totally unaware of the company's efforts. By informing the public, the media help serve as a balance, allowing the voice of the majority to be heard.

Acting As a Gatekeeper Keep in mind that the media—as information providers—also act as a gatekeeper. Because too much happens in the world for every topic to be covered completely the media must select which stories to report and how much importance to assign to them. For example, should an account of a hurricane in the Caribbean

Comparing Governments

The Cuban Press

Authoritarian governments around the world generally silence any criticism from the press. In Cuba, for example, all newspapers as well as radio and television stations are owned by the government. Journalists who criticize the policies of the nation's communist leaders are fired from their jobs. Many are arrested and imprisoned.

In October 1995, for example, Cuban police arrested journalist Olance Nogueras Roce for writing a story on safety problems at a nuclear plant. He was charged with "publishing false information contrary to international peace." Many other Cuban journalists also have been threatened and had their equipment and files seized.

Despite such harassment and the threat of arrest, some Cuban journalists have founded the Independent Press Bureau of Cuba to market stories outside the country. Independent journalist Yndamiro Restano hopes to establish a free press in Cuba. "It is the only way we can help change our system from an authoritarian government to a democratic one, without violence," he says.

be a newspaper's lead story instead of a report on newly released national economic statistics? How much broadcast airtime or front-page coverage should the passing of the federal budget receive in comparison to a plane crash in a foreign country? By making these decisions, the media direct the public's attention to areas they consider important. In the process, the media serve to promote the public good by enabling people to avoid sifting through mountains of detail just to find out what the big news stories are.

Criticisms of the Media

For the media to promote the public good, they must be fair in providing information and different viewpoints to the public. Many people question whether the media succeed in their roles as gatekeeper and watchdog. Some critics accuse members of the media of letting **bias**—personal judgment or prejudice—interfere with their role of informing the public. These critics believe that members of the media too often represent their own personal opinions. Actually, the way events are selected and covered, and with what kind of emphasis, does depend in large part on the judgment of the people who gather the news and decide which stories to publish or broadcast. In addition, some critics believe that by presenting too many negative stories, relying on visual imagery, and focusing on nonsubstantive issues, the media fail to promote the public good as well as they should.

Objectivity The ability to report both sides of an issue without bias is called **objectivity**. Being objective is essential if the media are to provide information fairly and accurately.

Some people question whether objectivity in the media is even possible. They point out that there are many facts connected with any story. At a presidential press conference, for instance, the facts include not only what the president says but also how he or she says it and what he or she avoids saying. In determining which parts of the conference to report, and what (if any) comments to make about them, the reporter has to decide what is important. This decision opens the door for bias to affect how a story is covered or even if it is covered at all.

Are the critics right? Are the media biased? Just as some members of the general population act on their biases, some members of the media allow their personal opinions to affect their reporting. Many other members of the media, however, do strive to report only what they believe to be newsworthy, based on general standards rather than personal bias, or what they believe their readers and viewers would want to know. In the end, citizens as well as the media are responsible for judging information. You, as a consumer of news, must be alert to the possible bias of a journalist, broadcaster, or other media figure, and keep it in mind when evaluating reported information.

Negative Focus Many critics also charge that the media focus on negative or sensational stories just to draw audience attention. A larger television audience or newspaper circulation usually means higher advertising revenues. Some people

"REMEMBER — THIS CHANNEL IS ALWAYS PLEASED TO GIVE AIR TIME TO A BROAD SPECTRUM OF EDITORIAL RESPONSES WHICH AGREE WITH US."

© 1999 by Sidney Harris.

PUBLIC GOOD *Although many members of the news media strive for objectivity in their reporting, critics argue that unbiased reporting may not be possible.* **Why might it be difficult for members of the media to be completely objective in their reporting?**

believe that to gain such revenue, the media concentrate too heavily on reporting bad news and problems and on exposing the flaws of politicians and officials.

For example, a study of election coverage of the 1992 presidential campaign concluded that all three candidates received more negative than positive coverage. In fact, according to one analysis, coverage of presidential candidates has become much more negative over the last 30 years. By making policies and institutions seem to work more poorly than they actually do, a negative focus can cause citizens to lose faith in government's ability to handle public problems.

Probably the major reason for the negative tone in journalism concerns newsworthiness—that is, whether or not an event makes a good story. The *unusual* is what is considered news. When social institutions are working as they should, they make no news. In most cases, they make news only when something goes wrong. Thus, the saying "No news is good news" is true: good news tends not to be news!

Though many people dislike this negative focus, others argue that it is necessary for keeping citizens informed about the problems surrounding public

GLOBAL CONNECTIONS

During the reign of communist leader Nicolae Ceausescu in Romania, the government rigorously censored the information the public recieved. Even typewriters had to be registered with the police. During the four hours of TV programming offered each day, Romanians received only positive news about their leader. This extraordinary bias in reporting made it difficult for Romanians to form accurate independent opinions about their government. It also meant that the media had little credibility with the public. With the collapse of communism, however, private television broadcasting, which strives for objectivity, has appeared in Romania. Many critics credit this development to a new sense of political awareness, increased voter participation, and a reduction in election fraud in Romania that accompanied the fall of communism. ■

officials and institutions. These people believe that the media's importance as a watchdog outweighs any effects of a negative focus in the media.

Visual Imagery Another criticism of television is that to gain reader or viewer interest, it relies too much on pictures instead of the ideas behind an issue. Because stories often seem more powerful when accompanied by strong imagery, some critics fear that important stories without good pictures might be ignored by television.

For example, the crisis in the savings and loan industry in the 1980s was not a very "visual" story. It could show no storm-ravaged coasts, no blazing fires, no dying victims. Thus, though the crisis ended up costing taxpayers almost $150 billion, it received little television news coverage. Some critics say that it might have received more attention if the story had been a visual one.

"Horse-Race Coverage" Other critics believe that reporters tend to focus on "horse-race coverage" of politics. By this they mean, for example, that a president's likely success in *passing* an energy policy proposal through Congress often receives more attention than what the policy actually *involves*. Coverage therefore focuses on which side is "winning"—the president or Congress. This, critics argue, draws attention from the ideas behind an issue and indicates media's failure to do their job.

Checks on the Media

Despite the above criticisms, the media do promote the public good in an important way. They provide information and, through the watchdog role, preserve a balance among government officials, institutions, and the public. At the same time, media's powerful influence on public opinion does have some natural limitations.

One limitation is that the media tend to reinforce the beliefs that people already hold rather than create new ones. For example, some researchers have found that people tend to expose themselves just to those media that support their opinions. Think again about where you find information about the subjects in which you are interested. *You* choose what magazines to read, what stations to listen to, and what shows to watch. In each of these cases you probably choose magazines, stations, and shows that reflect the tastes and opinions that you already hold.

Another limitation on any undue power of the media is that people do not always pay attention to what is on television or in the newspapers. One study found that as much as 40 percent of the time that a person's television set is on, he or she is doing other things. Many people talk with one another, read, or play games, while television merely serves as background noise. Regarding newspapers, most people pay close attention only to the stories that truly interest them.

If citizens are to take advantage of the media's role in promoting the public good, they must recognize the criticisms while working to remain informed. Taking the shortcomings of the media into account, you as a media consumer must analyze the information you receive and use it to make educated decisions about officials, policies, and institutions that affect your everyday life.

SECTION 3 REVIEW

1. Define and explain:
- censorship
- bias
- objectivity

2. Identifying Concepts:
Use the chart to the right to list and describe four criticisms of the media.

1.	2.
3.	4.

Homework Practice Online
keyword: SV3 HP16

3. **Finding the Main Idea**

a. How do the media influence public opinion?
b. What are the natural limitations on the media?

4. **Writing and Critical Thinking**

Drawing Conclusions: Does objectivity exist? If objectivity is impossible, do the media serve any purpose? Write a paragraph defending your ideas.
Consider the following:
- whether reporters are truly unbiased
- whether readers and viewers account for bias

GOVERNMENT
IN THE NEWS

Glory and Defeat

When Abraham Lincoln first ran for office, people thought him dull and non-descript. But underneath Lincoln's simplicity was vision and untold strength.

Between Lincoln's election and his inauguration, southern states began to secede from the Union. By March of 1861, eleven states had seceded. Lincoln was committed to saving the Union, though he hoped he would not have to use force to preserve it. Lincoln nevertheless ordered the provisioning of Fort Sumter. This provoked Confederates to fire on Fort Sumter, and the Civil War began.

As the brutal war remained deadlocked for two years, many in the North looked forward to replacing him in the next election. Only months before the election, Lincoln himself thought he would lose. When Union forces captured Atlanta, however, Lincoln regained enough popularity to win another term in office. Within months, the North had won, and Lincoln would be remembered as a hero.

Like Lincoln, Lyndon Baines Johnson assumed the presidency during tumultuous times, but unlike Lincoln, Johnson would be defeated by war. Johnson became president immediately following the assassination of President John F. Kennedy in 1963. The public did not instantly accept Johnson as president. With the increasing emphasis on television and the media, Johnson could not compete with Kennedy in showmanship or charm, but he was determined to win public favor.

Johnson embraced Kennedy's agenda, and his Great Society program initiated some of the greatest reforms in American history. Johnson became a champion of reform and equal rights for African Americans. In essence, Johnson completed what Lincoln had begun with emancipation during the Civil War. Johnson fought for and won the most comprehensive civil rights act to date, which

President Lyndon B. Johnson of Texas. Johnson's legacies include the Great Society and the Vietnam War.

prohibited discrimination in voting, education, and public facilities.

In 1965 Johnson escalated American involvement in Vietnam, turning the effort there into a full scale military conflict. In the following years the war consumed more and more resources, causing inflation to rise. To compensate, Congress slashed spending for Johnson's Great Society programs to pay for the war effort.

As television footage brought home the horror of the war, public opinion turned against Johnson. He did not run for reelection, and he left office distraught over the end of the Great Society and the length of the Vietnam war. He died at his Texas ranch four years later.

What Do You Think?

1. Compare public opinion of Lincoln and Johnson. How did it differ? How was it similar?

2. What advice do you think Lincoln would have given Johnson after Johnson first took office?

> **WHY IT MATTERS TODAY**
>
> Use CNNfyi.com or other **current events** sources to find information about the Vietnam War. How did the war change after Johnson left office? How long did it last?
>
> **CNN fyi.com**

Government in the News Answers

1. Both leaders were criticized for their involvement in war, but Lincoln ended up being perceived as a hero, and Johnson did not.

2. Students' answers will vary, but should focus on the difficulties of being president, waging war, or dealing with public opinion.

CHAPTER 16

Review Answers

Writing a Summary

Summaries should focus on the main points of each section. These may be found in the Read to Discover questions at the start of each section. Summaries should also use standard grammar, spelling, sentence structure, and punctuation.

Identifying Ideas

Refer to the following pages: pubic opinion (367), ideology (368), political socialization (368), polling (372), exit poll (373), sampling (374), sampling error (375), censorship (377), bias (379), objectivity (379).

Understanding Main Ideas

1. It influences the political process by serving as the voice of the people.

(Continued on page 382)

Review

(Continued from page 381)

2. ideology, political social-ization, and the media

3. The development of radio and television have increased media influence.

4. with polls

5. George Gallup

6. sampling, the wording and order of questions, and the timing of the poll

7. Based on exit polls, net-works have sometimes declared election winners incorrectly.

8. The media inform the public, serve as a watchdog, and act as a gatekeeper.

9. The media select from all the news in the world which stories the public will see and how they will see them.

10. By serving as a watch-dog, the media help pre-serve balance among peo-ple, government, and other institutions.

Reviewing Themes

1. Some people say the media are biased, have a negative focus, depend too much on visual imagery, engage in "horse-race" coverage, and tend to rein-force opinions rather than help viewers form new ones.

2. Answers will vary, but students should discuss the controversy over exit poll reporting and offer support for their reasoning.

3. Answers will vary, but students should discuss the media's role as an influence on public opinion.

(Continued on page 383)

Writing a Summary

Using standard grammar, spelling, sentence structure, and punctuation, write a summary of the information in this chapter.

Identifying People and Ideas

Identify the following terms or individuals and explain their significance.

1. public opinion

2. ideology

3. political socialization

4. polling

5. exit poll

6. sampling

7. sampling error

8. censorship

9. bias

10. objectivity

Understanding Main Ideas

SECTION 1 *(pp. 367–371)*

1. How does public opinion relate to the political process?

2. What are some of the factors that influence public opinion?

3. What has contributed to the increase in influence the media have over public opinion?

SECTION 2 *(pp. 372–376)*

4. How is public opinion measured?

5. Who pioneered the modern American poll?

6. What issues must one consider when conducting polls or examining poll results?

7. Why have exit polls been criticized?

SECTION 3 *(pp. 377–380)*

8. What are the most important roles of the media?

9. What does the media's gatekeeper function involve?

10. How do the media promote the public good?

Reviewing Themes

1. Constitutional Government The Constitu-tional guarantee of freedom of the press shows how much founders valued the role of the press. Why do some people say that the media fail to fulfill their role?

2. Political Processes Should television net-works broadcast exit polls while people are still voting? Why or why not?

3. Public Good Do you think the prominent media coverage given to sensational or scan-dalous stories promotes the public good? Why or why not?

Thinking Critically

1. Decision Making If you were a news director at a television station, which of the following stories would you run first and why? Footage of a violent fire burning an empty building; footage of a NASA shuttle launch, Congress cutting the health care budget with no video footage. Does your story choice promote the public good? How?

2. Identifying Points of View What points of view would it be important to consider when evaluating the validity of a poll?

3. Making Predictions Controversy surrounds the use of exit polls, and some predict that soon they will no longer exist. Do you think exit polls will cease to be used? Why or why not?

Writing about Government

Review what you wrote about your opinions in your Government Notebook. How do your opin-ions on such things as clothes or classes affect those around you? How did you form your opin-ions on these issues? Where did you get your information? Record your answers in your Notebook.

Interpreting the Chart

Study the chart below. Then use it to help you answer the questions that follow.

Goals Rated by Seniors as Extremely Important

PERSONAL GOALS	
Having a Good Marriage and Family Life	76%
Being Successful in My Line of Work	63%
Having Lots of Money	26%

SOCIAL GOALS	
Making a Contribution to Society	24%
Working to Correct Social and Economic Inequalities	14%
Being a Leader in My Community	14%

Source: Bachman, J. G.; Johnston, L. D.; and O'Malley, P. M. "Monitoring the Future: Questionnaire Responses from the Nations' High School Seniors," 1994

1. Which sentence offers an accurate interpretation of this chart?
  a. Most seniors consider having a good marriage and family life to be extremely important.
  b. Most seniors believe that having lots of money is extremely important.
  c. Most seniors believe that it is extremely important to contribute to society.
  d. Most seniors believe it is extremely important to correct social and economic inequalities.

2. Do you think these survey results accurately reflect the views of high school seniors you know? What would you have to know about the survey to evaluate its validity?

Analyzing Primary Sources

Read the following excerpt from pollster George Gallup, Jr., about public opinion on national service, and then answer the questions.

"As far as the American people are concerned, national service on a broad scale is an idea whose time is long overdue. Even greater enthusiasm is found for voluntary programs. In fact, a Gallup Poll found more than eight in ten Americans (83 percent) in favor of setting up a voluntary national program that would permit young people of both sexes to enroll in the military forces or in non-military service projects."

3. Which statement most accurately represents Gallup's view of public opinion?
  a. Most Americans would reject a proposal calling for mandatory national service.
  b. Most Americans favor mandatory or voluntary national service for young people.
  c. Young people in particular do not support voluntary national service.
  d. Young people should be required to enroll in a national service program.

4. What conclusion might a politician reach after seeing these poll results?

Alternative Assessment

Building Your Portfolio

Interview a classmate, a family member, and an adult about their ideology. Ask them questions about government, freedom, opportunity, justice, and equality. Write your questions out beforehand, and ask them all in the same order to each person. After you finish the interviews, write a paper comparing and contrasting respondents' ideologies.

☑ internet connect

Internet Activity: go.hrw.com
KEYWORD: SV3 GV16
Access the Internet through the HRW Go site to research the guidelines for conducting polls. Then prepare 5 questions on a political topic of your choice, and have a random sample of students respond to them. Then change the wording and order of the questions, and ask a different sample to respond. Compare the responses of each group and share the results with the class.

(Continued from page 382)

Thinking Critically

1. Students may choose any of the three stories, but they should explain why they chose the story they did and discuss whether and how their choice promotes the public good.

2. the points of view of the question writer, the person asking the questions, the person responding to the poll, and the person evaluating and reporting on the poll results

3. Answers will vary, but students should support their predictions with evidence from the text and from their own experiences.

Building Social Studies Skills

1. a.

2. Responses to the first part of the question will vary, but students might suggest that to evaluate the survey, they would have to know how the questions were worded and ordered, when the survey was taken, and the size and randomness of the sample.

3. b.

4. Given the overwhelming support shown in the poll results, an astute politician would propose a program of voluntary national service for young people.

Alternative Assessment

To assess this activity, see Acquiring Information and Writing to Inform in *Alternative Assessment Handbook.*

CHAPTER 17 INTEREST GROUPS

	OBJECTIVES	PACING GUIDE	REPRODUCIBLE RESOURCES
SECTION 1 ROLE OF INTEREST GROUPS (pp. 385–390)	▶ What is an interest group? ▶ What are the functions of interest groups? ▶ What are the types of interest groups?	**Regular** 1.5 days **Block Scheduling** .75 day	ELL Spanish Study Guide 17.1 ELL English Study Guide 17.1 PS Reading 14: NAACP: The Task for the Future PS Reading 52: *The Federalist* "No. 10"
SECTION 2 HOW INTEREST GROUPS WORK (pp. 391–395)	▶ In what ways are interest groups involved in the electoral process? ▶ What is lobbying? ▶ How do interest groups attempt to influence the political process through the legal system? ▶ How do interest groups try to shape public opinion?	**Regular** 1 day **Block Scheduling** .5 day	ELL Spanish Study Guide 17.2 ELL English Study Guide 17.2
SECTION 3 INTEREST GROUPS AND THE PUBLIC GOOD (pp. 396–400)	▶ What are the benefits of interest groups? ▶ Why are interest groups criticized? ▶ How is interest groups' influence on the political system limited?	**Regular** 1.5 days **Block Scheduling** .75 day	ELL Spanish Study Guide 17.3 ELL English Study Guide 17.3

Chapter Resource Key

PS	Primary Sources	**A**	Assessment		Video
RS	Reading Support	**REV**	Review		Videodisc
E	Enrichment	**ELL**	Reinforcement and English Language Learners		Internet
S	Simulations		Transparencies		Holt Presentation Maker Using
SM	Skills Mastery		CD-ROM		Microsoft ® Power Point ®

TECHNOLOGY RESOURCES	REINFORCEMENT, REVIEW, AND ASSESSMENT
One-Stop Planner: Lesson 17.1 Holt Researcher Online Homework Practice Online Transparency 35 Holt American Government Videodisc: Special Interests: Save Virginia City Global Skill Builder CD-ROM	**REV** Section 1 Review, p. 390 **A** Daily Quiz 17.1
One-Stop Planner: Lesson 17.2 Holt Researcher Online Homework Practice Online Transparency 36 Global Skill Builder CD-ROM	**REV** Section 2 Review, p. 395 **A** Daily Quiz 17.2
One-Stop Planner: Lesson 17.3 Holt Researcher Online Homework Practice Online Cartoon Transparency 18 E Challenge and Enrichment: Activity 17 E Simulations and Strategies for Teaching American Government: Activity 17 CNN Presents American Government	**REV** Section 3 Review, p. 400 **A** Daily Quiz 17.3

Chapter Review and Assessment

SM Global Skill Builder CD-ROM
HRW Go site
REV Chapter 17 Tutorial for Students, Parents, and Peers
REV Chapter 17 Review, pp. 402–403
Chapter 17 Test Generator (on the One-Stop Planner)
A Chapter 17 Test
A Chapter 17 Test Alternative Assessment Handbook

One-Stop Planner CD–ROM

It's easy to plan lessons, select resources, and print out materials for your students when you use the *One-Stop Planner CD-ROM with Test Generator.*

OBJECTIVES

▶ Explain what an interest group is.
▶ List and describe the functions of interest groups.
▶ Discuss the different types of interest groups.

MOTIVATE

Help students imagine the following scenario: The school board has recently approved a proposal to build a new football stadium for the following school year. Because of the proposal for this multimillion-dollar construction project, however, the board has also approved a motion to reduce funds for music, theater, and several other school clubs. The school board explains that these cuts are an attempt to keep the school from overspending its budget. Ask students, both those that will be affected by the recent board decision and those who may not, how they would respond. Help students create a plan that would allow them to express their opinions effectively. Have students discuss ways they would voice their concerns and who they should contact about their concerns. Point out to students that what they have done, essentially, is form an interest group. Explain that in this section students will learn what interest groups are, the different types of interest groups that exist, and the main functions of interest groups.

TEACH

Building a Vocabulary

In spiral notebooks, have students create a Political Dictionary to be used throughout the course. The dictionary may be used as an activity at the start of each new section; it may also be used as a modification device for students having difficulty or Sheltered English Students during tests and homework assignments. List words the students will be expected to know for this section on the chalkboard. Have students list, define, and give an example of each of the terms, using information provided in the text or on the *Researcher CD-ROM*.

Creating Charts

Discuss with students the different types of interest groups that exist and their purposes. Then, on the chalkboard, help students create a chart with two headings: *Types of Interest Groups* and *Functions of Interest Groups*. Have students take turns listing different interest groups as well as their functions in order to complete each column of the chart. Students may need to read about interest groups on the Internet or in newspapers or magazines to find the necessary information. Identify which interest groups are private and which are public interest groups, or citizens' groups. In addition, lead a discussion to predict the main goal of each interest group—trying to influence public opinion, working to affect the outcome of elections, lobbying those who make public policy, or some combination of each of these functions. Tell students that in the next activity they will learn about the functions of interest groups.

Acquiring Information

Discuss the concept that interest groups do not only influence the public but they also serve to lobby the government and to influence legislation. Organize students into small groups. Have each group find examples of advertisements sponsored by interest groups or articles written about interest groups in newspapers or magazines. Students should gather information from the materials to develop a presentation showing how interest groups inform both the public and the government. In addition, each presentation should clearly state what issues the interest groups are addressing and discuss any legislation that they have worked to enact. Students may wish to find additional information about interest groups in the National Organizations section on the *Holt Researcher Online*. Presentations may be written or given verbally or visually (e.g., a collage with detailed explanation). Tell students that in the next activity they will classify interest groups.

Categorizing Information/Conducting Research

Have students list the general types of interest groups, such as agricultural groups, business groups, labor unions, professional groups, social-action groups, and cause-based groups. As you write them on the chalkboard as different headings, students should list examples of different interest groups under each heading. Students may need to refer to this section of the text or to the National Organizations section on the *Holt Researcher Online* for help. After several types of interest groups have been listed for each category, organize the students into small groups. Assign each group the task of choosing one interest group to research and present to the rest of the class. Reports should include, but not be limited to, background information about the group (including when it was founded, its approximate membership); the interest group's major goals or main focus; and examples of the group's past and present influence on political decision making.

CLOSE

Refer back to the scenario presented in the Motivate activity. Remind students of their responses to the school board's plan to build a new football stadium and reduce funds in other areas. Have a handful of students volunteer to act as members of the school board. The rest of the class should form a student interest group. Each side should prepare statements that express their side of the issue and attempt to persuade the other side to agree with their position. Be sure that both sides of the issue are clearly explained during the meeting of the student interest group and the school board. The class may choose to elect someone to make a final decision about the board's construction project after listening to arguments for both sides. Afterward, lead a discussion about the function of the interest group and what type of group it represented. Have students identify other ways the interest group may have acted to achieve its goal.

OPTIONS

Gifted Learners

Have students prepare a short biography on Ralph Nader and his influence in helping people become more active citizens. Encourage students to focus on Nader's fight for auto safety in the 1960s, spearheaded by his best-selling book, *Unsafe at Any Speed*. Students should illustrate Nader's influence on consumer activism by citing government agencies and citizens' groups that were formed as a result of his crusades. Each student should prepare a presentation, either written or oral, to give to the class. Provide students with the option of working in pairs or in small groups if they choose.

Students Having Difficulty/ Sheltered English Students

Organize the class into small groups. Explain that their project is to design and produce a brochure for a new interest group that represents the needs of students. Working together, students should make a list of goals and a statement of policies for the new interest group. Each group should also design a symbol that expresses their particular group's goals and values. After the brochures are completed, have each team present its brochure to the rest of the class. Be sure to display the brochures throughout the classroom. Students may wish to use them as references as they learn about the different types of interest groups and the various functions performed by each.

REVIEW

Have students complete the Section 1 Review on page 390. Use the answers in the Annotated Teacher's Edition to assess student mastery of this section.

ASSESS

To assess student mastery of this section, have students complete Daily Quiz 17.1 in *Daily Quizzes with Answer Key*. For additional assessment options, see *Alternative Assessment Handbook* on the *One-Stop Planner CD-ROM*.

ADDITIONAL RESOURCES

Aeff, Robin Lee. *Environmental Action Groups*. 1993. Chelsea House.
Erickson, Judith. *Directory of American Youth Organizations: A Guide to 500 Clubs, Groups, Troops, Teams, Societies, Lodges, and More for Young People*. 1991. Free Spirit.

OBJECTIVES

▶ Discuss the ways in which interest groups are involved in the electoral process.

▶ Define lobbying.

▶ Explain how interest groups attempt to influence the political process through the legal system.

▶ List and describe how interest groups attempt to shape public opinion.

MOTIVATE

Inform students that their goal is to change the times that school begins and ends. Instead of the current system, in which school starts at 8:30 A.M. and ends at 3:30 P.M. each day, some students favor an earlier start, 8:00 A.M., and an earlier dismissal, 3:00 P.M. Guide students as they brainstorm ideas to help argue their case. Let students know that in addition to thinking of positive outcomes of this change in schedule, they should also consider the people or groups they will attempt to influence and how they plan to influence them. Allow 15 to 20 minutes for students to devise their plan. Have someone volunteer to act as spokesperson to make the presentation to the class. After the presentation remind students that they were serving as an interest group. Explain that in this section students will learn how interest groups participate in the electoral process, what lobbying is, how interest groups use the legal system to influence politics, and how interest groups try to shape public opinion.

TEACH

Building a Vocabulary

In their spiral notebooks, have students continue working on their Political Dictionary. List words the students will be expected to know for this section on the chalkboard. Have students list, define, and give an example of each of the terms, using information provided in the text or on the *Researcher CD-ROM*.

Debating Ideas

Discuss with students the various ways that interest groups are involved in the electoral process, which are discussed in this section of the chapter. Then organize the class into three groups. Two groups will serve as opposing teams in a debate, while the third group will evaluate the presentations of each team. Hold a class debate on the topic of whether interest groups should be allowed to donate money to political candidates, using examples from current elections. Encourage students to include the following topics of discussion in their debate: political action committee contributions vs. individual contributions; huge television fees and high campaign costs; and the influence of lobbying in politics. Have the group that acted as the judge for the debate explain their evaluations of each side. Point out positive statements made by each side, and make note of effective arguments that each side presented. Point out to students that in the next activity they will learn about ways that interest groups use the legal system to accomplish their goals.

Conducting Research/Taking a Stand

Discuss with students how interest groups have used the legal system to fight against the actions of government or business. Have students research examples of lawsuits brought by interest groups. Students may wish to use the Supreme Court Docket section on the *Holt Researcher Online* to help with their research. Students should write a short paper describing the circumstances surrounding the case, which interest group was involved, and the outcome of the case. Students should also give their opinions regarding whether or not they agree with the court's decision. Encourage students to share their findings and opinions on the case with the rest of the class. Tell students that in the next activity they will learn how interest groups work to shape public opinion.

Role-Playing/Solving Problems

Discuss with students the ways that interest groups attempt to shape public opinion. Have students imagine that they are staff members for an interest group that promotes programs to end hunger. Have them draft a memo to other staff members outlining their strategy for influencing public policy. Encourage students to include ideas for reaching the public, political candidates, and all levels of government. Be sure to have students prioritize which government agencies would be most important to influence in an attempt to change existing legislation. In addition, each group should describe the demographics of the public on which their strategy will focus and the political candidates (i.e., representatives of which states) their group's strategy will target.

CLOSE

Remind students of the plan they came up with during the Motivate activity and how they hoped to implement their plan in order to influence others. On the chalkboard write *The Public, The Candidates,* and *The Government.* Under each heading have students write the significance of each item to interest groups and various ways that interest groups may attempt to influence the opinions or beliefs of each of them. Lead a discussion about how and why interest groups use different techniques in attempting to influence each of the three different constituencies. As a class, try to decide which techniques appear to be the most effective for interest groups influencing the decision-making process of each of the three groups.

OPTIONS

Interpersonal Learners

 Ask the class to think of a current topic of debate they have seen on the news or read about in the newspaper. Organize the class into small groups. Have each group imagine that they are employed by an interest group. Their group is close to accomplishing their goal of passing new legislation in favor of their stance on the issue. There is one key member of Congress, however, who does not support the group's position. Have students list possible approaches they can use to influence the congressperson. Each group should choose an approach they feel will have the best chance of persuading the member of Congress to adopt their views. Have each group outline the approach their presentation would use and explain the content of their appeal to each of the other groups.

Encourage students to discuss which approach would be best to pursuade the member of Congress.

Students Having Difficulty/Sheltered English Students

 Refer students to resources where they can find information about the amount of money contributed to political candidates by political action committees (PACs). Have students research the past two decades to show how PACs have become an attractive funding source for political candidates after new legislation limited the amount of money allowed by individual campaign contributions. Students should create a graph that illustrates the dramatic increase in money contributed by PACs to federal candidates over the last 20 years. Students should be prepared to interpret their graphs and explain the results to the class.

REVIEW

Have students complete the Section 2 Review on page 395. Use the answers in the Annotated Teacher's Edition to assess student mastery of this section.

ASSESS

To assess student mastery of this section, have students complete Daily Quiz 17.2 in *Daily Quizzes with Answer Key.* For additional assessment options, see *Alternative Assessment Handbook* on the *One-Stop Planner CD-ROM.*

ADDITIONAL RESOURCES

Makinson, Larry. *The Cash Constituents of Congress.* 1994. Congressional Quarterly.

Birnbaum, Jeffrey. *The Lobbyists: How Influence Peddlers Get Their Way in Washington.* 1992. Times Books.

LESSON 17.3 | INTEREST GROUPS AND THE PUBLIC GOOD

TEXTBOOK PAGES 396–400

HOLT PRESENTATION MAKER
Access Illustrated LECTURE
NOTES using Microsoft®
Powerpoint® on the
One-Stop Planner CD-ROM

OBJECTIVES

▶ List and describe the benefits of interest groups.
▶ List and describe the criticisms of interest groups.
▶ Explain the limitations to interest groups' influence.

MOTIVATE

Present the following scenario to the class: The principal has recently informed each teacher that an additional $1,000 is allotted for each teacher to spend on improving their respective classrooms. The money may be spent on various educational resources, including books, computer software, educational films, art supplies, or educational field trips. In an attempt to resolve the issue of how to spend the money, explain that you would like to hear student input on how the money could be best put to use. Instead of merely taking a vote and letting majority rule, state that each student should tell how they think the money should be spent and should give a brief explanation as to why they believe that would be the most appropriate way to use the money. After students have given their feedback, compare the way the classroom situation was handled to the way a debate over a political issue may be handled. Explain the importance of allowing each student's views to be heard rather than simply taking a vote with majority opinion ruling. Briefly discuss that one of the functions interest groups serve is representing minority opinion. Ask students to give examples of why minority opinions are important to hear before making decisions. Explain that in this section students will learn some of the benefits of interest groups, some of the major criticisms of interest groups, and some ways in which interest groups' influence is limited.

TEACH

Judging Information/Organizing Ideas

 On the chalkboard write the headings *Top 10 Benefits of Interest Groups* and *Top 10 Criticisms of Interest Groups.* Organize the class into four groups. Assign two of the groups

the task of thinking of 10 ways that the current political system benefits from the existence of interest groups. Assign the remaining two groups the task of writing down 10 main concerns or criticisms people have of interest groups. Allow the groups time to brainstorm ideas for their list, and then have the groups working on the same topic agree on one final list. Then write students' ideas under the appropriate heading on the chalkboard. Number the items 1 to 20 (1 to 10 for the benefits, 11 to 20 for the criticisms). Write each number, 1 to 20, on a small piece of paper, and place the slips of paper in a hat or a box. Randomly pick a number and choose a student to explain the item on the list that corresponds to that number. Allow students to either describe or provide a political example of the benefit or criticism. Ask students to identify which list they agreed with. Tell students that in the next activity they will learn about how interest groups protect minority rights.

Demonstrating Understanding

Tell students that one of interest groups' most important roles is to ensure that minority opinions have a chance to be heard. Discuss what may happen if the majority view does not represent what is best for the public good. Ask students to provide examples of situations in real life when the opinion of the vast majority did not serve the public's best interests. Discuss ways in which the Constitution prevents minority rights from being violated. (Students may need a brief reminder of previous discussions about the Bill of Rights.) Have students describe additional ways in which the current political system allows for minority groups to express their views in an appropriate manner. Tell students that in the next activity they will learn about limitations on interest groups' influence.

Writing About Government/Taking a Stand

Have students write a draft of a bill aimed at regulating the influence of interest groups on government. Refer students to some of the criticisms of interest groups discussed in the earlier activity. For each criticism, have students suggest a method that may be used to offset any harmful effects from interest groups. As students make their suggestions, remind them of the constitutional guarantees of freedom of speech as well as other freedoms. Tell students to begin writing their bill with a statement explaining the purpose of the proposed legislation, followed by each of the provisions they identified for regulating the activities of interest groups. Allow students to work in small groups if they choose. Each student or group should draft a final copy to be presented to the class. Select a handful of final drafts to be displayed in the classroom throughout the remainder of the unit.

CLOSE

Refer students back to the discussion during the Motivate activity about how they came up with ways to spend the extra money for the classroom. Inform students that errors were made in calculating the school's budget, and as a result, there is no extra money for each teacher to spend on his or her classroom. The problem is that many teachers have already spent the money they thought they had. Explain that students are now faced with the dilemma of raising enough money to cover the overspending that has taken place. Have students think of the most efficient way of raising money to offset the additional costs incurred by the recent spending. Remind students to focus on the process of receiving input from all class members and arriving at a decision that best serves the school's needs.

OPTIONS

Students Having Difficulty/ Sheltered English Students

 Organize the class into an even number of groups. Assign half of the groups the task of creating a political cartoon describing the benefits of interest groups and their ability to serve the public good. Assign the other half of the groups the job of creating a political cartoon illustrating the major criticisms of interest groups and the problems they have helped to create. Have groups share their cartoons with each other when they are finished.

Students Having Difficulty/ Sheltered English Students

Review the benefits and criticisms of interest groups by creating two lists on the board. As students provide the information to complete each list, write each item under the appropriate heading. When each list is completed, organize students into small groups. Provide each group with a stack of index cards so they can create flash cards with the information on the board. Before taking the section quiz, students should take turns quizzing each other on the different benefits and criticisms of interest groups.

REVIEW

Have students complete the Section 3 Review on page 400. Use the answers in the Annotated Teacher's Edition to assess student mastery of this section.

ASSESS

To assess student mastery of this section, have students complete Daily Quiz 17.3 in *Daily Quizzes with Answer Key.* For additional assessment options, see *Alternative Assessment Handbook* on the *One-Stop Planner CD-ROM.*

RETEACH

For students having difficulty with the lessons, have them complete Reteaching Activity 17. This activity is located in *Reteaching Activities with Answer Key.*

ADDITIONAL RESOURCES

Phillips, Kevin. *Arrogant Capital: Washington, Wall Street, and the Frustration of American Politics.* 1994. Little, Brown and Co.

Makinson, Larry. *Open Secrets: The Encyclopedia of Congressional Money and Politics.* 1996. Congressional Quarterly.

Hirsch, H.N. *A Theory of Liberty: The Constitution and Minorities.* 1992. Routledge.

GOVERNMENT NOTEBOOK

The Government Notebook is a journal activity that encourages students to consider basic concepts of government that relate to their lives. A follow-up notebook activity appears on page 402.

WHY IT MATTERS TODAY

To find additional lesson plans dealing with interest groups, visit CNNfyi.com or have students complete the GOVERNMENT IN THE NEWS activity on page 401.

CNNfyi.com

INTEREST GROUPS

What do members of the American Frozen Food Institute and the National Hot Rod Association have in common? Probably very little. They do, however, have at least one common trait—they are both members of interest groups.

Like a team or club, interest group members have common goals and—often—intense concerns. Unlike teams or clubs, however, interest groups' goals often are far-reaching and political. In this chapter you will learn about the different types of interest groups, as well as the ways in which they promote their goals.

GOVERNMENT NOTEBOOK

In your Government Notebook, write a list of the kinds of groups you think qualify as interest groups. What do they have in common? Write your answer in your Notebook.

WHY IT MATTERS TODAY

Interest groups play a major role in shaping public policy. At the end of this chapter visit CNNfyi.com to learn more about interest groups.

CNNfyi.com

SECTION 1

ROLE OF
INTEREST GROUPS

READ TO DISCOVER

1. What is an interest group?
2. What are the functions of interest groups?
3. What are the types of interest groups?

POLITICAL DICTIONARY

agribusiness
trade association
labor union
public interest group

Throughout history, people have organized groups to promote their views on issues that concern them. As noted in Chapter 15, some such groups were made up of African Americans who came together to fight for their civil rights.

Such organized groups, or interest groups, give people a way to work together toward their common goals. As noted in Chapter 5, an interest group is a collection of people acting together to advance a shared concern in the political process. Interest groups serve several key functions in the United States and take several forms.

Functions of Interest Groups

As noted in Chapter 8, public opinion represents the voice of the majority in the political process. Interest groups, however, provide a means by which one segment of the population—typically a minority—can have its intensely held concerns represented in political decision making. They do so in three main ways—by

★ organizing people who share a concern,
★ providing a means of political participation, and
★ supplying information to the public and to policy makers.

Organizing People Interest groups provide a means of organization for people who share strong opinions about an issue. The issue might be one that affects members of the group personally or one that group members believe needs to be addressed to promote the public good. People with strong opinions typically join an interest group in the hope that working with others who have shared concerns will strengthen their cause.

Groups that have banded together to promote their common concerns include farmers, businesspeople, workers, environmentalists, feminists, civil rights activists, and students. People in the fishing industry who disagree with environmentalists over how much commercial fishing should take place may participate in interest groups to make their views heard. Likewise, joining an environmentalist group gives another sector of the population—in this case, citizens concerned about commercial fishing—political strength that they may not have as individuals.

Providing for Political Participation Often when citizens feel strongly about political issues, they want to do more than merely vote for candidates who will represent their concerns. Joining an interest group gives these citizens another way

POLITICAL PROCESSES *Members of the United Farm Workers of America gather at a convention in Fresno, California, to discuss issues concerning their group.* **What are some of the other types of groups whose members have banded together to promote their common cause?**

In the 1800s, farmers' organizations got together primarily for social purposes. Since rural life was harsh and isolated, when farmers organized they usually held picnics, dances, and other functions.

But agrarian organizations gained their strength from economic issues. An important example is the National Grange of the Patrons of Husbandry—usually called the Grange. Started in 1867 by Oliver Hudson Kelley, who had been a clerk in the U.S. Agriculture Department, the Grange began as a secret organization full of ritual and ceremony, but it encouraged the formation of independent political parties that ran on anti-monopoly platforms.

The Grange spread slowly at first, but when it successfully battled against unfair practices in various industries, it quickly attracted new members. Within eight years, enrollment had reached 850,000. In 1872 Montgomery Ward and Company was founded specifically to meet Grange members' needs for everything from household items to clothes and toys. ■

Caption Answer

because most businesses face heavy government regulation

---

to take part in the political process—particularly if they are part of a minority viewpoint that is not represented through majority-dominated elections. By working with like-minded people to make their views known to the public and to policy makers, interest group members can affect government actions. As you will learn in Section 2, interest groups have several ways of influencing the political process.

Supplying Information A third function of interest groups is to inform the public about their concerns. For example, if you are curious about a certain industry's effect on air quality, you can contact an environmental interest group. If you want to know what goods and services that industry provides, you can contact a business interest group that represents it. In both cases the interest groups are happy to provide information about their concerns. By doing so, groups that represent the concerns of a minority of the population can draw the attention of the majority to their viewpoints.

Interest groups supply information not only to the public but also to policy makers. In this way, interest groups hope to influence legislation that affects their areas of concern.

Types of Interest Groups

Thousands of interest groups operate in the United States. They range from small local groups to large national organizations, and they represent many concerns. Some seek to inform the public about the needs and concerns of museums, and some organize to support animal rights. These groups may have many members or only a few.

Many interest groups—such as agricultural groups, business groups, labor unions, and professional groups—are formed to address economic concerns. Others are based on social, cultural, or related causes.

Agricultural Groups Because government policies greatly affect agriculture, several interest groups have formed to represent the nation's farmers and agribusinesses. **Agribusinesses** are large companies that run farms, make and distribute farm equipment and supplies, and process, store, and distribute farm crops. Some agricultural interest groups, such as the American Farm Bureau Federation, represent farmers as a whole. Others, like the National Cotton Council of America, represent a particular section of the agricultural industry.

Business Groups Another element of society that operates under heavy government regulation is business. For this reason, businesses—like farmers and agribusinesses—have formed interest groups to advance their own concerns. For example, the Chamber of Commerce of the U.S.A. and the Business Roundtable are nationwide organizations that represent general business interests.

In addition, many businesses maintain specialized interest groups to represent their specific concerns. These interest groups, called **trade associations**, are organizations of business firms within an industry. For example, the snack food and trucking industries both have trade associations that represent their concerns. Though trade

PUBLIC GOOD *Members of the Columbia, Missouri, Chamber of Commerce tour the construction site of a stadium being built on the University of Missouri campus.* **Why have businesses formed interest groups such as the Chamber of Commerce to advance their own concerns?**

associations participate in non-political activities, such as developing product standards, their major function is to represent the political concerns of their industries.

Labor Unions Workers also have formed interest groups to represent them. These **labor unions** are organizations of workers acting together to gain better wages and working conditions. Labor organizations include those for educators and for office workers.

Major union activities involve representing member interests at the workplace, but most unions also are involved in politics. The American Federation of Labor–Congress of Industrial Organizations (AFL–CIO) is a huge collection of many unions that was established in 1955 and currently has more than 13 million members. The AFL–CIO works on a national level to raise the minimum wage, for example, and to secure greater health and other benefits for workers.

Professional Groups Some professions, such as law and medicine, also maintain interest groups to represent their concerns. Among the well-known professional organizations are the American Bar Association (ABA), which works to protect the interests of those in the legal profession, and the American Medical Association (AMA), a group representing those who practice medicine.

Professional groups perform several key functions. In addition to creating standards for the profession, holding meetings, and publishing journals and reports, these groups represent their members' concerns in the political system.

Societal Groups Another type of interest group represents societal groups, such as various ethnic groups, women, and veterans. Societal interest groups include the National Association for the Advancement of Colored People (NAACP), the Mexican-American Legal Defense Fund (MALDEF), the National Organization for Women (NOW), and the American Legion.

POLITICAL PROCESSES *The cartoon above provides an ironic look at how some people feel about environmental groups.* **What tools do cause-based groups use to promote their views?**

These groups are often powerful. The American Association of Retired Persons (AARP), which represents older Americans, has 34 million members. It is one of the largest organization in the United States.

Cause-Based Groups Some groups promote a broad cause, rather than the interest of a certain group of people or businesses. Such causes may include education, a particular field of research, and cultural goals. The National Association for the Advancement of Science promotes scientific research and funding for scientific endeavors. Like professional interest groups, such organizations often hold meetings and publish journals about their topics of concern. These organizations' political goals involve gaining funding for a project and influencing government regulation of the field in which they are interested.

CASE STUDY

Students Against Destructive Decisions

One growing cause-based interest group is Students Against Destructive Decisions (SADD). This group works to prevent teenage drinking and driv-

Holt American Government Videodisc

The videodisc segment Special Interests: Save Virginia City complements the Chapter 17 case study, Students Against Drunk Driving. Barcodes for the Spanish version of the video segment are available in the *Holt American Government Videodisc Teacher's Guide*.

PLAY SEGMENT

PAUSE

RESUME PLAY

PLAY OPTION A

PLAY OPTION B

PLAY EPILOGUE

In 1996 seven of eight state referendums to expand gambling were defeated. These defeats were cheered by the cause-based group, the National Coalition Against Legalized Gambling. The group's leader was especially pleased at the closing of a riverboat casino near his hometown in Illinois.

Yet observers note that the closing simply reveals that casinos have become ingrained in states where they are legal. Illinois did not revoke the license because the boat attracted gambling addicts or because the number of local bankruptcies doubled in 1997. The riverboat casino is being closed because the state wants to give the license to a more profitable casino. The state wants to do this because tax receipts increase with casino revenue.

Thus, in spite of referendum defeats, the Coalition may have difficulty closing down casinos in the 27 states where they already exist. ■

Caption Answer

because they believe that protecting the environment promotes the public good

---

ing by raising public awareness and by persuading teens to pledge not to drive under the influence of alcohol.

The organization was founded in 1981 by a high school coach and administrator in Wayland, Massachusetts, after two of his hockey players died in separate accidents. By the mid-1990s SADD had around 4 million members and 20,000 chapters in schools across the country.

Traffic accidents are the leading cause of death for 15 to 20 year olds. SADD works to spread awareness of the dangers facing teens on the road.

The National Highway Traffic Safety Administration (NHTSA) reports that 3,594 drivers in the U.S., ages 15 to 20, died in motor vehicle crashes in 2000, along with 348,000 injured. The use of alcohol was cited in 970 of these fatalities. After reaching a plateau in the mid 1990s, teen traffic deaths rose to their highest level in 1999, and then declined in 2000.

SADD chapters use a variety of strategies to prevent teen drinking and driving. Some chapters have staged public events such as mock crashes, with local police and emergency teams helping to simulate the aftermath of a car accident for a student audience. Many chapters sponsor alcohol-free events on prom or graduation night. One of the most unique SADD strategies is the Contract for Life. Under rules of the contract, teens promise to call their parents for a ride home if they or other drivers have been drinking. Parents agree to provide a ride home with no questions or punishment until the following day.

SADD also works with other organizations, such as Mothers Against Drunk Driving (MADD), to influence public policy regarding teen drinking and driving. Members of MADD's Youth in Action program, a group within the organization for people under 21, work with adults to change laws,

strengthen enforcement, and publicize efforts to stop teen drinking and driving.

Other groups promoting particular broad causes include religious groups, environmental groups, gun control groups, anti–gun control groups, and antiabortion and abortion rights groups. The Christian Coalition, the National Rifle Association (NRA), Planned Parenthood, and the National Catholic Welfare Council are all groups that promote causes.

Some cause-based groups refer to themselves as **public interest groups**, or citizens' groups, believing that the policies they pursue would benefit the general public rather than a narrow minority. Public interest groups thus represent people with strong beliefs about what would promote the public good.

The Sierra Club, one of the nation's oldest public interest groups, was founded in 1892 by environmentalist John Muir to work for the preservation of wilderness lands. Today the Sierra Club lobbies for environmentalist causes across the nation.

PUBLIC GOOD *Yosemite National Park, one of the country's oldest national parks, was established as federally protected land in 1890, due in large part to the efforts of Sierra Club-founder John Muir.* **Why might environmental interest groups also refer to themselves as public interest groups?**

Linking
Government and
Sociology

The Influence of Groups on Society

Do you closely follow the news about politics or other public issues? Have you ever passed out flyers or pamphlets to support a particular cause? Have you participated in a debate or discussion on an important political issue? Do you believe that once people reach the age of 18 they should register to vote and cast their ballot on election day? Your answers to these questions provide some insight into how you feel about political participation and how strong your opinions are on various issues that interest you. Why do you feel as you do? What factors are important in helping shape your political beliefs and behavior?

Sociologists believe that the groups we belong to have a strong influence on our attitudes and decisions. Sociologists define a group as two or more people who interact with each other, share expectations, and possess a degree of common identity. Sociologist Emile Durkheim believed that a group could be held together by one of two kinds of forces. The first type of group is held together by similarities, such as belonging to the same family. The second type of group is held together by complementary differences—for example, co-workers who each perform distinct tasks to achieve a shared goal.

Shared interests and desires also form the foundation for interest groups. Students, for example, might join together to support public policies that make it easier for them to afford a college education or to pursue certain degrees. They might try to persuade lawmakers to hold down tuition costs at public universities. They also might pressure Congress to provide more federal aid for those who want to attend college. One group of students at the University of Minnesota at Minneapolis–St. Paul formed Students Against Fee Excess. This organization works to influence school and public policy on

The League of Women Voters is a group of people who share the common goal of promoting political participation through voting.

student fees and tuition. It also educates students on fiscal responsibility in universities.

Groups influence the values, attitudes, and behavior of their members in a wide variety of ways. For example, parents who believe that voting is a civic duty often pass this belief on to their children. Friends planning to attend college may help one another with information about application deadlines or scholarships. The members of a soccer team might rally around a teammate to improve his or her performance.

People frequently do not share all the beliefs of their fellow group members. In addition, as people grow older and have more experiences, they may leave some groups and join others. Despite frequent changes in affiliation and disagreements among fellow members, groups do play an important role in shaping how people think and act.

What Do You Think?

1. Identify some groups to which you belong. How have members of these groups influenced your interests and attitudes?
2. How have your parents and other family members helped to shape your attitudes about government and political participation?

What Do You Think?
Answers
1. Answers will vary, but students should list groups they belong to. Students should list and explain how group members have influenced their interests and attitudes.
2. Answers will vary, but students should offer examples of their families' attempts to shape their political attitudes and explain how this influenced them.

internet connect

TOPIC: Lobbying
GO TO: go.hrw.com
KEYWORD: SV3 GV17

Have students access the Internet through the HRW Go site to find information about lobbying and lobbyists. Then ask students to determine how these groups try to influence legislation and elections, and to include both positive and negative viewpoints on the work of lobbyists. Then have students present a class skit portraying lobbyist activity.

Transparency

An overhead transparency of the chart on this page is available in *Transparency Resources*. See Transparency 35: Some Environmental Public Interest Groups.

Caption Answer

Answers will vary but should reflect the groups' interests.

SECTION 1
REVIEW ANSWERS

1. Refer to the following pages: agribusiness (386), trade association (386), labor union (387), public interest group (388).

2. Types include agricultural groups, business groups, labor unions, professional groups, societal groups, and cause-based groups. Examples will vary.

3a. Interest groups are groups of people who work toward a common goal. They provide a means of political participation and can supply information to the public and to policy makers

3b. Interest groups allow people to have an effect on politics without having to be an elected official.

4. Answers will vary, but students should clearly state their opinion and support it with evidence.

Some Environmental Public Interest Groups

Group	Year Founded	Membership In 2001	Purpose
American Rivers	1973	32,000	To preserve and protect America's river systems
American Wildlands	1977	2,800	To conserve the nation's wildland resources
Climate Institute	1986	1,500	To act as an international link between the scientific community and policy makers
Coast Alliance	1979	N/A	To increase public awareness of coastal ecology and the value of coastal resources
Ducks Unlimited, Inc.	1937	553,000	To conserve critical wetlands habitat in North America used by waterfowl and a wide variety of other wildlife
Friends of the Earth	1969	35,000	To protect the earth from environmental disaster
National Audubon Society	1905	600,000	To conserve and restore natural ecosystems with a focus on birds and other wildlife
Nature Conservancy	1951	1,000,000	To preserve biological diversity
Outdoors Unlimited	1965	4,000	To promote multiple-use resource management
Sierra Club	1892	550,000	To promote natural resource protection and conservation of wild areas
Trout Unlimited	1959	130,000	To conserve, protect, and restore trout (and other fish) by influencing the activities of governmental agencies

Source: *Associations Unlimited*

Public interest groups, such as the environmental organizations listed in the chart above, work to promote interests that they believe benefit the majority. **What are some of the interests promoted by the groups listed in this chart?**

Several citizens' groups have been formed by Ralph Nader, a consumer rights supporter. Nader became nationally known in the 1960s for writing *Unsafe at Any Speed,* a book that documented unsafe features of American automobiles. Later, he pioneered the consumer protection organization by forming groups such as the Center for Auto Safety and Public Citizen.

SECTION 1 REVIEW

1. Identify and Explain:
- agribusiness
- trade association
- labor union
- public interest group

2. Identifying Concepts: Copy the chart to the right. Use it to list the major types of interest groups. Provide an example of each type.

Interest Groups	
1.	2.
3.	4.
5.	6.

Homework Practice Online

keyword: SV3 HP17

3. **Finding the Main Idea**

a. What are interests groups, and what role do they play in the political process?
b. How does joining an interest group enable people to participate in the political process?

4. **Writing and Critical Thinking**

Making Predictions: What issues do you think interest groups will focus on in the future?
Consider the following:
- past changes brought about by interest groups
- current changes supported by interest groups

SECTION 2
HOW INTEREST GROUPS WORK

1. In what ways are interest groups involved in the electoral process?
2. What is lobbying?
3. How do interest groups attempt to influence the political process through the legal system?
4. How do interest groups try to shape public opinion?

POLITICAL DICTIONARY

endorsement
single-issue voting
lobbying
grassroots lobbying
class-action suit

H ow might you try to change a school policy that you have concerns about, such as one that keeps students from leaving campus during lunchtime? You might join with a group of students and approach the principal, other school administrators, or the student council.

Interest groups work in a similar way to make their political concerns known. Unlike other political players—such as members of Congress, the president, heads of government agencies, and judges—interest groups do not have the authority to make government decisions themselves. Instead, they seek to *influence* decisions others make. They do this by:

★ participating in the electoral process,
★ lobbying members of Congress and government agencies,
★ addressing their concerns through the legal system, and
★ trying to influence public opinion by using the media, demonstrating, and protesting.

Participating in the Electoral Process

Interest groups seek to influence the political system is by participating in the electoral process. Their political efforts include endorsing candidates with shared ideas and giving money to campaigns through political action committees.

Endorsing Candidates Interest groups' traditional method of influencing the political process has been through the **endorsement** of—or public declaration of support for—a certain candidate. An interest group will often make endorsements with the expectation of gaining some influence over the decisions of legislators it helps elect. Interest groups also may withhold support from and even work to defeat a candidate. This tactic was pioneered as early as 1917 by women's suffrage organizations that targeted a number of senators who were against giving the vote to women.

An interest group commonly keeps track of which elected officials vote for or against legislation that affects its concerns. Then, during elections, the group may tell its members which candidates to vote for—that is, which ones the interest group endorses. One study found that 44 percent of interest groups make congressional voting records known to the members.

How successful are endorsements? Many interest group members do indeed vote for or against a candidate solely based on his or her view on an issue of concern to the group. This practice is called **single-issue voting**. For example, members of the National Right-to-Life Committee oppose candidates who do not support a ban or limits on abortion, regardless of the candidates' positions on other issues. Members of the National Abortion Rights Action League also practice single-issue voting, opposing candidates solely because they support banning or limiting abortion.

Political Action Committees Interest groups also support political candidates by giving money to their campaigns. With the exception of labor unions, however, interest groups cannot use their own funds, such as members' dues, for campaign contributions. Instead, they contribute through political action committees (PACs).

As noted in Chapter 5, a political action committee is a separate political branch of an interest group that is set up to participate in politics and

Lesson Plans
For teaching strategies, see Lesson 17.2 located at the beginning of this chapter.

Political Dictionary
To reinforce the section's vocabulary terms, refer students to the Electronic Glossary on the *Researcher CD-ROM*.

Section Assessment
To assess students' mastery of this section, have them complete Daily Quiz 17.2 in *Daily Quizzes with Answer Key*.

THEMES IN GOVERNMENT

POLITICAL PROCESSES
During the 1980s feminist organizations began to endorse political candidates, often from the Democratic Party. In 1984 for the first time, the National Organization for Women (NOW) endorsed a presidential candidate, Democratic nominee Walter Mondale. ■

PUBLIC GOOD In 1999 there were 18.5 million licensed drivers over age 65 in the United States, which is 39 percent more than in 1989. As the number of older citizens has increased, concern has grown about drivers who may no longer be qualified to drive. Many states have begun to require behind-the-wheel tests for drivers 76 years of age and older. Other states, some of which have large and organized senior populations, have tended to avoid the issue.

Because of the lobbying efforts of senior groups, states are finding ways to help older people remain mobile. For instance, a driver education program developed by the American Association of Retired Persons (AARP) has trained more than 7.5 million people. Upon completing the course, drivers in the 34 states and the District of Columbia that offer the program are entitled to auto insurance discounts. Other ideas include more public transportation and technology to equip cars with driving aids. ■

Top 10 PAC Contributors to Federal Candidates in 1997–1998

1.	Realtors PAC	$2,474,133
2.	Association of Trial Lawyers of America PAC	$2,428,300
3.	American Federation of State, County, and Municipal Employees	$2,374,950
4.	American Medical Association PAC	$2,336,281
5.	Democratic Republican Independent Voter Education Committee	$2,183,250
6.	Dealers Election Action Committee of the National Automobile Dealers Association	$2,107,800
7.	United Auto Workers Voluntary Community Action Program	$1,915,460
8.	International Brotherhood of Electrical Workers Committee on Political Education	$1,884,470
9.	National Education Association PAC	$1,853,390
10.	Build PAC of the National Association of Home Builders	$1,807,240

Source: Federal Elections Commission

POLITICAL PROCESSES *PACs donate money to the campaigns of candidates who share their views.* **What is the maximum amount that a PAC may contribute to a candidate's campaign?**

give money to candidates. Many interest groups now have PACs. By giving money to candidates through a PAC, interest groups hope that the legislators an interest group helps elect will attempt to pass legislation favorable to its views.

Though PACs existed as early as the mid-1940s, they grew in number in the 1970s after a change in campaign finance laws. The new legislation limited individual campaign contributions in an attempt to prevent one person from having too much political influence. At the same time, the legislation authorized corporations and interest groups to set up PACs that could give more than individuals could. PACs thus became an attractive source of campaign funding for candidates.

Interest groups' importance in campaign fundraising has increased. Whereas PACs had contributed about 25 percent of the funds received in 1976 by winners of House races, the figure increased to about 41 percent by 1988. This number has begun to fall. In 1996, PACs contributed around 31 percent of the funds received by the winners of House races.

Individual PACs do not lavish vast sums of money upon single candidates. In fact, even though the maximum PAC donation is set at $5,000, the average donation by PACs in the 1992 congressional election was $1,600. In addition, given huge television fees and other campaign costs, even $5,000 is not a large amount of money. If many companies in the same industry each contribute $5,000 through several PACs, however, the total donations from that industry could be significant.

PACs tend to donate more money to incumbents because they have a greater chance of winning. In some elections, PACs have even paid off campaign debts of candidates who oppose their views, hoping to win these people's support.

Lobbying

A second way that interest groups participate in the political system is by trying to persuade government policy makers to make particular decisions regarding legislation. This **lobbying** is typically carried out by individual lobbyists who represent an interest group's concerns. Lobbyists' actions are protected by the First Amendment to the Constitution, which gives people the right to request that the government address their complaints.

History of Lobbying *Lobby* became a political term in the United States around 1830. It originated to describe the behavior of people who waited in

Careers in Government

Interest Group Director

Many interest groups rely on volunteers or part-time employees to do much of their work. Organizing and directing the personnel and resources of an interest group, however, often requires full-time professional managers. Such individuals must be knowledgeable about current politics, skilled at coordinating group efforts, and committed to the causes of the interest groups that employ them.

The role of organizing director for the Minnesota Public Interest Research Group (MPIRG) is an example of the talent required to handle this key position, and is typical of the level of experience required for other interest group directors.

MPIRG Director qualifications include:

- Experience in grassroots organizing
- Knowledge of organizing theories and implementation
- Strong track record in strategizing for political advancement of an issue through grassroots mobilization
- Demonstrated capacity to build coalitions
- Ability to negotiate and maintain the current funding structure through networking, coalition building, and organizing
- Knowledge of basic financial management processes

In addition to the above qualifications, interest group directors who have staff management experience and strong time management skills will have a competitive edge versus other individuals seeking this position.

Randy Tate, left, of the Christian Coalition with Ralph Reed, the former executive director, at a news conference.

Many interest groups are based in the nation's capital. The executives of these organizations look for job candidates who are dedicated to the principles of the organization and have the education and training necessary to carry out its work. For example, when the Christian Coalition—a conservative interest group that promotes public policies that support families and traditional values—needed a new executive director in 1997, it hired 31-year-old Randy Tate, who had earned a bachelor's degree in economics and political science from Western Washington University.

Tate was elected to Washington State's House of Representatives at 22, and served there for six years. He then served one full term in the U.S. House from 1995–1996 as a Republican in the 104th Congress. Tate viewed his job at the Christian Coalition as an opportunity to pursue causes in which he deeply believes.

the lobbies of government buildings to talk with legislators. Historically, lobbying has been a negative term, referring to secret meetings in which interest groups try to unfairly influence legislative decisions. Early political cartoons portrayed lobbyists as sinister people who held legislatures in their control. In the 1800s and early 1900s several states enacted strict regulations on lobbying.

Lobbying Today Today the interaction that lobbyists have with congressmembers takes place in private and during public meetings, or hearings. In both settings, lobbyists provide information about the legislation in which they are interested. Hearings are critical for lawmakers to obtain information previously unknown to them. Most lobbyists are experts on their subjects of concern and often have large staffs to perform their research.

Interest groups also lobby government agencies. After all, laws give only general guidance, leaving the agencies to hammer out the specifics. An environmental law passed by Congress, for instance,

Careers in Government

To help students learn about other careers in government, refer them to the Careers section on the *Holt Researcher Online*.

ACROSS THE CURRICULUM

SOCIOLOGY In the 1970s business groups began to pour increasing amounts of money into politics. Some of the funds were contributed through political action committees (PACs), but most of the donations were put into lobbying efforts.

Business groups began to institute new lobbying techniques. For example, they pioneered the use of organized grassroots lobbying.

Recognizing the power of information, business groups donated considerable amounts of money to think tanks such as the American Enterprise Institute. Scholars at such institutions wrote academic tracts criticizing government interference in free market activity. ■

POLITICAL PROCESSES *Lobbyists often wait in the halls of capital buildings for an opportunity to speak with certain legislators about policies concerning their group.* **What are some of the tools that lobbyists use to influence public opinion?**

sets general targets for clean air standards. Congress directs the Environmental Protection Agency (EPA) in the executive branch, however, to determine how much nitrogen oxide may be given off by coal-fired power plants or how much benzene may be given off by automobiles. Lobbyists thus talk not only to members of Congress about the legislation but also to officials at the EPA about its implementation.

Grassroots Lobbying In addition to providing information, many interest groups organize supporters to help further their cause. Much of this support is gathered through **grassroots lobbying**, an organized effort to urge local citizens to try to influence the decisions of Washington policy makers, particularly congressmembers. Because a district's residents choose whether or not to re-elect someone, congressmembers tend to listen to them.

Over the past 20 years, interest groups have become increasingly sophisticated at orchestrating grassroots efforts. This has resulted largely from technological advances. National organizations frequently use computers to forward information to citizens, urging them to contact their representatives about key issues. Lobbyists may even provide targeted "form letters," which computer users can print, sign, and send to their representatives with little effort. Form letters, however, are not considered as effective as other techniques.

Employing the Legal System

A third way interest groups try to influence public policy is through the legal system. In many instances, they file lawsuits regarding their issues of concern. Beginning in the mid-1930s, for example, civil rights interest groups tried to help bring an end to states' racist Jim Crow laws, such as those segregating schools, by filing lawsuits in state courts. (Jim Crow laws are more fully explained in Chapter 15.)

These efforts culminated in the early 1950s, when the National Association for the Advancement of Colored People (NAACP) and its legal arm, the Legal Defense and Education Fund, helped bring suit to integrate a racially segregated school district. The case, *Brown* v. *Board of Education of Topeka*, involved an African American student who was prevented from attending an all-white school. In its 1954 ruling the Supreme Court declared racial segregation of schools to be illegal.

Some legislation passed since the late 1960s, such as the Clean Air and the Clean Water Acts, has contained provisions allowing interest groups to sue government agencies. Typically, suits can be brought when an agency fails to perform some action the law requires it to perform. In a case regarding the habitat of the endangered spotted owl, an interest group called the Oregon Natural Resources Council sued the U.S. Forest Service for supposedly violating the Clean Water Act and other laws.

Interest groups also may initiate class-action suits. **Class-action suits** are brought by one or more plaintiffs on behalf of themselves and all others affected similarly by a particular wrong. Class-action suits allow individuals—each of whose suffering from an injury might be too small to go to court over—to band together to seek compensation. In a famous case in the 1980s, Vietnam War veterans claiming they were harmed by herbicides used by the U.S. Army won a class-action suit against the government and several chemical companies. In the mid-1990s cases were filed against tobacco companies on behalf of people with diseases thought to be linked to cigarette smoking.

Influencing Public Opinion

Another way in which interest groups work to achieve their goals is by influencing public opinion. Legislators frequently respond favorably to goals that have the support of the majority of the general public. The two main ways in which

POLITICAL PROCESSES *This 1992 Bush/Quayle campaign ad tried to persuade viewers that taxes would rise under rival Bill Clinton's economic plan.* **What other means do interest groups use to influence public opinion?**

interest groups try to influence the public are by sending out information through the media and by conducting demonstrations and protests.

Using the Media Interest groups commonly try to influence public opinion through the media, often through advertising. Business interest groups use newspaper and radio advertisements, mailings, and even inserts into monthly electric utility bills.

Today, television is the primary means of advertising. In 1994 an interest group representing health insurance companies used television advertising to combat President Bill Clinton's plan for rebuilding the nation's health-care system. One ad featured a couple named Harry and Louise. In the ad, Harry and Louise expressed concern that the Clinton plan might create several new levels of government. The ad helped defeat national health-care insurance.

Interest groups also encourage favorable stories about their issues of concern. This is called using "free media" (news stories) as opposed to the "paid media" (advertising).

Demonstrations and Protests Television airtime is expensive, so only around one third of all interest groups buy time on television as a means of reaching the public. Other groups stage demonstrations and protests in hopes that the media will cover their actions and bring their cause to the attention of the public.

For example, antiabortion activists have demonstrated in front of clinics that perform abortions. Likewise, environmentalists have made headline news by chaining themselves to trees to block logging trucks. Farmers gained significant media attention by parading down a major avenue in Washington, D.C., on their tractors. Such efforts are commonly rewarded with television news coverage, thus enabling interest groups to share their concerns with millions of viewers.

SECTION 2 REVIEW

1. Identify and Explain:
- endorsement
- single-issue voting
- lobbying
- grassroots lobbying
- class-action suit

2. Identifying Concepts: Copy the chart below. Use it to list examples of interest groups and the issues they target.

Interest group	Issues

3. Finding the Main Idea

a. How do interest groups try to promote their concerns through the electoral process?

b. What means do interest groups use to try to influence public opinion?

Writing and Critical Thinking

4. Evaluating: What do you think is the most effective method used by interest groups to influence public policy?

Consider the following:
- the effects of lobbying and class actions suits
- the goals of different interest groups

Homework Practice Online
keyword: SV3 HP17

Caption Answer
Interest groups use print resources, radio, and demonstrations.

SECTION 2 REVIEW ANSWERS

1. Refer to the following pages: endorsement (391), single-issue voting (391), lobbying (392), grassroots lobbying (394), class-action suit (394).

2. Examples will vary but may include the Right-to-Life Committee, which opposes abortion, and the NAACP, which fights for civil rights.

3a. They endorse candidates with shared ideas and give money to campaigns through political action committees.

3b. Interest groups use advertisements, protests, and demonstrations.

4. Answers will vary. Students should support their answers with evidence from the text.

SECTION 3

INTEREST GROUPS AND THE PUBLIC GOOD

SECTION 3

INTEREST GROUPS AND THE PUBLIC GOOD

READ TO DISCOVER

1. What are the benefits of interest groups?
2. Why are interest groups criticized?
3. How is interest groups' influence on the political system limited?

As noted in Chapter 16, public opinion is the collective opinion of the majority of the population. You may think that in a democracy, majority opinion should always win out over minority views. What if the *majority* view, however, does not represent what is best for the public good, which covers everyone?

Fearing unfair rule by the majority, the framers of the Constitution set up a framework preventing minority rights from being violated. A key to this framework is the establishment of specific protections for all people—for example, laws guaranteeing property rights and providing for religious freedom. In addition, the framers designed institutions to make it difficult for any group, even a majority, to establish unfair control over government. To accomplish this goal, the framers created a system that would be open to input from many sources. Thus, even interest groups that represent only a small minority have the opportunity to exert a significant influence on government actions. This gives interest groups the opportunity to promote the public good by pushing government to address minority concerns.

As you will see, however, interest groups do not always promote the public good. They sometimes attempt to advance the narrow interests of just a few at the expense of the general population. For this and other reasons, many citizens are critical of interest groups' role in the U.S. political system.

Benefits of Interest Groups

Interest group participation brings two main benefits to the U.S. political system. The first, as stated above, is that interest groups provide a voice for minority concerns in the political system. The second is that they supply information that lawmakers and the general public can use to make informed decisions about policies.

Representing Minority Concerns The major argument on behalf of interest groups is that majority views should not be the only factor that shapes public policy. Why might it be important that minority views be heard in the political system?

Suppose that a city is planning to build a highway. Much of the Oak Heights neighborhood would have to be destroyed to make room for the highway. Though the highway would make life more convenient for many commuters, it also would

PUBLIC GOOD *People representing minority interests can express their views in public meetings such as government hearings. **What is one major argument on behalf of interest groups?***

significantly disrupt the lives of the people living in Oak Heights. The number of commuters (the majority) is much greater than the number of neighborhood residents (the minority).

Even so, most citizens would probably say that the Oak Heights residents should have their views on the building of the highway considered. Forming an interest group, such as Save Oak Heights, allows the residents to try to convince policy makers and the majority of the public of the importance of protecting their homes.

In such a case, interest groups can perform a key role in promoting the public good, just as they have done throughout U.S. history. Civil rights leaders during the 1950s and 1960s, for example, created groups to bring the injustices of discrimination to the attention of the majority. During the years when it was led by Martin Luther King Jr., the basic strategy of the civil rights movement was to use demonstrations in the South to focus the attention of the country on the injustices of segregation. By giving minority concerns a voice in the political process through lobbying, filing lawsuits, and protesting, interest groups can temper majority rule with appropriate attention to minority concerns.

Providing Information As you learned in Section 1, a key interest group function is to provide information. In this way an interest group may promote the public good by increasing the awareness of officials and the public about its issues of concern. Without such a voice, these issues might not be heard, and the majority might not have the opportunity to lend support to a just minority cause.

As you also learned, members of interest groups often are experts on their subjects of concern and are able to provide detailed information that policy makers and the general public may not otherwise obtain. By providing information, interest groups enable policy makers and the general public to make more informed decisions about public policies.

Criticisms of Interest Groups

Perhaps you have heard someone in your family, your community, or the media say that a certain politician is overly influenced by "special interests." What that person means is that the politician gives interest groups too much control over

Comparing Governments

Restricting Interest Groups

In the United States, interest groups have relatively few government-ordered restrictions. In contrast, authoritarian governments often place tight restrictions on interest groups. Such restraints are usually an attempt to limit opposition to the government. Consider, for example, the experiences of interest groups under the communist governments of Poland and China.

Before the fall of communism in Eastern Europe in 1989, Polish workers could not legally join unions that were not sponsored by the government. In the 1980s, however, millions of workers defied this law and joined the independent Solidarity union. Union members demanded freedom of political and religious expression and the right to form free and independent unions. When Poland's first free elections in decades were finally held in 1989, Solidarity candidates received enough votes to take control of the government.

The recent efforts of prodemocracy interest groups in the People's Republic of China were less successful. In 1989 China's communist government ordered the military to put down massive student demonstrations calling for democracy and other reforms. In 1997 China also limited the influence of interest groups in the former British colony of Hong Kong, which had been turned over to Chinese control that year. The Chinese government-appointed Hong Kong legislature approved a law disbanding Hong Kong interest groups that receive political funds from overseas.

his or her policy decisions. Indeed, interest groups often are criticized for having too much sway over the political system. Critics believe that some of these groups gain this control through financial influence.

Financial Influence Interest groups have long been accused of attempting to improperly influence

POLITICAL PROCESSES *Some critics accuse interest groups of trying to influence government officials by providing them with entertainment such as tickets to sporting events.* **Why does entertaining no longer play a central role in lobbying?**

officials through favors, entertainment, and financial support. Many people believe that lobbyists actually get their way by buying congressmembers out-of-town trips, tickets to sporting events, and expensive meals. (During the 1800s a lobbyist supposedly remarked that "the way to a man's 'Aye' [vote of support] is through his stomach.") Along with these benefits supposedly come threats of retribution at the next election if members do not give in to the lobbyist's demands. Entertaining, however, played a more central role in earlier lobbying than it does today.

Interest groups' activities today more often come in the form of campaign contributions. Many people see this type of influence as more subtle and dangerous than entertainment. Specifically, many people resent what they see as businesses' and other wealthy groups' practice of providing financial support to elected officials in exchange for political influence. Wealthy and well-educated people can more easily form interest groups than can the disadvantaged, who may feel strongly about an issue but lack the resources to organize.

For example, even with the large increase in interest groups over the last three decades, no powerful interest groups exist exclusively for poor people. For this reason, critics charge that the disadvantaged do not receive the proper voice in the political process.

Excessive Power Many critics also believe that interest groups' financial and ideological influence gives them too much control over government. They believe that the balance between minority and majority views gets lost in U.S. politics. A small interest group that is wealthy, well organized, and vocal about its intense concerns might gain more political power than the majority. Part of the reason for this is that the majority often does not speak out as loudly as a focused minority. On many issues, critics argue, the voice of the majority hardly is heard at all, leaving *only* interest groups to exert influence. What would be a valid input if it were one voice among many, sometimes becomes the *only* voice.

According to some critics, the public policy-making system in the United States enables organized groups to gain excessive influence. For every major policy issue there is a congressional committee legislating on the subject, a government agency implementing the legislation, and one or more interest groups representing people and businesses with an intense concern in the subject. The congressmembers involved joined the committee because the issue at hand is important to them and their constituents. The government agency is staffed largely by people whose life's work centers on the subject. Of course, the interest group also is very concerned with the issue. With these three groups working together to create most public policy, the majority's viewpoint sometimes goes unheard.

An example is the price-support system for farm products such as corn, sugar, and peanuts. The agricultural committees in Congress are dominated by members from rural districts who want to help farmers. The mission of the Department of Agriculture is also to help farmers. Each price support program is backed by an organized farm interest group. These three groups work together to make agricultural policies, while consumers who may want lower food prices (the majority) have trouble being heard.

In such situations government officials certainly hear from several interest groups, but are unlikely to hear from many ordinary citizens. As a result, critics claim, the intense concerns represented by the interest groups gain more weight than the majority concerns represented by public opinion and elections.

This problem, however, usually develops only in fields of public policy that provide large benefits to a small group while the majority loses only a little. For example, tax dollars fund property development subsidies that provide significant new business for the real estate and construction industries in central cities, but cost each taxpayer only a few dollars a year. In such situations, government officials will most likely hear from an interest group in favor of such subsidies but are less likely to hear from many ordinary citizens. With a highly publicized issue that the public cares deeply about, elected officials are more likely to bow to the majority.

Campaign Finance Reform In recent years these criticisms of interest groups' influence over politics have led to demands for campaign finance reform. Congress has been working on campaign finance reform for years, but as of mid-2001 the House and the Senate still had not agreed on a substantive bill.

Some proposals limit the amount of money candidates can spend in campaigns. One problem here is that challengers cannot mount an effective campaign against a current officeholder without spending a great deal of money. Spending limits thus favor officeholders by making it more difficult for challengers to win. Many people believe that officeholders already enjoy many advantages in re-elections and that such legislation would unfairly strengthen their position.

Other proposals support financing elections with public funds, raised through the income tax on U.S. citizens. Public financing, however, has been criticized in light of government's already tight budgets.

Limitations on Interest Groups

Even though few campaign finance reform laws have been passed, there are limitations to interest groups' influence. First, though interest groups may donate money to a politician's campaign, elected officials often worry that support for "special interest" policies will hurt them with voters. For example, a politician who receives money from the tobacco industry but whose home state is passing significant antismoking legislation will likely be less concerned about tobacco interests than those of his or her state's registered voters.

Overall, evidence suggests that the influence of campaign contributions is less on issues of major significance. Campaign contributions certainly do not dominate congressional votes to the exclusion of other influences.

A second limitation on interest groups' influence is visibility. The increasing aggressiveness of media reporters over the past few decades has made it harder for policy issues to go unnoticed. Interest groups often can only dominate decisions on highly visible issues by gaining majority sympathy for their cause. As long as policy

POLITICAL PROCESSES *Congress has been working for years to pass a campaign finance reform bill that would limit interest groups' ability to influence policy by contributing large amounts of money to politicians' election campaigns.* **What is one of the criticisms of public financing of election campaigns?**

GLOBAL CONNECTIONS

In a 1993 referendum, only 4.4 percent of Puerto Rican voters chose independence from the United States. But a variety of interest groups have taken up the cause of 15 Puerto Ricans who fought for the island's autonomy during the 1970s and 1980s. The group claimed responsibility for bombings in the United States that killed five people. But none of the nationalists were charged with murder or with the bombing. Instead they were given 35- to 105-year prison terms for sedition and related charges.

Support for the nationalists is growing: church leaders in both countries, business groups, labor unions, winners of the Nobel Peace Prize, and leaders of Puerto Rico's statehood movement have argued that the prisoners' sentences were disproportionate to what they were charged with. In 1999 President Clinton granted them clemency. ■

Cartoon Transparency

An overhead transparency of the cartoon on this page is available in *Transparency Resources.* See Cartoon Transparency 18: Interest Groups Lobbying.

Caption Answer

Critics argue that the government's budget is already tight.

SECTION 3 REVIEW ANSWERS

1. benefits—represent minority concerns, provide information; criticisms—improper financial influence, excessive power

2a. They give voice to minority concerns and supply information that lawmakers and the public can use to make informed decisions.

2b. Interest groups often find that they are but one influence among many regarding important issues. The increasingly aggressive media, as well as competition among interest groups, also limit interest groups' influence.

3. Answers will vary, but students should state their opinion and provide examples from the text.

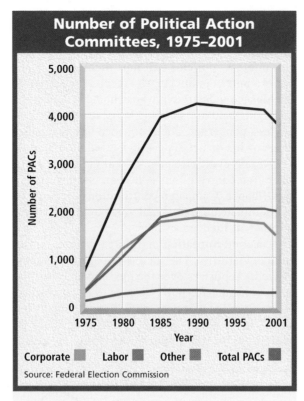

Number of Political Action Committees, 1975–2001

Source: Federal Election Commission

The number of PACs has increased dramatically over the last 20 years. **What has happened to the total number of PACs since 1990?**

concerns. When issues are visible, the ability of interest groups to control legislative decisions depends greatly on their ability to arouse public sympathy for a just cause. When a group is able to make a case for its position, the public will be much more likely to listen to the debate and go on to support that group's position.

Third, interest groups' influence is limited by the competition among them. The dramatic growth in the number and variety of interest groups over the past 30 years has meant that congressional committees and government agencies now hear from many more interest groups in more policy areas.

For example, if the U.S. government decides to set a tariff on imported luxury automobiles, many interest groups will become involved in the debate over the issue. Not only domestic car makers but also businesses who import and sell foreign cars will get involved on different sides of the issue. Even the foreign country where the automobiles are made may become involved in the debate.

Because of this kind of competition, some people believe that the enormous growth in interest groups has actually *decreased* individual groups' influence over U.S. politics. When fewer groups operated, they had more influence because they had less competition for policy makers' attention. As the number of groups competing in a policy area has increased, the ability of any one group to have significant influence over the system has declined.

arguments must be justified in terms of the public good and the debate proceeds completely in the open, interest groups will have trouble dominating the political system with purely selfish

SECTION 3 REVIEW

1. Identifying Concepts: Copy the graphic organizer below. Use it to list the major benefits and criticisms of interest groups.

Interest Group

Benefits

Criticisms

Homework Practice Online
keyword: SV3 HP17

2. **Finding the Main Idea**

   a. In what ways do interest groups promote the public good?

   b. What serves to limit interest groups' influence?

3. **Writing and Critical Thinking**

   Drawing Conclusions: Do you think interest groups have too much influence? Would you support campaign finance reform?

   Consider the following:
   • the impact interest groups have had on the political process
   • the ways interest groups influence public policy

Interest Groups: Past and Present

Often in American history interest groups have gathered together to fight for certain causes or rights. In 1848, Lucretia Mott and Elizabeth Cady Stanton called a women's rights forum, where they used the Declaration of Independence as a model in their fight for the vote. They said, "We hold these truths to be self-evident: that all men and women are created equal." Stanton and Susan B. Anthony formed the National American Woman Suffrage Association in 1890. In spite of tireless efforts to change legislation, though, women did not get the right to vote until 1920.

Another historic group led by women in the 1800s was the Women's Christian Temperance Union, an international organization endorsing total abstinence from alcoholic beverages.

By 1883, the organization grew more powerful by appealing to schools, churches and organized groups. In 1919, the 18th Amendment to the Constitution passed, prohibiting the sale, export and manufacture of alcoholic beverages. This amendment remained in place from 1920 to 1933.

Modern interest groups have been able to influence legislation by even more sophisticated measures, including mass media—television, print, and radio. They prepare detailed materials for legislators to lobby for their causes. They also address concerns through the legal system.

One of the most powerful interest groups is the American Association of Retired Persons (AARP). In 1958, Ethel Percy Andrus founded the organization as a non-profit, nonpartisan national organization devoted to "enriching the experience of aging." The AARP has around 30 million members, most of whom are retired or working people age 50 and over. The AARP advocates for older Americans on public policy issues such as social security and health care. It also provides a newsletter for mem-

Actress Debbie Reynolds addresses the national convention of the AARP.

bers on certain topics. It also actively lobbies for legislation benefiting its members.

Also in 1958, an ultraconservative, anti-Communist organization was formed in the United States. It was called the John Birch Society. Founded by Robert Welch, a manufacturer, it was named after John Birch, an American intelligence officer killed by Communists in China in August 1945. Known as an extreme right-wing group, it was formed to fight subversive Communism within the United States. Through advertising, billboards, and brochures, members tried to influence public opinion. They sought to get rid of the income tax, repeal social security legislation, and impeach certain government officials.

What Do You Think?

1. Describe the methods used by interest groups to influence public opinion.

2. What are some of the changes interest groups helped bring about in the past?

> **WHY IT MATTERS TODAY**
>
> How do interest groups help us today? Describe how they influence policy makers. What have they achieved? Use CNNfyi.com or other current events sources to find additional information about this subject.
>
> CNNfyi.com

Government in the News Answers

1. Methods include advertising, creating brochures, providing materials to legislators, and appealing to the public through the media.

2. Changes include women's right to vote and passing the 18th Amendment.

CHAPTER 17

Review Answers

Writing a Summary

Summaries should focus on the main points of each section. These may be found in the Read to Discover questions at the start of each section. Summaries should also use standard grammer, spelling, sentence structure, and punctuation.

Identifying Ideas

Refer to the following pages: agribusiness (386), trade association (386), labor union (387), public interest group (388), endorsement (391), single-issue voting (391), lobbying (392), grassroots lobbying (394), class action suit (394).

Understanding Main Ideas

1. a group of people who share a political concern; provide a means by which minority concerns can be represented in political decision making

(Continued on page 402)

(Continued from page 401)

2. labor unions, agricultural, business, professional, societal, and cause-based

3. participate in electoral process, lobby, make use of the legal system, influence public opinion

4. organize people who share a concern, provide a means of political participation, and supply information to the media and the public

5. They give voice to minority concerns and supply information. They may have too much influence on government, which they gain through campaign contributions.

6. They do not have total influence on major issues; the media make sure that the public hears about policy issues; competition among the various interest groups limits their power.

Reviewing Themes

1. Answers will vary, but students should give an example and explain the outcome.

2. Interest groups educate their members on issues of concern, so people can make informed political decisions. Interest groups feel that informed voters will enact political change favorable to their goals.

3. Students should state their opinion regarding financial resources. The extent of an interest group's influence depends on the significance of the issues, the media, and competition from other interest groups. Students should state their opinion and offer support for it.

Thinking Critically

1. Answers will vary, but students should choose a technique and offer an explanation of why they chose it.

Writing a Summary

Using standard grammar, spelling, sentence structure, and punctuation, write a summary of the information in this chapter.

Identifying Ideas

Identify the following terms and explain their significance.

1. agribusiness

2. trade association

3. labor union

4. public interest group

5. endorsement

6. single-issue voting

7. lobbying

8. grassroots lobbying

9. class-action suit

Understanding Main Ideas

SECTION 1 *(pp. 385–390)*

1. What are interest groups? Why do people form them?

2. What are the different types of interest groups?

SECTION 2 *(pp. 391–395)*

3. How do interest groups attempt to influence the political system?

4. What functions do interest groups fulfill in the political system?

SECTION 3 *(pp. 396–400)*

5. How might interest groups be beneficial to the political system? How might they be harmful?

6. What are the limitations on interest groups' influence?

Reviewing Themes

1. Political Processes Have you ever lobbied for something you wanted? Give an example of a time when you explained your point of view to a parent, teacher, or friend to try to change his or her decision about something. What was the outcome?

2. Principles of Democracy How can interest groups help their members become informed voters? Why do many interest groups spend their time and money educating citizens on legislative issues and candidates?

3. Public Good Do you think that financial resources play too large a role in politics? What limitations have been placed on interest groups' influence? Do you think that these limitations promote the public good? Explain your answer.

Thinking Critically

1. Comparing Recall the lobbying techniques discussed in section 2. Which one of these techniques do you think is the most powerful tool for influencing policy makers' decisions? Explain your answer.

2. Making Generalizations Do you think the changes brought about by interest groups have been beneficial to the country? Explain your answer.

3. Decision Making If you were to try to change a school policy, which one would it be? In what ways would you try to make your views known?

Writing about Government

Review the list of interest groups that you wrote in your Government Notebook at the beginning of the chapter. Now that you have studied the chapter, would you revise your list? Why or why not?

Interpreting the Visual Record

Examine the photograph below, which shows an interest group rallying in front of the Capitol. Then answer the questions that follow.

1. What is this group protesting?
   a. military spending
   b. pollution
   c. campaign financing
   d. corruption

2. What are some of the techniques used by this interest group to get media coverage of its rally?

Analyzing Primary Sources

The League of Women Voters of the United States, founded in 1920, is dedicated to educating voters and encouraging public participation in government. In June 1997 the league's president, Becky Cain, and several of the organization's leaders testified at a congressional hearing on campaign finance reform. Read the following excerpt from the testimony and answer the questions that follow.

"Do people discuss the independent expenditure loophole [law allowing interest groups to spend money in support of an election campaign without actually contributing money to a particular candidate] over coffee in the morning? No, probably not. But does this mean they don't care about campaign finance reform? . . .

They're joining coalitions [organizations], they're volunteering for initiative [proposed legislation] campaigns, they're voting for reform measures in large majorities: in short, citizens are engaging in the process of reforming how we finance campaigns. They care.

The message is that we, citizens, want reform. We deserve reform. We won't expect any less from Congress."

3. Which of the following statements best reflects Cain's point of view?
   a. citizens oppose campaign finance reform
   b. citizens expect too much from Congress
   c. citizens care about campaign finance reform
   d. citizens do nothing to promote reform

4. Why do you think that reform might be easier to achieve at a state level than at a federal level?

(Continued from page 402)

2. Answers will vary. Some students might suggest that interest groups benefit society by allowing minorities a voice in politics. Others might suggest that interest groups wield too much power because of campaign contributions.

3. Answers will vary but should reflect an understanding of the information about interest groups presented in the chapter.

Writing About Government

The Government Notebook is a follow-up activity to the notebook activity that appears on page 384.

Building Social Studies Skills

1. b
2. Answers will vary, but students might mention that the group is using demonstrations and protests to gain media coverage.
3. c
4. Answers will vary, but students may consider the influence of grassroots lobbying and the difficulty of operating at a national level.

Alternative Assessment

To assess this activity see Acquiring Information and Advertisements in *Alternative Assessment Handbook.*

Building Your Portfolio

With a group, make a poster illustrating of various types of interest groups including: labor unions, business groups, agricultural groups, professional groups, societal groups, and cause-based groups. Include membership statistics and a statement of purpose for each group you select. You may want to contact each group to request photos or other visual information such as brochures or pamphlets to attach to your poster.

☑ internet connect

Internet Activity: go.hrw.com
KEYWORD: SV3 GV17

Have students access the Internet through the HRW Go site to find information on an interest group from among selected business, labor, agricultural, professional, and environmental groups. Write a report about the activities of this group. As an extension, conduct a class debate on a particular interest group.

CHAPTER 18 POLITICAL PARTIES

	OBJECTIVES	PACING GUIDE	REPRODUCIBLE RESOURCES
SECTION 1 **ROLE OF POLITICAL PARTIES** (pp. 405–408)	▸ What are political parties? ▸ What functions do political parties serve? ▸ What are the different kinds of party systems?	**Regular** .5 day **Block Scheduling** .5 day	**ELL** Spanish Study Guide 18.1 **ELL** English Study Guide 18.1 **PS** Reading 21: *George Washington's Farewell Address*
SECTION 2 **THE U.S. TWO-PARTY SYSTEM** (pp. 409–415)	▸ Why did political parties develop in the United States? ▸ How do the main political parties in the United States today differ from each other? ▸ What role do third parties play in the U.S. two-party system?	**Regular** 1.5 days **Block Scheduling** .75 day	**ELL** Spanish Study Guide 18.2 **ELL** English Study Guide 18.2 **PS** Reading 22: *Thomas Jefferson's First Inaugural Address*
SECTION 3 **PARTY ORGANIZATION** (pp. 416–420)	▸ How were early political parties structured, and how did this structure change in the late 1800s? ▸ How did state parties change after the decline of local parties? ▸ How did national party organization change in the 1900s?	**Regular** 1.5 days **Block Scheduling** .75 day	**ELL** Spanish Study Guide 18.3 **ELL** English Study Guide 18.3
SECTION 4 **POLITICAL PARTIES AND THE PUBLIC GOOD** (pp. 421–424)	▸ What are the common criticisms of the U.S. two-party system? ▸ What are the benefits of the U.S. two-party system?	**Regular** .5 day **Block Scheduling** .25 day	**ELL** Spanish Study Guide 18.4 **ELL** English Study Guide 18.4

Chapter Resource Key

PS	Primary Sources	**A**	Assessment		Video
RS	Reading Support	**REV**	Review		Videodisc
E	Enrichment	**ELL**	Reinforcement and English Language Learners		Internet
S	Simulations		Transparencies		Holt Presentation Maker Using Microsoft ® PowerPoint ®
SM	Skills Mastery		CD-ROM		

TECHNOLOGY RESOURCES	REINFORCEMENT, REVIEW, AND ASSESSMENT
One-Stop Planner: Lesson 18.1 Holt Researcher Online Homework Practice Online Global Skill Builder CD-ROM	**REV** Section 1 Review, p. 408 **A** Daily Quiz 18.1
One-Stop Planner: Lesson 18.2 Holt Researcher Online Homework Practice Online Transparencies 37 and 38 Global Skill Builder CD-ROM	**REV** Section 2 Review, p. 415 **A** Daily Quiz 18.2
One-Stop Planner: Lesson 18.3 Holt Researcher Online Homework Practice Online Transparencies 39 Global Skill Builder CD-ROM	**REV** Section 3 Review, p. 420 **A** Daily Quiz 18.3
One-Stop Planner: Lesson 18.4 Homework Practice Online Global Skill Builder CD-ROM	**REV** Section 4 Review, p. 424 **A** Daily Quiz 18.4

Chapter Review and Assessment

SM Global Skill Builder CD-ROM
HRW Go site
REV Chapter 18 Tutorial for Students, Parents, and Peers
REV Chapter 18 Review, pp. 426–27
Chapter 18 Test Generator (on the One-Stop Planner)
A Chapter 18 Test
A Chapter 18 Test Alternative Assessment Handbook

One-Stop Planner CD–ROM

It's easy to plan lessons, select resources, and print out materials for your students when you use the *One-Stop Planner CD-ROM with Test Generator.*

OBJECTIVES

▶ Define and describe political parties.

▶ Discuss the functions of political parties.

▶ Identify and describe the different kinds of party systems.

MOTIVATE

Write the words *Democrat* and *Republican* on the chalkboard. Ask students to identify the importance of each of these two groups. Then have them come up with examples of how these groups participate in the U.S. political system. Explain to students that these are the two major political parties in the United States but that there are many other minor political parties. Ask students to identify other political parties that they have heard about, and list these parties on the chalkboard. Have students attempt to identify the characteristics of each of the political parties listed on the chalkboard, such as each party's stance on abortion or balancing the budget. Ask students to explain why so many parties are needed. Explain to students that political parties play an important role in U.S. government and that throughout this section they will learn what political parties are, what functions they perform, and what kinds of party systems exist throughout the world.

TEACH

Building a Vocabulary

In spiral notebooks, have students create a Political Dictionary to be used throughout the course. The dictionary may be used as an activity at the start of each new section; it may also be used as a modification device for students having difficulty or sheltered English students during tests and homework assignments. List words the students will be expected to know for this section on the chalkboard. Have students list, define, and give an example of each of the terms, using information provided in the text or on the *Researcher CD-ROM*.

Analyzing Information/Taking a Stand

Tell students that political parties are organized groups that seek influence over government. Explain to students that political parties have not always been welcome participants in the U.S. political system, although they have become an essential part of it. Have students read George Washington's Farewell Address in *From the Source: Readings in Economics and Government with Answer Key*. Have students write an essay commenting on whether George Washington's warning about political parties dividing the nation was true. Have students use other resources, such as newspapers, magazines, and the Internet, to find examples to support their stance. Encourage students to share their opinions with the rest of the class. Keep track of each student's opinion to figure out whether the class feels that political parties have divided the nation. Tell students that in the next activity they will learn about the functions of political parties.

Classifying Information

Explain to students that the role of political parties in the U.S. political process has grown substantially over the years. Organize the class into three groups. Each group will represent one of the roles of political parties: assisting the electoral process, organizing day-to-day running of the government, and nominating candidates. Have each group use information from the text, newspapers, magazines, and the Internet to find examples of ways that political parties fulfill the role they have been assigned. After each group has finished their research, have them present the information that they have found to the class. Have students create a list in their Government Notebooks that categorizes what role each action of the political parties fulfills. Tell students that in the next activity they will learn about the different types of party systems that exist throughout the world.

Conducting Research/Creating Maps

Tell students that there are different types of party systems throughout the world. Explain to students the differences between one-party systems, two-party systems, and multiparty systems. Assign each student to find out the type of party system that is used in several specific countries. Encourage students to use the Country Profiles section on the *Holt Researcher Online* and the Internet to conduct research on the countries they have been assigned. After students have finished their research, have the class create a large world map on butcher paper with a color-coded key to identify the type of party system that each country has. Have students color code the countries on the map that they researched. Display the finished map in the classroom for reference.

CLOSE

Review with students the functions of political parties and the different kinds of party systems that exist. Have students use information provided in this section of the text to hypothesize how the functions of political parties in the United States would be different if the United States operated under a different party system (e.g., how would committee membership be determined if the United States operated under a one-party system). Encourage students to share their ideas with the rest of the class.

OPTIONS

Students Having Difficulty/ Sheltered English Students

Discuss with students the functions of political parties. Give students copies of articles that describe the activities of a political party. Have students read the articles and write a few paragraphs describing the activity of the party and the function that it is serving. Encourage students to add these activities to the list they created during the Classifying Information activity.

Logical-Mathematical Learners/ Visual-Spatial Learners

Refer students to the map they created in the Conducting Research/Creating Maps activity in this section. Based on this map have students calculate the percentage of countries throughout the world with each type of party system. Students should then create a pie graph depicting the percentage of each type of party system. Encourage students to share their findings with the rest of the class, and display finished pie graphs throughout the classroom.

Gifted Learners

Remind students that different countries throughout the world have party systems and political parties different from those in the United States. Have students use the Country Profiles section on the *Holt Researcher Online* and other resources to research a political party from another country. Students should answer the following questions: What is the focus of the party? How much political power does it possess? How long has it existed? Have students share their answers with the the class.

REVIEW

Have students complete the Section 1 Review on page 408. Use the answers in the Annotated Teacher's Edition to assess student mastery of this section.

ASSESS

To assess student mastery of this section, have students complete Daily Quiz 18.1 in *Daily Quizzes with Answer Key*. For additional assessment options, see *Alternative Assessment Handbook* on the *One-Stop Planner CD-ROM*.

ADDITIONAL RESOURCES

McSweeney, Dean, and John Zvesper. *American Political Parties: The Formation, Decline, and Reform of the American Party System*. 1991. Routledge.

Johnson, Donald Bruce, and Kirk Porter. *National Party Platforms, 1840–1972*. 1973. University of Illinois Press.

To find information about the Democratic Party, see:
http://www.democrats.org

To find information about the Republican Party, see:
http://www.rnc.org

OBJECTIVES

▶ Explain why political parties developed in the United States.
▶ Describe the differences in the main political parties in the United States today.
▶ Describe the role of third parties in the U.S. two-party system.

MOTIVATE

Have students look through newspapers and magazines searching for articles that discuss political parties. Ask students to identify what party each article discusses. (The majority of articles will most likely discuss the Democratic and Republican Parties.) Ask students to give reasons why these are the most talked about parties. Explain to students that these two parties have not always been the major parties in the United States and that there have been many milestones in the development of political parties in the United States. Tell students that in this section they will learn about the development of political parties in the United States, how the main parties differ, and the role that third parties play.

TEACH

Building a Vocabulary

In their spiral notebooks, have students continue working on their Political Dictionary. List words the students will be expected to know for this section on the chalkboard. Have students list, define, and give an example for each of the terms, using information provided in the text or on the *Researcher CD-ROM.*

Creating Charts/Acquiring Information

Tell students that the first political parties in the United States were created as a result of differences in opinion between Alexander Hamilton and people who believed in his policies, and Thomas Jefferson and people who believed in his policies. Explain to students that political parties in the United States have undergone sig-

nificant changes since the first parties were formed. Organize the class into four groups, assigning each group one of these time periods to research: 1787–1850, 1851–1900, 1901–1950, and 1951–present. Have each group track the development of political parties in the United States for their time period. Students should identify significant changes in the major parties and any significant third parties or independent candidates that influenced politics. Each group should discuss their research with the class. Have each group complete part of a chart that shows the changes in the two-party system and when they occurred. Tell students that in the next activity they will learn about the major differences that exist today between the two major parties.

Navigating the Internet/Comparing and Contrasting

Discuss with students the major differences that exist today between the two main parties. The Democratic Party supports "more government" on behalf of disadvantaged groups, and the Republican Party supports "less government" to increase personal freedoms. Organize the class into an even number of small groups. Pair the groups up; one will research the Democratic Party, while the other will research the Republican Party. Assign each pair of groups specific issues to research, such as balancing the budget or funding for higher education. Have each group use the Internet and other resources to determine their party's stance on each issue. Have each pair of groups discuss the similarities and differences between the parties' stances on each issue with the rest of the class. As a transition to the next activity, tell students that they will learn about third parties.

Predicting Outcome

Tell students that at times in U.S. history third parties or independent candidates have had a significant impact on elections. Explain to students that sometimes these parties or candidates address specific issues, which are sometimes later incorporated into the party platforms of one of the two major parties. Have students review information from the text and the Elections section on the *Holt Researcher Online* to highlight the impact that certain independent candidates and third parties have had on elections. Ask students to think about significant issues that pose a problem to the nation. Have students write an essay predicting what impact third parties might have on these problems.

CLOSE

Ask students to discuss changes that have occurred in the two-party system in the United States. Have students keep in mind the contributions that third parties have made in changing the two-party system throughout U.S. history. Have students write a summary of these changes and give their opinion about what would happen if third parties and independent candidates were not allowed in the United States.

OPTIONS

Interpersonal Learners

Discuss with students that in recent years it has become more common for people to vote for candidates who support specific issues rather than for people to vote based solely on party affiliation. Tell students that sometimes it is difficult for people to stay informed about a party's stance on an issue. Develop a list of issues that are associated with the Democratic Party and a list of issues that are associated with the Republican Party. Have students interview several adults to see if they can identify which party is identified with each issue. Students should ask the questions in random order to avoid influencing the interviewee's responses. Once students have finished, have them figure out how many of the stances people could identify with each party. Discuss these results as a class.

Gifted Learners

Discuss with students the impact that ideological parties have had on politics in the United States. Create a list of ideological parties, both past and present, and allow students to choose the party that they would like to research. Students should write a short paper about the party that describes when it was formed, the type of issue that the party dealt with, the number of representatives it gained in Congress, and its overall impact on the two major parties. Encourage students to share their answers with the rest of the class.

Interpersonal Learners

Remind students of some of the differences between the Democratic and Republican Parties. Organize the class, or have students Organize themselves, into two groups, one representing the Democratic Party and one the Republican. Tell students that they will be conducting a debate to clarify each party's stance on some of the major issues facing the United States today. First, both groups will need to agree on the topics to be debated. Students may want to refer to the Navigating the Internet/Comparing and Contrasting activity or the previous Interpersonal Learners activity for ideas about topics to debate. The groups should then familiarize themselves with their party's respective stance on the chosen topics and then hold a debate. Correct any inaccuracies in the students' interpretation of their party's position. Finally, have the class create a chart that compares the main parties' views on each of the topics debated.

REVIEW

Have students complete the Section 2 Review on page 415. Use the answers in the Annotated Teacher's Edition to assess student mastery of this section.

ASSESS

To assess student mastery of this section, have students complete Daily Quiz 18.2 in *Daily Quizzes with Answer Key.* For additional assessment options, see *Alternative Assessment Handbook* on the *One-Stop Planner CD-ROM.*

ADDITIONAL RESOURCES

Kolbe, Richard. *American Political Parties: An Uncertain Future.* 1992. Harper & Row.

Reichley, James. *The Life of the Parties: A History of American Political Parties.* 1992. Free Press.

OBJECTIVES

▶ Describe the structure of early political parties and changes that occurred in their structure in the late 1800s.
▶ Explain how state parties changed after the decline of local parties.
▶ Describe how national party organization changed in the 1900s.

MOTIVATE

Ask students to imagine what they would do if they had just moved to the United States and members of one of the major political parties helped them find work and a place to live and then asked them to repay their good deeds by voting for their party on election day. Tell students that incidents such as these involving big-city party machines used to occur frequently. Ask students to identify reasons why this kind of action violates democratic principles. Explain to students that significant changes have occurred in the organization of political parties. Tell students that in this section they will learn more about party organization in the late 1800s, how state parties changed after the decline of local parties, and how the national party organization changed in the 1900s.

TEACH

Building a Vocabulary

In their spiral notebooks, have students continue working on their Political Dictionary. List words the students will be expected to know for this section on the chalkboard. Have students list, define, and give an example of each of the terms, using information provided in the text or on the *Researcher CD-ROM*.

Drawing Conclusions

Discuss with students that during the 1800s political parties were dominated at the local level by party machines. Explain to students that these machines were often very corrupt. Have students use information from this section of the textbook and other resources to identify ways that

party machines were corrupt. Students should then use information in the textbook regarding reforms such as the new split-ticket ballot system, voter registration, limiting the number of patronage jobs, and primary elections to write an essay that describes whether they feel these changes had a significant impact on controlling corruption in political parties during the late 1800s. Remind students to use standard grammer, spelling, sentence structure, and punctuation. Tell students that in the next activity they will learn about the impact that changes in local party organization had on state party organization.

Developing Life Skills

Explain to students that as local party organizations became weaker, state party organizations began to grow in power. Explain that national parties now provide significant funding to support the operation of state party activities. Organize the class into four groups. One group will conduct research on the organization of the Democratic Party from their state, and another will conduct research on the organization of the Republican Party from their state. The other two groups should write to each party's state headquarters to find out information about ways of becoming involved in party activities at the state or local level; one group should write the Democratic Party and the other the Republican Party. Each group should share the information they have learned about party organization with the rest of the class. As a lead-in to the next activity tell students that they will learn about how national party organization changed during the 1900s.

Writing About Government

Lead a class discussion on the growth of national party organization during the 1900s. Point out to students that the two major parties now have their own national headquarters, television studios, and schools for candidates, and that they are now capable of raising millions of dollars for candidates. Have students use information from this section of the text and other resources to write about the influence that a more powerful national party organization has had on local and state party organization and on the development of third parties. Encourage students to share their opinions with the rest of the class.

CLOSE

Have students work in groups to develop a time line that depicts changes in local, state, and national party organization in the United States. Students should be encouraged to include significant laws and events that have helped to shape these changes. Once groups have completed their time lines, they should discuss the events that they included and describe why they included them on the time line. Be sure to point out significant events that groups may have forgotten. Display the completed time lines throughout the classroom.

OPTIONS

Gifted Learners

Have students conduct research on corrupt party machines of the 1800s, such as Tammany Hall in New York City. Students should write a short paper describing the types of abuse that occurred, how widespread it was believed to be, and what actions were taken to stop the abuse. When students have finished writing their papers, encourage them to share the information they gathered with the rest of the class.

Students Having Difficulty/ Sheltered English Students

Discuss the modern organization of local party structures with students. Have students use the Internet and other resources to identify party organizations in their precinct, ward, city, and county. Have students create a list of the addresses and the phone numbers of these organizations. Display these lists throughout the classroom, and encourage students to contact the different levels of each party's organization to find out about activities that are being carried out at each level.

Visual-Spatial Learners

Organize the class into several small groups. Have each group develop a visual representation of the changes in structure of party organizations that have occurred at the various levels of government in the United States.

Students' charts should indicate how the change in one level of organization affected the other levels of party organization. Have groups compare their charts and check to ensure their accuracy.

Gifted Learners

Discuss with students the role of party activists in the political system. Have students read about activists in the Careers section on the *Holt Researcher Online* and then consult other sources for additional information. Students should find out if there are certain educational requirements for specific party positions, whether volunteer as well as professional positions are available, how a person can get involved as an activist, and whether there are any significant differences between the duties of Democratic and Republican Party activists. Encourage students to share the information that they find with the rest of the class. If possible, have a party activist speak to the class, so students can ask specific questions about his or her duties.

REVIEW

Have students complete the Section 3 Review on page 420. Use the answers in the Annotated Teacher's Edition to assess student mastery of this section.

ASSESS

To assess student mastery of this section, have students complete Daily Quiz 18.3 in *Daily Quizzes with Answer Key.* For additional assessment options, see *Altenative Assessment Handbook* on the *One-Stop Planner CD-ROM.*

ADDITIONAL RESOURCES

Gray, Virginia, Herbert Jacob, and Robert Allbritton, eds. *Politics in the American States: A Comparative Analysis.* 1990. Scott, Foresman and Company.

Riordan, William. *Plunkitt of Tammany Hall.* 1963. E.P. Dutton.

POLITICAL PARTIES AND THE PUBLIC GOOD

TEXTBOOK PAGES 421-424

HOLT PRESENTATION MAKER
Access Illustrated LECTURE NOTES using Microsoft® PowerPoint® on the One-Stop Planner CD-ROM

OBJECTIVES

▸ List and explain the common criticisms of the U.S. two-party system.
▸ Describe the benefits of the U.S. two-party system.

MOTIVATE

Discuss with students the government shutdowns that occurred during the 1990s because of the failure of both major parties to compromise over the budget. Ask students to think of times in their own lives when the failure to compromise with someone had negative consequences. Have students describe what the failure to compromise cost them and how it could have been avoided. Explain to students that one of the complaints about the two-party system is that the competition between the two parties has at times had negative effects on the public good. Tell students that in this section they will learn about some of the criticisms of the two-party system as well as some of the benefits of the two-party system.

TEACH

Role-Playing

Discuss with students the benefits of the two-party system that are mentioned in this section of the chapter: providing information about politics, offering varied opinions that help to balance the political system, discouraging sudden shifts in political trends, and encouraging political participation. Organize the class into four groups; each will represent one of these benefits. Have groups use information from this section of the text and other resources, such as newspapers and magazines, to come up with examples of how the two-party system achieves the benefit they were assigned. Once groups have come up with examples, have them role-play one of them for the rest of the class. Have students discuss the accuracy of these examples. Tell students that in the next activity they will further investigate the pros and cons of the two-party system.

Classifying Ideas

Discuss with students the common criticisms of the two-party system: parties are influenced too much by special interests, are full of self-serving office seekers, and lead to excessive politicking. Have students use newspapers, magazines, and the Internet to search for examples of each of these complaints against the two-party system. Students should write a short paper that explains these criticisms and offers examples of each. Once students have finished their papers, have them discuss examples of each type of criticism. Students should create a list of these examples in their Government Notebooks. As a lead-in to the next activity tell students that they will learn about some of the benefits of the two-party system.

Drawing Conclusions

Review with students some of the criticisms and benefits of the two-party system. Have students write a paper that discusses whether the benefits of the two-party system outweigh the criticisms of it. In their papers students should take a stand on the issue and use information presented in this lesson to support their opinions. If students feel that the criticisms of the system outweigh the benefits, have them discuss what kind of party system the United States should use and explain why they think that it would be a more appropriate choice. Encourage students to share their opinions with the rest of the class.

CLOSE

Ask students to think back to the discussion of the importance of the Democratic and Republican Parties from the Motivate activity in Lesson 18.1. Ask students if their opinions about the importance of these two major parties has changed. Have students write a paper that describes what they feel about the importance of these two parties to the U.S. two-party system. Students should be sure to consider the functions of the parties, how they have changed over time, and how they affect the public good. Encourage students to share their ideas on the subject with the rest of the class.

OPTIONS

Students Having Difficulty/ Sheltered English Students

   Discuss with students the wide variety of organizations that promote participation in the political system for young adults, such as the Young Democrats of America and the Young Republicans National Federation. Have students use information from the National Organizations section on the *Holt Researcher Online* and from other resources to find out more about one of these organizations. Have students write a few paragraphs describing the organization and its actions and how it promotes the public good. Encourage students to share the information that they find with the rest of the class.

Musical-Rhythmic Learners

Have students create a song or a poem in which they discuss the criticisms and benefits of the two-party system. Students should use examples from this lesson to emphasize their thoughts about the system. Encourage students to work with others who are proficient at a musical instrument to put the song to music. Have them perform their songs for the rest of the class. Videotape performances to use as an introduction to the subject of political parties for next year's students.

REVIEW

Have students complete the Section 4 Review on page 424. Use the answers in the Annotated Teacher's Edition to assess student mastery of this section.

ASSESS

To assess student mastery of this section, have students complete Daily Quiz 18.4 in *Daily Quizzes with Answer Key.* For additional assessment options, see *Alternative Assessment Handbook* on the *One-Stop Planner CD-ROM.*

RETEACH

For students having difficulty with the lessons, have them complete Reteaching Activity 18. This activity is located in *Reteaching Activities with Answer Key.*

ADDITIONAL RESOURCES

Aldrich, John. *Why Parties?: The Origin and Transformation of Political Parties in America.* 1995. University of Chicago Press.

Maisel, Sandy, ed. *Political Parties & Elections in the United States: An Encyclopedia.* 1991. Garland Publishing.

The Democratic Party. 1991. Aims Media, Inc. (Video)

The Republican Party. 1991. Aims Media, Inc. (Video)

To view the College Republican National Commitee's Web site, see: http://www.crnc.org

To view the College Democrats of America's Web site, see: http://www.collegedems.com/

GOVERNMENT NOTEBOOK

The Government Notebook is a journal activity that encourages students to consider basic concepts of government that relate to their lives. A follow-up notebook activity appears on page 426.

▶WHY IT MATTERS TODAY

To find additional lesson plans dealing with political parties in the United States, visit **CNNfyi.com** or have students complete the **GOVERNMENT** IN THE NEWS Activity on page 425.

CNNfyi.com

CHAPTER 18

POLITICAL PARTIES

If you have ever been a member of a team or club, you know that certain common goals and interests hold a group together. Members of a team share the desire to win a game. Members of a club experience the social bond that comes from interacting with people who share the same interest.

As noted in Chapter 17, interest groups are similar to organized teams and clubs. The reason that people in interest groups join together, however, is to take action on a specific political or social concern. One special kind of interest group is a political party. By belonging to a political party, people can influence elections and the running of government. In fact, political parties are a key way in which citizens participate in the U.S. political system.

GOVERNMENT NOTEBOOK

Think about a team or club to which you have belonged. What held the members of that group together? Was there a common set of rules? Were there standards for who could belong? Write a list of these factors in your Government Notebook.

▶WHY IT MATTERS TODAY

Political parties affect the political process every day. At the end of this chapter visit **CNNfyi.com** to learn more about issues related to political parties.

CNNfyi.com

SECTION 1

ROLE OF POLITICAL PARTIES

READ TO DISCOVER

1. What are political parties?
2. What functions do political parties serve?
3. What are the different kinds of party systems?

POLITICAL DICTIONARY

electorate
one-party system
two-party system
multiparty system

I magine this scene. Crowds are roaring. Bands are playing. Banners are waving in the air. Is this the Super Bowl? It could easily be. Or, it might be an election-night bash held by a political party to celebrate its winning candidate. For supporters of a political party, as for fans of a football team, winning is a thrill.

As noted in Chapter 3, political parties are organized groups that seek influence over government power. These parties serve many functions. The way in which they fulfill those functions, however, depends in large part on the kind of party system their country has.

Functions of Political Parties

When the framers were drawing up the Constitution, they did not include information about the functions of political parties. In fact, some parts of the Constitution even suggest that the framers did not intend for this country to have political parties. Many of the framers, including George Washington, feared that political parties might divide the nation by pursuing selfish interests.

Political parties began to form, however, during Washington's administration. In his Farewell Address, he warned the nation against the "baneful [harmful] effects of the spirit of party." He said that the spirit that motivates the formation of political parties creates in the community

❝ jealousies and false alarms, kindles the animosity [hatred] of one part against another, foments [causes] occasionally riot and insurrection [revolt against government]. **❞**

Despite Washington's warning, the United States developed what is today one of the oldest systems of popularly based, organized political parties in the world. Why did political parties develop in this country? What role do they play in the U.S. political system? Political parties serve three main functions:

★ assisting the electoral process,
★ organizing the day-to-day running of government, and
★ nominating candidates.

Assisting the Electoral Process As the nation's **electorate**—the body of people entitled to vote—grew, the country needed a system of organization to assist with the electoral process.

POLITICAL FOUNDATIONS *George Washington feared that political parties would divide the nation by pursuing selfish interests.* **What is the body of people who are entitled to vote called?**

The Granger Collection, New York

SECTION 1

ROLE OF POLITICAL PARTIES

Lesson Plans

For teaching strategies, see Lesson 18.1 located at the beginning of this chapter.

Political Dictionary

To reinforce the section's vocabulary terms, refer students to the Electronic Glossary on the *Researcher CD-ROM.*

Section Assessment

To assess students' mastery of this section, have them complete Daily Quiz 18.1 in *Daily Quizzes with Answer Key.*

Caption Answer

the electorate

How do political parties help provide the electorate with this organization?

First, political parties help citizens with the technical aspects of voting. Party workers encourage people to register to vote and to go to the polls on election day. They also raise money for political campaigns and go door to door distributing literature about their party's candidates.

Second, political parties provide a broad stance on major issues. Thus, when a candidate identifies him- or herself as a member of a particular party, voters immediately know much about his or her general political philosophy. For example, some people say that voting for a member of the Democratic Party is shorthand for "I want a government that takes a more active role in society." Voting Republican sends the message that you want government to be less involved in people's lives.

In this way, political parties act as a sort of team leader for voters. Think about how one person often guides a sports team's efforts. If every player on a team made his or her own plans and did not listen to the team captain, it would be difficult for the team to develop a winning strategy. In the same way, political parties provide a basic direction for voters. In doing so, parties gather together individuals with many different concerns by appealing to their broad common goals. This in turn helps the electoral process by making sure that the country is not splintered into so many competing groups that governing becomes impossible.

Third, political parties assist with the electoral process by closely examining the policies pursued by elected officials. In other words, the party out of power watches for any missteps by the party in power and offers alternative policies to voters. By doing so, the party out of power hopes to swing votes to its side during the next election.

Organizing the Government Another function of political parties is to help in the daily operation of the government. How do they do this? Political parties determine leadership in several areas of government. For example, as noted in Chapter 6, congressional leaders and committee members are chosen based on their party affiliation. The membership of committees is based on the number of seats each party holds in the House or the Senate. Therefore, if the Republicans hold more seats in the Senate, they receive more seats on each senatorial committee.

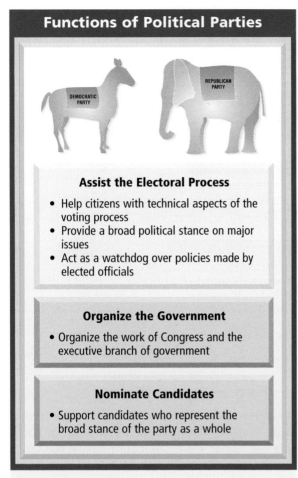

Functions of Political Parties

Assist the Electoral Process
- Help citizens with technical aspects of the voting process
- Provide a broad political stance on major issues
- Act as a watchdog over policies made by elected officials

Organize the Government
- Organize the work of Congress and the executive branch of government

Nominate Candidates
- Support candidates who represent the broad stance of the party as a whole

Political parties help to organize the electoral process by bringing together people who have common political interests. **What are the three main functions of political parties?**

Party membership also is important when it comes to filling positions in the executive branch. A president generally appoints people whose political viewpoints reflect his or her own and those of their political party.

Because their members actually participate in the running of government, political parties take responsibility for government decision making. In this way, the parties are distinct from other interest groups, which pressure the political process only from the outside. These other interest groups simply support a single group of concerns without taking the concerns of others into consideration. Political parties are different. Some of the process of weighing conflicting interests and listening to different ideas occurs within the parties themselves.

POLITICAL PROCESSES *The government of China is controlled by one party—the Communists.* **Why are some countries dominated by only one party even though other parties are free to participate in elections?**

Nominating Candidates

Nominating Candidates The third major function of political parties is to nominate candidates. When a political party nominates a candidate, it offers him or her its support. Although candidates have their own views about particular issues, they also represent both their party and its broad views, or ideology. The nomination process also reduces the number of candidates to a manageable size.

Types of Party Systems

The way in which a country's political parties fulfill these functions depends to a large degree on the type of party system the country has. There are three major types of party systems: one-party, two-party, and multiparty.

One-Party Systems A **one-party system** is one in which a single political party controls the government and clearly dominates political activity. In many cases, countries that have a one-party system are dictatorships. For example, the former Soviet Union had a one-party system. The Communist Party alone was allowed to participate in the government. Currently, China has a one-party system—the Communist Party is the only party permitted to take part in the government.

Some countries, such as Indonesia, have had one-party systems not because other parties are banned, but because no major opposition has arisen successfully during elections. Opposition does exist in these countries, but the party in power makes it difficult—through rules, and sometimes force—for the opposition to gain power. The party in power in these countries may continue to control the government for many years at a time.

Two-Party Systems Two major parties dominate the government in a **two-party system**. The United States, as you know, has a system dominated by two major parties—the Democrats and the Republicans. Other parties can exist, but two dominate the system.

In a two-party system each major party represents many diverse interests and opinions. Though a party's supporters may vary in their beliefs, they stand behind the overall party message. Voters in two-party systems tend to elect candidates with moderate political views.

As noted in Chapter 7, the United States has a plurality system, meaning that whoever receives the most votes in an election wins. A plurality electoral system generally promotes political moderation, for a party must appeal to a broad range of views to gain a plurality of the vote. To hold power in this system, a party must expand its base beyond the relatively small number of people who have very intense concerns about specific issues and move to satisfy the many people in the middle.

Multiparty Systems A third type of system is the **multiparty system**, in which several parties

SECTION 1 REVIEW ANSWERS

1. Refer to the following pages: electorate (405), one-party system (407), two-party system (407), multiparty system (407).

2. In a two-party system, two major parties dominate, voters tend to elect candidates with moderate political views, and each party represents many different interests and opinions.

3a. They assist the electoral process, organize the operations of the government, and nominate candidates for office.

3b. One party—one party controls the government and dominates political activity; two party—two major parties dominate the government; multiparty—several parties try to gain control of the government, are represented in the legislature based on the percentage of the vote they receive, and tend to represent specific interests.

4. Editorials will vary. Some students might mention nominating and supporting candidates for presidential and local elections. Others might mention the role parties play in determining committee membership in Congress.

Comparing Governments

Italy's Multiparty System

A strong two-party system has dominated U.S. politics since the early 1800s. Other democratic countries, however, have strong multiparty systems. Before and during World War II, Italy was dominated by dictator Benito Mussolini's Fascist Party. By the war's end, the Fascists had been thrown out. To prevent a return to totalitarianism, Italy adopted a multiparty system. Parties won seats in Parliament based on the percentage of votes they received in elections.

This electoral system encouraged the development of a number of smaller parties, making it difficult for stable coalitions, or combinations of parties, to control a majority of votes in Parliament. As a result, Italy has had almost 60 governments since World War II, even though most of those governments were dominated by the largest party, the Christian Democrats. In contrast, during the same time period the United States has had only 11 presidents, with majority control of the Senate having shifted only 8 times and majority control in the House only 5 times.

In 1993 three fourths of Italian voting districts adopted a new system for electing members of Parliament. Even so, Italy still has more than 20 political parties.

try to gain control of the government. In multiparty systems each party's representation in the legislature usually depends on the number of votes the party receives in an election. For example, a party that wins 15 percent of the vote receives roughly 15 percent of the seats in the legislature.

In a multiparty system each party tends to represent a specific region, concern, voter group, or ideology. A country's political landscape might include a Green Party, a Labor Party, or a Peasant Party, for example. By concentrating on a particular issue important to a portion of the population, these parties try to secure at least some representation in the legislature. For this reason, multiparty systems make it possible for a person to join and support a party that reflects his or her *specific* views. In fact, voters in multiparty systems often favor candidates with narrow views.

However, because so many parties share legislative power, multiparty systems sometimes cause government instability. The many parties form governing coalitions that can dissolve or change quickly because their interests are so varied. Think about the saying "Too many cooks spoil the broth." It implies that when too many people are involved in a task, such as making soup, competing visions may clash, resulting in a failed project. Similarly, the existence of many competing parties can make governing virtually impossible.

To reduce the number of parties in their legislatures, many countries with multiparty systems have passed laws requiring that a party receive a minimum percentage of votes before gaining representation. In Germany and some other countries, this minimum is set at 5 percent.

SECTION 1 REVIEW

1. Identify and explain:
• electorate
• one-party system
• two-party system
• multiparty system

2. Identifying Concepts: Copy the graphic organizer below. Use it to identify the characteristics of the two-party system.

> The Two-Party System

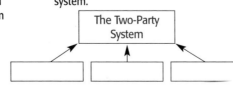

Homework Practice Online

keyword: SV3 HP18

3. Finding the Main Idea

a. What are the functions of political parties?
b. Describe the one-party, two-party, and multiparty systems.

4. Writing and Critical Thinking

Supporting a Point of View: What do you think are the most important function of political parties? Write an editorial explaining your opinion.
Consider the following:
• the role of parties play in elections
• how parties help organize the government

SECTION 2

THE U.S. TWO-PARTY SYSTEM

READ TO DISCOVER

1. Why did political parties develop in the United States?
2. How do the main political parties in the United States today differ from each other?
3. What role do third parties play in the U.S. two-party system?

POLITICAL DICTIONARY

realignment
independent
third party
splinter party
ideological party

Have you ever heard of the Natural Law Party of the United States or the U.S. Taxpayers Party? Probably not. Although these parties' presidential candidates received more than 100,000 popular votes in 1996, they are insignificant players in the U.S. political system.

You, like most citizens, are probably more familiar with the Republicans and the Democrats, the two parties that dominate the U.S. political system today. These two parties are the heirs of a long-standing two-party system in this country. These parties do not date back to the country's origins, however.

The U.S. party system has had five distinct periods, with each being characterized by a struggle between two parties. The first three periods involved the Federalists and Democratic-Republicans, the Democrats and Whigs, and the Republicans and Democrats. The two latest periods have been times when support has shifted decisively between Republicans and Democrats. Such periods of **realignment**—the

shifting of the parties' base of support among the electorate—generally are sparked by the development of issues of great public concern.

Early Political Parties

As noted in Section 1, the framers were concerned about the effect of self-interested groups on government. Despite such fears, however, political parties started to form not long after the new government began.

Unlike Congress, the presidency, and the Supreme Court, which were created by the Constitution, parties arose from the actual practice of political life. As the nation's first officials began to run the country and put the Constitution into effect, they differed about which policies the government should follow. The leaders of two major viewpoints organized their supporters into groups (political parties) to better pursue their goals. These groups soon became known as the Federalist and Democratic-Republican Parties.

Federalists and Democratic-Republicans

As noted in Chapter 2, the Federalists and Antifederalists were some of the first interest groups in the United States. Whereas the Federalists favored ratification of the Constitution, the Antifederalists opposed it. The Federalists

POLITICAL FOUNDATIONS *Conflict between Hamilton and Jefferson, both members of Washington's cabinet, led to the formation of the nation's first political parties.* **What were the names of these parties?**

The Granger Collection, New York

Lesson Plans

For teaching strategies, see Lesson 18.2 located at the beginning of this chapter.

Political Dictionary

To reinforce the section's vocabulary terms, refer students to the Electronic Glossary on the *Researcher CD-ROM*.

Section Assessment

To assess students' mastery of this section, have them complete Daily Quiz 18.2 in *Daily Quizzes with Answer Key*.

Caption Answer

Federalists and Democratic-Republicans

The founding fathers had not made any provisions for a party system in the Constitution because they believed that political parties were bad for democracy. They inherited this belief from British thinkers such as Jonathan Swift, who had declared, "Party is the madness of the many, for the gain of the few."

Benjamin Franklin accused parties of "tearing to pieces the best of characters," while John Adams maintained that a two-party system was "to be dreaded as the greatest political evil." The perception at the time that parties represented dangerous factionalism led the founding fathers to overlook the benefits that parties can bring to a democracy. ■

Transparency

An overhead transparency of the chart on this page is available in *Transparency Resources*. See Transparency 37: U.S. Political Parties.

Caption Answer

1884

---

succeeded in the struggle and in 1789 received many of the positions in the new government under President George Washington.

Soon, however, disagreements arose among the nation's leaders, particularly between Alexander Hamilton, the secretary of the treasury, and Thomas Jefferson, the secretary of state. Jefferson even resigned from Washington's cabinet in 1793 as the tensions mounted.

After his resignation, Jefferson eventually joined with James Madison (a former Federalist) and some of the original Antifederalists in opposition to the policies of Alexander Hamilton and the emerging Federalist Party. Jefferson and his followers included the Antifederalists, who were called Republicans or Democratic-Republicans.

The Federalists and the Democratic-Republicans disagreed about a number of issues. Generally, Hamilton's Federalist Party represented manufacturing and trade interests. Hamilton hoped to use the national government to aid the growth of industry by placing a tariff on foreign manufactured products. He also wished to provide government support for road and canal construction to lower transportation costs for manufactured goods.

In contrast, Madison, Jefferson, and the other Democratic-Republicans regarded farming, not manufacturing, as the backbone of the new nation. They disliked the industrialization and urbanization of the country. Thus, they also opposed government funding for policies and projects that furthered these developments.

Early on in the policy debate Hamilton began to organize congressional support for his programs. His activities were remarkably similar to those of political leaders today. Hamilton and his assistants helped allied congressmembers make their case in debates by providing them with arguments and statistics. He met in private with members, and quietly arranged informal conferences in which his followers could come together. Hamilton also tried to inform and organize nongovernment supporters of his programs.

Congressional opponents, led by Jefferson and Madison, quickly began similar efforts.

U.S. Political Parties

1787	Constitutional Convention takes place; Federalists back Constitution's ratification.
1800	Thomas Jefferson, a Democratic-Republican, defeats John Adams, the last Federalist president.
1828	Andrew Jackson becomes the first Democrat to win presidential election; Jackson's opponents become known as Whigs.
1850	Millard Fillmore succeeds the late Zachary Taylor, becoming the last Whig president.
1854	Republican Party formed as Whigs lose support.
1860	Abraham Lincoln becomes the first Republican to be elected president.
1884	Grover Cleveland becomes the first Democratic president to be elected since the Civil War.
1896	Republican William McKinley defeats Democrat William Jennings Bryan.
1932	Democrat Franklin D. Roosevelt wins the first of four presidential elections; Democrats begin a long domination of Congress.
1952	Dwight Eisenhower becomes the first Republican to be elected president since Herbert Hoover in 1928.
1968	Republican Richard Nixon wins presidency; until the 1992 election, Republicans control White House for all but four years.
1992	Democrat Bill Clinton elected president.
1994	Republicans become the majority party in both the House and Senate for first time since the 1954 elections.
2000	Republican George W. Bush elected president.

*The United States has a two-party political system, although the two parties in power have changed over time. **In what year did Grover Cleveland become the first Democratic president to be elected since the Civil War?***

Disagreements between the two young parties became so strong that by 1797 Jefferson wrote that "men who have been intimate [close friends] all their lives cross the street to avoid meeting, and turn their heads another way."

Jefferson and Madison continued to build their party and to fight the Federalist policies. In 1796 Jefferson ran for president against Federalist John Adams and was barely defeated. In 1800 he ran again and this time defeated Adams. With that defeat, the Democratic-Republicans established political domination that would last until 1829.

The Democratic-Republicans' control of the White House struck a tremendous blow to the Federalist Party. It suffered a gradual decline, with its original leaders dying and its policies representing an increasingly smaller portion of the population. By 1824 the Federalist Party had basically ceased to exist.

Democrats and Whigs By the 1824 election the Democratic-Republicans faced some of their own problems. The party had split into factions—those who supported candidate Andrew Jackson and those who supported candidates Henry Clay, John Quincy Adams, or William H. Crawford. Although Jackson won the most popular votes, Adams was chosen by the House of Representatives as president. A lack of popular support, however, plagued Adams's administration, and Jackson remained popular. Four years later, Jackson, leader of the newly named Democratic Party, won a stunning landslide victory in the election of 1828.

Jackson's win led to a new era of competing-party politics. Born in a remote area on the border of North Carolina and South Carolina, Jackson supported the interests of small-business owners, farmers, pioneers, and slaveholders. Opposition to Jackson's policies took form in a new party—the Whigs. The Whigs desired an active role for government, and they supported policies such as protective tariffs and federal improvement programs.

The Democratic Party at that time thought "the government is best that governs least." Party members believed that an active government would create inequality by taking actions that favored some people over others. For example, the Democrats attacked what they considered "special privileges" granted by government to some business interests at the expense of the population as a whole.

The Granger Collection, New York

POLITICAL PROCESSES *The 1858 debate between Democrat Stephen Douglas and Republican Abraham Lincoln helped Lincoln win the presidential election.* **What factors helped the Democrats hold power until the Civil War?**

Government aid to build canals and roads, they argued, came out of tax money paid by all, yet supported projects benefiting only business and industry. The Democrats also opposed tariffs, believing them discriminatory.

This Democratic philosophy appealed to immigrants and the many people developing the rapidly growing young nation's frontier. As a result, Democrats dominated the government most of the time until the Civil War.

During the 1840s and 1850s, however, political unrest began to rise. Democrats and Whigs continued to disagree over tariffs. They also disagreed over slavery, particularly about whether it was to be allowed in the country's newly settled areas. Slavery was in fact the main factor that led to the end of this period of competing-party politics. With southern and northern members present in both parties, tensions made it impossible for the old party system to continue.

After 1852 the Whig Party collapsed, and a new party opposed to slavery—the Republicans—arose in 1854. Many northern Whigs, as well as anti-slavery Democrats, joined the new Republican Party. Although the Democrats won the election of 1856, tensions over slavery, as well as divisions within the party itself, brought an end to Democratic control in 1860 and signaled the rise of the Republicans as the dominant power.

Enhancing the Lesson

For more information about Thomas Jefferson's political views, see Thomas Jefferson's First Inaugural Address in *From the Source: Readings in Economics and Government with Answer Key.*

ACROSS THE CURRICULUM

HISTORY Some historians argue that the Democrats of the Jackson era were traditionalists attempting to preserve an old way of life that revolved around individual initiative and states' rights, while the Whigs represented the coming forces of modernization and nationalism.

The Democrats' position was popular with U.S. voters, who gave Jackson's party control of the House and Senate 22 of 26 years between 1829 and 1855. The Democrats controlled both houses for 20 years during that same period. The Whigs, while not as successful as the Democrats, did manage to place two candidates in the White House: William Henry Harrison in 1841 and Zachary Taylor in 1849. Interestingly, both men were war heroes who died while in office. ■

Republicans and Democrats

The Republican Party elected its first president, Abraham Lincoln, in 1860. During Lincoln's term the brewing tensions between the North and South over slavery and other issues erupted into the Civil War in 1861. The changes brought by the election of 1860 signaled another realignment and began a long period of Republican domination that lasted until 1932. Only two Democrats were elected president during that period—Grover Cleveland in 1884 and 1892 and Woodrow Wilson in 1912 and 1916.

Party Support After the Civil War

For many years after the war, support for the Republicans and Democrats remained divided according to region and racial and financial concerns. Much of the Republican Party's support stemmed from its stance on slavery during the war. In general, former Whigs, newly freed African Americans, and antislavery Democrats supported the Republicans. The party also embraced the concerns of businesspeople, who wanted government aid for roads and canals, and from pioneers, who hoped for cheap government land.

The Democrats' support, on the other hand, rested with workers in the growing U.S. cities, including the many new immigrants. The party also received support from southerners who, still recovering from the war, resented the Republican stronghold in the North.

During this period, people identified strongly with their party of choice and remained fiercely loyal to it. Indeed, few citizens switched parties, and elections were extremely close. The parties created enough loyalty to produce higher voting turnouts among eligible voters than in any other period of U.S. history.

Election of 1896

The period after the Civil War was one of rapid economic growth and change, with large corporations appearing for the first time. Many farmers, meanwhile, faced difficult economic times.

Although the Democrats lost the election of 1896 and Republican domination continued, the election was a turning point because it brought this new period's economic issues to the forefront. It generally pitted farmers and small-business owners against big business and industry. In doing so, the election served to define the future roles of the Republican and Democratic Parties.

William Jennings Bryan, a congressmember from Nebraska, was nominated as the Democratic

POLITICAL PROCESSES *William Jennings Bryan was the Democratic nominee for the 1896 and 1900 presidential elections. Bryan's candidacy marked a turning point in Democratic Party policy.* **In what way was this period a political turning point?**

candidate for president after he dazzled his party's convention with an emotional endorsement of rural life. In his speech Bryan declared:

>❝ Burn down your cities and leave our farms, and your cities will spring up again as if by magic. But destroy our farms and the grass will grow in the streets of every city in this country. . . . You shall not press down upon the brow of labor this crown of thorns. You shall not crucify mankind upon a cross of gold. ❞

The Democrats had long been a voice for the poor but had rarely endorsed government action on their behalf. This tradition began to change, however, as the party moved away from its "government is best that governs least" stance.

Republicans were changing as well, adopting policies intended to pave the way for economic prosperity. High tariffs to protect U.S. industry, Republicans argued, would give workers "a full dinner pail."

Representing business and industry interests, Republican William McKinley won a big victory in 1896. Part of the reason for this, however, was a reaction against the economic depression of 1893, which had occurred during President Cleveland's Democratic administration.

The Great Depression With the exception of Democratic president Wilson's two terms, the Republican Party continued its domination of the presidency until the 1930s. The Great Depression, however, brought about another party realignment, which resulted in more than 30 years of Democratic presidents, with the exception of World War II hero General Dwight Eisenhower's presidency.

As the country sank further into the depression, the Democrats rose to power in an effort to help people deal with its painful effects. Franklin Roosevelt and other Democrats fostered their success by building up an electoral base of labor groups, southerners, farmers, and city political organizations.

In a series of bold moves, President Roosevelt sought a cure for the depression in increased governmental activism through a series of programs collectively called the New Deal. The government put millions of unemployed people to work building roads, bridges, and post offices. Roosevelt also sponsored legislation setting up Social Security (an old-age and disability pension system) as well as

legislation making it easier for workers to organize in labor unions. The New Deal programs inspired the new coalition of voters backing Roosevelt to give him even greater support. Republicans opposed Roosevelt's actions and accused him of overstepping the government's powers.

With the New Deal, the reversal of the two parties' traditional roles was complete. Whereas the Republicans (and the earlier Federalists and Whigs) had traditionally stood for big government and increased government expenditures, the Democrats (and the Democratic-Republicans) had always promoted minimal government. Democrats since Roosevelt have been supporters of an active government, and Republicans have favored smaller government.

Political Parties Today The Democrats, with the exception of President Eisenhower's two terms, controlled the presidency until 1968, when Republican Richard Nixon was elected. Though Democrats dominated the Congress until 1994, party control of the presidency has shifted a great deal since 1968. Republicans have won the White House in four out of the first seven presidential elections since Nixon left office.

Since the 1960s many political scientists have been predicting a new period of party politics. Evidence up to now, however, does not reveal a major realignment. The major distinction between the parties—with the Democrats supporting "more government" on behalf of disadvantaged groups and the Republicans supporting "less government"—has remained largely unchanged since the New Deal.

Third Parties and Independents

Despite the Republicans' and Democrats' control over the political system since the 1850s, voters in some elections have opted to give significant backing to independent and third-party candidates. An **independent** candidate is not associated with any party. In a two-party system a **third party** is any political party, besides the two dominant ones, seeking to directly participate in government.

Although independent and third-party candidates have enjoyed little success in U.S. political history, there have been times when they have had

For several decades after the Civil War, most African Americans were loyal to the Republican Party because it was the party of Abraham Lincoln, the president who had signed the Emancipation Proclamation. During the Great Depression, however, a large percentage of African American voters switched their allegiance to the Democratic Party.

Since then, historians have debated the cause of this realignment. Some argue that African Americans turned to Franklin Roosevelt because the New Deal offered at least limited relief from the economic hardship of the depression. Other historians claim that Roosevelt and other New Dealers, including First Lady Eleanor Roosevelt, offered some small civil rights gains that African Americans appreciated and wished to support. Both arguments are probably correct to some degree. ■

Significant Third-Party Presidential Candidates Since the Civil War

Party	Candidate	Year	Issues
Greenback	Peter Cooper	1876	currency reform, labor rights
Greenback	James B. Weaver	1880	currency reforms, labor rights
Prohibition	John P. St. John	1884	antiliquor
Populist	James B. Weaver	1892	currency reform, farm interests
Socialist	Eugene V. Debs	1900–12; 1920	public ownership of property
Progressive (Bull Moose)	Theodore Roosevelt	1912	political and business reform
Progressive	Robert M. La Follette	1924	farm interests, labor interests
Socialist	Norman Thomas	1928–48	public ownership of property
Union	William Lemke	1936	opposition to the New Deal
States' Rights (Dixiecrats)	Strom Thurmond	1948	segregation, states' rights
Progressive	Henry A. Wallace	1948	social reform, opposition to Cold War
American Independent	George Wallace	1968	states' rights
American	John Schmitz	1972	states' rights, crime
Libertarian	Various	1972–96	limited government
Reform	Ross Perot	1996	political and budget reform

Sources: *1997 World Almanac and Book of Facts; Dynamics of the Party System,* James L. Sundquist, copyright 1983, The Brookings Institution

Third-party candidates have run in presidential elections since 1872 but have never won an election. **In what year did Theodore Roosevelt run as the Progressive Party presidential candidate?**

a decisive influence on the outcome of elections. In 1912, when Theodore Roosevelt failed to gain the Republican Party's presidential nomination, he formed a third party called the Progressives to back his bid for the presidency. He did not win the election, but he took so many votes away from Republican candidate William Taft that Democrat Woodrow Wilson won.

In 1992 independent candidate Ross Perot rallied disenchanted voters and campaigned against Republican George Bush and Democrat Bill Clinton. Perot won 19 percent of the vote, more than any independent or third-party candidate had won since Roosevelt's bid for the presidency in 1912. Many people said that Perot's success contributed to Bush's loss in the election, as many Republicans voted for Perot. Perot ran again in 1996 as the Reform Party's candidate, but that time received only 8.5 percent of the vote. Of the third parties appearing during periods of realignment, the only one ever to replace one of the existing parties was the Republican Party, which replaced the Whigs before the Civil War.

CASE STUDY

The Reform Party

POLITICAL PROCESSES Ross Perot's independent campaign for president in 1992 and the organization he created to aid his bid were the motivations behind the founding of the Reform Party prior to the 1996 election. Although the party did not nominate candidates for congressional seats, it succeeded in getting its nominee for president—Perot—added to ballots across the country, a difficult task for any third party.

The Reform Party called for balancing the federal budget, reforming the way political campaigns are funded, and establishing term limits for members of Congress. The party also pressed for a new tax system and restrictions on lobbying government officials.

Ross Perot won 19 percent of the vote in 1992 and in 1996 was the nominee of a national party. As a result, his 1996 campaign received federal election funds. Although he lost the race, he won more than 5 percent of the vote, making the Reform Party was eligible for campaign funds in the 2000 election.

In August of 1996, the Reform Party had begun to reorganize itself. The goal was to establish the party as a self-governing national political party—without the influence of Ross Perot.

In June of 1997, the Reform Party National Steering Committee was renamed the National Reform Party Committee (NRPC). This committee voted for independence from Perot in order for the party to grow beyond the influence of a single person. They wanted the party open to participation from large numbers of citizens and candidates, without the control of Ross Perot.

With his outspoken manner, Minnesota Governor Jesse Ventura seemed a likely choice to lead the new party. But in February of 2000, Ventura broke away from the National Reform Party. Instead, he affiliated himself with the Minnesota Reform Party.

Third parties arise because of support for political stances that differ from those held by either major party. People have even formed parties over a single issue. For example, the Prohibition Party formed in 1869 and has nominated a presidential candidate in every election since then. Third parties usually form as a splinter party or as an ideological party.

Splinter Parties People who feel that their party has failed to address their concerns sometimes break off to form a **splinter party**. Examples include not only Roosevelt's Progressive Party but also the American Independent Party, founded by former Democrat George Wallace. Each man ran for president under the banner of his new party.

Ideological Parties The other type of third party is an **ideological party**—a group whose basic political views differ from those of the majority of the population. The Socialists became the only ideological party to gain more than 5 percent of the vote in a presidential election in 1912. The Socialists, who favor government takeover of industry, have run candidates in most presidential elections since then. The ideological Libertarian Party has fielded presidential candidates since 1972. The party promotes individual rights and less government interference in private lives and opposes taxes and U.S. involvement abroad.

SECTION 2 REVIEW

1. **Identify and explain:**
   - realignment
   - independent
   - third party
   - splinter party
   - ideological party

2. **Categorizing:** Copy the graphic organizer below. Use it to list the points of view of the Democratic and Republican Parties on the role of government in people's lives.

U.S. Political Parties

D: ———— R:

Homework Practice Online
keyword: SV3 GV18

3. **Finding the Main Idea**

   a. What were the first political parties in the U.S. two-party system? Why did they form?
   b. What are third parties, and why do people join them?

4. **Writing and Critical Thinking**

   Drawing Conclusions: Briefly review the history of political parties in the United States. In what ways have certain parties changed the United States? Write a one-page essay describing changes that were the result of a certain political party.
   Consider the following:
   - the effects of the Republican Party before and after the Civil War
   - the policies of the Democratic Party during the Great Depression

SECTION 2 REVIEW ANSWERS

1. Refer to the following pages: realignment (409), independent (413), third party (413), splinter party (415), ideological party (415).

2. Republicans tend to call for "less government," while Democrats favor more government services for the disadvantaged.

3a. The first political parties were the Federalists and the Democratic-Republicans, which formed because of Alexander Hamilton and Thomas Jefferson's disputes over various policies.

3b. A third party is any political party other than the two dominant ones. People generally join third parties either to support policies different from those supported by the dominant parties or to support a single issue.

4. Essays will vary, but students should mention that the Republican Party opposed slavery before the Civil War and supported African Americans' rights after, unlike the Democratic Party. During the Great Depression the Democratic Party supported governmental activism to help the poor directly, unlike the Republican Party.

SECTION 3

PARTY ORGANIZATION

Lesson Plans

For teaching strategies, see Lesson 18.3 located at the beginning of this chapter.

Political Dictionary

To reinforce the section's vocabulary terms, refer students to the Electronic Glossary on the *Researcher CD-ROM.*

Section Assessment

To assess students' mastery of this section, have them complete Daily Quiz 18.3 in *Daily Quizzes with Answer Key.*

Caption Answer

Local governments were dominated by party machines during the mid- to late 1800s.

SECTION 3

PARTY ORGANIZATION

READ TO DISCOVER

1. How were early political parties structured, and how did this structure change in the late 1800s?
2. How did state parties change after the decline of local parties?
3. How did national party organization change in the 1900s?

POLITICAL DICTIONARY

party machine
patronage
straight ticket
split ticket
primary election
general election
precinct
ward

Political parties are set up in tiers—national, state, and local organizations exist for each party. National and state party organizations are strongest today, while local parties are the weakest. This has not always been true, however. In earlier days of party politics, local parties were much stronger than those at the national or state level.

Local Parties

During the mid- to late 1800s, political parties were highly organized at the local level. In large cities, particularly in the North and Midwest, strong local political structures developed as immigration increased and municipal populations grew. By the end of the 1800s, however, many local party structures began to weaken.

Party Machines Local governments during the mid- and late 1800s were dominated by political structures called party machines. A **party machine** is an organized group of individuals who dominate a political party within a geographic area, usually a big city. These people typically use the party's resources to further their own power and control over the political system. Local party headquarters, such as the Democratic Party's Tammany Hall in New York City, have been located in municipal centers of power.

To gain support, party machines assigned small armies of workers to become familiar with residents of a neighborhood well in advance of an election. On election day these workers would urge supporters to go to the polls. Party machines recruited their workers by promising them government jobs as a reward if the party won the election. This system of awarding political favors in exchange for political support is called **patronage**, also referred to as the spoils system.

Big-city party machines also made a point of recruiting newly arrived immigrants. The machines hoped to gain these people's loyalty by helping them deal with unfamiliar bureaucracies and look for work and housing in their new city. The local parties also sought to stoke the pride of these new Americans by giving them leadership positions in the party or in the city.

The Granger Collection, New York

PRINCIPLES OF DEMOCRACY *The caption to this 1871 cartoon criticizing local party machines reads, "As long as I count the votes what are you going to do?"* **During what period were local governments dominated by party machines?**

Local Party Corruption Part of the reason that the party machines were able to maintain their mastery over the political system was through their control of the electoral process. For example, before 1888 the government did not provide a ballot with the names of all parties and candidates. Instead, a local party would print ballots with a list of only its own candidates. A person voted by placing one of these party-produced ballots in a voting box. Because the ballots listed only one party's candidates, the voter was forced to cast a **straight ticket**, or to vote only for candidates from a single party.

Party machines also engaged in illegal voting practices to maintain control over the system. For example, because there was no system of voter registration, party machines could pay supporters to vote several times. A common expression of the time was "Vote early and vote often." Such crooked practices almost guaranteed that a party's candidates would win office.

Elected officials' support and loyalty also helped strengthen early local political parties. In addition, local party organizations were in charge of nominating candidates and of providing the campaign workers to help candidates become elected. Indeed, during the 1800s many people thought it improper for candidates to campaign for themselves, so they relied on local parties to do so on their behalf. If the party machine helped a candidate become elected, he or she would more than likely support the party machine's members.

Party machines frequently financed their operations through crooked deals. In return for offering certain businesses government contracts, the machines would receive financial payments, often called kickbacks. For example, a city government might offer a contract for garbage removal to one business over another. The selected company would receive all of the city's garbage removal business in exchange for money given to the machine or its leaders.

Local Party Reform At the end of the 1800s, an attack on party machines weakened local parties for good. From about 1900 to 1920, a period known as the Progressive Era, reformers led an attack on powerful, self-interested organizations. Many saw big-city party machines as examples of such monster organizations. The reform spirit led to state legislation that severely cut back the power of local party organizations.

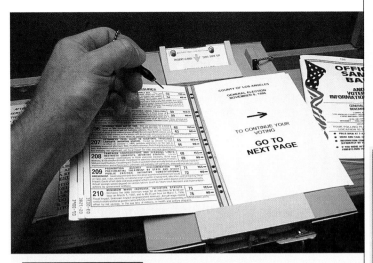

POLITICAL PROCESSES *During the early 1900s, state government officials replaced party-printed ballots with a government-printed ballot.* **What other reforms occurred during the Progressive Era?**

First, state laws introduced a new ballot system. Party-printed ballots were replaced with a government-printed ballot that listed all the parties and candidates. This made it possible for citizens to vote a **split ticket**, or to vote for candidates of different parties for different offices. By reducing the ability of local parties to support individual candidates, split-ticket voting helped to lessen the candidates' loyalty to the local party.

Second, voter registration was introduced. By requiring voters to register, election officials could exercise greater control over who voted—and how many times. This system was designed to make it difficult for party machines to engage in fraudulent election practices.

Third, reforms lowered the number of patronage jobs controlled by mayors and other local officials. This helped ensure that party machines could no longer gather support by securing jobs for their workers.

Last, states passed laws determining how a party could select its candidates. Previously, local party leaders had nominated party candidates for office. The new laws, however, required that party candidates be chosen in primary elections. **Primary elections**, often called primaries, are elections for nominating a party's candidate for office. The primary is held before the **general election**, in which voters actually choose their elected officials. (Types of elections are more fully explained in Chapter 19.)

While the president is often regarded as the leader of the national party, state governors are not always considered the leaders of their respective state parties.

Some governors do maintain strong relationships with the state's party chairperson, but others play only a small role in party operations. In a few cases, relationships have been hostile. Because many governors have little control over the legislators from their own party and often must rely on bipartisan cooperation to enact legislation, they often downplay party differences. ∎

Transparency

An overhead transparency of the chart on this page is available in *Transparency Resources.* See Transparency 39: Organization of Political Parties.

Caption Answer

National parties have channeled more money to state organizations to avoid violating campaign finance laws.

A party organization whose leadership could choose its candidates had a major tool for assuring candidate loyalty to the machine. Primaries eventually opened up the nominating process. Because the voters now nominated candidates through primaries, candidates were able to create their own election organizations, instead of relying strictly on the local party organization.

Local Parties Today In spite of their limited role, many party machines continued to operate into the 1900s. By midcentury, however, most of the long-established party machines, including New York's Tammany Hall, had ceased to exist.

Although party machines frequently operated at the municipal level, they were less common at the state level and rarely operated at the national level. Today, for the most part, local party organizations have been replaced by strong state and national party organizations and by candidates' personal election organizations.

Where they do survive, local party structures usually are broken up into precinct, ward, city, and county levels. **Precincts** are voting districts into which cities, towns, and counties are divided. In many cities, several precincts may make up a **ward**, a territorial division of city government. These divisions are helpful in organizing the administration of local services, which also may serve as legislative districts for city government elections. Each precinct, ward, city, or county has a distinct party organization or committee. These local political party divisions or committees are subject to the rules and regulations of the state party that oversees them.

State Parties

During the time when local party organization was strongest, national and state party organizations were weak. State parties, however, began to grow in power during the 1900s as the power of local party organizations slowly lost force.

Early State Parties Early state parties were weak and not as well organized as local parties. Instead of having a permanent building as a center of authority, as local parties often had, a state party's headquarters often were located in the home or office of its chief officer. The state party did not receive much funding or support because most citizens participated in politics at the local

level. As a result, state parties had little authority compared to local parties.

State Parties Today The growth of state parties during the 1900s coincided with, and in large part was created by, growth at the national party level. Stronger national parties have been able to provide funds and other support to state parties to help finance their operations.

For example, starting in the 1988 presidential campaign, national parties began channeling millions of dollars to state parties without violating any federal campaign finance laws limiting the amount a party could spend on an individual candidate's campaign. The laws allow state party organizations to spend unlimited amounts on "party-building activities." These activities include running voter registration drives, encouraging citizens to vote, and renting or buying facilities for party operations. Campaign finance laws allowed national parties to spend additional money for a presidential campaign by sending money raised at the national level to state party organizations for

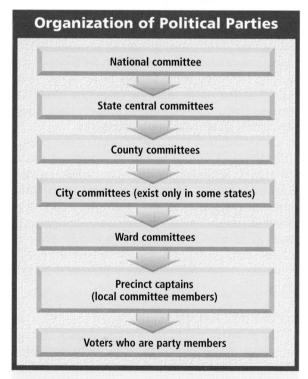

Organization of Political Parties

National committee

↓

State central committees

↓

County committees

↓

City committees (exist only in some states)

↓

Ward committees

↓

Precinct captains
(local committee members)

↓

Voters who are party members

State parties have recently progressed from weak, unorganized groups to powerful, well-funded political weapons. **Why have state parties received more funding from national parties since 1988?**

Careers in Government

Party Activist

Working in politics does not always mean running for office. For many people, working within a political party poses a challenge and an attractive alternative. It resembles working behind the scenes of a film or play. It requires stamina and vision. And, in the end, it can be quite rewarding.

A political party activist supports and works for their party of choice. One such position is that of a regional field coordinator. The regional field coordinator serves as the national party's contact person for voters, party candidates, and elected officials in a specific region. The regional field coordinator must also answer voter questions about the party and its various issues, and help candidates with research on key issues and available campaign resources.

Other duties of a political party activist may include: maintianing an accurate, up-to-date database of members and prospects; handling direct mailings involving current political information or membership renewals; continually prospecting for the organization in order to increase its size; publishing monthly newsletters to publicize current activities; and implementing a plan to raise campaign money.

Whether supporting state or local parties, some political party activists have earned college or post-graduate degrees in political science, pub-

Twenty-one year old Tammy Miller works in Washington, D.C., as a party activist for the Republican National Committee.

lic policy, and other applicable fields. Many party activists prepare for their jobs with internships at local, state, or national government levels.

A political party activist would be expected to uphold the tenets of their party, encouraging success, growth, and professionalism. An activist for any party might be expected to publicize meetings, plan strategy, make personal contacts, and further the goals of the party, while maintaining a vision of success. Party activists ensure that national parties are able to carry out their goals on a local level. Simply put, political parties would quickly fail without party activists.

---

such activities. Like national parties, however, state parties could not spend unlimited amounts on the campaign of any specific candidate.

As state parties grew, they began to raise funds through other means as well. Today, state-level political action committees (PACs) provide much of the money that state parties spend on their operations and on candidates. As noted in Chapter 17, a PAC is an organized group that gives funds to parties and candidates who support its interests.

As a result of greater financial strength, state party organization is much more powerful than it once was. Almost every state party has a permanent headquarters and a full-time chairperson, who is

chosen by a central committee of representatives from each county in the state.

Despite increased power, state party organizations have grown more dependent on national party committees. Because they receive funds from national parties, state parties are subject to national parties' rules and requests. Also, national party leaders sometimes try to persuade state parties to help fund important campaigns in other states.

National Parties

Like state parties, national parties lacked strong organization during the 1800s and early 1900s.

To help students learn about other careers in government, refer them to the Careers section on the *Holt Researcher Online.*

THEMES IN GOVERNMENT

POLITICAL PROCESSES

Parties struggle to dominate state politics just as they fight to control the national government. Using statistics concerning the proportion of success in elections and the length of time that a party has control over a state, political scientists have classified the states according to the ability of the major parties to control their governments.

During the 1980s one state, Mississippi, was rated as a Democratic one-party state. Twenty-one states had modified one-party Democratic systems, meaning that Democrats controlled state offices between 65 and 85 percent of the time. Twenty-two states struck a balance between the two parties, while the remaining six states were classified as modified one-party Republican. No state was completely dominated by the Republican Party. Republicans made gains during the 1990s. In Mississippi, for instance, they narrowed the gap between the two parties. They also made significant gains in other states. ■

However, during the mid- to late 1900s they transformed into the powerful organizations they are today.

Early National Parties Early national parties did little more than their basic duties—negotiating with the competing party over controversial issues and nominating presidential candidates. Until the early 1960s the Democrats and Republicans had no buildings to serve as permanent national headquarters. Instead, each party rented temporary office space in a building in Washington, D.C. In addition, national parties maintained much smaller staffs than they do today.

National Parties Today The Democratic and Republican Parties today have not only their own headquarters buildings but also television studios in which to record campaign commercials for party candidates and schools in which to teach candidates how to run for office. Each party is run by a national committee with a chairperson and a large staff.

Each party also has two congressional campaign committees, one for the House and one for the Senate, to channel funds to its congressional candidates. These committees are led by members of Congress, rather than by the party's national chair. The congressional committees have great freedom in deciding which candidates to support and how much money to give them. This makes the committees a possible source of party influence within Congress.

Larger national parties with bigger staffs have been able to raise millions of dollars for their

POLITICAL PROCESSES *Both the Republican and Democratic Parties own television studios in which they record campaign commercials.* **Until when, approximately, did both parties lack permanent headquarters buildings?**

candidates. In 1979–80 the national, state, and local Republican Party committees raised about $170 million for the party's candidates, beginning an era in which national political parties began raising a large portion of candidates' campaign funds. For the 1996 election, Democratic Party committees raised $221.6 million, while the Republican Party committees raised $416.5 million.

More money also has meant that national political party organizations have expanded the services they provide. National parties are able to provide candidates with assistance in polling and advertising, for instance. Through polling, parties can find out what voters think about the issues. Through media advertising, parties can make contact with and influence voters on candidates' behalf.

SECTION 3 REVIEW

1. Identify and explain:
- party machine
- patronage
- straight ticket
- split ticket
- primary election
- general election
- precinct
- ward

2. Sequencing: Copy the graphic organizer below. Use it to illustrate the shift in power from local parties to national parties.

Homework Practice Online
keyword: SV3 GV18

3. **Finding the Main Idea**

a. How has the national party organization changed? What is the role of the national party?

b. What role do state parties play in elections? What opportunities do they offer citizens?

4. **Writing and Critical Thinking**

Decision Making: In what ways would you spend a budget for a national election?

Consider the following:
- how state parties depend upon national parties
- the different ways national parties can spend money, including polling and advertising

SECTION 4

POLITICAL PARTIES AND THE PUBLIC GOOD

READ TO DISCOVER

1. What are the common criticisms of the U.S. two-party system?
2. What are the benefits of the U.S. two-party system?

Imagine that you are a registered voter in an election year but are undecided about how to cast your ballot. You have seen several commercials for the candidates on television, but the commercials are brief and do not provide enough information. To whom do you turn?

One way to start is by examining which party each candidate represents. By researching the programs a party supports and its politicians' voting records, you can determine much about the basic political beliefs of its candidates. Although the parties are much criticized, they do help promote the public good in several ways, such as by making it easier to figure out how to cast your ballot.

Criticisms of Political Parties

As noted in Chapter 17, several concerns exist about the effect of interest groups on the public good. Because of their visibility and size, political parties come under even closer scrutiny. The most common criticisms of political parties are that they too often represent special interests, that they are filled with selfish office seekers, and that they are too concerned with "politicking." On the other hand, some political scientists argue that U.S. political parties are too weak.

Special Interests Many people think that parties are influenced too much by special-interest groups. They believe that because these groups

provide money for political campaigns and other party activities, politicians and their parties will make decisions that benefit only the groups rather than promote the public good.

Self-Serving Office Seekers Critics of party politics also have charged that political parties are full of self-serving office seekers, or people interested in personal gain rather than sincerely working on issues. Many have said that politicians and their parties support certain policies only because doing so helps them get elected.

Politicking Many people feel that the frequent bickering between the two major parties is just "politics as usual." Some critics charge that congressional politicking—the posturing between the parties—is often less concerned with real issues and more about which party is winning the public relations race.

Weakness of U.S. Political Parties Finally, some political scientists criticize U.S. political

PUBLIC GOOD *Political parties are criticized for being strongly influenced by special interests rather than working to promote the public good.* **Why are political parties more closely scrutinized today than in years past?**

SECTION 4

POLITICAL PARTIES AND THE PUBLIC GOOD

Lesson Plans

For teaching strategies, see Lesson 18.4 located at the beginning of this chapter.

Section Assessment

To assess students' mastery of this section, have them complete Daily Quiz 18.4 in *Daily Quizzes with Answer Key.*

Caption Answer

because of their increased size and visibility

parties for being what they perceive as too weak. Although the United States has the oldest political parties in the world, it also has about the weakest of any democratic country. Parties in the United States lack strength in several important ways. The two major parties have weak organizations and low voter allegiance, and their elected officials often do not stick together on issues, giving voters the impression that each party lacks unity.

American political parties generally have few organized activities, and the activities they do offer involve a relatively small proportion of the population. By contrast, to join most interest groups, people must fill in application forms, pay dues, and receive a membership card. Only members of the organization may participate in the organization's governance. Even interest groups whose members do not help govern and who do not fill out membership applications or cards usually solicit members by mail.

Similarly, political parties such as the Liberal Democratic Party of Japan and the Christian Democratic Union of Germany have card-carrying, dues-paying members as well as ordinary voters who support the party at the polls. Members provide a core of party workers and loyal supporters who take the party's message to their neighbors or fellow workers. The two major U.S. parties, however, lack such a membership structure.

Furthermore, U.S. legislators of the same party stick together less often than those in most other countries. In many countries there is party discipline in the legislature, with all of a party's representatives voting together on important issues. This does not typically occur in the United States.

Why do political scientists think stronger political parties are important? One answer is voter turnout. A lower percentage of people vote in the United States than in countries with stronger political parties. The reason for this difference, theorize some political scientists, is that citizens with relatively low interest in politics are more apt to vote if exposed to strong parties. Strong parties thus promote high voter participation, whereas weak political parties do not.

PUBLIC GOOD *Youth organizations, such as the College Republicans, provide political information to young people.* **How can knowing the philosophy of a political party be helpful to voters?**

Benefits of the U.S. Two-Party System

Political parties do help promote the public good in four ways. They provide ready information about politics, help to balance the political system by taking into account varied opinions, discourage sudden shifts in political trends, and encourage political participation.

Providing Information Political parties help bring order to the political world. They present political information in a convenient form so that voters do not need to start over every time they encounter a political leader or a political proposal.

Parties provide a political "brand name," in much the same way a soft-drink company does for its products. Knowing the broad political philosophy of a party helps you understand where it will stand on certain issues. One reason you may vote for a candidate is that, overall, you support his or her party's views.

Accommodating Varied Opinions Parties help the political system do a better job of allowing for the expression of a wide range of opinions and interests, which is necessary if political decisions are to promote the public good. Each party is made up of both individual voters and organized groups. Therefore, each party must try to consider

Citizenship in Action

David Wade, former president of the College Democrats of America, worked to help inform college students about political issues and candidates.

Young Politicians

"The most important thing we could do is to make people care," says David Wade, who as a 21-year-old Brown University student served in 1997 as national president of the College Democrats of America. As a leader in this organization, Wade worked to further the Democratic Party's goals and elect its nominees to political office.

Other such organizations also focus on youth involvement in politics. Teen Republicans and Teen Democrats, for example, organize the efforts of teens who identify themselves as supporters of either the Republican or Democratic Party. The most well-known youth organizations, however, are the College Republicans National Committee, Young Republicans, Young Democrats of America, and College Democrats of America.

Although the College Republicans and the College Democrats limit membership to university students in the United States, the Young Democrats and Young Republicans include any partisans under the age of 36 (for the Democrats) and between the ages of 18 and 40 (for the Republicans). Each of the four organizations boasts tens of thousands of members who are working in thousands of chapters across the country.

The work of these youth organizations focuses on getting young people involved in the democratic process. Doing so helps address some people's concern that young people today care little about politics and the important issues of their time. For example, College Democrats and other youth-oriented political groups keep tabs on issues important to students, such as government policies on college financial aid, tuition rates, and access to education. Members then communicate that information—and the applicable positions of their parties—to other young people. At the same time, they encourage young voters to express their opinions and lobby government officials to support particular policies. "What we've found is that young people really respond to each other," Wade says.

The work of these youth organizations includes more than just keeping young people informed on important issues of the day, however. The organizations also work to register voters, get young people out to the polls on election day, raise money for party efforts, recruit volunteers for party work and campaigns, and provide a variety of community services.

In addition to their work in individual chapters around the country, members of some of these youth organizations also meet in national conventions. These gatherings give members the opportunity to debate issues, propose policies, and share ideas and experiences.

All of these efforts, Wade says, help educate students "so that they can cast a vote on election day or make a call to their congressperson that's reasoned, enlightened, and intelligent." In doing that, these young party members are setting a standard that all voters should follow.

What Do You Think?

1. How can Republican and Democratic youth organizations work together to promote participation in politics?
2. In what other ways can political parties reach out to young citizens and help them take part in the democratic process?

THEMES IN GOVERNMENT

CITIZENSHIP When do individuals develop a sense of identification with a political party? This is a question that many political scientists have asked. Some argue that values imparted by the family help determine a person's party affiliation and that the process of party identification begins in childhood. More recent research indicates that families play a much smaller role in determining the party loyalty of young adults. One study discovered that 40 percent of them affiliated with a party other than that of their parents. One source that might have a great deal of influence on party identification is a student's educational experience. Fellow students and teachers are now believed to have some impact on a young person's choice of political party. ■

SECTION 4
REVIEW ANSWERS

1. Criticisms—too influenced by special interests, full of self-serving office seekers, and engage in politicking; benefits—provide information to the public, balance varied opinions, discourage sudden shifts, and encourage political participation

2a. Answers will vary, but students should demonstrate knowledge of the points of view of each party on the issue chosen.

2b. Students might suggest that political parties allow diverse opinions to have a voice in politics, provide information to the public, balance varied political opinions, discourage sudden shifts in political trends, and encourage political participation.

3. Essays will vary. Students might suggest that unlike many nations, U.S. political parties are weak, have few organized activities, and stick together less often. Students might also mention that the two-party system discourages short-term political trends, unlike multiparty systems, and that competing political parties allow for diverse opinions to be expressed in the political system.

all of its supporters' interests if it is going to continue to receive their support. Including as many interests as possible is important because it means that more citizens are involved in the political system.

Discouraging Sudden Shifts Another benefit of political parties is that they serve as an anchor, making sudden political shifts in response to short-term trends more difficult. Think back to what you learned about multiparty systems in Section 1. By allowing many political parties, multiparty systems enable short-term trends to threaten government stability.

In the United States the two major political parties represent many issues, thus discouraging voters from giving up support for the party and elected officials just because of current trends on *one* political issue. Voters know that even if they disagree with a certain candidate on one issue, he or she represents the broader issues of his or her party. The resulting stability gives elected officials and parties more room to focus on the big picture. This is vital for wise public policies that take a long time to show they are working.

Encouraging Political Participation Many people think of competing political parties as a key part of democracy. In the nondemocratic Soviet Union, for example, only Communist Party members could participate in government. Indeed, the United States would cease to be a democracy if national leaders prevented people with opinions

PUBLIC GOOD *Although the two major U.S. parties each have a strong base of support, they are often criticized for holding similar views to each other on many issues.* **How do parties provide political stability in a two-party system?**

different from their own from organizing groups to try to affect government actions.

Participation in political parties is one way for U.S. citizens to take part in the political system—and in their own governing. The United States is a diverse country and political parties provide a way for this diversity to be expressed in the political system.

SECTION 4 REVIEW

1. Cause and effect: Copy the chart below. Use it to assess the criticisms and benefits of political parties.

Criticisms	Benefits

Homework Practice Online
keyword: SV3 GV18

2. **Finding the Main Idea**

a. What is one important present day issue that has caused great disagreement between the Democrats and Republicans? What was the point of view of each party on this issue?

b. In what ways do political parties benefit the public good? How effective are they at benefitting the public good?

3. **Writing and Critical Thinking**

Summarizing: How is the U.S. political party system different from other countries? Write an essay in response to this question.
Consider the following:
• the weakness of political parties in the U.S. system
• the ways in which political parties encourage participation in the U.S. electoral process

GOVERNMENT IN THE NEWS

Political Parties and Political Change

Political parties affect public policy through legislation. In Congress, each major party wrestles for the votes needed to pass legislation that will advance that party's agenda.

Some of the most dramatic changes in U.S. government have come when one party has been swept into office at a critical moment. With a mandate—perceived popular support for a legislative program—one party is free to enact rapid and far-reaching changes. In 1964 Democrat Lyndon B. Johnson won the presidency with one of the greatest landslides in U.S. history. Johnson combined this mandate, his political skills, and solid Democratic majorities in Congress to enact his Great Society program. Ronald Reagan's surprising landslide win in 1980 combined with Republican gains in Congress to give Republicans a mandate to pass broad measures, including a tax cut.

Sometimes neither major party dominates Congress; however, this does not prevent parties from trying to bring about change. Instead of relying on their majorities, parties must achieve compromises to pass legislation. The 2000 elections left Congress very evenly split: the Senate was made up of 50 Republicans and 50 Democrats, while the House comprised a slim Republican majority.

These rare circumstances demanded unprecedented compromises. In Congress the majority party determines committee assignments, giving its agenda an advantage. With the new Senate split evenly, Democratic leader Tom Daschle demanded equal representation on Senate committees. Republican leader Trent Lott resisted. When Democrats threatened to challenge the Florida presidential electoral vote, Lott relented. The split in Congress ended when in June 2001 Senator Jim Jeffords of Vermont left the Republican Party to

Senator Edward Kennedy and President George W. Bush celebrate the passage of the No Child Left Behind Act of 2001.

become an independent. This gave the Democrats a 50-to-49 advantage.

In 2001 the two parties worked together to pass President George W. Bush's education bill, named the No Child Left Behind Act of 2001. This act aims at ensuring that public schools have the ability and responsibility to see that each child receives quality education, regardless of income level, race or ethnicity, English proficiency, or disability.

An evenly divided Congress will probably not produce change as dramatic as the Great Society, but this is not necessarily a disadvantage for the country. Political scientist Michael Barone argues that legislation passed during one-party domination tends to produce a backlash that eventually pushes the dominant party out of power.

What Do You Think?

1. What are the effects of changes made when one party dominates Congress? when power in Congress is evenly split?

2. What methods must parties use when neither party dominates Congress?

> **WHY IT MATTERS TODAY**
>
> Congressional compromise is critical to passing legislation. Use **CNNfyi.com** or other **current events** sources to conduct research on recent examples of bipartisan legislation. **CNNfyi.com**

CHAPTER 18

Review Answers

Writing a Summary

Summaries should focus on the main points of each section. These may be found in the Read to Discover questions at the start of each section. Summaries should also use standard grammar, spelling, sentence structure, and punctuation.

Identifying Ideas

Refer to the following pages: electorate (405), one-party system (407), two-party system (407), multiparty system (407), realignment (409), independent (413), third party (413), splinter party (415), ideological party (415), party machine (416).

Understanding Main Ideas

1. organizations that seek to gain power in the political system; are the way in which many citizens become involved in politics.

2. assist the electoral process, organize the

(Continued on page 426)

(Continued from page 425)
day-to-day operations of the government, and nominate candidates for office

3. Hamilton and the Federalists hoped to use the national government to support manufacturing and trade interests. Madison, Jefferson, and the Democratic-Republicans supported farmers' interests.

4. Students might suggest the antislavery and civil rights laws passed by the Republican party after the Civil War, and the relief efforts passed by Democrats during the Great Depression.

5. Third parties have often altered the outcome of an election.

6. It was strongest at the local level. Since then, reforms weakened the local parties and allowed state and national organizations to grow in strength.

7. Perform "party-building activities,"voter registration drives, campaign fundraisers, and encouraging citizens to vote.

8. they are too influenced by special-interest groups and are full of self-serving office seekers interested in personal gain and politicking

9. Parties provide political information, balance varied opinions, discourage sudden shifts in political trends, and encourage political participation.

Reviewing Themes
1. Answers will vary, but students should evaluate the party system's influence on political participation and explain their reasoning.
2. Students might suggest that congressional committees are formed according to

(Continued from page 426)

Writing a Summary

Using standard grammar, spelling, sentence structure, and punctuation, write a summary of the information in this chapter.

Identifying Ideas

Identify the following terms and explain their significance.

1. electorate

2. one-party system

3. two-party system

4. multiparty system

5. realignment

6. independent

7. third party

8. splinter party

9. ideological party

10. party machine

Understanding Main Ideas

SECTION 1 *(pp. 405–408)*

1. What are political parties, and why are they important to political systems?

2. What are the primary functions of political parties in the United States?

SECTION 2 *(pp. 409–415)*

3. What issues led to the creation of the first political parties in the United States?

4. What are some significant changes caused by political parties?

5. What role have third parties played in the United States?

SECTION 3 *(pp. 416–420)*

6. Was the sphere of party influence strongest during the 1800s at the national, state, or local level? How has this changed?

7. What activities do state parties perform?

SECTION 4 *(pp. 421–424)*

8. What are some criticisms of political parties?

9. How do political parties promote the public good?

Reviewing Themes

1. **Principles of Democracy** Many people believe that the party system encourages political participation. Do you agree with this statement? Why or why not?

2. **Political Processes** One function of political parties is organizing the government. In what way does this process effect policy?

3. **Public Good** What reforms were made in the 1800s to stop corruption in local party machines? How have these reforms improved the voting process and helped voters today?

Thinking Critically

1. **Taking a Stand** Do you feel that political parties have too much influence in the political and electoral processes? Do they have more influence in one area than in another? What might happen if parties had less influence than they do? If they had more?

2. **Evaluating** How do parties provide citizens with opportunities to participate in the political process? How effective is this participation? What are some historical examples of changes brought about by parties?

3. **Identifying Cause and Effect** Do you think a third party candidate could ever be elected president in the United States? Why or why not? What might have been the appeal of Ross Perot and the Reform Party? Have the Reform Party's demands caused a change in the issues addressed by the major parties?

Writing about Government

Review the list you made in your Government Notebook about the rules and standards governing clubs or teams to which you have belonged. In what ways are political parties similar to your clubs or teams? How are they different? Would you change the rules and standards governing political parties? Why or why not? Explain your answers in your notebook.

Interpreting Political Cartoons

Study this political cartoon from the 1870s below. Then use it to help you answer the questions that follow.

IN COUNTING THERE IS STRENGTH

"THATS WHATS THE MATTER."

The Granger Collection, New York

1. What does this cartoon say about the electoral process and political parties at the time?

   a. Ballot boxes were protected against tampering by gruff individuals.

   b. Whoever counted the votes during an election was able to determine the winner.

   c. Political parties of the time ensured a fair vote was held.

   d. Because the electorate was uneducated, political parties had to tamper with the vote to ensure that qualified candidates would be elected.

2. How have the roles parties play in the electoral process changed since the 1800s?

Analyzing Primary Sources

In 1984, Democrat Geraldine Ferraro became the first female to be nominated for vice president by a major poitical party. Read the following excerpt from her campaign debate with then-vice president George Bush and answer the questions that follow.

"I wouldn't be standing here if [presidential candidate] Fritz [Walter] Mondale didn't have the courage and my party didn't stand for the values that it does, the values of fairness and equal opportunity. . . . Do you know when we find jobs for the eight and a half million people who are unemployed in this country, . . . that will be a patriotic act. . . . When we educate our children . . . they're going to be able to compete in a world economy and that makes us stronger and that's a patriotic act."

3. What is Ferraro trying to show voters about the values of the Democratic Party?

   a. The Democrats feel that patriotism is irrelevant in an election.

   b. Voting against the Democrats would be unpatriotic.

   c. The Democrats are no different from any other party.

   d. The Democrats value equal opportunity, patriotism, fairness, a strong economy, and education.

4. What might the Democrats have in common with other political parties?

Building Your Portfolio

Presidents and Political Parties

Choose any U.S. presidential candidate from the 1900s, and conduct reasearch on the political party to which he belonged. Find his acceptance speech, and imagine you are a convention delegate who has just heard the speech. Write a newspaper editorial comparing the speech to the goals of your party.

internet connect

go.hrw.com

Internet Activity: go.hrw.com
KEYWORD: SV3 GV18

Access the Internet through the HRW Go site to conduct research on a third party of the 20th century. Find reasons why the party came to exist. Then create a "party newspaper" in which you take the point of view of a member of the third party and publicize your candidates.

---

political party membership. This affects policies.

3. voter registration, split-ticket voting, a reduction of patronage positions, and primary elections; these helped reduce corruption and allow voters today a greater choice of candidates.

Thinking Critically

1. Answers will vary. Students should demonstrate knowledge of the roles political parties play in the political and electoral processes.

2. Answers will vary. Students might mention that parties provide citizens with access to politics, and that parties have often brought about great changes in society.

3. Answers will vary, but students might suggest that a third party president is unlikely in the U.S. Students might mention that Perot's Reform Party called for a balanced budget and campaign finance reform, issues of the 2000 presidential election campaign.

Writing About Government

The Government Notebook is a follow-up activity to the notebook activity that appears on page 404.

Building Social Studies Skills

1. b

2. Students might suggest that parties help register people to vote, nominate candidates for elections, raise campaign funds, and provide information about candidates to voters.

3. d

4. Students might suggest that most political parties value patriotism, fairness, education, and a strong economy.

CHAPTER 19 THE ELECTORAL PROCESS

	OBJECTIVES	PACING GUIDE	REPRODUCIBLE RESOURCES
SECTION 1 **NOMINATING CANDIDATES** (pp. 429–434)	▶ What is the first step in the electoral process? ▶ In what ways may candidates be chosen for an election? ▶ What types of primaries are held in the states?	**Regular** 1 day **Block Scheduling** .5 day	**ELL** Spanish Study Guide 19.1 **ELL** English Study Guide 19.1
SECTION 2 **CAMPAIGNS AND CAMPAIGN FINANCING** (pp. 435–439)	▶ How was early political campaigning different from political campaining today? ▶ What is the role of the media in today's political campaigns? ▶ How are campaigns financed? ▶ How is campaign financing regulated?	**Regular** 1.5 days **Block Scheduling** .5 day	**ELL** Spanish Study Guide 19.2 **ELL** English Study Guide 19.2
SECTION 3 **ELECTIONS AND VOTING** (pp. 440–446)	▶ What are the different types of elections? ▶ What determines where, how, and when people vote? ▶ What factors determine if a person may vote? ▶ What influences the way in which people vote?	**Regular** 1.5 days **Block Scheduling** 1 day	**ELL** Spanish Study Guide 19.3 **ELL** English Study Guide 19.3 **PS** Reading 24: *Susan B. Anthony on Women's Suffrage* **PS** Reading 45: *Voting Rights Act (1965)*
SECTION 4 **CAMPAIGNS AND THE PUBLIC GOOD** (pp. 447–450)	▶ Why do some people criticize the media's role in campaigns? ▶ What are the possible effects of negative campaigning? ▶ What are some of the benefits of political campaigns?	**Regular** 1.5 days **Block Scheduling** .5 day	**ELL** Spanish Study Guide 19.4 **ELL** English Study Guide 19.4

Chapter Resource Key

PS	Primary Sources	**A**	Assessment		Video
RS	Reading Support	**REV**	Review		Videodisc
E	Enrichment	**ELL**	Reinforcement and English Language Learners		Internet
S	Simulations		Transparencies		Holt Presentation Maker Using
SM	Skills Mastery		CD-ROM		Microsoft ® PowerPoint ®

TECHNOLOGY RESOURCES	REINFORCEMENT, REVIEW, AND ASSESSMENT
One-Stop Planner: Lesson 19.1 Holt Researcher Online Homework Practice Online Cartoon Transparency 19 Global Skill Builder CD-ROM	**REV** Section 1 Review, p. 434 **A** Daily Quiz 19.1
One-Stop Planner: Lesson 19.2 Holt Researcher Online Homework Practice Online Transparency 40 Cartoon Transparency 20 Global Skill Builder CD-ROM	**REV** Section 2 Review, p. 439 **A** Daily Quiz 19.2
One-Stop Planner: Lesson 19.3 Holt Researcher Online Homework Practice Online Global Skill Builder CD-ROM	**REV** Section 3 Review, p. 446 **A** Daily Quiz 19.3
One-Stop Planner: Lesson 19.4 Holt Researcher Online Homework Practice Online Cartoon Transparency 21 Global Skill Builder CD-ROM **E** Challenge and Enrichment: Activity 19 **E** Simulations and Strategies for Teaching American Government: Activity 19 CNN Presents American Government	**REV** Section 4 Review, p. 450 **A** Daily Quiz 19.4

Chapter Review and Assessment

SM Global Skill Builder CD-ROM
HRW Go site
REV Chapter 19 Tutorial for Students, Parents, and Peers
REV Chapter 19 Review, pp. 452–453
Chapter 19 Test Generator (on the One-Stop Planner)
A Chapter 19 Test
A Chapter 19 Test Alternative Assessment Handbook

One-Stop Planner CD-ROM

It's easy to plan lessons, select resources, and print out materials for your students when you use the *One-Stop Planner CD-ROM with Test Generator.*

internet connect

HRW ONLINE RESOURCES
Go To: go.hrw.com
Then type in a keyword.

TEACHER HOME PAGE
KEYWORD: SV3 Teacher

CHAPTER INTERNET ACTIVITIES
KEYWORD: SV3 GV19
Choose an activity on the electoral process to:
▶ learn about primary elections.
▶ make an oral presentation on voting methods.
▶ investigate polling practices.

CHAPTER ENRICHMENT LINKS
KEYWORD: SV3 CH19

HOLT RESEACHER ONLINE
KEYWORD: Holt Reseacher

ONLINE ASSESSMENT
Homework Practice
KEYWORD: SV3 HP19
Standardized Test Prep
KEYWORD: SV3 STP19
Rubrics
KEYWORD: SS Rubrics

ONLINE MAPS, CHARTS, AND GRAPHS
KEYWORD: SV3 MCG
▶ States' Candidate Selection Process
▶ Party Identification of U.S. Voters

CONTENT UPDATES
KEYWORD: SS Content Updates

HOLT PRESENTATION MAKER
KEYWORD: SV3 PPT19

ONLINE READING SUPPORT
KEYWORD: SS Strategies

CURRENT EVENTS
KEYWORD: S3 Current Events

LESSON 19.1 NOMINATING CANDIDATES

TEXTBOOK PAGES 429–434

OBJECTIVES

▶ Describe the first step in the electoral process.
▶ Discuss how candidates are chosen to run for elections.
▶ Identify the types of primary elections that are held in the states.

MOTIVATE

Ask students if they have ever aspired to be elected to an office of any kind (e.g., captain of a team or a class officer). Then, ask them how they became or could have become a candidate for that position. Discuss these methods with students, and list the ways they respond on the chalkboard. Explain to them that in the United States a systematic process has developed for nominating candidates. Tell students that there are many methods and that in this section they will learn about the first step in the electoral process, the various ways that an individual can become a candidate for elective office, and the types of primary elections that are held.

TEACH

Building a Vocabulary

In spiral notebooks, have students create a Political Dictionary to be used throughout the course. This dictionary may be used as an activity at the start of each new section; it may also be used as a modification device for students having difficulty or sheltered English students during tests and homework assignments. List words that students will be expected to know for this section on the chalkboard. Have students list, define, and give an example of each of the terms, using information provided in the chapter or on the *Researcher CD-ROM*.

Identifying the Main Idea

Organize the class into groups of three or four students each. Assign each group several states to research. On sheets of butcher paper each group should write the title *Methods of Nomination* and draw four columns under it. Label the columns *Method, Where Used, Advantages,* and *Disadvantages.* Using information from this section of the text and other resources students should fill in the first two columns of their charts. They should then discuss each method and record the advantages and disadvantages of each method as they understand them. Once students have finished, bring the class back together, and draw a similar chart on a large piece of butcher paper with enough room for all the states. Have students record the methods for each state they researched on the chart. Discuss each group's conclusions about the advantages and disadvantages of each method. Display the finished chart in the classroom. Tell students that in the next activity they will learn about the types of primary elections that are held.

Drawing Conclusions/Demonstrating Understanding

Tell students that the most common nomination procedure used is the primary. Identify and describe the types of primaries for students. If your state conducts a primary election write which type it holds on the chalkboard. Ask students to write an essay evaluating this method and the advantages and disadvantages it has relative to the other types of primaries. Students should also discuss whether or not their state should consider changing its type of primary. If your state does not hold a primary, have students write an essay describing how the nomination process of their state compares to the various types of primary elections. Students should also discuss whether they feel their state should change its nominating process. Encourage students to share their opinions with the class.

Learning From Visuals

Discuss with students some of the criticisms that have been made regarding the nomination process. On the overhead projector show students Cartoon Transparency 19: The Electoral Process. Have students write a short essay describing the problems with the electoral process that the cartoon points out. Students should be sure to comment on the way that the cartoon describes the media, the voter, and the electoral process itself. Encourage students to share their ideas about the cartoon with the class.

CLOSE

List the methods of nomination on the chalkboard. Now that students have studied the various methods of nomination each student should be asked which method they think is the fairest for the candidates. Have students discuss their opinions as a class. Students should offer support for their opinions based on material from the chapter and from discussions during the lessons. Keep a tally of their answers under each method, and discuss the final results with the class.

OPTIONS

Gifted Learners

 Ask students to find out what type of primary is held in each of the states that use primaries. They should then make a chart with the types of primaries written across the top of the page and list the appropriate states under each method. Finally, they should write a brief essay discussing the most dominant method and why they believe it is the most popular. Encourage students to share their opinion about the reasons for the method's popularity with the rest of the class.

Visual-Spatial Learners

 Have students use information from the Identifying the Main Idea activity and the Gifted Learners option to create a map of the United States that identifies the type of nomination procedure(s) used by each of the states. Students will need to include a color-coded legend that includes all of the nominating procedures used. Remind students that some states may use more than one method. Display the final product in the classroom.

Students Having Difficulty/ Sheltered English Students

  Discuss with students the nomination process that their state uses. Have some students draw cartoons in support of that nominating process and others draw cartoons criticizing it. Encourage students to consider how their nominating process compares to those used by other states when drawing their cartoons. Have students write captions for their cartoons that use vocabulary terms from this section. Encourage students to share their work with the rest of the class.

Musical-Rhythmic Learners/Interpersonal Learners

Organize the class into five groups. Assign each group one of the following topics: self-announcement, caucus, convention, petition, or primary election. Have each group write a song that describes the topic they were assigned. Students should be encouraged to research actual examples about their topic to use in their song and to use vocabulary from this section of the text in their lyrics. Have groups sing their songs to the rest of the class. Encourage groups to ask questions about the meaning of other groups' songs. Discuss any inaccuracies in students' songs.

REVIEW

Have students complete the Section 1 Review on page 434. Use the answers in the Annotated Teacher's Edition to assess student mastery of this section.

ASSESS

To assess student mastery of this section, have students complete Daily Quiz 19.1 in *Daily Quizzes with Answer Key.* For additional assessment options, see *Alternative Assessment Handbook* on the *One-Stop Planner CD-ROM.*

ADDITIONAL RESOURCES

Mayer, William, ed. *In Pursuit of the White House 2000: How We Choose Our Presidential Nominees.* 2000. Chatham House.

HOLT PRESENTATION MAKER
Access Illustrated LECTURE NOTES using Microsoft® PowerPoint® on the One-Stop Planner CD-ROM

OBJECTIVES

▶ Describe how early political campaigning was different from political campaigning today.

▶ Identify the role of the media in today's political campaigns.

▶ Discuss how campaigns are financed.

▶ Identify how campaign financing is regulated.

MOTIVATE

On the chalkboard write the question: *Why would you need to campaign if you were to run for an elected office?* Then, write a second question on the board, *Is the candidate who runs the best campaign necessarily the best candidate?* Allow students time to think about both of these questions; then as a class discuss students' answers. Encourage students to debate any differences in opinion that they may have on either topic. After the discussion tell students that in this section they will study the role of the media in campaigns, how campaigns are financed, how campaigning is regulated, and how early political campaigns differed from modern-day campaigning.

TEACH

Building a Vocabulary

In their spiral notebooks, have students continue working on their Political Dictionary. List words the students will be expected to know for this section on the chalkboard. Have students list, define, and give an example of each of the terms, using information provided in the chapter or on the *Researcher CD-ROM*.

Navigating the Internet/Creating Charts and Graphs

Describe for students how political campaigns have changed over the years, being sure to highlight the changes that have occurred during this century as a result of technology. Encourage students to use resources from the library to gather information. Students should record informa-

tion about the length of each campaign, the number of primaries held, and the amount of money spent on each election beginning with 1960. Have students create two charts. On one chart they should label one axis in years and the other in dollars (to illustrate the changes in campaign spending over the years); on a second chart they should label the year and the number of primaries held (to illustrate the changes in the nomination process over the years). Then, ask students to identify any trends they see and to evaluate the possible reasons for these trends. Conduct a class discussion based on student findings and reasoning. Tell students that in the next activity they will investigate the role of the media in modern political campaigns.

Demonstration

 Explain to students that the media has become a driving force behind major political campaigns. Ask students to remember ads and news coverage that they have seen in recent political campaigns, and have them describe how they perceived the candidate based on the ad. Explain to students that some people complain that people rely too much on what they see and hear in political ad campaigns rather than finding out what each candidate stands for. Organize the class into several small groups. Give all of the groups a list of attributes and political stances that an imaginary candidate will have. Have each group create an ad for the imaginary candidate. After each group has finished, have them share their ad with the rest of the class. Allow time for students to discuss the differences in the ads and the differences in the way they perceived the candidate after seeing each ad. As a lead-in to the next activity tell students that they will learn about people's opinions about campaign funding and regulation of these funds.

Developing Life Skills/Conducting Research

 Discuss with students the major issues concerning campaign financing. Ask students to interview at least five adults about their attitudes concerning contributing money to a political cause; their beliefs about whether or not there should be financial disclosures, contribution limits, spending limits, or donor restrictions, and why; and their opinions on whether too much money is spent on media campaigning and how influential they believe the media is.

After completing the interviews, students should write a multiple paragraph essay that summarizes their findings and gives their personal opinion on how campaigns should be financed. Following completion of the essays, lead a class discussion on students' findings and personal opinions.

CLOSE

Review with students the changes that have occurred in campaigning over the years. Have students write an essay describing these changes. Students should also be sure to give their opinion about whether the new methods by which campaigns are run are any better than earlier methods. Students should support their arguments using material from this section and from their research on campaigning. Encourage students to share their opinions with the class.

OPTIONS

Gifted Learners

 Have students conduct research on campaign controversies that have occurred in the United States. Students should identify who was involved in the controversy, when it took place, the type of issue that was involved, and any actions taken as a result of the controversy. Students should then write an essay describing how the controversy affected the election and the overall public good. Encourage students to share information that they have learned with the class.

Visual-Spatial Learners

 Have students create a chart entitled *Solutions to Campaign Controversies*. The horizontal axis of the graph should identify different types of problems associated with campaigning (e.g., people donating huge amounts of money to particular candidates' campaigns in an attempt to seek political influence). The vertical axis should list laws or policies that address these issues (e.g., contribution limits are established at $1,000 per individual). In the square where the problem addressed and the solution meet, students should identify the year that

the reform took effect. Encourage students to share their findings with the rest of the class.

Gifted Learners

 Encourage students to investigate the role of the media in influencing political campaigns by researching articles written about a specific candidate. Students should choose one newspaper and review campaign coverage from a recent election that deals with a specific candidate. Have students create a list of descriptive words that were used in articles about the candidate. Students should then consider whether the words used may have influenced readers' opinions about the candidate being discussed. Have students write a paper describing the effects that media coverage can have on an election.

REVIEW

Have students complete the Section 2 Review on page 439. Use the answers in the Annotated Teacher's Edition to assess student mastery of this section.

ASSESS

To assess student mastery of this section, have students complete Daily Quiz 19.2 in *Daily Quizzes with Answer Key*. For additional assessment options, see *Alternative Assessment Handbook* on the *One-Stop Planner CD-ROM*.

ADDITIONAL RESOURCES

Hail to the Candidate: Presidential Campaigns from Banners to Broadcasts. 1992. Smithsonian.

Legal History of the Presidential Election Campaign Fund Act. 1991. Federal Election Commission.

Woodward, Bob. *The Choice.* 1996. Simon and Schuster.

The Price of Power: Money in Politics. 1993. Cambridge Educational. (video)

LESSON 19.3 ELECTIONS AND VOTING

TEXTBOOK PAGES 440-446

OBJECTIVES

▶ Identify the different types of elections.
▶ Discuss the factors that determine where, how, and when people vote.
▶ Identify the factors that determine if a person may vote.
▶ Describe the influences on the way in which people vote.

MOTIVATE

Tell students that an election was held under the following circumstances: the polls opened at 10:00 A.M. and closed at 3:00 P.M.; it was a rainy day; there were 21 offices to be filled, but only 3 had more than one candidate running; it was in a year when a presidential election was not being held; only offices for the county and local government were to be filled. The election results showed that only 20 percent of the eligible voters actually voted. Discuss the reasons why voters did not vote given the circumstances listed. Ask students to identify the ways that the people running the election could have increased the voter turnout. Tell students that in this section they will learn more about the different types of elections and what influences voting patterns.

TEACH

Building a Vocabulary

In their spiral notebooks, have students continue working on their Political Dictionary. List words the students will be expected to know for this section on the chalkboard. Have students list, define, and give an example of each of the terms, using information provided in the chapter or on the *Researcher CD-ROM.*

Organizing Information

Discuss the differences between general elections and special elections with students. Organize the class into three groups. Have one group research state elections, another county elections, and another city elections, in order to determine when elections are scheduled for each level and what positions will be up for re-election. Each group should create a chart on butcher paper that gives these dates. Encourage groups to explain their charts to the rest of the class. Tell students that in the next activity they will learn about what factors determine where, how, and when people vote.

Acquiring Information

Organize the class into three groups. Assign each group one of these topics: where people vote, how people vote, and when people vote. Each group should use information from this section of the chapter and other research materials to prepare a presentation on the topic they have been assigned. Groups should be sure to identify changes in voting patterns that have occurred throughout U.S. history that apply to their topic. Have each group present their topic to the rest of the class, and encourage students to ask questions of the other groups. As a lead-in to the next activity tell students that they will learn about the factors that determine if a person is eligible to vote.

Analyzing Ideas/Writing About Government

Lead a class discussion concerning voting requirements and how they have changed over the years. Have students identify the current voting requirements. Then, have students take each of the current voting requirements and answer the following questions: "Why would this be required?" "What is the advantage of the requirement?" and "What are the disadvantages of the requirement?" Once students have finished, lead a class discussion dealing with students' answers to these questions. Tell students that in the next activity they will learn about the factors that influence the way people vote.

Conducting Research/Navigating the Internet

Discuss with students the influences that affect the way a person votes. Tell students that one of the main factors that influence the way a person votes is party identification. Organize the class into groups of four. Have each group identify five key issues that are important to voters. Two students in each group should be assigned the Democratic Party and the other two the Republican Party. They should then research the stance that the party takes on each of the five issues. Encourage students to use the Internet to find information about each party. After acquiring this information each group should prepare a chart that compares and contrasts the parties' views on each of the topics. After all groups have finished, have them compare the issues they researched and the parties' stances on these issues.

CLOSE

On the chalkboard write the names of several famous political figures. Then ask students to think back to the discussion of the influences on the way people vote. Have students identify whether people would most likely vote for the people listed on the chalkboard based on party identification, issues, or candidates' record and image. Review answers and encourage open discussion regarding these voting influences.

OPTIONS

Students Having Difficulty/ Sheltered English Students

 Ask students to review material from this section of the text dealing with the types of elections that are held and how they are conducted. On a sheet of paper students should write the title *Elections and Methods*. Have students draw a line down the left portion of the page. On the left side of the line, students should identify each type of election and the various ways that they are conducted. On the right side they should write two statements about each type. After the chart is completed students should discuss their answers.

Gifted Learners

 Tell students that women and African Americans did not always have the right to vote in the United States and that both groups had to fight for this right. Divide the class into small groups. Assign half of the groups the task of researching the struggle of African Americans to gain the right to vote and the other half of researching the women's suffrage movement. Each group should then prepare a time line identifying significant events in the struggle for the right to vote and key figures involved in these events. Have groups share their information with the rest of the class. Display time lines in the classroom.

REVIEW

Have students complete the Section 3 Review on page 446. Use the answers in the Annotated Teacher's Edition to assess student mastery of this section.

ASSESS

To assess student mastery of this section, have students complete Daily Quiz 19.3 in *Daily Quizzes with Answer Key*. For additional assessment options, see *Alternative Assessment Handbook* on the *One-Stop Planner CD-ROM*.

ADDITIONAL RESOURCES

Voting Behavior. At Issue series. 1996. Greenhaven.
Why Bother Voting? 1992. Public Broadcasting System. (video)

OBJECTIVES

▶ Explain why some people criticize the media's role in political campaigns.
▶ Identify the possible effects of negative campaigning.
▶ Describe the benefits of political campaigns.

MOTIVATE

Ask students if they believe everything they are told by their friends, parents, or teachers. Have students explain why their degree of trust varies for each of these groups. Tell students that election campaigns are meant to get a candidate elected and that sometimes candidates make promises that they cannot keep or do not intend to keep. Ask students if they would believe everything that is written or said about or by a candidate, and have them explain their reasoning. Explain to students that it is important for voters to think critically about accusations made about or claims made by people running for office if voters are to cast their ballots intelligently. Tell students that in this section they will learn about some of the criticisms of campaigns, the possible effects of negative campaigning, and the benefits of political campaigns.

TEACH

Building a Vocabulary

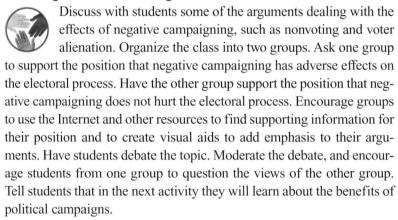

In their spiral notebooks, have students continue working on their Political Dictionary. List words the students will be expected to know for this section on the chalkboard. Have students list, define, and give an example of each of the terms, using information provided in the chapter or on the *Researcher CD-ROM*.

Demonstrating Understanding

Discuss with students that many people believe that the media plays too strong a role in political campaigns. Then, ask students to name the types of media that can influence a campaign (e.g., TV, radio, newspapers, magazines, the Internet). In an open class discussion ask students how these different forms of media are or can be used to promote or attack a candidate (e.g., testimonial, position statements, endorsements). Encourage students to discuss specific examples of the media either offering or discouraging support for a candidate. Remind students to think about these methods and their influence when choosing a candidate in the future. Finally, discuss with students whether these methods of promotion are assets or liabilities to the U.S. electoral process and why. Tell students that in the next activity they will learn about some of the possible effects that negative campaigning may have.

Debating Ideas/Conducting Research

Discuss with students some of the arguments dealing with the effects of negative campaigning, such as nonvoting and voter alienation. Organize the class into two groups. Ask one group to support the position that negative campaigning has adverse effects on the electoral process. Have the other group support the position that negative campaigning does not hurt the electoral process. Encourage groups to use the Internet and other resources to find supporting information for their position and to create visual aids to add emphasis to their arguments. Have students debate the topic. Moderate the debate, and encourage students from one group to question the views of the other group. Tell students that in the next activity they will learn about the benefits of political campaigns.

Analyzing Information

Tell students that although political campaigns are frequently criticized they do provide the benefits of encouraging debate and providing useful information about the candidates. Have students review articles in newspapers and magazines that deal with an election and to remember media coverage from previous elections. Have students write a short essay describing how the media either encouraged debate between the candidates (e.g., by pointing out that the candidates were dodging an issue) or provided information on a candidate (e.g., by uncovering a controversial fact about a candidate's background). Encourage students to share their examples with the rest of the class.

CLOSE

Encourage students to recall the criticisms of the media's role in election campaigns, the possible effects of negative campaigning, and the benefits of political campaigns discussed during this section. Have students evaluate these pros and cons to determine if the United States should maintain the system it currently uses. Have students write a paper offering either support for the current system or opposition to it. Encourage students to use examples to support their arguments. If students are in opposition to the current system, have them include suggestions for changing it in their papers. Encourage students to share their ideas with the rest of the class.

OPTIONS

Gifted Learners

 Assign students a specific presidential election to investigate. Have students research the top candidates in the election and the number of electoral votes they received. Students should then use outside resources to investigate any significant events during the campaign that may have altered the media's coverage of a candidate. They should then write a paper discussing whether or not they feel that the media's coverage of a candidate may have significantly altered the election. Students should offer support for their reasoning. Encourage students to share their research with the rest of the class.

Intrapersonal

Discuss with students the factors identified in the chapter as contributing to nonvoting. Have students write a descriptive essay describing their feelings about each of these factors and how these factors can have a negative influence on elections and on the United States. Encourage students to offer suggestions for eliminating these barriers to voter turnout. Discuss the plausibility of these ideas. Encourage students to share their ideas with the rest of the class.

REVIEW

Have students complete the Section 4 Review on page 450. Use the answers in the Annotated Teacher's Edition to assess student mastery of this section.

ASSESS

To assess student mastery of this section, have students complete Daily Quiz 19.4 in *Daily Quizzes with Answer Key*. For additional assessment options, see *Alternative Assessment Handbook* on the *One-Stop Planner CD-ROM*.

RETEACH

For students having difficulty with the lessons, have them complete Reteaching Activity 19. This activity is located in *Reteaching Activities with Answer Key*.

ADDITIONAL RESOURCES

Lewis, Michael. *Trail Fever: Spin Doctors, Rented Strangers, Thumb Wrestlers, Toe Suckers, Grizzly Bears, and Other Creatures on the Road to the White House*. 1997. Knopf.

The Media and Politics. At Issue series. 1996. Greenhaven.

Television and the Presidency (On the Air). 1984. Zenger Video. (video)

TOPICS INCLUDE

- ★ ways of nominating candidates
- ★ types of primary elections
- ★ candidate visibility
- ★ media involvement
- ★ polling
- ★ campaign financing
- ★ regulation of campaign financing
- ★ types of elections
- ★ administration of elections
- ★ voting requirements
- ★ voting behavior
- ★ criticisms of election campaigns
- ★ nonvoting
- ★ benefits of campaigns

GOVERNMENT NOTEBOOK

The Government Notebook is a journal activity that encourages students to consider basic concepts of government that relate to their lives. A follow-up notebook activity appears on page 452.

▶ WHY IT MATTERS TODAY

To find additional lesson plans dealing with the electoral process, visit CNNfyi.com or have students complete the GOVERNMENT IN THE NEWS Activity on page 451.

CNNfyi.com

THE ELECTORAL PROCESS

How are the candidates chosen for your school's student council elections? How do you choose from among the candidates? Do the candidates campaign for the student offices? What determines the winners of the elections?

More than likely, your class leaders are chosen in much the same way that U.S. political leaders are chosen by American citizens—through an established electoral process. In this chapter you will learn about the three steps in that process: nomination, campaigning, and election.

GOVERNMENT NOTEBOOK

In your Government Notebook, make a list of some of the times this school year that you and your friends or classmates have held a vote to decide a certain issue. On what kinds of things do you generally hold a vote? Explain why voting is an important part of making a decision about an issue.

▶ WHY IT MATTERS TODAY

The electoral process allows Americans to choose who will lead their government. At the end of this chapter visit CNNfyi.com to learn more about the electoral process.

CNNfyi.com

SECTION 1

NOMINATING CANDIDATES

READ TO DISCOVER

1. What is the first step in the electoral process?
2. In what ways may candidates be chosen for an election?
3. What types of primary elections are held in the states?

POLITICAL DICTIONARY

direct primary
closed primary
open primary
runoff primary
nonpartisan primary

When casting your vote during an election, you most likely choose from among the candidates listed. But how are the official candidates for an election selected?

As noted in Chapter 7, nominating candidates is the first step in the electoral process. Nomination procedures vary according to local, state, and national election rules. Candidates are nominated in five ways:

★ self-announcement,
★ caucus,
★ convention,
★ petition, and
★ primary election.

Self-Announcement

To nominate by self-announcement, a person simply declares publicly that he or she is running for office. Commonly practiced in the American colonies, this procedure is the oldest means of nomination in the United States.

Today, self-announcement is used most often at the local level. By announcing his or her candidacy,

a person enters the race for office, though there is usually some kind of officially required registration procedure as well.

In some cases a candidate at the national or state level might use self-announcement if he or she is unlikely to secure the nomination of either of the major parties or does not agree with the policies they support. For example, during the 1992 election Ross Perot declared himself an independent candidate for the presidency.

Most ballots are printed with a space for write-in candidates. A write-in candidate is a person who declares that he or she will run for office and then asks people to write his or her name on the ballot when they vote. In states whose official ballots do not provide such a space, voters can request a special ballot to vote for a write-in candidate. Write-in candidates usually fail to achieve a broad base of support and thus rarely, if ever, win.

Caucus

As noted in Chapter 7, the caucus is another long-standing means of nominating candidates in America. The earliest caucuses in what is now the United States date from around 1725. Community

POLITICAL PROCESSES *Most states stopped using caucuses as a means of nominating state and U.S. legislators by the mid-1800s.* **When were the first caucuses held in what is now the United States?**

Transparency

An overhead transparency of the cartoon on this page is available in *Transparency Resources.* See Cartoon Transparency 19: The Electoral Process.

Caption Answer

They stopped because of the corruption that was associated with conventions.

---

would gather in a home or an official town building to endorse candidates for local offices. Such groups were called caucus clubs. In his diary John Adams described an early caucus:

❝ This day learned that the Caucus Club meets, at certain times, in the garret [top-floor room] of Tom Dawes. . . . He has a large house . . . and the whole club meets in one room. . . . There they choose a moderator, who puts questions to the vote regularly; and selectmen [council members], assessors, collectors, wardens, fire-wards, and representatives are regularly chosen before they are chosen in the town. ❞

Caucuses were held at the state and national levels as early as the 1790s. State legislative caucuses chose candidates for state and local office, while national congressional caucuses chose presidential and vice presidential candidates.

Eventually, as political parties developed, caucuses became functions of the parties and were run by party officials. The meetings, which were not open to the public, were dominated by party leaders. Abuses of the system were frequent, as party leaders used caucuses to further their own interests. Gradually, many voters began to criticize the closed-door caucus meetings.

Because of a rise in voter dissatisfaction, party leaders in most states stopped using the caucus for nominating candidates to the U.S. Congress by the 1820s and for nominating candidates to state office by the 1840s. Today the caucus is still used at the local level in a few states. Some states, including Iowa, still hold caucuses for national office as well. These caucuses, however, are open to all members of a party—not just to party leaders and influential members of the community.

Convention

As noted in Chapter 7, a convention is a political party gathering held to nominate candidates, set party rules, and create a party platform. By the mid- to late 1800s, party conventions were common at the local, state, and national levels. The delegations were made up of people representing their town, city, county, or state.

Delegates to local conventions chose local candidates as well as delegates to the state convention. In turn, the state convention delegates would choose candidates for state offices and delegates to the national convention. Delegates from each of the states then assembled at the national convention to choose the presidential and vice presidential candidates.

As with caucuses, conventions eventually were subject to political corruption and control by party bosses, who tried to seat delegates favorable to their views. For this reason many states eventually gave up the convention system for nominating candidates. Today only a few states hold state and local nominating conventions, and these are heavily regulated to prevent abuses. Other states hold conventions only to nominate delegates to the national conventions. The presidential and vice presidential candidates also are still officially chosen by a national convention.

Petition

Another way that candidates are nominated is by petition. Supporters of someone seeking elected office but lacking the endorsement of a major

POLITICAL PROCESSES *Some critics think that the electoral process has become too expensive and time-consuming for candidates.* ***Why did many states stop using the convention system for nominating candidates?***

Campaign Worker

Political campaign workers focus on winning elections. Their job description includes: press and public relations, polling, opposition research, fund-raising, logistical organizing, and a wide range of other skills, such as dealing with crisis management concerning the campaign. Large campaigns combine the skills of several specialists to develop an integrated campaign. Smaller campaigns may use one or two people, utilizing various skills for the same purpose.

Campaign workers John McConnell, right, and Carol Thompson celebrate George W. Bush's victory in the 2000 presidential election.

Pollsters and researchers may work behind the scenes, but press and public relations specialists always work with the media. Rubbing shoulders with the media is part of the job. A good public relation specialist may rise to the highest level, later becoming a campaign manager.

Many pollsters or researchers have educational training in statistics, whereas many campaign aides have backgrounds in journalism. This enables them to use their knowledge of the print and broadcast news media to their advantage.

Campaign workers may range from students to recent college graduates to seasoned veterans from the campaign trail. Candidates often look for people who have experience, education, or training in politics that might be useful to the campaign. Whatever their backgrounds, however, campaign staff members share a common passion for politics and the candidates and ideals for which they work.

---

political party can circulate a petition requesting that the person's name be placed on the official ballot. A nominating petition is only valid if it has been signed by a certain percentage of people registered to vote in the election district in question.

Nomination by petition is most common in local elections. It also is widely used by independent and third-party state and national candidates who have some support from eligible voters.

Primary Election

Today the primary election is the most common way for candidates to gain a nomination for political office. As noted in Chapter 7, primary elections are held before the general election in order to determine the candidates for each party. The primaries give voters, instead of party leaders, the chance to do the nominating.

Nominations for the House and Senate and for state and local office occur through direct primaries. A **direct primary** is one in which the winner is named the party's nominee for the general election. Presidential primaries are not direct—they are followed by a national convention at which slates of delegates elected in the primaries choose a candidate based on the results of the primaries.

Political parties do not determine the rules for primary elections. The states do, just as they regulate other features of party organization. The states not only decide who may vote; they also regulate what party organizations may or may not

Careers in Government

To help students learn about other careers in government, refer them to the Careers section on the *Holt Researcher Online.*

THEMES IN GOVERNMENT

POLITICAL FOUNDATIONS
Robert M. La Follette decided to become a political reformer while serving in the House of Representatives. His decision was made when a Republican Party boss allegedly tried to bribe him.

La Follette, who won Wisconsin's race for governor as a Republican in 1900, proposed a direct primary law whereby popular elections rather than conventions run by party bosses would select party nominees.

This reform, which took effect in 1903, suited La Follette's political talents because those who opposed him were said to be more comfortable in the caucus room, while La Follette excelled when he could dramatize the issues to the public and thus generate grassroots support. Through his success with direct primaries, La Follette was able to lead the Republican Party in Wisconsin until his death in 1925. ∎

HISTORY Partly in opposition to President William Howard Taft's antitrust policy, Theodore Roosevelt announced in 1912 that he would run again for the Republican presidential nomination.

Roosevelt, who had been a popular Republican president, expected to receive more support for the Republican nomination, but Taft and his supporters held control of the national committee. With its affiliates, the committee controlled 254 contested seats at the Republican National Convention.

To gain leverage, Roosevelt's supporters tried passing legislation in some states that called for preferential primaries to be held for the nomination. In the end, only 13 states held preferential primaries, which gave 36 delegates to a third candidate, Robert M. La Follette; 48 to Taft; and 278 to Roosevelt. This made it appear that Roosevelt would win the nomination. But Taft's advantage with party leaders gave him 235 of 254 votes from the other states's delegates, which was enough to win the nomination. ■

Caption Answer
eight

---

do in primary campaigns. Each state also determines what kind of primary it will hold.

How much influence parties have on the outcome of primaries is also regulated by the states. In about one third of the states, party conventions are allowed to endorse primary candidates. In some states, only candidates running for a state office who receive a certain minimum percentage of the vote at a state party convention may appear on the primary ballot. In others, candidates endorsed by state party conventions appear first on the ballot or with asterisks next to their names. California and Florida go to the opposite extreme, prohibiting party conventions from backing primary candidates.

Closed Primary Fewer than 20 states have closed primaries. A **closed primary** is one in which only the members of a political party are permitted to vote in selecting the party's candidates. Under this system, separate but simultaneous primaries are held for both the Republican and Democratic Parties. Democrats wishing to vote Republican and Republicans wishing to vote Democrat must wait for a general election.

Many states with closed primaries, however, have more relaxed rules regarding party affiliation. On the day of the primary, citizens can register for

the party in whose nomination process they most want to participate.

Open Primary Most states have what are called open primaries. An **open primary** allows a registered voter to participate in either the Republican or Democratic nomination process just by choosing a party once he or she is in the voting booth. This means that a registered Republican, for example, may vote in a Democratic primary without giving up his or her Republican registration status. In some open primaries, voters may choose candidates from either party for each office open for election.

Runoff Primary Several states have a follow-up primary election if no candidate receives a majority of the votes. In these **runoff primaries**, voters choose between the top vote-getters from the first election. The winner of the runoff primary is then named the party's candidate for the general election.

Nonpartisan Primary A **nonpartisan primary** is one in which all candidates appear on the same ballot. In most cases these candidates are running for city- and county-level offices. For example,

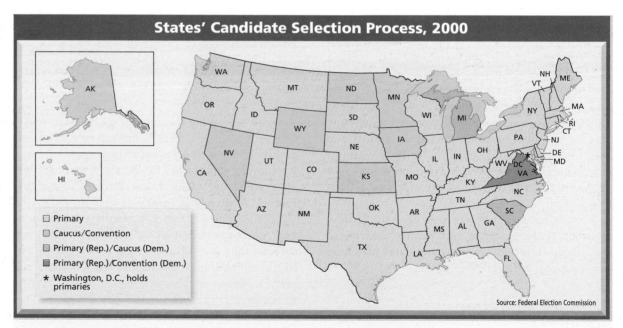

States' Candidate Selection Process, 2000

- ☐ Primary
- ☐ Caucus/Convention
- ☐ Primary (Rep.)/Caucus (Dem.)
- ☐ Primary (Rep.)/Convention (Dem.)
- ★ Washington, D.C., holds primaries

Source: Federal Election Commission

Primary elections are the most common way for candidates to gain nomination for political office. Several states, however, use other methods. **How many states use the caucus/convention system to nominate candidates?**

Citizenship in Action

Taking Part in Democracy

In a democracy such as the United States, citizens have many opportunities to get involved in the electoral process. In addition to debating issues, learning about candidates, and voting, they may choose to volunteer for campaign work. In fact, most successful campaigns might have failed were it not for the dedicated work of volunteers who kept the office operating smoothly, helped get out the vote, and provided other support for candidates and paid staff.

Some people choose to become directly involved in the electoral process by serving as delegates to party conventions. In some states, citizens attend precinct conventions to debate issues and support particular candidates. Citizens also work to become convention delegates at county, district, state, and national levels.

Jo Ann Strickler ran her own campaign to become a delegate to the 1992 Republican National Convention. Strickler, then a 22-year-old senior at Virginia Tech University, attended local county meetings, handed out buttons and signs, shook a lot of hands at the district convention, and organized a network of volunteers to help in her campaign. Her work paid off and she became one of her state's national convention delegates.

In 1992 Marc Glenn, then an 18-year-old high school graduate from Atlanta, worked hard to become a delegate to the Democratic National Convention. "The most interesting thing that I learned was that once I decided to get involved, it was relatively easy to become an active part of the American political system," Glenn says.

Dwayne C. Houston has been active in politics since his sophomore year at North Carolina Central University in Durham. After graduating in 1994, he entered the District of Columbia Law School. In 1996, at 23, Dwayne served as a page at the Democratic National Convention in Chicago. He also worked as a staff member for a candidate seeking the at-large City Council seat for the District of Columbia. By January 1999, his political ambitions resulted in his election to his first full term as the national committeeperson for the District of Columbia Young Democrats.

Strickler, Glenn, and Houston represent just three of the thousands of young people who take part in our nation's political process at various levels and in various roles. Others may attend debates or campaign rallies. Still others volunteer to work as clerks at polling places, or to transport people to vote, or to plan small gatherings in their homes where candidates can explain their positions on important issues.

Both major political parties offer opportunities for young people to get involved in the political process and to lend support to candidates running for political office whose views they share. In particular, the Young Republicans and Young Democrats specialize in this area. These organizations have local chapters across the country.

Tom Santaniello was 17 years old when he was selected as a delegate to the 2000 Democratic National Convention in Los Angeles.

What Do You Think?

1. Do you think it is important for citizens to get involved in the electoral process?
2. In what ways could you and your classmates become involved in the electoral process?

What Do You Think? Answers

1. Answers will vary, but students should discuss the importance of citizen involvement in the electoral process and should offer examples of how such involvement helps make people informed voters.

2. Answers will vary, but students may discuss attending debates, expressing concerns to representatives, and supporting political candidates' campaigns.

THEMES IN GOVERNMENT

CITIZENSHIP Volunteer organizations offer a variety of ways to get involved in the political process. Common Cause, for example, is a nonprofit organization committed to promoting government efficiency and honesty. The organization's main concerns are campaign finance reform and stronger ethics in government. Common Cause offers college students the chance to participate in the political process as interns, researchers, grassroots organizers, congressional monitors, magazine staff, and liaisons between the national office and local activists. ■

SECTION 1 REVIEW ANSWERS

1. Refer to the following pages: direct primary (431), closed primary (432), open primary (432), runoff primary (432), nonpartisan primary (432).

2. direct—winner named the party nominee for the general election; closed—only party members are permitted to vote; open—registered voters can vote in either party's primary without losing their previous party affiliation; runoff—second election in which voters choose between top vote-getters from the first election; nonpartisan—voters can choose someone from either party for office

3a. by self-announcement, caucus, convention, petition, primary election

3b. Candidates may need a certain percentage of the vote at a state party convention to run in the primary. Endorsed candidates may be required to appear first on the primary ballot.

4. Answers will vary but should reflect knowledge of the various methods of filling public offices.

Calvin and Hobbes
by Bill Watterson

WHEN I GROW UP, I'M NOT GOING TO READ THE NEWSPAPER AND I'M NOT GOING TO FOLLOW COMPLEX ISSUES AND I'M NOT GOING TO VOTE.

THAT WAY I CAN COMPLAIN THAT THE GOVERNMENT DOESN'T REPRESENT ME.

THEN, WHEN EVERYTHING GOES DOWN THE TUBES, I CAN SAY THE SYSTEM DOESN'T WORK AND JUSTIFY MY FURTHER LACK OF PARTICIPATION.

AN INGENIOUSLY SELF-FULFILLING PLAN.

IT'S A LOT MORE FUN TO BLAME THINGS THAN TO FIX THEM.

PUBLIC GOOD *Typically around half of the voting-age population does not vote in general elections.*
Is voter turnout usually greater for primary elections or general elections?

candidates for a local judgeship in some states must receive a nomination in a nonpartisan primary before being placed on a general election ballot.

In some states a candidate who receives the majority of the votes cast in a nonpartisan primary is automatically elected and does not have to run in the general election. If no one wins a majority in the primary, however, its two top vote-getters appear on the general election ballot.

Voter Turnout in Primaries

Turnout in primary elections is generally around one third to one half of that in the general election. Typically, a greater percentage of well-educated, upper-income voters participate in primaries. Some argue that primary voters also are ideologically more committed than voters in general elections—that Democratic primary voters are more liberal than Democratic voters and Republican primary voters more conservative than Republican voters in general. However, evidence gathered by political scientists does not consistently support this proposition. Sometimes primary voters are more extreme, other times not. Factors such as the economic situation might be more likely to inspire someone to vote in a primary than would his or her political ideology.

SECTION 1 REVIEW

1. Identify and explain:
- direct primary
- closed primary
- open primary
- runoff primary
- nonpartisan primary

2. Identifying Concepts:
Copy the chart below. Use it to identify and define the various types of primary elections.

Primary elections

3. **Finding the Main Idea**

a. What are the ways in which citizens can choose candidates to fill public offices?

b. What are some of the regulations states place on primary elections?

4. **Writing and Critical Thinking**

Comparing: Imagine that a new state is being admitted to the United States. How do you think local and state offices should be filled? Write an editorial expressing your point of view.

Consider the following:
- the various methods of filling public offices
- the benefits and drawbacks of elections and appointment

Homework Practice Online
keyword: SV3 HP19

SECTION 2

CAMPAIGNS AND CAMPAIGN FINANCING

READ TO DISCOVER

1. How was early political campaigning different from political campaigning today?
2. What is the role of the media in today's political campaigns?
3. How are campaigns financed?
4. How is campaign financing regulated?

Once candidates have been nominated, the second step in the electoral process—campaigning—begins. The fanfare surrounding political campaigns has been around for almost as long as the country itself. For example, during the 1800s supporters of both the Republicans and Democrats campaigned around the clock to promote their candidates. By day they marched with banners bearing candidates' slogans. At night they often held torchlight parades.

Why do people engage in such extravagant displays? Holding elected office is a high honor in the United States. Candidates must mount elaborate campaigns to convince the electorate that they are right for the job.

Though the reason for campaigning has not changed, the way campaigns are conducted has changed greatly since the 1700s and 1800s. During the 1900s, campaigns changed in three major ways:

★ candidates became more visible,
★ the role of the media became more pronounced, and
★ polling became a key tool.

In addition, campaign spending has skyrocketed to cover increasingly extensive campaigning.

Candidate Visibility

During the 1700s and early to mid-1800s, candidates, particularly those running for president,

were expected to maintain proper form during their campaigns. The political journal *The Nation* described what was generally considered appropriate behavior for a candidate:

66 Etiquette requires that the candidate shall rigidly abstain [keep] from any open efforts to promote his own election, and, indeed, from all discoverable complicity [participation] in such efforts on the part of others. Rigid propriety [properness] . . . seems even to require that he shall preserve complete silence during the [campaign] on all topics of the day, and the summit of dignity and decorum [good form] is only reached by a display of apparent ignorance that any [campaign] is going on, or if going on that he has any particular connection with it. 99

Gradually, as the nation grew, this attitude began to change. In 1896 Democratic presidential

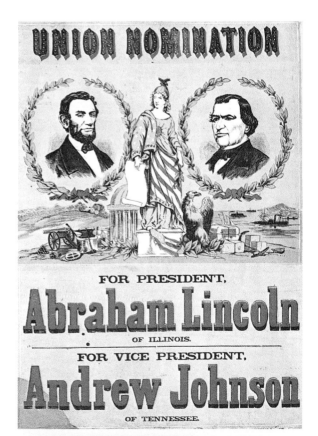

FOUNDATIONS OF DEMOCRACY *The poster above is from Lincoln's 1864 presidential campaign.* **Why do candidates engage in elaborate campaigns during an election year?**

Lesson Plans

For teaching strategies, see Lesson 19.2 located at the beginning of this chapter or the One-Stop Lesson Planner Strategy 19.2.

Section Assessment

To assess students' mastery of this section, have them complete Daily Quiz 19.2 in *Daily Quizzes with Answer Key*.

ACROSS THE CURRICULUM

PSYCHOLOGY Much of the debate over ratification of the Constitution centered on the distribution of powers and whether ambition would turn officeholders into tyrants. In the eighteenth and early nineteenth centuries, ambition was considered an undesirable trait, denoting a desire for rank and power. Thus, to avoid appearing ambitious, presidential candidates avoided participating in arguments over nomination. ■

Caption Answer

They hope to convince voters that they are right for the job.

candidate William Jennings Bryan undertook an unprecedented nationwide tour, giving rousing speeches along the way. A new trend in campaigning had begun.

Campaign Appearances By the first part of the 1900s, presidential candidates were engaging in stunts unheard of only a few years earlier. Woodrow Wilson, for example, got public attention by attending the yearly baby parade in Asbury Park, New Jersey. In 1924 Democratic presidential candidate John W. Davis tried to make points with voters by throwing a pitch to his vice presidential running mate at a baseball game.

Candidates toured large sections of the country by train in what became known as whistle-stop campaigning. While stopping along the way in small towns, candidates would address voters from the rear platform of a train. ("Whistle-stop" was a nickname that railroad workers gave to a town so small that the train stopped there only long enough for the whistle to blow.) According to some observers at the time, Harry Truman won the presidency in 1948 partly because of a vigorous whistle-stop campaign.

Campaigning in Person Today Campaigning today is a grueling activity that calls for constant travel, speaking, and handshaking. Candidates, particularly those running for president, often spend weeks away from home, traveling from city to city. It can be exhausting—most candidates catch very little sleep, especially during the intense campaigning right before an election. In the final week of the 1996 presidential campaign, for example, Bob Dole stayed up for 96 hours straight to speak at as many campaign rallies as possible before the election. Bill Clinton traveled the country by plane, train, and bus in the 1992 and 1996 campaigns, greeting supporters along the way.

Media Involvement

The early 1900s also brought a greater use of the media in promoting candidates. Presidential campaign organizations began pouring major resources into what were called literary bureaus, working units that generated literature and speeches, explored important issues, and maintained press relations.

With the introduction of new technology, campaigns could rely on not only print but also radio,

PUBLIC GOOD *During his 1952 presidential campaign, Dwight Eisenhower traveled to Mount Holyoke College to meet with students.* **Which presidential candidate of the late 1800s helped to change people's attitudes about campaigns?**

film, and television. When Woodrow Wilson ran for president in 1912, for example, his campaign team produced news reels and recordings about him. Radio and television have become very popular means of advertising in political campaigns.

Early Campaign Advertising Presidential candidates first used television advertising during the 1952 campaign. Dwight D. Eisenhower ran 30- and 60-second political ads, hoping that they would capture viewers' interest much like commercials for household goods, cars, and other products did. In contrast, Adlai Stevenson—Eisenhower's opponent—took a more traditional approach: he simply used television to air half-hour speeches. Unlike Eisenhower's shorter spots, these speeches failed to take advantage of a key feature of television—its ability to quickly and dramatically convey simple ideas and a sense of personality.

Media Campaigning Today Today presidential and senatorial campaigns are conducted largely through the media. The reason is simple: it is far easier to reach millions of voters through media messages than in person. A candidate for national or statewide office can never hope to meet or speak before more than a tiny fraction of a large state's voters, even during an extensive campaign. As political consultant Frank Luntz noted in 1988, "If the two Senate candidates in Florida . . . made ten speeches a day to audiences of 100 persons, it would take eight years to reach every voter."

Because the use of the media increases a candidate's reach, it has become a central campaign strategy. Political media consultants carefully tailor radio and television ads for targeted audiences and plan events whose primary purpose is to gain the candidate coverage on the evening news. In fact, candidates spend an increasing amount of time appearing at events that are staged solely for coverage by the media.

Polling

Polling also became a popular tool of political campaigns during the 1900s. As noted in Chapter 16, polling involves surveying a population on an issue. A major goal of campaign polling is to gain insight into voters' attitudes about a candidate's campaign and views.

For example, suppose that a campaign worker asks voters who oppose Senator Chen a series of questions, such as "Would learning that Senator Chen supports cuts in Social Security benefits lead you to vote for him?" By finding out which of his or her views generate the most voter support, a candidate can create a more effective campaign.

Campaign Financing

Today's extensive campaigns have become very expensive. Bumper stickers, campaign appearances, yard signs, direct mail, buttons, flyers, and above all, television advertising are just some of the campaign tools on which candidates spend money. During the 2000 presidential race the campaigns for George W. Bush and Al Gore spent over $143 million on advertising.

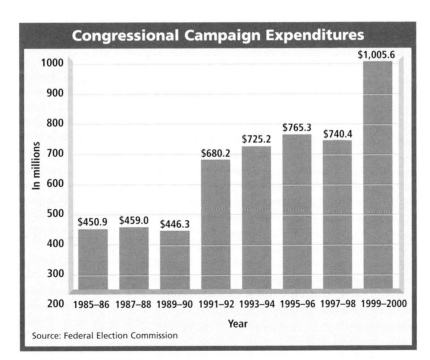

Congressional Campaign Expenditures

In millions

Year	Amount
1985–86	$450.9
1987–88	$459.0
1989–90	$446.3
1991–92	$680.2
1993–94	$725.2
1995–96	$765.3
1997–98	$740.4
1999–2000	$1,005.6

Source: Federal Election Commission

The amount of money spent on political campaigns increases each year to keep up with the rising costs of financing a campaign. **How much money was spent on political campaigns in 1991–92?**

ACROSS THE CURRICULUM

TECHNOLOGY As a politician in Arkansas, Bill Clinton used to stop at Harvey's, a country store near Chester, Arkansas, every two years when he was running for governor. He stopped at Geno's, a blue-collar restaurant in Philadelphia, when he ran for president in 1992. During his 1996 whistle-stop tour he paused at renovated little depots that resembled Norman Rockwell paintings. For each of these visits the backdrop was carefully planned. In Chester, cameras showed him as one of the folks; in Philadelphia, they saw him as having ties to the working people. The whistle-stop scenes are said to have made people feel good about Clinton.

Media experts say that campaigning all comes down to the candidate's image, and that in an era when marketing is crucial, the details cannot be taken for granted. They also claim that voters expect, and in fact do not mind, some gimmicks. ■

Transparency
An overhead transparency of the chart on this page is available in *Transparency Resources.* See Transparency 40: Congressional Campaign Expenditures.

Caption Answer
$680.2 million

As you can see, campaigning today requires huge sums of money. This is particularly true for a candidate challenging an incumbent—a person who already holds the elective office. How can a candidate raise this money? Political parties, political action committees, private donors, and the government supply most of the needed campaign funds. In addition, some candidates spend their own money on their campaigns.

Party Assistance As noted in Chapter 18, one duty of political parties is to raise funds for candidates and their campaigns. Parties do not give equally to all candidates. Rather, they concentrate most of their funds on helping those in the closest races. National party organizations, for example, generally give the most to strong challengers facing incumbent members of Congress or to candidates running for open seats, where the incumbent is not running for re-election.

Political Action Committees Also as noted in Chapter 18, political action committees (PACs) give funds to political parties and their candidates. A PAC contributes money to campaigns in hopes that a candidate who takes office will support the PAC's agenda.

Private Donors Private donors to campaigns vary greatly in their resources and their goals. Some give $5 to a single candidate, while others give thousands of dollars to several candidates. In some cases, wealthy people who give a great deal of money to a campaign may be hoping to influence the candidate's decisions if he or she is elected. In most cases, however, people are just trying to support a candidate who represents their views.

Public Funding Government in some instances provides public money for campaigns, though in limited amounts. Public funding occurs at both the state and the national level. Only presidential and vice presidential candidates receive public funds at the national level, however, and they must follow established fund-raising guidelines.

Personal Financing Some candidates, particularly those running for state or local office, use money out of their own pockets to finance their campaigns. In 2001 New York billionaire Michael Bloomberg spent about $69 million of his own money on his New York City mayoral campaign.

Regulation of Campaign Financing

With such large amounts of money changing hands during political campaigns, regulations are needed to make sure that funds are handled properly. These regulations were laid down in the Federal Election Campaign Act of 1972, which has since been amended several times. This act is enforced by the Federal Election Commission (FEC). Regulations that campaigns must follow include financial disclosure, contribution and spending limits, and donor restrictions.

Financial Disclosure Campaign committees are required by law to submit extensive financial reports explaining how much money they have raised and how it was spent. In federal elections these reports are submitted to Congress and the FEC. In state and local elections they are sent to the appropriate state officials. These reports enable officials to make sure that the money is being spent only for legitimate campaign purposes and that candidates do not receive any improper contributions.

Contribution Limits Contributions to a federal candidate's campaign, whether for a primary or general election, are limited to $1,000 for an individual and $1,000 or $5,000 for an organization such as a PAC. Organizations able to contribute as much as $5,000 must have at least 50 contributors, have been registered with the FEC for six months, and contribute to five or more candidates in the election at hand. In addition, an individual can give no more than $5,000 a year to a PAC and no more than $20,000 a year to a political party. Individuals can contribute no more than $25,000 overall in a given year, though PACs have no such limit. An important loophole in these restrictions is the ability to donate unlimited amounts of "soft money"— money that is given in support of a party that may not be used for specific candidates.

Contribution limits are established to prevent any one person or organization from gaining too much influence over candidates, and therefore over government. A person or an organization able to contribute vast amounts to a candidate or party might be able to influence elected officials to promote the interests of a few at the expense of the public good.

PUBLIC GOOD *Senators John McCain and Ross Feingold walk with campaign finance reform activist Doris Maddock.* **In the 2000 presidential primaries, what was the spending limit for candidates who received matching funds?**

Spending Limits Presidential candidates can receive federal funds if they meet certain requirements, including staying within set spending limits. In a presidential primary campaign, candidates may receive federal funds if they raise $5,000 or more in each of at least 20 states. The federal government matches funds for the first $250 of each contribution received. For example, if a candidate receives two contributions, one for $100 and one for $1,000, he or she would get $350 in matching funds. The federal government does not match PAC or political party donations. The spending limit for candidates receiving matching funds in the 2000 primary campaign was $40.5 million.

A candidate who wins a party's nomination is eligible for public funds for the general election campaign as well. Major-party candidates may not accept private contributions, however, if they receive public funding. A spending limit also applies to the general election campaign—for the 2000 election the limit was set at $67.6 million. The limits are adjusted for inflation. If a presidential candidate does not accept public funds, he or she is not bound by campaign spending restrictions.

Public funding is financed exclusively by a voluntary "check-off" on individual income tax returns, where taxpayers may indicate that $3 of their taxes be set aside for this purpose. (This donation does not increase someone's total tax bill.)

Unlike presidential campaigns, no spending limits have been set for congressional races. Congressional candidates, however, do not receive any public funding.

Donor Restrictions Several restrictions exist on the source of donations to an election campaign. Corporations are forbidden to give money directly, as are labor unions and government contractors. Corporations and other organizations, however, have been able to sidestep this restriction. They donate money to the PACs representing their industries, and the PACs are allowed to spend money on campaigns.

Finally, no campaign may accept donations from a foreign source. During the 1996 presidential election, the Democratic Party came under fire for accepting money from foreign sources. The questionable donations were returned, but led Congress to undertake a broad investigation of political fund-raising practices.

Caption Answer

The spending limit was $40.5 million.

SECTION 2 REVIEW ANSWERS

1. party assistance, political action committees, private donors, public funding, personal financing

2a. Early candidates did not promote their own election, relied only on print, and did not use polling. These became common practices in the 1900s.

2b. It led them to campaign personally and to rely on the media to reach more voters.

3. Answers will vary but students should clearly state their opinions and explain their reasoning.

SECTION 2 REVIEW

1. Identifying Concepts: Copy the chart below. Use it to identify the various sources of campaign financing.

Sources of Financing

Homework Practice Online
go.hrw.com
keyword: SV3 HP19

2. **Finding the Main Idea**

a. How were political campaigns in the late 1700s and 1800s different from campaigns in the 1900s?

b. How did the growth of the nation and changes in technology contribute to changes in the behavior of candidates?

3. **Writing and Critical Thinking**

Contrasting: How have leaders at the state and national level changed over the years? Write a paragraph explaining your answer.
Consider the following:
• the characteristics, style, and effectiveness of past leaders
• the characteristics, style, and effectiveness of present-day leaders

SECTION 3

ELECTIONS AND VOTING

READ TO DISCOVER

1. What are the different types of elections?
2. What determines where, how, and when people vote?
3. What factors determine if a person may vote?
4. What influences the way in which people vote?

POLITICAL DICTIONARY

single-member district
secret ballot
absentee ballot
suffrage

Campaigns run right into the final step of the electoral process—the election itself. Even on the day of the election, candidates and their workers continue to hand out flyers, call voters, make appearances, and run advertisements. State laws, however, regulate campaigning on election day as well as throughout the election. Laws made by the states and the federal government also determine the types of elections that may be held, how elections are administered, and who can vote.

Types of Elections

Besides primary elections, in which voters nominate candidates, there are two main types of elections. These are general elections and special elections.

General Elections As you have learned, U.S. citizens elect their local, state, and national leaders in general elections. The majority of these elections take place in **single-member districts**—electoral districts in which only one candidate can win election to a particular office. For example, in a city, several people from a particular ward or precinct might run for a place on the city council. Only one of the candidates, however, may be elected to the position.

In almost all single-member district elections, the candidate who receives a plurality of the votes is the winner. As noted in Chapter 7, a plurality is the largest number of votes received by a candidate in an election. Whereas races with only two major candidates are decided by a majority, races that typically have more than two candidates are decided by a plurality.

General elections are held on specific days determined by state or federal law. The winner of a general election takes office when the current officeholder's term expires.

Special Elections In addition to general elections, special elections are sometimes called at the state or local level to make a decision by popular vote. Such decisions include whether to institute a tax increase and whom to put into office to replace an official who has died or resigned before the end of his or her term. In some cases, special elections are called to give voters the opportunity to remove an elected official from office. (This process is more fully explained in Chapter 20.)

POLITICAL PROCESSES *George W. Bush and Dick Cheney, with their wives, at their inauguration in January 2001.* **When does the winner of the general election take office?**

Administration of Elections

What determines the types of elections that will be held? Local, state, and federal laws decide not only the types of elections but also when and how they are conducted.

When Elections Are Held

Congressional elections take place every even-numbered year. Congress determined that congressional and presidential elections will both be held on the first Tuesday following the first Monday in November. Presidential elections are held every four years.

The states set the dates for state and local elections. All states but Louisiana hold their statewide elections on the same date as that for federal elections. Several states, however, hold their elections on the first Tuesday after the first Monday in November in *odd*-numbered years. More than half of the states hold elections at the local level on the same date as that for federal elections. A few states hold these elections in other months.

How Elections Are Conducted

On election day, citizens go to their precinct's polling place—or voting site—to vote. Generally, two election judges, or inspectors, and several clerks oversee the election. These officials verify that each voter's name appears on the list of officially registered voters and then either distribute blank ballots or show voters to a voting machine.

Origins of the Ballot System

The United States has not always had the kind of ballot system. Citizens indicated their votes verbally at a public meeting, and their selections were recorded. Later, officials set rules dictating that ballots be printed for elections. However, each political party printed its own ballots. Because these ballots typically differed in size and shape according to party, anyone could tell at a glance for which party's candidates a citizen was voting. This system led to corrupt voting practices, as each political party could pressure voters into choosing its candidates.

Secret Ballot

The ballot system changed in 1888 with the introduction of the secret ballot. Also called the Australian ballot because it originated in Australia, the **secret ballot** allows voters to choose candidates in private. After stepping into a private voting booth, voters can record their votes on a paper ballot or by means of a voting machine.

Absentee Ballot

A person who is seriously ill or unable to go to the polls for some reason can vote by absentee ballot. An **absentee ballot** is a ballot requested by a voter prior to election day. The voter fills out this ballot and mails it in by a certain date. The main use of absentee balloting is by people in the military who are not living in their home district.

PRINCIPLES OF DEMOCRACY *In 2000 Republican Pete Sessions defeated Democrat Regina Montoya Coggins for the congressional seat in Texas's 5th district.* **How often do congressional elections take place?**

After the Fourteenth and Fifteenth Amendments were ratified, southern Democrats tried to find ways to take away blacks' political power, especially since African Americans tended to vote Republican.

Black voters who tried to reach distant polling places sometimes found roads blocked or ferries out of service on election days. Locations were changed without notifying African American voters, or those voters would be notified that a location changed when it really had not. Furthermore, because election laws were vague, many communities were able to avoid requiring uniform ballots. Thus, officials looked the other way as white Democrats cast extra ballots along with their original vote.

Ballot box stuffing was so widespread that one Democrat remarked that while black and white Republicans might outvote the Democrats, the Democrats could certainly outcount both groups. ∎

Caption Answer

They located polling places far from where African Americans lived, drew unfair voting districts, and required blacks to pay poll taxes and pass literacy tests.

Voting by Mail In a few states, such as Oregon, certain types of elections are conducted through the mail. Citizens receive their ballots in the mail, fill them out, and then mail them back to election officials.

Voting by mail has both pros and cons. On the up side, more people tend to vote in an election if they do not have to go to a polling place. Voting by mail might also reduce costs and streamline the voting process. This method does, however, raise the possibility that someone might tamper with the ballots. People might also mistake the ballots for junk mail and throw them away without realizing what they are. In addition, because some voters do not maintain permanent mailing addresses, not all ballots will reach their desired destinations.

Contested Elections Sometimes, once the ballots have been counted and the results are announced, someone challenges, or contests, the results of the election. For example, a candidate might contest an election if he or she suspects that the votes were miscounted or that the election was conducted improperly. A dispute over an election may be settled in court or by a legislature. In some cases the votes may be recounted.

Voting Requirements

Today, laws regarding who can vote are based on factors such as age, citizenship, residence, and registration status. This has not always been the case, however. At different times in U.S. history, people's **suffrage**, or right to vote, was restricted according to their ownership of property or their ability to pay a poll tax, as well as their race or sex.

Property and Tax Requirements When the Constitution was adopted, all 13 states had laws declaring that in order to vote, a person must own property. Political leaders thought that people had to have a stake in society, or concern for their property, to make wise choices about how the country should be governed. In addition, most states required that eligible citizens pay a poll tax—money paid to cast a ballot—before they could vote. Thus, voting in the late 1700s was restricted to fewer than one fourth of all adult white males.

During a period of political reform in the early 1800s, many states dropped their property requirements. In fact, by 1843, all states had removed all property requirements for voting, allowing almost all of the adult white male population to vote.

African Americans' Right to Vote Laws limiting suffrage to adult white males lasted until several years after the Civil War. Then, in 1870, the Fifteenth Amendment was passed, guaranteeing African American males the right to vote. However, white-run state governments, mostly in the South, made it increasingly difficult for blacks to participate in politics.

Southern leaders typically located polling places far away from where African Americans lived, drew election districts to prevent black majorities, created literacy tests that many blacks could not pass, and in many instances required voters to pay poll taxes. Legal loopholes allowed most adult white males to vote without passing such tests or paying poll taxes. Blacks who opposed the unfair restrictions placed on them were subject to harassment or worse by

CONSTITUTIONAL GOVERNMENT *African American males were guaranteed the vote with the passage of the Fifteenth Amendment.* **In what ways did some states make it difficult for blacks to vote despite the guarantees of the Fifteenth Amendment?**

CONSTITUTIONAL GOVERNMENT *Women parade through New York City in 1917 carrying a sign quoting President Woodrow Wilson's support of the suffrage movement.*
Which constitutional amendment guaranteed women the right to vote?

white supremacist groups such as the Ku Klux Klan. As noted in Chapter 15, barriers to black voting were not overcome until the civil rights movement of the 1950s and 1960s.

Women's Suffrage Women also were denied the right to vote for much of U.S. history. The movement for women's voting rights gained force after the Civil War. Supporters of women's suffrage, including Susan B. Anthony and Elizabeth Cady Stanton, organized parades, demonstrations, and protests to bring attention to the issue. These supporters often were criticized, arrested, and even imprisoned for their actions. Their opponents believed that women had no business being involved in politics and that they were not educated enough to vote.

During the late 1800s the Idaho and Colorado state constitutions were amended to give women the vote. By that time, Wyoming and Utah had already written women's suffrage into their territorial constitutions. These victories had little effect on the status of women's voting rights in the rest of the country, however. In 1911 an intense campaign for women's suffrage in California narrowly resulted in an amendment to that state's constitution. Many people, however, continued to push for an amendment to the U.S. Constitution.

In 1918 President Woodrow Wilson announced his support of the proposed Nineteenth Amendment to guarantee women's suffrage. A year later Congress passed the amendment. It was ratified by the required number of states in 1920.

Voting Requirements Today

Today voting requirements are based on four factors. These are

★ age,
★ citizenship,
★ residence, and
★ registration status.

Age Until 1971 all but four states (Alaska, Georgia, Hawaii, and Kentucky) set the minimum voting age at 21. During the 1960s, many people had argued to change the voting age. They said that if 18-year-olds could legally marry, as well as be drafted to serve in the armed forces, they should be allowed to vote as well.

WORLD AFFAIRS In Bosnia and Herzegovina, local elections held in 1997 reflected the war-torn country's ethnic divisions. Indeed, voters tended to see the elections as a chance to reclaim a territory or lay claim to a particular municipality for their ethnic group.

In Jajce—a town that had a population consisting of Croats, Serbs, and Muslims before the civil war in Bosnia—Croats began celebrating victory even before the election was held. Many Muslims had fled the town during a Serb occupation, and after Croat military forces reclaimed it, they refused to allow the Muslims to return.

Serb residents returned to another city to reclaim it with their votes. Croat officials slowed the registration process to discourage the voters, but Serb voters were willing to wait.

In Srebrenica, Muslims were expected to win a majority even though no Muslims lived there at the time of the elections. There and in other cities, displaced persons voted by absentee ballot. In fact, in eight municipalities, displaced candidates were expected to win, resulting in local governments being in exile. ■

Caption Answer

If registration is convenient, more people may vote.

In 1970 Congress passed a bill lowering the voting age to 18, but the Supreme Court ruled that the law was constitutional only for federal elections. Congress then proposed a constitutional amendment—the Twenty-sixth Amendment—establishing the voting age at 18. The amendment was quickly ratified and applies to *all* elections. In addition, some states allow 17-year-olds to register and vote in primary elections if they will turn 18 before the general election.

Citizenship All states have laws keeping non-citizens from taking part in elections. No voting laws, however, distinguish between native-born and naturalized citizens. On the other hand, many states do bar citizens convicted of serious crimes and those with serious mental illnesses from voting.

Residence Residency requirements for voting vary from state to state, but all states have them. The most common of these requirements says that a person must have been a legal resident in a state for at least 30 days to vote in its elections. Congress also determined in the Voting Rights Act of 1970 that 30 days' residence in a state was sufficient to allow people to vote in a presidential election.

Registration States do not allow any citizen to vote in elections unless he or she has registered. This requirement keeps citizens from voting twice. As voters come to cast their ballots, election workers officially record their names.

PUBLIC GOOD *The Motor Voter Law was passed to allow eligible voters to update their voter registration information in more convenient locations, such as at public assistance agencies. **How might this law encourage greater voter participation?***

To register, citizens fill out a form that provides information about themselves, such as their age and where they live. After the state checks to see that all voter eligibility requirements have been met, the person is registered.

Some states require that citizens reregister every few years. In most states a voter's registration remains valid unless he or she moves, dies, or does not vote in several consecutive elections.

CASE STUDY

Motor Voter Law

POLITICAL PROCESSES Many people have long argued that simplifying the voter registration process would encourage more citizens to go to the polls. In 1993 these citizens helped persuade Congress to pass and President Clinton to sign the National Voter Registration Act, which made it easier for people to register to vote.

The law, sometimes referred to as the Motor Voter Law, requires states to allow citizens to register to vote, or to update their registration information, when they apply for or renew their driver's licenses. In addition, the law requires that citizens be allowed to register at designated government agencies. These include public assistance agencies and agencies that provide services to people with disabilities. The law also states that citizens must be allowed to register by mail.

What impact has the law had thus far? In 1995, the first year it was implemented, more than 11 million citizens registered to vote or updated their voting addresses under the law. This marked the largest single increase in voter registration since the practice had begun. Young people were not forgotten in this movement. In 1996, arrangements were made so young people could register to vote at their local motor vehicle department.

Despite the new law, in 1996 it was reported that voter turnout declined by over 5 percentage points from 1992. After the 2000 presidential election, the Motor Voter law began to be

Party Identification of U.S. Voters

Year	Democrat	Republican	Independent/Apolitical
1970	54%	32%	14%
1972	52%	34%	14%
1980	52%	33%	15%
1984	48%	39%	13%
1988	47%	41%	13%
1990	52%	36%	12%
1992	50%	38%	13%
1994	47%	42%	12%
1996	52%	38%	10%
1998	51%	37%	13%
2000	50%	37%	13%

Source: National Election Studies, University of Michigan

The chart above shows party identification of U.S. voters during different periods. **In what year was the percentage of people identifying themselves as Democrats the largest?**

re-examined. At least 10 states sought to amend the law. One problem is that registering at motor vehicle bureaus and social service agencies can cause administrative mix-ups or possible fraud.

Critics say the Motor Voter law must change. Others seek change in Congress. But many feel that the Motor Voter law should not receive all the blame. "Generally, almost anything that goes wrong with voter registration anymore gets blamed on Motor Voter," says Gary McIntosh, Washington state's election director. Some states are also considering changes to same-day, Internet, and mail-in registration.

Voting Behavior

Now that you know how elections are conducted, you may be wondering why people vote the way they do. There are four main factors that influence the way people vote: party identification, personal opinions about the issues, a candidate's record and image, and the voter's personal background.

Party Identification Political party identification is one factor that influences how people vote. Some people absorb their family's political opinions and preferences as children. The party loyalties that are developed early in life may never change.

For others, however, party identification may change as they evaluate the performance of officeholders, or as they respond to certain events. Research now suggests that even voters who have supported one party for a long time may change their party loyalty if they are dissatisfied with their party's performance.

Yet other people choose not to back a particular political party. These people are called independents. (Independent voters are similar to independent candidates in an election. An independent candidate is one who does not represent a political party.) Research shows that the number of people who identify themselves as independents has risen significantly since the 1940s. According to statistics gathered by a series of National Election Studies, in 2000 about 13 percent of those polled identified themselves as independents.

Issues People's opinions on certain issues are another factor in how they vote. The issues that are "hot topics" change from decade to decade. Important issues of the 2000s, for example, include abortion rights and taxes. As you probably know, many citizens feel strongly about these two issues and their views about them can affect their party identification and choice of candidates.

Candidate's Record and Image A third factor influencing how people vote is a candidate's record and image. His or her past performance is particularly important. For example, in a presidential election, if people feel the country is headed on the right track, they are more likely to have a positive opinion of the incumbent candidate. If the economy is in a slump or unemployment has risen, however, voters are more likely to have a negative opinion of the incumbent.

Caption Answer

Voters would have the opportunity to evaluate the candidate's personality and character first-hand and might be convinced to vote for that candidate.

SECTION 3
REVIEW ANSWERS

1. Refer to the following pages: single-member district (440), secret ballot (441), absentee ballot (441), suffrage (441).

2. 1—citizens indicated their votes verbally; 2—ballots of differing shapes and sizes were used; 3—the secret ballot system was adopted in 1888.

3a. Restrictions were based on property ownership, ability to pay a poll tax, race, and sex.

3b. Voting requirements are based on age, citizenship, residence, and registration status.

4. Answers will vary but students should state their opinion and explain their reasoning.

PUBLIC GOOD *Typically, voters evaluate a candidate according to his or her personality and character.* **Why might a candidate believe that meeting with voters in person would help present a positive image?**

candidates according to a perception of their effectiveness, integrity, and leadership ability. In many cases a voter's feeling about the candidate's age and "style" also can affect his or her vote. A younger candidate might receive a greater number of votes from younger voters, for example.

Voter's Background

Studies of voting behavior show that a person's background is another important factor in how he or she votes. As noted in Chapter 16, people develop political opinions over the course of their lifetimes in a process called political socialization. People's individual backgrounds—their age, income, sex, race, education, and family beliefs—affect how they choose candidates. For example, people who have higher incomes may vote against a candidate who supports higher taxes for the middle to upper classes. Or, as noted above, younger voters might not support an older candidate if they feel he or she cannot relate to their concerns.

Voters in this situation are making their choices based on an overall evaluation of the state of the country rather than just focusing on the incumbent's positions on certain issues.

Research shows that voters' evaluations of a candidate's personality and character also are critical to voting decisions. Voters typically evaluate

SECTION 3 REVIEW

1. Identify and explain:
- single-member district
- secret ballot
- absentee ballot
- suffrage

2. Identifying Concepts: Copy the chart to the right. Use it to trace the development of the ballot system in the United States.

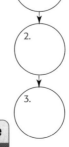

1.

2.

3.

3. **Finding the Main Idea**

a. How was suffrage limited in early U.S. history?

b. What voting requirements exist today?

4. **Writing and Critical Thinking**

Identifying Cause and Effect: How has government policy on voting rights affected American culture? Explain your answer.

Consider the following:
- past restrictions on voting
- the benefits of increased voter participation

 Homework Practice Online
keyword: SV3 HP19

READ TO DISCOVER

1. Why do some people criticize the media's role in campaigns?
2. What are the possible effects of negative campaigning?
3. What are some of the benefits of political campaigns?

As you have seen, elections serve an important role in U.S. government. By voting, citizens in effect give their opinions on how the country should be run and who should run it. Many critics, however, question the means by which candidates try to influence voters' opinions to win elections.

A campaign is meant not only to influence voters and get them more interested in an election but also to inform them about the candidate so that they can make educated choices. Critics believe, however, that campaigns' single-minded goal—to win—has led them to misinform more often than inform. In addition, many believe that this drive to win, along with registration requirements and the weakness of political parties, may reduce the level of voter turnout.

It can be argued, however, that campaigns bring issues to the attention of voters in a way that no other political events do. By presenting information about political issues in a format that will attract wide interest, campaigns promote the public good.

Criticisms of Election Campaigns

Campaigns are criticized chiefly for two reasons. First, many people believe that advertising in the media plays too strong a role in campaigns. Second, critics believe that there is too much negative campaigning in today's elections.

Role of Advertising in the Media Much of the criticism of the media's role in campaigns focuses on campaign advertising. In today's world of expensive airtime, campaigns choose to advertise most often in 30-second television and radio spots. How much substance, critics argue, can be communicated in a 30-second spot? A half-minute ad does not really argue a position; it only presents it. Furthermore, a commercial rarely gives a balanced account of what is involved in an issue.

Longer speeches allow for more substance, but they may lose some of the audience. A short spot, on the other hand, can make a point quickly without giving the viewer as much time to tune out. Many viewers, however, tuned in to watch a number of 30-minute infomercials, complete with charts and graphs that candidate Ross Perot ran to present his ideas in the 1992 presidential campaign. These segments differed a great deal from the typical spot format, and yet they received ratings that were competitive with regular network programs.

Negative Campaigning Negative campaigning is nothing new. Even during the country's early years, campaigns printed flyers and banners displaying the claimed faults of the opposing candidates. For example, during the election of 1796, Republicans in Pennsylvania supported

'...Political campaigns have become so simplistic and superficial ... In the 20 seconds we have left, could you explain why?...'

Courtesy of Clay Bennett, North America Syndicate.

PUBLIC GOOD *Some critics think that 30-second campaign ads do not contain much substance to help voters make an informed choice about a candidate.* **Why are long speeches not included in campaign advertisements?**

Lesson Plans
For teaching strategies, see Lesson 19.4 located at the beginning of this chapter or The One Stop Lesson Planner Strategy 19.4.

Section Assessment
To assess students' mastery of this section, have them complete Daily Quiz 19.4 in *Daily Quizzes with Answer Key.*

Transparency
An overhead transparency of the cartoon on this page is available in *Transparency Resources.* See Cartoon Transparency 22: The Way Media Cover Election Campaigns.

Caption Answer
Airtime is very expensive and candidates often lose some of the audience during long speeches.

PUBLIC GOOD Many people complain that the focus of political campaigns is too negative. But what preventive measures can be taken?

Here are some ideas to share with students that may help stop the negative focus of campaigns:

1) evaluate campaign advertising carefully to see if it is accurate;

2) praise candidates who have positive campaigns and protest campaigns that have a negative focus (both of these can be done by writing or calling);

3) speak out against candidates who use negative campaign techniques;

4) volunteer, and encourage your friends to volunteer, to work for candidates whose campaigns maintain a positive focus;

5) vote for, and encourage people you know to vote for, candidates who run positive campaigns. ■

Comparing
Governments

Media and Elections

Some people believe that the broadcast media, particularly television networks, should provide free airtime to political candidates. They think that this would make U.S. election campaigns more fair and more informative for voters.

Such is the case in Russia, where in the early 1990s the government passed a law requiring state-owned television and radio stations to provide one hour of free time each workday to political candidates. Government-subsidized mass media and mass media funded by public institutions must provide equal opportunities for candidates running for office in Russia's State Duma, or lower legislative branch. Political groups have the right to one appearance on state television and one on the state radio. These appearances are scheduled during the three weeks just before election day.

Although political groups each receive the same amount of free airtime, candidates and groups may purchase more. The fees for purchased time are regulated by the government to prevent bias. Even so, Russian political candidates continue to face the same problem of unequal media coverage that occurs in U.S. political campaigns.

Thomas Jefferson by passing out a leaflet that read:

" THOMAS JEFFERSON is a Firm REPUBLICAN, JOHN ADAMS is an avowed [self-declared] MONARCHIST. . . . Thomas Jefferson first drew the declaration of American independence;—he first framed the sacred political sentence that all men are born equal. John Adams says this is all a farce [an empty display] and a falsehood; that some men should be born Kings, and some should be born nobles. . . . Adams has sons who might aim to succeed their father; Jefferson, like Washington, has no son. "

Negative campaigning has become more prominent in recent decades. Although most voters tell pollsters that they oppose negative campaigning, it seems to work. Candidates subjected to it find themselves on the defensive, having to take time and effort away from presenting their own campaign themes in order to fend off attack.

Because of the success of negative campaigning, in many instances campaign workers search for embarrassing quotations, unethical behavior, or contradictory votes that could be used against opponents. By taking particular statements or votes out of context, this practice draws attention away from the opponent's record as a whole.

In many instances campaigns use this information to create negative ads (sometimes called attack ads) to run on television and radio. Some of these ads refer to a candidate's "flip-flops," pointing out how he or she has changed positions on an issue. "Not-on-the-job" ads point out missed legislative votes, while "negative-on-positive" ads dispute something positive an opponent has said about him- or herself, such as a claim about opposing special-interest groups. In recent years, candidates have even run negative ads attacking an opponent for negative campaigning.

Nonvoting

What effect do advertising and negative campaigning have on voters? Many critics feel that today's campaign techniques, along with registration procedures and the weakened condition of the political parties, have caused a decrease in voter turnout. In the 1992 presidential election, for example, only 55 percent of the voting-age population voted. By 2000 this number had shrunk to around 51 percent. This percentage has been decreasing steadily over the past few decades. Turnout is even lower for congressional elections that do not coincide with presidential elections (about 36 percent in 1998).

Voter Alienation Many nonvoters say that they feel alienated by the political system in this country. They feel powerless to change the system and think that their vote does not make a difference in the political process. In addition, some say that the strength of interest groups and contributions of the wealthy play too big a role in the political system.

Furthermore, although negative campaigning is intended to sway voters' opinions, one study reports that some people become less likely to vote after hearing and seeing negative ads. This result might occur because negative campaigning makes them distrust politicians and politics in general, not just the candidates being attacked. By causing fewer people to vote, negative ads detract from the contribution to the public good that campaigns otherwise make.

Registration Requirements

Some people believe that registration requirements discourage some citizens from voting. Before registration procedures were set up, some state governments maintained lists of eligible voters, but others allowed voters to just show up on election day and ask to vote. Registration makes the voting process more difficult because a person must take the time to register beforehand. About one fourth of the voting-age population fails to register by election day.

In 1993, Congress passed and President Bill Clinton signed into law the Motor Voter Law, which requires states to make registering to vote easier (see the case study on page 444–445). To meet the law's mandates, a state must permit citizens to register by mail or when applying for a driver's license or federal or state benefits.

Weakened Political Parties

Another reason for low voter participation is the apparently weakened state of the major political parties. During the late 1800s, when political parties were strong, voter participation was high, although fewer individuals had the right to vote. As political parties grew weaker, however, citizens became less involved in the electoral process. Statistics show that high levels of positive competition between the political parties increase voter turnout for the election in question. Increased competition sparks voters' interest.

VOTER REGISTRATION APPLICATION (SOLICITUD DE INSCRIPCION DE VOTANTE)

Caption Answer
about one fourth

PUBLIC GOOD *Voter registration helps the government keep the electoral process fair, but it also makes the voting process more difficult.* **Approximately what portion of the voting-age population is not registered?**

PUBLIC GOOD *John F. Kennedy and Richard Nixon participated in the first televised presidential debate during the 1960 presidential campaign.* **How does political debate help voters make more informed decisions?**

Benefits of Campaigns

Despite some criticisms, campaigns do benefit the political process. Campaigns encourage political debate and provide information to the electorate. Debate and accessible information promote the public good.

Encouraging Debate For voters to make decisions about political issues and candidates, they must be able to weigh conflicting points of view. Political campaigns expose people to opposing viewpoints, thus prompting them to seriously consider the issues. Some campaigns include public debates between the candidates, further fueling discussion among the citizenry.

Providing Information Political campaigns also provide information about candidates and their backgrounds. Some political ads expose information about an opposing candidate that he or she might not wish to have revealed. Though some of this injurious information may not relate to the issues, campaigns often provide facts that voters do need in order to be well informed.

Political campaigns provide information to voters in a variety of ways. Many candidates campaign in person—knocking on doors to speak with voters, distributing brochures, and speaking to small groups in homes or clubs. Candidates also mail out hundreds of letters directly to voters. These mailings usually contain information about a candidate's experience in government office and his or her positions on key issues. They may also point out the differences between a candidate's views about the issues and the views of his or her opponents.

Finally, campaign ads provide voters with significant information in a short period of time. Advertisements often focus on how a candidate's views differ from those of the opposition. By using a variety of campaign tools, a candidate can inform a variety of voters on key campaign issues.

SECTION 4 REVIEW

1. Identifying Concepts: Copy the graphic organizer to the right. Use it to describe the criticisms and benefits of campaigns.

Campaigns

Criticisms   Benefits

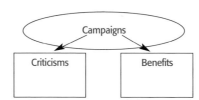

Homework Practice Online
keyword: SV3 HP19

2. Finding the Main Idea

a. Why is the role of the media in campaigns sometimes criticized?

b. What is negative campaigning, and why do campaigns use it?

3. Writing and Critical Thinking

Decision Making: Are campaigns beneficial or harmful to the public good? Write a paragraph explaining how you would change the system and the effect your changes would have on elections.

Consider the following:
• the criticisms of campaigns
• the benefits of campaigns

GOVERNMENT IN THE NEWS

The Media's Role in Politics

The media are so influential in politics that they have been referred to as the fourth branch of government. After the executive, legislative, and judicial branches, no institution has as much impact on American government as the media.

For hundreds of years, the printed word remained the only far-reaching media (other than word of mouth) upon which our country depended for news and views and opinions. In the 1900s newspapers were joined first by radio in the 1920s and then by television in the late 1940s and early 1950s to create the "big three" in political media circles.

KDKA of Pittsburgh became one of the nation's first radio stations in 1920. Almost immediately, the impact radio would have on politics was evident. That year in the presidential race, KDKA radio listeners learned that Warren Harding had defeated James Cox in the presidential election. In 1926, network radio appeared in the form of the National Broadcasting Company, which provided politicians and advertisers an even stronger means of communication.

Franklin Roosevelt was the first president to really take advantage of radio by holding a series of "fireside chats," in which he told Americans of his plans to energize the economy during the dark days of the Great Depression.

Harry Truman was the first president to broadcast a State of the Union address on television—his 1947 address was broadcast to the few Americans who were wealthy enough to own a television set. Dwight Eisenhower's 1952 campaign was the first to use TV as a political advertising medium in a national election. The World War II general won the White House that year, changing the way political campaigns were run.

President Ronald Reagan appeared comfortable in front of the camera because of his

George W. Bush meets with talk-show host Oprah Winfrey during the 2000 presidential campaign.

experience as an actor, earning him the nickname "The Great Communicator." Bill Clinton was able to gain a majority of young people's votes in the 1992 election in part because he appeared on MTV, and on *The Arsenio Hall Show* playing the saxophone.

In the late 1990s, the Internet had a quick and dramatic impact on both media coverage of politics and politicians. The 2000 presidential election witnessed an onslaught of political messages over the World Wide Web, aimed at affecting the views and opinions of U.S. citizens. The 2000 U.S. election, one of the closest in history, took the political center stage on TV and radio, in print, and on the Internet as George W. Bush defeated Al Gore.

What Do You Think?

1. How has the growth of the media affected the way political campaigns are conducted?

2. What are some examples of how politicians have used the media to their advantage?

> **WHY IT MATTERS TODAY**
>
> Research a historic political campaign in which the media played a prominent idea. Has the role of the media changed over time? Use CNNfyi.com or other current events sources to answer this question.
>
> **CNNfyi.com**

CHAPTER 19

Review Answers

Writing a Summary

Summaries should focus on the main section. These may be found in the Read to Discover questions at the start of each section. Summaries should also use standard grammar, spelling, sentence structure, and punctuation.

Identifying Ideas

Refer to the following pages: direct primary (431), closed primary (432), open primary (432), runoff primary (432), nonpartisan primary (432), single-member district (440), secret ballot (441), absentee ballot (441), suffrage (441)

Understanding Main Ideas

1. primary election; self-announcement, caucus, convention, petition

2. nomination, campaign, election

3. Candidates became more visible, media became

(Continued on page 452)

Review

(Continued from page 451)

more involved, and polling became more important.

4. Voters must be U.S. citizens, at least 18 years old, residents in a state for a specified period of time, and registered to vote in that state.

5. property ownership, ability to pay poll tax, race, sex

6. influence of the media and negative campaigning

Reviewing Themes

1. Delegates to local conventions chose delegates to state conventions, and then state convention delegates chose delegates to the national convention. These delegates then chose the presidential and vice presidential candidates. Students should state their opinion about local and state conventions and explain their reasoning.

2. Answers will vary, but students should discuss the importance of campaigning and the effect of seeing a candidate in person. Students should explain their opinions.

3. Descriptions will vary. Students should discuss age requirements and the elimination of discrimination in voter registration. Students should also offer support for their opinions.

Thinking Critically

1. Answers will vary, but students should offer support for their opinions.

(Continued on page 453)

Writing a Summary

Using standard grammar, spelling, sentence structure, and punctuation, write a summary of the information in this chapter.

Identifying Ideas

Identify the following terms and explain their significance.

1. direct primary

2. closed primary

3. open primary

4. runoff primary

5. nonpartisan primary

6. single-member district

7. secret ballot

8. absentee ballot

9. suffrage

Understanding Main Ideas

SECTION 1 (pp. 429–434)

1. What is the most common means of nominating candidates today? What are the other means of nominating candidates?

2. What are the three main steps in the electoral process?

SECTION 2 (pp. 435–439)

3. How did campaigns change during the 1900s?

SECTION 3 (pp. 440–446)

4. What are the requirements for voting in the United States today?

5. What limitations existed on voting in the past?

SECTION 4 (pp. 447–450)

6. Why are campaigns sometimes criticized?

Reviewing Themes

1. Principles of Democracy How were local concerns represented in the national conventions in the 1800s and early 1900s? Do you think local and state conventions should still exist?

2. Political Processes In campaigning for office, candidates of the past were much less visible than candidates today. How important is it for a candidate to campaign in person? If you were running for office, would you go on a campaign tour? Explain your answers.

3. Public Good Describe some of the discriminatory voting regulations in U.S. history. Do you think age requirements are discriminatory? How is the public good promoted by the elimination of discrimination in voter registration? Explain your answers.

Thinking Critically

1. Drawing Conclusions Imagine that you are running for political office. Is your goal to win at any cost or to inform the public about your platform? Do you think these two goals could go hand in hand? Explain your answers.

2. Evaluating In your opinion, is a candidate's image an important consideration in an election? How much would factors such as age affect your vote? Why?

3. Summarizing Has the elimination of voting restrictions promoted the public good? Use historical examples to support your opinion.

Writing about Government

Review the list you made in your Government Notebook at the beginning of the chapter. Why is it important that you have a voice in the decisions that you and your friends or classmates make? Write your answers in your Notebook.

Interpreting the Visual Record

Study the political cartoon below. Then use it to help you answer the questions that follow.

'...Political campaigns have become so simplistic and superficial ... In the 20 seconds we have left, could you explain why?..'

1. Which of the following statements best describes the cartoonist's point of view?
   a. Voters do not listen to politicians.
   b. Campaigns are very informative.
   c. The media has made campaigns better.
   d. The media has made campaigns worse.

2. Why do you think television plays such a large role in political campaigns?

Analyzing Primary Sources

Elizabeth Cady Stanton helped organize the women's rights movement of the 1800s. Read the excerpt below, from her book *Eighty Years and More,* which describes a time when Stanton attempted to cast a vote before women had the right to vote. Answer the questions that follow.

"When we entered the room it was crowded with men. . . .

The inspectors [men] were thunderstruck. . . . One placed his arms round it, with one hand close over the aperture [slot] where the ballots were slipped in, and said, with mingled surprise and pity, 'Oh, no, madam! Men only are allowed to vote.' I then explained that, in accordance with the Constitution of New Jersey, women had voted in New Jersey down to 1801, when they were forbidden the further exercise of the right by an arbitrary act of the legislature, and, by a recent amendment to the national Constitution, Congress had declared that 'all persons born or naturalized in the United States, and subject to the jurisdiction thereof, are citizens of the United States and of the State wherein they reside' and are entitled to vote. I told them that I wished to cast my vote, as a citizen of the United States. . . . The [inspector] held on to the box, and said 'I know nothing about the Constitutions, State or national. I never read either; but I do know that in New Jersey, women have not voted in my day, and I cannot accept your ballot."

3. Which of the following statements best reflects Stanton's point of view?
   a. only women should be allowed to vote
   b. all U.S. citizens should be able to vote
   c. men should not be allowed to vote
   d. property owners should be able to vote

4. What forbade women to vote in New Jersey after 1801?

(Continued from page 452)

2. Answers will vary, but students should explain why image is or is not a consideration and how much a candidate's age would affect their vote.

3. Answers will vary, but students should provide support for their reasoning.

Writing About Government

The Government Notebook is a follow-up activity to the notebook activity that appears on page 428.

Building Social Studies Skills

1. d

2. Answers will vary. Students might suggest that through television, candidates can reach huge amounts of potential voters fairly easily.

3. c

4. an act by the state legislature

Alternative Assessment

To assess this activity see Judging Information in *Alternative Assessment Handbook.*

Alternative Assessment

Building Your Portfolio

Make a list of some important issues such as education, taxes, and a balanced budget. Then answer the following questions: What do you think about each issue? Are the current laws concerning each issue effective? What laws do you think should be in place concerning each issue? Determine whether your answers are more in line with Democratic, Republican, or independent views.

🖥 internet connect

Internet Activity: go.hrw.com
KEYWORD: SV3 GV19

Have students access the Internet through the HRW Go site to conduct research on the way primary elections or caucuses are held in their state. Find information about turnout in these primaries. Then ask students to create a graph that shows voter turnout in primary and general elections in recent years.

go.hrw.com

LAB OBJECTIVES

The Unit 6 Public Policy Lab incorporates the following objectives:

▶ review information about important issues in a fictional presidential race.

▶ evaluate candidates' strengths and weaknesses, as well as their positions on important issues.

▶ use a problem-solving process to write a debate preparation paper for a presidential candidate.

Using the Lab

Before beginning the lab, organize students into groups and distribute copies of the Public Policy Lab Unit 6 Activity found in *Unit Tests and Unit Lab Activities with Answer Key*. Then have students read the assignment on this page. Discuss the assignment with students and point out the documents on pages 455–57 that students will use during the lab.

The What Do You Think? questions on pages 455–57 will help guide students during the project. In addition, the lab worksheet includes a step-by-step checklist for students to monitor their progress. For assessment guidelines, see the Problem Solving rubric in the *Alternative Assessment Handbook*.

PUBLIC POLICY LAB

You Solve the Problem

Campaign Consultant for a Day

*I*magine that you and other members of your group are campaign consultants. It is 2004 and presidential candidates are campaigning around the country. They have agreed to a nationally televised debate next month, two weeks before the general election. One candidate has hired you to help him or her prepare for the debate.

On the following pages is information you have gathered to help guide you in assessing the campaign's important issues. It also should provide some insight into the candidates' positions on those issues. This information includes statistical data from a national polling firm, the home pages of the candidates' Web sites, and a Voter's Guide from a special interest group. Use this information to draft a debate preparation paper for the candidate.

Government Notebook Assignment

Record your problem-solving process in your Government Notebook.

1. Review the documents and answer the WHAT DO YOU THINK? questions.

2. Identify the problem you are trying to solve with this paper.

3. Gather information on past presidential debates. Study the positions other presidential candidates have taken in other campaigns.

4. List and consider the options your group has with writing this paper. Consider the advantages and disadvantages associated with each of these options.

5. Choose and implement a solution by writing a debate preparation paper for your candidate. Include likely debate issues, the opponent's positions on these issues, and suggestions on how your candidate can address the issues to persuade the audience that his or her positions are superior.

6. As a class, evaluate the effectiveness of different debate preparation papers by contrasting papers written for opposing candidates.

Each year, PollStats, a national polling firm, conducts 1,500 telephone interviews, asking respondents to identify the country's most important issue. Each annual poll has a sampling error of plus or minus 5 points. The most recent poll was conducted last month in anticipation of the upcoming general election.

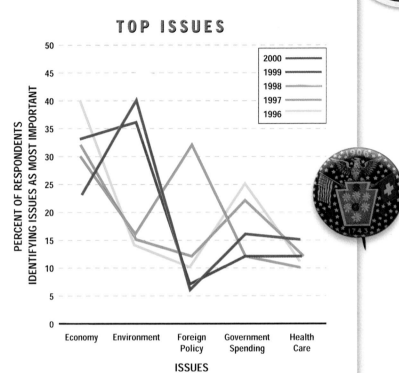

TOP ISSUES

2000	———
1999	———
1998	———
1997	———
1996	———

PERCENT OF RESPONDENTS IDENTIFYING ISSUES AS MOST IMPORTANT

Issues: Economy, Environment, Foreign Policy, Government Spending, Health Care

ISSUES

"Of these five issues, which do you believe is the most important facing the United States this year?"

WHAT DO YOU THINK?

1. Using the polling data as a guide, how have U.S. citizens attitudes changed over the last four years regarding which issues they believe are most important?

2. Why is the *Daily Post* editorial writer concerned about government spending?

3. Using the polling data and the editorial as guides, on what issues do you think the presidential nominees are most likely to be questioned in their upcoming debate? What might some of the questions be?

THE DAILY POST

Candidates Should Focus on Spending

As the general election approaches, we hope the Democratic and Republican nominees for president will focus their campaigns on issues that U.S. voters find important today. In addition, however, the nominees should focus on some issues that likely will become more important over the next four years.

A recent PollStats survey indicates that roughly 40 percent of potential voters believe that the environment is the most important issue facing the United States this year. Support for environmentalism began rising significantly last year, reflecting growing concern over air and water pollution. Congress has since been debating stricter regulations designed to lessen pollution.

At the same time, concern over foreign affairs is low, as it has been since U.S. intervention in the Ziberian civil war that ended two years ago. Even the economy is of relatively low concern to respondents, although nearly a quarter of them still identify it as the nation's top issue. As the economy continues to recover from the recession that preceded the Ziberian intervention, U.S. citizens should continue to feel better about their financial situation.

Unfortunately, Democratic presidential nominee George Jenkins and Republican nominee Bessy Smith have all but ignored another issue we believe will be a bigger concern over the next four years—government spending. After important progress was made toward a balanced budget in the late 1990s, leaders in both parties moved on to other issues. That was a mistake.

With many people in the baby boom generation soon reaching retirement age, government spending—particularly on programs for the elderly—is likely to rise rapidly. In their debate next month we hope the two major party nominees will tell the voters how they plan to address this difficult problem in the coming years.

What Do You Think? Answers

1. Foreign policy is becoming less important while environmental issues have risen in importance. Concern for economic issues remains somewhat steady.

2. Spending will increase as baby boomers reach retirement age and begin to receive government benefits.

3. Nominees should expect questions about the environment, the economy, and government spending. Examples of questions will vary, but students should base their questions on the data presented.

What Do You Think? Answers

1. Jenkins would probably appear strong on environmental and budget issues. Smith would appear strong on foreign policy and defense issues. Based on his experience, Jenkins would likely have an easier time addressing environmental questions than Smith would.

2. Smith could argue that Jenkins's approach to environmental issues would be less effective than hers would be. Jenkins could point out that foreign policy issues are not as important as they used to be.

3. Jenkins seems to support a strong central government to solve the nation's problems. Smith seems to believe in limiting government's power and spending, except when it comes to national defense.

4. Answers will vary. Students might point out that the Internet is becoming increasingly accessible to and popular with the general public. The Internet is also relatively inexpensive in terms of media advertising.

WHAT DO YOU THINK?

1. Judging from their backgrounds, on what issues does each candidate appear to have the most experience? Judging from their experience, which candidate might find it easier to address issues that poll respondents believe are the most important this year?

2. During the upcoming debate, what could each candidate do to counter the experience and advantages that the other candidate has in certain areas?

3. Judging from their backgrounds and their parties' platforms, how would you describe each candidate's general philosophy toward government?

4. Other political candidates have used Web sites to promote their campaigns. In fact, the Internet is an increasingly important source of information on politics. Why do you think this is so?

Democratic Presidential Nominee GEORGE JENKINS: Keeping America Working!

Find out more about the Democratic Party and how GEORGE JENKINS WILL KEEP AMERICA WORKING!

About the Democratic Party

Join the Democratic Party

Vice Presidential Nominee Olympia Martinez

Bills Sponsored by George Jenkins

Democratic Youth Organizations

Congressional Elections

State Elections

MEET U.S. SENATOR GEORGE JENKINS, the Democratic nominee for president of the United States. Here is a little background information on the senator who will keep America working!

★ Born: July 4, 1951
★ U.S. Senator, 1991–Present
★ Senate committees: Environment, Public Works, and Budget
★ Author of best-selling book: *The Environment: Making It Work for All of Us*

DEMOCRATIC PARTY PLATFORM

Delegates to the Democratic National Convention this summer adopted a party platform that serves the interests of all Americans. The platform calls for important measures designed to keep our environment clean and to keep workers on the job. These measures include:

★ stronger regulations designed to prevent air and water pollution;
★ a tax cut for the middle class;
★ more federal funding to improve roads, bridges, and railroads that need repair after years of neglect;
★ increased financial aid for students seeking college degrees to help them compete in the economy of tomorrow; and
★ laws that will make it easier for people to purchase health insurance.

Republicans for BESSY SMITH: Standing Up for AMERICA!

BESSY SMITH

✔ Former U.S. SECRETARY OF STATE
✔ Former U.S. TRADE REPRESENTATIVE
✔ Former U.S. congresswoman and chair of the House Foreign Affairs Committee
✔ Author of *Free Trade and Foreign Policy* and *Business and Environment: Finding Solutions Together*

BESSY SMITH AND THE REPUBLICAN PARTY ON THE ISSUES:

✔ Increase funding for a strong national defense.
✔ Empower the United States to act in its own interests internationally, without interference from foreign governments.
✔ Pass a balanced budget and keep a tight hold on overall government spending.
✔ Cut taxes for the middle class.
✔ Pass fewer regulations that tie the hands of business and hurt the economy.
✔ Encourage business and government to cooperate in finding solutions to pollution problems.

OTHER REPUBLICAN PARTY LINKS:

Vice Presidential Nominee & U.S. Sen. Danny O'Reilly

History of the GOP

Contacting the Republican Party

College Republicans

Young Republicans

Links to Local GOP Organizations

COALITION FOR A CLEAN ENVIRONMENT

The Coalition for a Clean Environment (CCE) works to promote policies that prevent air and water pollution and the wasting of our natural resources. To help inform U.S. voters about the major presidential nominees, we asked the candidates their positions on various environmental issues. Their responses are included in the following voter's guide.

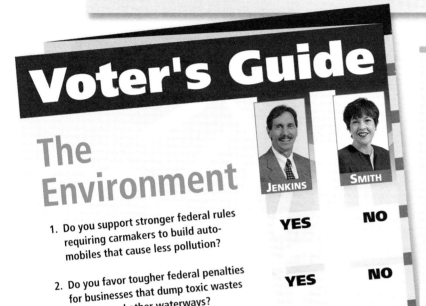

Voter's Guide

The Environment

JENKINS **SMITH**

1. Do you support stronger federal rules requiring carmakers to build automobiles that cause less pollution?

    YES   **NO**

2. Do you favor tougher federal penalties for businesses that dump toxic wastes in rivers and other waterways?

    YES   **NO**

3. Would you join other world leaders in seeking a ban on the manufacture of products that release gases damaging the earth's ozone layer?

    YES   **NO**

4. Would you support a summit of international leaders to agree on other ways to prevent the pollution of the world's air and water?

    YES   **NO**

WHAT DO YOU THINK?

1. Review the answers attributed to the candidates in this voter's guide. Which candidate would you expect the Coalition for a Clean Environment to support?

2. The Coalition for a Clean Environment is sending this voter's guide to members across the country. Why do you suppose the organization decided to send out this information?

3. What does this voter's guide really tell you about the candidates' positions? For example, does it tell voters what specific laws and actions Smith opposes and why? What might be some of Smith's reasons for opposing some of the proposals presented here? Does such opposition imply that Smith opposes a clean environment?

VOTE YES FOR BESSY

✓ YES BESSY SMITH

VOTE FOR BESSY SMITH

▸ internet connect

Internet Activity: go.hrw.com
KEYWORD: SV3 GVPL

Access the Internet through the HRW Go site to employ a problem-solving process to help prepare your candidate for an upcoming political debate. Research links and a problem-solving tutorial are provided.

What Do You Think? Answers

1. Jenkins

2. The coalition is trying to build support for Jenkins, whose answers would likely be favored by their members.

3. Answers will vary. Students should discuss how simple "yes" or "no" answers do not allow candidates to explain their responses or offer different ideas than the ones presented in the questionnaire. Smith may have other, perhaps better, ideas about how to deal with the problems addressed, but because of the format of the voter's guide, she could not express those ideas. Though the guide implies that Smith is opposed to a clean environment, she probably is not. As noted on her Web page, she has written a book about working with businesses to solve environmental problems.

Lesson Options

Suggestions for customizing the material in Unit 7 to fit the specific schedule and curriculum of your classroom are located at the beginning of each chapter.

Main Ideas

Ask each student to read the Main Ideas and briefly answer each question in writing. Later, when you have finished Unit 7, ask students to return to their original answers and revise them using what they learned in the unit.

PUBLIC POLICY LAB

The Unit 7 Public Policy Lab appears on pages 500–503. This project is a real-world assignment in which students working in groups will take on the roles of city council members in order to come up with a way to fund a city hall expansion. *Unit Tests and Unit Lab Activities with Answer Key* provides support materials to help students complete the lab.

CHAPTER 20

STATE GOVERNMENT

CHAPTER 21

LOCAL GOVERNMENT

Main Ideas

- *What is the basis of state governments' authority?*
- *How is state government structured and how is it funded?*
- *What kinds of communities comprise the United States and how did they develop?*
- *What kinds of local governments are there and how are they funded?*

PUBLIC POLICY LAB

How can students help fund construction of a new high school? Find out by reading this unit and taking the Public Policy challenge on pages 500–503.

STATE AND LOCAL GOVERNMENT

UNIT 7 OVERVIEW

Unit 7 presents the basic concepts necessary to introduce students to state and local governments, including state constitutions, the relationship between a state's government and its citizens, state legislatures, executive branches, and judicial branches, state budgets, taxes, and other forms of revenue, community size and makeup, types of local government, the effectiveness of local government, and the sources of local government revenues.

Teaching with Photographs

There are specific rules for displaying the U.S. flag with other flags, as in this photograph. When it is flown with flags of other nations, each flag should be on its own pole at the same height. When it is flown with flags of states or local governments, it should be higher than the other flags; the other flags may be smaller, but none may be larger; and the U.S. flag should be the first to be raised and the last to be lowered.

CHAPTER 20 STATE GOVERNMENT

	OBJECTIVES	PACING GUIDE	REPRODUCIBLE RESOURCES
SECTION 1 **THE STATES** (pp. 461–465)	▶ What is the basis of state governments' authority? ▶ In what ways do state governments answer to the people? ▶ How do state governments promote the public good?	**Regular** 2.5 days **Block Scheduling** 1 day	**ELL** Spanish Study Guide 20.1 **SM** English Study Guide 20.1 **E** Simulations and Strategies for Teaching Government: Activity 20 **PS** Reading 65: *Why Alaska Needs Statehood* **E** Challenge and Enrichment Activity 20
SECTION 2 **ORGANIZATION** (pp. 466–472)	▶ How are state legislatures structured? ▶ What are the responsibilities of a state's executive branch? ▶ How are state courts organized?	**Regular** 2 days **Block Scheduling** .75 day	**ELL** Spanish Study Guide 20.2 **SM** English Study Guide 20.2 **SM** Government Activities: Activity 20
SECTION 3 **STATE BUDGETS AND REVENUES** (pp. 473–476)	▶ How are state budgets created? ▶ What are the main sources of state revenue?	**Regular** 1.5 days **Block Scheduling** 1 day	**ELL** Spanish Study Guide 20.3 **SM** English Study Guide 20.3

Chapter Resource Key

PS	Primary Sources	**A**	Assessment		Video
RS	Reading Support	**REV**	Review		Videodisc
E	Enrichment	**ELL**	Reinforcement and English Language Learners		Internet
S	Simulations		Transparencies		Holt Presentation Maker Using
SM	Skills Mastery		CD-ROM		Microsoft ® PowerPoint ®

TECHNOLOGY RESOURCES	REINFORCEMENT, REVIEW, AND ASSESSMENT
<ul><li>One-Stop Planner: Lesson 20.1</li><li>Holt Researcher Online</li><li>Homework Practice Online</li><li>CNN Presents American Government</li><li>Holt Government Videodisc: Regulation: Watercraft in Washington</li><li>Transparency 42</li><li>Global Skill Builder CD-ROM</li></ul>	**REV** Section 1 Review, p. 465 **A** Daily Quiz 20.1
<ul><li>One-Stop Planner: Lesson 20.2</li><li>Holt Researcher Online</li><li>Homework Practice Online</li><li>Transparency 43, Transparency 44</li><li>Global Skill Builder CD-ROM</li></ul>	**REV** Section 2 Review, p. 472 **A** Daily Quiz 20.2
<ul><li>One-Stop Planner: Lesson 20.3</li><li>Holt Researcher Online</li><li>Homework Practice Online</li><li>Global Skill Builder CD-ROM</li></ul>	**REV** Section 3 Review, p. 476 **A** Daily Quiz 20.3

Chapter Review and Assessment

- Global Skill Builder CD-ROM
- HRW Go site
- **REV** Chapter 20 Tutorial for Students, Parents, and Peers
- **REV** Chapter 20 Review, pp. 478–479
- Chapter 20 Test Generator (on the One-Stop Planner)
- **A** Chapter 20 Test
- **A** Alternative Assessment Handbook

One-Stop Planner CD-ROM

It's easy to plan lessons, select resources, and print out materials for your students when you use the **One-Stop Planner CD-ROM with Test Generator.**

☑ internet connect

HRW ONLINE RESOURCES
Go To: go.hrw.com
Then type in a keyword.

TEACHER HOME PAGE
KEYWORD: SV3 Teacher

CHAPTER INTERNET ACTIVITIES
KEYWORD: SV3 GV20
Choose an activity on state government to:
- research initiative and referendum.
- compare salaries of state officials.
- learn about methods of generating revenue for states.

CHAPTER ENRICHMENT LINKS
KEYWORD: SV3 CH20

HOLT RESEARCHER ONLINE
KEYWORD: Holt Researcher

ONLINE ASSESSMENT
Homework Practice
KEYWORD: SV3 HP20
Standardized Test Prep
KEYWORD: SV3 STP20
Rubrics
KEYWORD: SS Rubrics

ONLINE MAPS, CHARTS, AND GRAPHS
KEYWORD: SV3 MCG
- States Allowing Initiatives, Referenda, and Recalls
- State Legislatures
- Terms of Office and Salaries of State Governors
- State Sales and Individual Income Taxes

CONTENT UPDATES
KEYWORD: SS Content Updates

HOLT PRESENTATION MAKER
KEYWORD: SV3 PPT20

ONLINE READING SUPPORT
KEYWORD: SS Strategies

CURRENT EVENTS
KEYWORD: S3 Current Events

OBJECTIVES

▸ Discuss the basis of state government's authority.
▸ List and describe the ways that state governments answer to the people.
▸ Explain how state governments promote the public good.

MOTIVATE

Pose the following situation to the class: The student body wants to suggest that the daily lunch period be lengthened by 10 minutes. Ask students who they would go to with their proposals. How would they go about getting their plan made into a school policy? Allow 10 to 15 minutes to develop their plan of action, including deciding to whom they would bring their proposal. Also encourage students to consider factors such as how lengthening the lunch period will affect the length of the school day and the pay of the cafeteria workers. After students have presented their plan, make the comparison between their school's administration level and the state legislature. Make students aware that state legislatures are responsible for making laws at the state level. Explain to the class that in this section they will learn about the authority that state governments have and the ways that state governments respond to the people and promote the public good.

TEACH

Building a Vocabulary

In spiral notebooks, have students create a Political Dictionary to be used throughout the course. This dictionary may be used as an activity at the start of each new section; it may also be used as a modification device for students having difficulty or Sheltered English Students during tests and homework assignments. List words that students will be expected to know for this section on the chalkboard. Have students list, define, and give an example of each of the terms, using information provided in the text or on the *Researcher CD-ROM*.

Conducting Research

Provide students with resources to conduct research about some of the different states in the United States. If possible, bring in a copy of your state's constitution and a copy of the U.S. Constitution. Explain to students that just as the federal government operates under the jurisdiction of the U.S. Constitution (the supreme law of the land), state governments and the people residing in those states function under their state constitutions. Also explain how state constitutions tend to vary greatly from one state to another just as each state varies significantly from the other states. Write the name of each of the 50 states on small pieces of paper and place them in a hat or a box. Have students (or small groups of students) choose a state and instruct them to find out as much general information about that state as they can in one class period. Students may wish to use the State Profiles section on the *Holt Researcher Online* to help gather the information. During the next class period, students should take the information they have gathered and draft a mock state constitution that reflects the history, population, and interests of that state. Tell students that in the next activity they will learn about how state governments answer to the people.

Predicting Outcome

Remind students that people's political beliefs and opinions on different issues tend to change over time. As a result, documents that were written many years ago, like state constitutions, need to be amended from time to time in order to remain current. For example, in the early nineteenth century, slavery was permitted in the South but was later abolished. Organize the class into several small groups. Using newspapers, magazines, textbooks, and other available resources, help students review significant changes to any state laws that have occurred over the years (e.g., raising the speed limit from 55 mph to 70 mph). Each group should list reasons for the change (e.g., a change in the federal law regarding speed limits). Have each group present the changes that took place in the state that they have researched to the rest of the class. Explain to students that in the next activity they will learn about how initiatives affect the public good of a state.

Debating ideas

Explain to students that initiatives are ways of changing laws, either adopting or repealing them through a direct vote of the people rather than by a vote of the legislature. Organize the class into two groups. Have one side list as many examples as they can about why initiatives are good for state government. Have the other side come up with reasons why initiatives should not be used to make public policy. (Remind students that currently only approximately half of the states allow initiatives to be used.) Allow each group 10 to 15 minutes to brainstorm ideas. Then hold a class debate on the issue. Rather than electing a spokesperson for each group, encourage all students to participate in the discussion. Have students attempt to predict whether more states will begin to adopt the initiative as an appropriate way to change legislation, or if the states that currently use this method will do away with it.

CLOSE

Refer students back to the Motivate activity and the discussion about their proposal to lengthen the time allotted for lunch. Ask them how they feel their ability to get their plan made into law may have changed if initiatives were allowed in deciding school policy. Have students create a list of advantages and disadvantages in allowing initiatives in school systems. Ask them to predict a scenario where initiatives voted on by the students could help their school form policies.

OPTIONS

Interpersonal Learners

Assign each student the task of interviewing a state employee. Some potential interviewees may include people working at the Department of Transportation, the License Bureau, or the State Highway Patrol. During class, help students prepare a list of questions they will ask during the interview. Encourage students to find out as much as they can about the position (e.g., job description) and how it serves the public good rather than about the person being interviewed. Students should share the information they gathered with classmates in a post-interview session. Encourage students to determine which jobs they may be interested in based on the information presented by their classmates.

Students Having Difficulty/ Sheltered English Students

Organize students into small groups (four in each group). Have students develop a campaign brochure for someone who is running for the state legislature. Students may want to assign group members different roles (e.g., copy writer, illustrator, presenter) based on their areas of interest. Remind students that the brochure should attempt to explain the candidate's understanding of the role of the legislature in state government, as well as promote the individual's ability to perform the role of legislator. Encourage students to list specific reasons why the candidate would want to serve in the position. Have students share their brochures with the other groups. Display each group's finished product on a bulletin board or classroom wall. Students may wish to include their brochures in their portfolios.

REVIEW

Have students complete the Section 1 Review on page 465. Use the answers in the Annotated Teacher's Edition to assess student mastery of this section.

ASSESS

To assess student mastery of this section, have students complete Daily Quiz 20.1 in *Daily Quizzes with Answer Key*. For additional assessment options, see *Alternative Assessment Handbook* on the *One-Stop Planner CD-ROM*.

ADDITIONAL RESOURCES

Beyle, Thad. *State Government.* 1992. Congressional Quarterly, Inc.

Kruman, Marc. *Between Authority and Liberty: State Constitution Making in Early America.* 1997. University of North Carolina Press.

Tarr, G. Alan. *Understanding State Constitutions.* 2000. Princeton University Press.

Weber, Ronald E. and Paul Brace. Editors. *American State and Local Politics: Directions for the 21st Century.* Chatham House Publishing.

LESSON 20.2 ORGANIZATION

TEXTBOOK PAGES 466–472

OBJECTIVES

▶ Explain how state legislatures are structured.
▶ Identify the responsibilities of a state's executive branch.
▶ Describe the way in which state courts are organized.

MOTIVATE

Write the name of your state's governor on the chalkboard. Ask how many students recognize the name and know specific details about that person's job. After students have identified that the individual is the governor, ask if they know when he or she was elected. When will the next election be held? Has the governor been in the news recently? If so, why? Tell students that in this section they will learn about the governor's role as chief executive of the state and how the state legislatures and state courts are organized.

TEACH

Building a Vocabulary

In their spiral notebooks, have students continue working on their Political Dictionary. List words the students will be expected to know for this section on the chalkboard. Have students list, define, and give an example of each of the terms, using information provided in the text or on the *Researcher CD-ROM*.

Role-Playing

Discuss with students the organization of state legislatures. Organize the class into three groups. Explain that each group will participate in the state legislative committee process. Tell students that a bill to change the usual time of road construction work from during the day to late at night has been proposed and has been approved in committee. Be sure to discuss any controversy surrounding the bill (e.g., noise pollution late at night, safety of the workers, increase in spending for late-shift employees). Assign one group to act as the state's upper house and another to act as the lower house. Have both groups debate the bill among themselves, make any necessary changes, and vote on its approval. When these tasks are completed, have each group send their version of the bill to a third group, which will act as a joint committee. The joint committee should then draft a compromise bill that both houses can agree on. Afterward, have students provide feedback about the process. Have them make suggestions about how the decision making could have been easier. Tell students that in the next activity they will be learning about the responsibilities of states' executive branches.

Demonstration

Discuss with students the main responsibilities of states' executive branches. Explain the various roles that a governor must fulfill. Tell students that one of the roles as the state's chief ambassador is to attract business to the state. Write the names of each of the 50 states on small pieces of paper. (You may want to reuse the pieces of paper from the first activity in Lesson 20.1.) Again, place the papers in a hat or a box and allow each student to choose one. Present the following scenario: Each student is the governor of the state he or she has chosen. Have students research what their state offers prospective businesses in regard to its economy, distribution of wealth, consumer needs, and availability of resources. Students may use the state profiles section on the *Holt Researcher Online* to assist them with this research. They should gather information, prepare a report or speech, and make a brief presentation to the class. Presentations should focus on promoting their state to outside businesses. Explain to students that in the next activity they will learn about how state courts are organized.

Organizing Information

Discuss with students the various levels of organization that make up state court systems. Organize the class into three groups, one to cover trial courts, another to cover appeals courts, and the final group to cover special courts. Have each group create a presentation on the type of court they were assigned that discusses the court's organization, responsibilities, and any significant cases that it has recently tried. Students may need to use outside resources such as the Internet to gather the necessary information. Once groups have finished their research, have them present their information to the rest of the class. Encourage students from other groups to ask questions about the various courts.

CLOSE

Make two separate columns on the chalkboard. Label one *U.S. Congress* and the other *State Legislatures*. Have students compare what they have previously learned about the U.S. Congress with what they learned in this chapter about state legislatures. Topics for discussion should include, but should not be limited to, similarities and differences in the size and structure of the legislatures, amount of pay each position receives, election procedures, and rate of turnover for these positions. Have students discuss why they believe differences between Congress and state legislatures exist. Ask them what explanations they can find for the differences among the various state legislatures. Lead a discussion about the different roles played by members of Congress and legislators. Have students debate which of these plays a more influential role in their daily lives and which they perceive as being more important. Encourage students to support their opinions with information from the chapter or lessons.

OPTIONS

Interpersonal Learners

Assign students the task of researching one or two recent messages or speeches delivered by the governor, such as the State of the State address. Allow students to use newspapers, television reports, the library and any other available resources to gather information. From these messages, students should be able to state a general overview of the governor's political agenda, the powers of the office, what he or she would like to see happen in the state in the near future, and any other important information. Students should prepare a report of their conclusions. Encourage students to present their research to the class.

Students Having Difficulty/ Sheltered English Students

  Ask each student to formulate a list of three to five questions that he or she has about the content of this lesson. Questions may be about unfamiliar vocabulary words, confusing concepts, or a general lack of understanding of a process. Encourage students who are having difficulty with the lesson to work with another student. Have pairs present their questions to each other and answer them. If a given pair of students cannot answer particular questions, allow other classmates to help provide the correct answers. Be sure to emphasize the importance of a collaborative effort from each of the students so that the exercise serves as a review session for everyone involved.

REVIEW

Have students complete the Section 2 Review on page 472. Use the answers in the Annotated Teacher's Edition to assess student mastery of this section.

ASSESS

To assess student mastery of this section, have students complete Daily Quiz 20.2 in *Daily Quizzes with Answer Key.* For additional assessment options, see *Alternative Assessment Handbook* on the *One-Stop Planner CD-ROM.*

ADDITIONAL RESOURCES

Behn, Robert. *Governors on Governing.* 1991. University Press of America.

Bosworth, Matthew H. *Courts As Catalysts: State Supreme Courts and Public School Finance Equity.* 2001. State University of New York Press.

Rosenthal, Alan. *Governors and Legislatures: Contending Powers.* 1990. Congressional Quarterly, Inc.

HOLT PRESENTATION MAKER Access Illustrated LECTURE NOTES using Microsoft® PowerPoint® on the One-Stop Planner CD-ROM

OBJECTIVES

▶ Explain the process of how state budgets are created.
▶ List and describe the main sources of state revenue.

MOTIVATE

Lead a discussion to discover students' viewpoints on the various taxes that states may impose on their citizens. Ask students if they believe there should be income taxes. Ask them if they think it is fair for states to place "sin taxes" on items such as cigarettes. Ask them whether they feel the state sales tax rate is reasonable. After students have given their answers to these questions, begin to pose additional questions about their opinions on some of the services the state provides. Ask students if their garbage gets collected on a regular basis, if they ever go to parks or recreational facilities, or whether they appreciate the ability to attend public schools for free. Explain to students that citizens pay taxes so that the states can provide such services.

TEACH

Building a Vocabulary

In their spiral notebooks, have students continue working on their Political Dictionary. List words the students will be expected to know for this section on the chalkboard. Have students list, define, and give an example of each of the terms, using information provided in the text or on the *Researcher CD-ROM*.

Applying a Model/Learning From Visuals

Explain to the class the process that states go through in preparing their budgets. Discuss the strain that is placed on a state's budget as it attempts to find ways to pay for new programs. On the chalkboard or on a large piece of paper, have the class create a list of expenses that would be included in a personal budget. Allot a set amount of money as income and have students decide how much money they would allocate to each category. When finished,

inform students that the budget needs to be readjusted because of a new category (e.g., car repairs, prom, college application fees). Allow time for the group to make the adjustments they need to balance their budget. Relate any difficulties the students may have in making the necessary changes to how the state must constantly adjust its budget when funding for new programs is required. Make students aware of the number of categories that are included in a state budget as compared to an individual's budget. As a lead-in to the next activity, tell students that they will learn about an issue that states are dealing with that can have a significant effect on their budgets.

Conducting Research/Writing About Government

Explain to students that legalizing gambling is a controversial issue that many state governments have recently faced. On the one hand, legalized gambling can raise millions of dollars for state governments through taxation, part of which can be used to fund education. On the other hand, legalized gambling has also been criticized for negatively affecting the lives of individuals living within the states, causing problems such as bankruptcy. Have students research the arguments both for and against legalized gambling and have them write a position paper stating whether they are for or against legalized gambling and their reasons for that position. Ask volunteers to share their papers with the rest of the class. Encourage students to send their papers to their representatives in the state legislature. Tell students that in the next activity they will investigate sources of state revenue.

Debating an Issue/Taking a Stand

Discuss with the class the main sources of revenue for states. Encourage students to ask questions about the differences in these sources of revenue. Explain to them that there are differences in the way that states collect some of these sources of revenue. Tell the class that a flat income tax rate is one in which all citizens are taxed at the same rate, regardless of their income, while a progressive tax rate is one in which an individual's tax rate rises as his or her income increases. Ask students to raise their hands in a vote to indicate whether they believe there should be a flat income tax rate or a progressive income tax rate. If the class appears to be split evenly on the issue, organize them into two teams to debate the issue. If teams need to be evened up, ask for volunteers to switch sides. Allow each team 15 to 20 minutes to discuss their viewpoints and construct their arguments. After conducting the debate, take a vote again to see if students' opinions have changed.

Have each student create a daily schedule of their life. Have them write down each of the activities they engage in on a "normal" day, everything from taking a bus to school to working a part-time job after school. Ask them to attempt to account for the entire 24 hours of a day. After students have finished accounting for all of their daily activities, generate a list on the chalkboard of as many of these activities as possible. As a class, go down the list and identify any activity in which the state has any influence (e.g., contributes funding or regulates in some manner). Put a check mark by each of these. Lead a discussion about the influence the state has on its residents' lives, most notably in providing services and funding for various programs. Ask students to try to imagine how life would be different if the state did not provide for these programs.

OPTIONS

Gifted Learners

 Explain to students that in an attempt by state governments to improve and expand services, states have seen a dramatic expansion of the state college system. The number of public colleges has increased, as well as the overall enrollment at most state institutions. Have students express their opinions, either in writing or orally, on how they feel this educational expansion of the state system will affect the state. Encourage students to discuss themes such as the accessibility of higher education, tuition costs, and the number and value of degrees awarded each year.

Students Having Difficulty/
Sheltered English Students

  Organize the class into small groups and have them find out the difference in tuition prices between public, state-funded colleges or universities, and private colleges or universities, in their state. Encourage students to use newspaper articles, the Internet, or magazine publications that list and rate academic institutions across the country to gather information about the schools. To narrow their research, have students choose two private and two public schools to research. When finished, have students present the information they have collected to the rest of the class. Lead a discussion about why public institutions are generally more affordable and describe the state's influence in maintaining reasonable tuition prices. Have students write a short essay that discusses whether states should fund universities.

Have students complete the Section 3 Review on page 476. Use the answers in the Annotated Teacher's Edition to assess student mastery of this section.

To assess student mastery of this section, have students complete Daily Quiz 20.3 in *Daily Quizzes with Answer Key*. For additional assessment options, see *Alternative Assessment Handbook* on the *One-Stop Planner CD-ROM*.

For students having difficulty with the lessons, have them complete Reteaching Activity 20. This activity is located in *Reteaching Activities with Answer Key*.

Hovey, Harold A. *The Devolution Revolution: Can the States Afford Devolution?* 1998. The Twentieth Century Fund/Century Foundation Report.

Zodrow, George. *State Sales and Income Taxes: An Economic Analysis (Texas A&M University Economics Series, No. 15)*. 1999. Texas A&M University Press.

STATE GOVERNMENT

In what state did you take your driving test? If you had sought your license in another state, you might have faced a different test and received a different score. You also might have been able to get your learner's permit at a younger age. Why is the driving test not the same across the country? States have the power to set their own rules for obtaining a driver's license as well as for many other actions, such as registering a car, regulating a public school, paying state college tuition, marrying, and more recently, setting welfare policy. In other words, when you cross state lines, you cross into another government's jurisdiction.

GOVERNMENT NOTEBOOK

What state laws affect you? Think about activities that require licenses, such as driving and fishing, or those that concern people's well-being and safety, such as attending school and wearing seat belts. In your Government Notebook, write a list of state laws that could affect you personally.

GOVERNMENT NOTEBOOK

The Government Notebook is a journal activity that encourages students to consider basic concepts of government that relate to their lives. A follow-up notebook activity appears on page 478.

WHY IT MATTERS TODAY

State government affects our lives in many ways. At the end of this chapter, visit CNNfyi.com to learn more about how state government affects you.

CNNfyi.com

WHY IT MATTERS TODAY

To find additional lesson plans dealing with state government, visit CNNfyi.com or have students complete the GOVERNMENT IN THE NEWS Activity on page 477.

CNNfyi.com

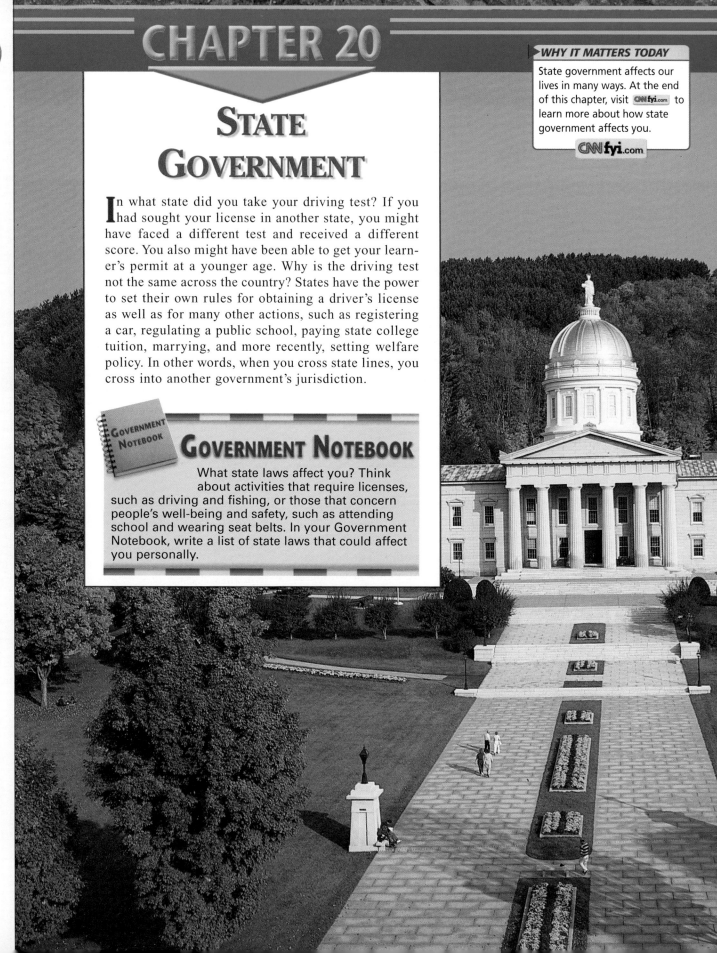

SECTION 1
THE STATES

READ TO DISCOVER

1. What is the basis of state governments' authority?
2. In what ways do state governments answer to the people?
3. How do state governments promote the public good?

POLITICAL DICTIONARY
initiative
referendum
recall

The 50 states are as diverse as any 50 people you might randomly pick from a crowd on the street. Alaska is 546 times as large in land area as Rhode Island. California has a population of 33.9 million, compared to Wyoming's population of around 494,000. The average annual precipitation in Las Vegas, Nevada, is 4 inches, compared to 67 inches in Mobile, Alabama.

In some ways, however, the states are quite similar. Like the federal government, they all receive their authority to govern from a constitution. In addition, the 50 state governments are all able to answer to the people more directly than can the federal government. The close relationship that a state government is able to maintain with the citizens is vital in its helping to promote the public good.

State Constitutions

Each state has its own constitution. The state constitutions, however, cannot conflict with the U.S. Constitution, which is the supreme law of the land.

Types of Constitutions Just as the U.S. Constitution reflects the concerns and events of the Revolutionary War period, state constitutions reflect the places and times in which they were written. In other words, both regional and historical traditions may affect a state's constitution. For example, Section XIII of Oklahoma's constitution requires the state legislature to "provide for the teaching of the elements of agriculture, horticulture, stock feeding, and domestic science" in public schools. Oklahoma's framers felt this provision was important, given the high number of people in the state who worked in agriculture when the constitution was drafted.

Each of the original colonies adopted its constitution before or shortly after U.S. independence. Like the U.S. Constitution, these constitutions strive to outline a social contract in the tradition of the political philosopher John Locke. That is, they list the state's responsibilities to the people and vice versa. They are mostly brief and have been revised less frequently than most state constitutions.

In contrast, many other states have constitutions that are quite long and have been revised frequently. In southern states such as Alabama and South Carolina, for example, government officials were forced in the aftermath of the Civil War to rewrite their existing constitutions.

POLITICAL FOUNDATIONS *Oklahoma's constitution requires the legislature to provide for teaching stock feeding in public schools.* **What might affect the contents of a state constitution?**

SECTION 1
THE STATES

Lesson Plans
For teaching strategies, see Lesson 20.1 located at the beginning of this chapter or the One-Stop Planner Strategy 20.1.

Political Dictionary
To reinforce the section's vocabulary terms, refer students to the Electronic Glossary on the *Researcher CD-ROM*.

Section Assessment
To assess students' mastery of this section, have them complete Daily Quiz 20.1 in *Daily Quizzes with Answer Key*.

Enhancing the Lesson
For more information on the states mentioned on this page, see the State Profiles section on the *Holt Researcher Online*.

Caption Answer
Regional and historical traditions can affect a state constitution.

The constitutions of most western states include provisions enabling the public to keep a relatively high degree of control over the government. For example, the western states established traditions allowing citizens to vote on some laws directly and to remove government officials from their positions before the end of their term. These processes—known as initiative, referendum, and recall—are explained more fully later in this section.

Constitutional Provisions Most state constitutions have been rewritten at least once and some, several times. In fact, since 1775 the 50 states have adopted more than 140 constitutions. Louisiana has had 11 since becoming a state, and Georgia has had 10. In the 1960s and 1970s, ten states adopted new constitutions, which are shorter and more focused than the documents they replaced. In 1982 Georgia became the most recent state to adopt a new constitution.

In addition, the current state constitutions have been amended more than 5,900 times, more than one amendment a year for each state. If the U.S. Constitution had been amended that often, it would have more than 250 amendments instead of just 27.

As a result of these amendments, many state constitutions are quite long—on average, 28,600 words. (The U.S. Constitution has only 7,800 words.) Alabama's constitution, the longest, has 174,000 words—the equivalent of a 687-page final exam essay!

Why are state constitutions so lengthy? Many are packed with details that seem inappropriate to such fundamental documents. One article of the Maryland constitution, for example, establishes conditions for off-street parking in the city of Baltimore. South Dakota's constitution authorizes the state legislature to assess hail insurance on agricultural land, and Minnesota's allows people to sell produce grown in their gardens without a license. The reason for including these detailed elements is often found in history. For instance, short-term events or conditions sometimes inspire provisions that later seem out of date.

C A S E   S T U D Y

Changing The Texas Constitution

CONSTITUTIONAL PRINCIPLES Texas's basic law is among the most amended and longest of the state constitutions. Between its adoption in 1876 and the end of 1999, the Texas Constitution was amended 390 times. In addition, state voters rejected 174 other proposed constitutional amendments.

As with other lengthy state constitutions, the Texas Constitution is overloaded with details and specific measures. It is not uncommon, for example, for Texas voters to be asked to approve an amendment affecting the local government of only one or a few specific counties.

Why is the Texas Constitution so lengthy? In part it reflects the suspicion with which many Texans have long regarded government. This suspicion was particularly strong when the current constitution was adopted in 1876—shortly after the end of Reconstruction and the withdrawal of federal troops that had helped keep a highly unpopular governor in office. As a result, Texas voters must approve constitutional amendments addressing a variety of specific issues, such as interest rates on state bonds, that might better be addressed by elected officials.

There have been a number of unsuccessful attempts to draft a more efficient state constitution. In 1974, state legislators meeting as delegates failed by just three votes to agree on a new constitution. After seven months of work and a dramatic vote that continued up until the final minute of the convention, they were unable to send it to the voters for their approval.

State Government and the People

You now know that each state's government, like the federal government, receives its governing authority from a constitution. Also like the federal government, a state's continued authority to rule rests firmly with the people. Many state governments, however, must answer to their citizens in ways that the federal government need not. In fact, citizens can become more directly involved in state legislative actions than in federal ones. In many states, citizens

Careers in Government

Librarian

For anyone doing research, a librarian can be an important source of information. Librarians train extensively to learn how to become guardians of information.

Consider, for example, Kevin Starr, who in 1997 was the state librarian of California. As head of the California State Library, the state librarian provides reference and information services that state officials need to draft legislation and do other important work. The state library also stores historical documents, books, and other materials, and provides other services for

Librarians must be able to select, store, and properly classify books, documents, software, and other library material and equipment.

use by the general public, government officials, and other libraries.

Starr's education and training prepared him well for his job as California's state librarian. He earned a bachelor's degree from the University of San Francisco, master's and doctoral degrees in American literature from Harvard University, and a master's degree in library science from the University of California, Berkeley.

Not all of this country's approximately 150,000 librarians need such extensive education. Most libraries require librarians to have a master's degree in library science. The degree often is earned through a one- or two-year program. This education helps prepare a librarian for a variety of tasks in public, school, and special libraries such as the California State Library and the Library of Congress. These tasks include selecting, ordering, storing, and properly classifying the books, documents, software, and other materials and equipment that best meet the needs of a library's patrons.

Librarians also help patrons in their research through reference services and by guiding them to appropriate library resources. Increasingly these library resources include access to computers, the Internet, and other electronic information. As a result, librarians are constantly working to further educate themselves so that they can provide the proper assistance needed in the information age.

Careers in Government
RESEARCHER ONLINE
go.
hrw
.com

To help students learn about other careers in government, refer them to the Careers section on the *Holt Researcher Online*.

THEMES IN GOVERNMENT

POLITICAL PROCESSES A successful 1978 constitutional initiative in California seems to have renewed citizens' interest in the initiative as a means of participating in legislative actions. The initiative in question is Proposition 13, a measure that reduced property taxes. After the initiative was passed, 12 other states followed California's lead and placed antitax initiatives before the voters.

In the early 1990s political activists turned to the initiative as a way of instituting term limits. In 1992, for example, voters in 14 states approved initiatives supporting term limits. By 1995, 23 states had established congressional term-limit legislation. The Supreme Court, however, ruled that laws placing term limits on federal lawmakers could only be made by amending the U.S. Constitution, not by passing laws in individual states. The Court did, however, allow term limits for state legislators to remain. ∎

can accomplish this by offering an initiative, holding a referendum, and recalling elected officials.

Initiatives Initiatives and referenda are both ways of adopting—or repealing—laws through a direct vote of citizens rather than by the vote of a legislature. (As noted in Chapter 1, such citizen actions are a form of direct democracy.) An **initiative** is a procedure for proposing and enacting state or local laws. If a certain minimum number of registered voters signs a petition backing the bill proposed by an initiative, the bill is placed on a ballot or sent to the state legislature. If voters or legislators approve the initiative, it becomes law. Around half of the states allow initiatives.

There are two kinds of initiatives: direct and indirect. A bill that is proposed by direct initiative is placed directly on a regular or special election ballot to be voted on by the people. A bill proposed by an indirect initiative, on the other hand, goes first to the legislature. If it passes the legislature, it becomes law. If it does not, the voters decide the matter. Only a few states use the indirect initiative.

Over the years almost every imaginable political issue has been the subject of an initiative. In 1918 Montana approved an initiative allowing chiropractors to practice within its borders. In 1972 Colorado passed an initiative to keep state funds from being spent on hosting the 1976 Winter

POLITICAL PROCESSES Each state has its own rules and regulations about conducting a referendum. The distinctions between these rules involve a number of factors.

One factor is the number of signatures needed to put a referendum on a ballot. North Dakota, for instance, requires the petition to bear the signatures of 2 percent of the state's population, while Wyoming requires the signatures of 15 percent of the number of citizens who voted in the last election.

Another factor involves the amount of time petitioners have to get the required number of signatures. Montana allows petitions to circulate for one year, while Colorado allows six months. Some states, such as Massachusetts and South Dakota, allow only 90 days. A petition that exceeds the applicable time limit is defunct.

Other factors include whether people are allowed to remove their name from a petition and which state official is to receive the list. ■

Caption Answer
direct and indirect

Olympics. (As a result, those Olympics were not held in Colorado, but in Innsbruck, Austria.) More recent initiatives have addressed issues such as lowering property taxes, denying government benefits to illegal immigrants, and repealing affirmative action programs.

Referenda A **referendum** is a popular vote on a proposal that has already been considered by the legislature. Referenda are submitted to the voters for several reasons. The constitutions of all states but Alabama require lawmakers to submit any constitutional amendments to the voters.

Sometimes a legislature chooses to submit a controversial proposed law to popular vote rather than deciding the matter itself. In addition, citizens may petition for a referendum to overturn a law the legislature has adopted. Forty-nine states allow some form of referendum.

Recalls Like initiatives and referenda, recalls allow citizens in some states to take direct governmental action. A **recall** is a special election to remove an elected official from office before the end of his or her term. Before a recall can be held, however, a certain number of registered

STATES ALLOWING INITIATIVES, REFERENDA, AND RECALLS

STATE	INITIATIVE	REFERENDA	RECALL	STATE	INITIATIVE	REFERENDA	RECALL
Alabama				Montana	X	X	X
Alaska	X	X	X	Nebraska	X	X	
Arizona	X	X	X	Nevada	X	X	X
Arkansas	X	X		New Hampshire		X	
California	X	X	X	New Jersey		X	X
Colorado	X	X	X	New Mexico		X	X
Connecticut		X		New York		X	
Delaware		X		North Carolina		X	
Florida	X	X		North Dakota	X	X	X
Georgia		X	X	Ohio	X	X	
Hawaii		X		Oklahoma	X	X	
Idaho	X	X	X	Oregon	X	X	X
Illinois	X	X		Pennsylvania		X	
Indiana		X		Rhode Island		X	X
Iowa		X		South Carolina		X	
Kansas		X	X	South Dakota	X	X	X
Kentucky		X		Tennessee		X	
Louisiana		X	X	Texas		X	
Maine	X	X		Utah	X	X	
Maryland		X		Vermont		X	
Massachusetts	X	X		Virginia		X	
Michigan	X	X	X	Washington	X	X	X
Minnesota		X	X	West Virginia		X	
Mississippi	X	X		Wisconsin		X	X
Missouri	X	X		Wyoming	X	X	

Source: *The Book of States: 2000–2001*

Initiatives, referenda, and recalls are all ways in which citizens, rather than legislatures, can adopt or repeal laws. **What are the two types of initiatives?**

voters must sign a petition requesting such an election.

Recall elections are rare, and the actual recall of an official is even more rare. Why? Elected officials who commit unethical acts are likely to resign or to be censured by their colleagues before a recall can take place. Besides, those who act in highly unpopular ways can be voted out of office in the next regular election, so citizens rarely feel compelled enough to organize a statewide petition drive.

State Government and the Public Good

Some critics of state governments charge that they are large, unresponsive bureaucracies that do not adequately address citizens' needs and concerns. Many people would argue, however, that these criticisms are unfounded. State governments have increased the quality and lowered the cost of some public services. For example, some states have opened offices in shopping malls to allow people to renew their car registration more easily.

Education is another area in which states have tried particularly hard to improve and expand services and opportunities. As a result, all 50 states have seen a dramatic expansion of their state college system. In fact, the research from one study suggests that by the year 2006 college enrollment in the United States will rise to 16.4 million, a 14 percent increase over 1996 college enrollment.

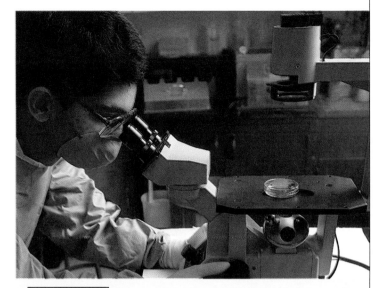

PUBLIC GOOD *Here a researcher at a state university examines a virus through a microscope. State governments have been working hard to improve educational research facilities at public schools.* **How do states determine how well public schools are educating their students?**

To improve their performance, many states also have developed tracking systems that assess how well their governments are fulfilling their responsibilities to citizens. Most states, for example, now use standardized tests to track how well public schools are educating their students. Through these and other inventive methods, states are striving to promote the public good.

Caption Answer

States measure schools' performance through standardized tests.

SECTION 1 REVIEW ANSWERS

1. Refer to the following pages: initiative (463), referendum (464), recall (464).

2. initiatives, referenda, and recalls

3. a. similar—reflect the historical circumstances under which they were written, many strive to outline a social contract based on Locke's philosophy; different—frequent revisions and rewrites of state constitutions and initiative, referendum, and recall in some state constitutions
b. Many states have increased the quality and lowered the cost of public services, expanded educational services, and developed tracking systems to assess the quality of their services.

4. Students should state their opinions and offer support for them. They should offer realistic examples of what might occur.

SECTION 1 REVIEW

1. Define and explain:
- initiative
- referendum
- recall

2. Identifying Concepts: Use the chart below to identify the three ways a citizen of a state can take direct action to influence the legislative process.

Citizen Action		

3. Finding the Main Idea

a. How are the U.S. Constitution and the constitutions of the states similar? How are they different?
b. How have states tried to improve the ways in which they deliver public services?

4. Writing and Critical Thinking

Drawing Conclusions: Why is it important that states have the power to establish laws for such things as driver's licences?
Consider the following:
- What problems might occur if the federal government rather than states established such laws?

Homework Practice Online
keyword: SV3 HP20

SECTION 2

ORGANIZATION

READ TO DISCOVER

1. How are state legislatures structured?
2. What are the responsibilities of a state's executive branch?
3. How are state courts organized?

POLITICAL DICTIONARY

governor
jury pool

Both federal and state governments divide power among legislative, executive, and judicial branches. The organization of the states' branches in many ways mirrors that of the federal government.

State Legislative Branches

Today's state legislatures are different from those of several decades ago. Since then, the powers and makeup of the legislatures have changed, sometimes dramatically.

Terms In most states, senators serve four-year terms, while members of the lower house serve two-year terms. These terms vary from state to state, however, with some senators serving just two years and some lower-house members serving as many as four.

Sessions About 30 years ago, only 20 state legislatures met every year. The other 30 met every two years, often for only three months. Making state law was a part-time job that legislators could perform while running a business, practicing law, or tending a ranch. Perhaps because of the part-time nature of the job, membership turnover was high—generally between 35 and 40 percent in each election.

Today the number of legislatures that meet annually has increased from 20 to 43. Being a legislator, however, still is a full-time job in only nine states (California, Illinois, Massachusetts, Michigan, New Jersey, New York, Ohio, Pennsylvania, and Wisconsin). Turnover among members has declined somewhat, although it is still much higher than the rate for Congress.

Qualifications Like members of Congress, state legislators must be U.S. citizens. They generally also must live in the district they represent. As with terms and sessions, however, age requirements for serving as a state legislator vary across the states. Many states require senators to be at least 25 years of age and lower-house members to be at least 21. In several states, however, the age requirement is only 18 for both houses.

Most state legislators are younger than the average member of Congress. Many politicians start their political careers in state legislatures, later becoming members of Congress, governors, or judges. Indeed, unlike in Congress, where it is not unusual for members to serve 20 years or more, few people choose to make a career out of serving in a state legislature.

How accurately do state legislatures reflect the population as a whole? As of 2001, 22 percent of

POLITICAL PROCESSES *State legislators need to devote a lot of time to their political positions in order to keep up with today's complex system of government.* **In how many states is being a legislator considered a full time job?**

State Legislatures

STATE	NUMBER OF MEMBERS		SESSIONS	MINIMUM AGE	STATE	NUMBER OF MEMBERS		SESSIONS	MINIMUM AGE
Alabama	Senate	35	Annual	25	Montana	Senate	50	Biennial—odd years	18
	House	105		21		House	100		18
Alaska	Senate	20	Annual	25	Nebraska	Senate	49	Annual	21
	House	40		21					
Arizona	Senate	30	Annual	25	Nevada	Senate	21	Biennial—odd years	21
	House	60		25		House	42		21
Arkansas	Senate	35	Biennial—odd years	25	New Hampshire	Senate	24	Annual	30
	House	100		21		House	400		18
California	Senate	40	Annual, full time	18	New Jersey	Senate	40	Annual	30
	Assembly	80		18		House	80		21
Colorado	Senate	35	Annual	25	New Mexico	Senate	42	Annual	25
	House	65		25		House	70		21
Connecticut	Senate	36	Annual	18	New York	Senate	61	Annual, full time	18
	House	151		18		House	150		18
Delaware	Senate	21	Annual	27	North Carolina	Senate	50	Annual—legal provisions for odd years only	21
	House	41		24		House	120		25
Florida	Senate	40	Annual	21	North Dakota	Senate	49	Biennial—odd years	18
	House	120		21		House	98		18
Georgia	Senate	56	Annual	25	Ohio	Senate	33	Annual, full time	18
	House	180		21		House	99		18
Hawaii	Senate	25	Annual	18	Oklahoma	Senate	48	Annual	25
	House	51		18		House	101		21
Idaho	Senate	35	Annual	18	Oregon	Senate	30	Biennial—odd years	21
	House	70		18		House	60		21
Illinois	Senate	59	Annual, full time	21	Pennsylvania	Senate	50	Annual, full time	25
	House	118		21		House	100		21
Indiana	Senate	50	Annual	25	Rhode Island	Senate	50	Annual	18
	House	100		21		House	100		18
Iowa	Senate	50	Annual	25	South Carolina	Senate	46	Annual	25
	House	100		21		House	124		21
Kansas	Senate	40	Annual	18	South Dakota	Senate	35	Annual	21
	House	125		18		House	70		21
Kentucky	Senate	38	Biennial—even years	30	Tennessee	Senate	33	Annual	30
	House	100		24		House	99		21
Louisiana	Senate	39	Annual	18	Texas	Senate	31	Biennial—odd years	26
	House	105		18		House	150		21
Maine	Senate	35	Annual	25	Utah	Senate	29	Annual	25
	House	151		21		House	75		25
Maryland	Senate	47	Annual	25	Vermont	Senate	30	Annual—legal provisions for odd years only	18
	House	141		21		House	150		18
Massachusetts	Senate	40	Biennial, full time	18	Virginia	Senate	40	Annual	21
	House	160		18		House	100		21
Michigan	Senate	38	Annual, full time	21	Washington	Senate	49	Annual	18
	House	110		21		House	98		18
Minnesota	Senate	67	Annual—legal provisions for odd years only	18	West Virginia	Senate	34	Annual	25
	House	134		18		House	100		18
Mississippi	Senate	52	Annual	25	Wisconsin	Senate	33	Annual	18
	House	122		21		House	99		18
Missouri	Senate	34	Annual	30	Wyoming	Senate	30	Annual	25
	House	163		24		House	60		21

Source: *The World Almanac:* 2001; *The Book of States:* 2000–2001

Transparency

An overhead transparency of the chart on this page is available in *Transparency Resources.* See Transparency 43: State Legislatures.

ACROSS THE CURRICULUM

HISTORY Almost all U.S. states currently have bicameral state legislatures. Vermont had a unicameral legislature until 1836, when it adopted a bicameral system.

Nebraska had a bicameral legislature until 1934, when, by a substantial majority, voters passed a measure to change the legislature to a unicameral system. The measure had the support of George Norris, a respected senator in the U.S. Congress. A feature that probably attracted many voters was the reduced cost of running the government with only one house, for the economic crisis of the Great Depression had made low costs attractive to many Nebraskans.

Though historical circumstances influenced the decision to adopt a unicameral legislature, the citizens of the state were pleased with the change and have not returned to a bicameral system. Thus, Nebraska is currently the only state with a unicameral legislature. ■

POLITICAL PROCESSES The number and nature of legislative committees in a state government depends on the needs of the state's citizenry. Alaska, which has a small population, has a senate with only nine standing committees, which cover concerns such as finances, resources, transportation, and the judiciary. On the other hand, New York's senate has 32 standing committees, most of which have no exact equivalent in Alaska. Examples include committees on aging, higher education, cities, crime victims, and consumer protection.

With its larger population, bigger cities, and more varied economy, New York places greater demands on its legislature than does Alaska. Alaska, however, requires each of its committees to cover a broader range of tasks than those covered by individual committees in New York. ∎

their members were women—a far higher percentage than in Congress (14 percent). About 7 percent of state legislators were African American. This figure does not differ much from the percentage in Congress in 2001 (7 percent) but is lower than the percentage of African Americans in the entire U.S. population (about 12 percent). About 2 percent of state legislators were Hispanic, compared with about 4 percent of Congress in 2001 and 12.5 percent in the U.S. population as a whole. The percentages of Asian Americans and American Indians serving as state legislators are also lower than their percentages in the population.

Salaries For many decades, state legislative salaries were low. As the job became more influential and time-consuming, however, legislators' salaries generally increased. California offers the highest salary at $99,000 a year, while New Hampshire legislators earn only $100 a year, and Alabama legislators earn just $10 a day.

Leadership Except for Nebraska, which has a nonpartisan, one-house legislature, all state legislatures are bicameral, or have two houses. In each house, there is a presiding officer with substantial leadership powers. As in Congress, these leaders assign bills to committees, make committee assignments, and control floor debates.

Committees Committees perform the main legislative work of the states, just as they do for the nation. That is, state legislative committees consider and report on proposed bills.

Bills undergo a legislative committee process similar to that in Congress. First, a member of the state legislature introduces a bill. It is then assigned to and considered in committee. If the bill is approved there, the full state senate and lower house debate it and vote on it.

If different versions of the bill are passed in the two houses, a joint committee will draft a compromise version. The compromise bill is then voted on in both houses and, if passed, sent to the executive branch, where it may be signed into law or vetoed.

Until fairly recently, state legislature committees had little power and no support staff, although today they have a great deal of power. Keep in mind, however, that the power of committees varies from state to state. In some states the legislative committees resemble congressional committees in their scope of influence. In other states, committees are not nearly as strong as in Congress, making it relatively easy to get a bill considered on the floor without committee approval.

As their power has increased, the state legislative committees' staff also has increased. By around 1990 the 50 state legislatures employed more than 33,000 staff members. In most states, committee staff is not divided along party lines, as it is in Congress. Instead, the entire staff serves the committee as a whole, regardless of the members' party affiliations. Gradually, however, partisan staffing is spreading to more states.

State Executive Branches

Every state has a **governor**, or elected chief executive. The qualifications for holding the governorship, as well as the position's terms, salaries, roles, and powers, vary from state to state.

Governors' Qualifications and Terms
Each state's constitution lists the requirements for becoming governor. Most states require that the governor be a U.S. citizen. He or she also must have resided in the state in question for a certain length of time. Age requirements vary from state to state, but typically a governor must be at least 30 years of age.

Governors in 48 states serve four-year terms. In New Hampshire and Vermont, however, they serve only two years. A number of states limit governors to serving two terms. Virginia is more extreme, allowing its governor to serve only one term.

Governors' Salaries
As with state legislators, the salaries of governors vary widely. The governor of New York, for example, receives $179,000 a year. In contrast, the governor of Nebraska earns $65,000. Most states also provide their chief executive and his or her family with a governor's mansion or other official residence in the state capital. In addition, due to the nature and requirements of their job, governors receive an allowance for travel and related expenses.

Governors' Roles
Governors, like presidents, generally take an active role in initiating legislation, preparing budgets, and setting an agenda for the state. In recent years, for example, governors

Linking

Government and History

Constitutional Change over Time

The constitutions of the United States and of each individual state have changed as a result of key events in history. Change in the U.S. Constitution is reflected in its 27 amendments, such as those ending slavery, extending the right to vote, and banning poll taxes. At the state level, change has been reflected in amendments and in complete revisions of some states' constitutions. In fact, some states have been governed by nearly a dozen different constitutions over the years.

What brought about some of these changes? How have historical events affected constitutional government in the states over time? Constitutional measures in the states often have reflected general attitudes and beliefs at the time in which they were adopted. Consider, for example, state constitutions that were adopted before 1820. Remembering more domineering governors that had been imposed on the colonies by the British crown before 1776, state leaders developed constitutions that put strong limits on executive power. Over time, however, amendments in various states brought a more even balance in power between the two branches of government.

Constitutional change in the decades after the Civil War also reflected the times and historical events, especially in the southern states of the former Confederacy. For example, after the war southern states, under federal occupation, adopted new constitutions that secured legal rights for former slaves. Under those constitutions, African Americans won elections to government offices across the South. For example, between 1869 and 1901 twenty African Americans represented Southern districts in the U.S. House. Mississippi sent two African Americans to the Senate during this period.

Following Reconstruction and the removal of federal troops, however, white southerners who opposed political rights for African Americans returned to power. This brought about another wave of constitutional change across the South. Revised constitutions allowed states to pass laws imposing a form of second-class citizenship on African Americans. These laws included measures for racial segregation and voting restrictions.

For example, Louisiana and six other southern states adopted measures that waived literacy and other eligibility requirements for people eligible to vote before Jan. 1, 1867. Those measures effectively barred most African Americans from voting. How? None had been eligible to vote before 1867, and few had ever received any formal education or could meet other requirements.

State constitutions today still reflect many attitudes that evolved in past eras. Primary and referendum elections, for example, gained popularity during the Progressive Era of the early 1900s. Both measures reflected the desire of many people at the time to expand democracy by allowing voters to bypass legislatures to enact popular laws.

The Granger Collection, New York

Pictured here is Hiram R. Revels, who in 1870 became the first African American elected to the U.S. Senate.

What Do You Think?

1. What are some historical events or general attitudes and beliefs that have been reflected in constitutional changes in the states?
2. Do you think that the changes made in state constitutions as a result of a key event in history have promoted the public good? Explain.

What Do You Think?
Answers

1. State constitutions written shortly after the Revolution usually placed strong limits on executive power. Southern constitutions written after Reconstruction included provisions designed to prevent African Americans from voting.

2. Answers will vary, but students should keep in mind that changes made in response to specific historic events must sometimes be changed again as time passes. Students should offer support for their answers.

THEMES IN GOVERNMENT

POLITICAL FOUNDATIONS

The colonial experience and the American Revolution influenced the drafters of the state constitutions in the eighteenth century. In addition to limiting the power of the executive, they sought to protect their newly gained liberty by including a list of enumerated rights. These drafters may also have remembered the role that the British Parliament played before and during the war, because they also placed many limits on legislative power, including residency requirements for legislators and scheduled elections so that the voters could remove politicians whom they feared or disliked. ■

THEMES IN GOVERNMENT

POLITICAL PROCESSES

Using various indicators, including veto power, influence over the budget process, and term length, some political scientists have created a scale to determine which state governors have the most power and which have the least.

The researchers conclude that the governors of the nine states of Hawaii, Iowa, Maryland, New Jersey, New York, Ohio, Pennsylvania, Tennessee, and West Virginia possess the most institutional power.

Terms of Office and Salaries of State Governors

STATE	LENGTH OF TERM (in years)	SALARY	STATE	LENGTH OF TERM (in years)	SALARY	STATE	LENGTH OF TERM (in years)	SALARY
Alabama	4	$94,655	Louisiana	4	$95,000	Ohio	4	$126,496
Alaska	4	$81,648	Maine	4	$70,000	Oklahoma	4	$101,140
Arizona	4	$95,000	Maryland	4	$120,000	Oregon	4	$88,300
Arkansas	4	$68,448	Massachusetts	4	$135,000	Pennsylvania	4	$105,035
California	4	$175,000	Michigan	4	$127,300	Rhode Island	4	$95,000
Colorado	4	$90,000	Minnesota	4	$120,303	South Carolina	4	$106,078
Connecticut	4	$78,000	Mississippi	4	$101,800	South Dakota	4	$92,602
Delaware	4	$107,000	Missouri	4	$119,982	Tennessee	4	$85,000
Florida	4	$120,171	Montana	4	$83,672	Texas	4	$115,345
Georgia	4	$122,998	Nebraska	4	$65,000	Utah	4	$96,700
Hawaii	4	$94,780	Nevada	4	$117,000	Vermont	2	$115,763
Idaho	4	$95,500	New Hampshire	2	$96,060	Virginia	4	$124,855
Illinois	4	$145,877	New Jersey	4	$85,000	Washington	4	$135,960
Indiana	4	$77,200	New Mexico	4	$90,000	West Virginia	4	$90,000
Iowa	4	$104,352	New York	4	$179,000	Wisconsin	4	$115,699
Kansas	4	$94,035	North Carolina	4	$113,656	Wyoming	4	$95,000
Kentucky	4	$99,657	North Dakota	4	$76,879			

Source: *World Almanac: 1997; The Book of States: 1994*

State constitutions outline many aspects of the office of governor such as the yearly salary and the number of terms an individual may hold the office. **What is the salary for the governor of Colorado?**

in several states have taken the lead on issues such as education and welfare reform. Their actions at the state level have often propelled them into leadership roles on these issues at the national level.

In addition, governors today often act as their states' chief ambassadors, working to attract business investment and to encourage the purchase of state exports. Governors frequently become personally involved in negotiations with large companies that are considering locating their offices and factories in the state. Governors even travel to other countries to promote their state to foreign investors and to find markets abroad for its products and businesses.

Governors' Powers As governors' roles have expanded, their powers have increased as well. As noted in Chapter 2, the constitutions of the newly independent American states created weak governorships. Remembering how strong colonial governors had abused their power, citizens of the young country worked to ensure that state

governors would not do the same. This legacy of limiting governors' powers continued well into the 1900s.

For example, most governors' appointment powers are restricted. Unlike presidents, governors seldom may appoint all the agency heads in the executive branch. In almost all states, for example, the attorney general is elected separately from the governor. In addition voters in many states also elect a lieutenant governor, secretary of state, treasurer, and state auditor or comptroller—whose job is to ensure that no public funds are paid out of the state treasury unless authorized by law.

Most governors do possess one power that traditionally has been withheld from the president—the line-item veto. As noted in Chapter 6, a line-item veto can be used to void specific parts of legislation or budget appropriations while signing the rest of the bill into law. By 1994, governors in 41 states held this power. In 1995 Congress also gave line-item veto power to the president, but a federal judge ruled the legislation unconstitutional. The case was appealed to the Supreme Court. In 1997 the Court ruled that the law's constitutionality could not be decided at that point because the president had not yet exercised the power. In 1998 the line-item veto was declared unconstitutional.

State Judicial Branches

As noted in Chapter 11, cases that involve federal laws or the federal government must go through the federal courts. Most legal rules that affect people's everyday lives are passed not by the federal government, however, but by the states. Therefore, most court cases take place in state courts. In addition, local courts also are established by states to handle matters of state law. During the mid-1990s state and local courts dealt with 99.7 percent of all cases filed in the United States.

Like the federal judiciary, the states maintain two basic types of courts: trial and appeals. The states have also established a number of special courts.

Trial Courts Most states' trial courts, though a part of state government, are organized at the county level. The office of the district attorney or the public prosecutor is in charge of investigating and prosecuting state criminal cases. In many states, criminal cases cannot be brought by the district attorney's office without a grand jury's approval. As noted in Chapter 12, a grand jury is a panel of citizens who determine if the government has enough evidence to put a person on trial.

As noted in Chapter 12, after a grand jury hands down an indictment, a trial—or petit (PEH-tee)—jury hears the case. In almost every state, juries in criminal cases consist of 12 jurors and in most states there can be no conviction in a criminal trial without a unanimous verdict.

As noted in Chapter 12, the jury selection process begins when potential jurors are chosen to come to court. Traditionally, potential jurors were selected using lists that included only one group of people, such as licensed drivers, car owners, or registered voters. This method, however, does a poor job of ensuring representative juries. For example, because poor people and young people are less likely to register to vote than others, they will have a relatively low chance of being called for jury duty in states that choose potential jurors from lists of registered voters only. As a result, 25

states have begun using multiple sources to compile their jury lists.

In many courts potential jurors sit around the courthouse for a long period of time as part of a **jury pool**, a group of people who might be chosen to serve in a trial. This waiting burdens people because they cannot work or attend classes while part of a jury pool. As a result, many people called as potential jurors ask to be excused from jury duty.

In recent years many state courts have introduced a system called one day, one trial. People selected under this system must appear as a potential juror for only one day. If not chosen as a juror on that day, he or she need not return. If chosen, the person need sit in only the trial for which he or she was selected. The one-day, one-trial system was first used in Houston in 1972. As of the

Comparing Governments

The Federal Republic of Nigeria

Federal governments in other countries have many similarities to the U.S. government. Oftentimes, however, those similarities appear only on the surface. Until recently this was the case with the Federal Republic of Nigeria.

A former British colony, Nigeria gained its independence in 1960. Although the country's constitution divided responsibility among federal, state, and local governments, the country was actually run by a series of military governments. Finally, after many years as a military dictatorship, Nigeria held its first free elections in 1999.

The difficulties did not end with the elections. Besides facing economic instability, coup threats, and regional tensions, new leaders also had to learn the fundamental elements of democracy. With the help of the United States, the new Nigerian government held training for all 10,300 newly elected officials. Training focused on the building blocks of a democratic government, including how to manage programs and resources, how to be accountable to citizens, and how to diffuse conflicts.

**SECTION 2
REVIEW ANSWERS**

1. Refer to the following pages: governor (468), jury pool (471).

2. State trial courts are usually organized at the county level and hear criminal cases brought by the public prosecutor or the district attorney. Appeals courts hear cases appealed within the state court system. Special courts found in 44 states include family courts, probate courts, and juvenile courts, and have limited jurisdiction.

3. a. First, bills are introduced, then assigned to a committee for consideration. Bills that are approved go to both houses for debate. If different versions are passed, a joint committee writes a compromise version and sends it to both houses for approval. If passed by both houses, it is then sent to the executive branch.

b. Governors' roles and powers have expanded to include handling issues such as education, welfare reform, and the line-item veto.

4. Students should state their opinions and show an understanding of the Missouri Plan. Students should explain how advantages outweigh the disadvantages.

Caption Answer
probate courts

POLITICAL PROCESSES *West Virginia Supreme Court judges look over the backlog of cases that have flooded their court.* **What courts handle the estates of deceased people?**

early 1990s, courts serving about 30 states were using this system.

Appeals Courts Cases under state law generally may be appealed only within the state court system. The highest court of appeals in a state is generally called the state supreme court. A state case can be appealed to the federal courts only if it involves a possible violation of the U.S. Constitution or other federal law.

Special Courts In 44 states there are also several special courts with limited jurisdiction, or that handle only specific types of cases. As with most state courts, these special courts usually are organized at the county level and sometimes at the city level. The most common special courts are

★ family courts, which handle divorces and child custody and support;
★ probate courts, which handle the estates of deceased people;
★ juvenile courts, which handle offenses committed by people legally too young to appear in adult criminal courts; and
★ traffic courts, which handle cases involving traffic violations.

The Judges Unlike the judges of the federal courts, who are appointed, county trial court judges are usually elected. Even state supreme court judges are elected in almost half of the states. In other states the governor appoints the judges, and in a few, the legislature selects them.

Twenty-seven states have adopted some form of the Missouri Plan for choosing state court judges. Introduced in Missouri in 1940, this plan empowers a nonpartisan commission led by the state bar association to develop a list of candidates qualified to serve as judges. The governor then selects judges from among those candidates, and voters decide at a regularly scheduled election, usually a year later, whether to retain the judges in office.

Most state judges serve limited terms—most often 6 to 10 years. Judges in only one state—Rhode Island—serve for life, as U.S. Supreme Court justices do. In two states—Massachusetts and New Hampshire—judges may serve until age 70, when they must retire. Seated judges in the other states, however, are often re-elected at the end of their terms, enabling many of them to retain their positions for life.

SECTION 2 REVIEW

1. Define and explain:
• governor
• jury pool

2. Identifying Concepts: Use the chart below to describe state trial, appeals, and special courts.

State Courts	
Trial Court:	
Appeals Court:	
Special Courts:	

Homework Practice Online
keyword: SV3 HP20

3. **Finding the Main Idea**
a. How do most state legislatures operate?
b. How have governors' roles and powers changed over time?

4. **Writing and Critical Thinking**
Taking a Stand: What are the advantages and disadvantages of the Missouri Plan for selecting state supreme court judges? Do you think that the advantages of this system outweigh the disadvantages? Write a paragraph describing and defending your ideas.

SECTION 3

STATE BUDGETS AND REVENUES

READ TO DISCOVER

1. How are state budgets created?
2. What are the main sources of state revenue?

POLITICAL DICTIONARY

sales tax
sin tax
income tax
severance tax
bond rating

As the trend toward less federal involvement in state affairs grows, state governments are taking on new responsibilities. Indeed, state governments are currently on the front lines of some of the nation's most difficult challenges, such as making policies dealing with education, drugs, welfare, and crime. As states formulate programs in these areas, they also must find ways to pay for them.

State Budgets

State legislatures generally play a role in the state budget process similar to that played by Congress in the federal budget process. The governor usually presents a budget to the legislature. The members of the legislature then debate the proposed budget and draft their own version, consulting with the executive branch in the process. The legislature draws up a final budget, votes on it, and sends it to the governor for his or her signature.

One key difference between the state and federal budget processes is that most states require by law that the budget be balanced. That is, state spending cannot exceed state revenues. Long before people began clamoring for a balanced-budget amendment to the U.S. Constitution, states had this requirement in place.

Achieving a balanced budget can be challenging during economic downswings, however. Therefore, some states, when revenues are up, hold money in "rainy day" funds set aside for tough economic times. The only exception to the balanced-budget requirement involves long-term bonds used to pay for expensive projects, such as the building of roads, bridges, schools, hospitals, and prisons. As noted in Chapter 9, a bond is a certificate issued by an institution (a government or corporation) in exchange for money borrowed from an investor.

Another difference between the federal and state budgets is the source of government revenue. Unlike the federal government, which depends on the income tax for the largest part of its revenue, states receive money from many sources, including various taxes, fees, federal grants, loans, and lotteries.

State Taxes

Most state governments have sales and income taxes. Some also have severance taxes. States try to keep their tax burdens down because a high tax rate often discourages businesses from locating their operations there.

Sales Taxes A **sales tax** is a tax placed on the sale of a good or service and is charged as a percentage of the sales price. West Virginia adopted the first sales tax in the United States in 1921. Today all but five states—Alaska, Delaware, Montana, New Hampshire, and Oregon—have a sales tax. Rates are generally the same for all goods and range from 2.9 percent in Colorado to 7 percent in Mississippi and Rhode Island.

Many states exclude some basic items from the sales tax. Half exclude food, and all but five exclude prescription drugs. Other states do not charge a sales tax on items such as clothing, and some do not tax the sale of college textbooks.

Special Sales Taxes Some states have additional sales taxes on certain categories of goods and services. For example, most states have special hotel sales taxes, which are often passed because they are paid largely by visitors from other states. Thus, a state can raise these tax rates without angering state residents. State officials must keep in mind, however, that if such taxes rise too high, businesses may decide to hold their conferences and other travel-related functions in

POLITICAL PROCESSES New Hampshire does not have a sales tax, and its income tax is only on dividends and interest. Gubernatorial candidates who have not taken "The Pledge," a promise not to institute a sales or income tax on other items, have not succeeded in winning office.

To raise money, the state has turned to other revenue sources. For example, it taxes business profits. New Hampshire also was the first state to establish a lottery. The state has found other unique ways of raising revenue as well. It has not only instituted high taxes on hotel rooms but also runs its own liquor store system, which generates over $40 million of revenue per year.

There are, however, costs to not having a sales tax or an income tax. New Hampshire's state services are minimal, and the state does not spend much money on education in comparison to other states. Partially because of the state's low revenue, local governments in New Hampshire find it necessary to impose high property taxes to operate social services. ■

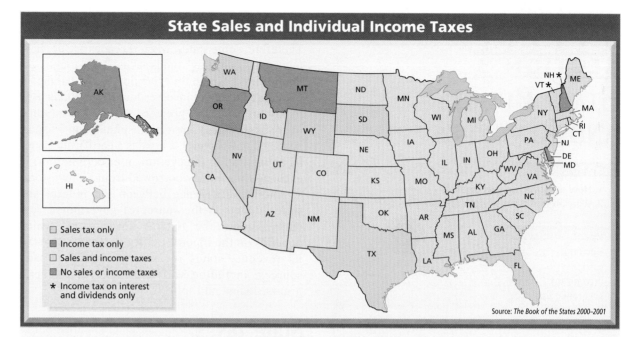

State Sales and Individual Income Taxes

Legend:
- □ Sales tax only
- ■ Income tax only
- □ Sales and income taxes
- ■ No sales or income taxes
- ★ Income tax on interest and dividends only

Source: *The Book of the States 2000–2001*

*Most states raise revenues by using a combination of sales and income taxes, but some states use either sales taxes or income taxes to raise revenue. **What is the only state that does not collect a sales tax or levy an income tax?***

states with lower taxes. Vacationers also might choose a less expensive destination.

Another kind of special sales tax are sin taxes. **Sin taxes** are meant to discourage the purchase of some types of goods, such as liquor and cigarettes. Some states charge as much as 81.5 cents in tax on a pack of cigarettes and $6.50 on a gallon of hard liquor. In 1991 California introduced a type of sin tax on snack foods. Although the state does not tax food, the passage of this law removed the sales tax exemption from snack foods.

Income Taxes An **income tax** is a tax placed on a variety of types of income, including profits, interest, and dividends, and can be levied on individuals and businesses. Wisconsin passed the first state income tax in 1911. Today 43 states have an individual income tax, although 2 of these only tax income from interest and dividends. All states but three—Nevada, Washington, and Wyoming—also have some form of tax on business income. In some states the income tax has a flat rate. That is, all people, regardless of how much money they earn, pay the same percentage of their income in taxes. In other states the rate is progressive, as with the federal income tax. This means that a person's income tax rate rises as his or her income rises.

The highest state income tax is in North Dakota, where people who earn more than $50,000 a year must turn over 12 percent of their incomes.

Severance Taxes **Severance taxes** are those placed on the extraction of nonrenewable resources, such as oil, coal, and natural gas. This type of tax is paid by a business when it removes such resources from the ground.

Most states raise less than 10 percent of their total tax revenue through severance taxes. States with large reserves of oil and minerals—such as Alaska, Louisiana, Montana, New Mexico, Wyoming, and North Dakota—earn a higher percentage of revenue than other states from severance taxes. In 1996 Alaska took in the highest amount from this source—around half of its total tax revenue.

State Fees

States also charge fees directly to the people who use a particular state service. These types of user fees include highway tolls, auto registration and driver's license fees, fishing and hunting license fees, and state park fees. One of the largest user fees in most states is tuition at state colleges. Some people support this method of financing a government service because user fees remove some of the monetary burden from the general tax payers and place it on those who actually use the service.

Federal Grants

A large revenue source for state governments is federal grants. As noted in Chapter 4, the federal government gives categorical and block grants to the states for many types of projects, such as building schools, roads, and bridges. In 1996 the federal government gave $227 billion in grants to state and local governments. By 2000, that figure had risen to a trillion dollars.

Rapid expansion of federal grants between 1960 and 1980 allowed state and local governments to increase their activities without significantly raising taxes. Many grant programs were set up during President Lyndon Johnson's administration. These grants differed from their predecessors in that they were intended to aid poor people rather than fund public works projects. Some grant programs established during the Johnson administration have been used to fund public education programs for poor students, provide health insurance for those in poverty, and aid in the construction of mass transit systems in cities. A number of the new programs, such as grants to public schools and to local police departments, involved policy areas traditionally reserved to state and local government.

During the early 1980s, however, cutbacks in federal grants created a funding crisis that sent state and local governments scrambling to develop new sources of revenue. Some states, often at the initiative of their governors, have raised taxes in recent years.

Borrowing

Having a mandate to create balanced budgets, most state governments cannot borrow money to fund a budget deficit, as the federal government does. They may, however, borrow in the short term to keep the government running until the budget's predicted tax revenue is collected.

States also may borrow money for longer periods of time to fund lengthy construction projects, such as roads, prisons, college dormitories, and hospitals. Because such construction projects have a long life, lawmakers typically spread their cost out over several years instead of funding them through a single year's budget.

PRINCIPLES OF DEMOCRACY *Toll roads, such as the one pictured here, charge user fees directly to those who actually use the service. **What are some other state services that charge a user fee?***

How do states borrow money? They do so by issuing bonds. A state bond indicates that the state is in debt to the bondholder for the amount listed on the certificate. In exchange for loaning money to the state, the bondholder receives interest on the bond. When the bond matures—typically after a number of years—the state returns the amount borrowed to the investor plus interest.

The interest rates a state offers on its bonds vary according to the state's bond rating. A **bond rating**—determined by independent, private organizations—is a measure of how much faith the financial community has in the issuer's (the state's) financial stability. Bond ratings vary from A3 to Aaa (the highest rating issued by Moody's Investors Service). In 1999, for example, Georgia, Maryland, Missouri, North Carolina, South Carolina, Tennessee, Utah, and Virginia all received Moody's highest rating. States with high bond ratings pay less money in interest because the bondholder is taking on less risk.

Lotteries and Gambling Revenues

In search of ways to raise funds "painlessly," without raising taxes, many states have turned to lotteries and other gambling revenues. In 1964 New

THEMES IN GOVERNMENT

PUBLIC GOOD Some critics have pointed to numerous problems generated by state lotteries. Advertising costs for lotteries in the United States reached half a billion dollars in 1996. This expense, combined with the cost of the prizes and of administration, means that only about 34 cents of every dollar spent on the lottery actually becomes part of a state's revenue.

Critics also charge that lottery advertising in many states is deceptive and does not reveal the real odds of winning big jackpots. These odds are sometimes 12 million to 1.

Scandals involving lottery operations have occurred in Texas, New Jersey, and other states. Though every state forbids gambling by minors, the easy availability of lottery tickets gives many teenagers the opportunity to play anyway. Although these problems have raised doubts in the minds of some Americans about the public good of lotteries as a revenue source, only Utah and Hawaii have no form of legalized gambling. ∎

POLITICAL PROCESSES *State-sponsored lotteries have become a source for additional income. State lotteries usually provide 2 to 3 percent of these states' revenues.* **What percent of Nevada's revenue is received from taxes on gambling?**

money in the hope of striking it rich. Early lottery advertising reflected this worry by trying to downplay that the lottery is a form of gambling. Instead, states stressed the worthy causes to which lottery revenues were being applied.

As state budgets grew tighter and tighter, however, and as the popularity of gambling increased, more states adopted lotteries. To maintain interest in the lotteries and to keep sales high, states turned from emphasizing the support of education to enticing buyers with the possibility of huge wealth. As a result, the size of the jackpots started rising astronomically. As of 2000 the largest prize awarded to a single ticket holder in a drawing was $181 million. States also began offering many additional games, particularly "instant winner" lotteries. To reach more people, the states began selling lottery tickets in additional places, including, in some cases, checkout lines at supermarkets.

Hampshire became the first state in the 1900s to establish a lottery. Today state-run lotteries exist in 38 states, providing about 2 to 3 percent of their total revenue.

At first, state lotteries spread slowly. Many critics objected to them on moral grounds, saying that the government should not encourage gambling among citizens. These critics charged that the lottery was not at all painless, that it encouraged citizens, particularly poor ones, to spend their

Casino gambling is a revenue source in several states, including Nevada and New Jersey. Taxes on gambling in Nevada provide the state with 40 percent of its revenue. In addition, six states have authorized riverboat gambling in dockside casinos. Some states also collect revenue from the horse- and dog-racing industries.

SECTION 3 REVIEW

1. Define and explain:
- sales tax
- sin tax
- income tax
- severance tax
- bond rating

2. Identifying Concepts:
Copy the chart below and use it to describe the advantages and disadvantages of each kind of tax.

TAXES			

Homework Practice Online
keyword: SV3 HP20

3. Finding the Main Idea
a. Why do states borrow money?
b. How is the state budget process similar to the federal budget process? How is it different?

4. Writing and Critical Thinking

Drawing Conclusions: Should states raise revenues through lotteries and other forms of gambling? Do you think lotteries are truly a painless way to raise money for state programs? Write a paragraph describing and defending your ideas.

GOVERNMENT IN THE NEWS

The States and Elections

When Americans awoke on the morning of Wednesday, November 8, 2000, they expected to find out, finally, who had won the presidential election held the previous day. By late Tuesday night the tally indicated that Vice President Al Gore was leading Texas governor George W. Bush in the popular vote, but in the all-important electoral vote, neither candidate had a clear majority. Rather than learn which man was now president-elect, however, Americans were confronted by debates over the complexity of election law.

Much of the debate concerned the election laws in Florida, the state that proved critical in the presidential election. The vote appeared too close to call, and whichever candidate won a majority of the Florida vote would gain the necessary majority of electoral votes and become the next president. The issue was complicated by the variety of voting methods—punch cards, paper ballots, and voting machines—employed across the state. Local judges, and eventually the Florida Supreme Court, ordered recounts in a number of counties.

Article II of the U.S. Constitution provides the mechanism for electing the president. Each state is allotted a slate of electors equal to the number of senators and representatives that state sends to Congress. Subsequent constitutional amendments and federal legislation have added further detail, but the states are still responsible for carrying out presidential elections.

As a result, the particulars of state election law are crucial in a close race. States have different requirements for the casting and counting of ballots, as well as for the recounting of disputed ballots. For example, Texas, which is home to NASA's Johnson Space Center, allows astronauts to cast ballots while on a space flight. The states also have many provisions for recounting ballots.

George W. and Laura Bush at the 2000 Republican National Convention.

Different procedures are required if the ballots were cast manually or mechanically, or if the initial tabulation was done by machine.

In 2000 it was five weeks before Americans knew which candidate had won the presidency. On Tuesday, December 12, The U.S. Supreme Court handed down its decision in *Bush* v. *Gore*, finding that the recount vote in Florida violated the Equal Protection Clause of the Fourteenth Amendment of the U.S. Constitution. George W. Bush became the forty-third president of the United States.

What Do You Think?

1. Why do the federal and state governments share powers in conducting elections? Do you think that the federal government should have more or less authority in national elections? Explain your answer.

> ▶ **WHY IT MATTERS TODAY**
>
> The 2000 presidential election revealed the importance of state election laws. Use **CNNfyi.com** or other **current events** sources to find more information about debates over election policies in the United States. Record your findings in your Government Notebook.
>
>
> CNNfyi.com

(Continued on page 478)

Government in the News Answers

1. Answers will vary. Students might suggest that states often have different needs when it comes to conducting an election. Students should explain their answers and support them with evidence from the text.

CHAPTER 20
Review Answers

Writing a Summary

Summaries should focus on the main points of each section. These may be found in the Read to Discover questions at the start of each section. Summaries should also use standard grammar, spelling, sentence structure, and punctuation.

Identifying People and Ideas

Refer to the following pages: initiative (463), referendum (464), recall (464), governor (468), jury pool (471), sales tax (473), sin tax (474), income tax (474), severance tax (474), bond rating (475).

Understanding Main Ideas

1. direct or indirect initiative

2. by submitting it to a vote in the form of a referendum

3. by getting enough voters to sign a petition requesting a recall election

(Continued from page 477)

4. As in the federal government, power in state government is divided among legislative, executive, and judicial branches.

5. because many members of Congress begin their careers in state legislatures

6. family courts, probate courts, juvenile courts, and traffic courts

7. Many state judges, especially county trial court judges, are elected, whereas federal judges are appointed.

8. Most states have laws that require their budgets to be balanced.

9. States can raise revenue by imposing taxes, charging fees, receiving federal grants, establishing lotteries, and issuing bonds.

10. So it could have a low interest rate on any bonds it issued.

Reviewing Themes

1. State governments promote the public good by providing public services, educational opportunities, and testing and tracking systems to assess the quality of services.

2. Students should state and explain their opinions regarding the usefulness of a recall and explain how they would initiate one.

3. A legislator introduces a bill, which is then considered by the committee. The committee performs the main legislative work by studying the bill and then voting on it. If the committee approves the bill, it is voted

(Continued on page 479)

CHAPTER 20
Review

Writing a Summary

Using standard grammar, spelling, sentence structure, and punctuation, write a summary of the information in this chapter.

Identifying People and Ideas

Identify the following terms or individuals and explain their significance.

1. initiative

2. referendum

3. recall

4. governor

5. jury pool

6. sales tax

7. sin tax

8. income tax

9. severance tax

10. bond rating

Understanding Main Ideas

SECTION 1 *(pp. 461–465)*

1. What procedure can voters in some states use to propose a new law?

2. How could a state legislature get direct citizen input on a controversial proposal it is considering?

3. How could dissatisfied voters remove an elected official from office before the official's term is over?

SECTION 2 *(pp. 466–472)*

4. Among what branches is power divided in state government? How does that compare with how power is divided in the federal government?

5. Why is the average age of state legislators younger than that of members of Congress?

6. What are the most common special courts?

7. What is one major difference in the way many state judges get their jobs compared with how federal judges get theirs?

SECTION 3 *(pp. 473–476)*

8. What is one key difference between state and federal budget processes?

9. What are several ways states raise revenues?

10. Why would a state want to maintain a high bond rating?

Reviewing Themes

1. **Public Good** Describe three ways in which state governments promote the public good.

2. **Political Processes** Imagine that an elected official in your state has committed an unethical act. As a registered voter, would you wait for the next election in hopes that the official would not be re-elected, or would you initiate a recall? How would you initiate a recall if you felt it necessary to do so?

3. **Constitutional Government** How is a bill introduced and passed by a state legislature? What part do legislative committees play in the passage of a bill?

Thinking Critically

1. **Drawing Conclusions** In addition to trial and appeals courts, the majority of states have a number of special courts. Do you think these courts help the judicial system run more smoothly or just make it more complicated? How might these special courts promote the public good?

2. **Sequencing** How are state budgets usually created?

3. **Supporting a Point of View** Do you think states should charge a flat income tax or a progressive income tax, like the federal government?

Writing about Government

Review the list of state laws you wrote in your Government Notebook. Now that you have studied this chapter, what other state laws do you know of that affect you personally? Add those laws to your list.

Interpreting the Political Cartoon

Study the cartoon below. Then use it to help you answer the questions that follow. Remember that the 2000 presidential election was not decided until the balloting in Florida had been settled.

SCHOT
ALGEMEEN DAGBLAD
Rotterdam
NETHERLANDS

1. Which sentence describes the cartoonist's point of view?

  a. The counting of ballots was fair.

  b. The counting of ballots was undemocratically influenced by party affiliation.

  c. Ballot counting is a technologically outmoded way to tally votes.

  d. The Flordia Supreme Court acted arbitrarily and did not live up to the ideals of American democracy.

2. Why do you think the cartoonist chose to portray the balloting in this manner?

Analyzing Primary Sources

Read the following excerpt from the inaugural address of Jeanne Shaheen, the first female governor of New Hampshire, then answer the questions.

"For too long, we have been paying the highest electric rates in the nation. They constitute a hidden tax, taking money away from families. . . .

Our task is clear: high electric rates are a threat to our economic future, and they must come down.

We must make sure quality healthcare is affordable and accessible to all our families. . . . And as our population ages, we must develop alternatives to costly nursing home care. . . .

I will make education a priority—in my budget, in my appointments, and in the full weight and visibility granted by this office."

3. According to the speech, what priorities has Shaheen set for her administration?

  a. Shaheen declares that electric rates are too low and outlines a proposal to raise rates.

  b. Shaheen vows to continue the work of her predecessors.

  c. Shaheen promises lower electric rates, affordable health care, alternatives to nursing homes, and better education.

  d. Shaheen promises to introduce a hidden tax that will mainly affect the elderly.

4. As governor, how can Shaheen make sure that her priorities are addressed?

(Continued on page 479)

on by the lower house of the senate. If the house and senate pass different versions of the same bill, a joint committee works out the differences.

Thinking Critically

1. Students should discuss the different special courts, take a position regarding the benefits or liabilities of special courts, and tell how those courts might promote the public good.

2. The governor usually presents a budget to the legislature, which then offers its own version. It confers with the governors office, drafts a final budget, votes on it, then sends it to the governor for approval.

3. Students should discuss the difference between a flat tax and a progressive tax, give their opinions of which would be better, and support their opinions with reasons and examples.

Building Social Studies Skills

1. d

2. Students opinions will vary, but they should discuss the delays caused by the 2000 Florida ballot count and offer and support an opinion about whether the Florida Supreme Court supported the ideals of American democracy.

3. c

4. Governors usually take an active role in initiating legislation, preparing the budget, and setting the agenda for the state. In general governors can use appointments and the line item veto.

Alternative Assessment

Building Your Portfolio

Imagine there are not enough candidates to run in your state's next election. To solve the problem, lawmakers have asked you—a clerk in the state government—to place help-wanted advertisements in the state's major newspapers. Write three want-ads describing the jobs of state legislator, governor, and state supreme court justice. In each ad, be sure to list the qualifications, duties, and term of office.

internet connect

Internet Activity: go.hrw.com
KEYWORD: SV3 GV20

Access the Internet through the HRW Go site to conduct research on the historical background and use of initiative and referendum. Find recent or current examples of a state referendum or initiative. Then write a sample initiative or referendum based on a current political issue. Finally, list the pros and cons of these measures: Should citizens have the power of initiative?

CHAPTER 21 LOCAL GOVERNMENT

	OBJECTIVES	PACING GUIDE	REPRODUCIBLE RESOURCES
SECTION 1 U.S. COMMUNITIES (pp. 481–484)	▸ What is a rural area? ▸ What historical factors led to the growth of cities? ▸ Why did suburbs develop outside of cities? ▸ What is a metropolitan area?	**Regular** .5 day **Block Scheduling** .25 day	**ELL** Spanish Study Guide 21.1 **ELL** English Study Guide 21.1 **PS** Reading 21: *George Washington's Farewell Address*
SECTION 2 LOCAL GOVERNMENT ORGANIZATION (pp. 485–492)	▸ What are the four main types of local government? ▸ What are the different types of municipal government? ▸ What are the functions of a county government? ▸ What services do special districts provide?	**Regular** 1.5 days **Block Scheduling** .75 day	**ELL** Spanish Study Guide 21.2 **ELL** English Study Guide 21.2
SECTION 3 REVENUE AND LOCAL SERVICES (pp. 493–496)	▸ What are the sources of revenue for local governments? ▸ What different types of taxes may local governments levy? ▸ How do federal and state grants help provide local governments with needed revenue? ▸ In what ways do local governments promote the public good?	**Regular** 1 day **Block Scheduling** .5 day	**ELL** Spanish Study Guide 21.3 **ELL** English Study Guide 21.3

Chapter Resource Key

PS	Primary Sources	**A**	Assessment		Video
RS	Reading Support	**REV**	Review		Videodisc
E	Enrichment	**ELL**	Reinforcement and English Language Learners		Internet
S	Simulations		Transparencies		Holt Presentation Maker Using
SM	Skills Mastery		CD-ROM		Microsoft ® PowerPoint ®

TECHNOLOGY RESOURCES	REINFORCEMENT, REVIEW, AND ASSESSMENT
💿 One-Stop Planner: Lesson 21.1 🖥 Holt Researcher Online 🖥 Homework Practice Online 💿 Global Skill Builder CD-ROM	**REV** Section 1 Review, p. 484 **A** Daily Quiz 21.1
💿 One-Stop Planner: Lesson 21.2 🖥 Holt Researcher Online 🖥 Homework Practice Online 🖌 Transparency 45 💿 Global Skill Builder CD-ROM	**REV** Section 2 Review, p. 492 **A** Daily Quiz 21.2
💿 One-Stop Planner: Lesson 21.3 🖥 Holt Researcher Online 🖥 Homework Practice Online 🖌 Transparency 46 🖌 Cartoon Transparency 23 E Challenge and Enrichment: Activity 21 E Simulations and Strategies for Teaching American Government: Activity 21 📼 CNN Presents American Government	**REV** Section 3 Review, p. 496 **A** Daily Quiz 21.3

Chapter Review and Assessment

SM Global Skill Builder CD-ROM
🖥 HRW Go site
REV Chapter 21 Tutorial for Students, Parents, and Peers
REV Chapter 21 Review, pp. 498–499
💿 Chapter 21 Test Generator (on the One-Stop Planner)
A Chapter 21 Test
A Chapter 21 Test Alternative Assessment Handbook

One-Stop Planner CD–ROM

It's easy to plan lessons, select resources, and print out materials for your students when you use the *One-Stop Planner CD-ROM with Test Generator.*

🔗 **internet** connect

HRW ONLINE RESOURCES
Go To: go.hrw.com
Then type in a keyword.

TEACHER HOME PAGE
KEYWORD: SV3 Teacher

CHAPTER INTERNET ACTIVITIES
KEYWORD: SV3 GV21
Choose an activity on local government to:
▸ create a chart or graph on population shifts.
▸ research metropolitan governments.
▸ create a diagram on local revenue.

CHAPTER ENRICHMENT LINKS
KEYWORD: SV3 CH21

HOLT RESEACHER ONLINE
KEYWORD: Holt Reseacher

ONLINE ASSESSMENT
Homework Practice
KEYWORD: SV3 HP21
Standardized Test Prep
KEYWORD: SV3 STP21
Rubrics
KEYWORD: SS Rubrics

ONLINE MAPS, CHARTS, AND GRAPHS
KEYWORD: SV3 MCG
▸ Basic Forms of Municipal Government
▸ Sources of local Government Revenues

CONTENT UPDATES
KEYWORD: SS Content Updates

HOLT PRESENTATION MAKER
KEYWORD: SV3 PPT21

ONLINE READING SUPPORT
KEYWORD: SS Strategies

CURRENT EVENTS
KEYWORD: S3 Current Events

LESSON 21.1 U.S. COMMUNITIES

TEXTBOOK PAGES 481–484

OBJECTIVES

▸ Define rural areas.
▸ Discuss the historical factors that led to the growth of cities.
▸ Explain why suburbs developed outside of cities.
▸ Define metropolitan areas.

MOTIVATE

Write the words *rural, urban, suburban,* and *metropolitan* on the chalkboard. Ask students to identify which of these terms describes the area in which they live. Then have students work to develop definitions for each of these terms. Tell students that the makeup of U.S. habitats has changed dramatically during the history of the United States. Tell students that in this section they will learn about rural and metropolitan areas, what factors led to the growth of cities, and why suburbs developed outside of cities.

TEACH

Building a Vocabulary

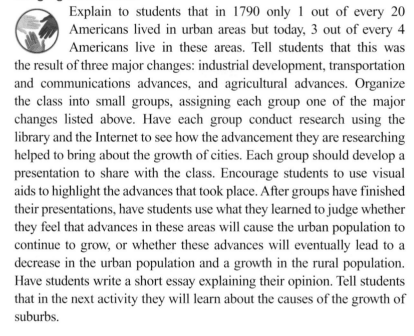

In spiral notebooks, have students create a Political Dictionary to be used throughout the course. The dictionary may be used as an activity at the start of each new section; it may also be used as a modification device for students having difficulty or sheltered English students during tests and homework assignments. List words the students will be expected to know for this section on the chalkboard. Have students list, define, and give an example of each of the terms, using information provided in the text or on the *Researcher CD-ROM*.

Distinguishing Fact from Opinion

Develop a list of facts and opinions, some of which apply to urban areas, others that apply to rural areas. Create an organizer that lists these facts and opinions and includes space so that students can identify whether each statement applies to urban or rural areas and whether the statement

is fact or opinion. Have students fill in the sheet, then discuss the characteristics of urban and rural areas with them. Ask students to explain how they knew a statement was an opinion rather than a fact, and discuss the importance of being able to discern fact from opinion. As a lead-in to the next activity, tell students that they will be learning about the historical factors that led to the growth of cities.

Judging Information

Explain to students that in 1790 only 1 out of every 20 Americans lived in urban areas but today, 3 out of every 4 Americans live in these areas. Tell students that this was the result of three major changes: industrial development, transportation and communications advances, and agricultural advances. Organize the class into small groups, assigning each group one of the major changes listed above. Have each group conduct research using the library and the Internet to see how the advancement they are researching helped to bring about the growth of cities. Each group should develop a presentation to share with the class. Encourage students to use visual aids to highlight the advances that took place. After groups have finished their presentations, have students use what they learned to judge whether they feel that advances in these areas will cause the urban population to continue to grow, or whether these advances will eventually lead to a decrease in the urban population and a growth in the rural population. Have students write a short essay explaining their opinion. Tell students that in the next activity they will learn about the causes of the growth of suburbs.

Identifying Cause and Effect

Tell students that many factors contributed to the growth of suburbs. Have students use materials from this section of the text and other resources to determine what caused this growth. Encourage students to investigate problems associated with large cities as well as the advances in transportation and communication that allowed people to move to suburban areas. You may wish to assign students specific problems to research, such as overcrowding of neighborhoods and high crime rates. After students have had time to conduct their research, discuss the cause-and-effect relationships that students were able to identify. Write students' ideas on the chalkboard.

Creating Maps/Learning from Visuals

 Explain to students that the growth of cities and their respective suburbs led to the growth of metropolitan areas. Organize the class into several small groups. Assign each group a time period after 1950 to investigate. Have each group use historical abstracts and almanacs to create a map identifying the 10 largest metropolitan areas in the United States during the time period they were assigned and the population of the area. Also have students identify the largest city in that area and list its population. After students have finished their maps, have groups compare them. Ask students to identify any trends in population distribution that they can determine from their research.

CLOSE

Have students recall the classification of their living area from the Motivate activity. Did their description of the area change or stay the same? Have students write a short essay describing the area in which they live. Students should correctly identify the area based on the terms used in the Motivate activity and should use material from the text and from the lessons to describe possible reasons for increases or decreases in population for their area.

OPTIONS

Students Having Difficulty/ Sheltered English Students

Give students a list of several cities that identifies the city's population and describes its location in respect to other cities. Have students classify each city as being rural, urban, suburban, metropolitan, and/or megalopolitan. Remind students that some of these cities may require more than one of these descriptive words. Have students discuss their reasoning for classifying each city the way they did.

Logical-Mathematical Learners/Gifted Learners

 Have students review information from the maps made in the Creating Maps/Learning From Visuals activity to study the changes in population between major cities and their surrounding metropolitan areas. Have students use this information along with outside resources to investigate the impact suburban population growth in a large metropolitan area has on congressional representation for the main city in that area. Did the city lose representatives as its suburbs grew? Did it gain representatives? Did it maintain the same number? Have students write a short report analyzing the changes in population and representation for these areas. You may wish to assign students specific metropolitan areas to investigate, so that the class can compare the results for different areas.

REVIEW

Have students complete the Section 1 Review on page 484. Use the answers in the Annotated Teacher's Edition to assess student mastery of this section.

ASSESS

To assess student mastery of this section, have students complete Daily Quiz 21.1 in *Daily Quizzes with Answer Key.* For additional assessment options, see *Alternative Assessment Handbook* on the *One-Stop Planner CD-ROM.*

ADDITIONAL RESOURCES

Jackson, Kenneth. "New York's Comeback." *U.S. News & World Report.* September 29, 1997.

Jacobs, James. "Get Out of Jail Free." *The City Journal.* Volume 1, Number 4. 1991.

OBJECTIVES

- List and describe the four main types of local government.
- Discuss the different types of municipal government.
- Describe the functions of a county government.
- Explain what services special districts provide.

MOTIVATE

Ask students to brainstorm about who was responsible for creating the following items: the roads that lead to school, the water system that provides them with clean drinking water, the public library, and the local swimming pool. Give students a few minutes to think about and discuss who was responsible for these items. Explain to students that all of these items were most likely established by one of the different levels of local government. Have students work together to create a list of other items that were most likely established by a local government. Encourage students to write this list in their Government Notebooks. Tell students that in this section they will learn about the types of local government, the types of municipal government, the functions of county government, and the purpose of special districts.

TEACH

Building a Vocabulary

In their spiral notebooks, have students continue working on their Political Dictionary. List words the students will be expected to know for this section on the chalkboard. Have students list, define, and give an example of each of the terms, using information provided in the chapter or on the *Researcher CD-ROM*.

Acquiring Information/Comparing and Contrasting

Explain to students that there are four main types of local governments: counties, towns or townships, municipalities, and special districts. Describe how these are generally classified according to the type of area that they govern. Organize the class into groups of four students. Have each member study a different type of local government to find out: the type of power that particular form of government holds; how common that type of government is in the United States; what areas of the country generally have that form of government; and what economic factors contribute to having that type of government. Once students have finished their research, have them share the information they gathered with the other students in their group. After all the groups have finished, have the class create a diagram that compares the four types of governments. Display the finished product in the classroom for later reference. As a lead-in to the next activity tell students they will learn about the three different types of municipal government.

Comparing and Contrasting/Drawing Conclusions

Tell students that the different forms of local governments vary within each type. Discuss with the class the different forms of municipal governments: council-manager, mayor-council, and commission. Then have students write an essay describing the similarities and differences between these types of governments. In their essays, students should consider: the distribution of power in the system; the duties of each level; the relationship between levels; and the way each system chooses its leaders. Students should also consider which one of these types of municipal government is currently used by or would be suited for their community. Encourage students to share their ideas with the class. Tell them that they will be learning about the functions of county government during the next activity.

Developing Life Skills

Have students read about county government in their textbooks. Discuss the services that county governments usually provide. Organize the class into several small groups. Encourage each group to come up with examples of the services provided by their county government (e.g., building a county hospital). Also have each group consult local newspapers and the Internet to see if they can find other examples of services provided by and the functions of their county government. Each group should create a list of the items they identified. When finished, have them share their lists with the rest of the class. Tell students that in the next activity they will learn about the need for special districts.

Practicing Skills: Creating Maps

 Discuss with students the need for special districts and the services that they perform. Organize the class into several small groups and assign each group an area of the country to research. Have students use the Internet and information from outside resources to identify special districts located in the area they were assigned. Be sure to tell students not to identify or research school districts in their assigned area. Students should identify the location of each district and its function. After all groups have finished, have them work together to create one large map that identifies the special districts of the United States. Each group should mark the location of some of the special districts in their assigned area on the map and should give a brief oral description of those districts' function.

CLOSE

Have students discuss the different types of local governments that exist in the United States. Students should identify the similarities and differences between each type, the area of the country where each type is most prominent, and the functions served by each level. Have students form groups to work at creating a study guide for this section. Allow time for each group to exchange study guides with another group and complete each other's questions.

OPTIONS

Students Having Difficulty/ Sheltered English Students

  Have students create a chart that identifies the type of municipal government used by various major cities throughout the country. Students can use the Internet to find the home pages of several large cities—you may wish to assign cities to specific students. Once students have researched the cities, have them create a chart identifying whether the city has a council-manager, mayor-council, or commission form of government.

Gifted Learners

 Discuss with students the type of municipal government that exists in their community. Identify it as being council-manager, mayor-council, or commission. Have students use the newspaper to conduct research on the distribution of power and the interactions between the main figures in their local government. Students should discuss the articles that they have read and should evaluate the effectiveness of their community's form of government. Have students consider whether alternative methods could be used to improve the effectiveness of government. Encourage students to write a summary of their findings and to send it to members of the municipal government for consideration.

REVIEW

Have students complete the Section 2 Review on page 492. Use the answers in the Annotated Teacher's Edition to assess student mastery of this section.

ASSESS

To assess student mastery of this section, have students complete Daily Quiz 21.2 in *Daily Quizzes with Answer Key.* For additional assessment options, see *Alternative Assessment Handbook* on the *One-Stop Planner CD-ROM.*

ADDITIONAL RESOURCES

The Municipal Year Book. 1997. International City Manager's Association.

Crotty, William. *Political Participation and American Democracy.* 1991 Greenwood.

LESSON 21.3 REVENUE AND LOCAL SERVICES

TEXTBOOK PAGES 493–496

OBJECTIVES

- Identify local governments' sources of revenue.
- Describe the types of taxes that local governments may levy.
- Discuss how federal and state grants provide local governments with needed revenue.
- Describe the ways that local governments promote the public good.

MOTIVATE

Tell students about an imaginary situation in which the local government has decided to improve the quality of life for local teenagers. Explain to students that the local government has decided to let students choose what major improvements need to be made or programs need to be started in their community. Give students 10 to 15 minutes to brainstorm on and to decide what changes they would recommend. (Students should be encouraged to suggest expensive ideas such as a new community recreation center, a community water park, or a community cultural center.) After students have suggested changes, have them decide on the one they would most like to enact. (Encourage students to cast secret ballots to determine the winner.) Explain to the class that one problem still exists—how the community will pay for this project. Tell students that in this section they will learn about how local governments raise money, what kind of taxes they can collect, and how grants help local governments.

TEACH

Building a Vocabulary

In their spiral notebooks, have students continue working on their Political Dictionary. List words the students will be expected to know for this section on the chalkboard. Have students list, define, and give an example of each of the terms, using information provided in the chapter or on the *Researcher CD-ROM*.

Classifying Information

On the chalkboard create a chart with the following headings: *taxes, fees, grants,* and *borrowing* located on the horizontal axis. For the vertical axis, write the following headings: *examples, advantages,* and *disadvantages*. Explain to students that these are the various ways that local governments can raise money. As a class, have students discuss the advantages and disadvantages of relying on each of these methods for revenue. Once students have finished this, have them brainstorm examples of how their local government uses these methods. Write students' ideas on the chalkboard under the appropriate heading. Encourage students to copy the chart in their Government Notebooks. Tell students that in the next activity they will be learning about the different types of taxes that local governments assess.

Debating Ideas/Making Decisions

Tell students that local governments most commonly raise money by levying taxes. Have the class read in their textbooks about the forms of taxation used at the local level. Then organize the class into several small groups. Have each group discuss the advantages and disadvantages of raising money through property taxes, sales taxes, and income taxes. After discussing the pros and cons of these taxes, have each group develop a presentation that describes which of these taxes they would like to levy to raise money for the project proposed during the Motivate activity. Allow time for each group to present its suggestion. Have students debate which group's proposal they would like to use. Encourage students to consider parts of each group's plan for raising the money needed to complete their project. As a lead-in to the next activity, tell students that they will be learning more about how grants can help a community.

Mastering Concepts

Remind students of the purposes of grants and of the different kinds of grants that they learned about in Chapter 4. Encourage students to examine local newspapers to identify grants that have benefited their local community. Students should write an essay describing the kind of grant given, whether it was issued by the national or state government, the purpose of the grant, and whether they feel the grant was necessary to successfully complete the project. Encourage students to share their ideas with the rest of the class.

CLOSE

Remind students about all of the different methods of raising revenue that local governments may use. Have students evaluate the advantages and disadvantages of each method. Then have them write an essay describing whether they feel each method would be suited for raising the money needed for the project discussed during the Motivate activity. Have students offer support for their reasoning based on materials covered in the text and during this lesson. Encourage students to share their opinions with the rest of the class.

OPTIONS

Linguistic Learners

 Videotape a segment of a local government meeting that discusses the need for raising revenue for a specific project and the methods available to raise that money. Have students view the videotape to identify what arguments if any were made for each of the methods of raising revenue discussed in this section. Have students discuss whether they feel the arguments presented were justified. Encourage students to calmly debate any differences in opinion.

Students Having Difficulty/ Sheltered English Students

 Have students work in pairs to create a study guide on the various methods that local governments use to raise revenue. Students should consider the different methods of taxation and the different sources of grants when creating their study guides. When each pair has finished, have them exchange their study guide with another pair and answer its questions. Once completed, each pair should give the finished guide back to the pair that made it to have their answers checked. Finally, have the two groups discuss any corrections that needed to be made, and have students make the necessary corrections.

REVIEW

Have students complete the Section 3 Review on page 496. Use the answers in the Annotated Teacher's Edition to assess student mastery of this section.

ASSESS

To assess student mastery of this section, have students complete Daily Quiz 21.3 in *Daily Quizzes with Answer Key.* For additional assessment options, see *Alternative Assessment Handbook* on the *One-Stop Planner CD-ROM.*

RETEACH

For students having difficulty with the lessons, have them complete Reteaching Activity 21. This activity is located in *Reteaching Activities with Answer Key.*

ADDITIONAL RESOURCES

Ehrenreich, Barbara. "Spinning the Poor into Gold." *Harper's Magazine.* August 1997.

Garreau, Joel. *Edge City: Life on the New Frontier.* 1991. Doubleday.

CHAPTER 21

GOVERNMENT NOTEBOOK

The Government Notebook is a journal activity that encourages students to consider basic concepts of government that relate to their lives. A follow-up notebook activity appears on page 498.

WHY IT MATTERS TODAY

To find additional lesson plans dealing with local government, visit **CNNfyi.com** or have students complete the **GOVERNMENT IN THE NEWS** activity on page 497.

CNNfyi.com

LOCAL GOVERNMENT

Local governments play an important role in providing essential services to the public. Take a look around your community—you may not even realize all of the services your local government provides. It may offer fire and police protection, public transit, airports and seaports, and public health services and hospitals.

Tens of thousands of local governmental units operate in the United States today. They vary a great deal in structure—so much so that some people have referred to the organization of local government in the United States as a "crazy quilt pattern" rather than a system. However, within most states, local governmental units share important similarities.

GOVERNMENT NOTEBOOK

In your Government Notebook, write a list of services that local government provides to your community.

WHY IT MATTERS TODAY

Local government has a direct impact on our daily lives. At the end of this chapter visit **CNNfyi.com** to learn more about local government.

CNNfyi.com

SECTION 1
U.S. COMMUNITIES

READ TO DISCOVER

1. What is a rural area?
2. What historical factors led to the growth of cities?
3. Why did suburbs develop outside of cities?
4. What is a metropolitan area?

POLITICAL DICTIONARY

rural area
urban area
suburb
metropolitan area
megalopolis

The size and makeup of a community largely determine its government. A city of 1 million residents would of course require many more services and a much larger government than would a town of 650. Governmental diversity is also widespread on the local level because the United States is home to many types of communities. Despite their many unique features, these communities all fit into one or more of the following categories—rural, urban, suburban, and metropolitan.

Rural Areas

Before 1920 a majority of Americans lived in rural areas. A **rural area** is an area with low population density where people live on farms, on ranches, or in small towns. Rural areas usually are dominated by agricultural production, mining, forestry, or ranching. Semirural areas—which make up a related subcategory—usually include a few more towns, sometimes of greater size, than rural areas.

Urban Areas

Today most people in the United States live in **urban areas**, or cities and their surroundings. The

first U.S. census, taken in 1790, revealed that only 1 out of every 20 Americans lived in an urban area. By 1920, however, more than 50 percent of Americans were living in urban areas. What sparked such a change?

In the late 1800s and early 1900s immigrants flocked to U.S. cities in search of jobs, which had been brought on by industrial development. Improvements in transportation and communications systems had also spurred the growth of cities, as had the advancement of technology in public works engineering, thus improving urban water supplies and electric utilities, as well as sewers, streets, and bridges. Meanwhile, advances in agricultural technology lessened the need for labor in rural areas, forcing many farmworkers to the cities in search of work. Today about 75 percent of all Americans live in urban areas.

Suburbs

An urban area generally includes **suburbs**—residential areas surrounding a city. While enabling urban areas to support an increasing population, new technology in transportation and communications allowed some people to move from the crowded central cities to the outskirts.

CITIZENSHIP *Today about 75 percent of all Americans live in urban areas such as New York City, pictured here.* **By the 1920s, what portion of the U.S. population lived in cities?**

SECTION 1
U.S. COMMUNITIES

Lesson Plans

For teaching strategies, see Lesson 21.1 located at the beginning of this chapter or the One-Stop Lesson Planner Strategy 21.1.

Political Dictionary

To reinforce the section's vocabulary terms, refer students to the Electronic Glossary on the *Researcher CD-ROM*.

Section Assessment

To assess students' mastery of this section, have them complete Daily Quiz 21.1 in *Daily Quizzes with Answer Key*.

Caption Answer

more than 50 percent

PUBLIC GOOD *New advances in communications and transportation technology made it more convenient for some people to move from the crowded central cities to suburbs that offered more space.* **What transportation developments helped to speed up suburbanization?**

The earliest commuter suburb, located just outside New York City, was Brooklyn Heights, which developed between 1815 and 1835. The largest U.S. cities, including Philadelphia and Boston, suburbanized rapidly during this period because of the Transportation Revolution, which ushered in widespread use of commuter trains.

With the development of automobiles, suburbanization occurred even more dramatically. Once they were able to afford cars, many people moved to the suburbs and drove to their jobs in the cities. The first large suburbs that catered to automobile commuters appeared around Los Angeles during the 1920s, after city residents voted to borrow money to build an extensive road system.

During the 1960s the country's suburban population began to exceed that of the central cities. By 1980 about 45 percent of the U.S. population lived in suburbs, while only 30 percent lived in central cities.

Suburban growth has been particularly pronounced in the states of the South and Southwest, known as the Sun Belt. Much of this growth has been caused by the arrival of vast numbers of people from the Northeast and Midwest. They hope to benefit from the Sun Belt states' mild climate, lower energy costs, lower taxes, and job opportunities created by newly developed industries and technologies.

Today Houston is one of the largest Sun Belt boomtowns. From 1945 to 1980, its population rose from 385,000 to almost 1.6 million. This tremendous growth was partly stimulated by the moving of a large number of oil and energy companies to Houston during the energy crisis of the mid-1970s. Abundant job opportunities drew thousands of new residents each month. In the late 1980s, however, oil prices dropped, triggering a decline in the growth of the city's economy. The economic downturn slowed the population growth rate in Houston and other Texas oil towns.

In contrast to the Sun Belt, during the mid- to late 1970s and early 1980s, cities in the northeastern and midwestern regions of the country experienced a decline in population growth. This area, sometimes called the Rust Belt because of its heavy concentration of steel and automobile

Citizenship in Action

Preserving Part of History

A core responsibility of local governments—rural and urban alike—involves the operation and funding of school systems. Many public school students in turn help promote the public good in their local communities by working to preserve important parts of history.

Students in Calallen Independent School District in Corpus Christi, Texas, for example, worked for more than 15 years to restore both a one-room schoolhouse built in the late 1800s and a farmhouse built in 1910. Sally Robeau, who taught Texas history in Calallen Independent School District, sponsored the Junior Historians club and helped its members recondition the two structures.

Work on restoring the schoolhouse, which had been constructed in Nuecestown—a ghost town near Corpus Christi—began in 1982. The building had been converted decades earlier into a residence. To return the schoolhouse to its original state, students raised money, helped remove pink stucco that had at some point been applied to the wooden exterior walls, replaced rotted boards, and painted the walls red. Students also worked hard to restore the old farmhouse, located in Calallen, installing insulation, building a back porch, wallpapering the interior, and replacing broken and rotted boards.

The students then raised thousands of dollars to move both structures to a common location in Corpus Christi. Some of the money raised for moving and restoring the buildings came from making and selling arts and crafts similar to those used in the late 1800s and early 1900s. The club also received small grants for its preservation work, but students have raised most of the at least $75,000 spent on the buildings, Robeau says. "Every one of the students seems to have a soft spot for the buildings," she says. "They have a sense of ownership."

The students exhibit the buildings during Pioneer Days, an annual two-day event organized by the Junior Historians. At that time, visitors can tour the buildings and view student-made clay pots and other artifacts that are similar to those made a century ago. The schoolhouse also is used for field trips. Students intended the farmhouse to be used as a center for researching local history. The house serves as a museum, and contains, historical files and other information that can be used in research.

Robeau's Junior Historians club is associated with an educational project sponsored by the Texas State Historical Association. The project encourages students to adopt an old building, research its history, restore it, and then apply to have it designated as an official historic site.

Students in one East Texas town adopted their own high school, which features the mission-style architecture that was popular in the 1930s, when it was built. More than 100 other Junior Historians clubs are working to preserve historic sites throughout Texas. Indiana and about six other states have similar programs.

Members of the Junior Historians club of Corpus Christi, Texas, work to restore a schoolhouse that was built in the late 1800s.

What Do You Think?

1. What values do you think students learn when working to preserve historic sites?
2. What historic sites in your community might be candidates for preservation?

What Do You Think?
Answers

1. Answers will vary, but students might suggest responsibility and the inherent benefits of serving the community.
2. Local historic sites will vary.

THEMES IN GOVERNMENT

GEOGRAPHY The early growth of cities in the United States often mimicked the growth of cities in Europe. Cities in both places were densely populated and usually covered small areas. Growing cities usually retained a sharp distinction between their formal boundaries and the surrounding countryside.

In the last half of the nineteenth century, however, these similarities began to disappear. Unlike their European counterparts, U.S. cities kept expanding beyond their formal boundaries to form what the census of 1910 began to call metropolitan areas.

U.S. cities remained congested, but their populations were not nearly as dense as those of European cities. In the 1890s fifteen of the largest U.S. cities averaged 22 people per acre. A comparable group of German cities averaged 158. With the U.S. urban population spread out, transportation became a more problematic issue in U.S. cities than it was in European cities. ∎

CITIZENSHIP *This aerial photograph shows Washington, D.C., which is part of a large megalopolis that stretches north 500 miles to Boston.* **How are megalopolises formed?**

industries, experienced the effects of high unemployment rates caused by the collapse of the steel industry and a declining demand for American-made automobiles. Many people from this region moved to the South and West in search of jobs.

Metropolitan Areas

By 1970 nearly two thirds of Americans lived in what the U.S. government categorizes as metropolitan statistical areas (MSAs), frequently referred to as metropolitan areas. **Metropolitan areas**—most of which have no single, overall unit of government—are urban areas made up of a central city of 50,000 or more people, its suburbs, and the surrounding counties that depend on it socially and economically. About one third of the metropolitan population of the United States lives in the nation's 12 largest metropolitan areas. These areas include New York; Los Angeles; Chicago; Washington, D.C.—Baltimore; San Francisco—Oakland; Philadelphia; Boston; Detroit; Dallas–Fort Worth; Houston; Atlanta; and Miami-Fort Lauderdale.

Fueled by high suburban growth, some metropolitan areas have spread far enough to border one another. Together, a group of bordering metropolitan areas constitute a **megalopolis**. Several megalopolises are already well developed in the United States, including one that stretches for 500 miles from Boston to the southernmost suburbs of Washington, D.C. Developing megalopolises include one running from Milwaukee to Pittsburgh and another from Santa Barbara, California, to San Diego and across the border to the southern areas of Tijuana, Mexico.

1. Identify and explain:
- rural area
- urban area
- suburb
- metropolitan area
- megalopolis

2. Identifying Concepts: Copy the chart below. Use it to list the advantages and disadvantages of living in a rural area and in an urban area.

Rural areas		
Urban areas		

Homework Practice Online

keyword: SV3 HP21

3. **Finding the Main Idea**

a. Why did urban areas grow in size during the late 1800s and early 1900s?

b. What developments spurred the growth of suburbs?

4. **Writing and Critical Thinking**

Decision Making: Would you rather live in a rural area or an urban area? Explain your reasoning.

Consider the following:
- the advantages and disadvantages of each area

SECTION 2

LOCAL GOVERNMENT ORGANIZATION

READ TO DISCOVER

1. What are the four main types of local government?
2. What are the different types of municipal government?
3. What are the functions of a county government?
4. What do special districts provide?

POLITICAL DICTIONARY

township
municipality
mayor-council system
council-manager system
city manager
commission
special district

Imagine that you are trying to cross the street near your house, but the street is so busy that you have to wait several minutes to cross. Whom would you contact about constructing a traffic light there? The answer most likely is your local government. As noted in Section 1, local governments provide a range of services—anything from installing signal lights to testing water quality. In these ways, local governments promote the public good by making people's lives easier and safer.

The first thing likely to strike someone studying local governments is just how numerous they are—over 87,000 at last count! Local governments provide several things to the citizens they serve, including a governing body, a legal system, and certain public services. In addition, they usually have the power to collect revenue to finance their operations. Local governments generally are classified according to the type of area they administer—counties, towns or townships, municipalities, and special districts. These governments differ widely in their structure and authority.

Authority of Local Government

In the American system of government, the balance between state and federal authority is a delicate one. The framers of the Constitution took great care to ensure that the states would retain the power to make their own laws.

The Constitution does not, however, address the relationship between state and local governments. Town, city, and county governments are created by the state in which they are located, and their powers are defined by state law.

Local governments generally are established by state charters—documents enacted by a state legislature to create a unit of local government. Localities may exercise only those powers expressly granted to them by the state. Local charters often are very long, because they must detail every local government power.

PUBLIC GOOD *One way in which local governments promote the public good is by establishing local law enforcement agencies to protect public safety.* **What defines the powers of town, city, and county governments?**

SECTION 2

LOCAL GOVERNMENT ORGANIZATION

Lesson Plans

For teaching strategies, see Lesson 21.2 located at the beginning of this chapter or the One-Stop Lesson Planner Strategy 21.2.

Political Dictionary

To reinforce the section's vocabulary terms, refer students to the Electronic Glossary on the *Researcher CD-ROM.*

Section Assessment

To assess students' mastery of this section, have them complete Daily Quiz 21.2 in *Daily Quizzes with Answer Key.*

Caption Answer

The powers of town, city, and county governments are defined by state law.

The word *county* is derived from a French term meaning "territory belonging to a count." After England was conquered by the French-speaking Normans in 1066, *county* slowly replaced the Saxon word *shire*, which described a sizable area ruled by a particular tribe.

Over time, counties came to be the largest administrative areas in England. Colonists took the idea of a county to the New World, and today, counties are the largest units of local government in the United States. Some states, however, do not use the term *county*. For example, Alaska refers to counties as boroughs, and Louisiana calls them parishes.

The number of counties in a state has little to do with a state's size or population. Arizona, for example, with a land area of more than 113,500 square miles and a population of 4 million, has only 15 counties. Iowa, with an area of not quite 56,000 square miles and a population of 2.8 million, has 99. ■

Caption Answer
the southern colonies

States often keep local governments on a short leash. Every state restricts in some way the ability of local governments to tax, frequently by specifying what kinds of taxes they may adopt. Some states even regulate the administration of local governments' finances. Around half of the states, however, grant local governments the power of home rule, which allows them to pass a wide range of legislation without state legislative approval. Home rule is now more common because city government has become much more complicated in today's world, and state legislators are unable to handle individual cities' complexities with the same expertise as local administrators.

County Government

All of the states are divided into counties. In every state but two, counties generally function as units of government over a particular area. In Rhode Island and Connecticut they serve only as judicial or electoral districts. (In Louisiana, counties are called parishes; in Alaska, they are called boroughs.) Counties play a strong role in the local governments of the South and West, which are more rural and less densely populated than some other regions. County government began in the

PUBLIC GOOD *Maintaining and repairing roads are primary responsibilities of county governments in many western states.* **In what region of the American colonies were the first counties established?**

largely agricultural southern colonies, where people often lived far away from one another, with few cities and few city governments.

In 1998 there were 3,043 counties in the United States (including parishes and boroughs). In New England, counties serve mostly as judicial districts, with the towns performing the legislative and executive duties that counties perform in other states. In the Middle Atlantic and midwestern states, counties and townships share the functions of local government. In rural and semirural areas, particularly in the South and West, the county may be the main body of local government.

Cities and towns are bound by state and county laws. Most cities—such as Minneapolis, in Hennepin County; Houston, in Harris County; and Los Angeles, in Los Angeles County—are located in a single county. Other large cities straddle several county boundaries. New York City, for example, sprawls across five counties.

In the states where counties play the strongest role, they generally hold mostly legislative and administrative powers. A county's legislative powers may include regulating the use of county property, establishing requirements for business licenses, and levying taxes. Administrative powers include operating welfare programs, hospitals, schools, and jails; keeping records of deeds, marriage licenses, and other legal documents; and supervising elections. Most county governments also maintain public roads, highways, and recreational facilities, as well as prosecute people accused of committing crimes anywhere within the county's borders, including in its cities.

Towns and Townships

In some parts of the country, particularly the Middle Atlantic and midwestern states, units of government called towns and townships provide services in areas outside major cities. In the United States the town form of government began during the colonial days in New England. Often, these small communities created a central government that combined the authority of the church with the lawmaking power of the community. The town included not only the community buildings but also the farms that the inhabitants established on the outskirts.

Early New England townspeople governed their communities through town meetings. The town's inhabitants would meet in a central

PRINCIPLES OF DEMOCRACY *Town meetings attended by all of the town's inhabitants, such as the one pictured here, have typically been replaced by representative town meetings.* **In what regions of the United States are township governments primarily found?**

location to discuss issues and problems and to vote on how they should be handled. Some small New England towns still operate in this manner. Because of population growth and poor attendance, however, many small towns have abolished the town meeting form of government. Others have moved to a representative town meeting, in which citizens elect representatives to attend the meetings and make decisions.

The town still serves as the major decision-making body in local government in New England. It provides many of the same services that are the responsibility of cities and counties in other parts of the country.

Outside of New England, in states such as New Jersey, New York, and Pennsylvania, communities called **townships** were established. Townships in these states were responsible for some of the same functions as towns in New England—providing roads, schools, and means for assisting the poor, for example. As settlers moved to the West, they established similar townships there to perform the services of local government.

Today, however, township government has generally decreased, as municipal and county governments have taken over many of their functions. Township governments are currently found in only 20 states, primarily in the Northeast and Midwest. They are usually governed by a town meeting and elected officers, or they may have a representative town meeting, as in some New England towns.

Municipalities

Most Americans make their homes in **municipalities**—cities, towns, and villages—with a state charter outlining their powers and responsibilities. Some of the nation's 19,000 incorporated municipalities are large, such as Houston or Chicago, while others are tiny, with nearly 90 percent having populations under 10,000. The smallest municipality is thought to be Valley Park, Oklahoma, which in 1994 had only one inhabitant. Another municipality, Hove Mobile Park, North Dakota, has only two residents.

Municipal governments generally provide services beyond those that county or township governments can provide. They are responsible for basic public services, such operating police and fire departments, initiating garbage collection, and constructing and maintaining sewer systems, streets, parks, and public buildings. Municipalities also adopt zoning laws, which restrict land use by area—so

PUBLIC GOOD *This photo shows a typical city zoning map. Municipalities adopt zoning laws that restrict land use by area.* **What services do municipal governments generally provide?**

ACROSS THE CURRICULUM

HISTORY During the colonial period, town meetings commanded high levels of attendance, which made it hard to get anything done. Executive boards with the power to decide most of the issues were formed to make government more efficient. The board decided the guilt or innocence of people accused of breaking the laws and settled thousands of questions concerning the public domain. For example, in 1667, when John Gay of Dedham, Massachusetts, wanted to build a barn and the best site was on public land, the town's board worked out a trade whereby Gay got the land in exchange for allowing a public road to run across his property.

These boards also enacted bylaws without citizens' approval and levied taxes at town meetings. Furthermore, the board had some control over calling town meetings. Members of the board called few meetings other than the one or two required by colonial law. ■

Transparency

An overhead transparency of the chart on this page is available in *Transparency Resources.* See Transparency 45: Basic Forms of Municipal Government.

> *Caption Answer*
>
> the council-manager form

Communities that govern by town meetings tend to have a weak-mayor plan and many more elected officers than do municipalities. Voters in one small Connecticut town, for example, choose candidates for 47 positions. Voters in, say, New York or Los Angeles may have far fewer choices to make on election day.

Most municipalities have adopted the strong-mayor-council structure, which restricts the number of officials who are chosen in popular elections. While county officials such as the prosecuting attorney and sheriff are chosen by popular election in other systems, the equivalent positions in most municipal governments are filled by appointment. ∎

Basic Forms of Municipal Government

MAYOR-COUNCIL

Elected mayor serves as chief executive while separately elected city council serves as legislative body.

COUNCIL-MANAGER

Elected city council and often a mayor appoint a professional city manager as chief executive.

COMMISSION

Elected commissioners set overall policy while each commissioner heads a city administrative department.

Different forms of municipal government place power into different officials' hands. ***In what form of municipal government is the chief executive appointed by an elected city council and often a mayor?***

that fish-processing plants are not located in residential neighborhoods, for example.

There are three basic forms of municipal government in the United States: mayor-council, council-manager, and commission. Although the overall structure of these systems is similar across the country, city governments do vary because each city's charter is designed to meet the specific needs of its various communities.

Mayor-Council Government The **mayor-council system** of city government consists of a separately elected legislature (city council) and chief executive (mayor). Mayors generally serve two- or four-year terms.

In some mayor-council systems the mayor does not play a substantial role. Mayors may lack such powers as veto and appointment, and may also lack the power to create budgets. Called the weak-mayor plan, this form of municipal government became common in the late 1800s and early 1900s, when people feared to give too much power to a single executive and wished to copy the executive branch structure set forth in the U.S. Constitution.

Other cities have what is called the strong-mayor plan, which developed in the late 1800s. This plan is structurally the same as the weak-mayor plan, but gives the mayor more authority. In the strong-mayor plan the mayor holds administrative responsibility and shares policy-making decisions with the council.

In a strong-mayor city the mayor may independently appoint and dismiss department heads without council approval. The mayor also is responsible for carrying out established policies, coordinating the efforts of various departments, preparing the annual budget, and administering it once it is adopted by the council.

City council members typically serve four-year terms and are elected in at-large elections—ones in which the entire city votes for all members. Some cities, however, hold ward elections, in which each ward's residents vote separately for their own council member. Most city councils meet part-time and require their members to attend only one meeting a week. Few councils outside of larger cities maintain any staff.

Council-Manager Government About one third of U.S. city governments operate under the **council-manager system**, in which the public does not elect an independent executive. Instead, the legislature (city council) appoints the chief of the executive branch. The council-manager system is most common in cities with populations between 25,000 and 500,000. About half of the cities with populations between 250,000 and 500,000 have an appointed executive. Many council-manager cities also have an elected mayor as well, but his or her role is generally limited to the heading of the city council.

The council-manager system executives—called **city managers**—are professionals trained to

City Manager

Experience and training in running the daily affairs of government are not formal job requirements for elected city officials. After all, elected city officials in many communities set general policies but turn over the daily work of municipal government to trained administrators called city managers. In cities that have a council-manager government, the city council appoints the city manager.

One of the most important jobs of a city manager is preparing a municipal budget for the mayor and city council to consider. A city manager's supervision extends to city departments that collect taxes and fees, purchase and maintain equipment, and perform other important duties. With help from the city staff, a city manager also plans for municipal growth by recommending zoning laws and expanding public facilities.

One of the jobs of a city manager is to prepare municipal budgets for the mayor and city council to consider.

In smaller cities, city managers often must tackle these and other tasks on their own. With a limited number of municipal employees, a small city may rely on its manager to help with such tasks as processing vehicle registration forms, fish and game permits, and other state documents. City managers also must research and write ordinances, respond to citizens' complaints and requests, and prepare reports of city operations.

Applicants for the job of city manager must have a college education and usually a graduate degree in public or business administration. Some positions require city government internships. City managers often start their careers as assistant managers or administrative assistants. City managers generally also need a knowledge of management techniques, experience with computers and various software programs that are used in urban planning and other work, and at least five years of experience working in the field.

manage city services in an expert, nonpartisan manner. Typically they have studied public administration in college or graduate school and have risen up the ranks of the city management profession.

City managers are wholly responsible to the council, which can dismiss them at any time. As an appointed official, the city manager is not a political leader, in that he or she does not participate in campaigns or party politics. The city manager does, however, play a role in policy making, which generally involves politics.

Though their roles vary, city managers usually possess the powers of a strong mayor for supervising and directing city government departments. Theoretically, a city manager's primary role is to administer the policies made by the city council. In practice, however, a city manager may become the most influential official in the city, depending on the limits placed on him or her by the city charter.

City managers usually have the right to appoint or remove the heads of various city departments without obtaining the council's approval. They may also act as chief ambassadors and handlers of emergencies (or share these roles with mayors), and prepare and submit executive budgets to city councils. Because city managers are not directly accountable to the voters, some people question whether their power in running city government is too great.

Commission Government A third type of municipal government is the **commission**, which is an elected body that holds both legislative and

Careers in Government

To help students learn about other careers in government, refer them to the Careers section on the *Holt Researcher Online.*

THEMES IN GOVERNMENT

PUBLIC GOOD In 1900 Galveston, Texas, was devastated by a hurricane. The work needed to rebuild the city was so extensive that the state government temporarily set aside Galveston's mayor-council government, replacing it with a commission made up of five members, each of whom took responsibility for a particular government function. Because the commission was so effective, Galveston continued to use it after recovering from the disaster, but with elected rather than appointed commissioners.

Other cities, following Galveston's lead, also adopted the plan. On the positive side, the commission system decreased political posturing. On the negative side, however, this did not prevent disruptions and delays when members of the commission disagreed with one another. Thus, many cities that embraced the commission plan have either gone back to the mayor-council structure or adopted the council-manager system. As of 1996 only about 125 cities in the United States used the commission plan. ■

SOCIOLOGY New York City's school system has more than a million students and more than 100,000 employees, including nearly 66,000 teachers. Of course, the cost of running such a big system is not cheap. From 1995 to 1997, New York City spent nearly $8 billion annually on education. This rose to $11.4 billion in 2001.

The good news for New York City's schools is that 1997 saw their most dramatic improvements in literacy in 10 years. Literacy tests revealed that the percentage of students reading at grade level had risen 3.6 percent between 1996 and 1997. The bad news is that, despite its improvements, still only 47.3 percent of the students could read at grade level. ■

internet connect

TOPIC: Metropolitan Government
GO TO: go.hrw.com
KEYWORD: SV3 GV21

Have students access the Internet through the HRW Go site to conduct research on metropolitan governments, such as Miami/Dade County. Ask students to assess how well these work. Then have students write an editorial that takes a position for or against having a metropolitan government. As an extension, have a local representative from a city or county government come to class to answer questions students may have on this topic after doing their research.

executive powers. City agencies are managed directly by the commission, which is usually made up of three to nine members. Each commissioner serves individually as the head of a city administrative department, while the commission as a whole makes city policy. Relatively few cities, many of them in Texas and most of them small, have this form of government. The only city with a population over 450,000 that currently has a commission form of government is Portland, Oregon.

Special Districts

About 34,000 local governments are **special districts**—units of government that perform a single service and are generally independent of other units of local government. The boundaries of some special districts coincide with those of a large city, with some special district boundaries extending into a city's suburbs or even into other states. Special districts include seaport facilities, such as the Port of Seattle District, or those in charge of transportation and other important aspects of an urban environment, such the Port Authority of New York and New Jersey.

The most familiar special districts are school districts, which run public schools. Other special districts provide services such as transportation, sewage disposal, and a water supply. These services often are not supplied by a central city because its outlying areas rely on them as well. In addition, special districts sometimes are formed to construct and manage low-rent housing and to undertake other types of urban renewal projects.

Special districts usually are run by commissioners. These public servants are either elected or are appointed by elected officials in city, county, or other local governments.

Metropolitan Government

For years some people have argued that metropolitan areas should have single units of government uniting cities and their suburbs. Supporters of this metropolitan organization argue that metropolitan governments are more cost-effective, can better handle shared problems, and can tax people living in the suburbs who enjoy city services without having to pay for them.

Supporters of metropolitan government have argued that some public services can be produced more efficiently on a large scale than on a small

scale. Large sewage disposal plants, for example, can process each pound of sewage for less money than can small plants. Because a metropolitan government can combine operations, it can provide services at a lower cost. Some people also argue that water and air pollution do not respect local boundaries and therefore should be regulated by metropolitan authorities. They also suggest that since transportation systems need to cover an entire metropolitan area, they should be organized under a single government.

Those who support the concept of metropolitan government also point out that it would increase the

Local Governments in Australia

Australia's local governments, like those in the United States, are often run by local councillors. About 8,300 council members serve in the country's more than 900 local governments. The governments of Australia's six states pass laws establishing and setting the responsibilities for these local councils. Most council seats are elected posts, though a state's governor can, if necessary, dismiss a council and appoint a local administrator.

Responsibilities for local councils are similar to those for local governments in the United States. For example, Australian councils are responsible for keeping track of such local services as road construction and garbage collection. To fund services, local councils levy property taxes. Since the early 1970s they also have received some funding from national and state governments.

Although local councils have some power to set rules for land use and urban planning, state governments generally establish uniform laws that guide the actions of local officials in such matters.

In addition, Australian state governments perform many functions normally handled by local governments in the United States. These functions include maintaining police forces, health services, educational facilities, and public transit systems.

number of people whose taxes go to pay for city expenses. Many suburban residents, particularly those who work in the city, use a variety of city services, such as streets and police protection. A metropolitan government, some people say, would require suburbanites to pay their fair share.

Opponents of metropolitan government disagree. Studies generally do not support the argument that consolidating services makes them cheaper. Opponents also argue that local areas should be allowed to retain their diverse character and not be required to provide the same level of services as other, nearby areas. When local jurisdictions differ in the services they provide and the taxes they impose, people in an area can "shop around" for a community whose services best suit them. In addition, competition for residents encourages local governments to be more responsive.

Only a small number of metropolitan governments have been established in the twentieth century. More frequently, metropolitan areas have established joint councils to discuss and act on common problems. Some proposals for forming metropolitan governments have been voted down by suburban residents who fear that they would be required to pay city taxes and that it would be harder to maintain a high level of public services in their own communities.

CASE STUDY

Consolidating Governments

POLITICAL PROCESSES The growth of suburbs and other communities surrounding large cities often complicates urban planning. As suburbs increase in size, central cities have less room to expand to accommodate their growing populations. In addition, a lack of coordination between governments of central cities and those of surrounding areas creates problems in planning roads, sewage facilities, and other services used by all metropolitan residents.

To ease such problems, some cities and counties have begun to share responsibilities. Several have even consolidated their governments into one metropolitan authority that serves all area residents. Some consolidated governments include Davidson County–Nashville, Tennessee;

POLITICAL FOUNDATIONS *Special districts are formed to provide a single service to the community in which they are located. School districts are the most common type of special district.* **What are some other services that special districts provide?**

Richmond County–Augusta, Georgia; and Duval County–Jacksonville, Florida. The city of Indianapolis, Indiana, and surrounding Marion County also have a unified government, but few services actually are consolidated.

Portland, Oregon, is another city that has consolidated some of the services in its metropolitan area to better serve residents. In 1977 the Oregon legislature created the Metropolitan Service District (Metro), which includes the city of Portland, 24 neighboring towns and cities, and three surrounding counties. As of 2001 the Metro had a population of more than 1.3 million.

Portland and surrounding communities each have their own governments, which provide police and fire protection, community development, and other services. An executive officer and a seven-member council—elected in district elections—set district policy and provide areawide services.

With a budget of $414 million in 2001, the Metro provided land use planning, solid waste management, and water and transportation services. In addition, it operates its own park system, the Oregon Zoo, the Oregon Convention Center, the Expo Center, and the Portland Center for the Performing

THEMES IN GOVERNMENT

CITIZENSHIP A responsible local government and an involved citizenry can better people's lives without dramatically increasing government expenditures. Currently, cities across the country are trying new ideas to put welfare recipients to work. This goal has broad appeal in cities with tight budgets that have cut back on hiring full-time employees.

In Chicago, for example, some welfare recipients recently began working as tutors in the public schools, helping children from poor families learn basic skills.

While some experts argue that requiring welfare recipients to work will not help them become self-sufficient, one tutor points out that contributing to the community gives her a feeling of personal satisfaction. To her, the money ($6 per hour) is not as important as the chance to help someone learn. Furthermore, this opportunity will provide experience for her future—she plans to study education and to teach. ■

Caption Answer

adequately meeting
the needs of their
community

1. Refer to the following
pages: township (487),
municipality (487), mayor-
council system (488),
council-manager system
(488), city manager (488),
commission (489), special
district (490).

2. mayor-council—separately elected legislature and
chief executive; council-
manager—an elected city
council that appoints the city
manager

3a. run welfare programs,
hospitals, schools, and jails;
keep legal records; super-
vise elections; maintain
roads and some recreational
facilities; prosecute persons
accused of breaking county
laws

3b. Metropolitan governments are cost-effective,
can better handle problems,
and can tax people in the
suburbs who benefit from
city services.

4. Answers will vary, but
students should clearly
state their opinion and provide support.

FRANK AND ERNEST

FRANK & ERNEST reprinted by permission of Bob Thaves

CITY HALL
PERMITS & LICENSES

MY GRANDFATHER HELPED BUILD A NATION. NOW, I NEED SIX PERMITS TO PUT UP A PORCH.

PUBLIC GOOD *Many citizens feel that local governments, although they attempt to provide for the public good, only make people's lives more difficult. **What is the biggest public service problem that local governments face?***

Arts. The state legislature also provided more than $135 million for parkland.

Local Government and the Public Good

Like state governments, most local governments have developed tracking systems to determine how well they are fulfilling their responsibilities to citizens. Some cities, for example, track how quickly potholes are repaired.

The biggest problem that local governments face in delivering services is in adequately meeting the needs of their many communities. Serving urban areas can be particularly difficult, because many solutions to urban problems require increased spending, and people often resist paying higher taxes.

However, some people hold that a more active and informed citizenry will produce local government leaders and alternative solutions that can help improve services without a dramatic increase in spending. The people who live in each local area or community depend on local government to serve them in a variety of ways but may take for granted many of the services local government provides. Though it might be possible for individuals in a community to hire someone to take away the trash, or to protect their neighborhoods from fire and crime, life would be much more difficult if they had to achieve these things alone. People generally find that by working together they receive better and more efficient services.

SECTION 2
REVIEW

1. Identify and explain:
- township
- municipality
- mayor-council system
- council-manager system
- city manager
- commission
- special district

2. Identifying Concepts: Copy the chart below. Use it to identify the differences between the mayor-council form of government and the council-manager form.

Local government

| Mayor-Council | Council-Manager |

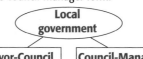

Homework Practice Online
keyword: SV3 HP21

3. **Finding the Main Idea**

a. What services do county governments provide?
b. What are the benefits of metropolitan governments?

4. **Writing and Critical Thinking**

Supporting a Point of View: Which form of local government do you think best serves the public good? Explain your answer.
Consider the following:
- the needs of the public
- the strengths and weaknesses of various forms of local government

SECTION 3

REVENUE AND LOCAL SERVICES

READ TO DISCOVER

1. What are the sources of revenue for local governments?
2. What different types of taxes may local governments levy?
3. How do federal and state grants help provide local governments with needed revenue?
4. In what ways do local governments promote the public good?

POLITICAL DICTIONARY

property tax

Unlike the federal government, which depends on federal income taxes for the bulk of its revenue, state and local governments receive most of their money from other sources. Two major sources of revenue are taxes and fees, but local governments also receive extensive state and federal grants. In many cases, local governments also may borrow money to fund major expenditures.

Taxes

The primary method that most local governments use to fund their operations is taxation. A local government's power to tax, however, is limited by the constitution of its state. While local governments' taxation power varies from state to state, citizens generally pay three types of local taxes: property taxes, sales taxes, and income taxes.

Property Taxes The most important source of local government tax revenue is the **property tax**, which is levied on the value of certain kinds of property. About half of property tax revenue goes to pay for schools. The bulk of this revenue is raised by taxes levied on land and buildings, especially homes, rather than on property such as clothes, furniture, cars, stocks, bonds, or jewelry.

There are two noteworthy features of property taxes. First, property taxes are levied on commercial as well as residential property, but usually not on property belonging to nonprofit or charitable organizations. Thus, a community's ease in raising revenue through the property tax depends on two factors: the value of the houses in the community (which is mostly a function of the community's wealth) and whether the community has a large shopping mall, a factory, or other business with substantial valuable real estate. A small town dominated by a university or other tax-exempt organization will have trouble raising tax revenues because there is not much taxable property. On the other hand, a community that attracts a major shopping mall or a new industry may have an easier time financing its government and meeting the needs of its citizens.

The second noteworthy feature of property taxes is that they generally are based on current property values. This can produce problems

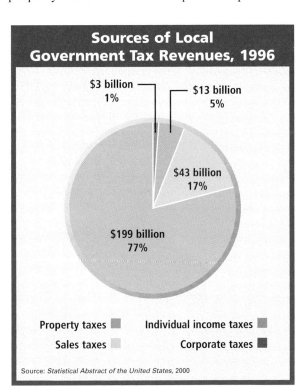

Sources of Local Government Tax Revenues, 1996

- $3 billion — 1%
- $13 billion — 5%
- $43 billion — 17%
- $199 billion — 77%

Property taxes
Sales taxes
Individual income taxes
Corporate taxes

Source: *Statistical Abstract of the United States, 2000*

State and local governments, while they depend heavily on property taxes, receive revenue from a variety of sources. **What source contributes the least to local government revenue?**

SECTION 3

REVENUE AND LOCAL SERVICES

Lesson Plans

For teaching strategies, see Lesson 21.3 located at the beginning of this chapter or the One-Stop Lesson Planner Strategy 21.3.

Political Dictionary

To reinforce the section's vocabulary term, refer students to the Electronic Glossary on the *Researcher CD-ROM.*

Section Assessment

To assess students' mastery of this section, have them complete Daily Quiz 21.3 in *Daily Quizzes with Answer Key.*

Transparency

An overhead transparency of the chart on this page is available in *Transparency Resources.* See Transparency 46: Sources of Local Government Tax Revenues, 1996.

> ***Caption Answer***
> corporate taxes.

THEMES IN GOVERNMENT

PUBLIC GOOD State and local tax amounts vary depending on where a person lives and how much money he or she makes. In 1994 a U.S. family of four with a combined income of $25,000 paid the least local and state taxes—$1,034 on average—if they lived in Jacksonville, Florida. Residents of Philadelphia, Pennsylvania, on the other hand, paid the most—$3,097.

For families with incomes of $100,000, Las Vegas, Nevada, had the lowest tax rate. The average family of four paid $4,698. Portland, Maine, had the highest tax rate at this income level, with $14,609 the average amount paid.

The state and local tax rate is just one factor that families should consider when relocating to a new community. They should also evaluate the services provided by the community for the amount of tax being paid. ■

Enhancing The Lesson

For more information on federal tax receipts, see the Federal Budgets section on the *Holt Researcher Online.*

Caption Answer

food, medicine, and clothing

---

when housing values rise. A family of modest means that bought a house 30 years ago may be hurt if soaring property values produce dramatically higher property tax bills.

A problem of property taxes in general lies in the fact that some citizens may own very little taxable property but have large incomes, while others may have low incomes but own a great deal of property. Many people argue that property taxes are regressive and therefore unfair—requiring lower-income people to hand over a larger percentage of their income in taxes than higher-income people are required to pay.

Sales Taxes As noted in Chapter 20, a sales tax is a tax charged as a percentage of the cost of

PRINCIPLES OF DEMOCRACY *To raise revenue, many state and local governments charge sales taxes on a variety of goods and services. **What items are sometimes exempt from sales taxes?***

---

services and retail goods. Many items are subject to the sales tax. The local sales tax is relatively new; New York City adopted its first local sales tax only in 1934. Today at least 29 states have authorized their county governments to impose a general sales tax. Some people oppose this tax for the same reason that people oppose the property tax—because it is regressive. Governments sometimes try to ease the effects of the sales tax by exempting essential items such as food, medicine, and clothing.

Income Taxes As noted in Chapter 9, an income tax is a tax levied on an individual's income, including wages or salaries, tips, interest, dividends, and money earned from property. Local governments rely less on personal income taxes than they do on other types of taxes, with only 11 states allowing income taxes at the local level in 1997.

Local governments choose to levy an income tax because it provides much-needed revenue, it is relatively easy and economical to administer, and it is considered by many people to be more equitable than the property or sales tax. In addition, income taxes are collected in the community where the income is earned rather than where the earner resides. This helps local governments—particularly in urban areas where many wage earners work but do not live—because they can collect taxes from both residents and nonresidents of the local community. A local government might, however, drive workers and, potentially, employers out of the city by imposing an income tax.

Fees

In recent years some local governments have come to rely increasingly on user fees, which are typically charged to citizens for the use of parks, recreation centers, other public facilities, parking spaces, mass transit, and utilities. While fees add to local government budgets, they may make services less available to citizens who cannot afford to pay.

On the other hand, some people argue that fees motivate communities to make more economical use of services, thus increasing efficiency and reducing waste. Such motivation does work particularly well for services such as water, which is used extravagantly if no fee or a flat fee—a fee that does not vary according to the level of use—is charged. However, when citizens are charged

PUBLIC GOOD *Many local governments raise revenue through user fees. Such fees may be charged for admission to county parks.* **For what other services may local governments charge user fees?**

individually for the amount of water they use, they are more likely to conserve.

Grants

As noted in Chapter 4, local governments—like state governments—receive extensive federal grants, called grants-in-aid. During the 1960s the Kennedy and Johnson administrations began increasing the number of grants directly available to local governments. Formerly, the federal government had allocated much more money to state governments to distribute among cities and counties for programs they chose to fund. This change in the administration of federal funding for local governments came partly as a response to lobbying efforts by both the United States Conference of Mayors and the National League of Cities.

Local governments do receive significant revenues through grants from state governments as well. About half of school district funding comes from state grants. Grants help pay for other services as well, including public welfare programs, highway construction and maintenance, and general government support.

As noted in Chapter 4, two types of grants are available to local governments: categorical and block. On a local level, categorical grants might

be used for specific purposes, such as vocational education, while block grants would cover public education in general.

Categorical grants can be further classified as project grants, formula grants, or open-ended reimbursements. The process by which the federal government distributes money varies according to the type of grant. To receive a project grant, a local government must submit an application to a federal agency, which can approve or deny the request. In contrast, the federal government distributes formula grants to local governments according to factors established in congressional legislation or administrative regulations. Open-ended reimbursements are federal payments to local and state governments for the expenses arising from the implementation of federal mandates. The federal government typically pays only a portion of the expenses incurred by the mandate; the remaining funds must be provided by the state or local government.

Borrowing

During the 1800s, local governments often managed their finances poorly. For this reason, many state constitutions heavily restrict local governments'

PUBLIC GOOD *Local governments borrow money to finance large projects, such as the Denver International Airport, which is shown under construction in this photograph.* **For what kinds of projects do local governments usually receive grants?**

THEMES IN GOVERNMENT

PUBLIC GOOD Fees may not always be easy to distinguish from other sources of revenue, particularly fines, license charges, tolls, and special assessments. Fees are distinct from these other revenue sources, however, in that they are related to the service provided and usually are for a nonessential service, such as entry into a national park. Fines, on the other hand, are imposed to deter law violations as well as to produce income. Besides generating revenue, licenses are regulatory in nature and serve to maintain order. Driver's licenses and auto registration, for example, make police work easier. Tolls are most often imposed to maintain highways that are managed by special districts. Special assessments are a means of charging for public necessities—for example, streets and sewers. ■

SECTION 3 REVIEW ANSWERS

1. Refer to page 493.

2. Sources include: property, sales, and income taxes; fees; and grants.

3a. to fund their operations

3b. advantages—add to local government revenue, prompt communities to make more efficient use of services; disadvantages—make services less available to people who cannot afford to pay for them

4. Answers will vary, but students should state their opinion and explain their reasoning.

496

PUBLIC GOOD *Citizens often have the opportunity to vote in bond elections.* **What are the two types of bonds issued by local governments?**

projects such as the building of schools. Popular referenda are usually required to authorize the use of general-obligation bonds. (As noted in Chapter 20, a referendum is a popular vote on a proposal.) Revenue bonds are often used to pay for convention centers, city-owned stadiums, utilities, toll roads, and toll bridges and are paid off from the revenue collected through user charges and tolls.

Bonds have been generally considered safe investments since the Great Depression, but they do carry a small element of risk. In late 1994, for example, Orange County, California, was suffering from financial troubles stemming from risky investments by Orange County officials. For some 18 months municipal bondholders were not sure that the county would be able to pay off its debts. In June 1996, however, their worries were over when the county got its finances in order.

In recent years some sellers of local bonds—including Orange County after its financial crisis—have offered insurance to bondholders. The interest rate for insured bonds generally is slightly lower than that for uninsured bonds, but bondholders receive a guarantee that they will be repaid.

ability to borrow money. Although local governments are supposed to maintain a balanced budget, they *can* borrow in anticipation of the revenue they will take in through taxes. They borrow this money through loans from a bank or they issue short-term tax anticipation notes.

Local governments usually issue bonds (which are defined and discussed in Chapter 20) to raise money for large expenditures. Local governments use two types of bonds: general-obligation bonds and revenue bonds. General-obligation bonds rely on the local government's taxing authority for repayment and are usually used to fund long-term

SECTION 3 REVIEW

1. Identify and explain:
• property tax

2. Identifying Concepts: Copy the chart below. Use it to identify the sources of funding for local government.

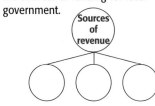

Sources of revenue

3. **Finding the Main Idea**

a. For what reasons do local governments need to tax citizens?

b. What are some of the advantages and disadvantages of charging fees for the use of public facilities?

4. **Writing and Critical Thinking**

Evaluating: Do you think that local government should issue bonds or find other ways to fund necessary services and projects? Explain your answer.
Consider the following:
• the function of local government
• sources of revenue available to local government

Homework Practice Online
keyword: SV3 HP21

GOVERNMENT IN THE NEWS

Global Problems, Local Action

Social-movement scholars have observed that during the late 1990s many activists around the world focused their energies at local government institutions. In the United States this rise in local activism can be attributed to the frustration with the federal government that grew during the 1990s.

In the late 1990s, the federal government delegated more responsibilities to the state and local levels—such as welfare services. Instead of waiting for a slow federal bureaucracy to act, many community organizations found that local governments were more responsive. Today many activists continue to seek change on the local level.

One of the most common concerns of local movements is the environment. While many activists agree that the global environment is in need of rescue, a growing number have found that immediate and effective change can be better made on the local level. Many groups have rallied to keep environmentally destructive projects out of their communities. Observers have dubbed this phenomenon the "Not in My Backyard" movement.

This movement is widely recognized as having been born during the Love Canal incident of the late 1970s. The town of Love Canal, New York, was the site of a toxic waste dump. The town's residents soon found that the dump was poisoning their children. Lois Gibbs, a Love Canal homemaker turned community activist, formed a neighborhood association and began protesting the dump at local, state, and national levels of government. Thanks in large part to Gibbs's efforts, the dump was eventually closed and a huge cleanup followed.

Gibbs has not stopped campaigning for a clean environment. Her latest effort also reflects a focus on local government. In 2001 Gibbs released a report revealing that many schools in the United States are built on contaminated sites that threaten

Activists demonstrate for the environment. In recent years many activists have worked for change on a local level.

students with illnesses and diseases, including cancer. Gibbs's movement, the Child Proofing Our Communities Campaign, wants to create state guidelines limiting where schools can be built. As of 2001, California was the only state with such rules.

Since there are practically no state or federal guidelines regarding where schools are built, working with local governments—specifically local school boards—is seen as the most effective way of bringing about change. The Child Proofing Our Communities Campaign report urges parents and community organizations to present local school boards with their concerns and initiatives for change. Using this type of local focus, activists anywhere can find ways to address national and even global problems.

What Do You Think?

1. Why are many activists focusing their energies for social change at the local level?

2. Identify a problem facing your community. How would you seek to change it? What areas of local government might you consult?

> ### WHY IT MATTERS TODAY
>
> Participating in recycling programs, paying property taxes, and attending public schools are just some of the ways in which citizens interact with their local government. Use **CNNfyi.com** or other **current events** sources to find out about issues currently facing the local government in your community.
>
> **CNNfyi.com**

Government in the News Answers

1. Students might suggest that many people derive their identity from their local community. Activists have found that local governments are more responsive to change, and Americans in general have grown frustrated with the federal bureaucracy.

2. Answers will vary but should present a realistic problem and a possible solution.

CHAPTER 21

Review Answers

Writing a Summary

Summaries should focus on the main points of each section. These may be found in the Read to Discover questions at the start of each section. Summaries should also use standard grammar, spelling, sentence structure, and punctuation.

Identifying Ideas

1. Refer to the following pages: suburb (481), metropolitan area (484), megalopolis (484), township (487), municipality (487), mayor-council sytem (488), council-manager system (488), city manager (488), special district (490), property tax (493)

Understanding Main Ideas

1. a central city of more than 50,000 people, its suburbs, and the surrounding counties that are economically and socially dependent on it

(Continued on page 498)

(Continued from page 497)

3. usually created by the state through state charters; by allowing local governments to exercise only the powers they are specifically granted

4. usually commissioners; services include running public schools, coordinating transportation, providing for sewage disposal, and maintaining a water supply

5. land and buildings, especially homes

6. property taxes and grants

Reviewing Themes

1. Answers will vary, but students should describe their local government, how its offices are filled, and if they feel it meets the community's needs. Students should offer support for each answer.

2. Answers will vary, but students may consider the suburban residents' use of city services when forming their opinion. Students should explain their reasoning regarding the suburban residents' sharing of these costs.

3. Answers will vary, but students should offer support for their opinions and support their opinions about successes and failures.

Thinking Critically

1. Answers will vary, but should demonstrate knowledge of how public offices are filled at the local level.

2. Answers will vary, but students should state their opinion and provide support.

(Continued on page 499)

CHAPTER 21
Review

Writing a Summary

Using standard grammar, spelling, sentence structure, and punctuation, write a summary of the information in this chapter.

Identifying Ideas

Identify the following terms and explain their significance.

1. suburb

2. metropolitan area

3. megalopolis

4. township

5. municipality

6. mayor-council system

7. council-manager system

8. city manager

9. special district

10. property tax

Understanding Main Ideas

SECTION 1 *(pp. 481–484)*

1. What makes up a metropolitan area?

2. Why has the population growth been particularly high in the Sun Belt?

SECTION 2 *(pp. 485–492)*

3. How are local governments established? How can state governments restrict the power of local governments?

4. Who runs special districts? What types of services do special districts provide?

SECTION 3 *(pp. 493–496)*

5. The bulk of property tax revenue comes from taxes on what kind of property?

6. Which sources of revenue do local governments rely on most to fund their schools?

Reviewing Themes

1. **Citizenship** What form of local government does your community have? How are its various offices filled? Do you think this form of government adequately serves the needs of the community? Explain your answer.

2. **Political Foundations** Why might some people argue that suburban residents should be required to share in the costs of running the central city on which they depend? Do you think that suburban residents should be forced to share these costs? Why?

3. **Public Good** Local government provides many necessary services, but some people criticize it for failing to meet the community's needs. In what ways do you think that local government succeeds in promoting the public good? In what ways do you think it fails?

Thinking Critically

1. **Comparing** Imagine that you have been asked to recommend a new form of government for your local community. Write a paragraph comparing the different the methods of filling public offices at the local level and explaining which method you would choose.

2. **Supporting a Point of View** Do you think people should have to pay to use a public park? Write a speech supporting or opposing fees for using local parks.

3. **Evaluating** Do you think a community's chief executive, such as a mayor or city manager, should be elected or appointed? Explain your answer.

Writing about Government

Review the list that you made in your Government Notebook at the beginning of this chapter. What other services does your local government provide to the community? Add to the list of services in your Notebook.

Interpreting the Visual Record

Examine the pie graph below. Then answer the questions that follow.

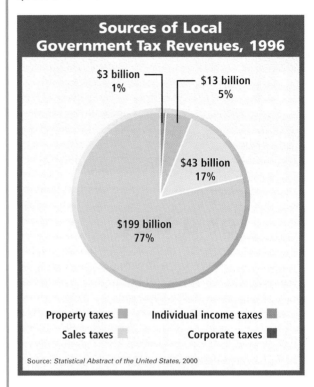

Sources of Local Government Tax Revenues, 1996

$3 billion — 1%
$13 billion — 5%
$43 billion — 17%
$199 billion — 77%

Property taxes
Individual income taxes
Sales taxes
Corporate taxes

Source: *Statistical Abstract of the United States*, 2000

1. What is the total dollar value of property taxes and sales taxes?
- **a.** $212 billion
- **c.** $242 billion
- **b.** $202 billion
- **d.** $199 billion

2. Why do you think property taxes represent the majority of revenue for local governments?

Analyzing Primary Sources

Henry Cisneros, the first Hispanic mayor of a major U.S. city (San Antonio), was appointed secretary of housing and urban development in 1993. In 1990 Cisneros and John Parr, a past president of the National Civic League, cowrote an article addressing the problem of a lack of public participation in government. Read the following excerpt and answer the questions that follow.

"In alarming numbers, citizens are becoming increasingly disengaged from public affairs, uninterested in the political process and public institutions, and skeptical that government has the talent, resources, and moral courage to solve problems. . . .

The problems confronting us as a nation and as communities require immediate attention. The solutions will not come from government alone. The society we want and can have will be achieved only through the combined effort of involved and concerned citizens and the public, private and voluntary sectors."

3. Which of the following best reflects the point of view of the authors?
- **a.** solutions will come from government
- **b.** citizens need to be more involved
- **c.** citizens are currently very involved
- **d.** citizens have great faith in government

4. Do the authors think that participation on a local level can solve problems facing the country? Do you agree? Explain your answer.

(Continued from page 498)

3. Answers will vary, but students should state their opinion and explain their reasoning.

Writing About History

The Government Notebook is a follow-up activity to the notebook activity that appears on page 480.

Building Social Studies Skills

1. c

2. Answers will vary, but students might suggest that by levying property taxes, local governments can ensure that only local residents pay for their own services.

3. b

4. Answers will vary, but students should explain their opinion.

Alternative Assessment

To assess this activity see Rubric 1: Acquiring Information I *Portfolio and Performance Assessment for Social Studies.*

Building Your Portfolio

Colonial New Englanders held town meetings in which they discussed and voted on issues and problems that affected them. Form three groups to research how New Englanders ran these meetings and what types of issues they addressed. Use the information you find to recreate a town meeting in your classroom. Costumes and props can make the re-enactment more believable. If possible, videotape the performance so that you can watch it as a class.

⧉ internet connect

Internet Activity: go.hrw.com
KEYWORD: SV3 GV21

Have students access the Internet through the HRW Go site to conduct research on the 2000 census. Have students find information on the fastest growing urban areas and on the movement of people from cities to suburbs. Then ask students to use the *Holt Grapher* to create a chart or graph that represents their research.

LAB OBJECTIVES

The Unit 7 Public Policy Lab incorporates the following objectives:

▶ review information about options for funding a city project.

▶ debate with other city-council members the course of action that should be taken.

▶ use a problem-solving process to draft legislation spelling out how the project will be funded.

Using the Lab

Before beginning the lab, organize students into groups and distribute copies of the Public Policy Lab Unit 7 Activity found in *Unit Tests and Unit Lab Activities with Answer Key*. Then have students read the assignment on this page. Discuss the assignment with students and point out the documents on pages 501–03 that students will use during the lab.

The What Do You Think? questions on pages 501–03 will help guide students during the project. In addition, the lab worksheet includes a step-by-step checklist for students to monitor their progress. For assessment guidelines, use the Problem Solving rubric in the *Alternative Assessment Handbook*.

PUBLIC POLICY LAB

You Solve the Problem

Council Member for a Day

*I*magine that you and other members of your group serve on a town council in a mayor-council form of government. The mayor and council members have decided to expand the town hall to accommodate the current staff and the new town employees whom the council expects to hire next year. Now you and other council members are searching for ways to pay for the construction. The town council must draft legislation to raise money for the town hall's expansion.

To help you in drafting the legislation, you and other council members should review the following documents: a newspaper clipping about local taxes, a letter about the project from the mayor to a local newspaper, a state law governing the taxing power of local governments, a rough town budget report, and public opinion polls.

Government Notebook Assignment

Record your problem-solving process in your Government Notebook.

1. Review the documents and answer the What Do You Think? questions.
2. Identify the problem you are trying to solve with this legislation.
3. Gather information on how local governments have funded projects and the advantages and disadvantages of different methods.
4. List and consider the options you have in drafting this legislation. Consider the advantages and disadvantages associated with each of these options.
5. Choose and implement a solution by meeting with other council members to debate a course of action. Prepare legislation that can win a majority of the votes on your council.
6. As a class, evaluate the effectiveness of different solutions by contrasting legislation prepared by different groups.

ANOTHER TAX INCREASE?

Last spring, for the third time in as many years, our property taxes went up. The increase was only slight, and Forest Park citizens bore it gladly for the sake of the new elementary school. However, with growing talk about a possible sales tax increase or a new local income tax to pay for construction to expand the town hall, people are beginning to grumble.

"We just had a tax increase! I, for one, am not ready to hand over more of my hard-earned money for some politician's pet project. They should cut some of their current spending to pay for their expansion if they really need it," commented Ronald Walker, a local businessperson.

Melanie Hopkins, a cashier at the grocery store, said, "I sure don't want to pay any more taxes. It seems like I hardly have any money left for my family as it is. But my aunt works for the town, and she says that the situation at the town hall is terrible. She has to share an office with three other people, and they can barely walk around all the filing cabinets and office equipment. I'm sure it's a fire hazard, among other things."

Fire Chief Tony Nguyen confirmed Hopkins's suspicion. "It's a fire hazard all right. By state law, I should shut down the town hall. But then who would be running things around here? We need the expansion, but I don't know how we're going to pay for it."

Citizens are largely resistant to a new tax, but according to town officials, the situation at the town hall is urgent. For more information on this issue, see Mayor Mason's letter to the editor on page 3B.

◀ WHAT DO YOU THINK?

1. What reason does the mayor give for the overcrowding in town hall?

2. What options does Mayor Mason offer readers for funding the town hall expansion?

3. Which options do you think would be best for town officials to pursue?

The Times 3B

Letters to the Editor

Mayor Urges Support of Town Hall Expansion

I am writing this letter to urge the citizens of Forest Park to support the town hall expansion effort. I hope you will take a few minutes to read my letter, because our community must understand the urgent need for more space in town hall.

The main reason the council has decided to expand the town hall is that the building is severely overcrowded. Built 80 years ago, it is designed to accommodate only about 20 employees. Currently, 45 employees are crowded into the building's offices. The town council expects to hire several new employees over the next year.

Why is the number of town employees increasing so quickly? More and more people move to Forest Park each month. Some do so because they like the peaceful lifestyle and beautiful countryside. Others choose Forest Park because it is within easy driving distance of their jobs in nearby cities.

Of course, most people already agree that we need to expand town hall. What is not clear is whether there is enough support to pay for the expansion. It will be expensive. Town officials estimate that it will cost about $300,000 a year to pay off general-obligation bonds for construction.

Forest Park residents will have to pay most of the cost. The choice, of course, is between raising taxes or cutting the budget. If we cut the budget, we must either lay off town employees or decrease the services that the town provides. The only other option is to put the expansion of the town hall on hold.

I believe we must be prepared to pay for construction through higher taxes. Higher taxes will be difficult for many people. Nevertheless, our community should have the facilities to continue to provide the services this town needs. Let's all pitch in and help make it happen. I encourage each of you to attend the upcoming town council meetings to let us know what you think about the issue.

Sheila Mason
Mayor

What Do You Think? Answers

1. Town hall was built 80 years ago for 20 employees; 45 employees now work in the building. Also, more people are moving to the town.

2. to raise taxes or to cut spending

3. Answers will vary, but students should offer their opinions and support them with information from the documents.

What Do You Think?
Answers

1. property taxes, sales taxes, income taxes

2. 5 percent

3. 15 percent

4. Answers will vary, but students might point out that, without such restrictions, a city government could unfairly tax its citizens for projects that the citizens do not necessarily support; or the government could overtax its citizens, thereby creating hardship for some.

5. no (2.6 percent)

PUBLIC POLICY LAB *continued*

Local Government: State Book of Laws

Taxing Authority for Local Governments

A. Municipal Improvements

1. Cities and towns throughout the state have the authority to levy the following taxes to pay for town improvements:

   a. property taxes,

   b. sales taxes, and

   c. income taxes.

2. City and town governments may set tax rates for funding municipal services and maintenance under the following conditions:

   a. revenue from tax rate increases in any one year may not exceed 5 percent of the city or town's current total budget without voter approval;

   b. general elections to decide a tax increase must be held between 30 and 90 days of the local government's approving it; and

   c. revenue from tax rate increases in any one year may not exceed 15 percent of the city or town's current budget with or without voter approval.

WHAT DO YOU THINK?

1. What kinds of taxes may town governments levy to pay for town services or improvements?

2. By how much may city governments raise tax rates annually before they must seek approval from local voters?

3. What is the upper limit of a tax rate increase, even with voter approval?

4. Why do you think state law requires voter approval for tax rate increases of more than 5 percent of the current budget and forbids them above a set limit?

5. You can see in the budget report that the estimated annual cost of paying off general-obligation bonds to expand the town hall is $300,000. Would those annual payments exceed 5 percent of the town's current budget?

 FROM THE OFFICE OF THE TOWN BUDGET DEPARTMENT

TO: Town Council Members
FROM: Jacqueline Soliz, Town Budget Department
RE: Budget Requirements for Town Growth

Per your request during the last council meeting, the Town Budget Department is preparing a report providing rough budget figures regarding current spending and the cost of the proposed expansion of the town hall. The following items are a summary of the main points included in the report:

a. Current annual town budget: $115.5 million

b. Estimated annual cost of proposed town hall expansion: $300,000

c. Possible sources of local revenue:
   • general-obligation bonds, to be paid off by new local sales or income taxes
   • property tax increase of 3 percent
   • decreased spending on an existing program [see below]

Currently, the budget is used to pay for public safety, town administrative services, public health, public recreation and culture, public works, social services, development, and municipal courts.

The full report will be available by the end of the week.

502

STATE UNIVERSITY
DEPARTMENT OF PUBLIC AFFAIRS

Dear Mayor Mason:

Thank you for asking me to poll residents in your area about expanding the town hall. I hope this information will help you in coming to a decision about how to pay for the construction.

To help me conduct the poll, I contacted graduate students in the Department of Public Affairs and the Department of Economics here at State University. With their help, I conducted two telephone polls in your community last month. The first poll asked respondents whether they believed an expansion of the town hall was needed. The second poll asked respondents their opinions about how the construction costs of the town hall expansion should be funded.

The poll results are shown in the attached two pie charts. If I can be of further assistance, please let me know.

Sincerely,

Peter Simek

Professor Peter Simek
Department of Public Affairs
State University

WHAT DO YOU THINK?

1. What percentage of poll respondents believes that town hall expansion is needed?

2. Review the results of both polls. How likely do you think voters are to approve the use of general-obligation bonds to fund the expansion of city hall?

"Town officials say that the Forest Park town hall does not have adequate space for the current town employees, and the town council expects to hire several new employees this year. To resolve this problem, the council is proposing to expand the town hall. In your opinion, is this expansion necessary?"

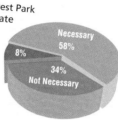

"In your opinion, how should the town pay for the expansion of the town hall?"

Internet Activity: go.hrw.com
KEYWORD: SV3 GVPL

Access the Internet through the HRW Go site to employ a problem-solving process to decide on a course of action regarding the expansion of the town hall. Research links and a problem-solving tutorial are provided.

What Do You Think?
Answers
1. 58%

2. Answers will vary, but students might state that voters are likely to approve the bonds because more than half of the poll respondents felt the city hall expansion was necessary. About half of the respondents would apparently accept a higher local tax rate to do it, and the other half would seemingly approve of the expansion if it were paid for by budget cuts.

UNIT 8

Lesson Options

Suggestions for customizing the material in Unit 8 to fit the specific schedule and curriculum of your classroom are located at the beginning of each chapter.

Main Ideas

Ask each student to read the Main Ideas and briefly answer each question in writing. Later, when you have finished Unit 8, ask students to return to their original answers and revise them using what they learned in the unit.

PUBLIC POLICY LAB

The Unit 8 Public Policy Lab appears on pages 552–55. This lab project is a real-world assignment in which students working in groups will take on the roles of ambassadors representing the five permanent member countries of the United Nations Security Council in order to prevent a potential conflict between two nations. *Unit Tests and Unit Lab Activities with Answer Key* provides support materials to help students complete the lab.

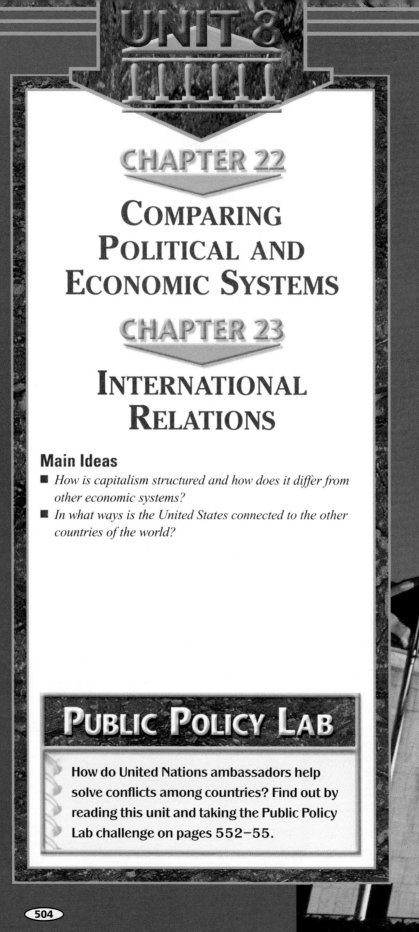

UNIT 8

CHAPTER 22
COMPARING POLITICAL AND ECONOMIC SYSTEMS

CHAPTER 23
INTERNATIONAL RELATIONS

Main Ideas

■ *How is capitalism structured and how does it differ from other economic systems?*

■ *In what ways is the United States connected to the other countries of the world?*

PUBLIC POLICY LAB

How do United Nations ambassadors help solve conflicts among countries? Find out by reading this unit and taking the Public Policy Lab challenge on pages 552–55.

THE UNITED STATES AND THE WORLD

Unit 8 presents the basic concepts necessary to introduce students to the theoretical basis and history of capitalism, socialism, and communism; to aspects of international relations, such as collective security; the causes of conflict; weapons proliferation; the United Nations; economic development; international trade; environmental interdependence; protecting natural resources; and U.S. relations with other countries.

While exploring the unit's concepts, students will find numerous examples relevant to their lives. In addition, they will have the opportunity to apply these concepts to events and issues around them.

Teaching with Photographs

The United Nations (UN) was founded in 1945—following the end of World War II—with the hope of preventing another world war by promoting world peace. Its main goal was and is to build peaceful cooperation among the world's nations. The UN General Assembly, in which all member nations have a voice, includes some 190 countries and uses five official languages—Chinese, English, French, Russian, and Spanish. Now more than 55 years old, the UN continues to promote universal human rights and global peace.

CHAPTER 22 COMPARING POLITICAL AND ECONOMIC SYSTEMS

	OBJECTIVES	PACING GUIDE	REPRODUCIBLE RESOURCES
SECTION 1 **CAPITALISM** (pp. 507–510)	▸ What are the four factors of production? ▸ In what way is a free-market economy an essential aspect of capitalism? ▸ How do supply and demand, competition, and the profit motive affect capitalist economies? ▸ How does the U.S. economy differ from Adam Smith's ideas of capitalism?	**Regular** 1.5 days **Block Scheduling** .75 day	**ELL** Spanish Study Guide 22.1 **ELL** English Study Guide 22.1 **PS** Reading 50: *The Wealth of Nations*
SECTION 2 **SOCIALISM** (pp. 511–514)	▸ What are some of the basic principles of socialism? ▸ What are some nations that have strong socialist traditions? ▸ What is a welfare state?	**Regular** 1 day **Block Scheduling** .25 day	**ELL** Spanish Study Guide 22.2 **ELL** English Study Guide 22.2 **PS** Reading 58: *Das Kapital* **PS** Reading 59: *Communist Manifesto*
SECTION 3 **COMMUNISM** (pp. 515–522)	▸ What are some of the basic principles of communism as described by Karl Marx? ▸ How did Vladimir Lenin's concept of communism differ from that of Marx? ▸ What changes occurred in the Soviet Union under Joseph Stalin? ▸ Why did the Soviet Union eventually dissolve?	**Regular** 2 days **Block Scheduling** 1 day	**ELL** Spanish Study Guide 22.3 **ELL** English Study Guide 22.3

Chapter Resource Key

PS	Primary Sources	**A**	Assessment		Video
RS	Reading Support	**REV**	Review		Videodisc
E	Enrichment	**ELL**	Reinforcement and English Language Learners		Internet
S	Simulations		Transparencies		Holt Presentation Maker Using
SM	Skills Mastery		CD-ROM		Microsoft ® PowerPoint ®

TECHNOLOGY RESOURCES	REINFORCEMENT, REVIEW, AND ASSESSMENT
One-Stop Planner: Lesson 22.1 Holt Researcher Online Homework Practice Online Transparencies 47 and 48 Global Skill Builder CD-ROM	**REV** Section 1 Review, p. 510 **A** Daily Quiz 22.1
One-Stop Planner: Lesson 22.2 Holt Researcher Online Homework Practice Online	**REV** Section 2 Review, p. 514 **A** Daily Quiz 22.2
One-Stop Planner: Lesson 22.3 Holt Researcher Online Homework Practice Online Cartoon Transparency 22: Class Struggle Between Working and Business Classes	**REV** Section 3 Review, p. 522 **A** Daily Quiz 22.3

Chapter Review and Assessment

SM Global Skill Builder CD-ROM
HRW Go site
REV Chapter 22 Tutorial for Students, Parents, and Peers
REV Chapter 22 Review, pp. 524–525
Chapter 22 Test Generator (on the One-Stop Planner)
A Chapter 22 Test
A Alternative Assessment Handbook

One-Stop Planner CD–ROM

It's easy to plan lessons, select resources, and print out materials for your students when you use the *One-Stop Planner CD-ROM with Test Generator.*

internet connect

HRW ONLINE RESOURCES
Go To: go.hrw.com
Then type in a keyword.

TEACHER HOME PAGE
KEYWORD: SV3 Teacher

CHAPTER INTERNET ACTIVITIES
KEYWORD: SV3 GV22
Choose an activity comparing political and economic systems to:
▸ write a report on transition economies.
▸ research interpretations of Adam Smith's theories.
▸ create a brochure on the fall of communism.

CHAPTER ENRICHMENT LINKS
KEYWORD: SV3 CH22

HOLT RESEARCHER ONLINE
KEYWORD: Holt Researcher

ONLINE ASSESSMENT
Homework Practice
KEYWORD: SV3 HP22
Standardized Test Prep
KEYWORD: SV3 STP22
Rubrics
KEYWORD: SS Rubrics

ONLINE MAPS, CHARTS, AND GRAPHS
KEYWORD: SV3 MCG
▸ Characteristics of Capitalism
▸ Four Factors of Production

CONTENT UPDATES
KEYWORD: SS Content Updates

HOLT PRESENTATION MAKER
KEYWORD: SV3 PPT22

ONLINE READING SUPPORT
KEYWORD: SS Strategies

CURRENT EVENTS
KEYWORD: S3 Current Events

LESSON 22.1 CAPITALISM

TEXTBOOK PAGES 507–510

OBJECTIVES

▶ List and define the four factors of production.
▶ Describe why a free-market economy is an essential aspect of capitalism.
▶ Explain how supply and demand, competition, and the profit motive affect capitalist economies.
▶ Describe how the U.S. economy differs from Adam Smith's ideas of capitalism.

MOTIVATE

Write the word *capitalism* on the chalkboard and tell the class that it is the type of economic system that is used in the United States. Ask students to identify other types of economic systems that exist throughout the world. Tell the class that they will be learning more about capitalism, communism, and socialism throughout this chapter. Have students attempt to identify factors that have led the United States to become a prosperous country. *(Students might mention rich natural resources or manufacturing.)* Then ask students to give examples of forces that they think drive the economy of the United States. After discussing their answers, tell students that in this section they will learn what makes capitalism function, the essential aspects of a free market, and how these systems work in the United States.

TEACH

Building a Vocabulary

In spiral notebooks, have students create a Political Dictionary to be used throughout the course. The dictionary may be used as an activity at the start of each new section; it may also be used as a modification device for students having difficulty or Sheltered English Students during tests and homework assignments. List words that students will be expected to know for this section on the chalkboard. Have students list, define, and give an example of each of the terms, using the text or the *Researcher CD-ROM*.

Demonstrating Understanding

Write the headings *private ownership, market economy, competition,* and *profit* on the chalkboard. Explain to students that these are the four principles that capitalism is based on. Then subdivide each category to include the headings *characteristics* and *examples.* Organize the class into several small groups. After having students read Section 1 of this chapter, have each group list the characteristics of each of these principles and as many examples as possible to illustrate what each principle means. Finally, ask each of the groups to write items from its list under the appropriate headings on the chalkboard and to explain its examples to the rest of the class. Allow time for groups to ask questions and to discuss each other's work. To lead into the next activity, tell students that they will be learning why a free-market economy is essential to capitalism.

Developing Life Skills

Remind students that a free-market economy is one of the essential aspects of capitalism. Ask students to name products that are currently very popular. *(Students might mention a new soft drink or video game.)* Then have students give examples of products that are not very popular, but that people may need anyway. *(Responses might include shoe laces or socks.)* Based on their knowledge of these products, ask students to consider the consumers' importance in determining how many of these products will be sold. Discuss the relationship between supply and demand and price with the class. Then ask students to discuss why consumers are critical to free-market economies. Tell students that in the next activity they will learn more about supply and demand and their effect on price.

Identifying Cause and Effect

Tell the class to imagine that they own a business that makes basketball shoes. Discuss with students the reasons that their company would want to make these shoes. Explain to students that the number of shoes they make (supply) will probably depend on how many shoes they can expect to sell (demand). Tell students that their factory can only produce one kind of shoe at a time. Explain to the class that the difference between the selling price and production cost of an item is the profit and that they will want to consider this factor when deciding which shoe to produce. Tell students that the shoe company has gathered the following data, which students will use to decide which shoe the company should make: approximately 10,000 people will buy shoe A (which costs $55 to make) for $75, and approximately 7,000 people will buy shoe B (which costs $65 to make) for $95. Have students discuss which shoe they would make and why.

Writing About Government

 Tell students that they are to write an essay in which they describe Adam Smith's idea of free-market capitalism, how the U.S. system of capitalism differs from the one Smith advocated, and which system they believe is better. They may wish to use the Biographies section on the *Holt Researcher Online* and information from the text to help support their opinions. Encourage students to share their ideas with the rest of the class.

CLOSE

Ask students to name a local or national business that has gone bankrupt or is having a difficult time surviving. Discuss with students how the factors studied throughout this section apply to such businesses. Then have students identify businesses that are thriving. Discuss with students how the factors studied throughout this section apply to these businesses as well. Finally, have students write a short essay describing how these economic factors can be applied to the failing and thriving businesses.

OPTIONS

Gifted Learners

Ask students to pick an American corporation and to research that company's activity during the last 10 years. Encourage students to focus on such issues as what the company produces and any changes that may have taken place in its corporate structure.

Students should also research financial reports for their chosen corporation to determine its profits or losses. Then have them graph those profits or losses. Next, they should analyze, based on their research, why the changes in the corporation's profits or losses have occurred over the time they researched. Discuss students' graphs and ideas as a class.

Students Having Difficulty/
Sheltered English Students

 Bring in articles or have students look through newspapers and magazines to find articles that feature businesses that are currently doing well financially. Have students identify the businesses' supply (what they are selling), their demand (how much they are selling), and their profit (how much money they are making). Encourage students to share their information with the rest of the class.

REVIEW

Have students complete the Section 1 Review on page 510. Use the answers in the Annotated Teacher's Edition to assess student mastery of this section.

ASSESS

To assess student mastery of this section, have students complete Daily Quiz 22.1 in *Daily Quizzes with Answer Key*. For additional assessment options see *Alternative Assessment Handbook* on the *One-Stop Planner CD-ROM*.

ADDITIONAL RESOURCES

Heilbroner, Robert. *The Worldly Philosophers: The Lives, Times, and Ideas of the Great Economic Thinkers*. 1999. Simon & Schuster.

LESSON 22.2 SOCIALISM

OBJECTIVES

▶ Describe some of the basic principles of socialism.
▶ List some nations that have strong socialist traditions.
▶ Define a welare state.

MOTIVATE

Ask students if all citizens are economically equal under the capitalist system. After they conclude this is not the case, tell students that in the 1700s, at the beginning of industrialization, such inequality was recognized and that theories were developed about how to make everyone economically equal. Write the word *socialism* on the chalkboard. Have students attempt to describe what it means for a country to be socialist. Then have them list countries that practice socialism. Tell students that in this section they will learn about socialism and countries that practice or have practiced a form of socialism.

TEACH

Building a Vocabulary

In their spiral notebooks, have students continue working on their Political Dictionary. List words that students will be expected to know for this section on the chalkboard. Have students list, define, and give an example of each of the terms, using information provided in the text or on the *Researcher CD-ROM*.

Comparing and Contrasting

On the chalkboard draw a chart with columns labeled *capitalism* and *socialism* and rows labeled *public services, nationalization, taxation,* and *nations.* Students should use information from this chapter, the Country Profiles section on the *Holt Researcher Online,* and other resources to find information about both systems. As a class, discuss the comparisons between the two systems. Discuss students' observations and write their conclusions under the appropriate section in the chart. Encourage students to copy the chart into their Government Notebooks for use as a study aid. To lead into the

next activity, tell students that they will be conducting research on countries that practice or have practiced a form of socialism.

Acquiring Information

Assign students different examples of historical or current socialist countries to research. Have students work in groups or pairs, depending on the size of the class. Have students use information from the Country Profiles section on the *Holt Researcher Online* and other resources to answer the following questions: When did socialism begin in the country? What industries have been nationalized? Has socialism made the nationalized industries more or less efficient? After groups have finished their research, have each of them work to develop a presentation that answers each of the questions. Have each group present its information to the entire class. Allow time for students to ask questions about the countries discussed. Refer students to the list created during the Comparing and Contrasting activity. Have them add the names of countries discussed in this activity that were not previously on the list. Tell students that they will be investigating the ideas of some of the political thinkers who fought to eliminate the differences in wealth between the social classes.

Identifying Cause and Effect

Explain to students that socialism developed as a result of the move from agricultural to industrial economies that occurred in many countries in the late 1700s. Tell students that this change often led to harsh working conditions and an uneven distribution of wealth between social classes. Encourage students to read about the ideas of political thinkers of the time—such as Robert Owen, Charles Fourier, Karl Marx, and Friedrich Engels—who pushed for the elimination of inequalities between social classes. Refer students to Reading 58: *Das Kapital* and Reading 59: *Communist Manifesto*, which may be found in *From the Source: Readings in Economics and Government with Answer Key*. Have students consider the arguments these thinkers made for reform. Have each student write a paper giving an opinion about whether the inequalities between social classes that existed in the late 1700s still exist today and whether the ideas for change suggested by these political thinkers affected the societies in which they lived. Encourage students to share their ideas about these discrepancies with the rest of the class.

CLOSE

Organize the class into four groups. The first group will examine the positive attributes of socialism. The second group will examine the negative attributes of socialism. The third group will examine the positive attributes of capitalism, and the final group will examine the negative aspects of capitalism. Have each group create a list of these attributes. When all groups have finished, have each discuss its list with the rest of the class. Students should be encouraged to discuss differences in opinion on these attributes and to create a list in their Government Notebook that includes the positive and negative aspects of each system.

OPTIONS

Students Having Difficulty/ Sheltered English Students

Discuss with students the differences between the bourgeoisie and the proletariat as well as Marx's idea of eliminating the differences between the two in order to create a classless society. Ask students to discuss whether they feel it is appropriate for one social class to violently rise up against another to achieve equality. Encourage students to explain their reasoning in a short paragraph.

Gifted Learners

Discuss with students the difference that exists in the percentage of income tax collected in socialist countries to that collected in capitalist countries.

Organize students into two groups, one to research the average rate of taxation in socialist countries, the other to research the same topic for capitalist countries. Encourage students to use the library, in-class resources, or the Internet to research this information. Once groups have finished, have them average the rate collected for all of the countries in their category. Have each group present its findings to the other group. As a class, discuss reasons for any discrepancy.

REVIEW

Have students complete the Section 2 Review on page 514. Use the answers in the Annotated Teacher's Edition to assess student mastery of this section.

ASSESS

To assess student mastery of this section, have students complete Daily Quiz 22.1 in *Daily Quizzes with Answer Key*. For additional assessment options see *Alternative Assessment Handbook* on the *One-Stop Planner CD-ROM*.

ADDITIONAL RESOURCES

McLellan, David. *Karl Marx*. 1975. Viking Press.
Karl Marx: The Specter of Marxism. 1985. The Media Guild. (video)
For information from the International Socialist Organization about its activities and socialism, see:
    http://www.internationalsocialist.org
For information on socialism including links, see:
    http://www.dsausa.org

OBJECTIVES

▶ List some of the basic principles of communism described by Karl Marx.

▶ Describe how Lenin's concept of communism differed from that of Marx.

▶ Identify and explain the changes that occurred in the Soviet Union under Joseph Stalin.

▶ Explain why the Soviet Union eventually dissolved.

MOTIVATE

List the following countries on the chalkboard: *Soviet Union, Poland, Romania, Hungary, Bulgaria, Cuba, China, North Korea,* and *Vietnam.* Tell students that each of these countries had a communist government sometime during the last 50 years but that today most have abandoned communism altogether or have modified it dramatically. Ask students to identify which countries abandoned communism, which modified it, and which still practice it. Tell students that in the next section, they will study how communism differs from capitalism and socialism.

TEACH

Building a Vocabulary

In their spiral notebooks, have students continue working on their Political Dictionary. List words that students will be expected to know for this section on the chalkboard. Have students list, define, and give an example of each of the terms, using information provided in the text or on the *Researcher CD-ROM.*

Identifying Cause and Effect/Evaluating Ideas

Draw an arrow from the left end of the chalkboard to the right end. Write the word *capitalism* at the left end and the word *communism* at the right end. As a class, discuss the steps that would need to occur to transform a capitalist society into a communist state. Students may wish to refer to Reading 58: *Das Kapital* and Reading 59: *Communist Manifesto* in

From the Source: Readings in Economics and Government with Answer Key to clarify Marx's position. Write on the chalkboard the steps necessary to transform a capitalist society into a communist state, listing the steps in the order that Marx described. Finally, discuss with students how each of these basic factors was supposedly necessary to achieve a communist government. Tell them that according to Marx, communism is the logical final stage in economic and governmental development. Tell students that in the next activity they will learn about some of the differences in philosophies about communism.

Comparing and Contrasting/Navigating the Internet

Tell students that even though many leaders came to support communism, these figures had different philosophies about how a communist state should be run. Organize the class into four groups. Assign one group to study each of the following: Marx, Lenin, Stalin, and Mao. Have each group use this section of the text as well as other resources to obtain as much information as possible about its figure's political ideas and the application of these ideas. Encourage students to utilize the Biographies section on the *Holt Researcher Online,* the Internet, and other resources to find the needed information. After they gather the information, have each group list its findings on a sheet of butcher paper. Each group should present its information to the entire class. Allow time for students to ask questions about each figure. Follow the presentations with a discussion of students' observations about similarities and differences between the four leaders and their philosophies.

Taking a Stand

Discuss with the class changes that occurred in the Soviet Union under Joseph Stalin. Have each student write a short essay stating an opinion on whether these changes actually benefited or hurt the Soviet Union. Encourage students to consult other resources to find support for their opinions. When students have finished, lead a class discussion about the opinions that students formed regarding Stalin and his methods. Tell students that in the next activity they will learn about the events that led to the collapse of the Soviet Union.

Writing About Government/Drawing Conclusions

Give students an article from a newspaper or magazine or have them find an article on the Internet that discusses the collapse of the former Soviet Union. Instruct students to read the article and to focus on the causes of the collapse. From this research, have each student write an essay expounding one aspect of the collapse of communism in the Soviet Union. Remind students to support their ideas with information from the article and the textbook.

CLOSE

Organize the class into two groups, with one group researching the positive aspects of communism and the other group covering the negative aspects. When both groups have researched their side of the issue, have them share their ideas with the other group. Remind students of the lists they created in the Close activity in Lesson 22.2 that describe the positive and negative attributes of socialism and capitalism. On a large sheet of butcher paper, create a chart that compares the positive and negative aspects of each of these systems. Display the chart for future reference.

OPTIONS

Interpersonal Learners

 Organize the class into three groups and have each group defend the position of either capitalism, socialism, or communism. Ask students to try to convince the other groups that their system is the best way to run an economy and/or a government. Students should refer to the charts created in the Close activity of this lesson and to any other information they need to defend their position. Lead the debate, making sure that students support their assertions with facts.

Gifted Learners

 Organize the class into several small groups and assign each group a Soviet leader to research (not including Stalin). Encourage groups to research the changes that occurred in the Soviet Union under their assigned leader, particularly those that contributed to communism's decline. Have each group discuss its findings with the rest of the class.

Gifted Learners

 Encourage students to learn more about the spread or the decline of communism by studying the similarities and differences of its rise and fall in various countries. Organize the class into groups. Then assign each group a different country to research. Try to include some countries in which communism has failed and others that still operate under a communist system. Have each group prepare a presentation on the fate of communism in the nation it studied. Have each group present its information to the rest of the class.

REVIEW

Have students complete the Section 3 Review on page 522. Use the answers in the Annotated Teacher's Edition to assess student mastery of this section.

ASSESS

To assess student mastery of this section, have students complete Daily Quiz 22.3 in *Daily Quizzes with Answer Key*. For additional assessment options see *Alternative Assessment Handbook* on the *One-Stop Planner CD-ROM*.

RETEACH

Instruct students having difficulty with the lessons to complete Reteaching Activity 22. This activity is located in *Reteaching Activities with Answer Key*.

ADDITIONAL RESOURCES

Tucker, Robert. *Stalin in Power: The Revolution from Above, 1928–1941.* 1992. Norton.

The End of the Soviet Union. 1992. Southern Center for International Studies. (video)

For information about the organization and actions of the Communist Party in the United States, see:
http://www.cpusa.org/

GOVERNMENT NOTEBOOK

The Government Notebook is a journal activity that encourages students to consider basic concepts of government that relate to their lives. A follow-up notebook activity appears on page 524.

▶ **WHY IT MATTERS TODAY**

To find additional lesson plans comparing political and economic systems, visit **CNNfyi.com** or have students complete the **GOVERNMENT IN THE NEWS** activity on page 523.

CNNfyi.com

CHAPTER 22

COMPARING POLITICAL AND ECONOMIC SYSTEMS

Two of the most dramatic events of the 1900s occurred when the Soviet Union dissolved and when the Berlin Wall was torn down. For many people around the world, these events showed the failures and successes of several major political and economic systems.

Varying political and economic systems have long been a feature of human societies. During the 1900s, democracy flourished in some nations, while authoritarian governments emerged in others. In some parts of the world, communist revolutionaries attempted to establish a social order without economic classes. In yet others, leaders worked to establish socialism. As the new millennium begins, capitalism is clearly the most prevalent economic system in the world. By studying the world's various political and economic systems, one can gain insight into these styles of governing and the cultures that have developed them.

GOVERNMENT NOTEBOOK

In your opinion, why might different societies and their leaders form different kinds of political and economic systems? What problems or difficulties might inspire the development of new systems? Write your answers in your Government Notebook.

▶ **WHY IT MATTERS TODAY**

The political and economic system a country follows dramatically affects the lives of its citizens. After reading this chapter, visit **CNNfyi.com** or other **current events** sources to learn more about issues related to political and economic systems around the world.

CNNfyi.com

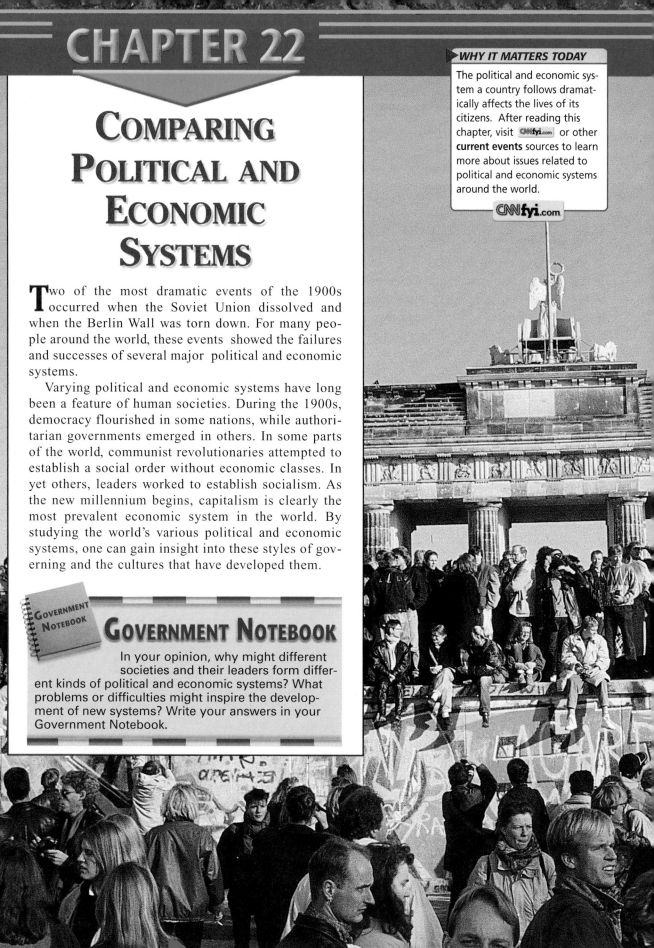

SECTION 1
CAPITALISM

READ TO DISCOVER

1. What are the four factors of production?
2. In what way is a free-market economy an essential aspect of capitalism?
3. How do supply and demand, competition, and the profit motive affect capitalist economies?
4. How does the U.S. economy differ from Adam Smith's ideas of capitalism?

POLITICAL DICTIONARY

entrepreneur
capitalist
factor of production
consumer
competition
supply and demand
profit
self-interest
mixed economy

Have you ever thought about starting your own company? If you bought a piece of land, built your own business there, and hired employees to work in the business, you would be an entrepreneur and a capitalist. An **entrepreneur** is a person who takes on the risk of starting, organizing, and operating a business, and a **capitalist** is a person who invests his or her money, land, or machinery in a business. Entrepreneurs and capitalists form the basis of the capitalist system, establishing and maintaining the businesses and industries that drive a free-enterprise economy.

Today the United States, Japan, Mexico, and Taiwan, for example, have some form of capitalist economy. To be classified as capitalist, a country must have an economy geared around some combination of the following principles—private ownership, a market economy, competition, and profit.

Private Ownership Central to the capitalist system is private, or nongovernmental, control over the factors of production. The **factors of production** are the basic resources needed for a country's economy. They include natural resources, human resources, capital resources—such as money and machinery needed to produce goods—and entrepreneurship. The factors of production for a shoe factory, for example, would include the land the factory occupies, the factory itself, the machines and materials required to make the shoes, the employees, and the person or people who started and manage the business.

Private ownership means that individuals and corporations—rather than the government—own or control the factors of production. In many capitalist societies, governments own some natural resources, such as land, as well as some basic public services, such as the postal system and public utilities. However, businesses in the United States and other capitalist nations are owned by individuals and corporations.

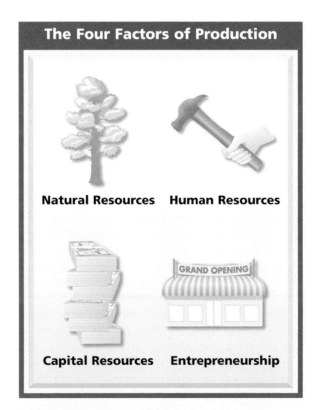

The Four Factors of Production

Natural Resources   **Human Resources**

Capital Resources   **Entrepreneurship**

GRAND OPENING

The basic resources needed for a country's economy are known as the factors of production. **What are some types of capital resources?**

SECTION 1
CAPITALISM

Lesson Plans

For teaching strategies, see Lesson 22.1 located at the beginning of this chapter or on the One-Stop Planner Strategy 22.1.

Political Dictionary

To reinforce the section's vocabulary terms, refer students to the Electronic Glossary on the *Researcher CD-ROM.*

Section Assessment

To assess students' mastery of this section, have them complete Daily Quiz 22.1 in *Daily Quizzes with Answer Key.*

Caption Answer

Answers will vary but may include money and machinery.

PUBLIC GOOD *The U.S. government controls certain basic public services in addition to owning some of the country's natural resources. This government-owned land near Jackson, Wyoming, is leased to ranchers for cattle grazing.* **What basic public services are controlled by the U.S. government?**

Market Economy A second principle of capitalism is the market economy. In precapitalist economies each family generally produced almost everything it needed, trading with others for items the family could not make itself. In this type of economy, individuals had to perform several jobs in order to make the things they needed. In a free-market economy, however, the products of an individual's labor are not for his or her use alone. Instead, for example, workers are paid by their employer, who then offers the products of their labor for sale in the market. In the market system, goods and services are bought or sold based not upon needs or traditions, but on individuals' desire to make money from the exchange. As noted in Chapter 9, goods and services are exchanged freely in a free-market economy, and the government has little say in what, how, and for whom they are produced.

Critical to free-market economies is the ability of **consumers**, or buyers of products, to choose freely from among goods offered for sale. Consumers therefore actively influence what and how much will be produced, through the pressures their buying decisions put on the market.

Competition and Profit Another essential element of capitalism is **competition**—the effort that sellers of similar goods or services exert to attract the business of consumers. When individuals and corporations must compete in the market economy, they are pressured to produce improved goods in order to attract buyers. In a competitive market the prices of goods are determined by two primary factors—supply and demand. Under the laws of **supply and demand**, goods that are in great supply and for which there is little demand tend to have low prices. Conversely, goods that are in low supply and for which there is high demand have high prices.

Another cornerstone of capitalist economies is **profit**—the difference between the revenue received from the sale of a good or service and the costs of producing it. A capitalist system works because the opportunity to earn profits lures people to invest their capital. Industries that generate particularly high profits encourage higher levels of investment. According to the laws of supply and demand, however, an increase in the supply of an industry's products forces down their prices and eventually decreases profits.

Roots of Capitalism

From about the 800s to the late 1300s, economic and social systems in Europe were dominated by feudal monarchies. Feudalism was based on the rule of an aristocratic class of titled landowners—such as barons, dukes, earls, and counts—who were loyal to a royal family headed by a monarch. As noted in Chapter 1, many people at that time believed that God chose monarchs and their heirs to rule over kingdoms and countries. In feudal societies, people's fates depended on the class into which they were born. Moving into a higher class was all but impossible. People who were born peasants almost always lived their entire lives as peasants, working the land for the benefit of the landowners and royal families.

Eventually, the feudal order was challenged by a middle class of entrepreneurs that first arose in cities. New theories of government and economics emerged as this rising business class gained influence. Writers and theorists such as Scottish economist Adam Smith, who published *An Inquiry into the Nature and Causes of the Wealth of Nations* in 1776, popularized ideas about how a free market could regulate economic activity.

Smith stated that in a capitalist economy everyone competes with everyone else to seek the greatest possible advantage from each market transaction. Thus, the primary motivation for

WORLD AFFAIRS *Scottish economist Adam Smith popularized ideas about how a free market regulates economic activity, creating maximum wealth.* **When did Smith publish his major writings?**

economic behavior is **self-interest**—the impulse that encourages the fulfillment of an individual's own needs and wants. Self-interest helps the economy grow as businesses compete with each other to provide goods and services to meet consumers' needs and wants. This competition brings about great efficiency because resources are used only to produce the goods and services for which people are most willing to pay. Individuals' pursuit of their own self-interest thus serves, in Smith's words, as an "invisible hand," guiding the market to promote the public good.

Smith argued that government efforts to regulate prices or restrict free trade interfere with this invisible hand's ability to satisfy consumer wants. He said that the laws of supply and demand would assure that enough goods would be produced to meet the needs of the population. In addition, competition among entrepreneurs would control profit levels and encourage both new and more-efficient production methods.

Capitalism in the United States and in Welfare States

The United States does not practice the pure market principles that Smith envisioned. Rather,

it has developed what can be called a **mixed economy**, one in which private enterprise and government action both play a role. The government of a capitalist nation may enact some regulations, but its role in the economy is limited.

As noted in Chapter 9, the government in a capitalist society such as the United States can encourage economic growth by means of fiscal policy—for example, by altering the federal budget or by increasing or decreasing taxes. Conversely, to regulate the nation's economy, the Federal Reserve may use monetary policy, raising or lowering interest

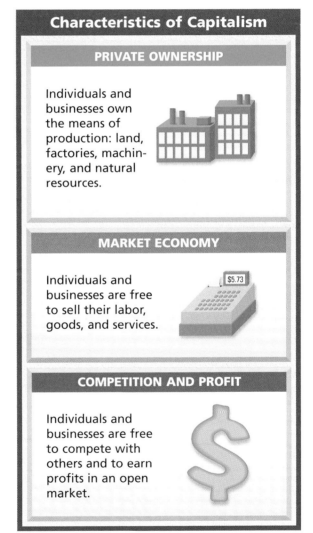

Characteristics of Capitalism

PRIVATE OWNERSHIP

Individuals and businesses own the means of production: land, factories, machinery, and natural resources.

MARKET ECONOMY

Individuals and businesses are free to sell their labor, goods, and services.

$5.73

COMPETITION AND PROFIT

Individuals and businesses are free to compete with others and to earn profits in an open market.

Capitalist economies are characterized by private ownership, free markets, competition, and profit. **In a capitalist economy, what assures that enough goods will be produced to meet the needs of the population?**

Caption Answer

Adam Smith published in the 1700s.

Transparency

An overhead transparency of the chart on this page is available in *Transparency Resources*. See Transparency 48: Characteristics of Capitalism.

Caption Answer

The laws of supply and demand ensure that enough goods will be produced.

⊿ internet connect

TOPIC: Adam Smith
GO TO: go.hrw.com
KEYWORD: SV3 GV22

Have students access the Internet through the HRW Go site to conduct research on the economic theories of Adam Smith. Then ask students to write a biography that outlines Smith's ideas on the free market and on competition. Students should outline the ways in which Smith's economic theories have been reinterpreted since *The Wealth of Nations* was first published.

SECTION 1 REVIEW ANSWERS

1. Refer to the following pages: entrepreneur (507), capitalist (507), factor of production (507), consumer (508), competition (508), supply and demand (508), profit (508), self-interest (509), mixed economy (509).

2. private ownership of the factors of production, a free market that allows consumer choice, competition between producers, and the ability to make a profit

3a. Smith did not believe in government intervention; the U.S. government encourages growth through fiscal policy

3b. The federal government owns some natural resources, runs some basic public services, and regulates industries, economic policy, and interactions between businesses.

4. Answers will vary, but students should give examples of how capitalism can both offer and limit economic freedom.

PUBLIC GOOD *In the U.S. capitalist economy, the government regulates industry, taxes citizens, and provides social services.* **In what other ways is the government involved in the economy?**

Otherwise, governments of countries with market economies pass few regulations on the operation of supply and demand. In a capitalist economy such as that of the United States, the government acts as a kind of referee. Although it helps regulate interactions among businesses, it generally does not interrupt the operations of capitalists, business owners, or the market economy. In the United States, private industries have great leeway in decision making, but the U.S. government influences the economy by regulating business practices, taxing citizens, and providing social services. The government also influences the economy in much the same way as a large business does through its purchases of goods and services from the private sector and as an employer of a significant portion of the population.

Many mixed economies today operate under what is called welfare state capitalism—government provides widespread social services financed by taxes. Examples of countries with welfare state capitalist economies include Brazil, Canada, Germany, Mexico, and the United Kingdom.

Welfare state capitalist governments differ from one another primarily in the extent to which they regulate industry, the rate at which they tax businesses and individuals, and the types of social services they provide. In mixed economies, taxes usually fund basic public services, social services such as monetary assistance to poor people, and health care, education, and public housing. Some mixed economies, particularly those in Europe, provide many additional services as well.

rates to discourage or encourage the borrowing of money. Taxing and spending policies enable the government to provide social services such as education, as well as provide for national defense. The government may also regulate health and safety standards in the workplace.

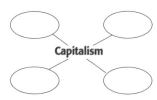

SECTION 1 REVIEW

1. Identify and Explain:
- entrepreneur
- capitalist
- factor of production
- consumer
- competition
- supply and demand
- profit
- self-interest
- mixed economy

2. Identifying Concepts: Copy the graphic organizer below. Use it to describe the essential elements of a capitalist economy.

Capitalism

3. **Finding the Main Idea**

a. How does the structure of the U.S. economy differ from Adam Smith's ideas of capitalism?

b. What role does the federal government play in the U.S. capitalist system?

4. **Writing and Critical Thinking**

In what ways do you think capitalism offers people more economic freedom? In what ways might it limit that freedoms for some people?
Consider the following:
- the role of consumers and competition in the market economy
- the role of self-interest in capitalism

Homework Practice Online
keyword: SV3 HP22

SECTION 2
SOCIALISM

READ TO DISCOVER

1. What are some of the basic principles of socialism?
2. What are some countries that have strong socialist traditions?
3. What is a welfare state?

POLITICAL DICTIONARY

socialism
democratic socialism
proletariat
bourgeoisie
communism
nationalization
command economy

As you have read, capitalism is based on private ownership, profit, competition, and the operation of the free market. In a capitalist system, people attain different levels of wealth and success, which produces inequality in their standards of living. Some people are quite wealthy, while others are very poor. Another economic system attempts to reduce these inequalities by redistributing wealth throughout society. Under this system, **socialism**, the government or the people as a whole own, or at least control, the factors of production and manage the distribution of goods. Various types of socialism have been developed to fit the unique cultural, social, economic, and political needs of different countries.

History of Socialism

Socialism as an organized political movement began in western Europe in the late 1700s and early 1800s after the Industrial Revolution—when Western countries moved from agricultural to industrial economies. Factory work subjected laborers to harsh conditions and worsened the unequal distribution of wealth. Some political thinkers, including Robert Owen and Charles Fourier, responded by calling for reforms to address these economic and social inequalities.

Early socialists sought to expand civil liberties and to secure greater economic equality. They concentrated on expanding voting rights and on establishing the ability of trade unions to bargain collectively with the management of corporations and other businesses. Following the ideas of **democratic socialism**, people sought to use these and other peaceful methods to eliminate capitalism. Industrial factory workers and intellectuals who favored socialism worked together in this movement's early political parties. Other political theorists, however, had more revolutionary ideas about political and social reform.

Karl Marx The founder of modern socialist thought is German political and economic theorist Karl Marx, who along with German social scientist Friedrich Engels wrote important works on socialism during the 1800s. These texts criticized capitalism, saying that free markets only enabled the wealthy to take advantage of the working class.

Marx urged the **proletariat**—the workers—to violently overthrow the **bourgeoisie**—the people

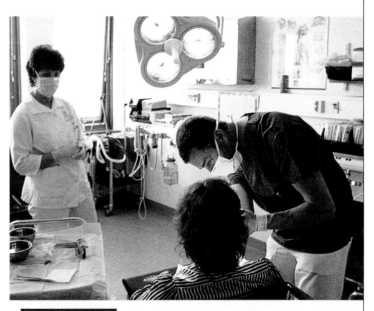

WORLD AFFAIRS *In Sweden, a democratic socialist country, the government provides citizens with health care.* **How did democratic socialists hope to eliminate capitalism?**

SECTION 2
SOCIALISM

Lesson Plans
For teaching strategies, see Lesson 22.2 located at the beginning of this chapter or on the One-Stop Planner Strategy 22.2.

Political Dictionary
To reinforce the section's vocabulary terms, refer students to the Electronic Glossary on the *Researcher CD-ROM.*

Section Assessment
To assess students' mastery of this section, have them complete Daily Quiz 22.2 in *Daily Quizzes with Answer Key.*

Caption Answer
through peaceful means such as by expanding voting rights

WORLD AFFAIRS *Karl Marx (pictured here) and Friedrich Engels wrote the* Communist Manifesto, *which urges workers to overthrow capitalist governments.* **Of what economic and political system do Marx and Engels's theories form the foundation?**

who own the means of production in a capitalist nation. Over time, his ideas formed the foundation of authoritarian socialism, or **communism**, which is based on government ownership or control of nearly all of the factors of production. (Communist doctrine is more fully explained in Section 3.)

Characteristics of Democratic Socialism

Democratic socialism has varied a great deal from nation to nation. In general, however, socialist economies all involve widespread social services and at least some **nationalization**, in which the government takes over industries. In most democratic socialist countries, government ownership is limited to industries of key national concern, such as electric utilities and transportation systems. Individuals are able to influence economic planning through the election of government officials. High taxes are

generally a feature of socialist economies as well. Socialist and communist economies make use of economic planning, where certain economic decisions are determined by a central authority. In most such economies, only certain sectors of the economy are planned, such as a key industry.

Many European nations, including Denmark, Austria, and Sweden, practice democratic socialism. In addition, economies of some less-developed countries, such as India, were traditionally based on democratic socialism. In recent years, many of these economies have moved closer to capitalism.

Social Services and the Welfare State Most socialists believe that government should ensure the equal distribution of certain basic social services. For this reason, nations with strong democratic socialist traditions—such as Israel, Sweden, and Australia—have enacted comprehensive social service programs, including old-age pensions, income supplements, health care, child care, unemployment compensation, and supplemental payments to people with children. Socialists have also attempted to expand educational opportunities for all people, eliminate discrimination, replan the layout of towns and cities, tear down slums and build new housing, and rebuild societies by cooperation instead of through competition for profits. As noted in Section 1, a government that provides widespread social services funded by taxes is a welfare state.

WORLD AFFAIRS *This textile-manufacturing plant belongs to the Egyptian government, which owns many of Egypt's major industries.* **Why do socialist countries nationalize industries?**

Careers in Government

International Broadcasting Bureau

In 1994 the U.S. International Broadcasting Bureau was established to coordinate all U.S. government international broadcast services. These services include U.S. and international news and programming for listeners around the world.

The most familiar of these broadcast services is Voice of America (VOA). VOA radio began airing on February 24, 1942, to provide news information to listeners in Germany and Nazi-occupied Europe during World War II. VOA remained on air after the war and today broadcasts in 53 languages to about 91 million listeners each week. Since October 1996 VOA has also broadcast television programs. Today, listeners can also hear VOA on the Internet. All VOA programming is produced in Washington, D.C.

Every VOA broadcaster must be a fluent speaker of his or her target audience's language.

Every Voice of America broadcaster must possess a wide variety of journalistic skills and be fluent in the language of his or her target audience.

Broadcasters must also possess a wide range of journalistic skills, such as interviewing, writing, and reporting for radio. Many VOA broadcasters have earned a college or graduate degree in print or broadcast journalism.

Most VOA broadcasting job applicants have experience reporting or editing for a news publication, a broadcaster, or a wire service, such as the Associated Press. In addition, applicants must pass an examination that tests their skills, experience, and foreign-language abilities.

A 24-hour hotline provides information about job openings throughout the federal government. Anyone interested in jobs with an International Broadcasting Bureau agency or with any other federal agency should submit a resumé or an official job application to the office in question.

Nationalization Although democratic socialists do not insist that government control of the means of production is always necessary, some socialist governments try to halt the concentration of wealth through the nationalization of basic industries and services such as banking, transportation, electric power, and mining. When a government operates such businesses, all citizens own them and collectively benefit from any of their profits.

Taxation Although all governments tax their citizens to help pay for government services and programs, under socialism, taxes are extremely high. For example, from the 1920s until 1991, Sweden was solidly socialist, and its taxes were among the highest in Europe. The Swedish government used the tax revenues to finance comprehensive health insurance, unemployment insurance, retirement benefits, public and college education, public housing, and child care. Although the Swedish standard of living was quite high, taxes were a source of great controversy. High taxes forced workers to demand higher wages. To cover the cost of these wage hikes, companies increased the prices of their goods. Moreover, tax revenues lagged behind the rising costs of social programs. As a result, the government ran deficits, borrowing heavily to meet its economic and social goals.

In Sweden's 1991 election, the Social Democrats lost control of the government, and a nonsocialist government was formed under the leadership of the Moderate Party. In 1994, however, the Social

SECTION 2 REVIEW ANSWERS

1. Refer to the following pages: socialism (511), democratic socialism (511), proletariat (511), bourgeoisie (511), communism (512), nationalization (512), command economy (514).

2. widespread social services, nationalized major industries, command economy, high taxes

3a. Socialist principles include the equal distribution of wealth, ownership of the factors of production by the government, and the nationalization of basic industries. Socialism aims to reduce the concentration of wealth in private hands and provide basic social services to all.

3b. Marx advocated violent revolution, but democratic socialism calls for the elimination of capitalism through reform and peaceful political methods.

4. Answers will vary, but students might suggest that the United States shares some policies in common with socialist countries, but rarely to the same degree.

POLITICAL PROCESSES *The Eastern European nation of Romania operated under a communist command economy before its communist government fell in the early 1990s. Today many of the country's formerly government-owned enterprises have come under private control.* **How much of the economy does the government control in a democratic socialist country?**

Command Economies

Both socialist and communist countries operate, wholly or in part, under what is called a command economy. In a **command economy**, government controls some or all of the major economic processes. Prices, for example, are determined by government regulations rather than by the interaction of supply and demand. Decisions about what, when, and by whom goods and services will be produced are made by government officials, often called central planners.

Although both democratic socialist countries and communist countries operate to some extent under command economies, the extent to which the government controls the economic activity varies significantly. In a democratic socialist economy, the government controls only a portion of the economy. For example, the government might own and operate public transportation, and postal and shipping services, and heavily regulate only a few industries. As you will learn in Section 3, in a communist country the government owns or controls all areas of the economy.

Democrats once again gained control of the government after winning the election. The government worked to ease some of the country's economic problems by restructuring government finances. It launched a government program to limit welfare benefits and turn over the operation of some government services to private firms. In 1995 Sweden joined the European Union in order to promote economic growth.

SECTION 2 REVIEW

1. Identify and Explain:
- socialism
- democratic socialism
- proletariat
- bourgeoisie
- communism
- nationalization
- command economy

2. Identifying Concepts: Copy the graphic organizer below. Use it to list the four main characteristics of democratic socialism.

Democratic Socialism
•
•
•
•

3. **Finding the Main Idea**

a. What are the two main principles of socialism, and why are they important?

b. How do Karl Marx's ideas differ from those of democratic socialism?

4. **Writing and Critical Thinking**

Comparing and Contrasting: What are some similarities and differences between the United States and socialist countries?

Consider the following:
- the role of taxation and social services in different economic systems
- the structure of command economies

Homework Practice Online
keyword: SV3 HP22

READ TO DISCOVER

1. What are some of the basic principles of communism as described by Karl Marx?
2. How did Vladimir Lenin's concept of communism differ from that of Marx?
3. What changes occurred in the Soviet Union under Joseph Stalin?
4. Why did the Soviet Union eventually dissolve?

POLITICAL DICTIONARY

class struggle
Communist Manifesto
forces of production
relations of production
vanguard
Bolsheviks
Communist Party

Beginning in 1917, communist revolutions promising sweeping political, economic, and social change took place in countries around the globe. Although most of the resulting communist governments no longer exist, communism powerfully shaped history and the way people look at power and politics around the world. Countries that have experienced communist rule include Bulgaria, Cuba, China, Hungary, North Korea, Poland, Romania, the Soviet Union, and Vietnam. In 1989 many of these countries abandoned communism. Others, such as China, have been slowly changing their economic and political systems to reflect some socialist and capitalist principles. Only Cuba and North Korea remain truly communist.

Communist Thought

As noted in Section 2, Karl Marx is considered the founder of modern socialist ideology; however, his more revolutionary views became the founding principles of the authoritarian style of social-

ism known as communism. Revolutionary leaders from around the world have based their policies and goals on Marxist thought.

Marx's View of History One of Marx's most important contributions to economic thought lies in his interpretation of past events. Marx stated that throughout history all societies have been characterized by **class struggle**—the ongoing competition between economic groups for resources and power. The class struggle in Europe between the 800s and the late 1300s took place between the feudal lords and their subjects. In the capitalist societies that followed feudalism, this struggle has taken place between the bourgeoisie and the proletariat.

In his ***Communist Manifesto,*** which he co-wrote with Friedrich Engels, Marx argued that economic factors have played the dominant role in shaping history. In an agricultural society, land is the basic means of production. Those who own it acquire prominence and make up the ruling class. According to Marx, these landowners had

WORLD AFFAIRS *Karl Marx argued that class struggle influenced the histories of all societies, as illustrated in this fifteenth-century painting showing property owners vowing service and allegiance to their feudal lord.* **According to Marx, what factors play the dominant role in shaping history?**

Lesson Plans

For teaching strategies, see Lesson 22.3 located at the beginning of this chapter or on the One-Stop Planner Strategy 22.3.

Political Dictionary

To reinforce the section's vocabulary terms, refer students to the Electronic Glossary on the *Researcher CD-ROM.*

Section Assessment

To assess students' mastery of this section, have them complete Daily Quiz 22.3 in *Daily Quizzes with Answer Key.*

Caption Answer
economic factors

more influence than any government or other formal organizations in shaping policy, social standards, and values.

Marx believed that because capitalists own the means of production in modern, industrial society, they hold the power. Capitalists not only rule society economically, they also determine its political destiny. In addition, they dominate the law, education, the press, and artistic and literary expression in order to maintain their property ownership.

Concepts of Production Two other concepts are central to Marx's idea of social change. First, Marx described what he referred to as **forces of production**, the various elements that fuel an economy. The greatest forces of production today are probably technological and scientific knowledge. Marx also discussed the **relations of production**, economic relationships that are affected by social institutions—for example, relations between buyers and sellers.

Marx argued that in a free-market economy the growth of technology and the other forces of production is hampered by capitalism's flawed relations of production. Workers do not get paid enough, and they therefore cannot buy the products the economy is able to produce. Economic crisis is the result.

POLITICAL PROCESSES *This Russian propaganda poster depicts the class struggle. The banner on the left reads, "Long live workers' and peasants' Soviet power!" The caption below it reads, "Death to capitalism." The banner on the right reads, "All power to capitalists and death to workers and peasants!" The caption below it reads, "Death under the heel of capitalism."* **What were Marx's primary objections to capitalism?**

Revolution Marx's primary objections to capitalism were to what he saw as its injustices and inefficiencies. To overcome these problems, Marx argued, workers must stage a violent revolution. Unlike democratic socialists, who believe in peaceful change through elections and participatory democracy, Marxists spoke of a war between the classes. Workers would have to rise up and seize the means of production from the capitalist class. Marx assumed that, over time, people of the working class would develop a consciousness, or awareness, that the capitalists were oppressing and taking advantage of them. Working-class leaders would then emerge to head revolutionary movements. Marx believed that working-class movements would then develop around the world to defeat capitalism.

Marx assumed that a global communist society would emerge after the revolution. There would be no social or economic classes and no private property, and workers would own the means of production, including railways and factories. In addition, the government would no longer serve as an agent of class rule. In a classless society, government would eventually wither away.

Marx's insights into the importance of material conditions and economic systems have helped modern scholars understand social forces much more thoroughly. However, Marx's economic interpretations have proved too general and too simplistic. Even though economic factors are critical to people's interactions with one another, they are not the key factors in all situations. Factors such as ideology, religious beliefs, and nationalism have often played more important roles in social and international conflicts. In addition, Marx's economic predictions about the increasing misery of the working class and the inability of capitalism to accommodate technological progress have proved wildly inaccurate. Furthermore, the governments of the Marxist states that have been established did not wither away, but rather turned totalitarian.

Proletarian Dictatorship Once a revolution took place, Marx believed that a "dictatorship of the proletariat" would be necessary to make the transition from capitalism to communism. During this transition, Marx thought that the workers would need to use force, even terror, to succeed in their communist revolution and abolish both the

POLITICAL PROCESSES *This 1886 painting by Robert Koehler titled* The Strike *shows workers protesting harsh working conditions.* **How did Marx believe that communism would be established?**

ruling classes and private ownership. Even though Marx hoped for a society in which no class ruled over another, he supported the use of violence by the working class against the ruling class to achieve this goal.

For Marx, who argued that a classless society could only exist under communism where capitalists could no longer dominate workers, economic equality would be achieved by the elimination of class privileges. Marx further believed that in the highest stage of communism all people would reach a state of full equality.

The World's First Communist Nation

Despite Marx's focus on overthrowing modern capitalism, the first communist nation was not to be a highly developed, industrial society. Instead, the first successful communist uprising occurred in Russia, an economically underdeveloped country.

Vladimir Lenin Vladimir Lenin, a Russian intellectual and revolutionary, was the most influential communist leader of the early 1900s. Although Lenin considered himself a faithful follower of Marx, he emphasized politics over economics. As a result, he stressed that a **vanguard**—the people he hoped would lead a communist revolution in his country—should form a professionally organized political party. In

working toward this aim, Lenin spent 17 years in exile leading and helping develop the **Bolsheviks**, a communist party organization in Russia.

Unlike Marx, Lenin did not believe that a country had to become a fully industrial society before a revolution could occur. He thought it would be smarter to smash capitalism where it was politically and organizationally weakest—for example, in economically underdeveloped Russia, Asia, and Africa. Also, while Marx believed in a temporary dictatorship *of* the proletariat, Lenin and the Bolsheviks established a dictatorship *over* the proletariat.

Russian Revolution Led by Lenin, the Bolsheviks successfully overthrew the Russian government in a bloodless revolution in November 1917. The Bolsheviks—who became known as the Russian **Communist Party**—gained support in the early 1900s through their rigorous opposition both to Russia's harsh monarchical government and to the country's bloody involvement in World War I. Opposition to the revolution led to civil war, which lasted until 1920, when the Communists defeated their opponents.

The Communists imposed policies throughout Russia that radically transformed political, economic, and social life. They nationalized banks and businesses and confiscated land, distributing it to peasants in the countryside.

WORLD AFFAIRS *In the early 1900s the Bolsheviks gained the support of Russian citizens by actively spreading propaganda.* **What organization did Lenin and the Bolsheviks form?**

Stalin's forced collectivization of the Soviet Union's agricultural enterprises was met with fierce opposition from much of the peasantry. Many perceived the collectivization policy as a move that would negatively alter their way of life.

Some peasants responded to collectivization by destroying their tools and burning their crops. They also destroyed their livestock, rather than allow them to be taken by the state. In all an estimated 21 million horses, 33 million cows, and 16 million hogs were killed.

Stalin retaliated with brutal laws, including the death penalty for destroying property. He also instituted the seizure of crops, which resulted in widespread famine in many parts of the country. Millions of Russians lost their lives during the 1930s because of Stalin's policies. Instead of increasing, agricultural production actually dropped during the 1930s. ■

Caption Answer

He disliked Lenin's move toward free enterprise.

By 1921, however, Lenin recognized that the communist society he had aspired to had not been created—poverty was rampant, and peasant revolts threatened the stability of the nation. Lenin then established what he called the New Economic Policy. This policy was designed to revive the nation's economy by promoting agriculture and industry, and by allowing some private ownership of land and limited free trade.

Spreading Communism Lenin had a more aggressive plan for the spread of communism than Marx had envisioned. Marx believed that economic crises in individual countries would inspire independent communist revolutions that would defeat capitalism. Lenin, however, believed that Russia should be used as a base for supporting communist revolutions in other countries. After seizing power in Russia, Lenin began to organize centers of communist activity throughout the world.

Lenin's ideas about freedom followed from Marx's ideas, but he set them aside in part when he came to power. Lenin believed that the proletariat should have political freedom to organize revolutionary parties before the fall of capitalism. Once the Communist Party took power during the revolution, however, it would have to govern the state ruthlessly and with iron discipline. After the Russian Revolution was complete, Lenin in fact maintained the dictatorship of the Communist Party while concentrating on building a communist nation. Only when the development of communism was complete, declared Lenin, would everyone gain genuine political freedom from the limitations imposed by poverty and inequality. Lenin emphasized that a classless society, not individual freedom, was his highest priority.

Joseph Stalin Vladimir Lenin died in 1924, two years after Russia had joined with other territories to form a new communist nation—the Union of Soviet Socialist Republics, or Soviet

Union. The Communist Party established itself as the Soviet Union's only political organization and did not tolerate opposition. Lenin's successor, Joseph Stalin, took the country's dictatorial government to new extremes. He ruled the Soviet Union with an iron fist for almost 30 years.

Disliking Lenin's move toward free enterprise, Stalin instituted his own economic strategies, the Five-Year Plans. Stalin focused on developing heavy industry, the military, science, and technology in order to demonstrate to other countries the Soviets' superiority in these areas. He also hoped that these actions would establish the Communists as a stable and accepted force.

Part of Stalin's new policy involved the forced collectivization of agriculture—the combining of small farms into large, government-owned agricultural enterprises. This system was imposed despite widespread peasant opposition. More than 5 million peasant households were eliminated, their property was taken, and millions of peasants were starved to death, killed, or were sent to forced-labor camps. About 7 million people died from 1929 to 1933 as a result of collectivization and brutality in the labor camps.

WORLD AFFAIRS *This historical photo shows a Soviet farm where peasants have gathered to hear a speaker talk about the advantages of collective farming.* **Why did Stalin institute his own economic plans?**

Results of the Five-Year Plans Because the Soviet Union had vast natural resources, the Five-Year Plans succeeded in transforming the nation into a world leader in the production of steel, iron, coal, and oil. However, the quality of life for the Soviet people was dismal. The development of agriculture and of consumer-goods industries under communist rule was weak. The Soviet Union also had difficulty providing adequate government-owned housing for many of its citizens. In the later years of the Soviet Union, health care also declined. For example, the infant mortality rate increased in the 1970s and 1980s.

In the area of education, however, the Soviet leadership effectively transformed an ill-educated nation into one with almost 100 percent literacy. At first, only 4 years of education were guaranteed for children in rural areas, but eventually, most areas provided 10 years. Adult education programs were common, and by the late 1970s, more than 5 million Soviet citizens attended institutions of higher education each year.

WORLD AFFAIRS *The Soviet Union created a highly effective system of education.* **What effect did the Soviet education system have on the country's literacy rate?**

The Failure of Communist States

More than 70 years after the Bolshevik Revolution, Communist Party rule in the Soviet Union and in Eastern Europe disintegrated in the late 1980s. Not only had the Communist Party failed to achieve its theoretical goal of abolishing economic and social classes, but at least three new classes had risen after the Russian Revolution. In the Soviet Union, the dominant class, made up of only a few hundred thousand families, included government officials, party leaders, military officers, industrial executives, scientists, and some artists and writers. The

Comparing Governments

Fascism

In contrast to democracy, the central principle of totalitarianism is government's absolute dominance of society. Two types of totalitarian governments, fascism and communism, arose in Europe after World War I. Fascism gained support in the 1920s and 1930s, a period that had been thrown into chaos first by the great economic and social costs of the war and then by a worldwide economic depression. Many people believed that an extremely powerful government was needed to restore political and economic order.

In this atmosphere, three fascist leaders emerged in Europe: Benito Mussolini in Italy in 1922, Adolf Hitler in Germany in 1933, and Francisco Franco in Spain in 1939. All three dictators came to power by using some degree of violence.

Once in power, Mussolini, Hitler, and Franco banned all political parties but their own and suspended basic rights and freedoms. In short, the three ruled as absolute dictators, demanding unquestioning obedience from the people, the press, and religious, civic, and social organizations. Today, with fascism a thing of the past in these countries, their citizens enjoy freedom. Germany and Italy are democratic republics and Spain is a constitutional monarchy.

internet connect

TOPIC: From Communism to Capitalism
GO TO: go.hrw.com
KEYWORD: SV3 GV22

Have students access the Internet through the HRW Go site to find information on a country in transition from communism to capitalism, such as Poland, the Czech Republic, or Yugoslavia. Ask students to find information on how pricing, production, and ownership have changed, and how this has affected the government. Then have them write a report on the transition economy they have selected. Students should include graphs and a bibliography page with their report

Linking Government and Journalism

The Foreign-Policy Debate

National leaders consider information and opinion from a variety of sources when deciding U.S. policy toward foreign countries. Among the official sources are military leaders, information-gathering organizations such as the Central Intelligence Agency, and elected federal officials. An important but unofficial source of policy influence is the media.

Professional and scholarly journals are particularly influential. Political scientists and other observers analyze foreign-policy issues and suggest courses of action in journals such as *Foreign Affairs* and *Foreign Policy.* These and other, similar journals are highly regarded by many policy makers. Many of the authors of journal articles have had substantial experience in developing foreign policy. Others have an established record of study in the field.

Perhaps the most famous journal article to influence foreign policy was a July 1947 piece in *Foreign Affairs*. The anonymous author, who signed the article "X," was George F. Kennan. Kennan had been a U.S. diplomat and State Department adviser on the Soviet Union. His diplomatic experience—particularly in the Soviet Union—made Kennan a respected authority on the issue of U.S.-Soviet foreign policy.

At the end of World War II, U.S. officials debated how the United States and its allies should deal with the Soviet Union. Soviet leaders were expanding their influence and control throughout Eastern Europe and in other regions. In his *Foreign Affairs* article, Kennan argued that the Soviet Union would eventually collapse under the weight of its unworkable system of communism and cooperate with the United States.

In the meantime, Kennan said, the U.S. government should work—patiently but firmly and over the long term—to contain, or block, the expansion of Soviet control and influence. This idea, which was known as containment, dominated official U.S. foreign policy for decades.

In 1947 George F. Kennan wrote an article in which he argued that the Soviet Union would collapse and eventually cooperate with the United States.

Like Kennan, other former government officials often publish articles and appear on television and radio news programs to contribute to foreign-policy debates after leaving office. For example, James A. Baker III, U.S. secretary of state under President George Bush, wrote an article for the *New York Times* that stressed the importance of strong U.S. ties with the former Soviet republic of Georgia. Some well-known and widely read columnists and commentators, such as William Safire—a former speechwriter for President Richard Nixon—Anthony Lewis, and George Will, regularly write on policy issues.

The media, then, provides an important national forum for debate on policy issues. In some instances, as with Kennan's 1947 article, journalism proves that the power of the pen can be quite persuasive.

What Do You Think?

1. In what ways does journalism contribute to the making of foreign policy? Why are journals such as *Foreign Affairs* highly regarded by policy makers?
2. Many observers debate public policy and social issues in newspapers and on television. What do you think makes a commentator persuasive?

second class, which was made up of about 4 to 5 million families, included the intermediary ranks of civilian and military officials, collective farm managers, and some of the better-paid skilled workers and technicians in industry. The third class included the bulk of the population—the common workers and the peasants—and was made up of more than 50 million families.

The Communist Party ruled everyday life in an authoritarian manner, controlling the military, police, mass media, and government-run enterprises. People who disagreed with the Communist Party's policies were incarcerated and sometimes tortured. The party's decisions had crippled the economy, while the standard of living for most Soviet people rose far more slowly than in major free-market nations. By the end of the 1980s, some leaders and disillusioned citizens in both the Soviet Union and Eastern European nations were openly challenging the failing communist system.

Eastern Europe The authoritarian governments that the Soviet Union had set up in Eastern Europe after World War II fell apart during the late 1980s. As anticommunist resistance in these nations grew, the governments allowed some political reforms. However, these reforms did not stop the demands for change. Movements such as those led by the Solidarity union in Poland demanded multiparty elections and hastened the disintegration of the Communist Party first in Poland, and then in Hungary, Czechoslovakia, the German Democratic Republic (East Germany), Bulgaria, and Romania.

Mikhail Gorbachev As noted in Chapter 10, in 1987 the Soviet government under Mikhail Gorbachev tried to ease some of the unrest in the Soviet Union by implementing perestroika, or "restructuring," and glasnost, or "openness." Gorbachev's policies included greater civil liberties, access to information, and legal restraints on government power. Some economic reforms were made to allow the influence of global capitalist markets. However, these changes only gave the Soviet people a clearer view of what life might be like if communism were abandoned.

WORLD AFFAIRS *Lech Walesa, leader of the Polish Solidarity movement in the 1980s, led his country's fight for government reform.* **In what other former communist nations did citizens organize movements to demand political reform?**

Gorbachev, believing that his country needed massive change, determined in 1989 that the Soviet Union would not block the political movements occurring in Eastern Europe. As a result, all of the communist governments there collapsed within months. In 1991, after the overthrow of Gorbachev, the Soviet Union dissolved.

Former Communist Nations Today The transition from communism to democratic, capitalist societies in Eastern Europe and the former republics of the Soviet Union has been filled with many difficulties. Political parties have been fragmented and unstable, and ethnic-religious strife in countries such as the former Yugoslavia has been a recurring problem. In some areas, political disorder and crime have grown particularly severe. Many of the existing industries in these countries had been inefficient by world standards and have therefore collapsed when forced to compete in the global capitalist economy. The nations of the former Soviet Union and Eastern Europe continue to struggle in their efforts to rebuild their societies. A new competitive economy seems to be taking root in some places. Nevertheless, the stability of these nations remain uncertain.

CULTURAL PERSPECTIVES

Relations between the United States and the former Soviet Union have come a long way. Consider, for example, the space race. In October 1957 the Soviets launched *Sputnik,* the first artificial satellite to orbit Earth. This event soon propelled the United States into the space race with the Soviets. In order to increase students' knowledge of science and math, the United States began providing scholarships and additional classes for study in these areas.

Since the fall of the Soviet Union, however, the United States has completed missions in space in cooperation with Russia. In 1997 the United States even helped the Russians work on their *Mir* space station. The missions were costly and dangerous because of the problems encountered on the craft, but NASA officials continued to send U.S. astronauts to *Mir* because they believed that the missions' scientific and symbolic importance outweighed the risks and expense. ∎

CASE STUDY

China: A Country with Two Economic Systems

WORLD AFFAIRS Like the nations of Eastern Europe and the former Soviet republics, China has experienced significant changes to its economic system in recent years. Great Britain's handing over of capitalist Hong Kong to communist China in 1997 marked the joining of two different economic systems. Some people believe that this transfer may have been the most dramatic moment in China's shift away from a communist economy that began in the 1970s.

For nearly 100 years, Hong Kong had been a British colony and had operated under a free-market system that enabled it to become an economic powerhouse. Before Britain gave up control of Hong Kong, China agreed to let this system remain in place.

China itself had already begun moving away from a communist command economy. China's leaders in 1978 introduced reforms that allowed private investment and trade. As a result, China's economy grew rapidly in the 1980s and 1990s.

This rapid economic growth created problems, however. For example, urban crowding increased as people moved from poor rural areas to search for economic opportunities in the cities. The benefits of growth were unevenly distributed, and prices skyrocketed.

China's leaders have continued to insist that a strong communist government is needed to keep the country stable during this period of change. Chinese citizens, on the other hand, have increasingly called for political reforms such as democratization and an end to political corruption. On one occasion in 1989, government leaders ordered soldiers to forcibly remove prodemocracy demonstrators from Tiananmen Square in China's capital city, Beijing. Hundreds were killed, and hundreds more were arrested.

In contrast, the Chinese government has remained uninvolved in the affairs of Hong Kong, now known as the Hong Kong Special Administrative Region (SAR) of China. At the same time, the SAR has been hesitant to integrate itself into the greater economy and culture of mainland China. Officials on both sides feel that the "one country, two systems" method of governing greatly benefits both the SAR and the rest of China.

SECTION 3 REVIEW

1. Identify and Explain:
- class struggle
- *Communist Manifesto*
- forces of production
- relations of production
- vanguard
- Bolsheviks
- Communist Party

2. Identifying Concepts: Copy the graphic organizer below. Use it to list the causes of the collapse of the Soviet Union.

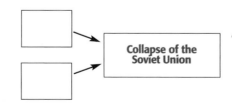

Collapse of the Soviet Union

3. Finding the Main Idea

a. In what ways did Marx think that communism would offer greater freedom and equality than capitalism?

b. How did Lenin go about putting communism into practice in Russia? What changes did Stalin bring to the Soviet Union?

4. Writing and Critical Thinking

Making Generalizations: Identify several communist countries, past and present. Do you think these examples show communism to be an effective political and economic system?
Consider the following:
- why people were attracted to communism
- why communist governments collapsed in many countries

Homework Practice Online
keyword: SV3 HP22

IN THE NEWS

A New Currency for Europe

On January 1, 2002, the European Union (EU) began the most complex economic transition in history by releasing its new currency, the euro, into full circulation. Of the 15 member countries of the EU, 12—Austria, Belgium, Finland, France, Germany, Greece, Ireland, Italy, Luxembourg, Netherlands, Portugal, and Spain—adopted the euro as their common currency. The design of euro coins and bills features bridges and windows on one side, symbolizing the new connections and openness between European countries. On the other side, each euro features one of several designs that are unique to each member country.

The transition to the euro involved a massive effort of coordination by the people and institutions in each participating country. Military troops transported the new bills and coins, businesses updated everything from computers to phone booths, and citizens exchanged their old currency for the new euro. Exchanging at a rate of 88 cents per dollar as of January 2002, the euro signified a new economic era in Europe.

The euro is just one aspect of the European Union, the alliance aimed at transforming Europe into an economic and political power on a level with the United States. To accomplish this, mechanisms of a free-market economy were integrated into the EU. The EU removed restrictions on trade and the movement of tourists, goods and services, workers, and capital between member countries.

The European Union also created a new political structure. The main decision-making and legislative body is called the Council of the European Union. The executive branch, called the European Commission; the judicial branch, called the European Court of Justice; and the European Parliament complete the EU government. The EU has plans to expand to 27 countries in the near future.

In Paris, a worker displays an oversized 10 euro cent coin. The symbol for the euro can be seen on the back of the worker's jacket. The design is based on the Greek letter epsilon, and the parallel lines symbolize stability.

Even as the EU brings most of Europe closer to a free-market economy like that of the United States, it is unlikely that member countries will give up the cherished tradition of the welfare state. One responsibility of the EU, in fact, is to aid its poorer members. Some Europeans regret that the transition to the euro has removed one of the physical manifestations of a country's identity: its currency. These critics also feel that the EU will erase many local identities. Some observers note, however, that Europeans already share many aspects of culture, including food and sport, and that the EU will only enhance this diversity.

What Do You Think?

1. If you were a citizen of a European country, would you support or oppose the European Union? Why?

2. How do the euro and the European Union enable Europe to compete economically with the United States?

> **WHY IT MATTERS TODAY**
>
> The euro has the potential to turn Europe into an economic superpower. Use CNNfyi.com or other **current events** sources to find out how the euro currently compares to the U.S. dollar.
>
>

CHAPTER 22

Review Answers

Writing a Summary

Summaries should focus on the main points of each section. These may be found in the Read to Discover questions at the start of each section. Summaries should also use standard grammar, spelling, sentence structure, and punctuation.

Identifying Ideas

Refer to the following pages: capitalist (507), competition (508), self-interest (509), mixed economy (509), democratic socialism (511), proletariat (511), nationalization (512), command economy (514), class struggle (515), *Communist Manifesto* (515)

Understanding Main Ideas

1. private ownership, a market economy, competition, profit

2. to act as a referee by regulating interactions among businesses but not (Continued on page 524)

Review

(Continued from page 523)
to interrupt operations of businesses or the market economy

3. widespread social services, nationalization of major industries, high taxes

4. Socialism is based on the notion that the greater good is more important than the individual good, and thus limits private ownership of the means of production. Socialism aims to limit individuals' economic freedom to increase social equality.

5. forces of production, relations of production

6. Lenin found it essential that the development of communism be complete before political freedom could be granted.

Reviewing Themes
1. democratic socialist—government controls only basic services; communist—government controls all forces of production.
2. Marx believed that a violent revolution by the workers was needed to seize the means of production from the capitalists.
3. Capitalists believe that in a market economy, competition ensures that producers will produce improved products in order to attract consumers.

Thinking Critically
1. Answers will vary, but students should state and explain their opinions about freedom of choice. Students might mention that in socialist economies, freedom of choice is limited by the nationalization of major industries.

2. Capitalist societies focus more on individual rights than
(Continued on page 525)

Writing a Summary

Using standard grammar, spelling, sentence structure, and punctuation, write a summary of the information in this chapter.

Identifying Ideas

Identify the following terms and explain their significance.

1. capitalist

2. competition

3. self-interest

4. mixed economy

5. democratic socialism

6. proletariat

7. nationalization

8. command economy

9. class struggle

10. *Communist Manifesto*

Understanding Main Ideas

SECTION 1 *(pp. 507–510)*

1. What are the four principles on which capitalist economies are based?

2. What is the government's role in a capitalist economy?

SECTION 2 *(pp. 511–514)*

3. Name three characteristics of a socialist economy.

4. On what principles is socialism based?

SECTION 3 *(pp. 515–522)*

5. What two concepts are central to Marx's theory of social change?

6. Why did Lenin establish a communist dictatorship after the Russian Revolution?

Reviewing Themes

1. **Political Processes** How does the operation of a command economy in a democratic socialist country differ from that of a communist country?

2. **Political Foundations** According to Karl Marx, how would revolution pave the way for a country to make the transition from a capitalist system to a communist system?

3. **Public Good** How is competition beneficial to the development of market economies?

Thinking Critically

1. **Drawing Inferences** Do you think that freedom of choice is important to a capitalist economy? How has freedom of choice been limited in some socialist economies?

2. **Drawing Conclusions** Are individual rights more of a focus in capitalist societies or socialist societies? What are some consequences of the focus of each system?

3. **Comparing and Contrasting** How do the basic principles of socialism and capitalism differ? What are some of the advantages and disadvantages of each system?

Writing about Government

Review what you wrote in your Government Notebook at the beginning of this chapter about the development of new political and economic systems. Now that you have studied this chapter, how would you revise your response? Explain your answer in your notebook.

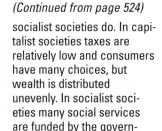
Interpreting the Visual Record

The Consumer Price Index, or cost-of-living index, measures the average change in prices of goods and services over time. Study the chart below and use it to help you answer the questions that follow.

Consumer Price Indexes, 1990–2000

Percent of Change (y-axis: 0–6)

Year (x-axis): 1990 1991 1992 1993 1994 1995 1996 1997 1998 1999 2000

Source: Bureau of Labor Statistics, U.S. Department of Labor

1. Which year had the lowest rate of increase?
- **a.** 1994
- **b.** 1995
- **c.** 1998
- **d.** 1992

2. Why might the Consumer Price Index be important in a capitalist economy?

Analyzing Primary Sources

Karl Marx and Frederich Engels published the *Communist Manifesto* in 1848 as a call for revolution. Read the excerpt and answer the questions that follow.

"The distinguishing feature of Communism is not the abolition of property generally, but the abolition of bourgeois property. Modern bourgeois private property is the final and most complete expression of the system of producing and appropriating products that is based on class antagonisms, on the exploitation [unfair use] of the many by the few.

In this sense, the theory of the Communists may be summed up in the single phrase: abolition of private property. . . .

Communists . . . openly declare that their ends can be attained only by the forcible overthrow of all existing social conditions."

3. Which of the following statements best reflects the point of view of Marx and Engels?
- **a.** Private property is an expression of class antagonism and the exploitation of the many by the few.
- **b.** Communists wish to abolish all property.
- **c.** Communists hope to maintain the current social and economic relations.
- **d.** Property is unimportant in society.

4. Why do you think the Communist Party never became a political force in the United States?

Building Your Portfolio

With a group, interview an owner of a small business in your community to find out about setting up a private business. What role do competition and supply and demand play in the operation of the business? What role does the government play? Do the local or state governments play a role? Prepare a presentation for your class. Include visual images such as charts, graphs, and photographs in your presentation.

☑ **internet** connect

Internet Activity: go.hrw.com
KEYWORD: SV3 GV22

Access the Internet through the HRW Go site to conduct research on the causes and effects of the decline of communism around the world. Then create a pamphlet that explains the reasons for the decline, the effect on world politics, and the struggle of former communist countries to rebuild their societies.

(Continued from page 524)

socialist societies do. In capitalist societies taxes are relatively low and consumers have many choices, but wealth is distributed unevenly. In socialist societies many social services are funded by the government and taxes are high, though wealth is distributed more evenly.

3. Socialism aims to increase equality, while capitalism aims to increase wealth and preserve freedom. Socialism features a planned economy with considerable government involvement; capitalism promotes private enterprise with minimal government interference. Answers will vary, but students should explain the advantages and disadvantages of each system.

Writing About Government

The Government Notebook is a follow-up activity to the notebook activity that appears on page 506.

Building Social Studies Skills

1. c
2. Answers will vary, but students might suggest that prices affect the purchasing power of consumers, whose choices are critical to free-market economies.
3. a
4. Answers will vary, but students might suggest that the United States has valued the principles of economic freedom.

Alternative Assessment

To assess this activity see Acquiring Information and Posters in *Alternative Assessment Handbook*.

CHAPTER 23 INTERNATIONAL RELATIONS

	OBJECTIVES	PACING GUIDE	REPRODUCIBLE RESOURCES
SECTION 1 **COLLECTIVE SECURITY** (pp. 527–532)	▸ Why is international collective security important? ▸ What causes conflicts that challenge collective security? ▸ How does growth in the production of weapons challenge collective security? ▸ In what ways does the United Nations help achieve collective security?	**Regular** 1.5 days **Block Scheduling** .75 day	**ELL** Spanish Study Guide 23.1 **ELL** English Study Guide 23.1
SECTION 2 **ECONOMIC INTERDEPENDENCE** (pp. 533–537)	▸ What is the difference between developing nations and developed nations? ▸ In what ways have nations worked to promote international trade? ▸ Why are U.S. trade deficits a problem?	**Regular** 1 day **Block Scheduling** .5 day	**ELL** Spanish Study Guide 23.2 **ELL** English Study Guide 23.2
SECTION 3 **ENVIRONMENTAL INTERDEPENDENCE** (pp. 538–542)	▸ How do air and water pollution challenge the international community? ▸ How can population growth and economic development strain the world's resources?	**Regular** 1.5 days **Block Scheduling** .5 day	**ELL** Spanish Study Guide 23.3 **ELL** English Study Guide 23.3 **PS** Reading 35: "Global Environmental Crisis" **PS** Reading 68: *Silent Spring*
SECTION 4 **U.S. RELATIONS WITH OTHER COUNTRIES** (pp. 543–548)	▸ How has the end of the Cold War affected the debate over U.S.-Japanese relations? ▸ What issues have dominated U.S.-European relations since the end of the Cold War? ▸ How have U.S. leaders addressed trade and human rights issues in relations with China? ▸ How have intervention and efforts to expand trade marked U.S. relations with Latin America? ▸ What has been U.S. policy toward Africa?	**Regular** 2 days **Block Scheduling** .75 day	**ELL** Spanish Study Guide 23.4 **ELL** English Study Guide 23.4

Chapter Resource Key

PS	Primary Sources	**A**	Assessment		Video
RS	Reading Support	**REV**	Review		Videodisc
E	Enrichment	**ELL**	Reinforcement and English Language Learners		Internet
S	Simulations		Transparencies		Holt Presentation Maker Using
SM	Skills Mastery		CD-ROM		Microsoft ® PowerPoint ®

TECHNOLOGY RESOURCES	REINFORCEMENT, REVIEW, AND ASSESSMENT
One-Stop Planner: Lesson 23.1 Holt Researcher Online Homework Practice Online Transparency 49 Global Skill Builder CD-ROM	**REV** Section 1 Review p. 532 **A** Daily Quiz 23.1
One-Stop Planner: Lesson 23.2 Holt Researcher Online Homework Practice Online Cartoon Transparency 25 Global Skill Builder CD-ROM	**REV** Section 2 Review p. 537 **A** Daily Quiz 23.2
One-Stop Planner: Lesson 23.3 Holt Researcher Online Homework Practice Online Transparency 50 Global Skill Builder CD-ROM	**REV** Section 3 Review p. 542 **A** Daily Quiz 23.3
One-Stop Planner: Lesson 23.4 Holt Researcher Online Homework Practice Online Holt American Government Videodisc: Trade Relations: Lifting the Embargo Global Skill Builder CD-ROM E Challenge and Enrichment: Activity 23 E Simulations and Strategies for Teaching American Government: Activity 23 CNN Presents American Government	**REV** Section 4 Review p. 548 **A** Daily Quiz 23.4

Chapter Review and Assessment

SM Global Skill Builder CD-ROM
HRW Go site
REV Chapter 23 Tutorial for Students, Parents, and Peers
REV Chapter 23 Review, pp. 550–551
Chapter 23 Test Generator (on the One-Stop Planner)
A Chapter 23 Test
A Chapter 23 Test Alternative Assessment Handbook

One-Stop Planner CD-ROM

It's easy to plan lessons, select resources, and print out materials for your students when you use the *One-Stop Planner CD-ROM with Test Generator.*

internet connect

HRW ONLINE RESOURCES
Go To: go.hrw.com
Then type in a keyword.

TEACHER HOME PAGE
KEYWORD: SV3 Teacher

CHAPTER INTERNET ACTIVITIES
KEYWORD: SV3 GV23
Choose an activity on international relations to:
▸ create a brochure on the impact of NAFTA.
▸ understand the relationship of world trade to developing countries.
▸ research environmentalism.

CHAPTER ENRICHMENT LINKS
KEYWORD: SV3 CH23

HOLT RESEARCHER ONLINE
KEYWORD: Holt Researcher

ONLINE ASSESSMENT
Homework Practice
KEYWORD: SV3 HP23
Standardized Test Prep
KEYWORD: SV3 STP23
Rubrics
KEYWORD: SS Rubrics

ONLINE MAPS, CHARTS, AND GRAPHS
KEYWORD: SV3 MCG
▸ Top 10 Countries in Military Spending
▸ World's Most Populous Urban Areas

CONTENT UPDATES
KEYWORD: SS Content Updates

HOLT PRESENTATION MAKER
KEYWORD: SV3 PPT23

ONLINE READING SUPPORT
KEYWORD: SS Strategies

CURRENT EVENTS
KEYWORD: S3 Current Events

OBJECTIVES

▶ Identify the reasons why worldwide collective security is so important.
▶ List and describe the causes of the conflicts that challenge the collective security of the world's nations.
▶ Explain how the growth in the production and ownership of weapons challenges collective security.
▶ Discuss the ways in which the United Nations contributes to worldwide collective security.

MOTIVATE

List the following scenarios on the board: 1) you had a fight with another student, 2) you lost something valuable, 3) you were hungry and had no money to buy something to eat, and 4) a group of students at school continued to harass you. Ask students to express how they think they would feel if they were faced with each situation. Have them state how they think they would initially respond in each case. Ask students whose help they would seek if they found themselves in one of the scenarios. Remind students that these types of situations exist in the world today. There are a number of countries that have great difficulty securing their borders, protecting themselves against other nations, and feeding their people. These developing countries, often look to the United States and other developed nations to provide the help they need. Explain to students why the collective security of all nations in the world is important. Tell students that in this section they will learn about some of the events taking place that challenge collective security and ways the UN contributes to the collective security of the world's countries.

TEACH

Building a Vocabulary

In spiral notebooks, have students create a Political Dictionary to be used throughout the course. The dictionary may be used as an activity at the start of each new section; it may also be used as a modification device for students having difficulty or sheltered English students during tests and homework assignments. List words the students will be expected to know for this section on the chalkboard. Have students list, define, and give an example of each of the terms, using information provided in the chapter or on the *Researcher CD-ROM*.

Acquiring Information/Navigating the Internet

Discuss with students the threats posed by nuclear weapons, chemical or biological weapons, and conventional arms. Have students use the Internet and other resources to find current articles dealing with either the use of or attempts at stopping the use of any of these weapons. Students should also research the effect that the use of these weapons has had on the people living in the areas where these weapons were used. Students should write a short paper that discusses the threat to world security that is posed by these weapons. Tell students that in the next activity they will be debating about the use of force to secure peace.

Debating Ideas/Writing About Government

Lead a discussion about the different ways in which peace is kept across the world. Have students cite examples of the various peacekeeping missions that are in progress and discuss their significance with the class. Explain that the UN serves as a forum for settling disputes, protecting human rights, and maintaining world peace. However, when the organization has been unsuccessful in preventing or stopping conflicts, it has occasionally authorized the use of force to stop the aggressive acts of a country. Allow 10 to 15 minutes for students to debate the issue of whether it is acceptable to use force in order to stop aggression and keep peace. After different student viewpoints have been discussed, ask each student to write a paper defending their position on this issue. Have students support their position by providing examples of situations in real life that illustrate their point of view. Ask for volunteers to share their papers with the rest of the class. As a lead-in to the next activity, tell students that they will be learning about how the UN contributes to the world's collective security.

Classifying Information

On a large piece of paper, write *The United Nations.* Divide the paper into seven columns. Write the heading for the first column *Descriptive Characteristics.* Each of the headings for the other six columns should be one of the sections of the UN: *The General Assembly, The Security Council, The Secretariat, The International Court of Justice, The Economic and Social Council,* and the *Trusteeship Council.* Review with students the role of the UN and some of the important work it has accomplished in the past 50 years. Explain that the task of this assignment is to describe, in as much detail as possible, each of the six sections that make up the UN as a whole and how each contributes to collective security. Students may use their textbooks and any other resources to answer questions such as: How many members are in each section? What (if any) are the length of terms served by each member? What types of problems does each section handle? Each question should be written in the first column under descriptive characteristics. Use student answers to complete the chart with the correct information under each of the other columns.

CLOSE

Remind students of the different scenarios they were faced with in the Motivate activity. Instead of placing themselves in each situation, ask students to give examples of countries that have found themselves in these situations. Lead a discussion about how these countries handled these difficulties, whom they sought out for help, and what kind of help they received.

OPTIONS

Students Having Difficulty/ Sheltered English Students

  Provide students with poster board and art supplies. Have students work together to create a political cartoon that illustrates the role of the United States in UN peacekeeping missions around the world. If necessary, assign group members to specific tasks, e.g., caption writer or illustrator. Remind them that many critics believe that the United States plays too large a part in UN missions in foreign countries. Have students share their cartoons with the other students and have students explain the significance of their drawing. Find a place in the classroom to display the cartoons.

Gifted Learners

 Have students pretend that they are the president of the United States running for re-election. Have them write a speech to be delivered to the UN and various heads of state in which they explain their view of U.S. foreign policy. Students may wish to prepare for the speech by researching and reviewing the foreign policy history of the United States, including its involvement in UN peacekeeping missions. Students should select the policies and principles that they feel will best serve the interests of the country and its allies. Have students explain why they feel it is so important for the country to have a clearly defined foreign policy. Ask volunteers to deliver their speeches to the class.

REVIEW

Have students complete the Section 1 Review on page 532. Use the answers in the Annotated Teacher's Edition to assess student mastery of this section.

ASSESS

To assess student mastery of this section, have students complete Daily Quiz 23.1 in *Daily Quizzes with Answer Key.* For additional assessment options, see *Alternative Assessment Handbook* on the *One-Stop Planner CD-ROM.*

ADDITIONAL RESOURCES

Cranna, Michael, ed. *The True Cost of Conflict.* 1995. New Press.
Enforcing Restraint: *Collective Intervention in Internal Conflicts.* 1993. Council on Foreign Relations Press.

OBJECTIVES

▶ Identify and discuss how some developing countries are closing the economic gap.

▶ List and describe the ways in which countries around the world have worked to promote international trade.

▶ Explain why trade deficits continue to be a problem for the U.S. economy.

MOTIVATE

Tell students that before they begin studying this section they need to create several world maps that the class will use as references throughout the chapter. Organize the class into small groups (two or three students in each). Provide two of the groups with poster board, colored pencils, and markers. Give another group poster board that already has the countries of the world outlined. Provide the remainder of the groups with a few blank pieces of paper and a couple of pencils. Apologize for the limited supplies, asking students to do the best they can with the resources they have. Allow 10 to 15 minutes at the end of class for students to give feedback on the activity. Ask those students who had limited art supplies how they felt about their ability to produce work that could compare to the other groups. Relate the activity to the economic climate of the world today in which poor, overpopulated countries struggle to compete with wealthy, industrialized nations. Tell students that in this section they will learn about attempts to promote trade and economic development and why trade deficits hurt the U.S. economy.

TEACH

Building a Vocabulary

In their spiral notebooks, have students continue working on their Political Dictionary. List words the students will be expected to know for this section on the chalkboard. Have students list, define, and give an example of each of the terms, using information provided in the chapter or on the *Researcher CD-ROM.*

Classifying Information/Using Charts

On the chalkboard, make two separate columns with the headings *Developed Countries* and *Developing Countries.* Have students create a list of categories that will best describe the two types of countries and highlight the differences between them. As students come up with categories, list them on the board in the left-hand margin. Some possible categories may include: examples of countries in each column, population growth rates, percentage of world population, and per capita GDP. After students have successfully completed the table, lead a discussion about the ways developing countries are closing the economic gap with wealthy nations and the roles that both developing countries and developed countries must play in order for this to happen. As a lead-in to the next activity, tell students that they will learn about how cooperative efforts have promoted international trade.

Demonstration

Tie a few pieces of rope or string from one side of the classroom to the other. (Be sure to move all chairs and desks out of the way or, if possible, do this activity outside where you can tie the ropes between two trees and have more space available.) Tie the ropes so that they are approximately two, three, and four feet above the ground. Explain to students that the goal is for all students to get from one side of the ropes to the other on their own without touching any of the ropes. Students must pass over or between the ropes, not go under or around. Allow some time for students to make individual attempts. After 10 minutes or so (or as soon as students start becoming frustrated) change the activity so that students are allowed to work together and help each other. After 10 to 15 minutes, lead a discussion about the importance of working together and helping one another accomplish a goal. Have students compare the group efforts with the difficulties they encountered while working on their own. Relate this activity to the many alliances and trading blocs that have been formed across the world and that are successfully improving the economies of several developing countries. Emphasize that this success is due largely to the cooperative efforts of nations working together as a team. Tell students that in the next activity they will learn about trade deficits.

Practicing Skill: Trade and Negotiations

Make up a list of as many goods or products that countries need in order to meet the wants and needs of their people. (The list may include items such as oil, coal, iron, wood, steel, electronics, fruit, vegetables, tobacco, coffee beans, and any other items of significance.) Write the name of each good on a small piece of paper or note card. For some items, make an excessive number of cards compared to the number of students in the class. For others, make too few cards for the number of students. Mix up the cards and randomly distribute them to each student, with each student receiving the same number of cards. Explain to students that the task is for each of them, through the process of trading with one another, to acquire one note card for each of the goods on the original list. Allow students approximately 10 to 15 minutes to conduct their trades. After they have completed their trading, see how many students were able to acquire a card for each of the products. Ask for student feedback on the difficult aspects of the activity. Relate the activity to the concept of comparative advantage discussed in the textbook. Lead a discussion about the importance of countries balancing the trade of their imports and exports and how a trade deficit can influence the economic well-being of the nation.

CLOSE

Ask students to recall the last time they gave something of theirs to someone else, or the last time they helped someone in need. Ask whether it is fair to then expect something in return. Have students describe situations in which they gave without expecting anything in return. Remind students that the United States must constantly extend a helping hand with the risk of receiving nothing in immediate return. Explain that the United States takes risks when providing aid to foreign countries, but the risks often foster the kind of interdependence and cooperation that must exist in the world today.

OPTIONS

Students Having Difficulty/ Sheltered English Students

  Have students make a list of as many countries as they can think of. Provide students with note cards and ask them to write the name of each country from their list on one side of a card. After they have listed the name of each country, have them write *developed* or *developing* on the back side of each card depending on the country's classification. Students may wish to use the Country Profiles section on the *Holt Researcher Online* to help them decide each countries status. Assign students to pair up and quiz each other on the different developed and developing countries, using the note cards as flash cards. Encourage students to review information on the countries they incorrectly identified.

Gifted Learners/Linguistic Learners

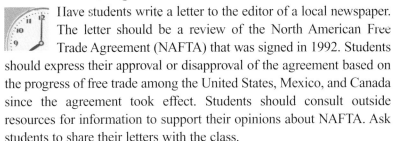 Have students write a letter to the editor of a local newspaper. The letter should be a review of the North American Free Trade Agreement (NAFTA) that was signed in 1992. Students should express their approval or disapproval of the agreement based on the progress of free trade among the United States, Mexico, and Canada since the agreement took effect. Students should consult outside resources for information to support their opinions about NAFTA. Ask students to share their letters with the class.

REVIEW

Have students complete the Section 2 Review on page 537. Use the answers in the Annotated Teacher's Edition to assess student mastery of this section.

ASSESS

To assess student mastery of this section, have students complete Daily Quiz 23.2 in *Daily Quizzes with Answer Key*. For additional assessment options, see *Alternative Assessment Handbook* on the *One-Stop Planner CD-ROM*.

ADDITIONAL RESOURCES

Creton, Marvin. *Crystal Glove: The Haves and Have-nots of the New World Order*. 1991. St. Martin's.

Naisbitt, John. *Global Paradox: The Bigger the World Economy, the More Powerful Its Smallest Players*. 1994. William Morrow.

LESSON 23.3 ENVIRONMENTAL INTERDEPENDENCE

TEXTBOOK PAGES 538–542

OBJECTIVES

▶ List and describe the ways in which air and water pollution challenge the world's countries.

▶ Identify how population growth and economic development can strain the world's resources.

MOTIVATE

Make a chart on the chalkboard. The horizontal axis should include a list of the 10 things that students feel pose the most serious threat to the health and safety of people in the world. After students have created their list, write the following headings on the vertical axis: *air pollution, water pollution, population growth,* and *deforestation.* Put a check in the square if terms from the horizontal axis also applied to the terms in vertical axis. If none of the terms from the vertical axis were also in the first column, ask students why they chose to leave these environmental concerns off the list. Ask students whether they consider these issues as serious problems on the world scene. Inform them that these environmental concerns are good examples of the need for cooperation among the world's countries because pollution in one country can affect another country's environment. Explain that in this activity students will learn about air and water pollution, population growth, and the depletion of natural resources and how these factors continue to threaten the environmental and economic security of countries all over the world.

TEACH

Building a Vocabulary

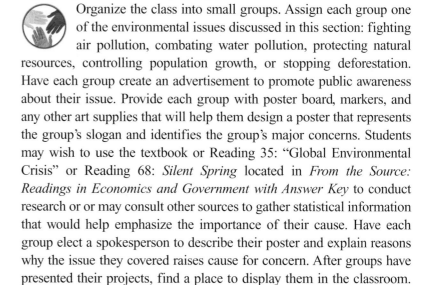

In their spiral notebooks, have students continue working on their Political Dictionary. List words the students will be expected to know for this section on the chalkboard. Have students list, define, and give an example of each of the terms, using information provided in the chapter or on the *Researcher CD-ROM.*

Applying a Model/Recognizing Point of View

Organize the class into small groups. Assign each group one of the environmental issues discussed in this section: fighting air pollution, combating water pollution, protecting natural resources, controlling population growth, or stopping deforestation. Have each group create an advertisement to promote public awareness about their issue. Provide each group with poster board, markers, and any other art supplies that will help them design a poster that represents the group's slogan and identifies the group's major concerns. Students may wish to use the textbook or Reading 35: "Global Environmental Crisis" or Reading 68: *Silent Spring* located in *From the Source: Readings in Economics and Government with Answer Key* to conduct research or or may consult other sources to gather statistical information that would help emphasize the importance of their cause. Have each group elect a spokesperson to describe their poster and explain reasons why the issue they covered raises cause for concern. After groups have presented their projects, find a place to display them in the classroom. Tell students that they will be studying population growth in the next activity.

Creating Graphs

Organize the class into several small groups. As a class, come up with a list of countries in which half are developed countries and the other half are developing countries. Provide each group with poster board or butcher paper and some art supplies. Assign each group one of the countries from the list and the task of creating a graph that illustrates that country's population growth over the last half of the twentieth century. Refer students to textbooks, almanacs, or the Internet in order to gather the information they need. Have groups compare their graphs. Ask students to identify which countries appear to have the most serious population growth problem. Lead a discussion about the adverse effect a rapidly growing world population can have on a country's resources. Display the graphs in the classroom as students continue to study this chapter. Tell students that in the next activity they will be mapping out environmental concerns in different areas of the world.

Creating Maps

Have students identify the major environmental concerns presented in this section. Write them on the chalkboard as they are given. Next to each term on the chalkboard, write a color. For example, *air pollution—yellow* or *population growth—red.* Assign each term a different color. Distribute markers and a black and white outline map of the world to students. Using their textbooks and additional resources, have students color code the various countries according to which environmental issues continue to pose the most serious threat to each nation's livelihood. After the maps have been colored, have the class discuss their observations. Ask them which regions of the world seem to be the most susceptible to various environmental hazards. Encourage students to provide suggestions to help relieve environmental problems in these countries.

CLOSE

Refer students to the list they created during the Motivate activity. Ask each student to develop a new list of the 10 things he or she feels pose the most serious threat to the health and safety of people in the world. Have students discuss whether their list changed at all from the Motivate activity until now. If so, ask students to explain why they changed their mind. Lead students in a discussion about the importance to human health of keeping the air we breathe and the water we drink clean.

OPTIONS

Gifted Learners

  Have students choose one of the environmental issues discussed in this section and find out more about what is being done to prevent further problems. Using the Internet or the National Organizations section on the *Holt Researcher Online* as resources, encourage students to gather a list of organizations that have been formed in order to create public awareness and raise money for research on each issue. After students have a list of organizations, have them draft a letter to one of those groups to gather more information about the issue they have chosen. Students may choose to put any pamphlets or brochures they may receive on a poster board. Each student can then share the information they have on their poster boards with the rest of the class.

Linguistic Learners

 Have students write a poem or song that discusses one or more of the world's environmental problems. Encourage students to focus on how these problems are affecting the world and what is being done to correct them. Have students share their poem or song with the rest of the class. Consider videotaping their performances as examples to show future classes and to track any changes over time in the nature of problems.

REVIEW

Have students complete the Section 3 Review on page 542. Use the answers in the Annotated Teacher's Edition to assess student mastery of this section.

ASSESS

To assess student mastery of this section, have students complete Daily Quiz 23.3 in *Daily Quizzes with Answer Key.* For additional assessment options, see *Alternative Assessment Handbook* on the *One-Stop Planner CD-ROM.*

ADDITIONAL RESOURCES

MacNeill, Jim. *Beyond Interdependence: The Meshing of the World's Economy and the Earth's Ecology.* 1991. Oxford University Press.

Kinlaw, Dennis. *Competitive and Green: Sustainable Performance in the Environmental Age.* 1993. Pfeiffer.

HOLT PRESENTATION MAKER
Access Illustrated LECTURE NOTES using Microsoft® PowerPoint® on the One-Stop Planner CD-ROM

OBJECTIVES

- Explain how the end of the Cold War has changed the debate over U.S.–Japanese relations.
- List and describe the issues that have dominated U.S.–European relations since the end of the Cold War.
- Discuss how U.S. leaders have addressed the issues of trade and human rights in relations with China.
- Describe how a history of intervention and efforts to expand have marked U.S. relations with Latin American countries.
- Identify the issues U.S. policy with Africa has focused on since the early 1990s.

MOTIVATE

Ask students to conduct an investigation of things in the classroom to find out where they were made. Have students inspect their shirt, shoes, watch, and anything else around them that can be identified as being made in the United States or another country. Generate a list to see how many products originated from this country and how many were imported from foreign nations. Have students speculate as to the percentage of products in the U.S. market that are made in the United States. Point out the importance of trade and how it links the United States with many countries. Explain that in this activity students will learn about the relationships the United States has formed with other countries, including Japan, China, and various European and Latin American countries.

TEACH

Building a Vocabulary

In their spiral notebooks, have students continue working on their Political Dictionary. List words the students will be expected to know for this section on the chalkboard. Have students list, define, and give an example of each of the terms, using information provided in the chapter or on the *Researcher CD-ROM.*

Practicing the Skill: Drafting a Proposal

Remind students that since the end of the Cold War, many people have expressed concerns over the current relationships the United States maintains with Japan and Eastern Europe. Organize the class into two groups (one will focus on Japan and the other on Eastern Europe) and explain that their task is to draft a proposal for a new policy outlining relations between the United States and their assigned country or region. Have students identify key issues influencing U.S. policy in each area. Then have them create their proposal paying close attention to the concerns that have been expressed by supporters and opponents of the current relationship. Have each group share their outlined proposal with the rest of the class. Lead a discussion about the importance of maintaining good relations with Japan and the countries of Eastern Europe and the changes in these relationships that have come about as a result of the end of the Cold War. Tell students that in the next activity they will learn about concerns surrounding trade with China.

Debating Ideas/Taking a Stand

Tell students that in 2000, the United States normalized trade relatons with China. Lead a discussion about the ongoing debate on whether the United States should continue trading with China. Explain that advocates of trade with China cite the large revenues and employment opportunities trade brings in, as well as economic reforms that China has recently instituted. On the other hand, opponents of the trade with China point to an authoritarian government that has at times been guilty of human rights violations. Have students write a position paper about their stance on this issue. Ask students to give their opinions on whether the relationship between the two countries should be predicated more on economics or politics, or a combination of both. The paper should attempt to settle the controversy of whether the economic benefits the United States gains from increasing exports to China outweigh concerns about the Chinese government's continued human rights violations against its citizens. Encourage students to share their ideas with the class. Tell students that in the next activity they will learn about U.S. relations with African and Latin American countries.

Demonstrating Understanding

Using their textbooks, the Internet or other resources, have students create a list of recent ways the United States has become involved in the affairs of countries in the Southern Hemisphere, such as expanding trade or offering aid. Lead a discussion about the outcome of each of these actions (both for the United States and the countries involved). Ask students to express their opinions about whether they agree or disagree with the United States's decision to become involved in each of the situations listed. Ask students to consider what kind of effect, if any, each situation has on the United States and its ability to carry out its foreign policy. Encourage students to do further research about one of the examples on the list. Have them report their findings to the class.

CLOSE

Remind students of some of the products they inspected in order to see where they were made. Ask students to make a list of three to four items that they cherish or use the most. Have students again investigate the countries in which these products were made. Explain to students that quality products can be manufactured throughout the world and that many of the countries these products come from have developed important trading links with the United States. Have students identify why trade is important to the U.S. economy. Encourage students to write about the importance of the relationship(s) the United States maintains with the country(ies) that their favorite products come from. Encourage students to think of ways the United States would be different if it did not.

OPTIONS

Students Having Difficulty/ Sheltered English Students

 Provide students with posterboard, scissors, glue, newspaper publications and current issues of different magazines. Have students look through the newspapers and magazines (and any other suitable reference guides) to locate as many articles as possible pertaining to U.S. foreign policy. Then have students cut out the articles and paste them on the posterboard. Above each article students should note the subject of the article and the date. Display the collages in the classroom as an example of the many different countries the United States encounters in maintaining its foreign relations.

Gifted Learners/Visual-Spatial Learners

 Organize students into small groups and provide them with posterboard and colored pencils or markers. Ask students to create a time line from the end of World War II to the present day that illustrates U.S. involvement in other countries around the world. Students should mark each intervention, as well as write a brief outcome of the mission. In addition, students may wish to color-code each occurrence according to the region of the world it took place (for example, yellow for Latin America, blue for Asia) in an attempt to discover any patterns in U.S. foreign policy. Display the finished products in the classroom.

REVIEW

Have students complete the Section 4 Review on page 548. Use the answers in the Annotated Teacher's Edition to assess student mastery of this section.

ASSESS

To assess student mastery of this section, have students complete Daily Quiz 23.4 in *Daily Quizzes with Answer Key.* For additional assessment options, see *Alternative Assessment Handbook* on the *One-Stop Planner CD-ROM.*

RETEACH

For students having difficulty with the lessons, have them complete Reteaching Activity 23. This activity is located in *Reteaching Activities with Answer Key.*

ADDITIONAL RESOURCES

Hammond, Victoria. *United States Foreign Policy in the Middle East: A Foreign Affairs Special Anthology.* 1991. Foreign Affairs.

United States Foreign Service Posts and Department of State Jurisdictions. 1996. U.S. Department of State.

TOPICS INCLUDE

★ collective security
★ spread of conflict
★ causes of conflict
★ weapons proliferation
★ United Nations
★ economic development
★ international trade
★ environmental challenges
★ protecting natural resources
★ U.S.-Japanese relations
★ U.S.-European relations
★ U.S.-Chinese relations
★ U.S.-Latin American relations
★ U.S.-African relations

GOVERNMENT NOTEBOOK

The Government Notebook is a journal activity that encourages students to consider basic concepts of government that relate to their lives. A follow-up notebook activity appears on page 550.

▶ WHY IT MATTERS TODAY

To find additional lesson plans dealing with international relations, visit **CNNfyi.com** or have students complete the **GOVERNMENT IN THE NEWS** activity on page 549.

CNNfyi.com

INTERNATIONAL RELATIONS

Why do you suppose that U.S. government leaders care what happens in other countries? After all, a nation such as North Korea is thousands of miles across the Pacific Ocean from the mainland United States. Similarly, why do efforts to develop forests in South America draw international concern? The answer lies in the recognition that no country is truly isolated from events outside its borders. This interconnectedness can be seen in issues concerning collective security, economics, and the environment.

GOVERNMENT NOTEBOOK

In your Government Notebook, write a short paragraph about the importance of understanding how events elsewhere in the world affect the United States.

▶ WHY IT MATTERS TODAY

The United States is closely tied to many nations throughout the world. At the end of this chapter visit **CNNfyi.com** to learn more about international relations.

CNNfyi.com

SECTION 1

COLLECTIVE SECURITY

READ TO DISCOVER

1. Why is international collective security important?
2. What causes conflicts that challenge collective security?
3. How does growth in the production and ownership of weapons challenge collective security?
4. In what ways does the United Nations help achieve collective security?

POLITICAL DICTIONARY

interdependence
refugee
nuclear proliferation
international law

Perhaps the most obvious example of the **interdependence**, or mutual reliance, of the world's countries is the struggle for collective security. As noted in Chapter 10, collective security involves ensuring peace by linking nations through mutual defense agreements. Because conflict and the spread of weapons of war are a global threat, many countries are constantly working together to maintain peace.

Working for Security

Why is security so important? Security is vital to a government's ability to perform its functions and promote the public good. A nation unable to secure its borders and protect its citizens may not be able to collect taxes effectively, provide services, protect communities from crime, or maintain a safe and clean environment. In today's interdependent world, security is a collective concern because conflicts often affect regions and countries that are not directly involved in them. Sometimes vast numbers of people cross international borders to flee war zones, and fighting spreads to regions outside the original area of conflict.

Refugees Conflicts often produce **refugees**—people who flee their community or country to escape war or for economic or political reasons. For example, in 1994 civil war erupted between ethnic groups in Rwanda in east central Africa. Fearing for their lives, hundreds of thousands of refugees fled to neighboring countries such as Zaire (now the Democratic Republic of the Congo).

Host countries usually have to help pay for the care of refugees, providing their food, shelter, and protection. Moreover, unsanitary conditions in crowded camps often raise fears about the spread of disease. Because of these burdens, host countries have an interest in helping to end the fighting so that refugees can return home. The U.S. Committee for Refugees estimated that despite all the efforts to restore peace and stability to war-torn regions, at the end of 1999 there were more than 14 million refugees in the world.

Spread of Conflict If fighting spreads within a nation or beyond national borders, it not only may create refugees but also threaten collective security. For example, in the early 1990s fighting broke out among various ethnic and religious

WORLD AFFAIRS *Refugees from Afghanistan at Jalozai refugees camp, near Pakistan.* **What problems might this refugee camp face?**

SECTION 1

COLLECTIVE SECURITY

Lesson Plans

For teaching strategies, see Lesson 23.1 located at the beginning of this chapter or the One-Stop Lesson Planner Strategy 23.1.

Political Dictionary

To reinforce the section's vocabulary terms, refer students to the Electronic Glossary on the *Researcher CD-ROM.*

Section Assessment

To assess students' mastery of this section, have them complete Daily Quiz 23.1 in *Daily Quizzes with Answer Key.*

Caption Answer

The camps might face unsanitary and overcrowded conditions and disease.

groups in the former Yugoslav republics, particularly in Bosnia and Herzegovina. European leaders feared that the fighting might spread to neighboring countries. In addition, many of the world's leaders were concerned about "ethnic cleansing"—attempts by the region's Serb population to eliminate local Muslims.

The mounting bloodshed and huge numbers of refugees led European countries and the United States to act. In 1992 troops under the jurisdiction of the United Nations (which you will learn about later in this section) were sent to maintain peace. Their efforts were unsuccessful, and fighting continued. In 1995, however, a peace agreement was signed in Dayton, Ohio. A UN-authorized peacekeeping force made up of members of the North Atlantic Treaty Organization (NATO) was sent in to help keep the peace and enforce a cease-fire.

In 1996 the NATO force was replaced by a UN stabilization force, which was still in place in late 2001. NATO, as noted in Chapter 10, is an alliance of nations originally formed to provide a unified defense of the North Atlantic area—Western Europe and North America. Today, NATO's focus is expanding to include political and military cooperation with new partners in Central and Eastern Europe.

Causes of Conflict

Today, world peace is still threatened by conflicts based on ethnic and religious intolerance, ideological rivalries, and other factors such as competing economic interests. Nations around the world are constantly challenged to contain and stop these conflicts.

Ethnic and Religious Intolerance Many fierce and bloody conflicts around the world have stemmed from ethnic or religious intolerance. Ethnic and racial differences have sometimes sparked violence in the United States. Considering that it has one of the world's most diverse populations, however, the United States has been relatively free of violence based on ethnicity or religion in recent history. Several other countries—particularly in southeastern Europe and in parts of Africa and Asia—have seen many more ethnic and religious clashes.

Persecution, typically fueled by prejudice and hatred, is a primary cause of such conflict. The

WORLD AFFAIRS *Soldiers patrol the border separating North and South Korea.* **How did China assist North Korea during the Korean War?**

Bosnian and Rwandan civil wars are just two recent examples of conflicts stemming from ethnic and religious differences.

Ideological Rivalries Differences in people's ideologies—basic belief systems—have inspired fierce rivalries. Such rivalries have been at the core of many conflicts around the world. In the mid- to late twentieth century, for example, the rivalry between the supporters of communism and those of capitalism and democracy led to a number of civil and regional wars.

Civil and regional conflicts based on ideological differences have at times drawn in countries from other parts of the world. During the 1950–53 Korean War, U.S. and allied troops aided South Korea, which had been invaded by communist North Korea. Communist China supported North Korea with hundreds of thousands of soldiers. Even today, despite the fall of communism elsewhere in the world, U.S. troops remain stationed on the Korean Peninsula, helping to maintain the tense peace on the border between North and South Korea.

Other Causes A violent change in the government of a nation may also threaten regional security. In 1997, for example, rebels overthrew President Mobutu Sese Seko (moh-BOO-too SAY-say SAY-koh)—the longtime dictator of the African country of Zaire—and created the Democratic Republic of the Congo. Supported by aid from neighboring countries, the rebels swept through much of Zaire, storming towns and crushing resistance by the state military. Such conflicts occur when people turn to violence to achieve political and economic aims. Similarly, government corruption and social unrest have often led to violence, as in several Central American nations during the 1970s and 1980s. Violent changes in government and other forms of civil unrest often have important international implications, forcing changes in countries' relationships.

Civil unrest in one country has at times led to international intervention. In 1994, for example, U.S. troops entered the Caribbean country of Haiti to reinstall a democratically elected president who had been overthrown by the military. The intervention came after thousands of Haitian refugees had fled to the United States to escape instability and violence in their country.

The 1990–91 Persian Gulf War is another instance of political and economic interests inspiring outside forces to intervene in a regional conflict. When Iraq invaded Kuwait—a small oil-producing country in the Middle East—the United States and other faraway nations quickly stepped in to defend it. Kuwait's strategic value as an important oil producer and a desire to punish Iraqi dictator Saddam Hussein for his launching of the invasion inspired their actions.

Weapons Proliferation

Another serious threat to international collective security is the increase in the production and ownership of weapons of mass destruction. These include nuclear weapons, chemical and biological weapons, and conventional arms.

Nuclear Proliferation A critical challenge to collective security is **nuclear proliferation**—the spread in the ownership of nuclear weapons. Currently, only the United States, Russia, Great Britain, France, and China acknowledge that they possess nuclear weapons. These nations are known as the nuclear powers. India and Pakistan have both exploded nuclear devices, although it is unknown if they currently have any nuclear weapons. Israel is also suspected of having the capability to produce nuclear weapons. Some other countries, including Iran, Iraq, and North Korea, have been suspected of seeking to acquire such weapons.

To assure that nuclear weapons will never again be used in a war, many nations—including the existing nuclear powers—have worked to stop their proliferation. In the 1968 Nuclear Nonproliferation Treaty, nuclear powers agreed not to transfer nuclear weapons to nonnuclear countries. In turn, nonnuclear signatories to the treaty have pledged not to try to produce or obtain such weapons. Nuclear powers also have worked to prevent nuclear-weapons material from being smuggled out of Russia and other former Soviet republics. World leaders fear that nonnuclear countries or even terrorist groups might purchase such material and attempt to produce nuclear weapons.

In addition, nuclear powers, most importantly the United States and Russia, have agreed to several treaties limiting the production and possession of nuclear weapons. World leaders also have signed treaties banning nuclear-weapons testing in hopes of eliminating potential environmental damage and the further development of such weapons.

Chemical and Biological Weapons Many countries also have worked to limit the production and possession of chemical and biological weapons. These weapons of mass destruction are much easier and more inexpensive to produce than nuclear weapons but are also capable of killing masses of people.

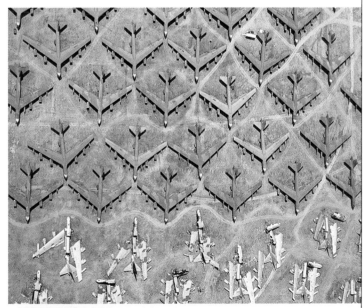

WORLD AFFAIRS *These American aircraft were destroyed in accordance with the U.S.-Soviet Strategic Arms Reduction Treaty.* **In what year did the nuclear powers agree to the Nuclear Nonproliferation Treaty?**

Caption Answer
They agreed to the Nuclear Nonproliferation Treaty in 1968.

THEMES IN GOVERNMENT

WORLD AFFAIRS The United States has faced stiff opposition to the Helms-Burton Act, which imposes sanctions on countries doing business with Cuba. The United States's position is based on the fact that during the Cuban Revolution, land was seized from U.S. companies that were operating in Cuba. They have never been compensated for the land that was confiscated. The European Union, Canada, and Mexico oppose the law, however, because it interferes with their right to conduct their own affairs, particularly free trade.

The European Union originally decided to challenge the Helms-Burton Act in the new court of world trade, a court that was created by the World Trade Organization, which the U.S. government helped to create. The court does not have the power to actually overturn a U.S. law, but it may authorize the countries filing suit to take action against the U.S.-imposed sanctions. In 1998 the European Union dropped its challenge. ∎

Countries first used chemical weapons on a large scale during World War I. In that war, mustard gas, which blisters the skin and lungs and causes blindness, killed and horribly wounded many soldiers. More recently, Iraq used chemical weapons in the 1980s in its war against Iran. Several countries also have produced biological weapons, which spread microbes that cause deadly diseases.

Over the years, the horror of chemical and biological weapons inspired a number of agreements to halt their production and use. Many nations agreed to the 1925 Geneva Protocol on Gas Warfare, which outlawed the use of chemical weapons in war. The 1972 Biological Weapons Convention, an agreement signed by some 140 nations, outlaws the development, production, and stockpiling of biological weapons.

The Chemical Weapons Convention, a similar agreement that went into effect in 1997, bans the production and stockpiling of chemical weapons. Although more than 160 countries signed the treaty, the United States was hesitant to join them. Some Americans believed that, as with other arms control agreements, ensuring other nations' compliance would be difficult. Nations that refused to sign were not limited by the ban. Signers would thus be at a disadvantage, because the nonsigners would be the only ones able to possess chemical weapons. Supporters of the treaty argued that ratifying it was necessary to maintaining U.S. prestige around the world and to preventing nations from producing and using such weapons. The U.S. Senate finally ratified the treaty in April 1997.

Conventional Arms Nations have long struggled to restrict the production and possession of conventional arms, such as tanks, artillery, warplanes, and naval ships. In the early 1920s, at the Limitation of Armaments Conference, for example, many of the world's most powerful countries agreed to limit the size of their naval forces. These and other early efforts, however, did not stop the peacetime stockpiling of weapons. During the Cold War, such stockpiling escalated. In 1987 alone, world military spending exceeded $1.3 trillion.

Military spending has declined since the end of the Cold War, however. By 1994 total world military expenditures had dropped to $840 billion, around $280 billion of which was spent by the United States. The decline occurred because of various military reduction agreements, such as the

Top 10 Countries in Military Spending

Country	Billions of U.S. Dollars
1. United States	$265.9
2. Russia	$53.9
3. France	$39.8
4. Japan	$37.0
5. China	$36.7
6. United Kingdom	$36.6
7. Germany	$32.4
8. Italy	$22.6
9. Brazil	$18.1
10. Taiwan	$13.9

(Figures are for 1998.)

Source: *World Almanac: 2001*

Although many countries have signed treaties to limit certain types of weapons, some countries still spend billions of dollars a year on their military. **How much did the United Kingdom spend on its military in 1998?**

1990 Treaty on Conventional Armed Forces in Europe. In spite of such treaties, the increasing level of military spending in some parts of the world, such as the Middle East and South Asia, continues to concern world leaders.

United Nations

As you have seen, the international community has worked in numerous ways to promote collective security. Another important key to collective security has been the work of the United Nations, a worldwide organization of countries that is based in New York City. The United States and 50 other countries founded the United Nations in 1945 after World War II. By 2001, UN membership had grown to 189 countries.

It is important to remember that the United Nations is not intended to be a world government. Rather, it serves as a forum for settling disputes and accomplishing other important goals, such as protecting human rights and promoting respect for international law. To organize its efforts to fulfill these goals, the UN Charter established six principal divisions:

- ★ the General Assembly,
- ★ the Security Council,
- ★ the Secretariat,
- ★ the International Court of Justice,
- ★ the Economic and Social Council, and
- ★ the Trusteeship Council.

The General Assembly is made up of all UN member nations. Each member has one vote in the assembly, which decides the UN's budget, member dues, and general policy issues. The assembly also plays a major role in choosing who will sit on various UN councils, including the Security Council.

The UN Security Council investigates international disputes and decides what actions to take to maintain peace or stop aggression. Actions could include the breaking off of diplomatic relations by UN members, the implementing of a trade embargo, or even the use of armed force. The Security Council is made up of 15 members. Five countries—the United States, Russia, China, Great Britain, and France—are permanent members, and each has the power to veto any council decision. The General Assembly elects 10 additional members for two-year terms.

The Secretariat, which is headed by the secretary-general, manages the day-to-day operations of the United Nations. The General Assembly elects the secretary-general for a five-year, renewable term. A nominee cannot assume the office of secretary-general without Security Council approval.

The International Court of Justice, or the World Court, hears legal disputes between countries and gives advisory opinions on international legal questions. The court is composed of 15 judges, each of whom is elected to a nine-year term by the General Assembly and approved by the Security Council.

The Economic and Social Council meets once a year to work on ways to improve people's lives. The council's work includes supervising and coordinating UN social, economic, cultural, health, and educational efforts.

The Trusteeship Council administers any trust territories under UN supervision. The council was formed to help run former colonies that had gained their freedom during World War II but had not yet set up independent governments. Currently, there are no trust territories under UN supervision.

In addition to these divisions, some specialized agencies work with the United Nations to provide its members with medical, agricultural, financial, humanitarian, and technical assistance. For example, the International Bank for Reconstruction and Development, or the World Bank, loans money to countries in need and gives them technical and economic advice to help improve their economies. Another agency, the World Health Organization (WHO), helps governments fight disease. The work of the WHO was instrumental in helping wipe out smallpox—one of the world's most feared and deadly diseases. Today the WHO is a leader in worldwide efforts against AIDS.

Maintain World Peace The primary mission of the United Nations is to maintain world peace by helping to build friendly relationships between countries. The United Nations provides a forum for countries to settle disputes peacefully. In addition, it has worked to keep the peace in a number of tense situations, though not always successfully. UN peacekeeping forces, for example, have intervened between the military forces of Israel and some of its Arab neighbors, with which it has

Judges of the International Court of Justice

Judges	Country
Gilbert Guillaume	France
Shi Jiuyong	China
Shigeru Oda	Japan
Raymond Ranjeva	Madagascar
Géza Herczegh	Hungary
Carl-August Fleischhauer	Germany
Abdul G. Koroma	Sierra Leone
Vladlen S. Vereshchetin	Russian Federation
Rosalyn Higgins	United Kingdom
Gonzalo Parra-Aranguren	Venezuela
Pieter H. Kooijmans	Netherlands
Francisco Rezek	Brazil
Awn Shawkat Al-Khasawneh	Jordan
Thomas Buergenthal	United States
Nabil Elaraby	Egypt

Source: International Court of Justice

The International Court of Justice, or the World Court, helps settle legal disputes between countries. **How long is the term of an elected World Court judge?**

Caption Answer
nine years

SECTION 1 REVIEW ANSWERS

1. Refer to the following pages: interdependence (527), refugee (527), nuclear proliferation (529), international law (532).

2. ethnic and religious intolerance, ideological rivalries, a violent change in government, the proliferation of weapons

3a. Kuwait's oil reserves are economically and politically important to the United States and other nations. The United States and many other nations also wished to punish Saddam Hussein.

3b. to maintain world peace, protect human rights, and promote respect for international law

4. Answers will vary, but students should state their opinion and provide support for it.

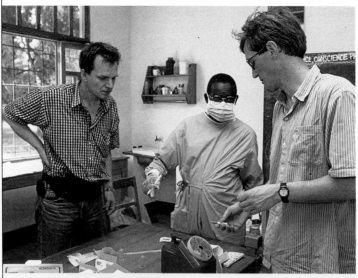

WORLD AFFAIRS *The World Health Organization (WHO), a United Nations agency, helps governments combat diseases. **What other types of assistance does the UN provide its members?***

fought several wars since 1948. The United Nations also authorized a peacekeeping force in Bosnia. In 2001 there were 15 such UN peacekeeping missions around the world.

The United Nations has even authorized the use of force to stop aggression. The organization authorized member countries to defend South Korea in 1950 and to drive Iraqi troops out of Kuwait in 1990–91.

Protect Human Rights The United Nations also works to protect human rights. In the Universal Declaration of Human Rights, the United Nations states that respect for human rights and human dignity "is the foundation of freedom, justice, and peace in the world." To that end, the United Nations helps forge international agreements on such things as the prevention of discrimination and promotion of human rights.

The United Nations also provides humanitarian assistance to victims of natural and human-caused disasters. In 2000 the UN's Office for the Coordination of Humanitarian Affairs raised more than $1.4 billion for disaster-relief programs that helped tens of millions of people worldwide.

Promote International Law In addition, the United Nations promotes respect for **international law**—the rules that govern the relationships among independent countries. International law is established through treaties and other agreements among nations and businesses. The UN's World Court provides a forum for resolving disputes over international law. Furthermore, the United Nations may enforce these rules. For example, it can call on members to limit trade with violators of international agreements.

SECTION 1 REVIEW

1. Identify and Explain:
- interdependence
- refugee
- nuclear proliferation
- international law

2. Identifying Concepts: Copy the chart below. Use it to describe the causes of conflict.

Conflict

3. Finding the Main Idea

  a. Why did the United States and other nations defend Kuwait against invasion by Iraq?

  b. What are the goals of the United Nations?

4. Writing and Critical Thinking

  Summarizing: What areas of the world are most important to the United States? Why do you think this is so? Explain your answer

  Consider the following:
  - the political significance of selected locations
  - the economic importance of certain places

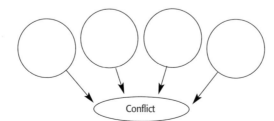

Homework Practice Online

keyword: SV3 HP23

SECTION 2

ECONOMIC INTERDEPENDENCE

READ TO DISCOVER

1. What is the difference between developing nations and developed nations?
2. In what ways have nations worked to promote international trade?
3. Why are U.S. trade deficits a problem?

POLITICAL DICTIONARY

developed nation
developing nation
comparative advantage
trading bloc
trade deficit

Interdependence among nations is evident not only in collective security but also in the world economy, where nations often cooperate to create healthy economic relationships. These relationships are strongly influenced by the economic development of the nations involved and the international trade in which they engage.

Economic Development

Nations are at different levels of economic development. The more developed a country is, the greater its influence is likely to be in the interdependent global economy.

Developed Nations Wealthy countries, commonly referred to as **developed nations**, share many characteristics. Among these are high levels of personal income, relatively low unemployment, and healthy manufacturing and industrial sectors. The wealthiest developed countries include the United States, Japan, Germany, France, and the United Kingdom, all of which have gross domestic products (GDPs) of more than a trillion dollars a year.

Developed nations' wealth enables them to strongly influence the economies of other countries around the world. For example, developed nations are the largest consumers of goods and services, making their markets important to producers elsewhere. They also largely determine international economic policies. Through organizations such as the World Bank, developed nations work to create policies and aid packages to improve the economies of poorer countries.

Developing Nations By 2000 about four fifths of the more than 6 billion people in the world were living in poorer countries, which are known as **developing nations**. In these countries most people spend much of their working lives just raising enough food to survive. Many of the world's poorest countries are in Africa, Asia, the Caribbean, and Central and South America.

The economic progress of developing and underdeveloped nations is often hindered by factors such as limited health services, poor and crowded schools, high rates of illiteracy, and poor productivity. These problems are often compounded by high rates of population growth. For example, the Democratic Republic of Congo (formerly Zaire), which had a per capita GDP of about $600 in 2000, is home to some 53 million people. This population is expected to reach 105 million by 2025.

WORLD AFFAIRS *These ships in a port near Mount Fuji carry Japanese imports and exports.* **How does a developed nation's wealth enable it to influence the economies of other countries?**

WORLD AFFAIRS *Many problems found in Kinshasa, the capital of the Democratic Republic of the Congo, are compounded by its rapidly growing population.* **What do experts predict the population of the Democratic Republic of the Congo will be in the year 2025?**

Making Progress Some developing nations have begun to close the economic gap that separates them from developed nations. Although some experienced a severe economic downturn in late 1997, the economies of the Asian countries of China, South Korea, Indonesia, Malaysia, Singapore, Thailand, and Taiwan have grown rapidly since the 1970s. In expanding their production and consumption, these countries have become increasingly important in the global economy. China's more than 1 billion people, for example, provide a huge market for businesses around the world. Chinese exports also have increased dramatically.

This economic expansion was largely brought about by reforms that freed markets and supported private industry. International aid also has helped some countries expand their economies. The World Bank, for example, has loaned billions of dollars for the development of industry.

One of the world's great economic success stories has been Japan. From 1953 to 1966 the country borrowed $857 million from the World Bank. Afterward, the Japanese economy grew rapidly, and by 1970 Japan had begun loaning money to the World Bank to finance development in other countries. However, economic stagnation has overtaken Japan over the last few years.

International Trade

International trade fuels the economic interdependence among nations. It is a major factor in the production and consumption of goods and services in developed and developing nations alike.

The United States strongly supports free trade. As noted in Chapter 10, free trade is the exchange of goods and services across national borders without restrictions, such as high tariffs. Free trade opens foreign markets to domestic businesses and gives consumers access to foreign-made goods.

By rewarding countries for specializing in what they do best, free trade tends to bring about lower-priced and higher-quality goods and services. For example, Kuwait has one of the world's largest reserves of oil. In fact, the Kuwaiti government—which controls most of the country's oil industry—generates much of its income from oil sales to other countries, such as the United States. This income has been used to pay for health care, education, defense, and other services, as well as for improvements necessary for further economic development.

Because Kuwait has no water resources and no land fit for agricultural use, however, it must depend almost wholly on food imports from foreign sources. One of Kuwait's largest food suppliers is the United States, which is the world's leading exporter of agricultural products. Kuwait's experience is an example of the economic principle of **comparative advantage** at work. This principle states that countries should primarily produce goods they can generate at a relatively low cost and purchase goods they cannot.

A great deal of international trade is conducted in regional **trading blocs**—groups of countries that ease trade among their members by setting various rules, such as the reduction of tariffs.

Europe One of the most successful trading blocs is the European Union (EU), which in 2001 had 15 members, including France, Germany, the United Kingdom, and other, mostly Western European countries. The EU grew out of the European Economic Community (EEC), which was established in 1957. Its goal was to create a common market in which goods, services, people, and capital could move freely, regardless of national borders. Member nations hoped that forming economic and political ties would prevent future conflict.

The EU has its own governmental institutions, including the European Parliament, which acts as

WORLD AFFAIRS *Trucks loaded with goods line up to cross the border of Mexico and the United States. In 1992, North American leaders established the NAFTA trading bloc.* **How does the debate over NAFTA illustrate the influence of international trade on U.S. economic policy?**

a public forum for debate of issues important to members. With the fall of communism in Eastern Europe, the EU also has strengthened economic relationships with countries there. In 1993 member countries approved the Maastricht Treaty. This created a common currency, the euro, that was launched on January 1, 1999.

North America The United States and two of its most important trading partners, Canada and Mexico, have formed a major trading bloc. In 1992, these countries' leaders signed the North American Free Trade Agreement (NAFTA). NAFTA removed tariffs and other barriers to the creation of a free market among the three countries.

The U.S. Senate ratified the agreement in 1993, but not without overcoming strong opposition. NAFTA opponents argued that tariffs, which raise prices on foreign goods sold in the United States, protect U.S. jobs by encouraging consumers to buy domestic products. In addition, they feared that eliminating tariffs would spur U.S. companies to move their facilities—and thus many jobs—to Mexico, where wages are lower. NAFTA supporters, on the other hand, argued that removing tariffs and allowing free trade would open markets for the sale of U.S. goods, thereby creating more jobs for U.S. workers.

Canadian, Mexican, and U.S. leaders signed NAFTA because they believed free trade would strengthen their countries' economies. Despite an economic crisis in Mexico shortly after NAFTA went into effect, that nation's economy has improved in recent years. NAFTA supporters are now considering expanding the agreement to include other countries in the Americas.

Asia Another important trading bloc is emerging among Asian countries that once were among the world's poorest. As you read earlier, although some experienced a downturn in 1997, the economies of Singapore, South Korea, Taiwan, Thailand, Malaysia, and Indonesia have grown rapidly in recent years. China too has experienced great economic growth since its communist government instituted free-market reforms.

To further encourage trade and economic development in the region, in 1989 many Southeast Asian countries joined with Japan, the United States, and other Pacific Rim countries—nations bordering the Pacific Ocean—to found the Asia-Pacific Economic Cooperation (APEC) group. Although it began as an informal group, APEC has become an important tool in promoting free trade and economic cooperation in Asia.

Asian countries have made other efforts to promote free trade. For example, in 1967 Thailand, Indonesia, Malaysia, the Philippines, and Singapore formed the Association of Southeast Asian Nations (ASEAN) to improve economic and

Careers in Government

U.S. Trade Office

The Office of the U.S. Trade Representative develops international trade and investment policy for the U.S. government. Congress created the office in 1962 and made it a cabinet-level agency in 1974. The head of the office, the U.S. trade representative, is the nation's chief trade negotiator.

Trade office staff members have considerable experience in economics and business. For example, consider the background of Robert B. Zoellick, who was appointed as the U.S. trade representative in 2001. In this role, Zoellick acts as the president's chief trade adviser and works to devise trade policies that will encourage growth in America and the world.

Before he became the U.S. trade representative, Zoellick served as an executive vice president for Fannie Mae, a housing finance investor. Zoellick also had plenty of government experience before serving as U.S trade representative. As an Under Secretary of State during the George H. W. Bush administration, Zoellick worked on NAFTA and on the U.S. role in Germany's reunification.

President Bush meets with Japanese Prime Minister Junichiro Koizumi. Strong trade ties with Japan are an important aspect of U.S.-Japanese relations.

Education also played a key role in preparing Zoellick for his post as head of the U.S. trade office. In 1975 he graduated from Swarthmore College and later received a law degree from Harvard Law School. He later completed a master's degree in public policy from Harvard University.

---

political cooperation among the nations of the region. After the group's formation, the nations of Brunei and Vietnam joined. The nations of Laos and Myanmar became members of ASEAN in 1997. Cambodia joined in 1999. The ASEAN nations have committed themselves to reducing tariffs and promoting free trade within their region.

Other Trading Blocs Central and South American and African countries also have made efforts to formalize trading relationships. In 1996 the South American countries of Argentina, Brazil, Paraguay, and Uruguay formed a free-trade association known by its Spanish acronym MERCOSUR. Chile and Bolivia have since joined the association. MERCOSUR's members hope to bring in other South American countries and eventually link up with NAFTA.

World Trade Organization Much trade takes place outside geographic trading blocs. The creation of the World Trade Organization (WTO) was an important effort to ease trade restrictions among all countries. Established in 1995, it replaced the General Agreement on Tariffs and Trade (GATT), which had pursued similar goals since 1947. More than 130 countries initially joined. To ensure that overall trade practices benefit all countries, the WTO requires governments to, among other things, lower tariffs and adopt fair trade practices with all other WTO members.

Trade and the United States

Historically, foreign trade played a relatively modest role in the U.S. economy. As a large, geographically diverse nation, the United States could meet most of its needs inside its borders. In the twentieth century, however, foreign trade has become increasingly important.

U.S. exports have grown by leaps and bounds, but since the mid-1970s they have consistently failed to keep pace with imports. This imbalance has created a **trade deficit**, meaning the total value of imports into the United States is higher than the total value of U.S. exports to other countries. Many Americans worry that the large trade deficit is a sign of the country's declining economic status in the world.

The trade deficit is caused by several factors, one of the most important of which involves federal budget deficits. Having run up large budget deficits over the last three decades, the U.S. government has had to borrow increasing amounts of money. Higher interest rates resulting from increased borrowing attracted increased foreign demand for American bonds. As a result of the increased demand for dollars, the dollar became more valuable—or "stronger"—which raised prices for U.S. exports but generally lowered prices for imports. With more expensive exports and cheaper imports, the trade deficit increased.

A large trade deficit raises two important concerns. First, it creates unemployment. Some things that would otherwise be produced by Americans are produced abroad, and some things the United States might have produced for export are not produced. Second, a large trade deficit indicates that the United States as a whole is living

© 1987 by Herblock in the *Washington Post.*

WORLD AFFAIRS *Some economists worry that the deficits, like the monsters in this cartoon, scare away potential foreign investors from investing in the U.S. economy.* **What two important concerns does a large trade deficit raise?**

beyond its means, since U.S. citizens consume more than the United States produces. In the short term, this makes for a higher standard of living. Eventually, however, foreigners could cash in the dollars they have accumulated. If this were to occur, a decline in the U.S. standard of living might follow.

SECTION 2 REVIEW

1. **Identify and Explain:**
   - developed nation
   - developing nation
   - comparative advantage
   - trading bloc
   - trade deficit
2. **Identifying Concepts:** Copy the chart to the right. Use it to list the major trading blocs in the world and their members.

Trading Bloc	Members

3. **Finding the Main Idea**
   a. What is the government's role in setting international trade policies?
   b. How does international trade promote healthy economies?

4. **Writing and Critical Thinking**
   Supporting a Point of View: Do you think NAFTA is beneficial or detrimental to the United States? Provide examples to support your opinion.
   Consider the following:
   - the importance of trade to the U.S. economy
   - the effect of trade on government policies

go.hrw.com Homework Practice Online
keyword: SV3 HP23

SECTION 3

ENVIRONMENTAL INTERDEPENDENCE

READ TO DISCOVER

1. How do air and water pollution challenge the international community?
2. How can population growth and economic development strain the world's resources?

POLITICAL DICTIONARY

global warming
renewable resource
nonrenewable resource
deforestation

The world's environmental challenges are yet another demonstration of international interdependence. Problems such as air and water pollution and the depletion of natural resources have significant global consequences.

Challenges of Shared Resources

Imagine that increasing temperatures caused polar ice to melt, raising ocean levels and gradually submerging highly populated coastal areas. Imagine also that deadly diseases such as cholera were being spread by contaminated rivers and other polluted water sources. Many people argue that these are potential consequences of air and water pollution and that they could affect people worldwide.

Air Pollution Researchers have warned of the dangers of air pollution for decades. In a 1992 study the United Nations reported that about 1 billion people around the world were breathing unhealthful air. Exhaust from cars and industrial pollution—which are plentiful in large, crowded cities—cause various respiratory ailments and contribute to disease.

Some scientists have warned that the release of certain chemicals into the air is having dangerous climatic and environmental effects. They believe that the chlorofluorocarbons (CFCs) used in air conditioner and refrigerator coolants, as well as in the manufacture of plastic foam products, damage the atmospheric ozone layer. This layer, which surrounds the earth, filters out harmful ultraviolet rays from the sun that can cause skin cancer. In addition, the burning of fossil fuels such as oil, coal, and natural gas adds carbon dioxide to the air. Some scientists believe that high levels of carbon dioxide and other so-called greenhouse gases can trap heat and thus cause **global warming**—a gradual rise in the world's average temperature. This could melt polar ice caps and thus cause the oceans to rise, flooding coastal areas and submerging tiny island-nations.

Water Pollution Another environmental challenge is water pollution, which threatens people's health by damaging drinking-water supplies and food resources. Industrial waste, pesticides, and

WORLD AFFAIRS *Mexico City, like many of the world's other major metropolitan areas, has an imposing air pollution problem. **According to UN experts, how many people were breathing unhealthful air in the early 1990s?***

Comparing Governments

International Cooperation

Cooperation on environmental issues often helps build goodwill between countries. For example, the governments of India and Bangladesh in South Asia have worked to overcome differences regarding management of the Ganges River. The Ganges—which flows through northern India, into Bangladesh, and then to the Bay of Bengal—is a major water source in the region.

In 1977 the Indian and Bangladeshi governments made an agreement fixing the amount of water to flow from the Ganges into Bangladesh. When that agreement expired in 1988, however, India began allowing more water to flow during wet seasons—adding to problems in flood-prone Bangladesh. During the dry season, India used more water to irrigate its farmland. As a result, farmers in Bangladesh did not receive enough water.

In 1996 the leaders of India and Bangladesh signed a new 30-year agreement on management of the Ganges. The two countries will receive equal amounts of water from the river, but Bangladesh will receive more of its water during the dry season.

other pollutants sometimes contaminate rivers and other water supplies. Many of these pollutants are suspected of causing various diseases, including cancer. In developing nations a lack of water-treatment facilities forces people to rely on impure water supplies, which often spread disease.

The oceans have long been used as dumping sites. Tons of discarded waste and oil spilled from damaged petroleum tankers have killed ocean life and spoiled large coastal areas. Decommissioned Russian nuclear submarines also threaten to spread radiation in parts of the Arctic Ocean north of Russia where the aging, rusty vessels were dumped.

Seeking Solutions The challenges of global pollution are not easily resolved, particularly since the scientific community does not agree about the potential consequences. Some experts, for example, have argued that the dangers of greenhouse gases and global warming have been exaggerated. This lack of agreement has sparked debate among world leaders over the best ways to maintain or improve the health of the global environment.

Nevertheless, most countries have begun to work together to reduce pollution. The Montreal Protocol of 1987, the first important international agreement addressing an environmental problem, sought to protect the ozone layer. Environmentalists credit the Montreal Protocol with helping reduce the production of CFCs by more than 75 percent.

In 1992 the United Nations held an "Earth Summit" in Rio de Janeiro, Brazil, to deal with issues including global warming and economic development. As a result of the conference, the United States and other countries agreed to reduce emissions, or discharges, of carbon dioxide. Though some nations have failed to reach the agreed-upon emissions levels, many environmentalists hope that more countries will meet the new goals agreed to at the second Earth Summit in 1997.

International negotiations about environmental issues raise difficult questions about how to distribute the burdens of pollution reduction. For example, in debates about limiting carbon dioxide emissions, poor countries argue that rich countries

WORLD AFFAIRS *Trudoya Bay in Russia has become a "cemetery" for nuclear submarines.* **How does water pollution threaten people's health?**

should bear most of the burden because they cause most of the emissions. Some developing nations also maintain that significantly restricting their emissions would set back their economic development. In turn, some developed nations point out that unless developing nations work to control their own pollution levels now, they will greatly expand emissions in trying to meet the needs of their rapidly growing populations.

Protecting Natural Resources

In addition to combating pollution, countries try to work together on another important environmental issue—protecting the world's natural resources. You are surrounded by examples of how natural resources are put to work—the paper in this book, the cotton or wool fibers in your clothing, and the wood used to construct your school or home. These are **renewable resources**, or natural resources that can be replaced. For example, people can grow trees to replace those used to produce paper and wood. Renewable energy resources are solar and wind power.

Many other important resources, however, are **nonrenewable resources**—natural resources that can be used only once. The gasoline that powered the car or bus that brought you to school this morning is refined from oil, a nonrenewable

PUBLIC GOOD *Many of the world's leaders attend summits, like the one shown in this photograph, to discuss solutions to global environmental problems.* **How are renewable resources different from nonrenewable resources?**

World's Most Populous Urban Areas	
City	**Population (2000)**
1. Tokyo, Japan	26,444,000
2. Mexico City, Mexico	18,131,000
3. Mumbai (Bombay), India	18,066,000
4. Sao Paulo, Brazil	17,755,000
5. New York City	16,640,000
6. Lagos, Nigeria	13,427,000
7. Los Angeles	13,140,000
8. Calcutta, India	12,918,000
9. Shanghai, China	12,887,000
10. Buenos Aires, Argentina	12,560,000
11. Dhaka, Bangledesh	12,317,000
12. Karachi, Pakistan	11,794,000
13. Delhi, India	11,695,000
14. Jakarta, Indonesia	11,018,000
15. Osaka, Japan	11,013,000
Source: *World Almanac: 2001*	

These urban areas are the most heavily populated in the world. If population projections are correct, by 2015 there will be 33 cities with populations that are more than 8 million. **Why are experts concerned about population growth?**

resource. The amounts of oil, coal, precious metals, and other minerals are limited. Once they are used up, they cannot be replaced. However, some nonrenewable resources may be recycled, or processed for reuse. Also, advances in exploration technology have dramatically increased estimated reserves of many nonrenewable resources. As a result of recycling and expanding access to resources, the price of many nonrenewable resources has actually been declining over time, despite increased demand.

Resources are unevenly distributed around the world. For example, many countries in the Middle East are rich in oil while others, such as Japan and most Western European countries, have virtually no oil and must import it. Such uneven distribution of resources sometimes has led to conflict, with countries going to war to take from others what they cannot produce for themselves.

Citizenship in Action

Peace Corps Volunteers

In Costa Rica and other Spanish-speaking countries in the Americas, the Peace Corps is called *Cuerpo de Paz.* In the African tongue of Swahili, the organization is known as *Watu Wa Amani.* People on the frozen plains of the former Soviet republic of Kazakhstan call it *Korpus Mira.* However it is identified, the Peace Corps is one of the key organizations for building ties between the United States and other countries around the world.

More than 163,000 people have served as Peace Corps volunteers since 1961, when Congress and President John F. Kennedy established the agency. Volunteers use their educational and professional experience to teach valuable skills to people in developing countries. Many of these skills are related to farming, business development, technology, and urban planning. Peace Corps volunteers also teach English as a foreign language, help improve health services, and provide aid and information for promoting healthy environments.

In 2001 more than 7,000 Peace Corps volunteers were doing such work in 77 countries.

Peace Corps volunteers teach many skills to people in developing nations. Here, a volunteer in Ecuador helps local residents plant trees.

Hundreds of such volunteers have worked throughout the former Soviet Union to ease the difficult transition from communism to democracy and capitalism.

Many Peace Corps volunteers discover that people in other countries—particularly in the former Soviet Union—are very curious about the United States. After being interviewed on Kazakh television and radio when she served as a Peace Corps volunteer at the age of 21, Michelle Ostrander found herself receiving phone calls from strangers wanting to talk to "the American."

"After I talked awhile and wanted to go, they'd say 'Don't hang up—you're the first American I've ever talked to,' " Ostrander says. Some Kazakhs, asking for "just a minute with the American," would go to the school where Ostrander taught English classes.

In fact, learning about the United States from these Peace Corps volunteers is helping to break down the barriers between old Cold War enemies. In the days of the Soviet Union, the communist government discouraged contact with foreigners, particularly Americans. Sometimes it was even a crime to make friends with a foreigner, says Kazakh teacher Irina Naumova.

Peace Corps volunteers often must endure difficult living conditions. In developing countries, for example, volunteers must learn to live without conveniences such as air-conditioning and central heating. Even indoor plumbing is an unknown luxury in some locations. Volunteers also must cope with the dangers of various diseases that plague some regions.

In Kazakhstan, Peace Corps volunteers have had to adjust to brutally cold winters, a smothering bureaucracy left over from the communist era, and other difficulties. Many volunteers, however, say that they are thrilled to have had the chance to experience this nation's culture and help its people.

What Do You Think?

1. How are Peace Corps volunteers helping build relations between the United States and other countries?
2. Why do you suppose that many Peace Corps volunteers take assignments in developing nations despite the sometimes difficult conditions?

SECTION 3
REVIEW ANSWERS

1. Refer to the following pages: global warming (538), renewable resource (540), nonrenewable resource (540), deforestation (542).

2. Renewable resources include wood, cotton, and paper. Nonrenewable resources include oil, coal, precious metals and other minerals.

3a. International trade is a peaceful way of acquiring needed resources.

3b. the burning of fossil fuels, car exhaust, industrial emissions, and chlorofluorocarbons

4. Answers will vary but students should clearly state their opinion and provide support.

International trade, on the other hand, is a means of peacefully acquiring needed resources.

A number of factors, such as population growth and economic development, are straining the world's resources. In some regions, drinking water is scarce, and overfishing greatly reduces the number of fish in the oceans. However, predictions made in the early 1970s about certain resources "running out" by the 1990s have proved false.

Population Growth

The demands of the world's rapidly increasing population place a great strain on natural resources. In 2001 there were 6.1 billion people living on earth. Experts say that this number will approach 8 billion by 2025.

The increase in the number of massive cities and their surrounding areas is evidence of this staggering growth. If population predictions are accurate, by 2015 there will be 28 "megacities," each with a population of more than 10 million. Already, some 26 million people live in the metropolitan area of Tokyo, Japan, while more than 17 million live in São Paulo, Brazil. In the coming years the people in these crowded cities will consume huge supplies of resources, such as gasoline, heating oil, electricity, wood, fresh water, and food.

The most rapid population growth is occurring in developing nations. Where economic growth is slow, it is increasingly difficult to feed growing populations. The World Resources Institute (WRI)

reports that some 800 million people worldwide currently suffer from malnutrition. The WRI predicts that in 2010 that number will fall to 680 million.

Economic Development

Nations need healthy economies to feed, house, educate, and employ their citizens. In some cases, however, unregulated economic development has come at great cost to natural resources.

For example, the rate of **deforestation**—the clearing of forests—has increased as people seek timber and land for economic development. Experts from the World Resources Institute estimate that from 1960 to 1990, one fifth of the world's tropical forest was lost. These forests are home to a wide variety of species of plants, insects, and animals—many of which are now threatened with extinction. Deforestation also contributes to the world's pollution problems by destroying plants, which take in carbon dioxide and give off oxygen, thereby helping to keep the atmosphere's gases balanced.

Economic development also consumes energy resources, increasing demand for the world's non-renewable supplies of fossil fuels. Because the strains on these resources affect all countries, world leaders are working together to improve resource conservation methods and to promote sustainable development—economic development that does not lead to further resource depletion.

SECTION 3 REVIEW

1. Identify and Explain:
- global warming
- renewable resource
- nonrenewable resource
- deforestation

2. Identifying Concepts: Copy the chart below. Use it to list examples of renewable and nonrenewable resources.

Nonrenewable resources	Renewable resources

Homework Practice Online
keyword: SV3 HP23

3. Finding the Main Idea

a. What role does international trade play in protecting natural resources?

b. What are the sources of air pollution?

4. Writing and Critical Thinking

Drawing Conclusions: Do you think pollution in other countries should be a concern for the United States? Explain your answer.

Consider the following:
- the economic impact of pollution
- the political importance of certain regions to the United States

SECTION 4

U.S. RELATIONS WITH OTHER COUNTRIES

READ TO DISCOVER

1. How has the end of the Cold War affected the debate over U.S.-Japanese relations?
2. What issues have dominated U.S.-European relations since the end of the Cold War?
3. How have U.S. leaders addressed trade and human rights issues in relations with China?
4. How have intervention and efforts to expand trade marked U.S. relations with Latin America?
5. What has been U.S. policy toward Africa?

As you have read, nations are interdependent in many ways. As a result, the international relationships of the United States—as one of the world's most powerful countries—are particularly important. As noted in Chapter 10, during the Cold War many U.S. relationships were based on the policy of containment—stopping the spread of communism. With the end of the Cold War, U.S relations with the rest of the world have undergone significant change.

U.S.-Japanese Relations

The relationship between the United States and Japan has changed a great deal since the end of World War II. After the war, the United States played an important role in the restructuring of Japan's government and economy. Throughout the Cold War, Japan concentrated on economic growth while its defense needs were managed by the United States. When the U.S.-Japan Mutual Security Treaty was signed after World War II, U.S. leaders insisted upon this policy because they wanted Japan to become a strong capitalist and democratic ally rather than to revert to its hostile military practices of the first half of the twentieth century. In addition, the United States wanted to establish a political presence in Asia. Since the end of the Cold War, there has been increased and unresolved debate in both countries over whether this defense policy should continue.

Debate in the United States Supporters of the current relationship note that Japan has a long warrior tradition and was an aggressive military power during the 50 years prior to the end of World War II. They warn that a deterioration of the close U.S.-Japanese relationship could produce a re-armed, militaristic Japan.

Other people argue that Japan has shown for more than 50 years that it no longer supports the warrior tradition. In addition, some say that Japan should pay more for its own military defense now that it is a great economic power. This view that Japan should no longer get a "free ride" from the United States is largely a result of frustration at the growing and longtime U.S. trade deficit with Japan. The first such trade deficit occurred in 1965 but created little tension because few Japanese imports at that time competed with major U.S. industries. The trade deficit has continued to widen since then, and since the late

WORLD AFFAIRS *In 1996 President Clinton, shown here with Japanese prime minister Ryutaro Hashimoto, made a state visit to Japan to discuss trade relations.*
In what year did the United States have its first trade deficit with Japan?

SECTION 4

U.S. RELATIONS WITH OTHER COUNTRIES

Lesson Plans

For teaching strategies, see Lesson 23.4 located at the beginning of this chapter or the One-Stop Lesson Planner Strategy 23.4.

Section Assessment

To assess students' mastery of this section, have them complete Daily Quiz 23.4 in *Daily Quizzes with Answer Key.*

Caption Answer
1965

After World War II and during the Cold War, the United States managed Japan's defense needs while Japanese leaders concentrated on the country's internal affairs and economy. In 1997 Japan announced that in the event of a crisis outside of its territory, it might offer noncombat support to U.S. military forces. This announcement came after more than a year's effort to strengthen the U.S.-Japanese military alliance.

The Japanese government may yet back out of this tentative agreement. Some Japanese citizens contend that the agreement oversteps the guidelines set up in Japan's constitution—a constitution drafted by the United States during the occupation that followed World War II. Still, despite local and regional concerns over Japan's expanded military role, most experts predict that Japan will find it advantageous to continue a close relationship with the United States. ■

Caption Answer
because the Cold War has ended

1970s friction has increased as the quality of Japanese products has improved and U.S. consumption of Japanese goods has grown.

Debate in Japan While many Japanese also wish to maintain their current relationship with the United States, an increasing number believe that Japan cannot remain economically powerful and politically weak. They argue that Japan is a significant economic world power and for this reason must play a more active role in world affairs.

In the early 1990s, Japan moved cautiously—sometimes at the prodding of U.S. leaders—toward a more significant role in world military and political matters. In response to U.S. pressure, for example, Japan contributed $13 billion toward the 1991 Persian Gulf War against Iraq, the largest contribution of any non–Middle Eastern country. Then in 1992–93, Japan sent a limited number of peacekeeping soldiers to supervise elections in Cambodia. Japanese leaders also have formally requested a permanent seat on the UN Security Council. Boutros Boutros-Ghali, UN secretary-general from 1992 to 1996, proposed Japan's membership to the council.

U.S.-European Relations

U.S. relations with European countries also are undergoing change. Some people argue that U.S. relations with Western Europe have significantly decreased in importance since the passing of the Cold War. During the Cold War, Western Europe was vital to U.S. military interests, for it helped balance the Soviet satellite nations. Western Europe remains an important focus of U.S. foreign policy, however, because of close cultural and economic ties.

With the exception of occasional difficulties, trade friction with the European Union has not been as severe as with Japan, mainly because the United States and Europe have had relatively balanced trade. Recently, U.S. leaders have concentrated on building new relationships with the former communist countries of Eastern Europe and in the countries of the former Soviet

Union to resolve conflict in the region. As noted in Chapter 10, this has meant enlarging the membership of the North Atlantic Treaty Organization (NATO). In 1999 three new members were added—the Czech Republic, Hungary, and Poland.

Promoting Stability In the early 1990s U.S. relations with Eastern Europe focused on helping the region make a stable transition from communism. Some U.S. leaders worried that dramatic changes in Eastern European governments would lead to chaos, particularly in Russia and the other former Soviet republics.

In addition, many people worried about the fate of the former Soviet Union's stockpile of nuclear weapons, which was under the control of various former Soviet republics. Many were afraid that the weapons would not be handled safely or would fall into the hands of terrorists. U.S. foreign-policy advisers strongly recommended that these weapons be removed from some of these newly independent countries—for example, Ukraine and Belarus. These countries have since disposed of the weapons or have transferred them to Russia, where they were dismantled.

Foreign-policy experts also supported sending economic aid to Russia to ease its transition to a market economy. They hoped that economic aid would help stabilize Russia and promote democracy there. Critics of this policy worry about aiding a nation that could potentially move away from

WORLD AFFAIRS *Capitalist reforms in Eastern Europe have enabled the development of privately owned businesses, such as this snack shop in Poland.* **Why do some people believe that U.S. relations with Western Europe are no longer as important as they once were?**

WORLD AFFAIRS *Leaders of the Group of Eight member nations pose for a picture at their 2001 summit in Genoa, Italy.* **What does U.S. membership in the G8 show about the role of the United States in the World?**

democracy and back toward authoritarianism. Russia has, however, held democratic elections for president and for its national legislature. In 2000 Vladimir Putin—a supporter of democratic and capitalist reforms—was elected as Russia's second president. Communists and other authoritarians, however, have made strong gains in parliamentary elections. The future of Russia's move to democracy is not yet clear.

Dealing with Conflict Foreign-policy experts are debating how the United States should deal with fighting in some nations in southeastern Europe, where tensions among ethnic groups have erupted in brutal domestic conflicts. Some who believe there are no vital U.S. interests at stake in these conflicts support a minimal U.S. role. Others believe the United States has an interest in maintaining stability and preventing human rights violations anywhere in the world.

One of the greatest challenges for U.S. policy in this region has been how to handle conflicts in the former republics of Yugoslavia. As you read earlier, the United States sent troops to Bosnia and Herzegovina as part of a multinational peacekeeping force. It is not yet clear if efforts to stabilize the region will be successful.

C A S E   S T U D Y

The Group of Eight

WORLD AFFAIRS Throughout the Cold War the United States, Japan, and the major Western European countries formed close relationships. To further strengthen these relationships, the leaders of the United States, Japan, Great Britain, Germany, France, Italy, and Canada began holding annual meetings in 1976. These industrial democracies collectively called themselves the Group of Seven, or G7.

The G7 held annual summits in a different member country every year. These summits featured discussions of important economic and political issues that affect their countries and the international community. In 1996, for example, G7 members meeting in Lyons, France, adopted a number of measures designed to combat international terrorism. G7 leaders also addressed ways to promote trade and economic cooperation.

In 1991 the leader of the Soviet Union first joined G7 leaders at a postsummit meeting. After the dissolution of the Soviet Union, Russia's president continued to meet with the G7. At the annual summit in 1997, Russia became an official member, causing a name change to the Group of Eight, or G8. Recently, the G8 has vowed to fight worldwide problems, including poverty and the AIDS epidemic.

U.S.-Chinese Relations

Relations between the United States and China are increasingly important as China's political influence

Holt American Government Videodisc

The videodisc segment Trade Relations: Lifting the Embargo complements the Chapter 23 case study, The Group of Eight. Barcodes for the Spanish version of the video segment are available in *Holt American Government Videodisc Teacher's Guide.*

PLAY SEGMENT

PAUSE

RESUME PLAY

PLAY OPTION A

PLAY OPTION B

PLAY EPILOGUE

In October 1997 President Clinton invited Chinese president Jiang Zemin and his wife, Wang Yeping, to the United States to help improve U.S.-Chinese relations. The goodwill meeting was the first state visit in 12 years between leaders of the two countries. Divisive issues remain to be resolved including China's human rights violations—the most well-known incident being the 1989 Tiananmen Square Massacre—as well as China's control of Tibet, which was annexed by China in 1950, and China's approach to controlling nuclear and chemical weapons. ■

Caption Answer

Answers will vary, but students might mention the placing of sanctions on China.

and economic development are on the rise. During the 1970s and 1980s the relationship often was intertwined with Cold War politics. Though for different reasons, each country viewed the Soviet Union as a threat to its security. Dispute between China and Taiwan over Taiwan's sovreignty also complicated U.S. China relations. Taiwan was once part of China, which has not ruled out using force to reclaim the island. Unofficial talks have improved this often-tense situation in recent years. The U.S. maintains cultural and economic ties with both China and Taiwan. The relationship between the United States and China began to revolve primarily around two major issues: trade and human rights.

Trade Trade between the United States and China has been growing since Chinese communist leaders embarked on a program of economic change at the beginning of the 1980s. These changes included allowing foreign investment, adopting free-market reforms, and even setting up a stock market. Since then, U.S. businesses have been eager to enter the huge Chinese market. By the early 1990s, China was the United States's sixth-largest trading partner. As with Japan, however, a growing U.S. trade deficit with China has created some tensions between the two countries.

Human Rights The Chinese government's treatment of its citizens also has led to tensions with the United States. While undertaking significant economic reforms, Chinese leaders have refused to allow substantial political change, such as permitting dissent, or criticism of government policies. The government has held thousands of political prisoners who, according to international organizations as well as the U.S. State Department, are often tortured. The Chinese government has been criticized for the high number of crimes punishable by death and for its use of executed prisoners as a primary source of organ transplants.

In 1989 Chinese leaders ordered troops to crush massive, weeks-long demonstrations by students and other Chinese citizens who were calling for democratic reforms and an end to government corruption. The resulting massacre at Tiananmen Square in the capital, Beijing, left hundreds—possibly thousands—dead and thousands injured. Thousands of others were imprisoned.

U.S. Debate As a result of the Tiananmen Square Massacre, the U.S. government placed some sanctions on China and canceled most weapons sales to the nation. However, China's relations with the United States—and the rest of the world—are now greatly influenced by economic considerations. The U.S. government has never revoked China's most-favored-nation trading status in spite of the nation's human rights violations.

China's dual policy of economic reform and political authoritarianism has led to great debate among U.S. leaders over U.S.-China relations. Some have demanded trade restrictions to protest the Chinese government's violations of human rights. Others—focusing on the gains from tapping the huge Chinese market—have opposed such measures, also pointing out that isolating the country will only lead to a deterioration of the political situation, while closer ties with the West will strengthen the movement toward democracy in China. Overall, U.S.-Chinese relations are frequently rocky. U.S. officials have pressed China to improve its human rights record, and Chinese leaders have resented such interference with their internal affairs. In addition, efforts to solve trade and economic disputes have been difficult, though some agreements have been reached.

WORLD AFFAIRS *Millions of Chinese political protesters march in front of Mao Zedong's tomb in 1989. Chinese troops later crushed the demonstrations in Tiananmen Square.* **What effect did such actions have on U.S. foreign policy toward China?**

WORLD AFFAIRS *Ships load and unload goods at the Bay of Valparaíso, Chile. Latin American countries have recently opened their markets and expanded trade with the United States.* ***Historically, why did the U.S. government intervene in Latin American countries?***

U.S.-Latin American Relations

U.S. relations with Latin American countries have been dominated by the principle of realism. As noted in Chapter 10, realist doctrine stresses placing U.S. interests above all other considerations when dealing with foreign countries. This has often led relations between the United States and Latin American countries to be marked by two things: U.S. intervention in Latin American affairs and efforts to expand trade.

An Interventionist Past Historically, the United States has intervened in Latin American countries when U.S. leaders decided that doing so was necessary to protect U.S. interests. For example, the U.S. government has sent troops to Cuba, Nicaragua, Haiti, Mexico, and the Dominican Republic to protect U.S. citizens and investments during various crises.

Such intervention created considerable resentment among Latin Americans. At times this resentment was reflected in revolutionary movements against U.S.-supported governments in the region. In addition, some Latin American governments pursued economic policies designed to limit U.S. influence.

Expanding Trade Since the late 1980s, Latin American countries have increasingly opened their markets and expanded trade with the United States. For the first time ever, more or less democratic governments are in power today in every Latin American country besides Cuba. These changes have come as Latin American leaders try to duplicate the success of East Asian governments in developing their economies. As you read earlier, several Latin American countries also have moved to improve their economies by forming a regional trading bloc.

Mexico is a dramatic example of changing attitudes. In the past the Mexican government feared U.S. domination, so it restricted the ability of foreigners to own Mexican companies, kept natural resource industries such as oil under government control, and shielded industry by keeping imports low. In the 1990s, however, Mexico reduced trade barriers under NAFTA and opened industry to foreign investment. After some initial economic difficulties, Mexico's economy improved and trade among the NAFTA countries boomed. U.S. leaders now are debating whether to open NAFTA to include other Latin American countries.

U.S.-African Relations

Compared to its activity in other parts of the world, the United States has been relatively uninvolved in African affairs, particularly in recent years. Some U.S. officials, however, believe the United States

SECTION 4 REVIEW ANSWERS

1. Charts will vary but should reflect an understanding of U.S. relations with other countries.

2a. China wants to regain control over Taiwan but the U.S. maintains cultural and economic ties to Taiwan.

2b. They have opened their markets and expanded trade with the United States.

3. Answers will vary, but students should clearly state their opinion and offer support for it.

WORLD AFFAIRS *South African protesters demonstrate outside of the AIDS Trial in South Africa. The trial focused on the right of the South African government to purchase generic versions of AIDS medicines.* **Since the early 1990s what has been the focus of U.S. policy toward Africa?**

should increase its efforts to help African nations overcome longtime poverty, political oppression, and other difficulties. This position has generally received strong support among African Americans. For example, in the 1980s African American and civil rights leaders were instrumental in pushing the U.S. government to impose sanctions on South Africa for its racist policy of apartheid.

In 1991 South Africa ended apartheid. Since then, U.S. policy toward Africa has largely focused on humanitarian aid. As you read in Chapter 10, U.S. troops were sent to Somalia in 1992–93 to help feed starving people caught in a chaotic civil war. In 1994 the United States offered assistance in Rwanda, although on a much smaller scale than in Somalia. In addition to humanitarian goals, the U.S. State Department's policy goals concerning Africa include

★ supporting democratic institutions,

★ promoting sustainable economic growth,

★ and gaining greater African participation in dealing with issues such as AIDS and drug trafficking.

The United States has begun to reconsider its longtime support of old Cold War allies in Africa. In 1997, for example, the United States did not support longtime dictator and former ally President Mobutu Sese Seko when rebels ended his rule in Zaire and created the Democratic Republic of the Congo.

SECTION 4 REVIEW

1. Identifying Concepts: Copy the chart below. Use it to list the issues you think are most important to U.S. relations with each country or region.

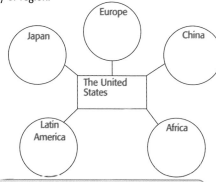

Homework Practice Online
keyword: SV3 HP23

2. **Finding the Main Idea**

a. How has China's relation to Taiwan complicated U.S.-Chinese relations?

b. How have many Latin American countries changed their economic and trade policies in recent years?

3. **Writing and Critical Thinking**

Evaluating: Do you think that U.S. relations with China and other countries should focus more on trade than on human rights? Explain your answer.

Consider:
• U.S. relations with Taiwan
• the importance of trade to the U.S. economy
• the government's role in creating trade policies

GOVERNMENT IN THE NEWS

Building a Coalition Against Terrorism

On September 11, 2001, in the most devastating attack ever on U.S. soil, terrorists hijacked four airliners, deliberately crashing two of them into the Twin Towers of the World Trade Center in New York City. A third plane crashed into the Pentagon in Washington, D.C., and the fourth went down in southern Pennsylvania. These coordinated attacks were soon linked to Osama bin Laden and a terrorist network known as al Qaeda, or "the Base." The ruling party of Afghanistan—known as the Taliban—had long harbored bin Laden and al Qaeda.

Less than a month later, President George W. Bush announced that the United States had begun air strikes aimed at destroying al Qaeda and the military capabilities of the Taliban regime in Afghanistan. In a television address to the country on October 7, Bush announced this latest effort against terrorism. "The battle is now joined on many fronts," he proclaimed. "We will not waver, we will not tire, we will not falter, and we will not fail."

The United States did not act alone. Great Britain announced the same day that it would send military troops to act in concert with the United States. The leaders of Australia, Canada, France, Germany, Italy, and Spain all vowed to cooperate with the U.S. military and to provide military assistance. The presidents of Mexico and Russia pledged moral support for the actions against terrorists.

While Western countries were quick to back U.S. efforts, U.S. officials needed to consult countries located near or next to Afghanistan in order to secure political support as well as the right to construct military bases in or fly over these countries. In the days before the announcement of air strikes, U.S. secretary of defense Donald Rumsfeld met with the leaders of Saudi Arabia, Oman, Egypt, Uzbekistan, and Turkey. Turkey, a member of NATO,

U.S. Secretary of Defense Donald Rumsfeld with Hamid Karzai. Karzai became Afghanistan's Interim Authority Chairman after the Taliban was driven from power.

gave the United States the full use of its airspace and military bases. Oman and Uzbekistan agreed to let the United States use their airspace and airfields. Saudi Arabia and Egypt pledged vocal—but not military—support for the U.S. actions. On October 10 Pakistan, which borders Afghanistan, permitted the United States to use two of its airfields.

After forming this coalition, the United States began air strikes against Afghanistan, targeting al Qaeda training camps and Taliban military sites. U.S. airplanes also dropped food packages over areas in Afghanistan that faced famine. Less than two weeks later, the U.S. armed forces launched the first operations using ground troops.

What Do You Think?

1. What political and geographic factors influenced the coalition formed by the United States?

2. How does the war on terrorism differ from other wars in U.S. history?

> **WHY IT MATTERS TODAY**
>
> The war on terrorism began with U.S. and British air strikes against bin Laden's al Qaeda network in Afghanistan. Use CNNfyi.com or other current events sources to find information on the progress of the war on terrorism.
>
> CNN fyi.com

Government in the News Answers

1. Students might suggest that the traditional political and military allies of the United States quickly lent their support to U.S. efforts against al Qaeda and the Taliban but that the United States had to work to obtain the support of countries located near or next to Afghanistan.

2. Students might suggest that unlike previous wars, the war on terrorism is not aimed at a country; instead it is aimed at those who commit or support terrorism, regardless of nationality.

CHAPTER 23
Review Answers

Writing a Summary
Summaries should focus on the main points of each section. These may be found in the Read to Discover questions at the start of each section. Summaries should also use standard grammar, spelling, sentence structure, and punctuation.

Identifying Ideas
Refer to the following pages: interdependence (527), refugee (527), nuclear proliferation (529), international law (532), developed nation (533), developing nation (533), comparative advantage (534), trading bloc (534), trade deficit (537), renewable resource (540)

(Continued on page 550)

Review

(Continued from page 549)

arise in the value of the U.S. dollar. Thus, U.S. exports become more expensive and the United States sells less, which may produce some unemployment.

3. opens markets to businesses, gives consumers access to foreign-made goods, lowers prices, raises quality

4. The problems of pollution and scarcity of resources have caused countries to try to work together to find solutions, even though scientists do not fully agree on the problems' causes and consequences.

5. to promote trade and protect human rights while preventing conflict between China and Taiwan

6. European—to help Eastern Europe achieve a peaceful transition from communism to capitalism; Africa—to supply humanitarian aid

Reviewing Themes
1. Answers will vary, but students may suggest that countries with economic ties are less likely to go to war with one another.
2. Answers will vary, but students should state their opinion and offer support for it.
3. Answers will vary, but students should state their opinions and offer logical explanations for them.

Thinking Critically
1. Answers will vary, but students should state their opinion and explain their reasoning.
2. Answers will vary, but students should explain the importance of the regions they choose.

(Continued on page 551)

Writing a Summary
Using standard grammar, spelling, sentence structure, and punctuation, write a summary of the information in this chapter.

Identifying Ideas
Identify the following terms and explain their significance.

1. interdependence
2. refugee
3. nuclear proliferation
4. international law
5. developed nation
6. developing nation
7. comparative advantage
8. trading bloc
9. trade deficit
10. renewable resource

Understanding Main Ideas
SECTION 1 *(pp. 527–532)*

1. How have nations around the world worked together to ease conflict?

SECTION 2 *(pp. 533–537)*

2. How might long-term trade deficits harm the U.S. economy?

3. In what ways does international trade help a country's economy?

SECTION 3 *(pp. 538–542)*

4. How do pollution and the scarcity of natural resources challenge the world's countries?

SECTION 4 *(pp. 543–548)*

5. What has been the focus of U.S. relations with China and Taiwan?

6. What has been the focus of U.S. relations with European and with African countries since the end of the Cold War?

Reviewing Themes
1. World Affairs In what ways do you think that promoting international trade also promotes worldwide collective security?

2. Political Processes The five permanent members of the UN Security Council have veto power. In some ways, that might be like giving California, Texas, and New York veto power over the actions of Congress. Why do you suppose these five countries have veto power?

3. Public Good Some people argue that the U.S. government can best promote the public good by concentrating on solving problems in this country before helping other countries through humanitarian aid and other assistance. Do you agree with this argument? Why or why not?

Thinking Critically
1. Decision Making Do you think the government should be involved in setting international trade policies? Explain your answer.

2. Making Predictions Which regions do you think will be of greatest economic and political importance to the United States in the future? Explain your answer.

3. Evaluating Do you think the world's developed countries have any responsibilities to poorer countries?

Writing about Government
Review in your Government Notebook how you answered the question at the beginning of the chapter about why it is important to understand how events elsewhere in the world affect the United States. Now that you have finished studying this chapter, would you change your answer? Respond in your Notebook.

Interpreting the Visual Record

Study the table below. Then use it to help you answer the questions that follow.

Population of Central America

Country	Population	Annual Rate of Growth	Pop. Per sq. mile
Belize	256,062	2.7	29
El Salvador	6,237,662	1.9	780
Guatemala	12,974,361	2.6	310
Costa Rica	3,773,057	1.7	193
Honduras	6,406,052	2.4	148
Nicaragua	4,918,393	2.2	106
Panama	2,845,647	1.3	97

Source: CIA World Factbook 2001

1. Which nation has the lowest population density?
- **a.** Belize
- **b.** Guatemala
- **c.** Honduras
- **d.** Panama

2. Which nation do you think is most likely to experience problems related to population growth?

Analyzing Primary Sources

THE UN SECRETARY-GENERAL'S ANNUAL REPORT

Kofi Annan of Ghana, the secretary-general of the United Nations, is responsible for generating an annual report on the work of the UN. The excerpt below, from the 1997 report, discusses the organization's desire to peacefully resolve conflict between countries. Read the excerpt and answer the questions that follow.

"The prevention of conflict both within and between States requires, first of all, ongoing attention to possible sources of tension and prompt action to ensure that tension does not evolve into conflict. During the past year, the Secretariat, in cooperation with other branches of the United Nations system, has worked to strengthen its global watch, which is designed to detect threats to international peace and security, enabling the Security Council to carry out or to foster preventive action.

Cooperation with regional organizations offers great potential. Close contacts with the Organization of African Unity (OAU) are a case in point. The two secretariats engage in almost daily consultations. . . . There is also increased cooperation between the United Nations and subregional organizations such as the Economic Community of West African States and the Southern African Development Community."

3. Which of the following statements best reflects Annan's point of view?
- **a.** conflict cannot be prevented
- **b.** only force can end conflict
- **c.** cooperation can prevent conflict
- **d.** only the UN can prevent conflict

4. What are some of the regional organizations that cooperate with the United Nations?

Alternative Assessment

Building Your Portfolio

Imagine that you have been chosen to develop a United Student World Assembly (USWA). Among the assembly's goals are promoting cooperation and understanding among students around the world. You must prepare a draft charter of the USWA. The charter should include a brief preamble explaining the goals of the USWA, the structure of the organization, the location(s) for assembly meetings, and the rules for making decisions. Present your charter to the class.

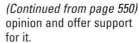

☐ internet connect

Internet Activity: go.hrw.com
KEYWORD: SV3 GV23

Have students access the Internet through the HRW Go site to conduct research on the effects of NAFTA on employment and the economy. Then ask students to create a brochure that illustrates the impact of NAFTA on business, workers, and global cultures. Use standard grammar, puctuation, spelling, and sentence structure in your brochure.

(Continued from page 550)
opinion and offer support for it.
3. Answers will vary, but students should state their opinions and offer logical explanations for them.

Thinking Critically
1. Answers will vary, but students should state their opinion and explain their reasoning.
2. Answers will vary, but students should explain the importance of the regions they choose.
3. Answers will vary, but students should state their opinions and provide support.

Writing About Government
The Government Notebook is a follow-up activity to the notebook activity that appears on page 526.

Building Social Studies Skills
1. a
2. Answers will vary, but students should suggest a link between a nation's rate of population growth and its population density.
3. c
4. Organization of African Unity (OAU), Economic Community of West African States, Southern African Development Community

Alternative Assessment
To assess this activity see Writing to Describe in *Alternative Assessment Handbook*.

The Unit 8 Public Policy Lab incorporates the following objectives:

▶ review information about a potential conflict between two fictional countries.

▶ develop a policy concerning the potential conflict.

▶ use a problem-solving process to prepare a report to the UN General Assembly outlining a plan to prevent the conflict.

Using the Lab

Before beginning the lab, organize students into groups and distribute copies of the Public Policy Lab Unit 8 Activity found in *Unit Tests and Unit Lab Activities with Answer Key.* Then have students read the assignment on this page. Discuss the assignment with students and point out the documents on pages 553–55 that students will use during the lab.

The What Do You Think? questions on pages 553–55 will help guide students during the project. In addition, the lab worksheet includes a step-by-step checklist for students to monitor their progress. For assessment guidelines, use the Problem Solving rubric in the *Alternative Assessment Handbook.*

PUBLIC POLICY LAB

You Solve the Problem

United Nations Ambassador for a Day

*I*magine that you are the ambassador representing the United States, Russia, China, France, or the United Kingdom on the United Nations Security Council. Work together with your group–the other Security Council members–to prevent a conflict between two fictional neighboring countries–Zelsa and Karnosh.

Review the supplied documents about the potential conflict and work with the other ambassadors to develop a policy for resolving the conflict. All five permanent members of the Security Council may veto any proposed action. Your policy must be approved by all the members of your group.

When your group has agreed upon a solution to this problem, prepare a formal report to the UN General Assembly. Your report should outline the specific steps that the Security Council authorizes member countries to take to prevent a conflict.

Government Notebook Assignment

Record your problem-solving process in your Government Notebook.

1. Review the documents and answer the WHAT DO YOU THINK? questions.

2. Identify the problem you are trying to solve with this policy.

3. Gather information on the types of actions the UN Security Council can take and how your assigned country might react to this type of situation.

4. List and consider the options you have in drafting this policy. Consider the advantages and disadvantages associated with each of these options.

5. Choose and implement a solution by meeting with your group to debate a course of action. Prepare a formal report describing the policy adopted by your group.

6. As a class, evaluate the effectiveness of different solutions by contrasting the formal reports prepared by different groups.

UNITED NATIONS
SECURITY COUNCIL

STAFF REPORT: History of Tensions Between Zelsa and Karnosh

The countries of Zelsa and Karnosh share a common border. Although they historically have been rivals, in the last few decades the two countries have been particularly hostile to each other. In part, this is because they have two very different political and economic systems. Zelsa has an authoritarian, communist government, while Karnosh has a democratic government and a capitalist economy.

In addition, the Zelsan government has demanded that Karnosh sacrifice control of the island of Casbah. The island, which lies off the coast of Karnosh near the border with Zelsa, belonged to Zelsa before it was seized by Karnosh following a war between the two nations 90 years ago. Before it lost control of Casbah, Zelsa had ruled the island for almost two centuries. The island still has a large Zelsan minority. Rich oil deposits also are believed to exist in the waters surrounding Casbah.

Over the years, each side has from time to time accused the other of hostile actions toward the other. Zelsan and Karnoshian troops have clashed in minor skirmishes along the border five times over the past quarter of a century. Two of those skirmishes have occurred in the last two years.

The following facts pertaining to each country further clarify the situation:

Karnosh
- Population: 23.2 million
- Political system: democratic
- Economy: capitalist, free-market
- Per capita GDP (in U.S. dollars): $19,200
- Military size: 300,000 (2.2 million reservists)

Zelsa
- Population: 17.9 million
- Political system: communist
- Economy: command economy
- Per capita GDP (in U.S. dollars): $8,800
- Military size: 900,000 (1.9 million reservists)

(1)

◀ WHAT DO YOU THINK?

1. What are the historic causes of tensions between Zelsa and Karnosh? What do you think is the chance that those tensions will erupt into war between the two countries?

2. How could war between Zelsa and Karnosh affect China, the United States, France, and the United Kingdom? How does Zelsa's friendship with China and Karnosh's friendship with the other three countries complicate the question of UN intervention?

UNITED NATIONS SECURITY COUNCIL

Zelsan officials claim that the Karnoshian government discriminates against the Zelsan minority on Casbah. In addition, Zelsan officials argue that rich oil deposits in the waters surrounding Casbah should belong to their country instead of to Karnosh.

The Zelsan government, therefore, has intensified its demands that Karnosh hand over the island. Those demands have been matched by increased military activity along the Zelsan-Karnoshian border. Two months ago a border skirmish between the countries' troops caused roughly 50 casualties on each side.

War between the two countries could have serious consequences for other countries. China, for example, has long been an ally of Zelsa and is one of that country's largest trading partners. On the other hand, the United States, France, and the United Kingdom have friendly trade and military relations with Karnosh. War between Karnosh and Zelsa, therefore, could pose economic problems for four members of the UN Security Council. In addition, a Zelsan-Karnoshian war could increase tensions between China and the three UN Security Council member countries allied with Karnosh.

The United Nations has a number of options:
1. insisting that Zelsa and Karnosh meet with an impartial body to decide how to protect the rights of Zelsans on Casbah and how to divide the revenue from any oil deposits,
2. sending peacekeeping troops to patrol the Zelsan-Karnoshian border,
3. threatening to cut off trade with Zelsa if its troops either invade Karnosh or try to take Casbah by force, or
4. sending UN forces to fight alongside Karnosh if it is invaded–an action similar to what happened in South Korea in 1950

What Do You Think?
Answers

1. The island of Casbah was seized by Karnosh from Zalsa following a war between the nations 90 years ago and now Zelsa claims Zelsans on the Karnoshian island of Casbah face official discrimination. Also, Zelsan officials claim oil deposits in waters around the island should belong to their country. Without outside intervention, war appears likely.

2. War could disrupt trade with countries friendly to Zelsa and Karnosh. Because they each—along with Russia—have veto power on the Security Council, China, the United States, France, and the United Kingdom must all agree on what action the UN should take.

PUBLIC POLICY LAB *continued*

U.S. and World News

Casbah Residents Brace for Conflict

By Evelyn Washington
Worldwide News Service

CASBAH, Karnosh—People on this Karnoshian island are anxiously waiting as Zelsan troops assemble across the border from Karnosh. War, Casbah residents say, would devastate the island and its economy.

"We've spent decades creating a good standard of living for our people, and now war threatens it all," said Lilal Heptat, mayor of Casbah City.

Many members of the Zelsan ethnic minority on Casbah, however, believe that the high standard of living for the majority of the island's residents has been purchased at their expense. In fact, ethnic Zelsans charge that they face discrimination by the Karnoshian majority, particularly in housing and employment.

"If it takes war to change the situation, then we should welcome it," said Metie Sax, a Zelsan community leader. Sax provides various examples of discrimination, such as Zelsans who have been refused jobs or been beaten by Karnoshian gangs.

Not all ethnic Zelsans agree, however. Some, who spoke on the condition that they not be identified, said that discrimination is not a big problem on the island. In fact, say some Zelsan sources, the beatings that Sax mentions are the work of criminal gangs who prey on Karnoshian victims as well as Zelsans.

Some Karnoshian officials say that the government in nearby Zelsa has encouraged ethnic Zelsans on Casbah to exaggerate their claims of discrimination.

"It's all a ploy to force Karnosh to turn over Casbah to the Zelsans," Mayor Heptat said. "Zelsa desperately wants control of the rich oil deposits in the waters that surround our island."

Meanwhile, demonstrations against the Karnoshian rule of Casbah are continuing in the Zelsan capital. An estimated 300,000 people marched through the streets of the capital yesterday, calling on the Zelsan military to seize the island. Zelsan media, all under government control, also have demanded that Casbah be returned to Zelsa. Casbah became a Karnoshian territory following a war between the two countries 90 years ago. Karnoshian officials have announced that military reservists may be called to active duty next week.

WHAT DO YOU THINK? ▶

1. What do Bellany officials fear would happen if war were to break out between Karnosh and Zelsa?

◀ WHAT DO YOU THINK?

1. Do you think that Zelsan media coverage might provide important clues about the intentions of the Zelsan government? Why or why not?

2. Because Karnosh took control of Casbah after a war nearly a century ago, do you think Zelsa has a right to demand the return of the island now? Why or why not?

The Republic of Bellany

United Nations Secretary-General
New York, New York

Dear Madame Secretary-General:

As you are aware, troops from Zelsa and Karnosh have been gathering along their common border. It appears that war may soon break out between the two countries. In fact, Zelsan officials have been threatening to send their troops to invade Karnosh and seize the island of Casbah.

War would be disastrous, not just for those two countries but also for my own country, Bellany. My people fear that if fighting breaks out, millions of Karnoshian and Zelsan refugees would flee to Bellany. Our country simply does not have the resources to feed and protect so many refugees. In addition, we fear that tensions between the citizens of Bellany and the refugees could erupt into violence.

Therefore, the government of Bellany urges the United Nations to act to prevent a war. Without strong UN action, we believe that war between Karnosh and Zelsa is certain.

Sincerely,

Layson Meiibus
Prime Minister
Republic of Bellany

UNITED STATES JOINT CHIEFS OF STAFF

POSSIBILITIES FOR INTERVENTION IN THE KARNOSHIAN-ZELSAN CONFLICT

Below are estimates of the resources needed should the UN Security Council decide to send troops as peacekeepers or to support Karnosh against a Zelsan invasion.

PEACEKEEPING

The United Nations has spent billions of dollars on a variety of peacekeeping missions. It spent $2.8 billion in 1995 on such missions and spent $1.4 billion in 1996. The drop in spending between these two years largely reflects the end of UN peacekeeping operations in Bosnia. In 1996, UN troops were replaced by about 60,000 troops from the North Atlantic Treaty Organization, sent to help maintain peace after years of civil war.

Based on past UN and NATO experiences, a peacekeeping mission along the Karnosh-Zelsa border could be expensive, both financially and in terms of personnel. In fact, UN member countries should be prepared to provide about 50,000 peacekeeping troops. Supporting this force likely would cost about $3–4 billion annually.

Supporting Karnosh

If the Security Council sends troops to Karnosh to stop a Zelsan invasion, costs will increase dramatically. Financial costs are difficult to estimate, but the number of troops needed for such a mission would likely exceed 100,000.

Sources of Support

The United States likely would play an important role in UN peacekeeping efforts in Karnosh. While the United States provided only about 3 percent of UN peacekeeping troops in 1996, it paid a full quarter of UN peacekeeping costs that year. As of mid-1997 the United States also kept a force of 37,000 on the Korean Peninsula, where UN forces went in 1950 to defend South Korea from a North Korean invasion.

The United States also has been an important part of non-UN peacekeeping efforts, such as those in Bosnia. U.S. forces made up nearly a third of the 60,000 NATO peacekeeping troops in Bosnia in 1996.

Nevertheless, since 1945 some 110 countries have contributed personnel to peacekeeping missions around the world. In addition, about three quarters of UN peacekeeping costs are paid by countries other than the United States. It is likely, then, that many UN members would be called on to support a peacekeeping mission in Karnosh or to help defend that country from a Zelsan invasion.

◀ WHAT DO YOU THINK?

1. According to the U.S. Joint Chiefs of Staff, how much might a peacekeeping mission to Karnosh cost the United Nations?

2. Why do you suppose that the United States has been an important source of financial and military support for peacekeeping missions and for the defense of countries such as South Korea?

3. Do you believe the United States should work with other UN members to prevent a war between Karnosh and Zelsa, or to defend Karnosh if needed? Why or why not?

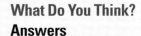

🖳 internet connect

Internet Activity go.hrw.com
KEYWORD: SV3 GVPL

Access the Internet through the HRW Go Site to use a problem-solving process to develop a policy that resolves the conflict between Zelsa and Karnosh. Research links and a problem-solving tutorial are provided.

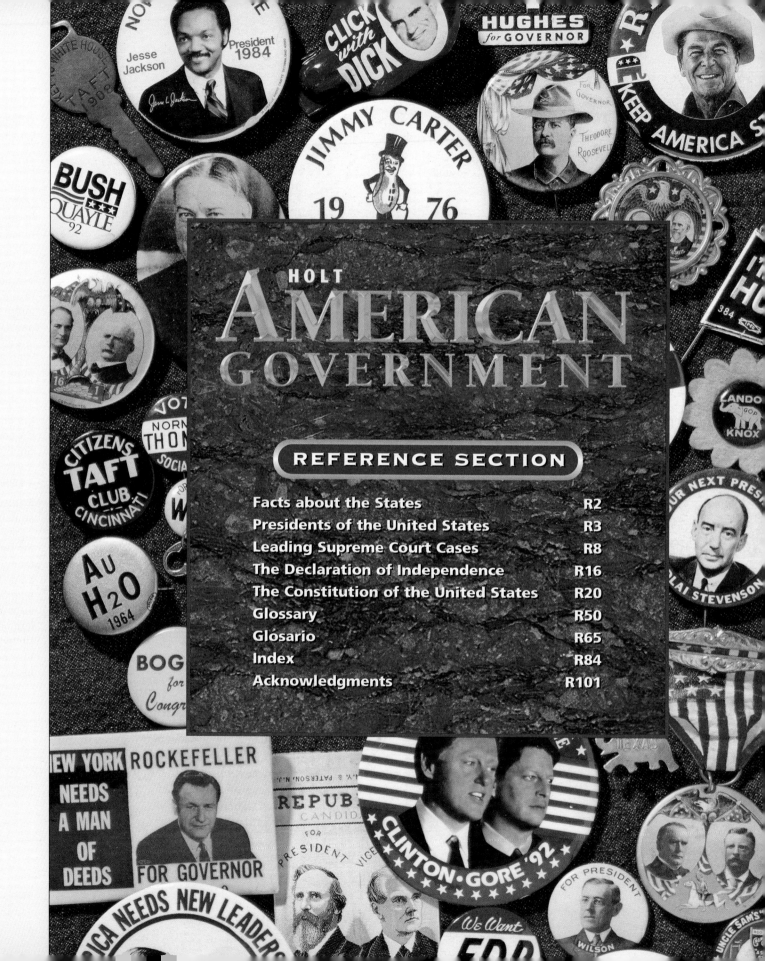

HOLT
AMERICAN GOVERNMENT

REFERENCE SECTION

FACTS ABOUT THE STATES

State	Year of Statehood	2000 Population	Reps. in the House	Area (sq. mi.)	Population Density (sq. mi.)	Capital
Alabama	1819	4,461,130	7	51,705	86.3	Montgomery
Alaska	1959	628,933	1	591,004	1.1	Juneau
Arizona	1912	5,140,683	8	114,000	45.1	Phoenix
Arkansas	1836	2,679,733	4	53,187	50.4	Little Rock
California	1850	33,930,798	53	158,706	213.8	Sacramento
Colorado	1876	4,311,882	7	104,247	41.4	Denver
Connecticut	1788	3,409,535	5	5,018	679.5	Hartford
Delaware	1787	785,068	1	2,057	381.7	Dover
District of Columbia	–	572,059	–	69	8,290.7	–
Florida	1845	16,028,890	25	58,664	273.2	Tallahassee
Georgia	1788	8,206,975	13	58,910	139.3	Atlanta
Hawaii	1959	1,216,642	2	6,471	188.0	Honolulu
Idaho	1890	1,297,274	2	83,557	15.5	Boise
Illinois	1818	12,439,042	19	56,400	220.6	Springfield
Indiana	1816	6,090,782	9	36,291	167.8	Indianapolis
Iowa	1846	2,931,923	5	56,275	52.1	Des Moines
Kansas	1861	2,693,824	4	82,277	32.7	Topeka
Kentucky	1792	4,049,431	6	40,395	100.2	Frankfort
Louisiana	1812	4,480,271	7	48,523	92.3	Baton Rouge
Maine	1820	1,277,731	2	33,265	38.4	Augusta
Maryland	1788	5,307,886	8	10,460	507.4	Annapolis
Massachusetts	1788	6,355,568	10	8,284	767.2	Boston
Michigan	1837	9,955,829	15	58,527	170.1	Lansing
Minnesota	1858	4,925,670	8	84,068	58.6	St. Paul
Mississippi	1817	2,852,927	4	47,689	59.8	Jackson
Missouri	1821	5,606,260	9	69,697	80.4	Jefferson City
Montana	1889	905,316	1	147,046	6.2	Helena
Nebraska	1867	1,715,369	3	77,355	22.2	Lincoln
Nevada	1864	2,002,032	3	110,561	18.1	Carson City
New Hampshire	1788	1,238,415	2	9,279	133.5	Concord
New Jersey	1787	8,424,354	13	7,787	1,081.8	Trenton
New Mexico	1912	1,823,821	3	121,593	15.0	Santa Fe
New York	1788	19,004,973	29	49,576	383.4	Albany
North Carolina	1789	8,067,673	13	52,669	153.2	Raleigh
North Dakota	1889	643,756	1	70,655	9.1	Bismarck
Ohio	1803	11,374,540	18	41,222	275.9	Columbus
Oklahoma	1907	3,458,819	5	69,956	49.4	Oklahoma City
Oregon	1859	3,428,543	5	97,073	35.3	Salem
Pennsylvania	1787	12,300,670	19	45,333	271.3	Harrisburg
Rhode Island	1790	1,049,662	2	1,212	866.1	Providence
South Carolina	1788	4,025,061	6	31,113	129.4	Columbia
South Dakota	1889	756,874	1	77,116	9.8	Pierre
Tennessee	1796	5,700,037	9	42,144	135.3	Nashville
Texas	1845	20,903,994	32	266,807	78.3	Austin
Utah	1896	2,236,714	3	84,899	26.3	Salt Lake City
Vermont	1791	609,890	1	9,609	63.5	Montpelier
Virginia	1788	7,100,702	11	40,767	174.2	Richmond
Washington	1889	5,908,684	9	68,192	86.6	Olympia
West Virginia	1863	1,813,077	3	24,181	75.0	Charleston
Wisconsin	1848	5,371,210	8	56,154	95.7	Madison
Wyoming	1890	495,304	1	97,914	5.1	Cheyenne

The Official Portraits

1 George Washington

Born: 1732   **Died:** 1799
Years in Office: 1789–97
Political Party: None
Home State: Virginia
Vice President: John Adams

2 John Adams

Born: 1735   **Died:** 1826
Years in Office: 1797–1801
Political Party: Federalist
Home State: Massachusetts
Vice President: Thomas Jefferson

3 Thomas Jefferson

Born: 1743   **Died:** 1826
Years in Office: 1801–09
Political Party: Republican*
Home State: Virginia
Vice Presidents: Aaron Burr, George Clinton

4 James Madison

Born: 1751   **Died:** 1836
Years in Office: 1809–17
Political Party: Republican
Home State: Virginia
Vice Presidents: George Clinton, Elbridge Gerry

5 James Monroe

Born: 1758   **Died:** 1831
Years in Office: 1817–25
Political Party: Republican
Home State: Virginia
Vice President: Daniel D. Tompkins

6 John Quincy Adams

Born: 1767   **Died:** 1848
Years in Office: 1825–29
Political Party: Republican
Home State: Massachusetts
Vice President: John C. Calhoun

7 Andrew Jackson

Born: 1767   **Died:** 1845
Years in Office: 1829–37
Political Party: Democratic
Home State: Tennessee
Vice Presidents: John C. Calhoun, Martin Van Buren

8 Martin Van Buren

Born: 1782   **Died:** 1862
Years in Office: 1837–41
Political Party: Democratic
Home State: New York
Vice President: Richard M. Johnson

* The Republican Party of the third through sixth presidents is not the Republican Party of Abraham Lincoln, which was founded in 1854.

9 William Henry Harrison
Born: 1773   **Died:** 1841
Years in Office: 1841
Political Party: Whig
Home State: Ohio
Vice President: John Tyler

10 John Tyler
Born: 1790   **Died:** 1862
Years in Office: 1841–45
Political Party: Whig
Home State: Virginia
Vice President: None

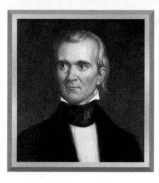

11 James K. Polk
Born: 1795   **Died:** 1849
Years in Office: 1845–49
Political Party: Democratic
Home State: Tennessee
Vice President: George M. Dallas

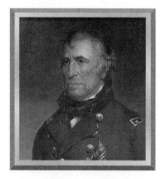

12 Zachary Taylor
Born: 1784   **Died:** 1850
Years in Office: 1849–50
Political Party: Whig
Home State: Louisiana
Vice President: Millard Fillmore

13 Millard Fillmore
Born: 1800   **Died:** 1874
Years in Office: 1850–53
Political Party: Whig
Home State: New York
Vice President: None

14 Franklin Pierce
Born: 1804   **Died:** 1869
Years in Office: 1853–57
Political Party: Democratic
Home State: New Hampshire
Vice President: William R. King

15 James Buchanan
Born: 1791   **Died:** 1868
Years in Office: 1857–61
Political Party: Democratic
Home State: Pennsylvania
Vice President: John C. Breckinridge

16 Abraham Lincoln
Born: 1809   **Died:** 1865
Years in Office: 1861–65
Political Party: Republican
Home State: Illinois
Vice President: Hannibal Hamlin, Andrew Johnson

17 Andrew Johnson
Born: 1808   **Died:** 1875
Years in Office: 1865-69
Political Party: Republican
Home State: Tennessee
Vice President: None

18 Ulysses S. Grant

Born: 1822 **Died:** 1885
Years in Office: 1869–77
Political Party: Republican
Home State: Illinois
Vice President: Schuyler Colfax,
Henry Wilson

19 Rutherford B. Hayes

Born: 1822 **Died:** 1893
Years in Office: 1877–81
Political Party: Republican
Home State: Ohio
Vice President: William A. Wheeler

20 James A. Garfield

Born: 1831 **Died:** 1881
Years in Office: 1881
Political Party: Republican
Home State: Ohio
Vice President: Chester A. Arthur

21 Chester A. Arthur

Born: 1829 **Died:** 1886
Years in Office: 1881–85
Political Party: Republican
Home State: New York
Vice President: None

22 Grover Cleveland

Born: 1837 **Died:** 1908
Years in Office: 1885–89
Political Party: Democratic
Home State: New York
Vice President: Thomas A.
Hendricks

23 Benjamin Harrison

Born: 1833 **Died:** 1901
Years in Office: 1889–93
Political Party: Republican
Home State: Indiana
Vice President: Levi P. Morton

24 Grover Cleveland

Born: 1837 **Died:** 1908
Years in Office: 1893–97
Political Party: Democratic
Home State: New York
Vice President: Adlai E. Stevenson

25 William McKinley

Born: 1843 **Died:** 1901
Years in Office: 1897–1901
Political Party: Republican
Home State: Ohio
Vice President: Garret A. Hobart,
Theodore Roosevelt

26 Theodore Roosevelt

Born: 1858 **Died:** 1919
Years in Office: 1901-09
Political Party: Republican
Home State: New York
Vice President: Charles W. Fairbanks

27 William Howard Taft

Born: 1857   **Died:** 1930
Years in Office: 1909–13
Political Party: Republican
Home State: Ohio
Vice President: James S. Sherman

28 Woodrow Wilson

Born: 1856   **Died:** 1924
Years in Office: 1913–21
Political Party: Democratic
Home State: New Jersey
Vice President: Thomas R. Marshall

29 Warren G. Harding

Born: 1865   **Died:** 1923
Years in Office: 1921–23
Political Party: Republican
Home State: Ohio
Vice President: Calvin Coolidge

30 Calvin Coolidge

Born: 1872   **Died:** 1933
Years in Office: 1923–29
Political Party: Republican
Home State: Massachusetts
Vice President: Charles G. Dawes

31 Herbert Hoover

Born: 1874   **Died:** 1964
Years in Office: 1929–33
Political Party: Republican
Home State: California
Vice President: Charles Curtis

32 Franklin D. Roosevelt

Born: 1882   **Died:** 1945
Years in Office: 1933–45
Political Party: Democratic
Home State: New York
Vice President: John Nance Garner,
Henry Wallace, Harry S Truman

33 Harry S Truman

Born: 1884   **Died:** 1972
Years in Office: 1945–53
Political Party: Democratic
Home State: Missouri
Vice President: Alben W. Barkley

34 Dwight D. Eisenhower

Born: 1890   **Died:** 1969
Years in Office: 1953–61
Political Party: Republican
Home State: Kansas
Vice President: Richard M. Nixon

35 John F. Kennedy

Born: 1917   **Died:** 1963
Years in Office: 1961–63
Political Party: Democratic
Home State: Massachusetts
Vice President: Lyndon B. Johnson

36 Lyndon B. Johnson

Born: 1908   **Died:** 1973
Years in Office: 1963–69
Political Party: Democratic
Home State: Texas
Vice President: Hubert H. Humphrey

37 Richard M. Nixon

Born: 1913   **Died:** 1994
Years in Office: 1969–74
Political Party: Republican
Home State: California
Vice President: Spiro T. Agnew,
Gerald R. Ford

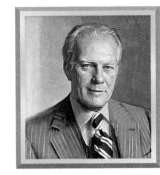

38 Gerald R. Ford

Born: 1913
Years in Office: 1974 77
Political Party: Republican
Home State: Michigan
Vice President: Nelson A.
Rockefeller

39 Jimmy Carter

Born: 1924
Years in Office: 1977–81
Political Party: Democratic
Home State: Georgia
Vice President: Walter F. Mondale

40 Ronald Reagan

Born: 1911
Years in Office: 1981–89
Political Party: Republican
Home State: California
Vice President: George Bush

41 George Bush

Born: 1924
Years in Office: 1989–93
Political Party: Republican
Home State: Texas
Vice President: Dan Quayle

42 Bill Clinton

Born: 1946
Years in Office: 1993–2001
Political Party: Democratic
Home State: Arkansas
Vice President: Al Gore

43 George W. Bush

Born: 1946
Years in Office: 2001–
Political Party: Republican
Home State: Texas
Vice President: Richard B. Cheney

LEADING SUPREME COURT CASES

1 *Marbury* v. *Madison*
1 Cranch (5 U.S.) 137 (1803)

What was this case about?

The story. The Federalist Party had been defeated in the election of 1800. However, President-elect Thomas Jefferson was not scheduled to take office until March 4, 1801. In the meantime, the outgoing president, John Adams, chose a number of Federalist supporters as justices of the peace in the District of Columbia. These justices received their appointments in the final hours of the Adams administration. However, they were unable to take office until their commissions were delivered. After the new president took over, he found that the previous secretary of state, John Marshall, had not had time to deliver all of the commissions. Jefferson immediately ordered his new secretary of state, James Madison, not to deliver the remaining commissions.

As one of the people whose commission was not delivered, William Marbury sued Madison. Marbury took advantage of a law passed by Congress that allowed him to make this kind of complaint directly to the Supreme Court. He asked the Court to order Madison to deliver the commission even though this request meant disobeying the president. Marbury probably expected the Court to do as he asked because John Marshall had been appointed Chief Justice of the United States.

The question. As Chief Justice Marshall saw it, the question before the Court had three parts. First, did Marbury have a right to receive the commission? Second, if he did have a right to the commission, was the government required to ensure that he received the commission? Finally, if the government was required to do so, would it have to order Madison to deliver Marbury's commission, as Marbury requested?

The issues. Chief Justice Marshall wanted the Court to be able to decide if laws passed by Congress were constitutional. Whether the Court had this power of judicial review—the power to decide if laws made by Congress are allowed by the Constitution—had not yet been decided. Marshall posed the question before the Court in three parts in order to discuss judicial review.

How was the case decided?

In 1803 the Court ruled against ordering Madison to deliver Marbury's commission.

What did the Court say about governmental powers?

The Court's reasoning passed through three stages:

Step 1. Pointing to a federal law that outlined the appointment process for District of Columbia justices of the peace, the Court said that Marbury had a right to the commission.

Step 2. The Court said that when government officials hurt people by neglecting legal duties, our laws require a remedy.

Step 3. Marbury had asked that the Supreme Court order Madison to deliver the commission. Here Chief Justice Marshall did something surprising. He declared that a court could issue such an order, but that the Supreme Court was not the right court to issue it.

Marbury had taken advantage of a federal law that allowed complaints such as his to be taken straight to the Supreme Court. However, Chief Justice Marshall declared this law unconstitutional. The Constitution mentions several kinds of cases that can be brought straight to the Supreme Court. All other kinds of cases must go through lower courts first. The chief justice explained that Marbury's lawsuit was one of the kinds of cases that must go through lower courts first. It did not matter that Congress had passed a law saying something different, because the Constitution is a higher law.

Marshall's cleverly written opinion excused the Supreme Court from hearing lawsuits such as the Marbury case before lower courts had heard them. Marshall accomplished this by claiming for the Court an even greater power—the power of judicial review.

What implications did this case have for the future?

If the Supreme Court did not have judicial review, Congress would decide for itself on the constitutionality of the laws it passed. Marshall's opinion in Marbury v. Madison removed that power from Congress. By deciding on the constitutionality of the other two branches' actions, the Supreme Court is the nation's final authority on the meaning of the Constitution.

2 *Martin* v. *Hunter's Lessee*
1 Wheaton (14 U.S.) 304 (1816)

What was this case about?

The story. In 1777, during the Revolutionary War, Virginia passed a law declaring that land owned by people who were still loyal to Great Britain no longer belonged to them. When Thomas Lord Fairfax died in England in 1782, his Virginia lands passed first to his American relative Denny Martin and then to Thomas Martin, Denny's nephew. However, Virginia gave Fairfax's land to David Hunter.

Thomas Martin considered himself the true owner of the land. Hunter disagreed and rented it to someone else. The renter (called the "lessee") tried to have Martin evicted. Virginia's highest court ruled that Hunter owned the land.

Martin appealed his case to the U.S. Supreme Court. He reminded the Court of the treaties between the United States and Britain. These treaties promised to protect the rights of British subjects who had owned property in America before the Revolution. Because of these treaties, he said, Virginia's 1777 law was not valid. The Supreme Court agreed. It sent the case back to the Virginia court with orders to change its decision.

However, the Virginia court denied that the Supreme Court had the authority to tell a state court what to do. Therefore, Martin asked the Supreme Court to reverse the Virginia court's judgment.

The question. In cases that involve the federal Constitution, laws, and treaties, does the Constitution give federal courts the power to reverse state court judgments?

The issues. In Marbury v. Madison the Supreme Court asserted the power of judicial review, but that did not settle the issue of how far the power of judicial review extends. In Marbury v. Madison one of the other branches of the federal government had been overruled, but in this case Martin was asking the Supreme Court to overrule one of the branches of a state government.

How was the case decided?
In 1816, in an opinion written by Justice Joseph Story, the Supreme Court did what Martin asked. It reversed the judgment of the Virginia court.

What did the Court say about governmental powers?
Justice Story thought that the Constitution gave the Supreme Court the power to reverse state courts in cases involving the federal Constitution, laws, and treaties. To explain his decision, he first tried to show why various objections to his view were mistaken. One such objection was that the Constitution does not affect state governments, but rather the people living in those states. Justice Story pointed out that the Constitution is "crowded" with conditions that affect the state governments. Another objection was that federal judges might abuse the power they had to decide the meaning of the

federal Constitution, laws, and treaties. Justice Story explained that the power of final decision has to be put somewhere and that it was placed with the Supreme Court.

Finally, Justice Story asserted the need for uniformity. If federal judges were not allowed to reverse state court judgments, then state courts all over the country might interpret the federal Constitution, laws, and treaties in different ways.

What implications did this case have for the future?
Under the Constitution, power is divided between two levels: state and national. U.S. history is full of various kinds of conflicts between the states and the national government. Usually, as in Martin v. Hunter's Lessee, the national government has won these conflicts. Thus, there has been a slow drift of power from the states to the national government. Justice Story, however, did not claim that federal courts could overrule state courts in all cases. He said only that they could overrule state courts in cases involving the U.S. Constitution, laws, and treaties.

3 *McCulloch* v. *Maryland*
4 Wheaton (17 U.S.) 316 (1819)

What was this case about?
The story. In 1791 Congress passed a law that set up the Bank of the United States. An attempt to renew the Bank's charter in 1811 failed. A number of states took advantage of this situation to charter their own banks.

After the War of 1812, the federal government needed money to pay for the war. Instead of being able to borrow money from one central bank, it had to deal with many state banks. Thus, Congress set up the Second Bank of the United States in 1816. The states generally opposed the National Bank, and several states passed laws that hindered it. For instance, they taxed branches of the Bank within their borders. When the Maryland branch of the Bank refused to pay the tax, Maryland sued the bank's cashier, James McCulloch. In 1819 the legal battle reached the Supreme Court.

The question. As Chief Justice John Marshall saw it, the question before the Court had two parts. Does the Constitution give Congress the power to establish a national bank? If so, does the Constitution allow a state to tax that bank?

The issues. The question of whether Congress had the power to establish a bank was not new. In 1791, after Congress had passed the bill that established the

First Bank of the United States, President George Washington had asked his cabinet for advice. He noted that although Article I, Section 8, of the Constitution lists the powers of Congress, it does not mention the power to charter a bank. Yet the article does state that in addition to the listed powers, Congress may also make all laws that are "necessary and proper" for carrying out the listed powers.

Alexander Hamilton and Thomas Jefferson presented Washington with sharply opposing views. Hamilton considered the power to charter a bank constitutional because it had "a natural relation" to the powers of collecting taxes and regulating trade. By contrast, Jefferson said that while the power to charter a bank may be "convenient" for carrying out this power, it was not "necessary," and thus was unconstitutional. Finding Hamilton's argument more convincing, Washington signed the bill. Maryland, however, wanted the Supreme Court to interpret the Constitution as Jefferson had done.

How was the case decided?

Led by Chief Justice Marshall, the Supreme Court ruled that the Constitution allowed Congress to establish the National Bank. The Court also asserted that the Constitution did not allow a state to tax the Bank.

What did the Court say about governmental powers?

Jefferson's argument against the First Bank of the United States had rested on a strict interpretation of the word "necessary" in the necessary and proper clause. The state of Maryland used the same argument. In deciding the first question, Marshall said that Maryland's interpretation of the Constitution was not broad enough. He explained that when the Constitution says that certain means are "necessary" to an end, it usually does not mean that the end cannot be achieved without them. Rather, it means that they are "calculated to produce" the end. The power to charter a bank is calculated to help carry out the other constitutional powers, so the Constitution permits it.

The second question before the Court was whether the Constitution allows a state to tax the National Bank. If the states could tax one of the federal government's activities, they could tax any of them. Marshall said that because "the power to tax involves the power to destroy," this could not be permitted. The supremacy clause in Article VI states that the Constitution and laws of the federal government come before state constitutions and laws.

What implications did this case have for the future?

As new cases arise, members of the Supreme Court try to settle them by using principles that have been established in earlier cases. This case involves the principles of implied powers and national supremacy. Some powers given to the federal government by the Constitution are listed. These are called enumerated powers. Others, called implied powers, are understood as given because they are needed to help carry out the enumerated powers. The federal government has only those powers that are enumerated and implied in the Constitution. However, when the federal government is using powers that do belong to it, the states must give way.

4 Scott v. Sandford
19 Howard (60 U.S.) 393 (1857)

What was this case about?

The story. In 1833 a slave named Dred Scott was purchased by John Emerson, an army doctor. As the army transferred Emerson from post to post, Scott went with him. First they went to Illinois; later they moved to Wisconsin Territory. When Emerson was transferred yet again, he sent Scott to Missouri, a slave state, to live with his wife, Eliza Irene Sanford Emerson. She inherited Scott when her husband died in 1843.

At this time, slavery was illegal in Illinois and in Wisconsin Territory. Scott believed that because he had lived on free soil for five years, he should be free.

In 1846 Emerson moved to New England and left Scott with sons of Scott's original owner. One son opposed the spread of slavery. He helped Scott file a lawsuit. In 1850 a Missouri court declared Scott free.

In 1852 the Missouri Supreme Court reversed the lower court's ruling. In 1854 lawyers who wanted the issue of slavery in the territories to be resolved filed Scott's lawsuit in federal court. Scott's case worked its way to the Supreme Court.

The question. As Chief Justice Roger B. Taney saw it, the case raised two questions. First, does the Constitution give an African American the right to file a suit in federal court? Second, does the Constitution allow Congress to pass a law that frees slaves who are brought into a free territory?

The issues. If African Americans were U.S. citizens, then they must have all of the rights of other citizens, including the right to sue in a federal court. Therefore, the first question before the court involved the Constitution's definition of a citizen.

The second question before the Court involved the kinds of limits the Constitution puts on laws about property. If slaves were property, then Congress faced the same limits when it made a law about slavery as when it made a law about property.

How was the case decided?
The Court ruled that the Constitution denied African Americans the right to sue in federal court and denied Congress the power to make a law abolishing or prohibiting slavery in the territories.

What did the Court say about constitutional rights?
The first theme of the Court's opinion was the relationship between race and citizenship. The opinion reflected the prejudices of the day. Taney said that African Americans had "none of the rights and privileges" of citizens. This statement was particularly startling because it applied to free African Americans as well as to slaves. Taney ignored the important fact that many states considered free African Americans to be state citizens. In addition, Article III, Section 2, of the Constitution gives the federal courts jurisdiction over various kinds of suits involving state citizens.

The other theme of the Court's opinion concerned slavery. The Fifth Amendment states that no one may be "deprived of life, liberty, or property, without due process of law." First, the chief justice reasoned that because slaves are "property," they could not be taken away without due process of law. Second, he reasoned that a law taking away citizens' property just because they entered a free territory cheated them of their due process of law. In addition, Taney ruled that the Missouri Compromise was unconstitutional.

What implications did this case have for the future?
By the time the Court made its decision, the Kansas-Nebraska Act had already canceled the Missouri Compromise's ban on slavery in certain federal territories. Therefore, it might seem that the Court's judgment did not matter. However, the Kansas-Nebraska Act was unpopular with people who opposed the spread of slavery. Many of them would have liked to have seen a return to something like the Missouri Compromise. The decision made such a return impossible and worsened the controversy over slavery in the territories.

Furthermore, this case established that merely freeing slaves was not enough to guarantee their U.S. citizenship. Not until 1868, when the Fourteenth Amendment was passed, did the Constitution guarantee that African Americans were U.S. citizens.

5 *Lochner* v. *New York*
198 U.S. 45 (1905)

What was this case about?
The story. In 1895 the New York legislature passed a law regulating the number of hours that bakery employees could be required or allowed to work. This law was necessary to prevent workers from having to agree to work long hours out of fear of losing their jobs. The legislature claimed that workers should not be allowed to work long hours because of potential harm to their health.

Joseph Lochner, a bakery owner convicted of violating the law, appealed. He said that the law was unconstitutional because it took away his liberty to make a contract. Lochner said that liberty of contract is promised by a clause in the Fourteenth Amendment that says that no state may "deprive any person of life, liberty, or property, without due process of law."

The question. Do limits on the number of hours an employee may work violate the Fourteenth Amendment?

The issues. State governments have a general power—called the police power—to make regulations that support the safety, health, morals, and general welfare of their citizens. The basic issue in this case is whether the Constitution can limit state governments' police power in some cases.

Various amendments set limits on the power of state governments, but the most general is the due process clause of the Fourteenth Amendment. To apply this clause to the New York bakery law, the Supreme Court had to decide what freedoms are meant by the word liberty and what is promised by the guarantee of due process of law.

How was the case decided?
The Court ruled that the law limiting the hours of labor in bakeries was unconstitutional.

What did the Court say about governmental powers?
Justice Rufus Wheeler Peckham argued that the New York legislature's interference with liberty of contract was improper. Peckham did not mean that the Constitution forbids all interference with liberty of contract. In fact, he stressed that the Court had approved a similar Utah law that said that no one could work more than eight hours a day in an underground mine except in cases of emergency. Such uses of the police power, he said, were "fair, reasonable, and appropriate." They regulate liberty without taking it away. By contrast, he argued, the New York law had nothing to do with safety, morals, or general welfare and was not necessary to protect health.

What implications did this case have for the future?
Even though the Court tries to rely on the same principles over and over, sometimes its members change their minds about controversial issues. Four justices dissented, or disagreed with the Lochner ruling. As the membership of the Supreme Court has changed, so have the attitudes of the justices. In 1937 the Court began to

reverse the precedent it had set in Lochner.

6 *Plessy* v. *Ferguson*
163 U.S. 537 (1896)
Brown v. *Board of Education*
347 U.S. 483 (1954)

What were these cases about?
The stories. These two cases illustrate a major change in the legality of racial segregation. Plessy v. Ferguson began with an 1890 Louisiana law that required all railway companies to provide "equal but separate" accommodations for white and African American passengers. A group of people who thought the law was unfair recruited Homer Plessy to get arrested in order to test the law. Plessy entered a train and took an empty seat in an all-white area. When he refused to move to an all-black section, he was arrested and jailed. In his defense, he said that the 1890 law was unconstitutional. The case eventually worked its way up to the Supreme Court.

More than 50 years later, an African American man named Oliver Brown and his family moved into a white neighborhood in Topeka, Kansas. The Browns assumed that their daughter Linda would attend the neighborhood school. Instead, the Board of Education ordered her to attend a distant all-black school that was supposedly "separate but equal." Charging that school segregation violated the Fourteenth Amendment to the Constitution, Mr. Brown sued the Board.

The question. The question raised by the Court was the same in both cases. Do racially segregated facilities violate the equal protection clause of the Fourteenth Amendment?

The issues. The state of Louisiana argued that separate railway carriages could be equal. For instance, they could be equally clean and equally safe. The state of Kansas said much the same thing, claiming that its all-black and all-white schools were equal in such features as teachers' skills and buildings' quality.

In the days of racial segregation, the claim that segregated facilities were equal in tangible, or measurable, features was almost always a terrible lie. The issue facing the Court, however, went deeper. Even if things were made equal in racially segregated facilities, was there something fundamentally unequal about segregation?

How were the cases decided?
In Plessy v. Ferguson, the Court ruled that the Fourteenth Amendment's equal protection clause allows racial segregation. In Brown v. Board of Education, however, the Court unanimously ruled that the clause does not allow racial segregation.

What did the Court say about constitutional rights?
Justice Henry Billings Brown wrote the Court's opinion in Plessy. He admitted that the purpose of the Fourteenth Amendment was "to enforce the absolute equality of the two races before the law." However, he said that this statement meant political equality, not social equality. Brown declared that there was no truth to the argument that separate facilities implied that African Americans were inferior.

In Brown the Court's opinion was written by Chief Justice Earl Warren. He said that separation of black schoolchildren from white schoolchildren of the same age and ability "generates a feeling of inferiority . . . that may affect their hearts and minds in a way unlikely ever to be undone." He said that when racial segregation is required by law, the harm is even greater. It makes no difference that "the physical facilities and other 'tangible' factors may be equal."

What implications did these cases have for the future?
In Brown v. Board of Education, the Court did not say that the "separate but equal" doctrine was completely invalid. It ruled that the doctrine had no place in public education. This statement, although limited, influenced future cases that eventually abolished all segregation. Taken together, Plessy and Brown show that interpretation of the Constitution's legal principles may change as society changes.

7 *Gideon* v. *Wainwright*
372 U.S. 335 (1963)

What was this case about?
The story. Clarence Earl Gideon was accused of breaking and entering a Florida poolroom. When Gideon's case came to trial, he could not afford a lawyer, so he asked that the court pay for one. The judge refused, the case proceeded, and Gideon was found guilty. While in prison, Gideon appealed to the U.S. Supreme Court. He claimed that by refusing to appoint him a lawyer, Florida had violated rights promised him by the Sixth and Fourteenth Amendments.

The question. Do the Sixth and the Fourteenth Amendments require that a poor person accused of a crime have access to an attorney free of charge?

The issues. The Sixth Amendment ensures certain rights to people accused of crimes. For example, "The accused shall enjoy the right .to have the Assistance of Counsel [a lawyer] for his defense." By itself, this amendment requires that poor people be provided with free lawyers in federal trials. Yet Gideon had been accused of breaking state laws and was tried in a state court. Still, the Fourteenth Amendment ensures that states cannot deprive people of life, liberty, or property without due process of law. Jailed, Gideon had been deprived of liberty. Had this liberty been taken away without due process of law?

How was the case decided?

In a unanimous opinion written by Justice Hugo Black, the Court ruled in Gideon's favor.

What did the Court say about constitutional rights?

Members of the Court based their decision on two different views of the Fourteenth Amendment. One is the incorporation view, which holds that the purpose of the due process clause is to incorporate most of the Bill of Rights into state court procedures. The second is the fundamental liberties view, which holds that "due process of law" means "whatever is necessary for justice." What is necessary for justice may not include every assurance in the Bill of Rights, but it may include assurances that go beyond anything in the Bill of Rights. In Gideon v. Wainwright the justices came to the same conclusion by different means.

In the Court's decision Justice Black accommodated both the incorporation view and the fundamental liberties view. The opinion was a compromise. It said that the Sixth Amendment's assurance of the "assistance of counsel" is necessary for a fair trial in any court, but it did not say that due process covers every other assurance in the first eight amendments.

What implications did this case have for the future?

Gideon v. Wainwright was one of several Supreme Court cases guaranteeing government payment to lawyers defending poor people accused of crimes. The Criminal Justice Act of 1964 established the defender services program.

8 Miranda v. Arizona
384 U.S. 436 (1966)

What was this case about?

The story. On March 13, 1963, a woman was kidnapped near Phoenix. Ernesto Miranda was arrested for the crime, and the victim identified him in a police lineup. Two officers then questioned him. Although at first Miranda denied the crime, after a short time he wrote out and signed a confession.

At the trial the officers testified that they had warned Miranda that anything he might say could be used against

him in court and that Miranda had understood. The officers also said that he had confessed without any threats or force. They admitted, however, that they had not told Miranda about his right to silence or legal assistance. Miranda was found guilty. Eventually, he appealed to the U.S. Supreme Court.

The question. Is it a violation of the Fifth, Sixth, or Fourteenth Amendment to use a confession to convict someone who has not been informed of the constitutional rights to silence and legal assistance?

The issues. The Fifth Amendment ensures a person the right to remain silent: "No person . . . shall be compelled [forced] in any criminal case to be a witness against himself." Without such a right, innocent people could be tortured into confessing to a crime they did not commit. The Sixth Amendment ensures the assistance of a lawyer to defendants in criminal trials in federal courts. The Fourteenth Amendment does the same for defendants in state courts.

One issue is the point at which Fifth and Sixth Amendment rights begin. Do they begin only at the trial? Or do these rights begin earlier?

A deeper issue concerns the meaning of being forced to be a witness against oneself. Perhaps keeping a person ignorant of his or her rights is a kind of force. If so, then it violates the Fifth Amendment.

How was the case decided?

By a 5-to-4 majority, the Supreme Court ruled that taking Miranda's confession without informing him of his rights to silence and legal assistance had violated his constitutional rights.

What did the Court say about constitutional rights?

The Court ruled that the Fifth and Sixth Amendment rights exist as soon as a person is in custody. The Court also ruled that failing to inform the accused of his or her rights is a violation of the right not to testify against oneself.

Today if prisoners are not informed of their rights, judges may rule that what the accused tells the police cannot be used as evidence in court. Furthermore, the court must disregard any evidence that is based on what the accused said.

What implications did this case have for the future?

The Miranda ruling has been controversial because it deals with the delicate balance between protecting the accused and protecting society. A hotly debated aspect of the decision has been the ruling that confessions given by accused people who have not been informed of their rights may not be used as evidence. The Court did this to prevent innocent people from being found guilty. Some people argue, however, that it prevents the guilty from being convicted.

9 Roe v. Wade
410 U.S. 113 (1973)

What was this case about?

The story. In 1970 Norma McCorvey, an unmarried pregnant woman living in Texas, sought to obtain a legal abortion in a medical facility. Because of Texas's antiabortion statute, no licensed physician would agree to perform the procedure. McCorvey was financially unable to travel to another state with a less-restrictive abortion law. She faced either continuing an unwanted pregnancy or having the procedure performed in a non-medical facility, which she believed would endanger her life.

McCorvey claimed that the Texas antiabortion law was unconstitutional because it interfered with her right of personal privacy that is protected by the Ninth and Fourteenth Amendments. She took legal action, naming the Dallas County district attorney, Henry Wade, in her lawsuit. Throughout the case, McCorvey used the pseudonym Jane Roe.

The question. Is it a violation of a person's right to privacy for a state to prevent a woman from terminating a pregnancy through an abortion?

The issues. The Fourteenth Amendment states that "no state shall make or enforce any law which shall abridge [diminish] the privileges . . . of citizens of the United States . . . nor deny to any person . . . the equal protection of the laws." The Ninth Amendment states that "the enumeration [naming] in the Constitution of certain rights shall not be construed [interpreted] to deny or disparage [reduce] others retained by the people." Do these amendments include and protect a woman's right to a legal abortion?

How was the case decided?

In an opinion written by Justice Harry Blackmun, the Court ruled that the Fourteenth Amendment's due process guarantee of personal liberty ensures the right to personal privacy. This guarantee protects a woman's decision about abortion and assures that a state's laws do not abridge this right. The vote was seven to two.

What did the Court say about constitutional rights?

In ruling that a state cannot prevent a woman from terminating a pregnancy during the first three months, the Court relied on the citizens' right to privacy. Justice Blackmun stated in his opinion that "[t]his right of privacy, whether it be founded in the Fourteenth Amendment's concept of personal liberty and restrictions upon state action, as we feel it is, or . . . in the Ninth Amendment's reservation of rights to the people, is broad enough to encompass [include] a woman's decision whether or not to terminate her pregnancy." In its ruling, however, the Court recognized the right of a state to regulate abortions as a pregnancy progressed. During the first three months of a pregnancy, a woman has a virtually unrestricted right to an abortion.

During the second trimester, a state can regulate abortions to protect a woman's health. Only in the final three months of a pregnancy can a state forbid an abortion, unless the procedure is necessary to protect a woman's life.

The ruling also said that a state cannot adopt a theory of when life begins. This prevents a state from giving a fetus the same rights as a newborn.

What implications did this case have for the future?

Since the 1973 ruling, related cases have been decided that some people claim weaken the legislative impact of Roe v. Wade. In Harris v. McRae (1980), the Court upheld a law that blocked the use of federal funds to pay for abortions for women on welfare. Critics of the ruling claimed that women who could not afford the procedure would, like Jane Roe, be faced with either continuing an unwanted pregnancy or resorting to dangerous measures to terminate it. The ruling in Webster v. Reproductive Health Services (1989) added more restrictions to the availability of abortions.

10 Regents of the University of California v. Bakke
438 U.S. 265 (1978)

What was this case about?

The story. A white man named Allan Bakke twice applied to the medical school at the University of California, Davis, during the years in which the medical school operated two different admissions programs. After the Civil Rights Act of 1964, schools and other institutions were under pressure to provide special admissions programs for minority students. There were, however, no specific guidelines on how to accomplish this.

At the University of California, Davis, medical school 84 of the 100 places in the incoming class were filled from the regular program. The remaining 16 spots were set aside for a special program that used a quota system. The regular program was for students of all races, as long as they met admission requirements, including a minimum grade point average. Only members of racial minorities could apply through the special program, and their grades did not have to meet the minimum.

Bakke applied through the regular program and was turned down. He thought he had been treated unfairly because in both years, students had been admitted through the special program whose grades and test scores were much lower than his. He sued the state university system. Bakke said the special program, established to fulfill the racial quota, violated his Fourteenth Amendment right to equal protection of the law.

The California Supreme Court made two rulings. One said that Davis's admission system was illegal and ordered Bakke admitted. The other ordered that in the future, admissions decisions must not take race into consideration. The California university system appealed to the U.S. Supreme Court.

The questions. First, does the use of a racial quota in admissions violate the Fourteenth Amendment's equal protection clause? Second, does this clause require that race be completely ignored in admissions?

The issues. Historically, most racial discrimination in our country has hurt members of racial minorities. Bakke complained of reverse discrimination, a type of discrimination that supposedly hurt members of the racial majority in order to help members of racial minorities.

The Fourteenth Amendment was primarily written because African Americans who had recently been freed from slavery needed protection from discrimination by the white majority. This fact suggests that the equal protection clause protects racial minorities more than the racial majority. On the other hand, what the amendment actually says is that no state may deny to any person the equal protection of the laws. This fact suggests that the equal protection clause gives the same protection to people of all races. The intent of the amendment seems to have been to protect minorities, but its wording does not specify this intent.

How was the case decided?

The U.S. Supreme Court agreed that racial quotas in admissions was unconstitutional and ordered that Bakke be admitted. It rejected the idea that an admissions system may never pay any attention to race.

What did the Court say about constitutional rights?

Justice Lewis Powell wrote the Court's opinion. He said that the equal protection clause does not completely prohibit states from taking race into account when they are making laws and official policies. However, it does make the consideration of race "suspect," or suspicious. When such a law or policy is challenged in court, judges must apply a two-part test. First, are the purposes of the law or policy legitimate? Second, is the consideration given to race necessary to achieve these purposes? California told the Court that its racial quota had four purposes.

Purpose 1. To correct the shortage of racial minorities in medical schools and among doctors. Justice Powell said that this purpose was not acceptable. "Preferring members of any one group for no reason other than race or ethnic origin is discrimination for its own sake."

Purpose 2. To counteract the effects of racial discrimination in society. Justice Powell said that this was an acceptable purpose. He approved of helping people who belong to groups that have been hurt by past discrimination. However, he said that helping them by hurting others is right only when it makes up for hurts caused by those other people. Bakke was not responsible for past discrimination against people of racial minorities.

Purpose 3: To increase the number of doctors who will be willing to practice medicine in communities where there are not enough doctors. This purpose was also acceptable. However, California had not shown that racial quotas were needed to accomplish this purpose.

Purpose 4. To improve education by making the student body more diverse. This purpose, too, was acceptable. However, Justice Powell pointed out that racial diversity is only one aspect of overall diversity and that racial quotas are not the only way to increase racial diversity.

What implications did this case have for the future?

This decision revealed that the members of the Court disagreed sharply about reverse discrimination. Furthermore, Powell stressed that the Court's decision concerned only reverse racial discrimination. He warned that reverse sexual discrimination may or may not have to be treated the same way as reverse racial discrimination. In the 1982 case Mississippi University for Women v. Hogan, however, the Court ruled that it was unconstitutional for a state-run school of nursing to refuse admission to men.

Thomas Jefferson wrote the first draft of the Declaration in a little more than two weeks. He drew upon the Virginia Declaration of Rights, written by George Mason, for the opening paragraphs.

★ Government

According to the first paragraph, why is it important for the signers to justify their political break with Great Britain?

impel: force
endowed: provided

"Laws of Nature" and "Nature's God" refer to the belief common in the Scientific Revolution that certain patterns are constant and predictable and that they come from a supreme being. Natural or "unalienable" rights (the rights to life, liberty, and the pursuit of happiness) cannot be taken away. English philosopher John Locke had argued that people create governments to protect their natural rights. If a government abuses its powers, it is the right as well as the duty of the people to do away with that government.

usurpations: wrongful seizures of power
evinces: clearly displays
despotism: unlimited power

The Declaration of Independence

In Congress, July 4, 1776
The unanimous Declaration of the thirteen united States of America,

When in the Course of human events, it becomes necessary for one people to dissolve the political bands which have connected them with another, and to assume among the Powers of the earth, the separate and equal station to which the Laws of Nature and of Nature's God entitle them, a decent respect to the opinions of mankind requires that they should declare the causes which impel them to the separation.

We hold these truths to be self-evident, that all men are created equal, that they are endowed by their Creator with certain unalienable Rights, that among these are Life, Liberty, and the pursuit of Happiness. That to secure these rights, Governments are instituted among Men, deriving their just powers from the consent of the governed, That whenever any Form of Government becomes destructive of these ends, it is the Right of the People to alter or to abolish it, and to institute new Government, laying its foundation on such principles and organizing its powers in such form, as to them shall seem most likely to effect their Safety and Happiness. Prudence, indeed, will dictate that Governments long established should not be changed for light and transient causes; and accordingly all experience hath shown, that mankind are more disposed to suffer, while evils are sufferable, than to right themselves by abolishing the forms to which they are accustomed. But when a long train of abuses and usurpations, pursuing invariably the same Object evinces a design to reduce them under absolute Despotism, it is their right, it is their duty, to throw off such Government, and to provide new Guards for their future security.— Such has been the patient sufferance of these Colonies; and such is now the necessity which constrains them to alter their former Systems of Government. The history

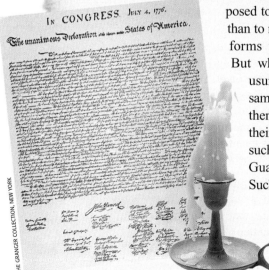

THE GRANGER COLLECTION, NEW YORK

The Declaration of Independence

of the present King of Great Britain is a history of repeated injuries and usurpations, all having in direct object the establishment of an absolute Tyranny over these States. To prove this, let Facts be submitted to a candid world.

He has refused his Assent to Laws, the most wholesome and necessary for the public good.

He has forbidden his Governors to pass Laws of immediate and pressing importance, unless suspended in their operation till his Assent should be obtained; and when so suspended, he has utterly neglected to attend to them.

He has refused to pass other Laws for the accommodation of large districts of people, unless those people would relinquish the right of Representation in the Legislature, a right inestimable to them and formidable to tyrants only.

He has called together legislative bodies at places unusual, uncomfortable, and distant from the depository of their Public Records, for the sole purpose of fatiguing them into compliance with his measures.

He has dissolved Representative Houses repeatedly, for opposing with manly firmness his invasions on the rights of the people.

He has refused for a long time, after such dissolutions, to cause others to be elected; whereby the Legislative Powers, incapable of Annihilation, have returned to the People at large for their exercise; the State remaining in the mean time exposed to all the dangers of invasion from without, and convulsions within.

He has endeavored to prevent the population of these States; for that purpose obstructing the Laws of Naturalization of Foreigners; refusing to pass others to encourage their migration hither, and raising the conditions of new Appropriations of Lands.

He has obstructed the Administration of Justice, by refusing his Assent to Laws for establishing Judiciary Powers.

He has made Judges dependent on his Will alone, for the tenure of their offices, and the amount and payment of their salaries.

He has erected a multitude of New Offices, and sent hither swarms of Officers to harass our people, and eat out their substance.

He has kept among us, in times of peace, Standing Armies without the Consent of our legislature.

He has affected to render the Military independent of and superior to the Civil Power.

He has combined with others to subject us to a jurisdiction foreign to our constitution, and unacknowledged by our laws; giving his Assent to their Acts of pretended legislation:

For quartering large bodies of armed troops among us:

For protecting them, by a mock Trial, from Punishment for any Murders which they should commit on the Inhabitants of these States:

For cutting off our Trade with all parts of the world:

---

tyranny: oppressive power exerted by a government or ruler
candid: fair

Beginning here the Declaration lists the charges that the colonists had against King George III.

relinquish: release, yield
inestimable: priceless
formidable: causing dread

annihilation: destruction

convulsions: violent disturbances

naturalization of foreigners: the process by which foreign-born persons become citizens
appropriations of land: setting aside land for settlement

tenure: term

a multitude of: many

⭐ **Government**

What wrongful acts stated in the Declaration have been committed by the king and the British Parliament?

quartering: lodging, housing

Tenure for Judges

The word *tenure* comes from the latin word *tenere*, which means "to hold." In English, the word often refers to a term of office. In the United States, it also refers to a guaranteed position, such as those held by professors at many universities. The authors of the Declaration did not approve of the king's ability to determine the length of a judge's tenure. After the Revolutionary War, the authors of the Constitution determined that Supreme Court justices would have lifetime appointments.

CRITICAL THINKING Why might the authors of the Constitution have wanted judges to have lifetime tenure?

ANSWER: Students might suggest that the authors wanted judges to be impartial and independent.

GOVERNMENT ANSWER
Students should note that the Declaration states that the king refused to obey the law and to establish judicial powers, among other offenses. The Declaration states that the British Parliament passed acts to quarter troops, among other offenses.

The Signers of the Declaration

The men who eventually signed the Declaration came from diverse backgrounds. Many, such as Arthur Middletown and Lewis Morris, grew up in wealthy families and received good educations. Others, such as Samuel Huntington and Roger Sherman, were from humble beginnings. One signer, George Taylor, had come to the colonies as an indentured servant. Taylor eventually received his freedom. He served the Continental Army during the Revolutionary War by producing munitions.

CRITICAL THINKING How might George Taylor's life have reflected the ideals of the Declaration and the Revolution?

ANSWER: Students might suggest that Taylor's life reflected the importance of equal opportunity for all.

GOVERNMENT ANSWER

Students should note that the colonists protested the king's taxes because they were imposed without due consent.

 Government

Why were the colonists protesting British tax policies?

The "neighboring Province" referred to here is Quebec.
arbitrary: not based on law
render: make

abdicated: given up

foreign mercenaries: soldiers hired to fight for a country not their own
perfidy: violation of trust

insurrections: rebellions

petitioned for redress: asked formally for a correction of wrongs

For imposing taxes on us without our Consent:

For depriving us in many cases, of the benefits of Trial by Jury:

For transporting us beyond Seas to be tried for pretended offences:

For abolishing the free System of English Laws in a neighboring Province, establishing therein an Arbitrary government, and enlarging its Boundaries so as to render it at once an example and fit instrument for introducing the same absolute rule into these Colonies:

For taking away our Charters, abolishing our most valuable Laws, and altering fundamentally the Forms of our Governments:

For suspending our own Legislature, and declaring themselves invested with Power to legislate for us in all cases whatsoever.

He has abdicated Government here, by declaring us out of his Protection and waging War against us.

He has plundered our seas, ravaged our Coasts, burnt our towns, and destroyed the lives of our people.

He is at this time transporting large armies of foreign mercenaries to complete the works of death, desolation and tyranny, already begun with circumstances of Cruelty & perfidy scarcely paralleled in the most barbarous ages, and totally unworthy the Head of a civilized nation.

He has constrained our fellow Citizens taken Captive on the high Seas to bear Arms against their Country, to become the executioners of their friends and Brethren, or to fall themselves by their Hands.

He has excited domestic insurrections amongst us, and has endeavored to bring on the inhabitants of our frontiers, the merciless Indian Savages, whose known rule of warfare, is an undistinguished destruction of all ages, sexes and conditions.

In every stage of these Oppressions We have Petitioned for Redress in the most humble terms: Our repeated Petitions have been answered only by repeated injury. A Prince, whose character is thus marked by every act which may define a Tyrant, is unfit to be the ruler of a free People.

This painting by Robert Pine and Edward Savage depicts the Continental Congress voting for independence.

Nor have We been wanting in attention to our British brethren. We have warned them from time to time of attempts by their legislature to extend an unwarrantable jurisdiction over us. We have reminded them of the circumstances of our emigration and settlement here. We have appealed to their native justice and magnanimity, and we have conjured them by the ties of our common kindred to disavow these usurpations, which, would inevitably interrupt our connections and correspondence. They too have been deaf to the voice of justice and of consanguinity. We must, therefore, acquiesce in the necessity, which denounces our Separation, and hold them, as we hold the rest of mankind, Enemies in War, in Peace Friends.

We, therefore, the Representatives of the united States of America, in General Congress, Assembled, appealing to the Supreme Judge of the world for the rectitude of our intentions, do, in the Name, and by Authority of the good People of these Colonies, solemnly publish and declare, That these United Colonies are, and of Right ought to be Free and Independent States; that they are Absolved from all Allegiance to the British Crown, and that all political connection between them and the State of Great Britain, is and ought to be totally dissolved; and that as Free and Independent States, they have full Power to levy War, conclude Peace, contract Alliances, establish Commerce, and to do all other Acts and Things which Independent States may of right do. And for the support of this Declaration, with a firm reliance on the Protection of Divine Providence, we mutually pledge to each other our Lives, our Fortunes and our sacred Honor.

John Hancock	Benjamin Harrison	Lewis Morris
Button Gwinnett	Thomas Nelson Jr.	Richard Stockton
Lyman Hall	Francis Lightfoot Lee	John Witherspoon
George Walton	Carter Braxton	Francis Hopkinson
William Hooper	Robert Morris	John Hart
Joseph Hewes	Benjamin Rush	Abraham Clark
John Penn	Benjamin Franklin	Josiah Bartlett
Edward Rutledge	John Morton	William Whipple
Thomas Heyward Jr.	George Clymer	Samuel Adams
Thomas Lynch Jr.	James Smith	John Adams
Arthur Middleton	George Taylor	Robert Treat Paine
Samuel Chase	James Wilson	Elbridge Gerry
William Paca	George Ross	Stephen Hopkins
Thomas Stone	Caesar Rodney	William Ellery
Charles Carroll of Carrollton	George Read	Roger Sherman
George Wythe	Thomas McKean	Samuel Huntington
Richard Henry Lee	William Floyd	William Williams
Thomas Jefferson	Phillip Livingston	Oliver Wolcott
	Francis Lewis	Matthew Thornton

unwarrantable jurisdiction: unjustified authority

magnanimity: generous spirit

conjured: urgently called upon

consanguinity: common ancestry

acquiesce: consent to

rectitude: rightness

Congress adopted the final draft of the Declaration of Independence on July 4, 1776. A formal copy, written on parchment paper, was signed on August 2, 1776.

 Government

From whom did the signers of the Declaration receive their authority to declare independence?

The following is part of a passage that the Congress took out of Jefferson's original draft: "He has waged cruel war against human nature itself, violating its most sacred rights of life and liberty in the persons of a distant people who never offended him, captivating and carrying them into slavery in another hemisphere, or to incur miserable death in their transportation thither." *Why do you think the Congress deleted this passage?*

ART
The Convention in Art

Howard Chandler Christy, the artist who painted the work to the right, was best known as an illustrator. He began work for *Scribners' Magazine* in 1898, illustrating current-events articles and stories. He also traveled to Cuba and Puerto Rico to provide the magazine with firsthand illustrations of the Spanish-American War. His illustrations eventually appeared on World War I recruitment posters. Christy began creating large oil paintings, mostly of historical scenes, late in his life. The painting to the right is huge—20 feet by 30 feet. It now hangs above the grand staircase in the Capitol in Washington, D.C.

CRITICAL THINKING In this painting, how does Christy show the importance of the Constitution?

ANSWER: Answers will vary. Some students might mention the men's serious expressions, George Washington's noble stance, the light on the document, or the grandeur of the room.

CONSTITUTION HANDBOOK

*T*he delegates who met in the spring of 1787 to revise the Articles of Confederation included many of the ablest leaders of the United States. Convinced that the Confederation was not strong enough to bring order and prosperity to the nation, they abandoned all thought of revising the Articles. Instead, they proceeded to draw up a completely new Constitution. Patrick Henry called this action "a revolution as radical as that which separated us from Great Britain." Out of their long political experience, their keen intelligence, and their great learning, the framers of the Constitution fashioned a blueprint for a truly united nation—the United States of America.

Delegates met in Independence Hall in Philadelphia to draft the Constitution.

The U.S. Constitution

Charles Pinckney

Some historians argue that Charles Pinckney of South Carolina played an important but forgotten role in the creation of the Constitution. During the convention, Pinckney submitted a plan to the Constitutional Convention. The later document incorporated some of his ideas. James Madison, who kept the only detailed notes at the convention, never mentioned the Pinckney plan, however. It became public only in 1818, when Pinckney sent a copy to John Quincy Adams. Historians have debated Pinckney's role ever since. Some claim that Madison, who hated Pinckney, attempted to squash evidence of his role. Others maintain that Pinckney faked the document he sent to Adams in order to inflate his role. The mystery remains.

CRITICAL THINKING What additional evidence might resolve the debate on Pinckney's role?

ANSWER: Answers will vary. Some students might suggest that an authenticated copy of the Pinckney plan from the Convention would resolve the dispute.

*U.S. Constitution
commemorative stamps*

*A*n unknown observer once referred to the U.S. Constitution as "the most wonderful work ever struck off at a given time by the brain and purpose of man." Revised, modified, and amended, the Constitution has served the American people for more than 200 years, becoming a model for representative government around the world. The Constitution has successfully survived the years for two reasons. First, it lays down rules of procedure and guarantees of rights and liberties that must be observed even in times of crisis. Second, it is a "living" document, capable of being amended to meet changing times and circumstances.

To Form a More Perfect Union

The framers of the Constitution wished to establish a strong central government, one that could unite the country and help it meet the challenges of the future. At the same time, however, they feared a government that was too strong. The memories of the troubled years before the Revolution were still fresh. They knew that unchecked power in the hands of individuals, groups, or branches of government could lead to tyranny.

The framers' response was to devise a system of government in which power is divided between, in the words of James Madison, "two distinct governments"—the states and the federal government—and then within each government. In *Federalist Paper* "No. 51," Madison described the advantages of such a system.

> ❝ In the compound republic of America, the power surrendered by the people is first divided between two distinct governments, and then the portion allotted to each subdivided among distinct and separate departments. Hence a double security arises to the rights of the people. The different governments will control each other, at the same time that each will be controlled by itself. ❞

The seven Articles that make up the first part of the Constitution provide the blueprint for this system. To help guard against tyranny and to keep any one part of the federal government from becoming too strong, the framers divided the government into three branches—the legislative branch (Congress), the executive branch (the president and vice president), and the judicial branch (the federal courts)—each with specific powers. As a further safeguard, the framers wrote a system of checks and balances into the Constitution. Articles I, II, and III outline the powers of each branch of government and the checks and balances.

Article IV outlines the relations among the states and between the states and the federal government. Among the issues addressed are each state's recognition of other states' public records and citizens' rights, the admission of new states, and the rights and responsibilities of the federal government in relation to the states.

Article V specifies the process by which the Constitution can be amended. The framers purposely made the process slow and difficult. They feared that if the process was too easy, the Constitution—the fundamental law of the land—would soon carry no more weight than the most minor law passed by Congress.

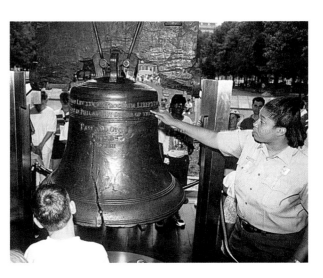

Quill pen belonging to constitutional delegate James Madison

Article VI includes one provision that addressed the immediate concerns of the framers and two that have lasting significance. The short-term provision promises that the United States under the Constitution will honor all public debts entered into under the Confederation. The two long-term provisions declare the Constitution the supreme law of the land and prohibit religion being used as a qualification for holding public office.

Article VII is the framers' attempt to ensure ratification of the Constitution. The Constitutional Convention was summoned by the Congress to amend the Articles of Confederation. Under the Articles of Confederation, amendments had to be approved by all 13 states. Realizing that it would be difficult to get the approval of all the states—Rhode Island, for example, had not even sent delegates to Philadelphia—the framers specified that the Constitution would go into effect after ratification by only 9 states, not all 13. (This provision led some opponents of the Constitution to claim that it had been adopted by unfair means.)

Protecting Individual Liberty

Opposition to a strong central government was in part a concern over states' rights. But it was also rooted in the desire to protect individual liberties. American colonists had always insisted on the protection of their civil liberties—their rights as individuals against the power of the government. The Constitution contains many important guarantees of civil liberties. On a broad level, the separation of powers and the system of checks and balances help safeguard citizens against the abuse of government power. But the Constitution also contains provisions that speak directly to an individual's right to due process of law. For example, Section 9 of Article I prohibits both *ex post facto* laws and bills of attainder.

An *ex post facto* law is a law passed "after the deed." Such a law sets a penalty for an act that was not illegal when it was committed. A bill of attainder is a law that punishes a person by fine, imprisonment, or seizure of prop-

The Liberty Bell has become a symbol of the ideas of individual liberty protected in the Constitution.

Religion and the Oath of Office

Article VI requires that many government officers, including some at the state level, take an oath in support of the Constitution. Some people, such as Quakers, cannot take oaths because of their religious beliefs, however. To accommodate this, Article VI allows for the option of affirming, or agreeing, to support the Constitution.

CRITICAL THINKING Why might the authors of the Constitution have required state officials to take an oath or to affirm support for the Constitution?

ANSWER: Students might suggest that the authors wanted to re-emphasize the supremacy of the Constitution. They may also have wanted to ensure that state officials understood their dual responsibility: to enforce the Constitution as well as the state laws.

Treason and the Supreme Court

The U.S. Supreme Court has heard only one case involving charges of treason. During World War II, German saboteurs entered the United States by submarine with the intent of destroying the American war effort. Authorities accused Anthony Cramer, a U.S. citizen with German ties, of aiding these saboteurs. When Cramer was found guilty of treason, he appealed to the Supreme Court. In its 1945 decision in *Cramer* v. *United States,* the court overturned his conviction. The court determined that witnesses could testify only that Cramer had met with the saboteurs, not that he had provided them with any aid or assistance.

CRITICAL THINKING What provision in Article III led the Supreme Court to overturn Cramer's conviction for treason?

ANSWER: Students should indicate that his case did not meet the constitutional standard of providing "Aid and Comfort" to the enemy.

erty without a court trial. If Congress had the power to adopt bills of attainder, lawmakers could punish any American at will, and that person could do nothing to appeal the sentence. Instead, the Constitution provides that only the courts can impose punishment for unlawful acts, and then only by following the duly established law.

Section 9 of Article I also protects citizens by guaranteeing the privilege of the writ of *habeas corpus*. The writ of *habeas corpus* is a legal document that forces a jailer to release a person from prison unless the person has been formally charged with, or convicted of, a crime. The Constitution states that "the privilege of the writ of *habeas corpus* shall not be suspended, unless when in cases of rebellion or invasion the public safety may require it."

The Constitution also gives special protection to people accused of treason. The framers of the Constitution knew that the charge of treason was an old device used by tyrants to get rid of persons they did not like. Such rulers might bring the charge of treason against persons who merely criticized the government. To prevent such use of this charge, Section 3 of Article III carefully defines treason.

> 66 Treason against the United States, shall consist only in levying War against them, or in adhering to their Enemies, giving them Aid and Comfort. No Person shall be convicted of Treason unless on the Testimony of two Witnesses to the same overt Act, or on Confession in open Court. 99

Article III also protects the innocent relatives of a person accused of treason. Only the convicted person can be punished. No penalty can be imposed on the person's family.

The signing of the Constitution

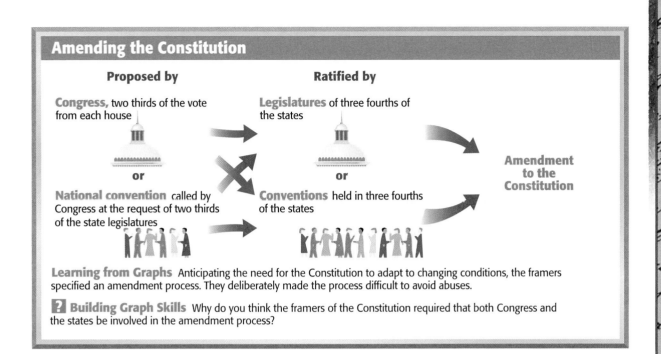

Amending the Constitution

Proposed by

Congress, two thirds of the vote from each house

or

National convention called by Congress at the request of two thirds of the state legislatures

Ratified by

Legislatures of three fourths of the states

or

Conventions held in three fourths of the states

Amendment to the Constitution

Learning from Graphs Anticipating the need for the Constitution to adapt to changing conditions, the framers specified an amendment process. They deliberately made the process difficult to avoid abuses.

? Building Graph Skills Why do you think the framers of the Constitution required that both Congress and the states be involved in the amendment process?

The Bill of Rights

Despite the safeguards written into the Articles of the Constitution, some states at first refused to ratify the framework because it did not offer greater protection to the rights of individuals. They finally agreed to ratification after they had been promised that a bill of rights would be added to the Constitution by amendment when Congress was called into session following ratification.

In 1789 the first Congress of the United States wrote some of the ideals of the Declaration of Independence into the Bill of Rights, the first 10 amendments to the Constitution. The Bill of Rights includes a protection for individuals against any action by the federal government that may deprive them of life, liberty, or property without "due process of law."

Among the guarantees of liberty in the Bill of Rights, several are especially important. The First Amendment guarantees freedom of religion, speech, press, assembly, and petition. The Fourth Amendment forbids unreasonable searches and seizures of any person's home. The Fifth, Sixth, and Eighth Amendments protect individuals from arbitrary arrest and punishment by the federal government.

The Bill of Rights was ratified by the states in 1791. It has remained one of the best-known features of the Constitution. The American people have turned to it for support whenever their rights as individuals have seemed to be in danger. No document in American history—except, perhaps, the Declaration of Independence—has been cherished more deeply.

GOVERNMENT
State Constitutions

Compared to certain state constitutions, the U.S. Constitution contains very few amendments. The California constitution has 493 amendments, while the South Carolina document contains 474 amendments. Alabama's constitution includes 618 amendments! The state requires that three fifths of the legislature approve proposed amendments.

CRITICAL THINKING Why might certain state constitutions have been amended so many times?

ANSWER: Answers will vary. Some students might suggest that it is relatively easy or simple to amend certain state constitutions.

THAT'S INTERESTING!
Several states have had more than one constitution. Louisiana has had 11 constitutions, and Georgia has had 10. Massachusetts, however, has had the same constitution since 1780.

CONTENTS OF THE CONSTITUTION

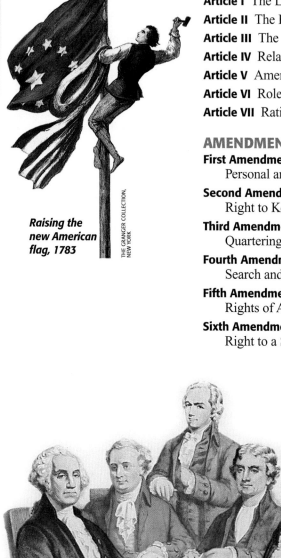

Raising the new American flag, 1783

THE GRANGER COLLECTION, NEW YORK

President George Washington (left) and his advisers

State seals of North Carolina, Massachusetts, and New York

The bald eagle, a symbol of the United States

George W. Norris, Constitutional Advocate

During his long congressional career, George W. Norris not only wrote the Twentieth Amendment and worked for its passage but also supported the introduction of presidential primaries and the direct election of senators. Although he was a Republican, Norris rarely voted along party lines. In defense of his independence, he claimed he "would rather be right than regular."

Activity:

Ask students to find examples of recent political reforms. Then have each student draft a bill or constitutional amendment that could be used to enact one of the reforms.

THAT'S INTERESTING!

The passage of the Fourteenth and Fifteenth Amendments dramatically increased African American political participation. Almost every institution of African American life, particularly the church, worked to mobilize the African American vote. So many African American workers attended the Republican state convention in Virginia that Richmond's tobacco factories had to close during the convention.

John Marshall in *The American Testament*

The Preamble

Chief Justice John Marshall cited the Preamble in his decision in the 1819 case of *McCulloch* v. *Maryland.* "The government proceeds directly from the people; is 'ordained and established' in the name of the people; and is declared to be ordained 'in order to form a more perfect union, establish justice, ensure domestic tranquility and secure the blessings of liberty' to themselves and to their posterity. . . . The government of the Union, then . . . is emphatically and truly, a government of the people. In form and substance it emanates from them. Its powers are granted by them and are to be exercised directly on them and for their benefit."

CRITICAL THINKING Why might Marshall have cited the Preamble?

ANSWER: Students might suggest that Marshall believed that the Preamble summarized the purpose of the U.S. Constitution and government.

Legislative Branch

Article I explains how the legislative branch, called Congress, is organized. The chief purpose of the legislative branch is to make the laws. Congress is made up of the Senate and the House of Representatives. The decision to have two bodies of government solved a difficult problem during the Constitutional Convention. The large states wanted membership in Congress to be based entirely on population. The small states wanted every state to have an equal vote. The solution to the problem of how the states were to be represented in Congress was known as the Great Compromise.

The number of members of the House is based on the population of the individual states. Each state has at least one representative. The current size of the House is 435 members, set by Congress in 1929.

The Constitution of the United States of America

PREAMBLE

W *e the People of the United States, in Order to form a more perfect Union, establish Justice, insure domestic Tranquility, provide for the common defense, promote the general Welfare, and secure the Blessings of Liberty to ourselves and our Posterity, do ordain and establish this Constitution for the United States of America.* *

ARTICLE I

Section 1. All legislative Powers herein granted shall be vested in a Congress of the United States, which shall consist of a Senate and House of Representatives.

Section 2. The House of Representatives shall be composed of Members chosen every second Year by the People of the several States, and the Electors in each State shall have the Qualifications requisite for Electors of the most numerous Branch of the State Legislature.

No Person shall be a Representative who shall not have attained to the Age of twenty-five Years, and been seven Years a Citizen of the United States, and who shall not, when elected, be an inhabitant of that State in which he shall be chosen.

Representatives and direct Taxes shall be apportioned among the several States which may be included within this Union, according to their respective Numbers, which shall be determined by adding to the whole Number of free Persons, including those bound to Service for a Term of Years, and excluding Indians not taxed, three fifths of all other Persons. The actual Enumeration shall be made within three Years after the first Meeting of the Congress of the United States, and within every subsequent Term of ten Years, in such Manner as they shall by Law direct. The Number of Representatives shall not exceed one for every thirty

*Parts of the Constitution that have been ruled through are no longer in force or no longer apply.

Thousand, but each State shall have at Least one Representative; and until such enumeration shall be made, the State of New Hampshire shall be entitled to choose three; Massachusetts eight; Rhode Island and Providence Plantations one; Connecticut five; New-York six; New Jersey four; Pennsylvania eight; Delaware one; Maryland six; Virginia ten; North Carolina five; South Carolina five; and Georgia three.

When vacancies happen in the Representation from any State, the Executive Authority thereof shall issue Writs of Election to fill such Vacancies.

The House of Representatives shall choose their Speaker and other Officers; and shall have the sole Power of Impeachment.

Section 3. The Senate of the United States shall be composed of two Senators from each State, chosen by the Legislature thereof, for six Years; and each Senator shall have one Vote.

Immediately after they shall be assembled in Consequence of the first Election, they shall be divided as equally as may be into three Classes. The Seats of the Senators of the first Class shall be vacated at the Expiration of the second Year, of the second Class at the Expiration of the fourth Year, and of the third Class at the Expiration of the sixth Year, so that one third may be chosen every second Year; and if Vacancies happen by Resignation, or otherwise, during the Recess of the Legislature of any State, the Executive thereof may make temporary Appointments until the next Meeting of the Legislature, which shall then fill such Vacancies.

No Person shall be a Senator who shall not have attained to the Age of thirty Years, and been nine Years a Citizen of the United States, and who shall not, when elected, be an Inhabitant of that State for which he shall be chosen.

The Vice President of the United States shall be President of the Senate, but shall have no Vote, unless they be equally divided.

The Senate shall choose their other Officers, and also a President pro tempore, in the Absence of the Vice President, or when he shall exercise the Office of President of the United States.

The Senate shall have the sole Power to try all Impeachments. When sitting for that Purpose, they shall be on Oath or Affirmation. When the President of the United States is tried, the Chief Justice shall preside: And no Person shall be convicted without the Concurrence of two thirds of the Members present.

Judgment in Cases of Impeachment shall not extend further than to removal from Office, and disqualification to hold and enjoy any Office of honor, Trust or Profit under the United States: but the Party convicted shall nevertheless be liable and subject to Indictment, Trial, Judgment and Punishment, according to Law.

Section 4. The Times, Places and Manner of holding Elections for Senators and Representatives, shall be prescribed in each State by the Legislature thereof; but the Congress may at any time by Law make or alter such Regulations, except as to the Places of choosing Senators.

Every state has two senators. Senators serve a six-year term, but only one third of the senators reach the end of their terms every two years. In any election, at least two thirds of the senators stay in office. This system ensures that there are experienced senators in office at all times.

The only duty that the Constitution assigns to the vice president is to preside over meetings of the Senate. Modern presidents have given their vice presidents more and varied responsibilities.

In an impeachment, the House charges a government official of wrongdoing, and the Senate acts as a court to decide if the official is guilty.

Congress has decided that elections will be held on the Tuesday following the first Monday in November of even-numbered years. The Twentieth Amendment states that Congress shall meet in regular session on January 3 of each year. The president may call a special session of Congress whenever necessary.

Impeachment

In December 1998 the House of Representatives impeached President Bill Clinton. The House brought two charges —perjury and obstruction of justice— against the president. In February 1999 the Senate voted on these charges. Forty-five senators voted to find him guilty on the perjury charge. Fifty-five voted not guilty. The senate vote was split 50-50 on the obstruction of justice charge. The votes did not reach the two-thirds majority required by the Constitution, and so the Senate acquitted Clinton of the impeachment charges.

CRITICAL THINKING Why might some observers have seen the Senate votes as a "humiliating defeat for the 13 House Republican 'managers' who had presented the case to the Senate"?

ANSWER: Students might suggest that neither charge garnered even a simple majority against Clinton, suggesting a weak initial case.

Tracking Congressional Votes

For many years, people learned about congressional proceedings in the *Congressional Record,* a bulky set of printed volumes. The Internet has allowed easier, faster access. The Library of Congress supports a Web site that covers every aspect of the government. In addition, independent organizations, such as Project Vote Smart, provide links to help track congressional votes.

CRITICAL THINKING Besides the *Congressional Record* and the Internet, how might citizens track votes or learn about congressional proceedings?

ANSWER: Answers will vary. Some students will suggest that citizens could call political offices, read newspapers, or watch television news programs.

CONSTITUTIONAL HERITAGE ANSWER

the House itself

Constitutional Heritage

According to the Constitution, who has the authority to judge elections, returns, and the behavior of congressmembers?

Congress makes most of its own rules of conduct. The Senate and the House each have a code of ethics that members must follow. It is the task of each house of Congress to discipline its own members. Each house keeps a journal, and a publication called the *Congressional Record* keeps records of what happens in congressional sessions. The general public can learn how their representatives voted on bills by reading the *Congressional Record.*

The framers of the Constitution wanted to protect members of Congress from being arrested on false charges by political enemies who did not want them to attend important meetings. The framers also wanted to protect members of Congress from being taken to court for something they said in a speech or in a debate.

The power to tax is the responsibility of the House of Representatives. Because members of the House are elected every two years, the framers felt that representatives would listen to the public and seek its approval before passing taxes.

The veto power of the president and the ability of Congress to override a presidential veto are two of the important checks and balances in the Constitution.

The Congress shall assemble at least once in every Year, and such Meeting shall be on the first Monday in December, unless they shall by Law appoint a different Day.

Section 5. Each House shall be the Judge of the Elections, Returns and Qualifications of its own Members, and a Majority of each shall constitute a Quorum to do Business; but a smaller Number may adjourn from day to day, and may be authorized to compel the Attendance of absent Members, in such Manner, and under such Penalties as each House may provide.

Each House may determine the Rules of its Proceedings, punish its Members for disorderly Behavior, and, with the Concurrence of two thirds, expel a Member.

Each House shall keep a Journal of its Proceedings, and from time to time publish the same, excepting such Parts as may in their Judgment require Secrecy; and the Yeas and Nays of the Members of either House on any question shall, at the Desire of one fifth of those Present, be entered on the Journal.

Neither House, during the Session of Congress, shall, without the Consent of the other, adjourn for more than three days, nor to any other Place than that in which the two Houses shall be sitting.

Section 6. The Senators and Representatives shall receive a Compensation for their Services, to be ascertained by Law, and paid out of the Treasury of the United States. They shall in all Cases, except Treason, Felony and Breach of the Peace, be privileged from Arrest during their Attendance at the Session of their respective Houses, and in going to and returning from the same; and for any Speech or Debate in either House, they shall not be questioned in any other Place.

No Senator or Representative shall, during the Time for which he was elected, be appointed to any civil Office under the Authority of the United States, which shall have been created, or the Emoluments whereof shall have been increased during such time; and no Person holding any Office under the United States, shall be a Member of either House during his Continuance in Office.

Section 7. All Bills for raising Revenue shall originate in the House of Representatives; but the Senate may propose or concur with Amendments as on other Bills.

Every Bill which shall have passed the House of Representatives and the Senate, shall, before it become a Law, be presented to the President of the United States; If he approve he shall sign it, but if not he shall return it, with his Objections to that House in which it shall have originated, who shall enter the Objections at large on their Journal, and proceed to reconsider it. If after such Reconsideration two thirds of that House shall agree to pass the Bill, it shall be sent, together with the Objections, to the other House, by which it shall likewise be reconsidered, and if approved by two thirds of that House, it shall become a Law. But in all such Cases the Votes of both Houses shall be determined by Yeas and Nays, and the Names of the Persons voting for and against the Bill shall be entered on the Journal of each House respectively. If any Bill shall not be returned by the President within ten Days (Sundays excepted) after it shall have been presented to him, the Same shall be a Law, in like Manner as if he had signed it, unless the Congress by their Adjournment prevent its Return, in which Case it shall not be a Law.

Every Order, Resolution, or Vote to which the Concurrence of the Senate and House of Representatives may be necessary (except on a question of Adjournment) shall be presented to the President of the United States; and before the Same shall take Effect, shall be approved by him, or being disapproved by him, shall be repassed by two thirds of the Senate and House of Representatives, according to the Rules and Limitations prescribed in the Case of a Bill.

Section 8. The Congress shall have Power To lay and collect Taxes, Duties, Imposts and Excises, to pay the Debts and provide for the common Defense and general Welfare of the United States; but all Duties, Imposts and Excises shall be uniform throughout the United States;

To borrow Money on the credit of the United States;

To regulate Commerce with foreign Nations, and among the several States, and with the Indian Tribes;

To establish an uniform Rule of Naturalization, and uniform Laws on the subject of Bankruptcies throughout the United States;

To coin Money, regulate the Value thereof, and of foreign Coin, and fix the Standard of Weights and Measures;

To provide for the Punishment of counterfeiting the Securities and current Coin of the United States;

To establish Post Offices and post Roads;

To promote the Progress of Science and useful Arts, by securing for limited Times to Authors and Inventors the exclusive Right to their respective Writings and Discoveries;

To constitute Tribunals inferior to the supreme Court;

To define and punish Piracies and Felonies committed on the high Seas, and Offenses against the Law of Nations;

To declare War, grant Letters of Marque and Reprisal, and make Rules concerning Captures on Land and Water;

To raise and support Armies, but no Appropriation of Money to that Use shall be for a longer Term than two Years;

To provide and maintain a Navy;

To make Rules for the Government and Regulation of the land and naval Forces;

To provide for calling forth the Militia to execute the Laws of the Union, suppress Insurrections and repel Invasions;

To provide for organizing, arming, and disciplining, the Militia, and for governing such Part of them as may be employed in the Service of the United States, reserving to the States respectively, the Appointment of the

Constitutional Heritage

How does Section 8 of Article 1 address some of the weaknesses of the Articles of Confederation?

The framers of the Constitution wanted a national government that was strong enough to be effective. Section 8 lists the powers given to Congress. The last sentence in the section contains the so-called elastic clause, which has been stretched— like elastic—to fit many different circumstances. The clause was first disputed when Alexander Hamilton proposed a national bank. Thomas Jefferson said that the Constitution did not give Congress the power to establish a bank. Hamilton argued that the bank was "necessary and proper" in order to carry out other powers of Congress, such as borrowing money and regulating currency. This argument was tested in the court system in 1819 in the case of *McCulloch* v. *Maryland,* when Chief Justice John Marshall ruled in favor of the federal government. Powers exercised by the government using the "elastic clause" are called implied powers.

GOVERNMENT
Suspending the Writ of Habeas Corpus

During the Civil War, President Abraham Lincoln suspended the writ of *habeas corpus.* Opposing his decision, Chief Justice Roger Taney argued that the authority to suspend the writ of *habeas corpus* belonged to Congress because that power was detailed in Article I, which is concerned with legislative matters. Lincoln, however, claimed that the Constitution was unclear on the matter. Congress resolved the dispute when it voted to approve the suspension. Presidents have suspended the writ of *habeas corpus* three times since the Civil War. Suspensions in 1871 and 1905 received congressional approval, but one instituted in 1941 did not. It was later ruled illegal by the Supreme Court.

CRITICAL THINKING Which branch of government has the authority to suspend the writ of *habeas corpus?*

ANSWER: Students might indicate that the history of suspensions indicates that presidents have the authority, with proper congressional approval.

CONSTITUTIONAL HERITAGE ANSWER

Students might answer that the Constitution prohibits many of these hereditary titles.

The delegates debated the articles of the Constitution in the Assembly Room of Independence Hall.

If Congress has implied powers, then there also must be limits to its powers. Section 9 lists powers that are denied to the federal government. Several of the clauses protect the people of the United States from unjust treatment. For instance, Section 9 guarantees the right of the writ of *habeas corpus* and prohibits bills of attainder and *ex post facto* laws.

 Constitutional Heritage

What prohibitions does the Constitution make against nobility and titles from monarchies?

Section 10 lists the powers that are denied to the states. In our system of federalism, the state and federal governments have separate powers, share some powers, and are denied other powers. The states may not exercise any of the powers that belong solely to Congress.

Officers, and the Authority of training the Militia according to the discipline prescribed by Congress.

To exercise exclusive Legislation in all Cases whatsoever, over such District (not exceeding ten Miles square) as may, by Cession of particular States, and the Acceptance of Congress, become the Seat of the Government of the United States, and to exercise like Authority over all Places purchased by the Consent of the Legislature of the State in which the Same shall be, for the Erection of Forts, Magazines, Arsenals, dock-Yards, and other needful Buildings;—And

To make all Laws which shall be necessary and proper for carrying into Execution the foregoing Powers, and all other Powers vested by this Constitution in the Government of the United States, or in any Department or Officer thereof.

Section 9. ~~The Migration or Importation of such Persons as any of the States now existing shall think proper to admit, shall not be prohibited by the Congress prior to the Year one thousand eight hundred and eight, but a Tax or duty may be imposed on such Importation, not exceeding ten dollars for each Person.~~

The Privilege of the Writ of Habeas Corpus shall not be suspended, unless when in Cases of Rebellion or Invasion the public Safety may require it.

No Bill of Attainder or ex post facto Law shall be passed.

No Capitation, or other direct, Tax shall be laid, unless in Proportion to the Census or Enumeration herein before directed to be taken.

No Tax or Duty shall be laid on Articles exported from any State.

No Preference shall be given by any Regulation of Commerce or Revenue to the Ports of one State over those of another: nor shall Vessels bound to, or from, one State, be obliged to enter, clear, or pay Duties in another.

No Money shall be drawn from the Treasury, but in Consequence of Appropriations made by Law; and a regular Statement and Account of the Receipts and Expenditures of all public Money shall be published from time to time.

No Title of Nobility shall be granted by the United States: And no Person holding any Office of Profit or Trust under them, shall, without the Consent of the Congress, accept of any present, Emolument, Office, or Title, of any kind whatever, from any King, Prince, or foreign State.

Section 10. No State shall enter into any Treaty, Alliance, or Confederation; grant Letters of Marque and Reprisal; coin Money; emit Bills of

Credit; make any Thing but gold and silver Coin a Tender in Payment of Debts; pass any Bill of Attainder, ex post facto Law, or law impairing the Obligation of Contracts, or grant any Title of Nobility.

No State shall, without the Consent of the Congress, lay any Imposts or Duties on Imports or Exports, except what may be absolutely necessary for executing its inspection Laws: and the net Produce of all Duties and Imposts, laid by any State on Imports or Exports, shall be for the Use of the Treasury of the United States; and all such Laws shall be subject to the Revision and Control of the Congress.

No State shall, without the Consent of Congress, lay any Duty of Tonnage, keep Troops, or Ships of War in time of Peace, enter into any Agreement or Compact with another State, or with a foreign Power, or engage in War, unless actually invaded, or in such imminent Danger as will not admit of delay.

ARTICLE II

Section 1. The executive Power shall be vested in a President of the United States of America. He shall hold his Office during the Term of four Years, and, together with the Vice President, chosen for the same Term, be elected, as follows.

Each State shall appoint, in such Manner as the Legislature thereof may direct, a Number of Electors, equal to the whole Number of Senators and Representatives to which the State may be entitled in the Congress: but no Senator or Representative, or Person holding an Office of Trust or Profit under the United States, shall be appointed an Elector.

~~The Electors shall meet in their respective States, and vote by Ballot for two Persons, of whom one at least shall not be an Inhabitant of the same State with themselves. And they shall make a List of all the Persons voted for, and of the Number of Votes for each; which List they shall sign and certify, and transmit sealed to the Seat of the Government of the United States, directed to the President of the Senate. The President of the Senate shall, in the Presence of the Senate and House of Representatives, open all the Certificates, and the Votes shall then be counted. The Person having the greatest Number of Votes shall be the President, if such Number be a Majority of the whole Number of Electors appointed; and if there be more than one who have such majority, and have an equal Number of Votes, then the House of Representatives shall immediately choose by Ballot one of them for President; and if no Person have a Majority, then from the five highest on the List the said House shall in like Manner choose the President. But in choosing the President, the Votes shall be taken by States, the Representation from each State having one Vote; A quorum for this Purpose shall consist of a Member or Members from two thirds of the States, and a Majority of all the States shall be necessary to a Choice. In every Case, after the Choice of the President, the Person having the greatest Number of Votes of the Electors shall be the Vice President.~~

governments have separate powers, share some powers, and are denied other powers. The states may not exercise any of the powers that belong solely to Congress.

 Constitutional Heritage

According to the Constitution, under what circumstances could a state engage in war?

Executive Branch

The president is the chief of the executive branch. It is the job of the president to enforce the laws. The framers wanted the president and vice president's terms of office and manner of selection to be different from those of members of Congress. They decided on four-year terms, but they had a difficult time agreeing on how to select the president and vice president. The framers finally set up an electoral system, which varies greatly from our electoral process today. The Twelfth Amendment changed the process by requiring that separate ballots be cast for president and vice president. The rise of political parties has since changed the process even more.

The Tyler Precedent

After President William Henry Harrison died only one month after taking office in 1841, Vice President John Tyler took the presidential oath of office. Some observers—and Tyler himself—believed that this was unnecessary. The vice presidential oath had established him as the president's successor. At the same time, however, Tyler wanted to emphasize his claim on the presidency. He regarded himself as the rightful president, entitled to serve until the end of Harrison's term. Although some critics disagreed, Tyler established an important precedent—that when the president died, the vice president assumed the higher office with all its powers.

CRITICAL THINKING On what grounds might Tyler's critics have objected to his position?

ANSWER: Students might note that critics might have objected on constitutional grounds.—Article II does not specify whether the vice president is an acting president or serves out the remaining term as president.

CONSTITUTIONAL HERITAGE ANSWER

It mentions the power that the president has to make treaties and appointments but also notes that Congress must approve them.

In 1845 Congress set the Tuesday following the first Monday in November of every fourth year as the general election date for selecting presidential electors.

Emolument means "salary, or payment." In 1999 Congress voted to set future presidents' salaries at $400,000 per year. The president also receives an annual expense account. The president must pay taxes only on the salary.

The oath of office is administered to the president by the chief justice of the United States. George Washington added "So help me, God." All succeeding presidents have followed this practice.

Constitutional Heritage

How does the description of the executive branch make clear the separation of powers established in the Constitution?

According to this section the president can form a cabinet of advisers. Every president, starting with George Washington, has appointed a cabinet.

Most of the president's appointments to office must be approved by the Senate.

~~But if there should remain two or more who have equal Votes, the Senate shall choose from them by Ballot the Vice President.~~

The Congress may determine the Time of choosing the Electors, and the Day on which they shall give their Votes; which Day shall be the same throughout the United States.

No Person except a natural born Citizen, ~~or a Citizen of the United States, at the time of the Adoption of this Constitution,~~ shall be eligible to the Office of President; neither shall any Person be eligible to that Office who shall not have attained to the Age of thirty-five Years, and been fourteen Years a Resident within the United States.

In Case of the Removal of the President from Office, or of his Death, Resignation, or Inability to discharge the Powers and Duties of the said Office, the Same shall devolve on the Vice President, and the Congress may by Law provide for the Case of Removal, Death, Resignation or Inability, both of the President and Vice President, declaring what Officer shall then act as President, and such Officer shall act accordingly, until the Disability be removed, or a President shall be elected.

The President shall, at stated Times, receive for his Services, a Compensation, which shall neither be increased nor diminished during the Period for which he shall have been elected, and he shall not receive within that Period any other Emolument from the United States, or any of them.

Before he enter on the Execution of his Office, he shall take the following Oath or Affirmation:—"I do solemnly swear (or affirm) that I will faithfully execute the Office of President of the United States, and will to the best of my Ability, preserve, protect and defend the Constitution of the United States."

Section 2. The President shall be Commander in Chief of the Army and Navy of the United States, and of the Militia of the several States, when called into the actual Service of the United States; he may require the Opinion, in writing, of the principal Officer in each of the executive Departments, upon any Subject relating to the Duties of their respective Offices, and he shall have Power to grant Reprieves and Pardons for Offenses against the United States, except in Cases of Impeachment.

He shall have Power, by and with the Advice and Consent of the Senate, to make Treaties, provided two thirds of the Senators present concur; and he shall nominate, and by and with the Advice and Consent of the Senate, shall appoint Ambassadors, other public Ministers and Consuls, Judges of the supreme Court, and all other Officers of the United States, whose Appointments are not herein otherwise provided for, and which shall be established by Law: but the Congress may by Law vest the Appointment of such inferior Officers, as they think proper, in the President alone, in the Courts of Law, or in the Heads of Departments.

The President shall have Power to fill up all Vacancies that may happen during the Recess of the Senate, by granting Commissions which shall expire at the End of their next Session.

Section 3. He shall from time to time give to the Congress Information of the State of the Union, and recommend to their Consideration such Measures as he shall judge necessary and expedient; he may, on extraordinary Occasions, convene both Houses, or either of them, and in Case of Disagreement between them, with Respect to the Time of Adjournment, he may adjourn them to such Time as he shall think proper; he shall receive Ambassadors and other public Ministers; he shall take Care that the Laws be faithfully executed, and shall Commission all the Officers of the United States.

Section 4. The President, Vice President and all civil Officers of the United States, shall be removed from Office on Impeachment for, and Conviction of, Treason, Bribery, or other high Crimes and Misdemeanors.

ARTICLE III

Section 1. The judicial Power of the United States, shall be vested in one supreme Court, and in such inferior Courts as the Congress may from time to time ordain and establish. The Judges, both of the supreme and inferior Courts, shall hold their Offices during good Behavior, and shall, at stated Times, receive for their Services, a Compensation, which shall not be diminished during their Continuance in Office.

Section 2. The judicial Power shall extend to all Cases, in Law and Equity, arising under this Constitution, the Laws of the United States, and Treaties made, or which shall be made, under their Authority;—to all Cases affecting Ambassadors, other public Ministers and Consuls;—to all Cases of admiralty and maritime Jurisdiction;—to Controversies to which

The U.S. Supreme Court in 2001

Every year the president presents to Congress a State of the Union message. In this message, the president explains the executive branch's legislative plans for the coming year.

This clause states that one of the president's duties is to enforce the laws.

⭐ Constitutional Heritage

What actions might lead to the impeachment of a president, vice president, or other civil officer?

Judicial Branch
The Articles of Confederation did not make any provisions for a federal court system. One of the first things that the framers of the Constitution agreed upon was to set up a national judiciary. With all the laws that Congress would be enacting, there would be a great need for a branch of government to interpret the laws. In the Judiciary Act of 1789, Congress provided for the establishment of lower courts, such as district courts, circuit courts of appeals, and various other federal courts. The judicial system provides a check on the legislative branch; it can declare a law unconstitutional.

Diplomatic Immunity.

Many nations offer foreign diplomats such as ambassadors immunity from prosecution for civil and, in some cases, criminal charges. Known as diplomatic immunity, this practice is an agreement made under international law and is not required by the Constitution. In fact, Article III empowers the judiciary to prosecute charges against diplomats.

CRITICAL THINKING Why might nations offer foreign diplomats immunity from prosecution?

ANSWER: Students might suggest that nations want to protect diplomats against politically motivated lawsuits.

**CONSTITUTIONAL
HERITAGE ANSWER**

that trials be by jury and that they be held in the state where the crimes were committed

Constitutional Heritage

What guidelines does the Constitution establish for criminal trials?

Congress has the power to decide the punishment for treason, but it can punish only the guilty person. Corruption of blood refers to punishing the family of a person who has committed treason. It is expressly forbidden by the Constitution.

The States
States must honor the laws, records, and court decisions of other states. A person cannot escape a legal obligation by moving from one state to another.

the United States shall be a Party;—to Controversies between two or more States;—between a State and Citizens of another State;—between Citizens of different States;—between Citizens of the same State claiming Lands under Grants of different States, and between a State, or the Citizens thereof, and foreign States, Citizens or Subjects.

In all Cases affecting Ambassadors, other public Ministers and Consuls, and those in which a State shall be Party, the supreme Court shall have original Jurisdiction. In all the other Cases before mentioned, the supreme Court shall have appellate Jurisdiction, both as to Law and fact, with such Exceptions, and under such Regulations as the Congress shall make.

The Trial of all Crimes, except in Cases of Impeachment, shall be by Jury; and such Trial shall be held in the State where the said Crimes shall have been committed; but when not committed within any State, the Trial shall be at such Place or Places as the Congress may by Law have directed.

Section 3. Treason against the United States, shall consist only in levying War against them, or in adhering to their Enemies, giving them Aid and Comfort. No Person shall be convicted of Treason unless on the Testimony of two Witnesses to the same overt Act, or on Confession in open Court.

The Congress shall have Power to declare the Punishment of Treason, but no Attainder of Treason shall work Corruption of Blood, or Forfeiture except during the Life of the Person attainted.

ARTICLE IV

Section 1. Full Faith and Credit shall be given in each State to the public Acts, Records, and judicial Proceedings of every other State. And the Congress may by general Laws prescribe the Manner in which such Acts, Records and Proceedings shall be proved, and the Effect thereof.

Section 2. The Citizens of each State shall be entitled to all Privileges and Immunities of Citizens in the several States.

A Person charged in any State with Treason, Felony, or other Crime, who shall flee from Justice, and be found in another State, shall on Demand of the executive Authority of the State from which he fled, be delivered up, to be removed to the State having Jurisdiction of the Crime.

~~No Person held to Service of Labor in one State, under the Laws thereof, escaping into another, shall, in Consequence of any Law or Regulation therein, be discharged from such Service or Labor, but shall be delivered up on Claim of the Party to whom such Service or Labor may be due.~~

Section 3. New States may be admitted by the Congress into this Union; but no new State shall be formed or erected within the Jurisdiction of any other State; nor any State be formed by the Junction of two or more States, or Parts of States, without the Consent of the Legislatures of the States concerned as well as of the Congress.

The Congress shall have Power to dispose of and make all needful Rules and Regulations respecting the Territory or other Property belonging to the United States; and nothing in this Constitution shall be so construed as to Prejudice any Claims of the United States, or of any particular State.

Section 4. The United States shall guarantee to every State in this Union a Republican Form of Government, and shall protect each of them against Invasion; and on Application of the Legislature, or of the Executive (when the Legislature cannot be convened) against domestic Violence.

ARTICLE V

The Congress, whenever two thirds of both Houses shall deem it necessary, shall propose Amendments to this Constitution, or, on the Application of the Legislatures of two thirds of the several States, shall call a Convention for proposing Amendments, which, in either Case, shall be valid to all Intents and Purposes, as Part of this Constitution, when ratified by the Legislatures of three fourths of the several States, or by Conventions in three fourths thereof, as the one or the other Mode of Ratification may be proposed by the Congress; Provided that no Amendment which may be made prior to the Year One thousand eight hundred and eight shall in any Manner affect the first and fourth Clauses in the Ninth Section of the first Article; and that no State, without its Consent, shall be deprived of its equal Suffrage in the Senate.

ARTICLE VI

All Debts contracted and Engagements entered into, before the Adoption of this Constitution, shall be as valid against the United States under this Constitution, as under the Confederation.

This Constitution, and the Laws of the United States which shall be made in Pursuance thereof; and all Treaties made, or which shall be made, under the Authority of the United States, shall be the supreme Law of the Land; and the Judges in every State shall be bound thereby, any Thing in the Constitution or Laws of any State to the Contrary notwithstanding.

The Senators and Representatives before mentioned, and the Members of the several State Legislatures, and all executive and judicial Officers, both of the United States and of the several States, shall be bound by Oath or Affirmation, to support this Constitution; but no religious Test shall ever be required as a Qualification to any Office or public Trust under the United States.

Section 3 permits Congress to admit new states to the Union. When a group of people living in an area that is not part of an existing state wishes to form a new state, it asks Congress for permission to do so. The people then write a state constitution and offer it to Congress for approval. The state constitution must set up a representative form of government and must not in any way contradict the federal Constitution. If a majority of Congress approves the state constitution, the state is admitted as a member of the United States of America.

The Amendment Process
America's founders may not have realized just how enduring the Constitution would be, but they did make provisions for changing or adding to the Constitution. They did not want to make it easy to change the Constitution. There are two different ways in which changes can be proposed to the states and two different ways in which states can approve the changes and make them part of the Constitution.

National Supremacy
One of the biggest problems facing the delegates to the Constitutional Convention was the question of what would happen if a state law and a national law conflicted. Which law would be followed? Who decided? The second clause of Article VI answers those questions. When a national and state law are in conflict, the national law overrides the state law. The Constitution is the supreme law of the land. This clause is often called the "supremacy clause."

William Short in *The Founders' Constitution*

Ratifying the Constitution

Article VII required nine states to ratify the Constitution before it took effect. William Short expressed concerns over this figure in a 1787 letter to James Madison. "I think the adoption by nine & refusal by four of the States is the worst possible situation to which the new plan can give birth; & it seems probable that that will be the situation. Would it not have been better to have fixed on the number eleven or twelve instead of nine? In that case the plan would have been either refused altogether or adopted by such a commanding majority as would almost necessarily have brought in the others in the end."

Activity:

Tell students to imagine that they are James Madison. Have each student write a half-page response to Short.

THAT'S INTERESTING!

Rhode Island initially refused to ratify the Constitution. In a popular vote just 237 people voted for it. 2,708 voted against ratification. The state finally ratified it in 1790, after the government created under the Constitution had already assumed control of the United States.

Ratification

The Articles of Confederation called for all 13 states to approve any revision to the Articles. The Constitution required that the vote of 9 out of the 13 states would be needed to ratify the Constitution. The first state to ratify was Delaware, on December 7, 1787. The last state to ratify the Constitution was Rhode Island, which finally did so on May 29, 1790, almost two and a half years later.

ARTICLE VII

The Ratification of the Conventions of nine States, shall be sufficient for the Establishment of this Constitution between the States so ratifying the Same.

Done in Convention by the Unanimous Consent of the States present the Seventeenth Day of September in the Year of our Lord one thousand seven hundred and Eighty seven and of the Independence of the United States of America the Twelfth. In witness whereof We have hereunto subscribed our Names.

George Washington—
President and deputy from Virginia

New Hampshire
John Langdon
Nicholas Gilman

Massachusetts
Nathaniel Gorham
Rufus King

Connecticut
William Samuel Johnson
Roger Sherman

New York
Alexander Hamilton

New Jersey
William Livingston
David Brearley
William Paterson
Jonathan Dayton

Pennsylvania
Benjamin Franklin
Thomas Mifflin
Robert Morris
George Clymer
Thomas FitzSimons
Jared Ingersoll
James Wilson
Gouverneur Morris

Delaware
George Read
Gunning Bedford Jr.
John Dickinson
Richard Bassett
Jacob Broom

Maryland
James McHenry
Daniel of St. Thomas Jenifer
Daniel Carroll

Virginia
John Blair
James Madison Jr.

North Carolina
William Blount
Richard Dobbs Spaight
Hugh Williamson

South Carolina
John Rutledge
Charles Cotesworth Pinckney
Charles Pinckney
Pierce Butler

Georgia
William Few
Abraham Baldwin

Attest: *William Jackson*, Secretary

THE AMENDMENTS

Articles in addition to, and Amendment of the Constitution of the United States of America, proposed by Congress, and ratified by the Legislatures of the several states, pursuant to the fifth Article of the original Constitution.

[The First through Tenth Amendments, now known as the Bill of Rights, were proposed on September 25, 1789, and declared in force on December 15, 1791.]

First Amendment

Congress shall make no law respecting an establishment of religion, or prohibiting the free exercise thereof; or abridging the freedom of speech, or of the press; or the right of the people peaceably to assemble, and to petition the Government for a redress of grievances.

Members of the Students Against Drunk Driving exercise their First Amendment right to expression by gathering in Washington, D.C., to speak out against drinking and driving.

Second Amendment

A well regulated Militia, being necessary to the security of a free State, the right of the people to keep and bear Arms, shall not be infringed.

The National Guard, which has replaced state militias, helps local citizens prevent a river from flooding.

Bill of Rights

One of the conditions set by several states for ratifying the Constitution was the inclusion of a bill of rights. Many people feared that a stronger central government might take away basic rights of the people that had been guaranteed in state constitutions. If the three words that begin the Preamble—"We the people"— were truly meant, then the rights of the people needed to be protected.

The First Amendment protects freedom of speech and expression, and forbids Congress to make any law "respecting an establishment of religion" or restraining the freedom to practice religion as one chooses.

Hugo Black in *Encyclope-
dia of the American Constitution*

Double Jeopardy

Justice Hugo Black
explained the Fifth Amendment's ban on double jeopardy in a 1957 ruling. "The
underlying idea . . . is that
the state with all its
resources and power
should not be allowed to
make repeated attempts to
convict an individual for an
alleged offense, thereby (1)
subjecting him to embar-
rassment, expense and
ordeal and (2) compelling
him to live in a continuing
state of anxiety and insecu-
rity, as well as (3) enhancing
the possibility that even
though innocent he may be
found guilty."

CRITICAL THINKING According to the excerpt, what did
Black perceive as the primary reason for the ban on
double jeopardy?

ANSWER: Students
should suggest that the
state could use repeated
prosecution to destroy
individuals it regarded
as enemies.

THAT'S INTERESTING!

The Third Amendment is
one of the least contro-
versial amendments to the
Constitution. It provoked
almost no debate in Con-
gress and it has never been
the subject of a Supreme
Court decision.

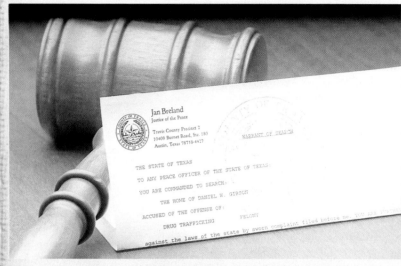

*Judges issue search warrants like this one to allow law enforcement
officials to legally search a suspected criminal's property.*

A police officer may enter a person's
home with a search warrant, which
allows the law officer to look for evidence that could convict someone
of committing a crime.

The Fifth, Sixth, and Seventh Amendments describe the procedures that
courts must follow when trying people accused of crimes. The Fifth
Amendment guarantees that no one
can be put on trial for a serious
crime unless a grand jury agrees
that the evidence justifies doing so.
It also says that a person cannot be
tried twice for the same crime.

The Sixth Amendment makes several promises, including a prompt
trial and a trial by a jury chosen from
the state and district in which the
crime was committed. The Sixth
Amendment also states that an
accused person must be told why
he or she is being tried and
promises that an accused person
has the right to be defended by a
lawyer.

Third Amendment

No Soldier shall, in time of peace, be quartered in any house, without
the consent of the Owner, nor in time of war, but in a manner to be prescribed by law.

Fourth Amendment

The right of the people to be secure in their persons, houses, papers,
and effects, against unreasonable searches and seizures, shall not be
violated, and no Warrants shall issue, but upon probable cause, supported
by Oath or affirmation, and particularly describing the place to be
searched, and the persons or things to be seized.

Fifth Amendment

No person shall be held to answer for a capital, or otherwise infamous
crime, unless on a presentment or indictment of a Grand Jury, except in
cases arising in the land or naval forces, or in the Militia, when in actual
service in time of War or public danger; nor shall any person be subject for
the same offense to be twice put in jeopardy of life or limb; nor shall be
compelled in any criminal case to be a witness against himself, nor be
deprived of life, liberty, or property, without due process of law; nor shall
private property be taken for public use, without just compensation.

Sixth Amendment

In all criminal prosecutions, the accused shall enjoy the right to a
speedy and public trial, by an impartial jury of the State and district
wherein the crime shall have been committed, which district shall have
been previously ascertained by law, and to be informed of the nature and
cause of the accusation; to be confronted with the witnesses against him;

to have compulsory process for obtaining witnesses in his favor, and to have the Assistance of Counsel for his defense.

Seventh Amendment

In Suits at common law, where the value in controversy shall exceed twenty dollars, the right of trial by jury shall be preserved, and no fact tried by a jury shall be otherwise reexamined in any Court of the United States, than according to the rules of the common law.

The Seventh Amendment guarantees a trial by jury in cases that involve more than $20, but in modern times, usually much more money is at stake before a case is heard in federal court.

Eighth Amendment

Excessive bail shall not be required, nor excessive fines imposed, nor cruel and unusual punishments inflicted.

Ninth Amendment

The enumeration in the Constitution, of certain rights, shall not be construed to deny or disparage others retained by the people.

The Ninth and Tenth Amendments were added because not every right of the people or of the states could be listed in the Constitution.

Tenth Amendment

The powers not delegated to the United States by the Constitution, nor prohibited by it to the States, are reserved to the States respectively, or to the people.

 Constitutional Heritage

How does the Tenth Amendment limit the powers of the federal government?

Eleventh Amendment

[Proposed March 4, 1794; declared ratified January 8, 1798]

The Judicial power of the United States shall not be construed to extend to any suit in law or equity, commenced or prosecuted against one of the United States by Citizens of another State, or by Citizens or Subjects of any Foreign State.

Many Americans consider attendance in free public schools a right of citizenship.

Cruel and Unusual Punishment

Do school disciplinary actions such as paddling constitute cruel and unusual punishment? After being roughly paddled, two Florida junior high students sued school officials on those grounds. In addition, they claimed that their right to due process had been violated because they had not received a hearing prior to the paddling. Their case eventually went to the Supreme Court. In *Ingraham* v. *Wright,* a 1977 ruling, the Supreme Court ruled that punishments such as paddling did not violate the Eighth Amendment rights of school students. In a 5-4 decision, the court determined that the Eighth Amendment applied to criminal punishments and not disciplinary actions such as school paddlings. Moreover, the court ruled that students who had been paddled could sue for damages, and therefore hearings were not necessary.

Activity:

Have students discuss *Ingraham* v. *Wright.* Then have each student write a one-page legal brief supporting or opposing the court's decision.

CONSTITUTIONAL HERITAGE ANSWER

gives non-delegated powers to the states or to the people

Ending Slavery

In 1863 President Abraham Lincoln freed slaves in certain areas—namely those in rebellion against the United States. Some observers questioned the president's power to end slavery, however, and many doubted that his proclamation would remain in effect after the Civil War. In order to ensure that slavery was forever banned in the United States, these people called for a constitutional amendment prohibiting slavery.

CRITICAL THINKING Why might a constitutional amendment banning slavery have been necessary?

ANSWER: Students should suggest that observers believed that an amendment was necessary due to the the legal questions surrounding Lincoln's actions. They might also have feared that white southerners would try to re-establish slavery after the war.

CONSTITUTIONAL HERITAGE ANSWER
the House of Representatives

The Twelfth Amendment changed the election procedure for president and vice president. Before this amendment, electors voted without distinguishing between president and vice president. Whoever received the most votes became president, and whoever received the next highest number of votes became vice president.

Constitutional Heritage

According to the Twelfth Amendment, who chooses the president if no candidate has received a majority of the electoral votes?

Poster commemorating President Abraham Lincoln's Emancipation Proclamation, which freed slaves in the Confederacy

---

Twelfth Amendment

[Proposed December 9, 1803; declared ratified September 25, 1804]

The Electors shall meet in their respective states and vote by ballot for President and Vice President, one of whom, at least, shall not be an inhabitant of the same state with themselves; they shall name in their ballots the person voted for as President, and in distinct ballots the person voted for as Vice President, and they shall make distinct lists of all persons voted for as President, and of all persons voted for as Vice President, and of the number of votes for each, which lists they shall sign and certify, and transmit sealed to the seat of the government of the United States, directed to the President of the Senate;—The President of the Senate shall, in the presence of the Senate and House of Representatives, open all the certificates and the votes shall then be counted;—The person having the greatest number of votes for President, shall be the President, if such number be a majority of the whole number of Electors appointed; and if no person have such majority, then from the persons having the highest numbers not exceeding three on the list of those voted for as President, the House of Representatives shall choose immediately, by ballot, the President. But in choosing the President, the votes shall be taken by states, the representation from each state having one vote; a quorum for this purpose shall consist of a member or members from two thirds of the states, and a majority of all the states shall be necessary to a choice. ~~And if the House of Representatives shall not choose a President whenever the right of choice shall devolve upon them, before the fourth day of March next following, then the Vice-President shall act as President, as in the case of the death or other constitutional disability of the President;~~ —The person having the greatest number of votes as Vice President, shall be the Vice President, if such number be a majority of the whole number of Electors appointed, and if no person have a majority, then from the two highest numbers on the list, the Senate shall choose the Vice President; a quorum for the purpose shall consist of two thirds of the whole number of Senators, and a majority of the whole number shall be necessary to a choice. But no person constitutionally ineligible to the office of President shall be eligible to that of Vice President of the United States.

Thirteenth Amendment

[Proposed January 31, 1865; declared ratified December 18, 1865]

Section 1. Neither slavery nor involuntary servitude, except as a punishment for crime whereof the party shall have been duly convicted, shall exist within the United States, or any place subject to their jurisdiction.

Section 2. Congress shall have power to enforce this article by appropriate legislation.

Fourteenth Amendment

[Proposed June 13, 1866; declared ratified July 28, 1868]

Section 1. All persons born or naturalized in the United States and subject to the jurisdiction thereof, are citizens of the United States and of the State wherein they reside. No State shall make or enforce any law which shall abridge the privileges or immunities of citizens of the United States; nor shall any State deprive any person of life, liberty, or property, without due process of law; nor deny to any person within its jurisdiction the equal protection of the laws.

Section 2. Representatives shall be apportioned among the several States according to their respective numbers, counting the whole number of persons in each State, ~~excluding Indians not taxed.~~ But when the right to vote at any election for the choice of electors for President and Vice President of the United States, Representatives in Congress, the Executive and Judicial officers of a State, or the members of the Legislature thereof, is denied to any of the ~~male~~ inhabitants of such State, ~~being twenty-one years of age, and~~ citizens of the United States, or in any way abridged, except for participation in rebellion, or other crime, the basis of representation therein shall be reduced in the proportion which the number of such male citizens shall bear to the whole number of male citizens twenty-one years of age in such State.

Section 3. No person shall be a Senator or Representative in Congress, or elector of President and Vice President, or hold any office, civil or military, under the United States, or under any State, who, having previously taken an oath, as a member of Congress, or as an officer of the United States, or as a member of any State legislature, or as an executive or judicial officer of any State, to support the Constitution of the United States, shall have engaged in insurrection or rebellion against the same, or given aid or comfort to the enemies thereof. But Congress may by a vote of two thirds of each House, remove such disability.

Section 4. The validity of the public debt of the United States, authorized by law, including debts incurred for payment of pensions and bounties for services in suppressing insurrection or rebellion, shall not be questioned. But neither the United States nor any State shall assume or pay any debt or obligation incurred in aid of insurrection or rebellion against the United States, ~~or any claim for the loss or emancipation of any slave;~~ but all such debts, obligations and claims shall be held illegal and void.

Section 5. The Congress shall have power to enforce, by appropriate legislation, the provisions of this article.

Fifteenth Amendment

[Proposed February 26, 1869; declared ratified March 30, 1870]

Section 1. The right of citizens of the United States to vote shall not be denied or abridged by the United States or by any State on account of race, color, or previous condition of servitude.

 Constitutional Heritage

According to the Fourteenth Amendment, who is a citizen of the United States, and what rights do citizens have?

In 1833 Chief Justice John Marshall ruled that the Bill of Rights limited the national government but not the state governments. The later effect of this ruling was that states were able to keep African Americans from becoming state citizens. If African Americans were not citizens, they were not protected by the Bill of Rights. The Fourteenth Amendment defines citizenship and prevents states from interfering in the rights of citizens of the United States.

The Fifteenth Amendment extended the right to vote to African American men.

CITIZENSHIP

American Indian Citizenship

In its 1884 decision in *Elk* v. *Wilkins,* the Supreme Court ruled that American Indians were not automatically U.S. citizens. The case began when John Elk, an Omaha Indian, attempted to register to vote in Nebraska. The local official refused to accept his application, arguing that he was not a citizen. Elk's case eventually went to the Supreme Court, which ruled that American Indians could only become citizens by treaty provisions or acts of Congress. Thus, the Fourteenth Amendment did not apply to American Indians. It was not until 1924 that Congress passed an act granting citizenship to all American Indians.

CRITICAL THINKING What did *Elk* v. *Wilkins* indicate about attitudes toward American Indians in the 1880s?

ANSWER: Students should suggest that the ruling indicated that many Americans viewed American Indians as "foreigners" in their own lands.

CONSTITUTIONAL HERITAGE ANSWER

all persons born or naturalized in the United States; all the rights of citizens, including life, liberty, and the equal protection of laws

---

GOVERNMENT
The Sixteenth Amendment

On the whole, Democrats tended to favor an income tax, while conservative Republicans generally opposed it. Ironically, Senator Nelson Aldrich of Rhode Island, a conservative millionaire Republican, introduced the constitutional amendment permitting an income tax. Aldrich assumed that his amendment would fail to gain adoption. He introduced the measure as a political move to forestall some Democrats from adding another income tax provision to a piece of tariff legislation. The Senate passed the Aldrich measure 77 to 0, however, and the House passed it 318 to 14. The necessary number of states approved it as well, and the amendment became part of the Constitution.

CRITICAL THINKING In what way might the history of the constitutional amendment process have given Aldrich the confidence that the income tax amendment would never be ratified?

ANSWER: Students should note that by 1913 the Constitution had only been amended 5 times.

CONSTITUTIONAL HERITAGE ANSWER

by allowing the citizens of each state to directly elect their senators

---

Expanding on the federal government's right to levy taxes, outlined in Article I of the Constitution, the Sixteenth Amendment gave Congress the power to issue the income tax.

Federal income tax form

Constitutional Heritage

How does the Seventeenth Amendment return authority to the people?

Although many people believed that prohibition was good for the health and welfare of the American people, the Eighteenth Amendment was repealed 14 years later.

Federal agents dispose of alcohol after the passage of the Eighteenth Amendment.

Section 2. The Congress shall have power to enforce this article by appropriate legislation.

Sixteenth Amendment
[Proposed July 12, 1909; declared ratified February 25, 1913]

The Congress shall have power to lay and collect taxes on incomes, from whatever source derived, without apportionment among the several States, and without regard to any census or enumeration.

Seventeenth Amendment
[Proposed May 13, 1912; declared ratified May 31, 1913]

The Senate of the United States shall be composed of two Senators from each State, elected by the people thereof, for six years; and each Senator shall have one vote. The electors in each State shall have the qualifications requisite for electors of the most numerous branch of the State legislatures.

When vacancies happen in the representation of any State in the Senate, the executive authority of such State shall issue writs of election to fill such vacancies: Provided, That the legislature of any State may empower the executive thereof to make temporary appointments until the people fill the vacancies by election as the legislature may direct.

This amendment shall not be so construed as to affect the election or term of any Senator chosen before it becomes valid as part of the Constitution.

Eighteenth Amendment
[Proposed December 18, 1917; declared ratified January 29, 1919; repealed by the Twenty-first Amendment December 5, 1933]

~~**Section 1.** After one year from the ratification of this article the manufacture, sale, or transportation of intoxicating liquors within, the importation thereof into, or the exportation thereof from the United States and all territory subject to the jurisdiction thereof for beverage purposes is hereby prohibited.~~

~~**Section 2.** The Congress and the several States shall have concurrent power to enforce this article by appropriate legislation.~~

~~**Section 3.** This article shall be inoperative unless it shall have been ratified as an amendment to the Constitution by the legislatures of the several States, as provided in the Constitution, within seven years from the date of the submission hereof to the States by the Congress.~~

Nineteenth Amendment

[Proposed June 4, 1919; declared ratified August 26, 1920]

The right of citizens of the United States to vote shall not be denied or abridged by the United States or by any State on account of sex.

Congress shall have power to enforce this article by appropriate legislation.

Women's suffrage button

Twentieth Amendment

[Proposed March 2, 1932; declared ratified February 6, 1933]

Section 1. The terms of the President and Vice President shall end at noon on the 20th day of January, and the terms of Senators and Representatives at noon on the 3rd day of January, of the years in which such terms would have ended if this article had not been ratified; and the terms of their successors shall then begin.

Section 2. The Congress shall assemble at least once in every year, and such meeting shall begin at noon on the 3rd day of January, unless they shall by law appoint a different day.

Section 3. If, at the time fixed for the beginning of the term of the President, the President elect shall have died, the Vice President elect shall become President. If a President shall not have been chosen before the time fixed for the beginning of his term, or if the President elect shall have failed to qualify, then the Vice President elect shall act as President until a President shall have qualified; and the Congress may by law provide for the case wherein neither a President elect nor a Vice President elect shall have qualified, declaring who shall then act as President, or the manner in which one who is to act shall be selected, and such persons shall act accordingly until a President or Vice President shall have qualified.

Section 4. The Congress may by law provide for the case of the death of any of the persons from whom the House of Representatives may choose a President whenever the right of choice shall have devolved upon them, and for the case of the death of any of the persons from whom the Senate may choose a Vice President whenever the right of choice shall have devolved upon them.

~~**Section 5.** Sections 1 and 2 shall take effect on the 15th day of October following the ratification of this article.~~

~~**Section 6.** This article shall be inoperative unless it shall have been ratified as an amendment to the Constitution by the legislatures of three fourths of the several States within seven years from the date of its submission.~~

Abigail Adams was disappointed that the Declaration of Independence and the Constitution did not specifically include women. It took almost 150 years and much campaigning by women's suffrage groups for women to finally achieve voting privileges.

In the original Constitution, a newly elected president and Congress did not take office until March 4, which was four months after the November election. The officials who were leaving office were called "lame ducks" because they had little influence during those four months. The Twentieth Amendment changed the date that the new president and Congress take office. Members of Congress now take office on January 3, and the president takes office on January 20.

⭐ **Constitutional Heritage**

According to the Twentieth Amendment, who becomes president if a president-elect dies before taking office?

Abigail Adams in *The Way We Lived: Essays and Documents in American Social History*

Abigail Adams on Women's Rights

Women finally gained universal suffrage in 1920. Abigail Adams expressed her views on women's rights in a 1776 letter to her husband. "In the new Code of Laws which I will suppose it will be necessary for you to make I desire you would Remember the Ladies, and be more generous and favourable to them than your ancestors. Do not put such unlimited power into the hands of the Husbands. Remember all Men would be tyrants if they could. If particular care and attention is not paid to the Laidies we are determined to foment a Rebellion, and will not hold ourselves bound by any Laws in which we have no voice, or Representation. . . . Men of Sense in all Ages abhor those customs which treat us only as the vassals of your Sex."

CRITICAL THINKING Why did Adams believe that women must be included in the laws of the new government?

ANSWER: Students should note that she argued that women had the right to representation in the nation's laws.

CONSTITUTIONAL HERITAGE ANSWER
the vice president–elect

The Twenty-first Amendment is the only amendment that has been ratified by state conventions rather than by state legislatures.

From the time of President Washington's administration, it was a custom for presidents to serve no more than two terms of office. Franklin D. Roosevelt, however, was elected to four consecutive terms. The Twenty-second Amendment made into law the custom of a two-term limit for each president.

Constitutional Heritage

How does the Twenty-second Amendment limit the years a president can remain in office?

Until the Twenty-third Amendment, the residents of Washington, D.C., could not vote in presidential elections.

Aerial view of Washington, D.C.

Twenty-first Amendment
[Proposed February 20, 1933; declared ratified December 5, 1933]

Section 1. The eighteenth article of amendment to the Constitution of the United States is hereby repealed.

Section 2. The transportation or importation into any State, Territory, or possession of the United States for delivery or use therein of intoxicating liquors, in violation of the laws thereof, is hereby prohibited.

~~**Section 3.** This article shall be inoperative unless it shall have been ratified as an amendment to the Constitution by conventions in the several States, as provided in the Constitution, within seven years from the date of the submission hereof to the States by the Congress.~~

Twenty-second Amendment
[Proposed March 24, 1947; declared ratified March 1, 1951]

Section 1. No person shall be elected to the office of the President more than twice, and no person who has held the office of President, or acted as President, for more than two years of a term to which some other person was elected President shall be elected to the office of the President more than once. ~~But this Article shall not apply to any person holding the office of President when this Article was proposed by the Congress, and shall not prevent any person who may be holding the office of President, or acting as President, during the term within which this Article becomes operative from holding the office of President or acting as President during the remainder of such term.~~

~~**Section 2.** This Article shall be inoperative unless it shall have been ratified as an amendment to the Constitution by the legislatures of three fourths of the several States within seven years from the date of its submission to the States by the Congress.~~

Twenty-third Amendment
[Proposed June 16, 1960; declared ratified April 3, 1961]

Section 1. The District constituting the seat of Government of the United States shall appoint in such manner as the Congress may direct:

A number of electors of President and Vice President equal to the whole number of Senators and Representatives in Congress to which the District would be entitled if it were a State, but in no event more than the least populous State; they shall be in addition to those appointed by the States, but they shall be considered, for the purposes of the election of President and Vice President, to be electors appointed by a State; and they shall meet in the District and perform such duties as provided by the twelfth article of amendment.

Section 2. The Congress shall have power to enforce this article by appropriate legislation.

Twenty-fourth Amendment

[Proposed August 27, 1962; declared ratified February 4, 1964]

Section 1. The right of citizens of the United States to vote in any primary or other election for President or Vice President, for electors for President or Vice President, or for Senator or Representative in Congress, shall not be denied or abridged by the United States or any State by reason of failure to pay any poll tax or other tax.

Section 2. The Congress shall have power to enforce this article by appropriate legislation.

Twenty-fifth Amendment

[Proposed July 6, 1965; declared ratified February 23, 1967]

Section 1. In case of removal of the President from office or of his death or resignation, the Vice President shall become President.

Section 2. Whenever there is a vacancy in the office of the Vice President, the President shall nominate a Vice President who shall take office upon confirmation by a majority vote of both Houses of Congress.

Vice President Lyndon Johnson was sworn in as president after John F. Kennedy's assassination.

Section 3. Whenever the President transmits to the President pro tempore of the Senate and the Speaker of the House of Representatives his written declaration that he is unable to discharge the powers and duties of his office, and until he transmits to them a written declaration to the contrary, such powers and duties shall be discharged by the Vice President as Acting President.

Section 4. Whenever the Vice President and a majority of either the principal officers of the executive departments or of such other body as Congress may by law provide, transmit to the President pro tempore of the Senate and the Speaker of the House of Representatives their written declaration that the President is unable to discharge the powers and duties of his office, the Vice President shall immediately assume the powers and duties of the office as Acting President.

Thereafter, when the President transmits to the President pro tempore of the Senate and the Speaker of the House of Representatives his written declaration that no inability exists, he shall resume the powers and duties of his office unless the Vice President and a majority of either the principal officers of the executive department or of such other body as Congress may by law provide, transmit within four days to the President pro tempore of

---

⭐ **Constitutional Heritage**

What practices does the Twenty-fourth Amendment outlaw?

The illness of President Eisenhower in the 1950s and the assassination of President Kennedy in 1963 were the events behind the Twenty-fifth Amendment. The Constitution did not provide a clear-cut method for a vice president to take over for a disabled president or in the event of the death of a president. This amendment provides for filling the office of the vice president if a vacancy occurs. It also provides a way for the vice president to take over if the president is unable to perform the duties of that office.

Gregory Watson, Constitutional Advocate

In 1982 Gregory Watson was a student at the University of Texas at Austin. In a paper for a political science class he argued that a proposed amendment regarding congressional pay, once part of the Bill of Rights, could still be ratified. Only six states had ratified the proposed amendment, which had then been ignored for more than 200 years. Watson received a "C" on his paper, but he was determined to prove that he was correct. He spent more than $5,000 of his own money in an effort to convince state legislatures throughout the nation to ratify the amendment. Watson was successful, and in 1992 the proposal became the Twenty-seventh Amendment.

CRITICAL THINKING Do you think that the proposed amendment should have become part of the Constitution? Explain your answer.

ANSWER: Some students might argue that it was not necessary, since the states had ignored it for more than 200 years. Others might argue that state legislatures ratified the amendment, and so it met all necessary qualifications.

CONSTITUTIONAL HERITAGE ANSWER

until an election of representatives had convened

Constitutional Heritage

According to the Twenty-seventh Amendment, if senators or representatives were to vote for a pay raise for themselves, when would it take effect?

The Voting Act of 1970 tried to set the voting age at 18 years old. However, the Supreme Court ruled that the act set the voting age for national elections only, not state or local elections. This ruling would make necessary several different ballots at elections. The Twenty-sixth Amendment gave 18-year-old citizens the right to vote in all elections.

the Senate and the Speaker of the House of Representatives their written declaration that the President is unable to discharge the powers and duties of his office. Thereupon Congress shall decide the issue, assembling within forty-eight hours for that purpose if not in session. If the Congress, within twenty-one days after receipt of the latter written declaration, or, if Congress is not in session, within twenty-one days after Congress is required to assemble, determines by two-thirds vote of both Houses that the President is unable to discharge the powers and duties of his office, the Vice President shall continue to discharge the same as Acting President; otherwise, the President shall resume the powers and duties of his office.

Twenty-sixth Amendment
[Proposed March 23, 1971; declared ratified July 5, 1971]

Section 1. The right of citizens of the United States, who are eighteen years of age or older, to vote shall not be denied or abridged by the United States or by any State on account of age.

Section 2. The Congress shall have power to enforce this article by appropriate legislation.

Twenty-seventh Amendment
[Proposed September 25, 1789; declared ratified May 7, 1992]

No law, varying the compensation for the services of the Senators and Representatives, shall take effect, until an election of Representatives shall have intervened.

These students are helping a local candidate campaign for office.

Amendments to the Constitution

Amendment	Year Enacted	Subject
1st	1791	Personal and political freedoms
2nd	1791	Right to keep weapons
3rd	1791	Quartering of troops
4th	1791	Search and seizure; search warrants
5th	1791	Rights of accused persons
6th	1791	Speedy trial
7th	1791	Jury trial
8th	1791	Bails, fines, punishments
9th	1791	Rights of the people
10th	1791	Powers of the states
11th	1798	Suits against the states
12th	1804	Election of president and vice president
13th	1865	Abolition of slavery
14th	1868	Rights of citizens; privileges and immunities, due process, and equal protection
15th	1870	Extension of suffrage to African American men
16th	1913	Income tax
17th	1913	Direct election of senators
18th	1919	Prohibition of liquor
19th	1920	Women's suffrage
20th	1933	Change in dates for presidential and congressional terms of office
21st	1933	Repeal of prohibition
22nd	1951	Two-term limit on presidential tenure
23rd	1961	Right to vote in presidential elections for residents of the District of Columbia
24th	1964	Poll tax banned in federal elections
25th	1967	Presidential disability and succession
26th	1971	Lowering of voting age to 18
27th	1992	Legislative salaries

The Bill of Rights

Slave chains

Voter registration form

Women's suffrage button

Failed Amendments

Only six proposed amendments that secured congressional approval failed to be ratified by the states. The first, a part of the original Bill of Rights, concerned congressional representation. Two amendments in the 1800s also failed. One regarded citizens who accepted titles of nobility from foreign governments and the other concerned slavery. During the 1900s amendments regarding child labor, equal rights, and congressional representation for the District of Columbia all failed. The Equal Rights Amendment and the District of Columbia amendment both contained deadlines, so they have no chance of being passed in the same manner as the Twenty-seventh Amendment.

CRITICAL THINKING Do you think that proposed amendments should include deadlines for ratification? Explain your answer.

ANSWER: Answers will vary. Some students might argue that deadlines place an unfair burden on the amendment's supporters.

GLOSSARY

This glossary contains terms you need to understand as you study government. After each term there is a brief definition or explanation of the term as it is used in *Holt American Government*. The page number refers to the page on which the term is introduced in the textbook.

Phonetic Respelling and Pronunciation Guide
Many of the key terms in this textbook have been respelled to help you pronounce them. The letter combinations used in the respellings throughout the narrative are explained in the following phonetic respelling and pronunciation guide. The guide is adapted from *Webster's Tenth New Collegiate Dictionary, Webster's New Geographical Dictionary,* and *Webster's New Biographical Dictionary*.

MARK	AS IN	RESPELLING	EXAMPLE
a	alphabet	a	*AL-fuh-bet
ā	Asia	ay	AY-zhuh
ä	cart, top	ah	KAHRT, TAHP
e	let, ten	e	LET, TEN
ē	even, leaf	ee	EE-vuhn, LEEF
i	it, tip, British	i	IT, TIP, BRIT-ish
ī	site, buy, Ohio	y	SYT, BY, oh-HY-oh
	iris	eye	EYE-ris
k	card	k	KAHRD
ō	over, rainbow	oh	oh-vuhr, RAYN-boh
ú	book, wood	ooh	BOOHK, WOOHD
ò	all, orchid	aw	AWL, AWR-kid
òi	foil, coin	oy	FOYL, KOYN
àu	out	ow	OWT
ə	cup, butter	uh	KUHP, BUHT-uhr
ü	rule, food	oo	ROOL, FOOD
yü	few	yoo	FYOO
zh	vision	zh	VIZH-uhn

*A syllable printed in small capital letters receives heavier emphasis than the other syllable(s) in a word.

A

absentee ballot   a ballot that a voter who will be unable to appear at his or her polling place on the day of an election can use to vote in advance by mail.   **441**

act of admission   an act of Congress that, when signed by the president, makes a territory a state.   **76**

administrative law   **1)** the rules and regulations that government agencies use to carry out statutory law, and the procedures through which those rules and regulations are created and practiced.   **2)** the body of laws that create government agencies and govern judicial review of actions taken by government agencies.   **272**

affirmative action   a program, supported by law, requiring American employers, labor unions, and other institutions to actively seek to eliminate discrimination against women and minorities and to increase the hiring, promotion, wage, training, and other opportunities for such persons.   **355**

agribusiness   the industry that is involved in producing, processing, or distributing agricultural products.   **386**

Albany Plan of Union   a plan to unite the thirteen colonies in 1754. Proposed by Benjamin Franklin, the Albany Plan of Union called for a council of representatives from each colony to levy taxes, handle military matters, and regulate affairs with American Indians. A president-general with veto power was head of the council, whose acts would be law throughout the colonies unless vetoed by the British monarch. Never approved by the British and colonial governments, the plan was never put into effect.   **26**

alien   a citizen of one nation who is temporarily or permanently living in another nation.   **298**

alliance   an agreement between two or more nations to work together toward some common (typically military or economic) goal.   **151**

ambassador   The highest-ranking diplomat who represents a nation to the government of another nation. An ambassador is the personal representative of his or her nation's head of state.   **224**

amendment   **1)** an addition to an already adopted constitution.   **51**   **2)** an addition to a bill that is under consideration by a legislature.   **126–27**

amicus curiae **brief**   a formal brief that reflects a group's concerns regarding a court decision.   **260**

amnesty   an act of forgiveness by a government for persons who have committed a crime, usually a political offense. Amnesty is granted to a group of people, in contrast to a pardon, which is granted to individuals.   **344**

anarchy   the absence of any legitimate governmental authority, resulting in political disorder and sometimes chaos and mob rule.   **14**

Antifederalist   someone who opposed the adoption of the U.S. Constitution in the late 1780s. Antifederalists feared the creation of a strong national government, preferring that state governments retain the greater share of power.   **40**

appellate jurisdiction   the requirement that an appeals court must hear cases that are appealed to it if the cases meet certain conditions set by law.   **253**

apportion   to determine how many legislators should represent a jurisdiction in a legislative body.   **99**

appropriations   **1)** funds assigned by a legislature to pay for something that has been authorized by law.   **2)** congressional legislation authorizing federal agencies to make payments out of the Treasury for specified purposes.   **118**

arraignment   in a criminal case, a court hearing in which the defendant is formally charged with a crime, informed of his or her rights, and required to enter a plea to the charge.   **277**

Articles of Confederation   a legal document to form a single national government in the United States. The Articles of Confederation went into effect in 1781 and created a "league of friendship" for the common defense and mutual welfare of the individual states.   **31**

attorney general   **1)** the head of the U.S. Department of Justice and the chief legal adviser to the president and federal government. The attorney general is a member of the president's cabinet and is appointed by the president, subject to approval by the Senate.   **2)** the primary legal official of a state, usually elected by the people.   **174**

authoritarianism   a system of government in which a dictator answers only to him- or herself.   **9**

authoritarian socialism   *See* communism.

autocracy   a government in which one person, a dictator, has unlimited political power.   **9**

B

---

bail   money that is paid to guarantee that a defendant will appear in court if he or she is released from jail while awaiting trial in a criminal case.   **276**

bench trial   a trial in which a judge, rather than a jury, decides an issue.   **331**

bias   **1)** a preference or prejudice, particularly one that hinders impartial judgment.   **2)** an unfair act or policy resulting from prejudice.   **379**

bicameral   having two houses or chambers. Bicameral legislatures were originally designed to represent both the elite and the common members of a society.   **22**

bilateral alliance   an agreement between two countries to help each other in time of war.   **238**

bill   proposed legislation that has been formally introduced into a legislature for consideration. A bill that is passed by Congress and signed by the president becomes a law.   **118**

bill of attainder   a law that convicts people of a crime and punishes them without a trial.   **108**

Bill of Rights   the first 10 amendments to the U.S. Constitution, which guarantee certain individual liberties, including property rights, the right to trial by jury, and freedom of expression and religion.   **53**

block grant   a payment that the federal government distributes to a state or local government and for which the recipient determines the specific use.   **73**

Bolsheviks   a revolutionary group that came to power following the Russian Revolution of 1917. *See also* Communist Party.   **517**

bond   **1)** a certificate that a government or corporation issues to a lender from whom it has borrowed money   **2)** bail money that is held as security to ensure that an accused person will not flee from the jurisdiction of the court if released. Bond money is returned when the accused person appears for the trial. *See also* bail.   **201, 276**

bond rating   a measure of the probability that a bond issuer will or will not pay its obligation to investors in its bonds.   **475**

bourgeoisie   the people who own the means of production in a capitalist system.   **511**

boycott a refusal to do business with or buy the products of a company, an industry, or a nation in order to pressure it into changing its policies. **28**

brief a written statement prepared by each side before a court hearing to summarize that side's view of the facts in the dispute and how the law should be applied. **253**

bureaucracy any management structure that carries out policy on a day-to-day basis, that is based on job specialization, uses standardized procedures, and continues its operations regardless of changes in leadership. **176**

bureaucrat a worker in a bureaucracy. **176**

cabinet an advisory board that is made up of the heads of the government's executive departments and reports to the chief executive. **58**

capital punishment the death penalty. Capital punishment can be ordered only for a defendant who has been convicted of a specified, very serious crime such as murder or treason. **282**

capitalist **1)** a person who supports or favors capitalism as an economic system. **2)** a person who has invested money in business, particularly someone who has a major financial interest in an important business venture. **507**

categorical grant a payment that the federal government distributes to a state or local government to fund specific activities. **73**

caucus a meeting of political party members to seek agreement on a course of action, nominate candidates for political office, or select delegates to a state or national nominating convention. **159**

censorship the legal act of determining if information or speech is suitable for the public, or if that information or speech should be banned. **377**

censure a legislature's formal expression of disapproval of one of its members. **117**

census a periodic, official counting of a population. Article 1, Section 2, of the Constitution requires a U.S. census every 10 years to use in apportioning seats in the House of Representatives among the states. **98**

change of venue the movement of a trial to a court in a different geographic location. **330**

charter **1)** a document that monarchs use to grant privileges to groups or individuals. **23** **2)** a record that defines the purposes and powers of a city government. **485**

checks and balances limitations placed on a branch of government's political power by giving the other branches some control over its affairs. **48**

circuit a geographic area over which a federal court of appeals has jurisdiction. **252**

citizen an officially recognized member of a state. **3**

city manager someone hired to run the daily operations of a municipality. **488–89**

civil law the body of law that governs relationships among individuals and that defines people's legal rights. **78**

civil liberty a basic individual right to which every human being is entitled. **297**

civil rights the rights that legally belong to a person because of his or her citizenship in a nation. **346**

civil rights movement the ongoing effort of women and minority groups to gain in practice the rights guaranteed to all citizens by the Constitution. **347**

civil servant any nonmilitary employee of government, particularly one who was awarded his or her job on the basis of the merit system. *See also* merit system. **178**

class-action suit a court action brought against an individual or a company by a person or small group for themselves and for all others who have been affected similarly by a particular wrong. **394**

class struggle according to Marxist theory, the ongoing competition between economic groups for resources and power. The idea of class struggle was introduced by German political theorists Karl Marx and Friedrich Engels in their 1848 work *Communist Manifesto*. **515**

closed primary a primary election in which only the members of a political party are permitted to vote in selecting the party's candidates. *See also* open primary. **432**

cloture a method for ending a filibuster in the U.S. Senate. **127**

collective security a multinational diplomatic and military arrangement to maintain peace by taking united action against any hostile and potentially hostile nation that is a threat to peace. **235–37**

command economy an economy in which government authorities control some or all of the major economic processes. **514**

commission a board that holds all executive, legislative, and administrative power in a municipality. **489–90**

common law a body of law that developed from traditions, customs, and precedents (or earlier judicial decisions). **271**

communism **1)** a theoretical economic system in which all land and capital is owned collectively by society. **2)** an economic system in which the government owns or controls nearly all factors of production; also known as authoritarian socialism. **512**

Communist Manifesto a book completed in 1848 by German political theorists Karl Marx (1818–1883) and Friedrich Engels (1820–1895) that presented the basic principles and beliefs of communism. **515**

Communist Party a political party formed by the Bolsheviks in Russia following the Russian Revolution of 1917. The party was originally led by Vladimir Lenin and was based on his interpretation of the writings of radical political thinkers Friedrich Engels and Karl Marx. **517**

commutation in law, the reduction of a punishment to a less severe one. **153**

comparative advantage the ability of a nation, region, or company to produce a certain good or service more cheaply than any other good or service. **534**

competition effort that sellers of similar goods or services exert in obtaining the business of consumers. Each seller tries to gain a larger share of a market and to increase profits. **508**

concurrent power a power or authority that is held by more than one level of government. **68**

concurring opinion in a court decision, a formal statement by a judge on a judicial panel. The person issuing the concurring opinion agrees with the decision of the majority but for different reasons than those cited in the majority opinion. **261**

confederal system a form of government in which independent states unite to accomplish common goals. **10**

conference committee a meeting of members from both the House and Senate to resolve differences over similar bills passed in both houses. **119**

Congressional Budget Office an agency created by Congress to provide legislators with data and technical assistance on financial policy, issues surrounding government programs, and other spending-related matters. **205**

constituent a resident of a district or state represented by an elected official. **94**

constitution the basic political and legal structures under which a government operates. **21**

constitutional interpretation a judicial function in which judges determine the meaning of a state's or the federal constitution as it relates to a case before the court. **272**

constitutional monarchy a government whose head of state inherits the position and holds it for life but either shares power with elected leaders or merely serves as the nation's symbolic leader, exercising no significant power. **8**

consul an official whose main function is to further his or her nation's business and trade interests in another country. A consul is thus distinct from the nation's ambassador, who furthers its diplomatic and political interests in the other country. **225**

consulate the office of a consul, from which he or she protects his or her nation's commercial interests. **223**

consumer buyer of goods or services for personal use. **508**

containment a basic U.S. foreign and military policy during the Cold War. Through containment, the United States sought to stop the spread of communism into nations that were not under communist control. **229**

convention an assembly of political party members gathered to perform some official duty, such as choosing candidates for elective office, adopting a party platform, or selecting delegates to a higher-level party meeting. **159**

council-manager system a system of municipal government in which an elected city council appoints a professional city manager to run the government's day-to-day affairs. **488**

county the unit of government directly below state government. Counties are generally governed by elected boards or commissions, although some are administered by a single elected or appointed official. **275**

court of appeals 1) a court established to hear appeals of trial court cases. In the court structure of most states, courts of appeals are midway between the trial courts and the state supreme court. **472** 2) one of 13 federal appeals courts, ranking just below the Supreme Court, that hear appeals from cases tried in federal district courts. **252**

criminal law the body of law that regulates the conduct of individuals as members of the state. **78**

customs duty a tax on imports that may be levied by a nation's government to raise revenue or to protect an industry within the nation from foreign competition. A customs duty is sometimes called a tariff. **193**

— **D** —

de facto **segregation** racial separation that exists not because of laws or government action, but because of social and economic factors and conditions. *See also de jure* segregation. **349**

de jure **segregation** racial segregation that is enforced by law. In the past, laws in many states required separate schools, parks, public transportation, and so on for whites and African Americans. *See also de facto* segregation. **348**

deduction in income tax policy, any business or personal expense or loss that reduces taxable income. **191**

defendant the party accused in a civil or criminal court of having committed a wrongful act. **274**

defense alliance an agreement in which countries come to one another's aid if any of them are attacked. **235**

deficit the amount by which a person's, business's, or a government's expenses exceed its income. **202**

deforestation the clearing of forests without replacing them. Deforestation results from the harvesting of timber and the clearing of land for agriculture, industry, or mining. **542**

delegate someone who is authorized to represent and act for others within a voting assembly, convention, or other meeting in which a small group of individuals makes decisions for a larger general group. **28**

democracy a system of government in which political authority is held by the people. Democracies typically feature constitutional governments with majority rule, a belief in individual worth and in equal rights for all people, freedom of expression, political freedom, and freedom of choice. **8**

democratic socialism an economic system in which some means of producing and distributing goods are owned or controlled by the government. The extent of the government's economic role is determined by elections rather than ideology. **511**

denaturalization the act of taking away a person's citizenship. **341**

deportation the act of officially returning an alien to his or her country of origin. **344**

détente a French word meaning "relaxation of tensions" that is used to describe U.S. foreign policy toward the Soviet Union in the early and mid-1970s. **232**

developed nation a nation with a high level of industrial development and technical expertise, as well as various established economic institutions such as banks and stock markets. The citizens of a developed nation enjoy a high standard of living with an average, annual per capita income of at least $9,266. **533**

developing nation a nation with little industry and that has a low standard of living in comparison with developed nations. The annual, average per capita income in a developing nation is less than $9,266. **533**

dictatorship a system of government in which one person or a small group of ruling elite has total political power. **9**

diplomacy 1) the art of negotiating, conducting, and maintaining relationships with other nations. 2) all formal relations and communications that nations maintain with one another. **144**

diplomatic recognition an acknowledgment by one nation's government that another nation's government is legitimate. Diplomatic recognition occurs when the chief executive of the acknowledging nation sends an ambassador or other diplomatic official to the nation being recognized. **151**

direct democracy a system of government in which decisions are made directly by the people rather than by their elected representatives. **15**

direct primary a primary election in which the winner becomes the party's candidate for elective office. **431**

discount rate the interest rate charged by the Federal Reserve for loans to member banks. **201**

discrimination the practice of treating a person or group

differently because of prejudice, such as that based on race, sex, religion, age, or physical characteristics. **345**

disposable income money that remains after taxes have been paid. Personal disposable income is a key factor in determining the level of consumption and savings in an economy. **198**

dissenting opinion in a court decision, a formal statement by a judge on a judicial panel. The person issuing the dissenting opinion disagrees with the decision of the majority and cites the reasons for disagreeing. **261**

district court a federal trial court in which issues involving federal law are heard. Each state has at least one district court. **252**

docket the list of cases to be heard by a court; also called a calendar of cases. **259**

double jeopardy trying someone more than once for the same criminal offense. The Fifth Amendment to the Constitution prohibits double jeopardy, but this protection is not absolute. If a mistrial has occurred because of some procedural error or if a deadlocked jury cannot reach a verdict, the prosecution may retry the accused. **331–32**

draft the practice of requiring civilians to serve in the military for a specified period of time. **310**

due process a constitutional protection that prevents the government from depriving individuals of their rights and freedoms without following established legal procedures. **319**

E

Elastic Clause a clause in Article I, Section 8, of the U.S. Constitution. Also called the Necessary and Proper Clause, it grants Congress the authority to enact all laws that are "necessary and proper" to carrying out its other powers. **68**

elector a member of the electoral college. **157**

electoral college a body of representatives from the 50 states and the District of Columbia who officially elect the president and vice president of the United States. **157**

electorate the total number of citizens who are eligible to vote in an election. **405**

embassy a diplomatic center that a nation maintains in a foreign country. **223**

enabling act a federal law that allows the residents of a territory to draft a constitution and take other steps necessary in preparing for statehood. **76**

endorsement official declaration of support for a candidate for political office by a political party, political action committee, newspaper, labor union, or other organization. **391**

English Bill of Rights a law passed by Parliament in

1689 that forms one of the foundations of Britain's unwritten constitution. The bill prohibited the monarchy from suspending laws, levying taxes, or maintaining an army in peacetime without consent of Parliament. **23**

entitlements benefits that federal law requires the government to give to individuals who meet established requirements. **209**

entrepreneur someone who undertakes and develops a new business enterprise at some risk of failure or loss. The entrepreneur typically invests capital and human resources in the hope of earning a profit. **507**

Establishment Clause the part of the First Amendment to the Constitution that prohibits Congress from passing any law that establishes a religion or that favors one religion over others. **300**

estate tax a tax levied on the estate, or property, of a person who has died. **193**

ethnic group a group of people within a nation who share certain characteristics, such as race, language, cultural heritage, religion, or national origin. **345**

ex post facto **law** a law that illegalizes specific acts that took place before it was passed. **108**

excise tax a tax placed by the federal government and some state governments on the manufacture, sale, or consumption of certain goods, often those considered to be luxury items or socially undesirable products. **193**

exclusionary rule a Supreme Court precedent establishing that illegally obtained evidence may not be used in a criminal trial. **322**

executive agreement an agreement between the president and the heads of other nations. **58**

executive order a rule or regulation issued by the president or another executive branch official on how to carry out and enforce legislation. **148**

executive privilege the principle that the executive branch may withhold information from Congress and the courts to preserve national security. **149**

exemption an amount of income on which the government does not levy a tax. **191**

exit poll a survey of selected voters as they leave polling places to determine how they voted. **373**

expatriation the voluntary giving up of one's citizenship. **341**

expressed power a governmental power that is specifically granted in a constitution; also called an enumerated or a delegated power. **67**

expulsion the removal by a legislature of one of its members for serious or criminal misconduct. Expulsion is the most serious disciplinary action that a legislature may take against a member. **117**

extradition the process by which one state or nation returns a person accused or convicted of a crime to the state or nation where the crime was committed. **79**

F

faction a group of people seeking to advance their own concerns. **60**

factor of production a resource used in the production process. The four factors of production are natural resources, human resources, capital resources, and entrepreneurship. **507**

federal budget the estimate of the revenues and expenses of the federal government for a fiscal year. **204**

federal mandate a federal requirement that state or local governments take a specific action, offer a particular program, or pay for a program the federal government establishes. **73**

Federal Reserve system the Fed; a system of 12 government banks and 25 branches across the United States run by a board that is appointed by the president. **200**

federal system a form of government in which power is shared among central, state, and regional levels. **10**

Federalist 1) someone who supported the proposed U.S. Constitution in the late 1780s and favored a strong national government. **40** 2) a member of the Federalist Party, an early political party in the United States. **409–10**

felony a major violation of criminal law that almost always calls for a minimum scheduled sentence of a year in prison. **273**

filibuster a delaying tactic that legislators sometimes use to prevent a vote on a bill they dislike. **127**

fiscal policy the overall government program that establishes levels of taxing, borrowing, and spending that promote the desired economic goals for the nation. **198**

floor leader a legislator chosen by members of his or her party to advance their political agenda through the legislative process. **116**

forces of production in Marxist terminology, the combination of the means of production and the potential productivity of workers. **516**

foreign aid any assistance granted by a nation's government or private organizations to another nation's government or people. **234**

foreign policy a nation's plans and procedures for dealing with other nations. **145**

foreign service a nation's professional diplomats, who carry out its foreign policy throughout the world. **225**

franking privilege the right of a member of Congress to send mail without paying postage. **101**

free enterprise a system in which private business operates with a minimal government regulation. **196**

Free Exercise Clause a clause in the First Amendment to the Constitution that prohibits government interference with the "free exercise" of religious practices. **302**

G

general election   an election in which voters choose from among candidates running for federal, state, or local elective office.   **159, 417**

gerrymandering   the redrawing of legislative district boundaries in order to strengthen the political power of one group or political party over another.   **100**

gift tax   a tax by the federal government and some state governments on large transfers of certain goods that are made without something of value being given in return.   **193**

glasnost   the Russian term for the late 1980s Soviet political reforms which permitted freer expression of political views. The term glasnost means "openness."   **233**

global warming   the theory that the world's climates are becoming dangerously warmer.   **538**

government   an institution that determines and enforces a society's laws. The size and nature of a government varies according to the society it governs.   **3**

government corporation   an independent agency that manages a self-supporting business.   **178**

governor   the chief executive of a state government who is elected by the state's voters.   **468**

Gramm-Rudman-Hollings Act   the Balanced Budget and Emergency Deficit Control Act of 1985. This law set maximum limits on yearly budget deficits and required automatic spending cuts whenever those maximums were exceeded.   **210**

grand jury   a panel of 12 to 23 citizens who review evidence that a prosecutor presents against a person accused of a crime. The grand jury determines if the government has enough evidence to issue an indictment and bring the person to trial.   **277**

grant-in-aid   a federal payment to a state, or a federal or state payment to a local government, for a specific purpose.   **72**

grassroots lobbying   a lobbying technique used to encourage large groups of citizens at the local level to try to influence legislators or other government officials.   **394**

Great Compromise   the agreement to establish a two-house U.S. legislature. The compromise was presented to the Constitutional Convention of 1787 by the Connecticut delegation. It combined elements of two plans. The Virginia Plan called for proportional representation determined by population and the New Jersey Plan proposed that each state have an equal vote in the legislative process. These two plans became the basis for the House of Representatives and Senate.   **38**

gross domestic product (GDP)   the total value of all goods and services produced within a country in a given year.   **208**

H

hate speech   words or symbols that can reasonably be expected to cause anger, fear, or resentment in others on the basis of race, color, creed, religion, or gender.   **311**

hung jury   a jury that is divided over a case and unable to reach a unanimous decision about a defendant's guilt or innocence.   **279**

I

idealism   in international relations, the belief that a nation's foreign policy should be guided by noble goals such as justice, equality, and world service instead of purely by national interest.   **220**

ideological party   a political party that forms around a political idea or point of view that is different from the majority of the population's view. Unlike many third parties, ideological parties tend to exist over long periods of time. *See also* splinter party.   **415**

ideology   an organized set of beliefs that a person or group holds about people, society, and the world.   **368**

illegal alien   a person from one country who is living or working in another country unlawfully.   **344**

immunity   a protection for certain government officials from being sued or prosecuted for actions that are part of their elective office.   **101**

impeach   the bringing of formal charges by a legislature against a public official. Impeachment is the first step in removing an official from office.   **106**

implied power   a power that is implied, or suggested, by the expressed powers in a constitution.   **68**

income tax   a tax applied on the earnings of an individual or a business.   **474**

incumbent   a political candidate who currently holds an elected or appointed office.   **113**

independent   a candidate with no political party affiliations who is running for a political office.   **413**

independent agency   a federal executive agency not included in a cabinet department. There are three types of independent agencies: regulatory commissions, government corporations, and independent executive agencies.   **177**

indictment   a formal document issued by a grand jury that names and charges an individual with a violation of criminal law, usually a felony.   **277**

inflation   an increase in overall prices that results from rising wages, an increased money supply, and increased spending relative to the supply of products.   **197**

information   a formal document—issued to a court by the state's prosecuting attorney—charging a specific individual with a violation of criminal law. This process is used in states that do not use the grand jury system. **277**

inherent power a power that is not specifically granted in or implied by a constitution, but that belongs to the governments of all sovereign nations. **68**

initiative a process in some states that allows citizens to propose and enact laws. **463**

interest group a group whose members hold common political beliefs and work to influence government officials, policies, and practices. Interest groups are also called pressure groups. **94**

interdependence mutual reliances between the world's countries. Countries' actions affect one another's economic growth and stability. **527**

international law the principles and rules that have been set up to guide the actions of nations in their relations with one another and in their dealings with other countries' citizens. **532**

internationalist a person who believes that nations should act as a community and should interact with one another peacefully and cooperatively. *See also* isolationist and neoisolationist. **219**

interstate compact a formal agreement approved by Congress between two or more states to jointly operate mutually beneficial programs. **79**

isolationist a person who believes that a nation should interact politically as little as possible with other nations so that it can exist peacefully by itself in the world. *See also* internationalist and neoisolationist. **218**

Jim Crow laws laws passed in the southern United States to require or permit racial segregation. Jim Crow laws are now unconstitutional. **348**

joint committee a congressional committee composed of members from both the Senate and the House of Representatives. **119**

judicial activism the practice of judges using their court decisions to make new public policy in order to advance what they believe to be desirable social goals. *See also* judicial restraint. **265**

judicial restraint the practice of judges narrowly interpreting laws and limiting their decisions in order to avoid making public policy. *See also* judicial activism. **264–65**

judicial review the power of a court to determine whether laws and other government actions are constitutional or otherwise lawful. **49**

jurisdiction the power of a court to interpret and administer the law. **250**

jury pool a group of people who are summoned to appear in court and from among which the actual jury in

a criminal or civil proceeding will be selected. Also called a jury panel. **471**

jus sanguinis the legal principle that a person's citizenship is determined by that of his or her parents rather than by his or her place of birth. *See also jus soli.* **339**

jus soli the legal principle that a person's citizenship is determined by where he or she was born rather than by the citizenship of his or her parents. *See also jus sanguinis.* **339**

juvenile delinquent a young person who is judged guilty of a criminal offense. The age of a juvenile may vary from under 16 to under 21 years of age, depending on the state. **283**

Keynesianism a school of thought pioneered in the 1930s by British economist John Maynard Keynes that calls for government to use fiscal policy and monetary policy to influence a nation's economy. **202**

labor union an organization of workers that negotiates with employers for better wages, improved working conditions, and job security. **387**

law a set of rules, issued and enforced by a government, that binds every member of society. **3**

legitimacy the legal and recognized right of a government to make decisions for the citizens of a nation, state, or locality. **4**

libel deliberately publishing false written or visual statements harming the reputation or business of an individual or group. **307**

line-item veto the power of a government's chief executive to reject specific parts of a bill passed by a legislative body, rather than having to veto the entire measure. **128**

lobbying the process by which an individual, a group, or an organization seeks to influence government policy makers. **392**

loose constructionist a person who believes that a constitution should be interpreted reasonably, but broadly, in order to meet the needs of changing times. *See also* strict constructionist. **250**

machine politics *See* party machine.

Magna Carta a document prepared by English nobles that granted certain rights to English citizens. The charter was signed under the threat of force by King John of England in 1215. **21–22**

majority opinion   a formal statement of the decision of a majority of members of a judicial panel hearing a case, giving the reasons for the decision. The majority opinion is the official opinion of the court. *See also* concurring opinion and dissenting opinion. **261**

majority party   a political party whose members make up the majority in a legislative house. **115**

majority rule   the principle that the will of the largest portion of a group should prevail in electing leaders and making policies. Majority rule is a basic characteristic of democratic systems of government. **15**

Marshall Plan   a massive U.S. foreign-aid program to help Europe recover from World War II. **235**

mayor-council system   a system of urban government in which power is shared by an elected chief executive (a mayor) and a separately elected legislature (a city council). **488**

megalopolis   a large, densely populated area made up of two or more cities and their suburbs. A megalopolis forms when metropolitan areas grow into one another. **484**

merit system   a system for hiring government workers based on demonstrated qualifications and competitive examinations. **180**

metropolitan area   an urban area made up of a city whose population is over 50,000 as well as its suburbs and all the surrounding counties dependant on the city. **484**

minority party   a political party whose members do not make up the majority in a legislative house. **115**

minority rights   political rights that cannot be abolished in a democracy, even though they are held by less than half of the population. **15**

Miranda Rule   an arresting officer's requirement to inform criminal suspects of their rights before questioning. **327**

misdemeanor   a minor violation of criminal law that is generally punishable by a fine or by a jail term of less than one year. *See also* felony. **273**

mixed economy   an economy that combines elements of the traditional, market, and command economic models. Almost all modern economies are mixed economies. **509**

monarchy   a system of government in which the head of state, usually a royal figure, is a hereditary position. **8**

monetarism   a school of thought pioneered by American economist Milton Friedman. Monetarism is based on the theory that if left alone, a market economy will operate at full employment and low inflation. **202**

monetary policy   a government's program for regulating a nation's money supply and the availability of credit in order to accomplish certain economic goals. **198**

Monroe Doctrine   a foreign-policy statement made by President James Monroe in 1823. Monroe declared that the United States would not allow European nations to further colonize or take any aggressive actions in the Western Hemisphere. **228**

multilateral treaty   a legal agreement among three or more nations to accomplish a common purpose. **237**

multiparty system   a political system in which several major and minor political parties compete for political power and government offices. **407–08**

municipality   a city or town with its own level of government. **487**

national debt   the total amount of money that a nation owes its creditors. It is the sum of each year's unpaid spending deficits—that is, the money borrowed to finance deficit spending that has not been repaid. **210**

national security   the freedom of a nation to protect its citizens from hostile or destructive forces or actions from within or outside its borders. **217**

nationalization   the government takeover of specific companies or of a major segment of a nation's private industry, such as manufacturing, agriculture, or transportation. **512**

natural right   a right that is considered to belong to all people, regardless of time or place. Being natural to everyone, these rights do not need to be granted by a government and should not be transferred or taken away. Natural rights are also known as inalienable rights. **4**

naturalization   the process by which a nation grants citizenship to an immigrant. **340**

neoisolationist   an individual opposed to the internationalism that has dominated American foreign policy since the end of World War II. Unlike a traditional isolationist, a neoisolationist does not oppose all U.S. entanglement with other nations. Neoisolationists support alliances and methods of furthering U.S. national interests abroad. *See also* internationalist and isolationist. **219–20**

New England Confederation   the first confederation of English colonies in North America. The confederation was formed in 1643 to unite four New England colonies, largely for defense against American Indians and England's European rivals. **25**

New Jersey Plan   a plan for establishing a one-house legislature in which each state would have an equal vote. The proposal was put before the Constitutional Convention in 1787 by William Paterson of New Jersey. **37–38**

no-contest plea   a formal answer in court in which a defendant states simply that he or she will not fight the charge, but neither proclaims innocence nor admits guilt. **277**

nominate to name a political party member as a candidate for a particular public office. **157**

nonpartisan primary a primary election in which candidates from all political parties are on the same ballot and in which all voters can participate, regardless of their political affiliation. **432**

nonrenewable resources any limited resource whose supply cannot be replenished in the short term. **540**

North Atlantic Treaty Organization (NATO) a collective security organization created by a multilateral treaty in 1949. NATO was originally created to protect the Western European and North American nations in the North Atlantic region against attack by the Soviet Union. **237**

Northwest Ordinance an act of Congress under the Articles of Confederation that set procedures for granting statehood to territories. The Northwest Ordinance allowed an area to become a territory once it had a population of at least 5,000 free males. It allowed a territory to apply for statehood once it reached a population of 60,000 free inhabitants. **32**

nuclear proliferation the spread of nuclear weapons to nations that did not previously have them. **529**

———————— **O** ————————

objectivity the ability to judge or present information factually, in a manner that is not influenced by emotions or prejudices, but that is instead based on evidence. **379**

obscenity printed or visual material that is not protected by the First Amendment because it is considered to lack serious social value and to be highly offensive. **307**

Office of Management and Budget (OMB) an executive branch agency within the Executive Office of the President that is responsible for preparing the president's budget request. **204**

oligarchy a system of government in which political power and control is held by a small group of political elite. The leaders of an oligarchy often govern for their own benefit or for the benefit of their social class. **9**

one-party system a political system in which one political party controls the government and clearly dominates political activity. **407**

open primary a primary election in which a voter may participate in the selection of a political party's candidates regardless of the voter's own political affiliation. **432**

open-market operations the purchasing and selling of securities—usually government securities—by the Federal Reserve system on the open market in order to help carry out monetary policy. **201**

original jurisdiction the requirement or authority of a court to be the first to hear a case. **250**

oversight the power of a legislature to review and monitor the activities of an executive branch agency to determine whether it is properly executing laws under its administration. **96**

———————— **P** ————————

pardon the official release of a person charged with or convicted of a crime, at the request of a chief executive. **153**

parliamentary system a system of government in which power is concentrated in a legislature. The legislature selects one of its members, usually called a prime minister, as the nation's principal leader and other legislative members serve as the leader's cabinet. **11**

parochial religious in nature, as in elementary and high schools run by churches and other religious organizations. **301**

parole the release of a prisoner before he or she has served a full sentence. **282**

party machine an organized group of individuals who dominate a political party within a geographic area and who use the party's resources to further their own power and to fight off challenges from other party members for party control. **416**

party platform a statement of a political party's position on issues. **161**

party whip a member of the Senate or House of Representatives who is chosen by his or her party colleagues to assist the party's floor leader in managing its legislative program. **116**

passport a document that a nation issues to its citizens that allows them travel to other nations, identifies them to government authorities in those nations, and gives them the right to return home. **225**

patronage the practice of elected officials rewarding political supporters with government contracts, appointments to office, jobs, and other benefits. **416**

peremptory challenge in choosing a jury for a trial, the right of either the defense or the prosecution to reject a possible juror without providing a reason. **279**

perestroika a Russian word meaning "restructuring." Perestroika was an effort by the Soviet Union to change its economy from communism to market socialism. **233**

petit jury a group of citizens who decide the verdict in a civil or criminal trial. **278**

Petition of Right a document drawn up by the English Parliament and signed by King Charles I in 1628. The Petition of Right, like Magna Carta, limited the ability of the monarch to act on his or her sole authority. **23**

picketing marching around in a specific area while carrying signs that communicate a message of protest. **313–14**

plaintiff the party who brings a legal action in a court of law. **274**

plank a political party's specific proposal for legislation or a statement of a short-term goal regarding a single issue. Planks are the components of a party platform. **161**

plea bargain in a criminal court case, an agreement negotiated between the prosecutor and the defendant and his or her attorney to avoid the time, expense, and uncertain outcome of a trial. **280**

plurality the greatest number of popular votes received by a candidate in an election. A plurality can be, but is not necessarily, a majority. **163**

pocket veto a method of preventing a bill from becoming a law. The pocket veto enables the president to dismiss a bill by simply refusing to sign it, without having to state his or her reasons for doing so. **128**

police power the power of a government to use force if necessary to control affairs within its jurisdiction in order to protect the health, safety, and welfare of its citizens. **322**

political action committee (PAC) an organization that is created to raise and distribute campaign money to candidates for elective political office. **94**

political party a formal organization of people who seek to influence government actions and policies by electing its members to public office. **58**

political socialization the process through which individuals obtain their political attitudes and values. **368**

politics the art and science of governing. Through politics, people express opinions about what government should or should not do. **6**

polling the process of systematically surveying the views of individuals within a selected group or groups in order to determine public opinion on an issue. **372**

popular sovereignty governing authority that comes from the people. **47**

popular vote the total votes cast by the general public in an election. **163**

pork-barrel spending legislative funding for unnecessary projects that favor the district of a particular legislator. **129**

precedent the legal principle of a court's ruling in a case serving as a model for future decisions in similar cases, unless for some reason it is specifically overruled by another case. **249**

precinct the smallest political subdivision of a U.S. city, town, or county for voting purposes and for political party organization. **418**

prejudice the holding of an opinion about a person, group, or thing without rational grounds or without having enough information upon which to base it. **345**

presentment a formal statement issued by a grand jury to authorize a trial for someone accused of a crime. **327**

president *pro tempore* the senator who presides over the Senate when its official presiding officer—the vice president of the United States—is absent. **116**

presidential doctrine a presidential statement that guides the nation's foreign policy—for example, the Monroe Doctrine or the Truman Doctrine. **222–23**

presidential succession the order in which the vice president or other designated official becomes president of the United States should the office become vacant. **147**

presidential system a system of government in which the legislative and executive branches operate independently of each other. **11**

primary election an election to choose a political party's candidates for an elective office. **159, 417**

prior restraint an action by a government to prevent the publication of something or to require approval before it can be published. Thus, prior restraint is a form of censorship. **306**

privatization the act of turning functions previously performed by government over to the private sector. **186**

probable cause reasonable grounds to accuse an individual of committing a specific crime. **322**

probation freedom granted to a person convicted of a crime, with the condition that he or she meet certain conditions of good behavior for a specified period of time. **281**

procedural due process the principle that the law must be applied fairly and evenly to all people, using established rules and procedures. *See also* substantive due process. **319**

profit the difference between the revenue received from the sale of a good or service and the costs of providing that good or service. **508**

proletariat the working class, whose members the radical political theorist Karl Marx believed were oppressed by the bourgeoisie. **511**

property tax government tax revenue levied on the value of certain kinds of property. **493**

public comment the opportunity for interested parties to react to a regulation that is proposed by a government agency before the regulation goes into effect. **176–77**

public good the common interests of the members of a society; also known as the public interest. **6**

public interest group an interest group that supports positions and causes that it believes to be in the general public good, as contrasted with interest groups that work for a particular social or economic interest. **388**

public opinion the collective opinion on a particular issue or group of related issues that is held by a large segment of society. **367**

public policy decisions and laws that a government makes in a particular area of public concern. **4**

───────── **Q** ─────────

quorum the minimum number of legislators who must be present to vote and conduct other formal business when Congress is in session. **113**

quota the minimum number of new hires to be made through an affirmative action program. **355**

───────── **R** ─────────

ratification the process of giving formal approval of an action by an agency or government. Ratification is generally the final step in accepting a treaty or a constitutional amendment. **31**

realignment a switching of political loyalties among the electorate or of political parties in a legislature. Realignment generally refers to significant and long-lasting changes in the attitudes of the electorate. **409**

realism in international relations, the belief that a nation's foreign policy should be based on the realities of human nature and history. Realists believes that foreign policy should be directed toward achieving power, maintaining national security, and pursuing other national interests. **219**

recall a procedure that allows the electorate to vote an elected official out of office before his or her term has expired. **464**

recession a substantial and general decline in overall business activity over a significant period of time. **197**

reconciliation a step in the federal budget process in which Congress adjusts the spending requests contained in the president's budget proposal. **207**

referendum a procedure in some states that gives voters the opportunity to approve or reject laws passed by the legislature or a local assembly. **464**

refugee a person who flees from a region, either voluntarily or by force, because of political, military, religious, social, or other conflict. **527**

regulatory commission an independent agency created by Congress with a greater degree of autonomy, or self-rule, than others. **177**

relations of production according to Marxist theory, the way people interconnect in the work process. The relations of production are determined by who owns the means of production, what position workers hold in relation to other groups involved in production, and how production and income are distributed among these groups. **516**

renewable resources resources that can be replenished in the short term through natural means. **540**

repeal to reverse or cancel an existing law or regulation. **52**

representative democracy a system of government in which the people choose political leaders to make policy decisions on their behalf. **16**

reprieve a postponement in the carrying out of a convicted person's sentence. **153**

republic a system of government in which governmental power comes from the people, who elect individuals to represent them in decision making. **8**

reserved power any power that the Constitution does not expressly or by implication give to Congress. The Tenth Amendment to the Constitution specifically reserves such powers to the states or to the people. **68**

reserve requirement a bank's financial reserve held either in its own vaults or in a district Federal Reserve bank. In essence, it is the bank's savings account. **201**

resolution a formal declaration or statement of policy concerning a specific issue or matter. **206**

revenue the total income of a business or a unit of government. **191**

revenue sharing the distribution by a government of a portion of its income to lower levels of government. **72**

roll-call vote a legislative procedure in which each legislator is called on individually to cast his or her vote. **127**

runoff primary a second election that is held in some states if no candidate in the primary election receives a majority of the votes. **432**

rural area a region of low population density where people live on farms or ranches or in small towns and where economic activities center around land-based enterprises such as agriculture or mining. **481**

───────── **S** ─────────

sales tax a tax on the sale of goods and services. **473**

sampling a procedure for choosing a small portion of a population to represent the population as a whole in a survey. **374**

sampling error an error in polling results caused by choosing a sample of individuals to poll that was not representative of the larger population being studied. **375**

search warrant a written authorization issued by a judge to allow law enforcement authorities to search a person's property for specified items and to seize those items if they are found. **322**

secret ballot the popular name for a voting system that allows voters to choose candidates in private. It originated in Australia and is now universally used in U.S. elections. **441**

secretary the head of a cabinet-level department within the executive branch of the U.S. government—for example, the secretary of defense, the secretary of state, and the secretary of the treasury. **174**

sedition language or actions that call for or encourage resistance or rebellion against a lawfully established government. *See also* treason. **305**

segregation the separation of people according to any specified identifying characteristic. **348**

select committee a House or Senate committee that is generally established for a limited time and for a specific, often investigative, purpose. **119**

self-interest the impulse that encourages people to fulfill their needs and wants. **508–09**

senatorial courtesy the practice that allows senators from the same political party as the president to approve or disapprove each potential nominee for certain appointed positions in their state before the official nominations are made. **254**

seniority system a system for granting congressional committee positions based on the length of time in service. **120**

separate-but-equal doctrine a legal precedent (established by the Supreme Court in the 1896 case *Plessy* v. *Ferguson*) that racial segregation was not a violation of the Equal Protection Clause of the Fourteenth Amendment as long as separate facilities for African Americans and whites were of equal quality. This principle remained in place until 1954, when the Supreme Court overturned it in *Brown* v. *Board of Education*. **348**

separation of powers the distribution of political power among the branches of government, giving each branch a particular set of responsibilities. **48**

sequester to isolate a jury from the public during a trial. **279**

shield law a law that protects reporters from having to reveal confidential sources of information. Shield laws allow people to provide information to the media without fear that they will be revealed as informants. **307**

sin tax a tax on products or activities that government authorities consider harmful or otherwise undesirable. **474**

single-issue voting a situation in which an individual chooses to support or reject a political candidate on the basis of just one factor, excluding all other issues. **391**

single-member district an electoral district in which only one candidate can win election to a particular office. **440**

slander deliberately making false spoken statements that might damage the reputation of a business, an individual, or a group. Slander is a criminal offense, but it generally is not prosecuted. However, the victims of slander often seek damages in civil lawsuits. **307**

social contract the theory that people give up their individual sovereignty in exchange for peace and order provided by the state. **4**

socialism an economic system in which the government owns or controls many of the means of production and directly provides for many of the people's needs. A socialist system may or may not be democratic. **511**

sovereignty the absolute authority that a government has over the citizens of a state. **3**

Speaker the presiding officer of the U.S. House of Representatives and second (after the vice president) in the line of succession to the presidency. The Speaker is elected by the House and has always been a member of the majority party. **115**

special district a unit of government, typically at the local level, that serves a specific function and that sometimes crosses existing political boundaries. **490**

splinter party a political party that is created when a group that is unhappy with the candidate, and sometimes the positions, of a major party breaks off from that party (or from both major parties). *See also* ideological party. **415**

split ticket the result of an individual voting for persons from different political parties for different political offices. **417**

spoils system the practice of government officials awarding public jobs and public contracts to political supporters rather than awarding them on the basis of job qualifications. *See also* merit system. **178–79**

Stamp Act a 1765 law passed by Parliament to raise money by taxing paper goods. However, because of violent protests in the colonies, the tax was repealed the year after it was introduced. **26**

standard of living people's economic well-being as determined by the quantity of goods and services they consume in a given time period. **195**

standing committee a regular or permanent committee created by a legislature to review bills within a specified subject area. **119**

stare decisis the legal principle and judicial practice of following precedents set in earlier legal decision. The Latin term means "let the decision stand." **261**

state 1) a territory whose population maintains an organized governmental body that regulates internal and external affairs. 2) a political unit in a federal system, such as a state within the United States. **3**

State of the Union address the president's annual message to Congress, in which he or she usually proposes the administration's legislative program. **143**

statutory interpretation a judicial function in which a judge decides a law's meaning in regards to a specific court case. **272**

statutory law all regulations put forth by a lawmaking government body. **272**

straight ticket the result of a voter's selecting only candidates from a particular party for every office on the ballot. **417**

strict constructionist a person who believes that a constitution should be interpreted rigidly and narrowly based only on what is written in the document. **249**

subcommittee **1)** a smaller, more specialized part of a committee. **2)** a group of committee members selected to work on specific categories of bills or other matters that come before the entire committee. **119**

subpoena a written order requiring a person to testify in court as a witness or to bring certain items to court as evidence. **279**

substantive due process the principle that a law must be fair and reasonable. The right to substantive due process requires a court to consider the fairness of the law itself. **320**

suburb a primarily residential community that is located near a city and whose residents largely depend on the city for jobs and other services. **481**

suffrage the right to vote. **442**

summit conference a meeting between the heads of state of two or more nations in order to discuss and conduct international relations. Summit conferences may involve military, economic, or diplomatic matters. **223**

supply and demand the forces that determine prices in a free market. **508**

suspect classification a potentially illegal basis for making distinctions between individuals or groups. **347**

symbolic speech messages that are communicated nonverbally. Symbolic speech can include articles worn on clothing, hand gestures, and certain types of actions. **310**

tax a required payment to a local, state, or national government, usually made on some regular basis. **191**

term limits legal limits on the number of terms certain elected officials can hold a particular office. **113**

third party a political party outside the dominant parties in a two-party system. **413**

totalitarianism a system of government in which a dictator or a small group of leaders exercise tremendous control over citizens' lives. **9–10**

township communities established in states such as New Jersey, New York, and Pennsylvania. Governments of townships served some of the same functions as New England town governments. **487**

trade association an organization formed by companies within an industry that represents the concerns of the industry. **386**

trade deficit a situation in which the total value of a country's imports is higher than the total value of its exports. **537**

trade embargo a government order that forbids trade with a specified nation. **218**

trading bloc a group of nations working together to provide trade benefits to its members. Trading-bloc members set import and export quotas, fix tariffs, and establish other trade controls. **534**

treason an act of disloyalty against one's own country. **304**

Truman Doctrine a 1947 foreign-policy statement made by President Harry Truman that pledged U.S. military and economic aid to nations that were trying to avoid a communist takeover. **229**

two-party system a system in which two political parties dominate the political system and compete for political power. **407**

unconstitutional a law or government action that violates provisions set forth in the U.S. Constitution. **49**

unicameral a legislative body that has one chamber or house. Nebraska is the only American state with a unicameral legislature. **30**

unitary system a system of government in which all legal power is held by the national, or central, government. **10**

urban area a region characterized by cities and other areas of high population density, and in which most of the working residents are involved in manufacturing, commercial, or other nonagricultural economic activities. **481**

U.S. Agency for International Development a U.S. government organization that carries out U.S. foreign-aid programs. The agency concentrates on five areas of foreign policy; promoting economic growth, advancing democracy, delivering humanitarian aid, promoting public health, and protecting the environment. **235**

value a basic quality, principle, or standard that is considered important or desirable and by which people live their lives. For example, humility is a value that many people consider important. **6**

vanguard the leading position in a movement, or those who occupy that position. In 1917 the Bolsheviks were the vanguard that led the Russian Revolution. **517**

veto the formal rejection of legislation by a chief executive. **48**

Virginia Plan a plan for establishing a one-house legislature in which each state would have proportional representation based on its population. The plan was submitted to the Constitutional Convention in 1787 by the Virginia delegation. Many of the plan's proposals were included in the U.S. Constitution. **36**

visa the permission that a nation gives to a citizen of another nation who wishes to visit it. **225**

voir dire the questioning of prospective jurors—by the judge and prosecuting and defense attorneys in a court case—to see if they are acceptable—to the judge and the attorneys—to serve on a jury. The phrase *voir dire* means "to speak truth." **278–79**

ward a territorial division of city government that is also often used as a voting subdivision and a unit of political party organization. **418**

writ of *certiorari* a formal order from an appeals court that requires a lower court to provide the record of a case for review. Most cases reaching the Supreme Court are heard because the Court has issued a writ of *certiorari*. **259**

writ of *habeas corpus* a judicial order directing law enforcement authorities to bring any prisoner before a court official and cite the reason for his or her imprisonment, to determine if that person is being held lawfully. **108**

GLOSARIO

Este glosario contiene los términos que necesitas para tu estudio sobre el gobierno. Después de cada término se incluye una breve definición o explicación del mismo, tal como se usa en *Holt American Government*. El número de página se refiere a la página en donde el término se presenta por primera vez en el libro de texto.

A

absentee ballot/boleta de ausencia boleta que permite a cualquier votante que no pueda presentarse en la casilla el día de la elección, enviar su voto por correo. **441**

act of admission/ley de admisión ley emitida por el Congreso que al ser firmada por el presidente, otorga a un territorio la condición de estado. **76**

administrative law/ley de administración 1) conjunto de disposiciones y reglamentos que las entidades del gobierno usan para aplicar el derecho estatutario, y procesos que crean y aplican dichas disposiciones y reglamentos. 2) conjunto de leyes que crea a las entidades del gobierno y regula la revisión judicial de las acciones que tales entidades llevan a cabo. **272**

affirmative action/acción afirmativa programa legalmente sustentado que obliga a empleadores, sindicatos y demás instituciones a intentar activamente eliminar la discriminación de mujeres y minorías, y a favorecer la contratación, promoción, salario, capacitación y demás oportunidades para esas personas. **355**

agribusiness/agroeconomía industria que participa en la producción, procesamiento y distribución de productos agrícolas. **386**

Albany Plan of Union/Plan Albany de la Unión plan propuesto por Benjamin Franklin en 1754 para unir a las trece colonias. Este plan convocaba la creación de un concejo de representantes de cada colonia para recaudar impuestos, resolver asuntos militares y regular las relaciones con los indígenas. Un presidente general con poder de veto presidía al concejo, cuyas leyes propuestas se aplicarían en todas las colonias, a menos que el monarca británico las vetara. Ni el gobierno británico ni el de las colonias aprobaron el plan, por lo que nunca entró en cfccto. **26**

alien/extranjero ciudadano de una nación que vive de manera temporal o permanente en otro país. **298**

alliance/alianza acuerdo entre dos o más naciones para trabajar conjuntamente hacia un fin común (militar o económico, por lo general). **151**

ambassador/embajador diplomático con el máximo rango que representa a una nación ante el gobierno de otra. Un embajador es el representante personal del jefe de gobierno de su país. **224**

amendment/enmienda 1) agregado a una constitución vigente. 2) agregado a un proyecto de ley a consideración de los legisladores. **126–27**

amicus curiae* brief/escrito *amicus curiae alegato formal que refleja la opinión de un grupo sobre una decisión de la corte. **260**

amnesty/amnistía perdón otorgado por un gobierno a personas que han cometido un delito, por lo general una falta de carácter político. La amnistía se otorga a grupos de personas. El indulto se otorga a individuos. **344**

anarchy/anarquía ausencia de toda autoridad gubernamental legítima, que conduce al desorden político y en ocasiones al caos y a los gobiernos de la plebe. **14**

Antifederalist/antifederalista personas que se oponían a la adopción de la constitución a finales de la década de 1780. Los antifederalistas temían la creación de un gobierno nacional demasiado fuerte y preferían que el gobierno de cada estado conservara la mayor parte del poder. **40**

appellate jurisdiction/jurisdicción de apelación solicitud legal de que una corte escuche la apelación de un caso, si éste reúne las condiciones que la ley determina. **253**

apportion/adjudicar determinar el número de legisladores que representarán a cada jurisdicción en un órgano legislativo. **99**

appropriations/consignaciones 1) fondos asignados a una legislatura para pagar bienes o servicios autorizados por la ley. 2) legislación del Congreso que autoriza a las entidades federales a realizar pagos con propósitos específicos, usando fondos de la tesorería. **118**

arraignment/proceso en un caso de delito, audiencia donde formalmente se acusa de un delito a una persona, se le informan sus derechos y se le pide que inicie su defensa. **277**

Articles of Confederation/Artículos de la Confederación documento legal que dictaminó la creación de un gobierno nacional en Estados Unidos. Los Artículos de la Confederación entraron en vigor en 1781, creando la "liga de la amistad" para la defensa común y el bienestar mutuo de los estados. **31**

attorney general/ministro de justicia 1) jefe del Departamento de Justicia de Estados Unidos y consejero legal del presidente y del gobierno federal. El ministro de justicia es parte del gabinete presidencial y su designación está a cargo del presidente, sujeta a la aprobación del senado. **2)** Principal funcionario legal de un estado, casi siempre elegido por el pueblo. **174**

authoritarianism/autoritarianismo sistema de gobierno en el que un dictador gobierna con base en sus propios intereses. **9**

authoritarian socialism/socialismo autoritario *Véase* communism/comunismo.

autocracy/autocracia gobierno en el que un individuo, un dictador, cuenta con poder político ilimitado. **9**

B

---

bail/fianza dinero dado en garantía de que un acusado se presentará ante la corte, aunque haya salido libre de prisión, en tanto espera el juicio en un caso de delito. **276**

bench trial/juicio de judicatura caso en que un juez y no un jurado da el veredicto de un juicio. **331**

bias/parcialidad 1) predilección o prejuicio, en particular cuando impide una decisión imparcial. **2)** acto o política injusta que es resultado de los prejuicios. **379**

bicameral/de cámara dual que tiene dos cámaras de representantes. Originalmente, las legislaturas de cámara dual se crearon para representar tanto a la élite como a los integrantes comunes de la sociedad. **22**

bilateral alliance/alianza bilateral acuerdo entre dos naciones para ayudarse mutuamente en tiempos de guerra. **238**

bill/proyecto propuesta de ley presentada formalmente a la legislatura para su consideración.

Los proyectos deben quedar aprobados por el Congreso y firmados por el presidente para convertirse en leyes. **118**

bill of attainder/escrito de proscripción y confiscación ley que acusa a una persona de un crimen y la castiga sin realizar un juicio. **108**

Bill of Rights/Declaración de derechos primeras 10 enmiendas de la constitución de Estados Unidos que garantizan ciertas libertades individuales, entre ellas los derechos de propiedad, de juicio formal y de libertad de expresión y elección religiosa. **53**

block grant/donación de bloque dinero del gobierno federal que los gobiernos de los estados reciben y deciden cómo utilizar. **73**

Bolsheviks/bolcheviques grupo revolucionario que tomó el poder de Rusia después de la Revolución Rusa de 1917. *Véase también* Communist Party/partido comunista. **517**

bond/bono 1) certificado emitido por un gobierno o corporación a cambio de un préstamo monetario. **2)** dinero usado como fianza para garantizar que una persona acusada de un crimen no evada la jurisdicción legal al ser liberada mientras se procesa su caso. Este dinero es devuelto cuando el acusado se presenta a su juicio. *Véase también* bail/fianza. **201, 276**

bond rating/reputación del bono medida de la probabilidad de que un emisor de bonos pague o no su obligación a los inversionistas de sus bonos. **475**

bourgeoisie/burguesía personas dueñas de los medios de producción en un sistema capitalista. **511**

boycott/sabotaje renuencia a negociar o comprar los productos de una compañía, industria o nación a modo de presión para que cambie sus políticas. **28**

brief/alegato declaración por escrito que la parte acusadora y la parte defensora presentan antes de un juicio, con la finalidad de resumir sus puntos de vista sobre la disputa y las posibilidades de aplicación de la ley. **253**

bureaucracy/burocracia estructura administrativa que diariamente lleva a cabo sus políticas, con base en la especialización laboral, y se vale de procedimientos estandarizados, operando sin interrupción aunque haya cambios de dirigencia. **176**

bureaucrat/burócrata persona que trabaja en la burocracia. **176**

C

cabinet/gabinete grupo de consejeros conformado por los jefes de los departamentos ejecutivos del gobierno, cuya función es asesorar al primer mandatario. **58**

capital punishment/pena capital pena de muerte. La pena capital se aplica a una persona acusada de algún delito grave, como asesinato o traición. **282**

capitalist/capitalista **1)** persona que apoya o favorece al capitalismo como sistema económico. **2)** persona que invierte su dinero en negocios, en especial la persona interesada en obtener grandes beneficios financieros en importantes empresas. **507**

categorical grant/transferencia categórica pago que el gobierno federal distribuye entre los gobiernos estatales o locales para cubrir gastos específicos. **73**

caucus/junta de dirigentes reunión de integrantes de un partido político para buscar el acuerdo en la trayectoria de acción, nominar candidatos a cargos políticos o seleccionar a los delegados de las asambleas estatales o nacionales. **159**

censorship/censura acto legal para determinar si la información o el discurso resulta adecuado para el público, o si debe prohibirse. **377**

censure/crítica expresión formal de desaprobación por parte de la legislatura hacia cualquiera de sus integrantes. **117**

census/censo conteo oficial de la población realizado periódicamente. El Artículo 1, Sección 2 de la Constitución indica que los censos nacionales deben realizarse cada 10 años para determinar el número de legisladores de cada estado en la Cámara de representantes. **98**

change of venue/cambio de tribunal pasar un juicio a una corte de diferente ubicación geográfica. **330**

charter/carta **1)** documento usado por los monarcas para garantizar privilegios a grupos o individuos. **23 2)** registro que define el propósito y el poder del gobierno de una ciudad. **485**

checks and balances/control y equilibrio limitaciones al poder político de una rama del gobierno, otorgando a las otras ramas cierto control sobre los asuntos de dicha rama. **48**

circuit/circuito zona geográfica sobre la que un tribunal federal de apelación tiene jurisdicción. **252**

citizen/ciudadano integrante de un estado reconocido oficialmente. **3**

city manager/administrador municipal persona contratada para realizar las operaciones cotidianas de una municipalidad. **488–89**

civil law/derecho civil cuerpo de leyes que gobierna la relación entre los individuos y que define los derechos legales de las personas. **78**

civil liberty/libertad ciudadana derecho individual básico al que todo ser humano tiene derecho. **297**

civil rights/derechos civiles derechos que legalmente pertenecen a una persona por ser ciudadana de una nación. **346**

civil rights movement/movimiento de derechos civiles esfuerzo continuo de mujeres y grupos minoritarios por ejercer los derechos que la Constitución garantiza para todos. **347**

civil servant/funcionario público empleado del gobierno que no pertenece a ningún cuerpo militar, en especial quien es reconocido por su desempeño con base en el sistema del mérito. *Véase también* merit system/sistema del mérito. **178**

class-action suit/litigio de clases acción de una corte en contra de un individuo o compañía, iniciada por una persona o grupo para defenderse a sí mismo o a todos los afectados de manera similar por un agravio particular. **394**

class struggle/lucha de clases según la teoría marxista, competencia entre clases económicas por la adquisición de recursos y poder. Esta idea fue presentada por los teóricos políticos alemanes Karl Marx y Friedrich Engels en la obra *Manifiesto comunista,* publicada en 1848. **515**

closed primary/primaria cerrada elección primaria en la que se elige a los candidatos de un partido político y en la que sólo se permite el voto a los integrantes de dicho partido. *Véase también* open primary/primaria abierta. **432**

cloture/límite de debate método usado para acabar con la obstrucción de la aprobación de una ley o una moción en el senado estadounidense. **127**

collective security/seguridad colectiva acuerdo diplomático y militar entre varias naciones, creado para mantener la paz mediante la acción conjunta frente a cualquier nación hostil y potencialmente hostil que represente una amenaza para la paz. **235–37**

command economy/economía dominante economía en la que las autoridades del gobierno controlan una parte o todos los principales procesos económicos. **514**

commission/comisión junta que reúne al poder ejecutivo, legislativo y administrativo en una municipalidad. **489–90**

common law/derecho consuetudinario conjunto de leyes desarrollado a partir de tradiciones, costumbres y antecedentes (de decisiones judiciales anteriores). **271**

communism/comunismo **1)** sistema económico teórico en el que las tierras y el capital son propiedad colectiva de la sociedad. **2)** sistema económico en que el gobierno posee o controla casi todos los factores de producción; también conocido como socialismo autoritario. **512**

Communist Manifesto/ Manifiesto comunista libro terminado en 1848 por los teóricos políticos alemanes Karl Marx (1818–1883) y Friedrich Engels (1820–1895) que presentó los principios y creencias básicas del comunismo. **515**

Communist Party/Partido Comunista partido político formado por los bolcheviques en Rusia al término de la Revolución Rusa de 1917. Originalmente estaba dirigido por Vladimir Lenin y estaba sustentado en la interpretación que éste daba a la obra de pensadores políticos radicales como Friedrich Engels y Karl Marx. **517**

commutation/conmutación en materia de derecho, intercambio de una pena por otra de menor severidad. **153**

comparative advantage/ventaja comparada capacidad de una nación, región o compañía para producir cierto producto o servicio a menor precio que cualquier otro producto o servicio. **534**

competition/competencia esfuerzo que los comerciantes de productos o servicios similares hacen por ganar las compras de los consumidores. Cada comerciante trata de obtener una mayor porción de un mercado y aumentar sus ganancias. **508**

concurrent power/poder conjunto poder o autoridad detentado por más de un nivel de gobierno. **68**

concurring opinion/opinión conjunta en una decisión de la corte, declaración formal de un juez en un jurado judicial. La persona que emite la opinión conjunta está de acuerdo con la mayoría, pero por razones diferentes de las establecidas en la opinión mayoritaria. **261**

confederal system/sistema confederal forma de gobierno en la que estados independientes se unen para lograr metas comunes. **10**

conference committee/junta de consulta reunión de integrantes de la cámara baja y el senado para resolver diferencias sobre proyectos similares recibidos en ambas cámaras. **119**

Congresional Budget Office/Ministerio de presupuesto del Congreso entidad creada por el Congreso para brindar a los legisladores información y apoyo técnico sobre políticas financieras, programas del gobierno y otros asuntos relacionados con el gasto público. **205**

constituent/constituyente residente de un distrito o estado representado por un funcionario electo. **94**

constitution/constitución estructuras políticas y legales básicas con las que opera un gobierno. **21**

constitutional interpretation/interpretación constitucional función judicial que permite a un juez determinar el significado de la constitución estatal o federal en relación con un caso del tribunal. **272**

constitutional monarchy/monarquía constitucional gobierno cuyo primer mandatario hereda de por vida su puesto, ya sea que comparta el poder con líderes electos o sea sólo una figura simbólica de la nación que no ejerce ningún poder. **8**

consul/ cónsul funcionario cuya labor principal es extender los intereses comerciales y de intercambio de su país a otra nación. En este sentido, un cónsul es diferente de un embajador, quien extiende los intereses diplomáticos y políticos de su país a otra nación. **225**

consulate/consulado oficina del cónsul, desde donde protege los intereses comerciales de su nación. **223**

consumer/consumidor comprador de productos o servicios para uso personal. **508**

containment/contención política exterior y militar básica de Estados Unidos durante la guerra fría. Mediante la contención, Estados Unidos buscaba evitar la expansión del comunismo a naciones que no estaban bajo el control comunista. **229**

convention/convención asamblea de los integrantes de un partido político convocada para desempeñar cierto deber oficial, como la elección de candidatos para puestos públicos, la adopción de plataformas partidistas o la selección de delegados para juntas de mayor nivel del partido. **159**

council-manager system/sistema de ayuntamiento sistema de gobierno municipal en el que un concejo municipal electo designa a un administrador para manejar los asuntos cotidianos de gobierno. **488**

county/condado unidad de gobierno bajo el mandato del gobierno estatal. La mayoría de los condados están gobernados por asambleas o comisiones electas, aunque algunos están administrados por un funcionario electo o designado. **275**

court of appeals/tribunal de apelación   1) tribunal establecido para atender apelaciones de los juicios. En la estructura de tribunales de la mayoría de los estados, el tribunal de apelación es la parte mediadora entre el tribunal estatal y la suprema corte del estado. **472   2)** uno de los 13 tribunales federales de apelación, bajo el mando directo de la suprema corte, que atiende los casos de apelación de los tribunales federales de distrito. **252**

criminal law/derecho penal conjunto de leyes que regula la conducta de los individuos como integrantes de un estado. **78**

customs duty/derecho de aduana impuesto aplicado a las importaciones recaudado por el gobierno del país con el propósito de reunir las rentas públicas o proteger de la competencia extranjera a un ramo industrial del interior. El derecho de aduana también se conoce como arancel. **193**

D

---

de facto **segregation/segregación** *de facto* separación racial que no se basa en leyes o acciones del gobierno, sino en factores y condiciones sociales y económicos. *Véase también de jure* segregation/segregación *de jure.* **349**

de jure **segregation/segregación** *de jure* segregación racial impuesta por la ley. En el pasado, las leyes de muchos estados exigían escuelas, parques, transportes públicos, etcétera separados para personas de raza blanca y afroestadounidenses. *Véase también de facto* segregation/ segregación *de facto.* **348**

deduction/deducción en políticas de impuesto sobre la renta, cualquier gasto o pérdida personal o empresarial que reduce la renta gravable. **191**

defendant/acusado parte acusada en un tribunal civil o penal de haber cometido acto ilegal. **274**

defense alliance/alianza de defensa acuerdo en que los países recurren unos a otros en caso de que cualquiera de ellos resulte atacado. **235**

deficit/déficit cantidad en la que los gastos de una persona, negocio o gobierno sobrepasan a sus ingresos. **202**

deforestation/deforestación tala de árboles sin plantar nuevos árboles. La deforestación es resultado del siego de árboles maderables y el desmonte de tierra para la agricultura, la industria o la minería. **542**

delegate/delegado persona autorizada para representar y actuar por otros en asambleas, convenciones y demás reuniones electorales donde un grupo reducido toma decisiones por un grupo mayor. **28**

democracy/democracia sistema de gobierno en el que la autoridad política recae en el pueblo. Por lo general, las democracias forman gobiernos constitucionales con gobernación de la mayoría, la creencia en el valor individual y la igualdad de derechos para todos, la libertad de expresión, la libertad política y la libertad de elección. **8**

democratic socialism/socialismo demócrata sistema económico en el que algunos medios de producción y distribución pertenecen o están controlados por el gobierno. El alcance del papel económico del gobierno está determinado por elecciones y no por la ideología. **511**

denaturalization/desnaturalización acto de quitar a una persona su ciudadanía. **341**

deportation/deportación acto de regresar oficialmente a un extranjero o extranjera a su país de origen. **344**

détente/*détente* término francés que significa "disminución de tensiones" y que se usa para describir la política exterior estadounidense hacia la Unión Soviética a principios y mediados de la década de 1970. **232**

developed nation/país desarrollado nación con un alto índice de industrialización y pericia técnica, así como con instituciones económicas establecidas, tales como bancos y mercados de valores. Los ciudadanos de un país desarrollado disfrutan un mayor nivel de vida y un ingreso per cápita promedio de al menos $9,266 al año. **533**

developing nation/país en vías de desarrollo nación con bajo índice industrial y nivel de vida menor en comparación con los países desarrollados. El ingreso per cápita promedio en un país en vías de desarrollo es menor a los $9,266 por año. **533**

dictatorship/dictadura sistema de gobierno en el que una persona o grupo pequéno tiene el poder político total. **9**

diplomacy/diplomacia 1) arte de negociar, dirigir y mantener relaciones con otras naciones. 2) relaciones y comunicaciones formales que los países mantienen entre sí. **144**

diplomatic recognition/reconocimiento diplomático confirmación del gobierno de un país de que el gobierno de otro país es legítimo. El reconocimiento diplomático se da cuando el primer mandatario del país que reconoce envía un embajador o cualquier funcionario diplomático a la nación a la que está reconociendo. **151**

direct democracy/democracia directa sistema de gobierno en el que el pueblo, y no sus representantes electos, es el que toma las decisiones de manera directa. **15**

direct primary/primaria directa elección primaria cuyo ganador se convierte en el candidato del partido para un cargo electivo. **431**

discount rate/tasa de descuento tasa de interés aplicada por la reserva federal en los préstamos a sus bancos afiliados. **201**

discrimination/discriminación trato diferente a personas o grupos debido a prejuicios, como los que se basan en raza, género, religión, edad o características físicas. **345**

disposable income/ingresos disponibles dinero restante después del pago de impuestos. Los ingresos disponibles personales son un factor clave para determinar el nivel de consumo y ahorro en una economía. **198**

dissenting opinion/opinión disidente en una decisión de la corte, declaración formal del juez en un jurado judicial. La persona que emite la opinión disidente no está de acuerdo con la decisión de la mayoría y cita las razones de su desacuerdo. **261**

district court/tribunal de distrito tribunal federal que atiende asuntos relacionados con juicios federales. En cada estado existe al menos un tribunal de distrito. **252**

docket/lista de causas lista de casos pendientes en un tribunal; también llamada agenda de casos. **259**

double jeopardy/doble exposición acción de juzgar a alguien dos veces por el mismo delito. Aunque la quinta enmienda constitucional prohíbe esta acción, la protección no es absoluta. Si existe un mal juicio debido a errores de procedimiento o si un jurado en empate no puede emitir un veredicto, la fiscalía puede volver a procesar al acusado. **331–32**

draft/servicio militar exigir a ciudadanos que presten servicio militar durante un periodo específico. **310**

due process/proceso establecido protección constitucional que prohíbe al gobierno la privación de derechos y libertades individuales sin haber cumplido con los procedimientos legales establecidos. **319**

Elastic Clause/cláusula elástica cláusula del Artículo 1, Sección 8 de la Constitución de Estados Unidos. También conocida como cláusula justa y obligatoria. Esta cláusula otorga al Congreso autoridad para aplicar las leyes "justas y obligatorias" que le permitan ejercer sus poderes. **68**

elector/elector integrante del colegio electoral. **157**

electoral college/colegio electoral cuerpo de representantes de los 50 estados y el Distrito de Columbia con capacidad oficial para elegir al presidente y al vicepresidente de Estados Unidos. **157**

electorate/electorado número total de ciudadanos aptos para votar en las elecciones. **405**

embassy/embajada centro diplomático de una nación en un país extranjero. **223**

enabling act/ley de facultad ley federal que permite a los residentes de un territorio redactar una constitución y tomar las medidas necesarias para adoptar la condición de estado. **76**

endorsement/respaldo declaración oficial emitida por un partido político, comité de acción, periódico, sindicato u otras organizaciones, para apoyar a un candidato a un cargo político. **391**

English Bill of Rights/Declaración británica de derechos ley aprobada por el parlamento en 1689 que es uno de los fundamentos de la constitución no escrita de la Gran Bretaña. Esta declaración prohibía a la monarquía suspender leyes, recaudar impuestos o formar agrupamientos militares en tiempos de paz sin el consentimiento del Parlamento. **23**

entitlements/autorizaciones beneficios que la ley federal exige al gobierno que otorgue a individuos que cumplen con las obligaciones establecidas. **209**

entrepreneur/empresario persona que inicia y desarrolla un nuevo negocio bajo cierto riesgo de fracaso o pérdida. Por lo general, un empresario invierte capital y recursos humanos con la confianza de obtener un beneficio. **507**

Establishment Clause/cláusula de establecimiento parte de la primera enmienda de la Constitución que prohíbe al Congreso aprobar cualquier ley que establezca una religión o favorezca a cierta religión sobre las demás. **300**

estate tax/impuesto testamentario impuesto recaudado de la herencia o propiedades de una persona fallecida. **193**

ethnic group/grupo étnico grupo de personas dentro de una nación que comparten ciertas características, como raza, idioma, herencia cultural, religión u origen nacional. **345**

ex post facto law/ley ex post facto ley que hace ilegales a ciertos actos que ocurricron antes de su aprobación. **108**

excise tax/impuesto al consumo impuesto aplicado por el gobierno federal y algunos gobiernos estatales a la fabricación, venta o consumo de ciertos productos, por lo general considerados como artículos de lujo u objetos socialmente indeseables. **193**

exclusionary rule/regla de exclusión precedente de la suprema corte que establece la imposibilidad de usar evidencias obtenidas ilegalmente en un juicio penal. **322**

executive agreement/acuerdo ejecutivo acuerdo realizado entre el presidente de un país y los dirigentes de otras naciones. **58**

executive order/orden ejecutiva disposición o reglamento emitido por el presidente u otro funcionario del poder ejecutivo que indica cómo aplicar y hacer cumplir una ley. **148**

executive privilege/privilegio ejecutivo principio que permite al poder ejecutivo reservarse información ante el Congreso y los tribunales de justicia para proteger la seguridad de la nación. **149**

exemption/exención parte de los ingresos no sujeta al cobro de impuestos. **191**

exit poll/votación de salida encuesta a ciertos electores realizada a la salida de las urnas electorales para determinar cómo votaron. **373**

expatriation/expatriación renuncia voluntaria de la nacionalidad. **341**

expressed power/poder expreso poder gubernamental otorgado específicamente en la Constitución; también llamado poder enumerado o delegado. **67**

expulsion/expulsión remoción de un integrante de cualquier legislatura por mala conducta grave o ilegal. La expulsión es la acción disciplinaria más severa que una legislatura puede ejercer contra uno de sus integrantes. **117**

extradition/extradición proceso mediante el cual un estado o nación entrega a una persona acusada de un delito a la nación donde se cometió el delito. **79**

F

---

faction/facción grupo de personas que busca exponer sus propios intereses. **60**

factor of production/factor de producción recurso del proceso de producción. Los cuatro factores de producción son los recursos naturales, los recursos humanos, el capital y la empresa. **507**

federal budget/presupuesto federal estimación de los ingresos y egresos del gobierno federal para el año fiscal. **204**

federal mandate/orden federal mandato federal que obliga a un gobierno estatal o local a tomar ciertas medidas, brindar algún programa o pagar un programa establecido por el gobierno federal. **73**

Federal Reserve System/sistema de la reserva federal el Fed; sistema de 12 bancos gubernamentales y sus 25 ramas administradas en todo el país por un concejo designado por el presidente. **200**

federal system/sistema federal forma de gobierno en que el poder se comparte entre las autoridades centrales, las estatales y las regionales. **10**

Federalist/federalista **1)** persona que apoyaba la creación de la Constitución a finales de la década de 1780 y la formación de un fuerte gobierno nacional. **40** **2)** integrante del partido federalista, uno de los primeros partidos políticos en Estados Unidos. **409–10**

felony/delito mayor violación mayor de derecho penal que casi siempre se castiga con una sentencia de por lo menos un año en prisión. **273**

filibuster/obstrucción táctica de postergación que a menudo usan los legisladores para evitar la votación por un proyecto de ley que no aprueban. **127**

fiscal policy/política fiscal programa gubernamental general que establece los niveles de recaudación de impuestos, gasto público y petición de créditos, que propician los objetivos económicos de la nación. **198**

floor leader/líder parlamentario legislador elegido por los integrantes de su partido político para presentar su agenda política mediante el proceso legislativo. **116**

forces of production/fuerzas de producción en terminología marxista, combinación de los medios de producción y la productividad potencial de los trabajadores. **516**

foreign aid/ayuda exterior ayuda otorgada por el gobierno de un país y organizaciones privadas a la población o gobierno de otra nación. **234**

foreign policy/política exterior planes y procedimientos de un país para relacionarse con otras naciones. **145**

foreign service/servicio exterior diplomáticos de carrera de una nación que dan a conocer las políticas de asuntos exteriores de su país al resto del mundo. **225**

franking privilege/derecho de franqueo derecho de los integrantes del Congreso para enviar correspondencia sin pagar servicios postales. **101**

free enterprise/libre empresa sistema en el que las empresas privadas operan con una mínima regulación del gobierno. **196**

Free Exercise Clause/cláusula de libre ejercicio cláusula de la primera enmienda de la Constitución que prohíbe al gobierno interferir en el "libre ejercicio" de prácticas religiosas. **302**

───────── **G** ─────────

general election/elecciones generales elección en la que los votantes eligen candidatos para puestos federales, estatales o locales. **159, 417**

gerrymandering/dividisión arbitraria nuevo trazo de los límites de los distritos políticos para fortalecer el poder político de un grupo o partido político sobre los demás. **100**

gift tax/impuesto de dote impuesto aplicado por el gobierno federal y algunos estados a grandes transferencias de ciertos productos, en las que no hay un valor de intercambio acorde. **193**

glasnost/glasnost término en ruso que se refiere a las reformas políticas soviéticas realizadas a finales de la década de 1980, que permitieron una expresión más libre de las opiniones políticas. En ruso, glasnost significa "apertura". **233**

global warming/calentamiento del planeta teoría de que el clima de la Tierra aumenta en proporciones peligrosas. **538**

government/gobierno institución que determina y aplica las leyes de una sociedad. El tamaño y naturaleza de un gobierno varía según la sociedad a la que regula. **3**

government corporation/corporación reguladora entidad independiente que administra un negocio autosustentable. **178**

governor/gobernador primer mandatario de un gobierno estatal elegido por los electores del estado. **468**

Gramm-Rudman-Hollings Act/Ley Gramm-Rudman-Hollings ley de presupuesto balanceado y de control de déficit de emergencia de 1985. Esta ley define el déficit máximo anual en el presupuesto y los recortes necesarios de gastos en caso de exceder el límite establecido. **210**

grand jury/gran jurado panel de 12 a 23 ciudadanos que revisan la evidencia presentada por la fiscalía en contra de una persona acusada de un delito. El gran jurado determina si existe evidencia suficiente para emitir un dictamen e iniciar un juicio. **277**

grant-in-aid/subvención de fondos públicos pago federal a un estado, o pago federal o estatal a un gobierno local, con un propósito específico. **72**

grassroots lobbying/cabildeo popular técnica de cabildeo para motivar a grandes grupos de ciudadanos locales a influir en los legisladores y otros funcionarios del gobierno. **394**

Great Compromise/Gran Compromiso acuerdo para establecer una legislatura de dos cámaras. La delegación de Connecticut presentó el compromiso en la Convención constitucional de 1787. En él se combinaban dos planes: el Plan de Virginia, que hacía un llamado a la representación proporcional con base en la población; y el Plan de Nueva Jersey, que solicitaba igualdad de voto en el proceso legislativo. Ambos planes formaron la base para la creación de la Cámara de representantes y el Senado. **38**

gross domestic product (GDP)/producto interno bruto (PIB) valor total de todos los productos y servicios producidos en un país durante un año. **208**

───────── **H** ─────────

hate speech/discurso incitador palabras o símbolos que se espera conscientemente que causan ira, temor o resentimientos en los demás, con base en cuestiones de raza, color, credo, religión o género. **311**

hung jury/jurado en desacuerdo jurado de opinión dividida que no puede llegar a una decisión unánime sobre la culpabilidad o inocencia del acusado. **279**

I

---

idealism/idealismo en las relaciones internacionales, creencia de que la política exterior de una nación deben basarse en factores de nobleza como la justicia, la igualdad y el servicio universal, en lugar de guiarse puramente por intereses nacionales. **220**

ideological party/partido ideológico partido político formado en torno a una idea o punto de vista diferente a la que expresa la mayoría de la población. A diferencia de terceros partidos, la existencia de los partidos ideológicos suele prolongarse por largos periodos. *Véase también* splinter party/partido separatista. **415**

ideology/ideología conjunto organizado de creencias que una persona o grupo sostiene acerca de la gente, la sociedad y el mundo. **368**

illegal allien/extranjero ilegal persona originaria de una nación que vive y trabaja de manera ilegal en otro país. **344**

immunity/inmunidad protección con que cuentan ciertos funcionarios del gobierno para no ser demandados o procesados por acciones que forman parte de su cargo público. **101**

impeach/denunciar presentación de cargos por parte de una legislatura en contra de un funcionario público. La denuncia es el primer paso para remover a un funcionario de su cargo. **106**

implied power/poder implícito poder implícito o insinuado por los poderes expresos en la Constitución. **68**

income tax/impuesto sobre ingresos un impuesto sobre los ingresos de un individuo o una impresa. **474**

incumbent/residente candidato político que por el momento ocupa un cargo público por elección o designación. **113**

independent/independiente candidato sin afiliación a algún partido político que se postula para un cargo político. **413**

independent agency/entidad independiente entidad ejecutiva federal no incluida en el gabinete. Existen tres tipos de entidades independientes: las comisiones reguladoras, las corporaciones reguladoras y las entidades ejecutivas independientes. **177**

indictment/auto de acusación documento formal formulado por el gran jurado en el que se definen los cargos en contra de una persona acusada de una violación de la ley, por lo general, un delito mayor. **277**

inflation/inflación aumento de los precios generales debido al incremento salarial, la sobreproducción de circulante y un mayor gasto relacionado con la demanda de productos. **197**

information/acusación por el fiscal documento formal dirigido a la corte y emitido por la fiscalía, en el que se acusa a un individuo específico de la violación del derecho penal. Este proceso se aplica en los estados en los que no se usa el sistema del gran jurado. **277**

inherent power/poder inmanente poder no otorgados específicamente ni implícitos en la constitución, pero que pertenecen a los gobiernos de todas las naciones soberanas. **68**

initiative/iniciativa proceso mediante el cual algunos estados permiten a los ciudadanos proponer nuevas leyes. **463**

interest group/grupo de intereses grupo cuyos integrantes sostienen creencias políticas comunes y trabajan para influir en los funcionarios, políticas y costumbres del gobierno. También se conoce como grupo de presión. **94**

interdependence/interdependencia relación entre los países del mundo. Las acciones de cada nación afectan el crecimiento y estabilidad económica de las demás. **527**

international law/derecho internacional principios y disposiciones establecidas para guiar las acciones de los países en sus relaciones entre unos y otros, y sus tratos con los ciudadanos de otros países. **532**

internationalist/internacionalista persona que cree que las naciones deben comportarse como una comunidad e interactuar de manera pacífica y cooperativa unas con otras. *Véase también* isolationist/partidario del aislamiento político y neoisolationist/opositor al aislamiento político. **219**

interstate compact/acuerdo interestatal acuerdo formal entre dos o más estados con la aprobación del Congreso para operar de manera conjunta en programas de beneficio común. **79**

isolationist/partidario del aislamiento político persona que cree que un país debe intervenir políticamente lo menos posible con las demás naciones, con la finalidad de que pueda existir pacíficamente en el mundo por sí misma. *Véase también* internationalist/internacionalista y neoisolationist/opositor al aislamiento político. **218**

J

Jim Crow laws/leyes de Jim Crow leyes aprobadas en el sur de Estados Unidos para exigir o permitir la segregación racial. Hoy en día, dichas leyes son anticonstitucionales. **348**

joint committee/comité mixto comité del congreso compuesto por legisladores del Senado y la Cámara de representantes. **119**

judicial activism/juez activista juez que se vale de sus decisiones en el tribunal para elaborar una nueva política pública que le permita presentar lo que considera metas sociales deseables. *Véase también* judicial restraint/juez limitado. **265**

judicial restraint/juez limitado juez que interpreta las leyes de manera estrecha y que limita sus decisiones a modo de evitar elaborar una nueva política pública. *Véase también* judicial activism/juez activista. **264–65**

judicial review/revisión judicial capacidad de un tribunal para determinar si las leyes y otras acciones del gobierno son constitucionales o bien legales. **49**

jurisdiction/jurisdicción capacidad de un tribunal para interpretar y administrar la ley. **250**

jury pool/banco de jurados grupo de personas a quienes se solicita su presencia en la corte y de entre las cuales se elige al jurado definitivo del juicio penal o civil. También conocido como panel de jurados. **471**

jus sanguinis/jus sanguinis principio legal que indica que la ciudadanía de una persona se determina con base en la ciudadanía de sus padres y no por su lugar de nacimiento. *Véase también jus soli.* **339**

jus soli/jus soli principio legal que indica que la ciudadanía de una persona se determina con base en su lugar de nacimiento y no por la ciudadanía de sus padres. *Véase también jus sanguinis.* **339**

juvenile delinquent/delincuente juvenil persona joven declarada culpable de haber cometido un agravio criminal. La edad de un delincuente juvenil varía desde 16 a 21 años, según el estado. **283**

K

Keynesianism/keynesianismo escuela de pensamiento creada en la década de 1930 por el economista británico John Maynard Keynes, quien pedía a los gobiernos que aplicaran una política fiscal y monetaria para influir en la economía de sus naciones. **202**

L

labor union/sindicato organización de trabajadores que realiza negociaciones con los empleadores por mejores salarios, condiciones de trabajo y seguridad. **387**

law/derecho conjunto de leyes emitidas y aplicadas por un gobierno, que abarca a todos los integrantes de la sociedad. **3**

legitimacy/legitimidad derecho legal y reconocido que tiene un gobierno para tomar decisiones para los ciudadanos de una nación, estado o localidad. **4**

libel/libelo publicación deliberada de declaraciones falsas escritas o visuales que dañan la reputación o empresa de un individuo o grupo. **307**

line-item veto/veto de renglón y párrafo poder que tiene el primer mandatario de un gobierno para rechazar partes específicas de un proyecto aprobado por un cuerpo legislativo, en vez de tener que vetar el proyecto completo. **128**

lobbying/cabildeo proceso mediante el cual un individuo, grupo u organización busca influir en los legisladores del gobierno. **392**

loose constructionist/interpretador abierto persona que cree que la constitución debe interpretarse de manera razonable, pero libremente con la finalidad de adaptarse a los cambios entre una época y otra. *Véase también* strict constructionist/interpretador estricto. **250**

M

machine politics/maquinaria política *Véase* party machine/maquinaria de partido.

Magna Carta/Carta Magna documento redactado por los nobles británicos para garantizar ciertos derechos a los ciudadanos británicos. La carta fue firmada bajo amenaza de uso de la fuerza por el rey John de Inglaterra en 1215. **21–22**

majority opinion/opinión mayoritaria declaración formal de la decisión de la mayoría de los integrantes de un jurado que atiende un caso, donde se expresan las razones en las que se basó la decisión. La opinión mayoritaria es la opinión oficial del tribunal. *Véase también* concurring opinion/opinión conjunta y dissenting opinión/opinión disidente. **261**

majority party/partido mayoritario partido político cuyos integrantes conforman la mayoría en una cámara legislativa. **115**

majority rule/gobierno por mayoría principio que indica que la voluntad de la mayor parte de un grupo debe prevalecer en la elección de sus líderes y la creación de sus políticas. El gobierno por mayoría es la característica básica de los sistemas democráticos de gobierno. **15**

Marshall Plan/Plan Marshall programa de asistencia exterior estadounidense de gran escala creado para ayudar a Europa a recuperarse de la Segunda Guerra Mundial. **235**

mayor-council system/sistema de alcaldía municipal sistema de gobierno urbano cuyo poder recae en un jefe de gobierno electo (alcalde) y una legislatura también electa (concejo municipal). **488**

megalopolis/megalópolis extensa área densamente poblada, formada por dos o más ciudades y sus suburbios. Una megalópolis se forma cuando las áreas metropolitanas crecen hacia adentro una de la otra. **484**

merit system/sistema del mérito sistema de contratación de empleados de gobierno con base en el grado de calificación demostrada y las pruebas de aptitud. **180**

metropolitan area/zona metropolitana área urbana formada por una ciudad cuya población es de más de 50,000 habitantes, así como por sus suburbios y todos los condados que dependen de la ciudad. **484**

minority party/partido minoritario partido político cuyos integrantes no representan la mayoría en una cámara legislativa. **115**

minority rights/derechos de las minorías derechos políticos que no pueden abolirse en una democracia, aunque sólo menos de la mitad de la población total los detente. **15**

Miranda Rule/disposición de Miranda acción en la que un oficial de policía está obligado a informar sus derechos a una persona sospechosa de acciones criminales antes de interrogarla. **327**

misdemeanor/delito menor violación menor del derecho penal que por lo general se castiga con una multa o prisión por un periodo menor de un año. *Véase también* felony/delito mayor. **273**

mixed economy/economía mixta economía que combina elementos de la economía tradicional, la de mercado y la dominante. La mayoría de las economías modernas son economías mixtas. **509**

monarchy/monarquía sistema de gobierno en el que el jefe de estado, por lo general una figura de la realeza, asume su cargo por herencia. **8**

monetarism/monetarismo escuela de pensamiento creada por el economista estadounidense Milton Friedman. El monetarismo se basa en la teoría de que, si no se interviene en la economía de mercado, puede generar por sí misma empleos para todos y bajar inflación. **202**

monetary policy/política monetaria programa gubernamental que regula la emisión de circulante de una nación y la disponibilidad de crédito para lograr ciertas metas económicas. **198**

Monroe Doctrine/Doctrina Monroe política exterior del presidente James Monroe, publicada en 1823. Monroe sostuvo que Estados Unidos no permitiría a ninguna nación europea continuar con la colonización ni con acciones en contra del hemisferio occidental. **228**

multilateral treaty/tratado multilateral acuerdo legal entre dos o más naciones para lograr un fin común. **237**

multiparty system/sistema multipartidista sistema político en el que varios partidos políticos, tanto mayoritarios como minoritarios, compiten por el poder político y puestos en el gobierno. **407–08**

municipality/municipalidad ciudad o pueblo que cuenta con su propio nivel de gobierno. **487**

Ⓝ

---

national debt/deuda nacional cantidad que una nación debe a sus acreedores. Es la suma de los déficits de gastos no pagados de cada año, es decir, el dinero que se ha pedido prestado para financiar el déficit de gastos que no se han reembolsado. **210**

national security/seguridad nacional libertad de una nación para proteger a sus ciudadanos de fuerzas o acciones hostiles o destructivas dentro o fuera de su territorio. **217**

nationalization/nacionalización acción del gobierno para tomar control de ciertas compañías o de un segmento importante de la industria privada, como la manufactura, agricultura o transportes. **512**

natural right/derecho natural derecho de todas las personas sin importar la época o el lugar donde vivan. Por ser naturales a todos estos derechos no tienen que ser otorgados por ningún gobierno y tampoco pueden transferirse ni enajenarse. Los derechos naturales también se conocen como derechos inalienables. **4**

naturalization/naturalización proceso mediante el cual una nación otorga la ciudadanía a un inmigrante. **340**

neoisolationist/opositor al aislamiento político individuo que se opone a la internacionalización que ha dominado la política exterior estadounidense desde el final de la Segunda Guerra Mundial. A diferencia del aislacionismo tradicional, el neoaislacionismo no se opone a los embrollos de Estados Unidos con otras naciones, sino que apoya las alianzas y métodos de expansión de los intereses estadounidenses hacia el exterior. *Véase también* internationalist/internacionalista y isolationist/partidario del aislamiento político. **219–20**

New England Confederation/Confederación de Nueva Inglaterra la primera confederación de colonias británicas en Estados Unidos. Fue formada en 1643 para unir a las cuatro colonias de Nueva Inglaterra y defenderse del ataque de los indígenas y demás naciones europeas rivales. **25**

New Jersey Plan/Plan de Nueva Jersey plan para establecer una legislatura de una sola cámara en la que cada estado tendría el mismo voto. William Peterson de Nueva Jersey presentó la propuesta antes de la Convención Constitucional en 1787. **37–38**

no-contest plea/alegato sin contienda respuesta formal en la que el acusado declara sencillamente que no se defenderá de los cargos, pero tampoco se declara inocente ni acepta la culpabilidad. **277**

nominate/designar nombrar a un integrante de un partido político como candidato para un cargo público en particular. **157**

nonpartisan primary/primaria independiente elección primaria en donde los candidatos de todos los partidos políticos están en la misma boleta. En estas elecciones pueden participar todos los electores, cualquiera que sea su afiliación política. **432**

non renewable resources/recursos no renovables recursos limitados cuyas reservas no pueden recuperarse por completo a corto plazo. **540**

North Atlantic Treaty Organization (NATO)/ Organización del Tratado del Atlántico Norte (OTAN) organización de seguridad colectiva creada mediante un tratado multilateral en 1949. La NATO/OTAN fue creada originalmente para proteger a las naciones de Europa Occidental y América del Norte en la región del Atlántico Norte de posibles ataques de la Unión Soviética. **237**

Northwest Ordinance/Ordenanza del Noroeste ley del Congreso de acuerdo con los Artículos de la Confederación para definir los procesos que garantizaban la calidad de estado a un territorio. La Ordenanza del Noroeste permitía que un área se convirtiera en territorio al contar con una población de al menos 5,000 varones libres. Permitía que un territorio solicitara la calidad de estado al alcanzar la cifra de 60,000 habitantes libres. **32**

nuclear proliferation/proliferación nuclear diseminación del uso de armas nucleares hacia las naciones que nunca habían hecho uso de ellas. **529**

O

objectivity/objetividad capacidad de un juez para presentar información verídica, sin recibir influencia de sus emociones o prejuicios y sólo con base en la evidencia. **379**

obscenity/obscenidad material visual o impreso no protegido por la primera enmienda por considerarse carente de valor social formal y sumamente ofensivo. **307**

Office of Management and Budget (OMB)/ ministerio de administración y presupuesto entidad del poder ejecutivo dentro de la oficina del presidente, responsable de la preparación de la solicitud de presupuesto presidencial. **204**

oligarchy/oligarquía sistema de gobierno en el que el poder político está controlado por un pequeño grupo de la élite política. Los líderes de una oligarquía suelen gobernar para su propio beneficio o en beneficio de su clase social. **9**

one-party system/sistema unipartidista sistema político en el que un partido político controla al gobierno y domina evidentemente la actividad política. **407**

open primary/primaria abierta elección primaria donde los electores pueden participar en la elección de candidatos de un partido político, cualquiera que sea su afiliación. **432**

open-market operations/operaciones de mercado abierto compra y venta de valores (por lo general del gobierno) en el mercado abierto por parte del sistema de la reserva federal, a fin de llevar a cabo la política monetaria. **201**

original jurisdiction/jurisdicción original obligación o autoridad de un tribunal para ser el primero en atender un caso. **250**

oversight/vigilancia capacidad de una legislatura para revisar y supervisar las actividades de una agencia del poder ejecutivo para determinar si ejecuta adecuadamente las leyes bajo su administración. **96**

pardon/indult liberación formal de una persona acusada o condenada por un delito, a solicitud del presidente de la nación. **153**

parliamentary system/sistema parlamentario sistema de gobierno en el que el poder está concentrado en una legislatura, la cual elige a uno de sus integrantes, denominado como primer ministro, como el líder principal de la nación y otros integrantes fungen como el gabinete del líder. **11**

parochial/parroquial religioso por naturaleza, como en las escuelas administradas por iglesias y otras organizaciones religiosas. **301**

parole/libertad bajo palabra liberación de un prisionero antes de haber cumplido su sentencia. **282**

party machine/maquinaria del partido grupo organizado de individuos que dominan un partido político en un área geográfica y que usan los recursos de ese partido para extender su poder y rechazar los desafíos de otros miembros del partido para tomar el control. **416**

party platform/plataforma de partido declaración de la posición de un partido político en los asuntos públicos. **161**

party whip/oficial de partido integrante del senado o de la cámara de representantes elegido por sus colegas para ayudar al líder parlamentario a organizar el programa de legislación. **116**

passport/pasaporte documento entregado por una nación a sus ciudadanos el cual les permite viajar a otros países, les sirve como identificación ante las autoridades de esas naciones y les da el derecho de regresar a su país de origen. **225**

patronage/prebenda costumbre de los funcionarios electos para compensar a sus simpati-

zantes mediante contratos, nombramientos, empleos y otros beneficios. **416**

peremptory challenge/objeción perentoria al elegir al jurado de un juicio, derecho que tiene la parte acusadora o la parte acusada de rechazar a cualquiera de los integrantes del jurado sin razón específica. **279**

perestroika/perestroika palabra de origen ruso que significa "reestructuración". La perestroika fue un esfuerzo de la Unión Soviética por modificar su economía pasando del comunismo al socialismo de mercado. **233**

petit jury/jurado de juicio grupo de ciudadanos que deciden el veredicto en un juicio civil o penal. **278**

Petition of Right/Petición de derechos documento redactado por el Parlamento británico y firmado por el rey Charles I en 1628. Al igual que la Carta Magna, esta petición limitaba la capacidad del monarca para actuar sólo con base en sus autoridad. **23**

picketing/piquete marcha alrededor de una zona determinada sosteniendo carteles que contienen un mensaje de protesta. **313–14**

plaintiff/demandante parte que presenta una acción legal en un tribunal. **274**

plank/punto de programa propuesta específica de un partido político para legislación, o declaración de una meta a corto plazo en relación con un asunto específico. Los puntos de programa son los elementos de la plataforma de un partido. **161**

plea bargain/convenio de alegato en un juicio penal, acuerdo que negocian la fiscalía y el acusado y su abogado defensor para evitar los gastos, la pérdida de tiempo y lo incierto de los resultados de un juicio. **280**

plurality/pluralidad el mayor número de votos populares a favor de un candidato en una elección. La pluralidad suele ser, pero no necesariamente, la mayoría. **163**

pocket veto/veto indirecto método para evitar que un proyecto se convierta en ley. De esta manera, el presidente puede rechazar un proyecto con el simple hecho de negarse a firmarlo, sin tener que presentar razones de ello. **128**

police power/fuerza pública autoridad del gobierno para usar la fuerza si es necesario a fin de controlar ciertos asuntos de su jurisdicción, protegiendo la salud, la seguridad y el bienestar de sus ciudadanos. **322**

political action committee (PAC)/Comité de acción política organización creada para recaudar y distribuir fondos de campaña para los candidatos a los cargos políticos. **94**

political party/partido político organización formal de personas que buscan influir en las acciones y políticas del gobierno mediante la postulación de sus candidatos a los cargos públicos. **58**

political socialization/socialización política proceso mediante el cual los ciudadanos adquieren su posición y valores políticos. **368**

politics/política arte y ciencia de gobernar. Mediante la política, las personas expresan su opinión sobre lo que el gobierno debe o no debe hacer. **6**

polling/escrutinio proceso de encuesta sistemática de los puntos de vista de los individuos dentro de un grupo o grupos selectos, a modo de determinar la opinión pública sobre cierto asunto. **372**

popular sovereignty/soberanía popular autoridad de gobierno que proviene del pueblo. **47**

popular vote/voto popular número total de votos emitidos por el público en general en una elección. **163**

pork-barrel spending/gastos por prebenda fondos públicos usados en proyectos innecesarios que favorecen al distrito de un legislador específico. **129**

precedent/precedente principio legal del veredicto de una corte que sirve como modelo para futuras decisiones en casos similares, a menos que por ciertas razones se anule específicamente con otro caso. **249**

precinct/barrio la menor de las subdivisiones políticas de una ciudad, población o condado estadounidense con propósitos electorales y de organización de partidos políticos. **418**

prejudice/prejuicio opinión acerca de una persona, grupo u objeto sin bases razonables ni suficiente información para sustentarla. **345**

presentment/denuncia declaración formal emitida por un gran jurado para autorizar el enjuiciamiento de una persona acusada de un delito. **327**

president *pro tempore*/**presidente** *pro tempore* senador que preside el senado cuando el presidente oficial, el vicepresidente de Estados Unidos, está ausente. **116**

presidential doctrine/doctrina presidencial declaración presidencial que guía la política exterior de la nación. La Doctrina Monroe y la Doctrina Truman son dos ejemplos. **222–23**

presidential succession/sucesión presidencial orden en el que el vicepresidente u otro funcionario designado se convierte en presidente de Estados Unidos si el cargo de presidente estuviera vacante. **147**

presidential system/sistema presidencial sistema de gobierno en el que los poderes legislativo y ejecutivo operan entre sí de manera independiente. **11**

primary election/elección primaria elecciones en las que se vota por los candidatos de los partidos políticos a los cargos públicos. **159, 417**

prior restraint/represión previa acción del gobierno que evita la publicación de cualquier material que no haya recibido su aprobación previa. La represión previa es una forma de censura. **306**

privatization/privatización acción en la que ciertas funciones anteriormente realizadas por el gobierno pasan a empresas del sector privado. **186**

probable cause/causa probable razonamientos en los que se basa la acusación criminal de un individuo. **322**

probation/libertad condicional libertad otorgada a una persona acusada de un delito con la condición de que cumpla con ciertos criterios de buena conducta durante un periodo específico. **281**

procedural due process/proceso establecido procesal principio que indica que la ley debe aplicarse de manera justa e imparcial para toda persona y con base en las normas y procedimientos establecidos. *Véase también* substantive due process/proceso conforme a derecho. **319**

profit/ganancia diferencia entre los ingresos de la venta de un producto o servicio y el costo original del mismo. **508**

proletariat/proletariado clase trabajadora cuyos integrantes, según la teoría del analista político Karl Marx, estaban oprimidos por la burguesía. **511**

property tax/impuesto sobre bienes impuesto aplicado por el gobierno sobre el valor de ciertas propiedades. **493**

public comment/exposición pública oportunidad para las partes interesadas de reaccionar ante una disposición propuesta por una entidad gubernamental antes de que dicha disposición entre en vigor. **176–77**

public good/bienestar público intereses comunes de los integrantes de una sociedad; también conocidos como interés público. **6**

public interest group/grupo de interés público grupo de interés que apoya las ideas y causas que considera para el bienestar público, en contraste con los grupos que apoyan intereses particulares, ya sean de índole social o económica. **388**

public opinion/opinión pública opinión colectiva sobre un tema o conjunto de temas relacionados, que sostiene un gran segmento de la sociedad. **367**

public policy/políticas públicas decisiones y leyes aprobadas por el gobierno acerca de un área particular del interés público. **4**

quorum/quórum cantidad mínima de legisladores que deben estar presentes para votar y llevar a cabo otros asuntos formales en las sesiones del Congreso. **113**

quota/contingente número mínimo de contrataciones necesarias en un programa afirmativo de acción. **355**

R

ratification/ratificación aceptación formal de una acción por parte de una entidad o gobierno. Por lo general, la ratificación es el paso final en la firma de un tratado o enmienda constitucional. **31**

realignment/realineación cambio de posición política en el electorado o de partido político de una legislatura. Por lo general, la realineación se refiere a los cambios significativos y duraderos en las actitudes del electorado. **409**

realism/realismo en las relaciones internacionales, creencia de que la política exterior de una nación debe basarse en la naturaleza e historia de la humanidad. Los realistas consideran que la política exterior debe dirigirse hacia la adquisición de poder, la conservación de la seguridad nacional y la búsqueda de otros intereses nacionales. **219**

recall/destitución procedimiento que permite al electorado votar para retirar a un funcionario de su cargo antes de que termine su periodo de servicio. **464**

recession/recesión reducción importante de las actividades comerciales generales durante un periodo significativo. **197**

reconciliation/conciliación parte del proceso del presupuesto federal en que el Congreso hace los ajustes necesarios a la propuesta de presupuesto presentada por la presidencia. **207**

referendum/referéndum procedimiento que en algunos estados da a los ciudadanos la oportunidad de votar para aceptar o rechazar las leyes aprobadas por la legislatura o la asamblea local. **464**

refugee/refugiado persona que escapa de una región por voluntad propia u obligada por causas políticas, militares, religiosas, sociales y otros conflictos. **527**

regulatory commission/comisión regulatoria entidad independiente creada por el Congreso que cuenta con mayor grado de autonomía o autogobierno que otras entidades. **177**

relations of production/relaciones de producción según la teoría marxista, es la manera en que las personas se relacionan en el proceso del trabajo. Las relaciones de producción dependen de quién posee los medios de producción, de lo que la posición de los trabajadores guarda en relación con otros grupos que participan en el proceso de producción, y de la distribución de la producción y los ingresos entre estas partes. **516**

renewable resources/recursos renovables recursos que pueden recuperarse a corto plazo por medios naturales. **540**

repeal/revocar revertir o cancelar una ley o disposición existente. **52**

representative democracy/democracia representativa sistema de gobierno en el que el pueblo elige a los líderes políticos que tomarán decisiones políticas a favor del pueblo. **16**

reprieve/suspensión retraso de la aplicación de la sentencia de una persona condenada. **153**

republic/república sistema de gobierno en el que el poder gubernamental proviene del pueblo, quien elige individuos para que lo represente en la toma de decisiones. **8**

reserved power/poderes reservados poderes que la Constitución no otorga expresa ni implícitamente al Congreso. La décima enmienda constitucional reserva estos poderes a los estados o al pueblo. **68**

reserve requirement/requerimiento de reserva reserva financiera que un banco guarda en sus propias arcas o en una reserva federal del distrito. En otras palabras, es la cuenta de ahorros del banco. **201**

resolution/resolución declaración formal o política relacionada con un tema o asunto específico. **206**

revenue/ingresos cantidad total de dinero recibida por un negocio o unidad de gobierno. **191**

revenue sharing/distribución de ingresos distribución que un gobierno hace de una parte de sus rentas a los niveles de gobierno inferiores. **72**

roll-call vote/ronda de votación procedimiento legislativo en el que cada legislador acude de manera individual a emitir su voto. **127**

runoff primary/primaria de eliminación segunda ronda de elecciones que se realiza en algunos estados cuando ningún candidato recibe la mayoría de los votos en las elecciones primarias. **432**

rural area/zona rural región de baja densidad de población en la que las personas habitan en granjas, ranchos o aldeas cuya actividad económica se basa en la tierra, como la agricultura o la minería. **481**

sales tax/impuesto sobre la venta impuesto aplicado a la venta de productos y servicios. **473**

sampling/muestreo selección de una pequeña parte de la población para representar a la población total en una encuesta. **374**

sampling error/error de muestreo error en los resultados de una votación ocasionado por la elección de una muestra de votantes que no representa a la población estudiada. **375**

search warrant/orden de cateo autorización escrita emitida por un juez que permite a las autoridades revisar la propiedad y las pertenencias de una persona en busca de objetos específicos, y a confiscar dichos objetos si se llegan a encontrar. **322**

secret ballot/voto secreto nombre popular del sistema de votación que permite a los votantes elegir a los candidatos en privado. Se usó por primera vez en Australia y hoy se usa las elecciones de Estados Unidos. **441**

secretary/secretario jefe de un departamento del gabinete presidencial dentro del poder ejecutivo del gobierno. Por ejemplo, el secretario de defensa, el secretario de estado, el secretario de la tesorería, etcétera. **174**

sedition/sedición lenguaje o acciones que propician o promueven la resistencia o rebelión en contra de un gobierno establecido de manera legal. *Véase también* treason/traición. **305**

segregation/segregación separación de personas de acuerdo con características específicas que las identifican. **348**

select committee/comité exclusivo comité del Senado o la Cámara de representantes que generalmente se establece de manera provisional y para propósitos específicos, especialmente de investigación. **119**

self-interest/interés propio impulso que motiva a las personas a satisfacer sus necesidades y deseos. **508–09**

senatorial courtesy/cortesía senatorial ejercicio que permite a los senadores del mismo partido político que el presidente, aprobar o rechazar a cualquier nominación a un cargo público antes de la presentación oficial de las nominaciones. **254**

seniority system/sistema de antigüedad sistema que otorga posiciones en el comité del Congreso según el tiempo de prestación de servicios. **120**

separate-but-equal doctrine/doctrina de igualdad con separación precedente legal (establecido por la suprema corte en el caso *Plessy vs. Fergusson* en 1896) de que la segregación racial no era una violación de la cláusula de protección de igualdad incluida en la Decimocuarta enmienda, siempre que las instalaciones para personas de raza blanca y personas de raza negra tuvieran las mismas características. Este principio permaneció en vigor hasta 1954, cuando la suprema corte lo anuló en el caso *Brown vs. Concejo de educación*. **348**

separation of powers/separación de poderes distribución del poder político que da a cada poder del gobierno un conjunto particular de responsabilidades. **48**

sequester/apartar aislar al jurado del público general durante un juicio. **279**

shield law/ley de protección ley que protege a los reporteros de tener que revelar fuentes confidenciales de información. Mediante esta ley, cualquier persona puede proporcionar información a los medios públicos sin temer que sean develados como informantes. **307**

sin tax/impuesto de actividades pecaminosas impuesto aplicado a las actividades consideradas por el gobierno como dañinas o no recomendables. **474**

single-issue voting/votación de una sola causa situación en que un individuo elige apoyar o rechazar a un candidato político con base en un solo factor, excluyendo a los demás. **391**

single-member district/distrito de un integrante distrito electoral en el que sólo un candidato puede ganar las elecciones para un cargo particular. **440**

slander/calumniar presentar intencionalmente falsas declaraciones que pueden dañar la reputación de un negocio, individuo o grupo. Aunque la calumnia es un delito, no se persigue de oficio en la mayoría de los casos. No obstante, las víctimas de la calumnia suelen buscan resarcir los daños en demandas civiles. **307**

social contract/contrato social teoría que indica que las personas ceden su soberanía individual a cambio de la paz y el orden establecidos por el estado. **4**

socialism/socialismo sistema económico en el que el gobierno posee la mayor parte de los medios de producción y satisface casi todas las necesidades del pueblo. Un sistema socialista puede o no ser democrático. **511**

sovereignty/soberanía autoridad absoluta de un gobierno sobre los ciudadanos de un estado. **3**

Speaker/presidente funcionario que preside la Cámara de representantes y ocupa el segundo lugar en la sucesión presidencial (después del vicepresidente). El presidente es elegido por la Cámara y siempre es un integrante del partido mayoritario. **115**

special district/distrito especial unidad de gobierno, por lo general a nivel local, que cumple una función específica y que en ocasiones no toma en cuenta las fronteras políticas. **490**

splinter party/facción de partido partido político creado por un grupo insatisfecho con el candidato elegido por su partido y que, a consecuencia de esto, rompe relaciones con el partido original (o con los partidos más importantes). *Véase también* ideological party/partido ideológico. **415**

split ticket/boleta dividida resultado de una votación individual por diferentes partidos políticos para distintos cargos públicos. **417**

spoils system/sinecuras como recompensa política retribución que ofrecen los funcionarios electos a sus simpatizantes en forma de empleos y contratos públicos, en lugar de otorgarlos con base en su calificación para el trabajo. *Véase también* merit system/sistema del mérito. **178–79**

Stamp Act/ley del timbre ley aprobada en 1765 por el Parlamento para recaudar dinero mediante la aplicación de impuestos a productos de papel. Debido a las violentas protestas de los colonos, este impuesto fue rechazado un año después de su aprobación. **26**

standard of living/estándar de vida bienestar económico de las personas, determinado por la cantidad de productos y servicios que éstas consumen en un periodo específico. **195**

standing committee/comité permanente comité permanente o regular creado por la legislatura para revisar los proyectos de un área temática específica. **119**

stare decisis/stare decisis principio legal y acción judicial que se basa en los precedentes de veredictos anteriores. El término en latín significa "decisión que permancce". **261**

state/estado 1) territorio cuya población mantiene un cuerpo organizado de gobierno que regula los asuntos internos y externos. **2)** unidad política en un sistema federal, como un estado de Estados Unidos. **3**

State of the Union address/Informe presidencial mensaje anual en el que el presidente propone al Congreso su programa administrativo. **143**

statutory interpretation/interpretación estatutaria función que permite a un juez determinar el significado de la ley en un caso especifico. **272**

statutory law/derecho estatutario disposiciones de las que se vale el organismo legislativo de un gobierno. **272**

straight ticket/boleta para elección de lista completa resultado de que un elector elija sólo a los candidatos de un partido político en particular para todos los cargos en la boleta. **417**

strict constructionist/interpretador estricto persona que cree que la constitución debe interpretarse con rigidez y con apego absoluto a sus artículos. **249**

subcommittee/subcomité 1) parte reducida y más especializada de un comité. **2)** grupo formado por integrantes de un comité, elegidos para revisar ciertas categorías de proyectos de ley antes de presentarse a todo el comité. **119**

subpoena/citación orden por escrito que exige a una persona que se presente como testigo en el tribunal o bien presente ciertos puntos en el tribunal a manera de evidencia. **279**

substantive due process/proceso conforme a derecho principio que declara que la ley debe ser justa y razonable. El derecho a un proceso conforme a derecho obliga al tribunal a considerar la equidad de la ley misma. **320**

suburb/suburbio comunidad principalmente residencial ubicada en los alrededores de una ciudad y cuyos residentes dependen en gran parte de la ciudad por sus empleos y otros servicios. **481**

suffrage/sufragio derecho al voto. **442**

summit conference/conferencia en la cumbre reunión de los jefes de estado de dos o más naciones para analizar y guiar las relaciones internacionales. Estas conferencias abarcan cuestiones militares, económicas y diplomáticas. **223**

supply and demand/oferta y demanda los factores que determinan los precios en el mercado libre. **508**

suspect classification/clasificación por sospecha base potencialmente ilegal de distinción entre individuos o grupos. **347**

symbolic speech/discurso simbólico mensajes que no son comunicados de manera verbal. El discurso simbólico abarca la vestimenta, las gesticulaciones con las manos y algunas acciones. **310**

trade embargo/embargo comercial orden de un gobierno que prohíbe el comercio con una nación específica. **218**

trading bloc/bloque comercial grupo de naciones que trabajan en conjunto para brindar beneficios comerciales a sus integrantes. Éstos definen sus propias cuotas de importación y exportación, aranceles y medios de control comercial. **534**

treason/traición acción desleal en contra de la nación propia. **304**

Truman Doctrine/Doctrina Truman declaración de política exterior planteada en 1947 por el presidente Harry Truman en la que ofecía ayuda económica y militar a las naciones que intentaba evitar una toma de control comunista. **229**

two-party system/sistema bipartidista sistema en el que dos partidos políticos dominan el sistema político en una nación y compiten por el poder político. **407**

T

---

tax/impuesto pago obligatorio de manera regular al gobierno local, estatal o nacional. **191**

term limits/límite de periodo límite legal en el número de periodos consecutivos en que un funcionario puede ocupar un cargo público. **113**

third party/tercer partido partido político independiente de los partidos mayoritarios en un sistema bipartidista. **413**

totalitarianism/totalitarianismo sistema de gobierno en el que un dictador o grupo pequeño de líderes ejerce un control muy grande sobre la ciudadanía. **9–10**

township/municipio comunidades establecidas en ciudades como Nueva Jersey, Nueva York y Pennsylvania. Los gobiernos de estos municipios tiencn las mismas funciones que los de los antiguos poblados de Nueva Inglaterra. **487**

trade association/asociación industrial organización formada por las compañías de un mismo ramo industrial para proteger sus intereses. **386**

trade deficit/déficit comercial situación en la que el valor total de las importaciones de un país es mayor que el valor total de sus exportaciones. **537**

U

---

unconstitutional/anticonstitucional ley o acción del gobierno que viola las disposiciones expuestas en la constitución. **49**

unicameral/unicameral cuerpo legislador con una sola cámara de representantes. Nebraska es el único estado de Estados Unidos con una legislatura unicameral. **30**

unitary system/sistema unitario sistema de gobierno en el que el gobierno nacional o central tiene todo el poder legal. **10**

urban area/zona urbana región caracterizada por ciudades y zonas de alta densidad de población y en la que la mayoría de los habitantes trabaja en actividades de manufactura, comerciales y demás actividades económicas no relacionadas con la agricultura. **481**

U.S. Agency for International Development/ Agencia Estadounidense para el Desarrollo Internacional organización del gobierno estadounidense para desarrollar programas de asistencia exterior. Esta agencia enfoca cinco áreas de política exterior: promoción del crecimiento económico, desarrollo de la democracia, ayuda humanitaria, promoción de la salud pública, y protección del medio ambiente. **235**

V

value/valor cualidad, principio o estándar básico que se considera importante o deseable, y con el que las personas viven su vida. Por ejemplo, la humildad es un valor que muchas personas consideran importante. **6**

vanguard/vanguardia puesto líder en un movimiento o las personas que ocupan ese puesto. En 1917, los bolcheviques fueron la vanguardia que encabezaron la Revolución Rusa. **517**

veto/veto rechazo formal de una legislación por parte del presidente. **48**

Virginia Plan/Plan de Virginia plan para establecer una legislatura unicameral de representación proporcional con base en la población de cada estado. La delegación de Virginia presentó el plan en la Convención Constitucional de 1787. Muchas de sus propuestas se incluyeron en la Constitución de Estados Unidos. **36**

visa/visa permiso que una nación otorga a un ciudadano extranjero que desea visitarlo. **225**

voir dire/voir dire interrogatorio del presunto jurado por parte del juez, el fiscal y el abogado defensor en un caso del tribunal, para ver si son aceptables para el juez y los abogados, para participar en un jurado. La frase *voir dire* significa "decir la verdad". **278–79**

W

ward/distrito división territorial del gobierno de una ciudad que con frecuencia también se usa como subdivisión electoral y unidad de organización de partido político. **418**

writ of *certiorari*/auto de avocación orden formal de un tribunal de apelación que solicita un tribunal de menor rango para que proporcione el registro de un caso a revisión. Muchos casos que llegan a la suprema corte se atienden gracias a que la corte emitió un auto de avocación. **259**

writ of habeas corpus/auto de habeas corpus orden judicial que instruye a las autoridades que ejecutan la ley para que lleven a un prisionero ante un funcionario del tribunal y cite la razón de su encarcelamiento, a fin de determinar si la persona está detenida de acuerdo con los procedimientos legales. **108**

INDEX

concurring opinion, 261

confederal system: *c10;* definition of, 10

conference committees, congressional, 119, 127

Congress, U.S.: *c102;* act of admission, 76; amending the Constitution, 265; appropriation committees, 118; appropriation of government funds, 227; approving presidential appointments, 106; under Articles of Confederation, 31–33; bicameral legislature, 48; borrowing power of, 105, *c105;* checks and balances, 48–49, *c49;* commerce power of, 105; committees system in, 118–22, *c119;* conference committees, 119; confirming presidential foreign-affairs appointments, 227; constituents' interests and, 94, 96–97; copyright and patent powers of, *c105;* currency power of, 105, *c105,* deciding presidential elections, 106; Due Process Clause, 306; enabling act, 76; Establishment Clause, 300; expressed powers of, 67, 105; *c105;* expulsion of members of, 117; federal spending and, 49; foreign-policy role of, 106; Free Exercise Clause, 302–303; home districts of, 129–31; immunity of, 101; impeachment powers of, 106, 253; implied powers of, 56–58, 68, 107; influence of personal beliefs on voting, 93–94; interest groups and, 94, 129; interpreting the Constitution, 57–58; investigatory powers of, 96; joint committees of, 119; judicial powers of, 265; lame ducks in, 113; lawmaking process in, 93–95, 123–28; leadership in, 115–16, *c116;* military powers of, 105, *c105;* minority representatives in, 104, *p104;* national sovereignty and, 105, *c105;* oversight function of, 96; party in control of, 115; "permanent," 114; political party loyalty and, 95; pork-barrel spending and, 129–31; postal power of, *c105,* powers denied to, 108, *c108;* powers of, 48–49, *c49;* privileges of members, 101; profiles of, 104; proposing constitutional amendments, 52; qualifications of members, 101, 104; resources of, 121–22; restrictions on pay raises, 54, 55; role of, 93–97; role in federal budget, 205–207, *c207;* role in U.S. foreign policy, 227; rules of conduct for, 116–17; salaries and benefits of members, 101, 104; select committees of, 118–19; seniority system in, 120; services to constituents, 96–97; special powers of, 105–106; staff of, 121–22, *p122;* standing committees in, 119, *c119;* taxing power of, 105, *c105,* 193; terms of office of members, 99, 102; terms and sessions, 113, *c114;* term limits, 113–15; treaty powers of, 106, 227; types of committees in, 118–19; types of congressional staff, 121–22, *p122;* voting influences of, 93–95; war powers of, 227; women in, 95, *p95,* 104. *See also* House of Representatives; legislation, congressional; Senate, U.S.

Congressional Budget and Impoundment Control Act of 1974, 204–205

Congressional Budget Office (CBO), 122, 205, 206

congressional districts, 99–100

congressional staffer, 120, *p120*

congressmember, 95

Congress of Racial Equality (CORE), 351, 394

Connecticut: as corporate colony, 24

Connecticut Plan. *See* Great Compromise

constituents, 94, 96–97

constitution, 21

constitution, state, 461–62

Constitution, U.S.: 10, 60–62, R20–R49; basic principles of, 47–50; bicameral legislature in, 38; bill of attainder, 327; checks and balances, 41, 48–50, *c48, c49;* concurrent powers in, 68, *c69;* creation of, 36–39, 40–42; custom and tradition, 58–59; Due Process Clause, 320–22; Elastic Clause, 68; electoral college in, 157–58, *c157;* Equal Protection Clause, 346–48; equal-representation guarantee, 60; *ex post facto* laws, 327; expressed powers in, 67, *c69,* 105, *c105;* federalism and, *c48,* 50, 67–71; foreign relations, 145; foreign relations and war powers in, 223–27; framers of, 35–36; Full Faith and Credit Clause, 76, *p76, 78;* implied powers in, 68, 107; influence of Roman Republic on structure of, 103; inherent powers in, 68; interpreting, 57; judicial powers, 250, 265; judicial review in, 49–50; limited government and, 48; loose constructionists' interpretation of, 250; Miranda Rule and, 327–28, *c328;* "necessary and proper" clause of, 68; opponents of, 40–41; popular sovereignty and, 47, *c48;* power to tax under, 193; powers denied to Congress in, 108, *c108;* powers denied to federal government in, 69; powers denied to states in, 50, 69; powers granted to Congress in, 48, 105–107, *c105;* powers granted to federal government in, 50; powers granted to the executive branch in, 48–49, 143, 145, 148–54; powers granted to states in, 68; Preamble to, 47; preparation of federal budget under, 206; presidential qualifications set by, 145; presidential selection in, 157–58, *c157;* presidential succession and, 146–47, *c147;* privileges and immunity clause of, 79; proposing amendments to, 52; protections for those accused of crimes, 326–28; *c326;* public good and, 60–62; public policies and, 61; ratification of, 41–42, *m41, p42;* ratifying amendments to, 52; reserved powers in, 68, *c69;* separation of powers under, 48; signing of, *p38,* 39; special powers of Congress in, 105–106; strict constructionists' interpretation of, 249–50; supporters of, 41; supremacy clause of, 50, 71; Supreme Court in, 48, 49–50; term of president in, 146; war powers, 143; writ of *habeas corpus,* 326–27. *See also* amendments; Bill of Rights; specific amendments

Constitutional Convention: 35–39, 107, 251; delegates of, 35–36; Great Compromise, 38; New Jersey Plan, *c36,* 37–38; election procedure of president, 39; slavery and trade issues, 38–39; Virginia Plan, 36–37, *c36*

constitutional interpretation, 272

constitutional law, 272

constitutional monarchy, *c9;* definition of, 8

consul, 224–25

consulate, 224

consumer, 508

Consumer Product Safety Commission (CPSC), 178

containment, 229–30, 520

contested elections, 442

Continental Congress: First, 28–29; Second, 29, 31

Contract with America, 95

convention, 159

conventions, national: 161–62; delegates to, 159–60; keynote speaker at, 161, *p161;* party caucuses and, 160; political nominations at, 430; presidential primaries and, 159–62, *p159, p162;* women as delegates to, *c167*

G

Philippines: American control of, 229; bilateral treaty with U.S., 238

picketing, 313–14

plaintiff, 274

plank: at national conventions, 161

Planned Parenthood: as a cause-based interest group, 388

plea bargain, 280

Pledge of Allegiance: and freedom of religion, 303

Plessy v. Ferguson, 348

plurality, 163

pocket veto, 128

Poland: interest groups in, 397

police powers: 275–76; due process and, 322–23; Miranda Rule, 327–28, *c328*

political action committees (PACs), 94, 391–92, *c392, c400*

political campaigns: 160, 435–39; benefits of, 450; criticisms of, 447–48; financing of, 437–38, *c437;* mass media in, 436–37; negative campaigning, 447–48; and the public good, 447–50; role of media, 447–48

political gridlock, 61–62

political parties: *c410;* criticisms of, 421–22; definition of, 58; function of, 405–407, *c406;* history of, 409–13; loyalty toward, 95; in multiparty system, 408; national machinery of, 419–20; nominating function of, 407; in one-party system, 407; organization of, 416–20, *c418;* organizing function of, 406; president as leader of, 145; and the public good, 421–24; state and local machinery, 416–20; in two-party system, 407, 422–24; types of, 407–15

political psychology, 369

political scientist, 5, *p5*

political socialization, 368

politics, 6

polling, 372, 437

pollster, 374

Pomeroy, Earl, 135

popular sovereignty, 47, *c48*

popular vote, 163, *c163*

pork-barrel spending, 129–31, *p131*

Postal Service, U.S., 178

Powell, Colin, *p217*

precedent, 249

precinct, 418

prejudice, 345

presentment, 327

president, U.S.: background of, 145–46; as chief agenda setter, 143; as chief executive, 143; as chief of state, 144; as commander in chief, 48,143, 151, 223; election by House of Representatives, 106, 158; election process of, 39, 157–64, *c157, c163;* Executive Office of the, 169–74, *c173;* executive privilege of, 149; financing campaign of, 437–39; as foreign policy leader, 145; formal titles of, 143; impeachment of, 106; lawmaking process and, 128; lobbying for legislation, 153–54; the media and, 150, 155, 182–83; nomination and election of, 429–34; as party leader, 145; and the public good, 182–83; qualifications for, 145; as representative of the nation, 143–44; role in federal budget, 205, *c207;* role in U.S. foreign policy, 222–23; roles of, 143–45; salary and benefits of, 146; speechwriting for, 169–70; and State of the Union address, 143, 153; succession of, 146–47, *c147;* terms of office of, 146

presidential aide, 183, *p183*

presidential awards, 171, *p171*

presidential doctrines, 222–23

presidential electors. *See* electoral college

presidential powers: appointing, 148–49, *p148,* 254, 257; criticism of, 156, *p156;* diplomatic, 149–51; executing the law, 148; executive, 148–49; executive agreements, 58; 151, 223; foreign relations, 149–52, 222–23; growth of, 154–56, 182; how presidents have viewed, 148; judicial, 152–53, 265–66; legislative, 128, 153–54; military, 151–52, 223; and the public good, 182–83; treaty making, 149–51, *p151,* 223; veto, 48, 128, 153; war, 151, 227

presidential primaries, 159–60

president *pro tempore,* 116, *c116*

president of the Senate, 116, *c116*

presidential succession, 146–47, *c147*

presidential system, 11

press. *See* freedom of press; mass media; newspapers

primaries: closed, 432; direct, 431; nonpartisan, 434; open, 432; presidential, 159–60; runoff, 432; voter turnout in, 434

primary election, 159, 417

prime minister, French, 144,

prior restraint, 306

privacy: right to, 324–25

private property: demonstrations on, 313–14

privatization, 186

privileges and immunity clause, 79

probable cause, 322

probation, 281

procedural due process, 319–20

profit, 508

Progressive Party, 415

prohibition, 55

Prohibition Party, 415

proletariat, 511

property tax: by local government, 493–94, *c493*

proprietary colony, 24

protests: freedom of assembly and petition, 312–14; interest groups and, 395

Public Citizen, 390

public comment, 176–77

public funding: of political campaigns, 438

public good: 15, 60–62; Aristotle's writings on the, 251; boot camps, 285–86; civil liberties and the, 298–99; congressional committees and, 131; definition of, 6–7; economic policy and, 202–03; federal court system and the, 263–66; federal government and, 131 32, 183–86; federalism and, 80–83; interest groups and the, 396–400; local government and the, 492; mass media and the, 377–80; political campaigns and the, 447–50; political parties and the, 421–24; pork-barrel spending and, 129–31; and the presidency, 182–83; state governments and the, 465; tax policy and, 195; U.S. foreign policy and, 221

public interest groups, 388, *c390*

public opinion: 366–80; definition of, 367; forms of, 367–68; interest groups and, 394–95; mass media and, 370, *c371,* 377–78, *p377;* measuring, 372–76; nature of, 371; role of, 367; role of schools in, 370

public opinion poll: 372–76, *c376;* conducting, 373–76; origins of, 372–73; types of, 373

public policy: 4, 61; interest groups and, 391–95

public property: demonstrations on, 312–13

public trial, 329–30

Puerto Rico: 98; U.S. control of, 229

Q

Quayle, Dan, 102

quorum, 113

quotas, 355

R

radio: freedom of speech and, 308; influence on public opinion, 370; Roosevelt's "fireside chats," 155

ratification, 31

rational basis test, 346–47

Reagan, Nancy, 173, *p182*

Reagan, Ronald, 154, *p182,* 198, 208, *p263*

realignment, 409

realism, 219

realpolitik, 219

reasonable distinction, 346

recall, 464–65, *c464*

recession, 197

reconciliation, 207

redistricting: 99; racial gerrymandering and, 100–01, *m101*

Reed, Ralph, 393

referendum, 464, *c464*

Reform Party, 414–15

refugee, 527

regulatory commissions, 177–78

relations of production, 516

religion. *See* freedom of religion

renewable resource, 540

repeal, 52

reprieve, 153

representation: population and, 99

representative democracy, 16

representative government, 22–23

republic: *c9;* definition of, 8

republican, 69–70

Republican Party: 409; domination of the government from 1860 to 1932, 412; rise of, 411; and tax policy, 194

reserve requirements, 201

reserved powers, 68, *c69*

resolution, 206

revenue: 191; nontax, 194. *See also* Taxes

revenue sharing, 72

Revolutionary War, 31, 72

Reynolds v. United States, 302–03

Rhode Island: as corporate colony, 24

Rio Pact, 237

Rockefeller, Nelson, 147

"Rock the Vote" campaign, 377–78

Roe v. Wade, 262, 325

roll-call vote, 127

Roman Empire, 103

Roosevelt, Eleanor, 174

Roosevelt, Franklin D., 58, *p59,* 146, *p146,* 150, 155, 174, 215, 229, 257–58, 413

Roosevelt, Theodore, 155, *p155,* 414, 415

Roth v. United States, 307

royal colony, 24

rule of law: concept of, 22

Rumsfeld, Donald, *p225*

runoff primary, 432

rural area, 481

Russia: communism in, 517–21; media and elections, 448; U.S. purchase of Alaska territory from, 77

Russian Revolution, 517–18

S

sales tax: 473–74; by local government, 494, *c493*

SALT treaty. *See* Strategic Arms Limitation Treaty

sampling, 374–75

sampling error, 375

Santaniello, Tom, *p433*

Schenck v. United States, 305

schools: federal government aid issue, 302; Pledge of Allegiance debate and, 303; prayer in, 301; religious activities in, 301; student religious groups in, 301

Schumer, Charles, *p121*

search and seizure, *c53,* 322–24, *p322, p324*

search warrant, 322

Second Continental Congress, 29, 31

secretaries: 174. *See also* cabinet, U.S., government departments by name

secret ballot, 441

Securities and Exchange Commission (SEC), 178

security of home and person, 322–24

sedition, 305

ACKNOWLEDGMENTS

For permission to reprint copyrighted material, grateful acknowledgment is made to the following sources:

Antonietta Barbieri: Quote by Antonietta Barbieri from "The Barn-Raising Spirit Still Thrives" by Alan Bunce from *The Christian Science Monitor,* April 26, 1996. Copyright © 1996 by Antonietta Barbieri.

Democratic National Committee: From Geraldine Ferraro's closing statement in "The Bush-Ferraro Debate: October 11, 1984," Online, World Wide Web, September 5, 1997. Copyright © 1984 by the Democratic National Committee. Available online http://wwwnetcapitol.com/Debates/vp84-1st.htm.

Dennis-Yarmouth Regional High School: Adapted from "Constitution of the Dennis-Yarmouth Regional High School Student Council" from World Wide Web, January 22, 1997. Copyright © 1995 by Dennis-Yarmouth Regional High School. Available at http://www.capecod.net/dystuco/const/constidx.html.

The Gallup Organization, Inc.: From speech by George Gallup on July 19, 1990, Online, September 8, 1997. Copyright © 1990 by The Gallup Organization, Inc. Available http://policy.gmu.edu/cif/gallup.html.

National Civic League: From "Reinvigorating Democratic Values: Challenge and Necessity," by Henry G. Cisneros and John Parr from *National Civic Review,* September/October 1990. Copyright © 1990 by National Civic League Press, Denver, Colorado.

The New York Times Company: From John Maynard Keynes's recorded thoughts on Roosevelt's plan, the New Deal, from *The New York Times,* June 10, 1934. Copyright © 1934 by The New York Times Company.

People Weekly: Quote by Gregory Watson from "The Man Who Would Not Quit" from *People Weekly,* June 1, 1992. Copyright © 1992 by People Weekly.

Governor Jeanne Shaheen: From the inaugural address of Governor Jeanne Shaheen of New Hampshire, January 9, 1997, Online, World Wide Web, August 12, 1997. Copyright © 1997 by Jeanne Shaheen. Available http://www.state.nh.us/governor/iaddress.html.

The Heirs to the Estate of Martin Luther King, Jr., c/o Writers House, Inc. as agent for the proprietor: From "Letter from Birmingham Jail" by Martin Luther King, Jr. Copyright © 1963 by Martin Luther King, Jr.; copyright renewed © 1991 by Coretta Scott King.

SOURCES CITED

Quote by an observer from *The Ring of Power: The White House Staff & Its Expanding Role in Government* by Bradley H. Patterson, Jr. Published by Basic Books, 1988.

Quote by a member of Congress from *Legislating Together: The White House and Capitol Hill from Eisenhower to Reagan* by Mark A. Peterson. Published by Harvard University Press, 1990.

Quote by anti-pork spokesman from "Congress" from *American Democracy and the Public Good.*

From *Showdown at Gucci Gulch* by Jeffrey H. Birnbaum and Alan S. Murray. Published by Random House, Inc., 1987.

Quotes by John Culver and George Smathers from *House and Senate* by Ross K. Baker. Published by W. W. Norton & Company, 1989.

From "The Casework Burden" from *To Serve the People: Congress and Constituency Service* by John R. Johannes. Published by University of Nebraska Press, 1984.

Quotes by Marc Glenn and Jo Ann Strickler from "Meet Two Student Delegates to the 1992 Presidential Conventions" from *American Democracy and the Public Good* by Steven Kelman. Published by Harcourt Brace College, 1996.

Quote by political consultant, Frank I. Luntz, about a hypothetical election in Florida from *Candidates, Consultants, and Campaigns* by Frank I. Luntz. Published by Basil Blackwell, 1988.

Quote by Sandra Murphy, owner of S. Buck Pizza, from "Getting by on minimum wage: What a little bit extra means," Online, World Wide Web, March 9, 1997. Published by The Associated Press. Available http://www2.nando.net/newsroom/ntn/nation/042596/nation5_19151_s1html.

From "The Supreme Court from Early Burger to Early Rehnquist" by Martin Shapiro from *The New American Political System,* 2nd version, edited by Anthony King. Published by AEI Press, 1990.

PHOTO CREDITS

Abbreviations used: (t) top, (c) center, (b) bottom, (l) left, (r) right, (bckgd) background, (bdr) border.

Front Cover: Chromosohm-Sohm/The Stock Market.

Table of Contents: Page xi(t), David Young-Wolff/PhotoEdit; (c), Martin Keene/"PA" Photo Library/The Image Works; (b), Andy Sacks/Tony Stone Images; (br), Library of Congress; xii(tl), Reproduced Courtesy of the Library and Information Centre, Royal Society of Chemistry; (tr), The Granger Collection, New York; (cl), The Granger Collection, New York; (bl), Uniphoto Picture Agency; (br), Superstock; xiii(tl), Bob Daemmrich/Stock, Boston; (tr), Paul Conklin/Photo Edit; (c), Tobias Everke/Gamma Liaison; (bl), M. Theiler/Washington Stock Photo, Inc.; (br), Jay Mallin Photos; xiv(tl), Dennis Brack/Black Star; (tr), Drew Harmon/Folio, Inc.; (c), Dirck Halstead/Gamma Liaison; (bl), Diana Walker/Gamma Liaison; (br), Luc Novovitch/AP/Wide World Photos; xix(l), Bob Daemmrich/Stock, Boston; (tr), Levick/Archive Photos; (c), © 1995 John Skowronski; (cr), Kenneth Jarecke/Contact Press Images; (br), Carlos Chavez/AP/Wide World Photos; xv(t), Joe Traver/Gamma Liaison; (c), Brown Brothers; (bl), Pamela Price/The Picture Cube; (br), Benelux Press/West Light; xvi(t), UPI/Corbis-Bettmann; (c), Topham Picturepoint/The Image Works; (bl), UPI/Corbis-Bettmann; (br), Collection, The Supreme Court Historical Society; xvii(tl), Alan Klehr/Tony Stone Images; (tr), Copyright (c) Larry Kolvoord; (c), J.B. Boykin/Photo Edit; (bl), from *Page One,* © 1987 by The New York Times Corporation, all rights reserved; (br), The Bettmann Archive; xviii(tl), © 1991 Stephen Shames/Matrix; (tr), Archive Photos; (cl), Bern Keating/Black Star; (bl), © Camerique/The Picture Cube; (br), David Woo/Stock, Boston; xx(tl), The Granger Collection, New York; (tr), Susan Sterner/AP/Wide World Photos; (cl), © M. Antman/The Image Works; (bl), Brown Brothers; (bc), The Granger Collection, New York; xxi(l), Steve Helber/AP/Wide World Photos; (tr), © Brian Yarvin '90/The Image Works; (cr), © E.J. Flynn/AP/Wide World Photos; (bl), © Mark C. Burnett/Stock, Boston; (br), © Pedrick/The Image Works; xxii(tl), Rhoda Sidney/PhotoEdit; (r), Earth Base/Gamma Liaison; (cl), Betty Press/Woodfin Camp & Associates, Inc.; (c), AKG Photo; (bl), Jeffrey Aaronson/Network Aspen; xxiii(l), © Bob Daemmrich/The Image Works; (tr), UPI/Corbis-Bettmann; (c), R. Rainford/Robert Harding Picture Library; (cr), Gary Braasch/Woodfin Camp & Associates, Inc.; (br), © Michelle Bridwell/Frontera Fotos; xxiv(tl), David Young-Wolff/PhotoEdit; (r), Amnesty International; (cl), Hank Walker/LIFE Magazine © TIME Inc.; (c), Phoebe Bell/Folio, Inc.; (bl), © Frank Fournier, Contact Press Images/Woodfin Camp & Associates, Inc.; xxv(l), Catherine Smith/Impact Visuals; (tr), Brown Brothers; (cr), The Granger Collection, New York; (br), Randy Duchaine/The Stock Market; xxvi(t), © Alan Schein/The Stock Market; (c), © 1997 Alex S. MacLean/Landslides; (b), © William Campbell/SYGMA; xxvii(t), Dick Durrancell/Woodfin Camp & Associates, Inc.; (c), © Alain Keller/SYGMA; (b), Photri.

Critical Thinking: Page xxix(bdr) , Peter Poulides/Tony Stone Images; (other), Ed Honowitz/Tony Stone Images;xxx(bdr), Peter Poulides/Tony Stone Images; (other), Christie's Images; xxxi (bdr), Jay Mallin Photos; (other), Peter Poulides/Tony Stone Images. **Skills Handbook:** Page xxxii (bdr), Peter Poulides/Tony Stone Images; (other), The Granger Collection, New York; xxxiii-xxxvi (bdr), Peter Poulides/Tony Stone Images; xxxvi(other), Steve Skjold/PhotoEdit; xxxvii-xxxix(bdr), Peter Poulides/Tony Stone Images; xxxix(other), GAMBLE reprinted with special permission of King Features Syndicate, Inc.; xl-xlv (bdr), Peter Poulides/Tony Stone Images; xlv (other), Gary A. Conner/PhotoEdit.

Unit 1: Page 0-1, © Matthew Borkoski/Stock, Boston. **Chapter 1:** Page 2, Telegraph Colour Library/FPG International Corp.; 3, Bernard Boutrit/Woodfin Camp & Associates; 4, Aaron Haupt/Stock, Boston; 5, Chip Henderson/Tony Stone Images; 6, Jose L. Pelaez/The Stock Market; 7, Photo 20-20; 8, Martin Keene/"PA" Photo Library/The Image Works; 11, Robert Trippett/Sipa Press; 12, ©Richard Pasely/Stock, Boston; 13(bdr), Brian Stablyk/Tony Stone Images, (other), Mark Richards/PhotoEdit; 14, David Young-Wolff/Tony Stone Images; 15, R. Rainford/Robert Harding Picture Library;16, Andy Sacks/Tony Stone Images; 18-19(bdr), Image Copyright © 1996 Photodisc, Inc. **Chapter 2:** Page 20, Superstock; 21, The Granger Collection, New York; 22(both), North Wind Picture Archives; 23, Colonial Williamsburg Foundation; 24, Courtesy, Winterthur Museum; 25, The Metropolitan Museum of Art, Bequest of Jacob Ruppert, 1939. (39.65.53); 26, Reproduced Courtesy of the Library and Information Centre, Royal Society of Chemistry; 27(bdr), Peter Poulides/Tony Stone Images; 28, HRW Photo Research Library; 29, Superstock; 31, From *The National Archives of The United States* by Herman J. Viola, courtesy Harry N. Abrams, Inc., New York; 33, Louis Schwartz; 37, David Young-Wolff/PhotoEdit; 38, Library of Congress; 40, The Granger Collection, New York; 42, The Granger Collection, New York; 44-45(bdr), Image Copyright c 1996 Photodisc, Inc.; 45, Superstock. **Chapter 3:** Page 46, The Granger Collection, New York; 51, Bob Daemmrich/Stock, Boston; 52, Arthur Grace/SYGMA; 54(bdr), Brian Stablyk/Tony Stone Images, (other), Zigy Kaluzny; 55, Cartoon by Grover Page, Louisville *Courier-Journal*/Brown Brothers; 56, The Granger Collection, New York; 57, Rick Buettner/Folio, Inc.; 58, Robert Trippett/Sipa Press; 59, UPI/Corbis-Bettmann; 60, National Portrait Gallery,Smithsonian Institution/Art Resource, NY; 61, Dennis Cook/AP/Wide World Photos; 64-65(bdr), Image Copyright © 1996 Photodisc, Inc. **Chapter 4:** Page 66, Randy Foulds/Washington Stock Photo, Inc.; 67, F. Figall/Washington Stock Photo, Inc.; 68, Peter Newark's American Pictures; 71, Todd Buchanan/Black Star; 73, Steve Leonard/Black Star; 74, Sam C. Pierson, Jr/The National Audobon Society Collection/Photo Researchers, Inc.; 75, © David Frazier Photolibrary; 76, Mary Kate Denny-Bim/PhotoEdit; 77(bdr), Peter Poulides/Tony Stone Images; (other), © Mark Kelley/Alaska Stock Images; 78, Ken Hawkins/SYGMA; 79, © Atlan/SYGMA; 80, David Muench Photography; 84-85(bdr), Image Copyright © 1996 Photodisc, Inc.; 86, Tony Freeman/PhotoEdit; 87, Larry Kolvoord.

Unit 2: Page 90-91, John Lawrence/Tony Stone Images. **Chapter 5:** Page 92, Jay Mallin Photos; 93, Tobias Everke/Gamma Liaison; 94, © 1984, Berke Breathed. Reprinted by permission; 95, Uniphoto Picture Agency; 96, Mark Richards/PhotoEdit; 97, Paul Conklin/PhotoEdit; 99, M. Theiler/Washington Stock Photo, Inc.; 103(bdr), Peter Poulides/Tony Stone Images; (other), Alexandra Avakian/Woodfin Camp & Associates; 104, Dennis Brack/Black Star; 106, Al Stephenson/Woodfin

Camp & Associates; 107, Superstock; 110-111(bdr), Image Copyright © 1996 Photodisc, Inc. **Chapter 6**: Page 112, Paul Conklin; 114, Mark Richards/PhotoEdit; 115, Drew Harmon/Folio, Inc.; 117, Greg Gibson/AP/Wide World Photos; 120, Jay Mallin Photos; 121, Dennis Cook/AP/Wide World Photos; 122, Paul Conklin/PhotoEdit; 123, Jay Mallin Photos; 124, Ashe/Folio, Inc.; 125(bdr), Brian Stablyk/Tony Stone Images; (other), Dennis Cook/AP/Wide World Photos; 126, National Cable Satellite Corporation; 127, UPI/Corbis-Bettmann; 128, Paul Conklin; 129, R. Bouchard/Washington Stock Photo, Inc.; 130, Dirck Halstead/Gamma Liaison; 131, Bob Galbraith/AP/Wide World Photos; 132, Jay Mallin Photos; 134-135(bdr), Image Copyright © 1996 Photodisc, Inc.; 136, Dallas & John Heaton/WestLight.

Unit 3: Page 140-141, M. Win/Washington Stock Photo, Inc. **Chapter 7**: Page 142, Dirck Halstead/Gamma Liaison; 143, ©1994 Robert A. Cumins/Black Star; 144, Greg Gibson /AP/Wide World Photos; 145, John Harrington/Black Star; 146, National Portrait Gallery, Smithsonian Institution/Art Resource, NY; 148, Diana Walker/Gamma Liaison; 150(bdr), Peter Poulides/Tony Stone Images; (other), Dennis Brack/Black Star; 151, Goksin Sipahioglu/Gamma Liaison; 152, Karl Gehring/Gamma Liaison; 153, Diana Walker/Gamma Liaison; 154(l), J. Scott Applewhite/AP/Wide World Photos; 154(r), The Granger Collection, New York; 155, Brown Brothers; 156, Cartoon by Bob Holland /Chicago Tribune, courtesy of Random House and the Foreign Policy Association; 158(l), The Granger Collection, New York; 158(r), The Bettmann Archive; 159, Luc Novovitch/AP/Wide World Photos; 160, ©Corbin M. Harris /AP/Wide World Photos; 161, Joe Traver/Gamma Liaison; 162, Joseph Sohm/ChromoSohm; 166-167(bdr), Image Copyright © 1996 Photodisc, Inc. **Chapter 8**: Page 168, ©Jeffery Markowitz /SYGMA; 169, Dirck Halstead/Gamma Liaison; 171(other), © RobertTrippett/Sipa Press; 171(bdr), Brian Stablyk/Tony Stone Images; 172, Yun Jai-Hyuoung/AP/Wide World Photos; 175, Dirck Halstead/Gamma Liaison; 176, Cleo Photography/The Picture Cube; 177, Chris Chapman/Gamma Liaison; 178, J. Blaustein/Woodfin Camp & Associates; 179(t), North Wind Picture Archives; 179(b), Benelux Press/WestLight; 181, Richard T. Nowitz/The National Audobon Society Collection/Photo Researchers, Inc.; 182, Pamela Price/The Picture Cube; 183, Tomas Muscionico/Contact Press Images; 184(t), © Tribune Media Services, Inc. All rights reserved. Reprinted with permission; 184(b), Gary Braasch/Woodfin Camp & Associates; 185, T. Campion/SYGMA; 186, Phil McCarten/PhotoEdit; 188-189(bdr), Image Copyright © 1996 Photodisc, Inc. **Chapter 9**: Page 190, G. Petrov/Washington Stock Photo, Inc.; 192(t), Kindra Clineff/The Picture Cube, Inc.; 192(b), Art Montes de Oca/FPG International Corp.; 193, R. Frasier/Folio, Inc.; 194, Paul Conklin/PhotoEdit; 195, Courtesy of David Horsey, Seattle *Post-Intelligencer*; 196, Mary Kate Denny-Bim/PhotoEdit; 199(bdr), Peter Poulides/Tony Stone Images; (other), W. B. Spunbarg/The Picture Cube; 202, courtesy Museum of American Financial History; 205, Denis Paquin/AP/Wide World Photos; 206, Dennis Brack/Black Star; 210, David Young-Wolff/PhotoEdit; 212, Jack Kustron/AP/Wide World Photos; 214-215(bdr), Image Copyright © 1996 Photodisc, Inc. **Chapter 10**: Page 216, Joseph Sohm /ChromoSohm; 217, Renault/Rieger/Gamma Liaison; 218, Brown Brothers; 219, UPI/Corbis-Bettmann; 220, Dennis Brack/Black Star; 222, John Ficara/SYGMA; 223, Peter Aaron/Esto Photographics; 224, Photo courtesy of the U.S. Department of State; 225(l), R. Foulds/Washington Stock Photo, Inc.; 225(r), Dennis Cook/AP/Wide World Photos; 226, ©Wilfredo Lee/AP/Wide World Photos; 227, Brown Brothers; 228, Nawrocki Stock Photo; 231, Photo # AR7522B, John F. Kennedy Library; 232, Sandra Baker/Liaison International; 233, UPI/Corbis-Bettmann; 235, Les Stone/SYGMA236(bdr), Brian Stablyk/Tony Stone Images;(other), Amnesty International; 238, UPI/Corbis-Bettmann; 240-241(bdr), Image Copyright © 1996 Photodisc, Inc.; 242(t), © 1990 David J. Sams/Stock, Boston; (b) The White House.

Unit 4: Page 246-247, ©Jeff Greenberg/The Picture Cube. **Chapter 11**: Page 248, Jane Rosenberg/AP/Wide World Photos; 251(bdr), Peter Poulides/Tony Stone Images; (other), The Granger Collection, New York; 254, UPI/Corbis-Bettmann; 255, Library of Congress/Theodore Horydczak Collection; 256, National Portrait Gallery, Smithsonian Institution/Art Resource, NY; 258, Collection, The Supreme Court Historical Society; 259, Michael Newman/PhotoEdit; 260, (c) 1997 John Skowronksi; 261, 262, Franz Jantzen/Collection of the Supreme Court of the United States; 263, © 1981 Fred Ward/Black Star; 264, Bob Daemmrich/Stock, Boston; 265, Don Smetzer/Tony Stone Images; 266, UPI/Corbis-Bettmann; 268-269(bdr), Image Copyright © 1996 Photodisc, Inc. **Chapter 12**: Page 270, Bob Daemmrich/Stock, Boston; 271, Topham Picturepoint/The Image Works; 272, HRW photo by Sam Dudgeon; 273, ©Danny Johnston/AP/Wide World Photos; 275, J.B. Boykin/PhotoEdit; 277, Alan Klehr/Tony Stone Images; 278, Los Angeles Times Photo by Bob Chamberlin; 279, © Fred Prouser/Sipa Press; 281, Michael Newman/PhotoEdit; 283, ©Mary Ann Chastain/AP/Wide World Photos; 284(bdr), Brian Stablyk/Tony Stone Images; (other), Copyright (c) Larry Kolvoord; 286, ©David Bundy/AP/Wide World Photos; 288-289(bdr), Image Copyright c 1996 Photodisc, Inc.; 290, H. Armstrong Roberts; 292, Corel Corporation.

Unit 5: Page 294-295, ©Joe Sohm, 1990 /ChromoSohm. **Chapter 13**: Page 296, The Granger Collection, New York; 297, The Bettmann Archive; 298, Paul Robertson Photography, photo courtesy the Southern Poverty Law Center, Birmingham, AL; 300, ©Camerique/The Picture Cube; 302, Gay Shackelford/*Texas Highways* Magazine; 304, ©1991 Stephen Shames/Matrix; 306, from *Page One*, © 1987 by The New York Times Corporation, all rights reserved; 307, Bob Daemmrich/Stock, Boston; 309(bdr), Brian Stablyk/Tony Stone Images; (other), UPI/Corbis-Bettmann; 310, ©1968 Dennis Brack/Black Star; 312, Jacques Chenet/Woodfin Camp & Associates; 313, ©Jeff Lowenthal/Woodfin Camp & Associates; 314, Gary Tramontina/AP/Wide World Photos; 316-317(bdr), Image Copyright © 1996 Photodisc, Inc. **Chapter 14**: Page 318, © Dave Bartruff/Stock, Boston; 319, ©Reinstein/The Image Works; 320, Alan Solomon/AP/Wide World Photos; 321(bdr), Peter Poulides/Tony Stone Images; (other), Gilles Bassignac/Gamma Liaison; 323, ©Bob Daemmrich/The Image Works; 324, David R. Frazier Photolibrary; 325, UPI/Corbis Bettmann; 329, David Woo/Stock, Boston; 330, © Jonathan Nourok/PhotoEdit; 331, ©Frank Fournier, Contact Press Images/Woodfin Camp & Associates; 332, © Jeff Robbins/AP/Wide World Photos; 334, UPI/Corbis-Bettmann; 336-337 (bdr), Image Copyright © 1996 Photodisc, Inc. **Chapter 15**: Page 338, © 1978 Matt Herron/Take Stock; 339, Randy Duchaine/The Stock Market; 341, Betty Press/Woodfin Camp & Associates; 342, Levick/Archive Photos; 343, Michael Grecco/Stock, Boston; 346, © Michelle Bridwell/Frontera Fotos; 347, Hank Walker/LIFE Magazine © TIME Inc.; 348, Bern Keating/Black Star; 349, © Michelle Bridwell/Frontera Fotos; 350, AP/Wide World Photos; 351, Archive Photos; 353, Bob Daemmrich/Stock, Boston; 354(bdr), Brian Stablyk/Tony Stone Images; (other), ©Denis Poroy/AP/Wide World Photos; 355, Brown Brothers; 356, Tom Stewart/The Stock Market; 358-359(bdr), Image Copyright © 1996 Photodisc, Inc.; 360, © Troy Maben/David R. Frazier Photolibrary.

Unit 6: Page 364-365, AP/Wide World Photos. **Chapter 16**: Page 366, Deborah Davis/PhotoEdit; 367, Louise Gubb/The Image Works; 369(bdr), Peter Poulides/Tony Stone Images; (other), Catherine Smith/Impact Visuals; 370, Mark Richards/PhotoEdit; 372, Bob Daemmrich/Stock, Boston; 373, Frank Siteman/The Picture Cube, Inc.; 374, Bob Daemmrich/Tony Stone Images; 377, Superstock; 379, © 1999 by Sidney Harris; 382-383(bdr), Image Copyright © 1996 Photodisc, Inc. **Chapter 17**: Page 384, Kenneth Jarecke/Contact Press Images; 385, Carlos Chavez/AP/Wide World Photos; 386, L.G. Patterson/AP/Wide World Photos; 388, © Larry Ulrich/Larry Ulrich Photography; 389(bdr), Peter Poulides/Tony Stone Images; (other) , © M. Antman/The Image Works; 393, Jay Mallin Photos; 394, ©Randy Squires/AP/Wide World Photos; 395, Goddard-Claussen/First Tuesday; 396, ©E.J. Flynn/AP/Wide World Photos; 398, Andy Hayt/NBA/Allsport; 402-403(bdr), Image Copyright © 1996 Photodisc, Inc.; 403, © 1995 John Skowronski. **Chapter 18**: Page 404, Dennis Brack/Black Star; 405, The Granger Collection, New York; 407, Forrest Anderson/Gamma Liaison; 408, Patrick Piel/Gamma Liaison; 409, 411, The Granger Collection, New York; 412, Brown Brothers; 416, The Granger Collection, New York; 417, Jonathan Nourok/PhotoEdit; 419, Jay Mallin Photos; 420, Photo courtesy GOP-TV; 421, Rick Friedman/Black Star; 422, ©1995 John Harrington/Black Star; 423(bdr), Brian Stablyk/Tony Stone Images; 423(other), Jay Mallin Photos; 424, John Jonik © 1997 from The Cartoon Bank. All rights reserved; 426-427(bdr), Image Copyright © 1996 Photodisc, Inc. **Chapter 19**: Page 428, Art by Mark Hess/The Image Bank, Inc.; 429, Bob Daemmrich Photography; 431, Phoebe Bell/Folio, Inc.; 433(bdr), Brian Stablyk/Tony Stone Images; (other), Allan Tannenbaum/SYGMA; 435, Peter Newark's American Pictures; 436, Brown Brothers; 439, Matthew McVay/Folio, Inc.; 440, Spencer Tirey/Liaison International; 441(l), Reed Saxon/AP/Wide World Photos; 441(r), Susan Sterner/AP/Wide World Photos; 442, The Granger Collection, New York; 443, Archive Photos; 444, Gary Gardiner/AP/Wide World Photos; 446, L. Dematteis/The Image Works; 449, Tom Pantages; 450, AP/Wide World Photos; 452-453(bdr), Image Copyright © 1996 Photodisc, Inc.; 454, HRW photos by Lance Schriner; 456, 457 (all), HRW Photo by Sam Dudgeon.

Unit 7: 458-459, © 1990, Joseph Sohm/ChromoSohm. **Chapter 20**: Page 460, Joseph Sohm/ChromoSohm; 461, ©Dennis MacDonald/PhotoEdit; 463, Rhoda Sidney/PhotoEdit; 465, © 1987 Rick Browne/The Stock Shop/Medichrome; 466, Steve Helber/AP/Wide World Photos;469(bdr), Peter Poulides/Tony Stone Images; (other), The Granger Collection, New York; 472, Bob Bird/AP/Wide World Photos; 475, © Brian Yarvin ©1990/The Image Works; 476, Jim McKnight/AP/Wide World Photos; 478-479(bdr), Image Copyright © 1996 Photodisc, Inc. **Chapter 21**: Page 480, Don & Pat Valenti/Tony Stone Images; 481, Donovan Reese/Tony Stone Images; 482, Dick Durrance II/Woodfin Camp & Associates; 483(bdr), Brian Stablyk/Tony Stone Images; (other), Photo courtesy of Sally Robeau; 484, Photri; 485, © Mark C. Burnett/Stock, Boston; 486, David R. Frazier Photolibrary; 487(t), © Paula Lerner/Woodfin Camp & Associates; 487(b), Mark E. Gibson; 489, © Bob Daemmrich/Tony Stone Images; 491, © Ian Shaw/Tony Stone Images; 494, © Charles Gupton/Stock, Boston; 495(t), Michelle Bridwell/Frontera Fotos; 495(b), © Kevin Horan/Stock, Boston; 496, ©Pedrick/The Image Works; 498-499(bdr), Image Copyright © 1996 Photodisc, Inc.; 500, Image Copyright © 1996 PhotoDisc, Inc.; 502, HRW Photo by Russell Dian.

Unit 8: Page 504-505, UN/Sygma. **Chapter 22**: Page 506, Eric Bouvet/Gamma Liaison; 508, © William Campbell/SYGMA; 509, The Granger Collection, New York; 510, © Alan Schein/The Stock Market; 511, Tomas Sodergen/MIRA/Impact Visuals; 512(t), E.T. Archive; 512(b), © '95 Josef Polleross/The Stock Market; 513, Voice of America/U.S. Information Agency; 514, © Andrei Iliescu/AP/Wide World Photos; 515, Giraudon/Art Resource, NY; 516, Sovfoto/Eastfoto; 517(both), AKG Photo;518, Ria-Novosti/Sovfoto; 519(bdr), Peter Poulides/Tony Stone Images; 519(other), Peggy Plummer/Black Star; 520, Sovfoto/Eastfoto; 521, © Alain Keller/SYGMA; 524-525(bdr), Image Copyright © 1996 Photodisc, Inc. **Chapter 23**: 526, Luc Novovitch/Gamma Liaison; 527, Betty Press/Woodfin Camp & Associates; 528, Nathan Benn/Woodfin Camp & Associates; 529, © 1997 Alex S. MacLean/Landslides; 532, © P. Robert/SYGMA; 533, Superstock; 534, © Stephen Ferry/Gamma Liaison; 535, Paul Howell/Gamma Liaison; 536, Diego Giudice/AP/Wide World Photos; 537, © 1987 by Herblock in The Washington Post; 538, Photri; 539, © Laski Diffusion/Gamma Liaison; 540, Earth Base/Gamma Liaison; 541(bdr), Brian Stablyk/Tony Stone Images; (other), Steve Maines/Stock, Boston; 543, FPIJ Pool/Sipa Press; 544, Peter Wilson/Sylvia Cordaiy Photo Library Ltd.; 545, Cynthia Johnson/The Gamma Liaison Network; 546, Jeffrey Aaronson/Network Aspen; 547, Mark Harvey/Network Aspen; 548, Wally McNamee/Woodfin Camp & Associates; 550-551(bdr), Image Copyright © 1996 Photodisc, Inc.; 552, Sandra Baker/Gamma Liaison; 553, Image Copyright © 1996 Photodisc, Inc.

Reference Section: Page 556, Uniphoto, Inc.